D0786317

COPYRIGHT LAW

LexisNexis Law School Publishing Advisory Board

Paul Caron
Charles Hartsock Professor of Law
University of Cincinnati College of Law

Olympia Duhart
Associate Professor of Law
Nova Southeastern University, Shepard Broad Law School

Samuel Estreicher
Dwight D. Opperman Professor of Law
Director, Center for Labor and Employment Law
NYU School of Law

Steve Friedland
Professor of Law
Elon University School of Law

Joan Heminway
College of Law Distinguished Professor of Law
University of Tennessee College of Law

Edward Imwinkelried
Edward L. Barrett, Jr. Professor of Law
UC Davis School of Law

Paul Marcus
Haynes Professor of Law
William and Mary Law School

John Sprankling
Distinguished Professor of Law
McGeorge School of Law

Melissa Weresh
Director of Legal Writing and Professor of Law
Drake University Law School

COPYRIGHT LAW

NINTH EDITION

Craig Joyce
Co-Director, Institute for Intellectual Property and Information Law,
& Andrews Kurth Professor of Law
University of Houston Law Center
http://www.law.uh.edu/faculty/main.asp?PID=21

Marshall Leaffer
Distinguished Scholar in Intellectual Property Law
University Fellow
Indiana University School of Law
http://www.law.indiana.edu/directory/sb/page/normal/1421.html

Peter Jaszi
Professor of Law & Director,
Glushko-Samuelson Intellectual Property Law Clinic
Washington College of Law, American University
http://www.wcl.american.edu/faculty/jaszi

Tyler Ochoa
Professor of Law
High Tech Law Institute
Santa Clara University School of Law
law.scu.edu/faculty/profile/ochoa-tyler.cfm

Michael Carroll
Professor of Law
Director, Program on Information Justice and Intellectual Property
American University, Washington College of Law
http://www.wcl.american.edu/faculty/mcarroll/

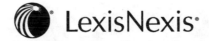 LexisNexis

ISBN: 978-0-7698-5924-8
Looseleaf ISBN: 978-0-7698-5943-9
eBook ISBN: 978-0-3271-8532-1
ISSN: 1932-6017

This publication is designed to provide authoritative information in regard to the subject matter covered. It is sold with the understanding that the publisher is not engaged in rendering legal, accounting, or other professional services. If legal advice or other expert assistance is required, the services of a competent professional should be sought.

LexisNexis and the Knowledge Burst logo are registered trademarks of Reed Elsevier Properties Inc., used under license. Matthew Bender and the Matthew Bender Flame Design are registered trademarks of Matthew Bender Properties Inc.

Copyright © 2013 Matthew Bender & Company, Inc., a member of LexisNexis. All Rights Reserved.

No copyright is claimed by LexisNexis or Matthew Bender & Company, Inc., in the text of statutes, regulations, and excerpts from court opinions quoted within this work. Permission to copy material may be licensed for a fee from the Copyright Clearance Center, 222 Rosewood Drive, Danvers, Mass. 01923, telephone (978) 750-8400.

NOTE TO USERS

To ensure that you are using the latest materials available in this area, please be sure to periodically check the LexisNexis Law School web site for downloadable updates and supplements at www.lexisnexis.com/lawschool.

Editorial Offices
121 Chanlon Rd., New Providence, NJ 07974 (908) 464-6800
201 Mission St., San Francisco, CA 94105-1831 (415) 908-3200
www.lexisnexis.com

MATTHEW◆BENDER

DEDICATION

For Will (25), Matt (21)
and Molly (ageless),
and for my parents, whose memory I cherish

For Joelle and Sarah

For Sabrina and Ned,
and for Sheryl,
whom we miss so much

In memory of my mother, Rosanne,
and for Karin, Marisa, Erik and Elizabeth

For Kristy, Madeleine, and Vivian

Anno Octavo

Annæ Reginæ.

An Act for the Encouragement of Learning, by Vesting the Copies of Printed Books in the Authors or Purchasers of such Copies, during the Times therein mentioned.

Hereas Printers, Booksellers, and other Persons have of late frequently taken the Liberty of Printing, Reprinting, and Publishing, or causing to be Printed, Reprinted, and Published Books, and other Writings, without the Consent of the Authors or Proprietors of such Books and Writings, to their very great Detriment, and too often to the Ruin of them and their Families : For Preventing therefore such Practices for the future, and for the Encouragement of Learned Men to Compose and Write useful Books ; May it please Your Majesty, that it may be Enacted, and be it Enacted by the Queens most Excellent Majesty, by and with the Advice and Consent of the Lords Spiritual and Temporal, and Commons in this present Parliament Assembled, and by the Authority of the same, That from and after the Tenth Day of April, One thousand seven hundred and ten, the Author of any Book or Books already Printed, who hath not Transferred to any other the Copy or Copies of such Book or Books, Share or Shares thereof, or the Bookseller or Booksellers, Printer or Printers, or other Person or Persons, who hath or have Purchased or Acquired the Copy or Copies of any Book or Books, in order to Print or Reprint the same, shall have the sole Right and Liberty of Printing such Book and Books for the Term of One and twenty Years, to Commence from the said Tenth Day of April, and no longer ; and that the Author of any Book or Books already Composed and not Printed and Published, or that shall hereafter be Composed, and his Assignee, or Assigns, shall have the sole Liberty of Printing and Reprinting such Book and Books for the Term of Four-

6   Ttt 2   teen

The Statute of Anne, 8 Anne, ch. 19 (1710)

THE STATUTE OF ANNE

When Anne was Queen of England, Parliament passed An Act . . . [M]en of letters and booksellers [had begun] to complain loudly of the evils of piracy. . . . It was in answer to these appeals that the [Act of] 8 Anne., c. 19, became a law, in 1710. This was the first English statute distinctly affirming copyright and providing for its protection. It was entitled "An Act for the Encouragement of Learning by vesting the copies of printed books in the authors or purchasers of such copies during the times therein mentioned." The preamble declares that "printers, booksellers and other persons have of late frequently taken the liberty of printing, reprinting, and published, or causing to be printed, reprinted, and published, books and other writings, without the consent of the authors or proprietors of such books and writings, to their very great detriment, and too often to the ruin of them and their families;" and that the object of the act is to prevent "such practices for the future, and for the encouragement of learned men to compose and write useful books."

— Eaton S. Drone,
A TREATISE ON THE LAW OF PROPERTY
IN INTELLECTUAL PRODUCTIONS
IN GREAT BRITAIN AND THE UNITED STATES
(Boston, 1879)

PREFACE

Time flies — not just in the publishing business, but in the history of the law. More than three hundred years have passed since April 10, 1710, the date on which the great-grandparent of all copyright laws — the Statute of Anne — became effective in England, the home of Anglo-American copyright. Now the United States, England, and the world have entered a new, distinctly high-tech, third millenium.

As always, in this edition of the casebook as in all of its predecessors, the one constant in copyright law is change. Speaking of history, even instructors who remember the advent of the present U.S. statute, the Copyright Act of 1976 (let alone those who have entered teaching or, like their students, been born since its passage!), must feel a degree of wonderment at how much, and how dramatically, copyright has evolved in only those (now almost) four decades. Since 1976, the United States has joined enthusiastically — and, indeed, taken a leadership role — in the process of internationalizing copyright protection. Congress has moved to harmonize U.S. domestic law with international norms. For the first time, the United States has recognized explicitly the existence, as to certain works at least, of authors' moral rights in the future and fate of their creations. And, most notably, new technologies have revolutionized the means of exploiting copyrighted works and challenged severely the theoretical integrity of the laws that protect them. Never has the study of copyright law been more challenging, or more enjoyable.

This casebook, then, is about copyright yesterday, today — and tomorrow. We have tried to locate the book in the midst of that dynamic tension that exists between copyright's history, including its most fundamental doctrines, and the future unfolding even as the students who use this work embark upon their careers as practitioners. The book deals comprehensively with the *technologies*, particularly digital technologies (the focus of the mammoth Digital Millennium Copyright Act of 1998), that are reshaping every aspect of our lives, from legal research to entertainment to the national economy. It integrates fully into traditional materials concerning domestic law the changes wrought by the *globalization* of copyright law, most notably (from this country's own perspective) through U.S. adherence to or adoption of the Berne Convention in 1989, NAFTA (the North American Free Trade Agreement) in 1994, TRIPS (the Agreement on Trade-Related Aspects of Intellectual Property Rights) in 1995, and the two World Intellectual Property Organization treaties in 1996. In addition, the book attempts to identify for students the variety of philosophical and practical approaches that today characterize our discourse about copyright and related bodies of law. And, as always (and in combination with frequent supplementation), this resource provides the most up-to-date information available on developments in the courts and in Congress that affect this ever-fascinating, ever-evolving field of study.

The book is organized in a straightforward way. Chapter 1 surveys the "landscape of copyright": it introduces the history and philosophy of copyright, differentiates copyright from related bodies of law (patents, trademarks, and state intellectual property law), and provides an overview of the international framework and the digital challenges (two closely related topics) to which the ancient body of copyright law must now adapt if it is to survive and prosper. Chapters 2 and 3 deal with the prerequisites (*i.e.*, originality and fixation in a tangible medium of expression) that *any* work must satisfy in order to be

PREFACE

copyrightable, and with what *types* of works (literature, music, etc.) are copyrightable. Chapters 4 through 6 explore what might be called the "mechanics" of copyright: ownership and transfer; duration and terminations; and publication and the statutory formalities. Chapter 7 considers the various exclusive rights recognized by the 1976 Act, and the statutory limitations on those rights. Chapters 8 and 9 canvass actions for infringement and the increasingly important issue of secondary liability. Chapter 10 explores fair use and affirmative defenses, while Chapter 11 focuses on remedies under federal and state law (if the latter remedies are not preempted). Finally, Chapter 12 attempts a look into copyright's future — its "horizon," so to speak — as we move well into the Digital Revolution and the Third Millennium.

Within each of the chapters other than 1 and 12 (the two "bookend" chapters), each major topic is introduced first by a concise scope note outlining the nature of the inquiry, followed by a specification of the relevant statutory provisions to be read in the Supplement, and finally an excerpt from the pertinent legislative history. The cases, with extensive notes and questions, follow this introductory material. The supplementary materials, both printed and on-line, provide constitutional, statutory, legislative and regulatory materials, recent cases, various relevant international treaties, materials concerning digital developments, and helpful bibliographies.

Both the selection of cases and the purpose of the notes and questions require special comment. By and large, the cases reproduced here are contemporary with the students who will read them. Over three-quarters of the principal cases have been decided since January 1, 1978, the effective date of the Copyright Act of 1976. In most instances, we have deleted doctrinal matter not germane to the topic at hand; but the facts of each case generally have been left to speak for themselves, on grounds that they assist in the learning process, are entertaining, and read rather quickly. Like the cases, the notes and questions emphasize heavily issues that have arisen, or may arise, under the present governing statute. We have made no attempt to "hide the ball." We hope that readers will find the notes to be systematic and informative in their exploration of current law. They should serve both to stimulate classroom discussion and to afford understanding of details that cannot be treated in class, due to time limitations.

Beyond this casebook, students will find many opportunities for further reading, including several multi-volume treatises: David and Melville Nimmer's NIMMER ON COPYRIGHT; William F. Patry's PATRY ON COPYRIGHT; Paul Goldstein's COPYRIGHT: PRINCIPLES, LAW AND PRACTICE; and Howard Abrams' THE LAW OF COPYRIGHT. A number of fine shorter treatises and handbooks are available, including Marshall Leaffer's UNDERSTANDING COPYRIGHT LAW, and Robert Lind's COPYRIGHT LAW: STUDENT STUDY GUIDE. The Copyright Society of the U.S.A. publishes its *Journal* on a bimonthly basis. Among the commercial services, CCH's *Copyright Law Reports* appears monthly, and BNA's *Patent, Trademark and Copyright Journal,* weekly.

Also, for those concerned to obtain an in-depth understanding of the revision process which led to the adoption of the Copyright Act of 1976, the two indispensable resources are the OMNIBUS COPYRIGHT REVISION LEGISLATIVE HISTORY (G. Grossman ed. 1976–77), which provides the official documents, and the KAMENSTEIN LEGISLATIVE HISTORY PROJECT: A COMPENDIUM AND ANALYTICAL INDEX OF MATERIALS LEADING TO THE COPYRIGHT ACT OF 1976 (A. Latman & J. Lightstone eds. 1981), which provides a roadmap through the process. Subsequent amendments to the 1976 Act are, of course, the subject of their own (but less extensive) legislative history, portions of which are reprinted in this casebook as warranted.

One other learning resource should be mentioned here: vigorous, informed interaction with others engaged in the study of this complex and fascinating subject. In that spirit, we look forward to receiving whatever comments or suggestions for improvements in these materials you may have to offer, based on your own experiences in using them.

Craig Joyce
Marshall Leaffer
Peter Jaszi
Tyler Ochoa
Michael Carroll

ACKNOWLEDGMENTS

Where to begin? Although there are many to whom we owe thanks, certainly none are more deserving than our students. In preparation for each new edition, they suffer through veritable mountains of photocopied materials, only to leave the fruits of the labors to future generations of students to enjoy. We hope, however, that our encounters both in and out of class have provided, and in the future as they enter the wide world of practice will continue to provide, both stimulation and satisfaction as the book evolves and improves.

In addition to the contributions of our students, we are grateful (with apologies in advance to those whose kind e-mails we may have mislaid in the compilation of the following list) to our colleagues at other schools, including Howard Abrams of Detroit-Mercy, Arthur Campbell of California Western, Dane Ciolino of Loyola-New Orleans, Anuj Desai of Wisconsin, Jay Dougherty of Loyola-Los Angeles, David Ensign of Louisville, Gordon Hylton of Marquette, Robert Lind of Southwestern, Joseph Liu of Boston College, Barry McDonald of Pepperdine, the late Ray Patterson of Georgia (a beloved friend), Phillip Page of South Texas, Pamela Samuelson of the University of California at Berkeley, Roger Schechter of George Washington, Jay Thomas of Georgetown, Russell VerSteeg of New England, and Alfred Yen of Boston College, whose thoughtful comments and other assistance have enhanced successive editions of this work.

Special thanks are due Paul M. Janicke, Greg R. Vetter, Jacqueline Lipton, Sapna Kumar, and Dean Raymond T. Nimmer, Professor Joyce's colleagues at the University of Houston Law Center's Institute for Intellectual Property & Information Law ("IPIL"), for their support and encouragement. Professor Joyce wishes to acknowledge also the generous assistance provided by Dean Nimmer, Associate Dean Richard Alderman, Andrews Kurth LLP, and the University of Houston Law Foundation.

We acknowledge with thanks, as well, the generosity of support personnel at each of our institutions, particularly Spencer Simons, Mon Yin Lung, Christopher Dykes, and Helen Boyce of the University of Houston's John M. O'Quinn Law Library, Scott Smith of the UHLC Legal Information Technology Department, and student assistants Jeffrey Adams, David Mika, Priya Prasad, and Courteney Taylor.

Professor Jaszi thanks Dean Claudio Grossman, the administration and the skilled library personnel of the Washington College of Law, American University.

A number of artists, attorneys and officials have been most helpful to us in completing the book, including Jean Murrell Adams, Andrew Baum, David O. Carson, J. Wesley Cochran, William Sloan Coats, John D. Deacon, Jr., David A. Einhorn, Andrew D. Epstein, Paul Fields, Tom Forsythe, Matthew Furton, Charles Gibbons, Suzanne Hines, Barbara T. Hoffman, Paul E. Kreiger, Annie Lee, Andrew Leicester, Jennifer E. Matthews, Bob McAughan, Charles D. Ossola, John Blair Overton, David Phillips, Charles Rembar, Faith Ringgold, Edward Samuels, Pamela Samuelson, Geraldine C. Simmons, Bion Smalley, Saul Steinberg, Philip H. Stillman, James P. White, Richard A. Williamson, and Adrian Zuckerman.

We are grateful, too, and beyond measure, to so many members of the LexisNexis Publishing team — including Cristina Gegenschatz, our tireless, cheerful and expert

ACKNOWLEDGMENTS

editor, as well as the ever-amazing Kelli Eagle, Sean Caldwell, Lisa Hughes, and Jennifer Bright — who have encouraged our work so steadfastly and done so much to bring it to fruition.

Lastly, particular thanks to Bob Dufford, S.J., John Foley, S.J., Tim Manion, Roc O'Connor, S.J., Dan Schutte, and Erich Sylvester for inspiration spanning more than nearly four decades, and not likely to end soon.

TABLE OF CONTENTS

| Chapter 1 | INTRODUCTION: THE LANDSCAPE OF COPYRIGHT . 1 |

§ 1.01   THE IMPORTANCE OF COPYRIGHT 1
§ 1.02   COPYRIGHT AND RELATED BODIES OF LAW 3
  [A]   An Introduction to Copyright 3
  [B]   Federal Intellectual Property Law 4
    [1]   In General 4
    [2]   Patent Law 4
    [3]   Trademark Law 9
  [C]   State Intellectual Property Law 11
    [1]   Unfair Competition and Trade Secrets 11
    [2]   Other State Law Theories 12
§ 1.03   HISTORY OF ANGLO-AMERICAN COPYRIGHT LAW 16
  [A]   The Beginnings to *Donaldson v. Beckett* (1774) 16
  [B]   From the Constitution to the Copyright Act of 1909 20
  [C]   The 1909 Act 22
    [1]   General Provisions of the 1909 Act 22
    [2]   The 1909 Act and the Berne Convention 22
    [3]   Legislative Attempts to Revise the 1909 Act 23
    [4]   The Continuing Importance of the 1909 Act 23
  [D]   The Copyright Act of 1976 23
    [1]   Important Changes Made by the 1976 Act 23
    [2]   Subsequent Developments Under the 1976 Act 25
    [3]   Trends in Copyright Legislation 27
§ 1.04   COPYRIGHT IN A CHANGING WORLD 28
  [A]   A Comparative Law Overview 28
  [B]   Major International Treaties Involving Copyright 31
    [1]   In General 31
    [2]   The United States and International Copyright 33
    [3]   The Berne Convention 34
  [C]   U.S. Entry Into Berne 37
    [1]   The Incentives for Entry 37
    [2]   The Berne Convention Implementation Act of 1988 38
    [3]   The Unfinished Business of the BCIA 38
  [D]   Neighboring and Related Rights Conventions 39
  [E]   Intellectual Property and International Trade 40
    [1]   NAFTA and TRIPS 40
    [2]   TRIPS and the Berne Convention 42
    [3]   The WTO Implementing Legislation 42

TABLE OF CONTENTS

[4]	Updating the Berne Convention	43
[5]	U.S. Participation in the New Order	44
§ 1.05	COPYRIGHT AND THE DIGITAL CHALLENGE	45
[A]	Looking Back	45
[B]	Digitization and the Revolution in Information Processing	45
[C]	Digital Networks and Their Importance	47
[D]	Digital Copyright at Home and Abroad	48
[E]	The Issues in Context	50
[F]	Looking Forward	50
§ 1.06	THINKING AND TALKING ABOUT COPYRIGHT LAW	52
[A]	In General	52
[B]	Copyright and "Interest Analysis"	53
[C]	"Rhetorics" of Copyright Jurisprudence	54
[1]	The "Utilitarian" and "Natural Law" Conceptions of Copyright	54
[2]	Other Rhetorics in Contemporary Copyright Discourse	60
[D]	Conclusion	64

Chapter 2	**PREREQUISITES FOR COPYRIGHT PROTECTION**	**65**
§ 2.01	FIXATION	66
[A]	Introduction	67
[B]	Development of Current Law	67
	White-Smith Music Publishing Co. v. Apollo Co.	68
	Notes and Questions	72
	Midway Manufacturing Co. v. Artic International, Inc.	75
	Notes and Questions	78
§ 2.02	ORIGINALITY	84
[A]	Introduction	84
[B]	Basic Originality Concepts	85
[C]	The Originality/Novelty Distinction	89
[D]	"Authors" and Their "Writings"	91
	Burrow-Giles Lithographic Co. v. Sarony	91
	Notes and Questions	95
	Bleistein v. Donaldson Lithographing Co.	99
	Notes and Questions	102
[E]	Originality Revisited	107
	Meshwerks, Inc. v. Toyota Motor Sales U.S.A., Inc.	107
	Notes and Questions	115
[F]	The Idea/Expression Dichotomy	118
	Baker v. Selden	118
	Notes and Questions	123
[G]	The Merger Doctrine	126

TABLE OF CONTENTS

Morrissey v. Procter & Gamble Co. 126

Notes and Questions 128

§ 2.03 OTHER PRELIMINARY CONSIDERATIONS 134

[A] National Origin 134

[B] U.S. Government Works 135

[C] The Reduced Role of the Statutory Formalities 137

Chapter 3   WORKS OF AUTHORSHIP 139

§ 3.01 ORIGINAL WORKS OF AUTHORSHIP UNDER § 102 140

[A] Introduction 141

[B] Literary Works, Including Computer Software 142

Miller v. Universal City Studios, Inc. 143

Notes and Questions 147

Apple Computer, Inc. v. Franklin Computer Corp. 154

Final Report of the National Commission on New Technological

Uses of Copyrighted Works (CONTU) at 28-30 (1979):

Dissent of Commissioner Hersey 162

Notes and Questions 163

[C] Musical Works, Dramatic Works, and Pantomimes and Choreographic

Works 171

[D] Pictorial, Graphic, and Sculptural Works 174

Mazer v. Stein 176

Pivot Point International, Inc. v. Charlene Products, Inc. 180

Notes and Questions 189

[E] Motion Pictures and Other Audiovisual Works 201

[F] Sound Recordings 203

[G] Architectural Works 207

Shine v. Childs 209

Notes and Questions 214

§ 3.02 DERIVATIVE WORKS AND COMPILATIONS UNDER § 103 220

[A] Introduction 221

[B] Derivative Works 222

Schrock v. Learning Curve International, Inc. 222

Notes and Questions 229

[C] Compilations 237

Feist Publications, Inc. v. Rural Telephone Service Company, Inc. . . 237

Notes and Questions 248

Chapter 4   OWNERSHIP AND TRANSFERS 261

§ 4.01 INITIAL OWNERSHIP 261

[A] Introduction 262

TABLE OF CONTENTS

[B]	Works Made for Hire		263
	Community For Creative Non-Violence v. Reid		263
	Notes and Questions		272
[C]	Joint Works		281
	Childress v. Taylor		281
	Notes and Questions		290
[D]	Collective Works and the *Tasini* Case		296
§ 4.02	TRANSFERS OF RIGHTS		299
[A]	Introduction		299
[B]	Preliminary Concepts		301
[1]	The Distinction Between Copyright and Material Object		301
[2]	The Bundle of Rights		302
[C]	Decisional Law		303
	Effects Associates, Inc. v. Cohen		303
	Notes and Questions		307
[D]	The "New Media" Problem		313
[E]	Recordation		315
[F]	Orphan Works		318

Chapter 5	**DURATION AND TERMINATIONS**		**323**
§ 5.01	DURATION OF COPYRIGHTS		323
[A]	Introduction		324
[B]	Duration Basics Under the CTEA		327
	Eldred v. Ashcroft		329
	Notes and Questions		338
[C]	The Law of Renewal		344
[1]	Renewal Basics		345
[2]	Renewal and Derivative Works		351
[3]	Automatic Renewal		354
[D]	Restored Copyrights		355
	Golan v. Holder		360
	Notes and Questions		368
§ 5.02	TERMINATIONS OF TRANSFERS		370
[A]	Section 203 Terminations: Post-1977 Transfers		371
[1]	Introduction		371
[2]	Summary of Provisions of § 203		372
[B]	Section 304(c) Terminations: Pre-1978 Transfers		375
[1]	Introduction		376
[2]	Summary of Provisions of § 304(c)		377
[C]	Section 304(d) Terminations		379
[D]	The Mechanics of Termination		380

TABLE OF CONTENTS

[1]	Summary	380
[2]	Decisional Law	383
	Siegel v. Warner Brothers Entertainment, Inc.	383
	Notes and Questions	392
[E]	The Derivative Works Exception	396

Chapter 6	**PUBLICATION AND FORMALITIES**	**399**
§ 6.01	PUBLICATION	400
[A]	Introduction	402
[B]	Publication in the Courts	403
	Academy of Motion Picture Arts and Sciences v. Creative House Promotions, Inc.	403
	Notes and Questions	408
[C]	Publication, Derivative Works, and the Public Domain	415
§ 6.02	NOTICE	416
[A]	Introduction	418
	House Report on the Berne Convention Implementation Act of 1988 (Excerpts)	419
[B]	Concepts and Procedures	420
	U.S. Copyright Office Circular 3: Copyright Notice (Excerpts)	420
	Notes and Questions	423
[C]	Notice for Compilations and Collective Works	427
§ 6.03	DEPOSIT AND REGISTRATION	428
[A]	Introduction	430
	Joint Explanatory Statement on Amendment to S. 1301 [the Berne Convention Implementation Act of 1988]	432
[B]	Concepts and Procedures	433
	U.S. Copyright Office Circular 1: Copyright Basics (Excerpts)	433
	Notes and Questions	437
[C]	Registration of Collective and Derivative Works	447
§ 6.04	THE COPYRIGHT OFFICE	448
[A]	Introduction	448
[B]	History and Functions of the Copyright Office	448
[C]	Combining the Copyright Office with the Patent and Trademark Office	450

Chapter 7	**EXCLUSIVE RIGHTS AND THEIR LIMITATIONS**	**453**
§ 7.01	OVERVIEW	454
[A]	Introduction	454
[B]	The "Architecture" of Rights and Limitations	455
[C]	Statutory (or "Compulsory") Licenses	456

TABLE OF CONTENTS

[D]		Exclusive Rights in the Networked Information Environment	459
[E]		Miscellaneous Rights: In and Beyond Copyright	460
[1]		In General	460
[2]		Copyright Management Information	461
§ 7.02		THE REPRODUCTION RIGHT	464
[A]		Introduction	464
[B]		Reproduction in Copies	465
		Walt Disney Productions v. Filmation Associates	465
		Notes and Questions	469
[C]		Reproduction in Phonorecords	474
[D]		Electronic Reproduction	478
		Cartoon Network v. CSC Holdings, Inc.	478
		Notes and Questions	484
§ 7.03		THE ADAPTATION RIGHT	490
[A]		Introduction	491
[B]		Case Law	492
		Lee v. A.R.T. Company	492
		Notes and Questions	496
§ 7.04		THE PUBLIC DISTRIBUTION RIGHT	505
[A]		Introduction	506
[B]		Domestic Distribution	508
		London-Sire Records, Inc. v. Doe 1	508
		Notes and Questions	514
[C]		Import and Export Rights	522
§ 7.05		THE PUBLIC PERFORMANCE RIGHT	526
[A]		Public Performances	526
[1]		Introduction	526
[2]		Case Law	528
		Columbia Pictures Industries, Inc. v. Aveco, Inc.	528
		Notes and Questions	532
[3]		Performing Rights Societies	539
[4]		Small and Grand Performing Rights	540
[5]		Synchronization Rights	542
[6]		Digital Network Transmissions	542
[7]		Performance Rights in Sound Recordings	544
		Notes and Questions	545
[B]		Secondary Transmissions	547
[1]		Introduction	547
[2]		The § 110(5) *Aiken* Exemption	549
		National Football League v. McBee & Bruno's, Inc.	549
		Notes and Questions	553

TABLE OF CONTENTS

[3]	The Cable System Limitations	558
[4]	The Satellite Carrier Limitations	560
[5]	Current Issues in the Law of Retransmission	561
§ 7.06	THE PUBLIC DISPLAY RIGHT	562
[A]	Introduction	563
[B]	Case Law	564
	Perfect 10, Inc. v. Amazon.com, Inc.	564
	Notes and Questions	570
§ 7.07	THE DIGITAL PERFORMANCE RIGHT IN SOUND RECORDINGS .	574
[A]	Introduction	574
[B]	Highlights of the DPRA	575
	Notes and Questions	579
§ 7.08	MORAL RIGHTS	580
[A]	A Comparative Overview	580
[B]	Protection Outside the Copyright Act	581
[C]	Copyright Protection: The Visual Artists Rights Act of 1990	585
[1]	Introduction	586
[2]	Case Law	588
	Phillips v. Pembroke Real Estate, Inc.	588
	Notes and Questions	597
Chapter 8	**INFRINGEMENT ACTIONS**	**607**
§ 8.01	INTRODUCTION	608
§ 8.02	FRAMING THE LAWSUIT	610
[A]	Jurisdictional Matters	611
	T.B. Harms Co. v. Eliscu	611
	Notes and Questions	614
[B]	Other Procedural Matters	623
	Righthaven LLC v. Wolf	623
	Notes and Questions	628
§ 8.03	PROVING THE CLAIM	635
[A]	Formulating a "General Test" for Infringement	635
[B]	Copying	637
	Bright Tunes Music Corp. v. Harrisongs Music, Ltd.	637
	Notes and Questions	641
	Ty, Inc. v. GMA Accessories, Inc.	644
	Notes and Questions	648
[C]	Improper Appropriation	652
[1]	By Way of Overview	652
[2]	Illustrative Cases	658
	Nichols v. Universal Pictures Corp.	658

TABLE OF CONTENTS

Peter Pan Fabrics, Inc. v. Martin Weiner Corp. 663
Notes and Questions 664
Laureyssens v. Idea Group, Inc. 670
Notes and Questions 676
Computer Associates Int'l, Inc. v. Altai, Inc. 684
Notes and Questions 697
Tufenkian Import/Export Ventures Inc. v. Einstein Moomjy, Inc. . 706
Notes and Questions 711
§ 8.04   EXTRATERRITORIALITY AND CONFLICTS OF LAWS 714
[A]   Extraterritoriality 715
           Subafilms, Ltd. v. MGM-Pathe Communications Co. 715
           Notes and Questions 721
[B]   Conflict of Laws 724
           Itar-Tass Russian News Agency v. Russian Kurier, Inc. 724
           Notes and Questions 729

Chapter 9   SECONDARY LIABILITY 733

§ 9.01   CONTRIBUTORY INFRINGEMENT AND VICARIOUS LIABILITY . 734
[A]   Introduction 734
[B]   Case Law 735
           Fonovisa, Inc. v. Cherry Auction, Inc. 735
           Notes and Questions 740
§ 9.02   COPYING DEVICES AND SOFTWARE 742
[A]   Case Law 743
           Sony Corp. of America v. Universal City Studios, Inc. 743
           Notes and Questions 749
[B]   The Audio Home Recording Act 751
[1]   Introduction 751
[2]   Highlights of the AHRA 752
           Notes and Questions 753
[C]   Peer-to-Peer File Sharing 755
           Metro-Goldwyn-Mayer Studios, Inc. v. Grokster, Ltd. 756
           Notes and Questions 764
§ 9.03   INTERNET SERVICE PROVIDERS 767
[A]   Introduction 767
[B]   Limitation of Liability for Service Providers 770
           Viacom International, Inc. v. Youtube, Inc. 772
           Notes and Questions 781
[C]   Other Online Issues 785
§ 9.04   TECHNOLOGICAL PROTECTION MEASURES AND
           CIRCUMVENTION DEVICES 787

TABLE OF CONTENTS

[A]	Anti-Circumvention Measures	787
	Notes and Questions	790
[B]	Case Law	792
	Universal City Studios, Inc. v. Corley	792
	Notes and Questions	800

Chapter 10   FAIR USE AND AFFIRMATIVE DEFENSES **809**

§ 10.01	INTRODUCTION: THE FAIR USE DOCTRINE	809
§ 10.02	THE FUNDAMENTALS OF FAIR USE	810
[A]	Judicial Origins	811
	Folsom v. Marsh	811
	Notes and Questions	813
[B]	Analyzing Fair Use Today	815
	Campbell v. Acuff-Rose Music, Inc.	815
	Notes and Questions	827
§ 10.03	CONCEPTUAL ISSUES IN FAIR USE	835
[A]	Copyright and the First Amendment	835
	Harper & Row, Publishers, Inc. v. Nation Enterprises	835
	Notes and Questions	842
[B]	The Meaning of "Transformative Use"	847
	Bill Graham Archives v. Dorling Kindersley Ltd.	848
	Notes and Questions	855
[C]	Actual and Potential Market Effect	860
	Notes and Questions	862
[D]	Photocopying, Guidelines, and "Personal Reproduction"	864
[1]	Photocopying	864
[2]	The Role of Guidelines	866
[3]	Modern Technology and "Personal Reproduction"	868
§ 10.04	FAIR USE AND TECHNOLOGY	872
[A]	Fair Use and Decompilation	872
[B]	Fair Use and the Internet	877
	Kelly v. Arriba Soft Corp.	877
	Notes and Questions	883
[C]	Fair Use and Technological Protection Measures Under the DMCA	888
§ 10.05	FAIR USE IN COMPARATIVE PERSPECTIVE	891
[A]	The Singularity of U.S. Fair Use	891
[B]	International Treaties and the Future of Fair Use	894
§ 10.06	AFFIRMATIVE COPYRIGHT DEFENSES	897

TABLE OF CONTENTS

Chapter 11	**REMEDIES, PREEMPTION, AND RELATED BODIES OF LAW**	**905**

§ 11.01   REMEDIES UNDER FEDERAL LAW 905
   [A]   Introduction 906
   [B]   Non-Monetary Relief 909
     [1]   Preliminary and Permanent Injunctions 909
        Salinger v. Colting 909
        Notes and Questions 916
     [2]   Impoundment and Disposition 921
   [C]   Damages 923
     [1]   Plaintiff's Damages and Defendant's Profits 923
        Polar Bear Productions, Inc. v. Timex Corporation 923
        Notes and Questions 931
     [2]   Statutory or "In Lieu" Damages 936
        Columbia Pictures Television v. Krypton Broadcasting of
        Birmingham, Inc. 936
        Notes and Questions 940
   [D]   Costs and Attorneys' Fees 945
   [E]   Federal Remedies and Rights Management 947
   [F]   Criminal Penalties 948
§ 11.02   PREEMPTION AND STATE LAW REMEDIES 952
   [A]   Introduction 953
   [B]   Misappropriation and the General Problem of Preemption 954
   [C]   Preemption Under the Supremacy Clause 958
        Bonito Boats, Inc. v. Thunder Craft Boats, Inc. 958
        Notes and Questions 961
   [D]   Preemption Under the 1976 Act 965
     [1]   Section 301: A Study in Confusion 965
     [2]   The Struggle in the Courts 968
        Katz, Dochtermann & Epstein, Inc. v. Home Box Office 968
        Notes and Questions 972
        Bowers v. Baystate Technologies, Inc. 978
        Notes and Questions 986
§ 11.03   RELATED BODIES OF FEDERAL AND STATE LAW 990
   [A]   Passing Off and the Protection of Trade Dress Under Federal Law 990
        Dastar Corporation v. Twentieth Century Fox Film Corporation ... 990
        Notes and Questions 997
   [B]   Idea Protection 1003
        Murray v. National Broadcasting Co., Inc. 1003
        Notes and Questions 1006
   [C]   The Right of Publicity 1008

TABLE OF CONTENTS

White v. Samsung Electronics America, Inc.   1008

White v. Samsung Electronics America, Inc.   1013

Notes and Questions   1017

Chapter 12   **EPILOGUE: THE HORIZON OF COPYRIGHT** **1023**

Table of Cases **TC-1**

**Table of Principal Discussions of the Copyright Act of 1976
As Amended** **TPD-1**

Table of Legislative History Excerpts **TLH-1**

Index **I-1**

Chapter 1

INTRODUCTION: THE LANDSCAPE OF COPYRIGHT

Once a relatively esoteric subject taught in only a few law schools, today copyright law is a key component of the regular curriculum. Both the legal academy and the practicing bar now recognize that copyright, and the industries it affects, are vitally important to the United States economy. But apart from this practical interest, copyright law is a challenging and theoretically intricate subject. As Justice Story put it, copyright law (along with patent law) "approaches nearer than any other class of cases . . . to what may be called the metaphysics of the law, where the distinctions are, or at least may be, very subtle and refined, and sometimes, almost evanescent." *Folsom v. Marsh*, 9 F. Cas. 342, 344 (C.C.D. Mass. 1841) (No. 4,901). Marked by both historical peculiarities and difficult policy dilemmas, copyright touches our artistic, cultural, and moral sensibilities.

This chapter introduces the concept of copyright and places it in historical, philosophical, and legal context. In addition, it differentiates copyright law from other bodies of law that confer intellectual property rights, such as patent law, trademark law, and related state causes of action.

Copyright is an exceptionally dynamic body of law. A major theme running through this introductory chapter (and the entire casebook) is that the law of copyright is a form of legal adaptation, a response to new technologies in the reproduction and distribution of human expression — or, more precisely, to the social, cultural, and economic trends unleashed by these technologies. We can observe the beginnings of this process in the pre-statutory antecedents of the law in the 16th Century. It is ongoing still. The changes wrought in our society by digital technology are forcing us to confront, once again, the most basic of questions: Should the law confer property rights in products of the mind? If so, to what extent? And how should intangible property rights be balanced against the public interest in access to knowledge? These questions have perplexed generations of legislators, judges, philosophers, economists, and law students. They are the subject of this casebook.

§ 1.01 THE IMPORTANCE OF COPYRIGHT

In a surprisingly short period of time, the United States has evolved from an industrial to an information- and services-based society. Our post-industrial era is marked by rapid technological change in which our ability to reproduce and receive information grows exponentially. It is hard to believe that many of our grandparents can remember a time when television was a suspect novelty, and cable and satellite communications belonged to a hazy future. Today, we are linked increasingly by digital networks, including the Internet, which defy physical distance to carry texts, images, and sounds with startling ease and rapidity. Who can predict what new information-based technologies lie ahead? From all indications, the communications revolution will only continue to gather speed as each year — each week! — goes by.

As the value of communicative expression grows, so does the legal structure that governs the rules concerning its ownership. Products of the mind are protected under three branches of federal law, known collectively as "intellectual property." *Patent law* provides a limited "monopoly" for new and inventive products, processes, and designs. *Trademark law* prohibits product imitators from passing off their goods or services as the products of others. *Copyright law* protects "original works of authorship." A separate body of state-created law provides additional protections.

From the first English copyright act, the Statute of Anne in 1710, the law of "copyright" has protected the exclusive right of authors to reproduce copies of their books and, by extension, other writings. Today, copyright covers much broader ground, including not only most literary, artistic, and musical works, but architectural works, computer software, and some kinds of databases as well.

The information industries are critically important to the American economy in its post-industrial state. The numbers are staggering, as a report issued in late 2011 (covering data from 2007 through 2010) demonstrates.[1] In 2010, the "core" copyright industries (including recorded music, TV programs, motion pictures, home videos, books, periodicals, newspapers, and computer software) accounted for 6.4% of the U.S. Gross Domestic Product, or $931.8 billion. For the entire period 2007–2010, and despite the financial crisis and U.S. recession of 2008–2009, the U.S. core copyright industries grew, in real terms, at an annual growth rate of 1.10%, compared with the U.S. economy's growth rate of only 0.05%. In terms of foreign exports, the core copyright industries generated $134.0 billion in sales in 2010 (with an annual growth rate of 3.8%), leading all major industry sectors, including chemicals, aircraft and aircraft parts, motor vehicles and parts, agriculture, food, and pharmaceuticals. It seems safe to predict that the importance of copyright to the U.S. economy will only grow in the years to come. At the same time, flexible limitations and exceptions to copyright owners' rights and safe harbors from certain forms of liability have proven important for U.S. technology companies, such as Internet service providers and developers of new communications platforms.

Such developments indicate clearly the growing international importance of intellectual property. The transfer of information has become an ever greater component of international trade and is the centerpiece of U.S. competitiveness. Unlike in other sectors of the economy, in the area of intellectual property the United States is a net exporter — indeed, the world's largest exporter by far. Whether old media (motion pictures, music, and the like) or new (computer software, for example), the United States is preeminent in the production and distribution of copyrighted works.

---

[1] *Copyright Industries in the U.S. Economy: The 2011 Report*, by Stephen E. Siwek of Economists Incorporated (prepared for the International Intellectual Property Alliance), *available at* www.iipa.com.

There is, however, a downside to this success. As their exports have increased, American copyright owners increasingly have become vulnerable to piracy abroad and to inadequate protection of their interests under foreign laws. Accordingly, the international aspects of copyright law no longer can be given secondary consideration in a serious study of the subject. They will receive full, integrated treatment in the pages that follow.

§ 1.02   COPYRIGHT AND RELATED BODIES OF LAW

[A]   An Introduction to Copyright

The term "copyright" is, or at least once was, a highly descriptive term. At the time of the Statute of Anne (1710), ownership of "copie" in a book amounted to the exclusive right to print and publish it. Today's copyright goes much farther than the copyright of centuries past, which protected only against reproducing the work — usually, by printing or reprinting it — and vending the copies so made. Much of what we protect in copyright law today — through derivative works rights, performance rights, and display rights — is really the right to *use* (and to *authorize* the use of) copyrighted works in a variety of ways.[1]

Conventional accounts of United States copyright law generally start with the proposition that, from the beginning, our statutes have reflected an assumption that unimpeded copying of those intangible products of the mind whose production we as a society wish to encourage would produce undesirable social consequences. According to this understanding, the focus of American copyright law is primarily on the benefits derived by the public from the labors of authors. Our law is concerned only secondarily on the desirability, in the abstract, of providing a reward to the author or copyright owner (often, but not always, the same person) in recognition of his or her creative accomplishment. So understood, the basic philosophy of our copyright law stands in tidy opposition to the underlying vision of the "authors' rights" statutes of civil-law countries, in Europe and elsewhere, at least as that vision is usually described.

As we will see in the succeeding sections of this chapter, however, the situation is considerably more complicated. In fact, there exist, in the legal materials both of the United States and of other countries with a developed jurisprudence on the subject, *many* theories about how and why copyright works — *all* of them rooted, to a greater or lesser extent, in the rich, untidy history of this curious body of law.

For the moment, however, our focus is on aspects of the American legal system that complement, reinforce or supplement copyright. Recently, federal law has begun to experiment cautiously with "neighboring" or "related" rights, which provide copyright-like protection for nontraditional subject matter, sometimes in an attempt to avoid the constitutional limitations which the courts have recognized with respect to protection based on the Copyright Clause itself. We will explore

---

[1] For a development of this idea, see Kernochan, *Imperatives for Enforcing Author's Rights*, 131 Revue Internationale de Droit D'Auteur [R.I.D.A.] 181 (1987). In addition, copyright today protects kinds of works — photographs, motion pictures, sound recordings, computer programs — not even imagined when the early statutes were enacted.

these developments in due course. For today, as always, anyone who seeks a thorough understanding of U.S. copyright law should become familiar also with *other* federal law protections for interests in intellectual property: specifically, the laws of patent and trademark.

[B]   Federal Intellectual Property Law

[1]   In General

Copyright, patent, and trademark law share certain basic similarities. First, by their nature, all three major areas of intellectual property law recognize property rights in intangible products of the mind: copyright (artistic and literary expression), patent (technological and other innovations), and trademark (symbolic information). Second, because these bodies of law concern federally recognized rights, they are governed by federal statutes and administered by federal agencies. (The federal role is exclusive as to the first two, while state law also has a role to play as to trademark.) Third, from an international perspective, intellectual property law is most fully developed in Western industrialized countries, and rights in such property frequently are the subject of international treaties.

On the other hand, copyright, patent and trademark law differ both theoretically and operationally, as the accompanying chart attempts to make clear.

[2]   Patent Law

Generally

Contrasted with copyright, patent is a form of intellectual property protection which is harder both to secure and to maintain, and shorter in duration, but relatively more robust while it lasts.[2] Generally speaking, the patent grant encourages investment in research and development to produce valuable techno-logical products and processes. It creates a limited "monopoly" (more properly described, a limited right to exclude) in return for public disclosure of the patentee's discovery. The patent becomes a public record upon issuance, and sometimes before issuance as an application, accessible to those wishing to learn from the information disclosed.

---

[2] Critics of the patent system sometimes argue that such robust protection is not needed to the degree currently provided by Title 35, or not needed at all, as an incentive to invention. More narrowly, others contend that patent law is too technology-specific (resulting, for example, in over-application of certain rules of patentability in biotechnology cases and under-application in software cases). *See* Burk & Lemley, *Is Patent Law Technology-Specific?*, 17 Berkeley Tech. L.J. 1155 (2002).

COMPARISON:
COPYRIGHT, PATENT, AND TRADEMARK

	COPYRIGHT	PATENT	TRADEMARK
SUBJECT MATTER	Literary, dramatic, and musical works; pantomimes and choreography; pictorial, graphic, and sculptural works; audiovisual works; sound recordings; architectural works	Utility patent: Functional features of products and processes Design patent: Ornamental designs for manufactured goods	Words, names, symbols, or devices
STANDARDS FOR VALIDITY	Originality and fixation in a tangible medium of expression	Utility patent: Utility, novelty, and nonobviousness Design patent: What is obvious to ordinary designer	Use of mark to distinguish one's goods or services
WHEN PROTECTION BEGINS	Upon fixation of original expression	When granted by U.S. Patent and Trademark Office	Upon use of mark
DURATION OF PROTECTION	Life of the author (or longest-lived joint author), plus 70 years; or 95 years from publication or 120 years from creation, whichever expires first	Utility patent: Until 20 years from date filed Design patent: 14 years from date issued	So long as properly used as trademark
STANDARDS FOR INFRINGEMENT	Copying and improper appropriation	Utility patent: Making, using, or selling something covered by the claim language Design patent: Similarity of the designs to the ordinary observer	Likelihood of confusion

[1] **Summary omits patents for distinct and new plant varieties asexually reproduced (*i.e.*, without using seeds) (same term of protection as utility patents). *See* 35 U.S.C. §§ 161-164.**

Patent law is the only branch of intellectual property law in which a claimant's rights depend wholly on a government grant — one made by the U.S. Patent and Trademark Office. In extreme contrast, a copyright does not spring into existence as the result of an official decision, but originates rather in the creative act of an author, which itself gives rise to the legal interest. Subsequent registration of a copyright with the Copyright Office enhances the value of an owner's right, but is not a source of it.

Likewise, trademark rights are based on use. They can spring directly from the claimant's qualifying use of a mark on a product, with or without the later confirmation of an official registration with the Patent and Trademark Office — and/or with an appropriate state government office. And even though an application to register a trademark may be filed prior to actual use, the substantive right to preclude others from using the mark vests only when use has been demonstrated, and registration can occur only then.

Not surprisingly, the differing roles of the various federal and state bureaucracies in the creation and confirmation of intellectual property rights can be a source of confusion to the non-specialist.

Procedures for Obtaining a Patent

As already noted, a patent is granted by a governmental agency: the U.S. Patent and Trademark Office ("PTO").[3] To handle patent applications before the PTO, a practitioner must have a technical background and must pass a special PTO examination. These special qualifications are intended to ensure that the patent application is drafted properly, and that its prosecution will be guided competently through the PTO's administrative procedures.

Generally, the term of a patent begins on the grant date and ends 20 years from the date on which the application for the patent was filed in the United States, provided required maintenance fees are paid during that term. The decision to grant the patent is made after the patent examiner evaluates the claims contained in the application to determine whether they meet the standards of patentability. The numbered claims, found at the end of the patent application document, determine the scope of the patent and are critical in deciding whether the patent has been infringed.

The administrative process leading to issuance of the patent can take years and cost thousands of dollars in legal fees.[4] Thus, patents should be sought only after careful consideration of the chances for successful issuance of commercially meaningful claim scope and the eventual validity of such scope if challenged in a court of law.

Kinds of Patents

A patent confers a legal right to exclude others for a limited time from making, using, selling, offering to sell, or importing the patented invention within or into the United States. There are three kinds of patents: a utility patent with a term running from the grant date until a date 20 years after filing, a plant patent with the same

---

[3] The "United States Patent and Trademark Office" is an agency within the Department of Commerce, and the Office's former Commissioner is its "Director" — and "Under Secretary of Commerce for Intellectual Property." Pub. L. No. 106-113 (1999).

[4] If corresponding patents are obtained in other countries — for example, Japan, Germany, and five other European countries — total costs for obtaining and maintaining such patents commonly exceed $100,000.

term, and a design patent with a 14-year term from the grant date.

Utility patents are granted for *new, useful, and nonobvious products and processes.* Plant patents may be given for discovering and asexually reproducing new and distinct plant varieties. Design patents are granted for new, original, and ornamental designs for articles of manufacture. Utility patents are those most often discussed and, overall, the most important economically.

Utility Patents: Eligibility and Requirements for Validity

The patent statute establishes the requirements for patent eligibility in § 101 of Title 35. A patent is conferred on one who "invents or discovers any new and useful process, machine, manufacture or composition of matter, or any new improvement thereof." 35 U.S.C. § 101. To obtain a patent, one must show eligible subject matter, novelty, nonobviousness, and usefulness — and must meet statutory invention disclosure requirements.

Eligible subject matter covers nearly the full range of technological innovations that can be physically implemented in a product or process. Products are things: machines, chemical compounds, or objects. A process is a method of achieving a result. In addition to the more familiar patents covering mechanical, electrical and chemical products or processes, patents have been granted for inventions in biotechnology (*e.g.*, human-altered microbes), *see Diamond v. Chakrabarty*, 447 U.S. 303 (1980), and certain processes involving computer software. *See Diamond v. Diehr*, 450 U.S. 175 (1981). Patents, however, may *not* be granted for abstract ideas, *see Bilski v. Kappos*, 130 S. Ct. 3218 (2010), mathematical algorithms, or laws of nature. *See Mayo Collaborative Servs. v. Prometheus Labs., Inc.*, 132 S. Ct. 1289 (2012). Generally speaking, the subject matter of utility patents and that of copyrights do not overlap, but (as we shall see) copyright law also has extended significant protection to software, creating the potential that a given program may be protected under both intellectual property schemes.

Requirements for validity imposed by statute ensure that not all products or processes are patentable. Thanks to the *novelty* requirement — that the invention be something new as compared with previously disclosed products or processes — one cannot patent a preexisting natural or synthetic substance, although one may be able to claim rights in an improved version of such a substance or in a process for its extraction or for a new use of it, such as in a medical treatment.

The novelty requirement also reveals a fundamental difference between patent law and the law of copyright, which requires only that a protected work be "original" — the author's own, not something copied from another work. Theoretically at least, two people who independently created identical works could both hold copyrights, and neither's use would infringe the other's rights. Thus, in order to recover for copyright infringement, a plaintiff always must prove that the defendant actually copied. By contrast, independent invention is not a defense in a patent infringement action: One who obtains a valid patent is entitled to enforce it against all who make, sell, or use the invention, whether or not they know about the work or the patent, or even if they independently developed the same technology. *See* 35 U.S.C. § 271(a).

In 2011, Congress passed a major patent reform bill, the America Invents Act ("AIA"). Among other goals, the AIA aims to reduce the disparity between the invention-date-related provisions of the prior United States law and the "first-to-file" systems of the rest of the world. Revised 35 U.S.C. § 102 provides that the first person to file a patent application is entitled to patent it, unless he or she derived the information from another inventor, or another person publicly disclosed the invention first and filed an application within one year of such disclosure. (In most other countries, a prior public disclosure before filing destroys patentability, *i.e.*, there is no grace period.) The new provisions apply only to applications filed on or after March 16, 2013. Applications filed before that date, and patents granted on such applications, will continue to be judged by the novelty provisions of the previous statute, which consider whether the invention was known or used in the United States (or patented or published anywhere in the world) before the applicant's date of invention; or whether the invention was in public use or on sale in the United States (or patented or published anywhere in the world) more than one year before the date of filing.

In the Patent Office, examiners search archives of "prior art" to assess an invention's novelty. But the statute requires them to look to this source for other determinations as well. Even if the subject matter is new, patentability is precluded if the invention would have been obvious to a person having ordinary skill in the art (sometimes referred to in shorthand as a PHOSITA). *See* 35 U.S.C. § 103. Applying the obviousness standard is one of the most troublesome tasks in patent law. Determination of obviousness is ultimately a question of law based on underlying factual observation. As such, it is a subjective evaluation.

To determine *nonobviousness*, first the scope and content of the prior art must be determined. Next, the differences between the prior art and the claim must be ascertained. Then, the level of ordinary skill of the worker in the pertinent discipline must be resolved. *See Graham v. John Deere Co.*, 383 U.S. 1 (1966). Secondary considerations — such as commercial success, long-felt needs, and failure of others to make the discovery — also are taken into account. *Id.* The Supreme Court, however, has rejected a rigid application of the so-called "teaching, suggestion, or motivation" test for determining obviousness. *KSR Int'l Co. v. Teleflex, Inc.*, 550 U.S. 398 (2007). It is easy to see why obviousness determinations frequently are lengthy proceedings involving battles of technical experts testifying why a certain invention was obvious or not.

Nothing in copyright or trademark approximates the obviousness standard. The same can be said for the *utility* requirement in patent law, requiring that the invention be useful. *See* 35 U.S.C. § 101. "Utility" means that the invention must work to accomplish some useful result.

Patent Infringement

The Patent Act allows for injunctions and up to three times actual damages for certain infringements. *See* 35 U.S.C. §§ 271–73, 281–94. Patent infringement suits brought in federal district court can be appealed only to the Court of Appeals for the Federal Circuit, a special appeals court created in 1982 in large part to handle the technicalities of patent litigation and to add a rational uniformity to patent law.

Although the patentee enjoys a statutory presumption of validity of her claims, courts can strike down a patent claim as invalid if the presumption is overcome by clear and convincing evidence. Thus, in litigation, the patentee runs the risk of having some or all claims of the patent invalidated after incurring the expense of obtaining the patent and asserting it in the litigation. The effect can be economically devastating for someone who has made substantial expenditures in the expectation that the claims would be enforceable.

[3]   Trademark Law

Generally

Unlike copyright and patent law, which are exclusively creatures of statute, the origins of trademark are in the common law. Indeed, the earliest British trademark decisions seem very distant from our modern notions of intellectual property. At its origins, trademark was a kind of "consumer protection" law, designed to prevent merchants from "passing off" inferior goods by using well-established signs or labels.

Trademark law has come a long way from its beginnings, and today federal statutes confer on proprietors of marks a broad range of rights to exclude others from using confusingly similar marks (brands) in association with the same or similar products or services or in ways that harm the mark.[5] A mark can be a word, a symbol, or a device used as a brand for a product or service, so long as it is used by a business to distinguish its goods or services from those of others. *See* 15 U.S.C. § 1127. Product and service brands surround us: Coca-Cola, the Pillsbury Dough Boy, and the Golden Arches of McDonald's are examples. These trade symbols are valuable to businesses as marketing devices and to consumers as aids to choice, not only nationally but worldwide.

As noted earlier, the essence of a trademark right is in use of the mark. Thus, while the design of a trademark may be the subject matter of a copyright, the basic theories of the two forms of protection are fundamentally different. Trademarks, unlike copyrights or patents, spring into existence upon use in commerce and have an indefinite duration, enduring so long as they continue to be used and effectively distinguish goods or services. Trademarks can be abandoned by non-use. They also can fall into the public domain if they no longer distinguish the goods or services, thereby becoming the generic name of a product (*e.g.*, cellophane, aspirin, escalator).

Unlike copyright and patent, trademark is not the exclusive domain of federal law. The first trademark statutes in the United States were state laws, and even today the federal role is a coordinate (and theoretically limited) one. *See The Trademark Cases*, 100 U.S. 82 (1879). Specifically, Congress's power to legislate is limited to marks used in interstate or foreign commerce — although this restriction

---

[5] Critics of trademark law, however, believe that trade symbols create irrational brand loyalty, permitting the owner of a well-known mark to set its price for the product above the competitive price of production, and that overly strong trademark law creates barriers to the entry of new competition from lower-priced products and more efficient competitors. *See, e.g.*, Lunney, *Trademark Monopolies*, 48 Emory L.J. 367 (1999).

on federal authority has not proved particularly constraining. Meanwhile, the states continue to apply their own independent trademark systems locally. Where appropriate, of course, federal courts may consider state law-based trademark claims along with federal ones, under the principle of supplemental jurisdiction.

Protection for Unregistered Marks

Under both federal and state law, the first user of a distinctive mark may have an action against one who offers goods or services marked in a confusingly similar manner, regardless of whether or not the mark has been registered. Section 43(a) of the Federal Lanham Act, codified in Title 15 of the United States Code, specifically provides for relief in cases where a word or symbol has been used in a confusing manner; and state laws provide general relief against "passing off" as a form of "unfair competition." In addition, the states and the federal government both offer facilities for trademark registration, and these (especially the latter) are important from a practical standpoint.

Federal Registration of Trademarks

The Lanham Act establishes a registration system in the U.S. Patent and Trademark Office for trademarks, and confers substantial procedural advantages, as well as access to enhanced remedies, in cases of infringement. These advantages are powerful inducements to register.

Federal registration of trademark is obtained by filing an application in the PTO. Once filed, an application is reviewed by a trademark examiner who verifies, among other things, that: (1) the mark is not deceptive, (2) the mark is not confusingly similar to another mark, and (3) the mark is not merely descriptive of the goods or deceptively misdescriptive of them. *See* 15 U.S.C. § 1052(a), (d), (e). After that verification, the mark is published for possible opposition. If unopposed, the mark will be registered. Although an applicant can base his application on an *intent to use* the mark in commerce as well as on *actual use*, registration will not issue until actual use of the mark is proved. *See* 15 U.S.C. § 1051(b)(1)(A).

The examination process for a trademark is usually neither as lengthy nor as costly as for a patent. The trademark application is relatively simple to draw up, as compared with the patent application. And although there are lawyers who have expertise in trademark registration, no special qualifications are required for trademark practice. Nevertheless, the trademark registration process can be much more intricate and costly than filing for registration of copyright — at least in part because, as we shall see, there is often more at stake!

Trademark Infringement

A trademark is infringed when a later third party, without authorization, uses a confusingly similar mark on similar goods or services. The ultimate test is whether the simultaneous use of the marks in connection with their respective goods or services would be likely to cause consumers to be mistaken or confused about the source of origin or sponsorship of the goods or services. Thus, the later mark does not have to be identical, or need to be used on an identical product, to be confusingly similar and hence infringing.

Trademark Dilution

Generally speaking, a successful action for trademark infringement requires that the plaintiff and the defendant be in competition. That is how confusion becomes likely. But the laws of some states have long provided the owners of protected marks with limited remedies against the non-competitive use of similar marks which "dilute" the distinctive quality (and, hence, the value) of the originals, even though no confusion is likely. In 1995, Congress also passed a provision (adding a new § 43(c) to the Lanham Act) to safeguard so-called "famous" marks against dilution. The statute contains some criteria for courts to use in assessing whether a mark is "famous," although the issue is by no means clear-cut. Only injunctive relief is available — unless the wrongful use was a "willful" one. After the Supreme Court interpreted the Act to require "actual dilution,"[6] Congress passed an amendment (the Trademark Dilution Revision Act of 2006) to clarify that only a likelihood of dilution is required.

[C] State Intellectual Property Law

In addition to federal law, a diverse system of state intellectual property law also plays a significant role in protecting intangible property. State protection of intangible property may supplement federal protection and fill gaps not addressed by federal law. On occasion, too, it may conflict with the purposes and particulars of federal intellectual property law — a topic dealt with in detail in Chapter 11.

[1] Unfair Competition and Trade Secrets

As already noted, state "unfair competition" laws are (among other things) a complement to the federal trademark statute, providing a cause of action when one company passes off its goods or services, or itself, as something or someone else. In this sense, an action for unfair competition may involve trademark infringement; use of confusingly similar corporate names; use of similar titles of literary works, products, or containers; or trade dress similarities. False representations and false advertising also fall under this definition of unfair competition.

Likewise, federal patent law is complemented by state trade secret laws. As defined by the original Restatement of Torts, a trade secret is:

> any formula, pattern, device, or compilation of information which is used in one's business, which gives [that person] an opportunity to obtain an advantage over competitors who do not know or use it. [A trade secret] may be a formula for a chemical compound; a process of manufacturing, treating or preserving materials; a pattern for a machine or other device; or a list of customers.

Restatement of Torts § 757, cmt. *b* (1939); *see also* Restatement, Third, of Unfair Competition (1995); Uniform Trade Secrets Act (1985).

---

[6] *See Moseley v. V Secret Catalogue, Inc.*, 537 U.S. 418 (2003) (requiring proof of harm in a case claiming that the mark "Victoria's Secret" was diluted by an adult-oriented shop using the name "Victor's Little Secret").

In other words, trade secret law can protect much the same technological information as does patent law, but trade secret is even broader in its subject matter, extending to customer lists, marketing plans, and other information not included within patentable subject matter. Moreover, a trade secret does not have to meet the rigorous standards of inventiveness required by patent law. For these reasons, some businesses decide not to seek patent protection if the risk of being rejected for lack of patent-eligible subject matter or inventiveness is substantial, so that the time and expense of the patent application process do not seem merited. In addition, trade secrets are a particularly appropriate form of protection for processes. By its nature, a process, such as the formula for making Coca-Cola, can be practiced secretly by a few people and often is difficult to determine by reverse engineering. Compared with the patent exclusivity that runs an average of about 17 years (beginning on grant date and ending 20 years from filing), a trade secret may exist indefinitely, so long as substantial secrecy is maintained.

Trade secrecy is, however, no general substitute for patent protection. One crucial limitation is that a valid trade secret exists only if its proprietor takes steps to maintain its secrecy, and if, in fact, it is substantially secret within the trade secret owner's industry.[7] In addition, both independent development and permissible reverse engineering are defenses to a trade secret claim.

Even where a valid trade secret exists, however, it may sometimes be worth less in practice than other forms of intellectual property. Trade secrets have the attributes of property and can be licensed, taxed, and inherited. But if an attribute of property is the right to exclude others from using it, the trade secret is a weak form of property protection. A trade secret can be enforced only against improper appropriation, such as theft by an industrial spy or breach of a contractual commitment not to divulge the trade secret. This is why it is often said that trade secret law protects a relationship rather than a property interest.

Many companies use a combination of patent and trade secret protection for a new product. This is permissible because the patent laws do not require every aspect of an invention to be disclosed in a patent application, and because secrets developed after filing the patent application need not be disclosed at all.[8]

[2]   Other State Law Theories

In addition to such traditional forms of state law protection, the right of publicity is a relatively new body of law, with similarities to copyright and trademark law. Misappropriation, an older and theoretically more dubious area of state law, may remain available, at least in certain limited factual situations. Finally, unlike trade secret law, which thrives despite the proximity of its subject matter to that of patent, so called "common-law copyright" is now almost entirely preempted by federal law.

---

[7] *See* R. Milgrim, MILGRIM ON TRADE SECRETS § 2.01 (2013).

[8] Typical examples of trade secrets remaining after patenting include the identities of reliable parts vendors, desirable dimensions and tolerances, and information developed post-filing on materials, catalysts, and product configurations.

The Right of Publicity

In 1953, a court recognized for the first time an intangible property right called the "right of publicity." *See Haelan Laboratories, Inc. v. Topps Chewing Gum, Inc.*, 202 F.2d 866 (2d Cir. 1953). A body of law already had developed around the right of privacy, prohibiting appropriation of a plaintiff's name or likeness for commercial benefit. If a private person's name or likeness is used to advertise a commercial product, for example, the law allows an injunction and damages for this invasion of a private citizen's right to be let alone. When the persona of an athlete, movie star, or other celebrity is exploited in this way, the argument that a privacy interest has been invaded is less persuasive. By implication, celebrities have waived many aspects of their privacy. The harm occurs because the celebrity has been deprived of a property right in the fruit of her labors: specifically, the ability to exploit her name or likeness commercially. While the right to privacy relates to dignitary harm, the right to publicity involves commercial harm.

Some states have statutes protecting the right of publicity, *e.g.*, Cal. Civ. Code § 3344 (2009); in other states, the right is protected under common law. *See, e.g., Hirsch v. S.C. Johnson & Son, Inc.*, 280 N.W.2d 129 (Wis. 1979). The right of publicity is not uniform from state to state. Jurisdictions take varying approaches to questions such as the availability of the right to non-celebrities and the descendibility of the right after the death of the individual depicted. *See, e.g., Martin Luther King, Jr., Center for Social Change, Inc. v. American Heritage Products, Inc.*, 694 F.2d 674 (11th Cir. 1983) (publicity right survives death under Georgia law); *Southeast Bank v. Lawrence*, 489 N.E.2d 744 (N.Y. 1985) (publicity right does not survive death under Florida law); Cal. Civ. Code § 3344.1 (statutory right of publicity limited to life of "personality" and 70 years after his or her death). Whatever its precise form and content, however, the right of publicity is a more absolute right than either trademark or general unfair competition rights, and is based on a theory of unjust enrichment. An action for invasion of the right of publicity does not require proof of confusion of source or sponsorship, or falsity — only proof of appropriation of goodwill by the defendant's unauthorized use of the plaintiff's name or likeness.

The policy favoring the right of publicity is debatable. Supporters maintain that there is a "natural right" to use one's likeness for commercial purposes, and that recognition encourages artistic creativity, much as federal copyright law does. Opponents argue that the right of publicity is too broad, and that other branches of intellectual property, such as trademark and unfair competition, adequately promote many of the same objectives.[9]

Such debates aside, the right of publicity continues to be a growth area in the law. Some decisions have extended protection under the right well beyond the core interests — name and likeness — to various other traits and attributes associated with a celebrity's "image." *See, e.g., White v. Samsung Electronics America, Inc.*,

---

[9] *See generally* Dogan & Lemley, *What the Right of Publicity Can Learn from Trademark Law*, 58 Stan. L. Rev. 1161 (2006); McKenna, *The Right of Publicity and Autonomous Self-Definition*, 67 U. Pitt. L. Rev. 225 (2005); Madow, *Private Ownership of Public Image: Popular Culture and Publicity Rights*, 81 Cal. L. Rev. 127 (1993); Coombe, *Authorizing the Celebrity: Publicity Rights, Postmodern Politics, and Unauthorized Genders*, 10 Cardozo Arts & Ent. L.J. 365 (1992).

971 F.2d 1395 (9th Cir. 1992) (reprinted in § 11.03 of this casebook, along with a remarkable dissent from the denial of rehearing *en banc* by Judge Alex Kozinski). Courts also have struggled with the proper standard for balancing the right of publicity against free speech. *See, e.g., ETW Corp. v. Jireh Publishing, Inc.*, 332 F.3d 915 (6th Cir. 2003) (lithographs of a painting of Tiger Woods); *Comedy III Prods., Inc. v. Gary Saderup, Inc.*, 21 P.3d 797 (Cal. 2001) (lithographs of a drawing of the Three Stooges).

Misappropriation

The misappropriation doctrine is the broadest, and also the vaguest, theory protecting intangible property under state law.[10] The doctrine traces its name to the Supreme Court's decision in *International News Service v. Associated Press*, 248 U.S. 215 (1918), a case involving two competing news services. There, INS systematically pirated the substance of "hot news" stories from the AP service and transmitted the rewrites to INS's West Coast affiliates, sometimes actually beating AP newspapers there to publication. INS's activities did not violate any traditional bodies of intellectual property law. AP had not copyrighted its stories; and, insofar as INS had gathered the news from public sources, there was no breach of trust on which to base an action for theft of trade secrets. Despite this lack of traditional intellectual property protection, the Supreme Court held that INS's activities constituted a new variety of unfair competition called "misappropriation." The Court enjoined INS from using AP news reports until the commercial value of the news (its "hotness," so to speak) had dissipated.

The decision in *Erie Railroad Co. v. Tompkins*, 304 U.S. 64 (1938), effectively invalidated many prior exercises in federal judicial law-making, including that in *INS*. But the misappropriation doctrine continues to exist on the fringes of state intellectual property law. The strong cases typically have arisen when (1) the plaintiff, by substantial investment, has created a valuable intangible not protected by patent, trademark, copyright, or trade secret law, which property is (2) appropriated by the defendant, a free rider, at little cost, thereby (3) injuring the plaintiff and jeopardizing her continued production of the intangible.[11] Under this theory, the Metropolitan Opera sought to enjoin the unauthorized recording of its broadcasts, *Metropolitan Opera Association v. Wagner-Nichols Recorder Corp.*, 101 N.Y.S.2d 483 (Sup. Ct. 1950), *aff'd*, 107 N.Y.S.2d 795 (1951); and, before sound recordings were given protection by federal law in 1971, record companies attacked pandemic record piracy in the state courts. *See Goldstein v. California*, 412 U.S. 546 (1973). In both situations, although the plaintiffs were unable to base their claims on traditional bodies of intellectual property law, they succeeded under the misappropriation doctrine.

---

[10] Note that conduct that violates state trade secret or right of publicity law is also referred to as "misappropriation," and that conduct that violates federal copyright law is sometimes referred to as "improper appropriation." It is important not to confuse the *doctrine* of misappropriation with other uses of the word, which may simply refer to a court's conclusion that a particular use of another's intellectual property is infringing.

[11] *See* 2 J.T. McCarthy, Trademarks and Unfair Competition § 10.51 (2013).

Some courts have expressed hostility toward the misappropriation doctrine, believing that it conflicts with the policy underlying federal patent and copyright law and therefore is preempted under the Supremacy Clause of the Constitution. In 1929, for example, Judge Learned Hand refused to apply the doctrine to dress-design piracy on this ground, *Cheney Bros. v. Doris Silk Corp.*, 35 F.2d 279 (2d Cir. 1929); and, in two 1964 decisions, the Supreme Court struck down Illinois unfair competition laws as clashing with the policies of federal patent law, *Sears, Roebuck & Co. v. Stiffel Co.*, 376 U.S. 225 (1964), and *Compco Corp. v. Day-Brite Lighting, Inc.*, 376 U.S. 234 (1964).

The more recent history of the doctrine in the courts is mixed. *Compare Board of Trade v. Dow Jones & Co.*, 456 N.E.2d 84 (Ill. 1983) (plaintiff's investment in stock index misappropriated), *with U.S. Golf Association v. St. Andrews Systems, Inc.*, 749 F.2d 1028 (3d Cir. 1984) (no misappropriation of formula for calculating golf handicaps). The continued vitality of the misappropriation doctrine apparently was confirmed in *Barclays Capital, Inc. v. Theflyonthewall.com, Inc.*, 650 F.3d 876 (2d Cir. 2011) (discussing misappropriation at length, although ultimately finding preemption on specific facts). The impact of § 301 of the 1976 Copyright Act on misappropriation is discussed below in § 11.02.

Misappropriation also has experienced something of a revival in the legislative arena, being pressed into service as a basis for proposals in Congress to confer protection on subject matter incapable of protection under the standards of copyright law (*e.g.*, computer databases). Not everyone is delighted. On the contrary, U.S. Court of Appeals Judge Richard Posner has urged that the tort be banished from the law books. Posner, *Misappropriation: A Dirge*, 40 Hous. L. Rev. 621 (2003). The future development of misappropriation, in Congress as in the courts, remains to be seen.

"Common-Law Copyright"

Under the 1909 Act, federal copyright protection generally began when an author *published* her work. With the exception of motion pictures and other works not intended for reproduction, *see* § 12 of the 1909 Act, *un*published works were given protection, if at all, under state law-based "common-law copyright" — a somewhat misleading label, because the right was codified in some jurisdictions, and because, historically, it was *not* entirely analogous to a federal statutory copyright.[12] In any event, the 1976 Act now protects works as of their *creation*, that is, from the moment that original expression becomes fixed in a tangible medium (paper, hard drive, etc.). *See* 17 U.S.C. § 102(a). In so doing, the 1976 Act specifically preempts any equivalent rights under state law. *See* 17 U.S.C. § 301.

Such state-created rights still may play a role if a work is not fixed in a tangible medium of expression. An example of such a work would be an extemporaneous

---

[12] The right at common law may more properly be described as the right to prevent an unauthorized publication of a previously unpublished manuscript. For a detailed discussion, see Joyce, *"A Curious Chapter in the History of Judicature"*: Wheaton v. Peters *and the Rest of the Story (of Copyright in the New Republic)*, 42 Hous. L. Rev. 325, 331 n.14 (2005). For an example of the persistence of the notion of a perpetual common-law copyright that survived public distribution of the work, see *Capitol Records, Inc. v. Naxos of America, Inc.*, 830 N.E.2d 250 (N.Y. 2005), discussed in § 3.01[F].

speech or jazz improvisation. The states are not precluded from protecting these non-fixed works under their own copyright laws. In practice, few courts have even considered copyright protection for oral works, but some have recognized its possibility. *See, e.g., Estate of Hemingway v. Random House, Inc.*, 244 N.E.2d 250 (N.Y. 1968) (discussed in § 2.01 below).

§ 1.03 HISTORY OF ANGLO-AMERICAN COPYRIGHT LAW

Understanding modern copyright law requires familiarity with its development. The process of adapting copyright to new economic and technological developments requires judges, lawyers, and legislators to return to first principles more often than with many other bodies of law. Understanding the history of how these principles have informed prior developments in the law is essential. Moreover, it is difficult to understand or explain numerous provisions and doctrines of current law without reference to the circumstances under which they were developed or adopted.

[A] The Beginnings to *Donaldson v. Beckett* (1774)

The development of copyright law has been a continuing response to the challenge posed by new technologies for the reproduction and distribution of human expression. Since the late 19th Century, for example, copyright in the United States has adapted to assimilate photography, motion pictures, and sound recordings. Today, at both the national and international levels, we are debating how best to modify copyright law to regulate use of digital information technology in general, and digital networks (such as the Internet) in particular. The connection between technological change and copyright is nothing new. Indeed, the first copyright statute was a reaction (albeit one delayed more than 200 years) to a new technology of the 15th Century: printing with movable type.

The relationship between technological stimulus and legal response is a complex one, intermediated by many other factors. Although we sometimes hear it said that developments in new information technology "demand" or "require" particular modifications in intellectual property doctrine, it probably is more accurate to say that such developments alter economic, cultural, and social relationships to create the conditions for change in copyright law. What form that change actually takes, in turn, is strongly influenced by both political and ideological considerations.

Introduced into England in 1476 by William Caxton, the modern printing press allowed large-scale reproduction of books for the first time. This new technology enriched printers and booksellers (although not necessarily authors). It also created, for the first time, significant competition among such publishers. "Competition over the right to publish a given text," it has been noted, "also introduced controversy over new issues involving monopoly and piracy."[1] And, not so incidentally, the new technology threatened the Crown, which shuddered at the thought of widespread dissemination of works advocating religious heresy and political dissent. The Crown's solution to the problem was a system of regulation

---

[1] E. Eisenstein, THE PRINTING REVOLUTION IN EARLY MODERN EUROPE 84 (Canto ed. 1993).

designed to control this "dangerous" art. In 1534, a royal decree prohibited anyone from publishing without a license and approval by official censors. In 1557, the Crown conferred a publishing monopoly on the Stationers' Company — a group of London printers and booksellers who could be relied upon to do the Crown's bidding while lining their own pockets.[2]

After a controversial and checkered career, during which the stationers' rights were used as an instrument of both monopoly and press control, official licensing to publish expired in 1694, leaving the Company unsheltered by regulation and vulnerable to competition from "upstart" publishers. Parliament heeded the Company's predictions of economic disaster and anarchy and, in response to these lobbying efforts, passed the first copyright act, the Statute of Anne,[3] 8 Anne, ch. 19, in 1710,[4] whose repercussions none in its own day could have anticipated fully[5] — and whose 300th anniversary this edition of the casebook continues to celebrate.[6]

The Statute of Anne, as even the stationers could see was inevitable, provided them lesser rights than had the late (and little-lamented) licensing acts. The new legislation maintained until 1731 the stationers' rights in works already printed. For new works, however, it granted protection to *authors themselves*, thereby seeming to break the stationers' historic monopoly. Prior to 1710, the stationers might have lobbied for a new statutory scheme which vested legal rights in, for example, the first individual to publish a given work. But they did not. For a variety of strategic and tactical reasons, they grudgingly put their weight behind a different approach, under which rights in new works would belong, in the first instance, to the "authors" who created them.

---

[2] B. Kaplan, An Unhurried View of Copyright 23 n.5 (1967).

[3] For the curious, Queen Anne, the second daughter of James II, succeeded to the throne in 1702 upon the death of William of Orange, who with Anne's elder sister, Mary, had ruled as joint sovereigns since the Glorious Revolution of 1688. When the crowns of England and Scotland were united in 1707, Anne became the first monarch of the United Kingdom of Great Britain. Upon her death without issue in 1714, she was succeeded by her second cousin, George I of the House of Hanover, whose grandson would live to see the American Revolution and the Constitution of the United States, including a certain clause on copyright patterned after the language of Anne's famous Statute.

[4] For an overview of the early development of copyright law, see L.R. Patterson, Copyright in Historical Perspective (1968).

[5] Indeed, "[w]hile the fundamental rationale for the [Statute of Anne] is identifiable and comprehensible, this does not necessarily mean that, at the time, there was any clear idea of appreciation as to what was meant by the concept of actually having a property in books. [The author of *Robinson Crusoe*, Daniel] Defoe, writing in his *Review*, at one point made reference to 'the miserable Havock that is made in this Nation, with the Property of the Subject, with Relation to Books.' " Ronan Deazley, On the Origin of the Right to Copy (2004).

[6] Exactly *which* date to celebrate presents a matter of at least modest difficulty, owing to calendrical revisions effected in Great Britain (and thus the American colonies) in 1752 in order to conform differing calendars in England and Europe. The details are recited in fascinating detail in W. Patry, Patry on Copyright § 1.9 n.18 (2010). For present purposes, however, the simplest solution seems the best. According to the Statute of Anne itself, its provisions became effective "from and after the tenth day of April one thousand seven hundred and ten" . . . whenever that may have occurred!

Queen Anne (1665-1714)

The printers' and booksellers' petitions to Parliament emphasized the attractively public-spirited argument that to secure authors' rights would serve the general good, because it would tend toward the "encouragement of learning." Moreover, because authors' copyrights, along with their manuscripts, could then be purchased by stationers, such legislation would provide the latter with a legal basis for combatting the outsiders whose activities threatened the economic health of the book trade. Once again, the public interest in receiving a steady flow of new printed materials would be advanced. In short, the stationers asked "that 'literary property' be secured to the writer or his assignee, or to the purchaser of the copy [that is, the exclusive right of reproduction]," and in doing so "managed to give prominence to the protection of authors without undermining their own position."[7]

Parliament took the public interest justifications for copyright seriously in adopting the Statute of Anne, as evidenced by the language of the enactment clause stating that the purpose of the new legislation was "the Encouragement of Learned Men to Compose and Write useful Books." It is apparent, as well, in the fact that the Statute, while rewarding authors for their creations, temporally limited their rights.[8] New books were given a first term of protection of 14 years for authors and

---

[7] Feather, *The Book Trade in Politics: The Making of the Copyright Act of 1710*, 8 Pub. Hist. 19, 30 (1980).

[8] *See* M. Rose, AUTHORS AND OWNERS: THE INVENTION OF COPYRIGHT 45-46 (1993); J. Feather, PUBLISHING,

their assigns, measured from the date of first publication, plus a second term of 14 years available to the author if he lived to its commencement. After that, the work entered what we know today as the "public domain" — a matter of no small consequence for learning and liberty.[9] The Act defined the "copyright" as including the liberties of printing, reprinting, and selling a book. Infringement occurred when a third party printed, reprinted, or imported the book without consent. The protection granted was basically no more than a prohibition against literal copying. To enforce these rights, a copyright owner (the author or — more likely — his or her assignee) had to register the title of the book with the Stationers' Company before its publication.

Notwithstanding the public interest features (like price controls on books, which proved short-lived, and mandatory library deposit, which did not), the Statute of Anne proved to be a boon to the stationers — at least in the short run. In the decades that followed, they continued to do business much as before, purchasing authors' new statutory rights for lump-sum payments and reaping whatever profits the success of those works in the marketplace might generate. One development that the stationers/publishers could not easily have foreseen, however, was that the powerful genie of "authorship," which they had conjured up in the years prior to 1710, ultimately might prove difficult to control and impossible to rebottle.

In fact, the stationers summoned that genie once again, later in the 18th Century, in their effort to defeat the limitations on copyright term which were a prominent feature of the Statute of Anne. The case was *Donaldson v. Beckett*, 2 Bro. P.C. 129, 1 Eng. Rep. 837, 4 Burr. 2408, decided in 1774. The plaintiff was an authorized publisher who argued to the House of Lords that he was entitled to relief on account of the defendant's unauthorized reprints — even though the statutory term of copyright in the work in question had expired. The plaintiff's theory was that, before the Statute of Anne, authors had enjoyed a perpetual copyright, and that, as the assignee of all of the author's rights, he should enjoy a right of action at common law notwithstanding the terms of the Statute. Although the idea of a perpetual common-law right found little support in history, it resonated sympathetically with the developing notion of "authorship" as a privileged category of human activity — and with the concomitant vision of authors' rights as "natural rights." *See* § 1.04 below. Although the plaintiff in *Donaldson* ultimately failed to carry the day,[10] the widely reported arguments about the "question of literary property" influenced future thinking about copyright and "authorship" on both sides of the Atlantic — as did the sympathetic treatment of the "natural rights" of "authors" in Blackstone's COMMENTARIES, arguably the most influential legal treatise of all time.[11] This was a notion which, if carried far enough, could prove inimical both to the interests of publishers and to the interests of the consuming public at large in "the encouragement of learning."

PIRACY AND POLITICS: AN HISTORICAL STUDY OF COPYRIGHT IN BRITAIN (1994).

[9] *See generally* Ochoa, *Origins and Meanings of the Public Domain*, 28 U. Dayton L. Rev. 215 (2003).

[10] *See* Rose, *The Author as Proprietor:* Donaldson v. Beckett *and the Genealogy of Modern Authorship*, 23 Representations 51, 69 & n.63 (1988).

[11] *See* W. Blackstone, 2 COMMENTARIES ON THE LAWS OF ENGLAND 405-06 (1766, facs. ed. 1979).

[B]   From the Constitution to the Copyright Act of 1909

Not surprisingly, in light of the background just outlined, the development of copyright law in the United States has been marked by a considerable measure of conceptual diversity. From Great Britain, the new republic had inherited a set of mixed messages about the purposes of copyright.[12] On the one hand, copyright was viewed as an instrument in the service of the public interest. On the other hand, it could be considered the natural due of those who engage in artistic creation.

Egged on, in part, by a resolution of the Continental Congress,[13] 12 of the new American states (excluding only Delaware) enacted or provisionally adopted copyright statutes shortly after the American Revolution. Many of these "pre-Constitutional" statutes placed heavy emphasis on the personal claims of "authors" like Noah Webster (of speller and dictionary fame).[14]

Soon thereafter, the Framers of the Constitution recognized the need for a uniform *federal* law for copyright and patents.[15] The result was Article I, Section 8, Clause 8, which creates the Federal Government's right to legislate regarding copyright and patent: "Congress shall have Power . . . To promote the Progress of Science and useful Arts, by securing for limited Times, to Authors and Inventors, the exclusive Right to their respective Writings and Discoveries."

Little is known about what precisely the Framers had in mind in adopting this provision, which was approved in final form without debate in a secret proceeding on September 5, 1787.[16] The constitutional language — which does not even employ the term "copyright" — seems to suggest that the dominant purpose of the Framers was to promote the creation (and, by implication, the dissemination) of knowledge, so as to enhance public welfare. This goal is to be achieved through provision of an *economic* incentive: a monopoly right given for "limited Times," whose direct beneficiary is the "Author." But it would be perilous to conclude that the Framers rejected entirely the ideology of "authorship." Why, for example, does the Copyright Clause speak of "securing" the rights of authors, unless those rights might be deemed, in some sense, preexistent?[17] And what are we to make of the statements of various of the Framers, seeming to endorse notions of "authors' rights"? In the end, the ambiguity of the constitutional language may be nothing

---

[12] *See generally* Jaszi, *Towards a Theory of Copyright: The Metamorphoses of Authorship*, 41 Duke L.J. 455 (1991).

[13] *Resolution passed by the Continental Congress, recommending the several States to secure to the Authors or Publishers of New Books the Copyright of such Books, May 2, 1783*, reprinted in U.S. COPYRIGHT OFFICE, COPYRIGHT ENACTMENTS: LAWS PASSED IN THE UNITED STATES SINCE 1783 RELATING TO COPYRIGHTS, BULL. NO. 3 (rev. ed. 1973).

[14] Ginsburg, *A Tale of Two Copyrights: Literary Property in Revolutionary France and America*, 64 Tul. L. Rev. 991, 1001 & n.44 (1990).

[15] *See generally* Crawford, *Pre-Constitutional Copyright Statutes*, 23 Bull. Copyright Soc'y 11 (1975).

[16] *See* Oman, *The Copyright Clause: "A Charter For A Living People,"* 17 U. Balt. L. Rev. 99, 103 (1987). *See generally* Ochoa & Rose, *The Anti-Monopoly Origins of the Patent and Copyright Clause*, 49 J. Copyright Soc'y 675 (2002); Oliar, *Making Sense of the Intellectual Property Clause: Promotion of Progress as a Limitation on Congress's Intellectual Property Power*, 94 Geo. L.J. 1771 (2006).

[17] *See generally* Walterscheid, THE NATURE OF THE INTELLECTUAL PROPERTY CLAUSE: A STUDY IN HISTORICAL PERSPECTIVE 133-39 (2002) (discussing The Federalist No. 43).

more than a reflection of the divided character of American thought — from the earliest times to the present day — about the purposes of the copyright system.

The First American Printing Press (Harvard 1640)
Corbis

In any event, the first federal copyright act was passed, pursuant to the new constitutional authority, in 1790. Its provisions, modeled on the Statute of Anne, set the tone for future statutes, securing to authors and their assigns the rights to print and sell maps, charts, and books for two 14-year terms — an original and a renewal term. Finally, in 1791, the several states ratified the Bill of Rights, including the free press (and speech) provisions drafted in the First Congress by many of the same founding generation who had participated in drafting the 1783 resolution of the Continental Congress, the Copyright Clause of the Constitution, and the 1790 Act. All of these matters have received recent scholarly consideration.[18]

Judicial construction of the new American copyright law, including most notably in *Wheaton v. Peters*, 33 U.S. (8 Pet.) 591, in 1834,[19] followed *Donaldson v. Beckett*

---

[18] *See, e.g.*, Lemley & Volokh, *Freedom of Speech and Injunctions in Intellectual Property Cases*, 48 Duke L.J. 147 (1998); Netanel, *Locating Copyright Within the First Amendment Skein*, 54 Stan. L. Rev. 1 (2001); Patterson & Joyce, *Copyright in 1791: An Essay Concerning the Founders' View of the Copyright Power Granted to Congress in Article I, Section 8, Clause 8 of the U.S. Constitution*, 52 Emory L.J. 101 (2003).

[19] The case is discussed at length in Joyce, *"A Curious Chapter in the History of Judicature"*:

in insisting upon the primacy of federal law, and punctilious compliance with its formalities, in the scheme of American copyright. General revisions of the applicable statutes in 1831 and 1870, as well as other important piecemeal amendments prior to the first comprehensive recodification of U.S. copyright law in 1909, greatly elaborated subject matter, rights, remedies, and administration.[20]

[C]   The 1909 Act

[1]   General Provisions of the 1909 Act

In 1905, President Theodore Roosevelt called for a complete revision of the copyright law to meet modern conditions. The result was the Copyright Act of 1909, which remained in effect until January 1, 1978, the effective date of the current law (as since amended many times): the Copyright Act of 1976.

The 1909 Act was hardly a model of clarity, coherence, or precision. But it did contain important new features. For instance, copyrightable subject matter was expanded to include "all the writings of an author." *See* 17 U.S.C. § 4 (1909 Act). The Act included a bifurcated durational system — a first term of 28 years from publication, plus a second 28-year renewal term — allowing copyright protection for a possible 56 years. *See* 17 U.S.C. § 24 (1909 Act). Under the Act, federal copyright protection began at the moment of publication (assuming affixation of a proper copyright notice), *see* 17 U.S.C. § 10 (1909 Act), rather than from the time the title of the work was filed for registration, as had previously been true. Except for works not intended for reproduction (such as speeches), unpublished works were not covered by the Act, resulting in a dual system of state protection for unpublished works and federal protection for published works.

[2]   The 1909 Act and the Berne Convention

Congress in 1909 chose not to amend U.S. law to conform to the terms of the then-relatively new Berne Convention for the Protection of Literary and Artistic Works. Concluded in 1886, the Berne Convention was the first and, for well more than a century now, has remained the most important treaty governing international copyright relations. By the mid-1980s, the parties to the treaty included every major producer and/or consumer of copyright works except China, the then-Soviet Union, and the United States. By its continuation of traditional American insistence on compliance with certain statutory formalities for copyright protection, its shorter term of protection, and other provisions, the 1909 Act delayed U.S. entry into the Berne Union for 80 years.[21] The eventual adherence of the U.S. to the Berne Convention is discussed further in § 1.04 below.

Wheaton v. Peters *and the Rest of the Story (of Copyright in the New Republic)*, 42 Hous. L. Rev. 325 (2005).

[20] For a more detailed history of the various statutory revisions to U.S. copyright law, see Chapter 1 of W. Patry, PATRY ON COPYRIGHT (2010).

[21] For a comprehensive study of the Berne Convention's origins, development, and provisions, see S. Ricketson & J. Ginsburg, INTERNATIONAL COPYRIGHT AND NEIGHBORING RIGHTS: THE BERNE CONVENTION AND BEYOND (2nd ed. 2005).

[3]   Legislative Attempts to Revise the 1909 Act

From 1909 until the passage of the 1976 Act, changing times and technologies forced Congress to amend the 1909 Act in major ways — a task Congress carried out sporadically. For example, motion pictures were added as a subject matter category in 1912, and in 1952 a right to authorize performance for profit was provided for nondramatic literary works. In 1954, the United States ratified the Universal Copyright Convention (the "U.C.C."). The U.C.C. provides nondiscriminatory protection in all member nations for works created by nationals of other treaty countries or first published within their borders. The minimum rights protected under the U.C.C. are less extensive than those of the Berne Convention; and the U.C.C., in contrast with the Berne Convention, permits signatories to require that published works bear a prescribed notice — a provision included to accommodate the United States.

After some years, it became apparent that the 1909 Act was beyond repair and should be replaced by new legislation. In 1955, Congress authorized a copyright revision project. Twenty-one years of reports and extensive hearings culminated in the passage of the Copyright Act of 1976. Act of October 19, 1976, Pub. L. No. 94-553, 90 Stat. 2541. *See also* H.R. Rep. No. 94-1476 at 47-50 (1976); S. Rep. 94-473 (1975); H.R. Rep. No. 94-1733 (1976) (Conference Report).

[4]   The Continuing Importance of the 1909 Act

Although the Copyright Act of 1976 became effective on January 1, 1978, and the Berne Convention Implementation Act on March 1, 1989, the 1909 Act remains relevant for several reasons. Most important, neither the 1976 Act nor any subsequent copyright legislation extends retroactive protection to domestic works. Copyright in a U.S. work which entered the public domain under the 1909 Act is not revived by these later acts. In addition, the 1976 Act specifically incorporated provisions of the prior law and retained standards developed in 1909 Act case law for important issues such as originality and infringement.

[D]   The Copyright Act of 1976

[1]   Important Changes Made by the 1976 Act

The 1976 Act made a number of innovative changes, in addition to clarifying various aspects of existing law.[22] Subsequently, certain of these innovations have themselves been subjected to modification. As enacted, however, the more important changes made by the Act included:

(1) *Attachment of protection.* Under the 1909 Act, most works that qualified for federal copyright protection did so on the basis of a publication in connection with which statutory requirements, such as the use of copyright notice, were observed. Under the 1976 Act, the event which qualifies a work for protection is its "fixation" in tangible form. One effect of this change was to expand dramatically the scope of

---

[22] For a provocative discussion of the innovations of the 1976 Act, see L.R. Patterson & S. Lindberg, The Nature of Copyright: A Law of Users' Rights (1991).

federal law: Only a minority of all works are ever published, but most (by far) are "fixed." The concomitant effect was to diminish dramatically the scope of "common-law copyright" under state law. As already noted, § 301 of the 1976 Act preempts common-law copyright, which had bedeviled administration of the 1909 Act. *See* 17 U.S.C. § 301.

(2) *Subject matter.* The 1976 Act protects "original works of authorship" — a rubric that we will consider in detail in Chapter 2. What constitutes sufficient originality for a valid copyright is governed, in the first instance, by precedent carried over from prior case law. For the first time, the Act established broad illustrative categories of copyrightable subject matter. These were (as of the date of enactment): (1) literary works; (2) musical works; (3) dramatic works; (4) panto-mimes and choreographic works; (5) pictorial, graphic, and sculptural works; (6) motion pictures and other audiovisual works; and (7) sound recordings. *See* 17 U.S.C. § 102(a). The last of these categories recapitulated a statutory innovation dating back to 1971, when, for the first time, sound recordings themselves were recognized as copyrightable works distinct from, and in addition to, the musical or literary works they embodied. The scope of protection provided for such works, however, was narrower than that afforded to works in the six preceding categories, excluding as it did any right against unauthorized broadcasting or other public performance. *See* 17 U.S.C. §§ 106 and 114. Although, according to the legislative history of the 1976 Act, all these categories are to be construed liberally, Congress deliberately declined to use the 1909 Act formulation — "all the writings of an author" — in order to avoid any suggestion that it had exhausted its constitutional authority.

(3) *Ownership.* The 1976 Act abolished any notion of the "indivisibility" of rights under copyright which had survived in the jurisprudence of the 1909 Act. Today, it is clear that an author or other owner can grant less than all of its whole "bundle of rights" to third parties who, in turn, can exploit those rights themselves, resell them, register claims of copyright in the work, and bring suits in their own names for infringement by others of the rights granted to them. *See* 17 U.S.C. §§ 201(d) and 408(a). The Act also makes explicit that ownership of the material object in which the work is fixed does not constitute ownership of copyright in the work itself, *see* 17 U.S.C. § 202, and added a new, statutory definition to the so-called "work for hire" doctrine. *See* 17 U.S.C. § 101.

(4) *Duration.* For works created after it took effect, the Act eliminated the prior statute's dual 28-year terms for copyright, commencing from the date of publica-tion, and replaced them with a basic single term of the life of the author plus 50 years. *See* 17 U.S.C. § 302(a). An alternate term of 75 years from publication or 100 years from creation, whichever was less, was provided for anonymous and pseud-onymous works, and works made for hire. *See* 17 U.S.C. § 302(c). All such terms were extended by 20 years in 1998.

(5) *Termination rights.* Individual authors, and in some instances their survivors, were given an inalienable option to terminate transfers of interest after specified periods of time. *See* 17 U.S.C. §§ 203, 304(c).

(6) *Formalities.* Formalities remained significant under the 1976 Act, as origi-nally enacted, although less so than under previous statutes. Notice continued to be

required for all published works, and it was possible to forfeit copyright by failure to affix notice. Registration of copyright and recordation of transfers of copyright ownership remained conditions to bringing suit for infringement. A requirement mandating the domestic manufacture of copies of copyrighted works — the so-called "Manufacturing Clause," a feature of American law since 1891 — was maintained in the 1976 Act (but expired in 1986).

(7) *The "exclusive rights" and their limitations.* Section 106 of the 1976 Act, as enacted, enumerated five exclusive rights of copyright ownership: the rights to reproduce and adapt the copyrighted work, and to distribute, perform and display it publicly. The sections following § 106 imposed various limitations on the exclusive rights. *See* 17 U.S.C. §§ 107-22.

(8) *Fair use.* For the first time, § 107 of the 1976 Act codified the broadest exception to the § 106 exclusive rights: the fair use doctrine, which had been developed in case law under previous statutes.

(9) *Statutory licenses.* The 1976 Act increased the number of compulsory (which Congress now has taken to calling "statutory") licenses, which allow access to copyrighted works upon payment of the statutory fees and compliance with formalities. As originally enacted, the Act contained four such licenses: the cable television license (§ 111), the mechanical recording license (§ 115), the jukebox license (§ 116), and the public broadcasting license (§ 118). The Act provided for administration of the compulsory licenses by an administrative agency, since abolished, called the Copyright Royalty Tribunal.

[2]   Subsequent Developments Under the 1976 Act

Technology — and copyright law — have continued to develop since 1978. Revisions to the newly enacted law began as early as 1980, when a completely amended § 117 was added to the Act, establishing protection for, and the scope of rights in, computer programs. Congress has created a new exclusive right under § 106 (*viz.*, the right to perform publicly a sound recording by means of a digital audio transmission), as well as enacting new limitations, in favor of such worthy enterprises as educational and nonprofit organizations, on rights already recognized. Existing statutory licenses have been revised, and new ones added. New technologies have been accommodated. Renewals, to the extent that they remain relevant under the present law of duration, have been made automatic. Copyright infringement has been criminalized to a degree heretofore unknown. And Congress has busied itself legislating *outside the Copyright Act* (*i.e.*, Chapters 1-8 of 17 U.S.C.) but still *within Title 17*, in an area that has come to be called "paracopyright" in acknowledgment of the reality that it is based on practical concerns and constitutional powers other than those found in Art. I, § 8, cl. 8. These, and many more highlights (and "lowlights") of copyright law revision, will receive detailed treatment in the chapters that follow.

Three sets of developments, however, deserve special mention here.

The first is adherence to the Berne Convention, effective March 1, 1989, by virtue of the Berne Convention Implementation Act of 1988 ("BCIA"). Under that legislation, required to place U.S. law in compliance with Berne treaty obligations, the United States dramatically weakened its historic regime of strict statutory formalities as an impediment to copyright protection while, on the other hand, not fully implementing all of the rights, particularly "moral rights," contemplated by Berne itself. (In 1990, Congress did further amend the Copyright Act to grant a limited moral right to visual artists and to provide more extensive protection for architectural works as an eighth subject matter category; and in 1994, as noted immediately below, Congress dealt statutorily with the problem of "restoring" copyright to foreign works that had fallen into the U.S. public domain through failure to comply with such formalities.) Besides the specific changes brought about by the Berne Convention implementing legislation, U.S. adherence to that agreement has had other, more subtle, effects as the author-centered "culture" of the Berne Union gradually becomes absorbed into American legal consciousness.[23]

Second, Congress has proceeded apace in revising U.S. copyright law to better serve the nation's international trade interests. Early in 1994, as part of the implementation of the North American Free Trade Agreement ("NAFTA"), Congress added to Title 17 a new § 104A, permitting foreign copyright owners to obtain "restoration" of their copyrights in certain Mexican and Canadian films which had fallen into the public domain in the United States for failure to comply with the notice provisions of the 1976 Act. This modest experiment in retroactivity soon was subsumed in the more dramatic developments which followed the conclusion of the Final Act of the Uruguay Round of the General Agreement on Tariffs and Trade ("GATT"). In December 1994, Congress enacted the Uruguay Round Agreements Act ("URAA"), which — in the midst of much, much more (including the creation of new rights and remedies against the "bootlegging" of live performances) — provides retroactive protection for large numbers of works of foreign origin in the U.S. public domain under a wide range of circumstances.

Finally, on consecutive days in late 1998 — "the apotheosis of American copyright law" or "two days that will live in infamy," depending on one's point of view — Congress enacted two landmark pieces of legislation. The first, the "Sonny Bono Copyright Term Extension Act" or "CTEA" (October 27, 1998), extended the term of copyright protection by 20 years (including, for works created by an individual on or after January 1, 1978, a term measured by the life of the author plus 70 years). The second, the "Digital Millennium Copyright Act" or "DMCA" (October 28, 1998), enacted an astonishing host of disparate measures. Most importantly, however, the DMCA implemented the two treaties — on copyright, and on performances and phonograms — adopted by the World Intellectual Property Organization in 1996 (and discussed in the following section of the casebook). The result is a schema of "technological protections" for digitized information to which we will devote considerable attention in § 1.05 and in Chapter 9. The importance of this development, viewed from the perspective of traditional copyright law, would be difficult to overstate.

All in all, it can be said without fear of contradiction that Congress has not been idle since enacting the Copyright Act of 1976.

---

[23] *See* Jaszi, *A Garland of Reflections on Three Copyright Topics*, 8 Cardozo Arts & Ent. L.J. 47, 58 (1989).

[3]   Trends in Copyright Legislation

We mention here only two trends in all of the foregoing activity, secure in the knowledge that we have an entire book in which to explore the subject in further detail.

One trend already is obvious to you. The pressures of operating in an increasingly interconnected world — particularly as regards exchanges of intellectual property and information generally, whether or not such information technically is protected by copyright law — has forced upon U.S. lawmakers the necessity of making rapid, and quite fundamental, changes in this ancient body of law. Berne. NAFTA. TRIPS. The 1996 WIPO treaties. All of these have impinged forcefully upon copyright as Anglo-American law has known it for five centuries. We will have more to say on all of this "internationalization" of the law in the very next section of this book.

The other trend on which we will remark here is the "complexification" of U.S. copyright law over the last 30 years. In the supplement accompanying this casebook, the Copyright Act of 1909 takes up barely 25 pages, while the 1976 Act, as amended to date, is *ten times* that long. In part, this dramatic difference in the length of the two statutes is attributable to the fact that the 1976 Act goes into significantly more detail than its predecessor on almost every topic it covers. In fact, there seems to be some risk that if this trend continues, the Copyright Act eventually will collapse under its own weight. Significantly, an important fraction of the additional bulk can be traced to the various sets of provisions dealing with cable television, secondary transmissions by satellite carriers, and secondary transmissions by superstations and network stations (all of which are lodged within the body of the Copyright Act), and to the provisions governing such matters as statutory royalties for digital audio recordings, copyright management information systems, and protection of certain original designs (each of which, although not within the Act itself, lies in the "neighboring provisions" of Title 17).

The approach taken in the six sets of provisions just mentioned differs significantly from that which characterizes the rest of copyright law, past and present. Whereas copyright traditionally has responded to the social, economic, and cultural stresses resulting from new information technology by elaborating and refining rules of general applicability, these provisions, in contrast, seek to legislate particular regulatory solutions to the short-term problems posed by particular technologies in minute (if not exquisite) detail. These solutions, in turn, are based not so much on any exercise of plenary legislative authority by Congress as they are on Congressional ratification of extra-legislative compromises struck between representatives of "stakeholders" or "interested parties" — meaning, in general, the various industries with financial stakes in the outcome.[24]

Although the final verdict is still out on this approach to copyright law revision, already there is ample reason to suspect that it threatens the very enterprise of such legislation, at least as that enterprise has conventionally been understood, by creating within Title 17 a series of highly specific "mini-statutes" whose content is

---

[24] *See generally* Litman, *Copyright Legislation and Technological Change*, 68 Or. L. Rev. 275 (1989).

not shaped by policy concerns but instead by the strength of the contending lobbies. Certainly, if this trend toward "Balkanization" in copyright legislation continues, it will only become more and more difficult for anyone — let alone a nonspecialist — to make coherent sense of the overall statutory scheme.[25]

The next two sections of this book will explore in greater detail two of the sources which are exerting pressure for further changes in U.S. copyright law: developments in international law, and developments in information technology (specifically, digital technology). How Congress responds to these pressures will be an indication of whether our copyright law can continue to grow by accretion, or whether, on the other hand, it will soon require another general revision, beginning from first principles.

§ 1.04   COPYRIGHT IN A CHANGING WORLD

As the foregoing history amply demonstrates, American copyright law today has been shaped by many forces. The most obvious among these influences, and historically the most important, have been the domestic ones, including the growing economic importance and political influence of the "copyright industries," on the one hand, and various powerful competing ideologies of intellectual property, on the other. In part because of these influences, the development of U.S. law has followed a path somewhat different from that taken by the laws of other nations. Today, however, our copyright law is increasingly subject to international pressures, and — partly as a result — its future path may converge with those of other nations. The present section of the casebook explores: (1) some of the discrepancies that appear when U.S. copyright is contrasted with the copyright law of other countries; (2) current U.S. treaty obligations regarding the law of copyright; and (3) the prospects for continued, and indeed increased, harmonization of U.S. copyright laws with those of the rest of the world, particularly our trading partners.

[A]   A Comparative Law Overview

As we have noted already, the classically dominant view of American copyright law is instrumental in character: Copyright is seen as a means by which the general welfare is advanced through the provision of economic incentives to creators (and, we might add, disseminators) of new works of the intellect.

The analogue of copyright in the civil-law world is known as *droit d'auteur* in France, *derecho de autor* in Spain, and *Urheberrecht* in Germany — all terms which, translated, mean "authors' rights." The difference in terminology between the common law ("copyright") and the civil law ("authors' rights") is more than linguistic happenstance. Rather, it suggests a fundamentally different emphasis between the two legal traditions in their attitudes about works of authorship.

There are, to be sure, important differences. Just as, in common-law "copyright" jurisdictions like the United States, the provision of protection to authors (individual or corporate) and their successors conventionally is justified as a means to promote the general welfare, in "authors' rights" jurisdictions the protection of

---

[25] *See* Litman, *Revising Copyright Law in the Information Age*, 75 Or. L. Rev. 19 (1996).

literary and artistic property is justified predominantly in terms of authors' inherent entitlements — indeed, as an extension of their personalities. And the laws of "authors' rights" countries embrace doctrines that clearly reflect such an emphasis. Thus, in the civil-law world, an author is deemed to have a moral entitlement to control and exploit the products of the author's intellect, including the right of association of the work with the author's name and the right to prevent the mutilation of the author's artistic vision. Likewise, many civil-law countries balk at the practice (familiar in common-law jurisdictions) of extending legal protection to the works of corporate "authors" as such, insisting that, to be eligible for protection, a creation must be designated as the work of one or more individual authors.

Like all dichotomies, however, the distinction between the animating philosophies which undergird the laws of literary and artistic property in "copyright" and "authors' rights" jurisdictions has its utility — and its limitations. Historically, the distinction may never have been as clear-cut as it is sometimes made out to be.

For one thing, there is evidence that, even in the countries most strongly associated with the civil-law "authors' rights" tradition, the true story of the origins and development of laws of literary and artistic property is far from mono-thematic. Although literary property rights in France had an interesting, albeit limited, pre-Revolutionary history, they took hold in earnest between 1791 and 1793, when the Revolution, having abolished the "privileges" of the Old Regime in 1789, proceeded to reinvent literary and artistic property. In a famous speech to the National Convention in 1793, Joseph Lakanal declared that "authors' rights" in the "productions of genius" were justified as being, "of all properties, the least disputable, the one whose growth can neither undermine republican equality nor offend freedom. . . ." Thus, the idea of "authorship" was invoked in justification of a "natural right" so obvious and important that it should survive even a revolutionary transformation of social life.

Still, the reestablishment of authors' rights in post-Revolutionary France was not justified on the basis of natural entitlement rhetoric alone. The author was not viewed solely as an atomistic individual responsible only to himself or herself and his or her art. In addition to the celebration of genius, the debates over the reestablishment of copyright in post-Revolutionary France also invoked a public purpose rationale: The artist deserves protection, in part, because he or she is a kind of *de facto* public servant who has consecrated his or her career to serving the information needs of the masses.

Closer to home, there is substantial evidence that the American law of literary and artistic property was itself shaped by the push-and-pull between competing visions of what such a body of doctrine could and should be designed to accomplish. One of those visions — stressing the instrumental basis of copyright — came to us as a highly specific element of our English legal heritage. The other — stressing the inherent entitlement of "authors" — is traceable to the general background of English and Continental social thought against which copyright laws everywhere in Europe developed, and specifically to the early modern vision of social life which has been described as "possessive individualism."

Before the emergence of 18th Century Romanticism, which was the specific literary and artistic correlate of "possessive individualism," most creative workers had been regarded — and had regarded themselves — as craftspersons laboring (along with others) toward the creation of a product.[1] As the 18th Century progressed, however, some creative workers were singled out for privileged treatment, a development illustrating the emerging "conception of the individual as essentially the proprietor of his own person or capacities."[2]

Throughout Western Europe, including Great Britain, writers and critics influenced by these trends developed a new, celebratory vision of "authorship" as a special calling, at once above and apart from ordinary human activity. The concept of "authorship," in turn, was the organizing concept around which new laws of intellectual property were articulated, and formed part of the heritage of United States copyright law. After literary Romanticism reached its zenith in England in the early 19th Century, its exponents (most notably William Wordsworth) became deeply involved in the Parliamentary campaign for the extension and expansion of copyright. But even decades earlier, the currents of thought which fed the Romantic movement were already flowing.

One such current was the emphasis on "originality," which marks much Romantic writing about the nature of "authorship." The Romantic "author" was expected to break with the past, and to offer something new and literally unprecedented as proof of genius.[3] The effect of this development was to celebrate certain kinds of creative enterprise, but also to denigrate other efforts as less worthy.[4] This emphasis has left its highly visible traces in the jurisprudence of common-law "copyright" laws, as well as that of civil-law "authors' rights."

Today the laws of common-law and civil-law countries are, as a doctrinal matter, converging to a significant degree. This trend is, in part, attributable to recent developments in the law of international copyright that stipulate the minimum standards to which our national laws must conform. In 1985, for example, France (an "authors' rights" country *par excellence*) introduced into its law a very "copyright"-like approach to the protection of computer software; and, in 1988, Great Britain (where "copyright" originated) revised its statute from top to bottom, going a long way toward achieving harmonization with the "authors' rights" laws of its Continental neighbors. As we will see, recent legislation in the United States, especially the enactment of "moral rights" for visual artists in 1990, also reflects this tendency toward convergence.

---

[1] *See* Woodmansee, *The Genius and the Copyright*, 17 Eighteenth Century Studies 425 (1984), *reprinted in* M. Woodmansee, THE AUTHOR, THE ARTS, AND THE MARKET (1993).

[2] C.B. MacPherson, THE POLITICAL THEORY OF POSSESSIVE INDIVIDUALISM 3 (1962).

[3] For a discussion of this development, see Woodmansee, *The Genius and the Copyright*, 17 Eighteenth Century Studies 425, 429 (1984); B. Kaplan, AN UNHURRIED VIEW OF COPYRIGHT 23 (1967); and Jaszi, *When Works Collide: Derivative Motion Pictures, Underlying Rights, and the Public Interest*, 28 UCLA L. Rev. 715, 730 n. 33 (1981).

[4] Jane Ginsburg has pointed out the "Romantic literary commonplace [that characterizes] the work drawn from nature or experience as a 'copy,' and the imitation of the original as the 'copy of a copy.'" Ginsburg, *Creation and Commercial Value: Copyright Protection for Works of Information*, 90 Colum. L. Rev. 1865, 1882 n.57 (1990).

In addition, the tendencies just remarked upon also are observable if we look still further afield, to countries whose cultural and legal arrangements are profoundly different from those of the West. In feudal China, for example, Confucian literary and artistic culture focused on interaction with the past and discouraged bold innovation. Similarly, after 1949, the new socialist legal culture of the People's Republic of China proved hostile to the development of a system of private proprietary rights in works of the mind. Global economic and diplomatic pressures have changed the landscape radically. In 1992, China became a party to the Berne Convention and has adopted a copyright law indistinguishable from that of Western nations.

[B]   Major International Treaties Involving Copyright

There is not now, nor has there ever been, a "universal" copyright system. Instead, an author who wishes to protect his work abroad typically must look to the pertinent national laws of the countries where protection is sought. These national laws, in turn, are stitched together by a series of international agreements prescribing the conditions under which countries must give recognition under their domestic laws to works of foreign origin.

The present section provides an overview of the major international conventions involving copyright, with particular emphasis on the provisions of the Berne Convention and on various implementing provisions of U.S. law. To keep yourself current on these matters as they develop, a good place to begin is U.S. Copyright Office *Circular 38a: International Copyright Relations of the United States* (revised regularly).

[1]   In General

Like the most recent international copyright treaties, the earliest examples of such agreements were responses to the phenomenon of cross-border "piracy." Beginning in 1827, a series of agreements among the various German states guaranteed what is sometimes called "formal reciprocity" of protection: that works originating in a signatory state would be assimilated, for purposes of domestic law, to those created by nationals of another signatory. Subject to certain qualifications, this approach was the basis, over the next half century, of a series of bilateral agreements which eventually covered most of Europe and parts of Latin America. And it remains the fundamental principle of international copyright today, under the rubric of "national treatment."

The protection that such a network of bilateral treaties could offer authors in countries *other than their own* was far from comprehensive or systematic.[5] It fell far short of being a truly universal scheme — and it was for just such a scheme that European authors' organizations began to campaign in earnest in the 1850s. Their goal was nothing short of establishing world-wide recognition that copyright is a natural and indefeasible right which arises in the first instance — without the intermediation of the state — from the very act of "authorship" itself. Soon the

---

[5] *See* S. Ricketson & J. Ginsburg, INTERNATIONAL COPYRIGHT AND NEIGHBORING RIGHTS: THE BERNE CONVENTION AND BEYOND (2nd ed. 2005).

drive for "universal copyright" was substantially co-opted by publishers, for whom a strong international legal regime represented an important precondition for the development of a world market in books.[6] The eventual result was the 1886 Act of the Berne Convention for the Protection of Literary and Artistic Works.

A Memorial
of
American Authors.

THE undersigned American citizens who earn their living in whole or in part by their pen, and who are put at disadvantage in their own country by the publication of foreign books without payment to the author, so that American books are undersold in the American market, to the detriment of American literature, urge the passage by Congress of an International Copyright Law, which will protect the rights of authors, and will enable American writers to ask from foreign nations the justice we shall then no longer deny on our own part.

American Authors Urge Berne Adherence (sample from 1886 Memorial)

In one sense, the Berne Convention fell short of meeting the expectations of those who had campaigned most earnestly to secure it. Neither the original Act of Berne, nor any of the five revisions of the Convention, created a universal law of copyright. Like the treaties that it supplanted, Berne is premised on the principle of "national treatment." At the same time, however, the Berne Convention, as it has evolved over more than a century, has greatly improved the level of protection for copyright worldwide. This has been accomplished in two ways: first, by establishing an international copyright regime which is truly multilateral (rather than bilateral or regional), and second, by introducing the concept of Convention "minima," which supplements the principle of national treatment by setting a "floor" below which signatory countries may not go in extending protection to qualifying foreign works. As we shall see, these minima deal with issues of subject matter, duration, formalities, and other crucial matters which help to determine the real substance of any regime of copyright protection.

---

[6] *See generally* N.N. Feltes, LITERARY CAPITAL AND THE LATE VICTORIAN NOVEL (1994).

[2]   The United States and International Copyright

A little more than a century ago, the United States was the world's most notorious "pirate" nation. Today, no country is more active in the diplomatic effort to develop an orderly and responsive international regime of copyright protection. The change has everything to do with economics, and little or nothing to do with ideology. As things now stand, the United States is the world's largest producer and exporter of copyrighted works — a bright spot in the otherwise unfavorable U.S. balance of payments. As a result of this development, the United States eventually (effective March 1, 1989) adhered to the Berne Convention, the oldest — and still the preeminent — multinational copyright treaty. Since then, the United States has become a leader in developing a series of important new international agreements in the field.

Until 1891, the United States had no international copyright relations. Indeed, the American publishing industry thrived during much of the 19th Century on the basis of unauthorized, "piratical" reprints of British "best-sellers." Not until the "elite" U.S. publishing establishment began to feel economic pressure from unregulated competition in the reprinting of British books would the laws undergo change.[7]

In 1891, the so-called "Chace Act," an amendment to U.S. copyright law, authorized the President to extend protection, by proclamation, to works originating in particular foreign countries, on the condition that those countries, in turn, provide adequate protection for the works of U.S. authors. Later, after a number of such proclamations had been issued, the United States began entering into a series of bilateral copyright agreements with other countries.[8] These piecemeal arrangements became increasingly less adequate, however, in an ever-shrinking world of new communication technologies and distribution mechanisms, and in the post-World War II era, when demand for U.S. works exploded. By the 1950s, when the United States emerged as a major exporter of copyrighted works, the need for American participation in a truly integrated system of international copyright had become apparent.

In response to these developments, a group of states convened by UNESCO between 1947 and 1952 developed a new treaty — the Universal Copyright Convention ("U.C.C.") — with the specific objective of drawing previously reluctant nations into the fold of international copyright. The United States joined in 1955 (and the Soviet Union in 1973). This "junior" version of the Berne Convention was distinguished primarily by the fact that U.C.C. minima were considerably less exacting. Nonetheless, it was (at least in part) the experience of the United States with the U.C.C. that eventually helped it muster the political will to take the larger step into the Berne Convention in 1988.

One important feature of the U.C.C. is the so-called "Berne Safeguard Clause," which prohibits a Berne Convention country from denouncing Berne and relying on

---

[7] *See* J. Barnes, AUTHORS, PUBLISHERS AND POLITICIANS: THE QUEST FOR AN ANGLO-AMERICAN COPYRIGHT AGREEMENT, 1815-1854 (1974).

[8] For a cumulative list of bilateral arrangements, along with other details on the position of the United States in the world copyright system, see *Copyright Office Circular 38a.*

the U.C.C. in its copyright relations with members of the Berne Convention. Art. XVII & App. Decl. This provision resulted from the efforts of Berne Union members who feared that the U.C.C. was a step backward and wanted to prevent Berne principles from being undermined by its members' adherence to the new treaty. Thus, the United States, now a member of Berne, cannot look to the U.C.C. for protection of any work originating from a Berne country, even though that country might have adhered also to the U.C.C. As a result, the U.C.C. is of relatively little practical importance in U.S. international copyright relations today, when almost all U.C.C. signatories are also parties to the Berne Convention and/or the Agreement on Trade-Related Aspects of Intellectual Property, or "TRIPS" (about which we have more to say below).[9]

[3] The Berne Convention

Administration of the Convention

The current text of the treaty, to which the United States has adhered (along with 165 other contracting parties as of January 25, 2013), is the Paris Act of 1971. The Berne Convention is administered by the World Intellectual Property Organization ("WIPO"), an intergovernmental organization with headquarters in Geneva, Switzerland.[10] WIPO is a specialized agency within the United Nations system. Its central role is to conduct studies and provide services designed to facilitate protection of intellectual property. Its Director General and staff oversee the "Berne Union," which was created by the Berne Convention.

Basic Provisions (Paris Text 1971)

The first article of the Paris Act recites (as has each Act of the Berne Convention since its inception): "The countries to which this Convention applies constitute a Union for the protection of the rights of authors in their literary and artistic works." This language clearly associates the Berne Union with the philosophy of "authors' rights," rather than the competing "copyright" approach to the conceptualization of literary and artistic property. In general, an aspiration toward improving and harmonizing the protection of literary and artistic property worldwide has driven the activities of the Berne Union since its inception.

Berne's substantive provisions are found generally in the Convention's next 20 articles, which are followed by administrative provisions and an appendix incorpo-

---

[9] Like the U.C.C., the Buenos Aires Convention, to which the United States and 17 Latin American nations adhere, is of little current practical importance. For an overview, see Rinaldo, *The Scope of Copyright Protection in the United States Under Existing Inter-American Relations: Abrogation of the Need for U.S. Protection Under the Buenos Aires Convention by Reliance Upon the U.C.C.*, 22 Bull. Copyright Soc'y 417 (1975). While many Latin American nations participated in a revision of the Buenos Aires Convention signed in Washington in 1948, the United States decided not to adhere to the new text and thus probably doomed the possibility of any effective inter-American copyright system. Publishers are cautious creatures, however, and old habits die hard. The casebook authors suspect that, if you turn to the back of this work's title page, you will find a Buenos Aires-inspired "All Rights Reserved" notice — just in case.

[10] For a full listing of treaties administered by WIPO, with current adherents to each, see *http://www.wipo.int/treaties/en/SearchForm.jsp?search_what=C.*

rating special provisions for developing countries. The substantive provisions include both specific and general obligations imposed on its membership. Other rules are optional with the member country. Like the U.C.C., the Berne Convention is based on national treatment and compliance with Convention minima. As the following summary will reveal, however, Berne has established Convention minima more substantial than those found in the U.C.C.:

(a) *Subject matter.* The scope of subject matter that a member country must protect under Berne is stated broadly. It encompasses "literary and artistic works [which] shall include every production in the literary and artistic domain, whatever may be the mode or form of its expression," Berne Convention Art. 2(1) (Paris Text), including — in addition to *belles lettres* — scientific works, architecture, and works of applied art. The Convention expressly excludes from obligatory protection "news of the day or . . . miscellaneous facts having the character of mere items of press information." Art. 2(8).

(b) *Basis of protection.* The Berne Convention requires that protection be given to published or unpublished works of an author who is a national of a member state. Berne protection also is required for a work of a non-national of a member state if the work is first published in a member state or simultaneously published in a non-member and a member state. A work is published "simultaneously" if it is published in a member country within 30 days of its first publication in a non-member country. Art. 3(4).

Even before U.S. entry into Berne, American authors were able to enjoy Berne privileges by simultaneously publishing their works in a Berne country — the so-called "back door to Berne." Simultaneous publication did not, however, prove to be the panacea it may have appeared at first glance. First, it could be costly, thereby precluding less wealthy authors from availing themselves of the privilege. Second, seeking protection under the simultaneous publication privilege involved various definitional and practical uncertainties.

(c) *Preclusion of formalities.* Berne requires that the work be protected without formalities outside the country of origin. Thus, if a work originates in a member country, it must be protected in all Berne countries without any prerequisite formalities. Art. 5(2). On the other hand, Berne does *not* govern protection of works *in their country of origin.* This means that formalities *can* be imposed on a work if it "originates" (in the special Berne sense of that term) within the country requiring compliance.

(d) *Minimum term of protection.* The Berne Convention has established a minimum term of protection of life plus 50 years, or 50 years from publication for cinematographic works and for anonymous and pseudonymous works. Art. 7(1)–(3). As is generally the case for all Berne provisions, the member country can grant a term of protection in excess of the minimum term. Art. 7(6).

(e) *Exclusive rights.* Berne requires that certain exclusive rights be protected under national law. These rights are, on the whole, quite similar to the array of economic rights found in § 106 of the Copyright Act of 1976. *See, e.g.*, Arts. 8(1) (the translation right); 9(1) (reproduction); 11(1) and 11[ter] (public performance); and 12 (adaptation). But the exclusive rights stipulated by Berne are, in other ways, not as extensive as those granted by American law. For example, Berne is silent on the public distribution and display rights, both of which are provided for specifically in the 1976 Act. *See* § 106(3),(5).

In addition to exclusive economic rights, Berne requires that certain "moral rights" be recognized "independently of the author's economic rights and even after the transfer of the said rights." The two rights recognized are the right of attribution and the right of integrity:

> [T]he author shall have the right to claim authorship of the work and to object to any distortion, mutilation or other modification of, or other derogatory action in relation to, the said work, which would be prejudicial to his honor or reputation.

Art. 6bis (1). Article 6bis (2) provides that these rights shall last at least until the expiration of the economic rights. This concept of "moral rights" is rooted in the civil-law tradition of literary and artistic property, and it is one which the United States has been slow to recognize.

(f) *Limitations and exceptions.* In addition to providing minima relating to exclusive rights, the Berne Convention also addresses the question of what conditions the laws of member nations may impose on the exercise of those rights. Article 10, for example, mandates exceptions for "fair quotation" from copyrighted works, and permits (although it does not require) broad national law exemptions in favor of illustrative uses of copyrighted works in education (including educational broadcasting). In addition to these provisions, which are specific as to the uses authorized but general in their application to the full range of authors' rights, the treaty articulates in Article 9(2) a general standard for exceptions to the reproduction right only: Under its so-called "three-part test" (also sometimes described as the "three-step test"), such exceptions are allowed "in *certain special cases*, provided that such reproduction does not conflict with a *normal exploitation* of the work and does not unreasonably prejudice the *legitimate interests* of the author." Quite a wide range of different national law practices, from the "fair use" doctrine in the United States to compulsory licensing in Europe and elsewhere, have been justified under the Article 9(2) formulation. Yet another Berne provision, Article 10bis, authorizes limitations on the musical works recording right of the sort found in § 115 of the U.S. Copyright Act.

(g) *Enforcement.* As noted above, the member countries of the Berne Convention constitute a "Union" for the protection of authors. This provision reflects a fundamental tenet of the Berne system: that the most important role of the treaty would be as the "constitution" of a "society" of states committed to the project of protecting copyright, rather than as a mechanism for mandating that particular states take particular domestic actions in their domestic laws. Accordingly, the treaty encompasses only one coercive provision, and it is largely (if not wholly) ineffectual. Article 33(1) provides for the submission of treaty compliance disputes among member states to the jurisdiction of the International Court of Justice in The Hague. Article 33(2), however, specifically permits an acceding country to declare that it is not bound by Article 33(1), and a number of states (including the United States) have so declared. The ICJ has never heard a case arising out of the interpretation of the Berne Convention. As a practical matter, each country is its own final arbiter in interpreting the Convention as applied to the field of domestic law.

Evaluating the Berne Convention

In 1986, the 100th anniversary of the first Act of the Berne Convention initiated a period of taking stock. On the one hand, the Convention and the Berne Union obviously had provoked world-wide upgrading and harmonization (if only partial) of laws relating to literary and artistic property. On the other hand, the Convention was — in the view of some — beginning to show its age. For one thing, it was silent on some of the most urgent current issues in copyright law: protection of computer programs, for example, and the treatment of sound recordings. For another, the very reliance on consensus-building and moral suasion which had contributed so much to the treaty's success began to look like a drawback in a world where some nations were ignoring Berne's precepts in their day-to-day practices. Of what use against copyright "piracy," some wondered, was a treaty which even signatory states could disregard with relative impunity? Finally, by no means were all of the countries with significant roles in the international intellectual property economy members of Berne: In particular, by 1986, the Convention had yet to attract the adherence of many developing countries, to say nothing of the United States, the Soviet Union, or the People's Republic of China. But this, at least, was soon to change.

[C] U.S. Entry Into Berne

[1] The Incentives for Entry

Before its entry into Berne on March 1, 1989, the United States was the only major Western country not a party to the Convention. By the late 1980s, however, the prospective advantages of U.S. membership in Berne were more apparent than ever. As the world's largest exporter of copyrighted works, the United States had a keen interest in stemming the rising tide of international piracy which threatened to engulf American copyright holders. The United States had, however, withdrawn from UNESCO, the U.N. organization which administers the U.C.C. Most (although not all) of America's major trading partners, meanwhile, were members of Berne. Despite (or because of) Berne's identified shortcomings, it appeared critically important for the United States to assume a major role in guiding the direction of international copyright matters by joining the world's preeminent copyright convention.

One obvious and immediate benefit of U.S. entry into Berne was that American authors and copyright owners would no longer have to rely on the costly and risky "back door to Berne" procedure to protect their works in the two-dozen Berne countries with which the United States had no other copyright relations. For the most part, however, the tangible benefits that Berne membership offered American copyright owners were ones which would not be felt immediately. Rather, they would manifest themselves over the long term, as the results of increasing U.S.

influence over the direction of international copyright policy.[11]

[2]   The Berne Convention Implementation Act of 1988

By 1988, major changes had transpired in American copyright law and attitudes, making it far easier for the United States to enter Berne than had formerly been possible. In particular, the provisions of the 1976 Act, especially with respect to copyright duration, had eliminated many of the impediments to Berne adherence by bringing U.S. law into compliance with some of the important minima of the Convention. The 1976 Act, however, still fell short of the goal of Berne compatibility. When Congress finally did take the step of preparing the implementing legislation necessary to place the United States in compliance with Berne, it took what has been termed a "minimalist" approach, meaning that it made only those amendments to American law that were deemed essential for compatibility with Convention obligations.[12] Even employing a minimalist approach, however, some important changes to U.S. law were seen as unavoidable.

The United States officially adhered to the Berne Convention on March 1, 1989. Section 2(1) of the BCIA, however, declares that the Berne Convention is not self-executing under U.S. law. This means that rights and responsibilities relating to copyright matters will be solely resolved under the domestic law — state and federal — of the United States, rather than pursuant to the terms of the treaty as incorporated into the body of federal law.

[3]   The Unfinished Business of the BCIA

Among other things, the minimalist approach taken by Congress in 1988 assured that some significant issues pertaining to the compatibility of U.S. law with Berne minima went unaddressed, namely, the issues of moral rights, architectural works, and retroactivity. In each instance, Congress took some time to address this "unfinished business." An example is the treatment of moral rights, recognized specifically in Article 6bis of the Berne Convention. Congress stated that the protection afforded by American copyright, unfair competition, defamation, privacy and contract law, taken together, were sufficient to meet the needs of Berne adherence. Nonetheless, only two years later, the Visual Artists Rights Act of 1990, amending the Copyright Act of 1976, gave limited recognition to moral rights under federal law.

Another example is the approach taken in 1988 and thereafter in the treatment of architectural works, which are specifically included within Berne's itemization of mandatory subject matter. Art. 2(1). In 1990, Congress added architectural works as another category of subject matter to § 102 of the Act.[13]

---

[11] *See* Jaszi, *A Garland of Reflections on Three International Copyright Topics*, 8 Cardozo Arts & Ent. L.J. 47 (1989); *Final Report of the Ad Hoc Working Group on U.S. Adherence to the Berne Convention, reprinted in* 10 Colum.-VLA J.L. & Arts 513 (1986).

[12] *See* 134 Cong. Rec. S14552 (daily ed. Oct. 5, 1988) (statement of Sen. Leahy).

[13] *See* Pub. L. No. 101-650 (Title VII), 104 Stat. 5089 (1990); H.R. Rep. No. 101-735 (1990).

A third delayed reaction to Berne concerned "retroactivity." Article 18 of Berne provides that, in general, "[t]his Convention shall apply to all works which, at the moment of its coming into force, have not yet fallen into the public domain in the country of origin through the expiry of protection." Despite Article 18, Section 12 of the BCIA provided that no retroactive protection would be available for any work that already had entered the public domain in the United States. As noted in § 1.03 above, Congress eventually resolved the retroactivity issue in 1994 in the Uruguay Round Agreements Act.

[D]　Neighboring and Related Rights Conventions[14]

A number of countries specifically recognize the concept of "related" or "neighboring rights" as a species of intellectual property which is, so to speak, adjacent to copyright, but not part of it.

Take, for example, the question of protection for sound recordings (or "phonograms"). Many, perhaps most, countries balk at recognizing the producers and performers associated with such works as "authors." As a result, the rights of such persons (and of broadcasters) are protected abroad under various schemes of "neighboring rights." The United States has entered into two such neighboring rights conventions: the Geneva Phonograms Convention and the Brussels Satellite Convention.

The 1971 Geneva Convention ("Convention for the Protection of Producers of Phonograms Against Unauthorized Duplication of Their Phonograms") provides international protection against the unauthorized manufacture, importation, and distribution of phonorecords. The United States adhered effective in 1974. As of January 25, 2013, the Geneva Convention had 78 adherents. In contrast, the 1961 Rome Convention ("International Convention for the Protection of Performers, Producers of Phonograms and Broadcasting Organizations") provides a significantly higher level of protection than the Geneva Convention and also protects performances, including those embodied in sound recordings. The United States has not ratified the Rome Convention (although 91 other nations have).

The Geneva and Rome conventions focus specifically on the performers and producers of recorded music. Actors and other performers whose work can be recorded as audiovisual works have long sought similar rights to control whether a live performance is recorded and whether or how recorded performances are broadcasted, communicated, or distributed to the public. On June 26, 2012, the WIPO Diplomatic Conference concluded the Beijing Treaty on Audiovisual Performances, which provides such rights. This treaty will not become effective in the United States unless and until Congress passes implementing legislation, which has not been proposed as of this writing.

The 1974 Brussels Convention ("Convention Relating to the Distribution of Programme-Carrying Signals Transmitted by Satellite") was ratified by the United States in 1984. Its purpose is to combat the misappropriation of satellite signals on

---

[14] For the latest list of member counties to the neighboring rights conventions, one should consult the WIPO website, *http://www.wipo.int/treaties/en/*.

an international level. The Convention itself creates no new rights for programs transmitted by satellite. Rather, member nations agree to provide adequate protection against satellite signal piracy in their domestic laws. The United States views its copyright and communication laws as adequate in this regard, and thus has seen no need for implementing legislation. The Convention focuses on the unauthorized distribution of signals, not their unauthorized reception. The private reception of signals for private use is not a regulated activity. Moreover, the object of protection is the signal itself, not the content of the material transmitted by the signal. Thus, the Convention is designed to protect the emitter or carrier, not the copyright owner of the program material. The United States is one of 35 adherents to the Brussels Satellite Convention.

[E] Intellectual Property and International Trade

[1] NAFTA and TRIPS[15]

Beginning in the early 1980s, the United States launched an initiative to tie international protection for intellectual property (including copyright) more closely to the developing law of international trade. Spurred by the recognition that revenues from intangible information products represented an increasingly important dimension of U.S. participation in the world economy, and by a perception that U.S. firms were losing huge amounts to foreign "piracy" as a result (in part) of the failure of existing international intellectual property agreements to provide mechanisms for the enforcement of the norms they proclaimed, a succession of U.S. administrations pursued policies based on the proposition that failure to adequately and effectively protect intellectual property — especially foreign intellectual property — is as much an unfair trade practice as are high tariffs, dumping, or governmental subsidies. The goal in the following pages is to describe briefly two important new international agreements rooted in this new way of conceptualizing intellectual property norms.

Along with many other aspects of the trilateral economic trade relationship among the United States, Canada and Mexico, intellectual property was addressed in the 1992 North America Free Trade Agreement ("NAFTA"). Where copyright and neighboring rights are concerned, NAFTA requires copyright protection for computer programs and data compilations as literary works, protection for sound recordings, recognition of a rental right for sound recordings, limitations on compulsory licensing, and recognition of rights against unauthorized importation of copies of protected works. In general, NAFTA puts a special emphasis on *effective* enforcement of intellectual property rights and, in particular, it requires signatories to make pretrial injunctive relief available in intellectual property cases — something Mexican courts had been reluctant to do in the past.

Subsequent to NAFTA, in April 1994, the "Agreement on Trade-Related Aspects of Intellectual Property Rights, Including Trade in Counterfeit Goods" — the

---

[15] Technically, the proper abbreviation for the Agreement on *T*rade-*R*elated Aspects of *I*ntellectual *P*roperty Rights would seem to be "TRIPs." But the WTO Agreement, and most commentators, use "TRIPS." The casebook authors surrender. Hereinafter, TRIPS!

so-called "TRIPS Agreement" — was adopted by 107 countries which had participated in the Uruguay Round of the General Agreement on Tariffs and Trade (the "GATT").[16] As of January 25, 2013, their number had risen to 157.[17] This agreement has enhanced international intellectual property protection, both substantively and procedurally.

Under the GATT regime, an ever-growing number of countries negotiated agreed-upon norms for freer international trade. When it was first organized following World War II, the GATT was concerned primarily with promoting the reduction of tariff barriers to the international movement of goods. Article XX of the original GATT Agreement treated copyright, along with patent and trademark, as an acceptable exception to the free trade commitments in the Agreement. Since then, the relationship between copyright and international trade agreements has shifted as periodic multilateral negotiations convened to revise the agreement (called "Rounds" in GATT terminology) have extended the scope of its norms to cover a variety of "non-tariff barriers." For example, the 1979 Code on Subsidies and Countervailing Duties limits the ability of governments to provide unfair economic advantages to local industries exporting in international commerce.

By analogy, advocates of the development of intellectual property provisions within the GATT framework argued that lax enforcement of the intellectual property rights of foreign proprietors also could be considered a means by which states shelter local companies from international competition. The costs of producing and disseminating a work of authorship are great, but the cost of copying is diminishing. The large disparity between the creator's costs and those of the pirate resulted, it was argued, in trade distortions which could appropriately be addressed by the GATT.

Inclusion of intellectual property on the agenda of the Uruguay Round was advocated by the intellectual property industries of the United States, Europe, and other regions. These talks produced a new international pact establishing the World Trade Organization ("WTO"), which superseded the GATT and to which TRIPS was annexed. The final TRIPS Agreement, in turn, incorporated many (although not all) of the provisions which the major intellectual property-producing nations sought to have included regarding a broad range of intellectual property rights. Where copyright and neighboring rights are concerned, signatories of the TRIPS Agreement commit themselves to the traditional principle of "national treatment." The TRIPS text incorporates by reference the bulk of minimum standards contained in Articles 1–21 of the 1971 Act of the Berne Convention, although it specifically excludes Art. 6bis (on moral rights) — a concession demanded by the United States.

On the other hand, the copyright norms of TRIPS go beyond the minima of Berne in a number of important respects. For example, the agreement mandates protection for computer programs under copyright, obligating parties to prohibit unauthorized commercial rentals of computer programs and audiovisual works. And

---

[16] Marrakesh Agreement Establishing the World Trade Organization, Annex 1C, Apr. 15, 1994, *reprinted* in THE RESULTS OF THE URUGUAY ROUND OF MULTILATERAL TRADE NEGOTIATIONS — THE LEGAL TEXTS 6–19 (GATT Secretariat ed. 1994).

[17] *http://www.wto.org/english/thewto_e/whatis_e/tif_e/org6_e.htm.*

where enforcement (a topic on which both Berne and existing neighboring rights treaties are largely silent) is concerned, TRIPS signatories commit themselves, in Articles 41–64, to a range of specific measures to effectuate intellectual property rights of all kinds.

Among the major attractions of the WTO approach to improving international protection for copyright (and other forms of intellectual property) is the fact that the basic WTO agreement provides procedures to resolve disputes over the application of its norms. As already noted, the possibility of sanctions arising out of particular disputes relating to intellectual property rights is one element that is missing from the traditional multilateral arrangements. Although these sanctioning mechanisms have not always worked well in the past, they do function. And many believe that the threat of their invocation has been effective in a number of instances in which the actual need to apply them never arose. Moreover, the negotiators who participated in the Uruguay Round devoted considerable attention to upgrading and refining the generic dispute-resolution procedures administered by WTO, adding provisions for more effective mediation and arbitration, tighter deadline structures, and greater use of non-governmental experts on dispute-resolution panels, as part of the Uruguay Round.

[2] TRIPS and the Berne Convention

One initial critique of the initiative to incorporate intellectual property standards into the GATT framework grew out of a fear that to do so would undermine the continuing effectiveness of existing multilateral intellectual property treaties, including the Berne Convention.[18] That concern is addressed in the TRIPS Agreement itself, which calls upon the newly-created Council for Trade-Related Aspects of Intellectual Property Rights to consult and cooperate with the World Intellectual Property Organization ("WIPO"), which functions as the Secretariat of the Berne Convention (and other international intellectual property agreements). How the norms of TRIPS will interact with those of the treaties administered by WIPO, and how WIPO itself will interact with the World Trade Organization and the TRIPS Council, will be worked out over the next decade.

[3] The WTO Implementing Legislation

Closer to home, the major follow-up to TRIPS was the enactment of the Uruguay Round Agreements Act ("URAA") in late 1994,[19] implementing the United States' obligations — and then some — under the TRIPS agreement. Two principles regarding the Uruguay Round Agreements in relation to U.S. law must be mentioned. First, with respect to the United States at least, the Agreements are not self-executing. They must be implemented in domestic legislation. Second, the Agreements are not a treaty. The U.S. Senate did not give its advice and consent.

---

[18] *See generally* Leaffer, *Protecting American Intellectual Property Abroad: Toward a New Multilateralism*, 74 Iowa L. Rev. 723 (1991); Jaszi, *A Garland of Reflections on Three International Copyright Topics*, 8 Cardozo L. & Ent. L.J. 47, 67-72 (1989); *GATT or WIPO? New Ways in the International Protection of Intellectual Property (Symposium at Ringberg Castle, July 13-16, 1989)* (F.K. Beier & G. Schricker eds., IIC Studies 1989).

[19] Pub. L. No. 103-465, 108 Stat. 4809 (Dec. 8, 1994).

Instead, the only action by Congress was passage of the implementing legislation.

The URAA included three components related to copyright. First, it made permanent the ban enacted by Congress in 1990 on the rental of computer programs for purposes of direct or indirect commercial advantage. Second, it added to Title 17, United States Code, a new Chapter 11 that provided a civil cause of action for performers to prevent the "bootlegging" of live performances. Third, it provided retroactive protection for works whose source country is a member of the Berne Convention or the World Trade Organization or is the subject of a presidential proclamation, if the subject works are in the public domain in the United States through failure to comply with U.S. formalities, lack of national eligibility, or, in the case of pre-1972 sound recordings, lack of subject matter protection. These provisions will be discussed at greater length in succeeding chapters of the casebook.

[4] Updating the Berne Convention

Over its 100-year-plus life, the Berne Convention has undergone several major revisions, the most recent being the Paris Act of 1971. The revision process, requiring the development of consensus among the differing interests of Berne members, has become increasingly difficult, if not impossible, to carry out. Beginning in 1995, the United States and a number of European countries pressed for the expansion of the ongoing discussions of possible new treaties to include a new so-called "digital agenda."

In December 1996, two new treaties, "The WIPO Copyright Treaty" ("WCT") and "The WIPO Performances and Phonograms Treaty," were concluded pursuant to a WIPO Diplomatic Conference. The Copyright Treaty provides for the protection of computer programs as literary works, and for copyright in original (as distinct from non-original) compilations of data. It obligates ratifying states to recognize a general right of distribution and a rental right limited to computer programs, movies and "works embodied in phonograms," and is itself subject to a number of significant exceptions. It also bars ratifying states from taking advantage of Berne Convention provisions which otherwise would permit them to allow lesser terms of protection to phonograms than to other copyrighted works. The Performances and Phonograms Treaty breaks significant new ground. In particular, performers fare better under the new treaty than under TRIPS. Not only are they afforded more extensive economic rights, but the text provides explicitly for the basic moral rights of the performer "as regards . . . live aural performances fixed in phonograms."

With respect to digital issues, the relevant provisions of the two treaties approved in December 1996 are substantially identical. The relevant obligations in the final acts of the treaties include a duty to recognize a right of "communication to the public," along with a limited mandate for the protection of "copyright management information" against tampering, and another relating to "circumvention" of technological safeguards.[20]

---

[20] For a detailed discussion of the Diplomatic Conference and its outcome, see Samuelson, *The U.S.*

In the United States, the Senate gave its advice and consent to the treaties on October 21, 1998. Implementing legislation, including provisions on "anti-circumvention" and "copyright management information" (but not moral rights of performers), was signed into law as the Digital Millennium Copyright Act ("DMCA") on October 28, 1998. The WCT entered into force on March 6, 2002. It has a total of 90 adherents. The WIPO Performances and Phonogram Treaty ("WPPT") entered into force on May 20, 2002. The current number of adherents to the WPPT is 91.

[5]   U.S. Participation in the New Order

The developments described in this chapter, of which the 1996 WIPO treaties are only the most recent, suggest that the character of the international copyright regime continues to undergo significant change. A system which traditionally has emphasized national treatment, supplemented by relatively few and easily satisfied treaty minima, is moving closer to one with an emphasis on true harmonization of national laws. Moreover, as a result of TRIPS and its dispute-resolution procedures, there now exists a procedure which will yield authoritative interpretations of international norms and conclusive adjudications of the compliance of particular countries with those norms.

More recently, however, a bit of a backlash against TRIPS has arisen among many developing countries, which assert that they made too many concessions regarding intellectual property without receiving much benefit. Negotiations on expanding existing rights have stalled, and a number of countries have called for a new agreement on exceptions and limitations to intellectual property rights. In the meantime, the United States has pressed ahead with its expansionist agenda by negotiating a number of bilateral "free trade agreements" with various countries that call for minimum levels of intellectual property protection greater than those required by Berne and TRIPS. The United States also has been a leading proponent of new plurilateral trade agreements, such as the Anti-Counterfeiting Trade Agreement ("ACTA") and the Trans-Pacific Partnership Agreement ("TPP"), aimed at strengthening enforcement of intellectual property rights in signatory countries.

The question is whether, by relinquishing the historical peculiarities of U.S. domestic copyright laws, the United States has gained the correspondingly greater benefits that international harmonization may offer U.S. works in the global marketplace.

Digital Agenda at WIPO, 37 Va. J. Int'l L. 369 (1997), and *Big Media Beaten Back*, WIRED 5.03, at 61 (1997).

§ 1.05   COPYRIGHT AND THE DIGITAL CHALLENGE

[A]   Looking Back

Over its several centuries of existence, copyright law has negotiated successfully a series of "crises" precipitated by changes in information distribution by adapting itself to new technological circumstances. In the last century or so, for example, copyright has proved flexible enough to deal effectively with the new media of photography, motion pictures, and sound recordings. The crisis of the moment, however, may pose a greater challenge by far to the adaptability of the copyright system.

As the term "copyright" itself suggests, the basic concepts of this body of law are rooted in the circumstances of print-on-paper information technology. At the beginning of this chapter, we suggested that the relationship between information technology and intellectual property law is a complex one. Advances in technology help to bring about changes in the life of society. These, in turn, generate demand for new legal regimes. As we also noted, the earliest copyright laws arose in response to the chaotic economic and cultural conditions caused in part by the spread of movable type throughout Europe. Because the crisis of that moment involved the multiplication and distribution of physical books, it was perhaps inevitable that these laws would be organized around the concept of publication: *First publication* was the act which caused copyright protection to attach, and the essential right of the copyright owner was the right to regulate *subsequent publications*. Even our ideas about limitations on and exceptions to the "copy" right — such as fair use and first sale — developed from the assumption that control over publication is central to copyright ownership.

Even today, despite the fact that the Copyright Act of 1976 has deprived publication of its function as the triggering mechanism for copyright protection, the jurisprudential superstructure of copyright doctrine remains based on the publication concept. Thus, at least until recently, unauthorized publication — the multiplication and distribution of physical copies — has been the most pressing practical concern of the U.S. copyright industries, against which most of their domestic and international enforcement campaigns have been directed.

[B]   Digitization and the Revolution in Information Processing

As copyright and the world move well into the Third Millennium, a development in information technology, which may have as much potential for social transformation as did movable type, is leading some to question the continued relevance of traditional copyright law. This development is the digitization of information — *i.e.*, its description by means of strings of binary code — which was ushered in by the invention and popularization of digital computers. The technology of digitization and the decentralized design of the Internet have produced a tide of economic and cultural trends which challenge many of copyright's most fundamental conceptions. Throughout this casebook, we will be highlighting digital technology and its implications for the law of intellectual property.

One consequence of digitization was to introduce an entirely new category of information products — computer programs — into the marketplace, with disquieting consequences for schemes of legal protection developed in response to earlier technologies. Yet another consequence of the advent of digital code was to create a powerful new means by which to store large amounts of information of all kinds. In fact, all the varieties of "works" previously known to human culture (and to the law of copyright) can be — and, increasingly, are being — expressed in digital form. On paper, digital code is expressed symbolically as zeros and ones; electronically, it is embodied in series of "on" and "off" settings. A variety of different media may be used to fix information in electronic form: magnetic tape, floppy disks, silicon chips, optical disks, flash drives, and so forth. A computer treats all forms of information expressed in binary code as data to be processed regardless of its content or form. Application programs, such as word processors, web browsers, and audio and video programs render this data as recognizable text, image, or sound.

For most of its development, copyright law was based on implicit assumptions about how analog technologies make it relatively difficult or expensive to engage in the activities that infringe a copyright owner's exclusive rights. Digital technologies and digital networks render many of these assumptions obsolete. What analog technologies such as prints, negatives, screen projections, and cathode tube displays have in common is that they represent an image — its shape, density, color, and so forth — directly to the human sense of sight. Copying or altering works in analog media requires the creation of new analogs. Consider the example of a photograph. If a magazine publisher wanted a photograph taken on film retouched to alter the texture of the background or the shape of a foreground object, a skilled retoucher would need hours or days to make the alterations because the process involves painstaking alteration of every affected portion of the picture.

Digital forms of creative works can be copied and altered with relative ease precisely because they are *descriptions* of how the computer should render them rather than analogous representations that must embody the characteristics of the work. Imagine digital photos stored on a DVD. No matter how hard one studies the surface of the disk, no matter at what magnification and no matter how bright the light, no representation of the image can be discerned there. What the disk contains is not a representation but an extraordinarily detailed description of the image, from which it can be rapidly rendered into familiar form by electronic means.

Retouching a digital photo is a process of changing the description of how the computer should render the image. The application program simply changes the sequence of 0s and 1s in response to the retoucher's commands. That such digital records describe rather than represent information gives rise to some of the most important implications of the new technology for the law of intellectual property, to be discussed at greater length below.

At the outset, then, it may be helpful to try to isolate the characteristics of digital information technology that require a response from the legal system. In

1990, Prof. Pamela Samuelson, *Digital Media and the Changing Face of Intellectual Property Law*, 16 Rutgers Computer & Tech. L.J. 323 (1990), presciently summarized these qualities as follows:

- ease of replication

- ease of transmission and multiple use

- plasticity of digital media

- equivalence of works in digital form

- compactness of works in digital form

- new search and link capacities

Copyright law must struggle to accommodate the consequences of a host of new realities that flow from the foregoing characteristics of digital information technology. These consequences include, for example, the ability to represent digitally, and to combine and recombine seamlessly, works of all kinds and categories, *i.e.*, the somewhat inaptly named "multimedia" phenomenon. Even more significantly, digital technology provides the means to communicate such information in new and unprecedented ways — through electronic networks in general, and through the Internet (the "network of networks") in particular — free from historic constraints of time and location.

[C] Digital Networks and Their Importance

If all digital devices (such as computers) were free-standing rather than interconnected, the impact of digitization — though significant — would be limited. In fact, however, this is not the case. Today, more and more devices are linked by wired and wireless connections to form small and large networks over which digitized information can be exchanged without any need for the transfer of a physical object. Digital networks can be designed in ways that allow for more or less control over communication flows by the network operator. Traditional understandings on which copyright law has been based are challenged both by the capabilities enabled by digitization and by the specific design of the Internet, which, to date, has minimized network operators' ability to control information flows.

The Internet's design reflects the public goal of providing a more robust communications network for the U.S. Government than the more vulnerable traditional telephone network. The Internet's design relies on voluntary adherence to a set of communication protocols that assign a numeric "address" to each device or network attached to the Internet and that specify how all digital communications are to be divided into standardized packets, regardless of the type of communication, *e.g.*, e-mail, web page, or telephone call. These packets are transmitted by a largely decentralized network of "routers" that can choose among multiple transmission routes. Ultimately the packets are received and reassembled by the receiving device. Additional protocols have been developed to standardize a range of Internet uses, most notably the graphical layer of the network that relies on protocols for creating, naming, and linking to pages on the World Wide Web.

Sir Tim Berners-Lee, Creator of the World Wide Web

Internet use is now ubiquitous. Good estimates of the extent of current use are hard to come by, but recent studies indicate over 245 million Internet users in the United States alone (three-quarters of the population), and nearly 2.4 billion worldwide.[1]

[D] Digital Copyright at Home and Abroad

Corporate providers of copyrighted content — the so-called "copyright industries" which produce motion pictures, make sound recordings, publish books, and distribute software — have had a mixed response to the growth trend in Internet usage. In their view, the network environment is a place of both great opportunity and tremendous risk. On the one hand, they have identified the Internet as a potential future source of vast profits: a distribution medium with the potential of delivering content of all kinds, on demand, to consumers without the high overhead associated with conventional distribution systems. On the other hand, they perceive the Internet as a present danger to their valuable intangible assets. Their aim, then, is to make the network environment "safe" for digital commerce in information and entertainment products.

---

[1] Statistics on Internet use as of July 1, 2012 are collected at *http://www.internetworldstats.com/top20.htm.*

To some extent, this goal can be achieved through self-help by means of "technological safeguards" which create barriers to infringement: scrambling, encryption, watermarking, use of secure passwords, and so forth. But content providers are quick to argue that any technological security measures can eventually be "hacked," and that, therefore, new legal protections for copyrighted works in the network environment are also required.

In August 1995, a working group of a special Clinton Administration Task Force issued its report, the so-called "White Paper" on *Intellectual Property and the National Information Infrastructure*. The report contained both (1) interpretations of how current copyright law could be applied in the network environment and (2) proposals for how the law could be updated to better serve the objective of securing intellectual property in cyberspace. The next year, the U.S. Administration took its campaign for copyright reform to an international forum: the Diplomatic Conference of the World Intellectual Property Organization, held that December in Geneva, Switzerland. *See* § 1.04 above. There, the United States joined with countries of the European Union to push for new legal restrictions on information use in cyberspace.

In 1997, the WIPO treaties were submitted to the U.S. Senate for ratification, and Administration-drafted legislation to "implement" the treaties (by bringing domestic law into conformity with their requirements) was introduced in both houses of Congress. This legislation contained provisions which would ban both the circumvention of technological safeguards and the making available of products or services which could be used to accomplish circumvention, along with other provisions to prohibit tampering with so-called "copyright management information." It also incorporated a schedule of civil and criminal penalties for the vindication of these new legal norms.

The centerpiece proposal on anti-circumvention drew fire from electronics and computer manufacturers, along with some commercial software developers, as well as from library, educational and consumer organizations. All of these interests insisted that the WIPO treaties required nothing more than the imposition of new penalties on those who circumvent technological safeguards in aid of copyright infringement, and that the United States should do no more than to provide for such penalties for circumvention. The same groups also faulted the proposals on copyright management information for their failure to provide unambiguous protections for the privacy of electronic information consumers. Other critics faulted the legislation for not going far enough to protect users in a digitally networked world by reinforcing such traditional pro-user protections as fair use, the first-sale doctrine, and exemptions for schools and libraries.

The legislation also incorporated what had been a separate proposal to limit the liability of Internet service providers for their users' infringing conduct on the Internet. We shall see in Chapter 9 that the legal regulation of the relationships among copyright owners, service providers, and end users has been a subject of rapid, significant, and ongoing legal developments. The WIPO treaties implementing legislation, as amended to include limits on Internet service provider liability, did ultimately pass Congress. On October 28, 1998, President Clinton signed into law the Digital Millennium Copyright Act ("DMCA").

Since passage of the DMCA, Congress has continued to consider and to enact copyright legislation covering a range of issues. With respect to the digital challenge, the 112th Congress considered controversial legislation known as the Stop Online Piracy Act ("SOPA") in the House and the Protect IP Act ("PIPA") in the Senate. These bills elicited a widely publicized response from Internet users and some Internet service providers. We will discuss this episode at greater length in § 9.03 below.

[E]   The Issues in Context

Even the issues summarized above do not fully reflect the breadth of the emerging debate, for there is the further question of how copyright and other bodies of law should interact in the new world of digital information products. In particular, licensing practices deserve attention. Anyone who has downloaded software or recently purchased a program on an optical disk knows from personal experience about the "click-through" or "shrink-wrap" licenses which the purchaser is required to "accept" as a condition of installing and utilizing the program. Often, these licenses include terms which run contrary to copyright law, restricting the purchaser's use of the program in ways which copyright doctrine does not, waiving "fair use" privileges, and so forth. The state of the law on the enforceability of such terms is still unsettled, both as a matter of contract doctrine and with respect to the law of copyright preemption (discussed below in Chapter 11).

One way or the other, the emergence of restrictive information licensing focuses new attention on the relationship between contract and copyright, and on the question of the extent to which our legal system should enable or abet the displacement of copyright rules by private arrangements.

Not all licensing practices in the digital environment raise these concerns. For example, public licenses such licenses for free and open source software or Creative Commons licenses, provide standard terms by which a copyright owner gives members of the public a non-exclusive license to make a range of uses of a copyrighted work beyond those allowed by fair use or other limitations on the copyright owners' exclusive rights. These licenses permit use of the work on a royalty-free basis, but they contain some conditions on use, such as requiring the user to give attribution as the copyright owner directs. One condition in some of these licenses, often referred to as "copyleft," provides that anyone who uses the licensed content to produce a new work must license the new work under the same license.

[F]   Looking Forward

This question, in turn, is part of a still larger set of issues that brings the discussion full circle. In the print-on-paper environment, today's information owners enjoy a more or less unfettered choice as to when they will choose to disclose their previously unpublished works to the public, whether for gain or glory. The manuscript in the desk drawer is protected against theft by criminal law, and its contents are protected against unauthorized use by copyright law — subject only to narrow exceptions. Once the manuscript has been commercialized or otherwise disclosed to the public, however, the situation is different. Would-be purchasers of additional copies, like would-be commercial adapters or performers of the work, still must deal with the copyright owner or its agent. But library patrons can read the work, libraries can lend it, critics or scholars can quote from it, teachers can photocopy it for classroom use or read it, students and actual or potential competitors can analyze it — all without obtaining permission or paying license fees, thanks to traditional limiting doctrines such as "first sale" and "fair use." Such a published work is not in the "public domain," in the technical sense of that term, but it is available to the public as part of the general "informational commons" — the existence of which has been regarded as crucial to the "Progress of Science and useful Arts."

The emergent business model for the distribution of copyrighted works in the network environment seems to challenge the survival of an "informational commons."[2] Many copyright industry spokespersons argue that copyright owners should enjoy an absolute right to control "access" to their works, without any limitations or qualifications, and that the law of copyright and contract should operate to guarantee this entitlement. So long as "access" controls are equated with the lock-and-key on the desk drawer containing an author's unpublished manuscript, the point seems noncontroversial. Access controls may, however, comprise far more. If information is published in a newspaper, a teacher can copy a paragraph to initiate a class discussion; if the same information is provided only on the Internet, it can be made available exclusively on a pay-per-use basis, protected by contractual restrictions and technological safeguards. Indeed, technology makes it possible for information proprietors to treat every use — even every reading — of a digital work available via the Internet as a new instance of "access." In this way, some fear, such proprietors could maximize economic returns while continuing to withhold their works from general public scrutiny, including critical "fair use."

In response, information proprietors argue that because their motive in making material available by way of digital networks is *precisely* to maximize profits, consumers should have no concern about being frozen out of "access." To the contrary, they assert that, in a network environment characterized by ubiquitous electronic licensing, all kinds of uses will be possible upon the payment of fees which will be individually trivial (although cumulatively significant). Clearly, a pay-per-use information environment may represent a dystopia or a utopia, depending on one's perspective.

Copyright policymakers today face issues beyond those that have arisen in the past in connection with new information technologies. Previously, it was enough to ask how traditional copyright principles applied to new media — or, at most, how those principles might be adapted to make such application more readily feasible. Digital technology in general, and digital networks in particular, invite us to undertake a more fundamental inquiry. Even if traditional copyright doctrines may not apply comfortably in cyberspace, we could, of course, work toward installing their functional equivalents, so as to assure the maintenance in this new

---

[2] For the geography of this concept, see Lessig, THE FUTURE OF IDEAS: THE FATE OF THE COMMONS IN A CONNECTED WORLD (2001).

environment of the balance of proprietary and user interests which traditionally has characterized this branch of our law of intellectual property.

§ 1.06 THINKING AND TALKING ABOUT COPYRIGHT LAW

[A] In General

The preceding sections of Chapter 1 trace the history of Anglo-American copyright law, seeking to place it in the context both of related bodies of U.S. law and of "authors' rights" laws elsewhere in the world, and to highlight the mechanisms and challenges that have made, and will continue to make, this ever-evolving field of study so fascinating and rewarding. Before proceeding, we take the liberty of raising one final topic: the practical and philosophical perspectives that inform and shape the "discourse" of copyright law.

Under the U.S. Constitution, Congress has the *power* to secure to authors for limited times exclusive rights in the creations of their minds. It has, on the other hand, no *obligation* to secure *any* such rights. Nor, for that matter, did the Parliament that enacted the Statute of Anne operate under any legal requirement to do so. Yet for over 300 years this body of law not only has continued to exist, but has continued to expand. Why?

Whether property rights should be recognized in products of the mind is a question which challenges fundamental assumptions about why society creates property rights in the first place. Few today would question the correctness of granting property rights in land or chattels, including manufactured products. But when the subject turns to intangible property, *i.e.*, to intellectual products, that consensus breaks down. There is, as we write, an on-going and lively disagreement about the very nature, and the proper scope, of the protections that are and should be made available under our law for the latter sorts of goods.[1]

Discomfort with recognizing property rights in products of the mind runs through the common law. Under common-law doctrine, property rights arose from possession. But intellectual products were quite unlike land or chattels because, once disseminated publicly, ideas and other intangibles were not subject to exclusive possession. Justice Brandeis reflected this view in a famous dissent:

> The general rule of law is, that the noblest of human productions — knowledge, truths ascertained, conceptions, and ideas — become, after voluntary communication to others, free as the air to common use.

International News Service v. Associated Press, 248 U.S. 215, 250 (1918).

This discomfort notwithstanding, intellectual property rights in general, and copyright in particular, have grown apace over the past three centuries. In the few

---

[1] *See, e.g.*, Boyle, *A Theory of Law and Information: Copyright, Spleens, Blackmail, and Insider Trading*, 80 Cal. L. Rev. 1413 (1992); Vaver, *Intellectual Property Today: Of Myths and Paradoxes*, 69 Can. Bar Rev. 98 (1990); Palmer, *Intellectual Property: A Non-Posnerian Law and Economics Approach*, 12 Hamline L. Rev. 261 (1989); Gordon, *An Inquiry into the Merits of Copyright: The Challenges of Consistency, Consent, and Encouragement Theory*, 41 Stan. L. Rev. 1343 (1989).

pages that follow, we address the question of why this should be so. Further discussion will appear in succeeding chapters.

[B]   Copyright and "Interest Analysis"

Like other kinds of property law, copyright serves several ends. It establishes the conditions for the existence of a market — in this case, a market in information — and, by defining specific rights, it performs the allocational function of helping to determine "who (in society) gets what" where information resources are concerned. The content of copyright law, like that of other bodies of legal doctrine, is the outcome of centuries of advocacy on behalf of various constituencies whose interests are affected by the laws governing artistic and literary property. One way of thinking about developments in copyright law — whether historical or contemporary, judicial or legislative — is to inquire who benefits from any particular development or set of developments.

Broadly speaking, the three groups in society who might stand to gain from any change in copyright law are:

- individual creators, who write, paint, photograph, compose, or program copyrighted works into existence;

- distributors (*i.e.*, booksellers, publishers, or disseminators), who facilitate the delivery of creative works to consumers; and

- consumers themselves.

This last "interest group," it should be noted, is a particularly diverse one, ranging as it does from end-consumers (readers, viewers, listeners) to those who re-use copyrightable content to create new works, and taking in along the way educators, researchers, journalists, *et al.* Or, to put the point differently, there is significant overlap among the various "interest groups" — and especially between creators and consumers.

Sometimes, the interests of some or all of these groups will be congruent. The decision to extend protection to some new, important and previously unrecognized form of creative production may be a net gain for all concerned. Sometimes, however, the interests of these groups may be divergent or even antithetical. For example, cutting back on "fair use" privileges may benefit distributors (and perhaps creators) at consumers' expense, while introducing "moral rights" principles into a copyright system is likely to benefit creators (and perhaps some consumers) at the cost of distributors.

Crude though this "interest analysis" approach may be, it gives us some basis for understanding the impact of trends in Anglo-American copyright law over the past 300 years. Generally speaking, the history of copyright since the Statute of Anne has been one of increase. Protection has been afforded to a progressively larger variety of works, for longer periods of time, against a wider range of unauthorized uses.

Likewise, the perspective of interest analysis may help us to appreciate the significance of the fact that copyright began in England with the efforts of the

Stationers' Company (whose members were neither creators nor consumers of works) to secure legal protection for the interests of the book trade, and that developments in U.S. copyright history often have resulted from the lobbying and litigation activities of latter-day distributors (publishing houses, movie studios, record companies, and other such entities), not so different from those ancient booksellers.

This is not to say, of course, that only distributors have benefited from these developments. Although commercial distributors seeking to establish information markets may drive the development of copyright law, everyone in society stands to gain from the establishment of such markets — up to a certain point. Beyond that point, however, the allocational effects of changes in copyright law may yield disparate consequences for various interest groups. We suggest, therefore, that such developments should be continually examined, individually and collectively, to determine their impact on the distribution of information resources within society.

[C] "Rhetorics" of Copyright Jurisprudence

In the previous paragraphs, we suggested that it may sometimes be useful to consider the contours of copyright law as the outcome of interest group politics operating through the institutions of the law. Obviously, however, the claims of various groups generally are not expressed so straightforwardly in legal scholarship or legal argument.

Rather, "interested" claims tend to be asserted in language that is less direct, and which is designed to appeal to values shared by broader segments of the general society — in short, through the deployment of a number of characteristic and variously compelling "rhetorics." These rhetorics, in turn, can take on lives of their own and become independent factors in the development of intellectual property law. In order to understand the materials in succeeding chapters, and to develop skills in making intellectual property policy arguments, students should learn first to recognize these rhetorics, and then to put them to work.

[1] The "Utilitarian" and "Natural Law" Conceptions of Copyright

The "Utilitarian" Conception

As has already been noted, early discussions of copyright law — including U.S. copyright — were dominated by two competing and, to a large extent, inconsistent rhetorics of justification. The first of these is the *rhetoric of incentives* — or, as it has been described in recent scholarship, the "utilitarian" position — which in the United States is strongly linked to the language of the Constitution's Copyright Clause. This conception of copyright remains dominant in American judicial opinions — especially Supreme Court opinions — today.[2]

---

[2] Justice Stewart, in *Twentieth Century Music Corp. v. Aiken*, 422 U.S. 151, 156 (1975), put the matter this way:

The immediate effect of our copyright law is to secure a fair return for an author's creative

Supreme Court Oral Argument
Courtesy of the Supreme Court Historical Society

The utilitarian position always has been premised, at least implicitly, on economic reasoning. In recent years, its economic foundations have become more and more explicit. Incentives in the form of legal protection are needed if works of the mind are to be brought to market, the argument runs, because of the special characteristics of such intangible commodities, which once created cannot be used up, and which can be used by large numbers of people at the same time. In other words, intellectual productions qualify as "public goods," because producers cannot appropriate their true value through sale. Accordingly, economic theory teaches, there is a risk that a suboptimal amount of information will be produced or disseminated.

Sometimes, of course, the problem vanishes because the producer's or distributor's natural "lead time" enables it to derive a sufficient profit to justify its investment and to encourage continued activity.[3] But where "lead time" does not

---

labor. But the ultimate aim is, by this incentive, to stimulate artistic creativity for the public good.

As noted by Justice O'Connor in *Harper & Row, Publishers, Inc. v. Nation Enterprises*, 471 U.S. 539, 558 (1985):

By establishing a marketable right to the use of one's expression, copyright supplies the economic incentive to create *and disseminate* ideas. (Emphasis added.)

[3] This argument is elaborated in Breyer, *The Uneasy Case for Copyright: A Study in Copyright of Books, Photocopies and Computer Programs*, 84 Harv. L. Rev. 281 (1970). *Cf.* Tyerman, *The Economic*

provide a sufficient return — as where investments in a work can only be recouped over time or through the exploitation of ancillary markets — the solution to the public goods problem is to provide special incentives for the desired activity — either in the form of direct government subsidies, or by granting limited monopoly rights to copyright owners.

Economists recognize, however, that the incentive solution can also be the source of new difficulties — at least when the solution takes the form of the creation of new property rights. Free market economics disfavors the creation of monopolies unless there is an economic justification. Because of the exclusionary rights she possesses, the owner of the copyright in a work can charge a higher-than-competitive price for her product, resulting in a less-than-optimal diffusion of information.

Thus, the rhetoric of incentives in copyright law, as it has been developed, has sought to embrace considerations of public welfare. Copyright law attacks the "public goods" problem by recognizing a property right in the work, but the exercise of that monopoly is carefully circumscribed through regulation. On the one hand, copyright provides the incentive to create new products and an economic motivation to distribute them. On the other hand, the copyright owner's monopoly right is limited in time and scope by such doctrines as originality, the idea/expression dichotomy, and fair use (all discussed in detail hereinafter). Viewed in this way, copyright law should represent an economic trade-off between encouraging the optimal creation and distribution of works of authorship through monopoly incentives, and providing for their optimal use through limiting doctrines.

The "utilitarian" conception of copyright gives us one vocabulary for discussing the ways in which our collective life may be affected, for good or ill, by changes in the law. While there is room for doubt about whether the scope of copyright protection affects significantly the behavior of individual poets, painters or computer programmers, there is little question that changes in the legal exclusivity which distributors enjoy in the works they distribute can affect their investment decisions and business planning. This insight, of course, does not necessarily extend by very much our practical ability to determine the desirability of particular changes in copyright law by assessing their impact on public welfare. Presumably, there is an optimal level of protection beyond which providing additional incentives to distributors will yield little or no net gains in the quantity or quality of works effectively available to be consumed by the public. But any attempt actually to quantify that level of protection raises difficult and probably insoluble methodological questions.

The "Natural Law" Conception

Competing with the "utilitarian" rhetoric in American copyright discourse, from the earliest era of the Republic down to the present day, is the alternative rhetoric of "natural rights" or "inherent entitlement." The natural law justification for

---

Rationale for Copyright Protection for Published Books: A Reply to Professor Breyer, 18 UCLA L. Rev. 1100 (1971); *see* Breyer, *Copyright: A Rejoinder*, 20 UCLA L. Rev. 75 (1972). For a general consideration of the strengths and limitations of the economic theory of copyright, see Gordon, *An Inquiry into the Merits of Copyright: The Challenges of Consistency, Consent, and Encouragement Theory*, 41 Stan. L. Rev. 1343 (1989).

recognizing property rights in works of authorship is based on the rights of authors to reap the fruits of their creations, to obtain rewards for their contributions to society, and to protect the integrity of their creations as extensions of their personalities.

Locke and the Labor Model. The proposition that a person is entitled to the fruits of her labor is a compelling argument in favor of property rights of any kind, tangible or intangible. The most famous proponent of this natural rights theory was John Locke, the 17th Century English philosopher, who reasoned that persons have a natural right of property in their bodies. Owning their bodies, he believed, people also own the labor of their bodies and, by extension, the fruits of their labor. *See* J. Locke, SECOND TREATISE OF GOVERNMENT, Ch. 5 (1690).

John Locke (1632-1704)
Corbis

In England itself, Lockean reasoning had little prominence in the campaign to establish the new law of copyright which culminated in the Statute of Anne in 1710. Across the English Channel, however, the emphasis on "authorship" and "authors' rights" provided the primary ideological justification for the recognition of new legal interests in literary and artistic creations in 18th Century European intellectual property law, and a convenient basis on which those interests could be allocated. Both of these developments were urgently required if the new statutes were to serve the needs of the emerging commercial marketplace in works of the imagination. Ultimately, the belief in the paramount importance of "authorship" was to take on a significance of its own, marking the doctrinal landscapes of national law systems which emerged in countries such as France and Germany.[4]

The natural law justification for copyright continues to enjoy considerable currency throughout the world. Perhaps most importantly, it has animated successive revisions of the Berne Convention for the Protection of Literary and Artistic Property, up to and including the 1971 Paris Revision,[5] to which the United States adhered in 1989.

It would be wrong, however, to regard the "natural rights" conception of copyright as a mere recent European import in England and the United States. The claims of "authorship" exerted a shaping influence in late 18th and 19th Century British copyright. Likewise, Lockean rhetoric has been part of the discourse of American copyright law since the 1790 Federal Copyright Act, and even before — in tension with the utilitarian conception discussed above.[6]

Lockean rhetoric remains a crucial part of the discourse in copyright jurisprudence today. In its present-day form and as applied to copyright, this view holds that an individual who has created a piece of music or a work of art should have the right to control its use and be compensated for its sale, no less than a farmer reaps the benefits of his crop. In addition, because the author has enriched society through his creation, the author has a fundamental right to obtain a reward commensurate with the value of his contribution.[7]

Like the rhetoric of incentives, the rhetoric of natural entitlement has struggled to incorporate considerations of what might be called the public interest in access. In particular, leading scholars have drawn on Locke's famous *proviso*, limiting property rights based on individual labor to situations "where there is enough and as good left in common for others," to suggest how a natural rights approach could be reconciled with the public's entitlement in the "informational commons."[8]

Like the utilitarian conception, the Lockean justification for copyright law provides a useful vocabulary but, in the end, is indeterminate insofar as its specific implications are concerned. The theory maintains that the author should have control over his work, but it indicates little about *how much* control the author should have, how long that control should last, who should benefit from the

---

[4] For general discussion of "authorship" as a legal concept, see Jaszi, *Toward a Theory of Copyright: The Metamorphoses of "Authorship,"* 41 Duke L.J. 455 (1991). *See also* Chartier, *Figures of the Author, in* OF AUTHORS AND ORIGINS 7 (B. Sherman & A. Strowel, eds. 1994).

[5] *See* § 1.04. Nor should one overlook the 1948 Universal Declaration of Human Rights, which at Article 27(2) reads: "Everyone has the right to the protections of the moral and material interests resulting from any scientific, literary, or artistic production of which he is the author."

[6] "Bracketing the slavery issue, there was perhaps no debate more insistent for writers in antebellum American than the issue of literary property." G. Rice, THE TRANSFORMATION OF AUTHORSHIP IN AMERICA 77 (1997).

[7] For an overview of natural law theory, see Yen, *Restoring the Natural Law: Copyright as Labor and Possession,* 51 Ohio St. L. Rev. 517 (1990).

[8] Gordon, *A Property Right in Self-Expression: Equality and Individualism in the Natural Law of Intellectual Property,* 102 Yale L.J. 1533, 1562–83 (1993).

copyrighted work, or what on any given set of facts constitutes just compensation for the author's contribution to society.

Hegel and the Personality Model. The most influential alternative to the labor-based Lockean model of natural law is one based on a personality justification. Associated with the German philosopher Hegel, and embodied in "moral rights" legislation, the personality model advances the idea that property provides a means for self-actualization, for personal expression, and for the dignity of the individual. Putting to one side Hegel's difficult concepts of human will and freedom, the personality theory of intellectual property has an immediate intuitive appeal. After all, is an idea not a manifestation of the creator's personality or self? As such, should it not belong to its creator?

One celebrated formulation of personality rights can be found in Article 6[bis] of the Berne Convention, which requires that member states protect an author's rights of "integrity" and "attribution." Despite the fact that Berne 6[bis] makes no distinction between literary, artistic or musical works, the personality justification applies better to some categories of copyrighted works than others. The arts are a prime example. In a work of art, the personality traits of the author are materialized in an external object. Consistent with this ready applicability of personality-based natural rights theory to art, the rights of "attribution" and "integrity" for certain visual artists are now specifically recognized in § 106A of the Copyright Act of 1976, as amended following U.S. admission to Berne in 1989. In addition to § 106A, American law, at the state level, recognizes personality interests in various bodies of law that overlap with copyright, such as unfair competition law, defamation, privacy, and right of publicity.

In contrast to the arts, other forms of expression, such as the structure of a database, tend to reflect little or no personality from individual creators. An intellectual property system based on personality interests will have trouble justifying a grant of exclusive rights to an individual who has little or no real personality stake in a particular object. Unlike Lockean labor theory, which may be applied across the range of intellectual property, a personality justification works less well when applied to intellectual products that are not suffused with what society would call "personal expression." Thus, a labor justification may be applied equally well to patent protection for a new chemical compound, a database, or a poem. On the other hand, personality theory cannot be conveniently applied to works of utility, computer programs, maps, or highly collaborative works, where individual personality is subsumed in a collective effort. In short, personality theory would exclude categories of works now recognized as integral parts of copyright law.

In addition to the category problems, personality theory shares some of the same conceptual problems found in a labor theory of property. Personality (or labor, for that matter) is not an on/off proposition but is found in varying amounts, depending on the particular work under consideration. Suppose one could say that a particular painting manifests the personality of the artist to a greater degree than another painting. If we accept this to be the case, should works be protected according to the amount of personality they manifest? If so, how should one make this measurement? In truth, Lockean labor theory also suffers from this conceptual dilemma, given that different works result from varying degrees of labor input.[9]

In summary, then, the utilitarian and natural law views (both of Locke and of Hegel) raise a good many questions to which they do not offer definitive answers. However, recognition of the ultimately indeterminate character of these contrasting rhetorics has not detracted from their popularity in the discourse of copyright law and policy. It is fair to say that, throughout the history of Anglo-American copyright, these rhetorics have been successfully deployed to explain or justify virtually every extension of the scope or intensity of copyright protection. They have also been invoked (usually with somewhat less success) in arguments against such expansionist developments.

The history of American copyright law has not reached an end, though — and there is more to the story.

[2] Other Rhetorics in Contemporary Copyright Discourse

In the scholarly literature and judicial decisions of recent years, a number of alternative ways of characterizing copyright and the purposes of the copyright system have begun to gain currency. Some of these rhetorics are new, while some have long and respectable, if not always extensive, histories. Some are offshoots, at least in part, in the traditional rhetorics described above, while others can claim a greater degree of autonomy. All of them add to the richness, if not necessarily the certainty, of copyright discourse.

The rhetoric of misappropriation. This characteristic rhetorical mode draws heavily on both utilitarian and natural law arguments, although invocations of it tend to appear in the guise of simple appeals to "fairness." How can it be right, the usual form of the argument begins, for one to profit (as a "free rider") from the outcome of the intellectual labor of another — to "reap where he or she has not sown"? Surely, the very fact that someone has cared enough to appropriate the products of another's mind must indicate that those products were worth something, and therefore deserving of legal protection.

The rhetoric of misappropriation has roots in the traditional doctrines of quasi-contract and restitution.[10] Moreover, the independent tort of misappropriation has a long, if somewhat checkered, history in both federal and state law, where it has sometimes been invoked in cases where copyright and patent law fail to provide remedies for the taking of mental creations. More recently, misappropriation rhetoric has provided an important part of the rationale for the development of new state causes of action for violation of the "right of publicity." The proliferation of state unfair competition law based on concepts of misappropriation has, in turn,

---

[9] For those wishing to brush up on their Hegel, see G. Hegel, PHILOSOPHY OF RIGHT 40-57 (T.M. Knox, trans., Oxford: Clarendon Press, 1965), and Netanel, *Copyright, Alienability Restrictions and the Enhancement of Author Autonomy: A Normative Evaluation,* 24 Rutgers L.J. 347 (1993). Hegelian property theory is examined in Radin, *Property and Personhood,* 34 Stan. L. Rev. 957 (1982). For application of the theory to intellectual property, see Hughes, *The Philosophy of Intellectual Property,* 77 Geo. L. Rev. 287, 330-65 (1988).

[10] *See generally* J. Dawson, UNJUST ENRICHMENT: A COMPARATIVE ANALYSIS (1951).

created difficult preemption issues which have yet to be satisfactorily resolved.[11]

Here, however, we want to note that the rhetoric of misappropriation has also found its way into the mainstream discourse of copyright itself. Courts invoke it in their decisions, and so do advocates for changes in copyright legislation. A good recent instance can be found in the (ultimately successful) arguments for the extension of the term of existing copyrights by an additional 20 years, to life-plus-70. Why, argue the children of deceased popular songwriters, should someone else benefit from the continued popularity of their parents' enduring hits, no matter how long ago they were composed?[12]

The difficulty with the rhetoric of misappropriation, at least where it is applied to copyright, may be apparent from the foregoing example. Powerful though it may be in its appeal to fundamental fairness, the tendency of misappropriation-based reasoning is infinitely expansive, insofar as the length, breadth and strength of rights are concerned. Put differently, the misappropriation justification, unlike those predicated on incentive-based or even natural entitlement principles, contains no internal checks. Without *external* checks, therefore, an intellectual property system based on ideas of misappropriation would protect every product of the mind, for an unlimited period, in the name of "fairness."

Obviously, copyright law is not likely to be remade along these lines any time soon. But the expansive pressure generated by the rhetoric of misappropriation is nonetheless a force to be reckoned with. Indeed, the next rhetoric to be discussed has gained currency (at least in part) because it seems to provide a basis for restraining the forces which misappropriation rhetoric has helped to release.

The rhetoric of the public domain. The core notion here has been stated as follows:

> [T]he existence of a robust, constantly enriched public domain of material not subject to copyright (or other intellectual property protection) is a good in its own right, which our laws should promote at the same time as they provide incentives or reward creativity.

Lange, *Recognizing the Public Domain*, 44 Law & Contemp. Probs. 147 (1981).[13]

Foregrounding the inescapable truth that all copyrightable works eventually become common property at the end of a period of protection, advocates of the public domain note further that durational limitations on copyright are part of the constitutional scheme itself, just as various other limitations on rights have been recognized in American copyright jurisprudence from its inception. They draw from this the conclusion that proposed modifications to contemporary intellectual property law should be tested against the standard of how well and fully they

---

[11] *See generally* Chapter 11.

[12] *See* § 5.01.

[13] *See also* J. Boyle, THE PUBLIC DOMAIN: ENCLOSING THE COMMONS OF THE MIND (2008); Litman, *The Public Domain*, 39 Emory L.J. 965 (1990); Aoki, *Authors, Inventors and Trademark Owners: Private Intellectual Property and the Public Domain* (Pts. 1 & 2), 18 Colum.-VLA J.L. & Arts 1, 191 (1994-95).

preserve these traditional values.[14]

Notably, a counter-rhetoric has developed in response to advocacy of the public domain. Increasingly, advocates of longer, stronger, and broader copyright protection take the position that the public domain is more an "information limbo" than an "informational commons," and that works in the public domain are likely to be lost to the public forever because no one has an economic incentive to exploit them.[15] In response, advocates of the public domain have begun to take up the challenge of explaining how, in concrete terms, the non-"propertyness" of some information actually promotes various good social and cultural ends.[16]

New economic rhetoric. The critique of the public domain advocacy just summarized represents an example of a relatively new strain in the discourse of copyright policy. By contrast, economic considerations have been part of the discussion from the beginning. With the rise of the "law and economics" movement in the United States, however, new claims are being made for the explanatory power of economic reasoning.

The traditional utilitarian rhetoric of copyright invokes economic concepts in its depiction of rewards to authors and distributors as incentives to make information goods available to the public. Incentive theory posits, as one observer has recently noted, "that copyright is necessary to prevent free riders from undermining the market in creative expression, notwithstanding a concern (usually) for 'copyright's social cost.' "[17]

Contemporary neoclassical economic theory, premised on faith in the power of the free market to allocate scarce resources, takes another, rather different approach to the economic analysis of copyright. Under the neoclassicist approach, copyright is not so much a system of incentives to production and distribution of new works as it is a mechanism "for market facilitation, for moving existing creative works to their highest socially valued uses . . . by enabling copyright owners to realize the full profit potential for their works in the market."[18]

Unlike the economic analysis underlying traditional incentive rhetoric, neoclassical "property rights" theory is not vulnerable to the charge of indeterminacy.

---

[14] Kastenmeier & Remington, *The Chip Protection Act of 1984: A Swamp or Firm Ground?*, 70 Minn. L. Rev. 417, 422-23, 440-42 (1985).

[15] These arguments appear to stem, at least in part, from comments made by Irwin Karp during hearings leading up to the enactment of the Copyright Act of 1976. *See* House Comm. on the Judiciary, 88th Cong., 1st Sess., Report of the Register of Copyrights on the General Revision of the U.S. Copyright Law: Discussion and Comments 316-17 (Comm. Print 1963).

[16] As Litman puts it, "The public domain [is] a device that permits the rest of the system to work by leaving the raw materials of authorship available for authors to use." *The Public Domain*, 39 Emory L.J. 968 n. 999 (1990). *See also* Jaszi, *Goodbye to All That — A Reluctant (and Perhaps Premature) Adieu to a Constitutionally-Grounded Discourse of Public Interest in Copyright Law*, 29 Vand. J. of Transnat'l L. 595 (1996); Heald, *Reviving the Rhetoric of the Public Interest: Choir Directors, Copy Machines and New Arrangements of Public Domain Music*, 1996 Duke L.J. 241; and Hamilton, *An Evaluation of the Copyright Extension Act of 1995: Copyright Duration Extension and the Dark Heart of Copyright*, 14 Cardozo Arts & Ent. L.J. 655 (1996).

[17] Netanel, *Copyright and a Democratic Civil Society*, 106 Yale L.J. 283, 308-09 (1996).

[18] *Id.* at 309.

Broadly speaking, its proponents conclude that the more broadly rights are defined, and the fewer exceptions to which they are subject, the more likely market mechanisms are to fulfill the function of promoting the valuation of resources through the pricing system. Viewed from this perspective, concepts like fair use (except in particular cases of "market failure")[19] and the existence of a public domain are inherently inefficient. Indeed, the critiques of public domain advocacy outlined above can be seen, in part, as anticipations or applications of neoclassical "property rights" theory. The true vulnerabilities of neoclassical economic rhetoric, when applied to copyright law, lie elsewhere: in theory, with its central assumption that market mechanisms do in fact promote efficient allocation, and in practice, with the many examples of ways in which real markets diverge from the ideal.[20]

Despite its vulnerabilities, however, neoclassical rhetoric has acquired considerable currency in copyright discourse, especially with respect to rights in the new digital information environment.[21]

The rhetoric of social dialogue and democratic discourse. Discussions of the future of copyright law in cyberspace also have given prominence to a powerful competing rhetoric in copyright discourse, in which the copyright system figures as a mechanism for promoting certain core values of the civil society — such as openness, freedom, and diversity of expression — which have long been prominent in discussions of First Amendment jurisprudence and policy, but which are a relatively new focus of attention in the domain of intellectual property.[22]

One important source of this rhetoric is the literature of political science, which recognized early on the liberatory potential of new international communications networks.[23] A number of scholars have argued specifically that the promotion of discourse in the civil society should be considered an important end of copyright policy in itself. Some have emphasized a perceived nexus between "social dialogue" and the creative process, arguing that if copyright is to fulfill its core cultural mission, it must reinforce rather than frustrate the elaboration of new communications technologies.[24] Others have stressed the structural function of copyright in maintaining the "independent expressive sector that is critical to democratic governance" — and which derives its independence from the fact that those who participate in it are supported by the market rather than being dependent on patronage or government largess.[25]

---

[19] *See, e.g.*, Landes & Posner, *An Economic Analysis of Copyright Law*, 18 J. Leg. Stud. 325 (1989).

[20] Netanel provides a good introduction to some of the critiques to which neoclassical theory is subject. 106 Yale L.J. at 332–36.

[21] *See generally* Hardy, *Property (and Copyright) in Cyberspace*, 1996 U. Chi. Leg. F. 217.

[22] For a discussion of the marginalized position of the First Amendment in traditional copyright jurisprudence, see Chapter 9.

[23] *See especially* I. de Sola Pool, TECHNOLOGIES OF FREEDOM: ON FREE SPEECH IN AN ELECTRONIC AGE (1983).

[24] *See, e.g.*, Chon, *Postmodern "Progress": Reconsidering the Copyright and Patent Power*, 43 DePaul L. Rev. 97 (1993); Elkin-Koren, *Copyright Law and Social Dialogue on the Information Superhighway: The Case Against Copyright Liability of Bulletin Board Operators*, 13 Cardozo Arts & Ent. L.J. 345 (1995).

[25] *See* Netanel, *Copyright and a Democratic Civil Society* 106 Yale L.J. 283, 358-59 (1996); Radin,

Whereas some exponents of this new rhetoric envision an electronically mediated space for social discourse which stands outside the commercial marketplace in information products, others believe that, if appropriately regulated, this marketplace itself could support the free, open, and diverse exchange which copyright was devised to promote. What both groups appear to share is a conviction that copyright exists, at least in part, to promote the collective life of society, and that mere reliance on an unregulated market in commodified expression will not necessarily further this end.

The rhetoric of "deference." In the judicial opinions you will read during this course, you also will encounter another characteristic set of arguments (or justifications) for results which sound in a somewhat different key from those we have considered up to this point. Taken altogether, however, these arguments do constitute a "rhetoric" in their own right: the rhetoric of judicial deference. Copyright law issues are fact-intensive, so you will not be surprised to see appellate courts deferring broadly to trial courts — although it also will be interesting to note the instances in which such deference is *not* afforded to determinations at trial. And copyright is, after all, a subject dominated by a complicated and detailed statute, so it is to be expected that judges sometimes will decline to second-guess Congressional judgments — even when there may be good arguments for doing so! We will encounter this aspect of the rhetoric of deference when (for example) we consider the Supreme Court's recent rulings on the constitutionality of copyright term extension, *Eldred v. Ashcroft*, 537 U.S. 186 (2003), and the "restoration" of foreign copyrights, *Golan v. Holder*, 132 S. Ct. 873 (2012), in Chapter 5. But this isn't the whole story of judicial deference. We also will have opportunity to observe, from time to time, how federal courts give way to interpretations of the statute from other sources, especially the U.S. Copyright Office, in recognition of their "expertise." *See Marascalco v. Fantasy, Inc.*, 953 F.2d 469, 473 (9th Cir. 1991). So we will want to ask, as we go along, how profoundly the rhetoric of "deference" works to shape copyright doctrine and policy.

[D] Conclusion

Your study of the body of law called "copyright" is only beginning. As this book proceeds, we will revisit some of the ways of thinking and talking about copyright which have been summarized in the foregoing pages. You may already have strong opinions about which of those approaches you prefer. You may develop such preferences as you go along. All we ask is that, as you read through the chapters that follow, you bear in mind that mastering the ability to make (and answer) arguments using the various rhetorics just summarized will help make you a more effective advocate for copyright clients in the years to come.

Regulation of Computer and Information Technology: Property Evolving in Cyberspace, 15 J.L. & Com. 509 (1996). For an historical argument that copyright law actually inhibited the development of civil discourse in the United States by "transforming printed texts from a practical means for assertive sociopolitical commentary into the more inert medium of property and commodity," see G. Rice, THE TRANSFORMATION OF AUTHORSHIP IN AMERICA 4 (1997).

Chapter 2

PREREQUISITES FOR COPYRIGHT PROTECTION

The title of the Statute of Anne provides a simple statement of purpose: Learning is to be encouraged by vesting the copyright "of printed books in the authors" of such works.[1] This purpose continues to be an animating principle of U.S. copyright law even to this day. We see it operative in the threshold requirements for copyrightability that appear early in Title 17. Section 102(a), establishing the two fundamental *prerequisites* for copyright protection, provides:

> Copyright protection subsists . . . in original works of authorship fixed in any tangible medium of expression, now known or later developed, from which they can be perceived, reproduced, or otherwise communicated, either directly or with the aid of a machine or device.

Although *originality* and *fixation* are not acknowledged by name in the Statute of Anne, they are recognized implicitly in the introductory phrase conferring protection to *authors* for their *printed books*. The concept of the "author," as creator, entails the notion of originality. And it is the author who fixes his or her words on the pages of a manuscript (or in digital form, on the hard drive of a computer), which in "printed" form becomes an object of commerce to the benefit of all concerned in the delicate bargain that is copyright law.

The Statute of Anne says little about limits on the scope of protection to be accorded to copyrighted works. These boundaries have been worked out through the years by case law and statutory amendment. The basic limitation is found today in § 102(b), which denies protection to "any idea, procedure, process, system, method of operation, concept, principle, or discovery . . . [that] is described, explained, illustrated, or embodied in" works otherwise satisfying the law's requirements of originality and fixation.

This chapter examines the meaning of the relevant provisions of modern-day U.S. law in an effort to understand what Congress can (and cannot) do pursuant to its constitutional empowerment "To promote the Progress of Science . . . by

---

[1] The statute refers also to the "purchasers" of authors' manuscripts. The purchasers in question were, of course, the "booksellers" of the day (or, as we might say today, the publishers and disseminators of copies of the work). The Copyright Clause of the U.S. Constitution makes no reference to such persons, but their existence, and their importance to the scheme of copyright, received quick acknowledgment in the first copyright act, enacted by Congress in 1790. We will hear more about American publishers and disseminators hereafter. They are the transferees whose interests are the subject of § 4.02 of this casebook ("Transfers of Rights"). For the moment, however, our concern is the central role of "authors" under both the Statute of Anne in England and the Constitution of the United States.

securing for limited Times to Authors . . . the exclusive Right to their . . . Writings . . ."[2]

In addition, we examine briefly other considerations — the work's national origin, and whether it is a "work of the United States Government" — that may, in individual instances, affect protectibility under U.S. law, and we offer a precautionary word about aspects of that law (the so-called "statutory formalities") on which protection once was, but no longer is, conditioned.

§ 2.01 FIXATION

Under the Copyright Clause of the U.S. Constitution, Congress may make laws to protect the "Writings" of authors. This "Writings" requirement has been construed by the Supreme Court to mean any "physical rendering" of the fruits of the author's creativity. *Goldstein v. California*, 412 U.S. 546, 561 (1973). Under the terminology of the present statute, a work is incapable of protection under federal law unless it is "fixed" in a "tangible medium of expression."

The first of the cases that follows — *White-Smith v. Apollo* — is not about copyrightability as such, but it reflects early reluctance to deal with copyright cases involving new modes of information storage. The 1976 Act aimed to correct this tendency by exploiting more fully the potential of the "Writings" requirement. The second case — *Midway v. Artic* — explores some of the ambiguities that still surround the concept of fixation under the statute. As you read the following materials, ask yourself: Why is federal power to confer copyright limited by the "Writings" requirement, and what is the connection between a "writing" and fixation?

Also, putting the constitutional question to one side: Does requiring that a work be physically embodied in order to be protected make sense as a matter of intellectual property policy? Suppose (and it is not so much of a supposition!) that Mozart was able to retain perfectly in his memory numerous compositions, writing them down as a purely ministerial chore whenever he had the spare time. Why should protection for such compositions be denied until Mozart committed them to paper, as distinguished from playing them from memory at a concert?

Or, to take a latter-day example: If you write and send an e-mail message containing an original literary work of real merit, should your copyright protection depend on the vagaries of current computer memory technology — *i.e.*, whether, technically and technologically, the fixation requirement is satisfied?

Assuming we are stuck with the fixation requirement, should Congress and the courts protect authors' original works even when the means of fixation are

---

[2] As to whether the writings of authors must promote "Science" or "useful Arts," even the Supreme Court has seemed uncertain. In *Bleistein v. Donaldson Lithographing Co.*, 188 U.S. 239 (1903), the Court assumed the latter. But in *Graham v. John Deere Co.*, 383 U.S. 1 (1966), the Court proceeded on the view that, in 18th-Century usage, "Science" (meaning "knowledge") referred to the works of authors and "useful Arts" to the products of inventors. In light of the order in which the Framers placed both "Authors and Inventors" and "Writings and Discoveries," the better view is that "Science and useful Arts" have the meanings attributed to them in *Graham. See, e.g., Eldred v. Ashcroft*, 537 U.S. 186, 193 (2003). Hence, the usage in the text above.

unfamiliar or new? If so, on what basis? If not, why not? And are the states preempted from according their own protections to such works? (Recall the discussion of "common-law copyright" in Chapter 1. The preemption doctrine is explored systematically in Chapter 11.)

[A] Introduction

Statutory References

1976 Act: §§ 101 ("copies," "created," "device, machine or process," "fixed," "phonorecords"), 102(a)

1909 Act: § 4

Legislative History

H.R. REP. No. 94-1476, 94th Cong., 2d Sess. at 52-53 (1976)[3]
reprinted in 1976 U.S.C.C.A.N. 5659, 5664-66

SECTION 102. GENERAL SUBJECT MATTER OF COPYRIGHT

. . . The two fundamental criteria of copyright protection — originality and fixation in tangible form — are restated in the first sentence of this cornerstone provision. . . .

Fixation in tangible form

As a basic condition of copyright protection, the bill [and, as enacted, the Copyright Act of 1976] perpetuates the existing requirement that a work be fixed in a "tangible medium of expression," and adds that this medium may be one "now known or later developed," and that the fixation is sufficient if the work "can be perceived, reproduced, or otherwise communicated, either directly or with the aid of a machine or device." This broad language is intended to avoid the artificial and largely unjustifiable distinctions, derived from cases such as *White-Smith [Music] Publishing Co. v. Apollo Co.*, 209 U.S. 1 (1908), under which statutory copyrightability in certain cases has been made to depend upon the form or medium in which the work is fixed. . . .

[*For a fuller excerpt from H.R. Rep. No. 94-1476, see Part Three of the Casebook Supplement.*]

[B] Development of Current Law

You may be wondering why we begin our exploration of "fixation" with a case that predates — and was partially overruled by — the 1909 Act, and that didn't deal with protectibility even when it was good law. The reason is that, although the *outcome* of the case was overruled by the 1909 Act, its *way of thinking* survived until the 1976 Act was passed — and even beyond. The House Report on the 1976 Act cited this case as an example of the "artificial and largely unjustifiable

---

[3] Hereinafter cited as "H.R. REP. No. 94-1476."

distinctions" that the fixation requirement in the 1976 Act was intended to avoid. Nonetheless, the legacy of *White-Smith* lives on in the 1976 Act's otherwise inexplicable distinction between "copies" and "phonorecords."

WHITE-SMITH MUSIC PUBLISHING CO. v. APOLLO CO.
Supreme Court of the United States
209 U.S. 1 (1908)

MR. JUSTICE DAY delivered the opinion of the court:

These cases . . . were brought to restrain infringement of the copyrights of two certain musical compositions, published in the form of sheet music, entitled respectively, "Little Cotton Dolly" and "Kentucky Babe." The appellee, defendant below, is engaged in the sale of . . . player pianos known as the "Apollo," and of perforated rolls of music used in connection therewith. The appellant, as assignee of Adam Geibel, the composer, alleged compliance with the copyright act, and that a copyright was duly obtained by it on or about March 17, 1897. The answer was general in its nature, and upon the testimony adduced a decree was rendered, as stated, in favor of the Apollo Company, defendant below, appellee here.

The action was brought under the provisions of the copyright act, § 4952 (U.S. Comp. Stat. Supp. 1907, p. 1021), giving to the author, inventor, designer, or proprietor of any book, map, chart, dramatic or musical composition the sole liberty of printing, reprinting, publishing, completing, copying, executing, finishing, and vending the same. . . .

Without entering into a detailed discussion of the[ir] mechanical construction . . . , it is enough to say that [the defendant sells] what has become familiar to the public in the form of mechanical attachments to pianos, such as the pianola, and the musical rolls consist of perforated sheets, which are passed over ducts connected with the operating parts of the mechanism in such manner that the same are kept sealed until, by means of perforations in the rolls, air pressure is admitted to the ducts which operate the pneumatic devices to sound the notes. This is done with the aid of an operator, upon whose skill and experience the success of the rendition largely depends. As the roll is drawn over the tracker board the notes are sounded as the perforations admit the atmospheric pressure, the perforations having been so arranged that the effect is to produce the melody or tune for which the roll has been cut. . . .

The learned counsel for the parties to this action advance opposing theories as to the nature and extent of the copyright given by statutory laws enacted by Congress for the protection of copyright, and a determination of which is the true one will go far to decide the rights of the parties in this case. On behalf of the appellant it is insisted that it is the intention of the copyright act to protect the intellectual conception which has resulted in the compilation of notes which, when properly played, produce the melody which is the real invention of the composer. It is insisted that this is the thing which Congress intended to protect, and that the protection covers all means of expression of the order of notes which produce the air or melody which the composer has invented.

Music, it is argued, is intended for the ear as writing is for the eye, and that it is the intention of the copyright act to prevent the multiplication of every means of reproducing the music of the composer to the ear.

On the other hand, it is contended that while it is true that copyright statutes are intended to reward mental creations or conceptions, that the extent of this protection is a matter of statutory law, and that it has been extended only to the tangible results of mental conception, and that only the tangible thing is dealt with by the law, and its multiplication or reproduction is all that is protected by the statute. . . .

Musical compositions have been the subject of copyright protection since the statute of February 3, 1831 . . . , and laws have been passed including them since that time. When we turn to the consideration of the act it seems evident that Congress has dealt with the tangible thing, a copy of which is required to be filed with the Librarian of Congress, and wherever the words are used (copy or copies) they seem to refer to the term in its ordinary sense of indicating reproduction or duplication of the original. . . .

What is meant by a copy? . . .

Various definitions have been given by the experts called in the case. The one which most commends itself to our judgment is perhaps as clear as can be made, and defines a copy of a musical composition to be "a written or printed record of it in intelligible notation." It may be true that in a broad sense a mechanical instrument which reproduces a tune copies it; but this is a strained and artificial meaning. When the combination of musical sounds is reproduced to the ear it is the original tune as conceived by the author which is heard. These musical tones are not a copy which appeals to the eye. In no sense can musical sounds which reach us through the sense of hearing be said to be copies, as that term is generally understood, and as we believe it was intended to be understood in the statutes under consideration. A musical composition is an intellectual creation which first exists in the mind of the composer; he may play it for the first time upon an instrument. It is not susceptible of being copied until it has been put in a form which others can see and read. The statute has not provided for the protection of the intellectual conception apart from the thing produced, however meritorious such conception may be, but has provided for the making and filing of a tangible thing, against the publication and duplication of which it is the purpose of the statute to protect the composer. . . .

After all, what is the perforated roll? The fact is clearly established in the testimony in this case that even those skilled in the making of these rolls are unable to read them as musical compositions, as those in staff notations are read by the performer. It is true that there is some testimony to the effect that great skill and patience might enable the operator to read this record as he could a piece of music written in staff notation. But the weight of the testimony is emphatically the other way, and they are not intended to be read as an ordinary piece of sheet music, which, to those skilled in the art, conveys, by reading, in playing or singing, definite impressions of the melody.

$10 Puts this Player Piano In Your Home

his Finest Windsor Player Will Delight Two Generations

HING has been spared to make this agnificent Windsor Player Piano all at you could wish in tone quality, nd beauty of finish.

n investment in enjoyment for your amily—for your children and their . Its resonant, sweet singing tone : outlast our guarantee. Expression automatic tracking device, balanced or easy playing, fiber-covered metal every single part is of the best pos-terials and workmanship. Compare any $600 player and see!

The case is built up layer on layer of thoroughly seasoned wood—it cannot warp. Genuine veneer of mahogany, burl walnut, or quartered oak, rubbed to a French polish. New Empire top. Brass hinges and pedals; genuine ivory keys. Height, 54 ½ inches; width, 60½ inches; depth, 28 inches. Bench and ten rolls of music included free. See "Estimated Freight Charges" below. Ship. weight, complete, 880 lbs.

Use Easy Payment Order Blank No. 1 on Page 721.

267 E 68—Mahogany.................$485.00
267 E 69—Walnut....................485.00
267 E 70—Oak.......................485.00

Shipped from Factory near Chicago

Early 20th Century Fixation — The Player Piano
Corbis

These perforated rolls are parts of a machine which, when duly applied and properly operated in connection with the mechanism to which they are adapted, produce musical tones in harmonious combination. But we cannot think that they are copies within the meaning of the copyright act.

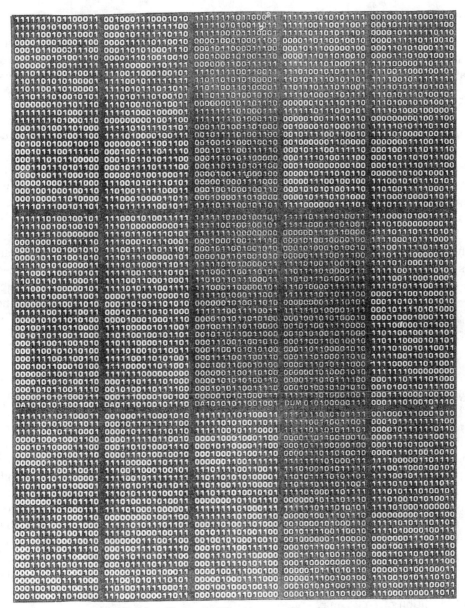

Early 21st Century Fixation — The Computer
Reproduced by courtesy of, and copyrighted by, 3M Company

It may be true that the use of these perforated rolls, in the absence of statutory protection, enables the manufacturers thereof to enjoy the use of musical compositions for which they pay no value. But such considerations properly address themselves to the legislative, and not to the judicial, branch of the government. As the act of Congress now stands we believe it does not include these records as copies or publications of the copyrighted music involved in these cases.

The decrees of the Circuit Court of Appeals are affirmed.

Mr. Justice Holmes, concurring specially.

In view of the facts and opinions in this country and abroad to which my brother Day has called attention, I do not feel justified in dissenting from the judgment of the court, but the result is to give to copyright less scope than its rational significance and the ground on which it is granted seem to me to demand. Therefore I desire to add a few words to what he has said.

The notion of property starts, I suppose, from confirmed possession of a tangible object, and consists in the right to exclude others from interference with the more or less free doing with it as one wills. But in copyright property has reached a more abstract expression. The right to exclude is not directed to an object in possession or owned, but is *in vacuo*, so to speak. It restrains the spontaneity of men where, but for it, there would be nothing of any kind to hinder their doing as they saw fit. It is a prohibition of conduct remote from the persons or tangibles of the party having the right. It may be infringed a thousand miles from the owner and without his ever becoming aware of the wrong. It is a right which could not be recognized or endured for more than a limited time and therefore, I may remark, in passing, it is one which hardly can be conceived except as a product of statute, as the authorities now agree.

The ground of this extraordinary right is that the person to whom it is given has invented some new collocation of visible or audible points, — of lines, colors, sounds, or words. The restraint is directed against reproducing this collocation, although, but for the invention and the statute, anyone would be free to combine the contents of the dictionary, the elements of the spectrum, or the notes of the gamut in any way that he had the wit to devise. The restriction is confined to the specific form, to the collocation devised, of course, but one would expect that, if it was to be protected at all, that collocation would be protected according to what was its essence. One would expect the protection to be coextensive not only with the invention, which, though free to all, only one had the ability to achieve, but with the possibility of reproducing the result which gives to the invention its meaning and worth. A musical composition is a rational collocation of sounds apart from concepts, reduced to a tangible expression from which the collocation can be reproduced either with or without continuous human intervention. On principle anything that mechanically reproduces that collocation of sounds ought to be held a copy, or, if the statute is too narrow, ought to be made so by a further act, except so far as some extraneous consideration of policy may oppose. . . .

NOTES AND QUESTIONS

(1) *Protectibility vs. infringement.* In thinking about copyright problems, keep in mind the difference between copyrightability analysis (which focuses on whether a work or an aspect of a work is protected) and infringement analysis (which is predicated on proof by the claimant of ownership of a valid copyright in the work and focuses on whether a copyright owner's exclusive rights have been violated by a particular act alleged to be an unauthorized use of a protected work). The two kinds of analysis — protectibility and infringement — serve different purposes and proceed along different lines. For example, while the addition of new material to a

preexisting work may entitle the author of the resulting "derivative work" to copyright protection if the preexisting work is in the public domain or its use has been authorized, the unauthorized use of a protected preexisting work is not thereby excused.

The issue of whether the work has been fixed in a tangible medium of expression always must be addressed as part of copyrightability analysis. The issue of fixation also arises in the infringement context because two of the copyright owner's exclusive rights are to reproduce and distribute fixed "copies" of the work. This issue receives more detailed treatment in § 7.02. For now, it is important to recognize that even where copyrightability analysis and infringement analysis share terms in common, those words may have distinct meanings in the two separate contexts. The term "copy," so important in *White-Smith*, provides an apt example.

Under the scheme of U.S. copyright laws before the 1976 Act, the attachment of protection under federal copyright law usually occurred when the work was "published" with a proper copyright notice. See the detailed discussion of this point in Chapter 6. "Publication" was accomplished by distributing "copies" of the work to the public. Also, under pre-1978 law as well as today, infringement of copyright could occur when unauthorized "copies" of a protected work were manufactured or sold.

White-Smith addressed the question of whether piano rolls were such "copies" for *infringement* purposes. It does not follow that the *White-Smith* definition of "copy" must (or even should) have been employed in the conceptually distinct setting of *copyrightability* analysis. But in fact, in later cases, that is just what occurred.

(2)   White-Smith *and its aftermath.* Justice Day himself does not always seem to be making with perfect clarity the distinction just described. Indeed, he seems to equate a "copy" for infringement purposes with the deposit "copy" that the statute required in order to gain copyright protection. But even assuming, *arguendo*, that a "copy" for one purpose is a "copy" for all, was there any *constitutional* justification for the requirement that it be "in a form which others can see and read"? Isn't Justice Holmes clearly correct in saying that the result "give[s] to copyright less scope than its rational significance and the ground on which it is granted seem . . . to demand"?

If so, whose job was it to fix the problem that Holmes perceived? Can the result be justified on the ground that Justice Day's opinion offers — namely, that "such considerations properly address themselves to the legislative, and not to the judicial, branch of the government"? And while Justice Day defers to Congress, Justice Holmes says he defers — concurring rather than dissenting — to other courts in the United States and abroad. Higher courts than his?

(3)   In 1909, Congress took some of the sting out of *White-Smith's* learning on infringement by enacting the provision codified as § 1(e) of the 1909 Act. Section 1(e) extended copyright protection to cover so-called "mechanical reproductions" of musical compositions (including piano rolls and the then-emergent technology of phonograph recordings), while at the same time providing a "compulsory license"

for mechanical reproduction on terms stipulated by the statute. (Incidentally, this device is preserved in the 1976 Act, as discussed in Chapter 7 below.) But Congress did *not* explicitly overrule *White-Smith*'s definition of "copy" itself. As a result, the absence of direct perceptibility continued to be a barrier to the protection of many kinds of works until January 1, 1978. Thus, for example, while motion pictures recorded on film stock were protected, there was a lingering question about the status of works fixed solely on videotape. This ambiguity disappeared only when the 1976 Act's new definition of a "copy" as a "material object . . . in which a work is fixed . . . and from which the work can be perceived, reproduced, or otherwise communicated, *either directly or with the aid of a machine or device*" took effect.

(4)   Recall that the legislative history of the 1976 Act referred to *White-Smith* as its primary example of "artificial and largely unjustifiable distinctions" which the courts had created in the fixation area under the 1909 Act and its predecessors. The drafters of the 1976 Act purposefully chose what the House Report calls "broad language" to avoid such line-drawing in judicial construction of the fixation requirement in the new Act. Thus, the current statute provides for protection of fixation in "*any* tangible medium of expression, *now known or later developed*" (emphasis added). As you read through the remainder of this casebook, be on the look-out for instances in which courts seem to carry out, or frustrate, this "open-ended" attitude of Congress toward new technologies.

(5)   *The limits of fixation.* Suppose your copyright professor forbids any recording or note-taking in her classes. As it turns out, however, one student has been taping them surreptitiously (for her own use), while another has taken advantage of his "photographic memory" to reproduce and sell the substance of the professor's lectures. When they both are discovered, the professor sues the latter for copyright infringement, alleging that the activities of the former satisfy the fixation requirement. On a motion to dismiss, what result? How sensible is the result you forecast? *See* Barnett, *"Profiting at My Expense": An Analysis of the Commercialization of Professors' Lecture Notes*, 9 J. Intell. Prop. L. 137 (2001).

(6)   *Computer software protection.* One area as to which even the 1976 Act failed to resolve issues arising from the constitutional "Writings" requirement was computer programs. Directions for the operation of a computer *can* be written out by their creator in a form "which others can see and read," although there seems to be little point in doing so. But the computer itself requires that these directions be translated into what might be called "machine language" in order to run them. (For a detailed explanation of computer programs, see *Apple Computer, Inc. v. Franklin Computer Corp.* in Chapter 3.)

Applying the 1909 Act, one District Court had held that computer programs, because they cannot be deciphered with the naked eye, are not "copies" of the programmers' original directions. On appeal, however, the Seventh Circuit affirmed for reasons seemingly inconsistent with the District Court's view. *See Data Cash Systems, Inc. v. JS&A Group, Inc.*, 480 F. Supp. 1063 (N.D. Ill. 1979), *aff'd on other grounds*, 628 F.2d 1038 (7th Cir. 1980).

Section 117 of the 1976 Act, as originally enacted, froze the law as it stood on December 31, 1977 with respect to computer programs, in order to permit further study of the issues by the Congressionally-mandated Commission on New Technological Uses of Copyrighted Works ("CONTU"). It was not until 1980 that, by enacting present § 117, Congress made the § 101 definition of "copy" applicable to computer programs. The next case in the book introduces the topic of computer software, the fixation requirement, and protectibility. But first, a cautionary note.

(7) The criterion of "perceptibility" laid down in *White-Smith* came to be applied across the board, whenever and however an issue arose as to whether a particular fixation constituted a "copy." Consequently, a decision of fairly restricted immediate importance, involving a technical question of infringement law relating to musical compositions, came to be a barrier to the availability of copyright protection for various kinds of works fixed by means of new technologies. Today, as one court has observed, the "sole purpose of [the] definition of 'copies' and 'fixed' is to explicate" the latter-day embodiment of the "Writings" of the Constitution by "defin[ing] the material objects in which copyrightable and infringing works may be embedded and . . . describ[ing] the requisite fixed nature of that work within the material object." *Matthew Bender & Co., Inc. v. West Publishing Co.*, 158 F.3d 693, 702 (2d Cir. 1998). But this inquiry still is sometimes less than completely straightforward.

MIDWAY MANUFACTURING CO. v. ARTIC INTERNATIONAL, INC.
United States District Court, Northern District of Illinois
547 F. Supp. 999 (1982),
aff'd on other grounds, 704 F.2d 1009 (7th Cir. 1983)

DECKER, DISTRICT JUDGE:

[Midway sued Artic for alleged infringement of Midway's copyrights in two coin-operated video games, Galaxian and Pac-Man. Designed for use in video arcades, the video games operate in two modes: "attract" mode, a fairly short animated sequence which repeats itself until the user deposits a coin or a token; and "play" mode, in which the audiovisual display responds to the operation of the controls by the player. The audiovisual displays of the two video games are generated by computer programs stored on computer chips called ROMs (for "read only memory"). The program instructions, contained in "program ROMs," instruct the microprocessor (or CPU, for "central processing unit") to retrieve images stored in "character ROMs" and to display those images at specified locations on the television screen. The CPU and the ROMs are attached to a printed circuit board inside the game cabinet.]

After a coin is inserted and the game goes into the play mode, the images generated by the character ROMs move on the screen in a finite but enormous number of sequences. . . . If a player were to move the controls of either a Pac-Man or Galaxian video game in exactly the same way in two different plays of the game, the images on the screen would all move in exactly the same way. . . .

The evidence presented at the hearing showed that defendant Artic sells two devices which Midway contends violate its rights in the Galaxian and Pac-Man games. The first of those items is a speed-up kit, which, when attached to the

Galaxian game, modifies the way the images move on the screen. . . .

The second item sold by Artic that is of interest in this litigation is a printed circuit board that is used to create a "Puckman" video game. . . .

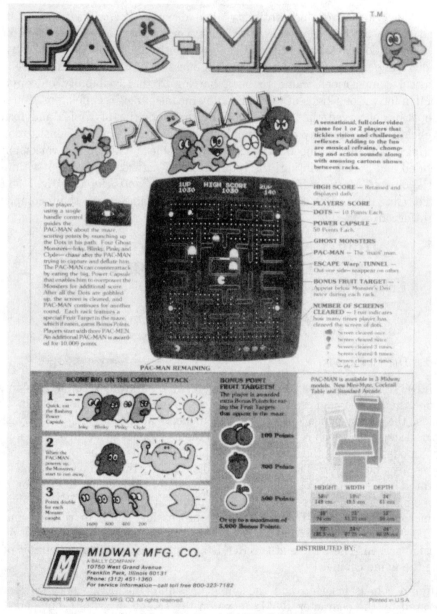

An Advertisement for PAC-MAN®
© 1980 NAMCO Ltd. All Rights Reserved. Courtesy of Namco Holding Corp.

Discussion

[Among what the court describes as a "massive scattershot of arguments against the validity and application of Midway's copyrights,"] Artic . . . contends that the audiovisual aspects of Midway's video games are not "fixed in any tangible medium of expression," 17 U.S.C. § 102(a), and so do not qualify for copyright protection at all. . . .

Before a copyright can attach in any original work of authorship, the work must be "fixed in any tangible medium of expression, now known or later developed, from which [it] can be perceived, reproduced, or otherwise communicated, either directly or with the aid of a machine or device." 17 U.S.C. § 102(a). The phrase is defined in the Copyright Act as follows:

> A work is "fixed" in a tangible medium of expression when its embodiment in a copy or phonorecord, by or under the authority of the author, is sufficiently permanent or stable to permit it to be perceived, reproduced, or otherwise communicated for a period of more than transitory duration.

17 U.S.C. § 101.

Artic contends that the audiovisual displays of Midway's games do not meet that requirement. Artic's argument is based on the specific technology by which the images that appear on the game screens are generated. Basically, Artic notes that the ROMs in the video game do not contain enough memory to store the entire picture that appears on the game's screen at any one instant. Rather, the ROMs contain a number of symbols or patterns which are combined in various ways by the microprocessor to make up the images seen on the screen. Artic argues, therefore, that the computer is simply generating a new set of pictures at all times, pictures that are themselves not fixed in any medium.

While Artic's argument has a certain facial validity, it nonetheless fails. The fixation requirement, as is clear from the statute, does not require that the work be written down or recorded somewhere exactly as it is perceived by the human eye. Rather, all that is necessary for the requirement to be satisfied is that the work is capable of being "reproduced . . . with the aid of a machine or device." 17 U.S.C. § 102(a). As was amply demonstrated by Midway at the hearing, the audiovisual features of its games may be reproduced over and over again, for extended periods of time. The attract modes of the two games, for instance, repeat themselves over and over again, in identical fashion, for as long as the games are turned on and no one is playing them. The copyrightable aspects of the play mode likewise repeat themselves whenever the game is played.

Artic attempts to draw support for its position from a statement in the Report of the House Judiciary Committee on the Copyright Act. The Judiciary Committee stated:

> [T]he definition of "fixation" would exclude from the concept purely evanescent or transient reproductions such as those projected briefly on a screen, shown electronically on a television or other cathode ray tube, or captured momentarily in the "memory" of a computer.

H.R. Rep. No. 94-1476, 94th Cong., 2nd Sess. 53. When read in context, however, the "purely evanescent or transient reproductions" referred to by Congress are those arising from live telecasts or performances that are nowhere separately recorded. Clearly, the lack of any recording of such events would preclude their ever again being identically reproduced. In the instant case, the copyrighted material is recorded in the ROMs and may be reproduced with the aid of the microprocessor. While the technology of the reproduction is different than that encountered with videotape, Congress has allowed for that eventuality by allowing for fixation in mediums of expression either "now known or later developed." 17 U.S.C. § 102(a). The technology used in the video games is one such later developed medium of expression. . . .

For the reasons stated above, the court finds that plaintiff has successfully demonstrated that all elements necessary for issuing a preliminary injunction are present in this case. Therefore, plaintiff's motion for preliminary injunction is granted . . .

NOTES AND QUESTIONS

(1) *Fixation and new technology, continued.* In an earlier proceeding in the same matter, the District Judge observed: "It seems clear that the framers of the [1976] Copyright Act did not consider the specific problems raised by advanced electronic games." *Midway Manufacturing Co. v. Artic International, Inc.*, 1981 U.S. Dist. LEXIS 16881, at *23 (N.D. Ill. 1981). If this is so, how can the court justify affording the plaintiff the protection of the copyright laws?

(2) In what sense is the plaintiff's work (assuming, for purposes of this chapter, that videogames qualify as "works" subject to copyright protection) "fixed" in a "tangible medium of expression" from which it can be "perceived, reproduced, or otherwise communicated," even "with the aid of a machine or device"? Precisely what is it that Midway claims to have fixed? Images? A computer program? And where is it fixed? Is a video screen, for example, a "tangible" medium of expression? The ROM chips?

(3) Shouldn't the court have paid closer attention to what occurs when the game is in the "play mode" (as distinct from the repetitive "attract mode")? Specifically, what is the effect of player participation? Does it prevent fixation of the sights and sounds of the game? Should variety in the audiovisual incidents and patterns experienced by a player or players on different occasions affect copyrightability, assuming that all of the sights and sounds are generated by the chip in which the computer program's creator has embodied the work? The matter is discussed more fully in *Stern Electronics, Inc. v. Kaufman*, 669 F.2d 852 (2d Cir. 1982), and *Williams Electronics, Inc. v. Artic International, Inc.*, 685 F.2d 870 (3d Cir. 1982).

(4) Does the court deal adequately with Artic's assertion that the Galaxian and Pac-Man images are not, as required by the definition of "fixed" in § 101, "sufficiently permanent or stable to permit [them] to be perceived, reproduced, or otherwise communicated for a period of more than transitory duration"? What exactly is "transitory duration," anyway?

One can imagine situations in which the "transitory" nature of a work might be an issue. Is a poem written in the sand "fixed"? Does it matter whether it is above or below the tide line? What about skywriting? Is a fireworks display "fixed" if it is meticulously scripted in advance? *See* Hopper, *Sky Power Producers Don't Take Copyright Law Lightly*, Hous. Chron., Sept. 20, 1998, at 37.

(5)   In a more practical vein, the fixation requirement plays an important role in defining which uses of digital technology fix copyrightable works in a tangible medium both for copyrightability and for infringement purposes. The easy cases are copies stored on a hard disk, a flash drive, or on some other digital medium in which they last until the user deletes them. These are sufficiently "permanent or stable to permit [them] to be perceived, reproduced, or otherwise communicated for a period of more than transitory duration." 17 U.S.C. § 101. But, what about all of the temporary copies that personal computers, smart phones, Internet routers, and all other manner of computing devices routinely make as part of their normal operation? The two forms of temporary copies where the fixation issue arises most commonly are with works that exist only in their complete form as temporary copies and works that are temporarily copied into "buffers" as streaming media or as packets of information repeatedly copied by the routers that make Internet communication possible.

Midway is an early case involving the first scenario, in which the constituent elements of a work of authorship are fixed as independent digital files that are then brought together "on the fly" to create a temporary copy of the complete work. The question usually is whether the work is fixed because its constituent elements are fixed or because the temporary copy lasts long enough to meet the definition of fixation. As we will see in other video game cases in § 7.03[B] of this book, this scenario also raises the question of whether these temporary copies infringe the copyright owner's right to prepare derivative works.

You also create temporary copies on the fly almost every time you surf the World Wide Web. The large majority of web pages are not stored as single complete files on a web server. Instead, many pages are "dynamic" or "active." When you click on a link to a dynamic web page, your computer receives and acts upon a set of instructions to compose the web page by pulling in content from both the website's server and, often, third-party advertisers' machines. Although each element of the web page, such as text, photos, and an advertisement, is independently stored in some lasting form, what about the compilation of these elements into the page you see on the screen? Unless saved to a hard disk, this copy is only temporary because it is stored in your computer's random access memory ("RAM"). RAM copies are those that the computer can act on, but they are deleted automatically when the device is turned off. (Anyone who has lost work in a word processing program when the computer crashed knows this truth all too painfully!) Whether such temporary copies are "fixed" for infringement purposes has been litigated. *See 1-800 Contacts, Inc. v. WhenU.com, Inc.*, 309 F. Supp. 2d 467, 486–87 (S.D.N.Y. 2003) (unwanted pop-up ads don't infringe a website owner's copyright), *rev'd on other grounds*, 414 F.3d 400 (2d Cir. 2005).

(6)   Whether RAM copies or buffer copies are fixed has received more attention in the infringement context. Initially, in *MAI Systems Corp. v. Peak Computer Inc.*, 991 F.2d 511 (9th Cir. 1993), the court held that the loading of the plaintiff's copyrighted software into RAM constituted a fixation and qualified as a "copy"

under the Copyright Act for purposes of infringement analysis because the copy could be "perceived, reproduced or communicated." Although the specific result of *MAI* was overturned in 1998 by Title III ("Computer Maintenance or Repair Copyright Exemption") of the Digital Millennium Copyright Act (codified at 17 U.S.C. § 117(c)), the court's reasoning was not rejected by Congress. To the contrary, Congress appeared to accept implicitly the holding of *MAI* in drafting other portions of the DMCA. See, for example, 17 U.S.C. § 512, discussed in § 9.03 of this casebook. Despite academic criticism of the *MAI* decision, courts have consistently accepted its holding that a work can be electronically "fixed" in RAM for purposes of the Act. *See, e.g., Stenograph L.L.C. v. Bossard Associates, Inc.*, 144 F.3d 96, 101–02 (D.C. Cir. 1998); *Tiffany Design, Inc v. Reno-Tahoe Specialty, Inc.*, 55 F. Supp. 2d 1113, 1121 (D. Nev. 1999); *Advanced Computer Services of Michigan, Inc. v. MAI Systems Corp.*, 845 F. Supp. 356, 362–64 (E.D. Va. 1994).

More recently, the Second Circuit held in *Cartoon Network v. CSC Holdings, Inc.*, 536 F.3d 121 (2d Cir. 2008), that a buffer copy of a video stream that lasted for only 1.2 seconds was not fixed because it did not last for "a period of more than a transitory duration." This case and discussion of the role of "fixation" for copyright law on the Internet is discussed in more detail in §§ 7.02 and 9.03 below.

(7)   Is a garden "fixed in a tangible medium of expression"? In *Kelly v. Chicago Park District*, 635 F.3d 290 (7th Cir. 2011), the court acknowledged that the pictorial design of a garden may be "fixed" (when printed on paper or stored in a computer), and that the living plants constituting the garden are "tangible and can be perceived for more than a transitory duration." Nonetheless, the court held that the garden itself was "not stable or permanent enough to be called 'fixed' " within the meaning of § 101, because "[s]eeds and plants in a garden are naturally in a state of perpetual change; they germinate, grow, bloom, become dormant, and eventually die. . . . [A garden] may endure from season to season, but its nature is one of dynamic change." Do you agree? If an elaborate design may be fixed on paper, why is the same design not "fixed" when it is replicated with plants? Is a topiary sculpture "fixed"? If so, why is a garden different?

(8)   Is the human body a "tangible medium of expression"? In *Whitmill v. Warner Bros. Entertainment, Inc.*, Civ. No. 11-cv-752 (E.D. Mo., filed Apr. 28, 2011), the plaintiff tattoo artist had "inked" former heavyweight boxer Mike Tyson with an image registered in the Copyright Office as *"Tribal Tattoo."* In the film *Hangover 2*, produced by the defendant, a character awakens to find that he now has a replica of the Tyson tattoo. Promotional materials for the film also prominently featured the character with the tattoo. The artist had given Tyson a license to be photographed with the tattoo, but Tyson had no rights to authorize other repro-ductions of the image. Warner Brothers submitted a Declaration from treatise author David Nimmer, who took the position that the human body could not serve as a medium of expression for fixation purposes. At the preliminary injunction hearing, the court allowed the movie to be released but was unimpressed by Warner Brothers' defense. The parties settled the case soon thereafter.

(9)   As we will see in the next chapter, original works of authorship fixed in tangible media of expression may take one of several forms — including, of particular relevance for a discussion of video games, "literary works" (a rubric that

comprehends, perhaps surprisingly, computer programs), and "audiovisual works" (which includes approximately what one would imagine). After *Midway* was decided, the Copyright Office reversed its previous practice of permitting separate registrations for the *display* of an electronic videogame as an audiovisual work, and for the underlying *computer program* as a literary work. The Office now allows only a single registration for display-generating programs: the proprietor must decide whether the "program" aspects or the "audiovisual" aspects predominate, and file for registration accordingly. *See Copyright Office Notice of Registration Decision*, 53 Fed. Reg. 21817 (June 10, 1988).

(10) *Live broadcasts and simultaneous recordings.* The final sentence of the definition of fixation in § 101 of Title 17 states: "A work consisting of sounds, images, or both, that are being transmitted, is 'fixed' for purposes of this title if a fixation of the work is being made simultaneously with its transmission." What types of works was this sentence intended to reach? You may want to look again at the legislative history reproduced in the Supplement. *See also Swatch Group Mgmt. Servs., Ltd. v. Bloomberg L.P.*, 808 F. Supp. 2d 634 (S.D.N.Y. 2011) (because a conference call between Swatch executives and outside securities analysts was being simultaneously recorded, call was "fixed" and unauthorized reproduction could be infringing).

[handwritten margin note: live TV NFL games?]

(11) Justifying the *"fixation" requirement.* In § 1.06, we outlined some ways of thinking and talking about copyright. How successfully can any of these be invoked to explain fixation? Are the utilitarian and natural law rationales for copyright relevant? Is the cult of the Romantic author? Isn't the fixation requirement in apparent tension with notions of creators' natural rights? Can't an unfixed work be misappropriated as thoroughly (and with as much harm to its creator) as a fixed one? What vision (if any) of the public interest is promoted by requiring fixation?

Can the fixation requirement be justified from an economic standpoint? One commentator has observed that, "[i]n the law of real property, physical boundaries are essential to organizing transactions. To have a market, the objects to be bought, sold, and licensed must be clearly identified. Outside the market sphere, boundaries function to keep an owner's rights within socially tolerable limits." See Gordon, *An Inquiry into the Merits of Copyright: The Challenges of Consistency, Consent, and Encouragement Theory*, 41 Stan. L. Rev. 1343, 1378–84 (1989), for elaboration.

Does the law of copyright impose boundaries that facilitate the organization of a market for copyrighted works and at the same time keep ownership rights within reasonable limits? Is the requirement of fixation one of those boundaries? Does the fixation requirement reduce the costs of litigation by providing evidence relevant to both copyright ownership and infringement? Might such lack of boundaries have influenced the courts in the *Hemingway* and *Falwell* cases described below to deny claims of common-law copyright? As you go through the following chapters, consider the other means by which the 1976 Act sets out boundaries that demarcate and delimit the grant of the statutory monopoly that copyright creates.

(12) *Unfixed works and common-law copyright.* In *Estate of Hemingway v. Random House, Inc.*, 244 N.E.2d 250 (N.Y. 1968), the New York Court of Appeals considered whether to recognize common-law copyright protection for certain "anecdotes, reminiscences, literary opinions and revealing comments" uttered, but never reduced to writing, by the late author Ernest Hemingway. Hemingway's

estate maintained that the author's utterances constituted "literary property" protectible under New York law, citing the late Prof. Melville B. Nimmer for the proposition that "the underlying rationale for common law copyright (*i.e.*, the recognition that a property right should attach to the fruits of intellectual labor) is applicable regardless of whether such labor assumes tangible form (Nimmer, Copyright, § 11.1, at 40)." 244 N.E.2d at 254.

Carried to extremes, the plaintiff's theory suggests that each of us (or, at least, every celebrated author) is entitled to legal protection for everything she says in the course of her day. Not surprisingly, *Hemingway* itself was decided on the ground that the author had not indicated an intention to claim the utterances in question as his property by somehow marking them off from the common run of his everyday speech.

See also *Falwell v. Penthouse International, Ltd.*, 521 F. Supp. 1204 (W.D. Va. 1981), involving the publication of unauthorized quotations from an interview, and noting that, because there had been "no defined segregation, either by design or by implication of any of plaintiff's expressions of his thoughts and opinions of the subjects discussed, which would aid in identifying plaintiff's purported copyrighted material," the complaint did not fall "within the narrow circumstances where a cause of action involving an oral expression can be sustained under a common law copyright theory." *Id.* at 1208.

How could "Old Man" Hemingway or the Reverend Falwell have marked off some of their oral expressions as literary property? If they had done so, how should the courts have ruled on the ultimate issue of protectibility? Would a state's rationale(s) for protecting, under the common law, unfixed works — *i.e.*, those which do not qualify as constitutional "Writings" — be the same as the justification(s) for extending copyright to fixed works under federal law? Would protection for unfixed works under state law run afoul of the "preemption doctrine" (explored in Chapter 11 of the book)?

(13)   In 1982, California amended its literary property law to extend protection to "any original work of authorship that is not fixed in any tangible medium of expression . . . as against all persons except one who originally and independently creates the same or similar work." Cal. Civ. Code § 980(a)(1) (2009). Are there any policy arguments *against* the California statute?

(14)   Discussions of the need for meaningful protection of at least some unfixed works frequently cite the example of jazz improvisations. Can you think of other examples? Consider the following situation.

At a comedy shop called "Politically Inexcusable," various groups regularly perform improvisational political skits lampooning unbeloved figures in government and politics. One evening, Hogge Wilde, a comedy writer attending the performances, copies material presented in a skit by Pigge Sloppe, a competing group. Are the improvisations at "Politically Inexcusable" protected by federal copyright law? If not, and assuming that state law does not protect "improvs" under its statutory or common law, what steps would you advise Pigge Sloppe to take to deal with the situation? *See also* Oliar & Sprigman, *There's No Free Laugh (Anymore): The Emergence of Intellectual Property Norms and the Transformation of*

Stand-Up Comedy, 94 Va. L. Rev. 1787 (2008).

(15) *Fixation, international protection, and "bootlegging."* The American requirement of "fixation" as a precondition for copyright protection is not characteristic of "authors' rights" laws around the world. Many countries protect fixed and unfixed works without differentiation. Neither the Berne Convention, to which the United States acceded effective March 1, 1989, nor the Universal Copyright Convention, to which the United States has been a party since 1955, limits member states to protecting fixed works.

Recall that a work is fixed only when embodied in a tangible medium "by or under the authority of the author." As a result, there are commercially valuable types of cultural artifacts — notably, live musical performances — which are not fixed when recorded without authorization but which the United States has an interest in protecting against unauthorized exploitation. For example, suppose an unauthorized recording (or "bootleg") of a live musical performance by a U.S. performer is made in a foreign country. A mechanical compulsory license fee might be paid for the musical composition, but no permission is sought from, nor royalties paid to, the performers. (Performances are not "works" within the meaning of the Berne Convention, and although the Rome Convention does protect performers, the United States is not a party to the latter.)

In response to international pressures and to fulfill its obligations under the Agreement on Trade-Related Aspects of Intellectual Property Rights ("TRIPS"), the United States amended Title 17 by adding § 1101 *outside* the Copyright Act (Chapters 1–8). The legislation gives performers a civil cause of action for unauthorized fixation of, or trafficking in, live musical performances. Criminal penalties under 18 U.S.C. § 2319A supplement the civil cause of action.

In *United States v. Moghadam*, 175 F.3d 1269 (11th Cir. 1999), the Eleventh Circuit rejected a constitutional challenge to 18 U.S.C. § 2319A, saying "the Copyright Clause does not envision that Congress is positively forbidden from extending copyright-like protection under other constitutional clauses, such as the Commerce Clause, to works of authorship that may not meet the fixation requirement inherent in the term 'Writings.' " *Id.* at 1280. In dicta, however, the decision stated that the "apparently perpetual" protection provided by the statute might prove "fundamentally inconsistent" with the "limited Times" restriction of the Copyright Clause. Because the criminal defendant in *Moghadam* had not raised that issue, the court reserved the question for another day. *Id.* at 1281.

More recently, another court reached the same result as *Moghadam*, but via very different reasoning. In *United States v. Martignon*, 492 F.3d 140, 151 (2d Cir. 2007), the court held that 18 U.S.C. § 2319A does not "secure" an exclusive right within the meaning of the Copyright Clause, because it "does not create and bestow property rights upon authors or inventors or allocate those rights among claimants to them," but instead is only a criminal prohibition. Because the law was therefore not a "copyright" law, it could be upheld under the Commerce Clause. *Id.* at 152-53. The court's reasoning strongly suggests that it might find the civil counterpart, § 1101, to be unconstitutional. *See id.* at 152 n.8 (reserving the question). *But see KISS Catalog v. Passport Int'l Prods.*, 350 F. Supp. 2d 823 (C.D. Cal. 2004), *on reconsideration*, 405 F. Supp. 2d 1169 (C.D. Cal. 2005) (holding on reconsideration that § 1101 is constitutional).

Putting the constitutional question to one side, is "bootlegging" merely commercial piracy that should be the subject of civil and criminal liability? Or is there a legitimate public policy argument to be made in favor of "bootlegging"? *See* Kozinn, *Bootlegging as a Public Service: No, This Isn't a Joke*, N.Y. TIMES, Oct. 8, 1997, at E3.

§ 2.02 ORIGINALITY

The second prerequisite for federal or statutory copyright protection, based upon the Copyright Clause's provision for protection of the writings of "Authors," is originality. You will search § 101 of the 1976 Act in vain for any definition of this key term. According to the House Report on the Act (a portion of which is reproduced below), this omission manifests a legislative intention to incorporate into the new statute the meaning of the term that had evolved in the case law construing prior acts. You will see that there are two aspects of originality as developed by the courts and now embodied in § 102(a): independent creation by the author, and a modest quantum of creativity. Another basic principle of copyright developed in the case law holds that copyright protects an author's expression of an idea, but not the idea itself. The Act codifies this latter principle in § 102(b).

What is the basis for these principles, and how have the courts applied them in practice? This section explores these fundamental issues of copyrightability.

[A] Introduction

Statutory References
> **1976 Act:** §§ 101 ("created"), 102(a) and (b)
> **1909 Act:** § 4

Legislative History

> **H.R. REP. NO. 94-1476 at 51-52, 56-57**
> *reprinted in* **1976 U.S.C.C.A.N. 5659, 5664-65, 5670**

> SECTION 102. GENERAL SUBJECT MATTER OF COPYRIGHT

"Original works of authorship"

. . . The phrase "original works of authorship," which is purposely left undefined, is intended to incorporate without change the standard of originality established by the courts under the [1909 Act]. This standard does not include requirements of novelty, ingenuity, or [a]esthetic merit, and there is no intention to enlarge the standard of copyright protection to require them. . . .

Authors are continually finding new ways of expressing themselves, but it is impossible to foresee the forms that these new expressive methods will take. The

bill does not intend either to freeze the scope of copyrightable technology or to allow unlimited expansion into areas completely outside the present congressional intent.
. . .

Nature of copyright

Copyright does not preclude others from using the ideas or information revealed by the author's work. It pertains to the literary, musical, graphic, or artistic form in which the author expressed intellectual concepts. Section 102(b) makes clear that copyright protection does not extend to any idea, procedure, process, system, method of operation, concept, principle, or discovery, regardless of the form in which it is described, explained, illustrated, or embodied in such work.

[*For a fuller excerpt from H.R. Rep. No. 94-1476, see Part Three of the Casebook Supplement.*]

[B] Basic Originality Concepts

Originality and the Constitution. The originality requirement was discussed extensively in the U.S. Supreme Court's landmark decision in *Feist Publications, Inc. v. Rural Telephone Service Company, Inc.*, 499 U.S. 340 (1991). *Feist* ranks effortlessly as one of the Court's truly great opinions on copyright. In a masterly opinion for a unanimous Court, Justice O'Connor emphatically declared originality to be an inescapable constitutional requirement for copyright protection for all works of authorship:

> The sine qua non of copyright is originality. To qualify for copyright protection, a work must be original to the author. *See* [*Harper & Row, Publishers, Inc. v. Nation Enterprises*, 471 U.S. 539, 547-49 (1985)]. "Original," as the term is used in copyright, means only that the work was independently created by the author (as opposed to copied from other works), and that it possesses at least some minimal degree of creativity. To be sure, the requisite level of creativity is extremely low; even a slight amount will suffice. . . .

> Originality is a constitutional requirement. The source of Congress' power to enact copyright laws is Article I, § 8, cl. 8, of the Constitution, which authorizes Congress to "secur[e] for limited Times to Authors . . . the exclusive Right to their respective Writings." In two decisions from the late 19th Century — *The Trade-Mark Cases*, 100 U.S. 82 (1879); and *Burrow-Giles Lithographic Co. v. Sarony*, 111 U.S. 53 (1884) — this Court defined the crucial terms "authors" and "writings." In so doing, the Court made it unmistakably clear that these terms presuppose a degree of originality.

> In *The Trade-Mark Cases*, the Court addressed the constitutional scope of "writings." For a particular work to be classified "under the head of writings of authors," the Court determined, "originality is required." 100 U.S., at 94. The Court explained that originality requires independent creation plus a modicum of creativity: "[W]hile the word writings may be liberally construed, as it has been, to include original designs for engraving,

prints, &c., it is only such as are *original*, and are founded in the creative powers of the mind. The writings which are to be protected are the fruits of intellectual labor, embodied in the form of books, prints, engravings, and the like." *Id.* (emphasis in original).

In *Burrow-Giles*, the Court distilled the same requirement from the Constitution's use of the word "authors." The Court defined "author," in a constitutional sense, to mean "he to whom anything owes its origin; originator; maker." 111 U.S., at 58 (internal quotations omitted). As in *The Trade-Mark Cases*, the Court emphasized the creative component of originality. It described copyright as being limited to "original intellectual conceptions of the author," *ibid.*, and stressed the importance of requiring an author who accuses another of infringement to prove "the existence of those facts of originality, of intellectual production, of thought, and conception." *Id.*, 111 U.S., at 59-60.

The originality requirement articulated in *The Trade-Mark Cases* and *Burrow-Giles* remains the touchstone of copyright protection today. *See Goldstein v. California*, 412 U.S. 546, 561-62 (1973). It is the very "premise of copyright law." *Miller v. Universal City Studios, Inc.*, 650 F.2d 1365, 1368 (CA5 1981). Leading scholars agree on this point. As one pair of commentators succinctly puts it: "The originality requirement is constitutionally mandated for all works." Patterson & Joyce, *Monopolizing the Law: The Scope of Copyright Protection for Law Reports and Statutory Compilations*, 36 UCLA L. Rev. 719, 763, n.155 (1989). . . .

499 U.S. 346–47.

We will examine *Feist* at length in Chapter 3, where the basic principles established (or rather, reiterated and constitutionalized) by the case can be considered in *Feist*'s immediate context: factual compilations. For the moment, bear in mind that *Feist* is, first and foremost, about the law of authorship, and that the Court's pronouncements on "originality," as quoted above, apply equally to claims of copyright protection for works of all descriptions.

Originality and amount of expression. Also in Chapter 3, we will return to the quantum requirement — the question of exactly how little (and what kind of) new authorship is needed to qualify a work as "original," especially in the context of copyright protection for "derivative works" (i.e., works like musical arrangements, artistic reproductions, and translations — that are based substantially on preexisting matter). Here, it is enough to note that while the copyright laws exist to encourage creative persons to produce new matter, there remains a narrow area in which admittedly independent efforts by an author are deemed too trivial or insignificant to warrant copyright protection and the rights that flow from it. "The standard of originality is low, but it does exist." *Feist*, 499 U.S. at 362. In *Atari Games Corp. v. Oman*, 888 F.2d 878 (D.C. Cir. 1989), then-Judge Ruth Bader Ginsberg noted that even "simple shapes, when selected or combined in a distinctive manner indicating some ingenuity, have been accorded copyright protection. . . ." But copyright nevertheless has been denied to short words and phrases, *Dobson v. NBA Properties, Inc.*, 1999 U.S. Dist. LEXIS 1834 (S.D.N.Y. 1999) ("Repeat Threepeat" in reference to Michael Jordan and the Chicago Bulls); slogans,

Alberto-Culver Co. v. Andrea Dumon, Inc., 466 F. 2d 705 (7th Cir. 1972) ("most personal sort of deodorant"); short musical phrases, *Newton v. Diamond*, 204 F. Supp. 2d 1244 (C.D. Cal. 2002) (three-note sequence), *aff'd on other grounds*, 349 F.3d 591 (9th Cir. 2003); slight variations of musical works, *Woods v. Bourne Co.*, 60 F.3d 978 (2d Cir. 1995) (piano-vocal arrangement of existing lead sheet); the insignia of a soccer team, *John Muller & Co. v. New York Arrows Soccer Team, Inc.*, 802 F.2d 989 (8th Cir. 1986); and the title of a song, *Acuff-Rose Music, Inc. v. Jostens, Inc.*, 155 F.3d 140 (2d Cir. 1998) ("You've Got to Stand for Something"), as not meeting the *de minimis* standard. *See* Hughes, *Size Matters (or Should) in Copyright Law*, 74 Fordham L. Rev. 575 (2005). On the other hand, one eminent jurist has suggested that copyright protection would be accorded such lines as "Euclid alone has looked on Beauty bare" and "'Twas Brillig and the slithy toves." *Heim v. Universal Pictures Corp., Inc.*, 154 F.2d 480 (2d Cir. 1946) (Jerome Frank, J.).

Originality and creativity. Remember, too, *Feist*'s requirement that an author's contribution reflect at least some *creativity*. The drafters of the 1976 Act deliberately avoided introducing the term "creativity" into the statute to avoid any suggestion that the new Act somehow increased the standard for copyrightability previously established in the cases. *See Supplementary Report of the Register of Copyrights on the General Revision of the U.S. Copyright Law: 1965 Revision Bill*, 89th Cong., 1st Sess., Copyright Law Revision Part 6, at 3 (House Comm. Print 1965). Nevertheless, "creativity" has become part of the common vocabulary of copyright analysis, suggesting that the inquiry into copyrightability has a qualitative as well as a quantitative dimension — and that some kinds of texts and images just don't count, even if they owe their origins to the person or firm claiming copyright. See *Incredible Techs., Inc. v. Virtual Techs, Inc.*, 400 F.3d 1007 (7th Cir. 2005), where on-screen graphics showing how to operate the controls for a "PGA Golf Tour" video game were deemed to be explanatory and utilitarian, rather than creative, as well as being subject to the *scènes à faire* doctrine (denying protection to features which "are as a practical matter indispensable, or at least standard in the treatment of a given topic," *id.* at 1014), which we consider in more detail in § 8.03.

Decisions about rights in catalogue numbers for replacement parts demonstrate the tendency of courts to discount authorship showing minimal creativity. *See Toro Co. v. R & R Products Co.*, 787 F.2d 1208, 1213 (8th Cir. 1986) (no copyright because "[t]he random and arbitrary use of numbers in the public domain does not evince enough originality to distinguish authorship"); *accord Mitel, Inc. v. Iqtel, Inc.*, 124 F.3d 1366, 1374 (10th Cir. 1997). Copyright protection has also been denied to part numbers which were assigned in a systematic way, rather than in a creative manner. *See Southco, Inc. v. Kanebridge Corp.*, 390 F.3d 276, 283 (3d Cir. 2004) (en banc); *ATC Distrib. Group, Inc. v. Whatever It Takes Transmissions & Parts, Inc.*, 402 F.3d 700, 708-09 (6th Cir. 2005). Nevertheless, some numerical classification schemes may still qualify for protection. *See American Dental Ass'n v. Delta Dental Plans Assn.*, 126 F.3d 977 (7th Cir. 1997) (taxonomy classifying dental procedures and assigning numbers to each was an original work of authorship). Is the decision about how to assign page numbers to a compilation of public domain judicial decisions original? *See* § 3.02 below for the full story.

Why originality? Stepping back, how can requiring a certain standard of originality be justified as a matter of policy? On the basis that we wish to reward only those who have truly enriched society? To protect potential defendants against unwarranted litigation by those claiming copyright in matters with little if any distinction from what society already owns as part of the public domain?

In *Emerson v. Davies*, 8 F. Cas. 615, 619 (C.C.D. Mass. 1845) (No. 4436), Justice Story offered the following practical reason for the originality standard in copyright:

> In truth, in literature, in science and in art, there are, and can be, few, if any, things, which, in an abstract sense, are strictly new and original throughout. Every book in literature, science and art, borrows, and must necessarily borrow, and use much which was well known and used before. . . . If no book could be the subject of copyright which was not new and original in the elements of which it is composed, there could be no ground for any copyright in modern times, and we would be obliged to ascend very high, even in antiquity, to find a work entitled to such eminence. Virgil borrowed much from Homer; Bacon drew from earlier as well as contemporary minds; Coke exhausted all the known learning of his profession; and even Shakespeare and Milton . . . would be found to have gathered much from the abundant stores of current knowledge and classical studies in their days.

More than one hundred years later, another commentator made the following observation:

> [T]o make the copyright turnstile revolve, the author should have to deposit more than a penny in the box, and some like measure ought to apply to infringement. Surely there is danger in trying to fence off small *quanta* of works or other collocations; these pass quickly into the idiom; to allow them copyright, particularly if aided by a doctrine of "unconscious" plagiarism, could set up untoward barriers to expression.

B. Kaplan, AN UNHURRIED VIEW OF COPYRIGHT 46 (1967).

Originality in court: fact or law?

Whether a work is original is treated by many courts as a question of fact, *Matthew Bender & Co. v. West Publishing Co.*, 158 F.3d 674, 681 (2d Cir. 1998); *Montgomery v. Noga*, 168 F.3d 1282, 1291 n.14 (11th Cir. 1999); *North Coast Indus. v. Jason Maxwell, Inc.*, 972 F.2d 1031, 1034 (9th Cir. 1992); by some as a question of law, *Superior Form Builders, Inc. v. Dan Chase Taxidermy Supply Co., Inc.*, 74 F.3d 488, 495 (4th Cir. 1996); *Newton v. Diamond*, 204 F. Supp. 2d 1244, 1253 (C.D. Cal. 2002); *Compaq Computer Corp. v. Ergonome, Inc.*, 137 F. Supp. 2d 768, 775 n.3 (S.D. Tex. 2001); and by others as a mixed question of fact and law, *Los Angeles News Service v. Tullo*, 973 F.2d 791, 793 (9th Cir. 1992). Attempting to harmonize these disparate views, the court in *CMM Cable Rep., Inc. v. Ocean Coast Properties, Inc.*, 97 F.3d 1504, 1517 (1st Cir. 1996), said (using *Feist* as an example):

> While we do not dispute that the question of originality can be a question of fact for the jury, it is not necessarily so. . . . [C]ourts clearly may

determine the question of originality and, in turn, copyrightability so long as they do so in accord with the familiar rules governing summary judgment: where there are no genuine issues of material fact as to the originality of the work, such that no reasonable trier-of-fact could find originality, then the movant is entitled to judgment as a matter of law.

By contrast, questions of idea versus expression are usually treated as matters of law for the court to decide. *See* § 2.02[F] below.

What practical difference does characterizing the issue as one of fact or law make? First, as noted in *CMM*, it affects the right to a jury trial on the issue of originality. Another consideration is the role of expert witnesses. If the question of originality is one of fact, the opinion testimony of expert witnesses may be appropriate — for example, as to whether the work contains original features. *See, e.g., Paul Morelli Design, Inc. v. Tiffany & Co.*, 200 F. Supp. 2d 482, 486-87 (E.D. Pa. 2002). If the question is one of law, however, expert witnesses may *not* be appropriate, because the issue is one for the court alone. Finally, the characterization may affect the standard of review to be applied by an appellate court in reviewing a trial court's originality determination. *Compare Matthew Bender*, 158 F.3d at 681 (clearly erroneous), *with Los Angeles News Service*, 973 F.2d at 793 (*de novo*).

Which characterization of the originality issue — fact or law — do you think better comports with general principles of law? As you read the cases reproduced in the present section, consider whether the courts are simply resolving factual issues as to originality (as distinguished from novelty), or whether they are making policy determinations as a matter of law.

[C]   The Originality/Novelty Distinction

In § 1.02, we explained that, to obtain a patent, an inventor must demonstrate that his or her invention is novel, nonobvious, and useful. Because patents and copyrights spring from the same constitutional clause, one might think the same requirements would be prescribed for a copyright as well. But, as we will explain, the "originality" requirement in copyright law is significantly different from the "novelty" requirement in patent law.

Neither the Constitution nor any of the copyright acts prior to 1976 mention "originality," although the House Report, as we have seen, claims that the 1976 Act, in requiring an "*original* work of authorship" as a prerequisite to federal copyright, merely "incorporates . . . the standard of originality established by the courts" in construing prior acts. On what basis may it be said that originality is constitutionally mandated as a precondition to statutory protection for intellectual creations? *Feist* locates the originality requirement in the words "Authors" and "Writings" in Art. I, § 8, cl. 8. This conclusion rests in large measure on the concept of the Romantic "author" discussed in § 1.04. Before the Romantic movement in art and literature, "authors" were lauded not necessarily for their originality, but for their imitation of existing material.

Another possible basis for interpreting the words "authors" and "writings" to require originality is the constitutional phrase "to Promote the Progress of

Science." If the purpose of copyright is to promote knowledge by providing an incentive for the creation and publication of new works, then should we require that a purported "author" demonstrate how his or her work improves upon, or is different from, works that have gone before? Such a requirement would be analogous to the novelty requirement in patent law, which, as implemented in the Patent Act of 1790, required an inventor to "distinguish the invention or discovery from other things before known and used."

In *Alfred Bell & Co. v. Catalda Fine Arts, Inc.*, 191 F.2d 99 (2d Cir. 1951), the defendants argued that "to be valid, a patent must disclose a high degree of uniqueness, ingenuity and inventiveness," and contended "that the same requirement constitutionally governs copyrights." *Id.* at 100. The court acknowledged that the word "original" was ambiguous: It *could* mean "startling, novel or unusual, a marked departure from the past." *Id.* at 102. Nonetheless, the court rejected that interpretation, concluding that "nothing in the Constitution commands that copyrighted matter be strikingly unique or novel." *Id.* The court reasoned that the First Congress, "legislators peculiarly familiar with the purpose of the Constitutional grant, . . . imposed far less exacting standards in the case of copyrights" than they did for patents. *Id.* at 101. It also contrasted the word "author" with the word "inventor," saying "the latter carries an implication which excludes the results of only ordinary skill, while nothing of this is necessarily involved in the former." *Id.* at 102. Rather, it explained:

> "Original" in reference to a copyrighted work means that the particular work "owes its origin" to the "author." No large measure of novelty is necessary. Said the Supreme Court in *Baker v. Selden*, 101 U.S. 99, 102-103: "The copyright of the book, if not pirated from other works, would be valid without regard to the novelty, or want of novelty, of its subject-matter. The novelty of the art or thing described or explained has nothing to do with the validity of the copyright. . . ."

Thus, in *Situation Mgmt. Sys., Inc. v. ASP Consulting LLC*, 560 F.3d 53 (1st Cir. 2009), the fact that the plaintiff's work was "filled with generalizations, platitudes, and observations of the obvious," contained "not-so-stunning revelation[s]," and "at its creative zenith" taught "common-sense" communication skills, did not render the work unoriginal, because "the district court erroneously treated copyright law's originality requirement as functionally equivalent to a novelty standard." *See also Kelly v. Chicago Park District*, 635 F.3d 290 (7th Cir. 2011) (holding that the District Court "mistakenly equate[d] originality with novelty" when it held that Wildflower Works, an arrangement of living plants, was not "original" because Kelley was not "the first person to ever conceive of and express an arrangement of growing wildflowers in ellipse-shaped enclosed area[s].").

The distinction between novelty and originality is often explained by saying that if a writer who has never known a previous work somehow creates an exact duplicate of that work or a substantial portion thereof, the second work is nonetheless copyrightable because, even though it is not "novel" or "unique," it "originated" with the second author. *See, e.g., Sheldon v. Metro-Goldwyn Pictures Corp.*, 81 F.2d 49, 54 (2d Cir. 1936) (L. Hand, J.) ("it makes no difference how far the [copyrighted work] was anticipated by works in the public demesne which the plaintiffs did not use"); *Alfred Bell*, 191 F.2d at 103 ("The 'author' is entitled to a copyright if he independently contrived a work completely identical with what went before; similarly, although he obtains a valid copyright, he has no right to prevent another from publishing a work identical with his, if not copied from his."); *Boisson v. Banian, Ltd.*, 273 F.3d 262, 270 (2d Cir. 2001) ("[A]n author is entitled to copyright protection for an independently created original work despite its identical nature to a prior work, because it is independent creation, not novelty, that is required.").

Except for the most simplistic and obvious writings, however, exact duplication of an entire work without copying is extremely unlikely. It beggars imagination that anyone could independently create an exact replica of Keats' "Ode On a Grecian Urn," any more than the proverbial monkey at a typewriter will bang out the Gettysburg Address. Does this mean that the distinction between originality and novelty lacks practical significance? The fact is that courts can, and often do, consider evidence of prior similar works in determining originality. *See, e.g., Acuff-Rose Music, Inc. v. Jostens, Inc.*, 155 F.3d 140 (2d Cir. 1998) ("prior usage of the saying was sufficiently widespread as to make it exceedingly unlikely" that plaintiff originated phrase "You've got to stand for something or you'll fall for anything"); *Paul Morelli Design, Inc. v. Tiffany & Co.*, 200 F. Supp. 2d 482, 487 (E.D. Pa. 2002) ("The jury also had before it evidence of other jewelry which bore on originality and creativity"); *Meade v. United States*, 27 Fed. Cl. 36 (1992) (relying on evidence that similar works "have existed for centuries"). Nevertheless, evidence of prior works will not always negate a finding of originality. *See Ulloa v. Universal Music and Video Distribution Corp.*, 2004 U.S. Dist LEXIS 6755 (S.D.N.Y., Apr. 19, 2004) (use of melody in which plaintiff claimed copyright in 14 prior works did not defeat copyrightability, because "originality does not signify novelty"). Can you think of other realistic situations in which it makes a difference that only originality, but not novelty, is required for copyright?

[D] "Authors" and Their "Writings"

BURROW-GILES LITHOGRAPHIC CO. v. SARONY
Supreme Court of the United States
111 U.S. 53 (1884)

Mr. Justice Miller delivered the opinion of the court.

This is a writ of error to the circuit court for the southern district of New York. Plaintiff is a lithographer, and defendant a photographer, with [a] large business in those lines in the city of New York. The suit was commenced by an action at law in which Sarony was plaintiff and the lithographic company was defendant, the plaintiff charging the defendant with violating his copyright in regard to a photograph, the title of which is "Oscar Wilde, No. 18." A jury being waived, the court made a finding of facts on which a judgment in favor of the plaintiff was rendered for the sum of $600 for the plates and 85,000 copies sold and exposed to sale, and $10 for copies found in his possession, as penalties under section 4965 of the Revised Statutes.

Among the finding of facts made by the court the following presents the principal question raised by the assignment of errors in the case:

(3) That the plaintiff, about the month of January, 1882, under an agreement with Oscar Wilde, became and was the author, inventor, designer, and proprietor of the photograph in suit, the title of which is "Oscar Wilde, No. 18," being the number used to designate this particular photograph and of the negative thereof; that the same is a useful, new, harmonious, characteristic, and graceful picture, and that said plaintiff made the same at his place of business in said city of New York, and within the United States, entirely from his own original mental conception, to which he gave visible form by posing the said Oscar Wilde in front of the camera, selecting and arranging the costume, draperies, and other various accessories in said photograph, arranging the subject so as to present graceful outlines, arranging and disposing the light and shade, suggesting and evoking the desired expression, and from such disposition, arrangement, or representation, made entirely by the plaintiff, he produced the picture in suit, Exhibit A, April 14, 1882, and that the terms "author," "inventor," and "designer," as used in the art of photography and in the complaint, mean the person who so produced the photograph.

The Portrait of Oscar Wilde by Napoleon Sarony

Other findings leave no doubt that plaintiff had taken all the steps required by the act of congress to obtain copyright of this photograph, and section 4952 names photographs, among other things, for which the author, inventor, or designer may obtain copyright, which is to secure him the sole privilege of reprinting, publishing, copying, and vending the same. That defendant is liable, under that section and section 4965, there can be no question if those sections are valid as they relate to photographs.

Accordingly, the two assignments of error in this court by plaintiff in error are:

(1) That the court below decided that congress had and has the constitutional right to protect photographs and negatives thereof by copyright.

[(2)] The second assignment related to the sufficiency of the words "Copyright, 1882, by N. Sarony," in the photographs, as a notice of the copyright of Napoleon Sarony, under the act of congress on that subject.

With respect to this latter question[, the Court concludes that] the notice is complete.

The constitutional question is not free from difficulty. The eighth section of the first article of the constitution is the great repository of the powers of congress, and by the eighth clause of that section congress is authorized "to promote the progress of science and useful arts, by securing, for limited times to authors and inventors the exclusive right to their respective writings and discoveries." The argument here is that a photograph is not a writing nor the production of an author. . . . It is insisted, in argument, that a photograph being a reproduction, on paper, of the exact features of some natural object, or of some person, is not a writing of which the producer is the author. Section 4952 of the Revised Statutes places photographs in the same class as things which may be copyrighted with "books, maps, charts, dramatic or musical compositions, engravings, cuts, prints, paintings, drawings, statuary, and models or designs intended to be perfected as works of the fine arts."

The first congress of the United States, sitting immediately after the formation of the constitution, enacted that the "author or authors of any map, chart, book, or books, being a citizen or resident of the United States, shall have the sole right and liberty of printing, reprinting, publishing, and vending the same for the period of fourteen years from the recording of the title thereof in the clerk's office, as afterwards directed." 1 St. p. 124, § 1. This statute not only makes maps and charts subjects of copyright, but mentions them before books in the order of designation. The second section of an act to amend this act, approved April 29, 1802, (2 St. 171), enacts that from the first day of January thereafter he who shall invent and design, engrave, etch, or work, or from his own works shall cause to be designed and engraved, etched, or worked, any historical or other print or prints, shall have the same exclusive right. . . .

The construction placed upon the constitution by the first act of 1790 and the act of 1802, by the men who were contemporary with its formation, many of whom were members of the convention which framed it, is of itself entitled to very great weight, and when it is remembered that the rights thus established have not been disputed during a period of nearly a century, it is almost conclusive. Unless, therefore, photographs can be distinguished in the classification of this point from the maps, charts, designs, engravings, etchings, cuts, and other prints, it is difficult to see why congress cannot make them the subject of copyright as well as the others. These statutes certainly answer the objection that books only, or writing, in the limited sense of a book and its author, are within the constitutional provision. Both these words are susceptible of a more enlarged definition than this. An author in that sense is "he to whom anything owes its origin; originator; maker; one who completes a work of science or literature." Worcester. So, also, no one would now claim that the word "writing" in this clause of the constitution, though the only word used as to subjects in regard to which authors are to be secured, is limited to the actual script of the author, and excludes books and all other printed matter. By writings in that clause is meant the literary productions of those authors, and congress very properly has declared these to include all forms of writing, printing, engravings, etchings, *etc.,* by which the ideas in the mind of the author are given visible expression. The only reason why photographs were not included in the extended list in the act of 1802 is, probably, that they did not exist, as photography, as an art, was then unknown, and the scientific principle on which it rests, and the chemicals and machinery by which it is operated, have all been discovered long since that statute was enacted. . . .

We entertain no doubt that the constitution is broad enough to cover an act authorizing copyright of photographs, so far as they are representatives of original intellectual conceptions of the author.

But it is said that an engraving, a painting, a print, does embody the intellectual conception of its author, in which there is novelty, invention, originality, and therefore comes within the purpose of the constitution in securing its exclusive use or sale to its author, while a photograph is the mere mechanical reproduction of the physical features or outlines of some object, animate or inanimate, and involves no originality of thought or any novelty in the intellectual operation connected with its visible reproduction in shape of a picture. That while the effect of light on the prepared plate may have been a discovery in the production of these pictures, and patents could properly be obtained for the combination of the chemicals, for their application to the paper or other surface, for all the machinery by which the light reflected from the object was thrown on the prepared plate, and for all the improvements in this machinery, and in the materials, the remainder of the process is merely mechanical, with no place for novelty, invention, or originality. It is simply the manual operation, by the use of these instruments and preparations, of transferring to the plate the visible representation of some existing object, the accuracy of this representation being its highest merit. This may be true in regard to the ordinary production of a photograph, and that in such case a copyright is no protection. On the question as thus stated we decide nothing. . . .

The third finding of facts says, in regard to the photograph in question, that it is a "useful, new, harmonious, characteristic, and graceful picture, and that plaintiff made the same . . . entirely from his own original mental conception, to which he gave visible form by posing the said Oscar Wilde in front of the camera, selecting and arranging the costume, draperies, and other various accessories in said photograph, arranging the subject so as to present graceful outlines, arranging and disposing the light and shade, suggesting and evoking the desired expression, and from such disposition, arrangement, or representation, made entirely by plaintiff, he produced the picture in suit." These findings, we think, show this photograph to be an original work of art, the product of plaintiff's intellectual invention, of which plaintiff is the author, and of a class of inventions for which the constitution intended that congress should secure to him the exclusive right to use, publish, and sell, as it has done by section 4952 of the Revised Statutes. . . .

The judgment of the circuit court is accordingly affirmed.

NOTES AND QUESTIONS

(1) *Copyrightability and technology.* How should the copyrightability of a photograph be assessed, especially when it was created using what was then a relatively new mechanical technique? The Court notes that the "mental conception" of the image that Sarony wished to create was given "visible" form in a new medium unknown to the Framers of the Copyright Clause and the early copyright acts. "The only reason why photographs were not included . . . in the act of 1802," says the Court, "is, probably, that they did not exist, as photography, as an art, was then unknown. . . ." But this begs the question of "originality."

In *Burrow-Giles*, the Court confronted a problem that had plagued courts in the United States and elsewhere during the early years of photography: Did a photograph have a human "author," or was it, in fact, just the product of a machine? *See* Farley, *The Lingering Effects of Copyright's Response to the Invention of Photography*, 65 U. Pitt. L. Rev. 385 (2004). Notice that this issue is the flipside of *White-Smith*. There, the Court considered whether a reproduction designed for a machine (a player piano) was a "copy" of the work. Here, the machine has rendered the copy for direct perception by a human audience. Congress overruled *White-Smith* in favor of expanding copyright to cover copies designed for machines, and *Burrow-Giles*, of course, resolved the problem of "authorship" for photographic works in favor of copyrightability. But the problem of "machine" authorship generally has not gone away.

Suppose, for example, that a *computer* had generated the image from a verbal description of Wilde's appearance. These days, increasing amounts of authorship can be automated through software or authoring tools. Computers can create respectable-sounding music and poetry, to say nothing of high-quality technical drawings; and they are being used more and more to generate new computer programs to meet stated specifications and requirements. How should these products be regarded for copyright purposes? In 1979, the Congressionally-mandated National Commission on New Technological Uses of Copyrighted Works ("CONTU") took up the issue of computer-generated works in its *Final Report*, concluding that, in such cases, it is "obvious" that the "author is one who employs the computer," *id.* at 45, rather than (for example) the author of the program which drives the computer. Is that conclusion still "obvious"? Is it obvious that such works have *any* "author"?

(2) *Photography specifically.* Congress added "photographs" to the list of subject matter eligible for copyright in 1865. 13 Stat. 540. Thus, the principal question before the Court in *Burrow-Giles* was whether photographs fall within the constitutional grant of power to Congress to secure exclusive rights to "Authors" for

their "Writings." How did the Court determine that photographs were within the constitutional meaning of "Writings"? Should the result have been different if photography had been known at the date of Congress' most recent amendments to the list of copyrightable subject matter, but had not been included?

Over the years, Congress has granted protection to an increasingly long list of types of writings that does not yet encompass everything that might constitute a "Writing" under the Copyright Clause. The current formulation used to describe this list is "works of authorship," a concept elaborated in § 102(a) of the Copyright Act and further examined in Chapter 3. At this point, however, can you think of any "writings" that may not be copyrightable subject matter?

(3)   Some of the very first items to which Congress granted copyright protection — for example, the "maps" and "charts" mentioned by the Court in *Burrow-Giles* — seem to exhibit little originality when compared with other items on the protected list, such as "designs" or "engravings." Where on this spectrum of writings do photographs fall?

(4)   What elements of Sarony's photograph caused the resulting picture to be a sufficiently original "intellectual invention" to justify copyright protection under the challenged statutory provision? Was it the simple act of selecting the subject? The artistic posing of the subject? The decisions concerning costume, lighting, exposure and shutter speed?

It would seem that a photographer can claim copyright protection only for those elements of a photograph over which she exercised creative control. Thus, for example, a photographer generally cannot claim copyright in her choice of subject matter, but she may be accorded protection for such aspects as lighting, shading, timing, angle and choice of film, where she made those decisions. *See Leigh v. Warner Bros., Inc.*, 212 F.3d 1210 (11th Cir. 2000) (photo of Bird Girl sculpture in Savannah cemetery, used on cover of book "Midnight in the Garden of Good and Evil," claimed to have been infringed by promotional images, etc., for movie based on the book); *Ets-Hokin v. Skyy Spirits, Inc.*, 225 F.3d 1068 (9th Cir. 2000) (photograph of vodka bottle for magazine ad). For the denouement of the latter case, see the notes after the next case.

What if the photographer merely happens to be in the right place at the right time? *See Time, Inc. v. Bernard Geis Associates*, 293 F. Supp. 130 (S.D.N.Y. 1968), holding that the Zapruder film of President Kennedy's assassination was sufficiently original, because:

> Zapruder selected the kind of camera (movies, not snapshots), the kind of film (color), the kind of lens (telephoto), the area in which the pictures were to be taken, the time they were to be taken, and (after testing several sites) the spot on which the camera would be operated.

Id. at 143. Should the result have been different if Zapruder had been an idle bystander who happened to be carrying a camera? *See also Los Angeles News Service v. Tullo*, 973 F.2d 791 (9th Cir. 1992) (videotape of sites of airplane crash and train wreck sufficiently original); *Los Angeles News Service v. KCAL-TV*, 108 F.3d 1119 (9th Cir. 1997) (videotape "creatively captured the [Reginald] Denny beating in a way that no one else did").

(5)   Are all photographs copyrightable, on the basis that, as Judge Learned Hand once famously observed, that "[n]o photograph, however simple, can be unaffected by the personal influence of the author, and no two will be absolutely alike"? *Jewelers' Circular Publishing Co. v. Keystone Publishing Co.*, 274 F. 932, 934 (S.D.N.Y. 1921), *aff'd*, 281 F. 83 (2d Cir. 1922). Is that true? Can you think of any photographs that do not possess the requisite "minimal degree of creativity"? *See, e.g.*, *Oriental Art Printing, Inc. v. Goldstar Printing Corp.*, 175 F. Supp. 2d 542 (S.D.N.Y. 2001) (photographs of Chinese food dishes on menu not sufficiently original). You may wish to reconsider this question after reading the *Meshwerks* case in § 2.02[E] below.

(6)   *Classifying the elements of originality?* In *Mannion v. Coors Brewing Co.*, 377 F. Supp. 2d 444 (S.D.N.Y. 2006), involving a dispute as to whether a billboard for defendant's Coors Light beer infringed the plaintiff's copyright in a photograph of basketball star Kevin Garnett, the court described photographs as being capable of originality in three (non-mutually exclusive) respects:

- *Rendition.* This comprises various aspects of the subject's depiction, including "angle of shot, light and shade, exposure, [and] effects achieved by means of filters [or] developing techniques." According to the *Mannion* court, "[u]nless a photograph replicates another work with total or near-total fidelity, it will be at least somewhat original in the rendition."

- *Timing.* This involves the photographer's decision to seize a moment in time and reduce it to an image ("being at the right place at the right time"). An example is Albert Eisenstadt's photo of a sailor kissing a young woman on World War II's V-J Day in New York's Times Square.

- *Creation of the Subject.* This aspect of photographic originality consists of contriving or "creat[ing] the scene or subject to be photographed." For example, the photographer may pose the subject in a particular setting, such as a couple on a park bench with eight puppies on their laps.

Is this typology helpful in explaining the originality in Sarony's image in *Burrow-Giles*? How about Mannie Garcia's Associated Press photo of then-candidate Barack Obama, used by artist Shepard Fairey during the 2008 presidential campaign to produce his iconic "Hope" poster? Are there aspects other than those catalogued in *Mannion* that might serve as a proper basis for finding originality in a photograph?

Would it be useful to formalize a multi-part originality analysis for *other types* of works of authorship, such as literary, musical, or architectural works? Or is there something special about photography that lends itself to such analysis?

(7) *The hidden issue of joint authorship.* In *Burrow-Giles*, were all of the relevant elements the result of Sarony's own creative artistry? Might not some of them have been more fairly attributed to the sitter himself? Would acknowledging Wilde's contributions have complicated the analysis or jeopardized its outcome? For a case in which the sitter's contribution is discussed (and dismissed), see *Olan Mills, Inc. v. Eckerd Drug of Texas, Inc.*, 1989 U.S. Dist. LEXIS 13768 (N.D. Tex., Apr. 21, 1989). We will reencounter the issue of joint authorship in § 4.01 below.

(8) *Higher authority.* Living creatures are composed of cells, which in turn contain within them the basic genetic information — packaged as deoxyribonucleic acid, or DNA — that provides a blueprint for constructing and operating the developed organism. The Human Genome Project, a collaboration of the U.S. Government and the private sector, produced a "map" of this information in support of long-term "genetic engineering" research, which holds great promise (and perhaps peril) for humanity. Are such "maps" protectible? Several alternative forms of protection have been suggested, among them copyright law. *See* Burk, *Copyrightability of Recombinant DNA Sequences*, 29 Jurimetrics J. 469 (Summer 1989). Can the two basic prerequisites for copyright protection be satisfied? Presumably, the "maps" themselves, being fixed, satisfy the first prerequisite. But what of originality? Who is the "Author" of the maps? The scientists who manipulate the DNA? The universities or companies that employ them? The U.S. Government, insofar as it funds the research? ("[W]orks of the United States Government" are barred from copyright protection by 17 U.S.C. § 105. *See* § 2.03 below). Do any of these persons or entities really qualify as "originators" of protectible expression in the sense contemplated by *Burrow-Giles*? By the way, no protection offered (or asked), to date, by the Supreme Author.

BLEISTEIN v. DONALDSON LITHOGRAPHING CO.
Supreme Court of the United States
188 U.S. 239 (1903)

MR. JUSTICE HOLMES delivered the opinion of the court.

. . . The alleged infringements consisted in the copying in reduced form of three chromolithographs prepared by employees of the plaintiffs for advertisements of a circus owned by one Wallace. Each of the three contained a portrait of Wallace in the corner, and lettering bearing some slight relation to the scheme of decoration, indicating the subject of the design and the fact that the reality was to be seen at the circus. One of the designs was of an ordinary ballet, one of a number of men and women, described as the Stirk family, performing on bicycles, and one of groups of men and women whitened to represent statues. The circuit court directed a verdict for the defendant on the ground that the chromolithographs were not within the protection of the copyright law, and this ruling was sustained by the circuit court of appeals. . . .

We shall do no more than mention the suggestion that painting and engraving, unless for a mechanical end, are not among the useful arts, the progress of which Congress is empowered by the Constitution to promote. The Constitution does not limit the useful to that which satisfies immediate bodily needs. *Burrow-Giles*

Lithographing Co. v. Sarony, 111 U.S. 53. It is obvious also that the plaintiff's case is not affected by the fact, if it be one, that the pictures represent actual groups, — visible things. They seem from the testimony to have been composed from hints or description, not from sight of a performance. But even if they had been drawn from the life, that fact would not deprive them of protection. The opposite proposition would mean that a portrait by Velasquez or Whistler was common property because others might try their hand on the same face. Others are free to copy the original. They are not free to copy the copy. . . . The copy is the personal reaction of an individual upon nature. Personality always contains something unique. It expresses its singularity even in handwriting, and a very modest grade of art has in it something irreducible, which is one man's alone. That something he may copyright unless there is a restriction in the words of the act.

An Original Wallace Shows Poster

If there is a restriction it is not to be found in the limited pretensions of these particular works. The least pretentious picture has more originality in it than directories and the like, which may be copyrighted. . . . The amount of training required for humbler efforts than those before us is well indicated by Ruskin. "If any young person, after being taught what is, in polite circles, called 'drawing,' will try to copy the commonest piece of real *work*, — suppose a lithograph on the title page of a new opera air, or a woodcut in the cheapest illustrated newspaper of the day, — they will find themselves entirely beaten." ELEMENTS OF DRAWING, first ed. 3. There is no reason to doubt that these prints in their *ensemble* and in all their details, in their design and particular combinations of figures, lines, and colors, are the original work of the plaintiffs' designer. If it be necessary, there is express testimony to that effect. It would be pressing the defendant's right to the verge, if not beyond, to leave the question of originality to the jury upon the evidence in this case. . . .

We assume that the construction of Rev. Stat. § 4952 (U.S. Comp. Stat. 1901, p. 3406), allowing a copyright to the "author, designer, or proprietor . . . of any engraving, cut, print . . . [or] chromo" is affected by the act of 1874 (U.S. Comp. Stat. 1901, p. 3412). That section provides that, "in the construction of this act, the words 'engraving,' 'cut,' and 'print' shall be applied only to pictorial illustrations or works connected with the fine arts." We see no reason for taking the words "connected with the fine arts" as qualifying anything except the word "works," but it would not change our decision if we should assume further that they also qualified "pictorial illustrations," as the defendant contends.

These chromolithographs are "pictorial illustrations." The word "illustrations" does not mean that they must illustrate the text of a book, and that the etchings of Rembrandt or Müller's engraving of the Madonna di San Sisto could not be protected today if any man were able to produce them. Again, the act, however construed, does not mean that ordinary posters are not good enough to be considered within its scope. The antithesis to "illustrations or works connected with the fine arts" is not works of little merit or of humble degree, or illustrations addressed to the less educated classes; it is "prints or labels designed to be used for any other articles of manufacture." Certainly works are not the less connected with the fine arts because their pictorial quality attracts the crowd, and therefore gives them a real use, — if use means to increase trade and to help to make money. A picture is none the less a picture, and none the less a subject of copyright, that it is used for an advertisement. And if pictures may be used to advertise soap, or the theatre, or monthly magazines, as they are, they may be used to advertise a circus. Of course, the ballet is as legitimate a subject for illustration as any other. A rule cannot be laid down that would excommunicate the paintings of Degas.

Finally, the special adaptation of these pictures to the advertisement of the Wallace shows does not prevent a copyright. That may be a circumstance for the jury to consider in determining the extent of Mr. Wallace's rights, but it is not a bar. Moreover, on the evidence, such prints are used by less pretentious exhibitions when those for whom they were prepared have given them up.

It would be a dangerous undertaking for persons trained only to the law to constitute themselves final judges of the worth of pictorial illustrations, outside of the narrowest and most obvious limits. At the one extreme, some works of genius would be sure to miss appreciation. Their very novelty would make them repulsive until the public had learned the new language in which their author spoke. It may be more than doubted, for instance, whether the etchings of Goya or the paintings of Manet would have been sure of protection when seen for the first time. At the other end, copyright would be denied to pictures which appealed to a public less educated than the judge. Yet if they command the interest of any public, they have a commercial value, — it would be bold to say that they have not an aesthetic and educational value, — and the taste of any public is not to be treated with contempt. It is an ultimate fact for the moment, whatever may be our hopes for a change. That these pictures had their worth and their success is sufficiently shown by the desire to reproduce them without regard to the plaintiffs' rights. . . . We are of opinion that there was evidence that the plaintiffs have rights entitled to the protection of the law.

The judgment of the Circuit Court of Appeals is reversed; the judgment of the Circuit Court is also reversed and the cause remanded to that court with directions to set aside the verdict and grant a new trial.

MR. JUSTICE HARLAN, dissenting:

Judges Lurton, Day, and Severens, of the circuit court of appeals, concurred in affirming the judgment of the district court. Their views were thus expressed in an opinion delivered by Judge Lurton:

> What we hold is this: That if a chromo, lithograph, or other print, engraving, or picture has no other use than that of a mere advertisement, and no value aside from this function, it would not be promotive of the useful arts, within the meaning of the constitutional provision, to protect the "author" in the exclusive use thereof, and the copyright statute should not be construed as including such a publication, if any other construction is admissible. If a mere label simply designating or describing an article to which it is attached, and which has no value separated from the article, does not come within the constitutional clause upon the subject of copyright, it must follow that a pictorial illustration designed and useful only as an advertisement, and having no intrinsic value other than its function as an advertisement, must be equally without the obvious meaning of the Constitution. . . .

Courier Lithographing Co. v. Donaldson Lithographing Co., 104 F. 993, 996.

I entirely concur in these views, and therefore dissent from the opinion and judgment of this court. The clause of the Constitution giving Congress power to promote the progress of science and useful arts, by securing for limited terms to authors and inventors the exclusive right to their respective works and discoveries, does not, as I think, embrace a mere advertisement of a circus.

Mr. Justice McKenna authorizes me to say that he also dissents.

NOTES AND QUESTIONS

(1) Bleistein *and copyrightability generally.* The impact of the decision in *Bleistein* was immediate and profound. As Diane Leenheer Zimmerman has noted, "Lower court judges both understood the case as setting the threshold for copyrightability at a very low level, and appreciated the pragmatic virtues of this approach. . . . [W]ithin thirty years, an appellate court could list dozens of decisions and cite to major treatises all agreeing that *Bleistein* required only 'a low degree of originality and artistic or literary merit' to obtain copyright." Zimmerman, *The Story of* Bleistein v. Donaldson Lithographing Company: *Originality as a Vehicle for Copyright Inclusivity*, in Intellectual Property Stories 77, 101–02 (J. Ginsburg & R. Dreyfuss eds. 2005) (hereinafter "*Bleistein Story*"), citing *Ansehl v. Puritan Pharmaceutical Co.*, 61 F.2d 131, 136 (8th Cir. 1932).

(2) *Artistic taste and Justice Holmes.* Is it useful, or just fun, to learn that Justice Holmes was fond of visiting art museums and, as a young man, "[h]e himself had created designs for advertising cards to publicize productions of the Hasty Pudding Club at Harvard"? Or that, looking back on the decision, Holmes noted ironically that "Harlan, that stout old Kentuckian, not exactly an esthete, dissented for high art"? *Bleistein Story* at 95.

(3) *The judiciary and aesthetic non-discrimination.* The proposition for which this case most often is cited — and one of the most famous lines in the annals of copyright jurisprudence — is Justice Holmes' comment that "[i]t would be a dangerous undertaking for persons trained only to the law to constitute themselves final judges of the worth of pictorial illustrations . . ." This self-effacing observation has been generalized into what is sometimes called (rather grandly) the principle of "aesthetic non-discrimination": judges evaluating issues of copyrightability should not take into account the aesthetic *quality* of the works under consideration. Like all useful general prescriptions, this one raises certain questions. For example, is it even *possible* to observe the prescription faithfully? As you read the cases in this book, you should ask yourself if judges really do steer clear of making qualitative assessments of works in issue as they go from case to case.

You should ask also whether the general principle of non-discrimination should be subject to any defined exceptions. In *Bleistein*, Justice Holmes continues the statement quoted above with these words: ". . . outside of the narrowest and most obvious limits." But what are those limits, and how obvious are they in fact? Would it have been possible for Justice Holmes to define a narrowly worded principle of exclusion that denied protection to the posters in *Bleistein* without leading the judiciary into the swamp of aesthetics?

(4) As already noted, Justice Holmes discusses at length the degree of originality required before an author may protect his or her writing under the copyright statute. But is this the real issue in the case? Surely, creation of the poster required much more than the minimal artistic effort that Justice Holmes describes as warranting copyright protection. Notice that the dissent focuses not on the amount of creative effort necessary to produce the poster, but on the argument that the sole function of the poster was commercial, and that, apart from its use as an advertisement, the poster had no value.

(5) *Discrimination on other grounds.* As *Bleistein* demonstrates, commercial speech, although arguably not "promotive of the useful arts" (to use Judge Lurton's phrase), receives at least a modicum of protection — and perhaps a good deal more than that — under copyright law. Note that the majority and dissenting Justices in *Bleistein* appear to share a dubious construction of the Constitution's Art. I, § 8, cl. 8. These days, the Copyright Clause is commonly read to mean that copyright is intended "To promote the Progress of Science" (meaning "knowledge" in 18th-Century usage). Does it matter? Or would the lines between majority and dissent have been similarly drawn under this alternative understanding of the constitutional grant of power?

(6) At the trial in *Bleistein*, the defendants objected (unsuccessfully) to one of the Wallace Shows posters (depicting ballet dancers in tights) because it constituted "an immoral picture." *Bleistein Story* at 87 n.49. Should all forms of expression

receive protection? What if the work can be demonstrated to have "negative social utility" in the eyes of the law, so that it could be successfully prosecuted as, for example, fraudulent, libelous, seditious, or obscene? Although two Courts of Appeals have held that obscenity is not a defense to copyright infringement, *see Jartech, Inc. v. Clancy*, 666 F.2d 403 (9th Cir. 1982); *Mitchell Bros. Film Group v. Cinema Adult Theater*, 604 F.2d 852 (5th Cir. 1979), some courts remain reluctant to extend copyright protection to such works. *See, e.g.*, *Devils Films, Inc. v. Nectar Video*, 29 F. Supp. 2d 174 (S.D.N.Y. 1998) (declining to order seizure of allegedly infringing films on grounds of obscenity). Why isn't it simply inconsistent to extend copyright protection to works containing material that is outside the zone of speech protected by the First Amendment?

One obvious problem with permitting an "obscenity defense" to claims of copyright infringement is that, under the Supreme Court's decision in *Miller v. California*, 413 U.S. 15 (1973), whether a particular work is obscene is to be decided, in part, according to local community standards. As the Ninth Circuit observed in *Jartech*, "[a]cceptance of an obscenity defense would fragment copyright enforcement, protecting registered materials in a certain community, while, in effect, authorizing pirating in another locale." 666 F.2d at 406. Would these problems disappear if a national standard were used to determine the copyrightability of obscene works? Or would the result be merely a different form of copyright fragmentation?

(7) A *perhaps* related issue is: Who is competent to make the judgment that works of a particular kind may advance the constitutional purpose, whatever that purpose is? Can a circus poster "Promote the Progress of Science"? Assume that Congress explicitly has made the decision to extend (or deny) protection to a particular class of works. Given the scope of the grant of power in the Copyright Clause, would the courts have any business second-guessing such a legislative choice? Under the language of the Copyright Clause, isn't Congress impliedly given almost *carte blanche* to make the tough decisions about which works to protect? For a discussion of the scope of Congressional power under the Clause, see the Supreme Court's opinion in *Eldred v. Ashcroft*, reproduced in § 5.01 below.

(8) Another issue at trial in *Bleistein* was whether the plaintiffs had filed the correct paperwork with the Library of Congress. Today, would-be copyright owners sometimes tangle with the Copyright Office during the registration process about whether their works are sufficiently "original." (The functions of the Office are described in greater detail in § 6.04.) How much deference should the Register of Copyrights be accorded in matters of law which Congress left to the courts? *See Paul Morelli Design, Inc. v. Tiffany & Co.*, 200 F. Supp. 2d 482 (E.D. Pa. 2002) (not error for District Court to instruct jury to give "some deference" to Register's denial of registration). In *Atari Games Corp. v. Oman*, 888 F.2d 878 (D.C. Cir. 1989), the majority in the Court of Appeals showed little deference to the Register's adverse determination, although the District Judge had referred repeatedly to the Office's "considerable expertise and experience" resulting from "having to make such determinations [of copyrightability] on a daily basis." What is the proper standard of judicial review in such cases: "abuse of discretion" or something else? *See* OddzOn Prods., Inc. v. Oman, 924 F.2d 346 (D.C. Cir. 1991) (affirming Register's denial of registration to a KOOSH ball, "a patented, trademarked product formed

of hundreds of floppy, wiggly, elastomeric filaments radiating from a core"). Is your conclusion affected by the fact that, under § 701(e) of the 1976 Act, registration decisions of the Copyright Office are reviewable as "agency actions" under the Administrative Procedure Act, 5 U.S.C. § 501 *et seq.*? Is there any other method by which a denial of registration may effectively be challenged? *See Syntek Semiconductor Co. v. Microchip Technology, Inc.*, 307 F.3d 775 (9th Cir. 2002) (action for declaratory judgment that copyright registration was invalid stayed to refer matter to Register of Copyrights under doctrine of primary jurisdiction).

(9) If courts don't defer extensively to Copyright Office decisions, why do refusals to register matter? Among the most common reasons behind attempts to register claims to copyright is the desire to initiate an infringement action. For U.S. works, § 411(a) of the 1976 Act provides, in part, that "no civil action for infringement of the copyright in any United States work shall be instituted until . . . registration of the copyright claim has been made." *See* Chapter 6. Given this, why doesn't refusal by the Copyright Office to register claims lead more often to court challenges of its registration decisions? *See OddzOn Prods., Inc.*, 924 F.2d at 350 n.6. And are there any other reasons, not related to litigation, why a copyright holder might want to seek registration? *See id.* at 347.

(10) *Originality and copying a copy.* At one point in his *Bleistein* opinion, Justice Holmes observes: "Others are free to copy the original. They are not free to copy the copy." What does this mean? Does it mean that, although Burrow-Giles could not reproduce Sarony's photograph of Oscar Wilde, it was free to make its own photograph of Oscar Wilde? What if Burrow-Giles posed Wilde in the same manner as did Sarony? *See Ets-Hokin v. Skyy Spirits, Inc.*, 323 F.3d 763 (9th Cir. 2003) (although plaintiff's photo of a vodka bottle was sufficiently original, the defendant's photo did not infringe under the "merger" doctrine). For more on the merger doctrine, see § 2.02 below.

(11) How should the "rule" quoted in the preceding note be applied when the artist making the second copy is the same person who made the first copy? Is he or she then copying the subject of the original study, or the study itself? Consider the facts of *Gross v. Seligman*, 212 F. 930 (2d Cir. 1914), as stated by the court:

> One Rochlitz, an artist, posed a model in the nude, and therefrom produced a photograph, which he named the "Grace of Youth." A copyright was obtained therefor; all the artist's rights being sold and assigned by the complainants. Two years later the same artist placed the same model in the identical pose, with the single exception that the young woman now wears a smile and holds a cherry stem between her teeth. He took a photograph of this pose, which he called "Cherry Ripe."

Id. at 930. The court carefully noted that the second photograph differed from the first, not only with respect to the smile and the cherry stem, but also because of differences in the background and slight changes in the model's figure. All the same, "[t]he identity of the artist and the many close identities of the pose, light, and shade, etc., indicate very strongly that the first picture *was used to produce the second.*" *Id.* at 931 (emphasis added). Had the artist infringed the copyright in the original photograph? The court held that he had. But what did Rochlitz copy: the copy or the original?

"Grace of Youth"

"Cherry Ripe"

Compare this with *Franklin Mint Corp. v. National Wildlife Art Exchange, Inc.*, 575 F.2d 62 (3d Cir. 1978), in which an artist painted a watercolor entitled "Cardinals on Apple Blossom," sold all rights in it to one of the parties to the eventual lawsuit, and then produced a similar painting, entitled "Cardinal," as part of a series published by the other party. In preparing the latter work, the artist used, among other aids, the same preliminary sketches, photographs, slides and working drawings (but not the "two stuffed cardinal specimens") that he had employed in creating the first work. The court noted that the two paintings contained "obvious similarities" but also "readily apparent dissimilarities." It concluded that the "similarity between the works necessarily reflected the common theme or subject and each painting was a separate artistic effort." *Id.* at 66.

Both of these cases raise the question of whether the *subject matter* of a photograph is subject to copyright protection. This question implicates an important limitation on copyright known as the idea/expression dichotomy, which we will examine in § 2.02[F] below.

(12) *A preview: the work-for-hire doctrine.* It sometimes goes unnoted that in addition to its fruitful pronouncements on the issue of "originality" in copyright, *Bleistein* also marked the first appearance of the rule that the employers should be considered the authors of works made by employees within the scope of their duties — applicable in this case (per Justice Holmes) if the posters were created by "persons employed and paid by the plaintiffs in their establishment to make those very things." 188 U.S. at 248–49. As Professor Zimmerman puts it, "[a]lthough the concept of works made for hire was not formally introduced into American copyright until 1909, modern commentators treat this language in *Bleistein* as the origin of the doctrine. . . ." Zimmerman, *Bleistein* Story at 91–92. For more on the work-for-hire doctrine, see § 4.01 below.

[E]   Originality Revisited

MESHWERKS, INC. v. TOYOTA MOTOR SALES U.S.A., INC.
United States Court of Appeals, Tenth Circuit
528 F.3d 1258 (2008)

Gorsuch, Circuit Judge. . . .

I.A.

In 2003, and in conjunction with Saatchi & Saatchi, its advertising agency, Toyota began work on its model-year 2004 advertising campaign. Saatchi and Toyota agreed that the campaign would involve, among other things, digital models of Toyota's vehicles for use on Toyota's website and in various other media. These digital models have substantial advantages over the product photographs for which they substitute. With a few clicks of a computer mouse, the advertiser can change the color of the car, its surroundings, and even edit its physical dimensions to portray changes in vehicle styling; before this innovation, advertisers had to conduct new photo shoots of whole fleets of vehicles each time the manufacturer made even a small design change to a car or truck.

To supply these digital models, Saatchi and Toyota hired Grace & Wild, Inc. ("G & W"). In turn, G & W subcontracted with Meshwerks to assist with two initial aspects of the project — digitization and modeling. Digitizing involves collecting physical data points from the object to be portrayed. In the case of Toyota's vehicles, Meshwerks took copious measurements of Toyota's vehicles by covering each car, truck, and van with a grid of tape and running an articulated arm tethered to a computer over the vehicle to measure all points of intersection in the grid. Based on these measurements, modeling software then generated a digital image resembling a wire-frame model. In other words, the vehicles' data points (measurements) were mapped onto a computerized grid and the modeling software connected the dots to create a "wire frame" of each vehicle.

At this point, however, the on-screen image remained far from perfect and manual "modeling" was necessary. Meshwerks personnel fine-tuned or, as the company prefers it, "sculpted," the lines on screen to resemble each vehicle as closely as possible. Approximately 90 percent of the data points contained in each final model, Meshwerks represents, were the result not of the first-step measurement process, but of the skill and effort its digital sculptors manually expended at the second step. For example, some areas of detail, such as wheels, headlights, door handles, and the Toyota emblem, could not be accurately measured using current technology; those features had to be added at the second "sculpting" stage, and Meshwerks had to recreate those features as realistically as possible by hand, based on photographs. Even for areas that were measured, Meshwerks faced the challenge of converting measurements taken of a three-dimensional car into a two-dimensional computer representation; to achieve this, its modelers had to sculpt, or move, data points to achieve a visually convincing result. The purpose and product of these processes, after nearly 80 to 100 hours of effort per vehicle, were two-dimensional wire-frame depictions of Toyota's vehicles that appeared three-dimensional on screen, but were utterly unadorned — lacking color, shading, and other details. . . .

With Meshwerks' wire-frame products in hand, G & W then manipulated the computerized models by, first, adding detail, the result of which appeared on screen as a "tightening" of the wire frames, as though significantly more wires had been added to the frames, or as though they were made of a finer mesh. Next, G & W digitally applied color, texture, lighting, and animation for use in Toyota's advertisements. . . . G & W's digital models were then sent to Saatchi to be employed in a number of advertisements prepared by Saatchi and Toyota in various print, online, and television media.

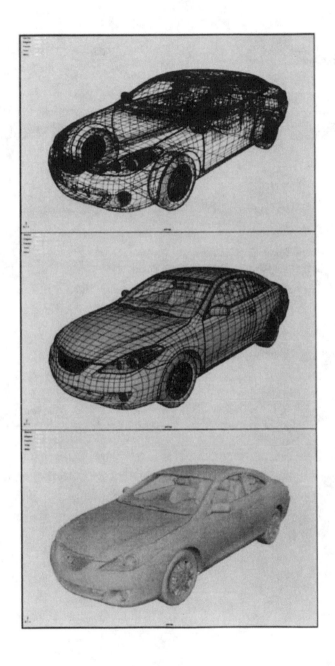

B.

    This dispute arose because, according to Meshwerks, it contracted with G & W for only a single use of its models — as part of one Toyota television commercial — and neither Toyota nor any other defendant was allowed to use the digital models created from Meshwerks' wire-frames in other advertisements. Thus, Meshwerks contends defendants improperly — in violation of copyright laws as well as the parties' agreement — reused and redistributed the models created by Meshwerks in a host of other media. In support of the allegations that defendants misappropriated its intellectual property, Meshwerks points to the fact that it sought and received copyright registration on its wire-frame models. Defendants moved for summary judgment on the theory that Meshwerks' wire-frame models lacked sufficient originality to be protected by copyright. . . . [The court granted summary judgment to the defendants.]

II.A.

. . . What exactly does it mean for a work to qualify as "original"? In *Feist* [*Publ'ns, Inc. v. Rural Tel. Serv. Co.*, 499 U.S. 340 (1991)], the Supreme Court clarified that the work must be "independently created by the author (as opposed to copied from other works)." *Id.* at 345; *see also Burrow-Giles Lithographic Co. v. Sarony*, 111 U.S. 53, 58 (1884) (the work for which copyright protection is sought must "owe[ ] its origin" to the putative copyright holder) (internal quotation omitted). In addition, the work must "possess[] at least some minimal degree of creativity," *Feist*, 499 U.S. at 345 . . .

The parties focus most of their energy in this case on the question whether Meshwerks' models qualify as independent creations, as opposed to copies of Toyota's handiwork. But what can be said, at least based on received copyright doctrine, to distinguish an independent creation from a copy? And how might that doctrine apply in an age of virtual worlds and digital media that seek to mimic the "real" world, but often do so in ways that undoubtedly qualify as (highly) original? . . .

. . . [P]hotography was initially met by critics with a degree of skepticism: a photograph, some said, "copies everything and explains nothing," and it was debated whether a camera could do anything more than merely record the physical world. . . . [In *Burrow-Giles*], the Supreme Court noted that photographs may well sometimes lack originality and are thus not *per se* copyrightable. *Id.* ("the ordinary production of a photograph" may involve "no protection" in copyright). At the same time, the Court held, . . . to the extent a photograph reflects the photographer's decisions regarding pose, positioning, background, lighting, shading, and the like, those elements can be said to "owe their origins" to the photographer, making the photograph copyrightable, at least to that extent. . . .

B.

Applying these principles, evolved in the realm of photography, to the new medium that has come to supplement and even in some ways to supplant it, we think Meshwerks' models are not so much independent creations as (very good) copies of Toyota's vehicles. In reaching this conclusion we rely on (1) an objective assessment of the particular models before us and (2) the parties' purpose in creating them. All the same, we do not doubt for an instant that the digital medium before us, like photography before it, can be employed to create vivid new expressions fully protectable in copyright.

1. Key to our evaluation of this case is the fact that Meshwerks' digital wire-frame

computer models depict Toyota's vehicles without any individualizing features: they are untouched by a digital paintbrush; they are not depicted in front of a palm tree, whizzing down the open road, or climbing up a mountainside. Put another way, Meshwerks' models depict nothing more than unadorned Toyota vehicles — the car *as* car. And the unequivocal lesson from *Feist* is that works are not copyrightable to the extent they do not involve any expression apart from the raw facts in the world. . . . [I]n short, its models reflect none of the decisions that can make depictions of things or facts in the world, whether Oscar Wilde or a Toyota Camry, new expressions subject to copyright protection.

The primary case on which Meshwerks asks us to rely actually reinforces this conclusion. In *Ets-Hokin v. Skyy Spirits, Inc.*, 225 F.3d 1068 (9th Cir. 2000) (*Skyy I*), the Ninth Circuit was faced with a suit brought by a plaintiff photographer who alleged that the defendant had infringed on his commercial photographs of a Skyy-brand vodka bottle. The court held that the vodka bottle, as a "utilitarian object," . . . was not itself (at least usually) copyrightable. *Id.* at 1080 (citing 17 U.S.C. § 101). At the same time, the court recognized that plaintiff's photos reflected decisions regarding "lighting, shading, angle, background, and so forth," *id.* at 1078, and to the extent plaintiff's photographs reflected such original contributions the court held they could be copyrighted. In so holding, the Ninth Circuit reversed a district court's dismissal of the case and remanded the matter for further proceedings.

But *Skyy I* tells only half the story. The case soon returned to the court of appeals, and the court held that the defendant's photos, which differed in terms of angle, lighting, shadow, reflection, and background, did *not* infringe on the plaintiff's copyrights. *Ets-Hokin v. Skyy Spirits, Inc.*, 323 F.3d 763, 765 (9th Cir. 2003) (*Skyy II*). Why? The only constant between the plaintiff's photographs and the defendant's photographs was the bottle itself, and an accurate portrayal of the unadorned bottle could not be copyrighted. Facts and ideas are the public's domain and open to exploitation to ensure the progress of science and the useful arts. Only original expressions of those facts or ideas are copyrightable, leaving the plaintiff in the *Skyy* case with an admittedly "thin" copyright offering protection perhaps only from exact duplication by others. *Id.* . . .

The teaching of *Skyy I* and *II*, then, is that the vodka bottle, because it did not owe its origins to the photographers, had to be filtered out to determine what copyrightable expression remained. And, by analogy — though not perhaps the one Meshwerks had in mind — we hold that the unadorned images of Toyota's vehicles cannot be copyrighted by Meshwerks and likewise must be filtered out. To the extent that Meshwerks' digital wire-frame models depict only those unadorned vehicles, having stripped away all lighting, angle, perspective, and "other ingredients" associated with an original expression, we conclude that they have left no copyrightable matter.

Confirming this conclusion as well is the peculiar place where Meshwerks stood in the model-creation pecking order. On the one hand, Meshwerks had nothing to do with designing the appearance of Toyota's vehicles, distinguishing them from any other cars, trucks, or vans in the world. . . . On the other hand, how the models Meshwerks created were to be deployed in advertising — including the backgrounds, lighting, angles, and colors — were all matters left to those (G & W [and] Saatchi) who came *after* Meshwerks left the scene. Meshwerks thus played a narrow, if pivotal, role in the process by simply, if effectively, copying Toyota's vehicles into a digital medium so they could be expressively manipulated by others.

Were we to afford copyright protection in this case, we would run aground on one of the bedrock principles of copyright law namely, that originality . . . means only that the work was independently created by the author (*as opposed to copied from other works*)." *Feist*, 499 U.S. at 345 (emphasis added). . . . *See also ATC Distr. Group, Inc. v. Whatever It Takes Transmissions & Parts, Inc.*, 402 F.3d 700, 712 (6th Cir. 2005) (denying copyright protection to catalog illustrations of transmission parts "copied from photographs cut out of competitors' catalogs"); *Bridgeman Art Library, Ltd. v. Corel Corp.*, 36 F. Supp. 2d 191, 197 (S.D.N.Y. 1999) (denying copyright protection to photographs that were " 'slavish copies' of public domain works of art"). . . .

It is certainly true that what Meshwerks accomplished was a peculiar kind of copying. It did not seek to recreate Toyota vehicles outright — steel, rubber, and all; instead, it sought to depict Toyota's three-dimensional physical objects in a two-dimensional digital medium. But we hold, as many before us have already suggested, that, standing alone, "[t]he fact that a work in one medium has been copied from a work in another medium does not render it any the less a 'copy.' " NIMMER ON COPYRIGHT § 8.01[B] . . . After all, the putative creator who merely shifts the medium in which another's creation is expressed has not necessarily added anything beyond the expression contained in the original. . . .

In reaching this conclusion, we do not for a moment seek to downplay the considerable amount of time, effort, and skill that went into making Meshwerks' digital wire-frame models. But, in assessing the originality of a work for which copyright protection is sought, we look only at the final *product*, not the process, and the fact that intensive, skillful, and even creative labor is invested in the process of creating a product does not guarantee its copyrightability. *See Feist*, 499 U.S. at 359-60. . . .

2. Meshwerks' intent in making its wire-frame models provides additional support for our conclusion. "In theory, the originality requirement tests the putative author's state of mind: Did he have an earlier work in mind when he created his own?" PAUL GOLDSTEIN, GOLDSTEIN ON COPYRIGHT § 2.2.1.1. If an artist affirmatively sets out to be unoriginal — to make a copy of someone else's creation, rather than to create an original work — it is far more likely that the resultant product will, in fact, be unoriginal. *See* Russ VerSteeg, *Intent, Originality, Creativity and Joint Authorship*, 68 Brook. L. Rev. 123, 133 (2002) ("[A] person's intent to copy . . . should be considered strong evidence that what that person has produced is not copyrightable."). Of course, this is not to say that the accidental or spontaneous artist will be denied copyright protection for not intending to produce art; it is only to say that authorial intent sometimes can shed light on the question of whether a particular work qualifies as an independent creation or only a copy.

In this case, the undisputed evidence before us leaves no question that Meshwerks set out to copy Toyota's vehicles, rather than to create, or even to add, any original expression. The purchase order signed by G & W asked Meshwerks to "digitize and model" Toyota's vehicles, and Meshwerks' invoice submitted to G & W for payment reflects that this is exactly the service Meshwerks performed. . . . Meshwerks itself has consistently described digitization and modeling as an attempt accurately to depict real-world, three-dimensional objects as digital images viewable on a computer screen. . . .

Other courts before us have examined and relied on a putative copyright holder's intent in holding that the resultant work was not original and thus subject to copyright protection. The Sixth Circuit, for example, held that a series of catalog illustrations depicting auto transmission parts were not independently copyrightable. *ATC Distrib. Group, Inc*, 402 F.3d at 712. The drawings had been copied by hand from photographs in a competitor's catalog. In denying copyright protection, the court emphasized that "[t]he illustrations were *intended* to be as accurate as possible in reproducing the parts shown in the photographs on which they were based, a form of slavish copying that is the antithesis of originality." *Id.* (emphasis added). In *Bridgeman Art Library*, the court examined whether color transparencies of public domain works of art were sufficiently original for copyright protection, ultimately holding that, as "exact photographic copies of public domain works of art," they were not. 36 F. Supp. 2d at 195. In support of its holding, the court looked to the plaintiff's intent in creating the transparencies: where "the *point of the exercise* was to reproduce the underlying works with absolute fidelity," the "spark of originality" necessary for copyright protection was absent. *Id.* at 197 (emphasis added). Precisely the same holds true here, where, by design, all that was left in Meshwerks' digital wire-frame models were the designs of Toyota's vehicles.

C.

. . . Digital modeling can be, surely is being, and no doubt increasingly will be used to create copyrightable expressions. Yet, just as photographs *can be*, but are not *per se*, copyrightable, the same holds true for digital models. There's little question that digital models *can* be devised of Toyota cars with copyrightable features, whether by virtue of unique shading, lighting, angle, background scene, or other choices. The problem for Meshwerks in this particular case is simply that the uncontested facts reveal that it wasn't involved in any such process, and indeed contracted to provide completely unadorned digital replicas of Toyota vehicles in a two-dimensional space. For this reason, we do not envision any "chilling effect" on creative expression based on our holding today, and instead see it as applying to digital modeling the same legal principles that have come, in the fullness of time and with an enlightened eye, to apply to photographs and other media.

* * *

Originality is the *sine qua non* of copyright. If the basic design reflected in a work of art does not owe its origin to the putative copyright holder, then that person must add something original to that design, and then only the original addition may be copyrighted. In this case, Meshwerks copied Toyota's designs in creating digital, wire-frame models of Toyota's vehicles. But the models reflect, that is, "express," no more than the depiction of the vehicles *as* vehicles. The designs of the vehicles, however, owe their origins to Toyota, not to Meshwerks, and so we are unable to reward Meshwerks' digital wire-frame models, no doubt the product of significant labor, skill, and judgment, with copyright protection. The judgment of the district court is affirmed, and defendants' request for attorneys' fees is denied.

NOTES AND QUESTIONS

(1) The "digital models" in *Meshwerks* are collections of digital data that represent a three-dimensional object in a way that can be manipulated by computer programs. Such digital models are used to create two-dimensional depictions of the objects that resemble traditional photographs. Unlike a still photograph, however, a digital model can be used to create an infinite variety of depictions of the object from many possible viewpoints.

(2) We discussed the copyrightability of photographs in connection with *Burrow-Giles*. If a photograph of Oscar Wilde is sufficiently original, what about a photograph of a Toyota car? In *Ets-Hokin I*, discussed in *Meshwerks*, the court held that photos of a vodka bottle made for a magazine ad were sufficiently original. *See also Schrock v. Learning Curve Int'l, Inc.*, 586 F.3d 513 (7th Cir. 2009) (photos that were "accurate depictions of the three-dimensional "Thomas and Friends' toys" were sufficiently original) (reprinted in Chapter 3). So, if an "accurate depiction" of a Toyota car is sufficiently original, why isn't a digital model of a Toyota car original? The court discusses *Ets-Hokin II*, in which the court held that another photographer's photo of the same vodka bottle did not infringe. But in *Meshwerks*, the defendants didn't make another digital model of the Toyota car; instead, they admittedly used the plaintiff's digital model. So how is *Ets-Hokin II* relevant?

(3) Is it helpful to apply the tripartite classification of *Mannion v. Coors Brewing Co.*, discussed in the notes following *Burrow-Giles*? Were the photos in *Ets-Hokin* original in their rendition, timing, or creation of the subject? Did the digital models in *Meshwerks* possess any of these types of originality?

(4) The *Meshwerks* court also relies on the plaintiff's intent, noting that the plaintiff "affirmatively set[ ] out . . . to make a copy of someone else's creation." But are deliberately imitative works always unoriginal? Compare *Meshwerks* with *Alfred Bell v. Catalda Fine Arts* (discussed earlier in connection with the originality/novelty distinction), involving the question of whether eight mezzotint engravings of old masters produced by Bell merited copyright protection. This is how the process of engraving was described by the trial court:

> Concededly, the subjects of the eight engravings are paintings by other persons than the mezzotint engravers, all of them being well-known paintings executed in the late eighteenth or early nineteenth centuries and all now in the public domain. The mezzotint method lends itself to a fairly realistic reproduction of oil paintings. It is a tedious process requiring skill and patience . . .
>
> . . . The work of the engraver upon the plate requires the individual conception, judgment and execution by the engraver on the depth and shape of the depressions in the plate to be made by the scraping process in order to produce in this other medium the engraver's concept of the effect

of the oil painting. No two engravers can produce identical interpretations of the same oil painting. . . .

74 F. Supp. 973, 974-75 (S.D.N.Y. 1947). On appeal, the Second Circuit applied the constitutional originality standard as follows:

> There is evidence that [the engravings] were not intended to, and did not, imitate the paintings they reproduced. But even if their substantial departures from the paintings were inadvertent, the copyrights would be valid. A copyist's bad eyesight or defective musculature, or a shock caused by a clap of thunder, may yield sufficiently distinguishable variations. Having hit upon such a variation unintentionally, the "author" may adopt it as his and copyright it.

191 F.2d 99, 104-05 (2d Cir. 1951).

(5) *Bridgeman Art Library, Ltd. v. Corel Corp.*, 25 F. Supp. 2d 421 (S.D.N.Y. 1998), *on reconsideration*, 36 F. Supp. 2d 191 (S.D.N.Y. 1999), cited in *Meshwerks*, also involved reproductions of oil paintings in the public domain, namely, photographic transparencies and digital images of public domain paintings. In its initial opinion, the court explained: "It is uncontested that Bridgeman's images are substantially exact reproductions of public domain works, albeit in a different medium. The images were copied from the underlying works without any avoidable addition, alteration or transformation. Indeed, Bridgeman strives to reproduce precisely those works of art." 25 F. Supp. 2d at 426. Accordingly, it held that the photographs and digital images were not original under the law of the United Kingdom.

On reconsideration, the court reached the same conclusion under U.S. law:

> There is little doubt that many photographs, probably the overwhelming majority, reflect at least the modest amount of originality required for copyright protection. "Elements of originality . . . may include posing the subjects, lighting, angle, selection of film and camera, evoking the desired expression, and almost any other variant involved." But "slavish copying," although doubtless requiring technical skill and effort, does not qualify. As the Supreme Court indicated in *Feist*, "sweat of the brow" alone is not the "creative spark" which is the *sine qua non* of originality. It therefore is not entirely surprising that an attorney for the Museum of Modern Art, an entity with interests comparable to plaintiff's and its clients, not long ago presented a paper acknowledging that a photograph of a two-dimensional public domain work of art "might not have enough originality to be eligible for its own copyright."
>
> In this case, plaintiff by its own admission has labored to create "slavish copies" of public domain works of art. While it may be assumed that this required both skill and effort, there was no spark of originality — indeed, the point of the exercise was to reproduce the underlying works with absolute fidelity. Copyright is not available in these circumstances.

34 F. Supp. 2d at 196-97. Is this consistent with *Alfred Bell*? With *Meshwerks*?

(6) Conversely, does "originality" require an intent on the part of the author to create a work of authorship? In an extensive scholarly treatment of the issue, David Nimmer (son of Melville Nimmer and present author of NIMMER ON COPYRIGHT) concludes that the answer is "yes." *See Copyright in the Dead Sea Scrolls, Authorship and Originality*, 38 Hous. L. Rev. 1, 205-06 (2001). Consider the following hypothetical from the article:

> After her careless brother breaks an old Barbie doll, Little Jane throws it into the garbage heap. There it sits, amidst bananas and other detritus of the household. By no stretch of the imagination has a copyrightable event occurred.
>
> Christu, the magnificent performance artist, decides to go the field of "readymades" one better: he buys a Barbie doll, smashes it with a hammer, perches it amidst banana peels and other household garbage, and displays the product at the newly refurbished Tate Gallery. Has a derivative work been created? It would seem so. The differing intent underlying Little Jane's and Christu's conduct would seem to vouchsafe their completely different treatment.

For a response contending that in some circumstances randomly-generated expression may warrant copyright protection, see Durham, *The Random Muse: Authorship and Indeterminacy*, 44 Wm. & Mary L. Rev. 569, 638 (2002): "Creativity can coexist with indeterminacy, and a mixture is probably the rule in authorship, rather than the exception."

(7) In *Kelly v. Chicago Park District*, 635 F.3d 290 (7th Cir. 2011), the court held that Wildflower Works, an arrangement of living plants, was "original" because it was "not copied" from any other work and "it plainly possesses more than a little creative spark." Nonetheless, the court held that Wildflower Works "lacks the kind of authorship . . . required to support copyright" because "gardens are planted and cultivated, not authored. . . . Most of what we see and experience in a garden — the colors, shapes, textures, and scents of the plants — originates in nature, not in the mind of the gardener." Do you agree? Didn't the Supreme Court in *Burrow-Giles* and *Feist* implicitly equate "originality" with "authorship"? Is it possible to have one without the other?

(8) Consider *Meshwerks* in terms of the rationales for copyright that we discussed in Chapter 1. A digital model takes a lot of time, effort, and money to create, and it can be copied easily. Does that mean that copyright should provide a financial incentive to foster the creation of such works? (Note that *Feist* rejected an argument based on "sweat of the brow"; *see* § 3.02[C] below.) Is there an "author" of the digital models who can claim a natural right to profit from their use? What are the arguments against recognizing a copyright in the digital models?

(9) The plaintiff in *Meshwerks* also pleaded a state-law breach of contract claim, but the District Court declined to exercise supplemental jurisdiction over the claim. If the plaintiff re-files the contract claim in state court, will that claim be preempted by federal copyright law? For an analysis of preemption, see § 11.02 below.

[F]   The Idea/Expression Dichotomy

BAKER v. SELDEN
Supreme Court of the United States
101 U.S. 99 (1880)

Mr. Justice Bradley delivered the opinion of the court.

Charles Selden, the testator of the complainant in this case, in the year 1859 took the requisite steps for obtaining the copyright of a book, entitled "Selden's Condensed Ledger, or Book-keeping Simplified," the object of which was to exhibit and explain a peculiar system of book-keeping. In 1860 and 1861, he took the copyright of several other books, containing additions to and improvements upon the said system. The bill of complaint was filed against the defendant, Baker, for an alleged infringement of these copyrights. The latter, in his answer, denied that Selden was the author or designer of the books and denied the infringement charged, and contends on the argument that the matter alleged to be infringed is not a lawful subject of copyright.

The parties went into proofs, and the various books of the complainant, as well as those sold and used by the defendant, were exhibited before the examiner, and witnesses were examined on both sides. . . .

The book or series of books, of which the complainant claims the copyright, consists of an introductory essay explaining the system of book-keeping referred to, to which are annexed certain forms or blanks, consisting of ruled lines and headings, illustrating the system and showing how it is to be used and carried out in practice. This system effects the same results as book-keeping by double entry; but, by a peculiar arrangement of columns and headings, presents the entire operation, of a day, a week or a month, on a single page or on two pages facing each other, in an account-book. The defendant uses a similar plan so far as results are concerned; but makes a different arrangement of the columns, and uses different headings. If the complainant's testator had the exclusive right to the use of the system explained in his book, it would be difficult to contend that the defendant does not infringe it, notwithstanding the difference in his form of arrangement; but if it be assumed that the system is open to public use, it seems to be equally difficult to contend that the books made and sold by the defendant are a violation of the copyright of the complainant's book considered merely as a book explanatory of the system. Where the truths of a science or the methods of an art are the common property of the whole world, any author has the right to express the one, or explain and use the other, in his own way. As an author, Selden explained the system in a particular way. It may be conceded that Baker makes and uses account books arranged on substantially the same system; but the proof fails to show that he has violated the copyright of Selden's book, regarding the latter merely as an explanatory work; or that he has infringed Selden's right in any way, unless the latter became entitled to an exclusive right in the system.

The evidence of the complainant is principally directed to the object of showing that Baker uses the same system as that which is explained and illustrated in

Selden's books. It becomes important, therefore, to determine whether, in obtaining the copyright of his books, he secured the exclusive right to the use of the system or method of book-keeping which the said books are intended to illustrate and explain. It is contended that he has secured such exclusive right, because no one can use the system without using substantially the same ruled lines and headings which he has appended to his books in illustration of it. In other words, it is contended that the ruled lines and headings, given to illustrate the system, are a part of the book and, as such, are secured by the copyright; and that no one can make or use similar ruled lines and headings, or ruled lines and headings made and arranged on substantially the same system, without violating the copyright. And this is really the question to be decided in this case. Stated in another form, the question is whether the exclusive property in a system of book-keeping can be claimed, under the law of copyright, by means of a book in which that system is explained. The complainant's bill and the case made under it, are based on the hypothesis that it can be.

It cannot be pretended and, indeed, it is not seriously urged, that the ruled lines of the complainant's account-book can be claimed under any special class of objects, other than books, named in the law of copyright existing in 1859. The law then in force was that of 1831, and specified only books, maps, charts, musical compositions, prints and engravings. An account-book, consisting of ruled lines and blank columns, cannot be called by any of these names, unless by that of a book.

There is no doubt that a work on the subject of book-keeping, though only explanatory of well known systems, may be the subject of a copyright; but, then, it is claimed only as a book. Such a book may be explanatory either of old systems, or of an entirely new system; and, considered as a book, as the work of an author conveying information on the subject of book-keeping and containing detailed explanations of the art, it may be a very valuable acquisition to the practical knowledge of the community. But there is a clear distinction between the book, as such, and the art which it is intended to illustrate. The mere statement of the proposition is so evident that it requires hardly any argument to support it. The same distinction may be predicated of every other art as well as that of book-keeping. A treatise on the composition and use of medicines, be they old or new; on the construction and use of ploughs or watches or churns; or on the mixture and application of colors for painting or dyeing; or on the mode of drawing lines to produce the effect of perspective, would be the subject of copyright; but no one would contend that the copyright of the treatise would give the exclusive right to the art or manufacture described therein. . . . That is the province of letters patent, not of copyright. . . .

[SELDEN'S FORM]

AUDITOR'S RECORD.

CONDENSED LEDGER.

DISBURSEMENTS.

County Fund.

Date.	No.	Amount.	To.	For.	Authority.

RECEIPTS.

Date.	No.	Amount.	Of.	For.	Authority.

CONDENSED LEDGER.

Date: from ...... to ...... inclusive.

	Bro't Forward.		Distri-bution.		Sundries to Sundries. TREASURER.			Total.		Balan-ces.	
	Dr.	Cr.	Dr.	Cr.	Dr. $	Cr. $	Dr.	Dr.	Cr.	Dr.	Cr.

County Fund.
Bridge Fund.
County Infirmary.
Building Fund.
Internal Fund.
Kind Fund.
Sale Redemptions.
Refunders.
Redemptions.
Tax Omissions.
Forfeitures.
Duplicate.
Section 16.
Section 29.
Peddlers' License.
Show License.
State Fund.
School Fund.
Corporation Fund.
Township Fund.
Treasurer's Fees.
State Relief Fund.
Soldiers' Fund.
Militia Fund.
Bounty Fund.
School Examiners' Fund.
CARRIED FORWARD.

Floating Order

RIGHT HAND PAGE

LEFT HAND PAGE

[BAKER'S FORM.]

AUDITOR'S REGISTER.

RECEIPTS.

Date.	No.	From.	For.	County.						Total.
			Total.							

BALANCE SHEET

FUNDS	Rec'd [Bar'd] to ___ 186_	To Rec. to ___ 186_	To Dis. to ___ 186_	Balance ___ 186_	Ov'r Pd. ___ 186_
County.					
Poor.					
Bridge.					
School.					
Township.					
Corporation.					
Redemption of Lands.					
Teachers' Institute.					
Show Licenses.					
Peddlers' Licenses.					
Volunteer Relief.					
Section 16.					
State Fund.					
Road Taxes.					
Building.					
Rail Road.					
Ministry.					
Soldiers' Pay.					
Bounty.					
Balance in Treasury.					
Total.					
County Treasurer-General Acct.					

ADDITIONAL RECEIPTS.

Floating Order.

RIGHT HAND PAGE

AUDITOR'S REGISTER.

DISBURSEMENTS.

Date.	No.	To.	For.	By.	County.	Poor.	Bridge.							Total.
			Total.											

ADDITIONAL DISBURSEMENTS.

Exhibit.

LEFT HAND PAGE

Reconstructed forms courtesy of Pamela Samuelson.

. . . The very object of publishing a book on science or the useful arts is to communicate to the world the useful knowledge which it contains. But this object would be frustrated if the knowledge could not be used without incurring the guilt of piracy of the book. And where the art it teaches cannot be used without employing the methods and diagrams used to illustrate the book, or such as are similar to them, such methods and diagrams are to be considered as necessary incidents to the art, and given therewith to the public; not given for the purpose of publication in other works explanatory of the art, but for the purpose of practical application. . . .

Recurring to the case before us, we observe that Charles Selden, by his books, explained and described a peculiar system of book-keeping, and illustrated his method by means of ruled lines and blank columns, with proper headings on a page, or on successive pages. Now, whilst no one has a right to print or publish his book, or any material part thereof, as a book intended to convey instruction in the art, any person may practice and use the art itself which he has described and illustrated therein. The use of the art is a totally different thing from a publication of the book explaining it. The copyright of a book on book-keeping cannot secure the exclusive right to make, sell and use account books prepared upon the plan set forth in such book. Whether the art might or might not have been patented, is a question which is not before us. It was not patented, and is open and free to the use of the public. And, of course, in using the art, the ruled lines and headings of accounts must necessarily be used as incident to it.

The plausibility of the claim put forward by the complainant in this case arises from a confusion of ideas produced by the peculiar nature of the art described in the books which have been made the subject of copyright. In describing the art, the illustrations and diagrams employed happen to correspond more closely than usual with the actual work performed by the operator who uses the art. Those illustrations and diagrams consist of ruled lines and headings of accounts; and it is similar ruled lines and headings of account which in the application of the art, the book-keeper makes with his pen, or the stationer with his press; whilst in most other cases the diagrams and illustrations can only be represented in concrete forms of wood, metal, stone, or some other physical embodiment. But the principle is the same in all. The description of the art in a book, though entitled to the benefit of copyright, lays no foundation for an exclusive claim to the art itself. The object of the one is explanation; the object of the other is use. The former may be secured by copyright. The latter can only be secured, if it can be secured at all, by letters patent. . . .

The conclusion to which we have come is that blank account-books are not the subject of copyright; and that the mere copyright of Selden's book did not confer upon him the exclusive right to make and use account-books, ruled and arranged as designed by him and described and illustrated in said book.

The decree of the Circuit Court must be reversed and the cause remanded, with instructions to dismiss the complainant's bill.

NOTES AND QUESTIONS

(1) *The idea/expression dichotomy. Baker v. Selden* generally is celebrated as an early, if quaintly worded, statement of what has become known as the idea/expression dichotomy — although, as will appear below, the relationship between the case and the principle is more complex, and indeed more problematic, than many have realized.

The basic point of the idea/expression dichotomy (or perhaps, more accurately, "distinction") is this: Copyright protects the expression of an idea, but not the idea itself. Once an author reveals his or her work to the public, any *ideas* contained in the work are released into the public domain, and the author must be content with protection for only the specific way in which he *expressed* those ideas. The protection provided by the copyright on the work as a whole extends only to the specific expressive form in which the author's ideas appear, leaving the substance of the ideas outside the scope of the copyright holder's monopoly. This is so even though the author may have spent vast amounts of time, energy and money developing his idea. There may be a possibility of protecting the *disclosure* of the idea to others under circumstances which suggest a confidential relationship or might imply a contract. But these are possibilities under state intellectual property protections (see Chapter 1), not federal copyright law (see Chapter 11 regarding preemption).

(2) The Supreme Court has identified the idea/expression distinction as one of two major copyright doctrines that protect the values of the First Amendment (the other being "fair use"). *See Eldred v. Ashcroft*, 537 U.S. 186, 219 (2003); *Golan v. Holder*, 132 S. Ct. 873, 890 (2012). Although it is sometimes viewed as a doctrine relating to the *scope* of copyright protection, the idea/expression dichotomy has significant implications for the analysis of *copyrightability* in general (and *originality* in particular). When looking at a work to see if the person claiming authorship contributed enough of, or the right kind of, value, one must concentrate not on ideas but on the way in which they are developed. Even coming up with a genuinely new and unusual idea — for example, by having been the first writer to imagine interplanetary space travel — doesn't count for copyright purposes.

(3) As we will see, Congress adopted and expanded the principle of the idea/expression (or fact/expression) dichotomy in § 102(b) of the 1976 Act. That provision denies protection to any "procedure, process, system, method of operation, concept, principle or discovery" as well. *See, e.g., Brooks-Ngwenya v. Indianapolis Public Schools*, 564 F.3d 804 (7th Cir. 2009) (ideas for better educating students are not protectible); *Hutchins v. Zoll Medical Corp.*, 492 F.3d 1377 (Fed. Cir. 2007) (method of treating victims using CPR or instructing others how to use CPR was not protected). For the moment, however, we will concentrate on how the principle plays out in *Baker v. Selden*.

(4) *Possible meanings of* Baker v. Selden. Along the way to exculpating *Baker*, the principal case offers us not one but several holdings. The most straightforward is its concluding statement that "blank account books are not the subject of copyright." Most courts, as well as the U.S. Copyright Office in its Regulations, 37 C.F.R. § 202.1(c) (barring protection for "blank forms . . . which are designed for recording information and do not in themselves convey information"), appear to

have accepted this proposition. There are, of course, problems in applying it. *Compare Utopia Provider Systems, Inc. v. Pro-Med Clinical Systems, LLC*, 596 F.3d 1313 (11th Cir. 2010) (denying copyright in hospital emergency room charts) *and Bibbero Systems, Inc. v. Colwell Systems, Inc.*, 893 F.2d 1104 (9th Cir. 1990) (denying copyright in medical claim forms) *with Kregos v. Associated Press*, 937 F.2d 700 (2d Cir. 1991) (blank form for recording nine pitching statistics was subject to copyright). For a comprehensive overview of the blank forms doctrine, see *Advanz Behavioral Management Resources, Inc. v. Miraflor*, 21 F. Supp. 2d 1179 (C.D. Cal. 1998).

Where it applies to bar protection, "[t]he Blank Form Doctrine is . . . simply an expression of the basic principle 'that originality . . . is the touchstone of copyright protection . . .' . . . Like the telephone directory white pages at issue in *Feist*, blank forms cannot be copyrighted because they are 'works in which the creative spark is utterly lacking or so trivial as to be virtually nonexistent. . . .' " *Hollister Inc. v. Uarco Inc.*, 39 U.S.P.Q. 2d (BNA) 1542 (N.D. Ill. 1996) (quoting *Feist*). In other words, however new and useful Selden's accounting system (the idea) may be, the forms (their expression) don't measure up.

But does the Supreme Court's opinion, read in its entirety, bear out the conclusion that this is the actual holding of *Baker*?

(5)   Elsewhere in its opinion, the Court seems to assume that Selden's book (consisting in substantial part of forms) *was* copyrightable. Nevertheless, it concludes that the copyright was not infringed. To explain the outcome, the opinion observes that where the useful information contained in a work is so intertwined with the particular way in which it is expressed that the information cannot be used without "employing the methods and diagrams used to illustrate [it], or such as are similar to them," then those "methods and diagrams" are free to the public for purposes of "practical application" — but not for the purpose of "publication in other works explanatory of the art."

This is the famous (or notorious) "use/explanation" distinction of *Baker v. Selden.* This distinction has had important ramifications in recent copyright jurisprudence for decisions involving works of utility, particularly those involving computer programs, for reasons that we will see shortly.

(6)   *Use/explanation and copyright/patent boundaries.* One possible under-standing of the language quoted in the preceding note is that the Court meant to refer to the different rights protected under the patent and copyright laws. Unlike copyright, patent law incorporates no "idea/expression" dichotomy to limit the scope of available protection. Thus, a patent gives the holder a right "to exclude others from making, *using* or selling" a patented invention, *including* its underly-ing idea, during the 20 years of the patent's existence. 35 U.S.C. § 154 (emphasis added). A copyright, on the other hand, confers upon its owner a handful of specifically enumerated rights, including "reproduction" and "adaptation," *see* 17 U.S.C. § 106, none of which encompasses the right to "use" the copyrighted work. According to Pamela Samuelson, the records of the Supreme Court argument suggest that at least one Justice (perhaps Bradley, the opinion's author) "perceived the case before the Court as an effort [by Selden's heirs] to misuse the copyrights in his books to get patent-like protection for the bookkeeping system." *See*

Samuelson, *The Story of* Baker v. Selden: *Sharpening the Distinction Between Authorship and Invention*, in INTELLECTUAL PROPERTY STORIES 158, 175 (J. Ginsburg & R. Dreyfuss eds. 2005) (hereinafter "*Baker Story*"). But wasn't Baker allegedly doing more than simply "using" the Selden system? Wasn't his publication of a competing form book exactly the kind of activity for which copyright *can* potentially provide redress?

(7) *Use/explanation and works of utility.* A somewhat different understanding of *Baker*'s "use/explanation" distinction may be stated as follows: Certain kinds of works, intended for practical application, are characterized by a high degree of integration between their ideas and the mode of expression. As to these works, *Baker* creates an exception to the general scope of copyright protection covering so-called "takings for application or use." In such instances, allowing the author's otherwise protected expression to be taken will facilitate utilization of the underlying idea by others. Obviously, this reading of *Baker* does not apply to copyrighted works across the board, but only to those containing material that can be "practically applied" — two key examples being blank accounting forms and computer programs. For a defense of this "pristine application" of *Baker* as a "species of 'fair use' devised for utilitarian works," drawing the contrast with Nimmer's interpretation (discussed in the note immediately below), see Reichman, *Computer Programs as Applied Scientific Know-How: Implication of Copyright Protection for Commercialized University Research*, 42 Vand. L. Rev. 639, 694 n.288 (1989).

(8) The Nimmer treatise urges restricting *Baker* to takings for "practical application" in situations "where the use of the 'art,' i.e., the idea, which a copyrighted work explains (or embodies) *necessarily* requires a copying of the work itself . . ." 1 NIMMER ON COPYRIGHT § 2.18[B] (2012) (emphasis added). Nimmer's notion of "necessity" may be summarized as follows. When there is only one way to express a given idea, the plaintiff's copyright in the work as a whole does not protect the idea against use by others. When, however, there is *more* than one way to express the idea, the author's precise manner of stating it can be protected (apparently, even if alternative modes of expression are not as straightforward or efficient as the expression chosen by the author of the copyrighted work). Knowing what you know about the facts of *Baker*, how good a fit is this interpretation?

(9) Baker's *backstory.* In *Baker*, the Court notes that Baker had "use[d] a similar plan so far as results are concerned; but makes a different arrangement of the columns, and uses different headings." In her recent investigation of *Baker*'s "backstory," Professor Samuelson notes:

> The Baker forms were similar to Selden's in some respects, for example, in enabling journal and ledger entries to be made on one page, in having columns for entering the date of a disbursement, its number, the recipient, the disburser, and by whose authorization, and in having space for balances to be carried forward. The principal difference between the Baker and Selden forms was in how they treated accounts. Baker's form featured several blank columns so that bookkeepers could label and then keep track of receipts and disbursements for each type of account; it also had space at the foot of each account column so that bookkeepers could calculate a total

period-to-date sum for each account at the foot of the form. With Baker's forms, [the trial record noted that] "you can enter your orders daily and tell just how your accounts stand." With Selden's forms, there was no space for entering orders sequentially or for calculating interim totals. Selden's system contemplated entering totals for each account at the end of the relevant period, so it was "hard to tell how your accounts [stood] during the month."

Baker Story at 161. In other words, Baker's system and forms may well have been independent creations rather than slavish copies — borrowing, at most, Selden's general principle of "condensing journal and ledger entries into one form" but displaying no other meaningful similarities. *Id.* at 169. So why wasn't the case dismissed on this ground alone, long before reaching the Supreme Court? (Samuelson's article sheds new light on the answer.)

(10) *Moving on:* Baker *and the merger doctrine.* One possible understanding of *Baker* remains to be considered. Might the *Baker* Court have decided the case as it did because it recognized intuitively, without saying so expressly, that there are a limited number of configurations of columns, rows and headings by means of which the idea of a week-, month- or year-at-a-glance ledger can be configured? More broadly, if an idea is capable of being expressed in only a few ways, should all such expressions be made nonprotectible on prudential grounds, lest, by copyrighting all usable expressions, an author might effectively copyright the idea itself? Keep reading!

[G] The Merger Doctrine

MORRISSEY v. PROCTER & GAMBLE CO.
United States Court of Appeals, First Circuit
379 F.2d 675 (1967)

ALDRICH, CHIEF JUDGE.

This is an appeal from a summary judgment for the defendant. The plaintiff, Morrissey, is the copyright owner of a set of rules for a sales promotional contest of the 'sweepstakes' type involving the social security numbers of the participants. Plaintiff alleges that the defendant, Procter & Gamble Company, infringed, by copying, almost precisely, Rule 1. In its motion for summary judgment, based upon affidavits and depositions, defendant denies that plaintiff's Rule 1 is copyrightable material, and denies access. The district court held for the defendant on both grounds. . . .

The second aspect of the case raises a more difficult question. Before discussing it we recite plaintiff's Rule 1, and defendant's Rule 1, the italicizing in the latter being ours to note the defendant's variations or changes.

'1. Entrants should print name, address and social security number on a boxtop, or a plain paper. Entries must be accompanied by * * * boxtop or by plain paper on which the name * * * is copied from any source. Official rules are explained on * * * packages or leaflets obtained from dealer. If you do not have a social security number you may use the name and number of any member of your immediate family living with you. Only the person named on the entry will be deemed an entrant and may qualify for prize.

'Use the correct social security number belonging to the person named on entry * * * wrong number will be disqualified.'

(Plaintiff's Rule)

'1. Entrants should print name, address and Social Security number on a Tide boxtop, or *on* [a] plain paper. Entries must be accompanied by Tide boxtop (*any size*) or by plain paper on which the name 'Tide' is copied from any source. Official rules are *available* on Tide Sweepstakes packages, or *on* leaflets at Tide dealers, *or you can send a stamped, self-addressed envelope to:* Tide 'Shopping Fling' Sweepstakes, P.O. Box 4459, Chicago 77, Illinois.

'If you do not have a Social Security number, you may use the name and number of any member of your immediate family living with you. Only the person named on the entry will be deemed an entrant and may qualify for a prize.

'Use the correct Social Security number, belonging to the person named on the entry — wrong numbers will be disqualified.'

(Defendant's Rule)

The district court . . . took the position that since the substance of the contest was not copyrightable, which is unquestionably correct, *Baker v. Selden*, 1879, 101 U.S. 99; and the substance was relatively simple, it must follow that plaintiff's rule sprung directly from the substance and 'contains no original creative authorship.' 262 F. Supp. at 738. This does not follow. Copyright attaches to form of expression, and defendant's own proof, introduced to deluge the court on the issue of access, itself established that there was more than one way of expressing even this simple substance. Nor, in view of the almost precise similarity of the two rules, could defendant successfully invoke the principle of a stringent standard for showing infringement which some courts apply when the subject matter involved admits of little variation in form of expression. . . .

Nonetheless, we must hold for the defendant. When the uncopyrightable subject matter is very narrow, so that 'the topic necessarily requires,' *Sampson & Murdock Co. v. Seaver-Radford Co.*, 1 Cir., 1905, 140 F. 539, 541; cf. Kaplan, An Unhurried View of Copyright, 64-65 (1967), if not only one form of expression, at best only a limited number, to permit copyrighting would mean that a party or parties, by copyrighting a mere handful of forms, could exhaust all possibilities of future use of the substance. In such circumstances it does not seem accurate to say that any particular form of expression comes from the subject matter. However, it is necessary to say that the subject matter would be appropriated by permitting the copyrighting of its expression. We cannot recognize copyright as a game of chess in which the public can be checkmated. Cf. *Baker v. Selden, supra.*

Upon examination the matters embraced in Rule 1 are so straightforward and simple that we find this limiting principle to be applicable. Furthermore, its operation need not await an attempt to copyright all possible forms. It cannot be only the last form of expression which is to be condemned, as completing defendant's exclusion from the substance. Rather, in these circumstances, we hold that copyright does not extend to the subject matter at all, and plaintiff cannot complain even if his particular expression was deliberately adopted.

NOTES AND QUESTIONS

(1) Conventionally, it is said that there are two aspects of the idea/expression dichotomy: first, the principle that an idea is not copyrightable, which we considered in connection with *Baker v. Selden*; and second, the so-called "merger doctrine." *Morrissey* is the most oft-cited description of the merger doctrine. Simply put, the merger doctrine is the principle that, when there exist only a very limited number of ways of expressing an idea, none of those expressions can enjoy protection. If they did, the theory runs, the result would be to allow the copyright holder(s) a potential effective monopoly on the underlying idea, because no one else could develop an independent expression of the idea that would differ sufficiently from the copyrighted expression(s). Since *Morrissey*, the doctrine has been alluded to often in the case law. *See, e.g., Ho v. Taflove*, 648 F.3d 489, 499 (7th Cir. 2011); *R.W. Beck, Inc. v. E3 Consulting, LLC*, 577 F.3d 1133, 1145 (10th Cir. 2009).

(2) *Rules and games.* In *Morrissey*, a notably efficient opinion, the court made short work of the issue before it. The plaintiff's sweepstakes rule was held unprotectible not because its expression manifested insufficient originality, but because that expression was too closely tied to the underlying idea. Along the same lines, see *Allen v. Academic Games League of America, Inc.*, 89 F.3d 614 (9th Cir. 1996) (the merger doctrine "is particularly applicable with respect to games since they consist of abstract rules and play ideas").

(3) *Mapping the merger doctrine.* Suppose that someone plotted out the most fuel-efficient way to drive from New York City to Los Angeles, using public domain maps. Could that mapmaker receive copyright protection for her work? At what point would there be sufficient authorship? *Compare Kern River Gas Transmission Co. v. Coastal Corp.*, 899 F.2d 1458 (5th Cir. 1990) (merger found), *with Mason v. Montgomery Data, Inc.*, 967 F.2d 135 (5th Cir. 1992) (no merger). The *Mason* court distinguished *Kern River*: "the idea in *Kern* was simply the placing on a map of Kern River's certain proposed location for a prospective pipeline." *Id.* at 140. By comparison, the idea in *Mason* was more diffuse and multifaceted: "to bring together available information on boundaries, landmarks, and ownership and to choose locations and effective pictorial expression of those locations." *Id.*

Speaking of maps, what is "original" about a map that is factually accurate? For a discussion, see § 3.01 below.

(4) *Recipes.* Recipes have long tried our understanding of the idea/expression distinction. How many different (and effective) ways are there in which to describe the preparation of a particular dish? *Compare Publications Int' l, Ltd. v. Meredith Corp.*, 88 F.3d 473 (7th Cir. 1996) (individual recipes not protected under § 102(b)), *with Barbour v. Head*, 178 F. Supp. 2d 758 (S.D. Tex. 2001) (declining to grant

summary judgment to defendants). The latter case also illustrates the dangers of relying too heavily on the Internet, which apparently is where the defendants had found the plaintiffs' uncredited recipes.

(5) *Copying merged expression.* Is it true, as at least some of the cases suggest, that copyright will protect against *identical* copying even when idea and expression merge? *Compare Apple Computer, Inc. v. Microsoft Corp.*, 35 F.3d 1435, 1444 (9th Cir. 1994) ("when an idea and its expression are indistinguishable, or 'merged,' the expression will only be protected against nearly identical copying"), *with Superior Form Builders, Inc. v. Dan Chase Taxidermy Supply Co.*, 74 F.3d 488, 493 (4th Cir. 1996) ("where idea and expression are indistinguishable, copying the expression would not be barred").

Consider *Herbert Rosenthal Jewelry Corp. v. Kalpakian*, 446 F.2d 738, 742 (9th Cir. 1971), in which the plaintiff charged the defendants with copyright infringement of a pin in the shape of a bee encrusted with jewels. The court assumed the validity of the plaintiff's copyright but refused to find actionable copying:

> What is basically at stake is the extent of the copyright owner's monopoly — from how large an area of activity did Congress intend to allow the copyright owner to exclude others? We think that the production of jeweled bee pins is a larger private preserve than Congress intended to be set aside in the public market without a patent. A jeweled bee pin is therefore an "idea" that defendants were free to copy. Plaintiff seems to agree, for it disavows any claim that defendants cannot manufacture and sell jeweled bee pins and concedes that only plaintiff's particular design or "expression" of the jeweled bee pin "idea" is protected under its copyright. The difficulty . . . is that on this record the "idea" and its "expression" appear to be indistinguishable. There is no greater similarity between the pins of plaintiff and defendants than is inevitable from the use of jewel-encrusted bee forms in both.

Compare *Herbert Rosenthal Jewelry Corp. v. Grossbardt*, 436 F.2d 315 (2d Cir. 1970), where the Second Circuit found an infringement of a jeweled bee pin (the same pin as in *Kalpakian*) when the defendant used a rubber mold to duplicate the pin. Why does such activity, however reprehensible, violate the *copyright* law, given the idea/expression dichotomy? Is the use of a rubber mold to copy a jeweled bee pin somehow more outrageous than the reproduction of an exact copy without benefit of such physical means? Should considerations of this sort influence the decisions of courts?

See also *Satava v. Lowry*, 323 F.3d 805 (9th Cir. 2003), in which the court ruled that allegedly protected elements of glass-in-glass jellyfish sculpture — "a vertically oriented, colorful, fanciful jellyfish with tendril-like tentacles and a rounded bell encased in an outer layer of rounded clear glass" — could not be protected under the idea/expression dichotomy, holding: "Satava possesses a *thin copyright* that protects against only virtually identical copying" (emphasis added). *But see Coquico, Inc. v. Rodriquez-Miranda*, 562 F.3d 62 (1st Cir. 2009) (although merger doctrine foreclosed copyright protection for idea of realistic depiction of a coquí, a Puerto Rican tree frog, plush toy featured combination of protected elements, including distinctive stitching, color combination, pose, placement of flag on underbelly, and dimensions).

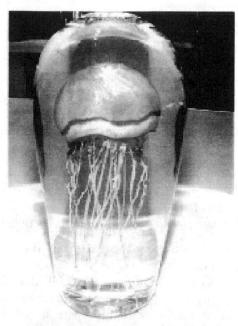

Satava Sculpture

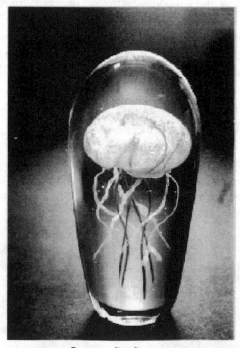

Lowry Sculpture

(6) *Litigating the merger doctrine.* A closely related question arises about the *timing* of the merger inquiry. Should it be considered in determining the copyrightability of a work as an initial matter, as a defense to infringement, or both? The Courts of Appeals are split on the issue. *Compare Kern River*, 889 F.2d at 1460 ("the maps at issue are not copyrightable"), *with Kregos v. Associated Press*, 937 F.2d 700, 705 (2d Cir. 1991) (merger is considered "in determining whether actionable infringement has occurred, rather than whether a copyright is valid"); *Ets-Hokin v. Skyy Spirits, Inc.*, 225 F.3d 1068, 1082 (9th Cir. 2000) (merger doctrine relates to infringement, not copyrightability), *on appeal after remand*, 323 F.3d 763 (9th Cir. 2003) (same). Attempting to reconcile these diverging views, the court in *Hart v. Dan Chase Taxidermy Supply Co.*, 86 F.3d 320, 322 (2d Cir. 1996), said:

> There may be highly unusual cases in which virtually all of an idea's possible expressions are before a district court at the copyrightability stage. In such rare cases it may perhaps be possible to determine the merger issue while deciding whether a given expression is copyrightable. But we agree with *Kregos* that this is very unlikely and therefore adhere to our strong preference that the question be decided only after all the evidence of substantial similarity is before the court.

See also W. Patry, PATRY ON COPYRIGHT § 4.46 (2012) ("[M]erger is merely a denial that defendant has copied protectible material. Like *scènes à faire*, merger, if applied at all, should be applied at the infringement, not at the originality stage of analysis").

For an example of the latter approach, see *Erickson v. Blake*, 839 F. Supp. 2d 1132 (D. Or. 2012), in which two composers assigned numbers to musical notes, and then wrote musical works based on the digits of the irrational number *pi* (3.14159). The court used the merger doctrine to reject the claim of infringement. You can listen to the two works (Erickson's "Pi Symphony" and Blake's "What Pi Sounds Like") on YouTube.

(7) *Burden of proof.* Who should have the burden of demonstrating that expression is "necessary" to express the underlying idea? In *Ho v. Taflove*, 648 F.3d 489 (7th Cir. 2011), plaintiffs' mathematical model for simulating the behavior of electrons was copied, without attribution, by a rival team of scientists. On defendant's motion for summary judgment, the court held that the model was an idea because it "attempts to represent and describe reality for scientific purposes." With regard to the merger doctrine, the court granted the motion because the plaintiffs "offered no evidence of how the Model could be expressed through other equations or figures" and "failed to refute" the assertion "that the allegedly copied text was 'one of only a few ways . . . to express'" the model. Given that the defendants concededly had copied the plaintiffs' text, was it proper to require the plaintiffs to show that the model could be expressed in other ways? Does the difficulty of "proving a negative" justify the court's action?

Note the distinction between plagiarism and infringement. Copying another person's ideas or expression without attribution constitutes plagiarism, a serious ethical violation and a punishable offense in the world of academia. Copyright law, however, allows the defendant to copy another's ideas, with or without attribution.

(8) *Judge or jury?* Given the purpose of the idea/expression dichotomy and the merger doctrine, should these questions be considered questions of law to be decided by the court or questions of fact to be submitted to a jury? In a thoughtful analysis of the issue, U.S. District Judge Robert Keeton said:

> The legal test for determining copyrightability . . . is a standard requiring an evaluative mixed law-fact determination, as distinguished from a bright-line rule calling for a finding about disputed historical facts such as who did what, where, and when. Moreover, this standard is far more heavily loaded with public policy implications than most other standards more commonly used in law, of which the negligence standard is an example. . . . The practical certainty of many outcomes inconsistent with the congressional accommodation among highly valued but conflicting interests, manifested in the Copyright Act, weighs heavily in favor of . . . treating copyrightability issues as exclusively for courts, not juries . . .

Lotus Development Corp. v. Borland Int' l, Inc., 788 F. Supp. 78, 95-96 (D. Mass. 1992); *see also Intervest Construction, Inc. v. Canterbury Estate Homes, Inc.*, 554 F.3d 914 (11th Cir. 2008) ("the ability to separate protect[i]ble expression from non-protect[i]ble expression is, in reality, a question of law, or at best, a mixed question of law and fact").

(9) *Justifying the merger doctrine.* Can you explain or justify the existence of this aspect of the idea/expression dichotomy using any of the approaches to copyright described in § 1.06 of this casebook? What place, if any, does such a distinction occupy within the contrasting "natural law" and "utilitarian" visions of intellectual property? From an economic standpoint, does the idea/expression dichotomy enhance consumer welfare by optimizing activity to create and disseminate works of authorship? *See* Landes & Posner, *An Economic Analysis of Copyright Law*, 18 J. Legal Stud. 325, 347-53 (1989). Does reasoning about justification help to explain how broadly or narrowly the doctrine should be applied?

(10) *Merger and originality.* Perhaps it may be said that, usually, the merger doctrine serves as a way of doing rough justice in copyright cases. Indeed, not infrequently, the doctrine has been applied by a court simply as a convenient way to administer the *coup de grace* against protection for a work exhibiting *dubious* originality. The point is nicely put in PATRY ON COPYRIGHT § 4.46:

> If an idea and its alleged expression are truly inseparable, there can be no selectivity sufficient to permit originality. This is also true if there are only a limited number of ways to "express" the idea. Such a conclusion is, in reality, a statement that the purported copyright owner's way of expressing the idea contains only a *de minimis* number of non-ideas. So understood, merger is merely a judgment that there is a lack of originality and thus, like the idea-expression dichotomy, merger merely reflects a judgment about where on the continuum of expression the work at hand lies.

See, for example, *Matthews v. Freedman*, 157 F.3d 25, 28 (1st Cir. 1998), holding that the plaintiff's t-shirt slogan, "Someone Went to Boston and got me this t-shirt because they love me Very much," was not infringed by a similarly worded text (with better capitalization) on competing apparel. The court observed: "Even if the sentiment were original with [plaintiff] — which is by no means clear — it would virtually give [him] a monopoly on the underlying idea if everyone else were forbidden from using a differently worded short sentence to express the same sentiment."

(11) *Avoiding the merger doctrine.* Sometimes the merger doctrine may appear to stand in the way of a satisfying result. When that happens, some courts have decided simply to "withhold" the application of the doctrine to specific facts. See, for example, *CCC Information Services, Inc. v. Maclean Hunter Market Reports, Inc.*, 44 F.3d 61 (2d Cir. 1994), which involved a claim of copyright in the "Red Book" of used car prices published by Maclean. Although the Red Book clearly was copyrightable as a compilation, the court concluded that the individual prices were "approximative statements of opinion" to which the merger doctrine should not apply. But is there any other effective way of expressing the "idea" of what a particular used car is worth? Is it appropriate to distinguish between, "on the one hand, those ideas that undertake to advance the understanding of phenomena and the solution of problems [as to which application of the merger doctrine is appropriate], . . . and those . . . that [instead] are infused with the author's taste or opinions [and as to which merger may appropriately be withheld]"? *Id.* at 71; *see also CDN Inc. v. Kapes*, 197 F.3d 1256 (9th Cir. 1999) (individual used coin prices were "compilations" rather than "ideas"). *But see New York Mercantile Exchange, Inc. v. IntercontinentalExchange, Inc.*, 497 F.3d 109 (2d Cir. 2007) (distinguishing *CCC* and holding NYMEX's futures contracts settlement prices were subject to the merger doctrine, in part because the incentive rationale for copyright did not apply to prices which NYMEX was required to make and report). For a spirited critique of both *CCC* and *CDN*, see Durham, *Speaking of the World: Fact, Opinion, and the Originality Standard of Copyright*, 33 Ariz. St. L.J. 791 (2001). For more on these cases, see § 3.02[C] below.

(12) *Merger, software, and compilations.* Merger analysis focuses on the range of possible choices there are for expressing an idea. For merger purposes, should the range of choice include all possible choices or should it be limited to those choices that are practical under the circumstances? The issue arises in relation to standards, particularly with respect to digital technology. Initially, an author may make expressive choices from a wide range of possibilities when selecting and arranging the elements in a database or in a software command menu. But, if this selection and arrangement becomes an industry standard such that it is the only practicable way for others in the industry to express the idea of organizing the database information or command structure, have idea and expression merged? Or should the fact that other possible forms of expression remain available grant the author copyright protection over the standard? The functionality of computer programs and the information-intensive nature of factual compilations means that copyright analysis of these two specialized categories of works often entails consideration of the merger doctrine. Be on the look-out for these issues in §§ 3.01 and 3.02 of the following chapter.

§ 2.03 OTHER PRELIMINARY CONSIDERATIONS

[A] National Origin

Statutory References

1976 Act: §§ 101 ("Berne Convention," "Geneva Phonograms Convention," "international agreement," "treaty party," "WIPO Copyright Treaty," "WIPO Performances and Phonograms Treaty," "WTO Agreement," "WTO member country"), 104, 104A

1909 Act: § 9

Summary of the Law

As we shall see in the notes immediately below and in § 8.04[B] on conflicts of law, certain legal consequences flow from the determination of a work of authorship's nation of origin. For example, until 1891, no work by a foreign author was entitled to copyright protection in the United States unless it was first published here. As a result, works by popular English authors such as Charles Dickens or Gilbert and Sullivan were in the public domain in the United States and, as a statutory matter, were free to be published without permission or payment of royalties even though these works were protected by copyright in England. Contractual arrangements between English and American publishers — the "Gentlemen's Agreement" — lessened this stark difference in practice.

After the 1891 Act, the United States entered into a number of bilateral treaties that provided reciprocal protection. Works of nationals of certain other countries became eligible for protection in the United States as the result of Presidential proclamations based on findings that those countries provided equivalent protection to the works of U.S. citizens under their national laws. In 1954, the United States signed its first multilateral copyright treaty, the Universal Copyright Convention. The U.C.C. provided yet another, and even more effective, means of protecting foreign authors in the United States (as well as U.S. authors overseas).

The 1976 Act, in § 104, codified these various bases for the protection of works of foreign origin: in effect, it recapitulated the history of U.S. international copyright relations up to that time. The list of circumstances which trigger U.S. protection for foreign works was amended and expanded in 1988 by the Berne Convention Implementation Act. (Under § 104(c), however, the Berne Convention is not "self-executing"; it is effective only to the extent it is implemented in domestic law.)

In 1994, the United States joined the World Trade Organization ("WTO"), and thus took on obligations under the Agreement on Trade-Related Aspects of Intellectual Property Rights ("TRIPS"). The TRIPS Agreement provides (at Article 3): "Each member shall accord to the nationals of other Members treatment no less favorable than it accords to its own nationals with regard to the protection of intellectual property . . ." Although § 104A of the Copyright Act was amended in 1994 to provide for the *restoration* of copyright in certain works of foreign origin (see § 5.01 of this casebook), § 104 itself was not altered. This problem was addressed in the 1998 Digital Millennium Copyright Act, which amended § 104 to cover works originating in WTO countries, as well as countries adhering to two new agreements, the WIPO Copyright Treaty and the WIPO Performances and Phonograms Treaty. In addition, the DMCA broadened the coverage of § 104A to provide copyright restoration for works originating in countries which are parties to the WIPO treaties. *See* § 5.01 below.

Under § 104(b), the availability of protection for published foreign works is based primarily on the citizenship of their authors, or on the place of first publication. For unpublished works, however, § 104(a) provides protection without regard to the author's nationality. Why should this be the case?

Be aware that determining the origin of a published work on the basis of place of first publication can be complicated. What if a work is published in several countries at about the same time, either on the same day or within a few days' time? If there is such multiple publication, and one or more of the countries where publication occurs does not have copyright relations with the United States, is U.S. protection available? Again, a careful reading of § 104 will provide some (if not all) of the answers.

You should review § 104 and the related definitions in § 101 (especially "treaty party" and "international agreement") to learn more of the details about how the "national origin" of a work may affect the availability of U.S. copyright protection. For a list of countries with whom the United States maintains copyright relations, see *Circular 38a, International Copyright Relations of the United States*, available from the U.S. Copyright Office.

[B] U.S. Government Works

Statutory References
  1976 Act: §§ 101 ("work of the United States Government"), 105
  1909 Act: § 8

Summary of the Law

Federal statutes, regulations, and judicial opinions are not subject to copyright protection in the United States. *See Wheaton v. Peters*, 33 U.S. (8 Pet.) 591 (1834); Joyce, *The Story of* Wheaton v. Peters: *A Curious Chapter in the History of Judicature, in* INTELLECTUAL PROPERTY STORIES 36, 49-76 (J. Ginsburg & R. Dreyfuss, eds. 2005). The prohibition extends only to the statutes, regulations, and opinions themselves. "Value-added" materials, such as summaries and headnotes, are subject to private copyright protection. *See, e.g., Matthew Bender & Co. v. West Publishing Co.*, 158 F.3d 674, 679-80 (2d Cir. 1998) (discussed in § 3.02); *State of Wisconsin v. Law Office Info. Systems, Inc.*, 603 N.W.2d 748 (Wis. Ct. App. 1999).

In addition to the case law authority cited above, the 1976 Act provides unambiguously, in § 105, that "[c]opyright protection under this title is not available for any work of the United States Government, but the United States Government is not precluded from receiving and holding copyrights transferred to it by assignment, bequest, or otherwise."

The definition of a "work of the United States Government" in § 101 is "a work prepared by an officer or employee of the United States Government as part of that person's official duties." The law regarding what constitutes an employee's scope of employment is a function of agency law. There is little unique about determining the scope of a U.S. Government employee's employment, except that it may be a bit easier to establish than the scope of a private sector employment, given the rigidity of U.S. Government personnel rules. *See Sherr v. Universal Match Corp.*, 297 F. Supp. 107 (S.D.N.Y. 1967) (sculpture created by enlisted persons on active duty is not a "work of the United States Government"); *Public Affairs Associates v. Rickover*, 268 F. Supp. 444 (D.D.C. 1967) (admiral entitled to copyright in speeches unrelated to official duties).

There is one explicit exception to the § 105 bar: 15 U.S.C. § 290e(a) specifically provides that the Secretary of Commerce may secure copyright on behalf of the United States in "standard reference data" compiled and evaluated by the National Institute of Technology and Standards in many different areas of science and engineering. The legislative history of the Standard Reference Data Act of 1967 indicates that the purpose of the exception is to promote the dissemination of this data by facilitating its licensing to private publishers.

In addition, § 105 does not bar copyright protection for works created for the Government by independent contractors. *See M.B. Schnapper Public Affairs Press v. Foley*, 667 F.2d 102 (D.C. Cir. 1981) (television documentary produced by public broadcasting entities); *United States v. Washington Mint, LLC*, 115 F. Supp. 2d 1089 (D. Minn. 2000) (design of Sacagawea dollar coin).

Below the Federal Government level, the matter stands somewhat differently. By its own terms, § 105 applies only to the Federal Government, so that there are no restraints placed on state and local government ownership of copyrighted works created by public officials *by § 105 itself. See, e.g., County of Suffolk v. First American Real Estate Solutions*, 261 F.3d 179 (2d Cir. 2001) (county could assert copyright in "tax maps" reflecting ownership, size and location of each parcel of real property; copyright was not abrogated by state freedom of information law). Provisions of state law, however, may dictate public availability of potentially protectible works. *See, e.g., County of Santa Clara v. Superior Court*, 89 Cal. Rptr. 3d 374 (Cal. App. 2009) (county is required to provide copies of its Geographic Information Systems (GIS) maps, and may not claim copyright or require an end-user license agreement); *Seago v. Horry County*, 663 S.E.2d 38 (S.C. 2008) (county must provide copies of GIS maps on request, but may pass ordinance or require license agreement to restrict commercial dissemination); *Microdecisions, Inc. v. Skinner*, 889 So.2d 871 (Fla. App. 2004) (tax maps produced by county employee within scope of his employment are public records not subject to copyright).

Certain types of government works, however, are part of the public domain and cannot be subject to copyright ownership by any government, whether state or federal — the most important instance, of course, being statutes and ordinances that are, themselves, the law. For example, in *Georgia v. Harrison Co.*, 548 F. Supp. 110 (N.D. Ga. 1982), *vacated by agreement between the parties*, 559 F. Supp. 37 (N.D. Ga. 1983), the court held that a new codification of Georgia statutes was not subject to copyright, in part because citizens must have free access to the laws governing them. The same logic holds, of course, for state court opinions. *See Banks v. Manchester*, 128 U.S. 244 (1888) (denying copyright to reporter of opinions of Ohio Supreme Court); Patterson & Joyce, *Monopolizing the Law: The Scope of Copyright Protection for Law Reports and Statutory Compilations*, 36 UCLA L. Rev. 719 (1989).

Somewhat more contentious is the situation in which the statute or ordinance is drafted by a private party. For example, in *Veeck v. Southern Building Code Congress Int'l*, 293 F.3d 791 (5th Cir. 2002), a model building code drafted by SBCCI was adopted by the towns of Anna and Savoy, Texas. Veeck purchased a copy directly from SBCCI and, notwithstanding the shrink-wrap license, posted the model code (as enacted) on his website. SBCCI sued, arguing that *Banks* could be distinguished on two grounds: first, that while judges' salaries are paid by the government, private parties need copyright to finance their code-drafting activities; and second, that public "access" to the law only required that copies be reasonably available for inspection. A majority of the Fifth Circuit, sitting *en banc*, disagreed, reversing a previous panel decision in favor of SBCCI. *Id.* at 795-800. Alternatively, the *Veeck* majority held that once the model code was enacted, it became a "fact" that could not be protected under the merger doctrine. *Id.* at 800-02; *see also Building Officials & Code Admins. Int'l v. Code Technology, Inc.*, 628 F.2d 730 (1st Cir. 1980) (vacating preliminary injunction; suggesting strongly that nonprofit organization's building code entered the public domain when enacted by Massachusetts). *But see Practice Management Info. Corp. v. American Medical Ass'n*, 121 F.3d 516 (9th Cir. 1997) (upholding trial court's ruling that AMA's medical procedure coding system did *not* enter the public domain when adopted by agreement with federal health care agency as sole permissible system for use by applicants for Medicaid reimbursement). For an analysis of these cases, see Hughes, *Created Facts and the Flawed Ontology of Copyright Law*, 83 Notre Dame L. Rev. 43 (2007).

Finally, note that § 105 was not intended to affect the U.S. copyright status of foreign government documents. Works of most other countries' governments are copyrighted in those countries and can be protected — when otherwise appropriate — here as well. Should a U.S. Government agency be able to claim copyright overseas? Why or why not?[1]

[C]   The Reduced Role of the Statutory Formalities

To put the matter simply, today copyright vests in the author(s) of a work at the moment of fixation. The statutory formalities of notice, registration, and deposit (all discussed at length in §§ 6.02 and 6.03 of this casebook) *are no longer, prerequisites* to copyright protection in the United States. This was a significant shift from a system that conditioned protection on an affirmative act by the beneficiary — at least, for published works — to one that grants protection automatically.

A slightly longer summary of the relevant history might run as follows. The reduced role of such formalities in U.S. copyright law is a phenomenon of relatively

---

[1] *See* Ringer & Flacks, *Applicability of the Universal Copyright Convention to Certain Works in the Public Domain in Their Country of Origin*, 27 Bull. Copyright Soc'y U.S.A. 157 (1980).

recent occurrence. Prior to the 1976 Act (effective January 1, 1978), as amended by the Berne Convention Implementation Act of 1988 (effective March 1, 1989), compliance with the statutory formalities determined the validity of copyrights, and non-compliance, for better or worse, placed works in the public domain.

Two examples will suffice to illustrate the point. First, the 1909 Act required notice on all copies of a work published in the United States. Failure to include such notice placed a work into the public domain. *See* 17 U.S.C. § 10 (1909 Act). Second, the 1909 Act, which had a bifurcated durational term (a 28-year first term with the possibility of a 28-year renewal term), required that a formal application for renewal be filed with the Copyright Office between the expiration of the 27th and 28th years of the original term, as measured from the date of publication of the work. Failure to effect renewal within the one-year period would inject the work into the public domain. *See* § 24 (1909 Act).

Formalities such as these served at least two purposes: They provided information about ownership, and they helped "filter" works for which copyright was desired from those for which it was not.[2] On the downside, such formalities often functioned as a trap for unwary authors and, by erecting barriers to protection, constituted a major stumbling block to U.S adherence to the Berne Convention. *See* Berne Convention for the Protection of Literary and Artistic Works, Art. 5(2) ("[t]he enjoyment and exercise of . . . rights [under the Convention] shall not be subject to any formality").

Generally speaking, it may be said that these problems have been addressed and resolved by recent revisions to U.S. copyright law, now that the United States has chosen to adhere to the Berne requirements. These developments will be considered in detail in later chapters: current durational requirements, and the restoration of foreign copyrights previously deprived of U.S. protection, in Chapter 5; the present, much diminished importance of the statutory formalities themselves, together with the closely related topic of general and limited publications, in Chapter 6; and certain remaining peculiarities of American law, involving litigation considerations and available remedies conditioned on the remaining vestiges of the formerly fearsome formalities, in Chapters 8 and 11 respectively. It is worth noting, however, that some scholars argue in favor of reintroducing formalities in a form that would avoid the problems caused by forfeiture while regaining the benefits of providing information and filtering protection.[3]

For the present, however, the important thing to remember is this. Much of what you will learn about modern copyright law in the pages that follow cannot be understood without reference to what came before — that is, developments in that body of law between 1787 and 1976. That history of two centuries, while it may not (as was once said of the old English writ system) rule us from its grave, still hovers about U.S. copyright law in the 21st Century, never to be forgotten — or, if so, only at our peril.

---

[2] Sprigman, *Reform(aliz)ing Copyright*, 57 Stan. L. Rev. 485 (2004).

[3] *Id. See also* Pamela Samuelson et al., *The Copyright Principles Project: Directions for Reform*, 25 Berkeley Tech. L.J. 1, 22–26 (2010) (recommending reintroduction of registration system).

Chapter 3

WORKS OF AUTHORSHIP

In the beginning was the Book. In the 21st Century, a dizzying array of media exist to enable the mass dissemination of creative expression. At the birth of Anglo-American copyright law, however, there was but one such medium — the printing press — which had been introduced in England by William Caxton in 1476; and that medium had but one product — the physical embodiments of authors' creativity described by the Statute of Anne as "books and other writings." In the United States, the first copyright act expanded the catalogue of copyrightable works to include "maps" and "charts" as well. Subsequent revisions of U.S. copyright law have continued and accelerated the process begun in 1790. Where do we stand today?

The preceding chapter explored what occurs when an "Author" creates a "Writing" — that is, fixes "original expression" in a "tangible medium of expression." The result, as the present chapter illustrates, is a "work of authorship." The Copyright Act of 1976 lists several specific but nonexclusive types or categories of such works. In the following pages, we consider why — and to what extent — individual works exemplifying those categories do or do not qualify for copyright protection.

One further preliminary note may be helpful. Modern copyright law distinguishes between the *work of authorship* itself and the *material object* in which the work is fixed. Under the 1976 Act, the product of the mind that is protected by copyright is not the tangible medium in which the work is expressed, but rather the intangible expression itself. For example, although all prior enactments from the Statute of Anne through the 1909 Act conferred protection (in some instances) by reference to tangible objects such as "books," § 102(a) of the 1976 Act instead protects intangible "literary works," which § 101 of the Act defines as "works . . . expressed in words, numbers, or other verbal or numerical symbols or indicia, *regardless of the nature of the material objects, such as books [etc.], in which they are embodied*" (emphasis added). This means that protection extends not to the material object — the book (or canvas or DVD) — *per se*, but only to the original expression actually fixed in the object.

This distinction between the material object and the work of authorship has important practical consequences that we will explore in Chapter 4 ("Ownership and Transfers"). For now, we will catalogue and consider the various types of "works" that are protected under the 1976 Act.

§ 3.01   ORIGINAL WORKS OF AUTHORSHIP UNDER § 102

Section 102(a) of the 1976 Act, as originally enacted, listed seven categories of "works of authorship," illustrating the types of subject matter eligible for the Act's protections. Congress added an eighth category — architectural works — in 1990. The present section considers all of the eight categories of works now protectible under § 102(a). All eight are, of course, subject to the limitations imposed by § 102(b).

All of the categories are both narrower and broader than they seem: narrower, in the sense that many works which fit within § 102(a) are denied protection by virtue of other statutory provisions, *e.g.*, §§ 102(b), 104 and 105 (already discussed in Chapter 2); broader, in the sense that works addressed by § 103(a) of the Act, namely, compilations and derivative works (discussed later in this chapter) are, on inspection, merely particular examples of the eight § 102(a) categories.

The legislative history says that the § 102(a) list, as indicated by the definition of "including" in § 101, is "illustrative and not limitative," to allow the courts as much flexibility as possible to adapt the law to new technologies and media.[1] This is not to say that Congress intended the courts to protect everything that might be considered the writing of an author. On the contrary, Congress in 1976 purposely chose the phrase "original works of authorship" to describe what it wanted to protect, after the courts had found it necessary to limit judicially the seemingly more expansive language of the 1909 Act, "all the writings of an author." As noted in § 2.01, however, Congress took pains to ensure that *qualifying* works would be protected regardless of their mode of fixation, whether or not the means of exploitation was known or developed when Congress passed the 1976 Act.

Section 102(a) of the 1976 Act improves upon its predecessor in at least one other important aspect already alluded to above. In § 5 of the 1909 Act, Congress listed 14 categories of writings as administrative categories for registration in the Copyright Office. Unfortunately, courts tended not to accept a work as copyrightable unless it fit into one of the specified categories — and sometimes to accept it uncritically if it did. Worse still, the list lacked logic and coherency. Some of the categories described not types of works but the material objects embodying them — *e.g.*, "books" and "prints" — while others, like the categories of the 1976 Act, more helpfully specified broad types of subject matter such as "motion pictures" and "musical compositions."

By comparison, § 102(a) of the present statute conceptually streamlines the categorization of copyrightable subject matter. It is consistent in separating works of authorship from the material objects — *i.e.*, the copies or phonorecords — in which they might be embodied. For instance, a literary work such as a novel can be embodied in a book or recorded on a CD; similarly, a musical work such as a ballad may be fixed in sheet music (a "copy") or in an MP3 file on a hard drive (a "phonorecord"). But regardless of the media in which they are embodied, the novel remains a "literary work" and the ballad remains a "musical work."

---

[1] Note, however, that the Copyright Office has issued a policy statement interpreting the 1976 Act to withhold protection from compilations that do not fit within one of the eight subject matter categories in § 102(a). *See* 77 Fed. Reg. 3760508 (June 22, 2012). What weight should be given this pronouncement?

In this section of the casebook, three of the § 102(a) categories — "literary works," "pictorial, graphic, and sculptural works," and "architectural works" — are explored through the use of cases, to illustrate generally how these categories work. You may or may not wish to examine all three in all of their particulars! For good and sufficient reasons (including the protection of old-growth forests), the remaining five categories are developed less extensively through textual material.

[A] Introduction

Statutory References

1976 Act: §§ 101 ("architectural work," "audiovisual works," "computer program," "including" and "such as," "literary works," "motion pictures," "pictorial, graphic, and sculptural works," "sound recordings," "useful article"), 102, 120

1909 Act: §§ 3-6

Legislative History

H.R. Rep. No. 94-1476 at 53-56,
reprinted in **1976 U.S.C.C.A.N. 5659, 5666-5669**

SECTION 102. GENERAL SUBJECT MATTER OF COPYRIGHT

Categories of copyrightable works[2]

The second sentence of section 102 lists seven [now eight] broad categories which the concept of "works of authorship" is said to "include." The use of the word "include," as defined in section 101, makes clear that the listing is "illustrative and not limitative," and that the seven categories do not necessarily exhaust the scope of "original works of authorship" that the bill is intended to protect. Rather, the list sets out the general area of copyrightable subject matter, but with sufficient flexibility to free the courts from rigid or outmoded concepts of the scope of particular categories. The items are also overlapping in the sense that a work falling within one class may encompass works coming within some or all of the other categories. . . .

Of the seven items listed, four [now five, including "architectural works"] are defined in section 101. The three undefined categories — "musical works," "dramatic works," and "pantomimes and choreographic works" — have fairly settled meanings. . . .

The four items defined in section 101 are "literary works," "pictorial, graphic, and sculptural works," "motion pictures and audiovisual works," and "sound recordings." In each of these cases, definitions are needed not only because the meaning of the term itself is unsettled but also because the distinction between "work" and

---

[2] The following excerpt from the House Report refers to "seven" categories of works of authorship. As a result of Public Law 101-650, 104 Stat. 5089, an eighth category — "architectural works" — was added to § 102 of the Act on December 1, 1990. Architectural works are considered at the conclusion of the present section. — *Eds.*

"material object" requires clarification. The term "literary works" does not connote any criterion of literary merit or qualitative value: it includes catalogs, directories, and similar factual, reference, or instructional works and compilations of data. It also includes computer data bases, and computer programs to the extent that they incorporate authorship in the programmer's expression of original ideas, as distinguished from the ideas themselves. . . .

The committee has added language to the definition of "pictorial, graphic, and sculptural works" in an effort to make clearer the distinction between works of applied art protectible under the bill and industrial designs not subject to copyright protection. . . .

In adopting this amendatory language, the committee is seeking to draw as clear a line as possible between copyrightable works of applied art and uncopyrighted works of industrial design. A two-dimensional painting, drawing, or graphic work is still capable of being identified as such when it is printed on or applied to utilitarian articles such as textile fabrics, wallpaper, containers, and the like. The same is true when a statue or carving is used to embellish an industrial product or, as in [*Mazer v. Stein*, 347 U.S. 201 (1954)], is incorporated into a product without losing its ability to exist independently as a work of art. On the other hand, although the shape of an industrial product may be aesthetically satisfying and valuable, the committee's intention is not to offer it copyright protection under the bill. Unless the shape of an automobile, airplane, ladies' dress, food processor, television set, or any other industrial product contains some element that, physically or conceptually, can be identified as separable from the utilitarian aspects of that article, the design would not be copyrighted under the bill. . . .

As defined in section 101, copyrightable "sound recordings" are original works of authorship comprising an aggregate of musical, spoken, or other sounds that have been fixed in tangible form. The copyrightable work comprises the aggregation of sounds and not the tangible medium of fixation. Thus, "sound recordings" as copyrightable subject matter are distinguished from "phonorecords," the latter being physical objects in which sounds are fixed. They are also distinguished from any copyrighted literary, dramatic, or musical works that may be reproduced on a "phonorecord."

[For a fuller excerpt from H.R. Rep. No. 94-1476, see Part Three of the Casebook Supplement.]

[B] Literary Works, Including Computer Software

The term "literary works," the initial category under § 102(a), would seem, at first blush, to require little or no explanation. The manuscripts of authors were among the first works to receive copyright protection both in England and in the United States; further, the necessity of encouraging the continued creation of those examples of literary works that spring most readily to mind — for example, poetry and fiction — is almost universally accepted.

Even this first and most obvious category of literary works, however, is not without its gray areas. Indeed, cases involving literary works often remind us of the important proposition that not everything in a copyrighted work is entitled to copyright protection. Suppose that an author writes an historical novel about a particular figure or period. Absent perhaps a fair use justification (discussed in Chapter 10), no subsequent writer may appropriate with impunity the precise words employed by the first author to communicate her thoughts to the reader. Does copyright law, however, protect the author's research? What about her fictional inventions? Are all of them protected, or only some?

At least equally intriguing are the questions posed by new technologies. Are computer programs, for example, protectible under existing law? If so, what *types* of programs, to what extent, and why? And what burdens on the public interest or practical difficulties in administration may such protection entail?

The following cases address these and other questions that make the "literary works" category surprisingly fluid and interesting.

MILLER v. UNIVERSAL CITY STUDIOS, INC.
United States Court of Appeals, Fifth Circuit
650 F.2d 1365 (1981)

RONEY, CIRCUIT JUDGE:

A sensational kidnapping, committed over a decade ago, furnishes the factual backdrop for this copyright infringement suit. The issue is whether a made-for-television movie dramatizing the crime infringes upon a copyrighted book depicting the unsuccessful ransom attempt. After careful and lengthy study and consideration, we conclude that the verdict for plaintiff must be reversed and the cause remanded for a new trial. . . .

Facts

 . . . In December 1968 the college-aged daughter of a wealthy Florida land developer was abducted from an Atlanta motel room and buried alive in a plywood and fiberglass capsule. A crude life-support system kept her alive for the five days she was underground before her rescue. Gene Miller, a reporter for the *Miami Herald*, covered the story and subsequently collaborated with the victim to write a book about the crime. Published in 1971 under the title 83 HOURS TILL DAWN, the book was copyrighted along with a condensed version in *Reader's Digest* and a serialization in the *Ladies Home Journal*. The co-author has assigned her interest in this litigation to Miller.

 . . . In January 1972 a Universal City Studios (Universal) producer read the condensed version of the book and thought the story would make a good television movie. He gave a copy of the book to a scriptwriter, who immediately began work on a screenplay.

Although negotiations for purchase of the movie rights to 83 HOURS TILL DAWN were undertaken by Universal, no agreement with Miller was ever reached. The scriptwriter was eventually advised that use of the book in completing the script was "verboten." The movie was completed, however, and aired as an ABC Movie of the Week, *The Longest Night*. . . .

Is Research Copyrightable?

The district court instructed the jury that if an author engages in research on factual matters, "his research is copyrightable." This instruction, at best confusing, at worst wrong, was given with some reluctance by the trial court over the strenuous objection of defendants on the urging by plaintiff, "That's the heart of the case."

As it develops on appeal, plaintiff may have won without the instruction, but later explanation by the trial court and the brief on appeal convince this Court that the idea conveyed to the jury by the court and trial counsel contained an erroneous view of the law. In context, the instruction is found in this portion of the extended jury charge:

> Copyrightability is best defined in terms of what can and cannot be copyrighted. Ideas can never be copyrighted. Only the particular expression of an idea can be copyrighted. . . .

> Similarly, in a case like the instant one, which deals with factual matters such as news events, the facts themselves are not copyrightable but the form of expression of the facts and their arrangement and selection are copyrightable. *Moreover, if an author, in writing a book concerning factual matters, engages in research on those matters, his research is copyrightable.* As was the case with ideas, if the expression, arrangement and selection of the facts must necessarily, by the nature of the facts, be formulated in given ways then they are not copyrightable. (Challenged instruction emphasized.)

It is well settled that copyright protection extends only to an author's expression of facts and not to the facts themselves. Under the Constitution, copyright protection may secure for a limited time to "Authors . . . the exclusive Right to their respective Writings." U.S. Const. Art. I, § 8, cl. 8. An "author" is one "to whom anything owes its origin; originator; maker; one who completes a work of science or literature." *Burrow-Giles Lithographic Co. v. Sarony*, 111 U.S. 53 (1884). Obviously, a fact does not originate with the author of a book describing the fact. Neither does it originate with one who "discovers" the fact. "The discoverer merely finds and records. He may not claim that the facts are 'original' with him although there may be originality and hence authorship in the manner of reporting, *i.e.*, the 'expression,' of the facts." 1 M. Nimmer, NIMMER ON COPYRIGHT § 2.03[E], at 2-34 (1980). Thus, since facts do not owe their origin to any individual, they may not be copyrighted and are part of the public domain available to every person.

The district court's charge to the jury correctly stated that facts cannot be copyrighted. Nevertheless, in its order denying defendants' motion for a new trial the court said it viewed "the labor and expense of the research involved in the obtaining of those uncopyrightable facts to be intellectually distinct from those facts and more similar to the expression of the facts than to the facts themselves." 460 F. Supp. at 987. The court interpreted the copyright law to reward not only the effort and ingenuity involved in giving expression to facts, but also the efforts involved in discovering and exposing facts. In its view, an author could not be expected to expend his time and money in gathering facts if he knew those facts, and the profits to be derived therefrom, could be pirated by one who could then avoid the expense of obtaining the facts himself. Applying this reasoning to the case at bar, the court concluded "[i]n the age of television 'docudrama' to hold other than [that] research is copyrightable is to violate the spirit of the copyright law and to provide to those persons and corporations lacking in requisite diligence and ingenuity a license to steal." *Id.* at 988.

Thus the trial court's explanation of its understanding of its charge undercuts the argument to this Court that the word "research" was intended to mean the original expression by the author of the results of the research, rather than the labor of research.

The issue is not whether granting copyright protection to an author's research would be desirable or beneficial, but whether such protection is intended under the copyright law.[2] In support of its instruction, the district court cited a number of cases, one of which involved the use of another's historical research in writing a literary work.

It is difficult to adequately distinguish some of the directory cases, and particularly the language of the opinions. . . . A copyright in a directory, however, is properly viewed as resting on the originality of the selection and arrangement of the factual material, rather than on the industriousness of the efforts to develop the information. Copyright protection does not extend to the facts themselves, and the mere use of the information contained in a directory without a substantial copying of the format does not constitute infringement. . . .

In any event, it may be better to recognize the directory cases as being in a category by themselves rather than to attempt to bring their result and rationale to bear on nondirectory cases. Under the 1909 Copyright Act, directories are specifically identified as copyrightable subject matter, 17 U.S.C. § 5(a) (1970),[4] and the rule is now well settled that they can be copyrighted . . . However appropriate it may be to extend copyright protection to the selection and arrangement of factual material in a directory if it involves originality and hence authorship, and however difficult it may be to reconcile these cases with the principle that facts are not copyrightable, . . . the special protection granted directories under the copyright law has generally not been applied to other factual endeavors. For example, the labor involved in news gathering and distribution is not protected by copyright although it may be protected under a misappropriation theory of unfair competition. *International News Service v. The Associated Press*, 248 U.S. 215 (1918). . . .

Although most circuits apparently have not addressed the question, the idea that

---

[2] The statutory law applicable to this infringement action is the Copyright Act of 1909. Although Congress revised and recodified the law in the Copyright Act of 1976, the legislative history indicates the revision was not intended to change the scope of copyright protection under the previous law: "Its purpose is to restate, in the context of the new single Federal system of copyright, that the basic dichotomy between expression and idea remains unchanged." House Report on the Copyright Act of 1976, H.R. Rep. 94-1476, 94th Cong., 2d Sess. 52.

[4] Under the Copyright Act of 1976, directories fall into the category of "compilations," copyrightable under 17 U.S.C.A. § 103. A compilation is defined as "a work formed by the collection and assembling of preexisting materials or of data that are selected, coordinated, or arranged in such a way that the resulting work as a whole constitutes an original work of authorship." 17 U.S.C.A. § 101.

historical research is copyrightable was expressly rejected by the Second Circuit in the . . . soundly reasoned case of *Rosemont Enterprises, Inc. v. Random House, Inc.*, 366 F.2d 303 (2d Cir. 1966), *cert. denied*, 385 U.S. 1009 (1967). In *Rosemont*, it was alleged that defendant's biography of Howard Hughes infringed the copyright on a series of *Look* articles about Hughes. The district court had asserted in sweeping language that an author is not entitled to utilize the fruits of another's labor in lieu of independent research. . . . The Second Circuit reversed . . . :

> We . . . cannot subscribe to the view that an author is absolutely precluded from saving time and effort by referring to and relying upon prior published material. . . . It is just such wasted effort that the proscription against the copyright of ideas and facts, and to a lesser extent the privilege of fair use, are designed to prevent.

366 F.2d at 310 (citations omitted).

The Second Circuit has adhered to its position in the most recent appellate case to address the question, *Hoehling v. Universal City Studios, Inc.*, 618 F.2d 972 (2d Cir.), *cert. denied*, 449 U.S. 841 (1980). *Hoehling* involved various literary accounts of the last voyage and mysterious destruction of the German dirigible Hindenberg. Plaintiff A.A. Hoehling published a book in 1962 entitled, WHO DESTROYED THE HINDENBERG? Written as a factual account in an objective, reportorial style, the premise of his extensively researched book was that the Hindenberg had been deliberately sabotaged by a member of its crew to embarrass the Nazi regime. Ten years later, defendant Michael McDonald Mooney published his book, THE HINDENBERG. While a more literary than historical account, it also hypothesized sabotage. Universal City Studios purchased the movie rights to Mooney's book and produced a movie under the same title, although the movie differed somewhat from the book. During the litigation, Mooney acknowledged he had consulted Hoehling's book and relied on it for some details in writing his own, but he maintained he first discovered the sabotage theory in Dale Titler's WINGS OF MYSTERY, also released in 1962.

Hoehling sued Mooney and Universal for copyright infringement. The district court granted defendants' motion for summary judgment and the Second Circuit affirmed, holding that, assuming both copying and substantial similarity, all the similarities pertained to categories of noncopyrightable material. The court noted the sabotage hypothesis espoused in Hoehling's book was based entirely on interpretation of historical fact and was not copyrightable. The same reasoning applied to Hoehling's claim that a number of specific facts, ascertained through his personal research, were copied by defendants. Relying on the *Rosemont* case, the court stated that factual information is in the public domain and "each [defendant] had the right to avail himself of the facts contained in Hoehling's book and to use such information, whether correct or incorrect, in his own literary work." 618 F.2d at 979. . . .

We find the approach taken by the Second Circuit in *Hoehling* and *Rosemont* to be . . . consistent with the purpose and intended scope of protection under the copyright law . . . The line drawn between uncopyrightable facts and copyrightable expression of facts serves an important purpose in copyright law. It provides a means of balancing the public's interest in stimulating creative activity, as embodied in the Copyright Clause, against the public's need for unrestrained access to information. It allows a subsequent author to build upon and add to prior accomplishments without unnecessary duplication of effort. As expressed by the Second Circuit in *Hoehling*:

> The copyright provides a financial incentive to those who would add to the corpus of existing knowledge by creating original works. Nevertheless, the protection afforded the copyright holder has never extended to history, be it documented fact or explanatory hypothesis. The rationale for this doctrine is that the cause of knowledge is best served when history is the common property of all, and each generation remains free to draw upon the discoveries and insights of the past. Accordingly, the scope of copyright in historical accounts is narrow indeed, embracing no more than the author's original expression of particular facts and theories already in the public domain.

618 F.2d at 974.

The valuable distinction in copyright law between facts and the expression of facts cannot be maintained if research is held to be copyrightable. There is no rational basis for distinguishing between facts and the research involved in obtaining facts. To hold that research is copyrightable is no more or no less than to hold that the facts discovered as a result of research are entitled to copyright protection. Plaintiff argues that extending copyright protection to research would not upset the balance because it would not give the researcher/author a monopoly over the facts but would only ensure that later writers obtain the facts independently or follow the guidelines of fair use if the facts are no longer discoverable. But this is precisely the scope of protection given any copyrighted matter, and the law is clear that facts are not entitled to such protection. We conclude that the district court erred in instructing the jury that research is copyrightable. . . . Reversed and remanded.

NOTES AND QUESTIONS

Scope of Protection

(1) *The problem generally.* In *Miller*, wasn't the plaintiff's work copyrighted? If so, why didn't the copyright protect everything *contained* in the work?

Is one who discovers a new insect species — and discloses it to the world in an important scientific article — entitled to "copyright" her discovery? What about an author whose book proposes a new theory concerning the true identity of Shakespeare or the assassination of President Kennedy? Is his theory or interpretation protectible under copyright law?

What is the general principle at work here? By limiting protection for the "original work of authorship," federal copyright law gives the public the freedom to copy certain aspects of creative works, such as the underlying ideas or facts expressed in the work. How general is this principle? Just as copyright law has its limits, so federal patent law refuses protection to fundamental scientific discoveries. What if a state were to extend statutory protection to such unpatentable discoveries? Or to some aspect of a copyrightable work to which copyright does not extend under § 102(b) of the 1976 Act? How vulnerable to challenge would such a state law be? We will review the technicalities of the doctrine of "preemption" in Chapter 11. But it is not too soon to consider what the result in such a situation *should* be.

(2) The court in *Miller* concludes that the fact/expression distinction would be imperiled "if research is held to be copyrightable." Most courts would probably agree. *See, e.g., Chase-Riboud v. Dreamworks, Inc.*, 987 F. Supp. 1222 (C.D. Cal 1997) (historical facts and theories, specifically those underlying Stephen Spielberg's film *Amistad*, may be copied, "as long as the defendant does not bodily appropriate the expression of the plaintiff"). Do you agree, or are you instead persuaded by the following observation:

> As the discipline of historiography instructs, a historical work may reveal more about the historian and his period than about the subject the historian described. Each historian may view a subject differently, and may devise different explanations of the same occurrence. The explanation, however intended to reveal the truth, in fact reveals the author's perceptions and inclinations. . . . [I]t should be equally clear that historical theories may be "original." By their nature, they derive from and reflect the author's personality and inspiration.

Ginsburg, *Sabotaging and Reconstructing History: A Comment on the Scope of Copyright Protection in Works of History after* Hoehling v. Universal City Studios, 29 J. Copyright Soc'y 647, 658-59 (1982). If an author's historical theories were copyrightable, would that "promote the Progress of Science" or knowledge?

(3) If labor and research, as such, are not protected, what about the other contributions made by the authors of factual works? Suppose Alphonse, a biographer, writes the 1,017th book-length account of the life and career of Napoleon. Following after so many other biographies, there is little for him to do except retell in his own words (and in chronological sequence) a series of already well-known tales about the great emperor. But Alphonse chooses to go into some of these episodes in detail, while summarizing others and passing over yet others altogether. Along comes Gaston, another biographer, who reads Alphonse's published book (along with many others) in preparation for writing *his* Napoleon biography. When that book appears, it details the same episodes as Alphonse's volume, in the same order, with the same degree of emphasis — although in Gaston's own words. Is there an infringement of *protected* matter?

(4) How persuasive an argument can you make that different *types* of factual works should be accorded different *levels* of protection? For example, do the historical facts in the principal case differ significantly from an expert's strategies and tactics for winning at Scrabble? For a negative answer, see *Landsberg v. Scrabble Crossword Game Players, Inc.*, 736 F.2d 485 (9th Cir. 1984), also holding that factual works may be infringed only by "verbatim reproduction or very close paraphrasing." What do you think?

(5) Besides ideas, facts, systems and so forth, are there other elements of a copyrighted work that should not be protected by the copyright on the work as a whole? What about protection for a distinct literary or pictorial *style*, which can

represent an author's or an artist's most valuable innovation? And what about titles? The regulations of the Copyright Office, at 37 C.F.R. § 202.1(a), state that "words and short phrases such as names, titles and slogans" are not "subject to copyright," and generally speaking the courts have gone along. Why not protect short phrases by copyright?

Whatever your answer to the immediately preceding question, you should not assume that, because a title (for example) is not protected in itself, it can be copied with impunity. Trademark or unfair competition law may apply, *see Charter Oak Fire Ins. Co. v. Hedeen & Cos.*, 280 F.3d 730, 736 (7th Cir. 2002). Even where copyright is concerned, the defendant's duplication of the plaintiff's title may be used to show that the defendant's work probably was copied from the plaintiff's, rather than independently created. Indeed, in some cases copying of a title may also be given some weight on the ultimate question of "substantial similarity." *See Shaw v. Lindheim*, 908 F.2d 531 (9th Cir. 1990).

(6)   There is a growing debate about to what extent, and in what way, intellectual property law should provide protection for songs, stories, designs and other items of cultural heritage that are transmitted from generation to generation within indigenous communities (in other words, derived from "traditional knowledge"). *See, e.g.,* SAFEGUARDING TRADITIONAL CULTURES: A GLOBAL ASSESSMENT (P. Seitle ed., Smithsonian Center for Folklife and Cultural Heritage, 2001); WIPO, INTELLECTUAL PROPERTY NEEDS AND EXPECTATIONS OF TRADITIONAL KNOWLEDGE HOLDERS (2001). But while this discussion continues, how should old-fashioned copyright law deal with new works that borrow or steal from traditional sources? *See Bell v. E. Davis International, Inc.*, 197 F. Supp. 2d 449 (W.D.N.C. 2002) (denying protection for plaintiff's miniature "War Bonnet" handicraft designs).

Characters: A Special Problem

(7)   One particular scope-of-protection issue has caused the courts special difficulty: the fictional character (for example, Sam Spade, James Bond, or Tarzan). Courts have had little trouble extending protection to characters in copyrighted cartoon strips or animated films. The line of cases goes back at least as far as *King Features Syndicate, Inc., v. Fleischer*, 299 F. 533 (2d Cir. 1924). But literary characters are another matter entirely. No one doubts that a literary work, if original and fixed in a tangible medium of expression, is protected by copyright. But the question of whether that copyright should prevent others from using the characters described in such works has bedeviled judges. Indeed, for decades every court presented with an opportunity to confront the issue contrived somehow to duck it instead.

Finally, in *Silverman v. CBS, Inc.*, 870 F.2d 40 (2d Cir. 1989), the Second Circuit apparently resolved the issue, albeit somewhat indirectly. The court decided that the defendant, who was planning to stage a musical comedy, had no right to imitate details of the characters featured on the "Amos 'n' Andy" television programs, to the extent that those details were original to those programs. On its way to this conclusion, however, the court also noted that the programs were derivative works, based on old radio scripts:

> With respect to the "Amos 'n' Andy" characters, which are at the heart of this litigation, we have no doubt that they were sufficiently delineated in the pre-1948 radio scripts to have been placed in the public domain when the scripts entered the public domain.

It seems unavoidable that, for the characters to have been "placed in the public domain," they must first have been protected!

(8)   Prior to *Silverman*, a number of courts which refused to rule squarely on literary character protection were unable to resist contributing *dicta* on the dependent question of *which* — if any — characters would be protected. *Silverman* itself refers to Judge Learned Hand's famous comments in *Nichols v. Universal Pictures Corp.*, 45 F.2d 119, 121 (2d Cir. 1930):

> If *Twelfth Night* were copyrighted, it is quite possible that a second comer might so closely imitate Sir Toby Belch or Malvolio as to infringe, but it would not be enough that for one of his characters he cast a riotous knight who kept wassail to the discomfort of the household, or a vain and foppish steward who became amorous of his mistress. These would be no more than Shakespeare's "ideas" in the play . . . It follows that the less developed the characters, the less they can be copyrighted; that is the penalty an author must bear for marking them too indistinctly.

In a society in which sequels, prequels, and other derivative works form an increasingly lucrative aspect of the entertainment business, delineating a character "too indistinctly" can become a matter of considerable economic consequence.

(9)   Some courts have enunciated a standard more restrictive than Judge Hand's in the *Nichols* case. In *Warner Bros. Pictures, Inc. v. Columbia Broadcasting System, Inc.*, 216 F.2d 945 (9th Cir. 1954), the Ninth Circuit suggested, arguably in *dicta*, that the copyright in a literary work covers only the fictional character that "really constitutes the story being told," rather than serving as merely a "chessman in the game of telling the story." *Id.* at 950. The case arose out of a contractual dispute over the rights to Dashiell Hammett's fictional detective Sam Spade. Having adopted a contract interpretation seemingly sufficient to dispose of the matter, the court further opined that, in assigning the motion picture, radio and television rights to the book THE MALTESE FALCON, the contract had failed to convey exclusive rights in the Sam Spade character because the character *per se* was not copyrightable.

How should one respond to this view? Judge Posner says flatly: "That decision is wrong, though perhaps understandable on the 'legal realist' ground that Hammett was not claiming copyright in Sam Spade — on the contrary, he wanted to reuse his own character but to be able to do so he had to overcome Warner Brothers' claim to own the copyright." *Gaiman v. McFarlane*, 360 F.3d 644, 660 (7th Cir. 2004). *See also Jim Henson Productions, Inc. v. John T. Brady & Associates, Inc.*, 16 F. Supp. 2d 259, 285–87 (S.D.N.Y. 1997) (noting that "[a]rtists . . . d[o] not customarily relinquish all rights in their characters," so that, "under both the 1909 and 1976 Copyright Acts, unless the author has given up his or her rights under copyright in a clear and unequivocal manner, he or she retains these rights").

More generally, assuming at least a modicum of originality, should a character need to be a separately registrable "work of authorship" in order to receive copyright protection? On the other hand, is there any basis for protecting stock characters of *de minimis* originality? *See Gaiman*, 360 F.3d at 660 ("If a drunken old bum were a copyrightable character, so would be a drunken suburban housewife, a gesticulating Frenchman, a fire-breathing dragon, a talking cat, [or] a Prussian officer who wears a monocle and clicks his heels . . . even though such stereotyped characters are the products not of the creative imagination but of simple observation of the human comedy.").

(10) The Ninth Circuit apparently retreated from the "story being told" standard, at least for cartoon characters, in *Walt Disney Productions v. Air Pirates*, 581 F.2d 751 (9th Cir. 1978). But the *Walt Disney* opinion suggests that, in the Ninth Circuit, that standard may still be viable where literary characters are concerned:

First Cover of "Air Pirates" Comics

In [*Warner Brothers*], Judge Stephens reasoned that it is difficult to delineate distinctively a literary character. When the author can add a visual image, however, the difficulty is reduced. Put another way, while many literary characters may embody little more than an unprotected idea, a comic book character, which has physical as well as conceptual qualities, is more likely to contain some unique elements of expression.

581 F.2d at 755 (citations omitted).

The court's distinction between literary and graphic characters has been relied upon in subsequent cases. *Compare Olson v. National Broadcasting Co.*, 855 F.2d 1446, 1452 (9th Cir. 1988) ("lightly sketched" characters described in unpublished screenplay were not protected by copyright), *with Gaiman*, 360 F.3d at 660 (characters from comic book "Spawn" were sufficiently distinctive to be copyrightable), *and Fleischer Studios, Inc. v. A.V.E.L.A., Inc.*, 654 F.3d 958 (9th Cir. 2011) ("There is no doubt that a separate Betty Boop character copyright exists."). The distinction is not dispositive, however. Sometimes one encounters an audiovisual character that "embod[ies] little more than an unprotected idea." *See, e.g., Rice v. Fox Broadcasting Co.*, 330 F.3d 1170 (9th Cir. 2003) (title character of "The Mystery Magician" video not protected by copyright); *cf. Halicki Films, LLC v. Sanderson Sales & Marketing*, 547 F.3d 1213 (9th Cir. 2008) (remanding for determination whether customized Ford Mustang "Eleanor" from movie *Gone in 60 Seconds* was a distinctive character that "displays consistent, widely-identifiable traits").

(11)   How should we deal with characters that have had a variety of different manifestations, visual and literary, over time? *See, e.g., Toho Co. v. William Morrow & Co.*, 33 F. Supp. 2d 1206 (S.D.N.Y. 1998) ("While Godzilla may have shifted from evil to good, . . . Godzilla is a well-defined character with highly delineated consistent traits"); *Metro-Goldwyn-Mayer, Inc. v. American Honda Motor Co.*, 900 F. Supp. 1287 (C.D. Cal. 1995) (James Bond character is protected by copyright, even though the character has changed "from year to year and film to film").

This issue has particular salience in the digital environment. While there has been little litigation over the practice, the explosive growth of fan-fiction websites raises issues about the relationship among copyright in narrative works, copyright in literary characters as distinct works of authorship, and the scope of fair use in either or both. For example, author E. L. James' erotic novel *50 Shades of Grey* started out as online fan fiction in the form of an X-rated reworking of the popular *Twilight* series by Stephanie Meyer. James removed the *Twilight* characters and other references to the story before publishing *50 Shades. See* Jason Boog, National Public Radio, *Fifty Shades Of Grey: Publishing's Sexiest Trend*, Mar. 15, 2012, at *http://www.npr.org/2012/03/15/148605287/fifty-shades-of-grey-publishings-sexiest-trend.*

Questions of copyright in characters as distinct works of authorship also arise in the context of videogames and virtual worlds. May a videogame maker incorporate literary or graphic characters into a game without a copyright license? *Cf. Marvel Enterprises, Inc. v. NCSoft Corp.*, 2005 U.S. Dist. LEXIS 8448 (C.D. Cal. Mar. 9, 2005). Does a player or user who creates a character or avatar with distinctive attributes, and perhaps a backstory, obtain copyright in the character or avatar? *See* Ochoa, *Who Owns an Avatar? Copyright, Creativity, and Virtual Worlds*, 14 Vand. J. Ent. & Tech. L. 959 (2012).

(12)   Assume a character that is indeed protected by a valid, subsisting copyright in the work containing the character; and assume further that the character, having achieved popular acclaim, appears in a series of copyrighted later works by the same author. What happens if somehow the initial work utilizing the

character passes into the public domain, while the other works exploiting the character remain under copyright?

Clearly, the initial work may be copied by a second author with impunity, but the later works of the first author, because they remain protected by copyright, may not be so copied. Does the right to copy the initial work encompass a right to copy the character, which also appears in the later works? It seems that, to the extent the character is delineated in the initial work, it passes into the public domain along with that work, and receives no continuing protection from the copyrights in the subsequent derivative works. This is the message of *Silverman* and of *Burroughs v. Metro-Goldwyn-Mayer, Inc.*, 683 F.2d 610 (2d Cir. 1982) ("Tarzan"). Where, however, the "initial" work was publicity material for a subsequently released motion picture, the court held that only the precise visual images in the publicity material entered the public domain. The characters themselves, and all other visual depictions of those characters, were protected by the valid copyrights in the "derivative" films. *See Warner Bros. Entertainment, Inc. v. X One X Prods.*, 644 F.3d 584 (8th Cir. 2011).

Conversely, what if a *derivative* work containing a particular protected character has entered the public domain (as the result, say, of a failure to renew the copyright under the 1909 Act's dual term provisions), while the copyright in the *initial* work in which that character was introduced continued in force? Can the derivative work be reproduced freely, or would this infringe the still-valid underlying copyright? *Burroughs* failed to resolve this question, though a majority of the panel seemed to lean towards permitting free reproduction. But the Supreme Court's subsequent decision in *Stewart v. Abend*, 495 U.S. 207 (1990), seems to indicate the contrary. We will consider this matter further when we encounter *Stewart* in Chapter 5.

(13)   On occasion, the copyrightability of characters gives rise to fascinating and poignant questions of ownership. *See, e.g., Gaiman v. McFarlane*, 360 F.3d 644 (7th Cir. 2004) (holding that certain characters in the comic book series "Spawn" were works of joint authorship); *Siegel v. National Periodical Publications, Inc.*, 508 F.2d 909 (2d Cir. 1974) (awarding renewal rights to the "Superman" character to its originator); *Archie Comics Publications, Inc. v. DeCarlo*, 258 F. Supp. 2d 315 (S.D.N.Y. 2003) (holding that artist's contributions to characters in "Sabrina, The Teen-Age Witch" were works made for hire). These cases, like others involving ownership of characters, turn on the Copyright Act's definitions of "joint works" and "works made for hire," which are covered at length in § 4.01.

(14)   Finally, always be alert to the possibility that a desired result may be achieved through means other than the copyright law. Isn't the *Sam Spade* case, for example, really a matter of contract law, in which the stronger party failed to bargain for particular rights? *See also Warner Bros., Inc. v. American Broadcasting Cos.*, 720 F.2d 231 (2d Cir. 1983) (unfair competition law); *Frederick Warne & Co. v. Book Sales, Inc.*, 481 F. Supp. 1191 (S.D.N.Y. 1979) (trademark law); *but see Fleischer* (finding insufficient evidence that "Betty Boop" character had acquired secondary meaning as a trademark). In addition, where a character has been played by a particular actor, the performer's right of publicity may come into play. *See, e.g., Wendt v. Host Int'l, Inc.*, 125 F.3d 806 (9th Cir. 1997) (Norm and Cliff from TV series "Cheers"). For fuller discussion of the right of publicity, see *White v.*

Samsung Electronics America, Inc., 971 F.2d 1395 (9th Cir. 1992) (the "Vanna White" case), in § 11.03.

APPLE COMPUTER, INC. v. FRANKLIN COMPUTER CORP.
United States Court of Appeals, Third Circuit
714 F.2d 1240 (1983)

SLOVITER, CIRCUIT JUDGE:

I. *INTRODUCTION*

Apple Computer, Inc. appeals from the district court's denial of a motion to preliminarily enjoin Franklin Computer Corp. from infringing the copyrights Apple holds on fourteen computer programs. . . .

In this case the district court denied the preliminary injunction, *inter alia*, because it had "some doubt as to the copyrightability of the programs." This legal ruling is fundamental to all future proceedings in this action and . . . has considerable significance to the computer service industry. Because we conclude that the district court proceeded under an erroneous view of the applicable law, we reverse the denial of the preliminary injunction and remand.

II. *FACTS AND PROCEDURAL HISTORY*

Apple, one of the computer industry leaders, manufactures and markets personal computers (micro-computers), related peripheral equipment such as disk drives (peripherals), and computer programs (software). . . . One of the byproducts of Apple's success is the independent development by third parties of numerous computer programs which are designed to run on the Apple II computer.

Franklin, the defendant below, manufactures and sells the ACE 100 personal computer. . . . The ACE 100 was designed to be "Apple compatible," so that peripheral equipment and software developed for use with the Apple II computer could be used in conjunction with the ACE 100. Franklin's copying of Apple's operating system computer programs in an effort to achieve such compatibility precipitated this suit.

Like all computers, both the Apple II and ACE 100 have a central processing unit (CPU) which is the integrated circuit that executes programs. In lay terms, the CPU does the work it is instructed to do. Those instructions are contained on computer programs.

When the World Was Young:
Steve Jobs, John Scully, and Steve Wozniak
with an Apple IIc Computer
Corbis

There are three levels of computer language in which computer programs may be written. High level language, such as the commonly used BASIC or FORTRAN, uses English words and symbols, and is relatively easy to learn and understand (*e.g.*, "GO TO 40" tells the computer to skip intervening steps and go to the step at line 40). A somewhat lower level language is assembly language, which consists of alphanumeric labels (*e.g.*, "ADC" means "add with carry"). Statements in high level language, and apparently also statements in assembly language, are referred to as written in "source code." The third, or lowest level computer language, is machine language, a binary language using two symbols, 0 and 1, to indicate an open or closed switch (*e.g.*, "01101001" means, to the Apple, add two numbers and save the result). Statements in machine language are referred to as written in "object code."

The CPU can only follow instructions written in object code. However, programs are usually written in source code which is more intelligible to humans. Programs written in source code can be converted or translated by a "compiler" program into object code for use by the computer. Programs are generally distributed only in their object code version stored on a memory device.

A computer program can be stored or fixed on a variety of memory devices, two of which are of particular relevance for this case. The ROM (Read Only Memory) is an internal permanent memory device consisting of a semi-conductor "chip" which is incorporated into the circuitry of the computer. A program in object code is embedded on a ROM before it is incorporated in the computer. Information stored on a ROM can only be read, not erased or rewritten.[3] . . . The other device used for storing the programs at issue is a diskette or "floppy disk," an auxiliary memory device consisting of a flexible magnetic disk resembling a phonograph record, which can be inserted into the computer and from which data or instructions can be read.

Computer programs can be categorized by function as either application programs or operating system programs. Application programs usually perform a specific task for the computer user, such as word processing, checkbook balancing, or playing a game. In contrast, operating system programs generally manage the internal functions of the computer or facilitate use of application programs. The parties agree that the fourteen computer programs at issue in this suit are operating system programs. . . .

After expedited discovery, Apple moved for a preliminary injunction to restrain Franklin from using, copying, selling, or infringing Apple's copyrights. . . .

Franklin did not dispute that it copied the Apple programs. . . .

Franklin's principal defense at the preliminary injunction hearing and before us is primarily a legal one, directed to its contention that the Apple operating system programs are not capable of copyright protection. . . .

III. *THE DISTRICT COURT OPINION*

. . . We read the district court opinion as presenting the following legal issues: (1) whether copyright can exist in a computer program expressed in object code, (2) whether copyright can exist in a computer program embedded on a ROM, (3) whether copyright can exist in an operating system program, and (4) whether independent irreparable harm must be shown for a preliminary injunction in copyright infringement actions.

IV. *DISCUSSION*

A. *Copyrightability of a Computer Program Expressed in Object Code*

Certain statements by the district court suggest that programs expressed in object code, as distinguished from source code, may not be the proper subject [of] copyright. We find no basis in the statute for any such concern. . . .

In 1976, after considerable study, Congress enacted a new copyright law to replace that which had governed since 1909. . . . Under the [1976 Act], two primary requirements must be satisfied in order for a work to constitute copyrightable subject matter — it must be an "original wor[k] of authorship" and must be "fixed in [a] tangible medium of expression." 17 U.S.C. § 102(a). . . .

---

[3] In contrast to the permanent memory devices, a RAM (Random Access Memory) is a chip on which volatile internal memory is stored which is erased when the computer's power is turned off.

Although section 102(a) does not expressly list computer programs as works of authorship, the legislative history suggests that programs were considered copyrightable as literary works. *See* H.R. Rep. No. [94-1476, at] 54 (" 'literary works' . . . includes . . . computer programs"). Because a Commission on New Technological Uses ("CONTU") had been created by Congress to study, *inter alia*, computer uses of copyrighted works, Pub. L. No. 93-573, § 201, 88 Stat. 1873 (1974), Congress enacted a status quo provision, section 117, in the 1976 Act concerning such computer uses pending the CONTU report and recommendations.[6]

The CONTU Final Report recommended that the copyright law be amended, *inter alia*, to make it explicit that computer programs, to the extent that they embody an author's original creation, are proper subject matter of copyright." National Commission on New Technological Uses of Copyrighted Works, *Final Report* 1 (1979) [hereinafter CONTU Report]. CONTU recommended two changes relevant here: that section 117, the status quo provision, be repealed and replaced with a section limiting exclusive rights in computer programs so as "to ensure that rightful possessors of copies of computer programs may use or adapt these copies for their use," *id.*, and that a definition of computer program be added to section 101. *Id.* at 12. Congress adopted both changes. Act of Dec. 12, 1980, Pub. L. No. 96-517, § 10, 94 Stat. 3015, 3028. . . .

The 1980 amendments added a definition of a computer program:

> A "computer program" is a set of statements or instructions to be used directly or indirectly in a computer in order to bring about a certain result.

17 U.S.C. § 101. The amendments also substituted a new section 117 which provides that "it is not an infringement for the owner of a copy of a computer program to make or authorize the making of another copy or adaptation of that computer program" or "for archival purposes only." 17 U.S.C. § 117. The parties agree that this section is not implicated in the instant lawsuit. The language of the provision, however, by carving out an exception to the normal proscriptions against copying, clearly indicates that programs are copyrightable and are otherwise afforded copyright protection.

We considered the issue of copyright protection for a computer program in *Williams Electronics, Inc. v. Artic International, Inc.*, [685 F.2d 870 (3d Cir. 1982),] and concluded that "the copyrightability of computer programs is firmly established after the 1980 amendment to the Copyright Act." [*Id.*] at 875. . . .

The district court here questioned whether copyright was to be limited to works "designed to be 'read' by a human reader [as distinguished from] read by an expert with a microscope and patience." The suggestion that copyrightability depends on a communicative function to individuals stems from the early decision of *White-Smith Music Publishing Co. v. Apollo Co.*, 209 U.S. 1 (1908), which held a piano roll was not a copy of the musical composition because it was not in a form others, except perhaps for a very expert few, could perceive. . . . However, it is clear from the language of the 1976 Act and its legislative history that it was intended to

---

[6] Section 117 applies only to the scope of protection to be accorded copyrighted works when used in conjunction with a computer and not to the copyrightability of programs. H.R. Rep. No. 1476, at 116.

obliterate distinctions engendered by *White-Smith*. . . .

Under the statute, copyright extends to works in any tangible means of expression *"from which they can be perceived,* reproduced, or otherwise communicated, either directly or *with the aid of a machine or device."* 17 U.S.C. § 102(a) (emphasis added). Further, the definition of "computer program" adopted by Congress in the 1980 amendments is "sets of statements or instructions to be used *directly or indirectly* in a computer in order to bring about a certain result." 17 U.S.C. § 101 (emphasis added). As source code instructions must be translated into object code before the computer can act upon them, only instructions expressed in object code can be used "directly" by the computer. . . . This definition was adopted following the CONTU Report in which the majority clearly took the position that object codes are proper subjects of copyright. *See* CONTU Report at 21. The majority's conclusion was reached although confronted by a dissent based upon the theory that the "machine-control phase" of a program is not directed at a human audience. *See* CONTU Report at 28-30 (dissent of Commissioner Hersey). . . .

The district court also expressed uncertainty as to whether a computer program in object code could be classified as a "literary work."[7] However, the category of "literary works," one of the seven copyrightable categories, is not confined to literature in the nature of Hemingway's FOR WHOM THE BELL TOLLS. The definition of "literary works" in section 101 includes expression not only in words but also "numbers, or other . . . numerical symbols or indicia," thereby expanding the common usage of "literary works." . . . Thus a computer program, whether in object code or source code, is a "literary work" and is protected from unauthorized copying, whether from its object or source code version. . . .

B. *Copyrightability of a Computer Program Embedded on a ROM*

Just as the district court's suggestion of a distinction between source code and object code was rejected by our opinion in *Williams* . . . , so also was its suggestion that embodiment of a computer program on a ROM, as distinguished from in a traditional writing, detracts from its copyrightability. In *Williams* [defendant] argued that there can be no copyright protection for the ROMs because they are utilitarian objects or machine parts. We held that the statutory requirement of "fixation," the manner in which the issue arises, is satisfied through the embodiment of the expression in the ROM devices. . . . [W]e reaffirm that a computer program in object code embedded in a ROM chip is an appropriate subject of copyright. . . .

---

[7] The district court stated that a programmer working directly in object code appears to think more as a mathematician or engineer, that the process of constructing a chip is less a work of authorship than the product of engineering knowledge, and that it may be more apt to describe an encoded ROM as a pictorial three-dimensional object than as a literary work. The district court's remarks relied in part on [authority concerning] "microcode"; Apple introduced testimony that none of the works in suit contain "microcode." Moreover Apple does not seek to protect the ROM's architecture but only the program encoded upon it.

C. *Copyrightability of Computer Operating System Programs*

We turn to the heart of Franklin's position on appeal which is that computer operating system programs, as distinguished from application programs, are not the proper subject of copyright "regardless of the language or medium in which they are fixed." . . . [W]e consider [this issue] as a matter of first impression.

Franklin contends that operating system programs are *per se* excluded from copyright protection under the express terms of section 102(b) of the Copyright Act, and under the precedent and underlying principles of *Baker v. Selden*, 101 U.S. 99 (1879). These separate grounds have substantial analytic overlap. . . .

1. *"Process," "System," or "Method of Operation"*

Franklin argues that an operating system program is either a "process," "system," or "method of operation" and hence uncopyrightable. Franklin correctly notes that underlying section 102(b) and many of the statements for which *Baker v. Selden* is cited is the distinction which must be made between property subject to the patent law, which protects discoveries, and that subject to copyright law, which protects the writings describing such discoveries. However, Franklin's argument misapplies that distinction in this case. Apple does not seek to copyright the method which instructs the computer to perform its operating functions but only the instructions themselves. The method would be protected, if at all, by the patent law, an issue as yet unresolved. *See Diamond v. Diehr*, 450 U.S. 175 (1981).

Franklin's attack on operating system programs as "methods" or "processes" seems inconsistent with its concession that application programs are an appropriate subject of copyright. Both types of programs instruct the computer to do something. Therefore, it should make no difference for purposes of section 102(b) whether these instructions tell the computer to help prepare an income tax return (the task of an application program) or to translate a high level language program from source code into its binary language object code form (the task of an operating system program such as "Applesoft"). Since it is only the instructions which are protected, a "process" is no more involved because the instructions in an operating system program may be used to activate the operation of the computer than it would be if instructions were written in ordinary English in a manual which described the necessary steps to activate an intricate complicated machine. There is, therefore, no reason to afford any less copyright protection to the instructions in an operating system program than to the instructions in an application program.

Franklin's argument, receptively treated by the district court, that an operating system program is part of a machine mistakenly focuses on the physical characteristics of the instructions. But the medium is not the message. . . . The mere fact that the operating system program may be etched on a ROM does not make the program either a machine, part of a machine or its equivalent. . . .

Franklin also argues that the operating systems cannot be copyrighted because they are "purely utilitarian works" and that Apple is seeking to block the use of the art embodied in its operating systems. This argument stems from . . . dictum in *Baker v. Selden* . . . that . . . has been rejected by a later Supreme Court decision[,] . . . *Mazer v. Stein*, 347 U.S. 201, 218 (1954), . . . [and by t]he CONTU majority. . . .

Perhaps the most convincing item leading us to reject Franklin's argument is that the statutory definition of a computer program as a set of instructions to be used in a computer in order to bring about a certain result, 17 U.S.C. § 101, makes no distinction between application programs and operating programs. . . .

2. Idea/Expression Dichotomy

Franklin's other challenge to copyright of operating system programs relies on the line which is drawn between ideas and their expression. *Baker v. Selden* remains a benchmark in the law of copyright for the reading given it in *Mazer v. Stein*, *supra*, where the Court stated, "Unlike a patent, a copyright gives no exclusive right to the art disclosed; protection is given only to the expression of the idea — not the idea itself." 347 U.S. at 217 (footnote omitted).

The expression/idea dichotomy is now expressly recognized in section 102(b) which precludes copyright for "any idea." This provision was not intended to enlarge or contract the scope of copyright protection but "to restate . . . that the basic dichotomy between expression and idea remains unchanged." H.R. Rep. No. 1476. The legislative history indicates that section 102(b) was intended "to make clear that the expression adopted by the programmer is the copyrightable element in a computer program, and that the actual processes or methods embodied in the program are not within the scope of the copyright law." *Id.*

Many of the courts which have sought to draw the line between an idea and expression have found difficulty in articulating where it falls. . . . We believe that in the context before us, a program for an operating system, the line must be a pragmatic one, which also keeps in consideration "the preservation of the balance between competition and protection reflected in the patent and copyright laws." *Herbert Rosenthal Jewelry Corp. v. Kalpakian*, 446 F.2d 738, 742 (9th Cir. 1971). As we stated in *Franklin Mint Corp. v. National Wildlife Art Exchange, Inc.*, 575 F.2d 62, 64 (3d Cir.), *cert. denied*, 439 U.S. 880 (1978), "Unlike a patent, a copyright protects originality rather than novelty or invention." In that opinion, we quoted approvingly the following passage from *Dymow v. Bolton*, 11 F.2d 690, 691 (2d Cir. 1926) (emphasis added):

> Just as a patent affords protection only to the means of reducing an inventive idea to practice, so the copyright law protects the means of expressing an idea; and it is as near the whole truth as generalization can usually reach that, *if the same idea can be expressed in a plurality of totally different manners, a plurality of copyrights may result*, and no infringement will exist.

We adopt the suggestion in the above language and thus focus on whether the idea is capable of various modes of expression. If other programs can be written or created which perform the same function as an Apple's operating system program, then that program is an expression of the idea and hence copyrightable. In essence, this inquiry is no different than that made to determine whether the expression and idea have merged, which has been stated to occur where there are no or few other ways of expressing a particular idea. *See, e.g., Morrissey v. Procter & Gamble Co.,* 379 F.2d 675, 678-79 (1st Cir. 1967); *Freedman v. Grolier Enterprises, Inc.,* 179 U.S.P.Q. 476, 478 (S.D.N.Y. 1973) ("[c]opyright protection will not be given to a form of expression necessarily dictated by the underlying subject matter"); CONTU Report at 20.

The district court made no findings as to whether some or all of Apple's operating programs represent the only means of expression of the idea underlying them. Although there seems to be a concession by Franklin that at least some of the programs can be rewritten, we do not believe that the record on that issue is so clear that it can be decided at the appellate level. Therefore, if the issue is pressed on remand, the necessary finding can be made at that time.

Franklin claims that whether or not the programs can be rewritten, there are a limited "number of ways to arrange operating systems to enable a computer to run the vast body of Apple-compatible software." This claim has no pertinence to either the idea/expression dichotomy or merger. The idea which may merge with the expression, thus making the copyright unavailable, is the idea which is the subject of the expression. The idea of one of the operating system programs is, for example, how to translate source code into object code. If other methods of expressing that idea are not foreclosed as a practical matter, then there is no merger. Franklin may wish to achieve total compatibility with independently developed application programs written for the Apple II, but that is a commercial and competitive objective which does not enter into the somewhat metaphysical issue of whether particular ideas and expressions have merged.

In summary, Franklin's contentions that operating system programs are *per se* not copyrightable is unpersuasive. The other courts before whom this issue has been raised [citing, *e.g., Apple Computer, Inc. v. Formula International, Inc.,* 562 F. Supp. 775 (C.D. Cal. 1983)] have rejected the distinction. Neither the CONTU majority [in CONTU Report at 21] nor Congress [in 17 U.S.C. § 101] made a distinction between operating and application programs. We believe that the 1980 amendments reflect Congress' receptivity to new technology and its desire to encourage, through the copyright laws, continued imagination and creativity in computer programming. . . .

V. [CONCLUSION]

For the reasons set forth in this opinion, we will reverse the denial of the preliminary injunction and remand to the district court for further proceedings in accordance herewith.

Final Report of the National Commission on New Technological Uses of Copyrighted Works (CONTU) at 28-30 (1979): Dissent of Commissioner Hersey

. . . Programs are profoundly different from the various forms of "works of authorship" secured under the Constitution by copyright. Works of authorship have always been intended to be circulated to human beings and to be used by them — to be read, heard, or seen, for either pleasurable or practical ends. Computer programs, in their mature phase, are addressed to machines.

All computer programs go through various stages of development. In the stages of the planning and preparation of software, its creators set down their ideas in written forms, which quite obviously do communicate to human beings and may be protected by copyright with no change in the present law. . . .

We take it as a basic principle that copyright should subsist in any original work of authorship that is fixed in any way (including books, records, film, piano rolls, videotapes, etc.) which communicates the work's means of expression. But a program, once it enters a computer and is activated, does not communicate information of its own, intelligible to a human being. It utters work. Work is its only utterance and its only purpose. So far as the mode of expression of the original writing is concerned, the matter ends there; it has indeed become irrelevant even before that point. The mature program is purely and simply a mechanical substitute for human labor.

The functions of computer programs are fundamentally and absolutely different in nature from those of sound recordings, motion pictures, or videotapes. Recordings, films, and videotape produce for the human ear and/or eye the sounds and images that were fed into them and so are simply media for transmitting the means of expression of the writings of their authors. The direct product of a sound recording, when it is put in a record player, is the sound of music — the writing of the author in its audible form. Of film, it is a combination of picture and sound — the writing of the author in its visible and audible forms. Of videotape, the same. But the direct product of a computer program is a series of electronic impulses which operate a computer; the "writing" of the author is spent in the labor of the machine. The first three communicate with human beings. The computer program communicates, if at all, only with a machine.

And the nature of the machine that plays the second recording is fundamentally and absolutely different from that of the machine that uses software. The record player has as its sole purpose the performance of the writing of the author in its audible form. The computer may in some instances serve as a storage and transmission medium for writings (but different writings from those of the computer programmer — i.e., data bases) in their original and entire text, in which cases these writings may be adequately secured at both ends of the transaction by the present copyright law. But in the overwhelming majority of cases, its purposes are precisely to use programs to transform, to manipulate, to select, to edit, to search and find, to compile, to control and operate computers and a vast array of other machines and systems, with the result that the preparatory writings of the computer programmer are nowhere to be found in recognizable form, because the program has been fabricated as a machine-control element that does these sorts of work. It is obvious that the means of expression of the preparatory writing — that which copyright is supposed to protect — is not to be found in the computer program's mechanical phase.

An appropriate analogy to computer programs, in their capacity to do work when passed over a magnetized head, would be such mechanical devices as the code-magnetized cards which open and close locks or give access to automated bank tellers. These are not copyrightable. . . .

To support the proposition that programs are works of authorship the report says that "the instructions that make up a program may be read, understood, and followed by a human being," and that programs "are *capable* of communicating with humans. . . ." Programmers may and sometimes do read each other's copyrightable *preparatory* writings, the early phases of software, but the implication of these statements is that programs in their machine form also communicate with human "readers" — an implication that is necessarily hedged by the careful choices of the verbs *could be* and *are capable of*; for if a skilled programmer can "read" a program in its mature, machine-readable form, it is only in the sense that a skilled home-appliance technician can "read" the equally mechanical printed circuits of a television receiver.

It is clear that the machine-control phase of a computer program is not designed to be read by anyone; it is designed to do electronic work that substitutes for the very much greater human labor that would be required to get the desired mechanical result. In the revealing words of the report, programs "are used in an almost limitless number of ways to release human beings from . . . diverse mundane tasks. . . ." The Commission report thus recommends affording copyright protection to a labor-saving mechanical device. . . .

NOTES AND QUESTIONS

(1)   Obviously, much of what the court in *Apple v. Franklin* has to say derives, directly or indirectly, from the work of the highly influential Commission on New Technological Uses of Copyrighted Works. For a critique of the CONTU Report, see Samuelson, *CONTU Revisited: The Case Against Copyright Protection for Computer Programs in Machine-Readable Form*, 1984 Duke L.J. 663. Do you find Commissioner Hersey's CONTU dissent persuasive? Do the CONTU-inspired amendments to the 1976 Act, at least as interpreted in the principal case, move copyright law dangerously close to patent law?

At the time of CONTU's deliberations, the circumstances under which inventions utilizing computer programs would be eligible for patent protection were uncertain. *See* Samuelson, Benson *Revisited: The Case Against Patent Protection for Algorithms and Other Computer Program-Related Inventions*, 34 Emory L.J. 1025 (1990). Today, however, patent protection for software is well established. Do you see a problem with this state of affairs? Critics of the existing legal regime for software often assert that our laws are "overprotective" and actually may discourage innovation rather than promoting it. Does the "patent/copyright overlap" contribute to this risk?

(2) *Protecting code.* We should be clear on what was the *exact* issue posed for decision in *Apple v. Franklin.* Sometimes the case is said to have decided the "copyrightability of computer programs." In one sense, that issue actually was not in controversy: Few then or now would dispute that a program expressed in human-readable "source code" (which would include such familiar programming "languages" as C++) is copyrightable. The problem, of course, is that the commercial value of a computer program is not in "source code" but in *machine*-readable "object code" form (as encoded on a hard disk, or on a semi-conductor chip, for example), and the hard question was whether copyright for programs extended this far. Today, for better or worse, the proposition that it does appears to be clearly established. *See Goldman v. Healthcare Mgmt. Systems, Inc.*, 628 F. Supp. 2d 748, 753-54 (W.D. Mich. 2008).

(3) To arrive at its conclusion, the court in *Apple* had to surmount a number of doctrinal hurdles. Exactly how many becomes clearer from a reading of the skeptical District Court opinion by Judge Newcomer, reported at 545 F. Supp. 812 (E.D. Pa. 1982). How does the Court of Appeals deal with each of them? What about the limitation on copyright for "useful articles" — something that is discussed further in § 3.01[C]? And what about *Baker v. Selden?* You will recall that there are several ways to interpret the holding of that famous, but far from lucid, decision. Which one does the Court of Appeals adopt, and why?

(4) Object code has been held copyrightable by the Ninth Circuit also. In affirming the grant of a preliminary injunction in *Apple Computer, Inc. v. Formula International, Inc.*, 725 F.2d 521 (1984), the court observed that the defendant had "provide[d] absolutely no authority for its contention that the 'expression' required in order for a computer program to be eligible for copyright protection is expression that must be communicated to the computer user when the program is run on a computer. . . . The computer program when written embodies expression; never has the Copyright Act required that the expression be communicated to a particular audience." 725 F.2d at 525.

(5) *"Second generation" issues.* The group of cases of which *Apple v. Franklin* is the most important sometimes is referred to as the "first generation" of software protection decisions: those concerned more or less exclusively with making a binary choice as to the protectibility of programs in machine-readable form. Once that choice had been made — in favor of protection — there arose a whole set of additional dilemmas, often referred to as "second generation" software protection issues. *See* Menell, *An Analysis of the Scope of Copyright Protection for Application Programs*, 41 Stan. L. Rev. 1045, 1048 (1989). One of the most important "second generation" issues was the extent to which computer programs would be protected against "non-literal" infringement. Initially, some courts expressed the view that computer programs should be given a wide scope of protection, like any other "literary work." Since 1992, however, most courts have taken a more cautious — even skeptical — approach to the scope of protection for computer programs. The key turning point was the opinion in *Computer Associates International, Inc.*

v. Altai, Inc., 982 F.2d 693 (2d Cir. 1992), which is reproduced and discussed in § 8.03.

(6)   Another "second generation" issue was the scope of copyright protection for computer screen displays. While no one doubted that the screen displays of a video game (for example) could be protected, there was considerable debate concerning the copyrightability of a "user interface" for an application program, such as a word processor or spreadsheet. Such user interfaces may contain attractive aesthetic features, but their principal function is to facilitate the efficient use of the computer. Moreover, popular formats for screen displays (such as menus) tend to become "standards" throughout the computer industry, which may enhance consumer welfare. Consider, by analogy, the confusion which would result if every typewriter or computer keyboard were legally required to be significantly different from all its predecessors.

After some early divergence of approaches to this problem in the lower courts, the First Circuit in 1995 decided *Lotus Development Corp. v. Borland International, Inc.*, 49 F.3d 807 (1995) (menu command structure was uncopyrightable "method of operation" within meaning of § 102(b)), a case affirmed in 1996 by an equally divided Supreme Court. For more on the *Lotus* case and user interfaces, see § 8.03 below.

(7)   Yet another "second generation" issue, directly related to the utilitarian nature of computer programs, is the extent to which copying is allowable for the purposes of "reverse engineering." In practice, reverse engineering usually involves "decompiling" or "disassembling" the "object code" form of a program to produce a version in a higher-level, human-readable language. The disassembled code is then analyzed to discover the unprotectible ideas underlying the program. While reverse engineering by means of decompilation necessarily involves making a copy of the program, in practice courts have carved out a substantial exception for such activity under the "fair use" doctrine. *See, e.g., Sega Enterprises Ltd. v. Accolade, Inc.*, 977 F.2d 1510 (9th Cir. 1992), which is discussed in § 10.04.

(8)   A final issue is that of "microcode," defined as "a series of instructions that tell a microprocessor which of its thousands of transistors to actuate in order to perform the tasks directed by the macroinstruction set." *NEC Corp. v. Intel Corp.*, 10 U.S.P.Q. 2d 1177 (N.D. Cal. 1989). Microcode fits the definition of a computer program, in that it is a set of statements used directly in a computer in order to bring about a certain result. Nonetheless, a programmer is far more constrained in creating microcode than he or she is, for example, in programming in a high-level language such as C++. As a result, although microcode has been held to be copyrightable, difficult issues involving the idea-expression dichotomy and the merger doctrine arise here as well. *See, e.g., Syntek Semiconductor Co. v. Microchip Technology, Inc.*, 307 F.3d 775 (9th Cir. 2002) (referring dispute over copyrightability of microcode to the Copyright Office under the doctrine of primary jurisdiction).

(9)   We have noted earlier that there now is a significant amount of overlap between the protection provided by software copyright, on the one hand, and software patent, on the other. This overlap suggests the question: Should software protection under federal law be rethought and legislatively rationalized, rather than

being permitted to continue to develop through the process of piecemeal judicial decision making?

In 1986, an advisory body to Congress — the Office of Technology Assessment — did take up the question of software protection, conducting a study culminating in a report entitled *Intellectual Property Rights in an Age of Electronics and Information*. The study concluded that copyright may *not*, after all, be the most appropriate form of legal protection for computer programs — and, for that view, it was widely criticized by the American software industry, among others. At about the same time, skepticism was being expressed about the appropriateness of the burgeoning trend toward software patents. See the 1990 Samuelson article cited in note (1) above.

One way to have avoided the difficulties inherent in the attempt to adapt existing forms of intellectual property protection to this new information technology would have been to create a new *sui generis* federal legislative scheme designed specifically to secure proprietary interests in software. *See* Samuelson, Davis, Kapor & Reichman, *A Manifesto Concerning the Legal Protection of Computer Programs*, 94 Colum. L. Rev. 2308 (1994). At least for the time being, however, this approach appears to be an idea whose time has come and gone.

(10) *Looking to the future*. A substantial basis for the preceding generalization is that Article 10 of the TRIPS agreement (discussed in Chapter 1) provides that "[c]omputer programs, whether in source or object code, shall be protected as literary works under the Berne Convention (1971)" — which, in turn, makes protection for qualifying "literary and artistic" works mandatory in its Article 2. For good measure, Article 4 of the WIPO Copyright Treaty concluded in Geneva in December 1996 specifies that "[c]omputer programs are protected as literary works within the meaning of Article 2 of the Berne Convention. Such protection applies to computer programs, whatever may be the mode or form of their expression."

ALTERNATIVE PROTECTIONS FOR COMPUTER SOFTWARE

Patent Protection

Although some uncertainties remain about the scope and protection of computer software under copyright law, cases like *Altai* and *Sega* left the scope of copyright protection for software narrower than some software developers had hoped in the wake of earlier decisions. Consequently, software developers have looked to other bodies of law to protect their creations.

At about the same time courts were cutting back on copyright protection for computer software, the Patent and Trademark Office was relaxing its historical antipathy to patent protection for software. Once viewed as a type of mathematical algorithm (a class of non-patentable laws of nature), patents for software inventions had been the object of a distinct hostility in the PTO and the courts, including the U.S. Supreme Court, prior to the 1980s. *See, e.g., Gottschalk v. Benson*, 409 U.S. 63 (1972) (method of programming a general-purpose digital computer to perform a mathematical algorithm was not patentable subject matter). This view persisted until the Supreme Court's decision in *Diamond v. Diehr*, 450 U.S. 175 (1981), which held that an industrial process controlled by software is patent-eligible under 35

U.S.C. § 101 if it is tied to a particular machine or apparatus or it transforms a particular article into a different state or thing. After *Diehr*, the U.S. Court of Appeals for the Federal Circuit progressively expanded the scope of patent protection for computer software. *See, e.g., In re Alappat*, 33 F.3d 1526 (Fed. Cir. 1994) (holding that a newly programmed general purpose computer could be patentable subject matter). In response, the PTO announced that, henceforth, computer programs embodied in a tangible medium would be considered patentable subject matter. *In Re Beauregard*, 53 F.3d 1583 (Fed. Cir. 1995); *Examination Guidelines for Computer-Related Inventions*, 61 Fed. Reg. 7478 (Feb. 28, 1996).

The net effect of the *Guidelines* and liberal court decisions was the issuance of more software patents and their effective immunity from challenge on subject matter grounds. The high point of this approach was *State Street Bank & Trust Co. v. Signature Financial Group, Inc.*, 149 F.3d 1368 (Fed. Cir. 1998), in which the Federal Circuit upheld a patent in a computerized accounting system. It rejected a "business method" exception to patentability, holding that a process is patentable so long as it leads to a "useful, concrete, and tangible" result, such as transforming data from one form to another form.

State Street's liberal attitude, however, is now on the wane. In *Bilski v. Kappos*, 130 S. Ct. 3218 (2010), the Supreme Court rejected patent claims involving a method of hedging risks in commodities trading. The Court held that "the machine-or-transformation test is not the sole test" for determining the patent eligibility of a process, but rather "a useful and important clue, an investigative tool, for determining whether some claimed inventions are processes under § 101." *Id.* at 3227. *See also CyberSource Corp. v. Retail Decisions, Inc.*, 654 F.3d 1366 (Fed. Cir. 2011) (rejecting a *Beauregard*-style claim to a "computer readable medium" containing software as an unpatentable mental process).

Given the limited scope of copyright protection afforded to software, patent protection has become the preferred alternative for protecting the functional aspects of computer programs, at least for companies with enough money to pursue it. Whether the recent limitations on patent protection for software render patent protection less desirable remains to be seen.

State Trade Secret Protection

State trade secret law provides a limited, albeit important, mode of protection for computer software in appropriate circumstances. Because a trade secret may be protected so long as it is not generally known, trade secret protection may play an important role for protecting source code and for software that is used "in-house," that is, not marketed to the general public. But once the software program is distributed to the public, trade secret protection becomes problematic. Anything that a third party can readily learn by "proper means" — for example, by testing or reverse engineering — is free for appropriation. And while secrets disclosed under circumstances of trust and confidence can be protected, it is doubtful whether end-user licenses (discussed below) purporting to prohibit reverse engineering create such a relationship. *See, e.g., DVD Copy Control Ass'n v. Bunner*, 116 Cal. App. 4th 241 (2004). In a public environment, trade secrets embodied in computer software tend to have a short shelf life.

State Contract Law

Software developers have also looked to contract law to provide protection where copyright might not. Normally, this is accomplished by the use of restrictive licensing agreements that prohibit disclosure and reverse engineering. One drawback to contract protection is that contract rights run between the parties to the contract. Copyright law, by comparison, gives the copyright owner rights against the world. For that reason, contract has proved to be most attractive as an alternative source of protection for "custom" software designed to be used in large computer systems.

Obviously, contract law is not as well-adapted to situations in which standardized software products are sold in large numbers to individual consumers. In such situations, copyright law permits consumers to engage in uses (such as resale and "fair use") which some copyright owners might prefer to restrict. In response, many copyright owners have attempted to circumvent the limits of copyright law through so-called "shrink-wrap" and "click-through" licenses.

"Shrink-wrap" licenses are form agreements packaged with consumer software products, the restrictive terms of which the consumer is said to "accept" by virtue of his or her decision to open the package and to remove (and utilize) its contents. Under the terms of a typical "shrink-wrap" license, various otherwise permissible or "fair" uses of the purchased program are prohibited contractually. Although questions linger about the enforceability of such agreements, case law suggests that they may indeed have the legal effect which software manufacturers have claimed for them. *See, e.g., Bowers v. Baystate Technologies, Inc.*, 320 F.3d 1317 (Fed. Cir. 2003) (reproduced in Chapter 11).

A close cousin to the "shrink-wrap" license, the "click-through" license (the terms of which the consumer typically acknowledges by clicking a computer mouse on a virtual "button" marked "OK" or "Accept") has become more familiar as various kinds of information products, including software, are sold over the Internet. Although such agreements generally have been held to be enforceable, *see Davidson & Associates v. Jung*, 422 F.3d 630 (8th Cir. 2005), at least one appellate court has raised questions about whether consumers can truly be said to assent to terms proposed in this manner. *See Specht v. Netscape Communications Corp.*, 306 F.3d 17 (2d Cir. 2002).

In light of doubts concerning the enforceability of such provisions, in 1999 the National Conference of Commissioners on Uniform State Laws ("NCCUSL") adopted the Uniform Computer Information Transactions Act ("UCITA," formerly proposed as new Article 2B of the Uniform Commercial Code), which was specifically intended to validate the use of "shrink-wrap" and "click-through" licenses under state law. UCITA drew fierce opposition from consumer advocates, however, and it failed to receive approval from the American Bar Association. As a result, NCCUSL decided in 2003 that it would not expend further resources to promote UCITA in state legislatures. Only two states, Maryland and Virginia, have enacted UCITA, and four states have enacted so-called "anti-UCITA" statutes (which purport to prohibit enforcement of UCITA against consumers in those states).

Technological Protection Measures

Despite the best efforts of trade organizations, such as the Software Publishers' Association, to inform the public about software copyright and to detect and prosecute software piracy, the very ease with which computer programs can be duplicated continues to make them easy prey. Moreover, as mentioned above, in some instances software providers would prefer to restrict activities which would be permitted under copyright law. (A good example is "reverse engineering," discussed above.) As a result, companies which make and sell computer programs have for some time been experimenting with various forms of technological and legal self-help, in an effort to protect their software against both outright piracy and unauthorized use or adaptation.

In the 1980s, various forms of "copy protection" frequently were applied to consumer software products in an effort to frustrate their casual reproduction. This approach, however, met with considerable resistance from customers, and as a result it was largely abandoned in favor of other alternatives (such as "shrink-wrap" and "click-through" licenses). Today, however, copyright owners once again are employing various technological safeguards, such as encryption and password protection, to assure that only those consumers who have agreed to specified conditions of use can gain access to their works, and to exercise control over the uses which can be made of those works once access has been granted.

One obvious problem with such measures, however, is that they can be avoided or "hacked" by relatively sophisticated computer users. As a result, copyright owners (including but not limited to software manufacturers) sought new federal statutory provisions (within Title 17, although technically outside the Copyright Act) imposing civil and criminal penalties on those who "circumvent" technological protection measures applied to copyrighted works — as well as prohibitions on equipment or services which can be used for purposes of "circumvention." These measures, which were included in the Digital Millennium Copyright Act of 1998, are described in detail in § 9.04. For the moment, suffice it to say that, as ultimately enacted, the DMCA is highly complex and deservedly controversial.

For a comprehensive and continually updated treatment of copyright and alternative protections for computer software, see R. Nimmer, THE LAW OF COMPUTER TECHNOLOGY (4th ed. 2009).

PROTECTION FOR SEMICONDUCTOR CHIP DESIGNS

As we have seen, the resolution of the controversy over copyrightability of computer programs was that such works are protectible under existing copyright law. A different solution was adopted by Congress with respect to another mini-marvel of the Information Age: semiconductor chip products (or, more familiarly, "chips").

Chips are small pieces of semiconductor material. As their name suggests, they are intermediate in function between conductors, which efficiently conduct electricity, and insulators, which do not appreciably conduct electricity. In essence, chips are tiny instances of complex electronic circuitry. The basic building block of a chip is an electronic switch, or "transistor," which controls or amplifies electronic signals.

These transistors are connected, or "integrated," to form circuits that perform specific electronic functions. Hundreds of thousands of such sophisticated switching mechanisms can be compacted on a wafer, typically of silicon, no larger than a baby's fingernail. The two principal types of chips that result are indispensable to American industry: "memory" chips, which store information for use in computers, databases, and the like; and "microprocessors," which serve as the brains of computers, smart phones, microwave ovens, robots, automobile ignition systems, and a myriad of other modern devices.

Chips are complex products to design and manufacture, but remarkably cheap and easy to pirate. The key process exposed to piracy is known as "photolithography" or "masking." After the two-and three-dimensional features of the shape and configuration of a chip have been determined, the layout or "topography" of the chip is fixed in pictorial form through a "composite" drawing of the various layers of the chip, shown in different colors on a very large sheet of paper. The same information can then be recorded in digital form by storing all of the relevant coordinates of points in the composite. The data is used to generate a series of "masks," which are basically stencils employed to manufacture the chips by etching or depositing materials away from or onto the silicon wafer. The patterns into which the etching and depositing processes configure the chip surface are called "mask works." The process of creation culminating in a mask work often takes the innovating chip firm years to accomplish and can cost up to $100 million. A competing firm, however, can photograph the chip and its layers, and in several months duplicate the mask work for a cost of less than $50,000.

Rather than classifying chips as "writings" protected by copyright, or as "discoveries" more suitable for patent protection, Congress chose an intermediate course. The Semiconductor Chip Protection Act of 1984 (or "SCPA") added "Chapter 9 — Protection of Semiconductor Chip Products" at the end of Title 17, *i.e.*, following the Copyright Act of 1976. The legislative history states that this chapter "is not a part of the Copyright Act, chapters 1-8 of title 17. Instead, the new chapter creates a *sui generis* form of intellectual property right, similar in many respects to existing copyright law but differing from copyright law in many ways." H.R. Rep. No. 98-781 (1984). The SCPA creates a 10-year term of protection for mask works; confers exclusive rights upon proprietors to reproduce such works and to make and sell chips embodying them; exempts innocent infringers from liability for use or resale of unauthorized chips occurring before receiving notice of infringement; and permits reverse engineering of mask works to teach, analyze or evaluate the concept or technique embodied therein.

The law has not generated a flood of litigation. In fact, during its first 20 years, the only reported case deciding the merits of an SCPA claim was *Brooktree Corp. v. Advanced Micro Devices, Inc.*, 977 F.2d 1555 (Fed. Cir. 1992) (holding that copying of any material portion of a chip was an infringement, even if the rest of the chip was independently created). The potential scope of the SCPA was broadened considerably, however, by the decision in *Altera Corp. v. Clear Logic, Inc.*, 424 F.3d 1079 (9th Cir. 2005), which held that the SCPA protects the overall architecture of a chip — *i.e.*, the placement of large groups of transistors on the chip — and not just the specific layout of transistors within those groups.

The SCPA has not proved to be a model for the rest of the world. The Washington Treaty (Treaty on Intellectual Property in Respect of Integrated Circuits), which was opened for signature on May 26, 1989, never entered into force due to insufficient ratifications. *See generally* Kastenmeier & Remington, *The Semiconductor Chip Protection Act of 1984: A Swamp or Firm Ground?*, 70 Minn. L. Rev. 417 (1985). Among the nations that ultimately refused to ratify the agreement was the United States!

Microprocessor chips protected under the SCPA may contain, among other things, computer programs. Although the subject matter of protection under the SCPA is not the program as such, and although works other than programs (such as databases) commonly are represented in semiconductor chip form, many protected chips do in fact embody programs. In effect, then, for such programs the SCPA provides a third, overlapping form of legal protection, in addition to whatever protection is provided to them by copyright and patent law.

[C] Musical Works, Dramatic Works, and Pantomimes and Choreographic Works

The legislative history to the 1976 Copyright Act states that the terms "musical works," "dramatic works," and "pantomimes and choreographic works" (treated in § 102(a)(2),(3), and (4) respectively) are left undefined because they have "fairly settled meanings." The appropriate use of these categories has not been the subject of extensive litigation.

Musical Works

Musical works include both the instrumental component of the work and any accompanying words.[3] Fixation may be accomplished in various media, including written notation on paper or electronic recording on audiotape, CD, or disk drive. The originality requirement may be satisfied through melody, harmony or rhythm, individually or in combination. *See, e.g., Newton v. Diamond*, 204 F. Supp. 2d 1244, 1249 (C.D. Cal. 2002), *aff'd*, 388 F.3d 1189 (9th Cir. 2004); *Tempo Music, Inc. v. Famous Music Corp.*, 838 F. Supp. 162 (S.D.N.Y. 1993) (dispute involving Duke Ellington, Billy Strayhorn and Johnny Mercer over rights in melody, harmony and lyrics of jazz classic "Satin Doll"). Originality is an issue, typically, in instances in which a musical work incorporates public domain sources or is "popular" in character (*i.e.*, is relatively so simple that the genre itself permits a limited and familiar number of usable elements).

A few cases have questioned whether taking either the lyrics or the music alone infringes a musical work. As might be expected, the answer is "yes." *See, e.g., Acuff-Rose Music, Inc. v. Jostens, Inc.*, 988 F. Supp. 289, 292 (S.D.N.Y. 1997) (country-western hit "You've Got to Stand for Something"), *aff'd on other grounds*,

---

[3] Historically, published music did not neatly fit copyright's protection of "books." In England, published music was formally recognized as protected subject matter under the Statute of Anne in *Bach v. Longman*, 98 Eng. Rep. 1274 (K.B. 1777). *See* Carroll, *The Struggle for Music Copyright*, 57 Fla. L. Rev. 907 (2005). Congress first expressly added musical compositions to the list of protected subject matter in 1831.

155 F.3d 140 (2d Cir. 1998). Obviously, the composite character of musical works may give rise to questions about their authorship; indeed, musical works have featured in many copyright decisions parsing the concept of "joint authorship," discussed below in Chapter 4. Note also that musical works can be incorporated into other, larger composite works, such as motion pictures, without losing their character as works in their own right. The machinery of copyright registration now takes account of this. The 1909 Copyright Act prohibited separate registration of musical works which had been first published as part of a motion picture. But the 1976 Act removed that bar. And although this topic is covered later in the chapter, it is worth noting here that arrangements of musical works are protected under § 103(a) as derivative works. *See Baron v. Leo Feist, Inc.*, 173 F.2d 288 (2d Cir. 1949).

Where musical works are concerned, one of the most valuable exclusive rights of the copyright owner is the right to prepare and distribute what used to be called "mechanical reproductions" — a category which, over time, has included recordings in forms ranging from piano rolls to compact discs. The 1976 Act refers to these as "phonorecords" and recognizes the rights of the musical work copyright owner in § 106. This section does not tell the whole story, however. Under some circumstances, uses of musical works which would be considered infringements if another category of work were involved are immunized from liability by the operation of the "compulsory licensing" provisions of § 115. *See* § 7.02[B] below. Under § 115, the copyright owner is allowed a statutory "first bite at the apple" of authorizing the creation and distribution of phonorecords. Thereafter, anyone who follows the procedures set down in the statute and pays the statutorily stipulated fees can "cover" the original recording without the express permission of the copyright owner — so long as the new version does not "change the basic melody or fundamental character of the work." This last limitation, incidentally, represented one of the few explicit recognitions of "moral right" in American copyright law before § 106A was inserted into the statute in 1990.

Of course, the commercial value of a phonorecord is not entirely attributable to the musical work (or literary work, as the case may be) which it fixes. Typically, the phonorecord will also reflect creative contributions by the performers, and by the engineers and producers who oversee the recording session itself and the post-recording "mix." Until February 1972, these contributions received no recognition under federal law, and it proved difficult to police effectively the phenomenon of "record piracy" under the distinctly non-uniform body of state laws that then governed. Accordingly, the Copyright Act was amended in 1971 to create a new category of protected works, "sound recordings," which arise out of the joint "authorship" of those who participate in the recording process — generally as employees of record companies which acquire the resultant copyrights by virtue of assignment or by operation of the "work for hire" doctrine (covered in the following chapter). These amendments were retained in the 1976 Act and are discussed at greater length below.

For present purposes, it is important to realize that, in the conceptual scheme of the copyright law, phonorecords may "fix" simultaneously a number of distinct and different works: musical works, literary works, and sound recordings.

Dramatic Works

The dramatic works category illustrates how various categories in the § 102(a) list may overlap one another. Music accompanying a dramatic work may be copyrighted separately rather than under the dramatic works category. The script for a dramatic work can be protected as a literary work. A film dramatization of a screenplay is protected as a motion picture.

Is this category really necessary? As a practical matter, probably not. But since the list of § 102(a) categories is designed to be illustrative and not limitative, specifically including the category of dramatic works serves the minimal purpose of making it clear that plays, screenplays and other dramatizations of works are protectible.

Additionally, some important legal and practical consequences attach to the categorization of a work as a dramatic work, rather than as a nondramatic literary or musical work. For example, § 110(2) of the 1976 Act exempts from liability for infringement certain performances by nonprofit or governmental entities, but only if the work is a nondramatic literary or musical work (or a "reasonable and limited portion[ ] of any other [type of] work"). The compulsory license to make sound recordings under § 115 is limited to nondramatic musical works. Also, performing rights societies, such as ASCAP and BMI, and licensing organizations, such as the Harry Fox Agency, limit their activities to nondramatic musical works. See § 7.05[A] below.

Pantomimes and Choreographic Works

Although protected under the decisional law of the 1909 Act, pantomimes and choreographic works were added to the statutory catalogue of copyrightable works for the first time in the 1976 Act. These works may be protected if the necessary prerequisites are met. First, the work must be fixed in a tangible medium. Normally, fixation occurs by making a videotape or movie of the performance, whether it be pantomime or choreography. *See Martha Graham School and Dance Foundation, Inc. v. Martha Graham Center of Contemporary Dance*, 380 F.3d 624, 632 (2d Cir. 2004). Choreography also may be fixed by using the Laban or Benesh systems, both forms of shorthand notation describing movements. *See Horgan v. MacMillan, Inc.*, 789 F.2d 157, 160 n.3 (2d Cir. 1986).

Second, the work must, of course, be original. Choreography may consist of original routines or original arrangements of preexisting routines. The House Report indicates, however, that folk dances or social steps are not protectible. *Horgan*, 789 F.2d at 161.

May an original sequence of established yoga poses be protected as a choreographic work? One court has acknowledged the possibility. *See Open Source Yoga Unity v. Choudhury*, 2005 U.S. Dist. LEXIS 10440 (N.D. Cal., Apr. 1, 2005) (finding triable issue as to whether yoga sequence consisting of 26 asanas was original). But the Copyright Office has issued a policy that "a compilation of exercises or the selection and arrangement of yoga poses" does not qualify as a choreographic work, with the result that claims for the protection of dance "will be refused registration." *See* 77 Fed. Reg. 37605–08 (June 22, 2012).

For pantomimes, originality is to be found in the performer's art in "imitating or acting out situations, characters, or some other events with gestures and body movement." Stock movements and styles, however, are not protectible. COMPENDIUM II OF COPYRIGHT OFFICE PRACTICES §§ 460-461. To be copyrighted, a choreographic work or pantomime must be described in sufficient detail to enable the work to be performed from that description. *Micro Star v. Formgen Inc.*, 154 F.3d 1107, 1112 (9th Cir. 1998) (citing COMPENDIUM II § 463).

[D] Pictorial, Graphic, and Sculptural Works

Section 102(a)(5) of the 1976 Act provides for the copyrightability of "pictorial, graphic, and sculptural works." This phrase is defined in § 101 by means of an illustrative list, which includes "two-dimensional and three-dimensional works of fine, graphic, and applied art, photographs, prints and art reproductions, maps, globes, charts, diagrams, models, and technical drawings . . ."

The foregoing language recalls the very first American copyright statute, which protected not only "books" — *i.e.*, what the present act terms "literary works" — but also "maps" and "charts" — all the key sources of information required, apparently, for exploration of the new nation's various frontiers. Almost prophetically, the case law that grew up around maps and charts evinces several of the problems associated with this category of works.

The principal issue, not surprisingly, has been originality rather than fixation. Maps generally are rearrangements or depictions of factual matter, accumulated most often in 1790 by first-hand observation of the terrain itself, but now more frequently by resorting to public domain sources of the information to be incorporated in a new map. Historically, the courts have experienced notable difficulty in identifying and specifying the elements of originality upon which copyright protection for maps is founded.

One strain of case law, developed by courts construing the 1909 Act, insisted that, to meet the standard of originality, the cartographer must engage in at least a modicum of direct observation — in other words, in actual surveying or calculation or investigation of the terrain that is the subject of the map. In *Amsterdam v. Triangle Publications, Inc.*, for example, the court opined that a map is incapable of copyright protection unless "the publisher of the map in question obtains originally some of that information *by the sweat of his own brow.*" 93 F. Supp. 79, 82 (E.D. Pa. 1950). The development of this peculiar — even aberrational — standard is traced in Gorman, *Copyright Protection for the Collection and Representation of Facts*, 76 Harv. L. Rev. 1569 (1963). The "sweat of the brow" standard for originality in map cases may have rested ultimately on a concern that a less onerous test would encourage the real or apparent monopolization of valuable factual information, while producing no countervailing public benefit.

Even before the Supreme Court categorically rejected the "sweat of the brow" criterion for copyrightability generally in the *Feist* case, which you will read in § 3.02, case law under the 1976 Act had begun to reject this approach in map cases, recognizing that originality analysis in this particular subject matter context requires reference not only to the character of maps as pictorial works, but also to the reality that such works are — in addition — factual "compilations" within the meaning of § 101.

A typical 1976 Act map case is *United States v. Hamilton*, 583 F.2d 448 (9th Cir. 1978) (opinion by Judge, now Supreme Court Justice, Anthony Kennedy), in which the Ninth Circuit rejected the defendant's argument that the map copied was not subject to copyright because it was simply a synthesis of information already in the public domain. The court treated maps the same as any other copyrightable work, requiring only that they display something original, and held that arrangements and combinations of facts are copyrightable so long as they are not merely trivial variations of information within the public domain. The elements of authorship provided by selection, design, and synthesis were found to satisfy the originality standard. *See also Rockford Map Publishers, Inc. v. Directory Service Co. of Colorado, Inc.*, 768 F.2d 145 (7th Cir. 1985). *But see Kern River Gas Transmission Co. v. Coastal Corp.*, 899 F.2d 1458 (5th Cir. 1990) (holding map of proposed pipeline unprotectible under the merger doctrine).

Post-*Feist* map cases continue to follow the general approach just described. *Compare Mason v. Montgomery Data, Inc.*, 967 F.2d 135 (5th Cir. 1992) (copyrightability found based on selection, coordination, and arrangement of material), *Streetwise Maps, Inc. v. Vandam, Inc.*, 159 F.3d 739 (2d Cir. 1998) (tourist map copyrightable but not infringed by competing map with similar content), *and County of Suffolk v. First American Real Estate Solutions*, 261 F.3d 179 (2d Cir. 2001) (New York State Freedom of Information Law does not abrogate copyright in county's tax maps), *with Darden v. Peters*, 488 F.3d 277 (4th Cir. 2007) (changes in color, shading and labeling made to U.S. Census maps were not sufficiently original to qualify for copyright).

The same principles apply to more specialized maps, such as site plans for development. In *Sparaco v. Lawler, Matusky, Skelly, Engineers LLP*, 303 F.3d 460 (2d Cir. 2002), for example, the court held that, while a surveyor's use of standard cartographic symbols to represent existing physical features was not original, detailed plans for proposed physical improvements (such as creation of parking lots, drives, curbs, and walkways; placement of utilities; creation of fire lanes, fences, walls, and security gates; and landscaping) constituted protected expression. In so holding, the court distinguished an earlier case rejecting copyright in plans that conveyed only general ideas about how a site might be developed. *See Attia v. Society of the New York Hospital*, 201 F.3d 50 (2d Cir. 1999); *see also Peter F. Gaito Architecture LLC v. Simone Development Corp.*, 602 F.3d 57 (2d Cir. 2010) (allegedly copied matter consisted solely of "generalized notions of where to place functional elements," and concepts and ideas "common to countless other urban high-rise residential developments.").

Maps are not the only, or even the most vexing, species of "pictorial, graphic, or sculptural works" that have puzzled and tormented the courts in recent years. At least since the Supreme Court's decision in *Mazer v. Stein*, 347 U.S. 201 (1954), there has been vigorous debate concerning the degree to which copyright protection should be available for works of art embodied in useful objects, fusing the functional with the aesthetic to create articles of everyday life — *e.g.*, telephones, lighting fixtures, automobiles, tableware — that are simultaneously beautiful and utilitarian. While the House Report to the 1976 Act clearly recognizes "works of art, in the traditional sense" as copyrightable subject matter, it also expresses Congress' clear intent *not* to impose or countenance any criterion "of artistic taste, aesthetic value, or intrinsic quality" in the application of § 102(a)(5).

We consider the merits of the various arguments for and against the copyrightability of useful articles by examining both *Mazer* and a more recent decision wrestling with developments since passage of the present statute. The Notes and Questions for both cases follow *Pivot Point*.

MAZER v. STEIN
Supreme Court of the United States
347 U.S. 201 (1954)

MR. JUSTICE REED delivered the opinion of the Court.

This case involves the validity of copyrights obtained by respondents for statuettes of male and female dancing figures made of semivitreous china. The controversy centers around the fact that although copyrighted as "works of art," the statuettes were intended for use and used as bases for table lamps, with electric wiring, sockets and lamp shades attached.

Respondents are partners in the manufacture and sale of electric lamps. One of the respondents created original works of sculpture in the form of human figures by traditional clay-model technique. From this model, a production mold for casting copies was made. The resulting statuettes, without any lamp components added, were submitted by the respondents to the Copyright Office for registration as "works of art" or reproductions thereof under § 5(g) or § 5(h) of the copyright law, and certificates of registration issued. . . . Thereafter, the statuettes were sold in quantity throughout the country both as lamp bases and as statuettes. The sales in lamp form accounted for all but an insignificant portion of respondents' sales.

Petitioners are partners and, like respondents, make and sell lamps. Without authorization, they copied the statuettes, embodied them in lamps and sold them. . . .

Petitioners, charged by the present complaint with infringement of respondents' copyrights of reproductions of their works of art, seek here a reversal of the Court of Appeals decree upholding the copyrights. Petitioners in their petition for certiorari present a single question:

> Can statuettes be protected in the United States by copyright when the copyright applicant intended primarily to use the statuettes in the form of lamp bases to be made and sold in quantity and carried the intentions into effect?

> Stripped down to its essentials, the question presented is: Can a lamp manufacturer copyright his lamp bases?

Statuette of a Balinese Dancer

The first paragraph accurately summarizes the issue. The last gives it a quirk that unjustifiably, we think, broadens the controversy. The case requires an answer, not as to a manufacturer's right to register a lamp base but as to an artist's right to copyright a work of art intended to be reproduced for lamp bases. As petitioners say in their brief, their contention "questions the validity of the copyright based upon the actions of respondents." Petitioners question the validity of a copyright of a work of art for "mass" production. "Reproduction of a work of art" does not mean to them unlimited reproduction. Their position is that a copyright does not cover industrial reproduction of the protected article. . . . It is not the right to copyright an article that could have utility under § 5(g) and (h) . . . that petitioners oppose. Their brief accepts the copyrightability of the great carved golden salt-cellar of Cellini but adds:

> If, however, Cellini designed and manufactured this item in quantity so that
> the general public could have salt cellars, then an entirely different
> conclusion would be reached. In such case, the salt cellar becomes an article
> of manufacture having utility in addition to its ornamental value and would
> therefore have to be protected by design patent.

It is publication as a lamp and registration as a statue to gain a monopoly in manufacture that they assert is such a misuse of copyright as to make the registration invalid. . . .

. . . [A] review of the development of copyright coverage will make clear the purpose of the Congress in its copyright legislation. In 1790 the First Congress conferred a copyright on "authors of any map, chart, book or books already printed." Later, designing, engraving and etching were included; in 1831 musical composition; dramatic compositions in 1856; and photographs and negatives thereof in 1865.

The Act of 1870 defined copyrightable subject matter as:

> . . . any book, map, chart, dramatic or musical composition, engraving, cut, print, or photograph or negative thereof, or of a painting, drawing, chromo, *statue, statuary, and of models or designs intended to be perfected* as works of the fine arts. (Emphasis supplied.)

The italicized part added three-dimensional works of art to what had been protected previously. In 1909 Congress again enlarged the scope of the copyright statute. The new Act provided in § 4:

> That the works for which copyright may be secured under this Act shall include all the writings of an author.

Some writers interpret this section as being coextensive with the constitutional grant, but the House Report, while inconclusive, indicates that it was "declaratory of existing law" only. . . . Significant for our purposes was the deletion of the fine-arts clause of the 1870 Act. Verbal distinctions between purely aesthetic articles and useful works of art ended insofar as the statutory copyright language is concerned.

The practice of the Copyright Office, under the 1870 and 1874 Acts and before the 1909 Act, was to allow registration "as works of the fine arts" of articles of the same character as those of respondents now under challenge. . . . The current pertinent regulation, published in 37 CFR, 1949, § 202.8, reads thus:

> Works of art (Class G) — (a) — In General. This class includes works of artistic craftsmanship, in so far as their form but not their mechanical or utilitarian aspects are concerned, such as artistic jewelry, enamels, glass-ware, and tapestries, as well as all works belonging to the fine arts, such as paintings, drawings and sculpture. . . .

So we have a contemporaneous and long-continued construction of the statutes by the agency charged to administer them that would allow the registration of such a statuette as is in question here. . . .

The successive acts, the legislative history of the 1909 Act and the practice of the Copyright Office unite to show that "works of art" and "reproductions of works of art" are terms that were intended by Congress to include the authority to copyright these statuettes. Individual perception of the beautiful is too varied a power to permit a narrow or rigid concept of art. . . .

The conclusion that the statues here in issue may be copyrighted goes far to solve the question whether their intended reproduction as lamp stands bars or invalidates their registration. This depends solely on statutory interpretation. Congress may after publication protect by copyright any writing of an author. . . .

But petitioners assert that congressional enactment of the design patent laws should be interpreted as denying protection to artistic articles embodied or reproduced in manufactured articles. They say:

> Fundamentally and historically, the Copyright Office is the repository of what each claimant considers to be a cultural treasure, whereas the Patent Office is the repository of what each applicant considers to be evidence of the advance in industrial and technological fields.

Their argument is that design patents require the critical examination given patents to protect the public against monopoly. . . . Petitioner urges that overlapping of patent and copyright legislation so as to give an author or inventor a choice between patents and copyrights should not be permitted. We assume petitioner takes the position that protection for a statuette for industrial use can only be obtained by patent, if any protection can be given. As we have held the statuettes here involved to be copyrightable, we need not decide the question of their patentability. Though other courts have passed upon the issue as to whether allowance by the election of the author or patentee of one bars a grant of the other, we do not. We do hold that the patentability of the statuettes, fitted as lamps or unfitted, does not bar copyright as works of art. Neither the Copyright Statute nor any other says that because a thing is patentable it may not be copyrighted. We should not so hold. . . .

The economic philosophy behind the clause empowering Congress to grant patents and copyrights is the conviction that encouragement of individual effort by personal gain is the best way to advance public welfare through the talents of authors and inventors in "Science and useful Arts." Sacrificial days devoted to such creative activities deserve rewards commensurate with the services rendered. Affirmed.

Opinion of MR. JUSTICE DOUGLAS, in which MR. JUSTICE BLACK concurs.

An important constitutional question underlies this case — a question which was stirred on oral argument but not treated in the briefs. . . . It is whether these statuettes of dancing figures may be copyrighted. . . .

Is a sculptor an "author" and is his statue a "writing" within the meaning of the Constitution? We have never decided the question. . . .

The interests involved in the category of "works of art," as used in the copyright law, are considerable. The Copyright Office has supplied us with a long list of such articles which have been copyrighted — statuettes, book ends, clocks, lamps, door knockers, candlesticks, inkstands, chandeliers, piggy banks, sundials, salt and pepper shakers, fish bowls, casseroles, and ash trays. Perhaps these are all "writings" in the constitutional sense. But to me, at least, they are not obviously so. It is time that we came to the problem full face. I would accordingly put the case down for reargument.

PIVOT POINT INTERNATIONAL, INC. v. CHARLENE PRODUCTS, INC.
United States Court of Appeals, Seventh Circuit
372 F.3d 913 (2004)

RIPPLE, CIRCUIT JUDGE:

Pivot Point International, Inc. ("Pivot Point"), brought this cause of action against Charlene Products, Inc., and its president Peter Yau (collectively "Charlene"), for copyright infringement pursuant to 17 U.S.C. § 501(b). The district court granted summary judgment for the defendants on the ground that the copied subject matter, a mannequin head, was not copyrightable under the Copyright Act of 1976 ("1976 Act"). For the reasons set forth in the following opinion, we reverse the judgment of the district court and remand the case for proceedings consistent with this opinion.

I. BACKGROUND

A. Facts

Pivot Point develops and markets educational techniques and tools for the hair design industry. It was founded in 1965 by Leo Passage, an internationally renowned hair designer. . . .

In the mid-1980s, Passage desired to develop a mannequin that would imitate the "hungry look" of high-fashion, runway models. Passage believed that such a mannequin could be marketed as a premium item to cutting-edge hair-stylists and to stylists involved in hair design competitions. Passage then worked with a German artist named Horst Heerlein to create an original sculpture of a female human head. Although Passage discussed his vision with Heerlein, Passage did not give Heerlein any specific dimensional requirements. From Passage's description, Heerlein created a sculpture in plaster entitled "Mara."

Wax molds of Mara were made and sent to Pivot Point's manufacturer in Hong Kong. The manufacturer created exact reproductions of Mara in polyvinyl chloride ("PVC"). The manufacturer filled the PVC form with a liquid that expands and hardens into foam. The process of creating the Mara sculpture and of developing the mannequin based on the sculpture took approximately eighteen months.

In February of 1988, when Pivot Point first inspected the PVC forms of Mara, it discovered that the mannequin's hairline had been etched too high on the forehead. The manufacturer corrected the mistake by adding a second, lower hairline. Although the first, higher hairline was visible upon inspection, it was covered with implanted hair. The early PVC reproductions of Mara, and Pivot Point's first shipment of the mannequins in May of 1988, possessed the double hairlines.

About the same time that it received its first shipment of mannequins, Pivot Point obtained a copyright registration for the design of Mara, specifically the bareheaded female human head with no makeup or hair. Heerlein assigned all of his rights in the Mara sculpture to Pivot Point. Pivot Point displayed the copyright notice in the name of Pivot Point on each mannequin. . . .

At a trade show in 1989, Charlene, a wholesaler of beauty products founded by Mr. Yau,[2] displayed its own "Liza" mannequin, which was very close in appearance to Pivot Point's Mara. In addition to the strikingly similar facial features, Liza also exhibited a double hairline that the early Mara mannequins possessed.

On September 24, 1989, Pivot Point noticed Charlene for copyright infringement. When Charlene refused to stop importing and selling the Liza mannequin, Pivot Point filed this action.

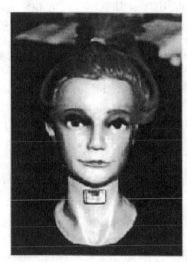

Mara   Liza

B. District Court Proceedings

[On cross-motions for summary judgment, the District Court ruled that Mara was a useful article, because "[s]tudents in beauty schools practice styling hair on Mara's head and may practice other skills by applying makeup to Mara's eyes, lips, and cheeks." 170 F. Supp. 2d 828, 831 (N.D. Ill. 2001). Noting that copyright for useful articles is limited by statute, the District Court adopted the following test: "a pictorial, graphic or sculptural feature incorporated in the design of a useful article is conceptually separable if it can stand on its own as work of art traditionally conceived, and if the useful article in which it is embodied would be equally useful without it." *Id.* at 833 (quoting 1 Paul Goldstein, COPYRIGHT: PRINCIPLES, LAW & PRACTICE § 2.5.3, at 109 (1989)). Applying this test, the District Court concluded that Mara cannot be copyrighted, because "even though one can conceive of Mara as a sculpture displayed as art, it would not be equally useful if the features that Pivot

---

[2] Mr. Yau was not unfamiliar with Pivot Point. Shortly before founding Charlene Products in 1985, Mr. Yau had worked for Pivot Point.

Point wants to copyright were removed." *Id.*]

II. ANALYSIS

. . .

B. Copyrightability

The central issue in this case is whether the Mara mannequin is subject to copyright protection. This issue presents, at bottom, a question of statutory interpretation. We therefore begin our analysis with the language of the statute. . . . The definition section . . . provides that "[a] 'useful article' is an article having an intrinsic utilitarian function that is not merely to portray the appearance of the article or to convey information. An article that is normally a part of a useful article is considered a 'useful article.' " 17 U.S.C. § 101. As is clear from the definition of pictorial, graphic and sculptural work, only "useful article[s]," as the term is further defined, are subject to the limitation contained in the [former definition]. If an article is not "useful" as the term is defined in § 101, then it is a pictorial, graphic and sculptural work entitled to copyright protection (assuming the other requirements of the statute are met).

1. Usefulness

Pivot Point submits that the Mara mannequin is not a "useful article" for purposes of § 101 because its "inherent nature is to portray the appearance of runway models. Its value . . . resides in how well it portrays the appearance of runway models, just as the value of a bust — depicting Cleopatra, for example . . . — would be in how well it approximates what one imagines the subject looked like." Pivot Point relies upon the decisions of the Fourth Circuit in *Superior Form Builders* [*v. Dan Chase Taxidermy Supply Co.*, 74 F.3d 488 (4th Cir. 1996)] and of the Second Circuit in *Hart* [*v. Dan Chase Taxidermy Supply Co.*, 86 F.3d 320 (2d Cir. 1996)] for the proposition that mannequins, albeit in those cases animal and fish mannequins, are not useful articles. Specifically, the Fourth Circuit explained that . . . any utilitarian aspect of the mannequin exists "merely to portray the appearance" of the animal. *Superior Form Builders*, 74 F.3d at 494; *see also Hart*, 86 F.3d at 323 ("The function of the fish form is to portray its own appearance, and that fact is enough to bring it within the scope of the Copyright Act."). Consequently, in Pivot Point's view, because the Mara mannequin performs functions similar to those of animal and fish mannequins, it is not a useful article and is therefore entitled to full copyright protection.

Charlene presents us with a different view. It suggests that, unlike the animal mannequins at issue in *Superior Form Builders* and in *Hart*, the Mara mannequin does have a useful function other than portraying an image of a high-fashion runway model. According to Charlene, Mara also is marketed and used for practicing the art of makeup application. Charlene points to various places in the record that establish that Mara is used for this purpose and is, therefore, a useful article subject to the limiting language of § 101.

Pivot Point strongly disputes that the record establishes such a use and argues that the district court's reliance on Charlene's alleged proof improperly resolves an issue of fact against the non-moving party . . . Indeed, our own review of the record leads us to believe that many of the documents cited by Charlene are susceptible to more than one interpretation.

Nevertheless, we shall assume that the district court correctly ruled that Mara is a useful article and proceed to examine whether, despite that usefulness, it is amenable to copyright protection.

2. Separability

. . . The statutory language provides that "the design of a useful article . . . shall be considered a pictorial, graphic, or sculptural work only if, and only to the extent that, such design incorporates pictorial, graphic, or sculptural features *that can be identified separately from and are capable of existing independently of*, the utilitarian aspects of the article." Although the italicized clause contains two operative phrases — "*can be identified separately from*" and "*are capable of existing independently of*" — we believe, as have the other courts that have grappled with this issue, that Congress, in amending the statute, intended these two phrases to state a single, integrated standard to determine when there is sufficient separateness between the utilitarian and artistic aspects of a work to justify copyright protection.

Certainly, one approach to determine whether material can be "identified separately," and the most obvious, is to rely on the capacity of the artistic material to be severed physically from the industrial design. *See Mazer v. Stein*, 347 U.S. 201 (1954) (holding that a statuette incorporated into the base of a lamp is copyrightable). When a three-dimensional article is the focus of the inquiry, reliance on physical separability can no doubt be a helpful tool in ascertaining whether the artistic material in question can be separated from the industrial design. As Professor Denicola points out, however, such an approach really is not of much use when the item in question is two-dimensional. *See* Denicola, [*Applied Art & Industrial Design: A Suggested Approach to Copyright in Useful Articles*, 67 Minn. L. Rev. 707 (1983)] at 744. Indeed, because this provision, by its very words, was intended to apply to two-dimensional material, it is clear that a physical separability test cannot be the exclusive test for determining copyrightability.

It seems to be common ground between the parties and, indeed, among the courts and commentators, that the protection of the copyright statute also can be secured when a conceptual separability exists between the material sought to be copyrighted and the utilitarian design in which that material is incorporated.[8] The

---

[8] Although the district court was skeptical that the statutory language encompassed both physical and conceptual separability, circuits have been almost unanimous in interpreting the language of § 101 to include both types of separability, [Cites to cases from the Second, Fourth and Eleventh Circuits deleted.] Only one appellate court has rejected the idea of conceptual separability. *See Esquire, Inc. v. Ringer*, 591 F.2d 796 (D.C. Cir. 1978). In that case, arising under the 1909 Act, the Copyright Office had refused to register a design for outdoor lighting fixtures. The court's focus in *Esquire* was a regulation adopted pursuant to the former law and its obligation to defer to the agency's interpretation of the law

difficulty lies not in the acceptance of that proposition, which the statutory language clearly contemplates, but in its application. As noted by Pivot Point, the following tests have been suggested for determining when the artistic and utilitarian aspects of useful articles are conceptually separable: 1) the artistic features are "primary" and the utilitarian features "subsidiary," *Kieselstein-Cord* [*v. Accessories by Pearl, Inc.*], 632 F.2d [989 (2d Cir. 1980)] at 993; 2) the useful article "would still be marketable to some significant segment of the community simply because of its aesthetic qualities," Melville B. Nimmer & David Nimmer, 1 Nimmer on Copyright § 2.08[B][3], at 2-101 (2004); 3) the article "stimulate[s] in the mind of the beholder a concept that is separate from the concept evoked by its utilitarian function," *Carol Barnhart* [*Inc. v. Economy Cover Corp.*], 773 F.2d [411 (2d Cir. 1985)] at 422 (Newman, J., dissenting); 4) the artistic design was not significantly influenced by functional considerations, *see Brandir* [*Int'l, Inc. v. Cascade Pac. Lumber Co.*], 834 F.2d [1142 (2d Cir. 1987)] at 1145 (adopting the test forwarded in Denicola, *supra*, at 741); 5) the artistic features "can stand alone as a work of art traditionally conceived, and . . . the useful article in which it is embodied would be equally useful without it," Goldstein, 1 COPYRIGHT § 2.5.3, at 2:67; and 6) the artistic features are not utilitarian, *see* William F. Patry, 1 COPYRIGHT LAW & PRACTICE 285 (1994).

Pivot Point submits that "the test for conceptual separability should reflect the focus of copyright law — the artistic, not the marketability, design process, or usefulness." According to Pivot Point, the central inquiry is whether the article is a "work of art." . . . This test, Pivot Point suggests, has the additional benefit of "satisf[ying] most, if not all, of the current definitions of conceptual separability." Charlene, by contrast, lauds the district court's adoption of Professor Goldstein's test. . . . Charlene contends that this approach mirrors that adopted by the majority in *Carol Barnhart Inc. v. Economy Cover Corp.*, 773 F.2d 411 (2d Cir. 1985), "the most closely related precedent to the case at bar."

Although both sides present thoughtful explanations for their proposed tests, we perceive shortcomings in the parties' choices. With respect to Pivot Point's focus on the article as a "work of art," it is certainly correct that Congress, in enacting § 101, attempted to separate the artistic from the utilitarian. However, this approach necessarily involves judges in a qualitative evaluation of artistic endeavors — a function for which judicial office is hardly a qualifier. With respect to the Charlene's approach, we believe that the test, at least when applied alone, is tied too closely to physical separability and, consequently, does not give a sufficiently wide berth to Congress' determination that artistic material conceptually separate from the utilitarian design can satisfy the statutory mandate. . . .

Among the circuits, the Court of Appeals for the Second Circuit has had occasion to wrestle most comprehensively with the notion of "conceptual separability." Its case law represents, we believe, an intellectual journey that has explored the key aspects of the problem. We therefore turn to a study of the key stages of doctrinal development in its case law. . . .

---

embodied in that regulation. Furthermore, the court acknowledged that the 1976 Act was "not applicable to the case before" it. *Id.* at 803. Given these differences, we do not believe that the D.C. Circuit would conclude that its decision in *Esquire* disposed of the issue of conceptual separability presently before this court.

[The court's discussion of prior case law is omitted. These cases are discussed in the Notes and Questions below.]

C. Application

Each of these cases differs in the object at issue and the method by which the court evaluated whether the object was entitled to copyright protection. Yet, each court attempted to give effect to "the expressed congressional intent to distinguish copyrightable applied art and uncopyrightable industrial design." *Kieselstein-Cord*, 632 F.2d at 993; *see also Carol Barnhart*, 773 F.2d at 417-18 (reviewing legislative history in detail and concluding that, although "copyright protection has increasingly been extended to cover articles having a utilitarian dimension," Congress did not intend all useful articles that are "aesthetically satisfying or valuable" to be copyrightable); *Brandir Int'l*, 834 F.2d at 1145 (adopting Professor Denicola's test that makes copyrightability dependent upon "the extent to which the work reflects artistic expression uninhibited by functional considerations" (internal quotation marks and citations omitted)); *Superior Form Builders*, 74 F.3d at 494 (distinguishing the animal mannequins at issue from "aesthetically pleasing articles of industrial design").

The Second Circuit cases exhibit a progressive attempt to forge a workable judicial approach capable of giving meaning to the basic Congressional policy decision to distinguish applied art from uncopyrightable industrial art or design. In *Kieselstein-Cord*, the Second Circuit attempted to distinguish artistic expression from industrial design by focusing on the present use of the item, i.e., the "primary ornamental aspect" versus the "subsidiary utilitarian function" of the object at issue. 632 F.2d at 993. In *Carol Barnhart*, the Second Circuit moved closer to a process-oriented approach:

> What distinguishes those [*Kieselstein-Cord*] buckles from the Barnhart forms is that the ornamented surfaces of the buckles were not in any respect required by their utilitarian functions; the artistic and aesthetic features could thus be conceived of as having been added to, or superimposed upon, an otherwise utilitarian article. The unique artistic design was wholly unnecessary to performance of the utilitarian function. In the case of the Barnhart forms, on the other hand, the features claimed to be aesthetic or artistic, e.g., the life-size configuration of the breasts and the width of the shoulders, are inextricably intertwined with the utilitarian feature, the display of clothes. Whereas a model of a human torso, in order to serve its utilitarian function, must have some configuration of the chest and some width of shoulders, a belt buckle can serve its function satisfactorily without any ornamentation of the type that renders the *Kieselstein-Cord* buckles distinctive.

773 F.2d at 419. Thus, it was the fact that the creator of the torsos was driven by utilitarian concerns, such as how display clothes would fit on the end product, that deprived the human torsos of copyright protection.

This process-oriented approach for conceptual separability — focusing on the process of creating the object to determine whether it is entitled to copyright protection — is more fully articulated in *Brandir* and indeed reconciles the earlier case law pertaining to conceptual separability.

> [T]he approach is consistent with the holdings of our previous cases. In *Kieselstein-Cord*, for example, the artistic aspects of the belt buckles reflected purely aesthetic choices, independent of the buckles' function, while in *Carol Barnhart* the distinctive features of the torsos — the accurate anatomical design and the sculpted shirts and collars — showed clearly the influence of functional concerns. Though the torsos bore artistic features, it was evident the designer incorporated those features to further the usefulness of the torsos as mannequins.

Brandir, 834 F.2d at 1145.

Furthermore, *Brandir* is not inconsistent with the more theoretical rendition of Judge Newman in his *Carol Barnhart* dissent — that "the requisite 'separateness' exists whenever the design creates in the mind of an ordinary observer two different concepts that are not inevitably entertained simultaneously." 773 F.2d at 422. When a product has reached its final form as a result of predominantly functional or utilitarian considerations, it necessarily will be more difficult for the observer to entertain simultaneously two different concepts — the artistic object and the utilitarian object. In such circumstances, *Brandir* has the added benefit of providing a more workable judicial methodology by articulating the driving principle behind conceptual separability — the influence of industrial design. When the ultimate form of the object in question is "as much the result of utilitarian pressures as aesthetic choices," "[f]orm and function are inextricably intertwined," and the artistic aspects of the object cannot be separated from its utilitarian aspects for purposes of copyright protection. *Brandir*, 834 F.2d at 1147.

Conceptual separability exists, therefore, when the artistic aspects of an article can be "conceptualized as existing independently of their utilitarian function." *Carol Barnhart*, 773 F.2d at 418. This independence is necessarily informed by "whether the design elements can be identified as reflecting the designer's artistic judgment exercised independently of functional influences." *Brandir*, 834 F.2d at 1145. If the elements do reflect the independent, artistic judgment of the designer, conceptual separability exists. Conversely, when the design of a useful article is "as much the result of utilitarian pressures as aesthetic choices," *id.* at 1147, the useful and aesthetic elements are not conceptually separable.

Applying this test to the Mara mannequin, we must conclude that the Mara face is subject to copyright protection. It certainly is not difficult to conceptualize a human face, independent of all of Mara's specific facial features, i.e., the shape of the eye, the upturned nose, the angular cheek and jaw structure, that would serve the utilitarian functions of a hair stand and, if proven, of a makeup model. Indeed, one is not only able to conceive of a different face than that portrayed on the Mara mannequin, but one easily can conceive of another visage that portrays the "hungry look" on a high-fashion runway model. Just as Mattel is entitled to protection for "its own particularized expression" of an "upturned nose[ ], bow lips, and widely spaced eyes," *Mattel*, [*Inc. v. Goldberger Doll Manufacturing Co.*,] 365 F.3d [133 (2d Cir. 2004)] at 136, so too is Heerlein (and, therefore, Pivot Point as assignee of the copyright registration) entitled to have his expression of the "hungry look" protected from copying.

Mara can be conceptualized as existing independent from its use in hair display or makeup training because it is the product of Heerlein's artistic judgment. When Passage approached Heerlein about creating the Mara sculpture, Passage did not provide Heerlein with specific dimensions or measurements; indeed, there is no evidence that Heerlein's artistic judgment was constrained by functional consider-ations. Passage did not require, for instance, that the sculpture's eyes be a certain width to accommodate standard-sized eyelashes, that the brow be arched at a certain angle to facilitate easy make-up application or that the sculpture as a whole not exceed certain dimensional limits so as to fit within Pivot Point's existing packaging system. Such considerations, had they been present, would weigh against a determination that Mara was purely the product of an artistic effort. By contrast, after Passage met with Heerlein to discuss Passage's idea for a "hungry-look" model, Heerlein had carte blanche to implement that vision as he saw fit. Consequently, this is not a situation, such as was presented to the Second Circuit in *Carol Barnhart*, in which certain features ("accurate anatomical design and the sculpted shirts and collars") were included in the design for purely functional reasons. *Brandir*, 834 F.2d at 1145. Furthermore, unlike "the headless, armless, backless styrene torsos" which "were little more than glorified coat-racks used to display clothing in stores," *Hart*, 86 F.3d at 323, the creative aspects of the Mara sculpture were meant to be seen and admired. Thus, because Mara was the product of a creative process unfettered by functional concerns, its sculptural features "can be identified separately from, and are capable of existing independently of," its utilitarian aspects. It therefore meets the requirements for conceptual separability and is subject to copyright protection.

[III.] CONCLUSION

The Mara mannequin is subject to copyright protection. We therefore must reverse the summary judgment in favor of Charlene Products and Mr. Yau; the case is remanded for a trial on Pivot Point's infringement claim. . . .

KANNE, CIRCUIT JUDGE, dissenting:

. . . As the district court noted, the statute requires, on its face, that sculptural features must be separately identified from the utilitarian aspects of the article ("conceptual separability") and they must exist independently from the utilitarian aspects of the article ("physical separability") in order to receive copyright protection. As to whether both conceptual and physical separability are required for copyrightability, most courts and commentators have concluded that only one or the other test is appropriate. But that issue is not presented here because Mara is not copyrightable regardless of whether both or either is applied.

Taking physical separability first, the district court used examples from case law to illustrate that the sculptural features in many useful items can be physically removed from the object and sold separately without affecting the functionality of the useful article. . . .

Mara, on the other hand, has only functional attributes. Thus, any physical separation of a portion of her would not be independent of her utilitarian aspects. She is sold to beauty schools as a teaching device; students style her hair and apply makeup as realistic training for such pursuits on live subjects. A mannequin head without a neck, or with different eyes and musculature, would not serve the utilitarian purpose of applying makeup or teaching the art of matching hair styles to facial features. As the district court explained: "Beauty students style hair to flatter the face, not to be worn on featureless ovoids. The use of a mannequin head in training students of beauty schools *lies in its aesthetic qualities*." There is nothing in Mara that we could physically remove that would not be part of Mara's utility as a teaching aid. . . .

Next, the district court considered various restatements of the meaning of "conceptual separability" (whether features can be identified or conceived of separately from the utilitarian aspects) and applied the most appropriate one to Mara. Professor Goldstein . . . presents a reasonable explanation of the statutory text: "a . . . sculptural feature incorporated in the design of a useful article is conceptually separable if it can stand on its own as a work of art traditionally conceived, and if the useful article in which it is embodied would be equally useful without it." Mara has no conceptually separable features to which copyright protection could be granted. Her features are incapable of being identified separately from the utilitarian use of those features. Without features, the mannequin's head and neck would be little more than an egg on a stick, useless for its intended purpose. Mara possesses neither physical nor conceptual separability. . . .

Problematically, the majority's test for conceptual separability seems to bear little resemblance to the statute. . . . The statute looks to the useful article as it exists, not to how it was created. I believe it simply is irrelevant to inquire into the origins of Mara's eyes, cheekbones, and neck. If such features have been fully incorporated as functional aspects of the mannequin, then copyright does not provide protection. Even if we were to look at the "process" that led to the creation of Mara, it is undeniable that, from the beginning, Pivot Point intended Mara to serve a functional purpose and commissioned her creation to fulfill that purpose (not to create a work of art for aesthetic beauty).

The majority, as evidenced by its emphasis on the fact that Charlene Products apparently copied Mara with its doll, "Liza," seems unduly concerned in this context with Charlene's questionable business practices. This is immaterial to the determination of whether the Mara doll is protected by copyright law. Importantly, other possible legal protections for Pivot Point's intellectual property — design patent, trademark, trade dress, and state unfair competition law — are available to address the majority's concerns.

Copyright does not protect functional products. Charlene is free, under its own brand name, to copy and sell copies of useful articles that do not have patent protection. *See, e.g., TrafFix Devices, Inc. v. Marketing Displays, Inc.*, 532 U.S. 23 (2001); *Bonito Boats, Inc. v. Thunder Craft Boats, Inc.*, 489 U.S. 141 (1989); *Sears, Roebuck & Co. v. Stiffel Co.*, 376 U.S. 225 (1964). I fear that the majority's opinion grants copyright protection to functional aspects of a useful article. I would, therefore, affirm the district court's grant of summary judgment in favor of Charlene Products and Mr. Yau.

NOTES AND QUESTIONS

Useful Articles

(1)   Nothing in pre-1976 American copyright law barred protection for otherwise qualified works that were also "useful articles." To the contrary, the 1909 Act may have been intended to rule out any discrimination on this basis. Nonetheless, the Copyright Office interpreted that Act narrowly, in a series of regulations culminating with the one in effect when the Supreme Court decided *Mazer*. That regulation, according to which protection was available for "works of artistic craftsmanship in so far as their form but not their mechanical or utilitarian aspects are concerned," in turn became the basis for the approach taken in the 1976 Act.

In *Mazer v. Stein*, the Court deferred broadly (as courts frequently do) to the interpretation placed on the statute by the Copyright Office. Why? Is it simply a matter of giving weight to expertise? When Justice Reed refers to the "practice of the Copyright Office" for guidance about the meaning of the terms "works of art" and "reproductions of works of art," is his reference to *current* practice only? If not, what is its scope?

Following *Mazer*, the Copyright Office adopted a regulation setting forth its understanding of the case. The regulation stated:

> If the sole intrinsic function of an article is its utility, the fact that the article is unique and attractively shaped will not qualify it as a work of art. However, if the shape of a utilitarian article incorporates features, such as artistic sculpture, carving, or pictorial representation, which can be identified separately and are capable of existing independently as a work of art, such features will be eligible for registration.

Former 37 C.F.R. § 202.10(c), quoted in *Esquire, Inc. v. Ringer*, 591 F.2d 796, 800 (D.C. Cir. 1978). This regulation also left its mark on the language adopted by Congress in the 1976 Act.

(2)   Whatever the background, did Congress have to adopt an approach that discriminated between "artistic" features and "mechanical or utilitarian" aspects when it legislated in 1976? Was it wise to do so? Why not grant copyright protection to all pictorial, graphic, and sculptural works embodied in useful articles? Does the Copyright Clause afford Congress the power to do so? How did the drafters of the 1976 Act differ from the drafters of the 1909 Act and the Copyright Office regulations in their treatment of the problem?

(3)   Be sure you understand the statutory basis for the separability limitation on copyright protection for useful articles. Section 102(a) provides copyright protection for "pictorial, graphic, and sculptural" works. The definition of that category in § 101 excludes "the design of a useful article," unless that design contains "pictorial, graphic, or sculptural *features*" (emphasis added) that are separable from "the utilitarian aspects of the article." If separable features exist, then "the design of a

useful article" qualifies as a "pictorial, graphic, and sculptural" work that is protected under the Act. But before we can apply the separability limitation, we must also look to the § 101 definition of "useful article" to determine *which* works are subject to that limitation.

(4)   Obviously, the concept of "utilitarian function" at work in the 1976 Act's definition of a "useful article" is a relatively specialized one. In some sense, all copyrightable works aspire to usefulness. What could be more profoundly "useful," for example, than the inspirational effect of great art or music? The Act carves out an exception in its own terms: By definition, an article is not "useful" if its only function is "to portray the appearance of the article." But what, exactly, does this mean?

In *Masquerade Novelty, Inc. v. Unique Industries, Inc.*, 912 F.2d 663 (3d Cir. 1990), the court considered the copyrightability of the plaintiff's "nose masks" (representing the characteristic proboscises of pigs, parrots, and so forth). The District Court had granted summary judgment on the ground that the animal shapes were "conceptually inseparable from the product's utilitarian purpose of creating humor." *Id.* at 670 (quoting District Court opinion). The Circuit Court agreed that, *if* the masks were considered "useful," effective separation of form and function would be difficult indeed, but it rejected the underlying premise:

> That nose masks are meant to be worn by humans to evoke laughter does not distinguish them from clearly copyrightable works of art like paintings. When worn by a human being, a nose mask may evoke chuckles or guffaws from onlookers. When hung on a wall, a painting may evoke a myriad of human emotions, but we would not say that the painting is not copyrightable because its artistic elements could not be separated from the emotional effect its creator hoped it would have on persons viewing it. The utilitarian nature of an animal nose mask or a painting of the crucifixion of Jesus Christ inheres solely in its appearance, regardless of the fact that the nose mask's appearance is intended to evoke mirth and the painting's appearance a feeling of religious reverence. Thus, Masquerade's nose masks are not "useful articles" for purposes of 17 U.S.C. § 101, and are copyrightable as sculptural works.

Id. at 671.

The reasoning in *Masquerade* seemed to conflict with a previous case involving Halloween costumes, *Whimsicality, Inc. v. Rubie's Costume Co.*, 891 F.2d 452 (2d Cir. 1989), in which the court stated bluntly: "[T]he Copyright Office considers costumes to be wearing apparel and consistently rejects applications to register them." *Id.* at 454. The conflict led the Copyright Office to clarify its position. In *Registrability of Costume Designs*, 56 Fed. Reg. 56530 (Nov. 5, 1991), the Register agreed that masks were not useful articles, but he maintained that costumes "serve a dual purpose of clothing the body and portraying their appearance." Since the former was "an intrinsic utilitarian function" of the costumes, the Register continues to treat "fanciful" costumes as "useful articles" subject to separability analysis. *See, e.g., Chosun Int'l, Inc. v. Chrisha Creations, Ltd.*, 413 F.3d 324, 329 & n.3 (2d Cir. 2005) (reversing District Court's holding that "Halloween costumes may not be copyrighted" and remanding for determination of separability). The Register also reaffirmed that "the general policy of nonregistrability of garment designs will be applied not only to ordinary wearing apparel, but also to period and historical dress, and uniforms." 56 Fed. Reg. at 56532; *see Galiano v. Harrah's Operating Co.*, 416 F.3d 411, 416 (5th Cir. 2005) (finding "little doubt" that casino uniforms were "useful articles").

(5)   The definition of a "useful article" contains another limitation: An article is not "useful" if its only function is "to convey information." The apparent purpose of this limitation is to exclude literary works, such as directories and textbooks, and some pictorial works, such as maps, from the definition. But what about computer programs? Aren't most application programs "useful" for something other than to convey information? Yet we know that *Apple v. Franklin*, and the decisions following it, have rejected the notion that protection for computer programs in object code form is limited because of their "utility." Is this because programs are considered "literary works" and the limitation on protection for "useful articles" is contained in the statutory definition of "pictorial, graphic, and sculptural" works? Whatever its legal merit, does such a distinction have any basis in common sense?

(6)   In *Pivot Point*, the court expresses doubt as to whether the Mara mannequin head is a "useful article" at all. Some human mannequins are used to display clothing, which may be considered to be a utilitarian purpose. *See Carol Barnhart Inc. v. Economy Cover Corp.*, 594 F. Supp. 364, 370 (S.D.N.Y. 1984) (discussed in more detail below). But in the two cases involving taxidermy forms discussed in *Pivot Point*, both the Fourth Circuit and the Second Circuit concluded that animal and fish mannequins, respectively, fell within the exception for articles whose only function is "to portray the[ir own] appearance." *See Superior Form Builders, Inc. v. Dan Chase Taxidermy Supply Co.*, 74 F.3d 488 (4th Cir. 1996); *Hart v. Dan Chase Taxidermy Supply Co.*, 86 F.3d 320 (2d Cir. 1996). The fact that the mannequins were used to display animal and fish skins was not sufficient to make them "useful articles." Does Mara have "an intrinsic utilitarian function" other than to portray her own appearance? The *Pivot Point* court dodged the issue, assuming without deciding that Mara was a useful article, and resting its decision instead on "conceptual separability."

"Conceptual Separability": A Potpourri of Analyses

(7)   By its definition of "pictorial, graphic, and sculptural works," § 101 of the 1976 Act indicates that the "design of a useful article" may itself qualify as such a copyrightable work only to the extent that it incorporates artistic features "that can be identified separately from, and are capable of existing independently of, the utilitarian aspects of the article." Just what does the last-quoted language mean?

In his District Court opinion in *Pivot Point*, Circuit Judge Easterbrook (sitting by designation) suggested that the statute requires *both* conceptual separability ("can be identified separately from") *and* physical separability ("is capable of existing independently of"), and that since the "plain language" of the statute was unambiguous, resort to the legislative history (which requires "some element that, physically *or* conceptually, can be identified as separable") was unnecessary. 170 F. Supp. 2d 828, 833 (N.D. Ill. 2001). Do you agree? Or does the word "capable" suggest that physical separability is not strictly necessary? On appeal, Judge

Easterbrook was overruled by two of his colleagues, who noted that all but one of the Circuit Courts to address the issue have concluded (based on the legislative history) that conceptual separability alone is sufficient.

(8) As noted in *Pivot Point*, the Second Circuit has taken the lead in interpreting, reinterpreting, and re-reinterpreting the statutory language and the supporting legislative history. The first court to address the issue, however, was the D.C. Circuit. In *Esquire, Inc. v. Ringer*, 591 F.2d 796 (D.C. Cir. 1978), the court considered the copyrightability of a lighting fixture (pictured nearby). The court held that the relevant portion of the House Report, when read "in its entirety," indicated "unequivocally that the overall design or configuration of a utilitarian object, even if it is determined by aesthetic as well as functional considerations, is not eligible for copyright." 591 F.2d at 803-04. The opinion implies that "conceptual separability" can exist only where the physical disaggregation of an object's useful and decorative features could be imagined but, for some practical reason, cannot be accomplished. The removal of an incised *bas relief* from the wall of a building might be an example.

The *Esquire* Lighting Fixture

Although *Esquire* arose under the 1909 Act, the court referred to the 1976 Act and its legislative history for guidance in interpreting the regulation quoted in note (1) above, on which the language of the 1976 Act was based. Given this linguistic connection, are you persuaded by *Pivot Point*'s rejection of *Esquire* (in its footnote 8) as precedential authority? *See Universal Furniture Int'l, Inc. v. Collezione Europa USA, Inc.*, 618 F.3d 417 (4th Cir. 2010) (citing *Esquire* with approval).

(9) The Second Circuit first took up the "separability" problem under the 1976 Act in *Kieselstein-Cord v. Accessories by Pearl, Inc.*, 632 F.2d 989 (1980), a case involving claims of copyright in decorative belt buckles, which the evidence showed were sometimes worn as jewelry in their own right. In holding that the belt buckles were copyrightable, the majority seems to have doubted that the buckles really had much to do with holding up anyone's trousers. The majority's analysis, however, is

less than helpful. It simply concludes that "the primarily ornamental aspect of the . . . buckles is conceptually separate from their subsidiary utilitarian function." *Id.* at 993.

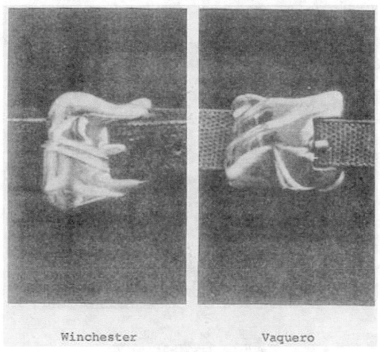

Winchester   Vaquero

The *Kieselstein-Cord* Buckles

What is meant by "primary" and "subsidiary"? The court apparently did not focus on the frequency of utilitarian versus nonutilitarian usage: The buckles were used most frequently to fasten belts and were only occasionally worn as pieces of ornamental jewelry. Does the majority's subjective approach provide sufficient guidance to the trier-of-fact, or the judge endeavoring to determine whether a triable issue of fact exists? And what has become of the *Bleistein* principle that judges are not to attempt any assessment of the artistic quality of works in determining their copyrightability?

(10)   The Second Circuit's next foray into the territory of "useful articles" was in *Carol Barnhart Inc. v. Economy Cover Corp.*, 773 F.2d 411 (2d Cir. 1985). *Barnhart* involved four life-size human torso forms made of styrene, each without neck, arms, or a back, which were designed and used to display sweaters, blouses and dress shirts. In a passage quoted in *Pivot Point*, the majority concluded that "the features claimed to be aesthetic or artistic . . . are inextricably intertwined with the utilitarian feature, the display of clothes." *Id.* at 419. How does this standard compare to the one used in *Kieselstein-Cord*? Isn't asking whether the decorative features of a work are "inextricably intertwined" with its utilitarian aspects an essentially subjective inquiry? Perhaps the inquiry into "conceptual separability" is *inherently* subjective, and the real question is *whose* subjectivity should control.

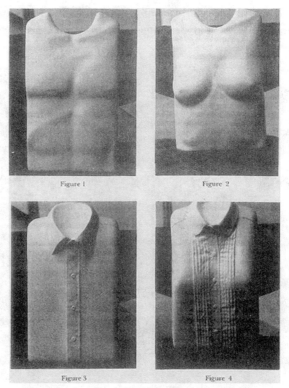

Figure 1 Figure 2

Figure 3 Figure 4

The Works in Suit:
The Four Torsos in *Barnhart*

Judge Newman, dissenting in *Barnhart*, answered that he thought "the relevant beholder must be that most useful legal personage — the ordinary, reasonable observer." But what, exactly, should the ordinary observer be asked to determine? Judge Newman suggested:

> I think the requisite "separateness" exists whenever the design creates in the mind of the ordinary observer two different concepts that are not inevitably entertained simultaneously. . . . [T]he example of the artistically designed chair displayed in a museum may be helpful. The ordinary observer can be expected to apprehend the design of a chair whenever the object is viewed. He may, in addition, entertain the concept of a work of art, but if this second concept is engendered in the observer's mind simultaneously with the concept of the article's utilitarian function, the requisite "separateness" does not exist. The test is not whether the observer fails to recognize the object as a chair but only whether the concept of the utilitarian function can be displaced in the mind by some other concept. . . . The separate concept will normally be that of a work of art.

Id. at 422-23. The majority in *Barnhart* criticized Judge Newman's standard as "so ethereal as to amount to a 'non-test' that would be extremely difficult, if not impossible, to administer or apply." *Id.* at 419 n.5. Other courts apparently agree, as no court has yet adopted Judge Newman's proposal.

(11)   The next case involved the copyrightability of a design for a bicycle rack constructed of metal tubing bent to create a serpentine form. In *Brandir International, Inc. v. Cascade Pacific Lumber Co.*, 834 F.2d 1142 (2d Cir. 1987), the court adopted a test for "conceptual separability" proposed by Professor Denicola in the article cited in *Pivot Point*. In the *Brandir* court's words:

> [I]f design elements reflect a merger of aesthetic and functional considerations, the artistic aspects of a work cannot be said to be conceptually separable from the utilitarian aspects. Conversely, where the design elements can be identified as reflecting the designer's artistic judgment exercised independently of functional influences, conceptual separability exists.

834 F.2d at 1145. Because the artist had modified his original sculpture in order to produce a more useful bike rack, the court concluded that the bike rack was not copyrightable.

The *Brandir* Bike Rack

Why does the court in *Pivot Point* prefer this test to the other tests it discusses? Is the requirement in the *Brandir*-Denicola test that the design elements be uninfluenced by functional considerations realistic or consistent with the statute? Is it consistent with the legislative history, which states that the overall configuration of a useful article will not be protected "even if the appearance of an article is determined by [a]esthetic (as opposed to functional) considerations"? *See* Perlmutter, *Conceptual Separability and Copyright in the Design of Useful Articles*, 37 J. Copyright Soc'y 339 (1990).

The *Brandir*-Denicola test has also been endorsed by the Fourth Circuit. In *Universal Furniture Int'l, Inc. v. Collezione Europa USA, Inc.*, 618 F.3d 417, 434 (4th Cir. 2010), the court held that the "decorative elements" on plaintiff's furniture, consisting of "three-dimensional shells, acanthus leaves, columns, finials, rosettes, and other carvings," were "conceptually separable from the furniture's utilitarian aspects." The court also relied on the House Report, which states that "even if the three-dimensional design contains some such element (for example, a *carving on the back of a chair or a floral relief design on silver flatware*), copyright protection would extend only to that element, and would not cover the over-all configuration of the utilitarian article as such." *Id., quoting* H.R. Rep. 94-1476, at 55 (1976) (emphasis added by the court).

(12)   Would it be satisfactory simply to inquire, with Nimmer, whether "there is any substantial likelihood that even if the article had no utilitarian use it would still be *marketable* to some significant segment of the community simply because of its aesthetic qualities"? *See* 1 NIMMER ON COPYRIGHT § 2.08[B][3] (2010) (emphasis added). How would *Pivot Point* and the other cases have been decided under the Nimmer standard? Subsequent to *Pivot Point*, the Fifth Circuit endorsed the Nimmer standard on the basis of its relative simplicity and ease of application, although for now it has limited the application of that standard to garment designs only. *See Galiano v. Harrah's Operating Co.*, 416 F.3d 411, 422 (5th Cir. 2005). Two other federal appellate courts have also used the Nimmer test — one in an unpublished disposition! *See Poe v. Missing Persons*, 745 F.2d 1238, 1243 (9th Cir. 1984); *Magnussen Furniture, Inc. v. Collezione Europa USA, Inc.*, 43 U.S.P.Q.2d (BNA) 1218 (4th Cir. 1997).

(13)   Both the District Court opinion and the dissent in *Pivot Point* endorse yet another test, this one proposed by Professor Goldstein in his treatise. Goldstein's test asks whether there is a pictorial, graphic, or sculptural feature that "can stand on its own as a work of art traditionally conceived," and whether "the useful article in which it is embodied would be equally useful without it." How does this test differ from the Nimmer test? From the Denicola test?

(14)   In the end, which standard do you prefer, and why? The ultimate choice is likely to matter greatly in years to come. The absence of specific industrial design legislation in the United States all but assures that manufacturers will continue to try to use copyright to redress allegedly unfair competitive practices in the field of commercial design.

(15)   *Additional limitations concerning useful articles.* In addition to the limitation on copyright protection for useful articles in § 101's definition of "pictorial, graphic, and sculptural" works, the Copyright Act contains two other limitations pertinent to useful articles. First, when the design of a useful article *does* qualify for copyright protection, § 113(c) still allows others to make, distribute, and display pictures or photos of such articles in advertisements, commentaries, or news reports. Second, when a pictorial, graphic, or sculptural work "portrays a useful article as such," then under § 113(b), the copyright owner has no greater or lesser rights in such a work than she did under the law, as interpreted by the courts, in effect on December 31, 1977. This section was intended to preserve pre-1978 case law holding that the copyright in a drawing of a useful article does not prevent others from manufacturing the useful article itself. *See, e.g., Niemi v. American Axle Mfg. & Holding, Inc.*, 2006 U.S. Dist. LEXIS 50153 (E.D. Mich., July 24, 2006).

In *Tire Engineering & Distribution, LLC v. Shandong Linglong Rubber Co.*, 682 F.3d 292 (4th Cir. 2012), both the parties and the court seem to have entirely overlooked the last of these limitations. Because the defendant had infringed the plaintiff's blueprints, which were protected pictorial works, in the United States, the court held that the plaintiff could recover damages for the subsequent manufacture in China of the useful articles (tires) depicted in those blueprints. Putting aside the problem of the extraterritorial reach of the Copyright Act (discussed in § 8.04), this holding gave the plaintiff more relief than it was entitled to under § 113(b).

ALTERNATIVE PROTECTIONS FOR ORNAMENTAL DESIGN

Although recent cases involving copyright protection for design indicate that U.S. law has become more receptive to such claims since 1976, there are still important areas of commercial design (clothing and furniture, to name two) which are largely untouched by copyright law, thanks to the "useful articles" doctrine. Some sentiment exists in favor of affording even broader copyright protection to the designs of useful articles. For example, the Copyright Act could be amended to relax or even eliminate the "separability" test. (One modest step in this direction — the 1990 revision of the Act to extend protection to "architectural works" — is discussed below.) Alternatively, protection could be provided for design by means of doctrines other than copyright. Which branch of law is best suited to the purpose, and what would be the scope of this broadened protection?

Design Patent Protection

One interesting question left undecided in *Mazer v. Stein* was whether a work remains eligible for copyright if a design patent for the work already has been obtained. The issue has yet to be resolved by the Supreme Court. Does the language of the Copyright Clause or the 1976 Act provide any support for denying copyright protection to a design-patented work? For now, both the Copyright Office and the lower courts have taken the position that an election is not required: A work may receive both copyright and design patent protection, regardless of which was obtained first. *See Application of Yardley*, 493 F.2d 1389 (C.C.P.A. 1974); 37 C.F.R. § 202.10(a).

A design patent may be obtained for "any new, original, and ornamental design for an article of manufacture." 35 U.S.C. § 171. A design patent lasts for 14 years from issuance and confers broad exclusionary rights on its owner: Any similar design, even if independently created, is strictly barred. Whether an accused design infringes a patented design is determined from the perspective of the ordinary observer. Thus, a design patent is infringed by a second design "[i]f, in the eye of an ordinary observer, . . . [the] two designs are substantially the same." In other words, infringement occurs if the resemblance "deceives such an observer, inducing him to purchase one [good,] supposing it to be the other." *Egyptian Goddess Inc. v. Swisa Inc.*, 543 F.3d 665, 670 (Fed. Cir. 2008).

For a variety of reasons, design-patent protection is less satisfactory than copyright protection.

First, the requirements for a design patent are stringent. As with utility patents, a design must be both novel and nonobvious to qualify for a patent. Copyright protection is afforded to works that are merely original.

Second, obtaining a patent is a cumbersome and expensive process because the Patent and Trademark Office must examine the design to determine if the above-mentioned requirements have been met. Copyright registration requires only filling out a simple form and paying a modest fee.

Third, design patent protection does not begin until the patent is issued. The interval between the time one seeks a patent and the issuance of that patent can be several months. A copyright, however, provides protection immediately upon creation, even though registration is required prior to filing suit. Waiting for protection can be costly in a volatile consumer marketplace, in which the commercial value of a design may be short-lived.

Nonetheless, design patents may prove useful in those cases in which copyright protection for the design of a useful article is not available, as demonstrated by the $1-billion jury verdict against Samsung for infringing, *inter alia*, certain design patents on Apple's iPhone.

Trademark Protection

Protection for ornamental designs of useful articles also may be available, in appropriate circumstances, under federal trademark and unfair competition law. Some courts have afforded quite robust protection to "product configurations" under the Lanham Act, 15 U.S.C. §§ 1051–1127. *See, e.g.*, *Kohler Co. v. Moen, Inc.*, 12 F.3d 632 (7th Cir. 1993) (holding that a faucet design was a protected trade dress). To meet the standards of protection under the Lanham Act, the manufacturer must show that the design in question is non-functional and that it has acquired secondary meaning. *See Wal-Mart Stores, Inc. v. Samara Bros., Inc.*, 529 U.S. 205 (2000). If these standards are met, the design is protected for as long as the design is used and maintains its origin-indicating significance. If, however, the product design is functional, trademark protection is unavailable even if consumers treat the design as a source identifier. *See Specialized Seating, Inc. v. Greenwich Industries, L.P.*, 616 F.3d 722 (7th Cir. 2010) (holding that design of folding chairs was functional even though alternative designs were available and the trademark registration in the design had become "incontestable"). The role of functionality as a limit on trademark protection has been under active development in the courts. We treat the subject in more detail in Chapter 11.

Protections Outside Federal Law

What other non-copyright alternatives exist for the product designer who believes that his creation (which we may assume has not been patented) has been unjustly imitated by a competitor? Could the aggrieved designer appeal for relief under a state law prohibiting commercial "misappropriation"? As we will see in Chapter 11, if the design is one that passes the separability test and qualifies for copyright, there will be significant preemption problems under § 301 of the Copyright Act. But suppose the design fails to meet the relevant separability standard. Could it be argued persuasively that, in this situation, a state-law claim should be permitted to proceed? The Supreme Court's unanimous decision in *Bonito Boats, Inc. v. Thunder Craft Boats, Inc.*, 489 U.S. 141 (1989) (reproduced in Chapter 11), suggests otherwise. There, it was held that *unpatentable* technologies (in this case, boat hull designs) could not be given patent-like protection under state law, even against direct, slavish imitation. The Court relied on general preemption doctrine, and on its view that intellectual property law should be designed to promote, rather than discourage, technological competition. Although *Bonito Boats* does not speak to copyright as such (and its specific result, as we will see momentarily, has been overtaken by new federal legislation), the decision's implications for the availability of state law protection for designs of useful articles unprotected under federal law seem clear enough.

"Sui Generis" Protection

Many countries provide for protection of ornamental designs under statutory schemes independent of, although in some instances overlapping with, copyright. *See, e.g.,* Levin & Richman, *A Survey of Industrial Design Protection in the European Union and the United States,* 25 E.I.P.R. 111 (2003). In the United States, there have been proposals — though, with one limited exception described below, no actual legislation to date — to provide protection for original designs of useful articles. If enacted, any *sui generis* design protection legislation would presumably be codified in a new chapter of Title 17. As such, like the 1984 Semiconductor Chip Protection Act, that protection would supplement copyright rather than modify it.

One of the most serious attempts to enact general design protection domestically occurred during consideration of the 1976 Act. The Senate approved legislation protecting designs under a *sui generis* regime appended as Title II of the Copyright Revision Bill, but the provision was deleted from the statute as enacted. The legislation would not have affected the availability of copyright protection for artistic features which are separable from the utilitarian function of an object. Nor would it have extended any protection to the design or shape of the article dictated by the utilitarian features of the article. The legislation would, however, have changed existing law by affording protection for a period of ten years to works in which the design aspects were (a) not separable from the work but (b) not determined by functional considerations.

Different forms of such legislation have been reintroduced periodically, although not in the last few years. Ultimately, the prospects of any such sweeping legislation depend, at least in part, on the effectiveness of the lobbying efforts for and against it. Foremost among the lobbying interests have been automobile manufacturers on one side, and insurers on the other, who believe that design protection will drive up the cost of spare parts. Some important design industries, such as the fashion industry, appear to be split on the merits of *sui generis* protection.

Design Protection for Vessel Hulls

Although there has been little recent progress toward *sui generis* protection for designs in general, one particular group of designs has fared better — and may provide a harbinger of things to come. The vulnerability of unpatented boat hull designs, which can be accurately and inexpensively copied by means of "plug molding" techniques, was recognized in the Supreme Court's decision in *Bonito Boats.* In response, in 1998 Congress enacted the "Vessel Hull Design Protection

Act" ("VHDPA") as Title V of the Digital Millennium Copyright Act.

The VHDPA added to Title 17 a new Chapter 13 entitled "Protection of Original Designs." Its provisions give 10 years of protection against manufacturing, importing, selling or distributing for sale articles duplicating protected designs, subject to certain exceptions. Protection is available only for original designs which have been registered with the Copyright Office and runs from the time the Office publishes the registration (an act which may trigger applications for cancellation from third parties) or the time when authorized merchandise incorporating the design is first exhibited, distributed or sold — whichever comes first. A design is "original" if it results from the designer's creative endeavor, "provides a distinguishable variation over prior similar works which is more than merely trivial," and was not copied from another source. By contrast, an unoriginal design is not subject to protection, nor is a design which is staple, commonplace, familiar, standard, prevalent, ordinary, or dictated solely by a utilitarian function of the article which embodies it. *See Maverick Boat Co. v. American Marine Holdings, Inc.*, 418 F.3d 1186 (11th Cir. 2005) (holding changes made to original design were merely corrections to a mistake and were not a "substantial revision" entitled to separate protection).

Despite its inclusion in the DMCA, the VHDPA clearly is not a mere extension of the Copyright Act. The protections afforded by new Chapter 13 are not subject to any of the general provisions of the Copyright Act (*i.e.*, Chapters 1-8). Nor do the VHDPA's specialized terms or definitions apply anywhere else in Title 17. And unlike copyright, the VHDPA expressly prohibits dual protection under Chapter 13 and design patent law; the issuance of a design patent will terminate any protection of the design provided by the VHDPA.

In November 2003, the U.S. Copyright Office issued a comprehensive report on the impact of the VHDPA. It found that in the five years since the VHDPA's enactment, 156 registrations were made and only one lawsuit was filed. It concluded that "it is too soon to tell whether the VHDPA has had a significant overall effect on the boat building industry." The report is available at *http://www.copyright.gov/reports/vhdpa-report.pdf*.

In 2008, the VHDPA was amended to "clarify" that its protection extended to a vessel hull or a deck, separately or together. Ultimately, however, the impact of the VHDPA may be much broader than now appears. As currently formulated, Chapter 13 is a detailed code protecting the "original design of a useful article" (§ 1301(a)(1)), a phrase which is qualified only by language which — somewhat artificially — defines a "useful article" as "a vessel hull or deck, including a plug or mold, which in normal use has an intrinsic utilitarian function that is not merely to portray the appearance of the article or to convey information." § 1301(b)(2). It requires little imagination to envision how this definition could be amended to broaden the scope of Chapter 13's coverage.

Furthermore, proprietors of other valuable industrial designs are now lobbying Congress for protection similar to that given to vessel hulls. Since 2006, Congress has been considering whether to extend protection to fashion design. The 112th Congress saw the re-introduction of a proposed "Innovative Design Protection and Piracy Prevention Act" that would grant protection for three years to fashion designs, defined as "the appearance as a whole of an article of apparel," including an original arrangement of original or non-original design elements. Apparel was defined broadly to include not only clothing, but also accessories such as gloves, footwear, headwear, purses, tote bags, belts, and eyeglass frames. *See* H. Rep. 2511 (introduced Jul. 13, 2011). Opponents claimed that *lack* of protection has led to greater innovation in the fashion industry, by making trends grow *passé* more quickly. *See* K. Raustiala & C. Sprigman, The Knockoff Economy: How Imitation Sparks Innovation (2012). Whether fashion designers will succeed in obtaining *sui generis* design protection similar to vessel hulls remains to be seen.

[E] Motion Pictures and Other Audiovisual Works

The beginnings of protection for "audiovisual works" (the genus in which motion pictures are by far the dominant species) was humble. In 1894, the Copyright Office registered its first claim to copyright in a motion picture — *Edison Kinetoscopic Record of a Sneeze, January 7, 1894*, better known as *Fred Ott's Sneeze* — under the nearest plausible category: "photographs." The 1909 Act did not protect motion pictures as such, although the Copyright Office continued to register them; and it was not until 1912, in the Townsend Amendment, that Congress provided express protection. During the 1909 Act's long life, television programs came to be registered as "motion pictures," while video tapes received protection as "addresses prepared for oral delivery." In the 1976 Act, Congress settled on the umbrella formulation in § 102(a)(6): "motion pictures and other audiovisual works."

Everyone has an idea of what a motion picture is, and the importance of movies both to the American economy and to American culture is widely appreciated. As one court observed, "[f]ilm has in many ways, as never before, replaced the written work as a vehicle for the transmission of ideas, viewpoints and opinions." *Amato v. Wilentz*, 753 F. Supp. 543 (D.N.J. 1990) (Politan, J.), *vacated on other grounds*, 952 F.2d 742 (3d Cir. 1991).

The 1976 Act, however, treats motion pictures as a subcategory of audiovisual works. What is an "audiovisual work"? Section 101 defines such works as consisting of:

> a series of related images which are intrinsically intended to be shown by the use of machines and devices such as projectors, viewers, or electronic equipment, together with accompanying sounds, if any, regardless of the nature of the material objects, such as films or tapes, in which the works are embodied.

The key language in the statutory definition — "a series of related images" — raises several interesting issues. First, is it necessary that the images be *presented* serially — *i.e.*, sequentially, in a fixed, invariable order — as they are in a motion picture? The answer is "no," as demonstrated in *Stern Electronics, Inc. v. Kaufman*, 669 F.2d 852 (2d Cir. 1982). There, the court sustained a copyright in the audiovisual display of a videogame, where the display was predetermined by a computer program embodied in a microchip memory device but the sequence of images was affected by player intervention. The Second Circuit held:

The repetitive sequence of a substantial portion of the sights and sounds of the game qualifies [the game] for copyright protection as an audiovisual work.

Id. at 856. Suppose, however, that a videogame program contains a randomizing feature that makes virtually the entire performance of the work nonrepetitive. Might there come a point at which any repeating series of images form too insubstantial a portion of an entire performance to warrant a copyright? Where would that point occur? Might the work still warrant a copyright under some heading other than "motion pictures and other audiovisual works"? Not surprisingly (because the issue was not presented there), *Stern* does not say.

A second issue arising in this category concerns the requirement that the images be *related*. In *WGN Continental Broadcasting Co. v. United Video, Inc.*, 693 F.2d 622 (7th Cir. 1982), the Seventh Circuit confronted this issue in connection with a work containing two sets of images — one, a television newscast, and the other, the TV station's program schedule — broadcast simultaneously as part of the same signal. Viewers could receive the second set of images only by pressing a decoder button, thereby causing the schedule to replace the newscast on their screens. Influenced, perhaps, by its perception that Congress wanted the courts "to interpret the definitional provisions of the new [1976 Act] flexibly, so that it would cover new technologies as they appeared, rather than to interpret those provisions narrowly and so force Congress periodically to update the act," the court held that the copyright in the newscast protected the embedded schedule as well, "provided the [schedule] is intended to be seen by the same viewers as are watching the nine o'clock news, during the same interval of time in which that news is broadcast, and is an integral part of the news program." *Id.* at 629. The court further observed, however, that the copyright in suit would *not* have protected a cartoon show for preschoolers broadcast simultaneously with the news. Why not? Where does one draw the line on "relatedness"?

A further issue involving audiovisual works is the proper approach to be adopted in determining whether a work satisfies the quantum-of-originality requirement considered in Chapter 2. Clearly, a work can qualify as an audiovisual work even though it consists of images which, individually, qualify for protection as pictorial, graphic, or sculptural works. What if, instead, the individual components of the "series of related images" are insufficiently expressive to merit protection, but their *combination* is claimed to be original? Recall the discussion of *Atari Games Corp. v. Oman* in § 2.02. On remand from the D.C. Circuit, the Copyright Office again denied protection to the plaintiff's videogame, saying:

> [M]any works that are made up of simple geometric shapes are nonetheless copyrightable, if the selection or arrangement [of such shapes and their interactions] is distinctive.
>
> . . . Viewing "Breakout" as a whole, one is confronted with flat, unadorned geometric shapes carrying out the action of the game. . . . [T]he graphic, visual display elements do not evince authorship in the nature of perspective, shading, depth or brushstroke which would significantly contribute to creative expression. "Breakout" consists of nothing more than a large rectangle comprising different colored bars, pieces of which

disappear in response to the manipulation of a small rectangle by the player of the game. The concept of the game, conveyed through the movement of the pieces, is not protectible. 17 U.S.C. § 102(b). While Breakout's visuals are a series of related images, we find no original authorship in either the selection or arrangement of the images or their components. Were the Copyright Office to register "Breakout" simply because it is a series of related images, then the Office would have no choice but to register *every* audiovisual work submitted.

As mentioned in Chapter 2, however, the D.C. Circuit's firm follow-up opinion, reported at 979 F.2d 242 (1992), did ultimately prompt registration notwithstanding the Register's marked reluctance.

Many hands may be involved in the production of an audiovisual work such as a motion picture. In theory, this fact can be the source of disputes about the identity of such a work's "author" or "authors" for copyright purposes. In the culture of the American film industry, the director would seem to have a claim to being considered the "author" of a movie, and there is even a case (decided under the 1909 Act) that so holds, on its own peculiar facts: *Epoch Producing Corp. v. Killiam Shows, Inc.*, 522 F.2d 737 (2d Cir. 1975). But does the director have the only claim — or should he be required to share "authorship" with others? And if a "joint authorship" solution is preferred, who will be included in the charmed circle? What about screen writers (whose scripts are, after all, independently copyrightable works), or cinematographers (whose creative efforts are reflected only in the motion picture itself)? Do actors' contributions ever rise to the level of "authorship"? These are hard questions, and American law has contrived to avoid answering them by taking refuge behind the "work for hire" doctrine. See the discussion in Chapter 4.

One final matter concerning audiovisual works deserves brief mention. Under the 1909 Act, the status of motion picture soundtracks was ambiguous. The present statute resolves the issue, making soundtracks an integral part of the copyright in a motion picture, by defining such audiovisual works to include "accompanying sounds, if any."

[F] Sound Recordings

Nature and ownership of the work. Sound recordings are defined by § 101 of the Copyright Act of 1976 as "works that result from the fixation of a series of musical, spoken, or other sounds, but not including the sounds accompanying a motion picture or other audiovisual work, regardless of the nature of the material objects, such as discs, tapes, or other phonorecords, in which they are embodied." Thus, the performance "captured" in the sound recording might be of a literary work (Robert Frost reciting one of his poems) or a dramatic work (Richard Burton declaiming "To be or not to be . . ."). The archetype, however, is a sound recording of a musical work.

Two distinctions are important here. First, it is easy to confuse a sound recording with the musical (or other) work captured therein, particularly since both works can be fixed in the same physical object, namely, a phonorecord (a tape, CD, or computer disk). But a sound recording and the musical work that underlies the sound recording are *not* the same. In the case of a popular song, for example, the *musical work* is the melody and harmony, plus any accompanying lyrics, as created by the composer. The *sound recording* is the "rendition" of the song as embodied in the phonorecord, including the way the song is sung by the vocalist, played by the instrumentalists, arranged by the musical director, and mixed by the recording engineer. The vocalist, instrumentalists, musical director and engineer, in other words, are the creators of a derivative work (see below as to who owns it), and their expression is the sound recording, *not the song itself* — which is the composer's expression, and a separately copyrighted work. The song is comprised of musical notes and words, while the sound recording is a *unique aggregate of sounds.*

The second distinction is easy, once the first is understood: § 102(a)(7) protects the particular aggregate of sounds collected in the copyrighted work called the "sound recording," *not* the song being recorded (the "musical work") nor the physical object in which the sound recording and the musical work are embodied (the "phonorecord"). Thus, if Sony issues a compact disc of Aaron Copland's *Third Symphony* performed by the New York Philharmonic, the copyright in the sound recording initially belongs jointly to Sony and the Philharmonic as co-authors; the copyright in the musical work belongs to Copland's estate; and the CDs themselves, which are physical fixations of both works, belong to the individuals who purchase them.

A sound recording must satisfy the ordinary prerequisites for a copyright: Besides being fixed in a tangible medium of expression, the sound recording must be original. The source of originality may be, for example, the lead performer's rendition (*e.g.*, compare "Sinatra Sings the Music of Cole Porter" with a similar work by Linda Ronstadt) or the record producer's or recording engineer's selection and mixing or adjusting of sounds. In addition, because a sound recording is also a derivative work of the musical (or other) work being performed, it is subject to the condition in § 103 that the underlying material must have been used lawfully. *See Palladium Music, Inc. v. EatSleepMusic, Inc.*, 398 F.3d 1193 (10th Cir. 2005) (holding karaoke sound recording copyrights invalid and unenforceable for failure to obtain compulsory or consensual licenses from the copyright owners of the underlying musical works).

Because the sound recording may arise from the varied contributions of several people — all of whom in a sense are its creators, and some or all of whom may be employees of others — one might inquire who owns the sound recording and in what proportions. Congress ducked this question, leaving the matter to be determined by "the employment relationship and bargaining among the interests involved." The issue of copyright ownership in a sound recording, therefore, is one that usually is resolved by contract. In addition to incorporating language assigning musical performers' rights in a sound recording (if any) to the recording company, contracts also designate those recordings as "works made for hire." Whether this designation is a legally apt one has been the subject of some controversy, as is explained more fully in §§ 4.01 and 5.02.

History of U.S. protection. The impetus for creation of the sound recording category was the alarming rise in record piracy in the decade or so immediately preceding passage of the 1976 Act. This is a form of "free-riding" to which record companies have always objected vigorously. By 1971, the problem had become acute enough so that they were willing to accept less-than-complete copyright protection in order to achieve an effective federal remedy against the unauthorized duplication and sale of their products.

In 1971, Congress passed the Sound Recording Amendment Act, effective February 15, 1972, which was then carried over into the 1976 Act. Under § 114, the *duplication* of a sound recording fixed on or after the effective date of the 1971 Act is an infringement, not only of the rights of the songwriter and the songwriter's publisher in the musical work, but also of all persons holding a copyright in the sounds recorded on the disc or tape (see the discussion of ownership above).

The protection accorded sound recordings under federal law differs, however, from that accorded other works listed in § 102(a), in important respects. For example, while unauthorized duplication of a sound recording is an infringement, imitation of the recording — by rerecording the musical work, even using the same artists and engineers — is not. *See* § 114(b). This possibility is dealt with by recording contract provisions in which the performer agrees not to rerecord a song done for that company for a set number of years.

Another important limitation is the lack of a general public performance right. When a radio station plays a record, it must pay a royalty to the copyright owner of the musical work; it does not pay a royalty to the copyright owner of the sound recording. This limitation was insisted upon by broadcasters and was an important part of the political compromise that made the 1971 Act possible. Not until the Digital Performance Right in Sound Recordings Act of 1995 did Congress finally enact a limited public performance right in sound recordings, applicable only to certain kinds of digital transmissions. The rationale offered at the time was that subscription-based and interactive services posed a special risk to recording companies, because music consumers who received them might be inclined to buy fewer CDs as a result. *See* H.R. Rep. No. 104-274, at 13 (1995). This legislation was significantly amended in 1998 by the Digital Millennium Copyright Act.

During the 110th and 111th Congresses, bills entitled "Performance Rights Act" were introduced to grant sound recording copyright owners a performance right that would include analog transmissions, such as terrestrial radio broadcasts. The recorded music industry is likely to continue seeking an expansion of sound recording performance rights, while broadcasters are likely to continue to resist such efforts.

One final matter of importance concerning the Sound Recording Amendment Act as carried over into the current statute is its effect on works fixed prior to February 15, 1972. There is *no* effect, or at least no immediate effect: § 301(c) provides that "any rights or remedies [with respect to such works] under the common law or statutes of any State shall not be annulled or limited . . . until February 15, 2067." Until then, therefore, rights in sound recordings fixed before February 15, 1972 are governed exclusively by state law. *See Capitol Records, Inc., v. Naxos of America, Inc.*, 372 F.3d 471 (2d Cir. 2004) (certifying questions of law concerning pre-1972 sound recordings to the New York Court of Appeals). By the same token, however, state-law protection for sound recordings fixed *after* the effective date of the Sound Recording Amendments *is* subject to preemption under § 301 of the Act, if the state-law right is "equivalent to any of the exclusive rights" provided by federal copyright law. But many state laws contain provisions which arguably are *not* equivalent to anything in the Copyright Act, such as prohibitions against unauthorized recording of live performances or labeling requirements. *See, e.g.*, Mass. Ann. Laws, ch. 266, §§ 143A-143C.

In responding to the certified questions in *Capitol Records*, the New York Court of Appeals held that, under New York law, there was a perpetual common-law copyright prior to publication of a work; and that because a sale of phonograph records was not considered a "publication" of the underlying musical work under the 1909 Copyright Act (*see* § 6.01), sound recordings distributed to the public in New York never had been "published" at all, even after the 1976 Act came into effect. *See Capitol Records, Inc., v. Naxos of America, Inc.*, 830 N.E.2d 250 (2005). The result is that, in New York, a common-law copyright for all sound recordings — even Edison cylinders recorded in the late 1870s — will remain in effect until February 15, 2067, even for sound recordings which are in the public domain in their country of origin (in this case, the U.K.). *Id.* In Chapter 6, we will consider whether the same definition of "publication" should apply to both musical works and sound recordings. Even assuming that is the case, however, how does it serve the public interest to protect such sound recordings beyond the term provided in their country of origin? And if a *perpetual* common-law copyright for sound recordings existed prior to 1972, why was it not a "taking" of private property for Congress to preempt such copyrights as of 2067?

The patchwork nature of state-law protection has generated uncertainties that have clouded efforts to digitize, preserve, and provide online access to pre-1972 sound recordings. At the direction of Congress, the Copyright Office conducted a study and issued a report in December 2011 recommending that federal copyright protection should displace state law protection of pre-1972 sound recordings to provide greater certainty and greater opportunities for preservation and access. As of this writing, Congress has not taken action in response to the report.

International protections and domestic legislation. The approach to the protection of sound recordings reflected in U.S. law is unusual, although not unique, among the national laws of the world. Of those countries which provide some form of protection for sound recordings, more have elected to do so by means of *sui generis* legislation than as part of the mainstream of copyright — one reason being the continued uncertainty in countries of the civil-law tradition as to whether production and performance represent eligible forms of creative "authorship." The divergent approaches of different national laws have made the development of effective international norms difficult.

Historically, there are three international treaties dealing specifically with the protection of sound recordings (or "phonograms" in international parlance): the 1961 Rome Convention for the Protection of Performers, Producers of Phonograms and Broadcasting Organizations (to which the United States is not a party, primarily because of its continued lack of a general public performance right); the 1971 Geneva Convention for the Protection of Producers of Phonograms Against Unauthorized Duplication of Their Phonograms (entered into force for the United

States in 1974); and the 1996 WIPO Performances and Phonograms Treaty ("WPPT") (entered into force for the United States in 2002). The latter provides comprehensive rights to sound-recording producers and performers (including rights of reproduction, distribution, rental, "making available to the public," and — where performers are concerned — moral rights). But the means by which these rights are to be implemented, whether by copyright or otherwise, are not specified. In addition, Article 14 of the TRIPS Agreement requires countries of the World Trade Organization to give sound-recording producers rights of reproduction, which again may be implemented by means of copyright or otherwise.

Apart from all of the foregoing, both TRIPS and the WPPT also require nations that are parties to recognize a right which, at least where the United States is concerned, clearly falls outside even the potential scope of copyright: the right of performers to control the fixation of their *unfixed performances* in the form of sound recordings and music videos. The United States enacted implementing legislation, codified at 17 U.S.C. § 1101 and 18 U.S.C. § 2319A, in December 1994. These "anti-bootlegging" provisions in some ways resemble the protections of copyright law, but in other ways are distinct from them. For example, although the civil portions of the legislation were incorporated into Title 17 and borrow the remedies that apply to copyright infringement, neither they nor the criminal provision mesh with the overall structure of the Copyright Act. In contrast to the six exclusive rights of a copyright owner spelled out in 17 U.S.C. § 106, the anti-bootlegging statute gives the performer a right to prohibit the unauthorized recording, transmission and/or communication to the public of his or her performance, as well as the distribution of copies or phonorecords of any such recording. 17 U.S.C. § 1101. Thus, it is unclear whether longstanding concepts generally applicable in copyright law — such as fair use, the work for hire doctrine, limited duration, and the statute of limitations — carry over to the anti-bootlegging provisions.

Finally, there is a serious constitutional question whether Congress may protect unfixed performances under the Commerce Clause without regard to the "Writings" requirement and the "limited Times" restriction of the Copyright Clause. *Compare United States v. Moghadam*, 175 F.3d 1269 (11th Cir. 1999) (upholding the criminal provision) *and KISS Catalog v. Passport Int'l Prods.*, 405 F. Supp. 2d 1169 (C.D. Cal. 2005) (upholding the civil provision) *with United States v. Martignon*, 492 F.3d 140 (2d Cir. 2007) (upholding the criminal provision, but casting doubt on the constitutionality of the civil provision). For more on these cases, see § 2.01 of this casebook regarding fixation.

[G] Architectural Works

While architectural plans traditionally have been (and continue to be) protected by copyright as pictorial or graphic works, the functionality doctrine (recall the discussion of functionality in the Notes and Questions concerning pictorial, graphic, and sculptural, or PGS, works) traditionally denied protection to the architectural design itself. The protection of architectural works was a side issue during debates concerning U.S. adherence to the Berne Convention for the Protection of Literary and Artistic Works, which became effective on March 1, 1989. In 1990, however, the

United States did enact protection for such works, albeit somewhat limited protection. You may wish to review Article 2(1) of Berne before considering the statutory references, legislative history, and case law that follow.

Statutory References

1976 Act: §§ 101 ("architectural work"), 102(a)(8), 120, 301(b)(4)
1909 Act: —

Legislative History

H.R. REP. No. 101-735 at 18-21 (1990)

[The Architectural Works Copyright Protection Act, or AWCPA] amends section 101 of title 17, United States Code, to provide a definition of the subject matter protected by the bill, "architectural works." . . .

The definition has two components. First, it states what is protected[: "the design of a building"]. Second, it specifies the material objects in which the architectural work may be embodied[: "a building, architectural plans, or drawings"]. . . . The term "design" includes the overall form as well as the arrangement and composition of spaces and elements in the design. The phrase "arrangement and composition of spaces and elements" recognizes that: (1) creativity in architecture frequently takes the form of a selection, coordination, or arrangement of unprotectible elements into an original, protectible whole; (2) an architect may incorporate new, protectible design elements into otherwise standard, unprotectible building features; and (3) interior architecture may be protected.

Consistent with other provisions of the Copyright Act and Copyright Office regulations, the definition makes clear that protection does not extend to individual standard features, such as common windows, doors, and other staple building components. A grant of exclusive rights in such features would impede, rather than promote, the progress of architectural innovation. The provision is not, however, intended to exclude from the copyright in the architectural work any individual features that reflect the architect's creativity. . . .

[The AWCPA] amends section 102, title 17, United States Code, to create a new category of protected subject matter: "architectural works." By creating a new category of protectible subject matter in new section 102(a)(8), and, therefore, by deliberately not encompassing architectural works as pictorial, graphic, or sculptural works in existing section 102(a)(5), the copyrightability of architectural works shall not be evaluated under the separability test applicable to pictorial, graphic, or sculptural works embodied in useful articles. There is considerable scholarly and judicial disagreement over how to apply the separability test, and the principal reason for not treating architectural works as pictorial, graphic, or sculptural works is to avoid entangling architectural works in this disagreement.

The Committee does not suggest, though, that in evaluating the copyrightability or scope of protection for architectural works, the Copyright Office or the courts should ignore functionality. A two-step analysis is envisioned. First, an architectural work should be examined to determine whether there are original design elements present, including overall shape and interior architecture. If such design elements are present, a second step is reached to examine whether the design elements are functionally required. If the design elements are not functionally required, the work is protectible without regard to physical or conceptual separability. As a consequence, contrary to the Committee's report accompanying the 1976 Copyright Act with respect to industrial products, the aesthetically pleasing overall shape of an architectural work could be protected under this bill.

[For a fuller excerpt from H.R. Rep. No. 101-735, see Part Three of the Casebook Supplement.]

SHINE v. CHILDS
United States District Court, Southern District of New York
382 F. Supp. 2d 602 (2005)

MUKASEY, DISTRICT JUDGE:

Plaintiff Thomas Shine sues David M. Childs and Skidmore, Owings & Merrill, LLP (SOM) for copyright infringement under the United States Copyright Act. . . . Shine alleges that he created designs for an original skyscraper which Childs saw and later copied in the first design plan for the Freedom Tower at the World Trade Center (WTC) site. Defendants move to dismiss the Complaint, or alternatively for summary judgment. For the reasons explained below, defendants' motion for summary judgment is granted in part and denied in part.

I.

The facts viewed in the light most favorable to the plaintiff . . . are as follows. In fall 1999, Shine was a student in the Masters of Architecture Program at the Yale School of Architecture. As part of the required curriculum in his program, he took a studio class on skyscrapers taught by renowned architect Cesar Pelli. The object of this studio was to create a design proposal for a monumental skyscraper that would be built on West 32nd Street in Manhattan and used by the media during the 2012 Olympic Games; the building was to be adjacent to the proposed West Side stadium.

During the first half of October 1999, Shine developed a preliminary model for his design, which he refers to as "Shine '99" for the purposes of this litigation. Plaintiff describes Shine '99 as a tower that tapers as it rises, with "two straight, parallel, roughly triangular sides, connected by two twisting facades, resulting in a tower whose top [is] in the shape of a parallelogram."

By the end of the fall 1999 semester, Shine had developed a more sophisticated model of his design, entitled "Olympic Tower." Shine describes this structure as "a twisting tower with a symmetrical diagonal column grid, expressed on the exterior of the building, that follows the twisting surface created by the floor plates' geometry." According to Shine, the column grid he designed gives rise to "an elongated diamond pattern, supporting a textured curtain wall with diamonds interlocking and protruding to create a crenelated appearance."

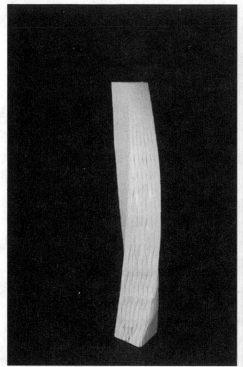

Olympic Tower   Freedom Tower

On or about December 9, 1999, Shine presented his designs for Olympic Tower to a jury of experts invited by the Yale School of Architecture to evaluate and critique its students' work. During a 30-minute presentation to the panel, Shine explained his tower's structural design, and displayed different structural and design models (including Shine '99), renderings, floor plans, elevations, sections, a site plan, and a photomontage giving a visual impression of the tower's exterior. Defendant Childs was on the panel, and he praised Olympic Tower during the presentation, as did the other luminaries evaluating Shine's work. When the review was completed, Shine was applauded by the jury and other visitors, which, according to Shine, is "highly unusual" at a student's final review.

[After the presentation, Childs complimented Shine's color pencil rendering of Olympic Tower. Childs' favorable reaction was documented in two Yale alumni publications, including a quote from Childs: "It is a very beautiful shape. You took the skin and developed it around the form — great!" Shine and Childs had no further contact.

Subsequently, Childs was brought into the WTC site redevelopment project and collaborated with Studio Daniel Libeskind on the original design for the Freedom Tower. As described by Shine, this version of the Freedom Tower "tapers as it rises and has two straight, parallel, roughly triangular facades on opposite sides, with two twisting facades joining them." "Shine allege[d] that this design was substantially similar to the form and shape of Shine '99, and that it incorporated a structural grid identical to the grid in Olympic Tower, as well as a facade design that is 'strikingly similar' to the one in Olympic Tower."

Shine registered Shine '99 and Olympic Tower as architectural works with the U.S. Copyright Office and filed suit for copyright infringement in 2004. "Defendants move[d] to dismiss the complaint, or alternatively for summary judgment, claiming that Shine's works are not original and not worthy of protection, and further arguing that there is no substantial similarity between either work and the Freedom Tower." In ruling on the defendants' motion, the court applied the summary judgment standard because the parties submitted, and relied upon, evidence outside the original pleadings.

The court explained that the allegedly infringing original design of Freedom Tower was subsequently substantially redesigned in June 2005 in response to objections from law enforcement authorities and others. Shine did not assert an infringement claim against the revised design.]

II.

. . . Defendants argue first that neither Shine '99 nor Olympic Tower qualifies as an architectural work under the Copyright Act. They argue also that both designs are unoriginal and functional, and therefore unworthy of whatever copyright protection they currently have. Finally, assuming that plaintiff's copyrights are valid, defendants deny that they copied plaintiff's designs, and assert that there is no substantial similarity between plaintiff's designs and the Freedom Tower. Plaintiff counters that Shine '99 and Olympic Tower are each original, copyrightable designs, that defendants actually copied each work, and that the Freedom Tower is substantially similar to each in different ways.

A. Architectural Works Under the Copyright Act

Prior to 1990, the United States did not allow structures to be copyrighted, except those few that did not serve any utilitarian purpose. *See* 1 Nimmer on Copyright § 2.20[A]. However, in 1989, the United States became a party to the Berne Convention for the Protection of Literary and Artistic Works, which required protection for " 'three dimensional works relative to . . . architecture.' " *See id.* (quoting Berne Convention for the Protection of Literary and Artistic Works, revised at Paris, July 24, 1971, art. 2). Membership in the Berne Convention required the United States to protect works of architecture; therefore, in 1990, Congress amended the Copyright Act, adding the Architectural Works Copyright Protection Act (AWCPA), which included architectural works as a new category of copyrightable material.

The AWCPA defines an architectural work as:

> the design of a building as embodied in any tangible medium of expression, including a building, architectural plans, or drawings. The work includes the overall form as well as the arrangement and composition of spaces and elements in the design, but does not include individual standard features.

17 U.S.C. § 101. Defendants cite various portions of the legislative history of the

AWCPA to argue that Shine's models are not architectural works meriting copyright protection. They claim that Shine's works are preliminary or conceptual, and do not meet the standard of a "design of a building." They argue also that plans for the "design of a building" may be protected only if a building actually could be constructed from the plans.

Defendants cite no cases to support their reading of the AWCPA. The statute nowhere states or implies that only designs capable of construction are worthy of protection. Although our Circuit has not specifically articulated the standard by which an architectural design is to be evaluated under the Copyright Act, when considering pictorial, graphic, and sculptural (PGS) works, also protected by the Act, *see* 17 U.S.C. § 101, it has twice noted that plans or designs not sufficiently detailed to allow for construction still may be protected. *See Attia v. Soc'y of the N.Y. Hosp.*, 201 F.3d 50, 57 (2d Cir. 1999) ("[W]e do not mean to suggest that, in the domain of copyrighted architectural depictions, only final construction drawings can contain protected expression."); *Sparaco v. Lawler, Matusky[,] Skelly Eng'rs LLP*, 303 F.3d 460, 469 (2d Cir. 2002) ("We do not mean to imply that technical drawings cannot achieve protected status unless they are sufficiently complete and detailed to support actual construction."). This reasoning should apply equally to architectural works, because our Circuit also has held that " '[i]n general, architectural works are subject to the same standards that apply to other copyrightable works.' " *Attia*, 201 F.3d at 53 n.3 (quoting 1 Nimmer § 2.20[A]). It is true that "generalized ideas and concepts pertaining to the placement of elements, traffic flow, and engineering strategies," or in other words, "ideas and concepts," are not worthy of protection. *Id.* at 57. However, once a design includes "specific expression and realization of . . . ideas," copying constitutes infringement. *Sparaco*, 303 F.3d at 469; *cf. Peter Pan Fabrics, Inc. v. Martin Weiner Corp.*, 274 F.2d 487, 489 (2d Cir. 1960) ("[N]o principle can be stated as to when an imitator has gone beyond copying the 'idea' and has borrowed its 'expression.' Decisions must therefore inevitably be ad hoc.") (L. Hand, J.).

Both Shine '99 and Olympic Tower are worthy of protection under the AWCPA. Shine '99 is a scale model of a twisting tower: Two of the tower's sides are smooth and taper straight toward the top creating a roughly triangular shape; the other two sides twist and taper as they rise, and one of those sides features four graded setbacks or levels that narrow as the tower rises. The top of the tower forms a parallelogram. Shine '99, although certainly a rough model, is more than a concept or an idea; it is a distinctive design for a building. As explained above, whether a tower actually could be constructed from this model is irrelevant. Defendants argue that the shape and form of Shine '99 are so rudimentary and standard that protecting it would be akin to protecting a particular geometric shape, such as "an ellipse, a pyramid, or an egg." However, the AWCPA protects "the design of a building as embodied in any tangible medium of expression . . . [including] the overall form as well as the arrangement and composition of spaces and elements in the design. . . ." 17 U.S.C. § 101. Individual arguably "standard" elements of Shine '99, such as its twist or its setbacks, might not be worthy of protection, but the arrangement and composition of the various elements in the model do at least arguably constitute the "design of a building" under the AWCPA.

The same is true for Olympic Tower, which is a much more intricate and detailed design than Shine '99. The copyrighted Olympic Tower materials include two models of the tower, one of the building's internal supports and one of its external appearance. Both models show that the building twists on all four sides; comparing the models reveals that the internal diamond-shaped grid supporting the tower is reflected and repeated in the external "skin" on its facade — a design that Childs commented on during his evaluation of Shine's work. Shine also copyrighted elevation sketches of the tower to display the building's core at different levels, a photomontage of what the building might look like against the New York sky, as well as what appears to be a sketch of the undulating triangular grid design for the exterior of the building. The detailed and specific materials Shine copyrighted for Olympic Tower certainly constitute the "design of a building," and qualify it as an architectural work under the AWCPA.

B. Originality

Defendants next claim that neither Shine '99 nor Olympic Tower is sufficiently original to warrant protection under the AWCPA. Using the House Committee Report on the AWCPA as their guide, defendants argue for a two-step analysis of the originality and functionality of an architectural work: First, the House Report noted, the work in question should be examined for the presence of original design elements. If such elements exist and are not functionally required, the Report concluded, then the work is protectable. Following this framework, defendants argue that no single part of Shine's work is original; that any parts that might be original are functionally required to support its design and therefore unprotectable; and that the arrangement of the various design elements featured in Shine's work is a compilation not meriting protection under existing law.

In this analysis, defendants fly high and fast over the large body of Supreme Court and Second Circuit case law on originality and copyright infringement, as well as the text of the AWCPA, which states that "the overall form as well as the arrangement and composition of spaces and elements in the design" of an architectural work may be the subject of a valid copyright. 17 U.S.C. § 101. First, defendants fail to acknowledge that plaintiff's "certificates of [copyright] registration constitute prima facie evidence of the validity not only of their copyrights, but also of the originality of [the] works." *Boisson v. Banian, Ltd.*, 273 F.3d 262, 268 (2d Cir. 2001); *see also* 17 U.S.C. § 410(c) (a copyright registration certificate, when issued within five years of the first publication of the work, is prima facie evidence of ownership of a valid copyright). It is also true, however, that originality is "the sine qua non of copyright," *Feist*, 499 U.S. at 345, and if a work is not original, then it is not protectable. If a certain element within a work is not original, that element is not protectable "even if other elements, or the work as a whole, warrant protection." *Boisson*, 273 F.3d at 268.

Plaintiff need not clear a high bar in order for his architectural works to qualify as original:

> In the copyright context, originality means the work was independently
> created by its author, and not copied from someone else's work. The level
> of originality and creativity that must be shown is minimal, only an

"unmistakable dash of originality need be demonstrated, high standards of uniqueness in creativity are dispensed with."

Folio Impressions, Inc. v. Byer California, 937 F.2d 759, 764-65 (2d Cir. 1991) (quoting *Weissmann v. Freeman,* 868 F.2d 1313, 1321 (2d Cir. 1989)); *see also Gaste v. Kaiserman,* 863 F.2d 1061, 1066 (2d Cir. 1988) (describing the requirement of originality as "little more than a prohibition of actual copying") (internal quotation marks omitted). Additionally, our Circuit has held that "a work may be copyrightable even though it is entirely a compilation of unprotectible elements." *Knitwaves* [*Inc. v. Lollytags Ltd.*, 71 F.3d 996, 1003-04 (1995)].

If the court followed defendants' suggestion and analyzed the elements of plaintiff's works separately, comparing only those elements that are copyrightable to those present in the designs for the Freedom Tower, as our Circuit noted, "we might have to decide that there can be no originality in a painting because all colors of paint have been used somewhere in the past." *Id.* at 1003 (internal quotation marks omitted) . . .

Following this analysis, both Shine '99 and Olympic Tower at least arguably are protectable and original. It is true that, as defendants' expert points out, twisting towers have been built before. Towers with diamond-windowed facades have been built before. Towers with support grids similar to the one in Olympic Tower have been built before. Towers with setbacks have been built before. But defendants do not present any evidence that the particular combinations of design elements in either Shine '99 or Olympic Tower are unoriginal. These works each have at least the mere "dash of originality" required for copyrightability, not to mention that they both have been copyrighted, and therefore are prima facie original.

Defendants argue also that any original aspect of Olympic Tower's facade is functionally required by the support grid utilized by Shine, and therefore unprotectable. However, Shine's expert disputes this contention. Therefore, even if certain of the original design elements of Olympic Tower are dictated by functionality and therefore not copyrightable — a proposition for which there is no apparent support in the case law or the AWCPA — a material issue of fact on this matter remains for trial.

C. Infringement

[With regard to infringement, the court granted the defendants' motion for summary judgment in part, finding a lack of probative similarity between Shine '99 and the proposed Freedom Tower, and denied it in part, finding that "reasonable jurors could disagree as to the substantial similarity between Olympic Tower and the Freedom Tower."]

NOTES AND QUESTIONS

(1) *Preliminary considerations.* In general, the law relating to architectural works serves to remind us that there is nothing inevitable about the "useful articles" doctrine, which we saw earlier in conjunction with pictorial, graphic, and sculptural works. As far as the Copyright Act is concerned, the useful articles doctrine could

be swept away, in whole or part, by a stroke of the legislative pen (although vestiges of it might still remain in the case law by virtue of the idea-expression dichotomy). Indeed, that is precisely what occurred in 1990, when the Copyright Act was amended by the Architectural Works Copyright Protection Act ("AWCPA") to provide protection for architectural works — which generally had been denied protection previously on the grounds that their utility was too closely integrated with their function.

(2) *The principal case.* The first issue raised in *Shine* is whether the plaintiff's sketches and models qualify as "architectural works." Is there any support for the defendant's view that only designs that are detailed enough to be constructed qualify? *See Scholz Design, Inc. v. Sard Custom Homes, LLC*, 691 F.3d 182 (2d Cir. 2012) (rejecting the argument that plaintiff's drawings "were not entitled to copyright protection because they lacked sufficient detail to allow for construction of the homes depicted."). If that standard was adopted, what types of designs (and designers) would receive or be denied copyright protection, in general?

(3) More generally, § 101 of the Copyright Act, as amended by the AWCPA, defines an "architectural work" as "the design of a building." The term "building," however, is *not* defined. The House Report indicates that the term includes habitable structures such as houses and office buildings, as well as "structures that are used, but not inhabited, by human beings," such as churches and gazebos. Not included are other three-dimensional structures such as dams and bridges. Does this excerpt clarify what is included in the term "building"?

(4) In *Yankee Candle Co. v. New England Candle Co.*, 14 F. Supp. 2d 154 (D. Mass. 1998), the court held that a store enclosed within a shopping mall was not an "architectural work" entitled to protection, even though the entire mall would qualify under the Act as a building. In other words, protection under the Act was held to extend to free-standing structures but not to individual units comprising a larger structure. The court reflected on the troubled meaning of the term "building": "The term's ambiguous nature might leave a structure like Fenway Park, one of the greatest architectural works ever designed, undeserving of copyright protection as a building without a roof over its baseball diamond (a space used for recreation, business, and some would say, religion)." *Id.*

Do you agree that the AWCPA should not be applied to structures within structures? Or to an uncovered ball park like Fenway Park? Incidentally, in the same case, the court found that the defendant had infringed the candle store's two-dimensional floor plans. Subsequently, however, the case was settled and the opinion vacated. 29 F. Supp. 2d 44 (D. Mass. 1998).

(5) The next issue in *Shine* is whether the plaintiff's designs were sufficiently "original" to qualify for copyright protection. The court notes that twisted towers, diamond-windowed facades, setbacks, and support grids similar to Shine's have all existed before. Are you persuaded by its conclusion that Shine's designs were nonetheless original? Note that the House Report states that "creativity in architecture frequently takes the form of a selection, coordination, or arrangement of unprotectible elements into an original, protectible whole." Does this explain the court's ruling? *See also Oravec v. Sunny Isles Luxury Ventures, L.C.*, 527 F.3d 1218, 1225 (11th Cir. 2008) ("while individual standard features and architectural ele-

ments classifiable as ideas are not themselves copyrightable, an architect's original combination or arrangement of such features may be").

You may want to compare the opinion in *Shine* with *Trek Leasing, Inc. v. United States*, 66 Fed. Cl. 8 (2005), a case involving alleged infringement by the U.S. Postal Service of the plaintiff's design for a post office. The court in *Trek Leasing* found that most of the plaintiff's design was not original, in part because the design was based upon an existing standard Postal Service design, and in part because many elements were standard in the "BIA Pueblo Revival" style of architecture. After eliminating these features from consideration, the court concluded that the remaining features were not infringed. Should a court "dissect" an architectural design in this manner, or should it take a more holistic view of the design, as in *Shine*? You may want to reconsider this question after you have studied infringement in Chapter 8.

(6)   The opinion in *Shine* refers to the two-step copyrightability analysis for architectural works envisioned by the passage in the House Report concluding: "If the [original] design elements are not functionally required, the work is protectible without regard to physical or conceptual separability." The court is skeptical, however, calling the lack of copyright protection for functional elements "a proposition for which there is no apparent support in the case law or the AWCPA." How much weight should the House Report be given in this situation? Should considerations of functionality limit copyright protection for architectural works? You may want to revisit this question after you have read the decision in *Computer Associates, Inc. v. Altai* in § 8.03.

(7)   *Additional issues.* Most architectural works cases deal with alleged infringement of designs less fanciful than the one involved in *Shine*. A good deal of litigation concerns competing plans for mass-produced "semi-custom" development homes, which consist of a combination of elements that might be called "standard features," incapable of copyright protection in themselves. In such cases, the issue of copyrightability may turn on whether the particular design in which rights are claimed represents a sufficient variation on preexisting structures. *See, e.g., Richmond Homes Management, Inc. v. Raintree, Inc.*, 862 F. Supp. 1517 (W.D. Va. 1994), *aff'd in relevant part, rev'd in part*, 66 F.3d 316 (4th Cir. 1995); *see also Watkins v. Chesapeake Custom Homes*, 330 F. Supp. 2d 563 (D. Md. 2004). The standard is not a particularly exacting one, as we will see in our more general discussion of derivative works in the following section of this chapter. But, of course, the resulting right is a relatively "thin" copyright, which a would-be copyist may be able to "design around," if he or she bothers to try. How big a problem is this? Doesn't it depend on what the owners of copyright in architectural designs are most concerned with protecting themselves against?

(8)   Like most architectural works cases, those just cited involve relatively "mundane" works. Is copyright protection really necessary to protect these works? For that matter, is copyright needed at all to encourage creativity in the field of architecture? How is it that the United States was at the forefront of architectural creativity for more than 100 years without such protection?

(9)   *Kootenia Homes, Inc. v. Reliable Homes, Inc.*, 2002 U.S. Dist. LEXIS 235 (D. Minn., Jan. 3, 2002), involves an interesting (but not atypical) "infringement"

scenario. A couple in the market for a new house toured a model designed by the plaintiff and passed on information about it to the builder who was creating a home design for them. The builder, in turn, incorporated some of this information into his design — but did not copy directly from the plaintiff's plans or structure. How do you imagine such a case is likely to come out?

(10) Under the relevant provisions of the AWCPA, discussed in detail in *Hunt v. Pasternack*, 192 F.3d 877 (9th Cir. 1999), protection of architectural works under the Copyright Act is limited to: (a) architectural works created on or after December 1, 1990 (the date of enactment of the Act); and (b) works that were unconstructed, but nonetheless embodied in unpublished plans or drawings, as of that date (protection for which, if not constructed by 2003, has now expired). This excludes from protection all those works of architecture embodied in existing buildings and published plans or drawings as of December 1, 1990. Thus, as often is the case in copyright law, one cannot forget prior statutes and case law: here, specifically, the law of "publication," which we will explore in depth in Chapter 6.

What about structures that were in the process of construction on Dec. 1, 1990? In *Richard J. Zitz, Inc. v. Dos Santos Pereira*, 232 F.3d 290, 292-93 (2d Cir. 2000), the Second Circuit held that AWCPA did not protect those works that were "substantially constructed" as of that date. The court explained:

> If we are to understand "constructed" as having the same significance as "publication" for purposes of copyright protection, then it seems more sensible to say that the equivalent of publication occurs when others can readily see — and copy — the work in question. On that basis, habitability and final completion seem much less significant, and whether the architectural work is substantially constructed is much closer to what Congress intended in the statute.

Is "substantially constructed" likely to prove a robust and reliable standard? Does the explanation provided by the court help?

(11) In the process of shaping the AWCPA, various industry groups (*e.g.*, real estate owners) and public domain lobbyists successfully pushed to impose limitations on the scope of protection for architectural works. The limitations are codified in § 120 of the Act. Under § 120(a), the copyright owner in a constructed architectural work cannot prevent the distribution or public display of pictures, paintings, photographs, or other pictorial representations of the work, if the building is located in or visible from a public place. Does the limitation make policy sense? Why should anyone be able to profit from selling images of someone else's design? Many other national laws, incidentally, don't go this far: They may exempt images in which protected designs appear incidentally, or in the background, but not ones where the design is the primary focus (so to speak).

(12) In *Leicester v. Warner Bros.*, 232 F.3d 1212 (9th Cir. 2000), the defendant relied on the § 120(a) exception in filming a building in downtown Los Angeles for use in the movie *Batman Forever*. The plaintiff, however, claimed that the five towers and gates that formed the "streetwall" of a courtyard adjacent to the building were part of a sculptural work he had created in the courtyard called the Zanja Madre. Because the § 120(a) exception on its face applies only to buildings,

and not to other works of public art, the court had to determine whether the "streetwall" portion of the sculpture was or was not part of the "building" itself.

"Zanja Madre"
Courtesy of Andrew Leicester, Public Artist

In a fractured ruling that elicited three opinions from the three-judge panel, the Ninth Circuit affirmed the District Court's ruling that the streetwall towers "have functional aspects designed to be part of the building plan and from their appearance are designed to match up with the architecture of the building . . . and are therefore an integrated part of the 'architectural work.' " *Id.* at 1215. In her lead opinion, Judge Rymer noted that the streetwall "was not a creative aspect of Leicester's work; it was an architectural element mandated by" the city planning agency." *Id.* at 1218. Moreover,

> The streetwall towers are designed to appear as part of the building. . . . The lanterns on the lantern towers match the lanterns attached to the building at its third floor level; they are made of the same material and are at the same height as those on the building. . . . In addition, the Zanja Madre streetwall serves the functional purpose of channeling traffic into the courtyard, as metal gates, which open and close for control, latch onto the lantern towers.

Id.

Leicester contended that the towers were nonetheless "conceptually separate" from the building and were thus protectable, relying on pre-1990 case law that had protected nonutilitarian sculptures (such as gargoyles and stained glass windows) incorporated into a work of architecture. Judge Rymer found it unnecessary to address this argument, agreeing with the District Court that the streetwall towers were not "conceptually separate" from the building. Concurring in the judgment, Judge Tashima read the AWCPA "as rejecting application of the conceptual separability test where the architectural work and the artistic work are so closely and functionally intertwined as in this case." *Id.* at 1222. Otherwise, he concluded,

Congress' intent in creating the § 120(a) exception would be rendered meaningless: "To require one to wade through the morass of conceptual separability before he can exercise the right granted by § 120(a) . . . cannot be what Congress intended." *Id.* Dissenting, Judge Fisher expressed the opinion that "[if] the towers can be seen as conceptually separate from the [building], then they are entitled to full copyright protection as a sculptural work under 17 U.S.C. § 102(5), despite being part of an architectural work." *Id.* at 1225. He explained: "While it is true that Congress did not want architects to have to survive the morass of separability in order to obtain copyright protection for their creations, there is nothing in the AWCPA that suggests Congress intended to prevent sculptors and other artists who created PGS works that were attached to buildings from attempting to satisfy the difficult separability test and thereby gain full PGS copyright protection for their works." *Id.* at 1232.

Is the concept of conceptual separability that divides the judges in *Leicester* the same one we encountered back in our examination of the copyrightability of pictorial, graphic and sculptural works, or a different one which happens to have the same name? Do the multiple tests for conceptual similarity discussed in connection with *Pivot Point* make sense in the present context?

(13) The concurrence and the dissent in *Leicester* both are concerned about the problem of predictability. How can a would-be user know in advance whether a particular artistic feature of a building design is or is not freely available for pictorial reproduction? The dissent's "conceptual separability"-based approach entails certain risks of uncertainty. Moreover, even if one concludes that a separate sculptural work exists, then the "fair use" doctrine comes into play, which, as we will see in Chapter 10, has its own uncertainties. The concurrence avoids these uncertainties by denying separate copyright protection for pictorial or sculptural elements embodied in architectural works. Which approach, broadly speaking, is likely to be the more protective of artists' creativity? Of the public interest?

(14) Section 120 includes another substantial limitation: Notwithstanding the right to prepare derivative works in § 106(2), § 120(b) allows the owner of a building to destroy or make alterations in a building embodying an architectural work. This provision also poses interesting questions. For example, does the building owner's right of alteration include the right to make plans that copy the design of the original? *See Javelin Investments, LLC v. McGinnis*, 2007 U.S. Dist. LEXIS 21472 (S.D. Tex., Jan. 23, 2007) (yes). More generally, does the perceived necessity for a destruction-and-alteration right imply that the copyright model for architectural works is an awkward fit in the real world of architectural design?

(15) Might protection for architectural works have a chilling effect on progress in the realm of architectural design? Will it discourage architects from incorporating certain stylistic ideas into their works, owing to fear of litigation? In considering this question, consider also the possibility of trade dress protection for the design of a building. *See, e.g., Rock & Roll Hall of Fame & Museum, Inc. v. Gentile Prods.*, 134 F.3d 749 (6th Cir. 1998).

(16) Finally, it is important to reiterate that protection for architectural works under the AWCPA *supplements*, rather than replaces the pre-existing protection for architectural plans, drawings, and models as pictorial, graphic, or sculptural

works. This point was made forcefully by the Second Circuit in *Scholz Design*, cited above: "[t]he fact that Scholz's drawings might or might not be protected under the AWCPA . . . does not deprive them of the protection they have as pictorial works." *See also T-Peg, Inc. v. Vermont Timber Works, Inc.*, 459 F.3d 97, 109–10 (1st Cir. 2006); *Oravec*, 527 F.3d at 1228 n.8.

As a result of this overlapping protection, the Copyright Office requires separate registrations if building plans are being claimed as both technical drawings and architectural works. 37 C.F.R. § 202.11(c)(4). *Cf. Home Design Services, Inc. v. Starwood Const., Inc.*, 801 F. Supp. 2d 1111 (D. Colo. 2011), in which the defendant initially registered its design as a "technical drawing," but amended the registration to "architectural work" before it discovered the alleged infringement. What should the result be if the amendment occurred *after* the alleged infringement was discovered? See Chapter 6 for more information on when errors in registration are considered "material."

§ 3.02   DERIVATIVE WORKS AND COMPILATIONS UNDER § 103

Section 103 of the 1976 Act extends copyright protection to "compilations and derivative works" as special forms of the "works of authorship" illustrated by the categories in § 102. Compilations and derivative works, although listed separately in § 103(a), nevertheless are types of literary works, musical works, or other § 102(a) works. A derivative work might take the form of a play or a movie, while a compilation might take the form of a literary anthology or a musical medley. The fixation and originality requirements apply to all works described by §§ 102(a) and 103(a); and the prohibition on copyrighting ideas, concepts, principles, and so on, imposed by § 102(b), applies just as forcefully to derivative works and compilations as it does to the works listed in § 102(a).

How, then, do § 103 works differ from § 102 works? The answer is that the latter typically are what might be called "first generation" works, composed essentially (although not, of course, exclusively) of materials created by their authors; derivative works and compilations, on the other hand, fundamentally are "second generation" works based on *preexisting matter*. The preexisting matter in the musical comedy *My Fair Lady*, for example, is the George Bernard Shaw stage play *Pygmalion*. Lerner and Loewe created the music and lyrics sung by Henry Higgins, Eliza Doolittle, and their fellow *My Fair Lady* characters. But the characters themselves, the key elements of the plot and much of the dialogue were Shaw's creations. Similarly, an anthology compiling Shakespeare's wit and wisdom is *based upon* Shakespeare's works, although the choice and editing of his words are the compiler's. The matter borrowed by the author of the derivative work or compilation may be nothing more than facts, as in an almanac bringing together data exclusively within the public domain. So long as the author of a derivative work or compilation incorporates preexisting matter and satisfies both the fixation and originality requirements, the work qualifies for copyright protection under § 103(a).

The remaining major issue concerning derivative works and compilations should come as no surprise. It is the *extent* to which the matter contained in the work —

both the preexisting matter and the matter contributed by the § 103 author — is protected by the copyright in the work as a whole. According to § 103(b):

> The copyright in a compilation or derivative work extends only to the material contributed by the author of such work, as distinguished from the preexisting material employed in the work, and does not imply any exclusive right in the preexisting material. The copyright in such work is independent of, and does not affect or enlarge the scope, duration, ownership, or subsistence of, any copyright protection in the preexisting material.

What all of this means, in the context of concrete cases, is the subject of the following section.

[A] Introduction

Statutory References

1976 Act: §§ 101 ("collective work," "compilation," "derivative work"), 103
1909 Act: § 7

Legislative History

H.R. REP. No. 94-1476 at 57-58,
reprinted in 1976 U.S.C.C.A.N. 5659, 5670-71

SECTION 103. COMPILATIONS AND DERIVATIVE WORKS

Section 103 complements section 102: A compilation or derivative work is copyrightable if it represents an "original work of authorship" and falls within one or more of the categories listed in section 102. Read together, the two sections make plain that the criteria of copyrightable subject matter stated in section 102 apply with full force to works that are entirely original and to those containing preexisting material. Section 103(b) is also intended to define, more sharply and clearly than does section 7 of the [1909 Act], the important interrelationship and correlation between protection of preexisting and of "new" material in a particular work. The most important point here is one that is commonly misunderstood today: copyright in a "new version" covers only the material added by the later author, and has no effect one way or the other on the copyright or public domain status of the preexisting material.

Between them the terms "compilations" and "derivative works," which are defined in section 101, comprehend every copyrightable work that employs preexisting material or data of any kind. There is necessarily some overlapping between the two, but they basically represent different concepts. A "compilation" results from a process of selecting, bringing together, organizing, and arranging previously existing material of all kinds, regardless of whether the individual items in the material have been or ever could have been subject to copyright. A "derivative work," on the other hand, requires a process of recasting, transforming, or adapting "one or more preexisting works"; the "preexisting work" must come within the general subject matter of copyright set forth in section 102, regardless of whether it is or was ever copyrighted.

The second part of the sentence that makes up section 103(a) deals with the status of a compilation or derivative work unlawfully employing preexisting copyrighted material. In providing that protection does not extend to "any part of the work in which such material has been used unlawfully," the bill prevents an infringer from benefiting, through copyright protection, from committing an unlawful act, but preserves protection for those parts of the work that do not employ the preexisting work. Thus, an unauthorized translation of a novel could not be copyrighted at all, but the owner of copyright in an anthology of poetry could sue someone who infringed the whole anthology, even though the infringer proves that publication of one of the poems was unauthorized. Under this provision, copyright could be obtained as long as the use of the preexisting work was not "unlawful," even though the consent of the copyright owner had not been obtained. For instance, the unauthorized reproduction of a work might be "lawful" under the doctrine of fair use or an applicable foreign law, and if so the work incorporating it could be copyrighted.

[For a fuller excerpt from H.R. Rep. No. 94-1476, see Part Three of the Casebook Supplement.]

[B] Derivative Works

SCHROCK v. LEARNING CURVE INTERNATIONAL, INC.
United States Court of Appeals, Seventh Circuit
586 F.3d 513 (2009)

SYKES, CIRCUIT JUDGE:

HIT Entertainment ("HIT") owns the copyright to the popular "Thomas & Friends" train characters, and it licensed Learning Curve International ("Learning Curve") to make toy figures of its characters. Learning Curve in turn hired Daniel Schrock, a professional photographer, to take pictures of the toys for promotional materials. Learning Curve used Schrock's services on a regular basis for about four years and thereafter continued to use some of his photographs in its advertising and on product packaging. After Learning Curve stopped giving him work, Schrock registered his photos for copyright protection and sued Learning Curve and HIT for infringement.

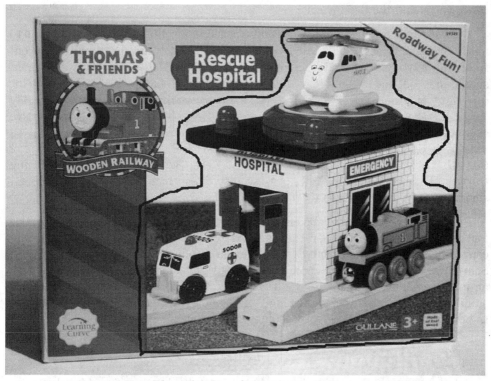

Photo by Dan Schrock (circled)

The district court granted summary judgment for the defendants, holding that Schrock has no copyright in the photos. The court classified the photos as "derivative works" under the Copyright Act — derivative, that is, of the "Thomas & Friends" characters, for which HIT owns the copyright — and held that Schrock needed permission from Learning Curve (HIT's licensee) not only to make the photographs but also to copyright them. Because Schrock had permission to make but not permission to copyright the photos, the court dismissed his claim for copyright infringement.

History *derivative* *work*

We reverse. We assume for purposes of this decision that the district court correctly classified Schrock's photographs as derivative works. It does not follow, however, that Schrock needed authorization from Learning Curve to copyright the photos. As long as he was authorized to make the photos (he was), he owned the copyright in the photos to the extent of their incremental original expression. In requiring permission to make *and* permission to copyright the photos, the district court relied on language in *Gracen v. Bradford Exchange*, 698 F.2d 300 (7th Cir. 1983), suggesting that both are required for copyright in a derivative work. We have more recently explained, however, that copyright in a derivative work arises by operation of law — not through authority from the owner of the copyright in the underlying work — although the parties may alter this default rule by agreement. *See Liu v. Price Waterhouse LLP*, 302 F.3d 749, 755 (7th Cir. 2002). Schrock created the photos with permission and therefore owned the copyright to the photos *provided* they satisfied the other requirements for copyright and the parties did not

Holding *reverse*

contract around the default rule.

We also take this opportunity to clarify another aspect of *Gracen* that is prone to misapplication. *Gracen* said that "a derivative work must be substantially different from the underlying work to be copyrightable." 698 F.2d at 305. This statement should not be understood to require a heightened standard of originality for copyright in a derivative work. We have more recently explained that "the only 'originality' required for [a] new work to be copyrightable . . . is enough expressive variation from public-domain or other existing works to enable the new work to be readily distinguished from its predecessors." *Bucklew v. Hawkins, Ash, Baptie & Co., LLP*, 329 F.3d 923, 929 (7th Cir. 2003). Here, Schrock's photos of Learning Curve's "Thomas & Friends" toys possessed sufficient incremental original expression to qualify for copyright.

But the record doesn't tell us enough about the agreements between the parties for us to determine whether they agreed to alter the default rule regarding copyright or whether Learning Curve had an implied license to continue to use Schrock's photos. Whether Schrock could copyright his photographs and maintain an infringement action against the defendants depends on the contractual understandings between Schrock, Learning Curve, and HIT. Accordingly, we remand to the district court for further proceedings consistent with this opinion. . . .

II. Discussion

Schrock argues that the district judge mistakenly classified his photos as derivative works and misread or misapplied *Gracen*. He contends that his photos are not derivative works, and even if they are, his copyright is valid and enforceable because he had permission from Learning Curve to photograph the underlying copyrighted works and his photos contained sufficient incremental original expression to qualify for copyright. HIT and Learning Curve defend the district court's determination that the photos are derivative works and argue that the court properly read *Gracen* to require permission to copyright as well as permission to make the derivative works. Alternatively, they maintain that Schrock's photographs contain insufficient originality to be copyrightable and that copyright protection is barred under the *scènes à faire* or merger doctrines. Finally, the defendants ask us to affirm on the independent ground that Schrock orally granted them an unlimited license to use his works. . . .

Much of the briefing on appeal — and most of the district court's analysis — concerned the classification of the photos as derivative works. A "derivative work" is:

> [A] work based upon one or more preexisting works, such as a translation, musical arrangement, dramatization, fictionalization, motion picture version, sound recording, art reproduction, abridgment, condensation, or any other form in which a work may be recast, transformed, or adapted. A work consisting of editorial revisions, annotations, elaborations, or other modifications which, as a whole, represent an original work of authorship, is a "derivative work".

17 U.S.C. § 101. The Copyright Act specifically grants the author of a derivative

work copyright protection in the incremental original expression he contributes as long as the derivative work does not infringe the underlying work. The copyright in a derivative work, however, "extends only to the material contributed by the author of such work, as distinguished from the preexisting material employed in the work." 17 U.S.C. § 103(b).

A. Photographs as Derivative Works

Whether photographs of a copyrighted work are derivative works is the subject of deep disagreement among courts and commentators alike. The district court held that Schrock's photos came within the definition of derivative works because they "recast, transformed, or adapted" the three-dimensional toys into a different, two-dimensional medium. For this conclusion the judge relied in part on language in *Gracen* and in the Ninth Circuit's decision in *Ets-Hokin v. Skyy Spirits, Inc.*, 225 F.3d 1068 (9th Cir. 2000), recognizing, however, that neither decision directly decided the matter. *Gracen* did not involve photographs at all, and although *Ets-Hokin* did, the Ninth Circuit ultimately sidestepped the derivative-works question and rested its decision on other grounds. Id. at 1081. . . .

We need not resolve the issue definitively here. The classification of Schrock's photos as derivative works does not affect the applicable legal standard for determining copyrightability, although as we have noted, it does determine the scope of copyright protection. Accordingly, we will assume without deciding that each of Schrock's photos qualifies as a derivative work within the meaning of the Copyright Act.

B. Originality and Derivative Works

. . . Federal courts have historically applied a generous standard of originality in evaluating photographic works for copyright protection. In some cases, the original expression may be found in the staging and creation of the scene depicted in the photograph. But in many cases, the photographer does not invent the scene or create the subject matter depicted in it. Rather, the original expression he contributes lies in the *rendition* of the subject matter — that is, the effect created by the combination of his choices of perspective, angle, lighting, shading, focus, lens, and so on. Most photographs contain at least some originality in their rendition, except perhaps for a very limited class of photographs that can be characterized as "slavish copies" of an underlying work, *Bridgeman Art Library, Ltd. v. Corel Corp.*, 25 F. Supp. 2d 421, 427 (S.D.N.Y. 1998) (finding no originality in transparencies of paintings where the goal was to reproduce those works exactly and thus to minimize or eliminate any individual expression).

Our review of Schrock's photographs convinces us that they do not fall into the narrow category of photographs that can be classified as "slavish copies," lacking any independently created expression. To be sure, the photographs are accurate depictions of the three-dimensional "Thomas & Friends" toys, but Schrock's artistic and technical choices combine to create a two-dimensional image that is subtly but nonetheless sufficiently his own.[3] This is confirmed by Schrock's deposition testimony describing his creative process in depicting the toys. Schrock explained how he used various camera and lighting techniques to make the toys look more "life like," "personable," and "friendly." He explained how he tried to give the toys "a little bit of dimension" and that it was his goal to make the toys "a little bit better than what they look like when you actually see them on the shelf." The original expression in the representative sample is not particularly great (it was not meant to be), but it is enough under the applicable standard to warrant the limited copyright protection accorded derivative works under § 103(b).

Aside from arguing that the works fail under the generally accepted test for originality, Learning Curve and HIT offer two additional reasons why we should conclude that Schrock's photographs are not original. First, they claim that the photos are intended to serve the "purely utilitarian function" of identifying products for consumers. The purpose of the photographs, however, is irrelevant. *See Bleistein v. Donaldson Lithographing Co.*, 188 U.S. 239, 251-52 (1903); *SHL Imaging, Inc. [v. Artisan House, Inc.]*, 117 F. Supp. 2d [301], 311 [(S.D.N.Y. 2000)] ("That the photographs were intended solely for commercial use has no bearing on their protectibility.").

The defendants' second and more substantial argument is that it is not enough that Schrock's photographs might pass the ordinary test for originality; they claim that as derivative works, the photos are subject to a higher standard of originality. A leading copyright commentator disagrees. The Nimmer treatise maintains that the quantum of originality required for copyright in a derivative work is the same as that required for copyright in any other work. *See* 1 NIMMER ON COPYRIGHT § 3.01, at 3-2, § 3.03[A], at 3-7. More particularly, Nimmer says the relevant standard is whether a derivative work contains a "nontrivial" variation from the preexisting work "sufficient to render the derivative work distinguishable from [the] prior work in any meaningful manner." *Id.* § 3.03[A], at 3-10. The caselaw generally follows this formulation. *See, e.g., Eden Toys, Inc. v. Florelee Undergarment Co.*, 697 F.2d 27, 34-35 (2d Cir. 1982) (holding that numerous minor changes in an illustration of Paddington Bear were sufficiently nontrivial because they combined to give Paddington a "different, cleaner 'look.'"). . . .

Learning Curve and HIT argue that our decision in *Gracen* established a more demanding standard of originality for derivative works. *Gracen* involved an artistic competition in which artists were invited to submit paintings of the character Dorothy from the Metro-Goldwyn-Mayer ("MGM") movie *The Wizard of Oz*. Participating artists were given a still photograph of Dorothy from the film as an exemplar, and the paintings were solicited and submitted with the understanding that the best painting would be chosen for a series of collector's plates. Plaintiff Gracen prevailed in the competition, but she refused to sign the contract allowing her painting to be used in the collector's plates. The competition sponsor commis-

---

[3] We note, however, that a mere shift in medium, without more, is generally insufficient to satisfy the requirement of originality for copyright in a derivative work. *Durham Indus., Inc. v. Tomy Corp.*, 630 F.2d 905, 910 (2d Cir. 1980) (noting that circuit's rejection of "the contention that the originality requirement of copyrightability can be satisfied by the mere reproduction of a work of art in a different medium"); *L. Batlin & Son, Inc. v. Snyder*, 536 F.2d 486, 491 (2d Cir. 1976) (same).

sioned another artist to create a similar plate, and Gracen sued the sponsor, MGM, and the artist for copyright infringement. We held that Gracen could not maintain her infringement suit because her painting, a derivative work, was not "substantially different from the underlying work to be copyrightable."

Gracen drew this language from an influential Second Circuit decision, *L. Batlin & Son, Inc. v. Snyder*, 536 F.2d 486 (2d Cir. 1976). Read in context, however, the cited language from *L. Batlin* did not suggest that a heightened standard of originality applies to derivative works. To the contrary, the Second Circuit said only that to be copyrightable a work must " 'contain some substantial, not merely trivial originality.' " *Id.* at 490. . . . The court explained that for derivative works, as for any other work, "[t]he test of originality is concededly one with a low threshold in that all that is needed is that the author contributed something more than a merely trivial variation, something recognizably his own." *Id.* . . .

The concern expressed in *Gracen* was that a derivative work could be so similar in appearance to the underlying work that in a subsequent infringement suit brought by a derivative author, it would be difficult to separate the original elements of expression in the derivative and underlying works in order to determine whether one derivative work infringed another. The opinion offered the example of artists A and B who both painted their versions of the Mona Lisa, a painting in the public domain. *See Gracen*, 698 F.2d at 304. "[I]f the difference between the original and A's reproduction is slight, the difference between A's and B's reproductions will also be slight, so that if B had access to A's reproductions the trier of fact will be hard-pressed to decide whether B was copying A or copying the Mona Lisa itself." *Id.*

No doubt this concern is valid. But nothing in the Copyright Act suggests that derivative works are subject to a more exacting originality requirement than other works of authorship. Indeed, we have explained since *Gracen* that "the only 'originality' required for [a] new work to b[e] copyrightable . . . is enough expressive variation from public-domain or other existing works to enable the new work to be readily distinguished from its predecessors." *Bucklew*, 329 F.3d at 929. We emphasized in *Bucklew* that this standard does not require a "high degree of [incremental] originality." *Id.*

We think *Gracen* must be read in light of *L. Batlin*, on which it relied, and *Bucklew*, which followed it. And doing so reveals the following general principles: (1) the originality requirement for derivative works is not more demanding than the originality requirement for other works; and (2) the key inquiry is whether there is sufficient nontrivial expressive variation in the derivative work to make it distinguishable from the underlying work in some meaningful way. This focus on the presence of nontrivial "distinguishable variation" adequately captures the concerns articulated in *Gracen* without unduly narrowing the copyrightability of derivative works. It is worth repeating that the copyright in a derivative work is thin, extending only to the incremental original expression contributed by the author of the derivative work. *See* 17 U.S.C. § 103(b).

As applied to photographs, we have already explained that the original expression in a photograph generally subsists in its rendition of the subject matter. If the photographer's rendition of a copyrighted work varies enough from the underlying work to enable the photograph to be distinguished from the underlying work (aside from the obvious shift from three dimensions to two, *see supra* n.3), then the photograph contains sufficient incremental originality to qualify for copyright. Schrock's photos of the "Thomas & Friends" toys are highly accurate product photos but contain minimally sufficient variation in angle, perspective, lighting, and dimension to be distinguishable from the underlying works; they are not "slavish copies." Accordingly, the photos qualify for the limited derivative-work copyright provided by § 103(b). . . . However narrow that copyright might be, it at least protects against the kind of outright copying that occurred here.

C. Authorization and Derivative Works

To be copyrightable, a derivative work must not be infringing. See 17 U.S.C. § 103(a). . . . The owner of the copyright in the underlying work has the exclusive right to "prepare derivative works based upon the copyrighted work," 17 U.S.C. § 106(2), and "it is a copyright infringement to make or sell a derivative work without a license from the owner of the copyright on the work from which the derivative work is derived," *Bucklew*, 329 F.3d at 930. This means the author of a derivative work must have permission to make the work from the owner of the copyright in the underlying work; *Gracen* suggested, however, that the author of a derivative work must *also* have permission to *copyright* it. The district court relied on this language from *Gracen* to conclude that Schrock has no copyright in his photos because he was not authorized by Learning Curve to copyright them. This was error.

. . . *Gracen's* language presupposing a permission-to-copyright requirement was dicta; the case was actually decided on nonoriginality grounds. More importantly, the dicta was mistaken; there is nothing in the Copyright Act requiring the author of a derivative work to obtain permission to copyright his work from the owner of the copyright in the underlying work. To the contrary, the Act provides that copyright in a derivative work, like copyright in any other work, arises by operation of law once the author's original expression is fixed in a tangible medium. . . . This principle applies with equal force to derivative works.

The leading treatise on copyright law confirms this basic understanding. "[T]he right to claim copyright in a noninfringing derivative work arises by operation of law, not through authority from the copyright owner of the underlying work." 1 NIMMER ON COPYRIGHT § 3.06, at 3-34.34. We have cited Nimmer with approval on this point. *See Liu*, 302 F.3d at 755. As we noted in *Liu*, however, there is an important proviso explained in the treatise: "[I]f the pertinent agreement between the parties affirmatively bars the licensee from obtaining copyright protection even in a licensed derivative work, that contractual provision would appear to govern." 1 NIMMER ON COPYRIGHT § 3.06, at 3-34.34; *see also Liu*, 302 F.3d at 755. . . .

In this case, the evidence submitted with the summary-judgment motion does not establish as a matter of law that the parties adjusted Schrock's rights by contract; . . . it may be a jury question. We say "may" because further development of the record might resolve the remaining liability questions as a matter of law. It is undisputed that Schrock was authorized to photograph the "Thomas & Friends" toys, and as the creator of the photos, Schrock's copyright arose by operation of law.

We cannot tell, however, whether the parties altered this default rule in their agreements. . . .

Learning Curve argues in the alternative that Schrock granted it an unlimited license to use his photos, but on this issue the record is also ambiguous. We leave it to the district court to sort out . . . whether the evidence requires a trial to determine liability among the parties.

Accordingly, for all the foregoing reasons, we REVERSE the judgment of the district court and REMAND for further proceedings consistent with this opinion.

NOTES AND QUESTIONS

(1) The court in *Schrock* "assume[s] without deciding that each of Schrock's photos qualifies as a derivative work within the meaning of the Copyright Act." Suppose, however, that *you* had to decide that question in a case which required its resolution. Where would you start? The Copyright Act defines a derivative work in § 101 as "a work *based upon one or more preexisting works*, such as a translation, musical arrangement, dramatization, fictionalization, motion picture version, sound recording, art reproduction, abridgment, condensation, or any other form *in which a work may be recast, transformed, or adapted*" (emphasis added). What does the emphasized language mean? Assuming that a second work is "based upon" a prior work and adds thereto whatever may be the requisite quantum of creativity (see the discussion below), isn't the second work, by definition, a derivative work? Or is something more than incremental originality required to "recast, transform[] or adapt[]" an underlying work?

Leaving aside for a moment the contested work in *Schrock*, would a painting based upon an image from a beloved motion picture, so long as it is not a slavish copy, qualify (albeit with protection only for the originality added by the painter)? How about a "lexicon" based upon a beloved children's fantasy book, which defines various people, places, and things (using quotes from the book) in alphabetical order? Should the answer turn upon whether the second creator had the permission of the copyright holder in the first work?

(2) The term "derivative work" serves two different functions in the Copyright Act. In § 103, it refers to a category of works which potentially are protectible under copyright law — provided that the constitutional and statutory prerequisites for protection are fulfilled. In § 106(2), by contrast, the term is used to help specify conduct (the "prepar[ation of] derivative works based upon the copyrighted work") which, when undertaken without a copyright owner's authorization, may constitute infringement. Both functions are implicated in *Schrock*. In deciding these issues, the Seventh Circuit ruled that the lower court had improperly relied on *Gracen v. Bradford Exchange*, 698 F.2d 300 (7th Cir. 1983). The following notes examine the issues of originality and lawful use in the derivative work context, and the court's rationale for rejecting *Gracen*.

Derivative Works and the Originality Requirement

(3)   Section 103(a) provides that "[t]he subject matter of copyright *as specified in section 102* includes . . . derivative works" (emphasis added). The House Report interprets this to mean that "the criteria of copyrightable subject matter stated in section 102 apply with full force to works . . . containing preexisting material." Thus, to qualify for copyright protection, a derivative work must meet the statutory criterion of originality. How should a court determine whether a work "containing preexisting material" is sufficiently original?

Schrock purports to adopt the standard in *L. Batlin & Son, Inc. v. Snyder*, 536 F.2d 486 (2d Cir. 1976) (en banc), which is discussed in the notes below. To meet the standard, according to *Schrock*, the derivative work must manifest "sufficient nontrivial expressive variation . . . to make it distinguishable from the underlying work in some meaningful way."

(4)   *Schrock* is first and foremost a rejection of Judge Posner's opinion in *Gracen v. Bradford Exchange*, which involved the copyrightability of paintings based on stills from *The Wizard of Oz*. In *Gracen*, MGM licensed Bradford Exchange to use characters and scenes from its beloved motion picture (itself based on a series of books by L. Frank Baum) to create a set of collector's plates. Bradford invited several artists to submit paintings of Dorothy as played by Judy Garland, with the understanding that the artist who submitted the best painting would be offered a contract for the entire series. Gracen won the competition but refused Bradford's proffered contract. Bradford then turned to another artist, who was given Gracen's painting as an aid in making his own. Gracen brought an action for copyright infringement against Bradford. The court held that Gracen's painting was not an original derivative work within the meaning of copyright law.

In *Gracen*, the court opined that the test for copyrightability of a derivative work must be whether the second work is "substantially *different*" from the first. Although Judge Posner cites *Batlin* respectfully, *Gracen*'s language appeared to represent a significant *departure* from the *Batlin* standard — and, as the court in *Schrock* indicates, has been the subject of considerable criticism.

Even before *Schrock*, however, there were indications that Judge Posner himself may have thought better of the *Gracen* test. In *Saturday Evening Post Co. v. Rumbleseat Press, Inc.*, 816 F.2d 1191 (7th Cir. 1987), involving porcelain copies of Norman Rockwell paintings, he stated in dictum that derivative works are "copyrightable provided the derivative work has some incremental originality," citing *Gracen*. And in *Gaiman v. McFarlane*, 360 F.3d 644 (7th Cir. 2004), he stated that "the question is simply whether Medieval Spawn is sufficiently distinct from Spawn also to be copyrightable as a derivative work." Is it parsing language too finely to inquire whether all of these formulations are distinct from one another? Or do they really represent the same test in different language?

Gracen's Painting and Dorothy/Judy Garland from "The Wizard of Oz"

(5) Judge Posner justified his *Gracen* rule as being necessary to avoid "overlapping claims." In a journal article, he explained how a relatively high threshold for derivative work copyrightability would serve the goal of minimizing "transaction costs": "Some courts have required that the increment [of new expression] be significant, worrying that if it is set too low, and if the original and derivative copyrights happen to be in different hands . . . , the costs of determining infringement could be prohibitive." Landes & Posner, *An Economic Analysis of Copyright Law*, 18 J. Legal Stud. 325, 356 (1989). Are these assumptions correct, or do they confuse copyrightability analysis with infringement analysis? Without a "substantial difference" standard, could the infringement problem be solved through the use of expert testimony?

(6) Judge Posner acknowledged that if Gracen's painting had been painted from life, it would be copyrightable. If that is the case, why is her painting uncopyrightable as a derivative work? One reason, of course, is the importance of avoiding "overlapping claims" discussed above. Is this concern also present when a painting or photograph is taken from life? If so, how does (or should) copyright law handle the problem? By comparison, *Schrock* simplifies matters by adopting a unitary standard: namely, that derivative works are subject to the same standard of originality as other works. But is this the end of the inquiry? Should the standard vary depending on whether the derivative work is based on a public domain work or copyrighted work?

(7) *Derivative works based on public domain works.* While the underlying work that is adapted to create a derivative work may itself be protected by copyright, as in *Schrock*, often the derivative work is based on a preexisting work or works incapable of copyright or in the public domain for some other reason (such as extreme age). In *Alfred Bell & Co. v. Catalda Fine Arts, Inc.*, 191 F.2d 99 (2d Cir. 1951) (discussed in Chapter 2), the works involved were mezzotint engravings based on "old masters," *i.e.*, famous paintings whose term of protection, if any, had long since expired. The plaintiff was free to adapt these prior works and to attempt to secure protection for the derivative works thereby produced. In determining whether the mezzotints contained the necessary quantum of originality to warrant protection as derivative works, Judge Frank opined:

> We consider untenable defendants' suggestion that plaintiff's mezzotints could not validly be copyrighted because they are reproductions of works in the public domain. Not only does the Act include "Reproductions of a work of art," but — while prohibiting a copyright of "the original text of any work . . . in the public domain" — it explicitly provides for the copyrighting of "translations, or other versions of works in the public domain." The mezzotints were such "versions." They "originated" with those who made them, and — on the trial judge's findings well supported by the evidence — amply met the standards imposed by the Constitution and the statute. . . . There is evidence that they were not intended to, and did not, imitate the paintings they reproduced. But even if their substantial departures from the paintings were inadvertent, the copyrights would be valid. A copyist's bad eyesight or defective musculature, or a shock caused by a clap of

thunder, may yield sufficiently distinguishable variations. Having hit upon such a variation unintentionally, the "author" may adopt it as his and copyright it.

Id. at 104. This is, of course, a very low threshold. Should anything *more* be required, on constitutional, statutory, *or policy* grounds?

(8)   Like *Alfred Bell*, the decision in *Batlin* (which both *Schrock* and *Gracen* cite) concerned an adaptation of a public domain work. In *Batlin*, the Second Circuit rejected as a protectible derivative work a plastic replica of a traditional cast-iron "Uncle Sam" bank. *Batlin*, however, held that, to demonstrate originality, the "author," as a statutory and constitutional matter, has to contribute "substantial, not merely trivial, originality" above and beyond the preexisting work. Since 1976, this standard has enjoyed considerable currency in the courts. How do the *Batlin* and *Alfred Bell* originality standards compare with each other and with the standard of originality we saw developed in Chapter 2 for *non*-derivative works? Is *Schrock* closer in spirit to *Batlin* or to *Alfred Bell*? Are all of these standards in fact identical (albeit "substantially different" from the *Gracen* standard)?

Metal Replica of Original Uncle Sam Mechanical Bank (left)
and Snyder's Plastic Replication for 1976 Bicentennial (right)
*Banks courtesy of Robert Faber, photos by Clarence Thorne, and
copyright permission courtesy of Edward Samuels*

(9)   *Derivative works based on copyrighted works.* In *Durham Industries, Inc. v. Tomy Corp.*, 630 F.2d 905, 909 (2d Cir. 1980), the court rejected a claim of copyright in licensed three-inch wind-up plastic toys based on Mickey Mouse,

Donald Duck, and Pluto — characters protected by subsisting copyrights. In that context, the *Durham* court expressed the standard for derivative work copyrightability as follows:

> First, to support a copyright the original aspects of a derivative work must be more than trivial. Second, the original aspects of a derivative work must reflect the degree to which it relies on preexisting material and must not in any way affect the scope of any copyright protection in that preexisting material.

The first prong of the test is familiar enough — coming straight from *Batlin*. But where does the second prong come from? The *Durham* court cites § 103(b), which provides that the copyright in a derivative work "extends only to the material contributed by the author of such work, as distinguished from the preexisting material employed in the work," and that it "does not affect or enlarge the scope . . . [of] any copyright protection in the preexisting material." Does the statute require an additional inquiry where the underlying work is copyrighted? *Durham* itself states that "[a]lthough in the instant case the preexisting works are themselves the subjects of copyrights and are therefore not in the public domain, the standard announced in *Batlin* by which the copyrightability of a derivative work is to be determined is fully applicable."

(10)   The Ninth Circuit endorsed the *Durham* test in *Entertainment Research Group, Inc. v. Genesis Creative Group, Inc.*, 122 F.3d 1211 (1997), in which it denied a claim of copyright in eight-foot high costume designs based on advertising characters such as the Pillsbury Doughboy, Geoffrey Giraffe, and Cap'n Crunch. The *ERG* court distinguished its previous decision in *Sunset House Distributing Corp. v. Doran*, 304 F.2d 251 (1962), which upheld a claim of copyright for a three-dimensional, inflatable representation of Santa Claus, in part on the ground that in *Doran*, the preexisting work was "taken from the public domain and not copyrighted itself," whereas the costumes at issue in *ERG* were "based on preexisting works that were copyrighted and owned by the ultimate purchasers." The difference was said to be "critical." But why?

The *ERG* court itself gave one answer. If derivative work copyright were granted too readily, "the owner of the underlying copyrighted work would effectively be prevented from permitting others to copy her work since the original derivative copyright holder would have a *de facto* monopoly due to her 'considerable power to interfere with the creation of subsequent derivative works from the same underlying work.'" 122 F.3d at 1220 (quoting *Gracen*). Is the risk of "*de facto* monopoly" any less where the underlying works are in the public domain? *See also Batlin*, 536 F.2d at 492 ("To extend copyrightability to minuscule variations would simply put a weapon for harassment in the hands of mischievous copiers intent on appropriating and monopolizing public domain work."). Where does all of this leave us: with a unitary derivative works standard, or different standards, based on the copyright status of the underlying work?

(11)   *Derivative work based on noncopyrightable objects.* As we saw in § 3.01[D], some designs that might otherwise be eligible for copyright protection as pictorial, graphic, or sculptural works fail to qualify because they are deemed to be utilitarian. Is a photograph of such an object a "derivative" work? Or does the fact

that the subject of the picture was noncopyrightable require a different analysis? *See Ets-Hokin v. Skyy Spirits, Inc.*, 225 F.3d 1068 (9th Cir. 2000) (holding an advertising photo of a vodka bottle was sufficiently original but was not a derivative work); H.R. REP. No. 94-1476 at 57 ("the 'preexisting work' must come within the general subject matter of copyright set forth in section 102, regardless of whether it is or was ever copyrighted"). Why should the characterization matter? Should the standard of copyrightability depend on it? In a subsequent appeal, the Ninth Circuit applied the idea-expression dichotomy and held that the plaintiff's photo was not infringed by a different photo of the same vodka bottle. 323 F.3d 763 (9th Cir. 2003).

(12) *Derivative works based on change in medium?* Schrock's photographs were based upon preexisting works (the Thomas & Friends toys) and, as such, arguably were "recast, transformed, or adapted" by the change in medium from three-dimensional sculptures to two-dimensional photographs. As the *Schrock* court indicates, in the course of that transformation the photographer made *expressive choices* sufficient to warrant copyright protection for the resulting work. But can a change in medium *by itself* constitute sufficient originality to qualify a work for protection? In *Batlin*, the court ruled that "the mere reproduction of a work of art in a different medium should not constitute the required originality, for the reason that no one can claim to have independently evolved any particular medium." *But see Doran v. Sunset House Distributing Corp.*, 197 F. Supp. 940 (S.D. Cal. 1961) (plaintiffs were entitled to copyright because they "were the first to reproduce the traditional character [Santa Claus] in this particular form [3D] and medium [plastic]"), *aff'd on other grounds*, 304 F.2d 251 (9th Cir. 1962). Is it possible, as Dustin Hoffman's character learned in *The Graduate*, for just one word — plastic — to be such a game-changer? What are the consequences for all later authors, and the public, if being "the first" to place a character in a new medium is sufficient to justify copyright?

The "Used Unlawfully" Limitation

(13)   Under § 103(a), copyright in a derivative work "does not extend to any part of the work in which [the preexisting] material has been used unlawfully." This provision sometimes denies copyright to a derivative work that otherwise would meet the standard of sufficient originality. *See, e.g., Palladium Music, Inc. v. EatSleepMusic, Inc.*, 398 F.3d 1193 (10th Cir. 2005) (holding karaoke sound recording copyrights invalid and unenforceable for failure to obtain compulsory or consensual licenses from the copyright owners of the underlying musical works). Note, however, that permission does not have to be granted in writing; an implied nonexclusive license (discussed in § 4.02 below) will suffice. *See Latimer v. Roaring Toyz, Inc.*, 601 F.3d 1224 (11th Cir. 2010) (assuming photos of custom-painted motorcycles were derivative works of the artwork, copyrights were nonetheless valid, because artist was aware that the motorcycles would be photographed for promotional purposes).

Under what circumstances is it possible to separate protected original material from unlawfully used preexisting material? Can copyright be claimed in a movie which uses the characters of a copyrighted movie without permission, but employs an entirely different plot? *See Anderson v. Stallone*, 11 U.S.P.Q.2d (BNA) 1161 (C.D. Cal. 1989). The House Report states that "an unauthorized translation of a novel could not be copyrighted at all, but the owner of copyright in an anthology of poetry could sue someone who infringed the whole anthology, even though the infringer proves that publication of one of the poems was unauthorized." Relying on this sentence, the *Anderson* court concluded that a compilation which unlawfully uses preexisting material could qualify for partial protection, but that a derivative work which does so could not. Do you agree? *See also Caffey v. Cook*, 409 F. Supp. 2d 484 (S.D.N.Y. 2006) (selection and arrangement of 32 songs was protected by copyright, even if songs were compiled without permission).

(14)   In *Schrock*, the court rejected the lower court's reliance on *Gracen* for the principle that the author must have permission both to make the derivative work and to "copyright" it. What do you think Judge Posner had in mind in *Gracen*? Who's right? Would this problem have been avoided if the *Gracen* court had properly used the word "copyright" only as a noun, instead of improperly, as a verb? (When used as a verb, to "copyright" a work usually means to "register" the copyright in a work.)

(15)   What if preexisting material is used subject to a limited permission — allowing the creation of a derivative work, but expressly prohibiting its creator from asserting a copyright in the result? If the maker of the derivative work chooses to ignore this prohibition and claim copyright anyway, he or she may (of course) be subject to liability for breach of contract. But is *validity* of the copyright claim affected?

In *Liu v. Price Waterhouse LLP*, 302 F.3d 749 (7th Cir. 2001), cited in *Schrock*, Waterhouse commissioned Yang to create a derivative work based on its copyrighted software. The letter agreement between the parties indicated that Waterhouse would own the resulting derivative work. With Waterhouse's approval, however, the actual programming was subcontracted to a Chinese software firm. As you will learn in Chapter 4, a transfer of copyright ownership must be in a signed writing in order to be valid. § 204(a). Does the letter agreement bind the Chinese programmers, even though they did not sign that agreement? Or does ownership of an authorized derivative work vest in its creators by operation of law, regardless of the intent of the owner of copyright in the underlying work?

In *Schrock*, the court approves of Nimmer's suggestion that the parties can "alter [the] default rule by their agreements." Because the parties' agreements were not before the court, however, it held that summary judgment on this basis was improper.

From Derivative Works to Compilations

(16)   Suppose that an artist were to create a collage made up of hundreds of small, partially superimposed pre-existing images. Suppose further that the artist had neglected to obtain permission from the owners of copyright in the images, but that all but a handful of the images were in the public domain. How would the extent of the artist's copyright protection be assessed? Is the collage a derivative work or a compilation (or both)? *See Jarvis v. K2 Inc.*, 486 F.3d 526 (9th Cir. 2007) (where images were altered and fused with other images rather than merely selected and arranged in order, collage was a derivative work rather than a compilation or collective work).

(17)   Our final case in this chapter, *Feist Publications, Inc. v. Rural Telephone Service Co.* (already encountered in § 2.02), deals with the question of what constitutes "originality" in the context of compilations. But its analysis has implications that reach much further. Consider *Earth Flag, Ltd. v. Alamo Flag Co.*, 153 F. Supp. 2d 349 (S.D.N.Y. 2001), in which the plaintiff's predecessor-in-interest had "the creative spark to take [a] NASA photograph [of the earth from space], place it on a flag, file[] a copyright in the U.S. Copyright Office and begin to make it a symbol of a movement for peace and later ecology." Let the *Earth Flag* court's rejection of the copyright claim serve an introduction to the final section of this chapter:

> Simply put, plaintiff seeks a reward for the hard work of its predecessors in developing and popularizing the Earth Flag. However, in *Feist*, 499 U.S. at 354, the Supreme Court rejected the "sweat of the brow" doctrine and emphasized that the doctrine "flout[s] basic copyright principles" — most notable of which is the originality requirement. . . .

> Plaintiff also argues that the holding in *Feist* should be limited to its subject matter of telephone directories. It is well established, however, that the underlying tenets of *Feist* inform the entire body of copyright jurisprudence. . . .

Id. at 355. Without further ado, then . . .

[C]   Compilations

FEIST PUBLICATIONS, INC. v. RURAL TELEPHONE SERVICE COMPANY, INC.
Supreme Court of the United States
499 U.S. 340 (1991)

JUSTICE O'CONNOR delivered the opinion of the Court.

This case requires us to clarify the extent of copyright protection available to telephone directory white pages.

I.

Rural Telephone Service Company is a certified public utility that provides telephone service to several communities in northwest Kansas. It is subject to a state regulation that requires all telephone companies operating in Kansas to issue annually an updated telephone directory. Accordingly, as a condition of its monopoly franchise, Rural publishes a typical telephone directory, consisting of white pages and yellow pages. The white pages list in alphabetical order the names of Rural's subscribers, together with their towns and telephone numbers. The yellow pages list Rural's business subscribers alphabetically by category and feature classified advertisements of various sizes. Rural distributes its directory free of charge to its subscribers, but earns revenue by selling yellow pages advertisements.

Feist Publications, Inc., is a publishing company that specializes in area-wide telephone directories. Unlike a typical directory, which covers only a particular calling area, Feist's area-wide directories cover a much larger geographical range. . . . The Feist directory that is the subject of this litigation covers 11 different telephone service areas in 15 counties and contains 46,878 white pages listings — compared to Rural's approximately 7,700 listings. Like Rural's directory, Feist's is distributed free of charge and includes both white pages and yellow pages. Feist and Rural compete vigorously for yellow pages advertising.

As the sole provider of telephone service in its service area, Rural obtains subscriber information quite easily. Persons desiring telephone service must apply to Rural and provide their names and addresses; Rural then assigns them a telephone number. Feist is not a telephone company, let alone one with monopoly status, and therefore lacks independent access to any subscriber information. To obtain white pages listings for its area-wide directory, Feist approached each of the 11 telephone companies operating in northwest Kansas and offered to pay for the right to use its white pages listings.

Justice Sandra Day O'Connor
Photograph by Dane Penland, Smithsonian Institution
Courtesy of the Supreme Court of the United States

Of the 11 telephone companies, only Rural refused to license its listings to Feist. Rural's refusal created a problem for Feist, as omitting these listings would have left a gaping hole in its area-wide directory, rendering it less attractive to potential yellow pages advertisers. In a decision subsequent to that which we review here, the

District Court determined that this was precisely the reason Rural refused to license its listings. The refusal was motivated by an unlawful purpose "to extend its monopoly in telephone service to a monopoly in yellow pages advertising." *Rural Telephone Service Co. v. Feist Publications, Inc.*, 737 F. Supp. 610, 622 (D. Kan. 1990).

Unable to license Rural's white pages listings, Feist used them without Rural's consent. Feist began by removing several thousand listings that fell outside the geographic range of its area-wide directory, then hired personnel to investigate the 4,935 that remained. These employees verified the data reported by Rural and sought to obtain additional information. As a result, a typical Feist listing includes the individual's street address; most of Rural's listings do not. Notwithstanding these additions, however, 1,309 of the 46,878 listings in Feist's 1983 directory were identical to listings in Rural's 1982-1983 white pages. Four of these were fictitious listings that Rural had inserted into its directory to detect copying.

Rural sued for copyright infringement in the District Court for the District of Kansas, taking the position that Feist, in compiling its own directory, could not use the information contained in Rural's white pages. Rural asserted that Feist's employees were obliged to travel door-to-door or conduct a telephone survey to discover the same information for themselves. Feist responded that such efforts were economically impractical and, in any event, unnecessary because the information copied was beyond the scope of copyright protection. The District Court granted summary judgment to Rural, explaining that "courts have consistently held that telephone directories are copyrightable" and citing a string of lower court decisions. 663 F. Supp. 214, 218 (1987). In an unpublished opinion, the Court of Appeals for the Tenth Circuit affirmed "for substantially the reasons given by the district court." . . . We granted *certiorari* to determine whether the copyright in Rural's directory protects the names, towns, and telephone numbers copied by Feist.

II.A.

This case concerns the interaction of two well-established propositions. The first is that facts are not copyrightable; the other, that compilations of facts generally are. Each of these propositions possesses an impeccable pedigree. That there can be no valid copyright in facts is universally understood. The most fundamental axiom of copyright law is that "no author may copyright his ideas or the facts he narrates." *Harper & Row, Publishers, Inc. v. Nation Enterprises*, 471 U.S. 539, 556 (1985). . . . At the same time, however, it is beyond dispute that compilations of facts are within the subject matter of copyright. Compilations were expressly mentioned in the Copyright Act of 1909, and again in the Copyright Act of 1976.

There is an undeniable tension between these two propositions. Many compilations consist of nothing but raw data — *i.e.*, wholly factual information not accompanied by any original written expression. On what basis may one claim a copyright in such a work? Common sense tells us that 100 uncopyrightable facts do not magically change their status when gathered together in one place. Yet copyright law seems to contemplate that compilations that consist exclusively of facts are potentially within its scope.

The key to resolving the tension lies in understanding why facts are not copyrightable. The *sine qua non* of copyright is originality. To qualify for copyright protection, a work must be original to the author. . . .

Originality is a constitutional requirement. [The Court's discussion of Article I, § 8, cl. 8 of the Constitution, and of its decisions in *The Trade-Mark Cases*, 100 U.S. 82 (1879), and *Burrow-Giles Lithographic Co. v. Sarony*, 111 U.S. 53, 58 (1884), is omitted. See the text introducing § 2.02 above.]

It is this bedrock principle of copyright that mandates the law's seemingly disparate treatment of facts and factual compilations. "No one may claim originality as to facts." [NIMMER ON COPYRIGHT] § 2.11[A], at 2-157. This is because facts do not owe their origin to an act of authorship. The distinction is one between creation and discovery: the first person to find and report a particular fact has not created the fact; he or she has merely discovered its existence. To borrow from *Burrow-Giles*, one who discovers a fact is not its "maker" or "originator." 111 U.S., at 58. "The discoverer merely finds and records." NIMMER § 2.03[E]. Census-takers, for example, do not "create" the population figures that emerge from their efforts; in a sense, they copy these figures from the world around them. Denicola, *Copyright in Collections of Facts: A Theory for the Protection of Nonfiction Literary Works*, 81 Colum. L. Rev. 516, 525 (1981) (hereinafter *Denicola*). Census data therefore do not trigger copyright because these data are not "original" in the constitutional sense. NIMMER § 2.03[E]. The same is true of all facts — scientific, historical, biographical, and news of the day. "They may not be copyrighted and are part of the public domain available to every person." *Miller* [*v. Universal City Studios, Inc.*, 650 F.2d 1365,] 1369 [(CA5 1981)].

Factual compilations, on the other hand, may possess the requisite originality. The compilation author typically chooses which facts to include, in what order to place them, and how to arrange the collected data so that they may be used effectively by readers. These choices as to selection and arrangement, so long as they are made independently by the compiler and entail a minimal degree of creativity, are sufficiently original that Congress may protect such compilations through the copyright laws. NIMMER §§ 2.11[D], 3.03; *Denicola* 523, n.38. Thus, even a directory that contains absolutely no protectible written expression, only facts, meets the constitutional minimum for copyright protection if it features an original selection or arrangement. *See Harper & Row*, 471 U.S., at 547. *Accord*, NIMMER § 3.03.

This protection is subject to an important limitation. The mere fact that a work is copyrighted does not mean that every element of the work may be protected. Originality remains the *sine qua non* of copyright; accordingly, copyright protection may extend only to those components of a work that are original to the author. [Patterson & Joyce, *Monopolizing the Law: The Scope of Copyright Protection for Law Reports and Statutory Compilations*, 36 UCLA L. Rev. 719, 800-802 (1989)]; Ginsburg, *Creation and Commercial Value: Copyright Protection of Works of Information*, 90 Colum. L. Rev. 1865, 1868, and n. 12 (1990) (hereinafter *Ginsburg*). Thus, if the compilation author clothes facts with an original collocation of words, he or she may be able to claim a copyright in this written expression. Others may copy the underlying facts from the publication, but not the precise words used to present them. In *Harper & Row*, for example, we explained that President Ford could not prevent others from copying bare historical facts from his autobiography, *see* 471 U.S., at 556-557, but that he could prevent others from copying his "subjective descriptions and portraits of public figures." *Id.*, at 563. Where the compilation author adds no written expression but rather lets the facts speak for themselves, the expressive element is more elusive. The only conceivable expression is the manner in which the compiler has selected and arranged the facts. Thus, if the selection and arrangement are original, these elements of the work are eligible for copyright protection. *See* Patry, *Copyright in Compilations of Facts (or Why the "White Pages" Are Not Copyrightable)*, 12 Com. & Law 37, 64 (Dec. 1990) (hereinafter *Patry*). No matter how original the format, however, the facts themselves do not become original through association. *See Patterson & Joyce* 776.

This inevitably means that the copyright in a factual compilation is thin. Notwithstanding a valid copyright, a subsequent compiler remains free to use the facts contained in another's publication to aid in preparing a competing work, so long as the competing work does not feature the same selection and arrangement. As one commentator explains it: "No matter how much original authorship the work displays, the facts and ideas it exposes are free for the taking. . . . The very same facts and ideas may be divorced from the context imposed by the author, and restated or reshuffled by second comers, even if the author was the first to discover the facts or to propose the ideas." *Ginsburg* 1868.

It may seem unfair that much of the fruit of the compiler's labor may be used by others without compensation. As Justice Brennan has correctly observed, however, this is not "some unforeseen byproduct of a statutory scheme." *Harper & Row*, 471 U.S., at 589 (dissenting opinion). It is, rather, "the essence of copyright," *ibid.*, and a constitutional requirement. The primary objective of copyright is not to reward the labor of authors, but "to promote the Progress of Science and useful Arts." Art. I, § 8, cl. 8. *Accord, Twentieth Century Music Corp. v. Aiken*, 422 U.S. 151, 156 (1975). To this end, copyright assures authors the right to their original expression, but encourages others to build freely upon the ideas and information conveyed by a work. *Harper & Row, supra*, at 556-557. This principle, known as the idea/expression or fact/expression dichotomy, applies to all works of authorship. As applied to a factual compilation, assuming the absence of original written expression, only the compiler's selection and arrangement may be protected; the raw facts may be copied at will. This result is neither unfair nor unfortunate. It is the means by which copyright advances the progress of science and art.

This Court has long recognized that the fact/expression dichotomy limits severely the scope of protection in fact-based works. [Discussion of *Baker v. Selden*, 101 U.S. 99, 103 (1880), and *Harper & Row, supra*, omitted.]

This, then, resolves the doctrinal tension: Copyright treats facts and factual compilations in a wholly consistent manner. Facts, whether alone or as part of a compilation, are not original and therefore may not be copyrighted. A factual compilation is eligible for copyright if it features an original selection or arrangement of facts, but the copyright is limited to the particular selection or arrangement. In no event may copyright extend to the facts themselves.

B.

As we have explained, originality is a constitutionally mandated prerequisite for copyright protection. The Court's decisions announcing this rule predate the Copyright Act of 1909, but ambiguous language in the 1909 Act caused some lower courts temporarily to lose sight of this requirement.

The 1909 Act embodied the originality requirement, but not as clearly as it might have. *See* NIMMER § 2.01. The subject matter of copyright was set out in § 3 and § 4 of the Act. Section 4 stated that copyright was available to "all the writings of an author." By using the words "writings" and "author" — the same words used in Article I, § 8 of the Constitution and defined by the Court in *The Trade-Mark Cases* and *Burrow-Giles* — the statute necessarily incorporated the originality requirement articulated in the Court's decisions. It did so implicitly, however, thereby leaving room for error.

Section 3 was similarly ambiguous. It stated that the copyright in a work protected only "the copyrightable component parts of the work." It thus stated an important copyright principle, but failed to identify the specific characteristic — originality — that determined which component parts of a work were copyrightable and which were not.

Most courts construed the 1909 Act correctly, notwithstanding the less-than-perfect statutory language. They understood from this Court's decisions that there could be no copyright without originality. *See Patterson & Joyce* 760-761. . . .

But some courts misunderstood the statute. *See, e.g., Leon v. Pacific Telephone & Telegraph Co.*, 91 F.2d 484 (CA9 1937); *Jeweler's Circular Publishing Co. v. Keystone Publishing Co.*, 281 F. 83 (CA2 1922). These courts ignored § 3 and § 4, focusing their attention instead on § 5 of the Act. Section 5, however, was purely technical in nature: it provided that a person seeking to register a work should indicate on the application the type of work, and it listed 14 categories under which the work might fall. One of these categories was "books, including composite and cyclopedic works, directories, gazetteers, and other compilations." § 5(a). Section 5 did not purport to say that all compilations were automatically copyrightable. Indeed, it expressly disclaimed any such function, pointing out that "the subject-matter of copyright is defined in section four." Nevertheless, the fact that factual compilations were mentioned specifically in § 5 led some courts to infer erroneously that directories and the like were copyrightable *per se*, "without any further or precise showing of original — personal — authorship." *Ginsburg* 1895.

Making matters worse, these courts developed a new theory to justify the protection of factual compilations. Known alternatively as "sweat of the brow" or "industrious collection," the underlying notion was that copyright was a reward for the hard work that went into compiling facts. The classic formulation of the doctrine appeared in *Jeweler's Circular Publishing Co.*, 281 F., at 88 (emphasis added):

> The right to copyright a book upon which one has expended labor in its preparation does not depend upon whether the materials which he has collected consist or not of matters which are *publici juris*, or whether such materials show literary skill *or originality*, either in thought or in language, or anything more than industrious collection. The man who goes

through the streets of a town and puts down the names of each of the inhabitants, with their occupations and their street number[s], acquires material of which he is the author.

The "sweat of the brow" doctrine had numerous flaws, the most glaring being that it extended copyright protection in a compilation beyond selection and arrangement — the compiler's original contributions — to the facts themselves. Under the doctrine, the only defense to infringement was independent creation. A subsequent compiler was "not entitled to take one word of information previously published," but rather had to "independently work out the matter for himself, so as to arrive at the same result from the same common sources of information." *Id.*, at 88-89 (internal quotations omitted). "Sweat of the brow" courts thereby eschewed the most fundamental axiom of copyright law — that no one may copyright facts or ideas. . . .

Decisions of this Court applying the 1909 Act make clear that the statute did not permit the "sweat of the brow" approach. The best example is *International News Service v. Associated Press*, 248 U.S. 215 (1918). In that decision, the Court stated unambiguously that the 1909 Act conferred copyright protection only on those elements of a work that were original to the author. International News Service had conceded taking news reported by Associated Press and publishing it in its own newspapers. Recognizing that § 5 of the Act specifically mentioned "periodicals, including newspapers," § 5(b), the Court acknowledged that news articles were copyrightable. *Id.*, at 234. It flatly rejected, however, the notion that the copyright in an article extended to the factual information it contained: "The news element — the information respecting current events contained in the literary production — is not the creation of the writer, but is a report of matters that ordinarily are *publici juris*; it is the history of the day." *Id.*[*]

Without a doubt, the "sweat of the brow" doctrine flouted basic copyright principles. Throughout history, copyright law has "recognized a greater need to disseminate factual works than works of fiction or fantasy." *Harper & Row*, 471 U.S., at 563. *Accord*, Gorman, *Fact or Fancy: The Implications for Copyright*, 29 J. Copyright Soc. 560, 563 (1982). But "sweat of the brow" courts took a contrary view; they handed out proprietary interests in facts and declared that authors are absolutely precluded from saving time and effort by relying upon the facts contained in prior works. In truth, "[i]t is just such wasted effort that the proscription against the copyright of ideas and facts . . . [is] designed to prevent." *Rosemont Enterprises, Inc. v. Random House, Inc.*, 366 F.2d 303, 310 (CA2 1966), *cert. denied*, 385 U.S. 1009 (1967). "Protection for the fruits of such research . . . may in certain circumstances be available under a theory of unfair competition. But to accord copyright protection on this basis alone distorts basic copyright principles in that it creates a monopoly in public domain materials without the necessary justification of protecting and encouraging the creation of 'writings' by authors.' " NIMMER § 3.04, at 3-23 (footnote omitted).

---

[*] The Court ultimately rendered judgment for Associated Press on noncopyright grounds that are not relevant here. *See* 248 U.S. at 235, 241–42.

C.

"Sweat of the brow" decisions did not escape the attention of the Copyright Office. When Congress decided to overhaul the copyright statute and asked the Copyright Office to study existing problems, the Copyright Office promptly recommended that Congress clear up the confusion in the lower courts as to the basic standards of copyrightability. The Register of Copyrights . . . suggested making the originality requirement explicit.

Congress took the Register's advice. In enacting the Copyright Act of 1976, Congress dropped the reference to "all the writings of an author" and replaced it with the phrase "original works of authorship." 17 U.S.C. § 102(a). In making explicit the originality requirement, Congress announced that it was merely clarifying existing law: "The two fundamental criteria of copyright protection [are] originality and fixation in tangible form. . . . The phrase 'original works of authorship,' which is purposely left undefined, is intended to incorporate without change *the standard of originality established by the courts under the present [1909] copyright statute.*" H.R. Rep. No. 94-1476, at 51 (1976) (emphasis added) (hereinafter *H.R. Rep.*); S. Rep. No. 94-473, at 50 (1975) (emphasis added) (hereinafter *S. Rep.*). . . .

To ensure that the mistakes of the "sweat of the brow" courts would not be repeated, Congress took additional measures. For example, . . . § 102(b) . . . identifies specifically those elements of a work for which copyright is not available: "In no case does copyright protection for an original work of authorship extend to any idea, procedure, process, system, method of operation, concept, principle, or discovery, regardless of the form in which it is described, explained, illustrated, or embodied in such work." Section 102(b) is universally understood to prohibit any copyright in facts. *Harper & Row, supra,* at 547, 556. . . .

Congress took another step to minimize confusion by deleting the specific mention of "directories . . . and other compilations" in § 5 of the 1909 Act. . . . In its place, Congress enacted two new provisions. First, to make clear that compilations were not copyrightable *per se,* Congress provided a definition of the term "compilation." Second, to make clear that the copyright in a compilation did not extend to the facts themselves, Congress enacted 17 U.S.C. § 103.

The definition of "compilation" is found in § 101 of the 1976 Act. It defines a "compilation" in the copyright sense as "a work formed by the collection and assembly of preexisting materials or of data *that* are selected, coordinated, or arranged *in such a way that* the resulting work as a whole constitutes an original work of authorship" (emphasis added).

The purpose of the statutory definition is to emphasize that collections of facts are not copyrightable *per se.* It conveys this message through its tripartite structure, as emphasized above by the italics. The statute identifies three distinct elements and requires each to be met for a work to qualify as a copyrightable compilation: (1) the collection and assembly of pre-existing material, facts, or data; (2) the selection, coordination, or arrangement of those materials; and (3) the creation, by virtue of the particular selection, coordination, or arrangement, of an "original" work of authorship. "This tripartite conjunctive structure is self-evident,

and should be assumed to 'accurately express the legislative purpose.' " *Patry* 51.
. . .

At first glance, the first requirement does not seem to tell us much. It merely describes what one normally thinks of as a compilation — a collection of pre-existing material, facts, or data. What makes it significant is that it is not the sole requirement. It is not enough for copyright purposes that an author collects and assembles facts. To satisfy the statutory definition, the work must get over two additional hurdles. In this way, the plain language indicates that not every collection of facts receives copyright protection. Otherwise, there would be a period after "data."

The third requirement is also illuminating. It emphasizes that a compilation, like any other work, is copyrightable only if it satisfies the originality requirement ("an original work of authorship"). Although § 102 states plainly that the originality requirement applies to all works, the point was emphasized with regard to compilations to ensure that courts would not repeat the mistake of the "sweat of the brow" courts by concluding that fact-based works are treated differently and measured by some other standard. As Congress explained it, the goal was to "make plain that the criteria of copyrightable subject matter stated in section 102 apply with full force to works . . . containing preexisting material." H.R. Rep., at 57; S. Rep., at 55.

The key to the statutory definition is the second requirement. It instructs courts that, in determining whether a fact-based work is an original work of authorship, they should focus on the manner in which the collected facts have been selected, coordinated, and arranged. This is a straightforward application of the originality requirement. Facts are never original, so the compilation author can claim originality, if at all, only in the way the facts are presented. To that end, the statute dictates that the principal focus should be on whether the selection, coordination, and arrangement are sufficiently original to merit protection.

Not every selection, coordination, or arrangement will pass muster. This is plain from the statute. It states that, to merit protection, the facts must be selected, coordinated, or arranged "in such a way" as to render the work as a whole original. This implies that some "ways" will trigger copyright, but that others will not. *See Patry* 57, and n.76. Otherwise, the phrase "in such a way" is meaningless and Congress should have defined "compilation" simply as "a work formed by the collection and assembly of preexisting materials or data that are selected, coordinated, or arranged." That Congress did not do so is dispositive. . . . [Thus,] we conclude that the statute envisions that there will be some fact-based works in which the selection, coordination, and arrangement are not sufficiently original to trigger copyright protection.

. . . [T]he originality requirement is not particularly stringent. A compiler may settle upon a selection or arrangement that others have used; novelty is not required. Originality requires only that the author make the selection or arrangement independently (*i.e.*, without copying that selection or arrangement from another work), and that it display some minimal level of creativity. Presumably, the vast majority of compilations will pass this test, but not all will. There remains a narrow category of works in which the creative spark is utterly lacking or so trivial as to be virtually nonexistent. . . .

Even if a work qualifies as a copyrightable compilation, it receives only limited protection. This is the point of § 103 of the Act. Section 103 explains that "the subject matter of copyright . . . includes compilations," § 103(a), but that copyright protects only the author's original contributions — not the facts or information conveyed:

> The copyright in a compilation . . . extends only to the material contributed by the author of such work, as distinguished from the preexisting material employed in the work, and does not imply any exclusive right in the preexisting material.

§ 103(b).

As § 103 makes clear, copyright is not a tool by which a compilation author may keep others from using the facts or data he or she has collected. . . . Rather, the facts contained in existing works may be freely copied because copyright protects only the elements that owe their origin to the compiler — the selection, coordination, and arrangement of facts.

In summary, the 1976 revisions to the Copyright Act leave no doubt that originality, not "sweat of the brow," is the touchstone of copyright protection in directories and other fact-based works. . . . The revisions explain with painstaking clarity that copyright requires originality, § 102(a); that facts are never original, § 102(b); that the copyright in a compilation does not extend to the facts it contains, § 103(b); and that a compilation is copyrightable only to the extent that it features an original selection, coordination, or arrangement, § 101.

The 1976 revisions have proven largely successful in steering courts in the right direction. A good example is *Miller v. Universal City Studios, Inc.*, [*supra*]. Additionally, the Second Circuit, which almost 70 years ago issued the classic formulation of the "sweat of the brow" doctrine in *Jeweler's Circular Publishing Co.*, has now fully repudiated the reasoning of that decision. . . . Even those scholars who believe that "industrious collection" should be rewarded seem to recognize that this is beyond the scope of existing copyright law. *See Denicola* 516 ("the very vocabulary of copyright is ill suited to analyzing property rights in works of nonfiction"); *id.*, at 520-521, 525; *Ginsburg* 1867, 1870.

III

There is no doubt that Feist took from the white pages of Rural's directory a substantial amount of factual information. At a minimum, Feist copied the names, towns, and telephone numbers of 1,309 of Rural's subscribers. Not all copying, however, is copyright infringement. To establish infringement, two elements must be proven: (1) ownership of a valid copyright, and (2) copying of constituent elements of the work that are original. *See Harper & Row*, 471 U.S., at 548. The first element is not at issue here; Feist appears to concede that Rural's directory, considered as a whole, is subject to a valid copyright because it contains some foreword text, as well as original material in its yellow pages advertisements.

The question is whether Rural has proved the second element. In other words, did Feist, by taking 1,309 names, towns, and telephone numbers from Rural's white pages, copy anything that was "original" to Rural? Certainly, the raw data does not satisfy the originality requirement. Rural may have been the first to discover and report the names, towns, and telephone numbers of its subscribers, but this data does not " 'owe its origin' " to Rural. *Burrow-Giles*, 111 U.S., at 58. Rather, these bits of information are uncopyrightable facts; they existed before Rural reported them and would have continued to exist if Rural had never published a telephone directory. The originality requirement "rules out protecting . . . names, addresses, and telephone numbers of which the plaintiff by no stretch of the imagination could be called the author." *Patterson & Joyce* 776.

Rural essentially concedes the point by referring to the names, towns, and telephone numbers as "preexisting material." Section 103(b) states explicitly that the copyright in a compilation does not extend to "the preexisting material employed in the work."

The question that remains is whether Rural selected, coordinated, or arranged these uncopyrightable facts in an original way. As mentioned, originality is not a stringent standard; it does not require that facts be presented in an innovative or surprising way. It is equally true, however, that the selection and arrangement of facts cannot be so mechanical or routine as to require no creativity whatsoever. The standard of originality is low, but it does exist. *See Patterson & Joyce* 760, n.144 ("While this requirement is sometimes characterized as modest, or a low threshold, it is not without effect") (internal quotations omitted; citations omitted). . . .

The selection, coordination, and arrangement of Rural's white pages do not satisfy the minimum constitutional standards for copyright protection. As mentioned at the outset, Rural's white pages are entirely typical. Persons desiring telephone service in Rural's service area fill out an application and Rural issues them a telephone number. In preparing its white pages, Rural simply takes the data provided by its subscribers and lists it alphabetically by surname. The end product is a garden-variety white pages directory, devoid of even the slightest trace of creativity.

Rural's selection of listings could not be more obvious: it publishes the most basic information — name, town, and telephone number — about each person who applies to it for telephone service. This is "selection" of a sort, but it lacks the modicum of creativity necessary to transform mere selection into copyrightable expression. Rural expended sufficient effort to make the white pages directory useful, but insufficient creativity to make it original.

We note in passing that the selection featured in Rural's white pages may also fail the originality requirement for another reason. Feist points out that Rural did not truly "select" to publish the names and telephone numbers of its subscribers; rather, it was required to do so by the Kansas Corporation Commission as part of its monopoly franchise. *See* 737 F. Supp., at 612. Accordingly, one could plausibly conclude that this selection was dictated by state law, not by Rural.

Nor can Rural claim originality in its coordination and arrangement of facts. The white pages do nothing more than list Rural's subscribers in alphabetical order.

This arrangement may, technically speaking, owe its origin to Rural; no one disputes that Rural undertook the task of alphabetizing the names itself. But there is nothing remotely creative about arranging names alphabetically in a white pages directory. It is an age-old practice, firmly rooted in tradition and so commonplace that it has come to be expected as a matter of course. It is not only unoriginal; it is practically inevitable. This time-honored tradition does not possess the minimal creative spark required by the Copyright Act and the Constitution.

We conclude that the names, towns, and telephone numbers copied by Feist were not original to Rural and therefore were not protected by the copyright in Rural's combined white and yellow pages directory. As a constitutional matter, copyright protects only those constituent elements of a work that possess more than a *de minimis* quantum of creativity. Rural's white pages, limited to basic subscriber information and arranged alphabetically, fall short of the mark. As a statutory matter, 17 U.S.C. § 101 does not afford protection from copying to a collection of facts that are selected, coordinated, and arranged in a way that utterly lacks originality. Given that some works must fail, we cannot imagine a more likely candidate. Indeed, were we to hold that Rural's white pages pass muster, it is hard to believe that any collection of facts could fail.

Because Rural's white pages lack the requisite originality, Feist's use of the listings cannot constitute infringement. This decision should not be construed as demeaning Rural's efforts in compiling its directory, but rather as making clear that copyright rewards originality, not effort. As this Court noted more than a century ago, " 'great praise may be due to the plaintiffs for their industry and enterprise in publishing this paper, yet the law does not contemplate their being rewarded in this way.' " *Baker v. Selden*, 101 U.S., at 105. The judgment of the Court of Appeals is reversed.

JUSTICE BLACKMUN concurs in the judgment.

NOTES AND QUESTIONS

Compilations Generally

(1)   A compilation, according to the § 101 definition, is a work formed "by the collection and assembly of preexisting materials or of data that are selected, coordinated, or arranged in such a way that the resulting work as a whole constitutes an original work of authorship." The preexisting materials brought together by the compiler may include separate and independently copyrightable works, such as articles collected in a periodical, poems selected for an anthology, or entries assembled in an encyclopedia. Such "collective works" (also defined in § 101) are one, but only one, type of compilation.

Other compilations bring together facts, data or public domain materials which in and of themselves are not copyrightable. The "white pages" directory in *Feist* represents the latter sort of compilation in perhaps its starkest form. Factual compilations — a category that includes directories of many types (not just telephone books), as well as catalogues and computer databases — strain the conceptual fabric of copyright law. Tugging from one end is a desire to protect the researcher against a free-riding defendant who has capitalized on the researcher's labor. Tugging from the other end is the doctrine that copyright law does not protect facts *per se*, but only original authorship.

(2) *Pre-Feist decisions.* Much of the trouble in this area traces its lineage directly to the "granddaddy" of the directory cases, *Leon v. Pacific Telephone & Telegraph Co.*, 91 F.2d 484 (9th Cir. 1937), which *Feist* expressly disapproves. In *Leon*, the court found Leon liable for producing a numerical telephone directory by making unauthorized use of the alphabetical directory prepared and published by the plaintiff, PT&T. Discussing the process of producing PT&T's directory, the Ninth Circuit observed:

> The San Francisco listings of the directory alleged to be infringed totaled 160,266, and the East Bay listings 97,512. The total cost of producing these directories was $295,222. One hundred persons are regularly employed by [PT&T] in its directory department.
>
> It is obvious from this evidence that the business of getting out a directory is an expensive, complicated, well-organized endeavor, requiring skill, ingenuity, and original research. Unless the product of such activity is by its very nature not subject to copyright, [PT&T's] directories are certainly entitled to copyright protection in the case at bar.

Id. at 485-86. Obviously, the *Leon* court concluded that the plaintiff's large expenditure of time, energy and money entitled it to the protection of the copyright laws — notwithstanding the fact that the plaintiff's efforts in collecting names, addresses and telephone numbers could not by any reasonable stretch of the imagination be said to meet the originality standard developed in the case law in Chapter 2.

Ironically, *Leon* itself, insofar as it depended on "sweat of the brow" analysis to justify its outcome, was rejected in the Circuit of its birth even before *Feist*. In *Worth v. Selchow & Righter Co.*, 827 F.2d 569 (9th Cir. 1987), the Ninth Circuit flatly discarded *Leon* "to the extent [it] suggests that research or labor is protectible." 827 F.2d at 573.

(3) Even courts disinclined to the "sweat of the brow" theory remained willing, however, to protect factual compilations in appropriate circumstances. For instance, in *Eckes v. Card Prices Update*, 736 F.2d 859 (2d Cir. 1984), the plaintiffs were the authors of a baseball card price guide (the "Guide") widely used by traders in such memorabilia. The Guide listed approximately 18,000 cards published between 1909 and 1979, arranging them by manufacturer and year and stating the current value of each card, depending on its condition. In addition, the Guide placed each card in one of two groups: premium or star cards (about 5,000, deemed by the guide's authors to be particularly valuable "because of the player featured on the card, . . . or because of the team on which he plays, or because of some characteristic of the card itself, such as an imperfection or the scarcity of the card"); and common cards (all of the rest).

The defendants published a monthly update (the "Update"), tracking price trends in baseball cards but listing separately only premium cards. The Update's premium card list was substantially similar to the Guide's; the defendants conceded access to the plaintiffs' work; and the Court of Appeals, finding clear error by the District Court, reversed its finding that there had been no copying. As to whether what the Update copied from the Guide was protected expression, the Second Circuit noted its relatively recent restrictive attitude toward protecting nonfiction literary works "absent, perhaps, wholesale appropriation," but continued:

> Nevertheless, our cases do not hold that subjective selection and arrangement of information does not merit protection. In fact, the definition of a compilation in the [1976] Act . . . suggest[s] that selectivity in including otherwise non-protected information can be protected expression. . . .
>
> We have no doubt that [plaintiffs] exercised selection, creativity and judgment in choosing among the 18,000 or so different baseball cards in order to determine which were the 5,000 premium cards. Accordingly, we believe that the Guide merits protection under the copyright laws.

736 F.2d at 862-63.

Do you suppose that the *Eckes* court would have found the exercise of sufficient "selection, creativity and judgment" if a subsequent copyright claimant had chosen data for inclusion in *his* guide based on mechanical application of an invariable formula (such as including all baseball cards depicting players with a lifetime batting average of 250 or better)? Does it matter whether the person doing the choosing has special expertise or articulable criteria of selection? What about a selection of baseball cards based solely on the compiler's belief that some cards are "prettier than others"? And does it matter if there are relatively few ways available to represent a particular kind of data? Some of these problems are taken up in *Kregos v. Associated Press*, 937 F.2d 700 (2nd Cir. 1991).

(4)   Despite the valiant efforts of the Second and Ninth Circuits — as well as the Fifth Circuit, commended in *Feist* for its decision in *Miller v. Universal City Studios, Inc.*, 650 F.2d 1365 (5th Cir. 1981), and the Eleventh Circuit, *see Southern Bell Telephone & Telegraph Co. v. Associated Telephone Directory Publishers*, 756 F.2d 801 (11th Cir. 1985) — "sweat of the brow" seemed to be a doctrine that would not die, living on in the Seventh, Eighth, and Tenth Circuits. See *Illinois Bell Telephone Co. v. Haines & Co., Inc.*, 905 F.2d 1081 (7th Cir. 1990); *Hutchinson Telephone Co. v. Fronteer Directory Co.*, 770 F.2d 128 (8th Cir. 1985); and, of course, the lower court opinion in *Feist*. Not until the Supreme Court decided to "reach out and touch someone" by granting *certiorari* to review the Tenth Circuit's two-paragraph, *unpublished* opinion in *Feist* did the prospects for finally interring the "industrious collection" doctrine really brighten.

(5)   *The* Feist *case and its aftermath.* After *Feist*, what constitutes the kind of "selection" of noncopyrightable data which will justify copyright protection for the resulting compilation? When is a choice of data "mere selection," *i.e.*, selection "so mechanical or routine" as to lack the requisite quantum of originality, and when (on the other hand) is it "copyrightable expression"? Is any method of sorting data which relies on "obvious" categories automatically suspect? Should protection be

denied for lists of the "100 Best" or "100 Worst" or "100 Oldest" or "100 Richest"? For example, what about an anthology of public domain poetry assembled on the principle that it contains the "100 most familiar poems in the English language"? *See Silverstein v. Penguin Putnam, Inc.*, 368 F.3d 77 (2d Cir. 2004) (remanding for a determination as to whether plaintiff's selection of unpublished poems by Dorothy Parker was original), *on remand*, 522 F. Supp. 2d 579 (S.D.N.Y. 2007) ("Silverstein's choices were obvious ones that required no creative judgment."); *Thornton v. J Jargon Co.*, 580 F. Supp. 2d 1261 (M.D. Fla. 2008) (finding genuine issue of material fact where defendant copied 24 of 29 trivia questions in order; 10 were identical, 10 had only minor differences, and 4 had some material removed).

(6)   In the aftermath of *Feist*, the distinction between the copyrightability, on the one hand, and the scope of copyright protection, on the other, takes on special importance in compilation cases. In *Key Publications, Inc. v. Chinatown Today Publishing Enterprises, Inc.*, 945 F.2d 509 (2d Cir. 1991), for example, the Second Circuit applied the *Feist* definition of originality to justify copyright protection for the selection and coordination of yellow pages data in a classified business directory for New York City's Chinese-American community. Ultimately, however, the court determined that the defendant had not infringed the plaintiff's protected expression. *See also Transwestern Publishing Co. v. Multimedia Marketing Associates, Inc.*, 133 F.3d 773 (10th Cir. 1998) (no infringement of yellow pages directory due to "thin" protection for such works); *Ross, Brovins & Oehmke v. Lexis Nexis Group*, 463 F.3d 478 (6th Cir. 2006) (although selection of 576 legal forms was original, it was not infringed by defendant's selection of 406 forms, even though 350 forms, or 61%, were common to both).

(7)   *Compare Key with Bellsouth Advertising & Publishing Corp. v. Donnelly Information Publishing, Inc.*, 933 F.2d 952 (11th Cir. 1991), *vacated on reh'g en banc*, 977 F.2d 1435 (11th Cir. 1993). The initial opinion in *Bellsouth* had concluded that the plaintiff's work did indeed contain sufficient "originality" in its selection and demarcation of geographical boundaries for the various directories it published, its selection of a closing date after which no more changes would be made in directory entries, its creation of selection-of-business classifications, its coordination of individual businesses' names with their addresses and phone numbers, and its assignment of businesses to the various classifications. After rehearing *en banc*, however, the Eleventh Circuit, while accepting that the "yellow pages" *may* be copyrightable in some instances, found insufficient originality in the actual work in suit. Did the court go too far in its application of *Feist? See also Warren Publishing, Inc. v. Microdos Data Corp.*, 115 F.3d 1509 (11th Cir. 1997) (*en banc*) (no compilation protection for facts compiled in factbook for the cable television industry because the copyright claimant's system for selecting data to list was insufficiently creative). The aggressive application of the *Feist* principle in the Eleventh Circuit has helped to fuel the complaints of database producers that they currently receive insufficient legal protection for their investments and should receive new statutory protection, as discussed in the note on "Database Protection" that concludes this chapter.

(8)   What is an original "arrangement" of data after *Feist*? In *Assessment Technologies of Wisconsin, LLC v. WIREdata, Inc.*, 350 F.3d 640 (7th Cir. 2003), plaintiff created a computer program to facilitate the collection and storage of real estate data by municipal tax assessors. The program sorted the data into 456 fields

grouped in 34 master categories. Judge Posner's opinion found this arrangement to be copyrightable, "because this structure is not so obvious or inevitable as to lack the minimal originality required." *Id.* at 643. Nonetheless, the court held that the underlying data was factual information that was not copyrightable under *Feist*, and therefore the plaintiff could not prevent the municipalities from extracting and copying the data for the defendant, so long as the defendant sorted the data in a different manner. The opinion begins: "This case is about the attempt of a copyright owner to use copyright law to block access to data that not only are neither copyrightable nor copyrighted, but were not created or obtained by the copyright owner. . . . It would be appalling if such an attempt could succeed." *Id.* at 641-42.

As noted in *Feist*, an arrangement also may lack originality if it is traditional or commonplace. Can this principle be applied if the arrangement is novel? *See ATC Distribution Group, Inc. v. Whatever It Takes Transmissions & Parts, Inc.*, 402 F.3d 700, 711-12 (6th Cir. 2005) ("a catalog that featured additional subheadings and a rearranged sequence of information was, while 'organized in a manner unknown to the industry prior to its publication,' and 'perhaps original,' nonetheless 'typical, if not inevitable,' and lacking in the 'requisite creativity for copyright protection.' "). Can a compilation be denied protection even though there are other ways in which the information could have been arranged? *See ATC*, 402 F.3d at 712 ("To be sure, ATC could have arranged the parts information in other ways that were potentially less clear or useful, but this fact alone is insufficient to demonstrate the creativity necessary for copyright protection."). *But see BUC Int'l Corp. v. Int'l Yacht Council, Ltd.*, 489 F.3d 1129 (11th Cir. 2007) (arrangement of subject headings was not subject to merger doctrine where there were different ways to present the information, and defendants used different organization before plaintiff's work existed).

(9) *"Soft" and "hard" facts.* The originality standard may be satisfied where the compiler's claimed "original" contribution is subjective and evaluative. For example, in a case we encountered in § 2.02, *CCC Information Services v. Maclean Hunter Market Reports, Inc.*, 44 F.3d 61 (2d Cir. 1994), plaintiff Maclean published the Red Book of estimated used car values, based on the professional judgment of its editors, who consulted a variety of sources. The court held that the estimated values were neither reports of historical prices nor mechanical derivations of such prices, and were therefore copyrightable. In so ruling, it distinguished between "building block" ideas (which are subject to the merger doctrine because they must be freed up to "assist the understanding of future thinkers"), and "approximative statements of opinion" (which are "infused with the author's taste or opinion" and thus need *not* be subject to the merger doctrine). *Id.* at 72-73.

CCC was applied in *CDN Inc. v. Kapes*, 197 F.3d 1256, 1260 (9th Cir. 1999), in which the court held that a collector's guide's estimates of wholesale prices for collectible U.S. coins were copyrightable "compilations of data" that were the product of a "creative process" in which CDN "extrapolates from . . . reported prices to arrive at estimates for prices for unreported coin types and grades." The opinion cites extensively to the letter of *Feist*. But is it true to the spirit of the Supreme Court's decision? Is it proper to treat each individual estimated value as a separate "compilation"? *See also Health Grades, Inc. v. Robert Wood Johnson University Hospital, Inc.*, 634 F. Supp. 2d 1226 (D. Colo. 2009) (hospital "ratings" developed by plaintiff were not "facts" or "ideas" but were original compilations entitled to copyright protection).

Both *CCC* and *CDN* were distinguished in *New York Mercantile Exchange, Inc. v. Intercontinental Exchange, Inc.*, 497 F.3d 109 (2d Cir. 2007), in which the court held that NYMEX's daily settlement prices for futures contracts were not copyrightable, based on the merger doctrine. The court noted that the incentive rationale for copyright did not apply, since NYMEX had to arrive at settlement prices to clear transactions, and it was required by law to report the settlement prices it reached. For an analysis of these cases, see Hughes, *Created Facts and the Flawed Ontology of Copyright Law*, 83 Notre Dame L. Rev. 43 (2007); Grimmelmann, *Three Theories of Copyright in Ratings*, 14 Vand. J. Ent. & Tech. L. 851 (2012).

Feist *and Copyright Claims in Judicial Reports*

(10)   From Day One of law school, every law student is required to learn the fine art of "reading cases." Practicing attorneys, of course, read cases, too — not from casebooks like this one, but online or from volumes of judicial reports. It has been generally recognized since *Wheaton v. Peters*, 33 U.S. (8 Pet.) 591 (1834) (discussed in Chapter 2) that the cases themselves are not subject to copyright protection. Headnotes, summaries of the case, and other matter added by the publishers *are* protectible; but the language of the opinions themselves is *not* protectible. The notes that follow deal with something else: the protectability of assembling, editing, and arranging judicial opinions in a post-*Feist* world.

(11)   *The decision in* West Publishing v. MDC. The trouble began back in 1986, in *West Publishing Co. v. Mead Data Central, Inc.*, 799 F.2d 1219 (8th Cir. 1986). There, West managed to obtain from the trial court a preliminary injunction prohibiting LEXIS from inserting into its online reports of cases "jump cites" to West's hardbound reports of the same cases, using the technique of "star pagination" (so-called because an asterisk and citation or page number are inserted in the text of a judicial opinion to indicate where a page break occurs in a different report of the case). The accompanying illustration shows a portion of the report of a decided case by LEXIS, with double asterisks indicating the pages on which the same (public domain) text is located in a volume of West's Supreme Court Reporter.

FEIST PUBLICATIONS, INC. v. RURAL TELEPHONE SERVICE CO.,
INC.

No. 89-1909

SUPREME COURT OF THE UNITED STATES

499 U.S. 340; 111 S. Ct. 1282; 1991 U.S. LEXIS 1856; 113 L.
Ed. 2d 358; 59 U.S.L.W. 4251; 18 U.S.P.Q.2D (BNA) 1275;
Copy. L. Rep. (CCH) P26,702; 68 Rad. Reg. 2d (P & F) 1513;
18 Media L. Rep. 1889; 121 P.U.R.4th 1; 91 Cal. Daily Op.
Service 2217; 91 Daily Journal DAR 3580

March 27, 1991, Decided

CERTIORARI TO THE UNITED STATES
COURT OF APPEALS FOR THE TENTH
CIRCUIT.

DISPOSITION: *916 F. 2d 718*, reversed.

OPINIONBY: O'CONNOR

OPINION: [*342] [**1286] This case
requires us to clarify the extent of copyright
protection available to telephone directory white
pages.

I

Rural Telephone Service Company, Inc., is a
certified public utility that provides telephone
service to several communities in northwest
Kansas. It is subject to a state regulation that
requires all telephone companies operating in
Kansas to issue annually an updated telephone
directory. Accordingly, as a condition of its
monopoly franchise, Rural publishes a typical
telephone directory, consisting of white pages and
yellow pages. The white pages list in alphabetical
order the names of Rural's subscribers, together
with their towns and telephone numbers. The
yellow pages list Rural's business subscribers
alphabetically by category and feature classified
advertisements of various sizes. Rural distributes
its directory free of charge to its subscribers, but
earns revenue by selling yellow pages
advertisements. [***6]

Feist Publications, Inc., is a publishing company
that specializes in area-wide telephone directories.
Unlike a typical [*343] directory, which covers

only a particular calling area, Feist's area-wide
directories cover a much larger geographical
range, reducing the need to call directory
assistance or consult multiple directories. The
Feist directory that is the subject of this litigation
covers 11 different telephone service areas in 15
counties and contains 46,878 white pages listings
— compared to Rural's approximately 7,700
listings. Like Rural's directory, Feist's is
distributed free of charge and includes both white
pages and yellow pages. Feist and Rural compete
vigorously for yellow pages advertising.

As the sole provider of telephone service in its
service area, Rural obtains subscriber information
quite easily. Persons desiring telephone service
must apply to Rural and provide their names and
addresses; Rural then assigns them a telephone
number. Feist is not a telephone company, let
alone one with monopoly status, and therefore
lacks independent access to any subscriber
information. To obtain white pages listings for its
area-wide directory, Feist approached [***7]
each of the 11 telephone companies operating in
northwest Kansas and offered to pay for the right
to use its white pages listings.

Of the 11 telephone companies, only Rural
refused to license its listings to Feist. Rural's
refusal created a problem for Feist, as omitting
these listings would have left a gaping hole in its
area-wide directory, rendering it less attractive to
potential yellow pages advertisers. In a decision
subsequent to that which we review here, the
District Court determined that this was precisely
the reason Rural refused to license its listings. The
refusal was motivated by an unlawful purpose "to

An Example of Star Pagination in LEXIS

(12) Although West had claimed copyright protection for individual page
numbers at the District Court level, in the Court of Appeals its claim metamor-
phosed into an infringement claim based on the entire case reporter volume. West's
argument was that by copying the pagination, LEXIS had copied the arrangement
of the volume. The majority in *West Publishing* concluded that the trial court had
been right to enjoin MDC's planned star pagination to West's volumes of reports:

> [T]he arrangement West produces through [its editorial] process is the result of considerable labor, talent, and judgment. . . . [T]o meet intellectual-creation requirements a work need only be the product of a modicum of intellectual labor; West's case arrangements easily meet this standard. Further, since there is no allegation that West copies its case arrangements from some other source, the requirement of originality poses no obstacle to copyrighting the arrangements. . . . We . . . hold . . . that MDC's proposed use of West page numbers will infringe West's copyright. . . .

799 F.2d at 1227. Concur?

(13)   *West Publishing* was sharply criticized in Patterson & Joyce, *Monopolizing the Law: The Scope of Copyright Protection for Law Reports and Statutory Compilations*, 36 UCLA L. Rev. 719 (1989) (cited with approval in *Feist*). The authors contended, *inter alia*, that "the result in *West Publishing* in theory gives one publisher veto power over whether the [legal] profession, and thus the public, shall enjoy the full benefits of enhanced access to the law which computer-assisted legal research offers, and to which the public is entitled." *Id.* at 727. Compare the District Court's observation in its opinion ordering the preliminary injunction: "the public need for access to the law, which is currently embodied in West's publications, should [not] reduce or eliminate West's exclusive rights in the material." 616 F. Supp. at 1583.

(14)   Subsequent to the Eighth Circuit's decision and the trial on the merits (but before judgment), West and MDC settled *West Publishing* and two other pending suits — one an antitrust action by MDC against West. MDC reportedly paid West "tens of millions of dollars," Labaton, *Westlaw and Lexis Near Truce*, N.Y. Times, July 19, 1988, at D5, for a license to employ star pagination in LEXIS. In the meantime, while the preliminary injunction was in place, West had introduced "star pagination" into WESTLAW. Each of the parties had indicated earlier that the matter would be fought all the way to the Supreme Court — which had denied *certiorari* when asked to review the Eighth Circuit opinion. What motives might have prompted each of the parties ultimately to settle?

(15)   *The decision in* HyperLaw. The uncertainty left in the wake of *West Publishing* was heightened by the Supreme Court's decision in *Feist*. But there was not another authoritative pronouncement on the subject until 1999, when the Second Circuit decided two companion cases: *Matthew Bender & Co. & HyperLaw, Inc. v. West Publishing Co.*, 158 F.3d 674 (1998) ("*HyperLaw*") and *Matthew Bender & Co. v. West Publishing Co.*, 158 F.3d 693 (2d Cir. 1998) ("*Bender*"). Between them, these two related decisions dealt with a range of issues raised by a declaratory judgment action brought against West by competitors in the law-reporting business who sought a judicial green light for their activities.

HyperLaw disposed of the question of whether West could claim rights in its case reports based on various kinds of value added during the editorial process, including: (1) inserting standardized case captions, court information, and date information; (2) including the names of the attorneys involved, along with their roles and affiliations; (3) providing references to subsequent developments in reported decisions; and (4) supplying parallel or alternative citations to authorities relied upon in those decisions. None of this data was routinely included in the court opinions that West collects to create its reporters, and all of it was information that HyperLaw (a supplier of legal information on CD-ROM) wished to incorporate into its products. Relying on *Feist*, however, the Second Circuit decided that West's editorial activities were comprehensively lacking in "originality," "creativity," or both — in part because, as a practical matter, the range of useful choices about how to express the information supplied were so limited. The court said that creativity in selection and arrangement is a function of (a) the total number of options available, (b) external factors that limit the viability of certain options and render others non-creative, and (c) prior uses that render certain selections "garden variety." Do you agree? Are there other ways to look at the problem?

(16) The *HyperLaw* opinion included an extended discussion of whether the works in suit should be treated as derivative works or compilations. Which party might have thought it had a stake in which characterization? Is it easier to hang one of the two labels — derivative work or compilation — on the individual cases considered in *HyperLaw*, and a different label on the National Reporter System volumes at issue in *HyperLaw*'s companion case, *Bender*? Was the *HyperLaw* court right in concluding that the label makes no difference, because the originality standard is the same for both?

(17) In deciding the originality issue, the *HyperLaw* court's method was one of dissection and then extrapolation. That is, the court dissected each element of West's editorial process and then extrapolated that the cumulative effect of their citation decisions was either obvious or trivial. According to the dissent, however, West's selection of particular annotations for each case should have been considered as a whole, not individually. Was the dissent correct in arguing that the majority's approach too tightly applied the standard of originality, even in a post-*Feist* world?

(18) *The decision in* Bender. *HyperLaw*'s companion case, *Bender*, dealt — once again — with the issue of "star pagination." In *Bender*, the Second Circuit, declining to follow the Eighth Circuit's lead, held that Bender and HyperLaw had not infringed (as to Bender) and would not infringe (as to HyperLaw, which was seeking a declaratory judgment prior to actually producing its product) West's copyright by including star pagination to West's case reporters in their own CD-ROM versions of the same judicial opinions. The majority explained:

> We differ with the Eighth Circuit's opinion in *West Publishing Co. v. Mead Data Central, Inc.*, 799 F.2d 1219 (8th Cir.1986). . . . The Eighth Circuit in *West Publishing Co.* adduces no authority for protecting pagination as a "reflection" of arrangement, and does not explain how the insertion of star pagination creates a "copy" featuring an arrangement of cases substantially similar to West's. . . .

> At bottom, *West Publishing Co.* rests upon the now defunct "sweat of the brow" doctrine [overruled by *Feist*]. Thus, the Eighth Circuit in *West Publishing Co.* erroneously protected West's industrious collection rather than its original creation. Because *Feist* undermines the reasoning of *West Publishing Co.*, we decline to follow it.

158 F.3d at 693. Note, however, that the *Bender* court stopped short of holding that West was entitled to *no* copyright protection for its arrangement. That issue remains for another day.

(19)   Judge Sweet dissented in *Bender*, as he had in *HyperLaw*. In his view, the pagination of a West National Reporter System volume "results from West's arrangements, selections, syllabi, headnotes, key numbering, citations and descriptions." Thus, "[t]he page number, arbitrarily determined, is the sole result of the West system, appears nowhere else, and is essential to its coordinated method of citation. It is, so to speak, an original fact resulting from West's creativity." 158 F.3d at 707. Are you persuaded that the "original facts" created by West — namely, the page numbers on which words of judicial opinions appear in a published volume — are protectible expression?

(20)   Whether or not you agree with Judge Sweet in *Bender*, clearly West has created a valuable product in its compilations of opinions. But this is true, perhaps even more so in certain instances, of compilations of mere data. Recall that, under the 17 U.S.C. § 101 definition of a compilation, the Copyright Act is capable of protecting works "formed by the collection and assembling of preexisting materials [such as judicial opinions] *or of data*," at least insofar as "the resulting work as a whole constitutes an original work of authorship." How do the principles of copyrightability embedded in the Copyright Act apply to databases? Can the Act provide meaningful protection for such works? Or, in light of the minimal creativity involved in most such collections of data, can they be more readily, and better, protected by *sui generis* legislation *outside* the Copyright Act? In concluding this chapter, we turn briefly to recent debates in Congress concerning database protection and piracy.

DATABASE PROTECTION

The practical implications of the *Feist* decision have been minimal for the vast majority of database producers. As *Feist*'s own facts suggest, most companies routinely cross-license their data to one another already. Many other users (like direct mail marketers) who, as a matter of law, might copy phone number information from directories freely after *Feist* probably will continue to pay in order to receive that data in more convenient formats, and to be assured of being provided current updates.

By contrast, compilers of other databases may be more profoundly affected. Consider the problem of *computerized* databases. These (often vast) storehouses of information — accessible to subscribers and purchasers via the Internet or in CD-ROM format — represent significant investments, to say the least. But they lack characteristics which would make them readily protectible under some interpretations of the copyright law relating to factual compilations. Although computerized databases have a kind of "structure" which permits users to access the information in which they are interested without having to scan through the compilation as a whole, that format is internal to the database itself and is not reproduced when information from the database is copied or "downloaded," even in quantity. Thus, a subscriber to LEXIS or WESTLAW could take all of the recent estate tax decisions and reproduce them in the form of, say, a newsletter, without copying the "organization" of those databases. At the same time, because many databases are valuable precisely due to their inclusiveness, it may be difficult or impossible to justify their protection on the ground of "selection."

Most database proprietors use contractual mechanisms for protecting their compilations, as we will see when we discuss *ProCD v. Zeidenberg* in Chapter 11. In addition, however, some continue to seek protection under federal statutes. On its face, *Feist* looked like the end of the trail for protection based on "sweat of the brow." But beginning in 1995, inspired in part by the "Database Directive" then working its way through the legislative process of the European Union — which required member countries, among other things, to adopt new intellectual property rights in non-original databases, 1996 O.J. (L 77) — U.S. database providers sought to make an end-run around *Feist*. The vehicle was a *sui generis* bill based not on Art. I, § 8, cl. 8 of the Constitution, but rather on the Commerce Clause. In your judgment, how complete is the constitutional grounding of *Feist*? Could Congress successfully, under the authority of the Commerce Clause, provide for protection of databases and other factual compilations which lack the sort of "authorship" and "originality" described in Justice O'Connor's opinion?

In answering this question, consider whether *Feist*'s comments about a constitutional right to copy uncopyrightable information were intended to preempt all Congressional activity, or were instead merely a statement about the scope of Congress's authority under the Copyright Clause of the Constitution. Should it matter which hat Congress wears? If the Supreme Court has declared that one may copy uncopyrightable material, may Congress change hats and say, "No, you can't," under the Commerce Clause? Wouldn't the policy sought to be furthered by such copying be equally impeded regardless of which power Congress legislated under? For a review of some of the thinking on this question, see Heald & Sherry, *Implied Limits on the Legislative Power: The Intellectual Property Clause as an Absolute Constraint on Congress*, 2000 U. Ill. L. Rev. 1119, and Pollack, *The Right to Know?: Delimiting Database Protection at the Juncture of the Commerce Clause, the Intellectual Property Clause, and the First Amendment*, 17 Cardozo Arts & Ent. L.J. 47 (1999). So far, at least, the issue hasn't been presented, because a series of database protection bills introduced in Congress have failed to become law, in part because of the vociferous opposition from a surprisingly wide range of sources.

Future prospects for database legislation in the United States may turn on the relative success (or lack thereof) of the European Union's 1996 Database Directive. In 2004, the European Court of Justice handed down its first four judgments in cases requiring interpretation of the Directive. In the leading case, *British Horseracing Board Ltd. v. William Hill Org. Ltd.*, Case No. C-203/02, [2005] 1 C.M.L.R. 15, the ECJ held that any investment made in "creating" data was not to be considered in determining whether a database maker has made a substantial investment in "obtaining, verifying or presenting" the contents of a database. Whether such a law would actually benefit the public interest is highly debatable, particularly after a 2005 European Union evaluation of the Directive. The E.U. report concluded that there was little evidence regarding the Directive's effectiveness in creating growth in the production of European databases. See Commission of The European Communities, DG Internal Market and Services Working Paper, First Evaluation of Directive 96/9/EC on the Legal Protection of Databases (Dec.

12, 2005), *available at http://ec.europa.eu/internal_market/copyright/docs/ databases/evaluation_report_en.pdf*. The paper, however, did not recommend that the Directive be abrogated, because it did not impose significant administrative or other regulatory burdens on the database industry or any other industries that depend on having access to data and information.

Chapter 4

OWNERSHIP AND TRANSFERS

Prior to the Statute of Anne, printing patents and other printing privileges were granted to the publisher of a work, rather than to its author. The Statute of Anne was revolutionary because it was the first statute to grant an exclusive right to "the author" rather than to a publisher directly (although the latter actors are indeed contemplated in the title of the Act as "purchasers" of authors' manuscripts, in whom copyrights also may be vested).

It is clear, however, that the rallying cry of "author's rights" was primarily a stalking horse for the true beneficiaries of the Statute — namely, the "assignee or assigns," who appeared by name in the first section of the Statute and to whom the newly-enacted copyright could be transferred. The same section also confirmed all existing privileges by conferring the exclusive right to print books already published upon the "booksellers, printers or other persons . . . who have purchased or acquired the copy or copies of any book or books, in order to print or reprint the same." In the United States, the 1976 Act continues to reflect these two important features of the Statute of Anne: the assignment of initial ownership to the "author or authors" of a work; and the ability of the author to transfer ownership of his or her rights to a third party.

That said, determining who is the author or transferee of a work is not always an easy task. This chapter explores who owns a copyright in the work as an initial matter, and how ownership of the copyright can be validly transferred to those who are interested in exploiting the copyright.

§ 4.01 INITIAL OWNERSHIP

Initial ownership of copyright is easy to determine when an individual creates a work at his own instance and expense. In such circumstances, the individual is the author of the work and the initial owner of the copyright.

Many works, however, are created in an employment relationship or through the combined efforts of several persons. These works may qualify for special treatment as "works made for hire" or "joint works" respectively. Under the 1909 Act, these two situations presented difficult problems in determining the nature and scope of copyright ownership. The 1976 Act did much to clarify some of the more unsatisfactory doctrines developed under its predecessor statute. Even with this added clarity, important questions concerning copyright ownership remain open. For this reason, case law developed under the 1909 Act sometimes is used to deal with issues not clearly resolved by the 1976 Act. Moreover, 1909 Act rules and case law apply in determining the ownership status of copyrights that arose before January 1, 1978, the effective date of the 1976 Act.

A less complex but distinct problem, involving protection for individual contributions to periodicals, anthologies, encyclopedias, and the like (generically called "collective works"), is dealt with briefly at the end of this section.

[A] Introduction

Statutory References

1976 Act: §§ 101 ("copyright owner," "joint work," "work made for hire"), 201(a)–(c)

1909 Act: § 26

Legislative History

H.R. Rep. No. 94-1476 at 120–22,
reprinted in 1976 U.S.C.C.A.N. 5659, 5736–38

SECTION 201. OWNERSHIP OF COPYRIGHT

Initial ownership

Two basic and well-established principles of copyright law are restated in section 201(a): that the source of copyright ownership is the author of the work, and that, in the case of a "joint work," the coauthors of the work are likewise co-owners of the copyright. Under the definition of section 101, a work is "joint" if the authors collaborated with each other, or if each of the authors prepared his or her contribution with the knowledge and intention that it would be merged with the contributions of other authors as "inseparable or interdependent parts of a unitary whole." The touchstone here is the intention, at the time the writing is done, that the parts be absorbed or combined into an integrated unit, although the parts themselves may be either "inseparable" (as in the case of a novel or painting) or "interdependent" (as in the case of a motion picture, opera, or the words and music of a song). The definition of "joint work" is to be contrasted with the definition of "collective work," also in section 101, in which the elements of merger and unity are lacking; there the key elements are assemblage or gathering of "separate and independent works . . . into a collective whole."

There is . . . no need for a specific statutory provision concerning the rights and duties of the co-owners of a work; court-made law on this point is left undisturbed. Under the bill, as under the [1909 Act], co-owners of a copyright would be treated generally as tenants in common, with each co-owner having an independent right to use or license the use of a work, subject to a duty of accounting to the other co-owners for any profits.

Works made for hire

Section 201(b) of the bill adopts one of the basic principles of the . . . law [under the 1909 Act]: that in the case of works made for hire the employer is considered the author of the work, and is regarded as the initial owner of copyright unless there has been an agreement otherwise. The subsection also requires that any agreement under which the employee is to own rights be in writing and signed by the parties.

The status of works prepared on special order or commission was a major issue in the development of the definition of "works made for hire" in section 101, which has undergone extensive revision during the legislative process. The basic problem is how to draw a statutory line between those works written on special order or commission that should be considered as "works made for hire," and those that should not. The definition now provided by the bill represents a compromise which, in effect, spells out those specific categories of commissioned works that can be considered "works made for hire" under certain circumstances. . . .

Contributions to collective works

Subsection (c) of section 201 deals with the troublesome problem of ownership of copyright in contributions to collective works, and the relationship between copyright ownership in a contribution and in the collective work in which it appears. The first sentence establishes the basic principle that copyright in the individual contribution and copyright in the collective work as a whole are separate and distinct, and that the author of the contribution is, as in every other case, the first owner of copyright in it.

The second sentence of section 201(c), in conjunction with the provisions of section 404 dealing with copyright notice, will preserve the author's copyright in a contribution even if the contribution does not bear a separate notice in the author's name, and without requiring any unqualified transfer of rights to the owner of the collective work. This is coupled with a presumption that, unless there has been an express transfer of more, the owner of the collective work acquires "only the privilege of reproducing and distributing the contribution as part of that particular collective work, any revision of that collective work, and any later collective work in the same series."

[*For a fuller excerpt from* H.R. REP. NO. 94-1476, *see Part Three of the Casebook Supplement.*]

[B]   Works Made for Hire

COMMUNITY FOR CREATIVE NON-VIOLENCE v. REID
Supreme Court of the United States
490 U.S. 730 (1989)

JUSTICE MARSHALL delivered the opinion of the Court.

In this case, an artist and the organization that hired him to produce a sculpture contest the ownership of the copyright in that work. To resolve this dispute, we must construe the "work made for hire" provisions of the Copyright Act of 1976 (Act or 1976 Act), 17 U.S.C. §§ 101 and 201(b), and, in particular, the provision in § 101, which defines as a "work made for hire" a "work prepared by an employee within the scope of his or her employment" (hereinafter § 101(1)).

I

Petitioners are the Community for Creative Non-Violence (CCNV), a nonprofit unincorporated association dedicated to eliminating homelessness in America, and Mitch Snyder, a member and trustee of CCNV. In the fall of 1985, CCNV decided to participate in the annual Christmastime Pageant of Peace in Washington, D.C., by sponsoring a display to dramatize the plight of the homeless. As the District Court recounted:

> Snyder and fellow CCNV members conceived the idea for the nature of the display: a sculpture of a modern Nativity scene in which, in lieu of the traditional Holy Family, the two adult figures and the infant would appear as contemporary homeless people huddled on a streetside steam grate. The family was to be black (most of the homeless in Washington being black); the figures were to be life-sized; and the steam grate would be positioned atop a platform "pedestal," or base, within which special-effects equipment would be enclosed to emit simulated "steam" through the grid to swirl about the figures. They also settled upon a title for the work — "Third World America" — and a legend for the pedestal: "and still there is no room at the inn."

"Third World America"

Snyder made inquiries to locate an artist to produce the sculpture. He was referred to respondent James Earl Reid, a Baltimore, Maryland, sculptor. In the course of two telephone calls, Reid agreed to sculpt the three human figures. CCNV agreed to make the steam grate and pedestal for the statue. . . . The parties agreed that the project would cost no more than $15,000, not including Reid's services, which he offered to donate. The parties did not sign a written agreement. Neither party mentioned copyright.

After Reid received an advance of $3,000, he made several sketches of figures in various poses. At Snyder's request, Reid sent CCNV a sketch of a proposed sculpture showing the family in a creche-like setting: the mother seated, cradling a baby in her lap; the father standing behind her, bending over her shoulder to touch the baby's foot. Reid testified that Snyder asked for the sketch to use in raising funds for the sculpture. Snyder testified that it was also for his approval. . . . While Reid was in Washington, Snyder took him to see homeless people living on the streets. Snyder pointed out that they tended to recline on steam grates, rather than sit or stand, in order to warm their bodies. From that time on, Reid's sketches contained only reclining figures.

Throughout November and the first two weeks of December 1985, Reid worked exclusively on the statue, assisted at various times by a dozen different people who were paid with funds provided in installments by CCNV. On a number of occasions, CCNV members visited Reid to check on his progress and to coordinate CCNV's construction of the base. CCNV rejected Reid's proposal to use suitcases or shopping bags to hold the family's personal belongings, insisting instead on a shopping cart. Reid and CCNV members did not discuss copyright ownership on any of these visits.

On December 24, 1985, 12 days after the agreed-upon date, Reid delivered the completed statue to Washington. There it was joined to the steam grate and pedestal prepared by CCNV and placed on display near the site of the pageant. Snyder paid Reid the final installment of the $15,000. The statue remained on display for a month. In late January 1986, CCNV members returned it to Reid's studio in Baltimore for minor repairs. Several weeks later, Snyder began making plans to take the statue on a tour of several cities to raise money for the homeless. Reid objected, contending that the [synthetic] material was not strong enough to withstand the ambitious itinerary. He urged CCNV to cast the statue in bronze at a cost of $35,000, or to create a master mold at a cost of $5,000. Snyder declined to spend more of CCNV's money on the project.

In March 1986, Snyder asked Reid to return the sculpture. Reid refused. He then filed a certificate of copyright registration for "Third World America" in his name and announced plans to take the sculpture on a more modest tour than the one CCNV had proposed. Snyder, acting in his capacity as CCNV's trustee, immediately filed a competing certificate of copyright registration.

Snyder and CCNV then commenced this action against Reid . . . , seeking return of the sculpture and a determination of copyright ownership. The District Court granted a preliminary injunction, ordering the sculpture's return. After a 2-day bench trial, the District Court declared that "Third World America" was a "work made for hire" under § 101 of the Copyright Act and that Snyder, as trustee for CCNV, was the exclusive owner of the copyright in the sculpture. The court reasoned that Reid had been an "employee" of CCNV within the meaning of § 101(1) because CCNV was the motivating force in the statue's production. Snyder and other CCNV members, the court explained, "conceived the idea of a contemporary Nativity scene to contrast with the national celebration of the season," and "directed enough of [Reid's] effort to assure that, in the end, he had produced what they, not he, wanted."

The Court of Appeals for the District of Columbia reversed and remanded, holding that Reid owned the copyright because "Third World America" was not a work for hire. . . . The court suggested that the sculpture nevertheless may have been jointly authored by CCNV and Reid, and remanded for a determination whether the sculpture is indeed a joint work under the Act.

We granted *certiorari* to resolve a conflict among the Courts of Appeals over the proper construction of the "work made for hire" provisions of the Act. We now affirm. . . .

II

A

The Copyright Act of 1976 provides that copyright ownership "vests initially in the author or authors of the work." 17 U.S.C. § 201(a). As a general rule, the author is the party who actually creates the work, that is, the person who translates an idea into a fixed, tangible expression entitled to copyright protection. § 102. The Act carves out an important exception, however, for "works made for hire." If the work is for hire, "the employer or other person for whom the work was prepared is considered the author" and owns the copyright, unless there is a written agreement to the contrary. § 201(b). Classifying a work as "made for hire" determines not only the initial ownership of its copyright, but also the copyright's duration, § 302(c), and the owner's renewal rights, § 304(a), termination rights, § 203(a), and right to import certain goods bearing the copyright, § 601(b)(1). . . . The contours of the work for hire doctrine therefore carry profound significance for freelance creators — including artists, writers, photographers, designers, composers, and computer programmers — and for the publishing, advertising, music, and other industries which commission their works.[4]

Section 101 of the 1976 Act provides that a work is "for hire" under two sets of circumstances:

> (1) a work prepared by an employee within the scope of his or her employment; or

> (2) a work specially ordered or commissioned for use as a contribution to a collective work, as a part of a motion picture or other audiovisual work, as a translation, as a supplementary work, as a compilation, as an instructional text, as a test, as answer material for a test, or as an atlas, if the parties expressly agree in a written instrument signed by them that the work shall be considered a work made for hire.

---

[4] As of 1955, approximately 40 percent of all copyright registrations were for works for hire, according to a Copyright Office study. *See* Varmer, *Works Made for Hire and On Commission*, in STUDIES PREPARED FOR THE SUBCOMMITTEE ON PATENTS, TRADEMARKS, AND COPYRIGHTS OF THE SENATE COMMITTEE ON THE JUDICIARY, Study No. 13, 86th Cong., 2d Sess. 139, n. 49 (Comm. Print 1960) (hereinafter Varmer, *Works Made for Hire*). The Copyright Office does not keep more recent statistics on the number of work for hire registrations.

The petitioners do not claim that the statue satisfies the terms of § 101(2). Quite clearly, it does not. Sculpture does not fit within any of the nine categories of "specially ordered or commissioned" works enumerated in that subsection, and no written agreement between the parties establishes "Third World America" as a work for hire.

The dispositive inquiry in this case therefore is whether "Third World America" is "a work prepared by an employee within the scope of his or her employment" under § 101(1). The Act does not define these terms. In the absence of such guidance, four interpretations have emerged. The first holds that a work is prepared by an employee whenever the hiring party[6] retains the right to control the product. *See Peregrine v. Lauren Corp.*, 601 F. Supp. 828, 829 (D. Colo. 1985); *Clarkstown v. Reeder*, 566 F. Supp. 137, 142 (S.D.N.Y. 1983). Petitioners take this view. A second, and closely related, view is that a work is prepared by an employee under § 101(1) when the hiring party has actually wielded control with respect to the creation of a particular work. This approach was formulated by the Court of Appeals for the Second Circuit, *Aldon Accessories Ltd. v. Spiegel, Inc.*, 738 F.2d 548 (1984), and adopted by the Fourth Circuit, *Brunswick Beacon, Inc. v. Schock-Hopchas Publishing Co.*, 810 F.2d 410 (1987), the Seventh Circuit, *Evans Newton, Inc. v. Chicago Systems Software*, 793 F.2d 889 (1986), and, at times, by petitioners. A third view is that the term "employee" within § 101(1) carries its common law agency law meaning. This view was endorsed by the Fifth Circuit in *Easter Seal Society for Crippled Children & Adults of Louisiana, Inc. v. Playboy Enterprises*, 815 F.2d 323 (1987), and by the Court of Appeals below. Finally, respondent and numerous *amici curiae* contend that the term "employee" only refers to "formal, salaried" employees. *See, e.g., . . . Brief for Register of Copyrights as Amicus Curiae* 7. The Court of Appeals for the Ninth Circuit recently adopted this view. *See Dumas v. Gommerman*, 865 F.2d 1093 (1989).

The starting point for our interpretation of a statute is always its language. . . . The Act nowhere defines the terms "employee" or "scope of employment." It is, however, well established that

> [w]here Congress uses terms that have accumulated settled meaning under . . . the common law, a court must infer, unless the statute otherwise dictates, that Congress means to incorporate the established meaning of these terms.

NLRB v. Amax Coal Co., 453 U.S. 322, 329 (1981). . . . In the past, when Congress has used the term "employee" without defining it, we have concluded that Congress intended to describe the conventional master-servant relationship as understood by common law agency doctrine. . . . Nothing in the text of the work for hire provisions indicates that Congress used the words "employee" and "employment" to describe anything other than "the conventional relation of employer and employee." . . . On the contrary, Congress' intent to incorporate the agency law definition is suggested by § 101(1)'s use of the term "scope of employment," a widely

---

[6] By "hiring party," we mean to refer to the party who claims ownership of the copyright by virtue of the work-for-hire doctrine.

used term of art in agency law. *See Restatement (Second) of Agency* § 228 (1958) (hereinafter *Restatement*).

In past cases of statutory interpretation, when we have concluded that Congress intended terms such as "employee," "employer," and "scope of employment" to be understood in light of agency law, we have relied on the general common law of agency, rather than on the law of any particular State, to give meaning to these terms. . . . Establishment of a federal rule of agency, rather than reliance on state agency law, is particularly appropriate here given the Act's express objective of creating national uniform copyright law by broadly pre-empting state statutory and common-law copyright regulation. *See* 17 U.S.C. § 301(a). We thus agree with the Court of Appeals that the term "employee" should be understood in light of the general common law of agency.

In contrast, neither test proposed by petitioners is consistent with the text of the Act. . . . Section 101 plainly creates two distinct ways in which a work can be deemed for hire: one for works prepared by employees, the other for those specially ordered or commissioned works which fall within one of the nine enumerated categories and are the subject of a written agreement. The right to control the product test ignores this dichotomy by transforming into a work for hire under § 101(1) any "specially ordered or commissioned" work that is subject to the supervision and control of the hiring party. Because a party who hires a "specially ordered or commissioned" work by definition has a right to specify the character- istics of the product desired at the time the commission is accepted, and frequently until it is completed, the right to control the product test would mean that many works that could satisfy § 101(2) would already have been deemed works for hire under § 101(1). Petitioners' interpretation is particularly hard to square with § 101(2)'s enumeration of the nine specific categories of specially ordered or commissioned works eligible to be works for hire, *e.g.*, "a contribution to a collective work," "a part of a motion picture," and "answer material for a test." The unifying feature of these works is that they are usually prepared at the instance, direction, and risk of a publisher or producer. By their very nature, therefore, these types of works would be works by an employee under petitioners' right to control the product test.

The actual control test . . . fares only marginally better when measured against the language and structure of § 101. Under this test, . . . work for hire status under § 101(1) depends on a hiring party's actual control, rather than right to control, of the product. *Aldon Accessories*, 738 F.2d, at 552. Under the actual control test, a work for hire could arise under § 101(2), but not under § 101(1), where a party commissions, but does not actually control, a product which falls into one of the nine enumerated categories. . . . Section 101 clearly delineates between works prepared by an employee and commissioned works. Sound though other distinctions might be as a matter of copyright policy, there is no statutory support for an additional dichotomy between commissioned works that are actually controlled and supervised by the hiring party and those that are not.

We therefore conclude that the language and structure of § 101 of the Act do not support either the right to control the product or the actual control approaches.[8] The structure of § 101 indicates that a work for hire can arise through one of two mutually exclusive means, one for employees and one for independent contractors, and ordinary canons of statutory interpretation indicate that the classification of a particular hired party should be made with reference to agency law.

This reading of the undefined statutory terms finds considerable support in the Act's legislative history. . . . The Act, which almost completely revised existing copyright law, was the product of two decades of negotiation by representatives of creators and copyright-using industries, supervised by the Copyright Office and, to a lesser extent, by Congress. *See Mills Music, Inc. v. Snyder*, 469 U.S. 153, 159 (1985); Litman, *Copyright, Compromise, and Legislative History*, 72 Cornell L. Rev. 857, 862 (1987). Despite the lengthy history of negotiation and compromise which ultimately produced the Act, two things remained constant. First, interested parties and Congress at all times viewed works by employees and commissioned works by independent contractors as separate entities. Second, in using the term "employee," the parties and Congress meant to refer to a hired party in a conventional employment relationship. These factors militate in favor of the reading we have found appropriate.

In 1955, when Congress decided to overhaul copyright law, the existing work for hire provision was § 26 of the 1909 Copyright Act, 17 U.S.C. § 26 (1976 ed.) (1909 Act). It provided that "the word 'author' shall include an employer in the case of works made for hire." Because the 1909 Act did not define "employer" or "works made for hire," the task of shaping these terms fell to the courts. They concluded that the work for hire doctrine codified in § 26 referred only to works made by employees in the regular course of their employment. As for commissioned works, the courts generally presumed that the commissioned party had impliedly agreed to convey the copyright, along with the work itself, to the hiring party. . . .[10]

In 1961, the Copyright Office's first legislative proposal retained the distinction between works by employees and works by independent contractors. After numerous meetings with representatives of the affected parties, the Copyright Office issued a preliminary draft bill in 1963. Adopting the Register's recommendation, it defined "work made for hire" as "a work prepared by an employee within the scope

---

[8] We also reject the suggestion of respondent and *amici* that the § 101(1) term "employee" refers only to formal, salaried employees. While there is some support for such a definition in the legislative history, *see* Varmer, *Works Made for Hire* 130, . . . the language of § 101(1) cannot support it. The Act does not say "formal" or "salaried" employee, but simply "employee." Moreover, the respondent and those *amici* who endorse a formal, salaried employee test do not agree upon the content of this test. . . . Even the one Court of Appeals to adopt what it termed a formal, salaried employee test in fact embraced an approach incorporating numerous factors drawn from the agency law definition of employee which we endorse. *See Dumas*, 865 F.2d, at 1104.

[10] *See* Varmer, *Works Made for Hire* 130; Fidlow, *The "Works Made for Hire" Doctrine and the Employee/Independent Contractor Dichotomy: The Need for Congressional Clarification*, 10 Hastings Comm. & Ent. L.J. 591, 600–01 (1988). Indeed, the Varmer study, which was commissioned by Congress as part of the revision process, itself contained separate subsections labeled "Works Made for Hire" and "Works Made on Commission." It nowhere indicated that the two categories might overlap or that commissioned works could be made by an employee.

of the duties of his employment, but not including a work made on special order or commission." . . .

In response to objections by book publishers that the preliminary draft bill limited the work for hire doctrine to "employees," the 1964 revision bill expanded the scope of the work for hire classification to reach, for the first time, commissioned works. The bill's language, proposed initially by representatives of the publishing industry, retained the definition of work for hire insofar as it referred to "employees," but added a separate clause covering commissioned works, without regard to the subject matter, "if the parties so agree in writing." S. 3008, H.R. 11947, H.R. 1254, 88th Cong., 2d Sess., § 54 (1964). Those representing authors objected that the added provision would allow publishers to use their superior bargaining position to force authors to sign work for hire agreements, thereby relinquishing all copyright rights as a condition of getting their books published.

In 1965, the competing interests reached an historic compromise which was embodied in a joint memorandum submitted to Congress and the Copyright Office, incorporated into the 1965 revision bill, and ultimately enacted in the same form and nearly the same terms 11 years later, as § 101 of the 1976 Act. The compromise retained as subsection (1) the language referring to "a work prepared by an employee within the scope of his employment." However, in exchange for concessions from publishers on provisions relating to the termination of transfer rights, the authors consented to a second subsection which classified four categories of commissioned works as works for hire if the parties expressly so agreed in writing: works for use "as a contribution to a collective work, as a part of a motion picture, as a translation, or as supplementary work." S. 1006, H.R. 4347, H.R. 5680, H.R. 6835, 89th Cong., 1st Sess., § 101 (1965). . . . The *Supplementary Report* emphasized that only the "four special cases specifically mentioned" could qualify as works made for hire; "[o]ther works made on special order or commission would not come within the definition." *Id.*, at 67-68.

In 1966, the House Committee on the Judiciary endorsed this compromise in the first legislative report on the revision bills. *See* H.R. Rep. No. 2237, 89th Cong., 2d Sess., 114, 116 (1966). . . . The House Committee added four other enumerated categories of commissioned works that could be treated as works for hire: compilations, instructional texts, tests, and atlases. *Id.*, at 116. With the single addition of "answer material for a test," the 1976 Act, as enacted, contained the same definition of works made for hire as did the 1966 revision bill, and had the same structure and nearly the same terms as the 1966 bill. . . .

Thus, the legislative history of the Act is significant for several reasons. First, the enactment of the 1965 compromise with only minor modifications demonstrates that Congress intended to provide two mutually exclusive ways for works to acquire work for hire status: one for employees and the other for independent contractors. Second, the legislative history underscores the clear import of the statutory language: only enumerated categories of commissioned works may be accorded work for hire status. The hiring party's right to control the product simply is not determinative. . . . Indeed, importing a test based on a hiring party's right to control or actual control of a product would unravel the "carefully worked out compromise aimed at balancing legitimate interests on both sides." H.R. Rep. No. 2237, *supra*, at 114 . . .

We do not find convincing petitioners' contrary interpretation of the history of the Act. They contend that Congress, in enacting the Act, meant to incorporate a line of cases decided under the 1909 Act holding that an employment relationship exists sufficient to give the hiring party copyright ownership whenever that party has the right to control or supervise the artist's work. . . .

We are unpersuaded. Ordinarily, "Congress' silence is just that — silence." *Alaska Airlines, Inc. v. Brock*, 480 U.S. 678, 686 (1987). Petitioners' reliance on legislative silence is particularly misplaced here because the text and structure of § 101 counsel otherwise. . . .

Finally, petitioners' construction of the work for hire provisions would impede Congress' paramount goal in revising the 1976 Act of enhancing predictability and certainty of copyright ownership. *See* H.R. Rep. No. 94-1476, *supra*, at 129. . . .

To the extent that petitioners endorse an actual control test, CCNV's construction of the work for hire provisions prevents such planning. Because that test turns on whether the hiring party has closely monitored the production process, the parties would not know until late in the process, if not until the work is completed, whether a work will ultimately fall within § 101(1). . . . This understanding of the work for hire provisions clearly thwarts Congress' goal of ensuring predictability through advance planning. Moreover, petitioners' interpretation

> leaves the door open for hiring parties, who have failed to get a full assignment of copyright rights from independent contractors falling outside the subdivision (2) guidelines, to unilaterally obtain work-made-for-hire rights years after the work has been completed as long as they directed or supervised the work, a standard that is hard not to meet when one is a hiring party.

Hamilton, *Commissioned Works as Works Made for Hire Under the 1976 Copyright Act: Misinterpretation and Injustice*, 135 U. Pa. L. Rev. 1281, 1304 (1987).

In sum, we must reject petitioners' argument. Transforming a commissioned work into a work by an employee on the basis of the hiring party's right to control, or actual control of, the work is inconsistent with the language, structure, and legislative history of the work for hire provisions. To determine whether a work is for hire under the Act, a court first should ascertain, using principles of the general common law of agency, whether the work was prepared by an employee or an independent contractor. After making this determination, the court can apply the appropriate subsection of § 101.

B

We turn, finally, to an application of § 101 to Reid's production of "Third World America." In determining whether a hired party is an employee under the general common law of agency, we consider the hiring party's right to control the manner and means by which the product is accomplished. Among the other factors relevant to this inquiry are the skill required; the source of the instrumentalities and tools;

the location of the work; the duration of the relationship between the parties; whether the hiring party has the right to assign additional projects to the hired party; the extent of the hired party's discretion over when and how long to work; the method of payment; the hired party's role in hiring and paying assistants; whether the work is part of the regular business of the hiring party; whether the hiring party is in business; the provision of employee benefits; and the tax treatment of the hired party. *See Restatement* [*of Agency*] § 220(2) (setting forth a nonexhaustive list of factors relevant to determining whether a hired party is an employee). No one of these factors is determinative. . . .

Examining the circumstances of this case in light of these factors, we agree with the Court of Appeals that Reid was not an employee of CCNV but an independent contractor. . . . True, CCNV members directed enough of Reid's work to ensure that he produced a sculpture that met their specifications. . . . But the extent of control the hiring party exercises over the details of the product is not dispositive. Indeed, all the other circumstances weigh heavily against finding an employment relationship. Reid is a sculptor, a skilled occupation. Reid supplied his own tools. He worked in his own studio in Baltimore, making daily supervision of his activities from Washington practicably impossible. Reid was retained for less than two months, a relatively short period of time. During and after this time, CCNV had no right to assign additional projects to Reid. Apart from the deadline for completing the sculpture, Reid had absolute freedom to decide when and how long to work. CCNV paid Reid $15,000, a sum dependent on "completion of a specific job, a method by which independent contractors are often compensated." *Holt v. Winpisinger*, 811 F.2d 1532, 1540 (1987). Reid had total discretion in hiring and paying assistants. "Creating sculptures was hardly 'regular business' for CCNV." 846 F.2d, at 1494, n. 11. Indeed, CCNV is not a business at all. Finally, CCNV did not pay payroll or social security taxes, provide any employee benefits, or contribute to unemployment insurance or workers' compensation funds.

Because Reid was an independent contractor, whether "Third World America" is a work for hire depends on whether it satisfies the terms of § 101(2). This, petitioners concede, it cannot do. Thus, CCNV is not the author of "Third World America" by virtue of the work for hire provisions of the Act. However, as the Court of Appeals made clear, CCNV nevertheless may be a joint author of the sculpture if, on remand, the District Court so determines that CCNV and Reid prepared the work "with the intention that their contributions be merged into inseparable or interdependent parts of a unitary whole." 17 U.S.C. § 101. In that case, CCNV and Reid would be co-owners of the copyright in the work. *See* § 201(a).

For the aforestated reasons, we affirm the judgment of the Court of Appeals for the District of Columbia. It is so ordered.

NOTES AND QUESTIONS

(1) *The "work made for hire" concept in context.* The "work for hire" doctrine, embodied in § 201(b) of the 1976 Act and § 26 of the 1909 Act, codifies a principle first recognized by the U.S. Supreme Court in *Bleistein v. Donaldson Lithographing Co.*, excerpted in Chapter 2. In an omitted portion of the opinion, Justice Holmes noted the plaintiffs' right to sue for infringement of the subject posters,

which had "been produced by persons employed and paid by the plaintiffs in their establishment to make those very things." 188 U.S. 239, 248 (1903). Given the doctrine's distinguished paternity, it seems almost churlish to question whether the Framers of the Copyright Clause contemplated that works protected thereby might be "authored" by multinational corporations. *Cf. Scherr v. Universal Match Co.*, 417 F.2d 497, 502 (2d Cir. 1969) (Friendly, J., dissenting) (questioning whether Congress can willy-nilly deem anyone an "author"); *Childress v. Taylor*, 945 F.2d 500, 506 n.5 (2d Cir. 1991) (the next case in this book).

(2)   As we discuss in more detail in the notes that follow, the 1976 Act provides two means by which a work is "made for hire": (1) if the work is created by one or more employees within the scope of employment; or (2) if a person other than an employee creates the work in response to a special order or commission, the work fits within one of the nine categories of work specified in § 101(2), and the parties expressly agree in a signed writing that the work is made for hire. If the work is made for hire, the employer or commissioning party is deemed to be the "author" and, as a default rule, owns all of the exclusive rights in the work (although the individual creator may own some or all of the rights if the parties expressly agree in writing). *See* § 201(b).

(3)   Before becoming bogged down in the practical application of the 1976 Act's provisions, one should realize that there are other plausible ways of working out ownership rights for works created by employees. For example, in U.S. patent law, only natural persons can be "inventors," although the invention (and the right to file a patent application) may be assigned to an employer by contract. Even absent assignment, an employer who contributes resources may obtain a common-law "shop right" to use the patented invention in its business. Similarly, most foreign nations limit authorship status to natural persons (at least where traditional literary and artistic works are concerned), providing implied (or statutory) presumptions permitting employers to use, for their own purposes, works created by employees. *See* P. Goldstein & B. Hugenholtz, INTERNATIONAL COPYRIGHT: PRINCIPLES, LAW & PRACTICE § 7.4 (2d ed. 2010). In the same "pro-author" spirit, many of the same countries explicitly recognize authors' "moral" rights and regard them (unlike "economic" rights) as inalienable. When we cover the "Visual Artists Rights Act of 1990" in Chapter 7, ask yourself whether American law now gives employees who create "works made for hire" any similar rights. (Hint: Don't bet on it.)

How might the U.S. work-for-hire doctrine, disdained by authors' rights advocates worldwide, be justified in policy terms? To its advocates, the doctrine promotes economic efficiency in the market for copyrighted works by avoiding transactions costs in the negotiation of contracts between employers and employees. And the savings are substantial, considering how many works are created in an employment setting. Similarly, by establishing ownership rights that clearly favor the employer, property rights covering the work are rendered certain, facilitating the sale of the work to others who might find a higher-valued use for it. In this analysis it is assumed that, as between the employee and employer, the latter is in a better position to exploit and enhance the value of the work. *See* Hardy, *An Economic Understanding of Copyright Law's Work-Made-For-Hire Doctrine*, 12 Colum.-VLA J.L. & Arts 181 (1988). Compare Hardy's views with Dreyfuss, *The Creative Employee and the Copyright Act of 1976*, 54 U. Chi. L. Rev. 590 (1987), attempting to synthesize the economic and author-based approaches to the work-for-hire doctrine. Does the work-for-hire doctrine represent the classic tradeoff between economic efficiency and equity — *i.e.*, fairness to authors?

(4) A number of consequences follow once a work is determined to have been made for hire, all flowing from the fact that the work-for-hire "author" owns the entire copyright interest in the work, and the actual creator, none. For example, a notice showing the owner of a copyright in a work for hire to be anyone other than the employer is defective, thereby providing a defense to an innocent infringer for pre-Berne works. § 406(a). The duration of the copyright in such a work created on or after January 1, 1978 is 95 years from the year in which the work was first published, or 120 years from the year in which it was created, whichever comes first. § 302(c). Grants of rights in works for hire, unlike most other types of grants, are immune from termination by operation of law under the provisions of the current statute. §§ 203, 304(c).

Also, the status and nationality of the "author" become important in a work-for-hire situation. If the work was created by an employee of the U.S. Government as part of her official duties, copyright cannot be claimed at all. § 105. How could the fact that a foreign work was created in an employment relationship affect its status in the United States? For a partial answer, see § 104(b)(1) and (6) and the *Itar-Tass* case in § 8.04 below.

(5) *The* CCNV *case.* As indicated later in these notes, the work-for-hire doctrine under the 1909 Act strongly favored employers. The provisions of the 1976 Act were widely viewed as an effort to correct this imbalance. To what extent did they succeed in achieving that result? Would the *Aldon Accessories* or *Dumas* approaches, both rejected by the *CCNV* Court, have been preferable? Would either of the latter two approaches have produced a different result in *CCNV*? Do you see any practical difficulties with the "formal, salaried employee" approach of *Dumas*? Consider a regular volunteer at a local church whose responsibilities include writing occasional musical compositions for worship services and preparing periodic financial reports for the church — responsibilities carried out using church resources and under the supervision of the church's ministers. Clearly, the volunteer is not a formal, salaried employee. But isn't this a situation in which the work-for-hire doctrine *should* apply?

(6) *Works by employees.* Neither "employee" nor "independent contractor" is defined by the 1976 Act. *CCNV* holds that courts should rely for enlightenment on the general common law of agency. Does it make sense to define these federal law terms, for copyright purposes, by reference to common-law notions of the employment relationship originally devised to allocate liability under state law? Are any concerns in that regard alleviated by *CCNV*'s use of the "federal common law" of agency, rather than state law?

Take another look at *CCNV*'s "nonexhaustive list of [*Restatement (Second) of Agency* § 220(2)] factors" which a court should take into account in determining whether someone is an employee or an independent contractor. Which factors (if any) should be weighted most heavily? *See, e.g., Carter v. Helmsley-Spear, Inc.*, 71 F.3d 77 (2d Cir. 1995) (looking, in particular, to payroll formalities); *Aymes v. Bonelli*, 980 F.2d 857 (2d Cir. 1992) (ranking factors and noting that "every case since *Reid* . . . has found the hired party to be an independent contractor where the hiring party failed to extend benefits or pay social security taxes"); *Kirk v. Harter*, 188 F.3d 1005 (8th Cir. 1999) (noting that no single factor is determinative, but treating financial relationship, including tax treatment, as highly probative). *But see JustMed, Inc. v. Byce*, 600 F.3d 1118 (9th Cir. 2010) (finding programmer was an employee, despite the fact that he worked at home, was not paid benefits, and did not have taxes withheld). Note that failing to identify the work as made "for hire" on the registration certificate is not dispositive. *See Pritchett v. Pound*, 473 F.3d 217 (5th Cir. 2006).

In the second sentence of Part II.B of its opinion, the *CCNV* Court appears to say that the above-named factors are relevant because they bear on the overarching issue of "the hiring party's right to control the *manner and means* by which the product is accomplished" (emphasis added). In the very next paragraph, it states that "the extent of the control the hiring party exercises over the details of the product is not dispositive." Can these statements be reconciled? If "control" is to be afforded special importance, what is the rationale for the Court's rejection of the "right to control the product" and the "actual control" approaches?

(7) A number of cases consider whether works created by salaried employees were made within the "scope of employment." Again, the courts have looked to the *Restatement (Second) of Agency* for the basic standard. The *Restatement* employs a tripartite test:

(1) whether the work was of the type the employee was hired to perform;

(2) whether the creation of the work in question occurred "substantially within the authorized time and space limits" of the employee's job; and

(3) whether the employee was "actuated, at least in part, by a purpose to serve" the employer's purpose.

Restatement (Second) of Agency § 228.

How should this test be applied when an employee has created a work at home, after hours, that is arguably related to the employer's business? For example, compare two Fourth Circuit cases decided the same day but with different results. In *Avtec Systems, Inc. v. Peiffer*, 67 F.3d 293 (4th Cir. 1995), the court held that a computer program written after hours at the employee's home was not created within the scope of employment, stating that "at the time of fixation, Peiffer was not being compensated for the Program by either a salary, hourly wages, or a bonus; the Program was not related to any particular project that Peiffer was charged with performing for Avtec; he was not working on a way to improve the efficiency of his job or Avtec's business; and he was not receiving any direction from Avtec." In *Cramer v. Crestar Financial Corp.*, 67 F.3d 294 (4th Cir. 1995), however, the court held that the computer program in question was a work for hire, because the plaintiff, as director of the defendant's information systems department, had written the program "substantially within the authorized time and space limits of his job — even if he did so at home, outside regular work hours, on his own initiative, and using his own equipment." The panel also noted that, "[w]hen the first element of the *Restatement* test is met — that the work is of a kind the employee is hired to perform — 'courts have tended not to grant employees authorship rights solely on the basis that the work was done at home on his off-hours' " (quoting *Avtec*). Are *Avtec* and *Cramer* in conflict?

As digital networks and technologies increase the capacity for employees to do their work outside of the traditional office or factory setting or during non-traditional work hours, delineating the scope of employment is likely to become increasingly complex. In *Fleurimond v. New York University*, 876 F. Supp. 2d 190 (E.D.N.Y. 2012), for example, the court applied the *Avtec* factors to determine that NYU's new mascot design, created by an hourly work-study student, was a work made for hire. The student had been hired as a graphic designer, had done other design work for the university from home on her personal computer, and created the design at the university's request. *See also U.S. Auto Parts Network, Inc. v. Parts Geek, LLC*, 692 F.3d 1009 (9th Cir. 2012) (finding triable issue of fact whether former employee acted within the scope of his employment in modifying software that he originally created prior to his employment); *cf. Mattel, Inc. v. MGA Entertainment, Inc.*, 616 F.3d 904 (9th Cir. 2010) (finding contract language "at any time during my employment by the Company" was ambiguous as to whether it "refer[s] to the entire calendar period Bryant worked for Mattel, including nights and weekends," or whether it "encompass[ed] only those inventions created during work hours," where Bryant's initial sketches for MGA's "Bratz" dolls had been made "on his own time and outside of his duties at Mattel.").

In light of these cases, how would you advise an employee or employer to act so that rights in the results of after-hours works are clearly understood? Is a statutory correction desirable or possible?

(8) How should the law treat the works of an author who forms a corporation for the express purpose of promoting and supporting her artistic vision? In *Martha Graham School and Dance Foundation, Inc. v. Martha Graham Center of Contemporary Dance, Inc.*, 380 F.3d 624 (2d Cir. 2004), the court considered whether dances created by choreographer Martha Graham were owned by her individually or by the Center which she founded. In a Solomonic decision, the court held that, under the 1909 Act, dances created when Graham was a part-time employee of the Center, with the title of Program Director and contractual responsibilities for teaching and education only, were not works made for hire; while dances created after Graham became a full-time employee, with the title of Artistic Director and contractual responsibilities for choreography as well as education, were made at the "instance and expense" of the Center. *Id.* at 637-41 (see the discussion of this legal standard in Note 15 below). Dances that Graham created between 1978 and her death in 1991 were found likewise to be works for hire under the 1976 Act, because they had been made within the scope of her employment. Does this decision place too much weight on the formal aspects of the relationship, and not enough on the practical reality of artistic control?

(9) Suppose a law school professor writes an article (on the law of copyright, just to pick a subject at random). Assuming there are no contractual complications with a publisher, who owns the copyright in the work: the professor or her institution? Does the Copyright Act of 1976 provide that academic writings are works made for hire? Does it provide that they are not?

The probable answer, according to two former law professors now sitting on the federal bench, is that an exception arose under 1909 Act case law and remains viable today. In *Hays v. Sony Corp. of America*, 847 F.2d 412, 415 (7th Cir. 1988), Judge Posner reasoned that a contrary conclusion would wreak "havoc . . . in the settled practices of academic institutions," and concluded (in *dicta*) that the exception survived the enactment of the 1976 Act. To the same effect, see Judge Easterbrook's opinion in *Weinstein v. University of Illinois*, 811 F.2d 1091, 1094 (7th Cir. 1987) (the teacher exception "has been the academic tradition since copyright law began"). In view of the fact that the alleged "teacher exception" was referred to previously in only one California state appellate opinion, give the judges an A for effort. Even if such an exception exists, however, it is likely limited to academic books and articles, as opposed to software with commercial applications, *see Rouse v. Walter & Assocs., LLC*, 513 F. Supp. 2d 1041 (S.D. Iowa 2007), or materials prepared specifically for classroom use, *see Shaul v. Cherry Valley-Springfield Central School Dist.*, 363 F.3d 177 (2d Cir. 2004), and *Vanderhurst v. Colorado Mountain College District*, 16 F. Supp. 2d 1297 (D. Colo. 1998) (plaintiff's Veterinary Technology Outline "was connected directly with the work [he] was employed to do and was fairly and reasonably incidental to his employment").

So what about a professor's lectures or course web sites? The Internet has created new opportunities for the commercialization of course content in distance education. Can professors take advantage of these opportunities without permission? For commentary, see Packard, *Copyright or Copy Wrong: An Analysis of University Claims to Faculty Work*, 7 Comm. L. & Pol'y 275 (2002), and Kwall, *Copyright Issues in Online Courses: Ownership, Authorship and Conflict*, 18 Santa Clara Comp. & High Tech. L.J. 1 (2001).

(10) *Commissioned works.* If, as the *CCNV* Court determined, "Third World America" was not the work of an "employee," why wasn't it a work for hire under the second part of the § 101 definition, which permits "commissioned works" to qualify in certain circumstances? The treatment of commissioned works by § 101(2) is markedly different from the treatment accorded 1909 Act works under the case law. Those decisions established a presumption that the parties intended ownership of the work to vest in the commissioning party. *See, e.g., May v. Morganelli-Heumann & Associates*, 618 F.2d 1363 (9th Cir. 1980). The 1976 Act reflects no such presumption.

(11) While the § 101(2) list of categories is largely self-explanatory, it does pose some problems of interpretation. Are paintings intended to be reproduced for sale in a boxed "collection" a "contribution to a collective work"? *See Kasten v. Jerrytone*, 2004 U.S. Dist. LEXIS 16540 (E.D. La., Aug. 17, 2004). And how broadly should the term "supplementary work" be interpreted? Would an abridgment or substantive revision of a literary work be included? Or, to take a different problem, is a commissioned film script "part of a motion picture or other audiovisual work"? Speaking of "other audiovisual work[s]," do advertising jingles qualify? *See Lulirama Ltd. v. Axcess Broadcast Services, Inc.*, 128 F.3d 872 (5th Cir. 1997) (where images necessary to supply "visual" element are nonexistent, no; result not changed by notation on parties' agreement referring to works as "for hire"). Questions of this sort will continue to arise as § 101(2) is construed by the courts.

(12) In addition to coming within one of the nine categories, § 101(2) also requires that the parties "expressly agree in a written instrument signed by them" that the work is a work made for hire. How formal does the "written instrument" have to be? Does a printed legend on the back of a check, just below the signature where the check was endorsed, qualify? *See Playboy Enterprises v. Dumas*, 53 F.3d 549 (2d Cir. 1995) (yes). Does it matter *when* the parties sign the written agreement? The courts are in conflict. In *Dumas*, the court held that the parties must agree before the work is created, but that the agreement may be either oral or implied, as long as it is later confirmed in a signed writing. *Compare Dumas with Schiller & Schmidt, Inc. v. Nordisco Corp.*, 969 F.2d 410 (7th Cir. 1992) (Posner, J.) ("The writing must precede the creation of the property in order to serve its purpose of identifying the (noncreator) owner unequivocally.").

Leaving aside *ex post facto* agreements, what about blanket agreements? Suppose in the foregoing situation that the photographer and the magazine enter into an agreement creating a work-for-hire relationship concerning all future pictures the photographer takes for the magazine. Are such agreements inherently unfair to freelancers? Are there any sound business justifications for blanket agreements?

(13) Of course, the employer can disavow its interest in what otherwise would be a work made for hire, but according to § 201(b) this also requires that the parties "expressly agree" in a signed written instrument. Courts have been fairly tough in enforcing the requirement. For example, in *Foraste v. Brown Univ.*, 248 F. Supp. 2d 71 (D.R.I. 2003), photographs taken by a University employee were held to be works made for hire, notwithstanding a written policy stating that "[i]t is the University's position that, as a general premise, ownership of copyrightable property which results from performance of one's University duties and activities will belong to the author or originator," because the policy was not signed by both parties.

(14) *The impact of* CCNV. The Supreme Court's decision in *CCNV* was hailed initially as a great victory for freelance authors (that is, authors who are independent contractors). But was it, really? And how far did the decision go in promoting predictability in connection with the work-for-hire doctrine?

In the case of a commissioned work, keep in mind that if the work is determined not to fit within one of the statutory categories, the work is not a work made for hire even when both parties clearly intended it to be. Who, then, is the initial owner of the copyright? Some courts have construed an invalid work-for-hire agreement as effecting an assignment. *See, e.g., Compaq Computer Corp. v. Ergonome, Inc.*, 210 F. Supp. 2d 839 (S.D. Tex. 2001). Many hiring parties try to ensure their ownership by drafting an agreement that expresses the parties' intent that the work is made for hire, but that if this is not possible, then the creator assigns the copyright to the commissioning party. Although an assignment provides a somewhat inferior ownership right compared with ownership as a work-for-hire "author," it probably meets the needs of most commissioning parties. The major drawback to an assignment, when compared with a work for hire, is that a transfer of copyright can be terminated between the 35th and 40th year of the grant, if the author or her heirs decide to do so. *See* § 203(a) of the 1976 Act, discussed below in Chapter 5. Will many employers be concerned by the prospect of such terminations? How many commissioned works — or noncommissioned works, for that matter — have a commercial life of more than 35 years? Consider, for example, advertising jingles, commercial artwork, and computer software.

(15) *"A ticking time bomb."* Sound recordings clearly can have long "shelf lives" (think Elvis). In the House Report to the 1976 Act, Congress characterized the typical sound recording as a collaboration — specifically, between the "performers and the record producer responsible for setting up the recording session, capturing and electronically processing the sounds, and compiling them and editing them to make the final sound recording." The typical sound recording could well be considered a work of joint *authorship* between these various creative contributors. *But see Forward v. Thorogood*, 985 F.2d 604 (1st Cir. 1993) (producer who merely arranged for the recording session and requested that specific songs be performed made "no musical or artistic contribution" and was not a joint author). But in the 1976 Act, Congress ducked the question of how rights would be *owned and shared*, leaving the matter to be determined by "the employment relationship and bargaining among the interests involved."

Until recently, the question has seemed obscure and theoretical at best. After all, many producers are full-time employees of record companies, and those who aren't typically sign away their rights. So do performing artists, often in contracts that also specify (in the best "belt and suspenders" fashion) that their recordings should be considered "works made for hire." Now, however, as the 1976 Act's novel mechanism for terminating copyright assignments after 35 years (discussed under "Termination of Transfers" in § 5.02 below) begins to kick in, the theoretical has become real. If recording artists and producers all are employees for hire, recording companies have nothing to worry about. But if most artists and some producers are in fact independent contractors, boilerplate language notwithstanding, the companies face a sea of troubles. In particular, they could be forced to renegotiate what are (from their perspective) the highly favorable royalty terms of many contracts.

Back in 1999, the recording industry moved to stave off the problems by lobbying successfully for a "technical amendment" to the Act that added sound recordings as a tenth category under the second part of the § 101 "work made for hire" definition. After a storm of protest, this "stealth" amendment was repealed, with language stating that no weight should be given to the fact that this addition to, and deletion from, the statute had taken place.

So we are faced with the question: Are sound recordings "works made for hire" under the 1976 Act? Are they, for example, "collective works" within the meaning of § 101(2) — one of the nine categories of commissioned work subject to the writing requirement? Or are sound recordings covered under a *CCNV* rationale? For a suggestion of some of the difficulties entailed in answering this question, see *Ulloa v. Universal Music & Video Distrib. Corp.*, 303 F. Supp. 2d 409 (S.D.N.Y. 2004); and *Staggers v. Real Authentic Sound*, 77 F. Supp. 2d 57 (D.D.C. 1999). In any event, expect judicial fireworks soon! For a review of the issues, see Nimmer & Menell, *Sound Recordings, Works for Hire, and the Termination of Transfers Time Bomb*, 49 J. Copyright Soc'y 387 (2001); and Jaffee, *Defusing the Time Bomb Once Again*

— *Determining Authorship in a Sound Recording*, 53 J. Copyright Soc'y 139 (2006).

(16) *"Works made for hire" under the 1909 Act: the continuing importance of prior law.* Unlike the 1976 Act, the 1909 Act did not specify the circumstances under which an employer becomes a work-for-hire author. It merely provided that "the word 'author' shall include an employer in the case of works made for hire." § 26. Accordingly, the courts were forced to create their own standards in construing the statute. In general, case law favored employers over creators, presuming employment-for-hire in many circumstances. Even a person who simply commissioned another on a one-time basis for the limited purpose of creating a single work might be deemed an employer, and thus the author-in-law, for work-for-hire purposes. *See, e.g., Estate of Hogarth v. Edgar Rice Burroughs, Inc.*, 342 F.3d 149 (2d Cir. 2003) (illustrator who created graphic novel adaptations of Tarzan novels worked at the "instance and expense" of the publisher); *Twentieth Century Fox Film Corp. v. Entertainment Distributing*, 429 F.3d 869 (9th Cir. 2005) (General Eisenhower's memoirs were created at the "instance and expense" of the publisher, despite tax treatment as sale of a capital asset rather than payment of salary).

In *Marvel Worldwide, Inc. v. Kirby*, 777 F. Supp. 2d 720 (S.D.N.Y. 2011), for example, the court found that freelance comic-book artist Jack Kirby created his work at the "instance and expense" of Marvel, because he did not create anything until he received an assignment from Stan Lee, and because he was paid on a per-page basis for what he created. The comics were therefore "works made for hire" under the 1909 Act, despite the absence of any written employment agreement. Does it make sense that a transfer of copyright ownership requires a signed writing (*see* § 4.02[C] below), but that "work for hire" status can exist without anything in writing?

(17) Because the 1976 Act is not applied retroactively to determine who is the owner of a copyright, the law of ownership under the 1909 Act and the cases applying it hold more than historical interest for lawyers today. Such retroactivity — whether applied to works for hire or, as we will see in the next section of the casebook, to joint works — would raise serious constitutional problems. *See Roth v. Pritikin*, 710 F.2d 934 (2d Cir. 1983) (1909 Act applies to recipes provided under an oral contract in 1977, before the January 1, 1978 effective date of the 1976 Act). Note, however, that *CCNV*'s construction of the work-for-hire doctrine applies to works created after the effective date of the 1976 Act, but before the Court's decision. *See Autoskill, Inc. v. National Educational Support Systems, Inc.*, 994 F.2d 1476 (10th Cir. 1993).

(18) *From "works made for hire" to "joint works."* In the D.C. Circuit's decision in *CCNV v. Reid*, Judge (now Justice) Ruth Bader Ginsburg suggested that, on remand, CCNV would likely be able to demonstrate its co-ownership of the work, based on the participation of CCNV's employees and members in the work's creation. In fact, she stated that the case "might qualify as a text book example of a jointly authored work." 846 F.2d at 1485. Judge Ginsburg suggested that merely supplying the general idea or conception for the statue might make one or more of the employees or members "joint authors": "We note . . . CCNV's contribution to the steam grate pedestal *added to its initial conceptualization and ongoing*

direction of the realization of [the work]." *Id.* at 1497 (emphasis added). The emphasized factors may well be relevant to a work-for-hire analysis. But should they bear on the issue of whether "Third World America" is a joint work? As you read the *Childress* case below, consider whether the foregoing *dictum* is analytically sound.

In *CCNV*, on remand, the joint authorship issue was submitted to mediation. The parties agreed that CCNV should have sole ownership of the actual sculpture, but that Reid was its sole author. Reid received the exclusive right to make three-dimensional reproductions, and either party can make two-dimensional reproductions (although Reid's are required to omit the base and inscription). Each party gets to keep the income from its reproductions. After a brief dispute over Reid's right to obtain temporary possession of the original sculpture in order to create a master mold for his reproductions (a dispute resolved in Reid's favor), the matter seems finally to have been put to bed.

[C] Joint Works

CHILDRESS v. TAYLOR
United States Court of Appeals, Second Circuit
945 F.2d 500 (1991)

NEWMAN, CIRCUIT JUDGE:

This appeal requires consideration of the standards for determining when a contributor to a copyrighted work is entitled to be regarded as a joint author. The work in question is a play about the legendary Black comedienne Jackie "Moms" Mabley. The plaintiff-appellee Alice Childress claims to be the sole author of the play. Her claim is disputed by defendant-appellant Clarice Taylor, who asserts that she is a joint author of the play. Taylor, Paul B. Berkowsky, Ben Caldwell, and the "Moms" Company appeal from . . . [a judgment] determining, on motion for summary judgment, that Childress is the sole author. We affirm.

Facts

Defendant Clarice Taylor has been an actress for over forty years, performing on stage, radio, television, and in film. After portraying "Moms" Mabley in a skit in an off-off-Broadway production ten years ago, Taylor became interested in developing a play based on Mabley's life. Taylor began to assemble material about "Moms" Mabley, interviewing her friends and family, collecting her jokes, and reviewing library resources.

In 1985, Taylor contacted the plaintiff, playwright Alice Childress, about writing a play based on "Moms" Mabley. Childress had written many plays, for one of which she won an "Obie" award. Taylor had known Childress since the 1940s when they were both associated with the American Negro Theatre in Harlem and had previously acted in a number of Childress's plays.

When Taylor first mentioned the "Moms" Mabley project to Childress in 1985,

Childress stated she was not interested in writing the script because she was too occupied with other works. However, when Taylor approached Childress again in 1986, Childress agreed, though she was reluctant due to the time constraints involved. Taylor had interested the Green Plays Theatre in producing the as yet unwritten play, but the theatre had only one slot left on its summer 1986 schedule, and in order to use that slot, the play had to be written in six weeks.

Taylor turned over all of her research material to Childress, and later did further research at Childress's request. It is undisputed that Childress wrote the play, entitled "Moms: A Praise Play for a Black Comedienne." However, Taylor, in addition to providing the research material, which according to her involved a process of sifting through facts and selecting pivotal and key elements to include in a play on "Moms" Mabley's life, also discussed with Childress the inclusion of certain general scenes and characters in the play. Additionally, Childress and Taylor spoke on a regular basis about the progress of the play.

Jackie "Moms" Mabley
The Everett Collection

 Taylor identifies the following as her major contributions to the play: (1) she learned through interviews that "Moms" Mabley called all of her piano players "Luther," so Taylor suggested that the play include such a character; (2) Taylor and Childress together interviewed Carey Jordan, "Moms" Mabley's housekeeper, and upon leaving the interview they came to the conclusion that she would be a good character for the play, but Taylor could not recall whether she or Childress suggested it; (3) Taylor informed Childress that "Moms" Mabley made a weekly trip to Harlem to do ethnic food shopping; (4) Taylor suggested a street scene in Harlem with speakers because she recalled having seen or listened to such a scene many times; (5) the idea of using a minstrel scene came out of Taylor's research; (6) the idea of a card game scene also came out of Taylor's research, although Taylor could not recall who specifically suggested the scene; (7) some of the jokes used in the play came from Taylor's research; and (8) the characteristics of "Moms" Mabley's personality portrayed in the play emerged from Taylor's research. Essentially, Taylor contributed facts and details about "Moms" Mabley's life and discussed some of them with Childress. However, Childress was responsible for the actual structure of the play and the dialogue.

Childress completed the script within the six-week time frame. Childress filed for and received a copyright for the play in her name. Taylor produced the play at the Green Plays Theatre in Lexington, New York, during the 1986 summer season and played the title role. After the play's run at the Green Plays Theatre, Taylor planned a second production of the play at the Hudson Guild Theatre in New York City.

At the time Childress agreed to the project, she did not have any firm arrangements with Taylor, although Taylor had paid her $2,500 before the play was produced. On May 9, 1986, Taylor's agent, Scott Yoselow, wrote to Childress's agent, Flora Roberts, stating:

> Per our telephone conversation, this letter will bring us up-to-date on the current status of our negotiation for the above mentioned project:
>
> 1. CLARICE TAYLOR will pay ALICE CHILDRESS for her playwriting services on the MOMS MABLEY PROJECT the sum of $5,000.00, which will also serve as an advance against any future royalties.
>
> 2. The finished play shall be equally owned and be the property of both CLARICE TAYLOR and ALICE CHILDRESS.
>
> It is my understanding that Alice has commenced writing the project. I am awaiting a response from you regarding any additional points we have yet to discuss.

Flora Roberts responded to Yoselow in a letter dated June 16, 1986:

> As per our recent telephone conversation, I have told Alice Childress that we are using your letter to me of May 9, 1986 as a partial memo preparatory to our future good faith negotiations for a contract. There are two points which I include herewith to complete your two points in the May 9th letter, *i.e.*:
>
> 1. The $5,000 advance against any future royalties being paid by Clarice Taylor to Alice Childress shall be paid as follows. Since $1,000 has already been paid, $1,500 upon your receipt of this letter and the final $2,500 to be paid upon submission of the First Draft, but in no event later than July 7, 1986.

2. It is to be understood that pending the proper warranty clauses
to be included in the contract, Miss Childress is claiming originality
for her words only in said script.

After the Green Plays Theatre production, Taylor and Childress attempted to
formalize their relationship. Draft contracts were exchanged between Taylor's
attorney, Jay Kramer, and Childress's agent, Roberts. During this period, early
1987, the play was produced at the Hudson Guild Theatre with the consent of both
Taylor and Childress. Childress filed for and received a copyright for the new
material added to the play produced at the Hudson Guild Theatre. In March 1987,
Childress rejected the draft agreement proposed by Taylor and the parties'
relationship deteriorated. Taylor decided to mount another production of the play
without Childress. Taylor hired Ben Caldwell to write another play featuring
"Moms" Mabley; Taylor gave Caldwell a copy of the Childress script and advised
him of elements that should be changed.

The "Moms" Mabley play that Caldwell wrote was produced at the Astor Place
Theatre in August 1987.[2] No reference to Childress was made with respect to this
production. However, a casting notice in the trade paper "Back Stage" reported the
production of Caldwell's play and noted that it had been "presented earlier this
season under an Equity LOA at the Hudson Guild Theatre."

Flora Roberts contacted Jay Kramer to determine whether this notice was
correct. Kramer responded:

> Ben Caldwell has written the play which I will furnish to you when a final
> draft is available. We have tried in every way to distinguish the new version
> of the play from what was presented at the Hudson Guild, both by way of
> content and billing.
>
> Undoubtedly, because of the prevalence of public domain material in
> both versions of the play, there may be unavoidable similarities. Please also
> remember that Alice was paid by Clarice for rights to her material which
> we have never resolved.

Kramer never sent a copy of Caldwell's play. Childress's attorney, Alvin Deutsch,
sent Kramer a letter advising him of Childress's rights in the play as produced at
the Hudson Guild and of her concerns about the advertising connecting Caldwell's
play to hers. For example, one advertisement for Caldwell's play at the Astor Place
Theatre quoted reviews referring to Childress's play. Other advertisements made
reference to the fact that the play had been performed earlier that season at the
Hudson Guild Theatre.

Childress sued Taylor and other defendants alleging violations of the Copyright
Act, 17 U.S.C. § 101 *et seq.* (1988), the Lanham Act, 15 U.S.C. §§ 1051, 1125(a)
(1988), and New York's anti-dilution statute, N.Y. Gen. Bus. Law § 368-d (McKinney
1984). Taylor contended that she was a joint author with Childress, and therefore
shared the rights to the play. Childress moved for summary judgment, which the
District Court granted. The Court concluded that Taylor was not a joint author of

---

[2] The Caldwell play was billed as being "based on a concept by Clarice Taylor." Taylor was not listed
as an author of that play.

Childress's play and that Caldwell's play was substantially similar to and infringed Childress's play. In rejecting Taylor's claim of joint authorship, Judge Haight ruled (a) that a work qualifies as a "joint work" under the definition section of the Copyright Act, 17 U.S.C. § 101, only when both authors intended, at the time the work was created, "that their contributions be merged into inseparable or interdependent parts of a unitary whole," and (b) that there was insufficient evidence to permit a reasonable trier to find that Childress had the requisite intent. The Court further ruled that copyright law requires the contributions of both authors to be independently copyrightable, and that Taylor's contributions, which consisted of ideas and research, were not copyrightable.

Discussion

In common with many issues arising in the domain of copyrights, the determination of whether to recognize joint authorship in a particular case requires a sensitive accommodation of competing demands advanced by at least two persons, both of whom have normally contributed in some way to the creation of a work of value. Care must be taken to ensure that true collaborators in the creative process are accorded the perquisites of co-authorship and to guard against the risk that a sole author is denied exclusive authorship status simply because another person rendered some form of assistance. Copyright law best serves the interests of creativity when it carefully draws the bounds of "joint authorship" so as to protect the legitimate claims of both sole authors and co-authors.

Co-authorship was well known to the common law. An early formulation, thought by Learned Hand to be the first definition of "joint authorship," *see Edward B. Marks Music Corp. v. Jerry Vogel Music Co.*, 140 F.2d 266, 267 (2d Cir. 1944) ("Marks"), is set out in *Levy v. Rutley*, L.R., 6 C.P. 523, 529 (Keating, J.) (1871): "a joint laboring in furtherance of a common design". . . .

Like many brief formulations, the language from *Levy v. Rutley* is useful in pointing an inquiry in the proper direction but does not provide much guidance in deciding the close cases. Many people can be said to "jointly labor" toward "a common design" who could not plausibly be considered co-authors. And beyond the fairly straightforward context of words and music combined into a song, whatever formulation is selected will not necessarily fit neatly around such varied fact situations as those concerning architectural plans, *see Meltzer v. Zoller*, 520 F. Supp. 847 (D.N.J. 1981), or computer programs, *see Ashton-Tate Corp. v. Ross*, 728 F. Supp. 597 (N.D. Cal. 1989), *aff'd*, 916 F.2d 516 ([9th] Cir. 1990). Though the early case law is illuminating, our task is to apply the standards of the Copyright Act of 1976 and endeavor to achieve the results that Congress likely intended.

The Copyright Act defines a "joint work" as

> a work prepared by two or more authors with the intention that their contributions be merged into inseparable or interdependent parts of a unitary whole.

17 U.S.C. § 101. As Professor Nimmer has pointed out, this definition is really the definition of a work of joint authorship. *See* 1 NIMMER ON COPYRIGHT § 6.01 (1991). The definition concerns the *creation* of the work by the joint authors, not the

circumstances, in addition to joint authorship, under which a work may be *jointly owned*, for example, by assignment of an undivided interest. The distinction affects the rights that are acquired. Joint authors hold undivided interests in a work, like all joint owners of a work, but joint authors, unlike other joint owners, also enjoy all the rights of authorship, including the renewal rights applicable to works in which a statutory copyright subsisted prior to January 1, 1978. *See* 17 U.S.C. § 304.

Some aspects of the statutory definition of joint authorship are fairly straight-forward. Parts of a unitary whole are "inseparable" when they have little or no independent meaning standing alone. That would often be true of a work of written text, such as the play that is the subject of the pending litigation. By contrast, parts of a unitary whole are "interdependent" when they have some meaning standing alone but achieve their primary significance because of their combined effect, as in the case of the words and music of a song. Indeed, a novel and a song are among the examples offered by the legislative committee reports on the 1976 Copyright Act to illustrate the difference between "inseparable" and "interdependent" parts. *See* H.R. Rep. No. 1476, 94th Cong., 2d Sess. 120 (1976) ("House Report"); S. Rep. No. 473, 94th Cong., 2d Sess. 103-04 (1975) ("Senate Report").

The legislative history also clarifies other aspects of the statutory definition, but leaves some matters in doubt. Endeavoring to flesh out the definition, the committee reports state:

> [A] work is "joint" if the authors collaborated with each other, or if *each* of the authors prepared his or her contribution with the knowledge and *intention* that it would be merged with the contributions of other authors as "inseparable or interdependent parts of a unitary whole." The touch-stone here is the *intention, at the time the writing is done,* that the parts be absorbed or combined into an integrated unit. . . .

House Report at 120; Senate Report at 103 (emphasis added). This passage appears to state two alternative criteria — one focusing on the act of collaboration and the other on the parties' intent. However, it is hard to imagine activity that would constitute meaningful "collaboration" unaccompanied by the requisite intent on the part of both participants that their contributions be merged into a unitary whole, and the case law has read the statutory language literally so that the intent requirement applies to all works of joint authorship. *See, e.g., Weissmann v. Freeman*, 868 F.2d 1313, 1317-19 (2d Cir. 1989); *Eckert v. Hurley Chicago Co., Inc.*, 638 F. Supp. 699, 702-03 (N.D. Ill. 1986).

A more substantial issue arising under the statutory definition of "joint work" is whether the contribution of each joint author must be copyrightable or only the combined result of their joint efforts must be copyrightable. The Nimmer treatise argues against a requirement of copyrightability of each author's contribution, *see* 1 *Nimmer on Copyright* § 6.07; Professor Goldstein takes the contrary view, *see* 1 Paul Goldstein, *Copyright: Principles, Law and Practice* § 4.2.1.2 (1989), with the apparent agreement of the Latman treatise, *see* William F. Patry, *Latman's The Copyright Law* 116 (6th ed. 1986). The case law supports a requirement of copyrightability of each contribution. . . . The Register of Copyrights strongly supports this view, arguing that it is required by the statutory standard of "authorship" and perhaps by the Constitution. . . .

The issue, apparently open in this Circuit, is troublesome. If the focus is solely on the objective of copyright law to encourage the production of creative works, it is difficult to see why the contributions of all joint authors need be copyrightable. An individual creates a copyrightable work by combining a non-copyrightable idea with a copyrightable form of expression; the resulting work is no less a valuable result of the creative process simply because the idea and the expression came from two different individuals. Indeed, it is not unimaginable that there exists a skilled writer who might never have produced a significant work until some other person supplied the idea. The textual argument from the statute is not convincing. The Act surely does not say that each contribution to a joint work must be copyrightable, and the specification that there be "authors" does not necessarily require a copyrightable contribution. "Author" is not defined in the Act and appears to be used only in its ordinary sense of an originator. The "author" of an uncopyrightable idea is nonetheless its author even though, for entirely valid reasons, the law properly denies him a copyright on the result of his creativity. . . .

Nevertheless, we are persuaded to side with the position taken by the case law and endorsed by the agency administering the Copyright Act. The insistence on copyrightable contributions by all putative joint authors might serve to prevent some spurious claims by those who might otherwise try to share the fruits of the efforts of a sole author of a copyrightable work, even though a claim of having contributed copyrightable material could be asserted by those so inclined. More important, the prevailing view strikes an appropriate balance in the domains of both copyright and contract law. In the absence of contract, the copyright remains with the one or more persons who created copyrightable material. Contract law enables a person to hire another to create a copyrightable work, and the copyright law will recognize the employer as "author." 17 U.S.C. § 201(b). Similarly, the person with non-copyrightable material who proposes to join forces with a skilled writer to produce a copyrightable work is free to make a contract to disclose his or her material in return for assignment of part ownership of the resulting copyright. *Id.* § 201(d). And, as with all contract matters, the parties may minimize subsequent disputes by formalizing their agreement in a written contract. *Cf.* 17 U.S.C. § 101 ("work made for hire" definition of "specially ordered" or "commissioned" work includes requirement of written agreement). It seems more consistent with the spirit of copyright law to oblige all joint authors to make copyrightable contributions, leaving those with non-copyrightable contributions to protect their rights through contract.

There remains for consideration the crucial aspect of joint authorship — the nature of the intent that must be entertained by each putative joint author at the time the contribution of each was created. The wording of the statutory definition appears to make relevant only the state of mind regarding the unitary nature of the finished work — an intention "that their contributions be merged into inseparable or interdependent parts of a unitary whole." However, an inquiry so limited would extend joint author status to many persons who are not likely to have been within the contemplation of Congress. For example, a writer frequently works with an editor who makes numerous useful revisions to the first draft, some of which will consist of additions of copyrightable expression. Both intend their contributions to be merged into inseparable parts of a unitary whole, yet very few editors and even fewer writers would expect the editor to be accorded the status of joint author, enjoying an undivided half interest in the copyright in the published work. Similarly, research assistants may on occasion contribute to an author some protectible expression or merely a sufficiently original selection of factual material as would be entitled to a copyright, yet not be entitled to be regarded as a joint author of the work in which the contributed material appears. What distinguishes the writer-editor relationship and the writer-researcher relationship from the true joint author relationship is the lack of intent of both participants in the venture to regard themselves as joint authors.[6]

Focusing on whether the putative joint authors regarded themselves as joint authors is especially important in circumstances, such as the instant case, where one person (Childress) is indisputably the dominant author of the work and the only issue is whether that person is the sole author or she and another (Taylor) are joint authors. . . . This concern requires less exacting consideration in the context of traditional forms of collaboration, such as between the creators of the words and music of a song.

In this case, appellant contends that Judge Haight's observation that "Childress never shared Taylor's notion that they were co-authors of the play" misapplies the statutory standard by focusing on whether Childress "intended the legal consequences which flowed from her prior acts." We do not think Judge Haight went so far. He did not inquire whether Childress intended that she and Taylor would hold equal undivided interests in the play. But he properly insisted that they entertain in their minds the concept of joint authorship, whether or not they understood precisely the legal consequences of that relationship. Though joint authorship does not require an understanding by the co-authors of the legal consequences of their relationship, obviously some distinguishing characteristic of the relationship must be understood in order for it to be the subject of their intent. In many instances, a useful test will be whether, in the absence of contractual agreements concerning listed authorship, each participant intended that all would be identified as co-authors. Though "billing" or "credit" is not decisive in all cases and joint authorship can exist without any explicit discussion of this topic by the parties,[7] consideration of the topic helpfully serves to focus the fact-finder's attention on how the parties implicitly regarded their undertaking. . . .

Examination of whether the putative co-authors ever shared an intent to be co-authors serves the valuable purpose of appropriately confining the bounds of joint authorship arising by operation of copyright law, while leaving those not in a true joint authorship relationship with an author free to bargain for an arrangement that will be recognized as a matter of both copyright and contract law. Joint

---

[6] In some situations, the editor or researcher will be the employee of the primary author, in which event the copyright in the contributions of the editor or researcher would belong to the author, under the "work made for hire" doctrine. But in many situations the editor or researcher will be an independent contractor or an employee of some person or entity other than the primary author, in which event a claim of joint authorship would not be defeated by the "work made for hire" doctrine.

[7] Obviously, consideration of whether the parties contemplated listed co-authorship (or would have accepted such billing had they thought about it) is not a helpful inquiry for works written by an uncredited "ghost writer," either as a sole author, as a joint author, or as an employee preparing a work for hire.

authorship entitles the co-authors to equal undivided interests in the work, *see* 17 U.S.C. § 201(a); *Community for Creative Non-Violence v. Reid*, 846 F.2d 1485, 1498 (D.C. Cir. 1988), *aff'd without consideration of this point*, 490 U.S. 730 (1989). That equal sharing of rights should be reserved for relationships in which all participants fully intend to be joint authors. The sharing of benefits in other relationships involving assistance in the creation of a copyrightable work can be more precisely calibrated by the participants in their contract negotiations regarding division of royalties or assignment of shares of ownership of the copyright, *see* 17 U.S.C. § 201(d).

In this case, the issue is not only whether Judge Haight applied the correct standard for determining joint authorship but also whether he was entitled to conclude that the record warranted a summary judgment in favor of Childress. We are satisfied that Judge Haight was correct as to both issues. We need not determine whether we agree with his conclusion that Taylor's contributions were not independently copyrightable since, even if they were protectible as expression or as an original selection of facts, we agree that there is no evidence from which a trier could infer that Childress had the state of mind required for joint authorship. As Judge Haight observed, whatever thought of co-authorship might have existed in Taylor's mind "was emphatically not shared by the purported co-author." There is no evidence that Childress ever contemplated, much less would have accepted, crediting the play as "written by Alice Childress and Clarice Taylor."

Childress was asked to write a play about "Moms" Mabley and did so. To facilitate her writing task, she accepted the assistance that Taylor provided, which consisted largely of furnishing the results of research concerning the life of "Moms" Mabley. As the actress expected to portray the leading role, Taylor also made some incidental suggestions, contributing ideas about the presentation of the play's subject and possibly some minor bits of expression. But there is no evidence that these aspects of Taylor's role ever evolved into more than the helpful advice that might come from the cast, the directors, or the producers of any play. A playwright does not so easily acquire a co-author.

Judge Haight was fully entitled to bolster his decision by reliance on the contract negotiations that followed completion of the script. Though his primary basis for summary judgment was the absence of any evidence supporting an inference that Childress shared "Taylor's notion that they were co-authors," he properly pointed to the emphatic rejection by Childress of the attempts by Taylor's agent to negotiate a co-ownership agreement and Taylor's acquiescence in that rejection. Intent "at the time the writing is done" remains the "touchstone," House Report at 120; Senate Report at 103, but subsequent conduct is normally probative of a prior state of mind. . . .

Taylor's claim of co-authorship was properly rejected, and with the rejection of that claim, summary judgment for Childress was properly entered on her copyright and unfair competition claims, and on defendants' counterclaim. The judgment of the District Court is affirmed.

NOTES AND QUESTIONS

(1) *Substantiality of the parties' contributions.* Any questions? Judge Newman's treatment of the criteria for "joint authorship" is nothing if not exhaustive. What do you think of the court's view that the "troublesome" question of whether copyrightable contributions should be required from all putative joint authors is essentially one of policy, to which the Copyright Act (to say nothing of the Constitution) does not speak directly? When Judge Newman speaks of this rule as being "more consistent with the spirit of copyright law," what might he mean? (*Childress* is a post-*Feist* decision, but it doesn't mention that Supreme Court precedent and its imperative of "*original* authorship." Should it have done so?)

(2) Recall the steam grate and pedestal supplied for "Third World America" by the commissioning party in *CCNV*, and Judge Ginsburg's *dictum* in the Court of Appeals, apparently giving weight not only to CCNV's contribution of the pedestal but also to its "conceptualization and . . . direction" of the work. Good enough for joint authorship? Considering the question as one of policy, is Judge Newman correct in endorsing a rule that *does* require copyrightable contributions by all putative joint authors?

Until recently, there was no substantial difference of opinion among the various courts which have decided "joint authorship" cases turning on this issue. The decisions quite consistently denied claims of joint authorship based on contributions that would not in themselves be copyrightable. *See, e.g., S.O.S., Inc. v. Payday, Inc.,* 886 F.2d 1081 (9th Cir. 1989). But in *Gaiman v. McFarlane,* 360 F.3d 644 (7th Cir. 2004), Judge Posner posited an "exception" to the "general rule" for situations in which uncopyrightable contributions combine to form a copyrightable work. In that case, writer/illustrator Todd McFarlane asked writer Neil Gaiman to contribute a script for the comic book series "Spawn" for a fee of $100,000. Gaiman's script (illustrated by McFarlane) included three new characters, whose presence greatly spurred sales of comics and spin-offs such as action figures. Gaiman later sued, asserting among other things, joint authorship of the characters to which he had contributed. One of McFarlane's defenses was that, even in their final form, the characters were uncopyrightable. *See* § 3.01[B].

Judge Posner disagreed, stating (for example) of the "Count Nicholas Cogliostro" character:

> Although Gaiman's verbal description . . . may well have been of a stock character, once he was drawn and named and given speech he became sufficiently distinctive to be copyrightable. Gaiman's contribution may not have been copyrightable by itself, but this contribution had expressive content without which Cogliostro wouldn't have been a character at all, but merely a drawing.

How does Judge Posner's theory differ from *Childress*? If Gaiman's contribution "had expressive content," why would it "not have been copyrightable by itself"? Note also that Judge Posner's comment arguably is *dicta* because, of the expressive elements he identifies as "combin[ing] to create a distinctive character" ("Cogliostro's age, obviously phony title, what he knows and says, his name, and his faintly Mosaic facial features"), all but the facial features were contributed by Gaiman.

(3)   More generally, what are the advantages and disadvantages of requiring each contribution to be copyrightable? One argument for the copyrightability requirement is that it leads to greater judicial and administrative efficiency. The test, according to *Erickson v. Trinity Theatre, Inc.*, 13 F.3d 1061, 1071 (7th Cir. 1994), "enables parties to predict whether their contributions to a work will entitle them to copyright protection as a joint author," and to protect themselves by contract if it appears that they would not enjoy the benefits accorded to authors of joint works under the Act. Are you persuaded that reliance on contract law is a practical solution? If so, why haven't more squabbles over "joint authorship" been resolved on this basis? Are the facts of *Childress* an object lesson here?

(4)   *The parties' intent.* Having disposed of the "substantiality of the contributions" issue, Judge Newman proceeds to what he terms "the crucial aspect of joint authorship — the nature of the intent that must be entertained by each putative joint author."

Section 101 of the 1976 Act defines a joint work as a work "prepared by two or more authors *with the intention that their contributions be merged . . .*" (emphasis added). The "intention" requirement had quite a history under the 1909 Act. Until 1955, the case law contemplated a preconcerted common design or intent on the part of the authors, *at the time of creation of the joint work*, that their contributions be merged into an indivisible whole. Such intent could be found even though the authors did not work together or even know each other, and despite the fact that each author's contribution and intent to engage in the creation of a joint work arose at a different time, so long as at some point their separate contributions and intents merged in a single work. *See Edward B. Marks Music Co. v. Jerry Vogel Music Co.*, 140 F.2d 266 (2d Cir. 1944); *Shapiro, Bernstein & Co., Inc. v. Jerry Vogel Music Co., Inc.*, 161 F.2d 406 (2d Cir. 1946) (the so-called *Melancholy Baby* case).

Then, in *Shapiro, Bernstein & Co., Inc. v. Jerry Vogel Music Co., Inc.*, 221 F.2d 569 (2d Cir.), *modified on rehearing*, 223 F.2d 252 (1955) (the *Twelfth Street Rag* case), the Second Circuit further relaxed the "preconcerted design" standard, holding that, even if at the time one element of a putative joint work was created there was no intent to contribute to such a work, if at any time thereafter the author *or his assignee* conceived and carried out that intention, the resulting combination became a joint work. In *Twelfth Street Rag* itself, a composer created an instrumental piano solo, not intending that it be accompanied by words. He assigned his rights to a publisher, which then commissioned lyrics. Was the song a joint work? The court held that it was, even though the composer never had any intention of creating one.

The major objection to *Twelfth Street Rag* was that it introduced an element of uncertainty into determining ownership rights in derivative works (and collective works, which are considered in the following subsection of the casebook). Does the 1976 Act's § 101 "joint works" definition overrule *Twelfth Street Rag*? *See Batiste v. Island Records, Inc.*, 179 F.3d 217 (5th Cir. 1999) (yes). What does the *Childress* court have to say on this question? The House Report?

(5) Should a court apply the *Twelfth Street Rag* rule, or the *Childress* rule, if the transaction in question, although being litigated today, took place before the effective date of the 1976 Act? We have seen, in the notes following *CCNV v. Reid*, that serious constitutional problems would attend any attempt to apply the 1976 Act's dramatically different work-for-hire rules retroactively to pre-1978 transactions. Would the same be true of the *Twelfth Street Rag* rule, given its somewhat aberrant status in the history of joint works law under the 1909 Act? *See Weissmann v. Freeman*, 684 F. Supp. 1248 (S.D.N.Y. 1988).

(6) At a minimum, *Childress* is clear that the would-be co-authors' respective intents regarding the work in suit must have been entertained "at the time the contribution of each was created." What does this mean, though? What result if Composer writes a tune in 2002, with intent eventually to merge it with words by Lyricist (who is unaware at that point of Composer's intent); and in 2003, Composer sent the tune to Lyricist, whereupon Lyricist not only formed an intent to merge the tune with words, but in fact put pen to paper and completed the work? What result if, instead of writing in 2003, Lyricist put the project on his "to do" list; in 2004, Composer changed her mind, deciding the tune is better on its own, but failed to communicate her change of mind to Lyricist; and in 2005, Lyricist finally penned the words, still with intent to merge?

(7) *Miscellaneous intent problems.* Now, suppose a creative process in which one author is dominant and the other subsidiary. Suppose, further, that the latter makes non-*de minimis* copyrightable contributions to the work, but that she cannot satisfy the "mutual intent" requirement because the dominant author "absolutely, vehemently and totally" rejects collaboration out of a steadfast determination to make the work "entirely his own project," all the while incorporating the nontrivial contributions of the subsidiary author into the work. No joint work, right? In such circumstances, however, would the subsidiary author, in the absence of a work-for-hire agreement or any explicit contractual assignment, retain any rights or interests in her own contributions? The question was broached, but (due to the plaintiff's failure to raise the question in the trial court) not decided, in *Thomson v. Larson*, 147 F.3d 195 (2d Cir. 1998) (dispute regarding authorship of the critically acclaimed Broadway musical "Rent"). How *should* these questions be resolved?

(8) Besides requiring simultaneity between intention and creation, *Childress* says that the putative coauthors' collective intent to create a joint work must have included not just a common "state of mind regarding the unitary nature of the finished work," but also an "intent . . . to regard themselves as co-authors." Is this the same as insisting, as the trial judge did (with the Second Circuit's retroactive blessing), that the parties have "entertain[ed] in their minds the concept of joint authorship, whether or not they understood precisely the legal consequences of that relationship"? What is the statutory basis for this elaboration of the intent standard, and how is it to be applied? *See, e.g., Gaylord v. U.S.*, 595 F.3d 1364 (Fed. Cir. 2010) (holding Gaylord was sole author of the Korean War Veterans Memorial sculpture, and that contributions of others were more in the nature of "suggestions and criticism").

How helpful is Judge Newman's gloss that, "[i]n many instances, a useful test will be whether, in the absence of contractual agreements concerning listed authorship, each participant intended that all would be identified as coauthors"? Realistically, how reliable is a test based on understandings about "billing" or "credit"? Imagine the case of a ghost-written memoir, published under the celebrity subject's name, to which the "ghost" contributes the greatest share of protectible expression. Would the *Childress* approach to intent assign sole authorship to the celebrity? *See Childress*, n.7.

(9)   In practice, of course, the "memoir" hypothetical posed in the previous question might be resolved not in terms of "joint authorship," but under the "work for hire" doctrine. The proposition that "work for hire" trumps "joint authorship" is amply demonstrated by *Richlin v. Metro-Goldwyn-Mayer Pictures, Inc.*, 531 F.3d 962 (9th Cir. 2008). In *Richlin*, the heirs of one of the co-authors of the treatment on which the 1964 movie *The Pink Panther* was based sued for an accounting. The Ninth Circuit held that Richlin's share of the common-law copyright in the treatment had been assigned to MGM, and that the statutory copyright in the movie belonged to MGM, because Richlin and his co-author wrote the screenplay as a work made for hire. (The case was decided under the 1909 Act, but the court applied the 1976 Act's definition of joint authorship, as a codification of 1909 Act case law.) *See also Philadelphia Orchestra Ass'n v. Walt Disney Co.*, 821 F. Supp. 341 (E.D. Pa. 1993) (holding the orchestra was not a co-author of the 1939 movie *Fantasia*, because its recorded performance was made "for hire" under the 1909 Act).

(10)   Take another look at the Supreme Court's early decision in *Burrow-Giles Lithographic Co. v. Sarony*, reproduced in Chapter 2. There, as you will recall, a portrait photograph of Oscar Wilde was found to be a protected "work of authorship" by virtue of the artistic contributions of Sarony, the photographer. Could it have been argued that, in fact, the portrait was the joint work of Sarony and Wilde, his notoriously creative photographic subject?

(11)   *Motion pictures and "joint authorship."* In *Childress*, the joint work issue arose in a dispute between two parties. The issue of determining who is a joint author is much more complicated in situations involving highly collaborative works like motion pictures.

In *Aalmuhammed v. Lee*, 202 F.3d 1227 (9th Cir. 2000), the plaintiff was hired to work on Spike Lee's movie *Malcolm X*. While on the set, he allegedly "created at least two entire scenes with new characters, translated Arabic into English for subtitles, supplied his own voice for voice-overs, selected the proper prayers and religious practices for the characters and edited parts of the movie during post-production." Aalmuhammed received compensation for his work but never had a written contract with either Lee or Warner Brothers. He sued Lee and others for a declaratory judgment of his joint ownership.

The Court of Appeals held that "authorship is not the same thing as making a valuable and copyrightable contribution." *Id.* at 1232. Instead, the court endorsed a three-factor test: who exercised control over the final product; objective manifestations of shared intent, such as credit; and the "audience appeal" of the contributions. "Control in many cases will be the most important factor." *Id.* at 1234. Here, although Aalmuhammed "could make extremely helpful recommendations, . . . Spike Lee was not bound to accept any of them." Lacking control and any objective manifestations of intent, the court affirmed a grant of summary judgment to the defendants (although it remanded the plaintiff's contractual claims).

Absent a contract, who *should* be the author of a movie? For an extensive analysis, see Dougherty, *Not a Spike Lee Joint? Issues in the Authorship of Motion Pictures Under U.S. Copyright Law*, 49 UCLA L. Rev. 225 (2001). Note that Art. L. 113-7 of France's Intellectual Property Code establishes a presumption that the joint authors of an audiovisual work are the director, screenwriters, and composer.

(12)   *Other highly collaborative works.* Are contributors to Wikipedia or programmers who contribute code to open-source software projects joint authors? The capacity to "crowd-source" production of material online calls into question how well-suited the tests of intent, control, and audience or market appeal are for determining copyright ownership in works that are both highly collaborative and highly iterative. If all contributors are joint authors, they share rights in a single copyright; whereas, if they are individual authors, the work is a "compilation" of multiple works of authorship. From a policy perspective, is one of these results better than the other? Why?

(13)   *Proof.* Assuming we now know all we need (or want) to know about the nature of the intention required of joint work authors, what kind of *proof* can be used to find it? The case law suggests that the "intention" can be proved by direct or circumstantial evidence or both.

Many courts, like the court in *Weissmann v. Freeman*, 868 F.2d 1313 (2d Cir. 1989), appear to place special weight on circumstantial objective factors such as the use of an individual by-line in place of a co-authorship credit, or arrangements between the parties for review of the work prior to publication. For example, in *Janky v. Lake County Convention & Visitors Bureau*, 576 F.3d 356 (7th Cir. 2009), plaintiff Janky composed a theme song for use by the Bureau. Farag, another member of the band, recommended revisions, resulting in changes to ten percent of the lyrics. Janky then obtained a new copyright registration, listing Farag as a co-author who provided "additional lyrics" to a "joint work." Janky also filed a document with ASCAP stating that Farag held a 10 percent "ownership share." Three years later, Janky filed another registration application that omitted Farag and listed herself as the sole author. Reversing a summary judgment in favor of Janky, the majority instead granted summary judgment to the defendant, holding that Janky could not create a triable issue of fact by contradicting her own previous written acknowledgments that the work was a "joint work." The dissent placed more weight on Janky's subjective testimony explaining her "mistake," and would have remanded the case for trial.

(14)   *"Inseparability" and "interdependence."* Section 101 defines joint works so as to require that the co-authors' contributions "be merged into inseparable or interdependent parts of a unitary whole." What does this mean?

The statute and the legislative history are silent as to the distinction between "inseparability" and "interdependence." Nimmer suggests that the dividing line is "analogous to" the distinction between derivative and collective works. 1 NIMMER ON COPYRIGHT § 6.04 (2012). *But see Childress*, 945 F.2d at 504 n.3 ("The analogy is inexact at best"). In other words, if, when *A* and *B*'s contributions are combined, the result is that one or both are recast, transformed, or adapted, in the resulting work (say, a play based upon a preexisting short story) the two contributions are inseparable. If, on the other hand, the process is simply one of assembling the contributions of *A* and *B* into a collective whole without altering the individual elements (for example, music and lyrics), the contributions may still be separable but they are now interdependent. *See also BTE v. Bonnecaze*, 43 F. Supp. 2d 619 (E.D. La. 1999) (providing definitions and examples).

There appears to be no domestic significance to whether a joint work consists of inseparable, as distinguished from interdependent, parts. For foreign purposes, the distinction may be important because, under most foreign laws, a joint work results *only* from the merger of inseparable parts. Thus, a song — being the combination of interdependent but separable parts — is not a joint work in the United Kingdom. *See, e.g., Chappell & Co., Ltd. v. Redwood Music, Ltd.* [1980] 2 All E.R. 817 (H.L.). The classification of a work as joint or nonjoint may result, for example, in a different period of copyright protection, as we will see in Chapter 5.

(15) *Other matters.* Do state marital property laws prevail over federal copyright law with respect to joint ownership of copyrights? One state appellate court has said yes, positing a transfer by operation of law that transmogrifies an author's rights into community property for the benefit of the spouse (or soon-to-be ex-spouse). *In re Marriage of Worth*, 195 Cal. App. 3d 768 (1st Dist. 1987). In *Rodrigue v. Rodrigue*, 218 F.3d 432 (5th Cir. 2000), however, the Fifth Circuit, in a truly Solomonic decision, (1) recognized the divorcing author's "continued entitlement [under Federal law] to the exclusive control and management of the [six § 106] exclusive rights in [the subject works]," subject to a duty to "manage prudently," but (2) held that the non-author spouse should receive "an undivided one-half interest in the *net economic benefits* generated by or resulting from copyrighted works created by [the spouse] during the existence of the community and from any derivatives thereof" (emphasis added). No co-ownership of the copyrights, but one-half of all the proceeds therefrom!

(16) There are other means by which co-ownership of copyright can arise, apart from initial joint authorship. For example, a transfer of the copyright by the author to more than one person produces joint ownership. The same is true when the work passes by will or intestacy to multiple owners. In addition, co-ownership is created when renewal rights or rights terminated under the 1976 Act's termination-of-transfer provisions (both discussed in the next chapter) vest in a class made up of two or more persons.

(17) Section 201(a) of the 1976 Act does not specifically describe the rights and duties of the co-owners of a joint work. As the House Report notes, "court-made law [regarding such matters] is left undisturbed." Thus, the pre-1976 rule remains valid: Neither a joint owner of a copyrighted work nor the licensees of such an owner can be liable to other co-owners for infringing the copyright in the work. In essence, the joint owners are treated as tenants in common. Assuming no subsequent transfer of any of the authors' interests, "[j]oint authorship entitles the co-authors to equal undivided interests in the whole work — in other words, each joint author has the right to use or to license the work as he or she wishes, subject only to the obligation to account to the other joint owner for any profits that are made." *Thomson v.*

Larson, 147 F.3d 195 (2d Cir. 1998). Normally, the profits will accrue as the result of licensing to third-party non-owners, but modern cases also hold that one joint owner is obliged to account to other joint owners even for his or her own use of the work. *E.g., Oddo v. Ries*, 743 F.2d 630 (9th Cir. 1984); *see also* Note, *Accountability Among Co-Owners of Statutory Copyright*, 72 Harv. L. Rev. 1550 (1959) (use by one owner depletes residual value of work to nonusing owners).

It is a truism that one co-owner may not make or authorize a use of the work which would lead to its destruction (or perhaps more precisely, in the instance of intangible property, the destruction of its worth). 1 NIMMER ON COPYRIGHT § 6.10[B] (2012). It is less than clear what this means in practice. See the notes to *Effects Associates, Inc. v. Cohen* in § 4.02 below.

[D] Collective Works and the *Tasini* Case

The first sentence of § 201(c) provides: "Copyright in each separate contribution to a collective work is distinct from copyright in the collective work as a whole and vests initially in the author of the contribution." Thus, in a periodical such as the *New York Times*, each article and photograph has a separate copyright, and there is an additional copyright in the collective work as a whole, *i.e.*, in the selection and arrangement of the contributions. The *Times* owns the copyright in the collective work as the publisher and compiler. The *Times* also owns the copyrights in the individual contributions created by its employees, as works made for hire. Freelance authors, however, are independent contractors, so their contributions are owned initially by the individual authors.

Frequently, however, a freelancer submits an article for publication and gets paid without signing a written agreement. Clearly, the publisher has acquired some sort of license; but the potential for future litigation over the scope of such an implied license is evident. Accordingly, the second sentence of § 201(c) sets forth a default rule: "In the absence of an express transfer of the copyright or of any rights under it, the owner of copyright in the collective work is presumed to have acquired only the privilege of reproducing and distributing the contribution as part of that particular collective work, any revision of that collective work, and any later collective work in the same series."

In the early 1990s, six freelance authors brought a test case concerning 21 articles that they had contributed to the *New York Times* and two other periodicals. Under agreements with the periodicals' publishers, but without the freelancers' consent, LEXIS/NEXIS and University Microfilms International (UMI) placed copies of the freelancers' articles — along with all other articles from the periodicals in which the freelancers' work appeared — in three electronic databases: NEXIS, NYTO (New York Times OnDisk), and GPO (General Periodicals OnDisk). The question presented was whether this use was authorized by the default privilege in § 201(c).

In the District Court, Judge (now Justice) Sonia Sotomayor ruled in favor of the publishers, holding that the databases preserved the "selection" of articles in the collective works, even if they did not preserve their "arrangement." *Tasini v. N.Y. Times Co.*, 972 F. Supp. 804 (S.D.N.Y. 1997). On appeal, the Second Circuit reversed, holding that § 201(c), as an exception to the exclusive rights of the individual authors, should be construed narrowly; and that by presenting individual articles without any of the surrounding material, the databases did not preserve the "selection and arrangement" of the collective works. 206 F.3d 161 (2d Cir. 2000). The Supreme Court took up the case in *New York Times Co. v. Tasini*, 533 U.S. 483 (2001).

In an opinion by Justice Ginsburg, a majority of the Supreme Court held that the databases did not constitute a "revision" of the collective works in which the articles were first published. The Court noted that, according to the legislative history, a "publishing company could reprint a contribution from one issue in a later issue of its magazine, and could reprint an article from a 1980 edition of an encyclopedia in a 1990 revision of it; [but] the publisher could not revise the contribution itself or include it in a new anthology or an entirely different magazine or other collective work." H.R. Rep. No. 94-1476 at 122-23. The majority viewed the databases as a "new anthology" or compendium, rather than as a "revision" of the individual periodical issues.

The New York Times' report of *Tasini*
Copyright 2001 by the New York Times Co. Reprinted with permission.

The majority also rejected the publishers' proffered analogy between the databases and microform publications, noting that microfilm and microfiche faithfully reproduce, page by page, all of the contents of the periodicals they record, whereas the databases reproduce individual articles without any of the surrounding context present in the original periodicals. The Court also considered the publishers' arguments in favor of so-called "media neutrality" — an appeal, in effect, not to discriminate against new digital media in applying traditional copyright principles — and concluded that "[i]n this case, media neutrality should protect the Authors' rights in the individual Articles to the extent those Articles are now presented individually, outside the collective work context, within the Databases' new media." Finally, the Court rejected the publishers' strongly expressed concerns about the consequences of a narrow reading of § 201(c):

The Publishers warn that a ruling for the Authors will have "devastating" consequences. The Databases, the Publishers note, provide easy access to complete newspaper texts going back decades. A ruling for the Authors, the Publishers suggest, will punch gaping holes in the electronic record of history. . . .

Notwithstanding the dire predictions from some quarters, it hardly follows from today's decision that an injunction against the inclusion of these Articles in the Databases (much less all freelance articles in any databases) must issue. The parties . . . may enter into an agreement allowing continued electronic reproduction of the Authors' works; they, and if necessary the courts and Congress, may draw on numerous models for distributing copyrighted works and remunerating authors for their distribution.

533 U.S. at 504-05. Dissenting, Justice Stevens (joined by Justice Breyer) opined that a disk containing all the files from a given issue of the *New York Times* constituted an electronic "revision" of that edition, and that there was no compelling reason to treat the same collection of files differently when it was combined with the contents of other editions. He also emphasized that copyright should strive to "promot[e] *broad public availability* of literature, music, and the other arts." *Id.* at 520 (emphasis in original; citation omitted).

At first blush, the Supreme Court's decision in *Tasini* may seem a nice victory for freelance journalists. In fact, it may be that the freelancers won the battle but lost the war. In the 1990s, publishers became fully aware of the possible risk of liability and began insisting on "all rights" agreements designed to allow them to reuse freelancers' contributions. Such contracts are standard now, and it is not clear whether freelancers were able to extract larger profits in exchange. Moreover, at least some of the publishers' dire predictions appear to have been realized. Some publishers, uncertain as to which articles in their archives were written by freelancers, or under what terms, deleted many items from their electronic databases. With media revenues continuing to decline, it remains to be seen whether a way can be found to protect the rights of freelance writers and the public interest at the same time.

Meanwhile, in 2005, the parties agreed to settle four consolidated class actions (including *Tasini*) by creating an $18 million fund to compensate freelancers for previous infringing uses. That settlement was threatened when the Second Circuit ruled that the District Court could not assert subject-matter jurisdiction over unregistered copyrights, even for settlement purposes. *See In re Literary Works in Electronic Databases Copyright Litigation*, 509 F.3d 116 (2d Cir. 2007). The Supreme Court, however, held that the lack of registration did not deprive the District Court of subject-matter jurisdiction. *See Reed Elsevier, Inc. v. Muchnick*, 559 U.S. 154 (2010). On remand, the Second Circuit overruled the District Court's class certification on the ground that authors of unregistered works had not been adequately represented. The case was remanded for the District Court to subdivide the class. *See In re Literary Works in Electronic Databases Copyright Litigation*, 654 F.3d 242 (2d Cir. 2011). For now, more than a decade after the Supreme Court's decision in *Tasini*, the freelancers have yet to receive a dime.

The *Tasini* decision also left behind some loose ends, exemplified by *Greenberg v. National Geographic Society*, 244 F.3d 1267 (11th Cir. 2001). There, in an action brought by a freelance photographer, the court held that a CD-ROM containing exact, page-by-page digital reproductions of all the contents of all issues of the magazine, along with a computer program enabling users to "navigate" the contents and an animated introductory sequence of "morphing" cover images, constituted a new "collective work" rather than a "revision" within the meaning of § 201(c). *Greenberg* was handed down three months before the Supreme Court's decision in *Tasini*.

The issue of *Greenberg*'s continued viability was raised in *Faulkner v. National Geographic Enterprises, Inc.*, 409 F.3d 26 (2d Cir. 2005). The Second Circuit first held that *Greenberg* did not have collateral estoppel effect on the § 201(c) issue because of the intervening Supreme Court decision in *Tasini*. Addressing the merits, the court then concluded that *Greenberg* was wrongly decided, because the *Complete National Geographic* preserved the "selection, coordination, and arrangement" of the underlying works and presented the contents to users "in the same context as they were presented to the users in the original versions of the Magazine." *Id.* at 38. The court viewed the CNG as an "electronic replica" that was more analogous to microfilm than to the electronic databases in *Tasini*.

Two years later, the saga continued when the *Greenberg* case returned to the Eleventh Circuit. A panel of that court initially held that its prior decision had been overruled by the intervening Supreme Court decision in *Tasini*, and that *Faulkner* reached the correct result as to everything except the animated introduction. 488 F.3d 1331 (11th Cir. 2007). After rehearing *en banc*, the full court confirmed the panel's conclusion by a narrow 7-5 vote. 533 F.3d 1244 (11th Cir. 2008).

Ultimately, the most long-lasting implications of *Tasini* may lie not in the field of electronic publication, but in its answers to more general questions of how old copyright principles should apply in new technological circumstances. For an early reflection on some of these implications, see Jaszi, Tasini *and Beyond*, 23 Eur. Intell. Prop. Rev. 595 (2001).

§ 4.02 TRANSFERS OF RIGHTS

Owning a copyright is one thing. Exploiting it may be quite another. In due course, the initial owner of the copyright — whoever he, she, they, or it may be, under the rules explored in the preceding section — may wish to transfer to another person one or more of the several rights which comprise the copyright (for example, the rights to reproduce and sell copies of the work or to prepare another work based upon it). The present section explores the concept and mechanics of transfer.

[A] Introduction

Statutory References
1976 Act: §§ 101 ("transfer of copyright ownership"), 201(d)–(e), 202, 204-05
1909 Act: §§ 27-32

Legislative History

H.R. REP. NO. 94-1476 at 123-24, 128-29,
reprinted in 1976 U.S.C.C.A.N. 5659, 5738-40, 5744-45

SECTION 201. OWNERSHIP OF COPYRIGHT

Transfer of ownership

The principle of unlimited alienability of copyright is stated in clause (1) of section 201(d). Under that provision the ownership of a copyright, or of any part of it, may be transferred by any means of conveyance or by operation of law, and is to be treated as personal property upon the death of the owner. Clause (2) of subsection (d) contains the first explicit statutory recognition of the principle of divisibility of copyright in our law. This provision, which has long been sought by authors and their representatives, . . . means that any of the exclusive rights that go to make up a copyright, including those enumerated in section 106 and any subdivision of them, can be transferred and owned separately. . . .

SECTION 202. DISTINCTION BETWEEN OWNERSHIP OF COPYRIGHT AND MATERIAL OBJECT

The principle restated in section 202 is a fundamental and important one: that copyright ownership and ownership of a material object in which the copyrighted work is embodied are entirely separate things. Thus, transfer of a material object does not of itself carry any rights under the copyright, and this includes transfer of the copy or phonorecord — the original manuscript, the photographic negative, the unique painting or statue, the master tape recording, etc. — in which the work was first fixed. Conversely, transfer of a copyright does not necessarily require the conveyance of any material object. . . .

SECTIONS 204, 205. EXECUTION AND RECORDATION OF TRANSFERS

. . . [Under s]ection 204[(a)], a transfer of copyright ownership (other than one brought about by operation of law) is valid only if there exists an instrument of conveyance, or alternatively a "note or memorandum of the transfer," which is in writing and signed by the copyright owner "or such owner's duly authorized agent." Subsection (b) makes clear that a notarial or consular acknowledgment is not essential to the validity of any transfer, whether executed in the United States or abroad. . . .

The recording and priority provisions of section 205 are intended to clear up a number of uncertainties arising [under prior law] and to make them more effective and practical in operation. Any "document pertaining to a copyright" may be recorded under subsection (a) if it "bears that actual signature of the person who executed it," or if it is appropriately certified as a true copy. However, subsection (c) makes clear that the recorded document will give constructive notice of its contents only if two conditions are met: (1) the document or attached material specifically identifies the work to which it pertains so that a reasonable search under the title or registration number would reveal it, and (2) registration has been made for the work. . . .

. . . The one- and three-month grace periods provided in subsection [(d)] are a reasonable compromise between those who want a longer hiatus and those who argue that any grace period makes it impossible for a *bona fide* transferee to rely on the record at any particular time.

Under subsection [(e)] of section 205, a nonexclusive license in writing and signed, whether recorded or not, would be valid against a later transfer, and would also prevail as against a prior unrecorded transfer if taken in good faith and without notice. . . .

[For a fuller excerpt from H.R. REP. No. 94-1476, see Part Three of the Casebook Supplement.]

[B] Preliminary Concepts

[1] The Distinction Between Copyright and Material Object

Section 202 states one of the fundamental principles of the 1976 Act: the distinction between ownership of the copyright in the work and ownership of the material object that embodies the work.

Putting this relationship into words is much like trying to explain the relationship between the body and the soul. All the same, many courts have tried. In *United States v. Smith*, 686 F.2d 234 (5th Cir. 1982), for example, the Fifth Circuit characterized a copyright as "nothing more than an incorporeal, intangible right or privilege" that "does not implicate any tangible embodiment of the work." "In other words," said the court (no doubt hoping to make the point more clear), "a copyright is independent of both its physical manifestation and the very thing that is copyrighted [*i.e.*, the work]." *Id.* at 239-40.

Fortunately, the courts have long since proved themselves equal to the task of implementing the copyright/material object distinction in practice — with but one significant exception. On the credit side, to provide a single illustration, numerous courts held over the years that the right to publish private letters belongs to the writer or his or her legal representative, not to the recipient. *See, e.g., Baker v. Libbie*, 97 N.E. 109, 111-12 (Mass. 1912); *Salinger v. Random House, Inc.*, 811 F.2d 90, 94-95 (2d Cir. 1987).

On the debit side, however, the distinction too frequently became blurred in cases involving works of art, in which the "original," embodied in canvas or stone, had an artistic uniqueness quite apart from its potential as a "master" for making reproductions. Indeed, the court in *Pushman v. New York Graphic Society, Inc.*, 39 N.E.2d 249 (N.Y. 1942), held, in contrast to the letter cases, that an artist selling a work of art may be presumed to transfer reproduction rights as well.

The legislative history of § 202, in a passage omitted above, indicates that this section was drafted in part to overturn *Pushman*. In actuality, the demise of the *Pushman* rule had begun well before 1976, when New York and California enacted statutes creating a presumption that sales of art works do *not* effect transfers of copyright. *See* N.Y. Gen. Bus. Law §§ 223-24 (McKinney 1968); Cal. Civ. Code

§ 982(c) (West 1976). But despite § 202 of the 1976 Act and any currently applicable state statutes, the *Pushman* doctrine cannot safely be ignored even today. The reason is that the 1976 Act, and quite possibly the state statutes, do not operate retroactively for transactions involving pre-January 1978 transfers. For post-1977 transfers, however, § 202 is the law, applying to transfers of every type of federally copyrighted work from the moment of fixation.

[2] The Bundle of Rights

Under the 1909 Act, a copyright was perceived as an indivisible *bundle of rights* incapable of being broken up into smaller rights and exercised by multiple owners. This "doctrine of indivisibility" was justified mainly as protecting those charged with infringement from harassment in successive lawsuits. At any given time, there could be only one owner of the bundle of rights in a given work; anyone else claiming an interest under the copyright could rise no higher than the status of licensee, and therefore was unable to bring suit. The ramifications of indivisibility, however, reached far beyond standing to sue, affecting ownership itself, notice, recordation of transfers, and taxes. The inconveniences of indivisibility, and not infrequently the injustices worked by the doctrine, were many.

In consequence, the courts whittled away at indivisibility, most notably in *Goodis v. United Artists Television, Inc.*, 425 F.2d 397 (2d Cir. 1970). There, the court based protection for the plaintiff author's copyright in a novel upon a notice of copyright by a publisher, in its own name, in connection with the novel's serialization in the publisher's magazine — under circumstances, in short, in which the act critical to protection of the author's interest had been taken by one who clearly held only a limited license.

The result in *Goodis* foreshadowed the total abrogation of indivisibility in the 1976 Act. As indicated in the House Report, the Act contains "the first explicit statutory recognition of the principle of divisibility of copyright," in American law. In § 106, which we consider in Chapter 7, Congress has enumerated six separate "exclusive rights" protected under the current statute. In its definitional section, the Act specifically contemplates that the term "copyright owner," "with respect to any one of the exclusive rights comprised in a copyright, refers to the owner *of that particular right.*" § 101 (emphasis added). And § 201(d)(2) provides that "[a]ny of the exclusive rights comprised in a copyright, *including any subdivision of any of the rights specified by section 106,* may be transferred[,] . . . owned separately [and protected] . . . to the extent of that right . . ." (emphasis added).

To take a simple example: Under the 1976 Act, *A* could grant an exclusive license in his novel to *B* to prepare a derivative screenplay, another to *C* to write a play based on the novel, and a third exclusive license to *D* to perform the work in the state of Texas during the month of July 2014 (preferably indoors). All of these conveyances would be transfers covered by the Act (see the § 101 definition of "transfers of copyright ownership") and would entitle the transferee to enjoy all the rights of a copyright owner — including the right to sue for infringement of the transferee's interest without having to join the copyright proprietor.

As you can well imagine, by "unbundling" the bundle of rights, the 1976 Act has greatly encouraged the exploitation of copyrighted works.

[C]   Decisional Law

EFFECTS ASSOCIATES, INC. v. COHEN
United States Court of Appeals, Ninth Circuit
908 F.2d 555 (1990)

KOZINSKI, CIRCUIT JUDGE:

What we have here is a failure to compensate. Larry Cohen, a low-budget horror movie mogul, paid less than the agreed price for special effects footage he had commissioned from Effects Associates. Cohen then used this footage without first obtaining a written license or assignment of the copyright; Effects sued for copyright infringement. We consider whether a transfer of copyright without a written agreement, an arrangement apparently not uncommon in the motion picture industry, conforms with the requirements of the Copyright Act.

Facts

This started out as a run-of-the-mill Hollywood squabble. Defendant Larry Cohen wrote, directed and executive produced "The Stuff," a horror movie with a dash of social satire: Earth is invaded by an alien life form that looks (and tastes) like frozen yogurt but, alas, has some unfortunate side effects — it's addictive and takes over the mind of anyone who eats it. Marketed by an unscrupulous entrepreneur, the Stuff becomes a big hit. An industrial spy hired by ice cream manufacturers eventually uncovers the terrible truth; he alerts the American people and blows up the yogurt factory, making the world safe once again for lovers of frozen confections.

In cooking up this gustatory melodrama, Cohen asked Effects Associates, a small special effects company, to create footage to enhance certain action sequences in the film. In a short letter dated October 29, 1984, Effects offered to prepare seven shots,[1] the most dramatic of which would depict the climactic explosion of the Stuff factory. Cohen agreed to the deal orally, but no one said anything about who would own the copyright in the footage.

Cohen was unhappy with the factory explosion Effects created, and he expressed his dissatisfaction by paying Effects only half the promised amount for that shot. Effects made several demands for the rest of the money (a little over $8,000), but Cohen refused. Nevertheless, Cohen incorporated Effects's footage into the film and turned it over to New World Entertainment for distribution. Effects then brought this copyright infringement action, claiming that Cohen (along with his production company and New World) had no right to use the special effects footage unless he paid Effects the full contract price. Effects also brought pendent state law claims for fraud and conspiracy to infringe copyright.

The district court initially dismissed the suit, holding that it was primarily a

---

[1] The price originally agreed to was $62,335; in an invoice dated January 10, 1985, Effects adjusted this amount upward to $64,033.92, because of additional expenses incurred in creating the shots.

contract dispute and, as such, did not arise under federal law. In an opinion remarkable for its lucidity, we reversed and remanded, concluding that plaintiff was "master of his claim" and could opt to pursue the copyright infringement action instead of suing on the contract. . . . We recognized that the issue on remand would be whether Effects had transferred to Cohen the right to use the footage. . . .

A Poster for *The Stuff*

On remand, the district court granted summary judgment to Cohen on the infringement claim, holding that Effects had granted Cohen an implied license to use the shots. Accordingly, the court dismissed the remaining state law claims, allowing Effects to pursue them in state court. We review the district court's grant of summary judgment *de novo*.

Discussion

A. Transfer of Copyright Ownership

The law couldn't be clearer: The copyright owner of "a motion picture or other audiovisual work" has the exclusive rights to copy, distribute or display the copyrighted work publicly. 17 U.S.C. § 106 (1988). While the copyright owner can sell or license his rights to someone else, section 204 of the Copyright Act invalidates a purported transfer of ownership unless it is in writing. 17 U.S.C.

§ 204(a) (1988).[2] Here, no one disputes that Effects is the copyright owner of the special effects footage used in "The Stuff,"[3] and that defendants copied, distributed and publicly displayed this footage without written authorization.

Cohen suggests that section 204's writing requirement does not apply to this situation, advancing an argument that might be summarized, tongue in cheek, as: Moviemakers do lunch, not contracts. Cohen concedes that "[i]n the best of all possible legal worlds" parties would obey the writing requirement, but contends that moviemakers are too absorbed in developing "joint creative endeavors" to "focus upon the legal niceties of copyright licenses." Thus, Cohen suggests that we hold section 204's writing requirement inapplicable here because "it [i]s customary in the motion picture industry . . . not to have written licenses." To the extent that Cohen's argument amounts to a plea to exempt moviemakers from the normal operation of section 204 by making implied transfers of copyrights "the rule, not the exception," we reject his argument.

Common sense tells us that agreements should routinely be put in writing. This simple practice prevents misunderstandings by spelling out the terms of a deal in black and white, forces parties to clarify their thinking and consider problems that could potentially arise, and encourages them to take their promises seriously because it's harder to backtrack on a written contract than on an oral one. Copyright law dovetails nicely with common sense by requiring that a transfer of copyright ownership be in writing. Section 204 ensures that the creator of a work will not give away his copyright inadvertently and forces a party who wants to use the copyrighted work to negotiate with the creator to determine precisely what rights are being transferred and at what price. *Cf. Community for Creative Non-Violence v. Reid*, 490 U.S. 730 (1989) (describing purpose of writing requirement for works made for hire). Most importantly, section 204 enhances predictability and certainty of copyright ownership — "Congress' paramount goal" when it revised the Act in 1976. *Community for Creative Non-Violence*, 490 U.S. at 749; *see also Dumas v. Gommerman*, 865 F.2d 1093, 1103-04 (9th Cir. 1989). Rather than look to the courts every time they disagree as to whether a particular use of the work violates their mutual understanding, parties need only look to the writing that sets out their respective rights.

Section 204's writing requirement is not unduly burdensome; it necessitates neither protracted negotiations nor substantial expense. The rule is really quite simple: If the copyright holder agrees to transfer ownership to another party, that party must get the copyright holder to sign a piece of paper saying so. It doesn't have to be the Magna Charta; a one-line *pro forma* statement will do.

Cohen's attempt to exempt moviemakers from the requirements of the Copyright Act is largely precluded by recent Supreme Court and circuit authority

---

[2] The Copyright Act defines "transfer of copyright ownership" as an "assignment, mortgage, exclusive license, or any other conveyance, alienation, or hypothecation of a copyright or of any of the exclusive rights comprised in a copyright . . . but not including a nonexclusive license." 17 U.S.C. § 101.

[3] Cohen concedes that he licensed Effects to prepare the footage as a derivative work incorporating other shots from "The Stuff," and that Effects has a valid copyright in this footage.

construing the work-for hire doctrine.[4] [Discussion of *Community for Creative Non-Violence* and *Dumas v. Gommerman* omitted.] [W]here a non-employee contributes to a book or movie, as Effects did here, the exclusive rights of copyright ownership vest in the creator of the contribution, unless there is a written agreement to the contrary. . . .

Thus, section 101 . . . afford[s] moviemakers a simple, straightforward way of obtaining ownership of the copyright in a creative contribution — namely, a written agreement. The Supreme Court and this circuit, while recognizing the custom and practice in the industry, have refused to permit moviemakers to sidestep section 204's writing requirement. Accordingly, we find unpersuasive Cohen's contention that section 204's writing requirement, which singles out no particular group, somehow doesn't apply to him. As section 204 makes no special allowances for the movie industry, neither do we.

B. Nonexclusive Licenses

Although we reject any suggestion that moviemakers are immune to section 204, we note that there is a narrow exception to the writing requirement that may apply here. Section 204 provides that all transfers of copyright ownership must be in writing; section 101 defines transfers of ownership broadly, but expressly removes from the scope of section 204 a "nonexclusive license." *See* note 2 *supra*. The sole issue that remains, then, is whether Cohen had a nonexclusive license to use plaintiff's special effects footage.

The leading treatise on copyright law states that "[a] nonexclusive license may be granted orally, or may even be implied from conduct." 3 M. Nimmer & D. Nimmer, NIMMER ON COPYRIGHT § 10.03[A], at 10-36 (1989). Cohen relies on the latter proposition; he insists that, although Effects never gave him a written or oral license, Effects's conduct created an implied license to use the footage in "The Stuff."

Cohen relies largely on our decision in *Oddo v. Ries*, 743 F.2d 630 (9th Cir. 1984). There, we held that Oddo, the author of a series of articles on how to restore Ford F-100 pickup trucks, had impliedly granted a limited non-exclusive license to Ries, a publisher, to use plaintiff's articles in a book on the same topic. We relied on the fact that Oddo and Ries had formed a partnership to create and publish the book, with Oddo writing and Ries providing capital. Oddo prepared a manuscript consisting partly of material taken from his prior articles and submitted it to Ries. Because the manuscript incorporated preexisting material, it was a derivative work; by publishing it, Ries would have necessarily infringed the copyright in Oddo's articles, unless Oddo had granted him a license. We concluded that, in preparing and handing over to Ries a manuscript intended for publication that, if published, would infringe Oddo's copyright, Oddo "impliedly gave the partnership a license to use the articles insofar as they were incorporated in the manuscript, for without

---

[4] Because Effects is not an employee and there is no written agreement stating that plaintiff's footage is a work made for hire, Cohen can't take advantage of this doctrine. In any event, Cohen has waived this argument by failing to raise it below.

such a license, Oddo's contribution to the partnership venture would have been of minimal value." *Id.* [at 632-34].[5]

The district court agreed with Cohen, and we agree with the district court: *Oddo* controls here. Like the plaintiff in *Oddo*, Effects created a work at defendant's request and handed it over, intending that defendant copy and distribute it. To hold that Effects did not at the same time convey a license to use the footage in "The Stuff" would mean that plaintiff's contribution to the film was "of minimal value," a conclusion that can't be squared with the fact that Cohen paid Effects almost $56,000 for this footage. Accordingly, we conclude that Effects impliedly granted non-exclusive licenses to Cohen and his production company to incorporate the special effects footage into "The Stuff" and to New World Entertainment to distribute the film.

Conclusion

We affirm the district court's grant of summary judgment in favor of Cohen and the other defendants. We note, however, that plaintiff doesn't leave this court empty-handed. . . . Effects . . . retains the right to sue [Cohen] in state court on a variety of [non-copyright] grounds, including breach of contract. Additionally, Effects may license, sell or give away for nothing its remaining [§ 106] rights in the special effects footage. Those rights may not be particularly valuable, of course: "The Stuff" was something less than a blockbuster, and it remains to be seen whether there's a market for shots featuring great gobs of alien yogurt oozing out of a defunct factory. On the other hand, the shots may have much potential for use in music videos. *See generally* Kozinski & Banner, *Who's Afraid of Commercial Speech?*, 76 Va. L. Rev. 627, 641 (1990). In any event, whatever Effects chooses to do with the footage, Cohen will have no basis for complaining. And that's an important lesson that licensees of more versatile film properties may want to take to heart.

NOTES AND QUESTIONS

(1)   *The writing requirement.* As *Effects Associates* makes clear, the Copyright Act of 1976 contains an invariable rule that a transfer of copyright ownership (other than by operation of law) must be made, or memorialized, in writing. This rule represents at least a partial departure from the law of the 1909 Act. Although § 28 of the earlier law provided that "copyright . . . may be assigned, granted, or mortgaged by an instrument in writing signed by the proprietor of the copyright," it did not apply to exclusive licenses of copyright interests, as distinct from assignments of a copyright itself. Note that, in § 101, the 1976 Act includes an "exclusive license" within the definition of a "transfer of copyright ownership," to which the writing requirement of § 204(a) applies.

(2)   Unlike § 28 of the 1909 Act, which referred to an "instrument in writing

---

[5] Oddo did nevertheless prevail, but on other grounds. Ries was unhappy with Oddo's manuscript and hired another writer to do the job right. This writer added much new material, but also used large chunks of Oddo's manuscript, thereby incorporating portions of Oddo's pre-existing articles. By publishing the other writer's book, Ries exceeded the scope of his implied license to use Oddo's articles and was liable for copyright infringement.

signed by the proprietor of the copyright," § 204(a) allows, in addition, for a "note or memorandum of the transfer." Just how liberally should this language be construed? As Judge Kozinski says in *Effects Associates*, the writing "doesn't have to be the Magna Charta [sic]; a one-line *pro forma* statement will do." Most courts have insisted, however, that "the terms of any writing purporting to transfer copyright interests, even a one-line statement, must be clear." *Papa's-June Music, Inc. v. McLean*, 921 F. Supp. 1154, 1159 (S.D.N.Y. 1996); *see, e.g., Radio Television Espanola S.A. v. New World Entertainment, Ltd.*, 183 F.3d 922 (9th Cir. 1999) (faxes that referred to a "deal," but did not include any further information about the deal, were insufficient). What if there is a signed writing that specifically mentions copyrights, but the writing is ambiguous as to *which* copyrights were transferred? *See SCO Group, Inc. v. Novell, Inc.*, 578 F.3d 1201 (10th Cir. 2009) (holding writing was sufficient; but admitting parol evidence to interpret the agreement and finding a triable issue of fact). Does this decision serve "Congress' paramount goal" of "enhanc[ing] predictability and certainty of copyright owner- ship"? *Compare SCO with Bieg v. Hovnanian Enterprises, Inc.*, 157 F. Supp. 2d 475 (E.D. Pa. 2001) ("any ambiguity concerning the alleged transfer must be inter- preted in favor of the original copyright holder" in order to avoid inadvertent transfers).

What if there is a signed writing that purports to confirm an earlier oral agreement? The courts are split. *See Billy-Bob Teeth, Inc. v. Novelty, Inc.*, 329 F.3d 586 (7th Cir. 2003) ("an oral assignment may be confirmed later in writing"); *Imperial Residential Design, Inc. v. Palms Development Group, Inc.*, 70 F.3d 96 (11th Cir. 1995) ("a copyright owner's later execution of a writing which confirms an earlier oral agreement validates the transfer *ab initio*"). *But see Konigsberg Int'l, Inc. v. Rice*, 16 F.3d 355 (9th Cir. 1994) (Kozinski, J.) (writing must be "substantially contemporaneous" with the oral agreement and be "a product of the parties' negotiations"). Is this consistent with the treatment of work-for-hire agreements as discussed in § 4.01?

Does it matter whether the person challenging the writing is the transferor or a third-party infringer? In *Eden Toys, Inc. v. Florelee Undergarment Co.*, 697 F.2d 27 (2d Cir. 1982), the court stated that if "the copyright owner appears to have no dispute with its licensee on this matter, it would be anomalous to permit a third-party infringer to invoke [§ 204] against the licensee." Thus, the court allowed the licensee to prove it had an "informal license" that was later confirmed in a signed writing. *But see Barefoot Architect, Inc. v. Bunge*, 632 F.3d 822 (3d Cir. 2011) (agreeing, but requiring extrinsic evidence of purported prior oral transfer). Similarly, in *Dean v. Burrows*, 732 F. Supp. 816 (E.D. Tenn. 1989), an endorsed check bearing a notation that it was for "molds and mold designs" was held to be sufficient against a third-party infringer, even though most courts have held ambiguous check legends to be insufficient. *See, e.g., Playboy Enterprises, Inc. v. Dumas*, 53 F.3d 549 (2d Cir. 1995) (check legend purporting to transfer "all right, title and interest" in painting was ambiguous and did not satisfy § 204). Compare the discussion in *Dumas* with the discussion of check endorsements and the work-for-hire doctrine in the notes following the *CCNV* case in § 4.01.

(3) To satisfy § 204(a), a writing must be signed by an owner of the copyright interest to be transferred. It need not necessarily be signed, however, by *all* of the

owners of that interest. One consequence of "joint" ownership of copyright, whether arising by virtue of joint authorship or otherwise, is that any one of a work's multiple owners may exercise the § 106 rights (reproduction, adaptation, etc.), and also may authorize third parties to do the same, subject to a duty to account to co-owners.

The only significant limitation on this authority derives from the general law of co-tenancy: one co-tenant may not (without the assent of the others) make or authorize a use which operates to destroy the common property or cause it to deteriorate. The exact contours of the rule, as applied to co-tenancy in copyright, are (to say the least) unclear. There is authority for the view that a transfer of rights (such as music publishing rights or motion picture rights) by one joint owner, which "practically precludes the other from a like use," should fall within the bar. *See Shapiro, Bernstein & Co. v. Jerry Vogel Music Co.*, 73 F. Supp. 165 (S.D.N.Y. 1947); *see also Davis v. Blige*, 505 F.3d 90, 101 (2d Cir. 2007) (because an exclusive license destroys the value of the copyright to the other owners, a co-owner cannot grant an exclusive license to others). One commentator, however, has taken the position that, "as a general matter [courts should] confine relief to situations in which a co-owner's conduct may place the work in the public domain." *See* P. Goldstein, 1 Copyright § 4.2.2.2 (2012).

(4)   Does the text of § 204(a) leave room for any implied exceptions to the writing requirement? In *Latin American Music Co. v. ASCAP*, 593 F.3d 95 (1st Cir. 2010), West Side Music Co. granted an exclusive license to LAMCO in 1982 in writing, but allegedly rescinded the transfer orally before ASCAP acquired West Side's copyrights in 1993. The court held that § 204(a) "applies to the transfer or grant of copyright ownership, *not* to the termination of such a transfer or grant" (emphasis in original). Because, under New York law, a contract with no stated duration may be terminated upon reasonable notice, the court held that the oral termination was sufficient. Does this decision give sufficient weight to the Congressional policy for requiring transfers of copyright ownership to be in writing?

(5)   *Transfers of common-law copyright.* Note that although an assignment of a federal statutory copyright must be in writing to be valid, some courts have held that assignments of common-law copyrights do not need to be made in writing. *See, e.g., Martha Graham School and Dance Foundation, Inc. v. Martha Graham Center of Contemporary Dance, Inc.*, 380 F.3d 624, 643-44 (2d Cir. 2004) (holding that unpublished dances created by Martha Graham prior to 1956 were assigned to the Center she founded, based on written and oral testimony of board members and the conduct of the parties), *on appeal after remand*, 466 F.3d 97 (2d Cir. 2006) (affirming finding that unpublished dances created between 1956 and 1965 were likewise assigned to the Center).

(6)   *Transfers of ownership and sublicenses.* In general, "a license is presumed to be non-assignable and nontransferable in the absence of express provisions to the contrary," because a contrary rule would "transform every licensee into a potential competitor of the patent or copyright holder." *Cincom Systems, Inc. v. Novelis Corp.*, 581 F.3d 431 (6th Cir. 2009) (discussing a non-exclusive license). As discussed above, however, the 1976 Act abrogated the doctrine of indivisibility, allowing exclusive rights to be subdivided and owned separately. Moreover, § 101 defines a

"copyright owner" as the owner of *any* exclusive right; and by definition, an exclusive licensee does not compete with the transferor. Arguably, therefore, an exclusive licensee should be able to assign or sublicense its rights freely without permission from the transferor.

In *Gardner v. Nike, Inc.*, 279 F.3d 774 (9th Cir. 2002), however, the Ninth Circuit held that an exclusive licensee does *not* have the right to sublicense its rights without the express consent of the licensor. The court pointed out that exclusive licensees could not sublicense their rights under the 1909 Act; and it rejected the argument that § 201(d)(2) of the 1976 Act changed that result. Instead, it declared that, under § 201(d)(2), an exclusive licensee is entitled to the "protection and remedies" afforded by the Act, but not to rights of a "copyright owner" (as specified under § 101) such as the right to transfer.

Are you convinced by the court's rationale? Should the right to sublicense follow from the divisibility of a copyright? Or is it better, from a policy standpoint, to require parties to negotiate explicitly the right to sublicense? Does the *Gardner* rule promote or complicate the exploitation of copyrighted works? For two cases explicitly rejecting the *Gardner* rationale, see *Traicoff v. Digital Media, Inc.*, 439 F. Supp. 2d 872 (S.D. Ind. 2006); and *In re Golden Books Family Entertainment, Inc.*, 269 B.R. 311 (Bankr. D. Del. 2001). *See also* 2 NIMMER ON COPYRIGHT § 10.02[B][4] (2012); 1 PATRY ON COPYRIGHT § 5:103 (2012) (criticizing the decision).

(7) *Retroactive transfers.* May a co-owner transfer his or her interest in a copyright retroactively, so as to extinguish the other co-owner's accrued cause of action for copyright infringement against the assignee? In *Davis v. Blige*, 505 F.3d 90 (2d Cir. 2007), the court held that an assignment or license operates prospectively only, and that such an assignment cannot function as a settlement of claims brought by a co-author who was not a party to the agreement. Do you agree? If a co-owner can grant a non-exclusive license prospectively, why should it not be able to do so retroactively? For an analysis, see Rothstein, *Unilateral Settlements and Retroactive Transfers: A Problem of Copyright Co-Ownership*, 157 U. Pa. L. Rev. 881 (2009). *See also* 1 NIMMER ON COPYRIGHT § 6.10[A][3] (2012); 1 PATRY ON COPYRIGHT § 5:103 (2012) (criticizing the decision).

(8) *Conflicting transfers.* What if a copyright owner executes conflicting transfers of ownership — granting exclusive motion picture rights in a novel to two different studios, for example? Obviously, a subsequent transferee who has knowledge of a prior conflicting transfer will lose out. But suppose that all transfers are taken in good faith. The statutory solution, if there is one, lies in the recordation provisions of § 205, which are discussed in § 4.02[E] below. Under § 205, any transfer of copyright ownership, along with other documents relating to copyrights, can be registered with the Copyright Office.

(9) *Implied licenses and choice of law issues.* What law determines whether an implied non-exclusive license exists? As *Effects Associates* indicates, non-exclusive licenses need not be in writing and may be granted orally or by implication. The writing requirement of § 204(a) of the 1976 Act is inapplicable because that provision applies only to transfers of ownership (assignments and exclusive licenses), not to non-exclusive licenses. The court in *Effects Associates* did not explicitly decide, however, which law — state or federal — is to be applied in

determining whether an implied non-exclusive license has been granted under the circumstances.

In *Foad Consulting Group, Inc. v. Musil Govan Azzalino*, 270 F.3d 821 (9th Cir. 2001), the court held that although the effect of an implied non-exclusive license may be based on federal law, state law determines the contract question of whether such a license was in fact granted. (This could be consequential. For example, California has a liberal parol evidence rule, permitting consideration of extrinsic evidence to explain the meaning of the terms of a contract even though the meaning appears unambiguous.) Judge Kozinski, in a concurring opinion, disagreed, arguing that the implied license is an incident of federal law. What makes sense from a copyright policy standpoint? *See also Cincom*, 581 F.3d at 436-37 (applying "federal common law" rule prohibiting assignment of non-exclusive licenses).

(10) *Existence and duration of implied licenses.* Although one court has stated that "implied licenses are found only in narrow circumstances," *Estate of Hevia v. Portrio Corp.*, 602 F.3d 34 (1st Cir. 2010), a growing number of cases have found implied licenses to exist. *See, e.g., Baisden v. I'm Ready Prods., Inc.*, 693 F.3d 491 (5th Cir. 2012) (upholding jury verdict that playwright had granted implied license to make and sell DVDs of stage production); *Estate of Hevia* (evidence that deceased architect granted implied license to development company that he co-owned was "compelling"); *Latimer v. Roaring Toyz, Inc.*, 601 F.3d 1224 (11th Cir. 2010) (artist granted implied license to make and display photos of custom motorcycle artwork, and photographer in turn granted an implied license to display photos at media event).

Note that although a gratuitous implied license remains valid until it is revoked, *see, e.g., Wilchombe v. Tee VeeToons, Inc.*, 555 F.3d 949 (11th Cir. 2009), an implied license supported by consideration may be irrevocable. *See, e.g., Asset Marketing Systems, Inc. v. Gagnon*, 542 F.3d 748 (9th Cir. 2008).

(11) *Scope of express and implied licenses.* In holding that Effects granted Cohen an implied license to use the footage, should the court also have held that the implied license was conditioned on payment of the agreed-upon price? In an omitted footnote, the court explained that "conditions precedent are disfavored and will not be read into a contract unless required by plain, unambiguous language." 908 F.3d at 559 n.7. Other courts have similarly held that a promise to pay royalties constitutes a covenant rather than a condition precedent, so that non-payment of royalties gives rise to a cause of action for breach of contract, rather than to a claim for copyright infringement. *See, e.g., Sun Microsystems, Inc. v. Microsoft Corp.*, 188 F.3d 1115, 1121 (9th Cir. 1999); *Graham v. James*, 144 F.3d 229, 236-38 (2d Cir. 1998).

Likewise, in *MDY Industries, LLC v. Blizzard Entertainment, Inc.*, 629 F.3d 928 (9th Cir. 2010), where the Terms of Use for the video game *World of Warcraft* prohibited the use of programs that automate play, or "bots," the court held that the prohibition was a covenant and not a condition, and that users therefore did not infringe by using such a program (although the prohibition could be enforced by a state-law claim for tortious interference with contract). Otherwise, said the court, a copyright owner "could designate any disfavored conduct during software use as copyright infringement, by purporting to condition the license on the player's abstention from the disfavored conduct. . . . This would allow software copyright owners far greater rights than Congress has generally conferred on copyright owners." *Id.* at 941.

(12) *Open-source licenses.* The free-software movement has encouraged the use of "open-source licenses," under which the source code of a computer program is publicly disclosed, accompanied by a non-exclusive license which permits others to freely copy and adapt the source code, provided that the user publicly discloses its own source code under an open-source license as well. Creative Commons similarly offers six options for granting royalty-free, non-exclusive licenses. Until recently, a key question concerning such licenses was whether they could be enforced. In *Jacobson v. Katzer*, 535 F.3d 1373 (Fed. Cir. 2008), the court held that the terms of an open-source license were conditions that could be enforced by an infringement action, rather than independent covenants that could only give rise to an action for breach of contract. (Nonetheless, on remand the District Court refused to issue a preliminary injunction, finding no evidence of imminent future harm. 609 F. Supp. 2d 925 (N.D. Cal. 2009).) *See also Wallace v. Int'l Business Machines Corp.*, 467 F.3d 1104 (7th Cir. 2006) (providing software under GPL open-source license does not violate antitrust laws). For more on open-source licenses, see the Open Source Initiative at *www.opensource.org.*

(13) *Involuntary transfers.* The limitations of § 204(a) apply to transfers of copyright ownership "other than by operation of law" — terminology also employed in § 201(d)(1). In *Soc'y of the Holy Transfiguration Monastery, Inc. v. Archbishop Gregory of Denver, Colo.*, 689 F.3d 29 (1st Cir. 2012), the court noted "a desert of case law on the issue of transfers by operation of law," when deciding whether copyright ownership in modern translations of ancient religious texts was trans-ferred under the terms of monastic statutes and regulations. Interpreting a clause providing that "in case of [a monastery's] closing or liquidation, its possessions will be handed over to the diocese," the court implicitly accepted that such language would be sufficient to effect a transfer of copyright ownership but held that the monastery had not closed or been liquidated. *Id.* at 41–44.

One obvious example of a transfer "by operation of law" is one which occurs through the operation of the bankruptcy system, *see, e.g., Thompkins v. Lil' Joe Records, Inc.*, 476 F.3d 1294 (11th Cir. 2007) (rejection in bankruptcy of contract to pay royalties did not result in reversion of copyright to author); *ITOFCA, Inc. v. Mega Trans Logistics, Inc.*, 322 F.3d 928 (7th Cir. 2003), or as a result of a mortgage foreclosure. Significantly, the legislative history of § 201(e), which bars governmen-tal action "to seize, expropriate, transfer or exercise rights of ownership" with respect to the copyright of an "individual author" (in an attempt to protect dissident foreign authors against actions by their own governments), makes it clear that this limitation did not apply to "traditional legal actions" such as those already noted; and the section later was amended to provide an explicit bankruptcy exception.

Does this language really bar all other "involuntary transfers"? Suppose it could be demonstrated that the author of a computer program was using it to aid in the distribution of illegal drugs. Under federal law, "any property used . . . to facilitate the commission" of a narcotics offense is subject to forfeiture. *See* 21 U.S.C. § 853; *cf.* 18 U.S.C. § 1963 (forfeiture provision of R.I.C.O. statute). Would such a provision apply to the copyright in the computer program? Note that if the owner of copyright in the computer program were not its author, any limits imposed by § 201(e) would be inapplicable.

(14) *Valuation of copyright.* As we have seen, the 1976 Copyright Act makes it fairly easy to sell and buy (or give and receive) copyright interests — both in the form of grants of an entire copyright interest or as transfers of some smaller slice of the whole. Undoubtedly, this development has helped to spur commerce in the field, and it certainly has contributed to the ongoing reconceptualization of copyrights as long-term assets rather than properties to be worked over a fairly short period. It also has raised a set of relatively new questions about how copyrights are to be valued in connection with various kinds of transactions.

Although copyrights can be valued on a cost basis, professional appraisers generally equate the fair market value of a copyright with the capitalized value of projected earnings from it — *i.e.,* the sum which, if invested at prevailing rates, would earn interest equivalent to the future stream of licensing and other revenues that the copyright can be expected to generate. This approach has been used extensively in the past with respect to the valuation of trademarks, although application to copyrights remains in its relative infancy. *See generally* INTELLECTUAL PROPERTY VALUATION (W. Anson ed., 2005); G. Smith & R. Parr, INTELLECTUAL PROPERTY: VALUATION, EXPLOITATION AND INFRINGEMENT DAMAGES (4th ed. 2005).

Another, related set of issues arises with respect to donations of copyrights to charitable organizations. *See generally* J. Maine & X. Nguyen, INTELLECTUAL PROPERTY TAXATION ch. 11 (2003 & annual supplements).

[D] The "New Media" Problem

On the whole, grants of rights to exploit a copyrighted work present no greater problems of legal drafting or interpretation than do similar grants in any other specialized area of the law. One issue of contract construction, however, recurs with some frequency in copyright law because of rapid technological developments in communications media: how to determine the scope of the media to which the transfer of copyright pertains.

The "new media" issue has been around a long time. Consider the following examples. Should an instrument drafted in 1912, at the dawn of the motion picture era, which by its terms granted "the sole and exclusive license and liberty to produce, perform, and represent" a stage play, be construed to allow the defendant to prepare a silent film based on that work? *See Manners v. Morosco,* 252 U.S. 317 (1920) (no). Should a grant of "exclusive motion picture rights" made in 1923, *i.e.,* before "The Jazz Singer" (the first "talking movie"), be deemed to include the right to produce the underlying work as a "talkie"? *See L.C. Page & Co. v. Fox Film Corp.,* 83 F.2d 196 (2d Cir. 1936) (yes). Or try the following queries: Is the term "photoplay" broad enough to encompass videocassettes? *See Muller v. Walt Disney Prods.,* 871 F. Supp. 678 (S.D.N.Y. 1994) (yes). Do rights to synchronize musical compositions with "motion pictures," granted in 1933 and 1939, allow for videocassette synchronization? *See Bourne v. Walt Disney Co.,* 68 F.3d 621 (2d Cir. 1995) (yes); *see also Welles v. Turner Entertainment Co.,* 503 F.3d 728 (9th Cir.

2007) (finding triable issue of fact as to whether contracts by which RKO acquired "motion picture and television rights" in *Citizen Kane* screenplay included home video distribution).

The case law reveals two rival approaches to issues of contract construction involving unknown new technologies. One approach holds that a license of rights in a given medium "includes only such uses as fall within the unambiguous core meaning of the term . . . and exclude[s] any uses which lie within the ambiguous penumbra . . ." This tends to favor authors. *See Cohen v. Paramount Pictures Corp.*, 845 F.2d 851 (9th Cir. 1988). The alternative approach holds that the licensee "may properly pursue any uses which may reasonably be said to fall within the medium as described in the license." This tends to favor grantees — that is, disseminators of works. *See Bartsch v. Metro-Goldwyn-Mayer, Inc.*, 391 F.2d 150 (2d Cir. 1968). Nimmer prefers the latter approach. *See* 3 NIMMER ON COPYRIGHT § 10.10[B] (2012). The two approaches are discussed at length in *Boosey & Hawkes Music Publishers, Ltd. v. Walt Disney Co.*, 145 F.3d 481 (2d Cir. 1998) (favoring the pro-dissemination approach).

What is the real problem here? In *Cohen v. Paramount*, for example, the court held that a 1969 license conferring the right to exhibit a film "by means of television" did not include the right to distribute videocassettes of the film. Irrespective of the merits of the holding, could the "new media" problem have been avoided (in this and in other cases) by the proper drafting of contractual language? In the context of a film distribution contract, would the following clause work: *"A grants to B the exclusive right to exhibit, distribute, market, and exploit the motion picture, throughout the world, by any means or methods now or hereafter known"*? Try your hand at improving the language or applying it to another endeavour, such as a book publishing contract.

Query whether the "authors" of collective works have the right to exploit the collective work in new media without obtaining the permission of the owners of each of the individual copyrighted works. This particular "new media" problem was anticipated by Congress, which provided a default statutory privilege for collective works in § 201(c). See the discussion of *New York Times Co. v. Tasini*, 533 U.S. 483 (2001), and related cases in § 4.01 above.

What about a publishing contract from (say) the 1960s, granting the right to "print, publish and sell the work in book form"? Does that mean "e-books" as well as the old-fashioned codex variety? In *Random House, Inc. v. Rosetta Books LLC*, 283 F.3d 490 (2d Cir. 2002), the court held that the District Court, in denying the motion for a preliminary injunction, did not abuse its discretion in finding that the most reasonable interpretation of the contractual language just quoted did *not* include the right to publish the work as an e-book. Do you agree with the court's restrictive view of the "new use" in this context? A similar issue is posed by lawsuits brought by members of many musical groups against various music industry defendants, alleging, *inter alia*, that the contracts under which these artists worked from the 1950s through the mid-1990s did not effectively transfer rights in digital versions of their musical works and sound recordings. *See Chambers v. Time Warner, Inc.*, 282 F.3d 147 (2d Cir. 2002) (vacating an order of dismissal). *But see Reinhardt v. Wal-Mart Stores, Inc.*, 547 F. Supp. 2d 346

(S.D.N.Y. 2008) (contract defining "records" to include "all forms of reproduction . . . now or hereafter known" unambiguously includes digital downloads).

[E]   Recordation

Section 205(a) of the 1976 Act permits recordation in the Copyright Office of any transfer of copyright ownership or other document pertaining to a copyright, including assignments, exclusive licenses, and non-exclusive licenses, provided that the document filed for recordation bears the actual signature of the person who executed it, or it is accompanied by a sworn statement or official certification that it is a true copy of the original, signed document. To enjoy fully the benefits of the 1976 Act, an owner of any such interest should accompany the recordation with a registration of the subject work, if it is not already registered. § 205(c)(2). (Registration and recordation are not the same. For a detailed discussion of registration, including its history and the Copyright Act's current requirements, see Chapter 6.)

What Should Be Recorded?

Section 204(a) provides that a transfer of ownership may be accomplished by a signed "instrument of conveyance, *or* a note or memorandum of the transfer" (emphasis added). Section 205(d), however, in stating the actual recordation requirement, refers somewhat opaquely to "the instrument of transfer." In applying these provisions, the courts have held that either of the indicia of transfer named in § 204(a) will satisfy the § 205(d) requirement. *See, e.g., Co-Opportunities, Inc. v. National Broadcasting Co.*, 510 F. Supp. 43 (N.D. Cal. 1981).

As discussed in the notes following *Effects Associates* in § 4.02[C], the note or memorandum of the transfer to be recorded need not have been created when the transfer itself occurred, so long as it is "substantially contemporaneous" with the transfer. The document recorded also need not reflect all the terms and conditions of the agreement pursuant to which the transfer took place. In practice, documents prepared especially for recordation often are "short form" instruments, which recite the names of the parties and the subject matter of the agreement, but omit, for example, any description of the consideration in exchange for which the transfer was given. In order for recordation to yield any of the benefits described below, however, it is essential that the document recorded refer to the titles of the specific works involved in any transfer. § 205(c)(1).

In addition to documents evidencing a transfer, the Act permits recordation of "[a]ny . . . other document pertaining to a copyright" if the document has "a direct or indirect relationship to the existence, scope, duration or identification of a copyright, or to the ownership, division, allocation, licensing, or exercise of rights under a copyright. The relationship may be past, present, future, or potential." 37 C.F.R. § 201.4(a)(2). Examples include contracts, mortgages, powers of attorney, wills, and division orders. *But see Broadcast Music, Inc. v. Hirsch*, 104 F.3d 1163 (9th Cir. 1997) (assignment of right to receive royalties from a licensee does not qualify).

Besides bearing an original signature (or proper certification of the photocopy), the Copyright Office requires that every document sought to be filed be complete on its own terms (*i.e.*, lacking any reference to an external document not submitted as an attachment), be legible and capable of being reproduced in legible imaged copies, and be accompanied by the correct fee. 37 C.F.R. § 201.4. While it is technically unnecessary that the document evidencing the transfer be notarized, notarization may provide *prima facie* evidence of the execution of the transfer and thus seems still to be advisable.

Detailed information regarding the mechanics of recordation, including Circular 12 ("Recordation of Transfers and Other Documents"), is available at the Copyright Office website, *www.copyright.gov*.

Why Record?

The rewards for prompt recordation are considerable, although less so than formerly.

First, for actions filed before March 1, 1989 (the effective date of the Berne Convention Implementation Act of 1988), recordation of a copyright interest was a prerequisite to bringing a suit for copyright infringement. For actions accruing on or after March 1, 1989, recordation is no longer a prerequisite to suit. *See Architectronics, Inc. v. Control Systems, Inc.*, 935 F. Supp. 425 (S.D.N.Y. 1996). But it remains important anyway. To the extent that recordation specifically identifies the subject work, and when recordation is combined with registration, even a person who did not have actual notice of the document is *presumed* to be on notice of its contents (*i.e.*, receives "constructive notice" thereof). § 205(c).

Second, recordation establishes priority of ownership between conflicting transfers of copyright, as well as between conflicting transfers and non-exclusive licenses. These priority issues are discussed in detail below.

Note that recordation, while providing constructive notice of the matters asserted in the document filed, does *not* affect the legal sufficiency of the document. Thus, whether a transfer is valid is a question for the law of contracts, not the law of copyright. "Recordation," in other words, *records* — it is not a magic cure-all for a defective document.

Priority Between Conflicting Transfers

Section 205(d) (as redesignated by the Berne Convention Implementation Act of 1988) establishes priorities of copyright ownership between conflicting transfers of copyrights, including any combination of conflicting assignments and exclusive licenses, taken in good faith. Suppose, for example, that A, a songwriter, assigned to B the copyright to his song in 1981, and then, in 1995, conveyed the same rights to C, who took without actual knowledge of the prior transfer to B. Who owns the copyright? Under the terms of § 205(d), the first transferee, B, will prevail if he records within one month after execution of the agreement (two months, if the agreement was executed outside the country). When the one-month grace period expires, the two transferees become competitors in a race to record. If B, the first transferee, loses and C is the first to record, C rather than B becomes the owner of the copyright in the song. *See, e.g.*, *Banco Popular de Puerto Rico, Inc. v. Latin American Music Co.*, 685 F. Supp. 2d 259 (D.P.R. 2010), *aff'd on other grounds sub nom. Banco Popular de Puerto Rico, Inc. v. Asociación de Compositores y Editores de Música Latinoamericana ("ACEMLA")*, 678 F.3d 102 (1st Cir. 2012).

These priority rules apply only if the work is registered in addition to being recorded. If the work has not been registered, the rules do *not* apply, and the court will decide priority based on proof submitted by the parties. As already indicated, the priority rules described above are subject to two exceptions. One is that a person cannot enjoy a priority if he has received a transfer in bad faith (for example, with actual or constructive knowledge of the prior transfer). *See, e.g.*, *Latin American Music Co. v. Archdiocese of San Juan*, 499 F.3d 32, 40-41, 43 (1st Cir. 2007) (first transferee registered before second transfer, providing constructive notice). The second exception involves a transfer given without valuable consideration, as by gift or bequest. In such a situation, the later transferee will not prevail over the first even if the first transferee fails to record his transfer.

In operation, the federal recordation scheme poses some problems. Under § 205, constructive notice takes effect as of the time a submission complies fully with the statutory requirements. But documents forwarded to the Copyright Office for recordation are not indexed and made accessible to search for some months afterwards. In the interim, a recorded transfer may have legal priority, even though a subsequent transferee of rights in the same work would have no means of discovering its existence from the public record.

Other problems are apparent when one considers that this system of priorities based on recordation affects, among other kinds of transfers, grants of security interests in copyrights. In a controversial bankruptcy decision, *In re Peregrine Entertainment, Ltd.*, 16 U.S.P.Q.2d (BNA) 1017 (C.D. Cal. 1990), Circuit Judge Kozinski (sitting by designation) held that federal law relating to copyright transfer recordation preempts alternative methods of perfecting such security interests through filings under state laws incorporating the Uniform Commercial Code ("UCC"), on the basis of the "step-back" provisions of UCC Article 9. *In re World Auxiliary Power Co.*, 303 F.3d 1120 (9th Cir. 2002), offered additional guidance, holding that the UCC governs perfection of security interests in *unregistered* copyrights, while the rule of *Peregrine* applies to *registered* copyrights. Prudent lawyers will continue to make parallel UCC filings anyway, until the issue is resolved authoritatively. If the *World Auxiliary Power* rule prevails, practice in entertainment industry project financing will be simplified; if not, lenders may find it difficult to perfect security interests until some time after their loans are disbursed — during which period the copyright owner may make conflicting transfers to other *bona fide* purchasers. *See* Note, *Transfers of Copyrights for Security Under the New Copyright Act*, 88 Yale L.J. 125 (1978). In an attempt to cope with the problem, some entertainment industry loan transactions have been structured to provide, *e.g.*, for the registration of liens on screenplays preliminary to a completed motion picture; but the degree of real security this device provides to lenders remains untested. Nor can such improvisations reduce the inevitable uncertainty introduced by the one-month and two-month "look-back" provisions of § 205(d). In the end, the dilemma which the

Peregrine decision raised probably will need to be resolved by legislation, possibly through some sort of hybrid state/federal system for the registration of security interests in copyrighted works through amendments to § 205. Ultimately, changes in state laws incorporating UCC Article 9 also may be required.

Priority Between Transfers and Non-exclusive Licenses

Section 205(e) of the 1976 Act (as redesignated in 1988) addresses priority between a transferee and a non-exclusive licensee. Under this section, a non-exclusive license will prevail over an assignment or exclusive license, but only in certain circumstances. First, the non-exclusive license must be evidenced by a written instrument signed by the copyright owner and must have been taken before execution of the transfer. Second, even if the non-exclusive license was taken after the transfer, it will prevail if it is evidenced by a writing and was taken in good faith before recordation of the transfer without notice thereof. For example, suppose that Playwright *A* assigns the copyright in her play to *B*, and one month later gives *C* a non-exclusive license, in writing, to perform the play. Here, the non-exclusive license will prevail if *B* fails to record in the Copyright Office and *C* took his non-exclusive license in good faith.

[F]   Orphan Works

In Chapter 5, you will encounter a number of developments (including automatic renewal and copyright term extension) that have increased dramatically the proportion of older works of authorship that must be presumed to enjoy copyright protection today, in the absence of any specific affirmative knowledge to the contrary. Whatever we may think of these developments in their own right, or about the 1976 Act's extension of federal copyright to unpublished works generally, they exacerbate what formerly had been a relatively minor irritation for scholars, artists, museums, publishers, and others into a major headache. In the past, would-be users of existing text, images, and sounds occasionally found themselves frustrated in their efforts to ascertain these works' true owners in order to negotiate licensing arrangements. But as copyright has grown in duration and extent, these so-called "orphan works" problems have become more and more common. Moreover, with growing public awareness of the risks of copyright infringement, the problem also has become more severe. Increasingly, the various gatekeepers under whose scrutiny works must pass on their way from the creator's desk or studio to the public (publishers for books, distributors or broadcasters for films, and so forth) have become positively skittish about allowing unlicensed material of any kind to appear in the products they make available. The result has been heightened frustration on the part of individual scholars and artists, as well as non-profit cultural institutions.

In 2005, the U.S. Copyright Office conducted an exhaustive inquiry into the "orphan works" issue, which included weighing two rounds of written comments (hundreds in all), holding live "roundtable" discussions, and performing extensive background research. The Office's thoughtful final report, which includes proposals for legislative reform, was published in January 2006 and is available at *www.copyright.gov/orphan*. Some highlights from its Executive Summary follow:

Conclusions and Recommendations

. . . Our conclusions are:

- The orphan works problem is real.

- The orphan works problem is elusive to quantify and describe comprehensively.

- Some orphan works situations may be addressed by existing copyright law, but many are not.

- Legislation is necessary to provide a meaningful solution to the orphan works problem as we know it today.

In considering the orphan works issue and potential solutions, the Office has kept in mind three overarching and related goals. First, any system to deal with orphan works should seek primarily to make it more likely that a user can find the relevant owner in the first instance, and negotiate a voluntary agreement over permission and payment, if appropriate, for the intended use of the work. Second, where the user cannot identify and locate the copyright owner after a reasonably diligent search, then the system should permit that specific user to make use of the work, subject to provisions that would resolve issues that might arise if the owner surfaces after the use has commenced. In the roundtable discussions, there seemed to be a clear consensus that these two goals were appropriate objectives in addressing the orphan works issues. Finally, efficiency is another overarching consideration we have attempted to reflect, in that we believe our proposed orphan works solution is the least burdensome on all the relevant stakeholders, such as copyright owners, users and the federal government.

The proposed amendment follows the core concept that many commenters favored as a solution to the orphan works problem: if the user has performed a reasonably diligent search for the copyright owner but is unable to locate that owner, then that user should enjoy a benefit of limitations on the remedies that a copyright owner could obtain against him if the owner showed up at a later date and sued for infringement. . . .

1. The Reasonably Diligent Search Requirement

. . . [Our legislative proposal] sets out the basic qualification the user of the orphan work must meet — he must perform a "reasonably diligent search" and have been unable to locate the owner of the copyright in the work. Such a search must be completed before the use of the work that constitutes infringement begins. . . .

The proposal adopts a very general standard for reasonably diligent search that will have to be applied on a case-by-case basis, accounting for all of the circumstances of the particular use. Such a standard is needed because of the wide variety of works and uses identified as being potentially subject to the orphan works issues, from an untitled photograph to an old magazine advertisement to an out-of-print novel to an antique postcard to an obsolete computer program. It is not possible at this stage to craft a standard that can be specific to all or even many of these circumstances. Moreover, the resources, techniques and technologies used to investigate the status of a work also differ among industry sectors and change over time, making it hard to specify the steps a user must take with any particularity. . . .

. . . [There are] several factors that commenters identified as being relevant to the reasonableness of the search, including

- the amount of identifying information on the copy of the work itself, such as an author's name, copyright notice, or title;

- whether the work had been made available to the public;

- the age of the work, or the dates on which it was created and made available to the public;

- whether information about the work can be found in publicly available records, such as the Copyright Office records or other resources;

- whether the author is still alive, or the corporate copyright owner still exists, and whether a record of any transfer of the copyright exists and is available to the user; and

- the nature and extent of the use, such as whether the use is commercial or non-commercial, and how prominently the work figures into the activity of the user.

Importantly, our recommendation does not exclude any particular type of work from its scope, such as unpublished works or foreign works. . . . [W]e believe that unpublished works should not be excluded from this recommendation, and [that] the unpublished nature of a work might figure into a reasonable search determination.

Our recommendation permits, and we encourage, interested parties to develop guidelines for searches in different industry sectors and for different types of works. Most commentators were supportive of voluntary development of such guidelines. . . .

2. The Attribution Requirement

We also recommend one other threshold requirement for a user to qualify for the orphan works limitations on remedies: throughout the use of the work, the user must provide attribution to the author and copyright owner of the work if such attribution is possible and as is reasonably appropriate under the circumstances. The idea is that the user, in the course of using a work for which he has not received explicit permission, should make it as clear as possible to the public that the work is the product of another author, and that the copyright in the work is owned by another. . . .

3. Other Alternatives Considered

[These included a public notice filing with the Copyright Office and payment into an escrow prior to use.]

4. Limitation on Remedies

If a user meets his burden of demonstrating that he performed a reasonably diligent search and provided reasonable attribution to the author and copyright owner, then the recommended amendment would limit the remedies available in that infringement action in two primary ways: First, it would limit monetary relief to only reasonable compensation for the use, with an elimination of any monetary relief where the use was noncommercial and the user ceases the infringement expeditiously upon notice. Second, the proposal would limit the ability of the copyright owner to obtain full injunctive relief in cases where the user has transformed the orphan work into a derivative work like a motion picture or book, preserving the user's ability to continue to exploit that derivative work. In all other cases, the court would be instructed to minimize the harm to the user that an injunction might impose, to protect the user's interests in relying on the orphan works provision in making use of the work.

. . . [Some commenters] expressed concern about the impact that *any* monetary remedy at all might have on their ability to go forward and use orphan works. First, with respect to the concern about a chilling effect of any monetary remedy, it must be noted that in nearly all cases where a diligent search has been performed, the likelihood of a copyright owner resurfacing should be very low, so that no claim for compensation is ever made. Second, it should be clear that "reasonable compensation" may, in appropriate circumstances, be found to be zero, or a royalty-free license, if the comparable transactions in the marketplace support such a finding. . . .

In addition, to make absolutely sure that the concerns of nonprofit institutions like libraries, museums and universities about monetary relief are assuaged, we recommend an additional limitation on monetary relief where the user is making a non-commercial use of the work and expeditiously ceases the infringement after receiving notice of the infringement claim. In that case, there should be no monetary relief at all. Libraries, archives and museums indicated that posting material on the Internet was a primary use they would like to make of orphan works, and that they would take down any material if a copyright owner resurfaced. . . .

How well the scheme envisioned by the Copyright Office would work in practice remains to be seen. Some advocates of reform who favored a "capped damages" approach to compensating owners of orphan works who resurface once a use has begun remain skeptical about whether the "reasonable compensation" approach advocated by the report actually will promote certainty. Another concern is that the proposed limitation on injunctive relief where the orphan work has been incorporated into a "derivative" work may not be broad enough to cover, for example, the situation in which an old photograph has been used in unmodified form as an illustration in a book or article. On the other hand, representatives of some creators' organizations have expressed concerns, *inter alia*, that illustrators or photographers might suffer if their works are erroneously treated as having been "orphaned." See the reaction of the American Society of Media Photographers at *www.asmp.org/news/spec2006/orphanworks.php*.

Legislation to implement the report's recommendations was passed by the Senate in 2008, but was not enacted by the House before the end of the session. Among the changes being considered by Congress to overcome objections by interested parties were a requirement that the user file a Notice of Use with the Copyright Office, describing the work, the search efforts made and the proposed use, in order to be eligible for the limitation on remedies; and establishment of a database to facilitate searches for pictorial, graphic, and sculptural works. No action was taken in the 112th Congress, but the Register of Copyrights continues to list the orphan-works problem as one of her priorities. *See* M. Pallante, Priorities and Special Projects of the United States Copyright Office, October 2011–October 2013, at 7 (2011). Should legislation be enacted, it would be the first significant modification of the statute specifically designed to compensate for the ever-lengthening reach of copyright protection.

Chapter 5

DURATION AND TERMINATIONS

An author creates and fixes an original work. As a reward for her contribution to the storehouse of human knowledge, she receives ownership of a copyright in the work. How long does such ownership endure?

Article I, § 8, cl. 8 of the Constitution empowers Congress to recognize grant rights "for limited Times" only. The original 1790 Act followed the Statute of Anne in prescribing an initial term of 14 years, with a second term of 14 years if the author survived to the commencement of that term (and complied with certain statutory formalities). The 1831 Act increased the initial term to 28 years, retaining a 14-year renewal term. Under the 1909 Act, the initial and renewal terms ran 28 years each. The current statute eschews the renewal device and provides a basic term, for an individual author, of the life of the author plus 70 years. For joint works, the term is the same, measured by the life of the last-surviving author. A separate term of 120 years from the date of creation or 95 years from first publication — whichever expires first — applies to works made for hire, and to anonymous and pseudonymous works.

This chapter covers duration of copyright ownership, including certain pre-1976 Act rules that will continue to haunt the law for years to come, and an additional topic: recapture of copyright ownership through termination of the author's prior transfer of her interest in a work. The materials that follow are complex, but highly important.

§ 5.01 DURATION OF COPYRIGHTS

How long should a copyright last? In a speech on copyright before the House of Commons in 1841, Lord Macaulay reflected on the length of the copyright term:

> It is good that authors should be remunerated; and the least exceptionable way of remunerating them is by a monopoly. Yet monopoly is an evil. For the sake of the good we must submit to the evil; but the evil ought not to last a day longer than is necessary for the purpose of securing the good.

1 T.B. Macaulay, MACAULAY'S SPEECHES AND POEMS 285 (A.C. Armstrong & Son 1874).

How long is too long? And how can Congress determine when protection becomes "a day longer than is necessary"? On an intuitive level, the current life-plus-70-years term may seem excessive if the aim is to encourage production of advertising jingles, computer programs, and commercial art, all of which fall within the broad range of copyrightable subject matter — but perhaps appropriate, if the purpose is to reward the author of the Great American Novel.

The fact is that it is impossible to determine the minimum duration sufficient to encourage the optimum amount of investment for the enormous range and variety of works of authorship. But even if the length of protection, in any given instance, exceeds the ideal from a consumer welfare standpoint, perhaps we need not fear the copyright monopoly with the same intensity as, for example, the patent monopoly, described in Chapter 1. Despite the length of the copyright term, the copyright monopoly — at least, as it has developed in American law to this point — is tempered by various limiting doctrines, including the requirement of originality and the idea/expression dichotomy (seen earlier in Chapter 2) and the "safety valve" of fair use (still to come in Chapter 10). On the other hand, fair use is a peculiarly American doctrine, and the other doctrines, while universally accepted, may be applied more narrowly in other countries.

Taken together, these considerations may well raise the following question. With respect to copyright duration, is it possible to have *too much* of a good thing? And if so, how would we know?

[A] Introduction

Statutory References

1976 Act: §§ 101 ("anonymous work," "children," "joint work," "pseudonymous work," "widow" and "widower," "work made for hire"), 302, 303, 304(a) and (b), 305; Transitional and Supplementary Provisions §§ 102-03, 107

1909 Act: §§ 22-25

Legislative History

H.R. Rep. No. 94-1476 at 133-40, 142-43,
reprinted in **1976 U.S.C.C.A.N. 5659, 5749-56, 5758-59**

Section 302. Duration of Copyright in Works Created after Effective Date

[The following excerpt from the House Report discusses the policy justifications for the since-extended basic term of copyright originally adopted in the 1976 Act: life-plus-50 years (together with a term of 75 years from publication or 100 years from creation, whichever is shorter, for certain works). In 1998, Congress enacted the Sonny Bono Copyright Term Extension Act ("CTEA"), extending the basic term of protection to life-plus-70 years (and bumping up the alternative term to 95 years from publication or 120 from creation, whichever is shorter). — *Eds.*]

In general

The debate over how long a copyright should last is as old as the oldest copyright statute and will doubtless continue as long as there is a copyright law. . . . [T]here appears to be strong support for the principle, as embodied in the bill, of a copyright term consisting of the life of the author and 50 years after his death. In particular, the authors and their representatives stressed that the adoption of a life-plus-50 term was by far their most important legislative goal in copyright law revision. . . .

Under the [1909 Act,] statutory copyright protection begins on the date of publication (or on the date of registration in unpublished form) and continues for 28 years from that date; it may be renewed for a second 28 years, making a total potential term of 56 years in all cases.[1] The principal elements of this system — a definite number of years, computed from either publication or registration, with a renewal feature — have been a part of the U.S. copyright law since the first statute in 1790. The arguments for changing this system to one based on the life of the author can be summarized as follows:

1. The present 56-year term is not long enough to insure an author and his dependents the fair economic benefits from his works. Life expectancy has increased substantially, and more and more authors are seeing their works fall into the public domain during their lifetimes, forcing later works to compete with their own early works in which copyright has expired.

2. The tremendous growth in communications media has substantially lengthened the commercial life of a great many works. A short term is particularly discriminatory against serious works of music, literature, and art, whose value may not be recognized until after many years.

3. Although limitations on the term of copyright are obviously necessary, too short a term harms the author without giving any substantial benefit to the public. The public frequently pays the same for works in the public domain as it does for copyrighted works, and the only result is a commercial windfall to certain users at the author's expense. . . .

4. A system based on the life of the author would go a long way toward clearing up the confusion and uncertainty involved in the vague concept of "publication," and would provide a much simpler, clearer method for computing the term. . . . All of a particular author's works, including successive revisions of them, would fall into the public domain at the same time, thus avoiding the present problems of determining a multitude of publication dates and of distinguishing "old" and "new" matter in later editions. . . .

5. One of the worst features of the [1909 Act] is the provision for renewal of copyright. A substantial burden and expense, this unclear and highly technical requirement results in incalculable amounts of unproductive work. In a number of cases it is the cause of inadvertent and unjust loss of copyright. Under a life-plus-50 system the renewal device would be inappropriate and unnecessary.

6. Under the preemption provisions of section 301 and the single Federal system they would establish, authors will be giving up perpetual, unlimited exclusive common law rights in their unpublished works, including works that have been widely disseminated by means other than publication. A

---

[1] Under Public Laws 87-668, 89-142, 90-141, 90-416, 91-147, 91-555, 92-170, 92-566, and 93-573, copyrights that were subsisting in their renewal term on September 19, 1962, and that were scheduled to expire before December 31, 1976, have been extended to that later date, in anticipation that general revision legislation extending their terms still further will be enacted by then.

statutory term of life-plus-50 years is no more than a fair recompense for the loss of these perpetual rights.

7. A very large majority of the world's countries have adopted a copyright term of the life of the author and 50 years after the author's death. . . . The need to conform the duration of U.S. copyright to that prevalent throughout the rest of the world is increasingly pressing in order to provide certainty and simplicity in international business dealings. . . . Without this change, the possibility of future United States adherence to the Berne Copyright Union would evaporate . . .

Basic copyright term

Under subsection (a) of section 302, a work "created" on or after the effective date of the revised statute would be protected by statutory copyright "from its creation" and, with exceptions to be noted below, "endures for a term consisting of the life of the author and 50 years after the author's death."

Joint Works

Since by definition a "joint work" has two or more authors, a statute basing the term of copyright on the life of the author must provide a special method of computing the term of "joint works." Under the system in effect in many foreign countries, the term of copyright is measured from the death of the last survivor of a group of joint authors, no matter how many there are. . . .

Anonymous works, pseudonymous works, and works made for hire

Computing the term from the author's death also requires special provisions to deal with cases where the authorship is not revealed or where the "author" is not an individual. Section 302(c) therefore provides a special term for anonymous works, pseudonymous works, and works made for hire: 75 years from publication or 100 years from creation, whichever is shorter. . . .

SECTION 303. PREEXISTING WORKS UNDER COMMON LAW PROTECTION

Under [section 303], every "original work of authorship" fixed in tangible form that is in existence would be given statutory copyright protection as long as the work is not in the public domain in this country.

Its basic purpose is to substitute statutory for common law copyright for everything now protected at common law, and to substitute reasonable time limits for the perpetual protection now available. . . .

A special problem under this provision is what to do with works whose ordinary statutory terms will have expired or will be nearing expiration on the effective date. Section 303 provides that under no circumstances would copyright protection expire before December 31, 2002, and also attempts to encourage publication by providing 25 years more protection (through 2027) if the work were published before the end of 2002. [The CTEA extended the minimum term of protection for works published by the end of 2002 by 20 years, *i.e.*, through 2047. — *Eds.*]

SECTION 304. DURATION OF SUBSISTING COPYRIGHTS

The arguments in favor of lengthening the duration of copyright apply to subsisting as well as future copyrights. The bill's basic approach is to increase the present 56-year term to 75 years in the case of copyrights subsisting in both their first and their renewal terms.

Copyrights in their first term

Subsection (a) of section 304 reenacts and preserves the renewal provision, now in section 24 of the [1909 Act], for all of the works presently in their first 28-year term. A great many of the present expectancies in these cases are the subject of existing contracts, and it would be unfair and immensely confusing to cut off or alter these interests. Renewal registration will be required during the 28th year of the copyright but the length of the renewal term will be increased from 28 to 47 years. [In 1992, renewal was made automatic by the Copyright Renewal Act, and in 1998, the CTEA extended the renewal term by another 20 years, all as described later in this section. — *Eds.*] . . .

Copyrights in their renewal term

Renewed copyrights that are subsisting in their second term at any time during the period between December 31, 1976, and December 31, 1977, inclusive, would be extended under section 304(b) to run for a total of 75 years. . . .

[Under the CTEA, any copyright secured during the period 1923-77 still in its renewal term on the effective date of the Act (October 27, 1998) was extended to run for a total of 95 years from the date copyright originally was secured. — *Eds.*]

SECTION 305. YEAR END EXPIRATION OF TERMS

Under section 305, which has its counterpart in the laws of most foreign countries, the term of copyright protection for a work extends through December 31 of the year in which the term would otherwise have expired. This will make the duration of copyright much easier to compute, since it will be enough to determine the year, rather than the exact date, of the event from which the term is based.

Section 305 applies only to "terms of copyright provided by sections 302 through 304," which are the sections dealing with duration of copyright. It therefore has no effect on the other time periods specified in the bill; and, since they do not involve "terms of copyright," the periods provided in section 304(c) with respect to termination of grants are not affected by section 305. . . .

[For a fuller excerpt from H.R. REP No. 94-1476, see Part Three of the Casebook Supplement.]

[B] Duration Basics Under the CTEA

On January 1, 1978, the life-plus-50-years basic term contemplated in the foregoing excerpt from the House Report became a reality when the Copyright Act of 1976 entered into effect. That was not the end of the story, however. Succeeding years saw considerable pressure brought to bear on Congress to lengthen even the generous term of protection provided by the 1976 Act.

Supporters made their case based largely on national economic policy. In 1993 the European Union directed its member states, many of them major consumers of U.S. works, to "harmonize" their terms of protection using a basic term of life-plus-70 years. Under the "rule of the shorter term," as provided in § 7(8) of the Berne Convention and adopted by the EU, member states are permitted, within their own territories, to provide a term of protection not exceeding the term fixed in a work's country of origin. Thus, once a U.S. work entered the public domain in the United States, it would be unprotected in EU member states, notwithstanding the new life-plus-70-years term in force in those jurisdictions.

Moreover, as the public domain loomed for works created in the 1920s and 1930s, key players in the United States (particularly large media companies like Disney and Time Warner) began to confront the reality of losing copyright protection for many valuable properties in their inventories, both here and abroad. To cite but one example: Without a further extension, Disney's "Steamboat Willie" (copyrighted in 1928), the first sound cartoon starring Mickey Mouse, would have entered the public domain in 2004. Not surprisingly, Disney and other copyright owners urged Congress to extend copyright terms.

Those opposing extension argued that life-plus-50 years was long enough already, or even too long, in comparison with the actual commercial life of most works. Moreover, the longer term, it was feared, would impede access to protected works both by the public and by future authors seeking to prepare new works. Opponents also pointed out that term extension would amount to a 20-year moratorium on works entering the public domain (apart from those governed by § 303) — a result difficult to justify on the basis of any incentive-based rationale for copyright.

On balance, Congress concluded that, as the world's largest exporter of copyrighted works, the United States would benefit significantly by providing an extra 20 years of protection for U.S. owners of copyrighted works. On October 27, 1998, President Clinton signed into law the Sonny Bono Copyright Term Extension Act, extending the basic term of protection to life-plus-70 years. As enacted, the CTEA provides as follows:

- For works created on or after January 1, 1978, copyright protection now extends for the life of the author plus 70 years. For a joint work, protection lasts for 70 years after the last surviving author's death. For anonymous and pseudonymous works and works made for hire, the term is 95 years from the year of first publication or 120 years from the year of creation, whichever expires first. § 302.

- For works created but not published or registered before January 1, 1978, the same terms apply. But if the work was subsequently published before December 31, 2002, the term will not expire before December 31, 2047. § 303.

- For pre-1978 works still in their original or renewal term of copyright, the renewal term is extended to 67 years, for a total maximum term of 95 years from the date that copyright originally was secured. § 304.

- For works already in the public domain on the effective date of the CTEA (*i.e.*, works published or registered before 1923), there was no restoration of protection.

The CTEA was challenged in court on the ground that it violated either the "limited Times" provision of the Copyright Clause or the First Amendment. The Supreme Court's opinion rejecting that challenge follows.

ELDRED v. ASHCROFT
Supreme Court of the United States
537 U.S. 186 (2003)

JUSTICE GINSBURG delivered the opinion of the Court.

This case concerns the authority the Constitution assigns to Congress to prescribe the duration of copyrights. The Copyright and Patent Clause of the Constitution, Art. I, § 8, cl. 8, provides as to copyrights: "Congress shall have Power . . . [t]o promote the Progress of Science . . . by securing [to Authors] for limited Times . . . the exclusive Right to their . . . Writings." In 1998, in the measure here under inspection, Congress enlarged the duration of copyrights by 20 years. Copyright Term Extension Act (CTEA), Pub. L. 105-298, §§ 102(b) and (d), 112 Stat. 2827-2828 (amending 17 U.S.C. §§ 302, 304). As in the case of prior extensions, principally in 1831, 1909, and 1976, Congress provided for application of the enlarged terms to existing and future copyrights alike.

Petitioners are individuals and businesses whose products or services build on copyrighted works that have gone into the public domain. They seek a determination that the CTEA fails constitutional review under both the Copyright Clause's "limited Times" prescription and the First Amendment's free speech guarantee. Under the 1976 Copyright Act, copyright protection generally lasted from the work's creation until 50 years after the author's death. . . . Under the CTEA, most copyrights now run from creation until 70 years after the author's death. 17 U.S.C. § 302(a). Petitioners do not challenge the "life-plus-70-years" time span itself. Congress went awry, petitioners maintain, not with respect to newly created works, but in enlarging the term for published works with existing copyrights. . . . As to the First Amendment, petitioners contend that the CTEA is a content-neutral regulation of speech that fails inspection under the heightened judicial scrutiny appropriate for such regulations.

In accord with the District Court and the Court of Appeals, we reject petitioners' challenges to the CTEA. In that 1998 legislation, as in all previous copyright term extensions, Congress placed existing and future copyrights in parity. In prescribing that alignment, we hold, Congress acted within its authority and did not transgress constitutional limitations.

I.A.

We evaluate petitioners' challenge to the constitutionality of the CTEA against the backdrop of Congress' previous exercises of its authority under the Copyright

Clause. The Nation's first copyright statute, enacted in 1790, provided a federal copyright term of 14 years from the date of publication, renewable for an additional 14 years if the author survived the first term. . . . The 1790 Act's renewable 14-year term applied to existing works (*i.e.*, works already published and works created but not yet published) and future works alike. . . . Congress expanded the federal copyright term to 42 years in 1831 (28 years from publication, renewable for an additional 14 years), and to 56 years in 1909 (28 years from publication, renewable for an additional 28 years). . . . Both times, Congress applied the new copyright term to existing and future works. . . .

In 1976, Congress altered the method for computing federal copyright terms. . . .

The measure at issue here, the CTEA, installed the fourth major duration extension of federal copyrights. Retaining the general structure of the 1976 Act, the CTEA enlarges the terms of all existing and future copyrights by 20 years. For works created by identified natural persons, the term now lasts from creation until 70 years after the author's death. 17 U.S.C. § 302(a). This standard harmonizes the baseline United States copyright term with the term adopted by the European Union in 1993. . . . For anonymous works, pseudonymous works, and works made for hire, the term is 95 years from publication or 120 years from creation, whichever expires first. 17 U.S.C. § 302(c).

Paralleling the 1976 Act, the CTEA applies these new terms to all works not published by January 1, 1978. §§ 302(a), 303(a). For works published before 1978 with existing copyrights as of the CTEA's effective date, the CTEA extends the term to 95 years from publication. §§ 304(a) and (b). Thus, in common with the 1831, 1909, and 1976 Acts, the CTEA's new terms apply to both future and existing copyrights.

B.

. . . We granted certiorari to address two questions: whether the CTEA's extension of existing copyrights exceeds Congress' power under the Copyright Clause; and whether the CTEA's extension of existing and future copyrights violates the First Amendment. . . . We now answer those two questions in the negative and affirm.

II.A.

We address first the determination of the courts below that Congress has authority under the Copyright Clause to extend the terms of existing copyrights. Text, history, and precedent, we conclude, confirm that the Copyright Clause empowers Congress to prescribe "limited Times" for copyright protection and to secure the same level and duration of protection for all copyright holders, present and future.

The CTEA's baseline term of life plus 70 years, petitioners concede, qualifies as a "limited Tim[e]" as applied to future copyrights.[4] Petitioners contend, however, that existing copyrights extended to endure for that same term are not "limited." Petitioners' argument essentially reads into the text of the Copyright Clause the command that a time prescription, once set, becomes forever "fixed" or "inalterable." The word "limited," however, does not convey a meaning so constricted. At the time of the Framing, that word meant what it means today: "confine[d] within certain bounds," "restrain[ed]," or "circumscribe[d]." S. Johnson, A Dictionary of the English Language (7th ed. 1785). . . . Thus understood, a time span appropriately "limited" as applied to future copyrights does not automatically cease to be "limited" when applied to existing copyrights. . . .

To comprehend the scope of Congress' power under the Copyright Clause, "a page of history is worth a volume of logic." *New York Trust Co. v. Eisner*, 256 U.S. 345 (1921) (Holmes, J.). History reveals an unbroken congressional practice of granting to authors of works with existing copyrights the benefit of term extensions so that all under copyright protection will be governed evenhandedly under the same regime. As earlier recounted, . . . the First Congress accorded the protections of the Nation's first federal copyright statute to existing and future works alike. 1790 Act § 1. Since then, Congress has regularly applied duration extensions to both existing and future copyrights. 1831 Act §§ 1, 16; 1909 Act §§ 23-24; 1976 Act §§ 302-303; 17 U.S.C. §§ 302-304.

Because the Clause empowering Congress to confer copyrights also authorizes patents, congressional practice with respect to patents informs our inquiry. We count it significant that early Congresses extended the duration of numerous individual patents as well as copyrights. . . . [S]ee generally Ochoa, *Patent and Copyright Term Extension and the Constitution: A Historical Perspective*, 49 J. Copyright Society 19 (2001). The courts saw no "limited Times" impediment to such extensions; renewed or extended terms were upheld in the early days, for example, by Chief Justice Marshall and Justice Story sitting as circuit justices. . . .

Congress' consistent historical practice of applying newly enacted copyright terms to future and existing copyrights reflects a judgment stated concisely by Representative Huntington at the time of the 1831 Act: "[J]ustice, policy, and equity alike forb[id]" that an "author who had sold his [work] a week ago, be placed in a worse situation than the author who should sell his work the day after the passing of [the] act." 7 Cong. Deb. 424 (1831) . . . The CTEA follows this historical practice by keeping the duration provisions of the 1976 Act largely in place and simply adding 20 years to each of them. Guided by text, history, and precedent, we cannot agree with petitioners' submission that extending the duration of existing copyrights is categorically beyond Congress' authority under the Copyright Clause.

Satisfied that the CTEA complies with the "limited Times" prescription, we turn now to whether it is a rational exercise of the legislative authority conferred by the Copyright Clause. On that point, we defer substantially to Congress. . . .

---

[4] We note . . . that JUSTICE BREYER makes no such concession. He does not train his fire, as petitioners do, on Congress' choice to place existing and future copyrights in parity. Moving beyond the bounds of the parties' presentations, and with abundant policy arguments but precious little support from precedent, he would condemn Congress' entire product as irrational.

The CTEA reflects judgments of a kind Congress typically makes, judgments we cannot dismiss as outside the Legislature's domain. As respondent describes, a key factor in the CTEA's passage was a 1993 European Union (EU) directive instructing EU members to establish a copyright term of life plus 70 years. EU Council Directive 93/98. . . . Consistent with the Berne Convention, the EU directed its members to deny this longer term to the works of any non-EU country whose laws did not secure the same extended term. *See* Berne Conv. Art. 7(8). By extending the baseline United States copyright term to life plus 70 years, Congress sought to ensure that American authors would receive the same copyright protection in Europe as their European counterparts. The CTEA may also provide greater incentive for American and other authors to create and disseminate their work in the United States. *See* Perlmutter, *Participation in the International Copyright System as a Means to Promote the Progress of Science and Useful Arts*, 36 Loyola L.A. L. Rev. 323, [332] (2002) . . . (the United States could not "play a leadership role" in the give-and-take evolution of the international copyright system, indeed it would "lose all flexibility," "if the only way to promote the progress of science were to provide incentives to create new works"). . . .

In addition to international concerns, Congress passed the CTEA in light of demographic, economic, and technological changes,[14] and rationally credited projections that longer terms would encourage copyright holders to invest in the restoration and public distribution of their works; *see* H.R. Rep. No. 105-452, p. 4 (1998) (term extension "provide[s] copyright owners generally with the incentive to restore older works and further disseminate them to the public"). . . .

In sum, we find that the CTEA is a rational enactment; we are not at liberty to second-guess congressional determinations and policy judgments of this order, however debatable or arguably unwise they may be. Accordingly, we cannot conclude that the CTEA — which continues the unbroken congressional practice of treating future and existing copyrights in parity for term extension purposes — is an impermissible exercise of Congress' power under the Copyright Clause.

B.

Petitioners' Copyright Clause arguments rely on several novel readings of the Clause. We next address these arguments and explain why we find them unpersuasive.

---

[14] Members of Congress expressed the view that, as a result of increases in human longevity and in parents' average age when their children are born, the pre-CTEA term did not adequately secure "the right to profit from licensing one's work during one's lifetime and to take pride and comfort in knowing that one's children — and perhaps their children — might also benefit from one's posthumous popularity." 141 Cong. Rec. 6553 (1995) (statement of Sen. Feinstein). Also cited was "the failure of the U.S. copyright term to keep pace with the substantially increased commercial life of copyrighted works resulting from the rapid growth in communications media." [144 Cong. Rec. S12377 (daily ed. Oct. 12, 1998)] (statement of Sen. Hatch).

1.

Petitioners contend that even if the CTEA's 20-year term extension is literally a "limited Tim[e]," permitting Congress to extend existing copyrights allows it to evade the "limited Times" constraint by creating effectively perpetual copyrights through repeated extensions. We disagree.

As the Court of Appeals observed, a regime of perpetual copyrights "clearly is not the situation before us." 239 F.3d at 379. Nothing before this Court warrants construction of the CTEA's 20-year term extension as a congressional attempt to evade or override the "limited Times" constraint.[16] Critically, . . . petitioners fail to show how the CTEA crosses a constitutionally significant threshold with respect to "limited Times" that the 1831, 1909, and 1976 Acts did not. . . . Those earlier Acts did not create perpetual copyrights, and neither does the CTEA. . . .

2.

Petitioners dominantly advance a series of arguments all premised on the proposition that Congress may not extend an existing copyright absent new consideration from the author. . . .

. . . [P]etitioners contend that the CTEA's extension of existing copyrights does not "promote the Progress of Science" as contemplated by the preambular language of the Copyright Clause. Art. I, § 8, cl. 8. The CTEA's extension of existing copyrights categorically fails to "promote the Progress of Science," petitioners argue, because it does not stimulate the creation of new works but merely adds value to works already created.

As petitioners point out, we have described the Copyright Clause as "both a grant of power and a limitation," *Graham v. John Deere Co. of Kansas City*, 383 U.S. 1, 5 (1966), and have said that "[t]he primary objective of copyright" is "[t]o promote the Progress of Science," *Feist* [*Publications, Inc. v. Rural Telephone Service Co.*, 499 U.S. 340 (1991)], at 349. The "constitutional command," we have recognized, is that Congress, to the extent it enacts copyright laws at all, create a "system" that "promote[s] the Progress of Science." *Graham*, 383 U.S. at 6.

We have also stressed, however, that it is generally for Congress, not the courts, to decide how best to pursue the Copyright Clause's objectives. *See* . . . *Graham*, 383 U.S., at 6 ("Within the limits of the constitutional grant, the Congress may, of course, implement the stated purpose of the Framers by selecting the policy which in its judgment best effectuates the constitutional aim."). The justifications we earlier set out for Congress' enactment of the CTEA, *supra*, provide a rational basis for the conclusion that the CTEA "promote[s] the Progress of Science."

On the issue of copyright duration, Congress, from the start, has routinely applied new definitions or adjustments of the copyright term to both future works

---

[16] The House and Senate Reports accompanying the CTEA reflect no purpose to make copyright a forever thing. Notably, the Senate Report expressly acknowledged that the Constitution "clearly precludes Congress from granting unlimited protection for copyrighted works," S. Rep. No. 104-315, p. 11 (1996), and disclaimed any intent to contravene that prohibition, *ibid.*

and existing works not yet in the public domain. . . . Congress' unbroken practice since the founding generation thus overwhelms petitioners' argument that the CTEA's extension of existing copyrights fails *per se* to "promote the Progress of Science."

Closely related to petitioners' preambular argument, or a variant of it, is their assertion that the Copyright Clause "imbeds a *quid pro quo*." They contend, in this regard, that Congress may grant to an "Autho[r]" an "exclusive Right" for a "limited Tim[e]," but only in exchange for a "Writin[g]." Congress' power to confer copyright protection, petitioners argue, is thus contingent upon an exchange: The author of an original work receives an "exclusive Right" for a "limited Tim[e]" in exchange for a dedication to the public thereafter. Extending an existing copyright without demanding additional consideration, petitioners maintain, bestows an unpaid-for benefit on copyright holders and their heirs, in violation of the *quid pro quo* requirement.

We can demur to petitioners' description of the Copyright Clause as a grant of legislative authority empowering Congress "to secure a bargain — this for that." But the legislative evolution earlier recalled demonstrates what the bargain entails. Given the consistent placement of existing copyright holders in parity with future holders, the author of a work created in the last 170 years would reasonably comprehend, as the "this" offered her, a copyright not only for the time in place when protection is gained, but also for any renewal or extension legislated during that time. . . .

We note, furthermore, that patents and copyrights do not entail the same exchange, and that our references to a *quid pro quo* typically appear in the patent context. . . . This is understandable, given that immediate disclosure is not the objective of, but is *exacted from*, the patentee. It is the price paid for the exclusivity secured. . . . For the author seeking copyright protection, in contrast, disclosure is the desired objective, not something exacted from the author in exchange for the copyright.

Further distinguishing the two kinds of intellectual property, copyright gives the holder no monopoly on any knowledge. A reader of an author's writing may make full use of any fact or idea she acquires from her reading. *See* [17 U.S.C.] § 102(b). The grant of a patent, on the other hand, does prevent full use by others of the inventor's knowledge. . . . In light of these distinctions, one cannot extract from language in our patent decisions . . . genuine support for petitioners' bold view. Accordingly, we reject the proposition that a *quid pro quo* requirement stops Congress from expanding copyright's term in a manner that puts existing and future copyrights in parity. . . .

III.

Petitioners separately argue that the CTEA is a content-neutral regulation of speech that fails heightened judicial review under the First Amendment. We reject petitioners' plea for imposition of uncommonly strict scrutiny on a copyright scheme that incorporates its own speech-protective purposes and safeguards. The Copyright Clause and First Amendment were adopted close in time. This proximity indicates that, in the Framers' view, copyright's limited monopolies are compatible with free speech principles. Indeed, copyright's purpose is to *promote* the creation and publication of free expression. As *Harper & Row* [*Publishers, Inc. v. Nation Enterprises*, 471 U.S. 539 (1985)] observed: "[. . .] By establishing a marketable right to the use of one's expression, copyright supplies the economic incentive to create and disseminate ideas." 471 U.S., at 558.

In addition to spurring the creation and publication of new expression, copyright law contains built-in First Amendment accommodations. *See id.*, at 560. First, it distinguishes between ideas and expression and makes only the latter eligible for copyright protection. . . . As we said in *Harper & Row*, this "idea/expression dichotomy strike[s] a definitional balance between the First Amendment and the Copyright Act by permitting free communication of facts while still protecting an author's expression." 471 U.S. at 556. . . .

Second, the "fair use" defense allows the public to use not only facts and ideas contained in a copyrighted work, but also expression itself in certain circumstances. . . . The fair use defense affords considerable "latitude for scholarship and comment," *Harper & Row*, 471 U.S. at 560.

. . . The First Amendment securely protects the freedom to make — or decline to make — one's own speech; it bears less heavily when speakers assert the right to make other people's speeches. To the extent such assertions raise First Amendment concerns, copyright's built-in free speech safeguards are generally adequate to address them. We recognize that the D.C. Circuit spoke too broadly when it declared copyrights "categorically immune from challenges under the First Amendment." 239 F.3d at 375. But when, as in this case, Congress has not altered the traditional contours of copyright protection, further First Amendment scrutiny is unnecessary. . . .

IV.

If petitioners' vision of the Copyright Clause held sway, it would do more than render the CTEA's duration extensions unconstitutional as to existing works. Indeed, petitioners' assertion that the provisions of the CTEA are not severable would make the CTEA's enlarged terms invalid even as to tomorrow's work. The 1976 Act's time extensions, which set the pattern that the CTEA followed, would be vulnerable as well.

As we read the Framers' instruction, the Copyright Clause empowers Congress to determine the intellectual property regimes that, overall, in that body's judgment, will serve the ends of the Clause. . . . [P]etitioners forcefully urge that Congress pursued very bad policy in prescribing the CTEA's long terms. The wisdom of Congress' action, however, is not within our province to second guess. Satisfied that the legislation before us remains inside the domain the Constitution assigns to the First Branch, we affirm the judgment of the Court of Appeals. It is so ordered.

JUSTICE STEVENS, dissenting.

. . . The issuance of a patent is appropriately regarded as a *quid pro quo* — the grant of a limited right for the inventor's disclosure and subsequent contribution to the public domain. . . . It would be manifestly unfair if, after issuing a patent, the Government as a representative of the public sought to modify the bargain by shortening the term of the patent in order to accelerate public access to the invention. The fairness considerations that underlie the constitutional protections against *ex post facto* laws and laws impairing the obligation of contracts would presumably disable Congress from making such a retroactive change in the public's bargain with an inventor without providing compensation for the taking. Those same considerations should protect members of the public who make plans to exploit an invention as soon as it enters the public domain from a retroactive modification of the bargain that extends the term of the patent monopoly. . . .

Neither the purpose of encouraging new inventions nor the overriding interest in advancing progress by adding knowledge to the public domain is served by retroactively increasing the inventor's compensation for a completed invention and frustrating the legitimate expectations of members of the public who want to make use of it in a free market. Because those twin purposes provide the only avenue for congressional action under the Copyright/Patent Clause of the Constitution, any other action is manifestly unconstitutional. . . .

We have recognized that these twin purposes of encouraging new works and adding to the public domain apply to copyrights as well as patents. . . .

The express grant of a perpetual copyright would unquestionably violate the textual requirement that the authors' exclusive rights be only "for limited Times." . . . [But] a categorical rule prohibiting retroactive extensions would effectively preclude perpetual copyrights. More importantly, as the House of Lords recognized when it refused to amend the Statute of Anne in 1735, unless the Clause is construed to embody such a categorical rule, Congress may extend existing monopoly privileges *ad infinitum* under the majority's analysis.

By failing to protect the public interest in free access to the products of inventive and artistic genius — indeed, by virtually ignoring the central purpose of the Copyright/Patent Clause — the Court has quitclaimed to Congress its principal responsibility in this area of the law. Fairly read, the Court has stated that Congress' actions under the Copyright/Patent Clause are, for all intents and purposes, judicially unreviewable. That result cannot be squared with the basic tenets of our constitutional structure. . . .

JUSTICE BREYER, dissenting. . . .

II.B.

This statute, like virtually every copyright statute, imposes upon the public certain expression-related costs in the form of (1) royalties that may be higher than necessary to evoke creation of the relevant work, and (2) a requirement that one seeking to reproduce a copyrighted work must obtain the copyright holder's permission. The first of these costs translates into higher prices that will potentially restrict a work's dissemination. The second means search costs that themselves may prevent reproduction even where the author has no objection. . . .

First, the present statute primarily benefits the holders of existing copyrights, *i.e.*, copyrights on works already created. And a Congressional Research Service (CRS) study . . . estimate[s] that 20 extra years of copyright protection will mean the transfer of several billion extra royalty dollars to holders of existing copyrights — copyrights that, together, already will have earned many billions of dollars in royalty "reward." . . .

. . . [Second,] the permissions requirement can inhibit or prevent the use of old works (particularly those without commercial value): (1) because it may prove expensive to track down or to contract with the copyright holder, (2) because the holder may prove impossible to find, or (3) because the holder when found may deny permission either outright or through misinformed efforts to bargain. . . .

C.

What copyright-related benefits might justify the statute's extension of copyright protection? First, no one could reasonably conclude that copyright's traditional economic rationale applies here. The extension will not act as an economic spur encouraging authors to create new works. . . . Using assumptions about the time value of money provided us by a group of economists (including five Nobel prize winners), Brief for George A. Akerlof et al. as *Amici Curiae* 5-7, it seems fair to say that, for example, a 1% likelihood of earning $100 annually for 20 years, starting *75 years into the future*, is worth less than seven cents today. . . .

What potential Shakespeare, Wharton, or Hemingway would be moved by such a sum? What monetarily motivated Melville would not realize that he could do better for his grandchildren by putting a few dollars into an interest-bearing bank account? . . . Or (to change the metaphor) is the argument that Dumas *fils* would have written more books had Dumas *pere*'s *Three Musketeers* earned more royalties?

. . . The present extension will produce a copyright period of protection that, even under conservative assumptions, is worth more than *99.8%* of protection *in perpetuity* . . .

Second, the Court relies heavily for justification upon international uniformity of terms. . . . Despite appearances, the statute does *not* create a uniform American-European term with respect to the lion's share of the economically significant works that it affects — *all* works made "for hire" and *all* existing works created prior to 1978. With respect to those works the American statute produces an extended term of 95 years while comparable European rights in "for hire" works last for periods that vary from 50 years to 70 years to life plus 70 years. . . .

Third, several publishers and filmmakers argue that the statute provides incentives to *those who act as publishers* to republish and to redistribute older copyrighted works. This claim cannot justify this statute, however, because the rationale is inconsistent with the basic purpose of the Copyright Clause — as understood by the Framers and by this Court. The Clause assumes an initial grant of monopoly, designed primarily to encourage creation, followed by termination of the monopoly grant in order to promote dissemination of already-created works. It assumes that it is the *disappearance* of the monopoly grant, not its *perpetuation*, that will, on balance, promote the dissemination of works already in existence. . . .

Fourth, the statute's legislative history . . . refers frequently to the financial assistance the statute will bring the entertainment industry, particularly through the promotion of exports. . . . In doing so, however, Congress has exercised its commerce, not its copyright, power. . . .

Finally, the Court mentions as possible justifications "demographic, economic, and technological changes" — by which the Court apparently means the facts that today people communicate with the help of modern technology, live longer, and have children at a later age. . . . The first fact seems to argue not for, but instead against, extension. . . . The second fact seems already corrected for by the 1976 Act's life-plus-50 term, which automatically grows with lifespans. . . . And the third fact — that adults are having children later in life — is a makeweight at best, providing no explanation of why the 1976 Act's term of 50 years after an author's death — a longer term than was available to authors themselves for most of our Nation's history — is an insufficient potential bequest. The weakness of these final rationales simply underscores the conclusion that emerges from consideration of earlier attempts at justification: There is no legitimate, serious copyright-related justification for this statute. . . .

NOTES AND QUESTIONS

Duration Basics Generally

(1)   Before examining the constitutional issues raised by *Eldred,* let us pause to consider the Copyright Term Extension Act's basic durational provisions. In addition to perusing the nearby chart captioned "Duration After the CTEA," you might want to take a look back at relevant passages from the House Report on the 1976 Act. That report cited a variety of reasons for changing the duration of copyright from a renewal basis to a life-plus-50-years basis. Do the same policy justifications apply with equal force to a life-plus-70 term? Which arguments for extending copyright terms do you find most compelling?

DURATION AFTER THE CTEA

	DATE OF PROTECTION	NATURE OF TERM	LENGTH OF TERM	
WORKS CREATED ON OR AFTER 1/1/78	When work was fixed in a tangible medium of expression	Unitary	<u>Basic term</u>: Life of the author plus 70 years <u>Alternative term</u> for anonymous or pseudonymous works, or works made for hire: 95 years from publication or 120 years from creation, whichever is shorter	
WORKS CREATED BUT NOT PUBLISHED BEFORE 1/1/78	Federal protection began on 1/1/78	Unitary	Same as above, at least through 12/31/2002, if the work remained unpublished as of that date, or until 12/31/2047 if the work was published before 1/1/2003	
WORKS PUBLISHED BETWEEN 1964 AND 1977	When work was published with notice	Dual term	28-year first term	Automatic renewal term of 67 years (renewal registration is optional but incentives attach to renewal registration)
WORKS PUBLISHED BETWEEN 1923 AND 1963	When work was published with notice	Dual term	28-year first term	Renewal term of 67 years, but only if renewal was properly obtained
WORKS PUBLISHED BEFORE 1923	N/A	N/A	Work is now in the public domain	

As to which of the foregoing categories of works does copyright extend through December 31 of the year in which the term would otherwise expire? (Note that this is a trick question!)

(2) If Congress wanted to, could it provide different terms of protection for different *types* of copyrightable works (*e.g.*, longer terms for literary works and shorter terms for data compilations)? If Congress could so provide, why hasn't it done so? Would such a system be any less complicated than one which determines the term of copyright based on the work's authorship (*e.g.*, single, joint, or for hire), as does § 302?

Outside the Copyright Act (*i.e.*, Chapters 1–8 of Title 17), Congress has undertaken to provide copyright-like protection for certain types of works for a lesser term of years. *See, e.g.*, 17 U.S.C. § 904 (10 years for semiconductor chip designs); 17 U.S.C. § 1305 (10 years for vessel hull designs). There have been legislative proposals to protect databases outside of Title 17 *altogether* (in Title 15). Where does Congress get its authority under the Constitution to enact such terms of protection, if not under the Copyright Clause?

(3)   How well does the Copyright Act anticipate possible *combinations* of authors? Suppose that Jack Employee (acting within the scope of his employment) and Jill Independent-Contractor collaborate on a video game for Jack's employer. What is the duration of the copyright in the resulting game?

(4)   What is the effect on the proprietor of a derivative work copyright when the copyright in the underlying work expires? Is any of the original matter in the derivative work swept into the public domain along with the borrowed matter from the underlying work? You may want to consider this question later in light of the discussion of "Publication, Derivative Works, and the Public Domain" in § 6.01 below.

(5)   One of the most notable features of the 1976 Act was that it shifted the moment for the investiture of federal copyright from the date of the work's first general publication to the date of its fixation in a tangible medium of expression. How did this change affect works which were created before 1978, but not published or registered before that date? *See* 17 U.S.C. § 303. Under the 1909 Act, such works had been protected by so-called "common-law copyright." The duration of such copyrights was (at least in theory) *perpetual*. On January 1, 1978, however, all previously unpublished works — no matter how old — were given a federal copyright of the same duration as new copyrights (now life-plus-70 years). To compensate for the loss of common-law copyright, Congress provided a minimum term of at least 25 years. Thus, for example, even a previously unpublished letter by Mark Twain (who died in 1910) was protected by federal copyright from 1978 through the end of 2002.

Furthermore, in order to encourage publication of previously unpublished works, § 303 (as amended by the CTEA) provides that, if the work was published before the end of 2002, the minimum term is extended to the end of 2047. In the case of Mark Twain, copyright protection for a letter first published between 1978 and 2002 would endure more than 137 years after the death of the author! On the other hand, on January 1, 2003, all *previously unpublished* works of authors who died before 1933 entered the public domain in the U.S. Note that the December 31, 2002 cut-off was a part of the original 1976 Act — and was *not* extended by the 1998 CTEA.

(6)   One of the reasons why duration is so complicated is that Congress tried to avoid disrupting the settled expectations of copyright owners by preserving the framework of existing law while making prospective amendments. Thus, in the 1976 Act, Congress preserved the renewal requirement for works first published or registered before 1978, but extended the renewal term to 47 years (resulting in a maximum duration of 75 years). In 1992, Congress made renewal automatic, but only for works first published or registered between 1964 and 1977. And in 1998, the CTEA extended the renewal term for pre-1978 works to 67 years (resulting in a

maximum duration of 95 years), but only for works that had not yet entered the public domain.

Because the CTEA did not revive any expired copyrights, any work first published or registered in the United States *before 1923* is now in the public domain. Under the CTEA, the maximum duration of copyrights secured between 1923 and 1977 is 95 years. How and whether that maximum duration is received, however, depends upon the date when the work first received federal copyright protection (the date of first publication for published works, or the date of registration for unpublished works):

Works copyrighted between January 1, 1923, and December 31, 1949. If properly renewed under the 1909 Act, these works were already in their renewal terms when the 1976 Act went into effect. Section 304(b) of the 1976 Act, as originally enacted, extended the duration of these copyrights to 75 years from the date that copyright originally was secured; and the current version of § 304(b), as enacted in the CTEA, further extends the duration of these copyrights to 95 years from the date when copyright originally was secured.

Works copyrighted between January 1, 1950 and December 31, 1963. As enacted in 1976, § 304(a) required that any copyright in its first 28-year term on the effective date of the 1976 Act be renewed at the end of its initial term in order to secure protection for a second term. If a renewal registration was not made within the statutory time limit, the work entered the public domain. If a valid and timely renewal registration was made, however, the person(s) entitled to renewal received a 47-year renewal term. Those works whose copyrights were renewed were in their second term when the CTEA was enacted in 1998, so the current version of § 304(b) further extends those copyrights to 95 years from the date copyright originally was secured.

Works copyrighted between January 1, 1964 and December 31, 1977. As amended in 1992, § 304(a) provided for *automatic* renewal for copyrights first secured between these dates. (The Copyright Renewal Act of 1992 is discussed in more detail in § 5.01[C] below.) At that time, the renewal term for these works was 47 years. Those works copyrighted between 1964 and 1969 were in their second term when the CTEA was enacted in 1998, so the current version of § 304(b) further extends those copyrights to 95 years from the date on which copyright originally was secured. Those works copyrighted between 1970 and 1977 were in their first term when the CTEA was enacted in 1998. The current version of § 304(a), as amended by the CTEA, provides for an automatic 67-year renewal term for such works, resulting in a total duration of 95 years from the date copyright originally was secured.

Copyright Duration and the Eldred Decision

(7)   The *Eldred* case received a great deal of attention from the national media because of its potential to affect a large segment of the American economy. Justice Breyer's dissenting opinion estimated that "20 extra years of copyright protection will mean the transfer of several billion extra royalty dollars to holders of existing copyrights." Despite (or perhaps because of) the huge potential impact of the case, a single example came to symbolize the battle over copyright term extension:

Disney's Mickey Mouse, whose first cartoon would have entered the public domain in 2004 had the CTEA been overturned. For an example, see the accompanying cartoon that was published shortly after the Supreme Court's decision.

FOXTROT © 2003 Bill Amend
Reprinted with permission of Universal Uniclick
All rights reserved

(8) Think back to Chapter 1 and the various "rhetorics" of copyright jurisprudence discussed there. Which "rhetoric" best characterizes Justice Ginsburg's approach to copyright in *Eldred*? Which "rhetorics" do Justice Stevens and Justice Breyer employ? Justice Breyer's economic approach is perhaps unsurprising in light of his previously published articles in the area. *See* § 1.06. Is it significant that Justice Ginsburg also wrote the majority opinion in *New York Times Co. v. Tasini*, in § 4.01 above, decided by the same 7-2 majority? Do these two cases signal a trend in the High Court's copyright thinking? For a prescient prediction along these lines, see Jaszi, *Goodbye to All That — A Reluctant (and Perhaps Premature) Adieu to a Constitutionally-Grounded Discourse of Public Interest in Copyright Law*, 29 Vand. J. Transnat'l L. 595 (1996).

(9) What should be the proper standard of review under the Copyright and Patent Clause? Justice Ginsburg's majority opinion is characteristically deferential to Congress. She concludes that whether copyright terms should be extended is a policy decision entrusted to Congress, with which the Court will not interfere so long as the legislation has a rational basis. Dissenting, Justice Breyer opined that copyright legislation should be reviewed "somewhat more carefully" because of its potential effect on free expression. Which view persuades you more?

(10) Even rational basis review requires that "the means chosen by Congress must be reasonably adapted to the end permitted by the Constitution." *Hodel v. Virginia Surface Mining & Reclamation Ass'n*, 452 U.S. 264, 276 (1981). According to the majority, how does extending the terms of *existing* copyrights "promote the Progress of Science"? Is it rational to strive to harmonize U.S. copyright terms with those of the European Union — a political entity that is not bound by our "limited Times" requirement?

(11) Justice Ginsburg and the dissenting Justices draw very different conclusions from the history of copyright terms. Is the English experience under the Statute of Anne, including *Donaldson v. Beckett*, irrelevant, or is it evidence of (in Justice Breyer's words) "the antimonopoly environment in which the Framers

wrote the Clause"? *See* Ochoa & Rose, *The Anti-Monopoly Origins of the Patent and Copyright Clause*, 49 J. Copyright Soc'y 675 (2002). Is it important that the 1790 Act protected existing works as well as future ones, or should that be considered merely a transitional measure from state to federal protection? Should it matter that Congress extended individual patents and copyrights in the 18th Century? What implications do these debates have for the use of historical sources to interpret the Constitution?

For a post-*Eldred* attempt to place American copyright law in historical perspective, see Patterson & Joyce, *Copyright in 1791: An Essay Concerning the Founders' View of the Copyright Power Granted to Congress in Article I, Section 8, Clause 8 of the U.S. Constitution*, 52 Emory L. J. 909 (2003).

(12)   Is the United States now engaged in a process of creating, by successive extensions of the term of protection, "perpetual copyright on the installment plan" (per Prof. Peter Jaszi in his Senate testimony opposing the CTEA)? Justice Ginsburg states that "[n]othing before this Court warrants [such a] construction." Justice Breyer, by contrast, quotes statements by members of Congress and witnesses *expressly advocating* a perpetual copyright.

Is there an outer limit to the term of copyright that Congress could enact? How about another 20 years in 2018 (call it the "Digital Methusaleh Copyright Act," or DMCA II)? Would a life-plus-1000-years term still pass muster under the "limited Times" provision of the Copyright Clause, if enacted incrementally?

(13)   Justice Breyer states (without contradiction) that the discounted present value of the current term of copyright is worth 99.8% of the value of a perpetual copyright. The majority rejects this calculation as a basis for finding the CTEA unconstitutional. Is the majority correct that such a conclusion would call the 1976 Act into question as well? If so, what problems would that create? Is there any persuasive way of distinguishing the terms set by the 1976 Act from those set by the CTEA? Consider the following additional facts: If one does not count the nine "interim" extensions passed while the Copyright Act of 1976 was pending, the CTEA marks the first time that Congress has extended copyrights that had already been extended previously, and the first time that term extension was enacted outside of a general revision of the copyright laws.

(14)   What, if any, are the implications of *Eldred* for other familiar copyright doctrines? Justice Ginsburg states that "copyright's limited monopolies are compatible with free speech principles," citing the idea/expression dichotomy and the fair use defense as examples of such principles. The Court further observes that "when, as in this case, Congress has not altered the traditional contours of copyright protection, further First Amendment scrutiny is unnecessary." Suppose that, under pressure from other nations, Congress decided to pare back fair use under domestic law. Would such a decision be "compatible with free speech principles" and "the traditional contours of copyright protection"? Would "further First Amendment scrutiny" be warranted? And how should Justice Ginsburg's observations be applied to the DMCA, which in certain circumstances erects barriers to access to copyrighted and public domain materials alike?

(15)   Despite the ruling in *Eldred*, opponents of term extension brought a new action challenging the 1992 amendment that made copyright renewal automatic, on the ground that the elimination of the renewal requirement "alter[ed] the traditional contours of copyright protection." The Ninth Circuit affirmed the dismissal of the action on the basis of *Eldred*. *See Kahle v. Ashcroft*, 487 F.3d 697 (9th Cir. 2007).

(16)   In 1994, Congress passed a law restoring the copyrights in certain works of foreign origin that were in the public domain in the U.S. for failure to comply with formalities such as notice or renewal. If Congress can extend copyrights under *Eldred*, can it restore the copyrights of works that have entered the public domain? This question will be considered in § 5.01[D] below.

(17)   *International treaties and duration.* One of the differences between copyright protection under the Berne Convention and the protection provided to sound recordings ("phonograms") under the Rome Convention, the Geneva Phonograms Convention, and the WIPO Performances and Phonograms Treaty is the duration of the rights. Berne provides a minimum term of life plus 50 years for most copyrighted works, a minimum term of 50 years for cinematographic works, and a minimum term of 25 years for photographic works and works of applied art. The Rome and Geneva Conventions provide a minimum term of only 20 years for sound recordings, while the WPPT provides a minimum term of 50 years for sound recordings. What happens when a country chooses to protect works for a longer period of time? Under Article 7(8) of Berne, countries are permitted (but not required) to adopt the "rule of the shorter term," which limits the duration of copyright in the protecting country to the term provided in the country of origin. The three phonogram treaties, however, say nothing at all about the "rule of the shorter term." *See Capitol Records, Inc., v. Naxos of America, Inc.*, 830 N.E.2d 250 (N.Y. 2005) (holding pre-1972 sound recordings are protected under state law even after they have entered the public domain in their country of origin). (Lest you were wondering why Capitol Records would litigate a state-law case involving obscure classical music recordings, consider that Capitol owns rights to sound recordings made by the Beatles in England in the 1960s, for which the 50-year term then provided by British law was about to expire.)

(18)   In September 2011, the European Union directed its member states to increase the duration of rights in sound recordings from 50 years to 70 years. *See* Directive 2011/77/EU. The Directive also contains provisions allowing performers to terminate certain agreements concerning sound recordings after the 50th year, and to obtain additional compensation for those agreements that remain in force. Can these measures be justified on any incentive-based theory of copyright? Is there any reason to believe that sound recordings by the Beatles will *ever* be allowed to enter the public domain in Europe? In the United States?

[C]   The Law of Renewal

As you will have noticed already, the legislative enactments of 1976 and 1998 did not render entirely irrelevant all of the "old" law regarding renewals. Rather, under the complicated statutory scheme now in place after the 1976 Act and the CTEA, the law of renewal under the 1909 Act retains significance for works first published or registered before 1978. The present section examines in greater detail how renewal operates in practice.

[1]   Renewal Basics

To renew a copyright for its second term, the 1909 Act required claimants to file for renewal in the Copyright Office during the 28th year of the initial copyright term. A renewal application could be filed by anyone, but it had to be filed in the name of the person or persons entitled to the renewal term. Timely filing was required to obtain the renewal term; failure to timely file dedicated the work to the public domain. These matters are discussed in more detail below.

The major benefits of renewal were that many works lacking commercial value entered the public domain after their first 28-year term, while authors of works which had become quite valuable were (at least in theory) given the opportunity to earn a greater share of that value during the second term. In practice, however, the renewal system was neither fair to authors nor easy to administer. Through inadvertence or ignorance, many authors forfeited their works to the public domain by failing to comply with renewal formalities; and case law (described below) thwarted Congress' intent to give authors of valuable works a "second bite at the apple." Despite these obvious drawbacks, the 1976 Act continued the 1909 Act's renewal system, faults included, with respect to works copyrighted before January 1, 1978. Congress perhaps did so less for paternalistic reasons than to avoid the unfairness of changing rules on which authors and copyright owners had relied. *See* H.R. Rep. No. 94-1476, at 139 (1976).

Understanding the renewal system under the 1909 Act, and the case law interpreting it, is important for determining whether works which otherwise would be currently in their renewal term in fact continue to be protected. Failure to renew placed a work into the public domain irrevocably, with one exception: Congress later "restored" copyright protection for certain works of foreign origin which were in the public domain in the United States prior to January 1, 1996. (For a detailed discussion, see § 5.01[D] below.) For works of U.S. origin, however, the basic principle stated above — irrevocable loss of protection — remains intact.

Life has become somewhat easier as far as renewal mechanics are concerned. First, in 1992 Congress made renewal automatic (for works first published in 1964 or later), thereby avoiding the problem of inadvertent failures to renew (but also preventing such works from entering the public domain at the end of their first term). The 1992 amendments are discussed in § 5.01[C][3] below. Second, works first published in 1977 were the last group of works to which renewal applied. In other words, the last day to file a *timely* application for renewal was December 31, 2005 (although registration of subsisting renewal terms is still permissible). But even though the need to apply for renewal has passed, the necessity of knowing the effect of renewals made under prior law, and long ago, will continue well into the 21st Century.

When Did the Application for Renewal Need to be Made?

Under § 24 of the 1909 Act, the claimant was required to register the renewal application "within one year prior to the expiration of the original term of copyright" (in other words, during the 28th year). For example, the proper time frame for the renewal of a copyright first published (or, in the case of an unpublished work, registered) on July 1, 1930 was the period between July 1, 1957 and June 30, 1958. *See Mayhew v. Gusto Records, Inc.*, 960 F. Supp. 1302 (M.D. Tenn. 1997) (attempted renewal of musical work copyrights was invalid because applications were filed three days before commencement of the one-year period prior to expiration of the original term).

Under § 304(a) of the 1976 Act, as that provision stood prior to the 1992 amendments, the renewal application and fee were required to be received by the Copyright Office "within one year prior to the expiration of the copyright." After January 1, 1978, however, all terms of copyright "run to the end of the calendar year in which they would otherwise expire." § 305. This means that all subsequent periods for renewal registration began on December 31st of the 27th year of the initial term of copyright and ended on December 31st of the following year. Thus, a work copyrighted on July 1, 1960 was eligible for renewal only between December 31, 1987 and December 31, 1988, and applications filed earlier or later would be ineffective.

Who Was Entitled to Renew?

In the absence of a claim made by an eligible claimant, there could be no valid renewal under § 24 of the 1909 Act or under § 304(a) of the 1976 Act, as originally enacted. So an important preliminary matter in assessing the validity of a pre-1992 renewal is the identification of the person or entity possessing the right to renew the copyright. The answer that immediately springs to mind — "the author" — is often, perhaps even usually, correct. But not always. Under § 24 (1909 Act) and § 304(a) (1976 Act), possession of the right to renew depends on the type of work which is the subject of the copyright.

There are four types of works in which the right to renew belongs not to the author or to the widow/widower and children of the author, but to the *proprietor* of the copyright at the time renewal is claimed:

a. *Posthumous works*. The definition of this category of works was somewhat confused under the 1909 Act. The lay or dictionary meaning of "posthumous" pertains to publication of a work after the death of its author. In *Bartok v. Boosey & Hawkes, Inc.*, 523 F.2d 941 (1975), however, the Second Circuit construed a "posthumous work" to be one *as to which no copyright assignment or other contract for exploitation occurred during an author's lifetime*. The House Report to the 1976 Act approved this meaning for use in construing § 304(a). Does this special definition help or hurt the interests of an author's heirs seeking to realize the greatest possible benefit from their decedent's literary, artistic, or musical estate?

b. *Periodic, cyclopedic, or other composite works*. Neither the 1909 nor the 1976 Act defines "composite work." The term probably refers to what the 1976 Act calls a "collective work." Even this definition, however, leaves thorny problems as to precisely which aspects of such a work may be presented by its proprietor for a renewal copyright. The individual author of any contribution to the collective work may renew the copyright in the contribution. *See Abend v. MCA, Inc.*, 863 F.2d 1465, 1470-72 (9th Cir. 1988), *aff'd sub nom. Stewart v. Abend*, 495 U.S. 207 (1990). What aspects of the composite work then remain for renewal by the proprietor thereof? *See, e.g., Self-Realization Fellowship Church v. Ananda Church of Self-Realization*, 206 F.3d 1322 (9th Cir. 2000).

c. *Works copyrighted by corporate bodies (other than as assignees or licensees of individual authors).* Because of the relatively broad sweep of the work-for-hire doctrine (see below), this clause is almost never relied upon as a basis for renewal claims. *But see Schmid Brothers, Inc. v. W. Goebel Porzellanfabrik KG*, 589 F. Supp. 497 (E.D.N.Y. 1984) (renewal copyright in Sister Hummel porcelain figurine designs awarded to nun's convent).

d. *Works copyrighted by employers for whom such work is made for hire.* In practical terms, this is by far the most significant of the categories of works in which the proprietor, not the author, is entitled to the renewal term. *See, e.g., Twentieth Century Fox Film Corp. v. Entertainment Distributing*, 429 F.3d 869 (9th Cir. 2005) (holding that Doubleday was entitled to the renewal term in General Eisenhower's memoirs); *Estate of Hogarth v. Edgar Rice Burroughs, Inc.*, 342 F.3d 149 (2d Cir. 2003) (holding that ERB, Inc., and not the illustrator, was entitled to the renewal term in two graphic novels based on *Tarzan of the Apes*). As to when a work is "made for hire," see Chapter 4.

For all works other than those in the foregoing four categories, the proper renewal claimant is:

a. *The author*, if living at the time for renewal. For the effect of an assignment of the renewal term by the author, see the material on "Transfer of the Renewal Term" below.

b. *The widow/widower and children*, if the author is deceased on the date when the renewal term would vest. For problems associated with this class of claimants under the provisions of the 1909 Act, see *DeSylva v. Ballentine*, 351 U.S. 570 (1956). Fortunately, the 1976 Act now defines "widow," "widower," and "children" in § 101. Are children who have been disinherited still "children" for renewal purposes? Can a divorced spouse be a "widow" or "widower"? Are there justifiable reasons for distinguishing between disinherited children and a divorced spouse? *See Saroyan v. William Saroyan Foundation*, 675 F. Supp. 843 (S.D.N.Y. 1987).

And what about illegitimate children? In *Stone v. Williams*, 970 F.2d 1043 (2d Cir. 1992), the plaintiff belatedly discovered that she was the natural child of Hank Williams, the famous country western singer. The plaintiff learned of her relationship in 1979 but did not file a claim for renewal rights until 1985. The court held, following *DeSylva*, that whether an illegitimate child was entitled to copyright renewal was to be determined by Alabama state law, and applied the later, more favorable, version of that law after concluding that fraudulent activity by the estate had prevented the plaintiff from learning about her claim in a timely fashion.

Finally, suppose that an author has died, leaving a widower and three children, one of whom makes a timely application for renewal in his or her own name. Although that child may be the only renewal claimant on record, and thus the owner of the legal title to the renewal copyright, the equitable title vests in all the members of the class as joint owners. *See* 3 NIMMER ON COPYRIGHT § 9.05[E] (2012). But if the foregoing is clear, something else is not. According to what principle should this joint interest be apportioned among the members of a numerous class of statutory successors? If a *per stirpes* rule is followed, the widower would be entitled to a half-interest and each of the children to 16⅔%; in a *per capita* distribution, each would have a one-quarter share. The statute is silent, although *Bartok* appears to assume that the *per capita* principle would apply. But in the case of termination of transfers under §§ 203 and 304(c) of the 1976 Act, discussed in § 5.02 of this casebook, reversion interests vest in the author's successors on a *per stirpes* basis. What *should* the rule be in the case of renewal? Nimmer has taken the position that a *per capita* distribution is appropriate. *See* 3 NIMMER ON COPYRIGHT § 9.04[A][1] (2012). Two Courts of Appeal have held, however, that renewal copyrights, like termination interests, should vest on a *per stirpes* basis. *See Broadcast Music, Inc. v. Roger Miller Music, Inc.*, 396 F.3d 762 (6th Cir. 2005); *Venegas-Hernandez v. Asociacion de Compositores y Editores de Musica Latinoamericana*, 424 F.3d 50 (1st Cir. 2005).

c. *The executors of the author*, if there is no surviving widow, widower or child, and the author left a will. In effect, an author is statutorily required to leave the right to claim renewal to his or her spouse and children, if any survive to the commencement of the renewal term. If none do survive, both the 1909 and the 1976 Acts allow the author to provide by will for the disposition of the renewal right. The executors claim as fiduciaries for the benefit of the legatees. *See Music Sales Corp. v. Morris*, 73 F. Supp. 2d 364, 375 (S.D.N.Y. 1999).

d. *The author's next of kin*, if there is no surviving widow, widower or child, the author left no will, or the executor has been dismissed. The composition of this final class of claimants is a matter of state law, and (as usual) the actual claimant or claimants must share beneficial ownership with all members of the class. *Silverman v. Sunrise Pictures Corp.*, 273 F. 909 (2d Cir. 1921), *aff'd on other grounds*, 290 F. 804 (2d Cir. 1923).

Transfer of the Renewal Term

In approving a continuance of two-term copyright protection in the 1909 Act, while expanding the renewal term from 14 to 28 years, Congress' purpose appears to have been to protect authors against unremunerative transfers by giving them a "second bite at the apple" if the work turned out to be a success. This paternalistic goal, however, was undermined by 1909 Act case law in *Fred Fisher Music Co. v. M. Witmark & Sons*, 318 U.S. 643 (1943). *Fisher* involved the validity of an assignment of the renewal term of an author of the hit tune "When Irish Eyes Are Smiling." The Supreme Court held that an assignment by an author of the renewal term, before the right thereto had vested, was binding on the author. A majority of the *Fisher*

Court, in a dubiously reasoned opinion by Justice Frankfurter (over a dissent by Justices Black, Douglas, and Murphy), rejected the argument that authors must be protected against bad deals. The majority observed: "It is not for the courts to judge whether the interests of authors clearly lie upon one side of this question rather than the other. If an author cannot make an effective assignment of his renewal, it may be worthless to him when he is most in need. Nobody would pay an author for something he cannot sell." *Id.* at 657. After *Fisher*, it became industry practice to require an assignment of the author's renewal rights in the initial contract. Thus, in order to sell his rights in a work during its *first* term of protection, an author was forced to convey his rights to the *second* copyright term, which he himself could then never enjoy.

An author's power to assign the renewal term was limited in one significant way: The author had to survive until the renewal term vested. In *Miller Music Corp. v. Charles N. Daniels, Inc.*, 362 U.S. 373 (1960), the Supreme Court held that an author's assignment of the renewal term was a *contingent* interest only, so that if an assigning author died before the renewal vested, the right to the second term vested not in the assignee of the first term but rather in the author's statutory successors under § 24 of the 1909 Act. To circumvent this risk, assignees of renewal rights often sought to obtain contingent assignments from *all* the potential statutory successors, beginning with the author's spouse. Again, contrary to the paternalistic objective of the renewal term, courts upheld these agreements so long as they were supported by consideration and expressly granted rights in the renewal term. In sum, *Fisher* and its progeny undermined the basic policy of the renewal grant, which was to protect the unequal bargaining position of many authors. At the same time, *Miller Music* left the assignee with an irreducible measure of uncertainty: no matter how many contingent assignments the assignee obtained, those assignments could still be defeated if, for example, the author divorced and remarried, or had additional children, before the renewal term vested.

Another source of uncertainty concerned the specific language of the assignment. On the whole, courts have been reluctant to construe an assignment to include the renewal term absent language expressly granting rights in the "renewal" or "extension" of the copyright's initial term. "[A] general transfer by an author of the original copyright without mention of renewal rights conveys no interest in the renewal rights without proof of a contrary intention." *Edward B. Marks Music Corp. v. Charles K. Harris Music Publishing Co.*, 255 F.2d 518, 521 (2d Cir. 1958). Thus, in *Marks*, even a transfer purporting to convey "all right, title and interest" in a work was held to be insufficient. By contrast, a grant of the "*perpetual* and exclusive right to distribute" a motion picture was held to be sufficient in *P.C. Films Corp. v. MGM/UA Home Video Inc.*, 138 F.3d 453 (2d Cir. 1998) (emphasis added). *See also Roger Miller Music, Inc. v. Sony/ATV Publishing, LLC*, 477 F.3d 383 (6th Cir. 2007) ("express use of the term 'renew' . . . evinces an intent to convey the renewal interest").

Litigation Concerning the Renewal Term

For a concrete example of the renewal rules in action, consider *Epoch Producing Corp. v. Killiam Shows, Inc.*, 522 F.2d 737 (2d Cir. 1976), which concerned the renewal term for D.W. Griffith's classic silent film *Birth of a Nation*. The movie was based on a novel, *The Clansman*, written by Thomas Dixon and published in 1904. In 1913, Dixon assigned the motion picture rights to the Majestic Motion Picture Company; but when the movie was released in February 1915, the copyright in the movie was registered by the David W. Griffith Corporation ("DWG Corp.") instead. (Griffith was the producer, director, and co-screenwriter for the film.) Later, in April 1915, DWG Corp. executed two assignments, each "contain[ing] broad general language purporting to convey to Epoch all of the DWG Corp.'s interest in the film."

The Birth of a Nation (1915)
Corbis

In June 1942, Epoch applied for the renewal copyright as "the proprietor of copyright in a work made for hire." The Second Circuit, however, held that this renewal was invalid. Because Epoch was not incorporated until February 1915, it could not have been Griffith's "employer" when the film was being made. In addition, "there is no evidence of any employer-employee relationship between Majestic or Epoch, on the one hand, and D.W. Griffith, on the other. There is no contract of employment, record of salary payments, or proof that Majestic or Epoch supervised or controlled Griffith in the making of the picture."

As for the assignments, the court noted that "there is no specific reference in either assignment to the renewal term" and held, in accordance with the general rule noted above, that "[t]his deficiency has generally been held as a matter of law, absent contrary evidence, to preclude a holding that a transfer of renewal rights was intended." Finally, although the presumption against assignment of the renewal term may not apply with the same force when the assignor is a corporation, *see, e.g.,* *Rohauer v. Friedman*, 306 F.2d 933 (9th Cir. 1962), the court held that this distinction did not apply "where the corporation was controlled by the author."

In an action to determine the validity of a renewal copyright, which party has the burden of proof? On this point, the *Epoch* court was clear: The claimant does, and the renewal registration certificate does not discharge that burden. The opinion notes that § 209 of the 1909 Act created a presumption of validity only with respect to the facts stated in the *original* certificate of registration for the *initial* term, and further points out that even "the minimal verification of the information supplied in connection with an application for an original copyright certificate is wholly absent in the case of a renewal application."

Under the 1976 Act, as originally enacted, the same result applied. Section 410(c) provides that a certificate of registration constitutes *prima facie* evidence of the validity of the copyright, but only if the registration is made "before or within five years after first publication." In 1992, however, when renewal was made automatic, Congress bestowed an additional presumption of validity on renewal certificates resulting from timely affirmative registrations in order to encourage such applications. *See* § 5.01[C][3] below.

[2]   Renewal and Derivative Works

Suppose that, during the first term of copyright, the author of an original story assigned both the initial term and the renewal term to a movie producer, who produced a motion picture based on the story. Suppose further that the author died before the renewal term began, rendering the assignment of the renewal term ineffective. See *Miller Music Corp. v. Charles N. Daniels, Inc.*, 362 U.S. 373 (1960), discussed above in connection with *Fisher v. Witmark*. May the producer nonetheless continue to exploit the movie during the renewal term of the copyright without the permission of the author's successor in interest?

The Supreme Court addressed this issue in *Stewart v. Abend*, 495 U.S. 207 (1990). The case involved the rights to reproduce and distribute the motion picture "Rear Window," directed by Alfred Hitchcock and starring James Stewart and Grace Kelly. The movie was based on the short story "It Had to Be Murder" by Cornell Woolrich, first published in 1942. Woolrich assigned the motion picture rights to the story in 1945; the movie was produced and released in 1954. Woolrich died in 1968, before the renewal term in the short story began. His executor, Chase Manhattan Bank, later renewed the copyright in the short story and assigned it to Abend for $650 plus 10% of any proceeds. When MCA, Inc. (the successors in interest to the copyright in the motion picture) re-released the movie in theaters and on video in 1983, Abend sued MCA, Stewart, and the Hitchcock estate for infringement.

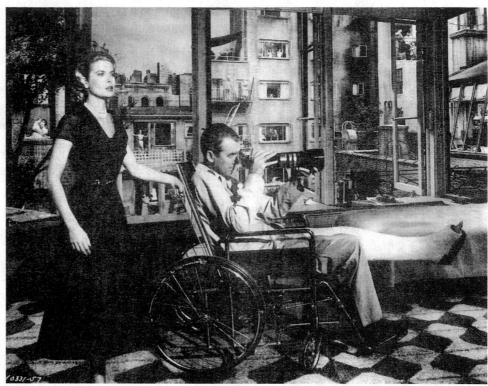

Grace Kelly and James Stewart in *Rear Window* (1954)
Corbis

The defendants relied on *Rohauer v. Killiam Shows*, 551 F.2d 484 (2d Cir. 1977), in which the Second Circuit held that the owner of the copyright in a derivative work may continue to use the existing derivative work according to the original grant from the author of the pre-existing work, even if the grant of rights in the pre-existing work had lapsed. The court reasoned that the author of the derivative work may have contributed as much or more to the derivative work than the author of the underlying story, and that "the purchaser of derivative rights has no truly effective way to protect himself against the eventuality of the author's death before the renewal period since there is no way of telling who will be the surviving widow, children or next of kin or the executor until that date arrives." *Id.* at 493.

The Supreme Court disagreed, holding that "if the author dies before the renewal period, then the assignee may continue to use the original work only if the author's successor transfers the renewal rights to the assignee." 495 U.S. at 221. The Court rejected the contrary holding in *Rohauer*, saying:

> When an author produces a work which later commands a higher price in the market than the original bargain provided, the copyright statute is designed to provide the author the power to negotiate for the realized value of the work. . . . At heart, petitioners' true complaint is that they will have to pay more for the use of works they have employed in creating their own works. But such a result was contemplated by Congress and is consistent

with the goals of the Copyright Act. . . . Absent an explicit statement of congressional intent that the rights in the renewal term of an owner of a pre-existing work are extinguished upon incorporation of his work into another work, it is not our role to alter the delicate balance Congress has labored to achieve.

Id. at 229-30. As we will see, in adopting automatic renewal in 1992, Congress limited the Supreme Court's decision in *Stewart* to those cases in which the person entitled to renew the underlying work timely registers the renewal term with the Copyright Office. Otherwise, the result in *Rohauer* applies. *See* § 5.01[C][3] below.

Justice Stevens' dissent in *Stewart* characterized the question as whether the copyright in an authorized derivative work ought to be considered "independent" from the copyright in the underlying work. What are the practical implications, beyond the precise issue posed in the case, of the majority's rejection of derivative work independence? Suppose, for example, that a motion picture has entered the public domain for failure to renew. May the former copyright owner prevent the distribution of the movie on the ground that the movie was based upon an unpublished screenplay, to which it still owns the rights? So far, both the Second and the Ninth Circuits have rejected this argument, holding that *Stewart* only applies to underlying works which were covered by federal statutory copyright, not common-law copyright. *See Shoptalk, Ltd. v. Concorde-New Horizons Corp.*, 168 F.3d 586 (2d Cir. 1999); *Batjac Prods., Inc. v. GoodTimes Home Video Corp.*, 160 F.3d 1223 (9th Cir. 1998) (discussed in § 6.02 below).

One way to view the substance of the dispute in *Stewart* is as a clash of two profoundly different understandings of the significance of "authorship." *See* Jaszi, *When Works Collide: Derivative Motion Pictures, Underlying Rights, and the Public Interest*, 28 UCLA L. Rev. 715 (1981). One of those visions derives directly from "Romantic" orthodoxy, described in Chapter 1, and elevates the interests of the creator of the "original" work (or his or her successors) over those of artists (or their successors) who devise subsequent, merely "derivative" works. The alternative "revisionist" vision would recognize the co-equal claims of all creators to legal (and nonlegal) recognition — as well as the public interest in fostering the creation and dissemination of such derivative works.

The Supreme Court in *Stewart* declined to consider any such public interest, noting: "Presumably, respondent is asking for a share in the proceeds because he wants to profit from the distribution of the work, not because he seeks suppression of it." 495 U.S. at 228. Could the public interest nonetheless be taken into account in deciding whether an injunction should issue? Although the Supreme Court did not address the question of what remedy would be appropriate, the Ninth Circuit's opinion below declared that the entry of an injunction in Abend's favor would cause "great injustice" and remanded for consideration of a court-ordered licensing scheme. *Abend v. MCA, Inc.*, 863 F.2d. 1465, 1479 (9th Cir. 1988). In a subsequent case, the Supreme Court cited this passage with approval. *See Campbell v. Acuff-Rose Music, Inc.*, 510 U.S. 569, 578 n.10 (1994), in Chapter 10 below. For more discussion on the question of remedies, see Chapter 11.

[3] Automatic Renewal

The renewal provisions of American copyright law were intended to enhance the rights of authors. In practice, however, the renewal requirements dispossessed many authors of rights in their works halfway through the maximum potential period of exploitation. The requirements became, in effect, a trap for authors who failed to file for timely renewal in the procedurally correct way, with the result that their works entered the public domain inadvertently.

In addition, the renewal provisions also generated uncertainty about copyright ownership, much of it traceable to unresolved questions about when the renewal term "vested." Suppose that an author granted an assignment of renewal rights and renewal was timely claimed, *i.e.*, during the 28th year; and suppose further that the author later died before the renewal term began. Who owned the rights to the renewal term: the author's statutory beneficiaries or the assignee of the renewal term? Under the case law, the answer depended on *when* the renewal term was deemed to have vested. Some courts held that renewal vested on the date of renewal registration, which could occur *at any time during* the 28th year of the initial term. *See, e.g., Frederick Music Co. v. Sickler*, 708 F. Supp. 587 (S.D.N.Y. 1989). Other courts held that the author had to survive *through the end of* the 28th year in order for the renewal term to vest in the author's assignee. *See, e.g., Marascalco v. Fantasy, Inc.*, 953 F.2d 469 (9th Cir. 1991).

Congress enacted the "Copyright Renewal Act of 1992" in an attempt to remedy the various difficulties associated with the prior renewal scheme. The Renewal Act featured three important changes in the law of renewal:

Permissive renewal. For works whose copyright was secured *between 1964 and 1977*, renewal occurred automatically when the first term ended. These works enjoy the 67-year renewal term without their proprietors having had to file for renewal registration. An author could still *actually file* for renewal after the 1992 Act, however, and many did so because of certain advantages that flowed from a renewal registration (see below). But such affirmative compliance with renewal formalities was permissive and did not affect the validity of the copyright.

On the other hand, *pre-1964* works were *not* affected by the 1992 legislation. The Renewal Act did not alter the status of pre-1964 works that had entered the public domain for failure to comply with the prior renewal requirements. *See, e.g., Martha Graham School and Dance Foundation, Inc. v. Martha Graham Center of Contemporary Dance, Inc.*, 224 F. Supp. 2d 567, 594–95 (S.D.N.Y. 2002), *aff'd in relevant part*, 380 F.3d 624, 637 n.26 (2d Cir. 2004) (holding that ten choreographic works first published before 1964 and not renewed were in the public domain).

Clarifying the vesting date. Under the Renewal Act, if a renewal application was filed during the 28th year by the person entitled to the renewal, *that is, the author or the author's statutory heirs*, then the renewal term vested, at the beginning of the 29th year, in that person, even if that person had died before the renewal term began — thereby validating any pre-existing assignments of the renewal term. *See, e.g., Roger Miller Music, Inc. v. Sony/ATVPublishing, LLC*, 672 F.3d 434 (6th Cir. 2012) (where author's assignee filed for renewal in author's name in January and April 1992, and author died in October 1992, renewal terms vested in assignee on

January 1, 1993, rather than in author's heirs). Alternatively, if no application was made, the renewal term vested in whoever was the appropriate renewal claimant on December 31st of the initial term's 28th year. 17 U.S.C. § 304(a)(2).

For example, suppose that the composer of a musical work secured copyright in 1977. The renewal term began automatically on January 1, 2006. The renewal term vested in the author (or the author's assignee) if she or he applied for renewal in 2005 or lived to December 31, 2005. If the author died before January 1, 2006 without having registered, the renewal term vested in those of the author's widow(er) or children alive when any of them obtained a 28th-year registration. If no registration was obtained, renewal vested in those who were alive on December 31, 2005. If none of the statutory beneficiaries was alive, the renewal term vested in the author's executor.

Incentives to register. In addition to the opportunity to "lock in" an early vesting date, the Renewal Act afforded powerful incentives to timely file for renewal.

The first incentive concerned derivative works prepared under an authorization granted during the original term of copyright. If a timely renewal was filed, the author's first-term grants of renewal rights to exploit such derivative works were nullified if the author died before the renewal term. Thus, the principles of *Stewart v. Abend*, 495 U.S. 207 (1990), still apply, but only if a renewal registration was obtained during the 28th year of the original term. If no registration was filed, a derivative work made pursuant to the grant still can be exploited during the renewal term, but no new derivative works could be made after the new term began. 17 U.S.C. § 304(a)(4)(A).

A second benefit of timely renewal registration concerned the evidentiary weight accorded the registration. If registration was made during the last year of the first term, the certificate of renewal registration constitutes *prima facie* evidence of the validity of the facts stated in the certificate — thus reversing what had been the rule on this issue. The evidentiary weight to be given to the certificate of registration made after the end of that one-year period is within the discretion of the court. 17 U.S.C. § 304(a)(4)(B).

Finally, under § 101 as revised, a renewal registration constitutes a registration for purposes of § 412, permitting the election of statutory damages and potentially an award of attorney's fees — a significant benefit for works that gained copyright by publication with notice but without a timely first-term registration.

[D]　Restored Copyrights

Restoration of Certain Foreign Copyrights Pursuant to NAFTA and TRIPS

Article 18 of the Berne Convention invites (if it does not actually require) new signatories to extend retroactive copyright protection to works originating in other Berne countries. Before 1992, however, U.S. representatives negotiating copyright issues with other governments consistently rejected demands for copyright recapture of foreign works in the U.S. public domain, while insisting on retroactivity for U.S. works under the laws of those countries. In 1988, for example, Congress rejected retroactivity in enacting the Berne Convention Implementation

Act. The most commonly given explanation for the avoidance of retroactivity was the desirability of avoiding constitutional conflicts — because recapture might run afoul of the Copyright Clause, the First Amendment, or the Fifth Amendment's Due Process Clause.

When the issue of retroactivity arose in the context of the negotiations over the North American Free Trade Agreement ("NAFTA"), 31 I.L.M. 997 (1992), however, the United States took a more flexible line. The final provisions of that agreement included an annex which stated that "[t]he United States shall provide protection to motion pictures produced in another Party's territory that have been declared to be in the public domain pursuant to 17 U.S.C. section 405. This obligation shall apply to the extent that it is consistent with the Constitution of the United States. . . ."

The NAFTA implementation legislation, which, like the treaty, went into effect on January 1, 1994, added a new § 104A to the Copyright Act. Section 104A, as enacted, provided for the recapture of copyright in motion pictures first fixed or published in a NAFTA country, and which entered the public domain in the United States between January 1, 1978 and March 1, 1989 because of an otherwise unexcused failure to comply with the then-applicable notice provisions of U.S. law.

Not long afterwards, however, § 104A was substantially amended (and broadened) by the Uruguay Round Agreements Act of 1994 ("URAA"), implementing the World Trade Organization Agreement that had been concluded earlier in the year, including the TRIPS Agreement on intellectual property rights. Congress later resolved some of the ambiguities of the 1994 legislation in the Copyright Clarifications Act of 1997. In addition, the Copyright Office issued useful regulations concerning the administrative details of restoration, which can be found at 37 C.F.R. § 201.33. The "highlights" of restoration mechanics are summarized for you below.

As you read what follows, you may want to ask yourself: Is this constitutional? How would one go about analyzing the constitutionality of legislation which has the effect of restoring copyright protection to works formerly in the public domain? The Supreme Court ultimately addressed the issue in *Golan v. Holder*, 132 S. Ct. 873 (2012), which concludes this section.

What Works Are Subject to Copyright Restoration?

The first, and most important, point is that restoration is automatic for qualifying works. Thus, there is simply no way of knowing how many works are subject to the URAA provisions. Presumably, however, the total number is immense, even though only a relatively small number of them are valuable enough to be the subjects of negotiation or litigation in the future.

In order to qualify, it is a necessary (although not a sufficient) condition that a work must have at least one author who is a national or domiciliary of a nation (other than the United States, of course!) which is a member of the WTO, or which adheres to the Berne Convention, the WIPO Copyright Treaty, or the WIPO Performances and Phonograms Treaty, or one named in a special proclamation (provided for in 17 U.S.C. § 104A(g)). In other words, countries with which the

United States has international copyright relations currently are "eligible," and any other country could be covered in the future.

A further requirement is that, to qualify, a work must be one that was in the public domain in the United States for one of several specified reasons, including noncompliance with formalities (such as notice, renewal, and the manufacturing requirement of former 17 U.S.C. § 601) or lack of national eligibility. Thus, the restoration scheme does not apply, for example, to works in which copyright has been abandoned or otherwise forfeited.

A special provision makes restoration available to foreign sound recordings dating from before February 15, 1972 (when protection was first extended to such works under U.S. law). By contrast, it appears that pre-1990 architectural works (for which protection was barred under the "useful articles" doctrine) do not qualify.

Works that would otherwise qualify may fail to do so on various specific grounds: because, if published, they were not first published in an eligible country, or were published in the United States within 30 days of their publication in such a country; because the term of their copyright protection has expired in their "source countries" (another term of art, defined in § 104A(h)(8) — essentially a localized version of the general international copyright concept of "country of origin"); or, for certain works, because the copyrights, if restored, would belong to the governments of the United States' World War II adversaries (§ 104A(a)(2)).

When Is Restoration Effective and How Long Do Restored Rights Last?

After providing the fodder for considerable debate and confusion, *see, e.g.*, *Cordon Art B.V. v. Walker*, 40 U.S.P.Q.2d (BNA) 1506 (S.D. Cal. 1996) (concluding that M.C. Escher engravings qualified as "restored works"), *order amended*, 41 U.S.P.Q.2d (BNA) 1224 (S.D. Cal. 1996) (correcting effective date of copyright restoration), this issue was statutorily resolved by the 1997 Copyright Clarifications Act. The effective date of the URAA restoration provisions is January 1, 1996. On that date, all qualifying works became protected under U.S. law. Of course, as additional works qualify in the future (because, for example, their source countries join the Berne Union or the World Trade Organization for the first time), they will be protected as well.

Whenever copyright in a given work is restored, however, protection lasts as long — and only as long — as U.S. law relating to copyright duration otherwise provides. Here, complete parity exists between the treatment of restored foreign works and that of protected domestic works.

Although Congress made sound recordings fixed before February 15, 1972 and first published in a foreign country eligible for copyright restoration, it neglected to amend § 301(c) to preempt state law for such foreign sound recordings. Hence, sound recordings first published in a foreign country may well be subject to state law protection as well — and that protection may not expire when the restored copyright does. *See Capitol Records, Inc., v. Naxos of America, Inc.*, 830 N.E.2d 250 (N.Y. 2005) (holding pre-1972 sound recordings are protected under state law even after they have entered the public domain in their country of origin).

Who Owns the Restored Copyright?

Here, the URAA provisions refer U.S. courts to foreign law. In general, under § 104A(b), ownership of a restored work vests initially in the "author"; where sound recordings are concerned, they may belong, alternatively, to the "rightholder." (The latter term, defined in § 104(h)(7), is included because, in some countries, a "sound recording" does not have an "author.") The identity of this initial owner is to be "determined by the law of the source country of the work." *See Alameda Films S.A. de C.V. v. Authors Rights Restoration Corp.*, 331 F.3d 472 (5th Cir. 2003) (under Mexican law, film production companies were "authors" of movies entitled to restored U.S. copyrights); *La Parade v. Ivanova*, 387 F.3d 1099 (9th Cir. 2004) (same). The initial owner may, of course, transfer the restored copyright by contract (although there remains the interesting question — to which § 104A does not speak — about the source of the law to be applied when an issue concerning a transfer of rights in a restored foreign work arises in a U.S. court). But may a restored U.S. copyright vest *initially* in an assignee who owns the foreign copyright? One District Court has concluded (somewhat dubiously) that the answer is "yes." *See Peliculas y Videos Internacionales, S.A. de C.V. v. Harriscope of Los Angeles, Inc.*, 302 F. Supp. 2d 1131 (C.D. Cal. 2004).

To What Special Limitations Are Rights in Restored Works Subject?

In general, the answer is: none. The owner of copyright in a restored work can proceed in all respects like any other copyright owner and is entitled to all the same remedies (and is subject to all the same restrictions) in cases of copyright infringement. *See, e.g., Cordon Holding, C.B. v. Northwest Publ. Corp.*, 2005 U.S. Dist. LEXIS 3860 (S.D.N.Y. 2005) (statutory damages for restored copyrights may be recovered only if the copyright was timely registered under § 412). There is an important exception, however, for so-called "reliance parties" (and their successors in interest). This term, defined in § 104A(h)(4), refers to those who own copies of restored works, or are engaged in exploiting those works, "before the source country of that work becomes an eligible country." *See Cordon Holding, B.V. v. Northwest Publ. Corp.*, 63 U.S.P.Q.2d (BNA) 1013 (S.D.N.Y. 2002) ("where the source country is an 'eligible country' before the date of the enactment of the statute [December 8, 1994], the allegedly infringing acts must have begun prior to that date"); *Troll Co. v. Uneeda Doll Co.*, 483 F.3d 150 (2d Cir. 2007) (holding defendant was not a reliance party where it had ceased production before restoration and reentered the market after restoration).

Among the objections raised to the retroactive extension of copyright protection was the concern that restoration would disadvantage those who, in good faith, had made investments premised on the public domain status of various works. The URAA seeks to address this objection by giving "reliance parties" a qualified immunity from liability. They can continue to exploit a restored work after copyright restoration, unless the copyright owner:

• Files a general notice of intention to enforce its rights with the Copyright Office within two years of the date of restoration, or

• Serves on a particular reliance party at any time a specific notice of intention to enforce its rights.

See, e.g., Hoepker v. Kruger, 200 F. Supp. 2d 340, 347 (S.D.N.Y. 2002) (granting motion to dismiss where plaintiff failed to file or serve the requisite notice). If appropriate notice has been given, the reliance party can exploit the work for a further year without liability, to the extent that it can do so without further reproduction of copies. In practice, this means that the reliance party would have a year in which to sell off its existing inventory.

The rules are still more complicated for one class of "reliance parties" — those who, prior to the date of enactment of the URAA, used a then-public domain work as the basis for a new "derivative work" containing additional copyrightable content. In an effort to preserve the value of adaptations made in good faith, the URAA provides that, if the reliance party pays the restored copyright owner "reasonable" compensation, it "may continue to exploit that derivative work for the duration of the restored copyright." § 104A(d)(3)(A). If the parties are unable to agree, § 104A(d)(3)(B) provides a mechanism for judicial determination of what constitutes reasonable compensation, based on "harm to the actual or potential market for or value of the restored work . . . as well as . . . the relative contributions of expression of the author of the restored work and the reliance party to the derivative work."

How should courts make the value-laden assessments called for in the just-recited formula? What types of "continued exploitation" should be permitted? *See Hoepker*, 200 F. Supp. 2d at 347 (exploitation "at the very least must include" the right to display and reproduce the derivative work, and arguably "might also include the right to create new derivative works from the existing derivative work" such as museum gift merchandise). And how substantial a change must the "reliance party" have made in order to qualify for the special treatment accorded derivative works? Presumably, the standard is the same one applied in determining the copyrightability of derivative works in general. In *Dam Things from Denmark v. Russ Berrie & Co.*, 290 F.3d 548 (3rd Cir. 2002), involving novelty "troll" figures (described by the court as "short, pudgy, plastic dolls with big grins and wild hair"), the Court of Appeals vacated a preliminary injunction and remanded with instructions to reconsider "whether the infringing works are derivatives of the restored work." *Id.* at 563. In particular, it directed the trial court to focus on the subtle but important difference between the "substantial similarity" standard for infringement and the "minimal creativity" standard for assessing whether a revision qualifies as a derivative work. "The fact that the two companies' dolls have the 'same aesthetic appeal' or 'are very similar in appearance' does not rule out the applicability of the safe harbor for derivative works." *Id.* at 565.

Is Copyright Restoration Unconstitutional?

What are the implications of the Supreme Court's opinion in *Eldred v. Ashcroft* (in § 5.01[B] above) for copyright restoration? If "justice, policy, and equity" permit Congress to extend existing terms, and if "longer terms would encourage copyright holders to invest in the restoration and public distribution of their works," would not the same considerations permit Congress to revive expired copyrights? Moreover, many of the cases upholding individual patents cited in *Eldred* involved revival of expired patents, not just extensions of existing ones. On the other hand, Congress has not revived expired copyrights each time the copyright term was lengthened. In fact, Congress consistently has avoided doing so, except in exigent circumstances (such as allowing retroactive compliance with formalities in wartime).

In *Golan v. Gonzales*, 501 F.3d 1179 (10th Cir. 2007), the court held that copyright restoration did *not* violate the Copyright Clause, because Congress had a "rational basis" for the legislation — namely, to bring the U.S. into compliance with Article 18 of the Berne Convention. With respect to the First Amendment, however, the Tenth Circuit held that copyright restoration "altered the traditional contours of copyright protection," because it "contravened a bedrock principle of copyright law that works in the public domain remain in the public domain." *Id.* at 1192. Accordingly, the Tenth Circuit remanded the case with instructions to address the merits of the First Amendment challenge.

On remand, the District Court held that § 104A burdened substantially more speech than was necessary to comply with Article 18, because Congress could have enacted a permanent exception for reliance parties. *Golan v. Holder*, 611 F. Supp. 2d 1165, 1172–75 (D. Colo. 2009). On appeal, however, the Tenth Circuit held that "the government has demonstrated a substantial interest in protecting American copyright holders' interests abroad, and [restoration] is narrowly tailored to advance that interest." *Golan v. Holder*, 609 F.3d 1076, 1083 (10th Cir. 2010). The Supreme Court granted *certiorari* to resolve the question of whether the Copyright Clause or the First Amendment prohibits the removal of works from the public domain. Its opinion follows.

GOLAN v. HOLDER
Supreme Court of the United States
132 S. Ct. 873 (2012)

JUSTICE GINSBURG delivered the opinion of the Court.

The Berne Convention for the Protection of Literary and Artistic Works (Berne Convention or Berne), which took effect in 1886, is the principal accord governing international copyright relations. Latecomer to the international copyright regime launched by Berne, the United States joined the Convention in 1989. To perfect U.S. implementation of Berne, and as part of our response to the Uruguay Round of multilateral trade negotiations, Congress, in 1994, gave works enjoying copyright protection abroad the same full term of protection available to U.S. works. Congress did so in § 514 of the Uruguay Round Agreements Act (URAA), which grants copyright protection to preexisting works of Berne member countries, protected in their country of origin, but lacking protection in the United States for any of three reasons: The United States did not protect works from the country of origin at the time of publication; the United States did not protect sound recordings fixed before 1972; or the author had failed to comply with U.S. statutory formalities (formalities Congress no longer requires as prerequisites to copyright protection). . . .

Petitioners include orchestra conductors, musicians, publishers, and others who formerly enjoyed free access to works § 514 removed from the public domain. They maintain that the Constitution's Copyright and Patent Clause, Art. I, § 8, cl. 8, and

First Amendment both decree the invalidity of § 514. Under those prescriptions of our highest law, petitioners assert, a work that has entered the public domain, for whatever reason, must forever remain there.

Petitioner Lawrence Golan
Photograph by Greg Rizzo

In accord with the judgment of the Tenth Circuit, we conclude that § 514 does not transgress constitutional limitations on Congress' authority. Neither the Copyright and Patent Clause nor the First Amendment, we hold, makes the public domain, in any and all cases, a territory that works may never exit. . . .

II.

A.

The text of the Copyright Clause does not exclude application of copyright protection to works in the public domain. Petitioners' contrary argument relies primarily on the Constitution's confinement of a copyright's lifespan to a "limited Tim[e]." "Removing works from the public domain," they contend, "violates the 'limited [t]imes' restriction by turning a fixed and predictable period into one that can be reset or resurrected at any time, even after it expires." . . .

Our decision in *Eldred* is largely dispositive of petitioners' limited-time argument. . . . The terms afforded works restored by § 514 are no less "limited" than those the CTEA lengthened. . . .

The difference, petitioners say, is that the limited time had already passed for works in the public domain. What was that limited term for foreign works once excluded from U. S. copyright protection? Exactly "zero," petitioners respond. . . . We find scant sense in this argument, for surely a "limited time" of exclusivity must begin before it may end.

Carried to its logical conclusion, petitioners persist, the Government's position would allow Congress to institute a second "limited" term after the first expires, a third after that, and so on. Thus, as long as Congress legislated in installments, perpetual copyright terms would be achievable. As in *Eldred*, the hypothetical legislative misbehavior petitioners posit is far afield from the case before us. In aligning the United States with other nations bound by the Berne Convention, and thereby according equitable treatment to once disfavored foreign authors, Congress can hardly be charged with a design to move stealthily toward a regime of perpetual copyrights.

B.

Historical practice corroborates our reading of the Copyright Clause to permit full U.S. compliance with Berne. Undoubtedly, federal copyright legislation generally has not affected works in the public domain. . . .

On occasion, however, Congress has seen fit to protect works once freely available. Notably, the Copyright Act of 1790 granted protection to many works previously in the public domain. Act of May 31, 1790, § 1, 1 Stat. 124 (covering "any map, chart, book, or books already printed within these United States"). . . . The First Congress, it thus appears, did not view the public domain as inviolate. As we have recognized, the "construction placed upon the Constitution by [the drafters of] the first [copyright] act of 1790 and the act of 1802 . . . men who were contemporary with [the Constitution's] formation, many of whom were members of the convention which framed it, is of itself entitled to very great weight." *Burrow-Giles Lithographic Co. v. Sarony*, 111 U.S. 53, 57 (1884).

Subsequent actions confirm that Congress has not understood the Copyright Clause to preclude protection for existing works. Several private bills restored the copyrights of works that previously had been in the public domain. . . . These bills were unchallenged in court. . . . Analogous patent statutes, however, were upheld in litigation. . . .

Congress has also passed generally applicable legislation granting patents and copyrights to inventions and works that had lost protection. An 1832 statute authorized a new patent for any inventor whose failure, "by inadvertence, accident, or mistake," to comply with statutory formalities rendered the original patent "invalid or inoperative." Act of July 3, § 3, 4 Stat. 559. An 1893 measure similarly allowed authors who had not timely deposited their work to receive "all the rights and privileges" the Copyright Act affords, if they made the required deposit by March 1, 1893. Act of Mar. 3, ch. 215, 27 Stat. 743. And in 1919 and 1941, Congress authorized the President to issue proclamations granting protection to foreign works that had fallen into the public domain during World Wars I and II. See Act of Dec. 18, 1919, ch. 11, 41 Stat. 368; Act of Sept. 25, 1941, ch. 421, 55 Stat. 732. . . .

Installing a federal copyright system and ameliorating the interruptions of global war, it is true, presented Congress with extraordinary situations. Yet the TRIPS accord, leading the United States to comply in full measure with Berne, was also a signal event. Given the authority we hold Congress has, we will not second-guess the political choice Congress made between leaving the public domain untouched and embracing Berne unstintingly.

C.

Petitioners' ultimate argument as to the Copyright and Patent Clause concerns its initial words. Congress is empowered to "promote the Progress of Science and useful Arts" by enacting systems of copyright and patent protection. U.S. Const., Art. I, § 8, cl. 8. Perhaps counter-intuitively for the contemporary reader, Congress' copyright authority is tied to the progress of science; its patent authority, to the progress of the useful arts.

The "Progress of Science," petitioners acknowledge, refers broadly to "the creation and spread of knowledge and learning." They nevertheless argue that federal legislation cannot serve the Clause's aim unless the legislation "spur[s] the creation of . . . new works." Because § 514 deals solely with works already created, petitioners urge, it provides no plausible incentive to create new works and is therefore invalid.

The creation of at least one new work, however, is not the sole way Congress may promote knowledge and learning. In *Eldred*, . . . we held that the Copyright Clause does not demand that each copyright provision, examined discretely, operate to induce new works. Rather, we explained, the Clause "empowers Congress to determine the intellectual property regimes that, overall, in that body's judgment, will serve the ends of the Clause." [537 U.S.,] at 222. And those permissible ends, we held, extended beyond the creation of new works. . . .

Even were we writing on a clean slate, petitioners' argument would be unavailing. Nothing in the text of the Copyright Clause confines the "Progress of Science" exclusively to "incentives for creation." *Id.*, at 324 n.5. Evidence from the founding, moreover, suggests that inducing *dissemination* — as opposed to creation — was viewed as an appropriate means to promote science. . . .

Considered against this backdrop, § 514 falls comfortably within Congress' authority under the Copyright Clause. Congress rationally could have concluded that adherence to Berne "promotes the diffusion of knowledge." A well-functioning international copyright system would likely encourage the dissemination of existing and future works. Full compliance with Berne, Congress had reason to believe, would expand the foreign markets available to U.S. authors and invigorate protection against piracy of U.S. works abroad. . . .

The provision of incentives for the creation of new works is surely an essential means to advance the spread of knowledge and learning. We hold, however, that it is not the sole means Congress may use "[t]o promote the Progress of Science." Congress determined that exemplary adherence to Berne would serve the objectives of the Copyright Clause. We have no warrant to reject the rational judgment Congress made.

III.

A.

We next explain why the First Amendment does not inhibit the restoration authorized by § 514. To do so, we first recapitulate the relevant part of our pathmarking decision in *Eldred*. . . .

Given the "speech-protective purposes and safeguards" embraced by copyright law, we concluded in *Eldred* that there was no call for the heightened review petitioners sought in that case. We reach the same conclusion here. Section 514 leaves undisturbed the "idea/expression" distinction and the "fair use" defense. Moreover, Congress adopted measures to ease the transition from a national scheme to an international copyright regime: It deferred the date from which enforcement runs, and it cushioned the impact of restoration on "reliance parties" who exploited foreign works denied protection before § 514 took effect.

B.

Petitioners attempt to distinguish their challenge from the one turned away in *Eldred*. First Amendment interests of a higher order are at stake here, petitioners say, because they — unlike their counterparts in *Eldred* — enjoyed "vested rights" in works that had already entered the public domain. The limited rights they retain under copyright law's "built-in safeguards" are, in their view, no substitute for the unlimited use they enjoyed before § 514's enactment. . . .

To copyright lawyers, the "vested rights" formulation might sound exactly backwards: Rights typically vest at the *outset* of copyright protection, in an author or rightholder. Once the term of protection ends, the works do not revest in any rightholder. Instead, the works simply lapse into the public domain. Anyone has free access to the public domain, but no one, after the copyright term has expired, acquires ownership rights in the once-protected works. . . .

. . . Petitioners protest that fair use and the idea/expression dichotomy are "plainly inadequate to protect the speech and expression rights that Section 514 took from petitioners, or . . . the public" - that is, the "unrestricted right to perform, copy, teach and distribute the *entire* work, for any reason." "Playing a few bars of a Shostakovich symphony," petitioners observe, "is no substitute for performing the entire work."

But Congress has not put petitioners in this bind. The question here, as in *Eldred*, is whether would-be users must pay for their desired use of the author's expression, or else limit their exploitation to "fair use" of that work. Prokofiev's *Peter and the Wolf* could once be performed free of charge; after § 514 the right to perform it must be obtained in the marketplace. This is the same marketplace, of course, that exists for the music of Prokofiev's U.S. contemporaries: works of Copland and Bernstein, for example that enjoy copyright protection, but nevertheless appear regularly in the programs of U.S. concertgoers. . . .

IV.

Congress determined that U.S. interests were best served by our full participation in the dominant system of international copyright protection. Those interests include ensuring exemplary compliance with our international obligations, securing greater protection for U.S. authors abroad, and remedying unequal treatment of foreign authors. The judgment § 514 expresses lies well within the ken of the political branches. It is our obligation, of course, to determine whether the action Congress took, wise or not, encounters any constitutional shoal. For the reasons stated, we are satisfied it does not. The judgment of the Court of Appeals for the Tenth Circuit is therefore *Affirmed.*

JUSTICE KAGAN took no part in the consideration or decision of this case.

JUSTICE BREYER, with whom JUSTICE ALITO joins, dissenting.

In order "to promote the Progress of Science" (by which term the Founders meant "learning" or "knowledge"), the Constitution's Copyright Clause grants Congress the power to "secur[e] for limited Times to Authors . . . the exclusive Right to their . . . Writings." Art. I, § 8, cl. 8. This "exclusive Right" allows its holder to charge a fee to those who wish to use a copyrighted work, and the ability to charge that fee encourages the production of new material. In this sense, a copyright is, in Macaulay's words, a "tax on readers for the purpose of giving a bounty to writers" — a bounty designed to encourage new production. . . .

The statute before us, however, does not encourage anyone to produce a single new work. By definition, it bestows monetary rewards only on owners of old works — works that have already been created and already are in the American public domain. At the same time, the statute inhibits the dissemination of those works, foreign works published abroad after 1923, of which there are many millions, including films, works of art, innumerable photographs, and, of course, books — books that (in the absence of the statute) would assume their rightful places in computer-accessible databases, spreading knowledge throughout the world. . . . In my view, the Copyright Clause does not authorize Congress to enact this statute. And I consequently dissent. . . .

II.

. . . The Act mainly applies to works first published abroad between 1923 and 1989. . . .

A.

The provision before us takes works from the public domain, at least as of January 1, 1996. It then restricts the dissemination of those works in two ways.

First, "restored copyright" holders can now charge fees for works that consumers previously used for free. . . . [A]s the Court recognizes, an orchestra that once could perform "*Peter and the Wolf* . . . free of charge" will now have to buy the "right to perform it . . . in the marketplace." But for the case of certain "derivative" works, the "restored copyright" holder, like other copyright holders, can charge what the market will bear. If a school orchestra or other nonprofit organization cannot afford the new charges, so be it. They will have to do without — aggravating the already serious problem of cultural education in the United States. . . .

Second, and at least as important, the statute creates administrative costs, such as the costs of determining whether a work is the subject of a "restored copyright," searching for a "restored copyright" holder, and negotiating a fee. Congress has tried to ease the administrative burden of contacting copyright holders and negotiating prices for those whom the statute calls "reliance parties," namely those who previously had used such works when they were freely available in the public domain. § 104A(h)(4). But Congress has done nothing to ease the administrative burden of securing permission from copyright owners that is placed upon those who want to use a work that they did not previously use, and this is a particular problem when it comes to "orphan works" — older and more obscure works with minimal commercial value that have copyright owners who are difficult or impossible to track down. . . .

B.

. . . Worst of all, "restored copyright" protection removes material from the public domain. In doing so, it reverses the payment expectations of those who used, or intended to use, works that they thought belonged to them. Were Congress to act similarly with respect to well-established property rights, the problem would be obvious. This statute analogously restricts, and thereby diminishes, Americans' preexisting freedom to use formerly public domain material in their expressive activities. . . .

. . . By removing material from the public domain, the statute, in literal terms, "abridges" a preexisting freedom to speak. In practical terms, members of the public might well have decided what to say, as well as when and how to say it, in part by reviewing with a view to repeating, expression that they reasonably believed was, or would be, freely available. Given these speech implications, it is not surprising that Congress has long sought to protect public domain material when revising the copyright laws. . . .

Moreover, whereas forward-looking copyright laws tend to benefit those whose identities are not yet known (the writer who has not yet written a book, the musician who has not yet composed a song), when a copyright law is primarily backward looking the risk is greater that Congress is trying to help known beneficiaries at the expense of badly organized unknown users who find it difficult to argue and present their case to Congress. . . .

Taken together, these speech-related harms . . . at least show the presence of a First Amendment interest . . . [that] is important enough to require courts to scrutinize with some care the reasons claimed to justify the Act in order to determine whether they constitute reasonable copyright-related justifications for the serious harms, including speech-related harms, which the Act seems likely to impose.

C.

1.

This statute does not serve copyright's traditional public ends, namely the creation of monetary awards that "motivate the creative activity of authors," *Sony*, 464 U.S., at 429, "encourag[e] individual effort," *Mazer*, 347 U.S., at 219, and thereby "serve the cause of promoting broad public availability of literature, music, and the other arts," *Twentieth Century Music*, 422 U.S., at 156. The statute grants its "restored copyright[s]" *only* to works *already produced*. It provides no monetary incentive to produce anything new. Unlike other American copyright statutes from the time of the Founders onwards, including the statute at issue in *Eldred*, it lacks any significant copyright-related *quid pro quo*.

The majority seeks to avoid this awkward fact by referring to past congressional practice that mostly suggests that Congress may provide new or increased protection *both* to newly created *and* to previously created works. . . . [But the] statutes to which the majority refers are private bills, statutes retroactively granting protection in wartime, or the like. . . . In fact, Congressional practice shows the contrary. It consists of a virtually unbroken string of legislation preventing the withdrawal of works from the public domain. . . .

2.

The majority . . . argues that the Clause does not require the "creation of at least one new work," but may instead "promote the Progress of Science" in other ways. And it specifically mentions the "dissemination of existing and future works" as determinative here. . . . But ordinarily a copyright — since it is a *monopoly* on copying — *restricts* dissemination of a work once produced compared to a competitive market. And simply making the industry richer does not mean that the industry, when it makes an ordinary forward-looking economic calculus, will distribute works not previously distributed. . . .

. . . [T]he majority [also] argues that this statutory provision is necessary to fulfill our Berne Convention obligations.

. . . I cannot find this argument sufficient to save the statute. For one thing, this is a dilemma of the Government's own making. The United States obtained the benefits of Berne for many years despite its failure to enact a statute implementing Article 18. But in 1994, [when] the United States and other nations signed the Agreement on Trade-Related Aspects of Intellectual Property Rights, . . . the Government, although it successfully secured reservations protecting other special features of American copyright law, made no effort to secure a reservation permitting the United States to keep some or all restored works in the American public domain. And it made no effort to do so despite the fact that Article 18 explicitly authorizes countries to negotiate exceptions to the Article's retroactivity principle. . . .

. . . Article 18(3) also states that "the respective countries shall determine, each in so far as it is concerned, *the conditions of application of this principle.*" Congress could have alleviated many of the costs that the statute imposes by, for example, creating forms of compulsory licensing, requiring "restored copyright" holders to provide necessary administrative information as a condition of protection, or insisting upon "reasonable royalties." . . .

III.

The fact that, by withdrawing material from the public domain, the statute inhibits an important preexisting flow of information is sufficient, when combined with the other features of the statute that I have discussed, to convince me that the Copyright Clause, interpreted in the light of the First Amendment, does not authorize Congress to enact this statute.

I respectfully dissent from the Court's contrary conclusion.

NOTES AND QUESTIONS

(1) *Son of* Eldred*?* In reading *Golan,* one gets the feeling, as the philosopher Yogi Berra said, of "déjà vu all over again." Justice Ginsberg, who wrote the *Eldred* opinion, used much the same reasoning in upholding copyright restoration under § 104A. As in *Eldred,* the Court deferred to the "wisdom" of Congress to draft a copyright law to comport with the multifaceted goal of the Constitutional Clause — to promote the progress of science and useful arts. The majority holds that the Clause not only provides incentives to create new works, but that it also aims to encourage the dissemination of works already created. *See* Malla Pollack, *What is Congress Supposed to Promote? Defining "Progress" in Article I, Section 8, Clause 8 of the U.S. Constitution, or Introducing the Progress Clause,* 80 Neb. L. Rev. 754 (2002). Moreover, membership in Berne facilitates the dissemination of U.S works in some 165 countries. The petitioners' First Amendment arguments received the *Eldred* treatment as well. The Court held that the "traditional contours of copyright protection" referred to in *Eldred* are limited to the idea/expression dichotomy and the fair use doctrine. Accordingly, as in Eldred, the court concluded that there was no necessity of heightened review under the First Amendment.

(2) *What promotes dissemination?* In his dissent, Justice Breyer acknowledges that the Copyright Clause is not limited to the incentive to create new works, but also aims to promote the dissemination of existing works. Nonetheless, he questions whether copyright restoration will encourage dissemination of existing works. One might come up with examples of little-known or forgotten public domain works that, once restored, will be effectively promoted and propagated through the efforts of their copyright owners. On the other hand, it seems unlikely that, on balance, copyright protection will encourage dissemination of the overwhelming number of restored works, given the administrative and transactional costs of clearing rights to them. Perhaps understandably, the majority did not wish to engage in speculation involving essentially empirical questions, but rather deferred to Congress in its fact-finding and policy-making role.

(3) *Historical precedent.* The Court emphasizes the fact that Congress has previously provided protection to existing works in several ways. First, the 1790 Copyright Act protected "previously published" works as well as new ones. (There

is evidence, however, that only a handful of previously published works were registered and protected under this Act.) Second, Congress occasionally gave special protection to specific copyrighted works and patented inventions. Third, Congress allowed works that had entered the public domain during World Wars I and II additional time to comply with the necessary formalities after the wars ended. Fourth, although Congress has added new subject matter only prospectively, it has sometimes expanded the scope of copyright (for example, in adding a public performance right) for existing works. But are any of these actions equivalent to restoring copyright to untold millions of works once in the public domain? The dissent thinks not. What's your opinion?

(4) *Term extension versus restoration.* Even though the majority in *Golan* treats both term extension and restoration as functionally similar for the purposes of the Constitution, the two concepts do have significant differences. Both term extension and restoration provide added protection to works already created that would have or have already entered the public domain. Unlike term extension, however, restoration of copyright not only plays havoc with users' expectations regarding the public domain, but it also complicates the economic lives of those who built their businesses around works that were once in the public domain. Do you think the provisions for "reliance parties" in § 104A are adequate to address the Due Process rights of those involved? Should the Court have addressed the differences between extension and restoration in a more systematic way?

(5) *Orphan works revisited.* Whatever one thinks about the constitutionality of restoration, it does impose costs in accessing copyrighted works. In particular, restoration compounds the orphan works problem, especially in the case of restored foreign works whose authors (or heirs) are unknown or whom cannot be located. Do you agree that restoration highlights the need for the orphan works initiative that has been stalled in Congress?

(6) *What does Berne Article 18 really require?* The majority makes U.S. obligations under Berne to restore copyright to certain foreign works a centerpiece of its argument in favor of restoration. The dissent, however, suggests the United States could have complied with Berne by less drastic means, for example, by establishing a compulsory licensing system or by negotiating an exception in the TRIPS Agreement (as we did with Article 6bis on moral rights). Can you envisage a better solution to the restoration dilemma brought about by our Berne obligation and the needs of user groups? These questions are examined in Gervais, Golan v. Holder: *A Look at the Constraints Imposed by the Berne Convention*, 64 Vand. L. Rev. En Banc 147 (2011).

(7) *What next?* Justice Ginsburg asserts that restoration "accord[ed] equitable treatment to once disfavored foreign authors." In fact, however, restoration treats foreign authors *more* favorably than domestic authors, in that it removes barriers to copyright protection once imposed by U.S. formalities, such as notice and renewal. One can imagine that domestic authors may soon lobby Congress to give them "equitable treatment" by restoring domestic copyrights as well. It has been estimated that up to 85% of works published between 1923 and 1963 were not renewed. Should Congress remove these works from the public domain? If they do, is there any reason to believe that the Court would not uphold that action as well?

What if Congress attempted to restore the copyrights of older works, those published before 1923? Many such works enjoyed the maximum period of copyright protection permitted at the time, but some never received any protection because of formalities. Would the Court permit Congress to restore copyrights to works by (say) Mark Twain? Does Justice Ginsburg's reference to "hypothetical legislative misbehavior" cover this situation?

§ 5.02 TERMINATIONS OF TRANSFERS

The preceding section of this casebook explored issues concerning the duration of copyright. You know from Chapter 4 that authors may, and very often do, transfer rights to others during the terms of their copyrights. When, subsequent to such a transfer, the work achieves a large commercial success, the author not infrequently feels undercompensated for the rights transferred. True, the disseminator of the work — *i.e.*, the transferee, in the typical case — contributes greatly to the popularity of the work by making it generally available to the public. But without the author, there would have been no work to exploit in the first place. At some point, should the author be entitled to recapture rights in the work and thus benefit more fully from his or her contribution to the public's enjoyment of it?

In enacting the 1909 Act, Congress considered this question and may well have thought that it had answered "yes." If, as the dissenters in *Fisher v. Witmark* believed, the 1909 Act Congress meant "to reserve the renewal privilege for the personal benefit of authors and their families," what Congress expected was that ownership of the copyright in a work would revert to the author at the beginning of the renewal term (assuming compliance with renewal formalities), notwithstanding claims by any transferee that the author had granted away all rights in the work forever by assignment during the first 28 years. The *Fisher* majority, however, read the legislative history of the 1909 Act differently and, by the Court's holding in that case, precluded authors in the *Fisher* plaintiff's circumstances from recovering exploitation rights in their creations.

The Congress that enacted the Copyright Act of 1976 took no chances in making plain its intent that authors who assign their copyright interests to others should be able, after a reasonable time, to regain those interests — *i.e.*, to "terminate" their transfers. The purpose of the 1976 Act's termination provisions is avowedly paternalistic: to protect authors from unremunerative transfers which may be given because of the author's "unequal bargaining position . . . , resulting in part from the impossibility of determining a work's value until it has been exploited." House Report at 124. However, both the creators and "authors" of "works made for hire" were excluded from this Congressional solicitude.

The 1976 Act's provisions regarding termination of transfers cover two different situations. Section 203 applies to transfers made on or after January 1, 1978 (the effective date of the Act), and permits termination at a specified interval after the date of the grant. In § 203, Congress was writing on a "clean slate," unencumbered by the rule in *Fisher v. Witmark*. (Note that a work *created* before January 1, 1978 might still be subject to § 203 termination: it is the date of the *transfer* that governs.) Section 304(c), which attempts to deal with the legacy of *Fisher*, applies to works that were in their first or renewal term on January 1, 1978, and allows the author or her surviving family to terminate transfers *made before that date,* so as to recover the 39-year "bonus" period (the 19 years added by the 1976 Act, plus the 20 years added by the CTEA in 1998) to the 1909 Act's 28-year renewal term. In addition, the CTEA added § 304(d), which in certain limited circumstances allows the author to recapture the 20-year period added by the CTEA.

Sections 203 and 304(c) and (d) give the author and her family a *right* to terminate if they wish, but require compliance with procedures established by statute and regulation in order to *effect* the termination. In other words, termination is not automatic: If the author or her family fails to take the necessary steps within the statutory time period, the transfer continues in accordance with the terms of the grant itself.

In either case, the right to terminate cannot be assigned in advance. Thus, the termination provisions of the present statute avoid recreating, in a new context, the problem created by *Fisher v. Witmark. Fisher* remains relevant in construing the effect of assignment of the renewal term for copyrights that arose prior to the effective date of the 1976 Act, but it does not apply to the author's right to terminate the extra 39 years of the extended renewal term nor to the author's right to terminate post-1977 transfers.

The following materials explore, in turn, the termination rights created by §§ 203 and 304(c) and (d).

[A]   Section 203 Terminations: Post-1977 Transfers

Section 203 is intended to provide an author and her family a second chance to reap the benefits of the author's creative accomplishments by furnishing the opportunity to terminate transfers made during the term of copyright. Terminations of transfers under § 203 apply to grants made *after 1977.* Another way to state the same important point is this: *when the copyright came into existence* is irrelevant for determining whether § 203 applies. All that matters is *the date of the transfer.* If the transfer itself occurred on or after January 1, 1978, the effective date of the 1976 Act, § 203 governs. If the work was created before January 1, 1978 *and* the transfer was made before that date, § 304(c) applies.

How important is § 203 for law students today? As we will see below, no termination under § 203 can take effect until 35 years from the date of the grant. Thus, the first terminations under § 203 will take effect in 2013. In addition, notices of termination must be served at least two and not more than 10 years before the effective date of the termination. Thus, notices of termination under § 203 already are being served; and we already have seen the first cases litigating the validity of such notices in the District Courts. As a result, you will need to be prepared to deal with § 203 terminations as soon as you begin the practice of law.

[1]   Introduction

Statutory References
   1976 Act: § 203
   1909 Act: —

Legislative History

H.R. REP. No. 94-1476 at 124-25,
reprinted in 1976 U.S.C.C.A.N. 5659, 5740

SECTION 203. TERMINATION OF TRANSFERS AND LICENSES

The problem in general

The provisions of section 203 are based on the premise that the reversionary provisions of the [1909 Act] section on copyright renewal (17 U.S.C. sec. 24) should be eliminated, and that the proposed law should substitute for them a provision safeguarding authors against unremunerative transfers. A provision of this sort is needed because of the unequal bargaining position of authors, resulting in part from the impossibility of determining a work's value until it has been exploited. Section 203 reflects a practical compromise that will further the objectives of the copyright law while recognizing the problems and legitimate needs of all interests involved.

Scope of the provision

Instead of being automatic, as is theoretically the case [when a renewal was claimed under the 1909 Act], the termination of a transfer or license under section 203 [of the 1976 Act] would require the serving of an advance notice within specified time limits and under specified conditions. However, although affirmative action is needed to effect a termination, the right to take this action cannot be waived in advance or contracted away. Under section 203(a) the right of termination would apply only to transfers and licenses executed after the effective date of the new statute [*i.e.*, January 1, 1978], and would have no retroactive effect.

The right of termination would be confined to *inter vivos* transfers or licenses executed by the author, and would not apply to transfers by the author's successors in interest or to the author's own bequests. The scope of the right would extend not only to any "transfer of copyright ownership," as defined in section 101, but also to non-exclusive licenses. The right of termination would not apply to "works made for hire," which is one of the principal reasons the definition of that term assumed importance in the development of the bill. . . .

[*For a fuller excerpt from H.R. REP No. 94-1476, see Part Three of the Casebook Supplement.*]

[2] Summary of Provisions of § 203

I. Grants Subject to Termination — § 203(a)[1]

Section 203 applies to any transfer or license of any right in any work, as long as (1) the grant is executed on or after January 1, 1978, and (2) the grant is made by

---

[1] An interesting question (in large part, but not wholly, a preemption question) arises with respect to contracts (usually oral, but sometimes written) that leave unspecified what one might have thought would be, to the parties, a key term: the duration of the license. Some states, *e.g.*, California, deem agreements of unspecified duration to be terminable at will. Section 203 provides that, with the exception of grants

the author. (Note that grants made by the author's heirs *cannot* be terminated under § 203.) There are two exceptions: § 203 does not apply to works made for hire or to dispositions made by will.

II. Persons Who May Exercise the Termination Right — § 203(a)(1) and (2)

If the author is still alive when the opportunity to terminate arises, only the author can terminate the grant. A grant made by joint authors may be terminated only "by a majority of the authors who executed it." In the first decision concerning the validity of a § 203 termination, however, the court ruled that "a joint author who separately transfers his copyright interest [*i.e.*, in a separate agreement] may unilaterally terminate that grant" without the consent of the other joint authors. *See Scorpio Music S.A. v. Willis*, 102 U.S.P.Q. 2d (BNA) 1606 (S.D. Cal. 2012) (termination by one member of the Village People of his interest in several musical works, including the anthem "YMCA").

When an author dies, his or her termination interest is owned by the author's surviving spouse and the author's surviving children. The interest is divided *per stirpes*, so that a surviving spouse receives a half interest, and the children divide the other half equally. (Children of any deceased child divide that child's interest equally, but they may exercise that child's interest only by majority action.) In all cases, a majority interest (*i.e.*, "a total of more than one-half of [the] author's termination interest") is needed to exercise the termination right. Thus, a surviving spouse must always participate in order to effect termination, and must be joined, for example, by one surviving child or by a majority of the children of any nonsurviving child.

If the author's widow or widower, children, and grandchildren are not living, the author's executor, administrator, personal representative, or trustee owns the author's entire termination interest.

A graphic representation of the mechanics of these rules, based on one of the hypotheticals in the House Report, may help to make the point more clear. Suppose, for example, that the author's widow and two of his three children are living, and a third child is deceased:

---

involving works made for hire or grants made by will, "the exclusive or nonexclusive grant of a transfer or license of copyright or any right under a copyright, executed by the author on or after January 1, 1978, *is subject to termination* . . ." (emphasis added). Surely, this means that all agreements not excluded from the statutory agreement have a maximum life as contemplated by § 203, provided only that the party with the power to terminate satisfies the statutory requirements for doing so. But does § 203 also prohibit the termination of a copyright license of unspecified duration *before* 35 years from the date the license was granted? In other words, does the statute establish 35 years as a minimum term of the grant? The cases are in conflict. *Compare Walthal v. Rusk*, 172 F.3d 481 (7th Cir. 1999), *and Korman v. HBC Florida, Inc.*, 182 F.3d 1291 (11th Cir. 1999) (holding that § 203 does not create a minimum term of 35 years for licenses of indefinite duration and state contract law governs), *with Rano v. Sipa Press, Inc.*, 987 F.2d 580 (9th Cir. 1993) (holding that § 203 *does* create such a term and California state contract law was preempted).

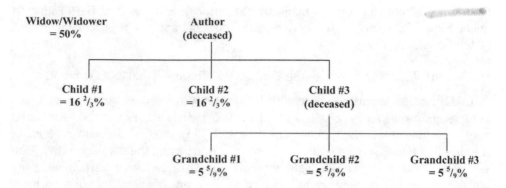

Graphic Representation of § 203 Provisions

In this example, the widow takes 50% and the children, as a class, take 50%. The share of each child is 16-2/3%, *i.e.*, one-third of 50%. Child 3, however, has died, leaving three children who are grandchildren of the deceased author. Each of the three grandchildren, therefore, takes 5-5/9%, *i.e.*, one-third of 16-2/3%. Because a majority interest is needed to terminate a grant, the widow must be joined by one of the children to terminate. If neither Child 1 nor Child 2 joins, the widow cannot exercise the termination right solely by obtaining the consent of one of Child 3's children — even though, in terms of pure addition, the combined ownership of the widow and the grandchild would constitute 55-5/9%. Because the interest of a deceased child can be exercised only by majority action of his or her surviving children, the widow must obtain the consent of at least *two* of the grandchildren in order to terminate the transfer.

III. Time to Exercise the Termination Right — § 203(a)(3)

The termination right may be exercised during a five-year period starting at the end of 35 years from when the grant was executed. There is an exception, however, if the grant covers the right of publication, in which case the five-year period begins at the earlier of 35 years after publication, or 40 years after the grant was made.

IV. Notice of Termination — § 203(a)(4)

The notice of termination must be signed by the persons entitled to terminate the grant, or by their agents. The notice must be served not less than two nor more than 10 years before the proposed date of termination. The notice must be served on the grantee or the grantee's successor(s) in title, at which point interests under the termination vest (even if one or more of the persons entitled to terminate dies before the effective date). The notice must comply with the regulations promulgated by the Copyright Office in 37 C.F.R. § 201.10 as to form, content, and manner of service; and the notice must be recorded in the Copyright Office prior to its effective date.

V. Effect of Other Agreements on Termination — § 203(a)(5)

Termination may be effected notwithstanding any agreement to the contrary, including an agreement to make any future grant or to make a will. (Be sure to distinguish between an *agreement to make a will* and a *grant made by will.*)

VI. Effect of Termination — § 203(b)

On the effective date of termination, the rights previously granted revert to the owners of the termination right in proportionate shares, whether or not they joined in invoking the termination. (Remember that the right need not be exercised unanimously by the owners.) There are two exceptions. First, a derivative work prepared under authority of the grant before its termination may continue to be exploited (although no new derivative works may be made after termination becomes effective). Second, the termination affects only rights arising under the Copyright Act and does not affect any rights under other federal, state, or foreign laws.

Once the right has been recovered, a majority of the owners, in the same number and proportion as under II. above, may make further grants which bind all owners. No new grant, or agreement to make one, may be made until termination becomes effective, except that owners of the termination interest and the original grantee or his/her successor in title may agree to such a new grant after notice of termination is served.

If termination is not effected at the proper time in accordance with the statutory procedures, the grantee retains all rights under the grant for the remainder of the copyright term (unless the grant itself provides otherwise).

[B] Section 304(c) Terminations: Pre-1978 Transfers

As originally enacted (and leaving aside for now the further 20-year extension enacted by Congress in 1998), § 304(a) and (b) of the 1976 Act added 19 years to the second or renewal term of protection for works copyrighted under the 1909 Act. The 1976 extension of the renewal term served many purposes, such as conforming the duration of subsisting 1909 Act copyrights (28 years plus 28 years plus 19 years, or 75 years altogether, prior to the 1998 amendments) to the duration of copyrights secured under the 1976 Act as originally enacted (life of the author plus 50 years, or approximately 75 years on an actuarial basis). In addition, the 19-year extension of the renewal term adopted in 1976 allowed Congress to mitigate, through the enactment of § 304(c), the effects on authors and their heirs of the Supreme Court's decision in *Fisher v. Witmark*. Through § 304(c), Congress created a "second chance" for such persons to benefit from the exploitation of commercially valuable works by permitting them to terminate virtually all grants of renewal term interests and thereby recapture the 19-year extension of the renewal term enacted in 1976. The 20-year extension of that term enacted by Congress in the 1998 amendments to the Act only enhanced this opportunity.

Two further preliminary notes should be added. First, while § 304(c) clearly was prompted by Congress's distaste for the result in *Fisher v. Witmark*, the reach of the provision is not limited to assignments of renewal expectancies. As will appear shortly, § 304(c), like § 203, extends to a variety of other grants, including both exclusive and nonexclusive licenses.

Second, as demonstrated by the example above and by the beginnings of a substantial body of case law concerning § 304(c), a good working knowledge of this provision will be vital well into the 21st Century for any attorney engaged in the practice of copyright law.

[1] Introduction

Statutory References
  1976 Act: § 304(c)
  1909 Act: —

Legislative History

H.R. REP. No. 94-1476 at 140-41,
reprinted in **1976 U.S.C.C.A.N. 5659, 5756-57**

SECTION 304. DURATION OF SUBSISTING COPYRIGHTS . . .

Termination of grants covering extended term

An issue underlying the [now 39]-year extension of renewal terms under both subsections (a) and (b) of section 304 is whether, in a case where their rights have already been transferred, the author or the dependents of the author should be given a chance to benefit from the extended term. . . . [This] term represents a completely new property right, and there are strong reasons for giving the author, who is the fundamental beneficiary of copyright under the Constitution, an opportunity to share in it.

. . . In the case of either a first-term or renewal copyright already subsisting when the new statute becomes effective, any grant of rights covering the renewal copyright in the work, executed before the effective date, may be terminated under conditions and limitations [provided in this subsection]. . . . [T]he 5-year period during which termination could be made effective would start 56 years after copyright was originally secured.

. . . [T]he right of termination under section 304(c) extends [both] to grants executed [by the author and to grants executed] by those beneficiaries of the author who can claim renewal under the [1909 Act]: his or her widow or widower, children, executors, or next of kin.

[The provision to permit termination of grants made by beneficiaries is necessary because,] under the present renewal provisions, any statutory beneficiary of the author can make a valid transfer or license of future renewal rights, which is completely binding if the author is dead and the person who executed the grant turns out to be the proper renewal claimant. Because of this, a great many contingent transfers of future renewal rights have been obtained from widows, widowers, children, and next of kin, and a substantial number of these will be binding. After the present 28-year renewal period has ended, a statutory beneficiary who has signed a disadvantageous grant of this sort should have the opportunity to reclaim the extended term. . . .

[2]   Summary of Provisions of § 304(c)

I. Grants Subject to Termination — § 304(c)

Section 304(c) applies to any transfer or license of the renewal term in a statutory copyright subsisting on the effective date of the 1976 Act, as long as (1) the grant was executed before January 1, 1978, and (2) the grant was made by the author, or by the widow, widower, or children of the author, or his or her executor or next of kin. As with § 203, § 304(c) does not apply to works made for hire or to dispositions made by will.

II. Persons Who May Exercise the Termination Right — § 304(c)(1) and (2)

If the author is still alive when the opportunity to terminate arises, the author can terminate the grant. In the case of grants made by joint authors, each author may terminate separately as to his or her interest in the work. If the grant was made by someone other than the author (*e.g.*, a successor renewal claimant), the grant may be terminated only by unanimous action by the surviving person or persons who executed it.

When an author dies, his or her termination interest is owned by the author's surviving spouse and the author's surviving children. The interest is divided *per stirpes*, so that a surviving spouse receives a half interest, and the children divide the other half equally. (Children of any deceased child divide that child's interest equally, but they may exercise that child's interest only by majority action.) In all cases, a majority interest (*i.e.*, "a total of more than one-half of [the] author's termination interest") is needed to exercise the termination right. Thus, a surviving spouse must always participate in order to effect termination, and must be joined, for example, by one surviving child or by a majority of the children of any nonsurviving child. (Recall the illustration provided in the summary of § 203. It works just as well here.)

If the author's widow or widower, children, and grandchildren are not living, the author's executor, administrator, personal representative, or trustee owns the author's entire termination interest.

III. Time to Exercise the Termination Right — § 304(c)(3) and (d)

The termination right may be exercised during a five-year period beginning at the end of 56 years from the date on which copyright was originally secured. (Works copyrighted in 1921 or earlier had a five-year period beginning on January 1, 1978; but the copyright in all such works has now expired.) Under the conditions specified in § 304(d), if the five-year period expired before the Sonny Bono Copyright Term Extension Act was enacted (October 28, 1998), and the termination right was not previously exercised, a second five-year period begins at the end of 75 years from the date copyright was originally secured. (Note that § 305, which extends the terms of copyrights to December 31 of the year in which they would otherwise expire, does not apply to termination periods.)

IV. Notice of Termination — § 304(c)(4)

The notice of termination must be signed by the persons entitled to terminate the grant, or by their agents. The notice must be served not less than two nor more than 10 years before the proposed date of termination. The notice must be served on the grantee or the grantee's successor(s) in title, at which point interests under the termination vest (even if one or more of the persons entitled to terminate dies before the effective date). The notice must comply with the regulations promulgated by the Copyright Office in 37 C.F.R. § 201.10 as to form, content, and manner of service; and the notice must be recorded in the Copyright Office prior to its effective date.

V. Effect of Other Agreements on Termination — § 304(c)(5)

Termination with respect to the 39-year extension to the duration of existing works which Congress created in the 1976 Act (as amended in 1998) may be effected notwithstanding any agreement to the contrary, including an agreement to make any future grant or to make a will. Do not confuse the ability to terminate the 39-year extension period (years 57–95) with the ability to transfer the second 28-year term (years 29–56). Under *Fisher v. Witmark*, a living author is bound by an advance assignment of the second 28-year term. Such an assignment is not binding on the author's heirs, although such persons may assign away their own interests in the second 28-year term in advance.

VI. Effect of Termination — § 304(c)(6)

On the effective date of termination, the rights previously granted by an author revert to the author, or (if the author is dead), to the owners of the author's termination right in proportionate shares, whether or not they joined in invoking the termination. Grants by persons other than the author likewise revert to all persons entitled to terminate. There are two exceptions. First, a derivative work prepared under authority of the grant before its termination may continue to be exploited (although no new derivative works may be made after termination becomes effective). Second, the termination affects only rights arising under the Copyright Act and does not affect any rights under other federal, state, or foreign laws.

Authors may, of course, re-grant rights as to which they have exercised a power of termination. When a grant made by an author's successor-in-interest is terminated, all those specified in the statute as having termination interests become tenants in common and may make grants of the interest in the work to which the terminated grant related (subject to the usual duty to account to co-owners and to other limitations on independent dealing in cases of joint copyright ownership). Where a dead author's rights are shared, further grants must be by majority action as to that author's share (see II. above) and the new grant binds all owners, including nonsigners. No new grant or agreement to make one may be made until termination becomes effective, except that owners of the termination interest and the original grantee or his/her successor in title may agree to such a new grant after notice of termination is served.

If termination is not effected at the proper time in accordance with the statutory procedures, the grantee retains all rights under the grant for the remainder of the copyright term (unless the grant itself provides otherwise).

[C]　Section 304(d) Terminations

In 1998, Congress significantly modified the termination provisions of the Copyright Act of 1976 in enacting the Sonny Bono Copyright Term Extension Act. First, besides extending the basic term of copyright to life-plus-70 years, the CTEA added an additional 20 years to the renewal term of pre-1978 copyrights. Thus, under the CTEA, the author or her successor, through timely termination within the five-year window specified in § 304(c), may recapture the last 39 years of the renewal term (*i.e.*, the original 19-year "bonus" period plus the 20 years added by the CTEA). Second, even if, prior to 1998, the author or successor did not timely exercise the right to recapture the initial 19 years of the extended term, the CTEA affords such a person a "second bite" at the termination apple. Under the CTEA, an author or successor may terminate a pre-1977 grant and recapture the last 20 years of the extended renewal period under the terms of § 304(d).

Section 304(d) sets forth three conditions: (1) the work must be subsisting in its renewal term on the date the CTEA was enacted (October 27, 1998); (2) the § 304(c) termination right must have expired by that date; and (3) the author or owner of the termination right must not have previously exercised her § 304(c) termination right. If those three conditions are met, all of the provisions of § 304(c) apply to § 304(d) terminations, except that the five-year period within which termination may be made effective begins at the end of the 75th year from the date on which copyright was originally secured.

How the two termination phases work may be illustrated as follows. Suppose an author published a novel in 1935 and assigned her rights to the renewal expectancy shortly thereafter to a movie company. Assume that the author survived until the renewal vested in 1963. Under these facts, the author (prior to enactment of the 1976 Act) would have had no rights in the copyrighted work during the second or renewal term that would have ended in 1991. Effective January 1, 1978, the 1976 Act (as originally enacted) extended the renewal term by 19 years; and, under § 304(c), the author and her heirs were given the opportunity to terminate the grant and recoup the extra 19 years, so long as they complied with the notice-of-termination procedures. If they did so, they would enjoy copyright in the work until it entered the public domain after 2010. Now, under the CTEA, the work will enter the public domain after 2030, and authors and heirs who have timely terminated under § 304(c) receive 20 more years of protection.

But what if the author or heirs failed to terminate the grant properly at the end of the second 28-year term? They would, of course, have missed their chance to benefit from the extended 19-year term. The CTEA, however, affords them an opportunity in § 304(d) to terminate and capture the remaining, newly added 20 years of the renewal term, if they properly observe the statutory notice provisions.

Schematically, the copyright terms referred to in the example above look like this:

COPYRIGHT TERMINATION TIME LINE

1935	1963	1991	2010	2030
Work is published.	Copyright renewed.	End of original 28-year renewal term.	19-year first extension ends.	Copyright ends.
28-year first term begins.	Second or renewal term begins.	First termination window opens. § 304(c).	Second termination window opens. § 304(d).	Work enters public domain.
FIRST TERM	67-YEAR RENEWAL TERM			

[D]   The Mechanics of Termination

[1]   Summary

In analyzing whether and how termination can be effected, it is helpful to go through a five-step process:

(1) Determine which section of the statute (§ 203, § 304(c), § 304(d)) applies to the grant to be terminated.

(2) Calculate when the termination window opens and closes.

(3) Select an effective date within the termination window.

(4) Serve notice at least two years and not more than ten years in advance of the effective date.

(5) Record a copy of the notice in the Copyright Office before the effective date.

The following discussion elaborates on these steps and explores some differences among the three statutes:

Step One — Which Statute Applies?

Sections 304(c) and 304(d) apply only to transfers of the renewal period, executed before January 1, 1978, in works copyrighted before January 1, 1978. Unlike § 203, § 304(c) and § 304(d) apply not only to grants made by the author, but also to those made by the author's widow, widower, or children, and his/her next of kin.

Because § 304(d) is limited to works in their renewal term on October 27, 1998 (the effective date of the CTEA), for which the termination right in § 304(c) had expired by such date, § 304(d) is limited to works whose copyright was first secured between January 1, 1923 and October 26, 1939. *See* 37 C.F.R. § 201.10. In addition, § 304(d) applies only if the owner of the § 304(c) termination right has not previously exercised that right.

Section 203 applies to all grants executed by the author on or after January 1, 1978. The fact that the work was created before 1978, or that copyright was secured before 1978, is irrelevant. It is the date of the transfer to be terminated that is determinative, not the date when copyright was secured.

As to any particular grant, § 304 and § 203 are mutually exclusive. But an interest which was the subject of a pre-1977 grant that has been terminated under § 304(c), and has been re-granted, may potentially be reclaimed once again by a termination under § 203.

A query, however. Suppose that, on December 31, 1977, Author ("*A*") signed an agreement with Publisher ("*P*") to write and deliver to *P* a work of nonfiction, granting to *P* "all of [*A*'s] right, title, and interest said work." In 1978, *A* wrote the work and duly delivered the manuscript to *P*, which promptly published it. If and when *A* wished to terminate the grant to *P*, which set of Title 17's termination provisions applies: § 304(c), § 304(d), or § 203?

In 2011, after a notice-and-comment rulemaking, the Copyright Office amended its regulations to provide:

> In any case where an author agreed, prior to January 1, 1978, to a grant of a transfer or license of rights in a work that was not created until on or after January 1, 1978, a notice of termination of a grant under section 203 of title 17 may be recorded if it recites, as the date of execution, the date on which the work was created.

37 C.F.R. § 201.10(f)(5). In so doing, however, the Office cautioned that such recordation is "without prejudice to how a court might ultimately rule on whether any particular document qualifies as a notice of termination." 76 Fed.Reg. 32320.

Step Two — Calculate the Termination Window

The focus of the § 304(c) termination right is not the first 56 years of a copyright obtained under the 1909 Act, but rather the 39 years added onto that period by the 1976 Act, as amended by the CTEA. Under § 304(c)(3), the five-year termination window opens at the end of the initial 56-year period. (Note that the termination window opens on the 56th anniversary of the date copyright was originally secured, and not on the following January 1; the House Report on § 305 specifically states that "the periods provided in section 304(c) with respect to termination of grants are not affected by section 305.") If, however, the 39-year period commenced before 1978, thus shortening or eliminating the window, the five years began to run on January 1, 1978 instead.

The focus of the § 304(d) termination right is the 20 years added onto the renewal term by the CTEA. Under § 304(d)(2), the five-year termination window opens on the 75th anniversary of the date copyright was originally secured.

Under § 203(a)(3), the five-year termination window generally opens 35 years after the date of the transfer to be terminated. If the transfer includes publication rights, however, the opening of the five-year termination window is postponed to the earlier of 35 years after publication or 40 years after the date of the transfer.

Step Three — Select an Effective Date

Under all three sections, termination "may be effected at any time during" the five-year termination window, and "[t]he notice shall state the effective date of the termination, which shall fall within the five-year period." Remember, however, that notice of termination must be served at least two years and not more than 10 years in advance of the effective date. Thus, in order to recapture the maximum period permitted by the termination provisions, the latest date notice may be served is two years before the date that the termination window opens. If the two-year advance date has already passed when your client consults you, make sure that you select an effective date that is at least two years after the date you plan to serve notice. If there are fewer than two years remaining in the termination window when your client consults you, it is too late to serve a termination notice.

Step Four — Serve a Termination Notice

Under all three sections, "[t]he termination shall be effective by serving an advance notice in writing upon the grantee or the grantee's successor in title." The notice must state the effective date of termination, and it must be served "not less than two or more than ten years before that date."

The termination notice must comply with Copyright Office regulations, and it must be signed by the number and proportion of persons entitled to terminate, as specified in each statute, or by "their duly authorized agents." The persons who are entitled to terminate under § 304(c) and (d) are set out in § 304(c)(1) and (2). Where the grant was made by joint authors, the authors are tenants in common and each may terminate separately to the extent of his/her interest. Under § 203(a)(1) and (2), a somewhat different list of persons is empowered to terminate grants made after 1977 (and grants made by joint authors must be terminated by majority vote), but the provisions for the exercise of the right by a deceased author's survivors are identical to those under § 304(c) and (d).

Step Five — Record the Termination Notice

Finally, a copy of the termination notice must be recorded in the Copyright Office before the effective date of termination, "as a condition to its taking effect."

Upon the effective date of termination, the rights covered by the terminated grant revert to those persons who were entitled to terminate on the date the notice of termination was served — even if they did not join in signing the notice. The same number and proportion of those people who are entitled to terminate may then make a further grant of the reverted rights — which, once again, is binding on all of the owners, even if they do not sign the further grant. A grant or promise that is made before the effective date is invalid, unless it is made to the original grantee or the grantee's successor in title. This, in effect, gives the original grantee or its successor an exclusive negotiation period between the time advance notice is served and the effective date.

There is one distinction between § 304(c) and § 203 with respect to who may make further grants in works of joint authorship. Under § 304(c), each author's interest is owned separately from the interests of any co-authors. Under § 203, it takes a majority vote of the joint authors to terminate or to make a further grant. If any of the authors of a joint work is deceased, that author's voting interest is exercised as a unit by the same number and proportion of heirs as are entitled to terminate.

[2] Decisional Law

SIEGEL v. WARNER BROTHERS ENTERTAINMENT, INC.
United States District Court, Central District of California
542 F. Supp. 2d 1098 (2008)

STEPHEN G. LARSON, DISTRICT JUDGE:

The termination provisions contained in the Copyright Act of 1976 have aptly been characterized as formalistic and complex, such that authors, or their heirs, successfully terminating the grant to the copyright in their original work of authorship is a feat accomplished "against all odds." 2 WILLIAM F. PATRY, PATRY ON COPYRIGHT § 7:52 (2007).

In the present case, Joanne Siegel and Laura Siegel Larson, the widow and the daughter of Jerome Siegel, seek a declaration from the Court that they have overcome these odds and have successfully terminated the 1938 grant by Jerome Siegel and his creative partner, Joseph Shuster, of the copyright in their creation of the iconic comic book superhero "Superman," thereby recapturing Jerome Siegel's half of the copyright in the same. No small feat indeed. . . .

[In 1934, Siegel conceived of the character "Superman," "who is sent as an infant to Earth aboard a space ship from an unnamed distant planet (that had been destroyed by old age) [and] who, upon becoming an adult, uses his superhuman powers . . . to perform daring feats for the public good." Siegel "also humanized his character by giving his superhero an "ordinary person" alter ego: Mild-mannered, big-city newspaper reporter Clark Kent . . . . [He also developed a] love 'triangle' between the character's dual identities and another newspaper reporter, Lois Lane."]

Shuster immediately turned his attention to giving life and color to Siegel's idea by drawing illustrations for the story. Shuster conceived of the costume for Siegel's Superman superhero — a cape and tight-fitting leotard with briefs, an "S" emblazoned on an inverted triangular crest on his chest, and boots as footwear. In contrast, he costumed Clark Kent in a nondescript suit, wearing black-rimmed glasses, combed black hair, and sporting a fedora. He drew Superman and his alter ego Clark Kent with chiseled features, gave him a hairstyle with a distinctive curl over his forehead, and endowed him with a lean, muscular physique. . . . The two shopped the character for a number of years to numerous publishers but were unsuccessful. . . .

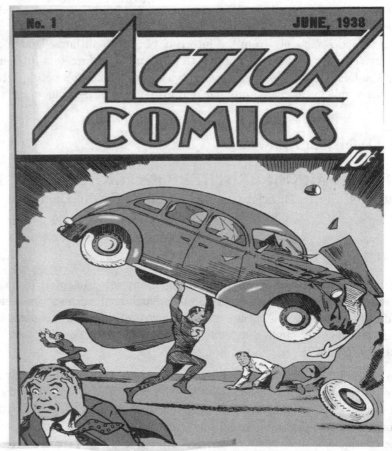

Cover of *Action Comics* No. 1

On December 4, 1937, Siegel and Shuster entered into an agreement with Detective Comics whereby they agreed . . . "that all of [the] work done by [them] for [Detective Comics] during said period of employment shall be and become the sole and exclusive property of [Detective Comics,] and [that Detective Comics] shall be deemed the sole creator thereof. . . ." . . .

Soon thereafter Detective Comics decided to issue a new comic book magazine titled *Action Comics* and began seeking new material. Detective Comics soon became interested in publishing Siegel and Shuster's now well-traveled Superman material . . . for release in its first volume of *Action Comics*. . . .

On March 1, 1938, prior to the printing of the first issue of *Action Comics*, Detective Comics wrote to Siegel, enclosing a check in the sum of $130 . . . and enclosing with it a written agreement for Siegel and Shuster's signatures. The agreement assigned to Detective Comics "all [the] good will attached . . . and exclusive right[s]" to Superman "to have and hold forever." Siegel and Shuster executed and returned the written assignment to Detective Comics. . . .

[In April 1938, Detective Comics published two promotional advertisements which contained a reduced-size black-and-white reproduction of the cover of the soon-to-be published first issue of *Action Comics.*]

Superman itself was published by Detective Comics on April 18, 1938, in *Action Comics*, Vol. 1, which had a cover date of June, 1938. . . . The Superman comic became an instant success, and Superman's popularity continues to endure to this day as his depiction has been transferred to varying media formats.

The Superman character has evolved in subsequent works since his initial depiction in *Action Comics*, Vol. 1. . . . For instance, absent from *Action Comics*, Vol. 1, was any reference to some of the more famous story elements now associated with Superman, such as the name of Superman's home planet "Krypton." Many of Superman's powers that are among his most famous today did not appear in *Action Comics*, Vol. 1, including his ability to fly [and his "x-ray" vision]. . . . [In addition,] it was later revealed that Superman's powers could be nullified by his exposure to Kryptonite, radioactive mineral particles of his destroyed home planet. . . .

. . . Some of the most famous supporting characters associated with Superman, such as Jimmy Olsen and rival villains LexLuthor, General Zod, and Brainiac, were created long after *Action Comics*, Vol. 1, was published. Moreover, certain elements contained in *Action Comics*, Vol. 1, were altered, even if slightly, in later publications, most notably Superman's crest. . . .

. . . Detective Comics oversaw the creation, development, and licensing of the Superman character in a variety of media, including but not limited to radio, novels, live action and animated motion pictures, television, live theatrical productions, merchandise and theme parks. From such promotional activity, Detective Comics came to "own dozens of federal trademark registrations for Superman related indicia . . . across a broad array of goods and services." The most notable of these marks that are placed on various items of merchandise are "Superman's characteristic outfit . . . , as well as certain key identifying phrases[,]" such as "Look! . . . Up in the sky! . . . It's a bird! . . . It's a plane! . . . It's Superman!" . . .

. . . [I]n 1947, Siegel and Shuster brought an action against Detective Comics' successor in interest in New York Supreme Court, Westchester County, seeking, among other things, to annul and rescind their previous agreements with Detective Comics assigning their ownership rights in Superman. . . .

. . . The parties eventually settled the Westchester action and signed a stipulation on May 19, 1948, whereby in exchange for the payment of over $94,000 to Siegel and Shuster, the parties reiterated the referee's earlier finding that Detective Comics owned all rights to Superman. Two days later, the referee entered a final consent judgment . . . reiterating the recitals contained in the stipulation.

The feud between the parties did not end after the Westchester action. . . . In 1969, Siegel and Shuster filed suit in federal district court in New York seeking a declaration that they . . . were the owners of the renewal rights to the Superman copyright. *See Siegel v. National Periodical Publications, Inc.*, 364 F. Supp. 1032 (S.D.N.Y. 1973), *aff'd*, 508 F.2d 909 (2d Cir. 1974). The end result of the litigation was that, in conformity with United States Supreme Court precedent at the time, *see Fred Fisher Music Co. v. M. Witmark & Sons*, 318 U.S. 643, 656–59 (1943), in transferring "all their rights" to Superman in the March 1, 1938, grant to Detective Comics (which was reconfirmed in the 1948 stipulation), Siegel and Shuster had assigned not only Superman's initial copyright term but the renewal term as well, even though those renewal rights had yet to vest when the grant (and later the stipulation) was made.

[In 1975, in exchange for further payment, "Siegel and Shuster re-acknowledged the Second Circuit's decision that 'all right, title and interest in' Superman ('including any and all renewals and extensions of . . . such rights') resided exclusively with DC Comics and its corporate affiliates."]

. . . With the passage of the Copyright Act of 1976 (the "1976 Act"), Congress changed the legal landscape concerning artists' transfers of the copyrights in their creations. . . . [T]he 1976 Act gave artists and their heirs the ability to terminate any prior grants of the rights to their creations that were executed before January 1, 1978, regardless of the terms contained in such assignments. . . .

It is this right of termination that Joanne Siegel and Laura Siegel Larson now seek to vindicate in this case. . . . On April 3, 1997, the two heirs served seven separate notices of termination under section 304(c) of the 1976 Act, purporting to terminate several of Siegel's potential grant(s) in the Superman copyright to defendants, including the March 1, 1938, assignment; the May 19, 1948, stipulation; and the December 23, 1975, agreement. The termination notices also specified that they covered hundreds of works, with the added proviso that the intent was for the termination notice to apply "to each and every work . . . that includes or embodies" Superman, and the failure to list any such work in the notice was "unintentional and involuntary." Each of the termination notices had an effective date of April 16, 1999. . . .

A. *Validity and Enforceability of Termination Notices*

The 1976 Act created a new right allowing authors and their heirs the ability to terminate a prior grant to the copyright in their creations. *See* 17 U.S.C. § 304(c). The 1976 Act also set forth specific steps concerning the timing and contents of the notices that had to be served to effectuate the termination of a prior grant. . . . Specifically, the "[t]ermination of the grant may be effected at any time during a period of five years beginning at the end of fifty-six years *from the date copyright was originally secured.*" 17 U.S.C. § 304(c)(3) (emphasis added). Moreover, the notice is required to be "served not less than two or more than ten years before" its effective date.

Taken together, someone seeking to exercise the termination right must specify the effective date of the termination, and that effective date must fall within a set five-year window which is at least fifty-six years, but no more than sixty-one years, from the date the copyright sought to be recaptured was originally secured, and such termination notice must be served two to ten years before its effective date. . . .

Additional procedures required to be followed to make the termination notice effective were specified as well: The author or his or her heirs had to serve "an advance notice in writing upon the grantee or the grantee's successor in title"; the notice had to be signed by the author or his or her heirs; the notice was required to "state the effective date of the termination"; and the notice must be "recorded in the Copyright Office before the effective date of termination." 17 U.S.C. § 304(c)(4).

Beyond these statutory requirements, the notice was also required to "comply, in form, content, and manner of service, with [the] requirements that the Register of Copyrights . . . prescribe[s] by regulation." 17 U.S.C. § 304(c)(4)(B). Toward that end, the Register promulgated regulations implementing this statutory proviso. *See* 37 C.F.R. § 201.10. Among those regulations was one requiring the terminating party to identify in the notice "each work as to which the notice of termination applies." 37 C.F.R. § 201.10(b)(1)(ii).

As one noted author has commented, "[i]t is difficult to overstate the intricacies of these [termination] provisions, the result of which is that they are barely used, no doubt the result desired by lobbyists for assignees." William Patry, *Choice of Law and International Copyright*, 48 Am. J. Comp. L. 383, 447 (2000). Those intricate provisions oftentimes create unexpected pitfalls that thwart or blunt the effort of the terminating party to reclaim the full measure of the copyright in a work of authorship. This case is no different.

1. *Promotional Announcements*

Plaintiffs gave notice that the effective date of the termination notices was April 16, 1999, meaning that, backdating from that date sixty-one years, the termination notices would leave unaffected (or better said, beyond their reach) any statutory copyright that had been secured in the Superman material before April 16, 1938. Defendants contend that the promotional announcements for *Action Comics*, Vol. 1, featuring a graphical depiction of Superman, fall just a few days outside the five-year effective window of plaintiffs' termination notices; therefore, they argue, any copyright material contained in those promotional announcements, notably the illustration of Superman on the cover of *Action Comics*, Vol. 1, is unaffected by the termination notices and remains theirs to exploit exclusively. . . .

Plaintiffs do not dispute the legal consequence section 304(c)'s five-year window has in this case on the effective reach of their termination notices. . . . A leading treatise supports such a calculation and the consequences flowing from it:

> The appropriate dates for termination notices are measured from "the date copyright was originally secured. . . ." In the case of pre-January 1, 1978 works, "secured" means the actual date the work was first published with notice (or in the case of unpublished works, the date of registration), e.g., April 15, 1970, not December 31, 1970. Failure to pay attention to the differences between the date the copyright was originally secured for purposes of section 304(c) termination of transfer and section 305 expiration of term may lead to an untimely notice of termination.

2 Patry on Copyright § 7:43. . . .

[The court found that the two promotional announcements contained proper copyright notices, and that they were published on April 5 and April 10, 1938.]

Here, the promotional announcements represent the first time Superman appeared to the public, and consequently, the first time any of Siegel and Shuster's Superman material was protected by statutory copyright. . . . Thus, all of the material in the promotional announcement (which included the graphic depiction of Superman later portrayed on the cover of *Action Comics*, Vol. 1) obtained statutory copyright protection before the earliest possible date covered by the plaintiffs' termination notices. The Court . . . finds that the publication date for at least one of the comics containing the promotional announcements falls outside the reach of the termination notice and, therefore, any copyrightable material contained therein (including that found in the cover to *Action Comics*, Vol. 1, as depicted in those announcements) remains for defendants to exploit.

This leads to the question of the scope of the copyrighted material remaining in defendants' possession by way of the promotional announcements. . . .

The Court begins by observing what is not depicted in the announcements. Obviously, nothing concerning the Superman storyline (that is, the literary elements contained in *Action Comics*, Vol. 1) is on display in the ads; thus, Superman's name, his alter ego, his compatriots, his origins, his mission to serve as a champion of the oppressed, or his heroic abilities in general, do not remain within defendants sole possession to exploit. Instead the only copyrightable elements left arise from the pictorial illustration in the announcements, which is fairly limited.

The person in question has great strength (he is after all holding aloft a car). The person is wearing some type of costume, but significantly the colors, if any, for the same are not represented, as the advertisement appears only in black and white. The argument that the "S" crest is recognizable in the promotional advertisement is not persuasive. What is depicted on the chest of the costume is so small and blurred as to not be readily recognizable. . . . The Court thus concludes that defendants may continue to exploit the image of a person with extraordinary strength who wears a black and white leotard and cape. What remains of the Siegel and Shuster's Superman copyright that is still subject to termination . . . is the entire storyline from *Action Comics*, Vol. 1, Superman's distinctive blue leotard (complete with its inverted triangular crest across the chest with a red "S" on a yellow background), a red cape and boots, and his superhuman ability to leap tall buildings, repel bullets, and run faster than a locomotive, none of which is apparent from the announcement.

2. *Work Made for Hire Aspect of Portions of* Action Comics, Vol. 1

Under the 1976 Act, an author's (or his or her heirs') ability to terminate a prior grant in the copyright to a creation does not apply to a "work made for hire," because the copyright in such a creation was never the artist's to grant, belonging instead to the one who employed the artist to create the work. *See* 17 U.S.C. § 304(c). . . .

Defendants argue that portions of the copyrightable material contained in *Action Comics*, Vol. 1, are unaffected by the termination notice because those portions belong exclusively to them as "works for hire," arguing that certain material found in the comic book was created by Detective Comics' in-house employees, or that the material was added to the underlying Superman material by Siegel and Shuster at the publisher's direction. . . .

The thrust of defendants' argument was made and rejected by the Second Circuit in the 1970s Superman copyright renewal litigation, and is thus precluded as a matter of collateral estoppel here. In that litigation, defendants' predecessors-in-interest presented much of the same evidence now submitted in this case to argue that this additional material transformed the entirety of Siegel and Shuster's pre-existing Superman material published in *Action Comics*, Vol. 1, into a work made for hire. The Second Circuit rejected this argument. *Siegel*, 508 F.2d at 914. This conclusion forecloses any further litigation on the point of whether Shuster's additional drawings when reformatting the underlying Superman material into a comic book format . . . rendered all or portions of the resulting comic book a work made for hire. . . .

In conclusion, the Court finds that . . . the Superman material contained in *Action Comics*, Vol. 1, is not a work-made-for-hire and therefore is subject to termination.

3. *Failure to Include 1948 Consent Judgment*

Among the regulatory requirements promulgated by the Register of Copyrights concerning the termination notice's "form, content, and manner of service," 17 U.S.C. § 304(c)(4)(B), is the requirement that the notice must "reasonably" identify "the grant" to which it applies. 37 C.F.R. § 201.10(b)(1)(iv). Thus, if the author entered into five separate grants of rights for the same work, and a notice of termination identifies only four of those grants, the fifth grant remains "intact," and the grantee's rights thereunder remain unaffected. . . .

Here, defendants argue that plaintiffs' failure to identify the 1948 consent judgment from the Westchester action is fatal to their attempts to terminate their grant to the copyright in Superman, as that consent judgment was among the grants leading to the transfer of ownership from the artists to Detective Comics. . . . The Court disagrees. . . .

The consent judgment at issue did not effectuate any transfer of rights from Siegel and Shuster to Detective Comics. If any rights were transferred as a result of the Westchester action, such a transfer was effectuated by the execution of the earlier stipulated agreement of the parties, not a document created two days later which simply memorialized the transfer that the stipulation itself had accomplished. The binding nature of the transfer contained in the stipulation was completed the moment that agreement was executed. The consent judgment was a mere formality whose execution (or lack thereof) did not detract from the otherwise binding nature of the parties' earlier agreement. It merely parroted what was already agreed to by the parties in the stipulation itself.

Finally, even if the 1948 consent judgment is a "grant" separate and apart from (or part and parcel with) the 1948 stipulation, the regulations recognize that not all errors in compliance with its terms impact the validity of the termination notice: "Harmless errors in a notice that do not materially affect the adequacy of the information required to serve the purposes of . . . section 304(c) . . . shall not render the notice invalid." 37 C.F.R. § 201.10(e)(1). . . .

Accordingly, the Court concludes that, even if the consent judgment is viewed as integral to the transfer of rights, plaintiffs' failure to identify it as a grant subject to the termination notice was a harmless error that did not diminish the notice defendants received regarding the nature of the grant (and resulting transfer of rights) that plaintiffs intended to terminate. . . .

B. *Limitations on Scope of Recaptured Rights*

The principal purpose behind the creation of the termination right was to give authors (and their heirs) a chance to retain the extended renewal term in their work and then re-bargain for it when its value in the marketplace was known. . . .

The need for such a second bite at the apple flowed from the fact that the 1909 Act created a dual term in the copyright to a work, one realized upon the work's publication and the second occurring twenty-eight years later with the copyright's renewal. Justification for this splitting of terms was based, in part, on the understanding that an author's ability to realize the true value of his or her work was often not apparent at its creation, but required the passage of time (and the marketing efforts by a publisher) to materialize. The renewal term in the copyright to the work thus served as a mid-course re-valuation tool allowing the author, by giving him or her the right of renewal in the work, leverage in re-negotiating a better deal with the original grantee or any other suitor who desired to continue to market the copyright. . . . This re-valuation mechanism provided by the renewal term under the 1909 Act was largely frustrated by the Supreme Court's decision in *Fred Fisher Music*, 318 U.S. at 656–59, allowing authors to assign away at the outset all of their rights to both the initial and the renewal term.

Although the termination right contained in the 1976 Act sought to correct the damage done by *Fred Fisher* to an author's ability to renegotiate through the reversion of rights, it did not revert to the author the full panoply of rights he or she would have enjoyed upon renewal under the 1909 Act. Owing in large measure to objections by publishers seeking to minimize the disruption to "existing contracts and authorized derivative works already in distribution" that such a recapture right would engender, *see* 2 PATRY ON COPYRIGHT § 7:43, Congress placed certain limitations on what authors (or their heirs) gained from exercising the termination right. . . .

1. *Foreign Profits*

Section 304(c)(6)(E) to the 1976 Act provides that "[t]ermination of a grant under this subsection affects only those rights covered by the grant that arise under this title [Title 17 of the United States Code, governing copyrights], and in no way affects rights arising under any other Federal, State, or foreign laws." Defendants read from this a statutory limitation on the scope of any accounting arising from the termination notices in this case to those profits realized by the domestic exploitation of the Superman copyright contained in *Action Comics*, Vol. 1, excluding those realized from foreign sources. The Court finds this argument persuasive. . . .

Accordingly, the Court holds that the termination notice affects only the domestic portion of Siegel's and Shuster's 1938 worldwide grant ("all rights") to Detective Comics of the copyright in the Superman material contained in *Action Comics*, Vol. 1. The termination notice is not effective as to the remainder of the grant, that is, defendants' exploitation of the work abroad under the aegis of foreign copyright laws. . . . As such, defendants must account to plaintiffs only for the profits from such domestic exploitation of the Superman copyright.

2. *Trademark Rights and Ownership of Pre-Termination Derivative Works*

As noted in the previous section, the right to termination leaves undisturbed the original grantee or its successors in interest's rights arising under [other] "federal law." 17 U.S.C. § 304(c)(6)(E). Among the rights based on federal law that defendants secured over the years were several trademarks that utilized or incorporated portions of the copyrighted material found in *Action Comics*, Vol. 1. Defendants seek a declaration from the Court that, even if successful in terminating the Superman copyright contained in *Action Comics*, Vol. 1, plaintiffs cannot share in defendants' profits "purely attributable to [Superman] trademark rights." Plaintiffs admirably concede the point in their briefs, but argue that they are "entitled to profits from mixed trademark uses to the extent such exploit recaptured copyright elements (e.g., 'Superman costume')."

Similarly, defendants seek a declaration that, to the extent plaintiffs are entitled to an accounting as a result of their successfully terminating the 1938 grant, it should not include any profits attributable to the "post-termination exploitation of derivative works [of *Action Comics*, Vol. 1] prepared prior to termination." Again, plaintiffs concede, as they should, this point. Section 304(c)(6)(A) provides that derivative works created during the grant (meaning up until the termination effective date) may continue to be exploited after termination. Again, however, plaintiffs hold out as a separate question the existence of pre-termination derivative works that are "altered so as to become post-termination derivative works." . . .

. . . Even though it is clear that these issues will impact the accounting of profits in some manner, they cannot be fully adjudicated based on the narrow record currently before the Court and absent a full briefing of the particular mixed uses or altered pre-termination derivative works that are specifically at issue. . . .

CONCLUSION

After seventy years, Jerome Siegel's heirs regain what he granted so long ago — the copyright in the Superman material that was published in *Action Comics*, Vol. 1. What remains is an apportionment of profits . . . and a trial on whether to include the profits generated by DC Comics' corporate sibling's exploitation of the Superman copyright.

NOTES AND QUESTIONS

(1)   The termination provisions are in many ways a poor substitute for the renewal opportunity that was largely thwarted by the Supreme Court's decision in *Fisher v. Witmark*. Whereas the renewal term *automatically* vested in the author or the author's heirs (unless assigned), termination requires that the author or the author's heirs take a series of formal steps in order to recapture the copyright. As the *Siegel* opinion demonstrates, in practice it can be quite difficult to identify the grant(s) to be terminated, to determine whether the work is made for hire, to calculate the proper termination window(s), and to complete all the steps necessary to terminate.

(2)   The first half of the analysis in the *Siegel* opinion concerns three objections to the validity of the termination notices. Consider the first of these objections. Can you explain why the copyrights in two of the promotional advertisements for *Action Comics*, Vol. 1, are not subject to termination? What was the plaintiffs' argument that the promotional announcements were immaterial, and why did the court reject that argument? What rights do the copyrights in the promotional announcements give to Detective Comics, according to the court? What could the plaintiffs have done in order to avoid the dispute concerning the promotional announcements?

(3)   Next, consider the work-made-for-hire objection to the validity of the termination notices. All of the work that Siegel and Shuster created *during* their employment with Detective Comics was work made for hire, meaning that most of the subsequent issues of Superman are not subject to termination. Only the fact that the material in *Action Comics*, Vol. 1, was created *before* Siegel and Shuster were hired by DC renders that material subject to termination. Does the work-for-hire exception create a big loophole in the termination provisions? Are works for hire any more or less likely to be the subject of unremunerative transfers than other works?

In a subsequent opinion, the District Court found that *Action Comics*, No. 4, pages 3-6 of *Superman*, No. 1, and the first two weeks of *Superman* newspaper strips also consisted of material that pre-existed the employment relationship with DC Comics, and were therefore also subject to termination. 658 F. Supp. 2d 1036 (C.D. Cal. 2009).

(4)   The third objection to validity of the termination notice concerns the identification of the grant to be terminated. Do you agree that the failure to list the 1948 consent decree in the notice of termination was "harmless error"? In actual practice, how often would you expect to encounter multiple grants of copyright in the same work to the same person? In a subsequent opinion, the District Court thoroughly explored the validity and effect of the "harmless error" regulation and reaffirmed its prior rulings. 690 F. Supp. 2d 1048 (C.D. Cal. 2009).

Note that because the case concerns pre-1978 grants, the same termination window applies to all potential grants in a single work, because the termination window is measured from the date copyright was first "secured." *See* § 304(c)(3). But for post-1978 grants, termination windows are measured instead from the date of the grant. *See* § 203(a)(3). If that section had been applicable to this case, when would the plaintiffs have had to serve their termination notices? Would termination effectively be defeated by a series of successive "re-grants" of the copyright, as occurred in this case? Or should any subsequent "grants" be considered mere "confirmations" that do not affect the validity of the termination of the original grant?

(5) Compare the "harmless error" analysis in *Siegel* to the opinion in *Burroughs v. Metro-Goldwyn-Mayer, Inc.*, 683 F.2d 610 (2d Cir. 1982), in which the heirs of author Edgar Rice Burroughs served a termination notice that covered 35 of Burroughs' *Tarzan* novels (including the first, *Tarzan of the Apes*), but that inadvertently omitted the titles of five sequels. Taking a "strict compliance" view of § 304(c), the majority held that the grant of rights in those five sequels had not been terminated, and that those rights implicitly included the right to use the character of Tarzan as he appeared in those sequels.

Johnny Weismuller and Maureen O'Sullivan
in *Tarzan, the Ape Man* (1932)
Bettman/Corbis

Concurring, Judge Newman opined that because the sequels were derivative works, the copyrights in those works included only the original material in those works, and thus did not include the character of Tarzan himself, assuming he was "sufficiently delineated" in the first book. Who has the better of this argument? Does the Supreme Court's subsequent decision in *Stewart v. Abend*, discussed in § 5.01 above, have any bearing on the issue?

Judge Newman nonetheless reached the same result as the majority, on the ground that the Burroughs heirs served their notice of termination only on ERB,

Inc., a corporation owned by Burroughs and his heirs, instead of serving notice on the real party in interest, MGM. Judge Newman agreed with the District Court that in serving ERB, Inc., the heirs were "essentially serving themselves." Are you persuaded that ERB, Inc. should, in effect, have been treated as the "alter ego" of Burroughs? In general, how should the holder of a termination interest determine who is the proper "grantee or successor in title" to be served? *See also Music Sales Corp. v. Morris*, 73 F. Supp. 2d 364 (S.D.N.Y. 1999) (holding executor was not required to serve corporation that purchased 50% interest in grantee after notice of termination was served).

(6)   The second half of *Siegel* concerns limitations on the scope of the termination. What exactly did the plaintiffs gain as a result of their successful notices of termination? As of April 19, 1999, plaintiffs became co-owners of the U.S. copyright in *Action Comics*, Vol. 1, for the remainder of the copyright term (as extended, through December 31, 2033). Exactly what rights does that share of the copyright give them? Can they license someone to make a Superman movie or to sell Superman merchandise? Do they need the consent of DC to do so, or can they license Superman works and products on their own?

(7)   At the very least, co-owners have a duty to account for any profits earned from any licensing of the jointly-owned work. The accounting at issue in the opinion concerns profits earned by DC between the effective date of termination (April 16, 1999) and the time of trial. To what works does this duty apply? What works are exempt from this accounting, and why? You may want to consider this question again after reading § 5.02[E] below.

How would you go about trying to apportion profits earned from the exploitation of post-termination derivative works? How much of the profit from a movie based on Superman, or from Superman merchandise, is attributable to the material in *Action Comics*, Vol. 1, and how much is attributable to other factors? Remember these issues when you examine the materials in § 11.01[C] below.

(8)   Any notice of termination must be served "not less than two nor more than ten years" before the date on which the grantee's rights are to be terminated. § 304(c)(4)(A). The requirement of notice is based on fairness, and may even be necessary to avoid violating the Due Process Clause of the Constitution. But what is the practical effect of § 304(c) notice? Might the requirement of providing "advance warning" to grantees, who often will be publishers, pose any danger to the interests of authors and their successors? And what happens if an author dies after the notice of termination has been served, but before the effective date of termination arrives? *See* § 304(c)(6)(B); *Range Road Music, Inc. v. Music Sales Corp.*, 76 F. Supp. 2d 375 (S.D.N.Y. 1999).

(9)   Section 304(c) provides that "the grant of a transfer or license of the renewal copyright or any right under it . . . otherwise than by will" is subject to termination. Does the phrase "otherwise than by will" include a devise of a contractual right to receive royalties? In *Larry Spier, Inc. v. Bourne Co.*, 953 F.2d 774 (2d Cir. 1992), Dreyer (a deceased songwriter) had left a will establishing a "testamentary trust" under which royalties from his copyrights and publishing contracts were paid to his widow, his children, and his mistress. Later, the widow and children attempted to exercise § 304(c) termination rights with respect to those

publishing contracts, in order to exclude the mistress from future participation. The Second Circuit concluded that the publishing contracts were not transfers "by will," because they had been in existence during the songwriter's lifetime, and that his family members, therefore, were entitled to terminate.

(10)   Can termination rights be alienated effectively prior to their "vesting," so as to frustrate the expectations of the successors designated in § 304? Obviously, the general answer is "no." Section 304(c)(5) provides that "[t]ermination of the grant may be effected *notwithstanding any agreement to the contrary*, including an agreement to make a will or to make any future grant" (emphasis added). But what, exactly, is an "agreement to the contrary"? Can an author and a publisher voluntarily agree to terminate an existing agreement and enter into a new agreement, even if the effect is to postpone or eliminate a future termination opportunity?

Congress apparently thought the answer was "yes." The House Report expressly states that "[s]ection 203 would not prevent the parties to a transfer or license from voluntarily agreeing at any time to terminate an existing grant and negotiating a new one, thereby causing another 35-year period to start running." What Congress did not anticipate, however, was that voluntary termination and renegotiation after 1978 of a grant made before 1978 could eliminate the future termination rights of an author's heirs altogether. Section 304 would not apply, because the new grant was made after 1978; and § 203 would not apply, because the new grant was not made by the "author," but by the author's heirs.

In both *Milne v. Stephen Slesinger, Inc.*, 430 F.3d 1036 (9th Cir. 2005) (which involved rights in *Winnie-the-Pooh*) and *Penguin Group (USA) Inc. v. Steinbeck*, 537 F.3d 193 (2d Cir. 2008), the courts held that a post-1978 renegotiation of a pre-1978 agreement was a new agreement to which neither § 304 nor § 203 applied. The courts reasoned that the purposes of termination had been served, because the author's son (in *Milne*) or widow (in *Steinbeck*) had used the threat of termination to negotiate a more favorable deal. Accordingly, they held that a renegotiated agreement was not an "agreement to the contrary," even though it had the effect of eliminating the later-enacted § 304(d) rights of the author's heirs (Milne's grand-daughter and Steinbeck's two sons), who were not parties to the renegotiated agreements.

By contrast, in *Classic Media, Inc. v. Mewborn*, 532 F.3d 978 (9th Cir. 2008), the court held that the daughter of author Eric Knight could terminate a 1976 agreement granting rights in her father's story *Lassie Come Home*, notwithstand-ing a 1978 agreement confirming and modifying the 1976 agreement. The court distinguished *Milne*, noting that although Milne used the threat of termination to negotiate a more favorable deal, Mewborn did not "intend to relinquish a known termination right" and did not receive any additional consideration.

Are you persuaded that the courts reached the right results in these three cases? Which, if any, is most questionable? Congress could ameliorate the situation by amending § 203 to permit grants made by an author's heirs to be terminated. Should it do so? Would such an amendment be constitutional?

(11) How should a court treat a settlement agreement that stipulates that a previously created work was a "work made for hire"? In *Marvel Characters, Inc. v. Simon*, 310 F.3d 280 (2d Cir. 2002), the court held that such an agreement constituted an "agreement to the contrary" which could not defeat the purported sole author's right of termination. Otherwise, "publishers would be able to utilize their superior bargaining power to compel authors to agree that a work was created for hire in order to get their works published." Thus, "[i]t is the relationship that in fact exists between the parties, and not their description of that relationship, that is determinative." *Id.* at 290-91, *quoting* 3 Nimmer on Copyright § 11.02[A][2] (2002).

Despite this holding, it is relatively easy for publishers to establish that works created under the 1909 Act were made "for hire." In *Marvel Worldwide, Inc. v. Kirby*, 777 F. Supp. 2d 720 (S.D.N.Y. 2011), for example, the court found that comics by freelance artist Jack Kirby were created at the "instance and expense" of Marvel and were therefore not subject to termination. The court found that a 1972 "assignment" of any copyrights that Kirby "may have" specifically acknowledged that the works were made for hire and was therefore consistent with the actual relationship and did not rebut the presumption that arose under the 1909 Act.

[E] The Derivative Works Exception

The preceding case and notes explore a variety of issues which commonly arise with respect to terminations under § 304(c) of the Copyright Act. The text which follows is focused on a particular set of problems involving the so-called "Derivative Works Exception" to terminations.

Section 304(c)(6)(A) provides:

> A derivative work prepared under authority of the grant before its termination may continue to be utilized under the terms of the grant after its termination, but this privilege does not extend to the preparation after the termination of other derivative works based upon the copyrighted work covered by the terminated grant.

Section 203(b)(1) contains identical language. For the sake of convenience, and because actual terminations under § 203 will not begin until 2013 (*i.e.*, 35 years after the first grants subject to § 203 were made in 1978), the following discussion is premised on attempted terminations of derivative works preparation grants made under § 304(c).

The impact of advance notice of termination. Recall that § 304(c)(4)(A) requires that any notice of termination — including the termination of a right to prepare derivative works — must be served on the grantee a minimum of two years before the termination itself is to take place. In light of the Derivative Works Exception, how would you expect the service of such "advance notice" of termination to affect the plans of a grantee who has not yet commenced the preparation of a derivative work under the grant? Provided that he/she still has time and the capacity to complete the work, what behavior is typically to be expected? Is there any way for the owner of the termination interest to prevent such behavior? Under the law of property, the holder of a remainder interest in real property may sue to prevent the holder of a temporary possessory interest from "wasting" the value of the property.

Might a similar concept be applied to termination interests?

Terminations and derivative works already "in preparation." What is the effect of the Exception on a derivative work which is "in preparation" at the moment of actual termination, but not yet "prepared" in the sense that it has been completed? Suppose, for example, that a motion picture based on a novel is in production but is not finished on the date when the termination takes effect. Defining "prepared" as "fixed," the Nimmer treatise contends that at least the portion of a derivative work already fixed as of termination is protected by the terms of the Exception. As to that portion of the motion picture remaining to be prepared, the treatise suggests that the later-added material may be used if, and only to the extent that, such material is not based on the underlying work in which the grantee's rights have been terminated. Thus, if the movie has been filmed but is still awaiting the addition of a musical score to the soundtrack on the effective date of the termination, the latter may be added under the terms of the Exception because the music itself is not based on the underlying novel. 3 NIMMER ON COPYRIGHT § 11.02[C] n.65 (2010); *see also* § 101 (definition of "creation"). Is this a persuasive position?

Termination and the exploitation of royalties. In *Mills Music, Inc. v. Snyder,* 469 U.S. 153 (1985), the Supreme Court decided the issue of whether an author's termination of a music publisher's interest in a copyright also terminated the publisher's contractual right to share in the royalties from those it had sublicensed to make derivative works. Ted Snyder, author of the song "Who's Sorry Now," had assigned the renewal term to Mills Music. As owner of the renewal term to the song, Mills had sublicensed the song to more than 400 record companies, each of which had prepared separate derivative works and paid royalties. The author's family served on Mills a notice of termination and demanded that royalties revert to them. The Supreme Court, reversing a decision in favor of Snyder, held that the use of the term "grant" three times in § 304(c)(6)(A) revealed a legislative intent to cover not only the original grant but any sublicenses made under that grant as well. The Court acknowledged that the principal purpose of § 304(c) was to benefit authors, but determined that this was not its sole rationale. Its other purpose was to enable continued public accessibility to derivative works after termination. The Court concluded that upholding the *status quo* did justice to both policies.

Justice White, in a dissenting opinion, sharply criticized the majority's reading of the statutory language and legislative history of § 304(c), concluding that a middleman assignee's right to receive continued royalties had nothing to do with continued public access to a work, but would undermine the other policy of the 1976 Act, which is to benefit authors. For other criticism of the majority opinion's rationale, see Abrams, *Who's Sorry Now? Termination Rights and the Derivative Works Exception,* 62 U. Det. L. Rev. 181 (1985). Note that the outcome in *Mills Music* impacts not just songwriters and music publishers, but all authors, book publishers, motion picture producers, and other creators, owners and users of copyrighted works and derivative works based thereon. Whatever the wisdom of the Court's decision, clearly it has had considerable significance to a whole host of interested parties.

As important as *Mills Music* may be for the point it decides, however, its reach is limited to that point. In *Mills Music* and similar situations, an author's termination is not wholly ineffective as to middlemen and their licensees. For example, after termination, Mills had no authority to authorize the preparation of any *additional* derivative works. If a license already issued by Mills to a record company had authorized the preparation of several derivative works, only one of which had been prepared at the time of the Snyders' termination, the remaining, unexercised portion of the license would have constituted part of the "terminated grant." Moreover, a middleman's right to continued royalties remains limited, even after *Mills Music*, by the terms of the grant, and will not extend to uses beyond its scope. *See, e.g., Fred Ahlert Music Corp. v. Warner/Chappell Music, Inc.*, 155 F.3d 17 (2d Cir. 1998) (terms of grant limited use of song to sale and distribution of phonograph records, and excluded use of song in motion picture soundtrack).

There is one further hurdle to be surmounted by a middleman seeking to benefit from the Derivative Works Exception after *Mills Music*: the derivative work must manifest sufficient originality to constitute an independently copyrightable work. *Woods v. Bourne Co.*, 60 F.3d 978 (2d Cir. 1995), concerned the termination of a grant involving the famous song "Red Red Robin." The defendant claimed that its piano-vocal version was a derivative work lawfully prepared under the grant of copyright, and that it could continue to claim royalties for both the sale of the sheet music and public performance of the song. The Second Circuit held that for the Derivative Works Exception to apply, the derivative work in question must contain at least some substantial variation from the underlying work. In *Woods*, the piano-vocal arrangements had been prepared in a mechanical way and, when compared to the "lead sheet," displayed nothing more than trivial changes, thus failing to meet the standard of originality.

Termination vs. restoration. The problem of how to treat pre-existing derivative works exists with respect to copyright restoration as well as with respect to termination. How are the solutions provided by the two statutes similar, and how do they differ? *Compare* § 203(b)(1), *and* § 304(c)(6)(A) (an existing derivative work "may continue to be utilized under the terms of the grant after its termination"), *with* § 104A(d)(3)(A) (a reliance party "may continue to exploit that derivative work for the duration of the restored copyright" upon payment of reasonable compensation). In particular, should the word "utilized" in the termination provisions be interpreted differently from the word "exploit" in the restoration provisions?

Chapter 6

PUBLICATION AND FORMALITIES

The twin topics of this chapter — publication and the formalities of registration, notice, and deposit — have a long and rich history in Anglo-American copyright law. In effecting the transition from the remnants of the stationers' copyright to the new statutory copyright, the Statute of Anne offered protection to two types of works: first, works already published before April 10, 1710, as to which pre-existing rights under the stationers' regime were merely extended (although not, as the booksellers had sought, in perpetuity) without need of further activity by their proprietors; and second, new works and previously unpublished works, which were afforded copyright protection *upon condition of compliance with certain formalities* prescribed by Parliament, namely, registration with the Stationers' Company before publication. The Statute of Anne also required the proprietor to deposit nine copies of the work for the use of various libraries, although such deposit was not a condition of copyright protection.

In the United States, the 1790 Act followed the Statute of Anne in requiring authors to register the work (with the clerk of a U.S. District Court) *before* publication, and to deposit a copy with the Secretary of State. In addition, the 1790 Act required that notice of the registration be published in a newspaper for four consecutive weeks. In 1802, Congress required that notice be printed in each published copy of the work. In 1834, in *Wheaton v. Peters*, the U.S. Supreme Court determined that strict compliance with these formalities was required to obtain copyright protection, meaning that non-compliance would place the work in the public domain. While the requirement of publication in a newspaper was later dropped, the formalities of registration, notice, and deposit were retained in some form in subsequent statutory revisions up to and including the 1909 Act.

All of that began to change with the passage of the Copyright Act of 1976, effective January 1, 1978. The 1976 Act anticipated, although it did not immediately accomplish, U.S. adherence to the Berne Convention by loosening, but not abrogating, many of the statutory formalities. An end to the formalities as conditions of copyright protection came finally with passage of the Berne Convention Implementation Act of 1988, effective March 1, 1989.

Yet, while they have been reduced in importance, the formalities remain very much a part of U.S. copyright law, both in their impact on the copyright status of works created before March 1, 1989 and as means whereby copyright owners, even today, may obtain certain important benefits, both statutory and practical. In short, publication and the statutory formalities are, and will remain for the foreseeable future, topics of considerable complexity and continuing relevance that require, and will reward, careful study.

§ 6.01   PUBLICATION

In the divided world of American copyright before the Copyright Act of 1976 took effect on January 1, 1978, "publication" was the central concept. Unpublished works were protected by "common-law copyright" under state law, while published works (and, to be scrupulously accurate, a very few unpublished works registered under § 12 of the 1909 Act) were protected only by "statutory" copyright under federal law. Generally speaking, copyright protection under state law ceased upon first publication. As of that moment, federal law *might*, but only might, extend protection to the work. We say "might" because, unlike the copyright protection which, under the 1976 Act, attaches automatically as of "fixation," copyright protection under the 1909 Act did not automatically ensue from the fact of publication itself. For protection to attach, the copyright claimant had to place copyright notice, in proper form and position, on published copies of the work.

Because so much depended on the concept of publication in pre-1978 American copyright law, a rich and detailed body of case law grew up, interpreting the statutory provisions relating to publication. In particular, the courts distinguished two kinds of publication. "General" publication was the genuine article for legal purposes: It *divested* perpetual "common-law" (that is, state-law) copyright in an unpublished work, and it had the potential to *invest* "statutory" (that is, federal) copyright, running for a limited time from the date of publication. "Limited" publication was publication only in lay terms — an event that left the legal *status quo* unaffected, even though the actor, in publishing, failed to observe the statutory formalities of copyright.

When does publication matter under the Copyright Act of 1976? Under the 1976 Act, as we saw in Chapter 2, the dividing line between protection and nonprotection is now the *fixation* of an original work. But although *publication* is no longer the event that "divests" a work of one kind of copyright and "invests" it with another, it is still necessary to understand what publication, whether "general" or "limited," means, both because many provisions of the 1976 Act still depend on the concept of "publication," and because practitioners will continue for years to encounter infringement actions in which the threshold issue is whether the work allegedly infringed had already lost its copyright, due to publication without notice, at a time when notice was still legally required.

The following categorization of domestic works[1] shows how the impact of publication depends on the period of time during which the publication occurred.

Works published prior to January 1, 1978

Before January 1, 1978, the effective date of the 1976 Act, unpublished works were protected by state law (so-called "common-law copyright"). Once a work was "published," state-law protection ended, and one of two things happened. If the work was published with proper copyright notice, it obtained a federal statutory copyright under § 10 of the 1909 Act. If the work was published without proper

---

[1] Section 104A, which "restores" U.S. copyright protection for many foreign works (see detailed discussion in § 5.01 above), renders some of the generalizations that follow inapplicable to many works of foreign origin.

copyright notice, it immediately entered the public domain. Publication, therefore, was the principal dividing line between state and federal protection, and the initial term of 28 years was measured from the date of first publication.[2]

If the copyrights in such works arose prior to 1964 and were not properly renewed, the works entered the public domain; if such copyrights *were* properly renewed, they acquired what is now an additional 67 years of protection. If the copyrights in such works arose between 1964 and 1977, they became subject to automatic renewal by virtue of the Copyright Renewal Act of 1992. All of these works, by definition, had been published *already* (or registered for federal copyright as unpublished works). But any *new* publication of such a work, without proper notice, had the effect of forfeiting copyright protection and placing the work in the public domain.

If a work remained unpublished (and unregistered) on January 1, 1978, its subsisting state-law copyright was transmuted into a federal copyright by § 303 of the 1976 Act. Under § 303, that federal copyright endures for the normal term of copyright given to post-1978 works, subject to a statutory minimum term whose duration depends on whether such works were *published* on or before December 31, 2002.

Works published between January 1, 1978 and February 28, 1989

For works created on or after January 1, 1978, publication has no investitive/divestitive effect, but it is still not without importance. For example, publication still matters in determining the eligibility of works of foreign origin, the ability to recover statutory damages and attorneys' fees, the duration of copyright for works made for hire, and the five-year termination window for all works. More importantly, copies of *any* work published between January 1, 1978 and March 1, 1989 (whether created before or after January 1, 1978) were required to bear a proper copyright notice. Failure to provide such notice forfeited all copyright protection and placed the work in the public domain, unless the copyright owner "cured" the omission of notice by complying with § 405 (as described in § 6.02 below).

Works published on or after March 1, 1989

As of March 1, 1989, the effective date of the Berne Convention Implementation Act, notice no longer is required when a work is published. But the use of proper copyright notice on published copies limits an infringer's ability to claim innocent infringement in mitigation of statutory damages (a point further explored in § 11.01 below). In addition, all of the consequences of publication described in the paragraph above, other than forfeiture, continue to apply.

Look back over the three categories above and note how often publication (or its absence) determined the copyright fate of a work whose status may still be relevant to 21st-Century attorneys and their clients. Although created to deal with copyright in a pre-1978 world, the law of publication remains highly relevant today.

---

[2] Authors could also secure federal statutory copyrights in certain kinds of unpublished works by registering them under § 12 of the 1909 Act. In such cases, state-law protection was terminated, and the initial 28-year federal term began, on the date of registration.

[A]   Introduction

Statutory References

1976 Act: §§ 101 ("treaty party," "publication"), 104(b), 304, 401-02, 405-07; Transitional and Supplementary Provisions § 103

1909 Act: §§ 2, 7, 10, 12-13, 22-23, 26

Legislative History[3]

H.R. Rep. No. 94-1476 at 129-30,
reprinted in 1976 U.S.C.C.A.N. 5659, 5745-46

Section 301. Federal Preemption of Rights Equivalent to Copyright

Single Federal system

Section 301, one of the bedrock provisions of the bill, would accomplish a fundamental and significant change in the present law [*i.e.*, the 1909 Act]. Instead of a dual system of "common law copyright" for unpublished works and statutory copyright for published works, which has been the system in effect in the United States since the first copyright statute in 1790, the bill adopts a single system of Federal statutory copyright from creation. Under section 301 a work would obtain statutory protection as soon as it is "created" or, as that term is defined in section 101, when it is "fixed in a copy or phonorecord for the first time." Common law copyright protection for works coming within the scope of the statute would be abrogated, and the concept of publication would lose its all-embracing importance as a dividing line between common law and statutory protection and between both of these forms of legal protection and the public domain.

By substituting a single Federal system for the present anachronistic, uncertain, impractical, and highly complicated dual system, the bill would greatly improve the operation of the copyright law and would be much more effective in carrying out the basic constitutional aims of uniformity and the promotion of writing and scholarship. The main arguments in favor of a single Federal system can be summarized as follows:

> 1. One of the fundamental purposes behind the copyright clause of the Constitution . . . was to promote national uniformity [in] determining and enforcing an author's rights. . . . Today, when the methods for dissemination of an author's work are incomparably broader and faster than they were in 1789, national uniformity in copyright protection is even more essential. . . .

> 2. "Publication," perhaps the most important single concept under the [1909 Act], also represents its most serious defect. Although at one time, when works were disseminated almost exclusively through printed copies, "pub-

---

[3] Do not bother, at this time, to read § 301 itself, which is treated in Chapter 11 in connection with federal preemption of state law. The present excerpt from the legislative history of § 301 is offered solely to assist you in understanding the concept of publication.

lication" could serve as a practical dividing line between common law and statutory protection, this is no longer true. With the development of the 20th-[C]entury communications revolution, the concept of publication has become increasingly artificial and obscure. . . .

3. Enactment of section 301 would also implement the "limited times" provision of the Constitution. . . . Common law protection in "unpublished" works is now perpetual, no matter how widely they may be disseminated by means other than "publication"; the bill would place a time limit on the duration of exclusive rights in them. . . .

4. Adoption of a uniform national copyright system would greatly improve international dealings in copyrighted material. No other country has anything like our present dual system. . . .

Under section 301, the statute would apply to all works created after [January 1, 1978], whether or not they are ever published or disseminated. With respect to works created before [that date] and still under common law protection, section 303 of the statute would provide protection from that date on, and would guarantee a minimum period of statutory copyright. . . .

[For a fuller excerpt from H.R. Rep. No. 94-1476, see Part Three of the Casebook Supplement.]

[B]   Publication in the Courts

ACADEMY OF MOTION PICTURE ARTS AND SCIENCES v. CREATIVE HOUSE PROMOTIONS, INC.
United States Court of Appeals, Ninth Circuit
944 F.2d 1446 (1991)

PREGERSON, CIRCUIT JUDGE:

Appellant-cross-appellee Academy of Motion Picture Arts and Sciences ("the Academy") brought an action in the district court for copyright . . . infringement . . . against appellee-cross-appellant Creative House Promotions, Inc. ("Creative House") for marketing the "Star Award," a gold figure closely resembling the Academy's famous "Oscar" statuette. The district court concluded after a bench trial that the Oscar was not entitled to copyright protection because it had previously entered the public domain. [The court also considered, and ruled against the Academy on, both trademark infringement and various related state law claims.]

The Academy appeals. . . . We have jurisdiction under 28 U.S.C. § 1291, and we reverse. . . .

BACKGROUND

. . . In 1929, the Academy began its annual awards ceremony, in which it recognizes industry artists for outstanding achievement in their fields and bestows upon them the coveted "Oscar" statuette. The awards ceremony has been televised annually since 1953. . . .

From 1929 through 1941, the Academy claimed common law copyright protection for the Oscar as an unpublished work of art. Each of the 158 Oscars awarded during that time bore its winner's name, but did not display any statutory copyright notice. In 1941, the Academy registered the Oscar with the United States Copyright Office as an unpublished work of art not reproduced for sale. All Oscars awarded since that time contained statutory copyright notices. In 1968, the statutory copyright was renewed.

After securing the original copyright registration in 1941, the Academy restricted the manner in which winners could advertise their Oscars. Specifically, any advertisements featuring the Oscar had to identify the year and category in which the recipient won the award. The Academy also required recipients to give the Academy rights of first refusal on any intended sale of their Oscar. Before this time, the Academy had not placed any express restrictions on the use or disposal of the award.

In 1950, the estate of post-mortem Oscar recipient Sid Grauman offered Grauman's Oscar for sale at a public auction. No Oscar had previously been offered for sale. An Academy representative ultimately purchased the award.

In 1976, Creative House . . . commissioned a trophy sculptor to design a striking figure holding a star in its hand. The finished product was a naked, muscular male figure closely resembling the Oscar, known as the "Star Award." Both the Star Award and the Oscar are solid metal with a shiny gold finish and stand on a circular gold cap mounted on a round base. The district court found only two significant differences between the two: the Star Award is two inches shorter than the Oscar, and holds a star rather than a sword. [Creative House marketed the Star Award to corporate buyers, who would present the award to their highest-performing salespeople.] . . .

After a bench trial, the district court ruled, in a published opinion, that the Oscar was not entitled to copyright protection because a divesting, general publication of the Oscar occurred before the 1976 Copyright Act's effective date of January 1, 1978, which triggered a loss of the pre-1941, common law copyright.[1] In concluding that the Oscar had "entered the public domain" through a general publication, the court rejected the Academy's argument that publication of the Oscar had been limited to a select group of persons for a limited purpose. . . .

---

[1] Because of differing protections between common law and statutory copyright under the 1909 Copyright Act, the concept of "publication" has become a legal word of art. A publication is deemed to occur "when by consent of the copyright owner, the original or tangible copies of a work are sold, leased, loaned, given away, or otherwise made available to the general public, or when an authorized offer is made to dispose of the work in any such manner even if a sale or other such disposition does not in fact occur." *American Vitagraph v. Levy*, 659 F.2d 1023, 1027 (9th Cir. 1981), quoting 1 Nimmer § 4.04 at 4-18 to 4-19. Under the Copyright Act of 1976, an act of publication which injects a work into the public domain before January 1, 1978 strips the work of its protection under both the common law and the 1976 Act.

"And the Winner Is . . ."
(Clark Gable at the 1935 Ceremonies)
The Everett Collection

DISCUSSION

I. Copyright Validity

Under the Copyright Act of 1976 ("the 1976 Act"), a copyrighted work is entitled to protection if it has not become part of the public domain prior to the Act's effective date of January 1, 1978. The district court ruled that the Oscar was not entitled to protection under the 1976 Act because it had entered the public domain through a general publication before it was protected by statutory copyright in 1941. The Academy attacks that ruling by arguing that the district court (1) failed to recognize and apply a presumption that the Oscar was a protected, unpublished work in light of its 1941 copyright registration certificate; and (2) erred in finding that a general publication of the Oscar occurred before January 1, 1978.

A. Statutory Presumption

The Academy maintains that the Oscar's 1941 copyright registration as a work "not reproduced for sale" under § 11 of the 1909 Copyright Act raised a statutory presumption of copyright validity. . . .

We agree that the district court erred in failing to afford the Academy's 1941 copyright a presumption of validity. Section 209 of the 1909 Act . . . creates a rebuttable presumption that the certificate holder has met all the requirements for copyright validity. In this case, the certificate of registration creates a rebuttable presumption that the Oscar was an unpublished work in 1941. As a result, Creative House bore the burden of showing that the Oscar entered the public domain before 1941.

B. General v. Limited Publication

Under the common law, the creator of an artistic work has the right to copy and profit from the work, and can distribute or show it to a limited class of persons for a limited purpose without losing that common law copyright. *Burke v. National Broadcasting Co.*, 598 F.2d 688, 691 (1st Cir. 1979). This sort of limited distribution is known as a "limited publication." If the creator exceeds the scope of a limited publication and allows the work to pass into the public domain, a "general publication" of the work occurs. At that point, unless the creator has obtained a statutory copyright,[2] anyone can copy, distribute or sell the work. *Id*. Although an artistic work may be exposed to the public by exhibition, by limited publication, or by general publication, only general publication triggers the loss of the creator's common law copyright. *Id*. The distinction between general and limited publication reflects an attempt by courts to mitigate the harsh forfeiture effects of a divesting general publication. *American Vitagraph, Inc. v. Levy*, 659 F.2d 1023, 1027 (9th Cir. 1981). As a result, "it takes more in the way of publication to invalidate any copyright, whether statutory or common law, than to validate it." *Id*. . . .

The district court correctly determined that the Oscar did not become part of the public domain merely by being publicly displayed or presented at the award ceremonies. In general under the common law, mere performance or exhibition of an artistic work does not amount to a publication. *Ferris v. Frohman*, 223 U.S. 424, 435 (1912). . . . Moreover, publishing pictures of the Oscar in books, newspapers, and magazines did not thrust the award into the public domain, because publishing two-dimensional pictures does not constitute a divesting publication of three-dimensional objects. . . .

Although merely displaying the Oscar to the public does not divest the award of common law copyright protection, Creative House argues that the Academy's distribution of the Oscar to 158 recipients between 1929 and 1941 without any express restriction on the use or sale of the award amounted to a divesting, general publication of the work. The Academy maintains that the Oscar's distribution was merely a limited publication.

A general publication occurs when a work is made available to members of the public regardless of who they are or what they will do with it. In contrast, a

---

[2] Once a creator obtains a statutory copyright, the common law copyright is extinguished. Here, the Academy's common law copyright in the Oscar was extinguished in 1941 when it obtained the copyright registration certificate. From that point on, the Oscar was protected by statutory copyright laws.

publication is "limited" — and does not trigger the loss of a common law copyright — when tangible copies of the work are distributed both (1) to a "definitely selected group," and (2) for a limited purpose, without the right of further reproduction, distribution or sale. *White v. Kimmell*, 193 F.2d 744, 746-47 (9th Cir. 1952). We consider each element of *White*'s two-part "limited publication" test separately.

1. Selected group

As the district court concluded, "There is no question that the Academy has awarded the Oscar only to a select group of persons." The Academy distributes the coveted Oscar to performers and members of the motion picture industry selected for outstanding achievement. . . . The majority of performers in the industry will never receive an Oscar. More importantly, the Academy has never sold or distributed the award to the general public.

2. Limited purpose

To meet the "limited purpose" prong of the *White* test, the Academy must show both (a) that the purpose of distributing the Oscar was limited; and (b) that Oscar recipients had no right of sale or further distribution — *i.e.*, that their right of distribution was expressly or impliedly limited. . . .

(a) *Limited purpose.* The district court ruled that the Academy's purpose in presenting the Oscar at its annual awards gala was not just to honor the distinguished recipients, but also to promote the film industry. The court noted that the Academy spends over $800,000 annually to promote the awards ceremony, and that recipients are allowed to advertise their Oscars, with certain limitations. . . . [T]he court concluded that the Academy's purpose was not sufficiently limited because the Academy "exploited the Oscar" to promote the movie industry. We disagree. . . .

The Academy . . . has never sold the Oscar to anyone. In addition, . . . the Academy has never distributed the Oscar to anyone other than the recipients. The fact that Oscar winners are permitted to advertise the fact they won their award, or display pictures of it, does not amount to a distribution. . . .

Moreover, . . . the Academy does not promote the Oscar for its own commercial benefit. While the film industry may benefit incidentally from the Oscar's promotion, indirect commercial benefits do not necessarily transform a limited distribution into a general publication where no direct sales of the work are involved. *See, e.g., Brewer v. Hustler Magazine, Inc.*, 749 F.2d 527, 529 (9th Cir. 1984) (business cards featuring a reproduced photograph distributed for employment purposes amounted to a limited publication); *Hirshon [v. United Artists Corp.]*, 243 F.2d [640,] 645-46 [(D.C. Cir. 1957)] (distribution of 2000 copies of song to broadcasting stations and musicians for "plugging" purposes was a limited publication); *American Vitagraph*, 659 F.2d at 1027 (screening movie to gauge audience reaction found to be a limited publication although small admission fee was charged). We therefore find that the Academy's purpose of advancing the motion picture arts and sciences is a limited one.

(b) *Right of further distribution*. Before 1941, the Academy did not expressly prohibit recipients from selling or disposing of their Oscars. After 1941, the Academy required recipients to give the Academy a right of first refusal on any sale of their award, and imposed various restrictions on advertising.

Although no express restrictions on recipients' use or distribution of the Oscar existed before 1941, we conclude that restrictions on further distribution were implied. . . . In *Hirshon*, the D.C. Circuit held that distributing copies of a song to radio stations for promotional purposes was a limited publication even though further distribution was not expressly restricted. The court noted that not a single copy of the song was ever sold, that no one had been given permission to use the song, and that nothing had been done to give any recipient the impression that he could use the song without first obtaining a license. *Id.* at 645.

Similarly here, neither the Academy nor any living Oscar recipient has ever offered to transfer an Oscar to the general public. Each Oscar trophy is personalized with the name of the individual winner, reflecting the Academy's expectation that the trophy will belong to the recipient alone. Although the Academy has given Oscar recipients permission to advertise their awards, it has never given them permission to sell or distribute their Oscars. Finally, the Academy has done nothing to suggest that recipients are free to make copies of the Oscars and distribute them. *Cf. Brewer*, 749 F.2d at 529 (distribution of business cards deemed a limited publication even though recipients were free to further distribute the cards); *King v. Mister Maestro, Inc.*, 224 F. Supp. 101, 107 (S.D.N.Y. 1963) (oral delivery of King's "I Have a Dream" speech to vast audience found to be a limited publication even though press was given copies of speech for reprinting).

From 1929 until the end of the Oscar's common law copyright protection in 1941, the Academy distributed personalized Oscar statuettes to a select group of distinguished artists. The Academy did not sell or directly profit from the award, nor did it encourage its further distribution. Under the *White* test, the Academy's actions constituted a limited publication that did not divest the Oscar of its common law protection. We therefore reverse the district court's contrary ruling, and remand to allow the Academy to present evidence of copyright infringement. . . .

NOTES AND QUESTIONS

(1) *Overview: 1909 Act considerations*. Under the 1909 Act, a work could receive common-law copyright protection, as a matter of state law, from the moment of creation. If the work was then published *with proper notice*, it received federal statutory copyright protection instead. Hence, the maxim: "Publication is divestitive of common-law copyright and investitive of statutory copyright." Absent proper notice, however, common-law copyright was lost without statutory copyright being gained.

The justification for this doctrine, which sometimes produced harsh results, is founded on the limited-monopoly concept underlying federal copyright law. The prior law allowed the author's right to the privacy of her manuscript to prevail over the public's right of access so long as the work remained unpublished. But "once an author elected to forego the privacy of his manuscript, preferring the more worldly rewards that come with exploitation of his work, he had to accept the limitations on his monopoly imposed by the public interest." *Brown v. Tabb*, 714 F.2d 1088, 1092 (11th Cir. 1983), quoting 1 NIMMER ON COPYRIGHT § 4.03 (1983). Upon general publication, compliance with the formalities of the federal statute would afford the author, in exchange for her perpetual rights under common law, a monopoly of defined duration and carefully prescribed scope. Noncompliance made the public's right of access complete by destroying the monopoly altogether and casting the work into the public domain.

In practice, many courts under the 1909 Act applied different standards in determining whether publication had occurred, depending on whether the issue at bar was divestiture or investiture. *See, e.g., Hirshon v. United Artists Corp.*, 243 F.2d 640, 645 (D.C. Cir. 1957); *American Visuals Corp. v. Holland*, 239 F.2d 740 (2d Cir. 1956) (observing that "[i]n each case the courts appear so to treat the concept of 'publication' as to prevent piracy"). For a more recent application of the investitive/divestitive distinction, see *Dolman v. Agee*, 157 F.3d 708 (9th Cir. 1998) ("under our case law, it takes 'more' publication to destroy a common-law copyright than to perfect a statutory copyright").

(2) As we saw in the principal case (from what Judge Alex Kozinski has called the "Court of Appeals for the Hollywood Circuit"), courts will have to interpret the significance of pre-1978 distributions of copies for years to come. One question that will continue to arise is whether, in distinguishing "general" and "limited" publication, any importance should be attached to the fact that copies of a work were given only to selected, identified individuals, with no copies being offered for sale to the public at large. *See, e.g., Warner Bros. Entertainment, Inc. v. X One X Prods.*, 644 F.3d 584 (8th Cir. 2011) (publicity materials for motion pictures *Gone with the Wind* and *The Wizard of Oz* were "published" without notice; although some agreements with theaters required that movie posters and lobby cards be returned or destroyed, publication was not "limited" because restriction was not enforced and redistribution and sale was encouraged and permitted); *Soc'y of the Holy Transfiguration Monastery, Inc. v. Archbishop Gregory of Denver, Colo.*, 689 F.3d 29 (1st Cir. 2012) (distribution of copyrighted translations of ancient texts to selected congregations for purpose of soliciting editorial feedback was a "limited" publication, and any further distributions were unauthorized and therefore immaterial).

If you think that the court in the *Academy* case stretched the notion of a "limited publication," consider *King v. Mister Maestro, Inc.*, 224 F. Supp. 101 (S.D.N.Y. 1963). In *King*, the court held that Martin Luther King, Jr.'s "I Have a Dream" speech was not in the public domain even though advance copies had been furnished to the press (and excerpts were later broadcast on national television and in movie newsreels). Although publication occurred when the text was given to the press, that publication was held to be "limited" and "non-divestive," rather than "general," because tangible copies were given only to a specific group to assist it in covering an event and were not offered to the public at large.

Martin Luther King Memorial in Washington, D.C.
Corbis

In a sequel decided 35 years later, a different court held that the speech *had* entered the public domain in 1963 and granted summary judgment to CBS, which had incorporated the speech into a TV documentary. The court held that "while performance itself may not be sufficient to constitute publication, performance coupled with such wide and unlimited reproduction and dissemination as occurred [at the time] can only be seen as a general publication which thrust the speech into the public domain." *Estate of Martin Luther King, Jr., Inc. v. CBS, Inc.*, 13 F. Supp. 2d 1347, 1353–54 (N.D. Ga. 1998). On appeal, however, the Eleventh Circuit reversed and remanded for further proceedings. 194 F.3d 1211 (11th Cir. 1999). Both judges in the majority (writing separately) faulted the District Court for failing to give sufficient weight to the principle that a public performance does not itself constitute a publication. If nothing else, the opinions illustrate the complexity of "publication" analysis under the 1909 Act.

   (3) *Fine arts.* How should the concept of "publication" be applied to works of fine art, which may be fixed in unique copies or limited editions? We know that the sale of a painting does not necessarily operate to *transfer* any intellectual property rights to the purchaser. But could it have operated, nonetheless, to *divest* such rights altogether, if it occurred without the notice required by the 1909 Act? See *Grandma Moses Properties, Inc. v. This Week Magazine*, 117 F. Supp. 348 (S.D.N.Y. 1953), where the unrestricted sale of a single copy (without copyright notice) forfeited common-law copyright in a work of art, without investing statutory copyright. Does such a result make any sense? What attitude toward the impor-

tance of copyright formalities does this result reflect? And what, exactly, is an "unrestricted" sale?

Under the 1909 Act, it was unclear whether a public display (say, for example, of a painting in a public art gallery) was a publication. *Compare American Tobacco Co. v. Werckmeister*, 207 U.S. 284 (1907) (public exhibition of a painting was not a publication, at least "where the greatest care was taken to prevent copying") *with Letter Edged in Black Press, Inc. v. Public Building Commission of Chicago*, 320 F. Supp. 1303 (N.D. Ill. 1970) (exhibiting a sculpture model without copyright notice in two museums, together with release of pictures of the model to the press at two press showings, constituted a general publication). By contrast, § 101 of the 1976 Act and Article 3(3) of the Berne Convention agree in excluding performance, broadcasting, and exhibition of works from their definitions of "publication."

(4) *Motion pictures.* Before the home video rental market exploded, it was the general practice of the American motion picture industry never to sell copies of commercially released films. Instead, prints were leased to exhibitors and, when a film was withdrawn from release, the prints of it were either destroyed or stored for future rental use. Although motion pictures usually bore copyright notices upon release, industry practice (especially in the early years) was less than uniform on this point. Would the omission of notice from the release prints of a motion picture have had any legal significance? Or did they continue to enjoy common-law copyright protection while being viewed by national audiences?

What constitutes "publication" of a motion picture? The answer is fairly clear under the 1976 Act, where either "rental, lease, or lending" or "offering to distribute copies . . . to a group of persons for further distribution [or] public performance" will suffice. But what was the rule under the 1909 Act? We know that mere performance or display of a motion picture did not constitute general publication. *Ferris v. Frohman*, 223 U.S. 424 (1912) (involving a dramatic work which had been extensively performed but never published). What *did* constitute publication, however, was never precisely defined until *American Vitagraph, Inc. v. Levy*, 659 F.2d 1023 (9th Cir. 1981), held that exhibition of a movie to paying customers over a one-week period for the limited purpose of gauging audience reaction to the film was a "limited" publication. The court held that publication of a motion picture does not occur "until the film is in commercial distribution — when copies of a film are placed in the regional exchanges for distribution to theatre operators." *Id.* at 1038; *see also Burke v. National Broadcasting Co., Inc.*, 598 F.2d 688 (1st Cir. 1979) (finding a "limited" publication where an individual gave a copy of his film footage to a professor to use in his lectures and on a noncommercial television program).

(5) *Choreography.* What constitutes "publication" of a work of choreography? *See Martha Graham School & Dance Foundation, Inc. v. Martha Graham Center of Contemporary Dance, Inc.*, 380 F.3d 624, 644-45 (2d Cir. 2004) (affirming finding of publication for choreographic works which were listed in business records as "filmed and sold" or "commercially produced films and videotapes," and for works listed in the catalog of the New York Public Library).

(6) *Phonorecords and musical works.* Under the 1909 Act, did the sale of a phonorecord constitute publication of the underlying musical composition? Over the years, this important question (just think about how many works the resolution of

the issue affects) has proved to be anything but simple to answer.

The problem traces its origin to the meaning of the term "copy" under the 1909 Act. Section 9 of that Act required that "notice shall be affixed to each *copy* [of the work] published or offered for sale in the United States." But phonorecords, like piano rolls (recall *White-Smith Music Publ'g Co. v. Apollo Co.*, 209 U.S. 1 (1908), in Chapter 2), generally were not regarded as *copies* of the underlying work. Thus, placing notice on a phonorecord would neither invest nor divest copyright. The leading case articulating this view is *Rosette v. Rainbo Record Mfg. Corp.*, 354 F. Supp. 1183 (S.D.N.Y. 1973), *aff'd per curiam*, 546 F.2d 461 (2d Cir. 1976). Other courts took the opposite view, holding that public sale or other distribution of phonorecords *did* constitute a publication, divesting common-law rights in the works recorded. *See* 1 NIMMER ON COPYRIGHT, § 4.05[B](2) (2010). In *La Cienega Music Co. v. ZZ Top*, 53 F.3d 950 (9th Cir. 1995), for example, the Ninth Circuit rejected *Rosette*, holding that musical works by John Lee Hooker embodied in phonorecords were injected into the public domain, upon sale of the phonorecords, for failure to affix proper notice.

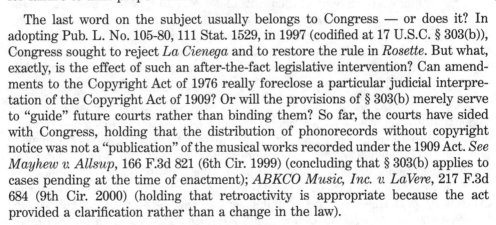

The last word on the subject usually belongs to Congress — or does it? In adopting Pub. L. No. 105-80, 111 Stat. 1529, in 1997 (codified at 17 U.S.C. § 303(b)), Congress sought to reject *La Cienega* and to restore the rule in *Rosette*. But what, exactly, is the effect of such an after-the-fact legislative intervention? Can amendments to the Copyright Act of 1976 really foreclose a particular judicial interpretation of the Copyright Act of 1909? Or will the provisions of § 303(b) merely serve to "guide" future courts rather than binding them? So far, the courts have sided with Congress, holding that the distribution of phonorecords without copyright notice was not a "publication" of the musical works recorded under the 1909 Act. *See Mayhew v. Allsup*, 166 F.3d 821 (6th Cir. 1999) (concluding that § 303(b) applies to cases pending at the time of enactment); *ABKCO Music, Inc. v. LaVere*, 217 F.3d 684 (9th Cir. 2000) (holding that retroactivity is appropriate because the act provided a clarification rather than a change in the law).

In 2010, Congress amended § 303(b) to extend it expressly to phonorecords of literary and dramatic works, as well as musical works.

(7) *Phonorecords and sound recordings.* How does the definition of "publication" for musical works for purposes of federal law affect the state-law protection accorded to sound recordings fixed before February 15, 1972? In *Capitol Records, Inc., v. Naxos of America, Inc.*, 830 N.E.2d 250 (2005), the New York Court of Appeals held that because pre-1972 musical works fixed in phonorecords sold to the public had never been "published" within the meaning of federal law (citing *Rosette* and similar cases), the "common-law copyright" provided by state law to the sound recordings themselves had never been divested and such recordings would remain protected by state law until February 15, 2067 — even if they had entered the public domain in their country of origin. *See* § 301(c) (providing that state-law protection for sound recordings is not preempted until February 15, 2067).

Assuming that a common-law copyright indeed existed prior to "publication," does it make sense to apply the same definition of "publication" to musical works (which *White-Smith* held were infringed only by "visually perceptible" copies) and to sound recordings (which, unlike musical works, can *only* be perceived aurally)?

If so, does it make sense to hold that publicly distributed sound recordings remained "unpublished" after January 1, 1978, when the 1976 Act (defining "publication" as the distribution of copies *or phonorecords* to the public) came into effect? For more on this case, see § 3.01[F] above.

(8) *Publication and the Internet.* Is the posting of a work to a publicly accessible website a "publication"? Does sending the work as an attachment to an e-mail message qualify? The answer would seem to depend (at least in part) on whether making a work in electronic form available to be downloaded, or transmitting that work over a network, constitutes a "distribution of copies." There have been relatively few cases on point. *Compare Getaped.com, Inc. v. Cangemi*, 188 F. Supp. 2d 398 (S.D.N.Y. 2002) (posting a work to a website constitutes "publication"), *with Einhorn v. Mergatroyd Prods.*, 426 F. Supp. 2d 189 (S.D.N.Y. 2006) (posting a video to a website does not constitute "publication"). A number of other cases, however, have noted that the definition of "publication" is broader than the definition of "distribution," in that the former also includes "offering to distribute copies or phonorecords to a group of persons for purposes of further distribution, public performance or public display." *See Atlantic Recording Corp. v. Howell*, 554 F. Supp. 2d 976, 984-85 (D. Ariz. 2008); *London-Sire Records, Inc. v. Doe 1*, 542 F. Supp. 2d 153, 168-69 (D. Mass. 2008). Does posting a work to a publicly accessible website meet the latter definition?

Assume for a moment that posting a work and/or e-mailing it as an attachment does indeed constitute "publication." If so, where does such a publication take place? Where the person posting the work or sending the message resides? Or somewhere else? The answer may be crucial not only for domestic venue purposes, but also for analyzing whether foreign works are protected in the United States or, if protected, whether they must be registered here. *See Moberg v. 33T, LLC*, 666 F. Supp. 2d 415 (D. Del. 2009) (assuming Swedish author's photos were "published" when posted on German website, they were not simultaneously "published" in the United States and were therefore not "United States works" for purposes of the registration requirement); *Kernal Records Oy v. Mosley*, 694 F.3d 1294 (11th Cir. 2012) (suggesting in dicta that posting photos on a publicly available website could effect simultaneous worldwide publication).

(9) *Intent.* What role should the author's intent play in determining whether there was a limited or general publication before 1978? *See Data Cash Systems, Inc. v. JS & A Group, Inc.*, 628 F.2d 1038 (7th Cir. 1980) ("dedication is a question of law, not the intent of the proprietor"); *Public Affairs Associates, Inc. v. Rickover*, 284 F.2d 262 (D.C. Cir. 1960) (holding that the distinction between "general" and "limited" publication is one of degree and depends less on an author's intentions than on his actions).

(10) *Forfeiture and abandonment.* Most courts distinguish between forfeiture and abandonment. Forfeiture typically occurred through publication without proper notice and, as indicated above, was accomplished by operation of law, regardless of the proprietor's intent. Abandonment requires intent, usually evidenced by an overt act such as a statement appearing on copies of the work that anyone who wishes to reproduce, perform, or display the work is free to do so. Sometimes, the distinction between these two ways of losing protection could blur.

For example, before March 1, 1989, if an author wanted to abandon all rights in a work, he simply could have committed the overt act of distributing large numbers of copies without a copyright notice. Today, however, the copyright owner can no longer forfeit copyright, either deliberately or inadvertently, by publishing without notice. For further discussion, see Chapter 10.

(11) Does the distinction between "limited" and "general" publication survive where works first distributed today are concerned? Although no court has squarely addressed the issue, some courts have applied the concept of "limited" publication to publications occurring after the effective date of the 1976 Act. *See, e.g., John G. Danielson, Inc. v. Winchester-Conant Properties, Inc.*, 322 F.3d 26 (1st Cir. 2003) (discussing whether display of architectural plans at meetings open to the public was a limited publication); *Aerospace Servs. Int'l v. LPA Group, Inc.*, 57 F.3d 1002 (11th Cir. 1995). Such a distinction had very real significance prior to March 1, 1989, when failure to affix notice to a work upon publication could still work a forfeiture of copyright. Today, however, notice is optional, although the date of publication still retains importance for other purposes.

(12) *Publication and international copyright law.* Publication is an important concept not only under U.S. law, but under international law as well. The Berne Convention, and other treaties incorporating its norms, commits each member nation to provide protection to the published and unpublished works of all authors who are nationals (or, in some cases, domiciliaries) of other member nations, equal to the protection the member provides for similarly situated works of its own nationals. In addition, Berne countries must protect foreign works by authors who are not nationals or domiciliaries of treaty states, if those works are "first published" in a treaty state. This so-called "back door" to protection stands fairly wide open, especially because, under Article 3(1)(b) of the 1971 Paris Act of the Berne Convention, "simultaneous publication" (that is, publication within 30 days) is equated with "first publication."

The foregoing rule regarding the *timing* of the publication is reflected in 17 U.S.C. § 104(b). But the § 101 definition of "publication" is somewhat broader than the corresponding provision of the Berne Convention. Under Berne, publication does not occur unless enough copies of the work have been made available to "satisfy the reasonable requirements of the public." Suppose that, within 30 days of a work's first appearance in his or her home country, an author who was a resident of a non-Berne country caused 15 copies of that work to be offered for sale at one bookstore in Los Angeles. Later, the author claimed protection in the United States on a "back door to Berne" basis. Which definition of publication — Article 3(3) of the Berne Convention or § 101 of the Copyright Act — would control the determination of that claim? Does § 104(c) provide a conclusive answer to the question?

The TRIPS Agreement requires members of the World Trade Organization to extend copyright protection to the works of nationals of WTO countries. Although it is not clear that this provision required that protection be extended, in addition, to works first published in the territory of such countries, legislative implementation of the TRIPS Agreement had this effect. *See generally* § 2.03 above. In addition, the legislation generalized the Berne-derived concept of "simultaneous" publication to apply to all works for which protection in the United States is claimed on the basis of publication in "treaty parties" (a category including members of Berne and the U.C.C., as well as WTO countries). *See* § 104(b).

[C]   Publication, Derivative Works, and the Public Domain

This note concerns a copyright conundrum under the 1909 Act, the nature of which can best be illustrated by a hypothetical. Suppose that, in 1975, the author and copyright owner of a properly copyrighted novel — one, that is, which previously had been published with appropriate copyright notice — decided to revise the work by adding a new conclusion, changing the gender of one of the principal characters throughout, and eliminating some extraneous dialogue from passages in several chapters. When the new version was completed, it was generally published — but without proper copyright notice. As we know from the preceding discussion of publication, this act injected the new version (or, as it would be called in 1976 terminology, the "derivative work") into the public domain. The question is this: After the "divestitive publication" of the derivative work, what is the copyright status of the underlying work?

In answering the question, reconsider the topic of "derivative work independence," already discussed in a very different context in connection with *Stewart v. Abend* in Chapter 5. Because the copyright in an authorized derivative work covers only the new material added to the underlying work, it might well be argued that, while the circumstances in which such a derivative work is published could affect its own copyright status, they would not alter the legal position of the underlying work. That is the position taken in *Rushton v. Vitale*, 218 F.2d 434 (2d Cir. 1955) (publication of a photograph of a three-dimensional doll did not dedicate the figure itself to the public) and *National Council of Young Israel, Inc. v. Feit, Co.*, 347 F. Supp. 1293 (S.D.N.Y. 1972) (lack of notice on licensee's catalog was no defense where defendant copied same drawings from plaintiff's copyrighted catalog). This understanding arguably gives force to the command of § 7 of the 1909 Act, which provided that "the publication of any . . . new work[ ] shall not affect the force or validity of any subsisting copyright. . . ." For the opposing view, see 1 NIMMER ON COPYRIGHT § 4.12[A] (2012) ("any authorized publication of a derivative work must necessarily also constitute a publication of the preexisting work on which it is based").

Some guidance may be found in cases that actually addressed the effect on underlying works of the forfeiture of derivative work copyright by means other than dedicatory publication. In *Grove Press, Inc. v. Greenleaf Publishing Co.*, 247 F. Supp. 518 (E.D.N.Y. 1965), rights in an authorized English translation of a French novel (itself validly copyrighted under American law) were lost through failure to comply with the *ad interim* provisions of the 1909 Copyright Act. Arguing that the copyright on the underlying work remained valid in all respects and that the defendant's republication of the now unprotected word-for-word translation would infringe the still-protected "pattern" of the French novel, the owner of the underlying work brought suit — and won. By contrast, both *Shoptalk, Ltd. v. Concorde-New Horizons Corp.*, 168 F.3d 586 (2d Cir. 1999), and *Batjac Productions, Inc. v. GoodTimes Home Video Corp.*, 160 F.3d 1223 (9th Cir. 1998), held that common-law copyright in an unpublished screenplay was lost to the extent that the screenplay was disclosed in a motion picture, with the result that the screenplay entered the public domain simultaneously with the motion picture. *Shoptalk* and *Batjac* construed the language of § 7 of the 1909 Act as referring to *statutory*, not common-law, protection.

An interesting twist occurs when a work that would otherwise be considered a derivative work is published before the work from which it is derived, so that the derivative must be treated as the underlying work for purposes of federal copyright law. For example, in *Warner Bros. Entertainment, Inc. v. X One X Prods.*, 644 F.3d 584 (8th Cir. 2011), the court found that certain publicity materials for the motion pictures *Gone with the Wind* and *The Wizard of Oz* had been published without notice before the movies were released, and were in the public domain. The defendant was allowed to reproduce the public domain materials in whole or in part, but the court held that *combining* images from those public domain materials in a way that "evoked" the "incremental expression" added in the later-copyrighted movies was infringing. The court also held that three-dimensional figurines based on the two-dimensional publicity materials were infringing, because the artists added the missing visual details by referring to the movies. *See also Siegel v. Warner Bros. Entertainment, Inc.*, 542 F. Supp. 2d 1098 (C.D. Cal. 2008) (in § 5.02[D] above), in which two black-and-white promotional ads for the first issue of *Action Comics* No. 1 (featuring Superman) received federal statutory copyright before the issue itself was published, leaving the court to ponder the effect of a termination notice that was timely only for the latter, and not the former.

The issues discussed here are matters of both intellectual interest and practical importance. For one thing, copyright lawyers will continue to be confronted with cases turning on the consequences of events that took place before January 1, 1978. In addition, forfeiture remained a possibility under the 1976 Act until March 1, 1989. In short, although the conundrum outlined by this note may have receded, it has by no means disappeared.

§ 6.02 NOTICE

Reliance on copyright formalities — including notice, registration, and deposit — has been a characteristic (some would say a defect) of American copyright law from its inception. Initially, some courts entertained substantial doubt concerning the rigor with which Congress intended them to enforce the various statutory formalities. The earliest American copyright case excused certain prerequisites to federal copyright as merely "directory." *Nichols v. Ruggles*, 3 Day 145 (Conn. 1808). The second decision, however, held that the formalities were "mandatory," not "directory," and that any departure from the strict requirements of the applicable statutes was fatal to the author's rights. *Ewer v. Coxe*, 8 F. Cas. 917 (C.C.E.D. Pa. 1824).

In 1834, the Supreme Court settled the matter by deciding in favor of the "mandatory" view. *Wheaton v. Peters*, 33 U.S. (8 Pet.) 591. *See generally* Joyce, *"A Curious Chapter in the History of Judicature":* Wheaton v. Peters *and the Rest of the Story (of Copyright in the New Republic)*, 42 Hous. L. Rev. 325 (2005). Both the 1909 Act and, to a lesser extent, the 1976 Act reflect this long-settled principle that the price of federal copyright is punctilious observance of the statutory formalities.

For much of the history of American copyright, our national preoccupation with formalities has been focused, in particular, on copyright notice. The Copyright Act of 1790 required publication of notice in a newspaper for four consecutive weeks. The requirement of notice on all published copies was introduced in 1802. The prescribed form of notice ran to 100 words, more or less, depending on the particulars of the work in question. The familiar short form of notice (consisting of the word "Copyright," the year of registration, and the name of the author) was not introduced until 1874.

In the 1909 Act, the form of the notice required to comply with the statute was redefined (once and for all), and the rule relating to noncompliance became what it would remain until 1978: failure to satisfy notice requirements when a work was published would cause immediate, permanent forfeiture of all copyright protection under both state and federal law. Although judge-made law under the 1909 Act showed some tendency toward the amelioration of this harsh principle in its actual application, the changes were, at most, marginal ones.

Passage of the 1976 Act did not produce the changes in the law of notice that might have been expected in light of other differences between that statute and its predecessor. Under the 1909 Act, terms of copyright ran from the date of publication, so that notice had an obvious utility. By contrast, most works created after the effective date of the 1976 Copyright Act are protected for fixed terms related to the lengths of their authors' lives, rendering a calculation of the term based on the date of the copyright notice impossible. *See generally* Chapter 5 above. Even so, the notice formality was retained in the 1976 legislation. And although that Act moved further away from rigorous enforcement of the notice requirement (providing, for example, limited means for curing an omission or defect in copyright notice after the fact of publication, so as to avoid forfeiture), even under this new scheme, works continued to fall into the public domain as a result of their proprietors' failures to comply fully with notice formalities.

The U.S. approach to formalities was drastically out of step with practice in most other nations of the world, which permitted copyright to be claimed without requiring compliance with any formalities as a condition to protection. Indeed, Article 5(2) of the Berne Convention *prohibits* the imposition of formalities such as notice as a prerequisite to protecting (a) works by the nationals of other signatory states or (b) works first or simultaneously published in such states. Thus, the United States could not adhere to the Berne Convention *and* maintain its traditional approach to copyright notice.

Although the United States could have modified its law so as to provide for a "two-tier" approach — that is, an approach requiring notice for domestic works but not for works claiming protection by way of Berne (the approach taken, as we will see, in accommodating U.S. law on copyright registration to the Berne *minima*) —

it did not. Instead, as of March 1, 1989, the use of copyright notice *ceased to be mandatory* under American law for *all* works. But although the Berne Convention Implementation Act retained a token incentive to the voluntary use of notice, the most significant incentive is a practical one: Many laypeople still believe notice is required, so the use of notice may deter law-abiding people from infringing. Thus, no prudent lawyer, even today, would advise a client that it was wise to dispense with notice.

[A] Introduction

Statutory References

1976 Act: §§ 101 ("best edition," "publicly"), 401-06; Transitional and Supplementary Provisions § 108

1909 Act: §§ 8, 10, 19-21

Legislative History

H.R. REP. No. 94-1476 at 143-44,
reprinted in 1976 U.S.C.C.A.N. 5659, 5759-60

SECTION 401. NOTICE ON VISUALLY-PERCEPTIBLE COPIES

Under the [1909 Act,] the copyright notice serves four principal functions:

(1) It has the effect of placing in the public domain a substantial body of published material that no one is interested in copyrighting;

(2) It informs the public as to whether a particular work is copyrighted;

(3) It identifies the copyright owner; and

(4) It shows the date of publication.

Ranged against these values of a notice requirement are its burdens and unfairness to copyright owners. One of the strongest arguments for revision of the [1909 Act] has been the need to avoid the arbitrary and unjust forfeitures now resulting from unintentional or relatively unimportant omissions or errors in the copyright notice. . . .

The fundamental principle underlying the notice provisions of the bill is that the copyright notice has real values which should be preserved, and that this should be done by inducing use of notice without causing outright forfeiture for errors or omissions. Subject to certain safeguards for innocent infringers, protection would not be lost by the complete omission of copyright notice from large numbers of copies or from a whole edition, if registration for the work is made before or within 5 years after publication. Errors in the name or date in the notice could be corrected without forfeiture of copyright.

Sections 401 and 402 set out the basic notice requirements of the bill, the former dealing with "copies from which the work can be visually perceived," and the latter covering "phonorecords" of a "sound recording." . . .

Subsections (a) of both section 401 and section 402 require that a notice be used whenever the work "is published in the United States or elsewhere by authority of the copyright owner." The phrase "or elsewhere," which does not appear in the [1909 Act], makes the notice requirements applicable to copies or phonorecords distributed to the public anywhere in the world, regardless of where and when the work was first published. . . .

[The following sections of the House Report have been omitted entirely here: § 402 (Notice on Phonorecords of Sound Recordings); § 403 (Notice for Publications Incorporating United States Works; § 404 (Notice for Contributions to Collective Works); § 405 (Omission of Copyright Notice); and § 406 (Error with Respect to Name or Date in Notice). These matters are covered in Copyright Office Circular No. 3 below, and in the Notes and Questions following the Circular.]

[For a fuller excerpt from H.R. REP. No. 94-1476, see Part Three of the Casebook Supplement.]

House Report on the Berne Convention Implementation Act of 1988 (Excerpts)
H.R. REP. No. 100-609 at 26, 45-46 (1988) (footnotes omitted)

. . . [T]he [BCIA] amends [the 1976 Act as originally enacted] in several areas. The intent of all these changes is to make the law with respect to the use of copyright notice . . . compatible with Berne while simultaneously doing no more to the present law than is absolutely necessary. The amendments to sections 401 and 402 make use of the copyright notice voluntary — a work will no longer fall into the public domain at any time because it is published without notice. At the same time, if a copyright owner elects to use a notice, its form is specified in the law. . . .

Sections 405 and 406 of current law, which deal with omissions of and errors in the copyright notice[,] are amended so as to apply only to works published . . . [,] with or without a copyright notice[,] before the effective date of the [BCIA]. Works created before the effective date of the [BCIA] but only first published after the effective date are subject to the voluntary provisions of the Act and not the mandatory provisions of prior law. . . .

**NOTICE PROVISIONS FOR PUBLISHED WORKS
UNDER THE 1909, 1976, AND
BERNE CONVENTION IMPLEMENTATION ACTS**

FOR WORKS PUBLISHED BEFORE 1/1/78	FOR WORKS PUBLISHED ON OR AFTER 1/1/78 AND BEFORE 3/1/89	FOR WORKS PUBLISHED ON OR AFTER 3/1/89
Federal protection began upon general publication with proper notice. Publication without proper notice placed work in public domain. §§ 10, 19 (1909 Act). See also § 104A (1976 Act) regarding restoration of foreign copyrights under TRIPS.	Notice required for all published works. If work published without notice, copyright owner had to comply with five-year cure provisions to avoid placing work in public domain. § 405(a). See also § 104A regarding TRIPS restoration of foreign copyrights.	Notice is optional. §§ 401-404. Lack of notice may allow reduction in amount of statutory damages for innocent infringer defense. §§ 401(d), 402(d).

[B]   Concepts and Procedures

U.S. Copyright Office
Circular 3: Copyright Notice (Excerpts)
(Aug. 2011)

U.S. law no longer requires the use of a copyright notice, although it is often beneficial. Prior law did, however, contain such a requirement, and the use of a notice is still relevant to the copyright status of older works. This circular describes the copyright notice provisions enacted in the 1976 Copyright Act (title 17, *U. S. Code*), which took effect January 1, 1978, and the effect of the 1988 Berne Convention Implementation Act, which amended the law to make the use of a copyright notice optional on copies of works published on and after March 1, 1989.
. . .

Works published before January 1, 1978, are governed by the previous copyright law. Under that law, if a work was published under the copyright owner's authority without a proper notice of copyright, all copyright protection for that work was permanently lost in the United States. . . .

Uruguay Round Agreements Act

For certain foreign works, the Uruguay Round Agreements Act (URAA) of 1994 modifies the effect of publication without notice. The act restores copyright automatically for certain foreign works that were placed in the public domain because they lacked proper notice or failed to comply with other legal requirements. Although restoration is automatic, if a copyright owner wants to enforce rights against reliance parties (those who, relying on the public domain status of a work, were already using the work before the copyright was restored), the copyright owner must either file a Notice of Intent to Enforce a Restored Copyright with the Copyright Office or serve such a notice on the reliance party. . . .

Use of the Copyright Notice

Copyright is a form of protection provided by U.S. law to authors of "original works of authorship." When a work is published under the authority of the copyright owner . . . , a notice of copyright may be placed on all publicly distributed copies or phonorecords. The use of the notice is the responsibility of the copyright owner and does not require permission from, or registration with, the Copyright Office.

Use of the notice informs the public that a work is protected by copyright, identifies the copyright owner, and shows the year of first publication. Furthermore, in the event that a work is infringed, if the work carries a proper notice, the court will not give any weight to a defendants use of an innocent infringement defense — that is, to a claim that the defendant did not realize that the work was protected. An innocent infringement defense can result in a reduction in damages that the copyright owner would otherwise receive.

For works first published on or after March 1, 1989, use of the copyright notice is optional. Before March 1, 1989, the use of the notice was mandatory on all published works. Omitting the notice on any work first published before that date could have resulted in the loss of copyright protection if corrective steps were not taken within a certain amount of time. . . .

The Copyright Office does not take a position on whether reprints of works first published with notice before March 1, 1989, that are distributed on or after March 1, 1989, must bear the copyright notice. . . .

Form of Notice

The form of the copyright notice used for "visually perceptible" copies — that is, those that can be seen or read, either directly (such as books) or with the aid of a machine (such as films) — is different from the form used for phonorecords of sound recordings (such as compact discs or cassettes).

Visually Perceptible Copies

The notice for visually perceptible copies should contain all three elements described below. They should appear together or in close proximity on the copies.

1. *The symbol* © (letter C in a circle), or the word "Copyright," or the abbreviation "Copr."

2. *The year of first publication.* If the work is a derivative work or a compilation incorporating previously published material, the year date of first publication of the derivative work or compilation is sufficient. Examples of derivative works are translations or dramatizations; an example of a compilation is an anthology. The year may be omitted when a pictorial,

graphic, or sculptural work, with accompanying textual matter, if any, is reproduced in or on greeting cards, postcards, stationery, jewelry, dolls, toys, or useful articles.

3. *The name of the owner of copyright in the work*, an abbreviation by which the name can be recognized, or a generally known alternative designation of the owner.[1] *Example* © 2007 Jane Doe.

The "C in a circle" notice is used only on "visually perceptible" copies. Certain kinds of works, for example, musical, dramatic, and literary works, may be fixed not in "copies" but by means of sound in an audio recording. Since audio recordings such as audio tapes and phonograph disks are "phonorecords" and not "copies," the "C in a circle" notice is not used to indicate protection of the underlying musical, dramatic, or literary work that is recorded.

Phonorecords of Sound Recordings

[The Circular discusses the analogous requirements for notice of works embodying sound recordings. *Example* ℗ 2007 X.Y.Z. Records, Inc. — *Eds.*] . . .

Publications Incorporating U.S. Government Works

Works by the U.S. Government are not eligible for copyright protection. For works published on and after March 1, 1989, the previous notice requirement for works consisting primarily of one or more U.S. Government works has been eliminated. However, use of a notice on such a work will defeat a claim of innocent infringement as previously described provided the notice also includes a statement identifying either those portions of the work in which copyright is claimed or those portions that constitute U.S. Government material. Example "© 2007 Ann Doe. Copyright claimed in Chapters 7–10, exclusive of U.S. Government maps."

Copies of works published before March 1, 1989, that consist primarily of one or more works of the U.S. Government should have a notice and the identifying statement.

Position of Notice

The copyright notice should be placed on copies or phonorecords in such a way that it gives reasonable notice of the claim of copyright. The notice should be permanently legible to an ordinary user of the work under normal conditions of use and should not be concealed from view upon reasonable examination.

The Copyright Office has issued regulations . . . concerning the position of the notice and methods of affixation. [*See* 37 C.F.R. § 201.20] . . .

---

[1] The United States is a member of the Universal Copyright Convention (the UCC), which came into force on September 16, 1955. To guarantee protection for a copyrighted work in all UCC member countries, the notice must consist of the symbol © (the word "Copyright" or the abbreviation is *not* acceptable), the year of first publication, and the name of the copyright proprietor. *Example* © 2007 John Doe. For information about international copyright relationships, read Circular 38a, *International Copyright Relations of the United States.*

Omission of Notice and Errors in Notice

The 1976 Copyright Act attempted to ameliorate the strict consequences of failure to include notice under prior law. It contained provisions that set out specific corrective steps to cure omissions or errors in notice. Under these provisions, an applicant had five years after publication to cure omission of notice or certain errors. Although these provisions are technically still in the law, their impact is limited by the Berne Convention Implementation Act, making notice optional for all works published on and after March 1, 1989. There may, however, still be instances, such as the defense of innocent infringement, where the question of proper notice may be a factor in assessing damages in infringement actions. . . .

NOTES AND QUESTIONS

(1) *The notice requirement: an overview.* As we saw in its legislative history, the Copyright Act of 1976 retained the notice requirement that had so long been part of U.S. law (typically, the symbol ©, the year of first publication, and the name of the copyright owner). It took eleven more years, until passage of the Berne Convention Implementation Act of 1988, for Congress to abrogate notice as a formal requirement for copyright protection. Nonetheless, the House Report on the BCIA states that "in deference to the utility of notice[,] . . . the legislation [is] designed to stimulate voluntary notice. . . ." H.R. Rep. No. 100-609, at 45. What purposes were served by the notice requirements of the 1976 Act? To what extent had notice under the 1976 Act already outlived the usefulness it possessed under the 1909 Act? And how did the notice requirements of those two Acts differ?

(2) One innovation was introduced into the law by the Sound Recording Amendments Act of 1971 and has been maintained in subsequent revisions — the ℗ notice for sound recordings. "℗" stands for "phonogram," an internationally used synonym for "sound recording," which term one should always distinguish from "phonorecord," the term that § 101 uses to designate the physical object in which a sound recording is fixed. The required form of notice is set forth in § 402(b). Under § 402(b)(3), the ℗ notice may omit the name of a copyright claimant if the producer of the phonorecord in question is identified elsewhere on the phonorecord or its packaging. (The ℗ notice applies only to the sound recording itself — and not to the musical or literary work which also may be fixed in a phonorecord. Such works normally would be protected by the © symbol if published, for example, in sheet music or book form, but § 401(a) imposes no such requirement with respect to their publication in phonorecords.)

(3) Just how conspicuous or easy to read must a copyright notice be? Overall, courts have been liberal in their interpretations of the legibility requirement embodied in § 401(c) of the Copyright Act. A copyright owner is required to affix notice "to the copies in such manner and location as to give reasonable notice of the claim of copyright." 17 U.S.C. § 401(c). The general rule is that any location is sufficient to satisfy the legibility requirement if it is such as to notify a person seeking to copy the work of the existence of copyright. *Coventry Ware, Inc. v. Reliance Picture Frame Co.*, 288 F.2d 193, 195 (2d Cir. 1961). What about a copyright notice placed on the back of a computer chip so that the copyright symbol

is not noticeable by a person observing the chip while it is properly inserted in the circuit board? *See Forry, Inc. v. Neundorfer, Inc.*, 837 F.2d 259, 267 (6th Cir. 1988).

How about a digital music file, that is, a digital phonorecord? Most digital file formats allow for the attachment of metadata, such as the "Properties" information in a Microsoft Word file, that could be used to make copyright notices machine-readable. Should copyright owners be required to attach metadata to serve effective notice? As we will see in Chapter 7, when a copyright owner does include notice in the metadata as part of the file's "copyright management information", *see* 17 U.S.C. § 1202(c)(3), it is illegal for a third party to remove or alter such information.

(4)   The Copyright Office has promulgated extensive regulations on the "methods of affixation and positions of notice on various types of works," which are found in 37 C.F.R. § 201.20. As § 401(c) indicates, the regulations are not designed to be exhaustive, but to specify examples of methods of affixation and positions of the copyright notice that will satisfy the notice requirements of the statute. Nonetheless, it is desirable as a practical matter to comply whenever possible, and courts afford the regulations considerable weight.

(5)   From January 1, 1978 to March 1, 1989, the Act required copyright owners to satisfy the Act's notice requirements whenever and wherever publication of their works occurred — even if that publication took place outside the United States. What was the law on this question under the Act of 1909? The answer to the question could be of considerable significance, even today. Remember that 1909 Act case law was relatively unforgiving where omissions or defects of notice were concerned; and because most countries in the world do not require notice, many works first published abroad probably were not published with the notice required by § 10 of the 1909 Act.

Although early district court cases were in conflict on this important question, both the Second and Ninth Circuits now have expressed the view that publication in a foreign country without notice did *not* place the work in the public domain in the United States. *See Heim v. Universal Pictures Co.*, 154 F.2d 480 (2d Cir. 1946); *Twin Books Corp. v. Walt Disney Co.*, 83 F.3d 1162 (9th Cir. 1996). But the two courts still disagree as to effect of such a publication. In *Heim*, the Second Circuit held that where the work was published in a country with which the United States had treaty relations, the mere publication of the work (even with an improper notice, or no notice at all) was sufficient to obtain a U.S. copyright. In *Twin Books*, however, the Ninth Circuit held that although the literary work "Bambi, A Life in the Woods" had been published in Germany in 1923 without notice, no federal statutory copyright was obtained until the book was republished in Germany in 1926 with proper notice. What was the status of the work during the intervening three years? The Ninth Circuit seemingly left the work in a kind of copyright limbo, indicating that it could have been freely copied in the United States during that time but that it was not placed permanently in the public domain. *See also Société Civile Succession Richard Guino v. Renoir*, 549 F.3d 1182 (9th Cir. 2008) (holding sculptures published in France in 1917 with no notice were neither "in the public domain [n]or copyrighted" in 1978, and were entitled to the life-plus-70-years term of § 303). What do you think the rule should be? For an extensive analysis, see Ochoa, *Protection for Works of Foreign Origin Under the 1909 Copyright Act*, 26

Santa Clara Computer & High Tech. L.J. 285 (2010).

(6) *Cure of omissions and defects: generally.* Unlike the 1909 Act, the 1976 Act, in § 405, provided for the "curing" of omissions of notice and serious notice defects which are treated as tantamount to omissions (less serious defects being governed by the terms of § 406). The most extensively litigated provision relating to cure is § 405(a)(2). This section provides that a copyright is not invalidated by failure of notice if registration is made within five years of publication and "a reasonable effort is made to add notice to all copies or phonorecords that are distributed to the public in the United States after the omission has been discovered." The notes which follow explore the ambiguities of the cure provisions.

(7) *Cure and the "discovery" issue.* As to unintentional (inadvertent) omissions, the discovery issue presents a question of fact: When did the copyright claimant become aware of the omitted notice? But what about deliberate omissions? How can one "discover" something that she was aware of doing at the time? Disregarding a certain logical inconsistency in the answer, the courts generally have held that deliberate omissions, too, can be cured. *See, e.g., Hasbro Bradley, Inc. v. Sparkle Toys, Inc.,* 780 F.2d 189 (2d Cir. 1985) (deliberate omission by assignor or licensor could be "discovered" by assignee or licensee). When is such a deliberate omission discovered? *Compare Charles Garnier, Paris v. Andin International, Inc.,* 36 F.3d 1214 (1st Cir. 1994) (deliberate omission is "discovered" when party is apprised of the legal significance of failure to provide notice) *with O'Neill Developments, Inc. v. Galen Kilburn, Inc.,* 524 F. Supp. 710 (N.D. Ga. 1981) (discovery occurs when a copyright holder finds out that someone else is copying the work).

(8) *Cure and the "reasonable effort" requirement.* What constitutes "reasonable effort" under the curative provision in § 405(a)(2) of the Copyright Act? Section 405(a)(2) requires a reasonable effort to add notice only for copies and phonorecords "distributed to the public" after the omission is discovered. Obviously, this requirement applies to copies and phonorecords still in the plaintiff's possession. But can the statutory language properly be stretched to require curative action as to copies already shipped to retailers but not yet sold to consumers? Generally, courts have held "yes." *See, e.g., Garnier,* 36 F.3d at 1224 (holding that the Act required notice to be applied to copies of plaintiff's earrings remaining in retail inventories).

(9) The statute requires a "reasonable effort," not necessarily a successful one. The copyright owner may not be able to force cooperation from those further down the distribution chain to add notice, but it must seek it. *See Lifschitz v. Walter Drake & Sons, Inc.,* 806 F.2d 1426 (9th Cir. 1986). Might it ever be "reasonable" not even to make an effort? The general rule is that a copyright owner who can establish impracticality is excused. What kinds of evidence would the copyright owner need in order to establish impracticality? *See Shapiro & Son Bedspread Corp. v. Royal Mills Associates,* 764 F.2d 69 (2d Cir. 1985) (overturning dismissal for failure to add notice to bedspreads shipped to retailers in heat-sealed plastic bags).

(10) What is the minimal amount of information that will suffice as proper notice for purposes of a cure? Consider the fancy Swirled Hoop earrings in the *Garnier* case cited above. How would one go about adding copyright notice to a pair of earrings from which it had been omitted (or, for that matter, apply proper notice

in the first instance)? The *Garnier* court mentioned "hang tags" as a possibility, but wouldn't these interfere materially with the aesthetic appeal and wearability of the items? *See* 37 C.F.R. § 202.2(b)(9) (notice on a detachable tag is insufficient).

Garnier's Swirled Hoop Earring

(11)   *Other issues concerning cure.* As to § 405(a)(2), once the omission of notice has been discovered, the copyright owner must move promptly to add proper notice to all copies or phonorecords distributed to the public "in the United States." As already noted, however, § 401 required the affixation of notice to all copies or phonorecords publicly distributed anywhere in the *world*. Is this a contradiction?

(12)   In addition to § 405(a)(2), the Copyright Act provides two other circumstances under which the omission of notice may be excused. One is the omission of notice "from no more than a relatively small number of copies or phonorecords distributed to the public." § 405(a)(1). Although the Act does not define precisely what "a relatively small number" means, most courts approach the question in percentage terms. *See, e.g., Original Appalachian Artworks, Inc. v. Toy Loft, Inc.,* 684 F.2d 821 (11th Cir. 1982) (400 out of 40,000 dolls, or 1%, meets § 405(a)(1) test); *but see Donald Frederick Evans & Associates, Inc. v. Continental Homes, Inc.,* 785 F.2d 897, 910 (11th Cir. 1986) (2,500 copies, comprising 2.4% of the total number of copies, is "more than a relatively small number," in part because it "is a significant number in the absolute sense").

The other circumstance under which omission of notice may be excused is when the copyright proprietor's written agreement for the public distribution of the copies or phonorecords expressly required the statutory notice, but the distributor nonetheless omitted it. § 405(a)(3).

(13)   Section 406 provides that if the person named in the copyright notice is not the owner of the copyright, "the validity and ownership of the copyright are not affected," but any person who innocently infringes "has a complete defense" if he or she was misled by the notice (on authorized copies) and obtained a license from the person erroneously named, unless registration has been made in the name of the true owner. *See, e.g., Bagdadi v. Nazar,* 84 F.3d 1194 (9th Cir. 1996) (where author gave licensee a copy with copyright notice in the licensee's name, § 406 applied to third party who received an unauthorized copy from the licensee). Section 406 also deals with errors in the date in the notice. What is the effect if the date is more than

one year too early? More than one year too late?

(14) *Notice and attempts to "cure" defects after the BCIA.* In the Berne Convention Implementation Act of 1988, the provisions of §§ 405(a) and 406 were preserved, but they now apply only to works first published before March 1, 1989. Suppose a work had been distributed with defective notice beginning in January 1989, but that the defect in question was not discovered until January 1990. In this situation, was the copyright owner required to make "reasonable efforts" with respect to the January and February 1989 copies only, or with respect to all copies made available to the public thereafter? *See Garnier* (holding, dubiously, that § 405(a)(2) requires an attempt to "cure" the notice defect in all the copies — even those distributed at a time when there was no affirmative statutory requirement to apply notice of any kind).

(15) The BCIA notice provisions which took effect on March 1, 1989 — §§ 401(d) and 402(d) — provide copyright owners with an incentive to use notice routinely by negating "innocent infringement" if proper notice appears on the copies or phonorecords "to which a defendant . . . had access." Innocent infringement is not a defense to infringement, but it may reduce the amount of statutory damages. *See* § 504(c). Do you think that these provisions effectively encourage the use of notice?

In *BMG Music v. Gonzalez*, 430 F.3d 888 (7th Cir. 2005), the court held that § 402(d) was satisfied where notice was used on commercially available CDs, even though the defendant downloaded an electronic file lacking such notice. *Accord Maverick Recording Co. v. Harper*, 598 F.3d 193 (5th Cir. 2010). Justice Alito, however, expressed the opinion that "a person who downloads a digital music file generally does not see any material object bearing a copyright notice, and accordingly there is force to the argument that § 402(d) does not apply." *Harper v. Maverick Recording Co.*, 131 S. Ct. 590 (2010) (Alito, J., dissenting from the denial of *certiorari*). Which interpretation would better serve the purposes of § 402(d)?

[C] Notice for Compilations and Collective Works

As we saw in Chapter 3, the compiler of a collective work or other compilation may be entitled to a copyright protecting the compiler's original contributions to the work (*e.g.*, an original selection or arrangement), irrespective of the copyright status of the work's individual constituent elements. Until March 1, 1989, the compiler (or that compiler's successor-in-interest) was required to provide notice on all published copies to safeguard that copyright, and such persons would be well-advised to do so even today.

Section 404 of the 1976 Act deals with notice issues concerning the *separate contributions* in collective works. Under this section, both the collective work and a pre-existing work incorporated into it may bear their own notices of copyright. If this were done systematically, unnecessary problems might be avoided. Often, however, the proprietors of the copyright in the collective work do not provide individual notices for the component parts. When both the pre-existing work and the collective work share the same ownership and the same year of first publication, omission of notice for the pre-existing constituent work scarcely matters in a practical sense. But what if the copyrights in the two works are owned by different persons, or the works were first published in different years, or the works differ in both respects?

Cases decided under the 1909 Act reached conflicting results. Some courts concluded that a properly affixed general or "masthead" copyright notice, in the name of the proprietor of a collective work, would be sufficient to secure or maintain copyright protection for all contributions contained in that work. *See Goodis v. United Artists Television, Inc.*, 425 F.2d 397 (2d Cir. 1970). Other courts, however, held that under the doctrine of indivisibility, "when a copyright notice appeared only in the publisher's name, the author's work would fall into the public domain, unless the author's copyright, in its entirety, had passed to the publisher." *New York Times Co. v. Tasini*, 533 U.S. 483, 494 (2001) (describing the problem).

In the 1976 revision, Congress acted to "clarify and improve [this] confused and frequently unfair legal situation with respect to rights in contributions." H.R. Rep. No. 94-1476, at 122 (1976). Thus, § 404 of the 1976 Act provides that a single copyright notice in a collective work, as a matter of law, protects all of the contributions contained therein.

For the one exception, see § 404(a) (advertisements inserted in a collective work on behalf of persons other than the collective work copyright holder cannot claim the benefit of a copyright notice applicable to the work as a whole). What is the purpose of this exception? *See TransWestern Publishing Co. v. MultiMedia Marketing Associates, Inc.*, 133 F.3d 773 (10th Cir. 1998).

§ 6.03 DEPOSIT AND REGISTRATION

Copyright registration, as mentioned at the outset of this chapter, was crucial to the scheme of the first American copyright statute, the Act of 1790. In particular, a copyright claimant was required to register the title of the work, *before publication*, with the clerk of the federal court in the district where he or she resided, to publish a copy of that registration record in a newspaper for four weeks *within two months of publication*, and to deposit a copy of the work with the U.S. Secretary of State *within six months of publication*. These deposit copies were intended for the purpose of preserving a legal record of the identity of works in which protection was claimed.

Even after the requirement of copyright notice was added, the formalities of registration and deposit retained their central importance. In fact, the burden of compliance with these formalities increased with time. After 1846, for example, copyright owners were required to submit additional deposit copies to the librarian of the Smithsonian Institution and the Library of Congress. After the Library of Congress beat out the Smithsonian in the competition for designation as the "national library," the Act of 1865 made the copyright owner's exclusive right of publication contingent on deposit with the Library.

The 1909 Copyright Act significantly affected the registration and deposit formalities. Although under the 1909 Act it was publication with the proper notice which caused federal copyright protection to attach, § 13 made registration a prerequisite for bringing an infringement action. The 1909 Act also imposed a universal, mandatory deposit requirement. Under § 13, deposit was to occur "promptly" after the publication of any work with copyright notice. Deposit had a dual function, providing a basis for Copyright Office processing of registration applications and a source of materials for the collection of the Library of Congress. Thus, submission of the prescribed number of deposit copies was made a precondition both for securing copyright registration (in § 11) and for the commencement of an infringement action (in § 13). The 1909 Act also created (in § 14) a procedure by which the Register of Copyrights could demand deposit of copies of *any* published work, and could impose fines and penalties — including, most notably, forfeiture of copyright — when a proprietor refused to comply with the Register's demand.

Judicial administration of this statutory scheme was not as harsh as it might have been. For example, the Supreme Court held that a 14-month delay in making a deposit, where there had been no request served on the copyright proprietor, did *not* work a forfeiture. *Washingtonian Publishing Co. v. Pearson*, 306 U.S. 30 (1939). Similarly, in *Shapiro, Bernstein & Co. v. Jerry Vogel Music Co., Inc.*, 161 F.2d 406 (1946), the Second Circuit excused a *27-year delay* and, in so doing, implicitly adopted the view that, absent a demand by the Register of Copyrights, registration and deposit might be made at any time during the first term of the copyright.

Unlike the 1909 Act, the 1976 Act described the procedures for copyright registration in detail and conferred extensive authority on the Register of Copyrights to implement those procedures. The 1976 Act also streamlined the deposit requirement. Section 408(b) prescribes one form of deposit as mandatory for registration applications. Separately, § 407 requires deposit of copies or phonorecords "for the Library of Congress," enforceable by the Register of Copyrights through written demands, backed by the threat of fines and other financial penalties. Copies submitted for § 407 purposes can be, and frequently are, used to satisfy the § 408(b) obligation (in connection with registration). In addition, the 1976 Act gave the Register the authority to provide complete or partial exemptions to the deposit requirements.

Probably the 1976 Act's most important innovation relating to deposit was its decoupling of the deposit requirement from the right to copyright protection. Under the 1909 Act, copyright could be forfeited for failure to comply with a demand for deposit, while the 1976 Act specifies that deposit is not a "condition of copyright." Motivating this change was a perception that maintaining a linkage between deposit and the enjoyment of copyright would put the United States very much out of step with the world community.

If the 1976 Act's reform of the deposit requirement is considered along with abolition of the notice requirement by the Berne Convention Implementation Act of 1988, the net practical effect is that a copyright owner need now take no formal steps — by way of notice, registration, or deposit — to secure or preserve her right under American law. Of course, notice has its uses, and deposit still can be compelled. Moreover, various incentives to register (with the requisite accompanying deposit) are built into the scheme of the Copyright Act. In particular, the availability of statutory damages and attorneys' fees to a successful copyright plaintiff is conditioned (in § 412) on the timely filing of a registration application.

Unlike the across-the-board abolition of the mandatory notice requirement, Congress adopted a so-called "two-tier" approach as to registration in the BCIA. Prior to the BCIA, § 411(a) required that a copyright owner register with the Copyright Office (or have an application for registration refused by it) before initiating an infringement action. The BCIA waived this requirement as of March 1, 1989 for one class of works: "Berne Convention works," which had as their "country of origin" Berne member countries other than the United States. Since the BCIA, Congress has further (and significantly) revised the Act, so that the § 411(a) pre-infringement registration requirement now applies *only* to "United States work[s]." The definition of "United States work[s]" contained in § 101 is not nearly as straightforward as the uninitiated might imagine.

[A] Introduction

Statutory References

1976 Act: §§ 101 ("best edition," "country of origin," "treaty party," "United States work"), 407-12; Transitional and Supplementary Provisions §§ 109-10

1909 Act: §§ 5-6, 14

Legislative History

H.R. Rep. No. 94-1476 at 150-58,
reprinted in 1976 U.S.C.C.A.N. 5659, 5766-74

Section 407. Deposit for the Library of Congress

The provisions of section[s] 407 through 411 of the bill mark another departure from the [1909 Act]. Under [that law], deposit of copies for the collections of the Library of Congress and deposit of copies for purposes of copyright registration have been treated as the same thing. The bill's basic approach is to regard deposit and registration as separate though closely related: deposit of copies or phonorecords for the Library of Congress is mandatory, but exceptions can be made for material the Library neither needs nor wants; copyright registration is not generally mandatory, but is a condition of certain remedies for copyright infringement. Deposit for the Library of Congress can be, and in the bulk of cases undoubtedly will be, combined with copyright registration. . . .

Section 408. Copyright Registration in General

Permissive registration

Under section 408(a), registration of a claim to copyright in any work, whether published or unpublished, can be made voluntarily by "the owner of copyright or of any exclusive right in the work" at any time during the copyright term. The claim may be registered in the Copyright Office by depositing the copies, phonorecords, or other material specified by subsection (b) and (c), together with an application and fee. Except where, under section 405(a), registration is made to preserve a copyright that would otherwise be invalidated because of omission of the notice, registration is not a condition of copyright protection. . . .

SECTION 410. REGISTRATION OF CLAIM AND ISSUANCE OF CERTIFICATE

. . . Subsection [410](c) deals with the probative effect of a certificate of registration issued by the Register under subsection (a). Under its provisions, a certificate is required to be given *prima facie* weight in any judicial proceedings if the registration it covers was made "before or within five years after first publication of the work"; thereafter the court is given discretion to decide what evidentiary weight the certificate should be accorded. . . .

It is true that, unlike a patent claim, a claim to copyright is not examined for basic validity before a certificate is issued. On the other hand, endowing a copyright claimant who has obtained a certificate with a rebuttable presumption of the validity of the copyright does not deprive the defendant in an infringement suit of any rights; it merely orders the burdens of proof. The plaintiff should not ordinarily be forced in the first instance to prove all of the multitude of facts that underlie the validity of the copyright unless the defendant, by effectively challenging them, shifts the burden of doing so to the plaintiff. . . .

SECTION 411. REGISTRATION AS PREREQUISITE TO INFRINGEMENT SUIT

. . . [A] copyright owner who has not registered his claim can have a valid cause of action against someone who has infringed his copyright, but he cannot enforce his right in the courts until he has made registration. . . .

. . . [A] rejected claimant who has properly applied for registration [and been refused] may maintain an infringement suit if notice of it is served on the Register of Copyrights. . . .

SECTION 412. REGISTRATION AS PREREQUISITE TO CERTAIN REMEDIES

. . . [A] copyright owner whose work has been infringed before registration would be entitled to the remedies ordinarily available in infringement cases: an injunction on terms the court considers fair, and his actual damages plus any applicable profits not used as a measure of damages. However, section 412 would deny any award of the special or "extraordinary" remedies of statutory damages or attorney's fees where infringement of copyright in an unpublished work began before registration or where, in the case of a published work, infringement commenced after publication and before registration (unless registration has been made within a grace period of three months after publication). These provisions would be applicable to works of foreign and domestic origin alike. . . .

[For a fuller excerpt from H.R. REP. No. 94-1476, see Part Three of the Casebook Supplement.]

Joint Explanatory Statement on Amendment to S. 1301
[the Berne Convention Implementation Act of 1988]
134 Cong. Rec. S14544, 14554-55 (1988),
reprinted in 36 J. Copyright Soc'y 16 (1988) at 24-26

[Editors' note: In the months leading up to the enactment of the BCIA, the requirement that an application for copyright registration must precede the initiation of an action for infringement, contained in § 411(a) of the 1976 Act, proved to be a particular bone of contention. Some argued that this requirement was unlikely to be compatible with Article 5(2) of Berne, which requires that, where works protected by way of the Convention (as distinct from domestic works) are concerned, "[t]he enjoyment and exercise of [copyright] shall not be subject to any formality." *See Final Report of the Ad Hoc Working Group on U.S. Adherence to the Berne Convention* at 60-62 (1986), *reprinted in* 10 COLUM.-VLA J.L. & ARTS 513, 572-74 (1986). By contrast, the Register of Copyrights took the position that the notice provisions of § 411(a) *were* Berne-compatible. *See* S. REP. No. 100-352, at 14-25 (1988). In the end, Congress reached a compromise which is reflected in the following "Joint Explanatory Statement" to the so-called Leahy-DeConcini-Hatch amendment.]

. . . [T]he elimination of section 411(a) . . . is not, strictly speaking, the most minimal change that may be made in the Copyright Act in order to comply with Berne. All Berne requires is the elimination from U.S. law of formalities applicable to works originating in Berne countries other than the United States.

. . . [T]he amendment . . . establishes a so-called "two-tier" system with respect to the requirements of section 411. Works whose country of origin is a foreign nation adhering to the Berne Convention are exempt from the registration prerequisite; infringement suits may be brought with respect to such works even if they have never been submitted for registration with the Copyright Office. All other works remain subject to existing section 411(a). . . .

[T]his amendment . . . minimizes the policy objection . . . that modification of the registration prerequisite will degrade the quality of the registration system and hamper the acquisition activities of the Library of Congress. . . . The Copyright Office estimates that 95 percent of all registrations are made with respect to domestic works, a category which largely overlaps with the tier of works of United States origin as defined in this amendment. For these works, the incentives for registration are substantially increased, not decreased, by this bill, which maintains the registration prerequisite for infringement suits with respect to works of United States origin, and also doubles the statutory damages available to redress infringement. . . .

The creation of a two-tier system with respect to the registration prerequisite of section 411(a) is not, and should not be regarded as, a precedent for established two-tiered approaches to any other area of copyright law in which the United States theoretically remains free, even after adherence to Berne, to treat copyrighted works differently based on their country of origin. . . .

DEPOSIT PROVISIONS FOR PUBLISHED WORKS
UNDER THE 1909, 1976 AND
BERNE CONVENTION IMPLEMENTATION ACTS

DATE OF PUBLICATION	WORK PUBLISHED BEFORE 1978	WORK PUBLISHED ON OR AFTER 1/1/78 AND BEFORE 3/1/89	WORK PUBLISHED ON OR AFTER 3/1/89
PREREQUISITE TO BRING SUIT FOR INFRINGEMENT OF COPYRIGHT?	Yes. § 13 (1909 Act).	Yes. § 411(a).	Yes, for works of U.S. origin. No, for non-U.S. Berne works. § 411(a).
SANCTIONS FOR FAILURE TO DEPOSIT?	Yes. § 14 (1909 Act).	Yes. § 407(d).	Yes, for both U.S. works and non-U.S. Berne works. § 407(d).

[B]   Concepts and Procedures

U.S. Copyright Office
Circular 1: Copyright Basics (Excerpts)
(May 2012)

Copyright Registration

In general, copyright registration is a legal formality intended to make a public record of the basic facts of a particular copyright. However, registration is not a condition of copyright protection. Even though registration is not a requirement for protection, the copyright law provides several inducements or advantages to encourage copyright owners to make registration. Among these advantages are the following:

- Registration establishes a public record of the copyright claim.

- Before an infringement suit may be filed in court, registration is necessary for works of U.S. origin.

- If made before or within five years of publication, registration will establish prima facie evidence in court of the validity of the copyright and of the facts stated in the certificate.

- If registration is made within three months after publication of the work or prior to an infringement of the work, statutory damages and attorney's fees will be available to the copyright owner in court actions. Otherwise, only an award of actual damages and profits is available to the copyright owner.

- Registration allows the owner of the copyright to record the registration with the U.S. Customs Service for protection against the importation of infringing copies. . . .

Registration may be made at any time within the life of the copyright. Unlike the law before 1978, when a work has been registered in unpublished form, it is not necessary to make another registration when the work becomes published, although the copyright owner may register the published edition, if desired.

REGISTRATION PROVISIONS FOR PUBLISHED WORKS UNDER THE 1909, 1976, AND BERNE CONVENTION IMPLEMENTATION ACTS

DATE OF PUBLICATION	WORK PUBLISHED BEFORE 1978	WORK PUBLISHED ON OR AFTER 1/1/78 AND BEFORE 3/1/89	WORK PUBLISHED ON OR AFTER 3/1/89
NATURE OF REQUIREMENT	Optional, but no renewal for second term without original registration.	Optional. § 408.	Optional. § 408.
PREREQUISITE TO BRING SUIT FOR INFRINGEMENT OF COPYRIGHT?	Yes, during both terms of copyright.	Yes. § 411.	Yes, for U.S. works, except for actions brought under § 106A(a). § 411. No, for non-U.S. Berne works. § 411.
INCENTIVES TO REGISTER	Prerequisite to suit (see above).	Prerequisite to suit (see above). Also, except for actions under §§ 106A(a) or 411(b), statutory damages and attorneys' fees are not available unless work was registered before infringement began, or work is infringed after first publication and registration is made within three months after first publication. § 412.	Same as for works published between 1/1/78 and 3/1/89 for both U.S. and non-U.S. Berne works. § 412.

Registration Procedures

Filing an Original Claim to Copyright with the U.S. Copyright Office

An application for copyright registration contains three essential elements: a completed application form, a nonrefundable filing fee, and a nonreturnable deposit — that is, a copy or copies of the work being registered and "deposited" with the Copyright Office.

If you apply online for copyright registration, you will receive an email saying that your application was received. If you apply for copyright registration using a paper application, you will not receive an acknowledgment that your application has been received (the Office receives more than 600,000 applications annually). With either online or paper applications, you can expect:

- a letter, telephone call or email from a Copyright Office staff member if further information is needed or

- a certificate of registration indicating that the work has been registered, or if the application cannot be accepted, a letter explaining why it has been rejected . . .

You can apply to register your copyright in one of two ways.

Online Application

Online registration through the electronic Copyright Office (eCO) is the preferred way to register basic claims for literary works; visual arts works; performing arts works, including motion pictures; sound recordings; and single serials. Advantages of online filing include:

- a lower filing fee

- the fastest processing time

- online status tracking

- secure payment by credit or debit card, electronic check, or Copyright Office deposit account

- the ability to upload certain categories of deposits directly into eCO as electronic files . . .

Basic claims include (1) a single work; (2) multiple unpublished works if the elements are assembled in an orderly form; the combined elements bear a single title identifying the collection as a whole; the copyright claimant in all the elements and in the collection as a whole is the same; and all the elements are by the same author or, if they are by different authors, at least one of the authors has contributed copyrightable authorship to each element; and (3) multiple published works if they are all first published together in the same publication on the same date and owned by the same claimant. . . .

Paper Application

You can also register your copyright using forms TX (literary works); VA (visual arts works); PA (performing arts works, including motion pictures); SR (sound recordings); and SE (single serials). To access all forms, go to the Copyright Office website and click on *Forms*. On your personal computer, complete the form for the type of work you are registering, print it out, and mail it with a check or money order and your deposit. Blank forms can also be printed out and completed by hand, or they may be requested by postal mail or by calling the Forms and Publications Hotline at (202) 707-9100 (limit of two copies of each form by mail). Informational circulars about the types of applications and current registration fees are available on the Copyright Office website at *www.copyright.gov* or by phone. . . .

[Certain applications must be completed on paper and mailed to the Copyright Office with the appropriate fee and deposit, including Form D-VH for vessel hull designs; Form MW for mask works (semi-conductor chip designs); Form CA for corrections or amplifications to applications; Form GATT for restored copyrights; Form RE for renewal registrations; and one of three versions of Form GR for registration of group submissions. See *www.copyright.gov* for details.]

Filing a Renewal Registration

To register a renewal, send the following:

1   a properly completed application Form RE and, if necessary, Form RE Addendum, and

2   a nonrefundable filing fee* for each application . . .

Deposit Requirements

If you file an application for copyright registration online using eCO, you may in some cases attach an electronic copy of your deposit. If you do not have an electronic copy or if you must send a hard copy or copies of your deposit to comply with the "best edition" requirements for published works, you must print out a shipping slip, attach it to your deposit, and mail the deposit to the Copyright Office. . . .

The deposit requirements vary in particular situations. The general requirements follow. . . .

- If the work is unpublished, one complete copy or phonorecord.

- If the work was first published in the United States on or after January 1, 1978, two complete copies or phonorecords of the best edition.

- If the work was first published in the United States before January 1, 1978, two complete copies or phonorecords of the work as first published.

---

* NOTE: For current fee information, check the Copyright Office website at *www.copyright.gov*, write the Copyright Office, or call (202) 707-3000 or 1-877-476-0778.

- If the work was first published outside the United States, one complete copy or phonorecord of the work as first published. . . .

Who May File an Application Form?

The following persons are legally entitled to submit an application form:

• **The author.** This is either the person who actually created the work or, if the work was made for hire, the employer or other person for whom the work was prepared.

• **The copyright claimant.** The copyright claimant is defined in Copyright Office regulations as either the author of the work or a person or organization that has obtained ownership of all the rights under the copyright initially belonging to the author. This category includes a person or organization who has obtained by contract the right to claim legal title to the copyright in an application for copyright registration.

• **The owner of exclusive right(s).** Under the law, any of the exclusive rights that make up a copyright and any subdivision of them can be transferred and owned separately, even though the transfer may be limited in time or place of effect. The term "copyright owner" with respect to any one of the exclusive rights contained in a copyright refers to the owner of that particular right. Any owner of an exclusive right may apply for registration of a claim in the work.

• **The duly authorized agent of such author, other copyright claimant, or owner of exclusive right(s).** Any person authorized to act on behalf of the author, other copyright claimant, or owner of exclusive rights may apply for registration.

There is no requirement that applications be prepared or filed by an attorney. . . .

[For further information regarding current registration procedures, see the Copyright Office website at *www.copyright.gov*.]

NOTES AND QUESTIONS

Deposit

(1) *Section 407 deposit.* Basically, § 407 of the 1976 Act requires "the owner of [the] copyright or of the exclusive right of publication" in a visually perceptible work to deposit, within three months after it is "published with notice of copyright in the United States," two complete copies of the "best edition" of the work (or, if the work is a sound recording, two complete phonorecords of the best edition of the sound recording, along with all accompanying printed material). The deposit provision is a long-standing requirement of our copyright law and has survived constitutional challenge. *See Ladd v. Law & Technology Press*, 762 F.2d 809 (9th Cir. 1985) (deposit requirement does not violate Fifth Amendment prohibition against taking of private property for public use without just compensation).

The Copyright Office has promulgated detailed regulations concerning deposit for the Library of Congress and for registration purposes in 37 C.F.R. §§ 202.19 and 202.20, respectively. Copyright Office Circulars also provide information on a range of copyright topics. They are written in clear language with the general public in mind and are particularly helpful on subjects, such as registration and deposit, in which the Office plays a significant role. They can be obtained by contacting the Copyright Office and are also accessible on the Office website.

Another important resource to be consulted is the Copyright Office publication COMPENDIUM II: COMPENDIUM OF COPYRIGHT OFFICE PRACTICES, first issued by the Office in 1984 and periodically updated since then. COMPENDIUM II (which is to be distinguished from COMPENDIUM I, describing Copyright Office practices under the 1909 Act) is a valuable, if somewhat outdated, source of detailed information about the Office's internal rules and policies and its working interpretations of the statutes and regulations that govern its operations. A digitized version of COMPENDIUM II is available at *www.copyrightcompendium.com*. Be advised that the Copyright Office website indicates that as of October 2011, COMPENDIUM II is undergoing substantial revision.

(2)   What constitutes the "best edition" of a work? According to the definition in § 101, the term means "the edition, published in the United States at any time before the date of deposit, that the Library of Congress determines to be most suitable for its purposes." This highlights the important fact that, while the copies or phonorecords required under § 407 must be deposited in the Copyright Office (where they may be examined in connection with registration proceedings), they are intended by Congress "for the use or disposition of the Library of Congress." § 407(b).

(3)   Unpublished works need not be deposited under the Act unless they are registered. In addition, a work published *outside of the United States* need not be deposited, unless it is submitted for registration or is imported or published in an American edition. § 407(a). The deposit requirement *does* apply, without exception, to works of foreign origin when they are published *in this country. Id.* Although the Berne Convention Implementation Act of 1988 excuses certain works from compliance with the § 408 registration formality (and the specific deposit requirements which accompany it), that legislation does not affect the operation of the deposit provisions of § 407.

(4)   The Register of Copyright is authorized to exempt from the § 407 deposit requirement any categories of material deemed appropriate, *e.g.*, sculptural works and automated databases; to reduce to one the required number of copies or phonorecords for any category; and to provide for alternative forms of deposit in the case of pictorial, graphic, and sculptural works. § 407(c). The results of the Register's exercise of this authority are reflected in 37 C.F.R. § 202.19(c). The Copyright Office also has developed special procedures for certain categories of works, including motion pictures. *See* 37 C.F.R. § 202.19(d)(2).

(5) Deposit under the 1976 Act, as under the 1909 Act, is mandatory, and is enforced as specified in § 407(d). If deposit is not made voluntarily upon publication, the Register of Copyrights may demand deposit in writing. The copyright holder then has three months to comply before sanctions may be imposed. In comparing the penalties available under § 407(d) with those in § 14 of the 1909 Act, note § 407(d)'s provision against willful or repeated failures to comply with the Register's demand and the absence from the 1976 Act of any threat of voiding the copyright in the work. Only a handful of cases have been referred by the Copyright Office to the Department of Justice for enforcement under § 407(d).

(6) *Section 408(b) deposit.* Often materials submitted for § 407 archival purposes also satisfy the § 408(b) requirement of deposit in connection with registration — something for which that section specifically provides. But copies of various kinds of works exempted from § 407 deposit must nevertheless be deposited under § 408(b) in order to accomplish registration. *Compare* 37 C.F.R. § 202.19(c) *with* § 202.20(c). In some cases, registrants are permitted or required to submit so-called "identifying material" — typically, photographic reproductions — rather than original copies. *See* 37 C.F.R. § 202.21.

Although deposit copies may not be copied without the permission of the copyright owner unless the works involved are the subject of pending litigation, *see* 37 C.F.R. § 201.2(d)(2), records of copyright deposits generally are open to public inspection. This creates a dilemma for copyright proprietors who wish to maintain secrecy for the contents of their works. Accordingly, the Copyright Office has developed special deposit procedures for so-called "secure tests" (such as standardized achievement and aptitude examinations) and for computer programs containing trade secret material. *See* 37 C.F.R. § 202.20(c)(2)(vi) and (vii). *But cf. Compuware Corp. v. Serena Software Int'l, Inc.*, 77 F. Supp. 2d 816 (E.D. Mich. 1999) (failure to utilize redaction procedure for computer program did not result in loss of trade secret status). The Office also permits registrants to petition for "special relief" from the otherwise applicable deposit requirements. *See* 37 C.F.R. §§ 202.19(e), 202.20(d).

(7) Note that for the registration to be valid, the § 408 deposit must be a *bona fide* copy of the work as it was originally fixed. In a series of cases, courts have held that an after-the-fact "reconstruction" of a work alleged to have predated the allegedly infringing work does not suffice to meet the deposit requirement. *See, e.g., Coles v. Wonder*, 283 F.3d 798 (6th Cir. 2002) (Stevie Wonder's song *For Your Love*); *Kodadek v. MTV Networks, Inc.*, 152 F.3d 1209 (9th Cir. 1998) (drawings of Beavis and Butthead); *Seiler v. Lucasfilm, Ltd.*, 808 F.2d 1316 (9th Cir. 1986) (Imperial Walkers from *The Empire Strikes Back*). *But see Nova Design Build, Inc. v. Grace Hotels, LLC*, 652 F.3d 814 (7th Cir. 2011) (although plaintiff had to reconstruct computer files of its designs to deposit with registration, deposit copy was a *bona fide* copy of the original where reconstructed files could be checked against hard copies that plaintiff retained).

(8) What happens to copyright deposits submitted in connection with applications for registration? Some, of course, are selected for inclusion in the collection of the Library of Congress, but many others eventually must be discarded. This may pose a problem for a copyright owner who anticipates the possibility of litigation in

connection with his or her work, and therefore desires that the Copyright Office maintain the deposit copy or copies as part of its records. This problem is addressed by 37 C.F.R. § 202.23, which provides a procedure under which a copyright owner may request so-called "full-term retention" of deposit copies — for a fairly hefty additional fee.

Registration

(9) *Generally.* Why is registration permissive, *see* § 408(a), whereas deposit of published works is mandatory? According to the legislative history of the 1976 Act, registration and deposit are "separate though closely related." What does that mean? Clearly, the functions of the two requirements can be distinguished. Registration creates a written record of each copyright's ownership, and thus facilitates transfers of rights in the work by means of assignments and licenses. Deposit under § 407 assures that the Library of Congress (through the Copyright Office) has access to copies and phonorecords of all works published in the United States.

In theory, deposit may be accomplished without registration, but registration necessarily requires an accompanying deposit. *Compare* § 407, *with* § 408. There would seem to be little point to depositing a work without simultaneously registering it, particularly in view of the fact that a deposit solely for § 407 purposes cannot be utilized retroactively to satisfy the deposit aspect of the § 408 registration requirement. *See* § 408(b).

(10) The reach of the registration requirement is significantly broader than that of the § 407 deposit requirement. For example, § 408 permits the registration of unpublished works and works published abroad, as well as works published in the United States. And, while the Copyright Office may exempt various categories of works from the § 407 deposit requirement altogether, the Register has no power to exempt particular types of works from the operation of § 408 — although regulations may vary the nature of the deposits required under § 408(b).

A further distinction is that § 408 allows registration by any owner of any of the "exclusive rights" in the work, whereas only the owner of the *copyright* or of the *right of publication* may make a deposit under § 407.

(11) *Incentives to register.* Although permissive, registration is rewarded handsomely under the 1976 Act. The most important incentive is that registration is a prerequisite to the filing of a civil action for infringement for United States works. As amended in 2008, the language of § 411(a) seems straightforward enough: "no civil action . . . shall be instituted until . . . registration of the copyright claim has been made. . . ."

Certificate of Registration

This Certificate issued under the seal of the Copyright
Office in accordance with title 17, United States Code,
attests that registration has been made for the work
identified below. The information on this certificate has
been made a part of the Copyright Office records.

Marybeth Peters

Register of Copyrights, United States of America

FORM TX
For a Literary Work
UNITED STATES COPYRIGHT OFFICE

REG'

TX 4-879-549

EFFECTIVE DATE OF REGISTRATION

11	13	98
Month	Day	Year

DO NOT WRITE ABOVE THIS LINE. IF YOU NEED MORE SPACE, USE A SEPARATE CONTINUATION SHEET.

TITLE OF THIS WORK▼
HARRY POTTER AND THE SORCERER'S STONE (35340-3)

PREVIOUS OR ALTERNATIVE TITLES▼

PUBLICATION AS A CONTRIBUTION If this work was published as a contribution to a periodical, serial, or collection, give information about
the collective work in which the contribution appeared. **Title of Collective Work ▼**

If published in a periodical or serial   Volume ▼   Number ▼   Issue Date ▼   On Pages ▼

NAME OF AUTHOR▼
J.K. ROWLING

DATES OF BIRTH AND DEATH
Year Born ▼   Year Died ▼

Was this contribution to the work
"work made for hire"?
☐ Yes
☒ No

AUTHOR'S NATIONALITY OR DOMICILE
Name of Country
OR { Citizen of ▶ USA
{ Domiciled in ▶

WAS THIS AUTHOR'S CONTRIBUTION TO THE WORK
Anonymous?   ☐ Yes ☒ No   If the answer to either
Pseudonymous? ☐ Yes ☒ No   of these questions is "Yes," see detailed instructions.

NATURE OF AUTHORSHIP Briefly describe nature of the material created by this author in which copyright is claimed.   TEXT

NOTE
Under the law,
the "author" of a
"work made for
hire" is generally
the employer,
not the em-
ployee (see in-
structions). For
any part of this
work that was
"made for hire"
check "Yes" in
the space pro-
vided, give the
employer (or
other person for
whom the work
was prepared)
as "Author" of
that part, and
leave the space
for dates of birth
and death blank.

NAME OF AUTHOR▼

DATES OF BIRTH AND DEATH
Year Born ▼   Year Died ▼

Was this contribution to the work
"work made for hire"?
☐ Yes
☐ No

AUTHOR'S NATIONALITY OR DOMICILE
Name of Country
OR { Citizen of ▶
{ Domiciled in ▶

WAS THIS AUTHOR'S CONTRIBUTION TO THE WORK
Anonymous?   ☐ Yes ☐ No
Pseudonymous? ☐ Yes ☐ No

NATURE OF AUTHORSHIP Briefly describe nature of the material created by this author in which copyright is claimed.

NAME OF AUTHOR▼

DATES OF BIRTH AND DEATH
Year Born ▼   Year Died ▼

Was this contribution to the work
"work made for hire"?
☐ Yes
☐ No

AUTHOR'S NATIONALITY OR DOMICILE
Name of Country
OR { Citizen of ▶
{ Domiciled in ▶

WAS THIS AUTHOR'S CONTRIBUTION TO THE WORK
Anonymous?   ☐ Yes ☐ No
Pseudonymous? ☐ Yes ☐ No

NATURE OF AUTHORSHIP Briefly describe nature of the material created by this author in which copyright is claimed.

YEAR IN WHICH CREATION OF THIS WORK WAS COMPLETED This information must be given in all cases.
1998 ◀ Year

DATE AND NATION OF FIRST PUBLICATION OF THIS PARTICULAR WORK Complete this information ONLY if this work has been published.
Month ▶ 10   Day ▶ 01   Year ▶ 1998
USA ◀ Nation

COPYRIGHT CLAIMANT(S) Name and address must be given even if the claimant is
the same as the author given in space 2.
J.K. ROWLING C/O
CHRISTOPHER LITTLE LITERARY AGENCY C/O
LLOYDS BANK, 3Y
MOORGATE LONDON, EC2R 6DN

See instructions
before completing
this space.

TRANSFER If the claimant(s) named here in space 4 are different from the author(s)
named ▼

APPLICATION RECEIVED
OCT 21 1998
ONE DEPOSIT RECEIVED

TWO DEPOSITS RECEIVED
OCT 21 1998
REMITTANCE NUMBER AND DATE
FUNDS RECEI'   NOV 1 3 1998

DO NOT WRITE HERE
OFFICE USE ONLY

MORE ON BACK ▸ • Complete all applicable spaces (numbers 5-11) on the reverse side of this page.
• See detailed instructions.   • Sign the form at line 10.

DO NOT WRITE HERE
Page 1 of 2 pages

EXAMINED BY _wkb_   FORM TX

CHECKED BY

☐ CORRESPONDENCE
Yes

FOR COPYRIGHT OFFICE USE ONLY

DO NOT WRITE ABOVE THIS LINE. IF YOU NEED MORE SPACE, USE A SEPARATE CONTINUATION SHEET.

PREVIOUS REGISTRATION Has registration for this work, or for an earlier version of this work, already been made in the Copyright Office?
☐ Yes   ☒ No   If your answer is "Yes," why is another registration being sought? (Check appropriate box:)
a. ☐ This is the first published edition of a work previously registered in unpublished form.
b. ☐ This is the first application submitted by this author as copyright claimant.
c. ☐ This is a changed version of the work, as shown by space 6 on this application.
If your answer is "Yes,"   Previous Registration Number ▼   Year of Registration ▼

DERIVATIVE WORK OR COMPILATION Complete both space 6a & 6b for a derivative work; complete only 6b for a compilation.
a. Preexisting Material Identify any preexisting work or works that this work is based on or incorpor.▼:s.

b. Material Added to This Work Give a brief, general statement of the material that has been added to this work and in which copyright is cla▼med.

See instructions before completing this space.

---space deleted---

REPRODUCTION FOR USE OF BLIND OR PHYSICALLY HANDICAPPED INDIVIDUALS A signature on this form at space 10, and a check in one of the boxes here in space 8, constitutes a non-exclusive grant of permission to the Library of Congress to reproduce and distribute solely for the blind and physically handicapped and under the conditions and limitations prescribed by the regulations of the Copyright Office: (1) copies of the work identified in space 1 of this application in Braille (or similar tactile symbols); or (2) phonorecords embodying a fixation of a reading of that work; or (3)
a ☒ Copies and Phonorecords   b ☐ Copies Only   c ☐ Phonorecords Only

See instructions.

DEPOSIT ACCOUNT If the registration fee is to be charged to a Deposit Account established in the Copyright Office, give name and number of
Name ▼   SCHOLASTIC INC.   Account Number ▼

CORRESPONDENCE Give name and address to which correspondence about this application should be   Name/Address/Apt/City/State/ZIP ▼
MARIAN STEFFENS/SCHOLASTIC INC.
555 BROADWAY
NEW YORK, NY 10012

Be sure to give your daytime phone number.

Area Code & Telephone Number ▶

CERTIFICATION* I, the undersigned, hereby certify that I am
Check only one ▶
☐ author
☐ other copyright claimant
☐ owner of exclusive right(s)
☒ authorized agent of   SCHOLASTIC INC.
Name of author or other copyright claimant, or owner of exclusive right(s) ▲

of the work identified in this application and that the statements made by me in this application are correct to the best of my

Typed or printed name and date ▼ If this application gives a date of publication in space 3, do not sign and submit it before that
MARIAN STEFFENS   date ▶ 10-13-98

Handwritten signature (X) ▼
SIGNATURE REDACTED

MAIL CERTIFICATE TO

Name ▼
MARIAN STEFFENS'SCHOLASTIC INC.
Number/Street/Apartment Number ▼
555 BROADWAY
City/State/ZIP ▼
NEW YORK, NY 10012

Certificate will be mailed in window envelope

YOU MUST
• Complete all necessary spaces
• Sign your application in space 10
SEND ALL 3 ELEMENTS IN THE SAME PACKAGE
1. Application form
2. Nonrefundable $20 filing fee in check or money order payable to Register of Copyrights
3. Deposit material
MAIL TO
Register of Copyrights
Library of Congress
Washington, D.C. 20559

The Copyright Office has the authority to adjust fees at 5-year intervals, based on changes in the Consumer Price Index. The next adjustment is due in 1996. Please contact the Copyright Office after July 1996 to determine the actual fee schedule.

*17 U.S.C. § 506(e): Any person who knowingly makes a false representation of a material fact in the application for copyright registration provided for by section 409, or in any written statement filed in connection with the application, shall be fined not more than $2,500.

This form was electronically produced by Elite Federal Forms, Inc.

Registration Certificate for
Harry Potter and the Sorcerer's Stone

But what, exactly, is meant by "has been made"? An interesting split has developed on this question. Some courts treat the submission of an application, accompanied by payment of the required fee and deposit of the requisite copies, as sufficient compliance. *See, e.g., Apple Barrel Productions, Inc. v. Beard*, 730 F.2d 384 (5th Cir. 1984); *Cosmetic Ideas, Inc. v. IAC/Interactive Corp.*, 606 F.3d 612 (9th Cir. 2010). Other courts hold that the prerequisite is not satisfied until the

Copyright Office has acted on the application. *See, e.g., LaResolana Architects v. Clay Realtors Angel Fire*, 416 F.3d 1195 (10th Cir. 2005) (collecting cases); *M.G.B. Homes, Inc. v. Ameron Homes, Inc.*, 903 F.2d 1486 (11th Cir. 1990). The dispute turns, in part, on § 410(d), which provides that the effective date of a copyright registration is the date on which the application and supporting materials are received by the Copyright Office, rather than the later date on which the application is determined to be acceptable for registration. Many of the courts adhering to the latter position, however, allow the plaintiff to file an amended complaint once the registration in fact issues, thus curing the jurisdictional problem. *See, e.g., M.G.B. Homes*, 903 F.2d at 1489. Some courts adhering to the former position have taken an even more generous approach. *See, e.g., Positive Black Talk, Inc. v. Cash Money Records, Inc.*, 394 F.3d 357 (5th Cir. 2004) (finding defect cured when Copyright Office received complete application four days after action was filed, despite the fact that plaintiff never filed an amended or supplemental pleading). The dispute could make a difference if, for example, the statute of limitations expires before the amended complaint is filed. *See Morgan v. Hanna Holdings, Inc.*, 635 F. Supp. 2d 404 (W.D. Pa. 2009).

Despite the near-unanimous opinion of the Courts of Appeals to the contrary, the U.S. Supreme Court recently held that § 411(a) is not "jurisdictional," so that failure to register does not deprive the trial court of subject-matter jurisdiction. *Reed Elsevier, Inc. v. Muchnick*, 559 U.S. 154 (2010). The ruling revived a proposed settlement of a class action that included both registered and unregistered copyrights; and it gives a boost to those courts that have held that a lack of registration may be "cured." The Court did not expressly resolve the circuit split noted above, however; and it also specifically "decline[d] to address whether § 411(a)'s registration requirement is a mandatory precondition to suit that . . . district courts may or should enforce *sua sponte* by dismissing copyright infringement claims involving unregistered works."

(12)   If the application for registration is denied, the applicant may seek judicial review under the Administrative Procedure Act, pursuant to § 701(e) of the Copyright Act. *See, e.g., Darden v. Peters*, 488 F.3d 277 (4th Cir. 2007) (reviewing denial for abuse of discretion). Alternatively, § 411(a) allows the rejected applicant to file an action for infringement, so long as the Register of Copyrights is given notice and an opportunity to intervene. *See, e.g., Paul Morelli Design, Inc. v. Tiffany & Co.*, 200 F. Supp. 2d 482 (E.D. Pa. 2002) (giving "some deference" to Register's decision, rather than abuse of discretion or *de novo* review); *Brooks-Ngwenya v. Indianapolis Public Schools*, 564 F.3d 804 (7th Cir. 2009) (although notice rule is mandatory, failure to notify does not deprive court of jurisdiction).

What if, for no good reason, the Copyright Office simply fails to act on an application, one way or the other? It has been held that, unlike the situation that prevailed under the 1909 Act, the availability of judicial review as specified above renders a writ of mandamus under 28 U.S.C. § 1361 no longer available to compel registration. *See Nova Stylings, Inc. v. Ladd*, 695 F.2d 1179 (9th Cir. 1983). Ordinarily, however, judicial review cannot occur until there is a final agency action, including the exhaustion of available administrative appeal procedures. *Cf. Proulx v. Hennepin Technical Centers Dist. No. 287*, 1982 Copr. L. Dec. (CCH) ¶ 25,389 (D. Minn. 1981) (one must exhaust administrative remedies and obtain a final refusal to register before proceeding with infringement claim in federal court). Does this render the expectant applicant powerless? Or is mandamus still available to compel the Register to act on a completed application, even though it is not available to compel registration itself?

(13) There are, of course, other incentives to register. Under § 410(c), a certificate proving a registration made before or within five years after first publication of a work constitutes *prima facie* evidence of the validity both of the copyright and of the facts stated in the certificate, thereby shifting the burden of producing evidence to the defendant. But the presumption is rebuttable, and if evidence sufficient to demonstrate invalidity is introduced, the burden of production shifts back to the plaintiff, who retains the ultimate burden of persuasion. *See, e.g.*, Fed. R. Evid. 301; *Estate of Hogarth v. Edgar Rice Burroughs, Inc.*, 342 F.3d 149, 166-67 (2d Cir. 2003); *Entertainment Research Group, Inc. v. Genesis Creative Group, Inc.*, 122 F.3d 1211, 1217-18 (9th Cir. 1997); *Fonar Corp. v. Domenick*, 105 F.3d 99, 104 (2d Cir. 1997).

Another important incentive to register is § 412, which provides that a court may not award statutory damages or attorneys' fees for any infringement of an unpublished work occurring before registration or for any infringement of a published work commenced before registration (unless registered within three months of publication). Other notable benefits of registration include availability of the "cure" provision for works published without notice prior to March 1, 1989, § 405(a)(2), and protection of the actual owner's interest when the notice erroneously names another as the proprietor of the copyright. § 406(a)(1).

(14) The scheme described in the preceding paragraphs, under which the copyright owner still may derive significant benefits from choosing to register, has been subject to considerable criticism. In particular, the conditioning of statutory damages and attorneys' fees on registration (or pre-registration) has been denounced as an imposition on "small creators," who may be unaware of the benefits of registration until it is too late to secure them, or for whom the mechanics of the registration system may be excessively burdensome. As described in the following paragraphs, however, the Copyright Office has attempted in a number of ways to reduce the burdens imposed by the registration requirement on at least some copyright owners.

(15) *Registration mechanics.* In recent years, the Copyright Office has transitioned to a primarily online registration system from a primarily paper-based system. In either case, in order to register a work, the claimant must submit to the Copyright Office a properly completed application form, the appropriate fee, and the required deposit of the work. Under § 408(c), the Register has administrative authority to classify works for purposes of registration and to prescribe appropriate forms.

Obviously, the cost of compliance with registration formalities can be significant for an author who creates many works. Imagine, for example, a freelance photographer who takes hundreds of photos each week and circulates them widely to possible buyers. Not knowing in advance which will have commercial value, she wishes to have as much legal protection as possible — but obviously cannot afford to register each photograph individually. Accordingly, the Copyright Office has exercised its authority under § 408(c) to provide by regulation for a single registration for a "collection" of unpublished works, and for group registrations of certain "related works": automated databases (and revisions to them), serials, newspapers, periodicals, newsletters, and published photographs. *See* 37 C.F.R. § 202.3(b)(3)–(8).

(16)   The preferred method of registration is through the Electronic Copyright Office (eCO) system at the Copyright Office's website. In most cases a hard-copy deposit must still be submitted (except for certain works that are published only in electronic form or are unpublished). The eCO system reduces processing time and is less expensive; the fee for online registration is $35 and the fee for processing traditional paper forms is $65. For current fees, visit the Copyright Office website at *www.copyright.gov*.

Suppose that you have a client who has not registered its copyright but wishes to commence an infringement suit immediately. Ordinarily, the process of copyright registration may take several months, but the Copyright Office, at its discretion, may agree to conduct an expedited process, known as "special handling," by which applications usually can produce final action within five working days. The fee for "special handling" is currently $760. Should registrations secured by this means be entitled to less evidentiary weight than those processed at the normal administrative pace? *See Carol Barnhart, Inc. v. Economy Cover Corp.*, 594 F. Supp. 364 (E.D.N.Y. 1984); Compendium II at § 605.07.

(17)   The provisions of § 412 sometimes made it difficult for motion picture companies to recover statutory damages or attorneys' fees: A motion picture could not be registered as a published work until it had been released, and it was impractical to register a film as an unpublished work until it was edited for release. Congress responded to these concerns in 2005 by requiring the Copyright Office to establish a procedure for "pre-registration" of an unpublished work "being prepared for commercial distribution," for any "class of works that the Register determines has had a history of infringement prior to authorized commercial distribution." § 408(f)(1), (2). The Register's regulations identify six classes of works eligible for pre-registration: motion pictures, sound recordings, musical works, literary works, computer programs, and advertising or marketing photos. 37 C.F.R. § 202.16(b)(1). Pre-registration allows a copyright owner to file suit for infringement before formal registration is made. A copyright owner who pre-registers a work, however, is required to register the completed work within three months after first publication, or within one month of learning of the alleged infringement (if the infringement commenced no later than two months after first publication), or else the action must be dismissed. § 408(f)(4). Statutory damages may be recovered for infringement of a pre-registered work if these time limits are met. § 412.

(18)   Pre-registration of a work can be made only after some portion of the work has been "fixed." 37 C.F.R. § 202.16(b)(2). Note, however, that § 411(c) permits an action for alleged infringement of a live broadcast which will be fixed to be filed "before or after such fixation takes place," and before any registration has been made. To take advantage of § 411(c), a copyright owner must have some idea in advance who is likely to engage in infringing conduct, because the statutory procedure involves serving at least 48 hours in advance of the broadcast a notice

identifying the work and declaring an intention to assert copyright in it. *See Football Ass'n Premier League, Ltd. v. YouTube, Inc.*, 633 F. Supp. 2d 159 (S.D.N.Y. 2009) (discussing notice requirement). How can such a provision, providing a right of action with respect to infringements of live broadcasts, be squared with the "fixation" requirement, which (in turn) is rooted in the Constitution?

(19) The Copyright Office's application forms demand detailed information about the nature of the authorship on the basis of which copyright in a particular work is claimed, including the relationship (in the case of derivative works) between the new authorship and the contents of the underlying work upon which it builds. An applicant who wishes to secure registration may be tempted to answer certain queries less than completely, in the hope of concealing the vulnerability of the claim. Besides being improper, this procedure is risky as a practical matter, because many courts have followed the Second Circuit in holding that "knowing failure to advise the Copyright Office of facts which might have occasioned a rejection of the application constitute[s a] reason for holding the registration invalid and thus incapable of supporting an infringement action." *Whimsicality, Inc. v. Rubie's Costume Co.*, 891 F.2d 452, 456 (2d Cir. 1989). In response to such cases, Congress enacted what is now § 411(b), which requires a showing "that the inaccuracy of the information, if known, would have caused the Register of Copyrights to refuse registration." § 411(b)(1)(B). See Chapter 10 for further discussion of "fraud on the Copyright Office" as an affirmative defense.

(20) *Registration and the BCIA.* Under the "two-tier" approach to registration adopted in the Berne Convention Implementation Act of 1988, as amended by the Uruguay Round Agreements Act of 1994, only "United States works" must be registered before an infringement suit is commenced. § 411(a). Works from a Berne or WTO nation other than the United States are excused from compliance with the registration formality for § 411 jurisdictional purposes, but continue to be subject to it for purposes of gaining the benefits available under §§ 406, 410, and 412. Is this consistent with Article 5 of the Berne Convention, which bars conditioning the "exercise" or "enjoyment" of copyright, as to works for which protection is claimed under the treaty, on compliance with any national law formality? *Cf. Elsevier, B.V. v. UnitedHealth Group, Inc.*, 93 U.S.P.Q.2d (BNA) 1408 (S.D.N.Y. 2010) (§ 412 is not inconsistent with the Supremacy Clause, because the Berne Convention is not a self-executing treaty and is therefore valid only to the extent implemented in domestic law).

The § 101 definition of "United States works" depends not only on the nationality or domicile of the author, but also on whether the work was first published in the United States or "simultaneously" published in the United States at the time of first publication. How should this definition be interpreted when a work is first published on the Internet? *Compare Moberg v. 33T LLC*, 666 F. Supp. 2d 415 (D. Del. 2009) (assuming Swedish author's photos were "published" when posted on German website, they were not simultaneously "published" in the United States and were therefore not "United States works" for purposes of § 411(a)), *with Kernal Records Oy v. Mosley*, 694 F.3d 1294 (11th Cir. 2012) (plaintiff failed to meet its burden of proving that its sound recording was first published in Australia and was not simultaneously published in the United States).

[C] Registration of Collective and Derivative Works

As we saw in § 6.02[C], a single copyright notice on a collective work is sufficient to preserve rights both in the collective work and in the individual contributions to that collective work. But does *registration* of a collective work also constitute registration of the individual contributions, so that the owners of rights in the individual component works are able to bring suit for copyright infringement?

In *Morris v. Business Concepts, Inc.*, 283 F.3d 502 (2d Cir. 2002), the Second Circuit held that if the copyright claimant for both the individual contribution and the collective work was the same (*i.e.*, if all rights in the individual contribution had been transferred to the collective work copyright owner), then the registration for the collective work would suffice to cover the individual contribution as well. But where the copyright claimants for the individual contribution and the collective work were *not* the same (as in *Morris* itself, in which the magazine was granted an exclusive license only for 90 days), then the registration for the collective work does *not* apply to the individual contributions. *Accord Xoom, Inc. v. Imageline, Inc.*, 323 F.3d 279 (4th Cir. 2003); *Educational Testing Services v. Katzman*, 793 F.2d 533 (3d Cir. 1986).

On a (perhaps) related matter: Can the owner of copyright in a *derivative work* rely on the registration of the underlying work for § 411(a) purposes? In *Montgomery v. Noga*, 168 F.3d 1282 (11th Cir. 1999), the court held that where the plaintiff owns both the copyright in the derivative work and the copyright in the underlying work, and the plaintiff alleges infringement of elements in the (unregistered) derivative work that also existed in the underlying work, registration of the underlying work will suffice. In *Well-Made Toy Mfg. Corp. v. Goffa Int'l Corp.*, 354 F.3d 112 (2d Cir. 2003), however, the court held that registration of the underlying work does *not* suffice with respect to alleged infringement of an unregistered derivative work, where the defendant allegedly copied expressive elements found *only* in the derivative work and not in the underlying work. *Accord Murray Hill Publications, Inc. v. ABC Communications, Inc.*, 264 F.3d 622 (6th Cir. 2001).

Conversely, can the owner of copyright in the underlying work rely on the registration of the derivative work for § 411(a) purposes? Remember that § 103(b) provides that the copyright in a derivative work "extends only to the material contributed by the author of such work, *as distinguished from* the preexisting material employed in the work," which strongly suggests that registration of the derivative work does not cover the pre-existing material. Nonetheless, *Murray Hill* suggests (in dicta) that where the same person owns both copyrights, registration of the derivative work will support an action for infringement of the underlying work, and at least one Court of Appeals has so held. *Streetwise Maps, Inc. v. VanDam, Inc.*, 159 F.3d 739 (2d Cir. 1998). *But see Oravec v. Sunny Isles Luxury Ventures, L.C.*, 527 F.3d 1218 (11th Cir. 2008) (principle does not apply where registration certificate does not properly identify the pre-existing work upon which the infringement claim is based).

The court in *Murray Hill* characterized the requirements of § 411(a) as adding clarity and certainty to the enforcement of copyrights. In your view, do the rules articulated in cases such as *Murray Hill* and *Morris* in fact foster the admirable qualities of certainty and clarity?

§ 6.04 THE COPYRIGHT OFFICE

[A] Introduction

Statutory References
  1976 Act: §§ 701-10
  1909 Act: §§ 201-16

Legislative History

[The legislative history concerning these sections is set forth at H.R. REP. No. 94-1476 at 171-73, *reprinted in* 1976 U.S.C.C.A.N. 5659, 5787-89. For a detailed excerpt, see Part Three of the Casebook Supplement.]

[B] History and Functions of the Copyright Office

The first federal copyright statute, enacted in 1790, provided for registration of each work to be made not in a central office, but rather in the office of the clerk of the federal judicial district where the author resided. In addition, within six months after publication of the work, the author was required to deposit a copy thereof with the Department of State. While the place of deposit was changed a number of times in the early years, the place of registration remained the same until 1870, when Congress revised the law to centralize both registration and deposit in the Library of Congress.

The impetus for the 1870 Act derived largely from the unusual vision of Ainsworth Rand Spofford, the sixth Librarian of Congress. Appointed by President

Lincoln in 1864, Spofford saw the potential for creating, in effect, a national library, by obtaining for the Library of Congress virtually the entire cultural output of the United States — books, periodicals, music, works of art, and other works — through a centralized copyright deposit system. With the adoption of Spofford's proposal in 1870, the Library began its transformation into the largest library in the world, an institution with over 3,600 employees in three large buildings containing approximately 650 miles of shelving and holding more than 150 million items in its collections.

In 1897, the growth of the Library's collections forced it to move out of the Capitol Building and into what is now called the Thomas Jefferson Building. In that same year, Congress decided to address the problem of the enormous additional workload created by centralized registration and deposit. The Act of February 19, 1897 created a separate department of the Library — the Copyright Office — to discharge these responsibilities, and provided for a new appointee of the Librarian — the Register of Copyrights — to administer the Office. Thorvald Solberg, a recognized authority in the field of literary property, became the first Register two weeks later.

Today, the Copyright Office has a staff of about 475 employees housed in the James Madison Building on Capitol Hill in Washington, D.C. In fiscal year 2010, the Office registered over 636,000 claims to copyright.[1] While not all of the copies deposited to make these registrations can be retained permanently due to space limitations, more than half are used by the Library to enrich its collections or to carry out other functions, such as its gift programs and exchanges with other libraries and learned institutions.

In addition to these responsibilities, the Copyright Office provides assistance to visiting members of the public seeking information about particular works, and answers more than 300,000 letters, e-mails and telephone inquiries annually. The Copyright Office contains the record of more than 33 million copyright registrations (including renewals), and constitutes a truly unique index of authorship. Registrations made beginning in 1978 are available for electronic searching on the Copyright Office website. Registrations made before 1978 are currently available only in paper form, but the Office plans to convert these records into electronic form when funding becomes available.

A further and important activity of the Copyright Office is its role in the formulation of national and international policy on copyright and related subjects. The Register of Copyrights is among the principal advisors to Congress and the Executive Branch on international copyright matters. In order to carry out these duties, the Copyright Office has assembled a staff of attorneys and other experts with special competence in copyright. In addition, the Office actively solicits the input of authors, publishers, librarians, and other users of copyrighted works.

The general information number at the Copyright Office is (202) 707-3000 or (877) 476-0778 (toll-free). The Office's address on the World Wide Web is *www.copyright.gov*.

---

[1] The latest available on-line Annual Report of the Register of Copyrights covers FY 2010. For updates, see *www.copyright.gov/reports/*.

[C]   Combining the Copyright Office with the Patent and Trademark Office

The placement of the Copyright Office in the Library of Congress would appear to make it part of the Legislative Branch, and for many purposes it is treated as such. For Constitutional purposes, however, the Register is appointed by the Librarian of Congress, who in turn is appointed by the President, with the advice and consent of the Senate, as a "Head of Department" under Article II. *See Intercollegiate Broad. Sys. v. Copyright Royalty Bd.*, 684 F.3d 1332 (D.C. Cir. 2012); *accord Eltra Corp. v. Ringer*, 579 F.2d 294 (4th Cir. 1978).

Were it not, some commentators have suggested that regulations promulgated by the Register of Copyrights would be constitutionally suspect. *See* Brylawski, *The Copyright Office: A Constitutional Confrontation*, 44 Geo. Wash. L. Rev. 1 (1975); Jiles, *Copyright Protection in the New Millennium: Amending the Digital Millennium Copyright Act to Prevent Constitutional Challenges*, 52 Admin. L. Rev. 443 (2000). It is extremely unlikely, however, that the Supreme Court would invalidate an arrangement that has stood for more than a century.

During the Clinton Administration, the increased influence of international trade considerations in formulating U.S. intellectual property law and policy prompted serious consideration of reform in the structure of the Copyright Office and its companion agency, the U.S. Patent and Trademark Office. In 1999, the PTO, which has been part of the Commerce Department since 1925, was reorganized. Whereas previously the PTO was led by a single Commissioner of Patents, there are now separate Commissioners of Patent and Trademarks, under the supervision of the "Under Secretary of Commerce for Intellectual Property and Director of the United States Patent and Trademark Office." In creating the position of "Under Secretary for Intellectual Property," Congress at least implicitly raised the question of whether the Copyright Office would (or should) be consolidated with the PTO.

What are the pluses and minuses of the suggestion that the United States should have a single agency which is (1) responsible for all of patent, trademark, and copyright law and (2) lodged in the Executive Branch rather than the Legislative Branch? One way to approach the question might be to ask yourself: If you were designing a system for the administration of U.S. intellectual property law from scratch, what would it look like? How important is it that the various bodies of federal intellectual property law be coordinated by a single agency? Should such an agency, if created, report to the Legislative Branch, which enacts intellectual property laws, or to the Commerce Department, which helps negotiate treaties that increasingly require revisions to those laws? Is there anything special about copyright law that justifies the current administrative regime?

One response might be that copyrights traditionally have been treated differently from patents and trademarks in international law. While copyrights are governed by the Berne Convention, patents and trademarks fall under the Paris Convention for the Protection of Industrial Property. Moreover, because the Berne Convention prohibits mandatory formalities, most countries lack any kind of registration system for copyrights, even though it is common to require government examination and registration for patents and trademarks. This fact alone makes the existence of *any* Copyright Office tasked with important regulatory responsibilities unusual in the international sphere.

The question of consolidation arose in part because TRIPS broke with tradition in addressing copyrights in the same agreement with patents and trademarks. The spirit of consolidation can also be detected in the Prioritizing Resources and Organization for Intellectual Property (PRO-IP) Act of 2008, which created an Intellectual Property Enforcement Coordinator (or "IP Czar"), whose principal duty is to chair an interagency intellectual property enforcement committee consisting of representatives from the Copyright Office and various agencies, including the PTO, the Department of Justice, and the U.S. Trade Representative. The committee was charged by Congress with creating and implementing a Joint Strategic Plan for, among other things, "reducing counterfeiting and infringement in the domestic and international supply chain" and "disrupting and eliminating domestic and international counterfeiting and infringement networks."

It remains to be seen whether the creation of the IP Czar will lead to substantive changes in the administration of copyright and other intellectual property laws. For now, however, despite the PRO-IP Act, the push for formal consolidation has subsided. Both inertia and tradition suggest that the Copyright Office will remain where it is for the foreseeable future.

Chapter 7

EXCLUSIVE RIGHTS AND THEIR LIMITATIONS

This chapter's contents lie at the very heart of copyright, both historically and in the digital millennium.

Historically, the Statute of Anne gave the copyright owner the rights to "print[] and reprint[]" the copyrighted work, but provided also to such owner (as we will see in Chapter 11) a panoply of remedies against any person who might "print, reprint, or import, . . . [or] sell, publish, or expose to sale" the copyrighted work "without the consent of the proprietor."[1] These rights and remedies correspond generally with the exclusive rights to "reproduce" and "distribute" the copyrighted work accorded to the copyright owner today.[2] In the three centuries since 1710, however, the scope of copyright has expanded to include additional rights in the subject work, including the exclusive rights to prepare derivative works based on the copyrighted work and to perform and display such works publicly.

Chapter 7 is concerned principally with examining the six "exclusive rights" currently recognized in § 106 of the 1976 Act, and with the complex array of limitations on those rights (especially those necessitated by modern technologies) which follow in §§ 107 to 122. After establishing the basic architecture of the exclusive rights and their limitations, we consider each of the rights in sequence, treating the relevant statutory limitations in connection with the specific right or rights to which they apply. We conclude with a discussion of the limited "moral rights" recognized in § 106A of the Copyright Act.

Because the violation of an exclusive right constitutes copyright infringement, these materials set the stage for the following four chapters. Chapter 8 examines infringement from both procedural and substantive standpoints; Chapter 9 considers secondary liability; Chapter 10 focuses on defenses to infringement, including fair use; and Chapter 11 treats the remedies available in actions for infringement

---

[1] Statute of Anne, 1710, 8 Ann., c. 10, § I (England). For an extended discussion of the Statute's curious lack of congruence between the rights of copyright and the acts of infringement, see L. Ray Patterson & Stanley F. Birch, Jr., *A Unified Theory of Copyright*, Ch. 8 (Craig Joyce ed., 2009), originally published in 46 Hous. L. Rev. 215 (2009).

[2] The absence from the Statute of Anne of any specification of other rights beyond those named above should come as no surprise. The entire pre-history of the Statute had concerned the rights of sellers of books in the English language. Indeed, by its own terms, the Statute of Anne excluded any liability for the "importation, or selling of any books in Greek, Latin, or any other foreign language printed beyond the seas . . ." § VII. Equitable relief to discourage unauthorized reproductions of unpublished plays, as performed, apparently was available at common law. *See, e.g.*, *Macklin v. Richardson*, 27 Eng. Rep. 451 (1770) (injunction against magazine publication of the second act of 18th Century farce, "Love a la Mode," following publication of first act based on notations made at live performances). Most possibilities for the exploitation of literary works through alternative media of the sort so familiar in the modern era remained in the distant future.

and in related actions for non-preempted, state-created claims. Together, these materials reflect the importance and complexity of defining and defending the "exclusive Right[s]" which the Copyright Clause of the Constitution is meant to "secur[e]."

§ 7.01 OVERVIEW

[A] Introduction

Statutory References
   1976 Act: § 106
   1909 Act: § 1

Legislative History

H.R. REP. No. 94-1476 at 61,
reprinted in 1976 U.S.C.C.A.N. 5659, 5674

SECTION 106. EXCLUSIVE RIGHTS IN COPYRIGHTED WORKS[1]
GENERAL SCOPE OF COPYRIGHT

The five [now six] fundamental rights that the bill gives to copyright owners — the exclusive rights of reproduction, adaptation, publication, performance, and display [plus the new digital performance right in § 106(6)] — are stated generally in section 106. These exclusive rights, which comprise the so-called "bundle of rights" that is a copyright, are cumulative and may overlap in some cases. Each of the [six] enumerated rights may be subdivided indefinitely and, as discussed below in connection with section 201, each subdivision of an exclusive right may be owned and enforced separately.

The approach of the bill is to set forth the copyright owner's exclusive rights in broad terms in section 106, and then to provide various limitations, qualifications, or exemptions in the [16] sections that follow. Thus, everything in section 106 is "made subject to sections 107 through [122]," and must be read in conjunction with those provisions . . .

[For a fuller excerpt from H.R. REP. No. 94-1476, see Part Three of the Casebook Supplement.]

---

[1] This excerpt from the House Report refers to the "five fundamental rights" under § 106, and to the several sections following § 106 in Chapter 1 of the 1976 Act as "sections 107 through 118." Subsequent amendments to the Act have added a new right under § 106 (the § 106(6) right to perform sound recordings by means of digital audio transmission), and four new limitations on the § 106 rights (in §§ 119 through 122). This chapter of the casebook deals with these post-enactment amendments to the 1976 Act, as well as the provisions referred to in the legislative history. — *Eds.*

[B] The "Architecture" of Rights and Limitations

Section 106 of the 1976 Act provides: "Subject to sections 107 through 122, the owner of copyright under this title has the exclusive rights to do and to authorize any of the following." Former Register of Copyrights David Ladd has described what Congress intended to accomplish in enacting § 106 and §§ 107-22 as follows:

> The statute sets forth [the copyright owner's] rights in broad terms, unlimited by general requirements of commerciality or profit, and then provides express and specific limitations, qualifications, and exemptions to these rights in the [16] sections that follow. The very architecture of the statute thus has compelling advantages in explicitly demarcating the legislature's balance between the rights of ownership and the rights of use. By the same token, the statute avoids wholesale exceptions, such as "not for profit" uses, which entail too great a risk of eroding the copyright monopoly. *Specific claims for additional limitations, qualifications, or exemptions thereby must be subjected to the legislative process and assessed on the whole evidence from all interests, instead of a limited litigation record among a few private parties.*

Ladd, *Home Recording and Reproduction of Protected Works*, 68 A.B.A. J. 42, 43 (Jan. 1982) (emphasis added). The courts have agreed with this analysis. For example, in the famous *Betamax* case (addressing whether a VCR manufacturer was liable for infringement committed by home users), the Ninth Circuit stated:

> The statutory framework is unambiguous; the grant of exclusive rights is only limited by the statutory exceptions. Elementary principles of statutory construction would indicate that the judiciary should not disturb this carefully constructed statutory scheme in the absence of compelling reasons to do so. That is, we should not, absent a clear direction from Congress, disrupt this framework by carving out exceptions to the broad grant of rights apart from those in the statute itself.

Universal City Studios, Inc. v. Sony Corp. of America, 659 F.2d 963, 966 (9th Cir. 1981), *rev'd on other grounds*, 464 U.S. 417 (1984). (We will consider the Supreme Court's reasons for exonerating Sony from liability in Chapters 9 and 10.)

Consequently, in analyzing whether a copyright owner's rights have been violated, one must first consider whether there has been an unauthorized exercise of one or more of the copyright owner's exclusive rights, as specified in § 106. Once a *prima facie* case has been established, one must then consider whether any of the exceptions or limitations in §§ 107 through 122 applies. In an infringement action, these exceptions or limitations are treated as affirmative defenses.

Initially, the author owns the six "exclusive rights" granted by § 106 (as limited by §§ 107-122), meaning that the author has the right to exclude all other persons from engaging in any of those six activities without permission. Of course, the "bundle of rights" may be transferred by the author to others, or the rights may be "unbundled" and transferred individually. Furthermore, each right may be subdivided, and, upon transfer, such subdivided rights may be separately owned and enforced by others. *See* Chapter 4.

Note that § 106 gives the copyright owner the right "to do *or to authorize*" each of the activities listed in subsections (1) through (6). The House Report states that the italicized language was "intended to avoid any questions as to the liability of contributory infringers." How would you define the concept of "contributory infringement"? For there to be a contributory infringer, must there be a primary infringer? The concept of contributory infringement (on which the outcome in the *Betamax* case turned) is explored in detail in Chapter 9.

[C] Statutory (or "Compulsory") Licenses

Normally, to use a copyrighted work, one must obtain from the copyright owner a license whose terms are determined through private bargaining. If *A*, for example, wishes to reproduce *B*'s copyrighted painting in a poster or perform *B*'s copyrighted song on stage, he must obtain *B*'s authorization for the specific use of the work. The terms of the ensuing agreement will depend on market conditions and the bargaining positions of the parties.

In seven instances, however, the Copyright Act supersedes the normal market mechanism for negotiating a license and replaces it with a statutory license. Under such a "compulsory" license, a third party can use a copyrighted work without the copyright owner's permission, so long as he complies with the statutory procedure and pays the established royalties. The seven compulsory licenses now recognized in the Copyright Act (not counting a "jukebox" license repealed in 1993) are:

1. *The Cable Television License* (§ 111), which establishes a statutory license for secondary transmissions by cable television systems;

2. *The Ephemeral Recordings License* (§ 112(e)), which establishes a statutory license for ephemeral recordings used to facilitate the digital transmissions permitted under § 114;

3. *The Digital Performance Right in Sound Recordings License* (§ 114), which establishes a statutory license for some operators of noninteractive digital transmission services;

4. *The Mechanical License* (§ 115), which establishes a statutory license for the reproduction and distribution of phonorecords of nondramatic musical works, and now includes provisions which apply to authorized "digital phonorecord delivery" of such musical works;

5. *The Public Broadcasting License* (§ 118), which establishes a statutory license for the use of certain copyrighted works by noncommercial broadcasting entities;

6. *The General Satellite Retransmission License* (§ 119), which establishes a temporary (for now) statutory license for satellite retransmissions to the public for private viewing; and

7. *The Local-to-Local Satellite Retransmission License* (§ 122), which establishes a statutory license for satellite retransmissions of local television stations' broadcasts into their local markets.

In addition, the Audio Home Recording Act of 1992 (or "AHRA," *see* § 9.02 below), establishes immunity from liability for copyright infringement for manufacturers and importers of digital audio recording equipment in connection with the imposition of a duty to pay statutory "royalties" into a fund for the benefit of copyright owners. Failure to pay these royalties does not, however, subject the manufacturer or importer to an infringement action, but only to an action for statutorily prescribed penalties.

In any scheme of compulsory licensing, some authority is needed to resolve two kinds of recurrent issues: to set the statutory royalty rates for licenses, and (with respect to some licenses, most notably the license for cable retransmission) to settle disputes concerning the distribution of the monies collected.

Under the 1976 Act, a Copyright Royalty Tribunal ("CRT") was established to administer the compulsory licenses. The CRT also administered the royalty system established by the AHRA. From its beginnings, the CRT was controversial. Part of the controversy was attributable to the Copyright Act itself. Although the Act provides relatively clear direction for ratemaking activities in connection with compulsory licensing, it did nothing to spell out how to distribute the royalties generated, in particular, by the complicated cable television compulsory license. Thus, partly as a result of its vague mandate, the CRT's activities became embroiled in a constant stream of litigation and criticism.

In addition, however, the CRT suffered from criticism directed at the tribunal itself. Some concerns related to the commissioners' lack of copyright experience and the CRT's efficiency, or lack thereof; also, at congressional hearings in 1993, two commissioners volunteered the view that the CRT's continued existence could not be justified by its workload. But the most serious concerns arose from dissatisfaction with the CRT's work product. An example of the endless controversies concerning the CRT in its ratemaking capacity is *Recording Industry Association of America v. Copyright Royalty Tribunal*, 662 F.2d 1 (D.C. Cir. 1981) (mechanical license for nondramatic musical work under § 115).

The Copyright Royalty Tribunal Reform Act of 1993 eliminated the CRT and transferred its functions to "Copyright Arbitration Royalty Panels," or CARPs. (Why not "Copyright Royalty Arbitration Panels"?) CARPs were convened from time to time by the Librarian of Congress, on the advice of the Register of Copyrights, to consider particular rates or resolve particular disputes over royalty distribution that could not be settled through private negotiation. The goal was to reduce the cost of administering the statutory licenses, while shifting the remaining costs entirely onto interested copyright owners and users. Like rulings of the CRT, the decisions of the CARPs, once adopted by the Librarian of Congress, were subject to judicial review.

In 2003, the CARPs themselves came under fire after a controversial rate-setting proceeding that was partially rejected by the Librarian of Congress and later superseded by Congress itself. *See* § 7.07[B]. As with the CRT, CARP proceedings were criticized as too lengthy and expensive. It was said that *ad hoc* arbitrators lacked experience and familiarity with the substantive law and with the economics of the industries involved, and their decisions were criticized as unpredictable and inconsistent. The criticism resulted in the enactment of the

Copyright Royalty and Distribution Reform Act of 2004, which replaced the CARPs with three full-time Copyright Royalty Judges ("CRJs"). Each of the CRJs must have at least seven years of legal experience, and the Chief Judge must have at least five years of experience in adjudications, arbitrations, or court trials. One of the other two judges must have "significant knowledge" of copyright law, and the other must have "significant knowledge" of economics. 17 U.S.C. § 802(a)(1). The three CRJs serve staggered six-year terms. § 802(c). The role of the CRJs is limited to fact-finding and rate determinations; the Judges are required to request a decision from the Register of Copyrights on any "novel material question of substantive law." § 802(f)(1)(B). The Register also may review and comment on the CRJs' resolution of any "material question of substantive law" (without regard to novelty), and the Register's interpretations of substantive law are binding on the CRJs in any subsequent proceedings. § 802(f)(1)(D).

Decisions of the CRJs are subject to judicial review in the U.S. Court of Appeals for the D.C. Circuit (as CARP decisions had been). § 803(d)(1). The applicable standard of review, however, has changed. Under the 1993 amendments, decisions of the Librarian of Congress taken on the basis of a determination by a CARP could be set aside or modified only if the court found "on the basis of the record before the Librarian, . . . the Librarian acted in an arbitrary manner." Under the 2004 amendments, the CRJs' decisions are subject to review under the Administrative Procedure Act, which provides that a court should allow an agency determination to stand unless it is "arbitrary, capricious, an abuse of discretion, or otherwise not in accordance with law." Is this change in the standard of review significant? Will it result in more or less litigation over statutory licenses?

In 2012, the D.C. Circuit held that appointment of the CRJs by the Librarian of Congress violates the Appointments Clause of the Constitution, which requires that officers with significant authority be appointed by the President with Senate confirmation. The court's remedy, however, was to sever and invalidate only the statutory language restricting the Librarian of Congress' authority to fire the CRJs, thus making them "inferior officers" who can lawfully be appointed by the Librarian (a "Head of Department") under the Appointments Clause. *See Intercollegiate Broad. Sys. v. Copyright Royalty Bd.*, 684 F.3d 1332 (D.C. Cir. 2012). While the rate-making determination under review had to be vacated and remanded, the court's solution effectively insulates future rate-making decisions from constitutional challenge.

If the statutory licenses are a major departure from the ordinary way of obtaining the right to use a copyrighted work, how did they come to exist — and are they justifiable? The statutory licenses essentially are the result of political compromise in which certain user groups obtained cheaper access to copyrighted works than was available by a private bargaining process. The cable television statutory license, considered in detail in § 7.05[B], provides a clear example of the outcome of this process of political compromise. As embodied in § 111, it reflects the intense negotiations between powerful interest groups (copyright owners versus cable television providers) that have struggled for favorable governmental treatment. The result of this heated clash of conflicting interests is a complicated system of regulation.

Supporters of statutory licensing justify the preemption of an author's control over the use of her work on economic grounds. The rationale is that a well-constructed statutory license can serve both owners and users by reducing the transaction costs involved in negotiating licenses. In certain instances, these transaction costs could be so high that negotiations would not take place at all, resulting in market failure and thereby impoverishing owners, users, and the public. Ideally, a well-conceived and administered statutory license scheme would increase net revenues for both users and creators of copyrighted works and facilitate the dissemination of copyrighted works to the public. Is this rationale valid today, given the merger frenzy in the communications industry?

Ironically, the switch to full-time CRJs came just as three of the seven statutory licenses were being called into question. In 2005, the Register of Copyrights recommended to Congress that the § 115 compulsory license be eliminated. *See* § 7.02[C]. And in 2008, the Register reported that the § 111 and § 119 cable and satellite retransmission licenses "have outlived their original purposes" and should be "phased out." *See* § 7.05[B][5]. As you read the materials below, consider whether these complicated regulatory provisions still play a valuable role, or whether the public would be better served by eliminating them in favor of free-market transactions.

[D] Exclusive Rights in the Networked Information Environment

In September 1995, the Clinton Administration's Information Infrastructure Task Force's Working Group on Intellectual Property issued its final report, titled "Intellectual Property and the National Information Infrastructure." The report (or "White Paper") recognized that new computer and communications technologies were having an enormous impact on the creation, reproduction, and dissemination of copyrighted works. Documents similar to the White Paper also emerged from Canada, Australia, Japan, and the European Union.

One recurrent question concerning copyright in the networked digital environment has been whether the rights of copyright owners, as recognized by existing legislation, are adequate as they stand or require revision. For example: When a copyrighted work in digital form is sent by means of e-mail, or posted to the World Wide Web, or streamed over the Internet, what exactly has occurred? A "reproduction"? A "performance"? A "distribution" of "copies"? Or something else? The White Paper proposed amendments to § 106 and the related definitions in § 101 to make clear that digital "transmissions" of works constitute a form of public distribution. This did not come to pass, however.

In December 1996, a Diplomatic Conference of the World Intellectual Property Organization produced two new international agreements: the WIPO Copyright Treaty and the WIPO Performances and Phonograms Treaty. Each calls on parties to recognize under their national laws a "right of communication to the public" by "wire or wireless means," including "the making available to the public of [copyright owners'] works in such a way that members of the public may access these works from a place and at a time individually chosen by them." WIPO Copyright Treaty, Art. 8. Obviously, this provision was designed to deal with circumstances created by the new digital technologies.

In the end, Congress concluded that U.S. copyright law measured up to the mandate of the new treaties in this respect. The Digital Millennium Copyright Act of 1998, enacted to "implement" the treaties, included no modifications to or clarifications of § 106. By contrast, the European Union's "Directive on the harmonization of certain aspects of copyright and related rights in the information society" (Directive 2001/29/EC of 22 May 2001) prominently featured a new exclusive right, in Article 3(1), tracking the language of the 1996 WIPO treaties.

We will be dealing with the implications of digital technology for the rights of copyright owners throughout the chapter to come. By way of background, you may wish to review the discussion of the "Digital Challenge" provided earlier in this casebook in § 1.05.

[E] Miscellaneous Rights: In and Beyond Copyright

In addition to the various exclusive rights traditionally protected by copyright law, Congress has been busy in recent years considering, and in some instances enacting into law, what might be called "miscellaneous rights." What these miscellaneous rights have in common is that each is a nontraditional protection produced by the interaction of new technologies, modes of commerce, and the "interest politics" by which much of contemporary copyright law and policy is shaped. This subsection explores that phenomenon.

[1] In General

Once upon a time, it might have made sense to speak of a "unified field" theory of copyright — one body of rules, that is, broadly applicable to all kinds of works and all kinds of uses. Indeed, the 1909 Copyright Act, as originally drafted, was a relatively straightforward document with only a few embellishments (like the provisions for "mechanical licenses," the great-granddaddy of today's statutory licenses). The 1971 Sound Recording Amendments, which brought in new subject matter while curtailing the exercise of rights with respect to it, marked a significant departure — the beginning of a tendency to incorporate special-purpose legislation into the law of copyright. The 1976 Act also was significantly shaped by this tendency. One needed to look no further than § 111 for a clear indication that, in the future, copyright law would increasingly be pressed into service as a vehicle for detailed regulation of new communications and information technologies. This trend continued with the addition of the digital performance right in sound recordings, a highly specialized right limited to a single type of work of authorship, that Congress enacted in 1995 and codified as § 106(6). (This right will be considered in § 7.07.)

In addition, there has been a related trend toward the inclusion in Title 17 of new provisions which are specifically designed to interact with and affect the operation of copyright law, even though technically speaking they are codified *outside* the Copyright Act itself (*i.e.*, outside the first eight chapters of Title 17). One example is the provisions on copyright management information (or "CMI"), enacted in 1998 as part of the Digital Millennium Copyright Act, but codified in § 1202 of Chapter 12 ("Copyright Protection and Management Systems") of Title 17. We will examine

CMI momentarily below. Before doing so, however, we hasten to add that there are many other examples of miscellaneous rights discussed elsewhere in this casebook. Indeed, all five chapters of Title 17 that lie outside the Copyright Act have received, or will receive, consideration at an appropriate juncture:

- Chapter 9 of Title 17, codifying the Semiconductor Chip Protection Act of 1984, was discussed in § 3.01;

- Chapter 10 of Title 17, codifying the Audio Home Recording Act of 1992, will be treated in § 9.02;

- Chapter 11 of Title 17, codifying rights granted in the 1994 Uruguay Round Agreements Act against unauthorized fixation of live musical performances, was noted in § 2.01;

- Chapter 12 of Title 17, insofar as it concerns the anti-circumvention measures enacted (along with CMI) as part of the DMCA in 1998, will be considered in detail in §§ 9.04 and 10.04; and

- Chapter 13 of Title 17, codifying the vessel hull design protection provisions of the DMCA, appeared in § 3.01 in connection with the discussion of various means for protecting ornamental designs.

Add to these the wide array of other miscellaneous rights protections (*e.g.*, for databases) regularly proposed for enactment and it becomes clear that, in this area at least, there is potentially no end to the creativity of the U.S. Congress.

[2] Copyright Management Information

If a person wishes to use a copyrighted work in a way that comes within any of the six exclusive rights in § 106, and that use is not authorized by any of the exceptions or limitations in §§ 107 through 122, then that person must "clear the rights" by obtaining the permission of the copyright owner. Clearing rights is often easier said than done; one must first determine who owns the rights and where to locate them. Formalities such as notice and registration (discussed in Chapter 6) can help by providing a written record of copyright ownership. In addition, there are vehicles for the collective licensing of rights, such as performing rights societies for musical works (*see* § 7.05[A][3]) and the Copyright Clearance Center for certain literary works (*see* § 7.02[A]).

Digital technology, with its ability to encode significant amounts of data, can greatly facilitate rights clearance. All pertinent information, such as name, contact information, and licensing rates, can be encoded with the work and displayed to a potential customer. For works available over digital networks, embedded links to the copyright owner can make electronic licensing even more convenient. As more and more works become available in electronic form, this sort of rights management information ("RMI") or — the synonym we will prefer here — copyright management information ("CMI") could significantly reduce the transaction costs associated with copyright licensing.

At the urging of many copyright owners, the 1996 WIPO treaties, which we introduced in § 1.04 and § 7.01[D], went beyond encouraging the voluntary provision of CMI. In addition, they mandate that party states provide penalties for failing to transmit, or for deleting, such information. *See* WIPO Copyright Treaty, Art. 12; WIPO Performances and Phonograms Treaty, Art. 19.

The Digital Millennium Copyright Act of 1998 implemented this portion of the WIPO treaties by adding § 1202 to Title 17. Section 1202(a) prohibits providing, distributing, or importing CMI that is false, if done "knowingly and with the intent to induce, enable, facilitate, or conceal infringement." Section 1202(b) prohibits (1) intentionally removing or altering CMI, (2) distributing or importing CMI knowing that CMI has been unlawfully removed or altered, or (3) distributing, importing, or publicly performing works, or copies or phonorecords of works, knowing that CMI has been unlawfully removed or altered. Any of these acts must be done "knowing or . . . having reasonable grounds to know that it will induce, enable, facilitate, or conceal an infringement."[2]

CMI is defined to include the title, author, rights owner, performer, "terms and conditions for the use of the work," identifying numbers or symbols, and "such other information as the Register of Copyrights may provide by regulation." § 1202(c). This definition of CMI raised a red flag for electronic privacy advocates, who feared that information about individuals' use of digital information (such as the embedded records of usage patterns on the World Wide Web known as "cookies") might be swept into the category of protected CMI, thus making it unlawful for consumers to correct or even delete their personal data. To protect consumer privacy, Congress excluded from the definition of CMI "any personally identifying information about a user of a work" and added the caveat that "the Register of Copyrights may not require the provision of any information concerning the user of a copyrighted work." In addition, § 1202 is subject to § 1205, which provides:

> Nothing in this chapter abrogates, diminishes, or weakens the provisions of, nor provides any defense or element of mitigation in a criminal prosecution or civil action under, any Federal or State law that prevents the violation of the privacy of an individual in connection with that individual's use of the Internet.

The plain language of § 1202(c) ("including in digital form") indicates that it covers analog as well as digital uses of CMI. *See Murphy v. Millennium Radio Group, LLC*, 650 F.3d 295 (3d Cir. 2011). In so holding, the Third Circuit expressly rejected two lower court decisions that had held that § 1202 was limited to CMI that "functioned as a component of an automated copyright protection or management system." *IQ Group, Ltd. v. Wiesner Publishing, LLC*, 409 F. Supp. 2d 587, 598 (D.N.J. 2006); *see also Textile Secrets Int'l v. Ya-Ya Brand, Inc.*, 524 F. Supp. 2d 1184 (C.D. Cal. 2007). Thus, in *Murphy*, allegations that the defendants scanned a magazine photo and posted it on the Internet, while omitting the photographer's credit that appeared in the "gutter" of the magazine, sufficed to state a cause of

---

[2] Note that both the Audio Home Recording Act (*see* § 9.02) and the Digital Performance Right in Sound Recordings Act (*see* § 7.07) also require that any digitally encoded identifying information be preserved when digital works are reproduced or transmitted pursuant to the statutory licensing provisions of those statutes. Both the AHRA and DPRA, however, carve out an exception to this requirement for information relating to the copyright status of works. This information is now required to be preserved as part of CMI. In addition, § 506(d) of the Copyright Act penalizes fraudulent removal of a copyright notice with a $2,500 fine.

action under § 1202. Other courts, however, have held that CMI must have been "removed from a plaintiff's product or original work," rather than simply omitted from a reproduction. *See, e.g., Faulkner Press, LLC v. Class Notes, LLC*, 756 F. Supp. 2d 1352 (N.D. Fla. 2010).

A handful of other decisions have addressed the "intent" requirements of § 1202. In *Kelly v. Arriba Soft Corp.*, 77 F. Supp. 2d 1116 (C.D. Cal. 1999), *aff'd in part and rev'd in part on other grounds*, 336 F.3d 811 (9th Cir. 2003), the defendant operated a "visual search engine" that located photographs posted on the World Wide Web and displayed "thumbnail" and full-sized versions of them to users, along with links to the sites where the original images appeared. (The Court of Appeals' decision in the case, which doesn't discuss the CMI issue, is reproduced in Chapter 10.) Kelly, a photographer, filed a complaint alleging, among other things, that CMI had been stripped from the original images, in violation of § 1202. The court first held that the prohibition against intentional removal of CMI had not been violated:

> Section 1202(b)(1) does not apply to this case. Based on the language and structure of the statute . . . this provision applies only to the removal of copyright management information on a plaintiff's product or original work. Moreover, even if Sec. 1202(b)(1) applied, Plaintiff has not offered any evidence showing Defendant's actions were intentional, rather than merely an unintended side effect of the [web] crawler's operation.

77 F. Supp. 2d. at 1122. The court also found that the requisite knowledge was not present:

> To show a violation of [§ 1202(b)(3)], Plaintiff must show Defendant makes available to its users . . . copies of Plaintiff's work separated from their copyright management information, even though it knows or should know this will lead to infringement of Plaintiff's copyrights. There is no dispute the [web] crawler removed Plaintiff's images from the context of Plaintiff's Web sites where their copyright management information was located. . . . There is also no dispute the search engine allowed full-size images to be viewed without their copyright management information.
>
> [But] Defendant's users could obtain a full-sized version of a thumbnailed image by clicking on the thumbnail. A user who did this was given the name of the Web site from which Defendant obtained the image, where any associated copyright management information would be available, and an opportunity to link there. Users were also informed on Defendant's Web site that use restrictions and copyright limitations may apply to images retrieved by Defendant's search engine.

Id. Do these facts really negate a finding of the requisite "knowledge"? How important, practically, is such a disclaimer? Should it matter how easy (or difficult) it was to print or download images retrieved by the Arriba Soft service? *See also Gordon v. Nextel Communications*, 345 F.3d 922 (6th Cir. 2003) (even though defendant intentionally removed notice, it did not have reasonable grounds to know that it would facilitate infringement, because it believed a license had been obtained to use the work); *Keogh v. Big Lots Corp.*, 2006 U.S. Dist. LEXIS 29496 (M.D. Tenn., Apr. 27, 2006) (§ 1202(b)(3) requires actual knowledge that CMI was removed or altered, but only constructive knowledge that actions will facilitate infringement). Litigation about CMI issues has been fairly sparse to date, but it can be expected to increase as courts and litigants become more familiar with § 1202's provisions.

§ 7.02 THE REPRODUCTION RIGHT

The reproduction right recognized by § 106(1) is the most fundamental of the exclusive rights: the right to reproduce the copyrighted work in copies and phonorecords. Historically, this "copyright" is the product of the technology — the printing press — that produced the first copyright statute, the Statute of Anne, in 1710. *See* Chapter 1. The other exclusive rights in § 106 — adaptation, distribution, performance, display, and the § 106(6) digital performance right — also could be said to concern "copying" in a broader sense, but probably they should be viewed more as rights to use the copyrighted work than as rights to copy it.

The present section, then, examines the archetypal right in the bundle of rights that constitute copyright. We examine first, and in detail, the right to reproduce in copies. You will see that Congress carefully hedged the copyright holder's "exclusive right" under § 106(1) with a variety of limitations, qualifications, and exemptions in many (although not all) of the 16 sections of the Act that follow, beginning with the § 107 fair use privilege (consideration of which appears in detail in Chapter 10). After examining reproduction in copies, we will discuss reproduction in phonorecords, with emphasis on two limitations focused particularly on reproductions of sound recordings (§ 114) and of musical works (§ 115). Finally, we will consider electronic reproductions, including reproductions on the Internet.

[A] Introduction

Statutory References
1976 Act: §§ 106(1), 108, 112-15, 117, 121
1909 Act: § 1(a) and (f)

Legislative History

H.R. REP. No. 94-1476 at 61,
reprinted in 1976 U.S.C.C.A.N. 5659, 5674-75

SECTION 106. EXCLUSIVE RIGHTS IN COPYRIGHTED WORKS[1]

Rights of reproduction, adaptation, and publication

The first three clauses of section 106, which cover all rights under a copyright except those of performance and display, extend to every kind of copyrighted work.

---

[1] As before, we note that the House Report, dating from 1976, assumes the existence of five rights under § 106 and twelve limitations thereon under §§ 107 through 118. Be aware that the Copyright Act now contains a sixth right in § 106(6) (the right to perform sound recordings by means of digital audio transmissions) and four new limitations concerning satellite transmission, architectural works, repro-

The exclusive rights encompassed by these clauses, though closely related, are independent; they can generally be characterized as rights of copying, recording, adaptation, and publishing. A single act of infringement may violate all of these rights at once, as where a publisher reproduces, adapts, and sells copies of a person's copyrighted work as part of a publishing venture. Infringement takes place when any one of the rights is violated: where, for example, a printer reproduces copies without selling them or a retailer sells copies without having anything to do with their reproduction. The references to "copies or phonorecords," although in the plural, are intended here and throughout the bill to include the singular (1 U.S.C. § 1).

Reproduction. — Read together with the relevant definitions in section 101, the right "to reproduce the copyrighted work in copies or phonorecords" means the right to produce a material object in which the work is duplicated, transcribed, imitated, or simulated in a fixed form from which it can be "perceived, reproduced, or otherwise communicated, either directly or with the aid of a machine or device." As under the [1909 Act], a copyrighted work would be infringed by reproducing it in whole or in any substantial part, and by duplicating it exactly or by imitation or simulation. Wide departures or variations from the copyrighted work would still be an infringement as long as the author's "expression" rather than merely the author's "ideas" [is] taken. An exception to this general principle, applicable to the reproduction of copyrighted sound recordings, is specified in section 114.

[The legislative history of the various statutory limitations on the reproduction right has been omitted. They have been much amended since the 1976 Act was enacted. The limitations, in their present form, are discussed in detail in the notes following the principal case below.]

[B] Reproduction in Copies

WALT DISNEY PRODUCTIONS v. FILMATION ASSOCIATES
United States District Court, Central District of California
628 F. Supp. 871 (1986)

STOTLER, DISTRICT JUDGE:

INTRODUCTION

In this action, plaintiff Walt Disney Productions ("Disney") asserts claims for violation of its copyright, trademark, and state-created rights in certain animated character depictions, full-length animated films, and industry marks.

Defendants Filmation Associates, Group W Cable, Inc., Westinghouse Broadcasting and Cable, Inc., and Westinghouse Electric Corporation (collectively, "Filmation") have moved for summary judgment on all counts of the First Amended Complaint. . . .

---

ductions for persons with disabilities, and local-to-local satellite retransmissions (in §§ 119, 120, 121 and 122, respectively). — *Eds.*

By this Order, the Court denies defendants' motion, concluding: (1) the preliminary works created in production of defendants' motion picture can constitute infringing copies within the meaning of the 1976 Copyright Act; (2) the issue of infringement of Disney's copyrights remains a question for the trier of fact. . . . [Discussion of the Lanham Act and unfair competition claims has been deleted.]

FACTS AND PROCEDURAL HISTORY

Plaintiff Disney is a corporation that produces, among other things, animated films. Beginning in 1937, Disney produced a series of feature-length motion pictures, which it refers to as the "Disney Classics." Included among these are pictures entitled "Pinocchio," "Alice in Wonderland," and "The Jungle Book." The story of each of these pictures is based in part upon a preexisting work, much of which is in the public domain.

Filmation is also in the business of producing animated films. In or prior to February 1985, Filmation announced its intention to produce and distribute a series of fully animated feature-length films which it refers to as its "New Classics Collection." Included among these are films entitled "The New Adventures of Pinocchio," "Alice Returns to Wonderland," and "The Continuing Adventures of the Jungle Book." Filmation's works are based in part upon the same preexisting sources as are Disney's. . . .

DISCUSSION

. . . In Count Six, Disney alleges that Filmation has infringed Disney's exclusive right to reproduce its copyrighted works in copies. *See* 17 U.S.C. § 106(1).

Disney owns the copyrights to a fully-animated feature-length motion picture entitled "Pinocchio" and to a series of original designs and drawings of certain characters — named Pinocchio, Geppetto, and Stromboli — portrayed therein. These copyrights are valid and duly registered. Filmation has begun production of a fully-animated motion picture entitled "The New Adventures of Pinocchio," which, contends Disney, utilizes a substantial amount of the aforesaid copyrighted materials. In the course of production, Filmation has produced a script, "story board," "story reel,"[2] models, and designs, which are said to be tangible and permanent reproductions of characters and scenes, "constituting copies of material" copyrighted by Disney.

It is undisputed that Filmation has generated a substantial body of work preliminary to a "finished film." It is also undisputed, however, that it has not completed its film "The New Adventures of Pinocchio." Filmation contends that Count Six is not actionable until it has completed work on its motion picture.

---

[2] A "story reel" is a working model used to create the final animated product. To create a story reel, Filmation first records a reading of the script. It then creates a "story board" comprising sketches of the various scenes in the film set in the order in which they will be portrayed and "shoots" the sketches to synchronize with the recorded dialogue track and a rough music track. By viewing the reel, the director can get a "feel" for the story line and pacing of the anticipated picture and can begin allocating responsibility for its animation.

Alternatively, Filmation asserts it is entitled to judgment because any articles so far produced are not substantially similar to Disney's copyrighted expressions.

Pinocchio
© *Disney Enterprises, Inc. Reprinted by permission.*

1. Actionable "Copies"

Filmation argues that the materials so far created are only transitory steps en route to a fixed product, and that until its film is completed and ready for distribution, there exists no article that could be said to infringe any of Disney's copyrights.

Filmation's argument is refuted by the provisions of the 1976 Copyright Act, 17 U.S.C. §§ 101-914 (the "Act"). Under the Act, " '[c]opies' are material objects . . . in which a work is fixed by any method now known or later developed, and from which the work can be perceived, reproduced, or otherwise communicated, either directly or with the aid of a machine or device." 17 U.S.C. § 101. The definition "includes the material object . . . in which the work is first fixed." *Id.* Further, a work is " 'fixed' in a tangible medium of expression when its embodiment in a copy . . . is sufficiently permanent or stable to permit it to be perceived, reproduced, or otherwise communicated for a period of more than transitory duration." *Id.* When the work is "prepared over a period of time, the portion of it that has been fixed at any particular time constitutes the work as of that time, and where the work has been prepared in different versions, each version constitutes a separate work." *Id.* [(definition of "created")]. To constitute an actionable copy, therefore, an expression need only be a material object permanently cast in some intelligible form. *See* 2 NIMMER ON COPYRIGHT, § 8.02[B], pp. 8-22-8-25 (1985).

The articles created by Filmation in the production of its film, including a script, story board, story reel, and promotional "trailer," satisfy this definition, and thus can constitute copies for purposes of the Act. Because the right of reproduction affords a copyright owner protection against an infringer even if he does not also infringe the § 106(3) right of distribution, *Sony Corp. v. Universal City Studios, Inc.*, 464 U.S. 417, 474 (1984) (Blackmun, J., dissenting); House Report No. 94-1476, 94th Cong., 2d Sess. (1976), p. 61, the fact that the articles may never be published or, indeed, may be prepared only for the use of Filmation's animators, does not obviate the possibility of infringement. . . . As explained by Professor Nimmer, "subject to the privilege of fair use, and subject to certain other exemptions, copyright infringement occurs whenever an unauthorized copy . . . is made, even if it is used solely for the private purposes of the reproducer." 2 NIMMER, § 8.02[C], pp. 8-26. It is thus irrelevant that Filmation has not concluded or "realized" what it considers to be a final motion picture: the Act prohibits the creation of copies, even if the creator considers those copies mere interim steps toward some final goal.

It is similarly no defense to copying that some of Filmation's expressions may be embodied in a medium different from that of plaintiff's. *Berkic v. Crichton*, 761 F.2d 1289, 1292 (9th Cir. 1985) ("in comparing . . . a film with a written work, the proper question . . . is whether the ordinary, reasonable audience would recognize the defendant's work as a 'dramatization' or 'picturization' of the plaintiff's work"). *See also Eden Toys, Inc. v. Florelee Undergarment Co.*, 697 F.2d 27 (2d Cir. 1982) (copying from gift wrapping paper to clothing actionable). *But see Sid & Marty Krofft Television v. McDonald's Corp.*, 562 F.2d 1157, 1164 (9th Cir. 1977) (observing, in *dicta*, that a painting of a nude would not infringe a statue of a nude). Thus, Filmation's materials, including scripts and story outlines, can infringe Disney's copyright on "Pinocchio" even though they are not rendered as a motion picture. . . .

Finally, the absence of a completed motion picture does not preclude meaningful comparison of Disney's character depictions and film with Filmation's materials. Although Filmation contends that copyright infringement of a cartoon character cannot be based on a mere sketch that is not part of a story, there is no support for this proposition. It is true that courts generally have considered "not only the visual resemblances but also the totality of the characters' attributes and traits," 1 NIMMER § 2.12, p. 175, n.16.2, and, thus, that the trier of fact would ordinarily evaluate a character in the context of a story. But where the work sued upon is not a "completed" story, but a series of depictions and other works, comparison of the expressions may be made in the form in which they are presented. *Walt Disney Productions v. Air Pirates*, 581 F.2d 751, 756 (9th Cir. 1978) (comparison of graphic images of cartoon characters sufficient to allow action for copyright infringement).

2. Substantial Similarity

Filmation's alternative argument — that its creations are not substantially similar as a matter of law — is unconvincing. . . . [Substantial similarity, and other infringement issues, are discussed in Chapter 8.]

CONCLUSION

Defendants' motion for summary judgment is denied. . . .

NOTES AND QUESTIONS

(1) Under § 501(a), "[A]nyone who violates any of the exclusive rights of the copyright owner as provided by sections 106 through 122 . . . is an infringer of the copyright . . ." Infringement actions are treated in Chapter 8. Here, we concentrate on understanding one specific right — the right to reproduce — and the limitations imposed on that right by the 1976 Act.

(2) The scope of each particular right in § 106 depends in part upon other provisions of the Act, particularly the definitions contained in § 101. The § 106(1) reproduction right discussed in *Disney* provides an example of this point. Section 101 defines the terms "copies" and "phonorecords" to include material objects in which the words, images, sounds, etc., subject to copyright are fixed "by any method *now known or later developed,* and from which the [copyrighted works] can be perceived, reproduced, or otherwise communicated, either directly *or with the aid of a machine or device*." The emphasized language in these definitions makes the rights in § 106 notably open-ended insofar as new technologies are concerned.

(3) As indicated in the legislative history reproduced at the beginning of this section, three of the rights recognized by the 1976 Act — the § 106(1) reproduction right, the § 106(2) adaptation right,[2] and the § 106(3) public distribution right — apply to *all* of the various kinds of copyrightable works described in §§ 102 and 103 of the Act. And, as the House Report says, "a single act of infringement may violate all of these rights at once."

The *Disney* case, however, demonstrates that it is possible to infringe the reproduction right without infringing any of the other exclusive rights. Typically, the distribution right is infringed along with the reproduction right because reproducing the work without distributing it (usually by sale) is rarely of interest from a financial standpoint. The distribution of the copy is what causes a financial loss to the copyright owner. Nonetheless, the reproduction right stands on its own — and protects even against private, nondistributed reproductions of copyrighted works. Later in this chapter, we will see that only *public* performances and displays of copyrighted works are prohibited under § 106(4) and (5): a private performance or display will *not* infringe copyright. Is there reason to provide a reproduction right more inclusive than the performance and display right?

(4) Given that "intermediate copying" may give rise to a technical violation of the reproduction right without a corresponding breach of the distribution right, should that violation ever be excused? This question assumes some importance in connection with the operation of digital technologies that function by making intermediate copies. This question also concerns the "decompilation" procedures employed by some software developers to ascertain the logical structure and other nonprotected characteristics of copyrighted programs which have been distributed only in machine-readable form. Should this practice be permitted as a form of "fair

---

[2] We follow the House Report in referring to the exclusive right "to prepare derivative works based on the copyrighted work" (§ 106(2)) by the shorthand phrase "the adaptation right." You should note, however, that the definition of "derivative work" in § 101 includes "any other form in which a work may be recast, transformed, or adapted," arguably making § 106(2) broader than mere "adaptation." *See* § 7.03 below.

use"? If so, should the "fair use" privilege apply always, or only sometimes? We will return to these questions in Chapter 10 in our discussion of *Sega Enterprises, Ltd. v. Accolade, Inc.*, 977 F.2d 1510 (9th Cir. 1993).

(5)   *Disney* reconfirms the rule that the reproduction right covers reproduction in other media, such as the defendants' sketch of an animated Disney character. Other examples might include making a three-dimensional rendition of a two-dimensional cartoon figure, or a movie version of a novel. Copyright law generously provides the copyright owner with the power to control the reproduction of the work in diverse media. This topic will be reexamined later in this chapter under the adaptation right — a right closely, sometimes inextricably, related to the reproduction right.

Limitations on the Reproduction Right

(6)   The granddaddy of the exclusive rights, the reproduction right, is broad in scope but, as is the case for all of the exclusive rights, it is limited by §§ 107-22. The following notes and questions examine these limitations on the reproduction right — except for the fair use privilege of § 107, which is given special treatment in Chapter 10.

(7)   Photocopying is the focus of § 108, which provides a limited exception to the § 106(1) reproduction right (as well as to the § 106(3) distribution right) in favor of libraries and archives. The § 108 exemption was modified significantly by Title IV of the Digital Millennium Copyright Act. Here is a quick summary of this relatively complex exception as it now stands.

A. A library or archive can reproduce and distribute a work only if all the following necessary (but not sufficient) conditions are met:

1. its purposes do not include direct or indirect commercial advantage; and

2. its collections are open to the public, or generally open to qualified researchers; and

3. any copies reproduced include a reproduction of the copyright notice on the original, or (if no notice is present) a general notice stating that the work may be protected by copyright.

B. If the foregoing conditions are satisfied, a library or archive can make up to three copies, in any format, of an unpublished work for purposes of preservation or deposit in another qualifying library or archive, or of a published work for purposes of replacement, if:

1. in the case of a preservation copy or copies to be deposited in another institution, the copy to be reproduced is in the collection of the library or archive in question; and

2. in the case of replacement copies, the library or archive's own copy is damaged, deteriorating, lost, or stolen, or the existing format in which the work is stored is obsolete (as, for example, when no appropriate reading or playback equipment is reasonably available),

and the library or archive has determined that an unused replacement cannot be obtained at a fair price; and

3. copies made in digital (as distinct from analog facsimile) formats are not made available (*e.g.*, on-line) outside the "premises" of the institutions in lawful possession of them.

C. Likewise, an otherwise qualifying library or archive can make a single copy, in any format, of part (and sometimes even all) of a work at the request of one of its own patrons, or of a patron at another qualifying institution, if:

1. the copy is to be owned by the patron (rather than added to the collection of the institution), the institution is not on notice that the patron will use the copy for purposes other than private study or research, and the institution displays a warning prescribed by the Register of Copyrights; and

2. the request is for no more than a single contribution to a collective work or a small part of another copyrighted work; or

3. if the extent of the request exceeds the limits just stated, the library or archives has made a reasonable determination that a copy is not otherwise available to the patron at a fair price.

D. During the last 20 years of copyright in a published work, a library or archive may reproduce (and distribute, perform, or display) a single copy or phonorecord of a work for purposes of preservation, scholarship, or research, if it has made a reasonable determination that the work is not subject to normal commercial exploitation, and that a copy or phonorecord cannot be obtained at a reasonable price.

E. The library or archive claiming any of the exemptions just described must not be engaged in a systematic practice of reproduction so as to avoid having to buy copies of books or subscribe to periodicals, and must not have substantial reason to believe that it is making multiple copies of the same materials for patrons or groups of patrons.

F. The exception in § 108 does not:

1. impose liability on the library or archive for unsupervised use of copying equipment by others, if the equipment displays a notice that making a copy may be subject to the copyright law;

2. excuse from liability any individual who utilizes a copy in a manner not contemplated by the exception; or

3. alter rights under the fair use doctrine or contracts.

G. Caution: Generally speaking, when making copies for patrons, § 108 does not apply to musical works, to pictorial, graphic or sculptural works, or to motion pictures or other audiovisual works other than those dealing with news.

What considerations justify the "special treatment" afforded to libraries and archives under § 108? In what circumstances, if any, might the benefit of § 108 be available to the library of a large oil company? The library of a government agency? The library of the law firm where you plan to work this summer? In addition to the House Report, you may wish to review as background the decision in *Williams & Wilkins Co. v. United States*, 487 F.2d 1345 (Ct. Cl. 1973), *aff'd by an equally divided Court*, 420 U.S. 376 (1975) (involving photocopying by the National Institutes of Health and the National Library of Medicine), which provided an important impetus to the enactment of original § 108.

(8)   The provisions of the DMCA that revised § 108 represented an effort to bring the law up to date with new technology. Through those provisions, Congress recognized that many libraries and archives now use digital technology to preserve materials in their collections, and that good library practice often involves making multiple copies of scarce or fragile items in the collection — for on-site use, for on-site backup, and for secure storage at a remote location. It also confronted the problem of obsolescence in data recording formats. (Have you priced a Beta format videotape player recently?)

Inevitably, the revisions of § 108 also introduce some new uncertainties. How should one define the "premises" to which use of digital preservation and replacement copies are restricted? What about a university library with multiple sites on a single campus, or a state-wide university library system with sites on multiple campuses? And how difficult (or expensive) need it be to obtain equipment for a data recording format to be considered "obsolete"?

(9)   In March 2008, a Study Group convened by the Library of Congress issued a report recommending additional legislative changes to § 108. Among the changes suggested by the group were: expanding § 108 to include museums as well as libraries and archives (but tightening the eligibility requirements); allowing these groups to "outsource" copying to independent contractors; replacing the three-copy limit with a "reasonably necessary" standard; and allowing preservation copies to be made before deterioration occurs. For more information, see *www.section108.gov*.

(10)   As discussed above, § 106(1) extends to all reproductions of copyrighted works, whether distributed publicly or not. But a legal right is only as valuable as one's ability to enforce it. Thanks to photocopy machines and computers, massive unauthorized reproductions of copyrighted works take place every day at copy shops and libraries. In principle, each of these unauthorized reproductions represents a lost royalty (assuming, of course, that what is being copied is protected expression). In reality, however, policing the reproduction right, even if possible, would be prohibitively expensive for the copyright owner.

The Copyright Clearance Center ("CCC"), a nonprofit organization, was founded in 1978 to serve as an intermediary between publishers and users in the photocopying of protected works. CCC has transcended its origins in the technology of photocopying and also grants case-by-case permissions for digital reproduction and distribution of copyrighted materials. Users may request permission to photocopy, e-mail, or fax materials or to post them on their Internet sites. CCC licenses the right to copy for a fee and distributes the collected revenues to copyright owners whose works were copied. For further information on CCC licenses, see *www.copy-right.com* (a pretty amazing URL, if you think about it).

(11) To illustrate the interplay of exclusive rights and their limitations, broadcasting and transmissions of audio and audiovisual works implicate the exclusive right of public performance. But, these performances also often involve or require a recorded copy of the program. Must each of these copies be the subject of a negotiated license? No. Section 112 limits the reproduction right with respect to so-called "ephemeral recordings." Although the Act does not define the term, its core meaning is self-evident. Basically, such recordings are permitted, notwithstanding § 106(1), in three types of situations. Under § 112(a), a broadcaster entitled to transmit to the public a performance or display of a copyrighted work (other than a motion picture or other audiovisual work) may make a single recording of that work if necessary to facilitate a delayed broadcast. Unless the recording is preserved solely for archival purposes, it must be destroyed within six months from the date of the original broadcast. Section 112 also provides similar, but not identical, exemptions for instructional broadcasts under § 110(2), religious broadcasts, and transmissions to the blind and deaf under § 110(8). Finally, § 112(e) provides a statutory license (rather than an outright exemption) for ephemeral recordings used to facilitate the digital transmissions of sound recordings that are permitted under § 114.

(12) Keep in mind that the reproduction right is limited by its definition: reproduction of the work in "copies" or "phonorecords." Logically, this limit should be considered before considering the effect of limitations or exceptions on the scope of the reproduction right. These issues arise with respect to other kinds of reproductions which are, on the one hand, temporary or transient (or "ephemeral") in nature and, on the other, essential to the operation of a particular information technology. What is their legal status? The question arises because a computer must transfer digital data temporarily into its "random-access memory" (or "RAM") in order to process that data. Should such temporary electronic reproductions constitute "copies" within the meaning of § 106(1)? This issue (and the § 117 exemption which addresses it) is discussed in more detail in § 7.02[D] below.

(13) Section 113 of the Act concerns reproductions of pictorial, graphic, and sculptural works in useful articles. In essence, subsection (a) provides that a copyright in these types of works will protect against all unauthorized reproductions of the work, whether in useful or nonuseful articles. The sole function of subsection (b) is to leave intact pre-1978 case law holding that a copyright in a work depicting a useful article does not include the right to prevent others from making the useful article as such. Subsection (c) exempts photographs or other depictions of copyrighted designs in useful articles, in the context of advertising, commentaries, or news reports. See § 3.01[D] above, for more details on these limitations in practice.

(14) Additional limitations on the reproduction right appear in §§ 114 and 115, which concern sound recordings and the compulsory phonorecord license for musical works, respectively. These are considered below in § 7.02[C].

(15) The Architectural Works Copyright Protection Act of 1990 ("AWCPA") added a new exception in § 120(a), which permits the reproduction, distribution, and

display of pictorial representations of a building that is located in or ordinarily visible from a public place. For details, see the notes following *Shine v. Childs* in § 3.01 above.

(16)   Narrowly drafted special limitations on the exclusive rights continue to proliferate. In 1996, Congress added § 121 to allow certain nonprofit and governmental agencies the right to reproduce or distribute copies and phonorecords of a published nondramatic literary work for use by blind persons or others with disabilities. The copies must be reproduced or distributed in specialized formats for use by the blind or disabled, *e.g.*, as Braille, audio, or digital texts. (In 2005, Congress amended § 121 to permit authorized publishers of elementary and secondary textbooks to provide electronic copies for conversion into specialized formats, including large print editions.) Section 121 does not apply to certain tests and testing material. In addition, computer programs are excluded, except for those portions existing in human language and displayed to users in the ordinary course of using the program.

International Obligations

(17)   Article 9(2) of the Berne Convention states that "[i]t shall be a matter for legislation in the countries of the Union to permit the reproduction of [literary and artistic] works in *certain special cases*, provided that such reproduction does not conflict with a *normal exploitation* of the work and does not unreasonably prejudice the *legitimate interests* of the author" — a formula sometimes referred to as the "three-part" or "three-step" test for exceptions to the reproduction right. Do the provisions limiting the reproduction right in U.S. law, itemized above, conform to the Berne formula? Is it significant that most of them were already firmly in place at the time of U.S. adherence to Berne in 1989?

Whatever your answers to the foregoing questions, you should be aware that Article 13 of the TRIPS Agreement generalizes this test to apply to exceptions and limitations on any right under copyright — not just the reproduction right — and that the formula is also adopted in the WIPO Copyright Treaty and WIPO Performances and Phonograms Treaty, which deal with (among other things) digital copyright issues. Accompanying these treaties are so-called "Agreed Statements" to the effect that "[i]t is understood that the [treaties] permit Contracting Parties to carry forward and appropriately extend into the digital environment limitations and exceptions in their national laws which have been considered acceptable under the Berne Convention. Similarly, [the treaties] should be understood to permit Contracting Parties to devise new exceptions and limitations that are appropriate to the digital network environment."

[C]   Reproduction in Phonorecords

In addition to the right to make or authorize reproductions of copyrighted works in "copies," the copyright holder owns the right to control reproductions in "phonorecords" — material objects such as tapes or compact discs that embody sound recordings. *See* 17 U.S.C. § 101 (definition of "phonorecords"). The right to reproduce in phonorecords is limited, in common with the right to reproduce in copies, by §§ 107, 108, 112, and 121. Besides these limitations, the right to reproduce in phonorecords is subject to specialized limitations, contained in §§ 114 and 115, which are discussed below.

Sections 114 and 115 compared. Recall that § 102(a)(7) specifically identifies sound recordings as works of authorship, and that § 106 specifies six types of exclusive rights in copyrighted works. How do §§ 114 and 115 interact with these provisions? In short, § 114 limits reproduction, adaptation and performance rights in *sound recordings.* By contrast, § 115 limits the reproduction, adaptation, and distribution rights in certain *musical works* (nondramatic musical works) through the creation of a compulsory license.

The § 114 limitation. Under § 114(a), the holder of a copyright in a sound recording owns the exclusive right of reproduction in the work — as well as the right to adapt and distribute it. But the sound recording copyright owner's reproduction and adaptation rights do not extend as far as those of other copyright owners. In particular, they do not reach the making of new sound recordings by others — no matter how slavishly these may imitate the protected works. *See* § 114(b). As to the remaining § 106 rights, obviously the display right provided by § 106(5) is inapplicable in the case of sound recordings. As to § 106(4), Congress decided in 1976 to exclude from that section a public performance right for sound recordings. It did direct the Register of Copyrights to prepare a report exploring the possibility of affording that right to the owner of the copyright, *and to the performers who created the work*, at a later date. In the end, Congress did not see fit to create the comprehensive right urged in the Register's 1976 report, but in 1995 it did create a limited public performance right for sound recordings by means of digital audio transmission only. *See* §§ 7.05[A] and 7.07 below.

Consider the following situations:

(a) Suppose Able composes a song called "Law School Blues" and authorizes Brown Records to make a recording of it. Brown has its staff musicians play Able's song, Brown's technical staff records the performance, and Brown manufactures CDs, which Brown then distributes to retail stores. Who owns which copyright? The answer: Able owns the copyright on the musical work and Brown owns the copyright on the sound recording.

(b) If Crown Records makes unauthorized copies of the recording, whose copyright(s) has it infringed? Crown has infringed both Able's reproduction right in the musical work and Brown's reproduction right in the sound recording.

(c) If, instead, Crown Records hires its own musicians and technical people to record Able's music and distributes the work to the public, has it infringed Able's copyright? Crown has not infringed Able's copyright if it complied with the terms of the compulsory license under § 115.

(d) If, in (c), Crown produced a sound recording that sounds identical in its stylistic and technical aspects to Brown's, has it infringed Brown's copyright? It has not, because § 114(b) limits infringement of a sound recording to a mechanical reproduction. Imitations and simulations are excluded from the scope of protection.

(e) If Downs plays Brown's recording on FM broadcast radio, whose rights have been infringed? Here, Able's copyright in the musical work has been infringed but Brown's copyright in the sound recording has not. Section 106(4) provides a public performance right in musical works, but not in sound recordings. *See also* § 114(c).

(f) If Edgar plays Brown's recording on Internet radio, whose rights have been infringed? Here, both Able's copyright in the musical work and Brown's copyright in the sound recording have been infringed. Section 106(6) provides a public performance right in sound recordings by means of digital audio transmission. Edgar, however, may be able to take advantage of the compulsory license for public performance of sound recordings in § 114(d). See § 7.07 of this casebook.

Remember that § 114 applies only to sound recordings protected under federal law, *i.e.*, sound recordings fixed on or after February 15, 1972. Sound recordings fixed before that date continue to be protected, if at all, under state law until February 15, 2067. *See* § 301(c).

The § 115 limitation. The so-called "mechanical license" under § 115 — a limitation on the reproduction right for nondramatic musical works (as well as the adaptation and distribution rights) — is the oldest of the compulsory licenses. Musicians sometimes refer to this as the "cover right" because it authorizes the recording and distribution of copies of a "cover version" of a musical work subject to the license's terms. First adopted in the 1909 Act because Congress feared monopoly control of recorded music by powerful turn-of-the-century music companies, it has survived now for over a century.[1]

Here's how it works. When the copyright owner distributes phonorecords of a *nondramatic* musical work (a qualification that excludes, for example, the score of an opera or musical) to the public in the United States, the copyright owner's rights to reproduce and distribute the musical work are subject to the compulsory licensing provisions of § 115. The compulsory licensee's use of the underlying work (typically, a popular song) is limited to making and distributing recordings of the same composition for private use by members of the public. § 115(a)(1). Thus, the composition may not be recorded by the licensee for primarily commercial purposes, such as use by a background music service; and the compulsory license does not permit any use other than in a recording, *e.g.*, a public performance of the composition by the licensee.

The rights conferred by the § 115 mechanical license do not, at least normally, include reproducing and distributing the original sound recording itself (as distinct from the musical composition). Unless those acts are authorized by the owner of the sound recording copyright, the licensee must assemble its own singers, instrumentalists, recording engineers, etc., and produce a new recording of the composition that is the subject of the license. § 115(a)(1). In conjunction with this effort, the licensee may make its own arrangement of the composition "to the extent necessary to conform it to the style or manner of interpretation of the performance involved,"

---

[1] *See* Abrams, *Copyright's First Compulsory License*, 26 Santa Clara Computer & High Tech. L.J. 215 (2010).

but the licensee may not "change the basic melody or fundamental character of the work" in the process. Although in form the new arrangement is a derivative work, it cannot receive protection as such except with the express consent of the copyright owner. § 115(a)(2).

The procedure for obtaining a license is set out in § 115(b). Within 30 days after making the new recording, and before distributing any phonorecords embodying the work, the person seeking the license must serve a "notice of intention" on the owner of the copyright in the musical work. If the owner's name and address cannot be determined from Copyright Office records, the notice may be filed there instead. Unless the notice is served or filed as required, there is no compulsory license and the new recording infringes the copyright owner's § 106(1) and (3) rights. *See 24/7 Records, Inc. v. Sony Music Entertainment, Inc.*, 429 F.3d 39 (2d Cir. 2005).

Section 115(c) extends the rights acquired under the "mechanical license" to include the right to authorize the distribution of the licensed sound recording by means of a digital transmission and creates a mechanism to determine compulsory licensing rates applicable to such "digital phonorecord deliveries." For more regarding this subsection, see § 7.07 below.

The current royalty rate, and various procedures for the collection and distribution of such royalties, are administratively determined. The current system is based on voluntary negotiations, immune from the antitrust laws, between interested parties affected by the compulsory license, *e.g.*, owners of copyright in nondramatic musical works and those desiring to make sound recordings of such works. If no agreement can be reached by voluntary negotiation, the statutory rate will be determined by the three Copyright Royalty Judges under Chapter 8 of the Act (§§ 801-805). *See* 7.01[C] above.

The § 115 compulsory licensing system has served as a backdrop for a voluntary system administered by a private organization, the Harry Fox Agency. This company, founded by a person of the same name, represents copyright owners and musical publishers in licensing mechanical reproductions of copyrighted music. The Agency has a form document that provides the terms of the license, which streamlines some of the cumbersome reporting and accounting procedures that otherwise would be required by the statute. *See, e.g.*, § 115(c)(5). Some courts have held that case law requiring only "substantial compliance" with § 115 also applies to Harry Fox licenses. *See EMI Entertainment World, Inc. v. Karen Records, Inc.*, 603 F. Supp. 2d 759 (S.D.N.Y. 2009) (defendant properly acquired mechanical licenses by faxing forms with non-material errors to the Harry Fox Agency). For more information on the services provided by the Harry Fox Agency, see *www.harryfox.com*.

In 2005, the Register of Copyrights recommended to Congress that the § 115 compulsory license be eliminated. *See* Statement of Marybeth Peters before the House Subcommittee on Courts, the Internet and Intellectual Property (June 21, 2005), available at *www.copyright.gov/docs/regstat062105.html*. What are the arguments for and against such a change? Are you confident that voluntary licenses, like those provided by the Harry Fox Agency, would continue to be provided if the alternative of a compulsory license did not exist? Instead of eliminating the license, why not extend it to drama, dance, and the other performing arts?[2]

[D] Electronic Reproduction

CARTOON NETWORK v. CSC HOLDINGS, INC.
United States Court of Appeals, Second Circuit
536 F.3d 121 (2008)

JOHN M. WALKER, JR., CIRCUIT JUDGE:

Defendant-Appellant Cablevision Systems Corporation ("Cablevision") wants to market a new "Remote Storage" Digital Video Recorder system ("RS-DVR"), using a technology akin to both traditional, set-top digital video recorders, like TiVo ("DVRs"), and the video-on-demand ("VOD") services provided by many cable companies. Plaintiffs-Appellees produce copyrighted movies and television programs that they provide to Cablevision pursuant to numerous licensing agreements. They contend that Cablevision, through the operation of its RS-DVR system as proposed, would directly infringe their copyrights both by making unauthorized reproductions, and by engaging in public performances, of their copyrighted works. . . . [The District Court awarded summary judgment to the plaintiffs and enjoined Cablevision from operating the RS-DVR system without licenses from its content providers. *See Twentieth Century Fox Film Corp. v. Cablevision Sys. Corp. (Cablevision I)*, 478 F. Supp. 2d 607 (S.D.N.Y. 2007). After describing the RS-DVR system in greater detail below, the Court of Appeals reversed.]

BACKGROUND

. . . In March 2006, Cablevision, an operator of cable television systems, announced the advent of its new "Remote Storage DVR System." As designed, the RS-DVR allows Cablevision customers who do not have a stand-alone DVR to record cable programming on central hard drives housed and maintained by Cablevision at a "remote" location. RS-DVR customers may then receive playback of those programs through their home television sets, using only a remote control and a standard cable box equipped with the RS-DVR software. Cablevision notified its content providers, including plaintiffs, of its plans to offer RS-DVR, but it did not seek any license from them to operate or sell the RS-DVR. . . .

Cable companies like Cablevision aggregate television programming from a wide variety of "content providers" — the various broadcast and cable channels that produce or provide individual programs — and transmit those programs into the homes of their subscribers via coaxial cable. At the outset of the transmission process, Cablevision gathers the content of the various television channels into a single stream of data. Generally, this stream is processed and transmitted to Cablevision's customers in real time. Thus, if a Cartoon Network program is scheduled to air Monday night at 8pm, Cartoon Network transmits that program's

---

[2] *See* Carroll, *Copyright's Creative Hierarchy in the Performing Arts*, 14 Vand. J. of Ent. & Tech. L. 797 (2012).

data to Cablevision and other cable companies nationwide at that time, and the cable companies immediately re-transmit the data to customers who subscribe to that channel.

Under the new RS-DVR, this single stream of data is split into two streams. The first is routed immediately to customers as before. The second stream flows into a device called the Broadband Media Router ("BMR"), which buffers the data stream, reformats it, and sends it to the "Arroyo Server," which consists, in relevant part, of two data buffers and a number of high-capacity hard disks. The entire stream of data moves to the first buffer (the "primary ingest buffer"), at which point the server automatically inquires as to whether any customers want to record any of that programming. If a customer has requested a particular program, the data for that program move from the primary buffer into a secondary buffer, and then onto a portion of one of the hard disks allocated to that customer. As new data flow into the primary buffer, they overwrite a corresponding quantity of data already on the buffer. The primary ingest buffer holds no more than 0.1 seconds of each channel's programming at any moment. Thus, every tenth of a second, the data residing on this buffer are automatically erased and replaced. The data buffer in the BMR holds no more than 1.2 seconds of programming at any time. While buffering occurs at other points in the operation of the RS-DVR, only the BMR buffer and the primary ingest buffer are utilized absent any request from an individual subscriber.

As the district court observed, "the RS-DVR is not a single piece of equipment," but rather "a complex system requiring numerous computers, processes, networks of cables, and facilities staffed by personnel twenty-four hours a day and seven days a week." To the customer, however, the processes of recording and playback on the RS-DVR are similar to that of a standard set-top DVR. Using a remote control, the customer can record programming by selecting a program in advance from an on-screen guide, or by pressing the record button while viewing a given program. A customer cannot, however, record the earlier portion of a program once it has begun. . . .

DISCUSSION

. . . "Section 106 of the Copyright Act grants copyright holders a bundle of exclusive rights. . . ." [*Bill Graham Archives v. Dorling Kindersley Ltd.*, 448 F.3d 605, 607-08 (2d Cir. 2006).] This case implicates two of those rights: the right "to reproduce the copyrighted work in copies," and the right "to perform the copyrighted work publicly." 17 U.S.C. § 106(1), (4). . . . [T]he district court found that Cablevision infringed the first right by 1) buffering the data from its programming stream and 2) copying content onto the Arroyo Server hard disks to enable playback of a program requested by an RS-DVR customer. In addition, the district court found that Cablevision would infringe the public performance right by transmitting a program to an RS-DVR customer in response to that customer's playback request. We address each of these three allegedly infringing acts in turn.

I. The Buffer Data

It is undisputed that Cablevision, not any customer or other entity, takes the content from one stream of programming, after the split, and stores it, one small piece at a time, in the BMR buffer and the primary ingest buffer. As a result, the information is buffered before any customer requests a recording, and would be buffered even if no such request were made. The question is whether, by buffering the data that make up a given work, Cablevision "reproduce[s]" that work "in copies," 17 U.S.C. § 106(1), and thereby infringes the copyright holder's reproduction right.

"Copies," as defined in the Copyright Act, "are material objects . . . in which a work is fixed by any method . . . and from which the work can be . . . reproduced." *Id.* § 101. The Act also provides that a work is "fixed in a tangible medium of expression when its embodiment . . . is sufficiently permanent or stable to permit it to be . . . reproduced . . . *for a period of more than transitory duration." Id.* (emphasis added). We believe that this language plainly imposes two distinct but related requirements: the work must be embodied in a medium, *i.e.*, placed in a medium such that it can be perceived, reproduced, etc., from that medium (the "embodiment requirement"), and it must remain thus embodied "for a period of more than transitory duration" (the "duration requirement"). *See* 2 Melville B. Nimmer & David Nimmer, *Nimmer on Copyright* § 8.02[B][3], at 8-32 (2007). Unless both requirements are met, the work is not "fixed" in the buffer, and, as a result, the buffer data is not a "copy" of the original work whose data is buffered.

The district court mistakenly limited its analysis primarily to the embodiment requirement. As a result of this error, once it determined that the buffer data was "[c]learly . . . capable of being reproduced," *i.e.*, that the work was embodied in the buffer, the district court concluded that the work was therefore "fixed" in the buffer, and that a copy had thus been made. In doing so, it relied on a line of cases beginning with *MAI Systems Corp. v. Peak Computer Inc.*, 991 F.2d 511 (9th Cir. 1993). . . .

The district court's reliance on cases like *MAI Systems* is misplaced. In general, those cases conclude that an alleged copy is fixed without addressing the duration requirement; it does not follow, however, that those cases assume, much less establish, that such a requirement does not exist. Indeed, the duration requirement, by itself, was not at issue in *MAI Systems* and its progeny. As a result, they do not speak to the issues squarely before us here: If a work is only "embodied" in a medium for a period of transitory duration, can it be "fixed" in that medium, and thus a copy? And what constitutes a period "of more than transitory duration"?

In *MAI Systems*, defendant Peak Computer, Inc., performed maintenance and repairs on computers made and sold by MAI Systems. In order to service a customer's computer, a Peak employee had to operate the computer and run the computer's copyrighted operating system software. The issue in *MAI Systems* was whether, by loading the software into the computer's RAM[1] the repairman created

---

[1] To run a computer program, the data representing that program must be transferred from a data storage medium (such as a floppy disk or a hard drive) to a form of Random Access Memory ("RAM") where the data can be processed. The data buffers at issue here are also a form of RAM.

a "copy" as defined in § 101. The resolution of this issue turned on whether the software's embodiment in the computer's RAM was "fixed," within the meaning of the same section. The Ninth Circuit concluded that

> by showing that Peak loads the software into the RAM and is then able to view the system error log and diagnose the problem with the computer, MAI has adequately shown that the representation created in the RAM is "sufficiently permanent or stable to permit it to be perceived, reproduced, or otherwise communicated for a period of more than transitory duration."

Id. at 518 (quoting 17 U.S.C. § 101).

The *MAI Systems* court referenced the "transitory duration" language but did not discuss or analyze it. The opinion notes that the defendants "vigorously" argued that the program's embodiment in the RAM was not a copy, but it does not specify the arguments defendants made. This omission suggests that the parties did not litigate the significance of the "transitory duration" language, and the court therefore had no occasion to address it. This is unsurprising, because it seems fair to assume that in these cases the program was embodied in the RAM for at least several minutes.

Accordingly, we construe *MAI Systems* and its progeny as holding that loading a program into a computer's RAM *can* result in copying that program. We do not read *MAI Systems* as holding that, as a matter of law, loading a program into a form of RAM *always* results in copying. Such a holding would read the "transitory duration" language out of the definition, and we do not believe our sister circuit would dismiss this statutory language without even discussing it. It appears the parties in *MAI Systems* simply did not dispute that the duration requirement was satisfied; this line of cases simply concludes that when a program is loaded into RAM, the embodiment requirement is satisfied — an important holding in itself, and one we see no reason to quibble with here. . . .

Nor does the Copyright Office's 2001 DMCA Report, also relied on by the district court in this case, explicitly suggest that the definition of "fixed" does not contain a duration requirement. However, as noted above, it does suggest that an embodiment is fixed "[u]nless a reproduction manifests itself so fleetingly that it cannot be copied, perceived or communicated." [U.S. Copyright Office, *DMCA Section 104 Report* 111 (Aug. 2001).] As we have stated, to determine whether a work is "fixed" in a given medium, the statutory language directs us to ask not only 1) whether a work is "embodied" in that medium, but also 2) whether it is embodied in the medium "for a period of more than transitory duration." According to the Copyright Office, if the work is capable of being copied from that medium *for any amount of time*, the answer to both questions is "yes." The problem with this interpretation is that it reads the "transitory duration" language out of the statute. . . .

In sum, no case law or other authority dissuades us from concluding that the definition of "fixed" imposes both an embodiment requirement and a duration requirement. *Accord CoStar Group Inc. v. LoopNet, Inc.*, 373 F.3d 544, 551 (4th Cir. 2004) (while temporary reproductions "may be made in this transmission process, they would appear not to be 'fixed' in the sense that they are 'of more than transitory duration' "). We now turn to whether, in this case, those requirements are met by the buffer data.

Cablevision does not seriously dispute that copyrighted works are "embodied" in the buffer. Data in the BMR buffer can be reformatted and transmitted to the other components of the RS-DVR system. Data in the primary ingest buffer can be copied onto the Arroyo hard disks if a user has requested a recording of that data. Thus, a work's "embodiment" in either buffer "is sufficiently permanent or stable to permit it to be perceived, reproduced," (as in the case of the ingest buffer) "or otherwise communicated" (as in the BMR buffer). 17 U.S.C. § 101. The result might be different if only a single second of a much longer work was placed in the buffer in isolation. In such a situation, it might be reasonable to conclude that only a minuscule portion of a work, rather than "a work" was embodied in the buffer. Here, however, where every second of an entire work is placed, one second at a time, in the buffer, we conclude that the work is embodied in the buffer.

Does any such embodiment last "for a period of more than transitory duration"? No bit of data remains in any buffer for more than a fleeting 1.2 seconds. And unlike the data in cases like *MAI Systems*, which remained embodied in the computer's RAM memory until the user turned the computer off, each bit of data here is rapidly and automatically overwritten as soon as it is processed. While our inquiry is necessarily fact-specific, and other factors not present here may alter the duration analysis significantly, these facts strongly suggest that the works in this case are embodied in the buffer for only a "transitory" period, thus failing the duration requirement.

Against this evidence, plaintiffs argue only that the duration is not transitory because the data persist "long enough for Cablevision to make reproductions from them." As we have explained above, however, this reasoning impermissibly reads the duration language out of the statute, and we reject it. Given that the data reside in no buffer for more than 1.2 seconds before being automatically overwritten, and in the absence of compelling arguments to the contrary, we believe that the copyrighted works here are not "embodied" in the buffers for a period of more than transitory duration, and are therefore not "fixed" in the buffers. Accordingly, the acts of buffering in the operation of the RS-DVR do not create copies, as the Copyright Act defines that term. Our resolution of this issue renders it unnecessary for us to determine whether any copies produced by buffering data would be *de minimis*, and we express no opinion on that question.

II. Direct Liability for Creating the Playback Copies

In most copyright disputes, the allegedly infringing act and the identity of the infringer are never in doubt. These cases turn on whether the conduct in question does, in fact, infringe the plaintiff's copyright. In this case, however, the core of the dispute is over the authorship of the infringing conduct. After an RS-DVR subscriber selects a program to record, and that program airs, a copy of the program — a copyrighted work — resides on the hard disks of Cablevision's Arroyo Server, its creation unauthorized by the copyright holder. The question is *who* made this copy. If it is Cablevision, plaintiffs' theory of direct infringement succeeds; if it is the customer, plaintiffs' theory fails because Cablevision would then face, at most, secondary liability, a theory of liability expressly disavowed by plaintiffs.

Few cases examine the line between direct and contributory liability. Both parties cite a line of cases beginning with *Religious Technology Center v. Netcom On-Line Communication Services*, 907 F. Supp. 1361 (N.D. Cal. 1995). In *Netcom*, a third-party customer of the defendant Internet service provider ("ISP") posted a copyrighted work that was automatically reproduced by the defendant's computer. The district court refused to impose direct liability on the ISP, reasoning that "[a]lthough copyright is a strict liability statute, there should still be some element of volition or causation which is lacking where a defendant's system is merely used to create a copy by a third party." *Id.* at 1370. Recently, the Fourth Circuit endorsed the *Netcom* decision, noting that

> to establish *direct* liability under . . . the Act, something more must be shown than mere ownership of a machine used by others to make illegal copies. There must be actual infringing conduct with a nexus sufficiently close and causal to the illegal copying that one could conclude that the machine owner himself trespassed on the exclusive domain of the copyright owner.

CoStar Group, Inc. v. LoopNet, Inc., 373 F.3d 544, 550 (4th Cir. 2004). . . .

When there is a dispute as to the author of an allegedly infringing instance of reproduction, *Netcom* and its progeny direct our attention to the volitional conduct that causes the copy to be made. There are only two instances of volitional conduct in this case: Cablevision's conduct in designing, housing, and maintaining a system that exists only to produce a copy, and a customer's conduct in ordering that system to produce a copy of a specific program. In the case of a VCR, it seems clear — and we know of no case holding otherwise — that the operator of the VCR, the person who actually presses the button to make the recording, supplies the necessary element of volition, not the person who manufactures, maintains, or, if distinct from the operator, owns the machine. We do not believe that an RS-DVR customer is sufficiently distinguishable from a VCR user to impose liability as a direct infringer on a different party for copies that are made automatically upon that customer's command.

The district court emphasized the fact that copying is "instrumental" rather than "incidental" to the function of the RS-DVR system. While that may distinguish the RS-DVR from the ISPs in *Netcom* and *CoStar*, it does not distinguish the RS-DVR from a VCR, a photocopier, or even a typical copy shop. And the parties do not seem to contest that a company that merely makes photocopiers available to the public on its premises, without more, is not subject to liability for direct infringement for reproductions made by customers using those copiers. They only dispute whether Cablevision is similarly situated to such a proprietor.

The district court found Cablevision analogous to a copy shop that makes course packs for college professors. [*See, e.g., Princeton Univ. Press v. Mich. Document Servs.*, 99 F.3d 1381 (6th Cir. 1996) (en banc).] . . .

But because volitional conduct is an important element of direct liability, the district court's analogy is flawed. In determining who actually "makes" a copy, a significant difference exists between making a request to a human employee, who then volitionally operates the copying system to make the copy, and issuing a command directly to a system, which automatically obeys commands and engages in no volitional conduct. In cases like *Princeton University Press*, the defendants operated a copying device and sold the product they made using that device. . . . Here, by selling access to a system that automatically produces copies on command, Cablevision more closely resembles a store proprietor who charges customers to use a photocopier on his premises, and it seems incorrect to say, without more, that such a proprietor "makes" any copies when his machines are actually operated by his customers. *See Netcom*, 907 F. Supp. at 1369. . . .

Our refusal to find Cablevision directly liable on these facts is buttressed by the existence and contours of the Supreme Court's doctrine of contributory liability in the copyright context. . . . Most of the facts found dispositive by the district court . . . seem to us more relevant to the question of contributory liability. . . . [For discussion of that issue, see the *Sony Betamax* case, reproduced in § 9.02[A] below.]

We conclude . . . that on the facts of this case, copies produced by the RS-DVR system are "made" by the RS-DVR customer, and Cablevision's contribution to this reproduction by providing the system does not warrant the imposition of direct liability. Therefore, Cablevision is entitled to summary judgment on this point, and the district court erred in awarding summary judgment to plaintiffs. . . .

[The court also held that transmission of recorded programs from Cablevision's server to the individual homes of the users that recorded those programs did not violate the public performance right. This aspect of the case is discussed in § 7.04[A] below.]

NOTES AND QUESTIONS

(1) Generally speaking, computers make two types of electronic reproductions of copyrighted works. Electronic reproductions may be made in some permanent form, such as a hard disk or "flash" memory. These reproductions persist, even when the power to the computer is turned off. It is clear that these permanent reproductions are fixed "copies" that are subject to the § 106(1) reproduction right. But computers cannot directly manipulate the digital data stored in such media. Instead, digital information must be downloaded from permanent storage into the "random-access memory" (or "RAM") of the computer for processing. Unlike other electronic media, RAM requires electricity to function. While the power is on, data held in RAM can be "perceived, reproduced, or otherwise communicated" (*e.g.*, by transmitting the data to a monitor, a permanent storage medium, or the RAM of a networked computer), but when the power is turned off, any data remaining in RAM disappears.

The first part of *Cartoon Network* involves a specific type of RAM known as a "buffer." A buffer is working memory that temporarily holds a stream of data while it is being processed; but, as noted in the case, the data in the buffer automatically is overwritten by new data entering the buffer in real time. Thus, although an entire data stream representing a copyrighted work passes through the buffer, only a small amount of the data (in this case, up to 1.2 seconds of the work) is contained in the buffer at any one time. The question is whether the temporary electronic embodiment of the data in RAM should be considered a fixed "copy" of the work that comes within the reproduction right in § 106(1). Before addressing that question, however, a little background is in order.

"RAM Copies" Computer Programs, and § 117

(2) Congress was aware of the "RAM" issue in 1976. The House Report accompanying the 1976 Act stated that "the definition of 'fixation' would exclude from the concept purely evanescent or transient reproductions such as those projected briefly on a screen . . . or captured momentarily in the 'memory' of a computer." With regard to computer programs, however, Congress temporarily preserved the status quo in § 117 of the 1976 Act, awaiting the final report of the Commission on New Technological Uses of Copyrighted Works ("CONTU"), as discussed in *Apple v. Franklin* in § 3.01[B] above. Despite the language in the House Report, CONTU took the position that data held in RAM is a fixed "copy" subject to the reproduction right. Consequently, it recommended that a new exception be enacted, so that "[o]ne who rightfully possesses a copy of a [computer] program . . . [is] provided with a legal right to copy it to that extent which will permit its use by that possessor." CONTU Final Report, at 13.

In 1980, Congress accepted CONTU's recommendation and replaced former § 117 with what is now § 117(a) and (b). Section 117(a)(1) permits one who owns a copy of a computer program to make or authorize the making of another copy or adaptation of that program if, but only if, "such a new copy or adaptation is created as an essential step in the utilization of the computer program." *See Vault Corp. v. Quaid Software Ltd.*, 847 F.2d 255, 261 (5th Cir. 1988) ("Congress recognized that a computer program cannot be used unless it is first copied into a computer's memory, and thus provided the § 117[(a)](1) exception to permit copying for this essential purpose."). This subsection permits both temporary RAM "copies" and permanent copies, such as uploading a program distributed on CD-ROM onto a hard disk. (§ 117(a)(1) also permits adaptations, such as a translation of the program from one language to another; this aspect will be discussed in § 7.03.)

Section 117(a)(2) permits a new copy of the program (or a new copy of a subsection (a)(1) adaptation) to be made for archival (rather than utilization) purposes. While some courts have construed this section narrowly to permit archival copies only "to guard against destruction or damage by mechanical or electrical failure," *see, e.g., Atari, Inc. v. JS & A Group, Inc.*, 597 F. Supp. 5, 9 (N.D. Ill. 1983), other courts have rejected such a limitation. *See, e.g., Vault*, 847 F.2d at 266-67.

Section 117(b) governs the further distribution of copies or adaptations made pursuant to subsection (a). It permits a subsection (a)(1) utilization copy to be sold, leased, or otherwise transferred, but only together with the initial copy from which it was made and as part of a transfer of all rights in the program. An adaptation made under subsection (a)(1) may also be transferred, again together with all rights in the program, but only with the copyright owner's permission. Archival copies made under subsection (a)(2), whether of the original program or an adaptation, must be destroyed upon transfer of the program under subsection (2)'s own terms.

(3) In enacting § 117, Congress made one significant change to CONTU's recommendation. CONTU had proposed an exception in favor of the "rightful possessor" of a copy of a computer program, but Congress changed the language so that the exception applied only to the "owner" of a copy. Because many software providers purport only to "license" their software to users, rather than "selling" it, this amendment threatened to defeat the purpose of § 117. *See, e.g., WallData, Inc. v. Los Angeles County Sheriff's Dept.*, 447 F.3d 769, 784-86 (9th Cir. 2006) (Department was not an "owner" of software subject to click-through licenses, and copies of software were not "essential" but were made for convenience). *But see Krause v. Titleserv, Inc.*, 402 F.3d 119, 124 (2d Cir. 2005) ("absence of formal title may be outweighed by evidence that the possessor of the copy enjoys sufficiently broad rights over it to be sensibly considered its owner").

(4) In *MAI Systems Corp. v. Peak Computer, Inc.*, 991 F.2d 511 (9th Cir. 1993), the court held that a company that provided service for computer hardware systems was guilty of copyright infringement when it "booted up" computers running the plaintiff's copyrighted operating system software without its permission. Apparently, MAI wanted to achieve an effective monopoly over the lucrative after-sales service market with respect to the machines it sold. It succeeded in doing so on the theory that in turning on the machine, the defendant had created a "copy" of the program in RAM, and had therefore infringed the reproduction right. The defendant argued that its activities were authorized by § 117, but the court held that the defendant's client was only a "licensee" of the program and was not the "owner" of a copy entitled to take advantage of § 117.

The *MAI* decision was widely criticized, both for its controversial reading of the statute and for its apparent failure to take into account the commercial/technological context. *See, e.g.*, Litman, *The Exclusive Right to Read*, 13 Cardozo Arts & Ent. L.J. 29, 40 (1994); Reese, *The Public Display Right: The Copyright Act's Neglected Solution to the Controversy Over RAM "Copies,"* 2001 U. Ill. L. Rev. 83. Despite this academic criticism, however, most courts have accepted *MAI'*s holding that transferring data into RAM constitutes a reproduction that must be authorized by the copyright owner. *See, e.g., Stenograph L.L.C. v. Bossard Assocs., Inc.*, 144 F.3d 96, 101-02 (D.C. Cir. 1998).

(5) The Digital Millennium Copyright Act overruled the specific holding of *MAI* by amending § 117 to authorize the making of ephemeral reproductions for purposes of computer repair and maintenance. *See* § 117(c); *Storage Technology Corp. v. Custom Hardware Engineering & Consulting, Inc.*, 421 F.3d 1307 (Fed. Cir. 2005) (under § 117(c), temporary RAM copies may be erased at the end of the maintenance contract, rather than every time a repair is made). In so doing, however, Congress appeared to implicitly accept the more controversial proposition that technologically necessary temporary reproductions in RAM may constitute "copies" for purposes of § 106(1).

(6) By its terms, § 117 is limited to a copy of a "computer program," defined in § 101 as "a set of statements or instructions to be used directly or indirectly in a computer in order to bring about a certain result." Is there an argument that the digital data in *Cartoon Network* could be considered a "computer program" under this definition? Perhaps, but only if the "result" to be achieved is the display of the

audiovisual work that the data represents. Moreover, it is doubtful that Cablevision would be considered the "owner" of a "copy" of the data. Thus, another approach to the problem of RAM was needed.

Cartoon Network *and "Transitory Duration"*

(7) Recall that § 106(1) is the exclusive right "to reproduce the copyrighted work in copies or phonorecords," and that "copies" and "phonorecords" are defined in § 101 as "material objects" in which a work is fixed. What is the "material object" in cases such as *MAI* and *Cartoon Network*? How does that "material object" differ from more traditional "copies," such as books and DVDs?

(8) *Cartoon Network* distinguishes *MAI* by emphasizing the requirement that data in the RAM buffer be embodied "for a period of more than transitory duration." Are you persuaded by the court's reasoning? Grammatically, does the "transitory duration" clause (in the definition of "fixed" in § 101) modify the noun "embodiment," the adjectives "permanent or stable," or the verbs "perceived, reproduced, or otherwise communicated"? Which view did the Copyright Office take in its *DMCA Section 104 Report*?

(9) In *CoStar Group, Inc. v. LoopNet, Inc.*, 373 F.3d 544 (4th Cir. 2004), cited in *Cartoon Network*, the court expressed a somewhat different view of the meaning of "fixed," in a case involving customers who posted infringing photos on the defendant's website:

> While temporary electronic copies may be made in this transmission process, they would appear not to be "fixed" in the sense that they are "of more than transitory duration." . . . "Transitory duration" is thus both a qualitative and quantitative characterization. It is quantitative insofar as it describes the period during which the function occurs, and it is qualitative in the sense that it describes the status of transition. Thus, when the copyrighted software is downloaded onto the computer, because it may be used to serve the computer or the computer owner, it no longer remains transitory. This, however, is unlike an ISP, which provides a system that automatically receives a subscriber's infringing material and transmits it to the Internet at the instigation of the subscriber.

373 F.3d at 551. Should the definition of "fixed" depend on the use to which an alleged reproduction is put? Is the only alternative a world in which all electronic reproductions are infringing, in the absence of an express statutory exception?

(10) How long must data remain embodied in RAM to be fixed "for a period of more than transitory duration"? In *SimplexGrinnell LP v. Integrated Systems & Power, Inc.*, 642 F. Supp. 2d 167 (S.D.N.Y. 2009), the court noted that *Cartoon Network* "suggested that the duration requirement would be satisfied where the program remained in the RAM for at least several minutes, or where the program remained in the RAM until the computer is shut off." Given that suggestion, how useful will *Cartoon Network* be in limiting the scope of the § 106(1) reproduction right?

The Reproduction Right and the Internet

(11)   But for the controversy over RAM "copies," digital network information technology seems to present no particular challenge to traditional concepts of the reproduction right. If an electronic message containing a copyrighted work is sent from one point to another, via the Internet or an intranet, it is possible (perhaps even likely) that the work will be reproduced in permanent form upon the message's arrival — as, for example, if the message is saved on the hard drive of the recipient's computer. If the transmission was an unauthorized one, the recipient of the message might be liable for infringement as the result of making such a copy, and the sender might be liable for violating the distribution right, or for inducing or facilitating an infringing reproduction.

Problems begin to appear, however, when one considers the ubiquity of temporary or ephemeral digital copies in the network environment. For example, an e-mail message may pass through dozens or even hundreds of separate "servers" on its way from origin to destination and, at each of these locations, a relatively short-lived reproduction of that message, or some portion of it, is created — only to be deleted or overwritten when that particular machine's role in facilitating the transmission is complete. Does this mean that, if the message contains unauthorized copyrighted material, the owner or operator of each and every one of those servers has some potential exposure to liability for infringement, along with the original sender and ultimate recipient of the message?

Or consider the routine activity of "browsing" the World Wide Web. Suppose that, in your virtual wanderings, you encounter a site where copyrighted material has been posted without permission. Obviously, you may be in trouble if you "download" content from that site. But what if you merely read it on the screen of your computer? Are you an infringer nonetheless? Before rushing to answer, remember that words and images appear on your screen only because a digital version of the web site's content resides temporarily in your computer's RAM. *See Intellectual Reserve, Inc. v. Utah Lighthouse Ministry, Inc.*, 75 F. Supp. 2d 1290, 1294 (D. Utah 1999) (holding browsing of infringing websites is itself an infringement). Consider, further, that the performance of Internet "browser" programs (like Microsoft's Internet Explorer) is enhanced by their capacity to create so-called "caches" (temporary copies that reside on the hard disk).

All of these forms of reproduction are either absolutely essential, or at least highly desirable, for the operation of digital network technology. And all of them are temporary, in the sense that they are technologically destined to be expunged, although the actual duration of their existence may range from milliseconds to weeks. Nevertheless, if we follow the reasoning of the *MAI* decision, discussed above, all of these examples implicate the § 106(1) reproduction right. And even under *Cartoon Network*, copies that persist for more than a few minutes are likely to be fixed "for a period of more than transitory duration." The result is widespread potential liability for infringement for any Internet-based use of a copyrighted work.

(12)   Even when it is clear that a copyrighted work has been reproduced in "copies," who bears legal responsibility for the making of the copy — the owner of

the device programmed to make copies or the person who causes the copy to be made? Some courts have adopted creative solutions to this issue. A leading case is *Religious Technology Center v. Netcom On-line Communication Services, Inc.*, 907 F. Supp. 1361 (N.D. Cal. 1995), discussed in *Cartoon Network*. In *Netcom*, the Church of Scientology sued various parties who had provided a former Church member with the electronic means to disseminate proprietary Church documents. The bulk of the court's opinion concerned Netcom's potential liability for direct infringement, contributory infringement, and vicarious liability. (Discussion of the latter two issues is deferred to § 9.03 below.)

With regard to direct infringement, the court noted that Netcom's computers automatically copied any messages posted to the Usenet, and stored them for eleven days; and it was bound by *MAI's* holding that any messages stored in RAM were sufficiently "fixed" to constitute "copies" within the meaning of the Act. Nonetheless, the court held that Netcom was not directly liable for copyright infringement, stating that "[a]lthough copyright is a strict liability statute, there should still be some element of volition or causation which is lacking where a defendant's system is merely used to create a copy by a third party." *Id.* at 1370.

(13) Title II of the Digital Millennium Copyright Act, codified at § 512 of Title 17, followed *Netcom's* approach in creating four new limitations on liability for copyright infringement by Internet service providers. For the sake of comprehensibility, discussion of this aspect of the DMCA will be taken up — at length! — in § 9.03 below. While providing comfort for ISPs, however, the enactment of § 512 carried the negative implication that temporary electronic copies that were *not* covered by the statute would be considered infringing.

In *CoStar*, however, the court rejected the argument that *Netcom* had been superseded by the enactment of § 512. Instead, the court endorsed and expanded *Netcom's* holding. Note that *Netcom* and *CoStar* are not limited to RAM "copies" but apply also to automated copies that are stored temporarily on a hard disk. Note also *CoStar's* further (and more questionable) holding that having an employee briefly review images for obvious copyright violations before posting them did not constitute the "element of volition or causation" held to be lacking in *Netcom*.

(14) *Netcom*'s holding that direct infringement requires some element of volition has proven influential in subsequent cases. *See, e.g., Field v. Google, Inc.*, 412 F. Supp. 2d 1106 (D. Nev. 2006); *Parker v. Google, Inc.*, 422 F. Supp. 2d 492 (E.D. Pa. 2006), *aff'd*, 242 Fed. Appx. 833 (3d Cir. 2007). Thus, in *Cartoon Network*, the court relied on both *Netcom* and *CoStar* in holding that Cablevision was not directly liable for setting up a RS-DVR system for its customers, because it was the customers, and not Cablevision, who made copies for later viewing. Note that *Netcom* ordinarily does not result in a finding of no liability, but only serves to distinguish direct infringement from secondary liability. (We will consider secondary liability in Chapter 9.) In *Cartoon Network*, however, plaintiffs made a strategic decision not to plead secondary liability, because the U.S. Supreme Court had held (in the *Sony Betamax* case considered below in § 9.02) that it is a "fair use" for viewers to make copies of television programs for later viewing. Thus, once the court decided that direct liability was not appropriate in *Cartoon Network*, Cablevision was entitled to summary judgment.

(15)   Another alternative to the problem of temporary electronic reproductions may be to rely on the "fair use" doctrine, treated in Chapter 10. As an example, consider *Ticketmaster Corp. v. Tickets.Com, Inc.*, 2000 U.S. Dist. LEXIS 12987 (C.D. Cal., Aug. 10, 2000), *aff'd without opinion*, 248 F.3d 1173 (9th Cir. 2001), in which the defendant used automated search programs (charmingly designated as "spiders") to search the World Wide Web for information about tickets for sale to sporting events, concerts, etc. In denying preliminary injunctive relief, the court concluded that 10-15 seconds of temporary copying (to extract the unprotected factual data from plaintiff's webpages) was likely to be a "fair use." The court later granted summary judgment on the same grounds. 2003 U.S. Dist. LEXIS 6483 (C.D. Cal., Mar. 7, 2003); *see also Kelly v. Arriba Soft Corp.*, 336 F.3d 811 (9th Cir. 2003) (reproduced in § 10.04 below).

(16)   The issue of "temporary reproduction" was discussed at the December 1996 WIPO Diplomatic Conference, but the results of that discussion were profoundly inconclusive. "Agreed Statements" (much like domestic legislative history) which accompany the two treaties concluded at the Conference say only that "the reproduction right . . . fully [applies] in the digital environment [and it] is understood that the storage of a protected work in digital form in an electronic medium constitutes a reproduction . . ." The ambiguity of this statement is self-evident, but given the context in which this language was negotiated, the term "storage" probably should be understood to refer only to the making of permanent copies (such as those on a computer's hard drive).

More recently, the European Union took a bold initiative in this area. Article 5(1) of the EU "Directive on the harmonisation of certain aspects of copyright and related rights in the information society" (2001/29/EC), reproduced in the casebook supplement, provides: "Temporary acts of reproduction . . . which are transient or incidental, which are an integral and essential part of a technological process whose sole purpose is to enable (a) a transmission in a network between third parties by an intermediary or (b) a lawful use of a work . . . and which have no independent economic significance, shall be exempted from the reproduction right. . . ." Do you think that the EU Directive offers an adequate solution to the problem?

§ 7.03 THE ADAPTATION RIGHT

Section 106(2) — the adaptation right — secures to the copyright owner the exclusive right "to prepare derivative works based on the copyrighted work." This right is infringed when a third party makes an unauthorized derivative work in which a preexisting work is "recast, transformed, or adapted." *See* § 101 (definition of derivative work). Examples of derivative works are translations, musical arrangements, and motion picture versions of popular novels. Through the adaptation right, American law has expanded the concept of "copying" to cover a much broader ground than the lay meaning of that term might suggest. In one sense, to recast, transform, or adapt a work is to copy it. But the derivative work author, in translating a novel or adapting it for the silver screen, is doing more than merely copying the work. She is transforming it, sometimes adding her own substantial authorship to the underlying work with which she began. Without recognition of the right to prepare derivative works, implicitly or explicitly, the copyright owner would have recourse only against verbatim copying in the same medium.

The principal case presents a situation in which the plaintiff copyright owner's grievances against the maker of the unauthorized alleged adaptation are *commercially motivated*. Consideration of the legal treatment of *offensive deforming changes* — that is, ones to which the creator of the work might object for reasons more aesthetic than economic — are deferred until we examine "moral rights" later in this chapter.

[A]   Introduction

Statutory References

1976 Act: §§ 106(2), 110(11), 114, 117, 120
1909 Act: § 1(b)

Legislative History

H.R. Rep. No. 94-1476 at 62,
reprinted in 1976 U.S.C.C.A.N. 5659, 5675

Section 106. Exclusive Rights in Copyrighted Works

Preparation of derivative works. — The exclusive right to prepare derivative works, specified separately in clause (2) of section 106, overlaps the exclusive right of reproduction to some extent. It is broader than that right, however, in the sense that reproduction requires fixation in copies or phonorecords, whereas the preparation of a derivative work, such as a ballet, pantomime, or improvised performance, may be an infringement even though nothing is ever fixed in tangible form.

To be an infringement the "derivative work" must be "based upon the copyrighted work," and the definition in section 101 refers to "a translation, musical arrangement, dramatization, fictionalization, motion picture version, sound recording, art reproduction, abridgment, condensation, or any other form in which a work may be recast, transformed, or adapted." Thus, to constitute a violation of section 106(2), the infringing work must incorporate a portion of the copyrighted work in some form; for example, a detailed commentary on a work or a programmatic musical composition inspired by a novel would not normally constitute infringements under this clause.

[B]   Case Law

LEE v. A.R.T. COMPANY
United States Court of Appeals, Seventh Circuit
125 F.3d 580 (1997)

EASTERBROOK, CIRCUIT JUDGE:

Annie Lee creates works of art, which she sells through her firm Annie Lee & Friends. Deck the Walls, a chain of outlets for modestly priced art, is among the buyers of her works, which have been registered with the Register of Copyrights. One Deck the Walls store sold some of Lee's notecards and small lithographs to A.R.T. Company, which mounted the works on ceramic tiles (covering the art with transparent epoxy resin in the process) and resold the tiles. Lee contends that these tiles are derivative works, which under 17 U.S.C. sec. 106(2) may not be prepared without the permission of the copyright proprietor. She seeks both monetary and injunctive relief. Her position has the support of two cases holding that A.R.T.'s business violates the copyright laws. *Munoz v. Albuquerque A.R.T. Co.*, 38 F.3d 1218 (9th Cir. 1994), *affirming without published opinion*, 829 F. Supp. 309 (D. Alaska 1993); *Mirage Editions, Inc. v. Albuquerque A.R.T. Co.*, 856 F.2d 1341 (9th Cir. 1988). *Mirage Editions*, the only full appellate discussion, dealt with pages cut from books and mounted on tiles; the court of appeals' brief order in *Munoz* concludes that the reasoning of *Mirage Editions* is equally applicable to works of art that were sold loose. Our district court disagreed with these decisions and entered summary judgment for the defendant. 925 F. Supp. 576 (N.D. Ill. 1996).

Now one might suppose that this is an open and shut case under the doctrine of first sale, codified at 17 U.S.C. sec. 109(a). A.R.T. bought the work legitimately, mounted it on a tile, and resold what it had purchased. Because the artist could capture the value of her art's contribution to the finished product as part of the price for the original transaction, the economic rationale for protecting an adaptation as "derivative" is absent. *See* William M. Landes & Richard A. Posner, *An Economic Analysis of Copyright Law*, 17 J. Legal Studies 325, 353-57 (1989). An alteration that includes (or consumes) a complete copy of the original lacks economic significance. One work changes hands multiple times, exactly what sec. 109(a) permits, so it may lack legal significance too. But sec. 106(2) creates a separate exclusive right, to "prepare derivative works," and Lee believes that affixing the art to the tile is "preparation," so that A.R.T. would have violated sec. 106(2) even if it had dumped the finished tiles into the Marianas Trench. For the sake of argument we assume that this is so and ask whether a card-on-a-tile is a "derivative work" in the first place.

"Derivative work" is a defined term:

> A "derivative work" is a work based upon one or more preexisting works, such as a translation, musical arrangement, dramatization, fictionalization, motion picture version, sound recording, art reproduction, abridgment, condensation, or any other form in which a work may be recast, transformed, or adapted. A work consisting of editorial revisions, annotations,

elaborations, or other modifications which, as a whole, represent an original work of authorship, is a "derivative work."

17 U.S.C. § 101.

The district court concluded that A.R.T.'s mounting of Lee's works on tile is not an "original work of authorship" because it is no different in form or function from displaying a painting in a frame or placing a medallion in a velvet case. No one believes that a museum violates sec. 106(2) every time it changes the frame of a painting that is still under copyright, although the choice of frame or glazing affects the impression the art conveys, and many artists specify frames (or pedestals for sculptures) in detail. *Munoz* and *Mirage Editions* acknowledge that framing and other traditional means of mounting and displaying art do not infringe authors' exclusive right to make derivative works. Nonetheless, the ninth circuit held, what A.R.T. does creates a derivative work because the epoxy resin bonds the art to the tile. Our district judge thought this a distinction without a difference, and we agree. If changing the way in which a work of art will be displayed creates a derivative work, and if Lee is right about what "prepared" means, then the derivative work is "prepared" when the art is mounted; what happens later is not relevant, because the violation of the sec. 106(2) right has already occurred. If the framing process does not create a derivative work, then mounting art on a tile, which serves as a flush frame, does not create a derivative work. What is more, the ninth circuit erred in assuming that normal means of mounting and displaying art are easily reversible. A painting is placed in a wooden "stretcher" as part of the framing process; this leads to some punctures (commonly tacks or staples), may entail trimming the edges of the canvas, and may affect the surface of the painting as well. Works by Jackson Pollock are notoriously hard to mount without damage, given the thickness of their paint. As a prelude to framing, photographs, prints, and posters may be mounted on stiff boards using wax sheets, but sometimes glue or another more durable substance is employed to create the bond.

Lee wages a vigorous attack on the district court's conclusion that A.R.T.'s mounting process cannot create a derivative work because the change to the work "as a whole" is not sufficiently original to support a copyright. Cases such as *Gracen v. The Bradford Exchange, Inc.*, 698 F.2d 300 (7th Cir. 1983), show that neither A.R.T. nor Lee herself could have obtained a copyright in the card-on-a-tile, thereby not only extending the period of protection for the images but also eliminating competition in one medium of display. After the ninth circuit held that its mounting process created derivative works, A.R.T. tried to obtain a copyright in one of its products; the Register of Copyrights sensibly informed A.R.T. that the card-on-a-tile could not be copyrighted independently of the note card itself. But Lee says that this is irrelevant — that a change in a work's appearance may infringe the exclusive right under sec. 106(2) even if the alteration is too trivial to support an independent copyright. Pointing to the word "original" in the second sentence of the statutory definition, the district judge held that "originality" is essential to a derivative work. This understanding has the support of both cases and respected commentators. *E.g.*, *L. Batlin & Son, Inc. v. Snyder*, 536 F.2d 486 (2d Cir. 1976); Melville B. Nimmer & David Nimmer, 1 NIMMER ON COPYRIGHT sec. 3.03 (1997). Pointing to the fact that the first sentence in the statutory definition omits any reference to originality, Lee insists that a work may be derivative despite the mechanical nature of the transformation. This view, too, has the support of both cases and respected commentators. *E.g.*, *Lone Ranger Television, Inc. v. Program Radio Corp.*, 740 F.2d 718, 722 (9th Cir. 1984); Paul Goldstein, COPYRIGHT: PRINCIPLES, LAW AND PRACTICE § 5.3.1 (2d ed. 1996) (suggesting that a transformation is covered by sec. 106(2) whenever it creates a "new work for a different market").

"Blue Monday" by Annie Lee
Reproductions courtesy of Annie Lee & Friends, Inc.

Fortunately, it is not necessary for us to choose sides. Assume for the moment that the first sentence recognizes a set of non-original derivative works. To prevail, then, Lee must show that A.R.T. altered her works in one of the ways mentioned in the first sentence. The tile is not an "art reproduction"; A.R.T. purchased and mounted Lee's original works. That leaves the residual clause: "any other form in which a work may be recast, transformed, or adapted." None of these words fits what A.R.T. did. Lee's works were not "recast" or "adapted." "Transformed" comes closer and gives the ninth circuit some purchase for its view that the permanence of the bond between art and base matters. Yet the copyrighted note cards and lithographs were not "transformed" in the slightest. The art was bonded to a slab of ceramic, but it was not changed in the process. It still depicts exactly what it depicted when it left Lee's studio. *See* William F. Patry, COPYRIGHT LAW AND PRACTICE 823-24 (1994) (disapproving *Mirage Editions* on this ground).[1] If mounting works a

---

[1] Scholarly disapproval of *Mirage Editions* has been widespread. Goldstein sec. 5.3 at 5:81-82;

"transformation," then changing a painting's frame or a photograph's mat equally produces a derivative work. Indeed, if Lee is right about the meaning of the definition's first sentence, then any alteration of a work, however slight, requires the author's permission. We asked at oral argument what would happen if a purchaser jotted a note on one of the note cards, or used it as a coaster for a drink, or cut it in half, or if a collector applied his seal (as is common in Japan); Lee's counsel replied that such changes prepare derivative works, but that as a practical matter artists would not file suit. A definition of derivative work that makes criminals out of art collectors and tourists is jarring despite Lee's gracious offer not to commence civil litigation.

The Corresponding Tile
As mounted by A.R.T. Company

If Lee (and the ninth circuit) are right about what counts as a derivative work, then the United States has established through the back door an extraordinarily broad version of authors' moral rights, under which artists may block any modification of their works of which they disapprove. No European version of *droit moral* goes this far. Until recently it was accepted wisdom that the United States did not enforce any claim of moral rights; even bowdlerization of a work was permitted unless the modifications produced a new work so different that it

---

Nimmer & Nimmer sec. 3.03; Gordon, *On Owning Information: Intellectual Property and the Restitutionary Impulse*, 78 Va. L. Rev. 149, 255 n.401 (1992).

infringed the exclusive right under sec. 106(2). *Compare WGN Continental Broadcasting Co. v. United Video, Inc.*, 693 F.2d 622 (7th Cir. 1982), *with Gilliam v. American Broadcasting Companies, Inc.*, 538 F.2d 14, 24 (2d Cir. 1976). The Visual Artists Rights Act of 1990, Pub. L. 101-650, 104 Stat. 5089, 5123-33, moves federal law in the direction of moral rights, but the cornerstone of the new statute, 17 U.S.C. sec. 106A, does not assist Lee. Section 106A(a)(3)(A) gives an artist the right to "prevent any intentional distortion, mutilation, or other modification of that work which would be prejudicial to his or her honor or reputation". At oral argument Lee's lawyer disclaimed any contention that the sale of her works on tile has damaged her honor or reputation. What is more, sec. 106A applies only to a "work of visual art," a new term defined in sec. 101 to mean either a unique work or part of a limited edition (200 copies or fewer) that has been "signed and consecutively numbered by the author." Lee's note cards and lithographs are not works of visual art under this definition, so she could not invoke sec. 106A even if A.R.T.'s use of her works to produce kitsch had damaged her reputation. It would not be sound to use sec. 106(2) to provide artists with exclusive rights deliberately omitted from the Visual Artists Rights Act. We therefore decline to follow *Munoz* and *Mirage Editions.*[2] Affirmed.

NOTES AND QUESTIONS

The Adaptation Right Generally

(1) *History and function of the adaptation right.* The right now found in § 106(2) was not recognized in the 1790 Act, which gave the copyright owner the exclusive right to "print, reprint, publish, or vend" the copyrighted work, or indeed in anything like its present form for much of the 19th Century. At least through the mid-1800s, abridgments, digests, and the like were *not* considered infringements. Thus, in *Stowe v. Thomas*, 23 F. Cas. 201 (C.C.E.D. Pa. 1853) (No. 13,514), the court held that the defendant's German translation of Harriet Beecher Stowe's English-language work, UNCLE TOM'S CABIN (1852), did not infringe her copyright because the defendant did not use the same "language in which the conceptions of the author are clothed." 23 F. Cas. at 207. The decision in *Stowe* prompted creation of a statutory right to control translations in 1870. Congress, in due course, recognized a fairly broad adaptation right, protected in § 1(b) of the 1909 Act and now, more comprehensively still, in § 106(2) of the 1976 Act.

(2) The adaptation right protects the author's incentive to exploit markets other than the one in which the original work was published. Thus, in *Midway Mfg. v. Artic Int'l, Inc.*, 1981 U.S. Dist. LEXIS 16881 (N.D. Ill., June 2, 1981), the court observed: "By forbidding [others] from creating a work based on a pre-existing copyrighted work, the author is assured that he will reap the profits from his artistic contribution in accordance with the policies of the [1976] Act." Today, such derivative markets often are more valuable than the market for the original work. Motion picture rights to a successful novel, or merchandising rights for characters in a

---

[2] Because this opinion creates a conflict among the circuits, it has been circulated to all judges in active service. See Circuit Rule 40(e). No judge requested a hearing en banc.

motion picture, are examples of these highly lucrative markets.

In granting this economic incentive to the author of the original work, however, does the Copyright Act give sufficient incentive to the potential creators of derivative works? In patent law, for example, an inventor who improves upon an existing patented invention can receive a patent on his or her improvement, resulting in "blocking patents," so that neither the original inventor nor the improver can practice the improved invention without the permission of the other (giving both parties a strong incentive to settle). In copyright law, however, if a subsequent author creates a derivative work without authorization, the first author can appropriate the second author's expression without compensation. *See, e.g., Anderson v. Stallone*, 11 U.S.P.Q.2d (BNA) 1161 (C.D. Cal. 1989). Does copyright law need a doctrine of "blocking copyrights"? For a discussion, see Lemley, *The Economics of Improvement in Intellectual Property Law*, 75 Tex. L. Rev. 989 (1997).

(3)   Like the reproduction right in § 106(1), the right to prepare derivative works under § 106(2) applies to *all* types of copyrightable works. Moreover, infringement of the adaptation right usually also infringes the reproduction right, the performance right, or both. Thus, if *A* writes a play based on a novel without permission of *B*, the copyright owner, and the play is substantially similar to the copyrighted work, *B* could bring an action for infringement of both the adaptation and reproduction rights. If the play were publicly performed, the performance right also would be infringed. We will return to the question of infringing performances later in this chapter.

(4)   *Derivative works and originality, revisited.* We noted in § 3.02 that in addition to being lawfully prepared, a derivative work must possess some incremental "originality" in order to be entitled to a separate copyright. But must a derivative work also be "original" in order to be infringing? Or are there some derivative works that are not sufficiently "original" to qualify for copyright, but which nonetheless violate § 106(2)?

In many cases, the answer may not matter, because of the overlap between the reproduction and adaptation rights. Suppose that *C* publishes a book that makes only trivial changes to a book written by *D*. If the new book is deemed to be a "derivative work," it would violate the adaptation right; if not, it would still violate the reproduction right. But the answer might make a difference if, for example, the reproduction right and the adaptation right were owned by different parties. And in *Lee*, the answer matters because the defendant did not reproduce the underlying work at all; instead, the defendant purchased authorized copies of the work, but used them in a way that was alleged to have violated § 106(2).

The trial court in *Lee* "held that 'originality' is essential to a derivative work," pointing to the § 101 statutory definition. Presumably, the reasoning must run as follows: The translations, dramatizations, motion picture versions, etc., referred to in the first sentence of the definition implicitly have been "recast, transformed, or adapted" in some original way, while the revisions, annotations, etc., in the second sentence of the definition, taken "as a whole," expressly are required to be "original works of authorship."

The plaintiff in *Lee* insisted that the defendant's work need not contain originality, and could still constitute a derivative work based solely on "mechanical transformation" of the underlying work. The statutory basis apparently is that the first sentence (unlike the second) does not expressly refer to originality. Accordingly, Professor Goldstein asserts that a derivative work results from any transformation that creates a "new work for a different market."

Judge Easterbrook says that the Seventh Circuit doesn't have to "choose sides." Does or doesn't the opinion in *Lee* implicitly reject the latter view of what constitutes a derivative work, along with the holding of *Mirage Editions*?

(5)   What are the implications if *Lee* is wrong and *Mirage Editions* is right about what "recast, transformed, or adapted" means? Would that mean that anyone who prepares a scrapbook of clippings from newspapers and magazines technically is a copyright infringer? If so, are we satisfied that, in practice, such technical infringers always would be insulated from liability? Suppose that an art dealer buys a single small print and frames it in a double matte, together with an autographed letter written by the artist and purchased independently by the dealer. Has the artist's § 106(2) right been violated by the act of associating these two items? *Compare National Bank of Commerce v. Shaklee Corp.*, 503 F. Supp. 533 (W.D. Tex. 1980) (addition of advertising material to text of book was infringing), *with Paramount Pictures Corp. v. Video Broadcasting Systems, Inc.*, 724 F. Supp. 808 (D. Kan. 1989) (addition of advertising material to the blank "lead-in" on purchased copies of videocassettes was not infringing).

(6)   *"Incorporation" of the underlying work.* The House Report states that "the infringing work must incorporate a portion of the original work in some form," noting that "a programmatic musical composition inspired by a novel" would not be infringing. In many cases, this requirement is easily satisfied. *See, e.g., Grove Press, Inc. v. Greenleaf Publishing Co.*, 247 F. Supp. 518 (E.D.N.Y. 1965) (translation of a novel); *Metro-Goldwyn-Mayer, Inc. v. Showcase Atlanta Cooperative Productions, Inc.*, 479 F. Supp. 351 (N.D. Ga. 1979) (musical stage production based on *Gone With the Wind*). On the other hand, some courts have found infringement of the adaptation right where the underlying work did not appear at all in the derivative work. See, *e.g., Addison-Wesley Publishing Co. v. Brown*, 223 F. Supp. 219 (E.D.N.Y. 1963), in which the court (in a questionable decision) found infringement in the publication of a manual providing the answers to questions presented in a well-known physics textbook. Is this decision consistent with the 1976 Act? Is this an example of a court using copyright as a substitute for unfair competition law?

(7)   *More from the Seventh Circuit.* In *Ty, Inc. v. Publications Int'l, Ltd.*, 292 F.3d 512 (7th Cir. 2002), a case we also will discuss in § 10.03, Judge Posner felt called upon to decide whether a "collectors' guide" to the plaintiff's Beanie Baby toy line constituted a derivative work based on the designs of those stuffed animal figures. He concluded that it did not:

> We cannot find a case on the point but the Copyright Act is clear. . . . A derivative work . . . must either be in one of the forms named [in § 101] or be "recast, transformed, or adapted." *Lee v. A.R.T. Co.*, 125 F.3d 580, 582 (7th Cir. 1997). The textual portions of a collectors' guide to copyrighted works are not among the examples of derivative works listed in the statute,

and guides don't recast, transform, or adapt the things to which they are guides. A guide to Parisian restaurants is not a recasting, transforming, or adapting of Parisian restaurants. Indeed, a collectors' guide is very much like a book review, which is a guide to a book and which no one supposes is a derivative work. Both the book review and the collectors' guide are critical and evaluative as well as purely informational; and ownership of a copyright does not confer a legal right to control public evaluation of the copyrighted work.

Id. at 520. Do you agree with Judge Posner's characterization of the holding in *Lee*?

(8) *Transformation without adaptation?* In *Warner Bros. Entertainment, Inc. v. RDR Books*, 575 F. Supp. 2d 513 (S.D.N.Y. 2008), author J.K. Rowling sued the author and publisher of *The Lexicon*, an unauthorized encyclopedia guide to the Harry Potter books. The court held that *The Lexicon* violated the reproduction right by including direct quotations, paraphrases, plot details, and summaries of scenes in its definitions; but it held that *The Lexicon* was *not* a derivative work, because (quoting Judge Posner) "guides don't recast, transform, or adapt the things to which they are guides."

Does this result make any sense to you? If *The Lexicon* had been authorized by the copyright owners, wouldn't it have received a separate copyright as a "derivative work"? Isn't it clear that the author of *The Lexicon* added "substantial, not merely trivial, originality" in "condensing, synthesizing, and reorganizing the preexisting material in an A-to-Z reference guide"? Strangely, the District Court seemed to think that *The Lexicon* added *too much* originality, because it was more than a mere "abridgment" or "condensation," and did not merely retell the story of Harry Potter in another medium. The court seemed to believe that "transformative uses" (which are favored in fair use analysis, see § 10.03) could not also be "derivative works" within the meaning of the Act. It remains to be seen whether this bizarre departure from the usual analysis under § 106(2) finds favor with other courts.

(9) *Cross-media infringement.* Infringement of § 106(2) often occurs in different media. For example, a three-dimensional sculptural work may be infringed by its incorporation in a two-dimensional photograph. *See Ty*, 292 F.3d at 519 (photos of Beanie Babies are derivative works). How far the concept of cross-media infringement can be pushed raises interesting conceptual problems regarding the scope of the adaptation right. For example, in *Horgan v. Macmillan, Inc.*, 789 F.2d 157 (2d Cir. 1986), the court considered whether a book containing still photographs of the New York City Ballet Company's production of *The Nutcracker* infringed the copyright in the choreography for the ballet, created by George Balanchine. Remanding for reconsideration of a preliminary injunction, the court held that the photos might indeed have infringed the choreographic work, capturing the flow of some of the steps of the ballet, even if it did not enable the recreation of the stage performance. Does this go too far in protecting a choreographic work against "copying" by means of photography? Would the incentive to create choreographic works be seriously undermined if this kind of copying were allowed?

(10) *The "first-sale" doctrine and the § 106(3) public distribution right. Lee* makes mention early on of the "first-sale" doctrine, codified in § 109(a), under which the copyright owner "exhausts" her economic rights in a particular copy of a work

— and thus loses control of the copy — by selling it. The first-sale doctrine is a defense to a claim of infringement of a copyright holder's § 106(3) right to publicly distribute copies of the work — or more precisely, as we will see in § 7.04, it is a limitation on the very *scope* of the public distribution right itself. The first-sale issue is disposed of quickly in *Lee* precisely because it so clearly applies. The defendant's acts cannot plausibly be said to infringe the public distribution right. Instead, the plaintiff is forced to claim infringement of the § 106(2) adaptation right.

(11)   *The "lurking" moral rights issue.* What may well be at stake in some cases decided under § 106(2) is what Judge Easterbrook refers to in his final paragraph: so-called "moral rights," *i.e.*, the artist's ability to control the conditions under which a work is resold and viewed — and thus, to some extent, to control the ways in which that work will be understood and appreciated. Is this a power that artists *should* possess?

Traditionally, American copyright law has not recognized the "moral rights" of authors and artists, as least in explicit terms. In § 7.08, however, we will consider the limited "moral rights" protection afforded under the Visual Artists Rights Act of 1990 (or "VARA"). By its terms, VARA gives artists the power to prevent "any distortion, mutilation, or other modification of [a covered] work which would be prejudicial to the [artist's] honor or reputation." § 106A(a)(3)(A). When we get to VARA, you'll discover that the new legislation would not apply to cases like *Lee*. Should the § 106(2) adaptation right be employed as a surrogate for moral rights?

Interoperability and the Adaptation Right

(12)   *The role of fixation.* We saw that the § 106(1) right involves reproduction in "copies" and "phonorecords" and is therefore infringed only when a new fixation has been made. The right to prepare derivative works under § 106(2), however, does not refer to "copies" or "phonorecords." It also avoids using the term "created," which is similarly defined in terms of fixation. Does a derivative work have to be "fixed" in order to be infringing?

The issue was raised in *Lewis Galoob Toys, Inc. v. Nintendo of America, Inc.*, 964 F.2d 965 (9th Cir. 1992), a case involving the Game Genie, a device designed to alter the play of video games made for the Nintendo Entertainment System. The Game Genie functioned by intercepting data sent from the game cartridge to the NES console and replacing selected bytes of data with new values input by the user. The Game Genie temporarily altered the audiovisual screen display generated by the game, but it did not alter the original computer program stored in the game cartridge.

The House Report states that "the preparation of a derivative work . . . may be an infringement even though nothing is ever fixed in tangible form." The *Galoob* court concurred, noting that "a derivative work must be fixed to be protected under the Act, but not to infringe." 964 F.2d at 968. In a seemingly contradictory statement, however, *Galoob* also held that "a derivative work must incorporate a protected work in some *concrete or permanent* form." *Id.* at 967 (emphasis added). What is the basis for this requirement? The House Report states that a derivative work must incorporate the copyrighted work in *some* form, but it does not use the words "concrete or permanent." Isn't this just "fixation" by another name?

If "fixation" (or its equivalent) is not required as a necessary element of other kinds of infringing uses (such as public performance or display), why should we insist on it as a component of an infringing adaptation? Doesn't doing so significantly limit the scope of protection available to the copyright owner? For a discussion, see Ochoa, *Copyright, Derivative Works and Fixation: Is* Galoob *a* Mirage, *or Does the* Form(Gen) *of the Alleged Derivative Work Matter?*, 20 Santa Clara Computer & High Tech. L.J. 991 (2004).

(13)   *Galoob* was cited with approval in *Micro Star v. Formgen, Inc.*, 154 F.3d 1107 (9th Cir. 1998). *Micro Star* involved another video game, Duke Nukem 3D (D/N-3D), a first-person "shooter" game that comes with 29 "levels" of play. The game also included a "Build Editor" which allowed users to design their own levels. Formgen, the copyright owner, encouraged users to post new levels to the Internet for others to download for free. Micro Star downloaded 300 user-created levels and stamped them onto a CD, which it then sold commercially as Nuke It (N/I). Judge Kozinski described how the game worked as follows:

> The game consists of three separate components: the game engine, the source art library and the MAP files. . . . In order to create the audiovisual display for a particular level, the game engine invokes the MAP file that corresponds to that level. Each MAP file contains a series of instructions that tell the game engine (and, through it, the computer) what to put where. . . . The MAP file describes the level in painstaking detail, but it does not actually contain any of the copyrighted art itself; everything that appears on the screen actually comes from the art library. . . . When the player selects one of the N/I levels, the game engine references the N/I MAP files, but still uses the D/N-3D art library to generate the images that make up that level.

Id. at 1110. Micro Star argued that the MAP files were like the Game Genie, in that they only temporarily altered the play of the game. The court disagreed, holding that the MAP files which defined the new audiovisual displays were sufficiently "concrete or permanent" to qualify as derivative works. *Id.* at 1111-12. Micro Star also argued that the new MAP files did not incorporate any of the protected expression of the original work, because although the MAP files referenced the D/N-3D art library, they did not themselves contain any images. Again the court disagreed, saying: "a copyright owner holds the right to create sequels, and the stories told in the N/I MAP files are surely sequels, telling new (though somewhat repetitive) tales of Duke's fabulous adventures. A book about Duke Nukem would infringe for the same reason, even if it contained no pictures." *Id.* at 1112. Do you agree? Are the MAP files different from the Game Genie in this regard?

"Nuke It" Advertisement

(14)   The lack of fixation played an important role in three cases holding that the unauthorized display of "pop-up" advertisements while browsing the Internet does not result in a "derivative work" of the website that is temporarily covered by the advertisement. *See 1-800 Contacts, Inc. v. WhenU.com, Inc.*, 309 F. Supp. 2d 467 (S.D.N.Y. 2003), *rev'd on other grounds*, 414 F.3d 400 (2d Cir. 2005); *Wells Fargo & Co. v. WhenU.com, Inc.*, 293 F. Supp. 2d 734 (E.D. Mich. 2003); *U-Haul Int'l, Inc. v. WhenU.com, Inc.*, 279 F. Supp. 2d 723 (E.D. Va. 2003).

(15)   The cases discussed in the preceding notes are specific examples of a more general and important phenomenon. More and more computer programs are being written to "interoperate" with, and thus enhance, existing software and hardware systems. Although they may not reproduce the codes of those systems, these new programs do — of necessity — refer to the existing works and depend upon them for the "interoperative" works' own functionality. *See generally* Black & Page, *Add-On Infringements: When Computer Add-Ons and Peripherals Should (and Should Not) be Considered Infringing Derivative Works Under* Lewis Galoob Toys, Inc. v. Nintendo of America, Inc. *and Other Recent Decisions*, 15 Hastings Comm. & Ent. L.J. 615 (1993). Should a software designer be allowed to create new applications that operate in the "Windows" environment, so long as the applications do not actually reproduce any copyrighted elements of Microsoft's software? If so, how is that different from creating new levels for a copyrighted video game? Does the answer depend on whether the enhancement can be used with more than one

copyrighted work?

(16)   Interoperability questions are not limited to computer technology. Suppose plaintiff produces a doll shaped like a bear, into which specially designed tapes manufactured by plaintiff are inserted. One track of the tape operates as an audio program telling stories in a high-pitched male voice. Another track contains a signal which causes the eyes, nose and mouth of the bear to move in synchronized fashion, giving a life-like animation to the doll. Defendant manufactures and sells compatible tapes, telling different stories in a high-pitched male voice and animating the bear's movements similarly. Has an infringing derivative work been created? *See Worlds of Wonder, Inc. v. Vector Intercontinental, Inc.*, 653 F. Supp. 135 (N.D. Ohio 1986); *Worlds of Wonder, Inc. v. Veritel Learning Systems, Inc.*, 658 F. Supp 351 (N.D. Tex. 1986) (yes). What is the copyrighted "work" in these cases? In what way does the defendant's work "incorporate" a portion of the copyrighted work?

Limitations on the Adaptation Right

(17)   *Software "masks" and § 110(11).* If fixation is not required for a derivative work to be infringing, does that mean that using the fast-forward button on your remote control violates the exclusive right to "prepare" a derivative work? In *Huntsman v. Soderbergh*, 2005 WL 1993421 (D. Colo. 2005), eight Hollywood studios filed infringement claims against two companies that provide software "masks" (software that instructs a DVD player to skip over certain scenes or to mute certain words when playing a specific motion picture). The software is popular with parents who wish to see Hollywood movies but don't want to expose themselves or their children to allegedly gratuitous sex and violence. Is such software more like the device in *Galoob*, which modified a work only temporarily, or more like the MAP files in *Micro Star*, which were held to be fixed? *See* Ochoa, *Copyright, Derivative Works and Fixation*, at 1033-40.

While summary judgment motions were pending in *Huntsman*, Congress enacted the Family Entertainment and Copyright Act of 2005. Title II of the Act added § 110(11), which exempts technology that makes limited portions of the audio or video content of a motion picture imperceptible at the direction of a home viewer, if no fixed copy of the altered version of the motion picture is created. Finding that the amendment covered the technology at issue, the District Court dismissed the infringement claims as moot. Assuming that § 110(11) was designed to preempt the *Huntsman* litigation, is it wise for Congress to intervene in a specific pending action in this manner?

(18)   *Digital "sampling" and § 114.* Recall that while most copyrighted works (including musical works) can be infringed by imitation or simulation, § 114 provides that a sound recording is infringed only by use of the actual fixed sounds. In particular, the adaptation right in a sound recording "is limited to the right to prepare a derivative work in which the actual sounds fixed in the sound recording are rearranged, remixed, or otherwise altered in sequence or quality." § 114(b). In limiting the adaptation right in this manner, do you think that Congress intended that any such electronic manipulation would *automatically* infringe the § 106(2) right to prepare derivative works? The question arises in the context of digital "sampling."

Digital sampling, a technique frequently used in the recording industry, is particularly prevalent in rap and hip-hop music. A recording artist copies or "samples" a short segment of an existing sound recording, electronically manipulates the sample, and incorporates it into a new sound recording. Generally, record producers license the right to use samples from the owners of copyright in particular sound recordings (as well as the musical compositions performed in those recordings). But sometimes, for a variety of reasons, sampling occurs without authorization. Does unlicensed sampling violate the right to prepare derivative works?

While some courts have shown little sympathy for unauthorized sampling, *see, e.g., Grand Upright Music Ltd. v. Warner Bros. Records*, Inc. 780 F. Supp. 182 (S.D.N.Y. 1991) (granting motion for preliminary injunction); *Jarvis v. A&M Records*, 827 F. Supp. 282 (D.N.J. 1993) (denying defendants' motion for summary judgment in relevant part), other courts have granted summary judgment for the defendant on grounds that the amount sampled was *de minimis* and the two works were not "substantially similar" as a matter of law. *See Newton v. Diamond*, 349 F.3d 591 (9th Cir. 2003). In *Bridgeport Music, Inc. v. Dimension Films*, 410 F.3d 792 (6th Cir. 2005), however, the Sixth Circuit held that because § 114(b) is limited to the manipulation of fixed sounds, *any* sampling of an existing sound recording is an infringement of copyright *per se*, without regard to whether the amount sampled was *de minimis* or whether the allegedly infringing work was "substantially similar." The court reasoned that sampling was unnecessary because, under § 114(b), a second comer could always make a new recording that imitated the original. *Id.* at 800-02. Do you find this rationale persuasive? The requirement of "substantial similarity" will be examined at greater length in Chapter 8.

(19)	*Computer programs and § 117.* Recall that § 117 permits the owner of a copy of a computer program to make a new copy or adaptation of that program, if "such a new copy or adaptation is created as an essential step in the utilization of the computer program in conjunction with a machine." § 117(a)(1). By including adaptations, § 117 makes it clear that the exception goes beyond the creation of copies in the random-access memory ("RAM") of a computer, as discussed in § 7.02[D]. Instead, the owner of a copy can modify the program if such modifications are necessary, for example, to permit the program to function with another operating system. But just how far does this privilege extend?

In *Krause v. Titleserv, Inc.*, 402 F.3d 119 (2d Cir. 2005), the court took an expansive view of the meaning of § 117. First, the court held that the former employer of the plaintiff, which still had a lawful copy of the computer program in its possession, had sufficient incidents of ownership to be considered an "owner" of that copy, even if it lacked formal title. In so holding, the court opined that the license terms conditioned ownership of the copyright only, and not ownership of the particular copy. The court then held that fixing bugs, updating client information, incorporating the program into its new Windows-based system and adding additional functional capabilities to the program were all "essential steps" in utilizing the program under § 117. The court rejected the narrow view that "essential" meant only those steps without which the program would not function, and instead took the broader, more practical view that "essential" included "the addition of features so that a program better serves the needs of the customer for which it was created." *Id.* at 128.

Similarly, in *Vault Corp. v. Quaid Software Ltd.*, 847 F.2d 255 (5th Cir. 1988), the court permitted the defendant to make "intermediate" copies of the plaintiff's diskette security software ("PROLOK") in developing a program ("RAMKEY") designed to "unlock" the plaintiff's software. The court held that "[e]ven though the copy of Vault's program made by Quaid was . . . made for the express purpose of devising a means of defeating its protective function, the copy made by Quaid *was* 'created as an essential step in the utilization' of Vault's program. Section 117[(a)](1) contains no language to suggest that the copy it permits must be employed for a use intended by the copyright owner . . ." *Id.* at 261.

What sense does the *Vault* court's expanded (if not exploded) reading of the "utilization" exception make? Even reading § 117 in isolation, do you find it plausible that Congress intended to allow users of software to employ other people's copyrighted works to enter into direct commercial competition with them? The answer may be that the court believed that the plaintiff had been using its security program to protect functional aspects of the program that were not protected by copyright. With computer programs, it would be difficult to analyze the unprotected aspects of the program without such intermediate copying. You may want to revisit *Vault* after reading about *Sega Enterprises Ltd. v. Accolade, Inc.* in Chapter 10.

One way to close any gap opened by the *Vault* court's reading of § 117 would be to prohibit interference with security programs and other "technological safe-guards" for the purposes of gaining "access" to a copyrighted work that has been "locked up" in this fashion — even where the ultimate goal of such "circumvention" is to make what would otherwise be a lawful use of that work. For better or worse, provisions of the Digital Millennium Copyright Act of 1998, codified in § 1201, took an important step in this direction. These provisions are discussed in § 9.04.

(20) *Architectural works and § 120.* As noted above, a two-dimensional photograph of a three-dimensional work is a derivative work. Thus, the exemption in § 120(a) that permits making, distributing, and displaying pictorial representations of an architectural work embodied in a building that is visible from a public place is implicitly a limitation on the § 106(2) right to prepare derivative works. Section 120(b) contains an express limitation on the § 106(2) right, permitting the owners of a building to modify the building without the consent of the architectural work copyright owner. These exemptions are discussed in more detail in § 3.01 above.

§ 7.04   THE PUBLIC DISTRIBUTION RIGHT

Section 106(3) establishes the copyright owner's exclusive right "to distribute copies or phonorecords of the copyrighted work to the public by sale or other transfer of ownership, or by rental, lease, or lending." Sometimes called the "right of publication" or the "right to vend," this provision gives the owner the right to control the first public distribution of any material embodiment of the work, whether or not the copy or phonorecord was lawfully made.

The right to distribute is distinct from the right to reproduce the work — in whole, in part, or by adaptation. Rather, § 106(3) provides the copyright owner the ability to control the transfer of physical copies or phonorecords of the work. Clearly, the distribution right is a necessary complement to the other § 106 rights. It would be difficult to defend a statute which, for example, prohibited public distribution of a work when the offending copies or phonorecords were obtained through unauthorized reproduction, but which permitted distribution when copies made or authorized by the owner had been stolen by the offending party. If for no other reason than efficiency of judicial administration, it is necessary that the Copyright Act provide the wronged party a remedy — in addition to whatever other sanctions may be available for conversion or for the violation of criminal statutes.

Like other § 106 rights, however, the distribution right is not absolute. Section 109 limits § 106(3) by creating a basic exception — the "first-sale" doctrine — which restricts the copyright owner's control over the dissemination of copies of the work to their first sale or transfer. Note also that § 602 prohibits importation into the United States of copies of a work acquired abroad without authority from the copyright owner. The proper limits of the first-sale doctrine and the relationship of § 602 to the first-sale doctrine and to the public distribution right itself — as well as the impact of the Internet on these rights — are considered in the materials below.

[A] Introduction

Statutory References
1976 Act: §§ 106(3), 108, 109(a), (b), and (d), 115, 117, 602–03
1909 Act: § 1(a)

Legislative History

H.R. Rep. No. 94-1476 at 62, 79-80, 169,
reprinted in 1976 U.S.C.C.A.N. 5659, 5675-76, 5693-94, 5785

 SECTION 106. EXCLUSIVE RIGHTS IN COPYRIGHTED WORKS

Public distribution. — Clause (3) of section 106 establishes the exclusive right of publication: the right "to distribute copies or phonorecords of the copyrighted work to the public by sale or other transfer of ownership, or by rental, lease, or lending." Under this provision, the copyright owner would have the right to control the first public distribution of an authorized copy or phonorecord of his work, whether by sale, gift, loan, or some rental or lease arrangement. Likewise, any unauthorized public distribution of copies or phonorecords that were unlawfully made would be an infringement. As section 109 makes clear, however, the copyright owner's rights under section 106(3) cease with respect to a particular copy or phonorecord once he has parted with ownership of it.

SECTION 109. EFFECT OF TRANSFER OF PARTICULAR COPY OR PHONORECORD

Effect on further disposition of copy or phonorecord

Section 109(a) restates and confirms the principle that, where the copyright owner has transferred ownership of a particular copy or phonorecord of a work, the person to whom the copy or phonorecord is transferred is entitled to dispose of it by sale, rental, or any other means. Under this principle, . . . the copyright owner's exclusive right of public distribution would have no effect upon anyone who owns "a particular copy or phonorecord lawfully made under this title" and who wishes to transfer it to someone else or to destroy it.

Thus, for example, the outright sale of an authorized copy of a book frees it from any copyright control over its resale price or other conditions of its future disposition. A library that has acquired ownership of a copy is entitled to lend it under any conditions it chooses to impose. This does not mean that conditions on future disposition of copies or phonorecords, imposed by a contract between their buyer and seller, would be unenforceable between the parties as a breach of contract, but it does mean that they could not be enforced by an action for infringement of copyright. Under section 202, however, the owner of the physical copy or phonorecord cannot reproduce or perform the copyrighted work publicly without the copyright owner's consent. . . .

[New subsection (b), added and amended since passage of the 1976 Act, is discussed in § 7.04[B] below. Old subsection (b), now denominated (c), is considered in § 7.06.]

Effect of mere possession of copy or phonorecord

Subsection (c) [now (d)] of section 109 qualifies the privileges specified in subsections (a) and [(c)] by making clear that they do not apply to someone who merely possesses a copy or phonorecord without having acquired ownership of it. Acquisition of an object embodying a copyrighted work by rental, lease, loan, or bailment carries with it no privilege to dispose of the copy under section 109(a) or to display it publicly under section 109[(c)]. To cite a familiar example, a person who has rented a print of a motion picture from the copyright owner would have no right to rent it to someone else without the owner's permission. . . .

SECTION 602. INFRINGING IMPORTATION

Scope of the section

Section 602 . . . deals with two separate situations: importation of "piratical" articles (that is, copies or phonorecords made without any authorization of the copyright owner), and unauthorized importation of copies or phonorecords that were lawfully made. The general approach of section 602 is to make unauthorized importation an act of infringement in both cases, but to permit the United States Customs Service to prohibit importation only of "piratical" articles. . . .

[For a fuller excerpt from H.R. REP. No. 94-1476, see Part Three of the Casebook Supplement.]

[B] Domestic Distribution

LONDON-SIRE RECORDS, INC. v. DOE 1
United States District Court, District of Massachusetts
542 F. Supp. 2d 153 (2008)

GERTNER, DISTRICT JUDGE:

This case consists of numerous actions consolidated under *London-Sire Records, Inc. v. Does 1-4*, Civil Action No. 04-cv-12434. The plaintiffs include several of the country's largest record companies. The defendants, the plaintiffs claim, are individual computer users — mainly college students — who use "peer-to-peer" file-sharing software to download and disseminate music without paying for it, infringing the plaintiffs' copyrights. . . .

I. *BACKGROUND*

A. *Facts*

[The plaintiffs alleged that each defendant had taken part in an infringing peer-to-peer file transfer. Plaintiffs relied on evidence gathered by their trade association, the Recording Industry Association of America, or "RIAA," which retained a third-party investigator, MediaSentry, Inc. ("MediaSentry"). MediaSentry acts as an undercover user of peer-to-peer networks by connecting to a network and searching for the plaintiff record companies' copyrighted files. Upon finding the files, MediaSentry downloads them and gathers information about the sending computer, such as the date and time at which the files were downloaded and the sending computer's Internet Protocol ("IP") address. Using this information, plaintiffs sought subpoenas to identify the names of anonymous users alleged to have infringed. Defendants filed motions to quash the subpoenas, arguing that plaintiffs failed to state a claim upon which relief could be granted. The court also granted the Electronic Frontier Foundation ("EFF") leave to file an amicus brief supporting the motions to quash.]

IV. [*DISCUSSION*]

A. *Factor One: Prima Facie Claim of Actionable Harm*

1. *Whether the Plaintiffs Have Asserted a Claim Upon Which Relief Can Be Granted*

. . . The plaintiffs claim that "each [d]efendant, without the permission or consent of [p]laintiffs, has . . . download[ed] or distribut[ed] to the public" music files to which the plaintiff holds the copyright. Two rights reserved to the copyright holder are at issue in this case: the right "to reproduce the copyrighted work in copies or phonorecords," 17 U.S.C. § 106(1), and the right "to distribute copies or phonorecords of the copyrighted work to the public by sale or other transfer of ownership, or by rental, lease, or lending," *id.* § 106(3).

The movants and the amicus present two broad arguments. . . . First, they contend that the copyright laws require an actual dissemination of copyrighted material; merely making copyrighted material available for another person to copy, they argue, is only an attempt at infringement — which is not actionable. Second, they contend that . . . the copyright owner's rights are limited to tangible, physical objects, and purely electronic transmissions over the internet fall outside those rights. . . .

a. *Whether the Copyright Holder's Right Extends Only to Actual Distributions*

The first question the Court must address is whether the distribution right under 17 U.S.C. § 106(3) requires an actual dissemination to constitute an infringement.[16] . . . MediaSentry, posing as just another peer-to-peer user, can easily verify that copyrighted material has been made available for download from a certain IP address. . . . [The court suggests that evidence of MediaSentry's own downloads would not be considered infringing because the plaintiffs authorized them.]

The plaintiffs suggest two reasons why an actual distribution might not be required. First, the statute reserves to the copyright owner the right "to do *and to authorize* . . . [the distribution of] copies or phonorecords of the copyrighted work to the public." § 106(3) (emphasis added). The language appears to grant two distinct rights: "doing" and "authorizing" a distribution. Making the copyrighted material available over the internet might constitute an actionable "authorization" of a distribution. Second, if mere authorization is not enough, the plaintiffs argue that in appropriate circumstances . . . "making available" copyrighted material is sufficient to constitute an act of actual distribution. Neither argument has merit.

The First Circuit has squarely considered and rejected the proposition that copyright liability arises where the defendant authorized an infringement, but no actual infringement occurred. *See Venegas-Hernandez v. Ass'n De Compositores & Editores de Música Latinoamericana*, 424 F.3d 50, 57-58 (1st Cir. 2005). It noted that Congress' intent in adding "authorize" to the statute was to "avoid any questions as to the liability of contributory infringers." *Id.* at 58 (internal quotation marks omitted) (quoting H.R. Rep. 94-1476 ("House Report") at 52 (1976)). Authorization is sufficient to give rise to liability, but only if an infringing act occurs after the authorization. . . .

Thus, to constitute a violation of the distribution right under § 106(3), the defendants' actions must do more than "authorize" a distribution; they must actually "do" it. The Court therefore moves to the plaintiffs' second argument:

---

[16] The plaintiffs have also alleged a violation of their reproduction rights under § 106(1). Under that statute, a copyright owner's rights are infringed whenever an unauthorized person "reproduce[s] the copyrighted work in copies or phonorecords." The plaintiffs have alleged that the defendants downloaded music, as well as distributed it, and that they did not have authorization to do so. . . . [T]he plaintiffs thus appear to have alleged a legally sufficient harm under § 106(1). It is still appropriate to address briefly the distribution right under § 106(3), however; it was the focus of the parties' briefing and arguably constitutes the crux of the alleged infringement in this case. . . .

Merely making copyrighted works available to the public is enough where, as in this case, the alleged distributor does not need to take any more affirmative steps before an unauthorized copy of the work changes hands. Other courts have split over whether that is a valid reading of the statute. . . .

To suggest that "making available" may be enough, the plaintiffs rely primarily on the Fourth Circuit's decision in *Hotaling* [v. *Church of Jesus Christ of Latter-Day Saints*, 118 F.3d 199 (4th Cir. 1997)]. In that case, a library had an unauthorized copy of a book, which it "made available" to the public; the defendant argued that without a showing that any member of the public actually read the book, it could not be liable for "distribution." The district court agreed and granted summary judgment to the defendant. The Fourth Circuit reversed:

> When a public library adds a work to its collection, lists the work in its index or catalog system, and makes the work available to the borrowing or browsing public, it has completed all the steps necessary for distribution to the public. At that point, members of the public can visit the library and use the work. Were this not to be considered distribution within the meaning of § 106(3), a copyright holder would be prejudiced by a library that does not keep records of public use, and the library would unjustly profit by its own omission.

Id. [at 203]; *see also id.* at 204.

The plaintiffs contend that this case is analogous to *Hotaling*, and suggest that the Court should reach the same conclusion as the Fourth Circuit. But the EFF correctly points out a lacuna in the Fourth Circuit's reasoning. Merely because the defendant has "completed all the steps necessary for distribution" does not necessarily mean that a distribution has actually occurred. It is a "distribution" that the statute plainly requires. *See* 17 U.S.C. § 106(3).

The plaintiffs encourage the Court to adopt a much more capacious definition of "distribution." They argue that the Supreme Court has held that the "terms 'distribution' and 'publication' . . . [are] synonymous in the Copyright Act." They further note, correctly, that the statutory definition of publication can include offers to distribute. *See* 17 U.S.C. § 101. And sharing music files on a peer-to-peer network does, at least arguably, constitute an offer to distribute them. . . .

To the contrary, even a cursory examination of the statute suggests that the terms are not synonymous. "Distribution" is undefined in the copyright statutes. "Publication," however, is defined, and incorporates "distribution" as part of its definition:

> 'Publication' is the distribution of copies or phonorecords of a work to the public by sale or other transfer of ownership, or by rental, lease, or lending. The offering to distribute copies or phonorecords to a group of persons for purposes of further distribution, public performance, or public display, constitutes publication. A public performance or display of a work does not of itself constitute publication.

17 U.S.C. § 101. By the plain meaning of the statute, all "distributions . . . to the public" are publications. But not all publications are distributions to the public —

the statute explicitly creates an additional category of publications that are not themselves distributions. For example, if [an] author offers to sell [her] manuscript to a publishing house "for purposes of further distribution," but does not actually do so, that is a publication but not a distribution.

Plainly, "publication" and "distribution" are not identical. And Congress' decision to use the latter term when defining the copyright holder's rights in 17 U.S.C. § 106(3) must be given consequence. In this context, that means that the defendants cannot be liable for violating the plaintiffs' distribution right unless a "distribution" actually occurred. . . .

[The court then holds that the plaintiffs provided sufficient evidence to support the inference that files were actually downloaded from defendants' computers. Therefore, plaintiffs met their burden to state a claim for infringement of the distribution right.]

b. *Whether the Distribution Right Is Limited to Physical, Tangible Objects*

Next, the movants and the EFF contend that the distribution right under 17 U.S.C. § 106(3) is limited to physical, tangible objects. By its terms, the distribution right only extends to distributions of "phonorecords of the copyrighted work to the public by sale or other transfer of ownership, or by rental, lease or lending." In turn, 17 U.S.C. § 101 defined "phonorecords" as "material objects in which sounds . . . are fixed." The movants and the EFF focus on the phrase "material object," as well as the meaning of "sale or other transfer," and conclude that purely electronic file sharing does not fall within the scope of the [distribution] right. . . .

The movants' argument is sweeping, carrying substantial implications for a great deal of internet commerce — any involving computer-to-computer electronic transfers of information. Indeed, this case is an exemplar. The plaintiffs have not alleged a physical distribution. To the contrary, it is clear that their harm comes from the purely electronic copying of music files. After carefully considering the parties' and the EFF's arguments, the Court concludes that § 106(3) confers on copyright owners the right to control purely electronic distributions of their work. . . .

Before squarely addressing the parties' arguments, however, the Court briefly revisits an important foundational issue — whether the electronic files at issue here can constitute "material objects" within the meaning of the copyright statutes. Doing so will help the Court explain the scope of the distribution right and frame the application of the Copyright Act to an electronic world.

(1) *Electronic Files Are Material Objects*

Understanding Congress' use of "material object" requires returning to a fundamental principle of the Copyright Act of 1976. . . . Congress drew "a fundamental distinction between the 'original work' which is the product of 'authorship' and the multitude of material objects in which it can be embodied. Thus, in the sense of the [Copyright Act], a 'book' is not a work of authorship, but is a particular kind of 'copy.' " House Report at 53. . . .

. . . [A]ny object in which a sound recording can be fixed is a "material object." That includes the electronic files at issue here. When a user on a peer-to-peer network downloads a song from another user, he receives into his computer a digital sequence representing the sound recording. That sequence is magnetically encoded on a segment of his hard disk (or likewise written on other media.) With the right hardware and software, the downloader can use the magnetic sequence to reproduce the sound recording. The electronic file (or, perhaps more accurately, the appropriate segment of the hard disk) is therefore a "phonorecord" within the meaning of the statute. *See also New York Times Co. v. Tasini*, 533 U.S. 483, 490-91 (2001) (appearing to assume that electronic-only distributions constitute material objects). . . .

With that background, the Court turns to the movants' and the EFF's arguments.

(2) *The Transmission of an Electronic File Constitutes a "Distribution" Within the Meaning of § 106(3)*

The movants and the EFF present two reasons why the Court should decline to find that purely electronic transmissions are a violation of the distribution right. First, they note that the distribution right is limited to "phonorecords of the copyrighted work," 17 U.S.C. § 106(3), and that part of the definition of "phonorecords" is that they are "material objects," *id.* § 101. They focus on the phrase "material objects" to suggest that a copyright owner's distribution right only extends to "tangible" objects. Because there was no exchange of tangible objects in this case — no "hand-to-hand" exchange of physical things — they argue that the plaintiffs' distribution right was not infringed by the defendants' actions.

The movants' second argument focuses on a different phrase in § 106(3): "distribution" is limited to exchanges "by sale or other transfer of ownership, or by rental, lease, or lending." They note, correctly, that an electronic download does not divest the sending computer of its file, and therefore does not implicate any ownership rights over the sound file held by the transferor. Therefore, they conclude, an electronic file does not fit within the defined limits of the distribution right.

. . . Electronic transfers generally involve the reading of data at point A and the replication of that data at point B. Whenever that is true, one person might be stationed at point A and another at point B, obviating the need for a "hand-to-hand" transfer. Similarly, because the data at point A is not necessarily destroyed by the process of reading it, the person at point A might retain ownership over the original, forestalling the need for a "sale or other transfer of ownership," as stated in § 106(3).

. . . But the "point A-to-point B" characterization is no less apt for an older technology, such as a fax transfer over a phone line. And it also applies to cases in which point A and point B are very close together — even in the same room.[24] The

---

[24] Suppose someone has a copy of a copyrighted poem on a single sheet of paper. He announces, "I'm going to be at the copy machine with the poem pressing the 'Copy' button, but I'm not going to touch the

movants' argument thus pivots on the *nature* of the transfer, in which the copyrighted work is read by a machine, translated into data, transmitted (in data form), and re-translated elsewhere.

After carefully considering the parties' and the EFF's arguments, the Court concludes that 17 U.S.C. § 106(3) does reach this kind of transaction. First, while the statute requires that distribution be of "material objects," there is no reason to limit "distribution" to processes in which a material object exists throughout the entire transaction — as opposed to a transaction in which a material object is created elsewhere at its finish. Second, while the statute addresses ownership, it is the newly minted ownership rights held by the transferee that concern it, not whether the transferor gives up his own. . . .

Read contextually, it is clear that this right was intended to allow the author to control the rate and terms at which copies or phonorecords of the work become available to the public. . . .

An electronic file transfer is plainly within the sort of transaction that § 106(3) was intended to reach. Indeed, electronic transfers comprise a growing part of the legitimate market for copyrighted sound recordings.[26] What matters in the marketplace is not whether a material object "changes hands," but whether, when the transaction is completed, the distributee has a material object. The Court therefore concludes that electronic file transfers fit within the definition of "distribution" of a phonorecord.

For similar reasons, the Court concludes that an electronic file transfer can constitute a "transfer of ownership" as that term is used in § 106(3). As noted above, Congress wrote § 106(3) to reach the "unauthorized public distribution of copies or phonorecords that were unlawfully made." House Report at 62. That certainly includes situations where, as here, an "original copy" is read at point A and duplicated elsewhere at point B. Since the focus of § 106(3) is the ability of the author to control the market, it is concerned with the ability of a transferor to create ownership in someone else — not the transferor's ability simultaneously to retain his own ownership.

This conclusion is supported by a comparison to the "first sale" doctrine, codified at 17 U.S.C. § 109. The "first sale" doctrine provides that once an author has released an authorized copy or phonorecord of her work, she has relinquished all control over that particular copy or phonorecord. *See id.* § 109(a); House Report at 79-80. The person who bought the copy — the "secondary" purchaser — may sell it to whomever she pleases, and at the terms she directs. The market implications are clear. The author controls the volume of copies entering the market, but once there, he has no right to control their secondary and successive redistribution. . . .

---

new copies that come out in the tray." If another person takes one of the new copies, no hand-to-hand transfer of a tangible object has occurred, and the person who presses the copy button has not been divested of ownership in his original.

[26] It is perhaps in recognition of this fact of internet-era life — and in recognition of the fact that copyrighted material can be "distributed" electronically — that Congress has made available compulsory licenses "to distribute [phonorecords] to the public for private use, including by means of a digital phonorecord delivery." 17 U.S.C. § 115.

Conversely, where ownership is created through an illegal copy, the first sale doctrine does not provide a defense to a distribution suit. *See Quality King Distrib., Inc. v. L'anza Research Int'l, Inc.*, 523 U.S. 135, 148 (1998). The distinction makes sense: where ownership is created through an illegal copy, the copyright holder has never had the chance to exercise his market rights over the copy. That is precisely the situation here.

2. *Whether the Plaintiffs Have Adduced Prima Facie Evidence of Infringement*

The plaintiffs have satisfied their burden for a prima facie case. As noted above, merely exposing music files to the internet is not copyright infringement. The defendants may still . . . contest the nature of the files, or present affirmative evidence rebutting the statistical inference that downloads occurred. But these are substantive defenses for a later stage. Plaintiffs need not prove knowledge or intent in order to make out a prima facie case of infringement. *See Feist*, 499 U.S. at 361. . . . As noted above, [plaintiffs] are not required to win their case in order to serve the defendants with process. . . .

[The court granted the motion to quash on other grounds but allowed the plaintiffs to serve a modified subpoena.]

NOTES AND QUESTIONS

(1)   Section 106(3) contemplates a "book model" of distribution, in which a work is first fixed in tangible "copies" or "phonorecords" and those copies or phonorecords are then distributed to the public. On the Internet, however, distribution occurs in the opposite order: A work is first transmitted to the public in the form of intangible digital information, and it is then fixed (if at all) on the receiving end. The economic effect is the same as a traditional distribution, *i.e.*, copies or phonorecords of the work end up in the hands of the public. One of the issues in *London-Sire Records* is whether such electronic dissemination of a work should be considered a "distribution."

As the court notes, both "copies" and "phonorecords" are defined as "material objects" in which a work is fixed. What is the "material object" in *London-Sire Records*? The court asserts that "material object" does *not* mean "a tangible object with a certain heft." Why, then, does the statute use the phrase "fixed in any *tangible* medium of expression" (emphasis added)? The definitions of "literary works" and "sound recordings" list several examples of "material objects" in which such works can be fixed, including "tapes" and "disks." Thus, as the court later concludes, it seems that the "phonorecord" is not the electronic file *per se*, but "perhaps more accurately, the appropriate segment of the hard disk" in which the electronic file (the "sound recording") is fixed.

(2)   Closely related to the identification of the "material object" is the argument that no material object has changed hands, and therefore, there has been no "sale or other transfer of ownership" nor any "rental, lease, or lending." The argument suggests that the reproduction and distribution rights are mutually exclusive. In the course of a digital transmission, either a new copy has been made (a reproduction)

or an existing copy has been transferred from one person to another (a distribution). The argument is clever, relying on the fact that the alleged "distributor" retains ownership of his or her original electronic file and hard disk, and therefore there has been no "transfer of ownership" or possession. In other words, read literally, an electronic transfer may be a distribution of the "work" (an intangible), but it is not a distribution of a "copy" or "phonorecord" (a "material object") of the work. Instead, the transaction may be more properly characterized as a "reproduction" (by the downloader) instead of a "distribution" (by the defendants).

It is entirely possible that, in 1976, Congress intended such a result. At the time, people commonly used "material objects" such as tapes or removable "floppy" disks to transfer information from one computer to another. Recognizing (but disagreeing with) the argument, the 1995 "White Paper" on *Intellectual Property and the National Information Infrastructure* recommended, at p. 213, "that the Copyright Act be amended to expressly recognize that copies or phonorecords of works can be distributed to the public by transmission, and that such transmissions fall within the exclusive distribution right of the copyright owner." Legislation to that effect failed in the 104th Congress; however, as the court notes (in fn. 26), Congress did amend the § 115 compulsory license to include the right "to distribute . . . a phonorecord of a nondramatic musical work by means of a digital transmission which constitutes a digital phonorecord delivery." Moreover, the legislative history of the 1998 Digital Millennium Copyright Act is replete with references making clear the shared assumption involved that digital transmission to the public *does* constitute "distribution" within the meaning of § 106(3).

(3) But why does it matter whether an electronic transmission is or is not a "distribution"? Even if we characterize the transaction as a "reproduction" by the downloader, wouldn't the defendant still be contributorily liable? In order to understand why the parties are fighting so hard over what appears to be mere semantics, one must consider the litigation strategy of the parties.

Beginning in 2003, the RIAA filed literally thousands of suits against individuals who made copyrighted sound recordings available for downloading on peer-to-peer networks. In order to make such suits economically viable, the RIAA needed a legal theory that could be successful on summary judgment, without extended legal proceedings. A case for "contributory infringement" not only requires proof of direct infringement (as the court notes), but it also requires knowledge of the infringement. *See* § 9.01 below. Knowledge is a question of fact that rarely can be resolved on summary judgment. Moreover, the downloader might raise the question of whether the "fair use" doctrine includes personal use (discussed in Chapter 10). Similarly, pursuing the file-sharing defendant for unlawful "reproduction" (in posting the electronic file in the first place) might involve a claim that the copy was lawfully acquired, or that it was a "fair use" to "rip" a lawfully acquired CD. By contrast, a claim of direct infringement (for violating the distribution right) does not require any showing of knowledge and does not raise the question of personal use.

(4) Litigation strategy also explains the principal issue in the case: Namely, whether merely making a copyrighted work available for others to download violates the distribution right. The evidence of MediaSentry is sufficient to establish

that the defendants made copyrighted works available; but proving that anyone actually downloaded one of the files is more problematic.

The plaintiff's first argument on this issue is that the phrase "to do *and to authorize*" (emphasis added) in § 106 includes offers to distribute. The court follows the House Report in holding that this language was intended to refer to contributory infringement, which requires proof of a direct infringement.

(5) The plaintiff's second argument is based on *Hotaling*, in which the Fourth Circuit held 2-1 that making an unauthorized copy available to patrons of a library violated the distribution right, even absent any evidence that anyone actually had used the copy. What arguments can you make to support this interpretation of the statute? Why does the *London-Sire Records* court disagree? A majority of courts and commentators have expressly disagreed with *Hotaling* on this point. *See, e.g., Atlantic Recording Corp. v. Howell*, 554 F. Supp. 2d 976, 981 (D. Ariz. 2008) (citing *inter alia* the Nimmer, Patry, and Goldstein treatises); *Capitol Records, Inc. v. Thomas*, 579 F. Supp. 2d 1210, 1223 (D. Minn. 2008); *see also Capitol Records, Inc. v. Thomas-Rasset*, 692 F.3d 899 (8th Cir. 2012) (declining to address the issue as moot); *National Car Rental Systems, Inc. v. Computer Associates Int'l, Inc.*, 991 F.2d 426, 434 (8th Cir. 1993) (§ 106(3) "requires an actual distribution of either copies or phonorecords") (quoting Nimmer).

(6) The plaintiff's third argument is that "distribution" is synonymous with "publication," and that the definition of "publication" in § 101 includes "offering to distribute copies or phonorecords to a group of persons *for purposes of* further distribution, public performance, or public display" (emphasis added). The first sentence of § 101 defines "publication" as "the distribution of copies or phonorecords to the public" by the same means specified in § 106(3). Thus, a public distribution of copies is a publication. But is the converse true?

Some courts, relying on the House Report's reference to "the exclusive right of publication," have held that Congress intended the terms "publication" and "distribution" to be synonymous. *See, e.g., Elektra Entertainment Group, Inc. v. Barker*, 551 F. Supp. 2d 234, 241-42 (S.D.N.Y. 2008). But most courts have agreed with *London-Sire Records* that the "plain language" of § 101 distinguishes between "publication" (which includes some offers to distribute) and "distribution" (meaning actual distribution). *See Thomas*, 579 F. Supp. 2d at 1219-20; *Howell*, 554 F. Supp. 2d at 984-85.

(7) Yet another argument made in similar cases is that the 1996 WIPO treaties require that signatory nations prohibit the unauthorized "making available to the public" of copyrighted works. WIPO Copyright Treaty Art. 6(1); WPPT Art. 12(1). In *Thomas*, the RIAA argued that requiring "actual distribution" would cause the United States to violate its treaty obligations. Instead, it urged the court to adopt the principle that "an Act of Congress ought never to be construed to violate the law of nations if any other possible construction remains." *Murray v. Schooner Charming Betsy*, 6 U.S. (2 Cranch) 64, 118 (1804). The court, however, rejected the argument, on the ground that the WIPO treaties are not self-executing and were contradicted by "unambiguous" domestic law. 579 F. Supp. 2d at 1225-26.

(8)   Finally, consider the evidentiary issue: How does one prove that an "actual distribution" occurred? Some courts have allowed the copy downloaded by Media-Sentry to serve as direct evidence of "actual distribution." *See, e.g., Thomas*, 579 F. Supp. 2d at 1215-16; *Howell*, 554 F. Supp. 2d at 985; *see also Olan Mills, Inc. v. Linn Photo Co.*, 23 F.3d 1345, 1348 (8th Cir. 1994). Why does the court in *London-Sire Records* express doubt about this theory? What circumstantial evidence does the court point to instead? Why might the RIAA be dissatisfied with this theory? Other courts have agreed with *London-Sire Records* that circumstantial evidence is sufficient. *See Thomas*, 579 F. Supp. 2d at 1225.

(9)   Unlike the reproduction and adaptation rights, the statutory language in § 106(3) refers to the distribution of copies "to the public." The *London-Sire* court avoids tackling head-on the meaning of "public" in the § 106(3) distribution right context. How would you do so? Consider two possibilities. First, one might borrow meaning for "to the public" from the Act's definition of the seemingly similar term "publicly," defined in § 101 and applied in §§ 106(4), (5), and (6) to the copyright holder's performance, display, and (in the instance of sound recordings) digital audio transmission rights. Second, one might borrow the meaning given the term "publication" at common law — that is, a distribution "to the public" could be accomplished through distribution to "only one member of the public." *See Ford Motor Co. v. Summit Motor Products, Inc.*, 930 F.2d 277, 299-300 (3d Cir. 1991). In your opinion, which formulation constitutes the more appropriate interpretation of "to the public" in the § 106(3) context? Courts and commentators have criticized *Ford* on this point. *See, e.g., Cartoon Network L.P. v. CSC Holdings, Inc.*, 536 F.3d 121, 139 (2d Cir. 2008) (citing 2 NIMMER ON COPYRIGHT, § 8.11[A] (2008)).

The 1995 "White Paper" states that "transmission of a copyrighted work from one person to another in a private e-mail message would not constitute a distribution to the public" (p. 215). Nonetheless, such a transmission likely violates the reproduction right of § 106(1), unless it can be characterized as a "fair use." For more on "personal use" as a fair use, see § 10.03 below.

The First-Sale Doctrine

(10)   Under the so-called first-sale doctrine, codified in § 109(a) of the 1976 Act, the owner of the copyright in a work is entitled to control the first public distribution of particular copies or phonorecords of the work, but thereafter "the owner of [the particular] copy or phonorecord . . . is entitled, without authority of the copyright owner, to sell or otherwise dispose of the possession of that copy or phonorecord." The first-sale doctrine thus attempts to strike a balance between assuring a sufficient reward to the copyright owner and permitting unimpeded circulation of copies of the work.

The first-sale doctrine was first established by the Supreme Court in *Bobbs-Merrill Co. v. Straus*, 210 U.S. 339 (1908). In *Bobbs-Merrill*, a book publisher inserted into its books a notice purporting to prohibit resale for less than $1. The Court held that the exclusive right to "vend" a copyrighted work did not include the right to impose conditions on future resale. The doctrine was later codified at § 27 of the 1909 Act, and then in § 109(a) of the 1976 Act.

Under § 109(d), the copyright owner can avoid application of the first-sale doctrine by retaining *title* to the copy or phonorecord, even if possession is transferred by rental, lease, or loan. By contrast, any transfer of ownership, even a gratuitous transfer, brings the doctrine into play. *See UMG Recordings, Inc. v. Augusto*, 628 F.3d 1175 (9th Cir. 2011) (resale of free promotional CDs on eBay was permitted under first-sale doctrine; label on CDs with alleged resale restriction did not create a license). Transfers of copies that imply a shift in ownership (for example, transfer of possession of a film print without time limitation) can qualify. *See United States v. Wise*, 550 F.2d 1180 (9th Cir. 1977). Even involuntary transfers, such as a judicial sale to satisfy creditors, may qualify. *See Platt & Munk Co. v. Republic Graphics, Inc.*, 315 F.2d 847, 854 (2d Cir. 1963); *Bryant v. Gordon*, 483 F. Supp. 2d 605 (N.D. Ill. 2007) (first-sale doctrine applies to copies sold in bankruptcy, where copyright owner had notice and did not object). *But see Denbicare U.S.A., Inc. v. Toys R Us, Inc.*, 84 F.3d 1143, 1150 (9th Cir. 1996) (stating in *dicta* that a bankruptcy trustee's sale of copies without authorization of the copyright owner would be an infringement).

The first-sale doctrine is a limitation on a copyright holder's distribution and display rights only. § 109(a), (c). If the claim is that the owner of the copy or phonorecord has attempted to reproduce or adapt the work, the first-sale doctrine is not implicated (although other rights and limitations may be).

(11) Would anything in the first-sale doctrine, or in copyright law generally, prevent the original owners of copies or phonorecords from imposing supplementary restraints on their distribution after sale by way of contract? Obviously, such restraints are highly desirable in certain circumstances, if they can be enforced. The issue has arisen in the context of software licenses. The second-hand trade in genuine (as distinct from counterfeit) software products is a "big little business," and it is coming under increasing legal fire from major software vendors. Typically, these enterprising resellers invoke the first-sale doctrine, asserting that the firms and individuals from whom they bought their wares were themselves lawful purchasers. The manufacturers respond that the copies in question were never sold, merely "licensed." As evidence, they point to various terms in the "shrink-wrap" agreements that accompany these software products when they are made available by or under the authority of their copyright owners — including the sorts of EULAs ("end user license agreements") with which you are (or should be) familiar.

Different courts have taken dramatically different approaches to sorting out this conundrum. In *Vernor v. Autodesk, Inc.*, 621 F.3d 1102 (9th Cir. 2010), the Ninth Circuit resolved a split among the district courts within the Circuit, holding that "a software user is a licensee rather than an owner of a copy where the copyright owner (1) specifies that the user is granted a license; (2) significantly restricts the user's ability to transfer the software; and (3) imposes notable use restrictions." Because Autodesk's EULA specified that it was only granting a license, prohibited transfer without Autodesk's consent, and prohibited use or transfer outside the Western Hemisphere, the court held that Vernor did not own copies he had purchased and could not resell them under the first-sale doctrine. In so holding, the court rejected an approach that looked to the "economic realities" of the transaction, under which a transfer of permanent possession of a copy in exchange for a single payment is deemed to be a "sale," notwithstanding the existence of a EULA.

See, e.g., Softman Products Co. v. Adobe Systems, Inc., 171 F. Supp. 2d 1075 (C.D. Cal. 2001); *cf. Krause v. Titleserv, Inc.*, 402 F.3d 119, 124 (2d Cir. 2005) ("absence of formal title may be outweighed by evidence that the possessor of the copy enjoys sufficiently broad rights over it to be sensibly considered its owner"). Is *Vernor* consistent with the Supreme Court's decision in *Bobbs-Merrill?* We will consider the legal status of "shrink-wrap" and "click-through" licenses further in Chapter 11.

(12) Note that the first-sale doctrine applies only to copies that are "lawfully made under this title," and that according to the House Report, "the burden of proving whether a particular copy was lawfully made or acquired should rest on the defendant." May a copy that was *not* lawfully made ever be resold without violating the distribution right? In *Christopher Phelps & Assoc. v. Galloway*, 477 F.3d 128 (4th Cir. 2007), the plaintiff sought an injunction against the future lease or sale of a house found to be infringing. The Fourth Circuit rejected this request, initially holding that once a judgment for damages was satisfied, the house "became a lawfully made copy" for purposes of the first-sale doctrine. On rehearing, however, the court removed this language, holding instead that an injunction should not issue because it would encumber real property. The court also drew an analogy to the law of conversion, in which satisfaction of a judgment for damages gives the defendant good legal title. 492 F.3d 532 (4th Cir. 2007). Should this holding be extended to infringing copies of other copyrighted works? Or is there something special about architectural works that justifies a departure from the "plain language" of the statute?

(13) How does the first-sale doctrine apply to electronic distribution? Suppose you have lawfully purchased an electronic file containing a copyrighted work and installed it on a device (such as an iPod or a Kindle). Can you transfer the possession of that file to someone else without giving them the device itself? According to the 1995 White Paper, at p. 92, the answer is "no":

> [T]he first sale doctrine limits only the copyright owner's distribution right; it in no way affects the reproduction right. Thus, the first sale doctrine does not allow the transmission of a copy of a work (through a computer network, for instance), because, under current technology the transmitter retains the original copy of the work while the recipient of the transmission obtains a reproduction of the original copy (*i.e.*, a *new* copy), rather than the copy owned by the transmitter.

This reasoning, of course, would appear to contradict the conclusion that electronic transmission is a distribution of copies or phonorecords (instead of, or in addition to, a reproduction). But assuming, for the moment, that this analysis is correct, doesn't it raise the question of whether there *should* be a digital equivalent to the first-sale doctrine? A bill introduced in the 105th Congress proposed amending § 109 to allow such a transmission if the sender "erases or destroys his or her copy or phonorecord at substantially the same time." Would such a provision make good policy sense? How easy (or difficult) would it be to enforce? Could you draft a better "digital equivalent" to the first-sale doctrine?

Alternatively, can the fair-use doctrine effectively substitute for the first-sale doctrine in the digital environment? In 2011, a website called ReDigi, billing itself as "the first pre-owned digital marketplace," chose to test this proposition. At the time this book went to press, the site allows users to store music files that were lawfully purchased and downloaded on ReDigi's servers, and then to resell those music files by changing the ownership data associated with the file, rather than by reproducing it. One large recording company promptly sued, seeking a preliminary injunction. The district court denied the motion for lack of irreparable harm, despite finding a likelihood of success on the merits. *See Capitol Records LLC v. ReDigi, Inc.*, No. 12-cv-00095 (S.D.N.Y., Feb. 6, 2012).

(14)   The first-sale doctrine constitutes a significant limitation on a copyright owner's ability to control certain secondary markets for copies of the work. And it applies to all varieties of copyrightable subject matter. As one might expect, exceptions to the doctrine have been created by Congress to meet a few special meritorious needs — and other such needs, according to their proponents, remain to be met. The following notes examine a few of the more interesting problems.

(15)   *The Record Rental Amendment Act of 1984.* Enacted at the behest of the music industry, this legislation added § 109(b) (and amended § 115). It was designed to curtail the burgeoning record rental business, in which, after purchasing its own phonorecord of a copyrighted work and thereby triggering the first-sale doctrine, a store would rent that phonorecord to a customer (who often purchased a blank audio tape at the same time) for the mutually understood purpose of unauthorized duplication. Congress concluded that this process functioned as "a direct displacement of a sale." S. Rep. No. 98-162, at 2 (1983). The 1984 legislation prohibits the rental, lease, or loan of phonorecords for commercial gain without the consent of the copyright owners of both the sound recording and the musical composition that it embodies. Note that this legislation applies only to sound recordings of musical works, and not to sound recordings of literary works, *see Brilliance Audio, Inc. v. Haights Cross Comms., Inc.*, 474 F.3d 365 (6th Cir. 2007), nor to motion pictures or other audiovisual works.

(16)   *The Computer Software Rental Amendments Act of 1990.* This legislation extended § 109(b) to prohibit the rental of computer software for direct or indirect commercial advantage. § 109(b)(1)(A). These restrictions are not absolute. For example, the amendments do not apply to the lending of a copy by a nonprofit library for nonprofit purposes, provided that the library has affixed an appropriate copyright warning. § 109(b)(2)(A). In addition, § 109(b) exempts "a computer program which is embodied in a machine or product and cannot be copied during the ordinary operation or use of the machine or product," as well as "a computer program embodied in or used in conjunction with a limited purpose computer that is designed for playing video games and may be designed for other purposes." § 109(b)(1)(B). Moreover, case law holds that the work must be registered as a computer program, and not in some other category, such as a "work of visual art." *See Action Tapes, Inc. v. Mattson*, 462 F.3d 1010 (8th Cir. 2006). Violations of § 109(b) constitute copyright infringement, but are not subject to criminal liability. § 109(b)(4).

(17)   *Restored copyrights and the first-sale doctrine.* The Uruguay Round Agreements Act ("URRA," discussed in Chapter 5) automatically restored copyright in certain foreign works that had entered the public domain in the United States. These restored copyrights will endure for the remainder of the term of

copyright as if they had not entered the public domain. Once copyright is restored in these works, it is illegal for third parties to make or distribute copies or phonorecords of the works.

But what about copies or phonorecords that were made before restoration? As amended by the URAA, § 109(a) provides that copies or phonorecords of restored works made or manufactured before the date of restoration — or, in the case of reliance parties, before notice — may be disposed of for "direct or indirect commercial advantage" *only* during the one-year sell-off period allowed for reliance parties.

(18) *Resale royalty legislation.* Not all claimants to relief from the first-sale doctrine seek a ban on rentals of copies of their works. Consider the situation of fine artists. A painter may sell a work for a moderate amount, only to see it resold later for many times the original price. The painter doesn't necessarily wish to see such resale barred, but he or she would like a share of the increase in value of the work (or the total sales price). This concept — a right allowing artists to benefit financially each time the original embodiments of their works pass into another purchaser's hands — is called the *"droit de suite,"* and to date it has been recognized primarily in Europe. In 2001, the European Union harmonized *droit de suite* laws, after much hesitation by the United Kingdom. *See* Directive 2001/84/EC of the European Parliament and of the Council of 27 September 2001 on the resale right for the benefit of the author of an original work of art.

There has been some pressure for recognition of the *droit de suite* in the United States, especially from organizations representing visual artists. In 1992, however, a report of the Register of Copyrights, *Droit de Suite: The Artist's Resale Royalty*, concluded that the right may not be appropriate as an element of U.S. copyright law, because it is "not clear that [resale] is actually a new exploitation of the work" and because the "concept fits awkwardly within a free market economy." The report also noted the argument that "the royalty benefits only successful, well-established artists, and that most artists, who lack a resale market, will suffer in the primary market as prices are depressed, anticipating the future royalty payment." What do you think of these grounds for rejecting a federal right to resale royalties?

(19) One state, California, does recognize the *droit de suite*. The California Resale Royalties Act ("CRRA"), enacted in 1976 and amended in 1982, requires payment upon the resale of "a work of fine art," defined as "an original painting, sculpture, or drawing or an original work of art in glass." Either the seller must be a resident of California at the time of the resale, or the resale must take place in California. Upon resale, the artist (or his/her successors for 20 years after the artist's death) is entitled to be paid by the seller or the seller's agent a royalty equal to five percent of the gross resale price (unless that price is under $1,000 or less than the price previously paid by the seller). If payment is not made, the artist may bring an action for damages within three years of the date of resale, or one year after discovery of the resale, whichever is later. An artist's royalty rights are not transferable and may not be waived except "by a contract in writing providing for an amount in excess of five percent of the amount of such sale." Cal. Civ. Code § 986 (2009). Practically speaking, what would you expect the effect of the CRRA to be on the art market? On the artists whom the Act seeks to benefit?

Is the CRRA preempted by the Copyright Act, on the ground that it directly interferes with the purchaser's § 109 right to distribute lawfully purchased copies of a work? *See Morseburg v. Balyon*, 621 F.2d 972 (9th Cir. 1980) (holding the CRRA was not preempted under the 1909 Act, on the doubtful theory that California merely supplemented the federal statute by providing an additional right). More recently, a District Court held that the CRRA violated the dormant Commerce Clause, because it attempted to regulate transactions taking place wholly outside the state. *See Estate of Graham v. Sotheby's, Inc.*, 860 F. Supp. 2d 1117 (C.D. Cal. 2012). For more details, see Chapter 11 below.

(20)   *The "public-lending right."* Another exception to the first-sale doctrine, called the "public-lending right," is found in the United Kingdom, Germany, Netherlands, the Scandinavian countries, and Australia. The public-lending right entitles an author of a book to royalties any time a book is borrowed from a public library. The public-lending right has its ardent supporters in the United States but never has come close to adoption here. Do writers of books deserve any less compensation than record or software producers — or, for that matter, fine artists? What would be the pros and cons of creating a public-lending right?

[C]   Import and Export Rights

In today's global marketplace, "parallel importation" of so-called "gray market" goods raises important policy questions. The gray market arises due to various economic factors, particularly fluctuations in currency exchange rates around the world. These fluctuations result in price differentials which may exceed tariff, freight and related importation costs. The differentials often are great enough to permit entrepreneurs to purchase goods outside the United States, import them, and sell them at less than the current domestic price and still turn a profit. Gray market importation has been estimated at various times at several billion dollars annually.

Gray market goods are a curse to authorized domestic distributors. Gray marketeers typically incur lower overhead costs than competing authorized distributors, because they take a free ride on the advertising provided by the domestic suppliers and rarely service the warranties accompanying the goods. On the other hand, consumer advocates maintain that the public should be able to buy the lower-priced authentic goods, that in many cases the goods do not have warranties already, and that consumers should have the option of foregoing warranty protection in exchange for a lower purchase price, should they so choose.

Clearly, these matters are not classically the province of copyright law, but rather of the related body of trademark law. The problem is that trademark law has provided uncertain protection against the gray market. *See* Leaffer, *The Gray Market in International Intellectual Property Law*, *in* 1 INTERNATIONAL INTELLECTUAL PROPERTY LAW AND POLICY (H. Hansen ed., 1996). As a result, owners of brand name goods faced with gray market problems sometimes turn to copyright law for relief.

Section 602(a)(1) of the Copyright Act provides that the unauthorized "importation into the United States . . . of copies or phonorecords of a work that have been acquired outside the United States, is an infringement of the exclusive right to distribute copies or phonorecords under section 106." If the copies would have been infringing "if this title had been applicable," then their importation is prohibited under § 602(b). If the copies were unlawfully made, they can be (and often are) seized at the border by U.S. Customs. Where the copies or phonorecords were lawfully made, however, the Customs Service is not authorized to seize the goods.

In 2008, § 602(a)(2) was added, providing:

> Importation into the United States or exportation from the United States, without the authority of the owner of copyright under this title, of copies or phonorecords, the making of which either constituted an infringement of copyright, or which would have constituted an infringement of copyright if this title had been applicable, is an infringement of the exclusive right to distribute copies or phonorecords under section 106, actionable under sections 501 and 506.

The provisions on importation in § 602(a)(2) are redundant, because former § 602(a) (now § 602(a)(1)) already prohibited importation. What is new is infringement by exportation, and the express reference to criminal penalties for unauthorized importation and exportation.

There are three narrow statutory exceptions: copies or phonorecords imported or exported by or for the use of the U.S. Government or the government of any state or political subdivision (except for audiovisual works or works for use in schools); a single copy or phonorecord of a work imported or exported in a person's personal baggage for private use; and no more than five copies or phonorecords of a work (or one copy of an audiovisual work for archival purposes only) imported (but not exported) by a scholarly, educational, or religious organization for library lending or archival purposes.

On its face, § 602(a)(1) would appear to clash with the first-sale doctrine, which permits the resale of "lawfully made" copies and phonorecords. The issue is whether § 602(a) creates an affirmative right to bar all unauthorized importation, or whether § 109(a) limits the reach of § 602(a), thus permitting the resale of at least some "lawfully made" imported copies. Proponents of the former view point to § 501, which appears to treat unauthorized importation in violation of § 602 separately from violations of the exclusive rights under §§ 106-122. Proponents of the latter view point out that § 602(a), by its own terms, defines unauthorized importation as an infringement of the copyright owner's public distribution right under § 106. Section 106, in turn, is limited by §§ 107-122, and § 109 explicitly limits § 106(3), meaning that § 109 must provide a limitation of some sort on § 602(a) as well.

After much conflict in the case law, the Supreme Court confronted the issue of whether goods imported from abroad are subject to the first-sale defense in *Quality King Distributors, Inc. v. L'Anza Research Int'l, Inc.*, 523 U.S. 135 (1998). In *Quality King*, plaintiff L'Anza manufactured hair care products (with copyrighted labels) for sale in the United States and abroad. L'Anza's distributor in the United Kingdom sold the L'Anza products to a distributor in Malta. The products reentered the United States, without L'Anza's permission, and were sold by unauthorized retailers who bought them at discounted prices from Quality King. L'Anza sued Quality King for copyright infringement, asserting that the importation and resale of its products infringed its exclusive rights under the Copyright Act to import and distribute its copyrighted works.

Both the District Court and the Ninth Circuit held that Quality King was liable for infringement, concluding that the import restriction provision in § 602 would be meaningless if the first-sale defense applied. In a unanimous decision, the Supreme Court reversed in favor of the distributors. The Court held that where a product is lawfully manufactured in the United States for export and is subject to a valid first sale, its subsequent reimportation is permissible under § 109 and thus does not fall within the prohibition of § 602(a) (now § 602(a)(1)). The Court accepted the argument that § 602(a) "does not categorically prohibit the unauthorized importation of copyrighted materials," but instead provides "that such importation is an infringement of the exclusive right to distribute copies" under § 106(3). As such, the importation right is limited by §§ 107 through 122 — including § 109(a), the first-sale doctrine.

In response to the argument that this interpretation would render the importation right a nullity, the Court noted that § 109(a) is limited to copies and phonorecords "lawfully made under this title." "Lawfully made" means made either with the permission of the copyright owner or under some exemption, such as the § 115 compulsory license or fair use. "Under this title" must refer to Title 17, because that is the title in which § 602(a) is codified; and, because the Copyright Act generally is not extraterritorial in its application (*see* § 8.04 below), the phrase "lawfully made under this title" must mean goods lawfully manufactured in the United States. On this logic, gray market copies manufactured outside the United States might be lawfully made, either by the copyright owner or a licensee, but they would not be lawfully made under Title 17. Rather, they would be lawfully made under the copyright laws of the other country, and the first-sale doctrine would therefore not limit the importation right for such copies. *See Omega S.A. v. Costco Wholesale Group*, 541 F.3d 982 (9th Cir. 2008), *aff'd by an equally divided Court*, 131 S. Ct. 565 (2010); *see also John Wiley & Sons v. Kirtsaeng*, 654 F.3d 210 (2d Cir. 2011) (questioning this result on policy grounds, but following *Quality King* as binding authority), *cert. granted*, 132 S. Ct. 1905 (2012).

This resolution makes sense, particularly when one compares the phrase "lawfully made under this title" in § 109 with the phrase "if this title had been applicable" in § 602(b) (and in newly enacted § 602(a)(2)). But does that mean that copies lawfully manufactured abroad can *never* be subject to the first-sale doctrine, even if lawfully imported and sold in the United States with the permission of the copyright owner? When faced with this dilemma, most courts have ignored the "plain language" of the statute, suggesting that "§ 109(a) can apply to copies not made in the United States so long as an authorized first sale occurred here." *Omega*, 541 F.3d at 986, citing *Denbicare U.S.A., Inc. v. Toys R Us, Inc.*, 84 F.3d 1143, 1150 (9th Cir. 1996).

The conflict between the plain language of the statute and the property rights of foreign purchasers who wish to resell authorized foreign editions prompted the

Supreme Court to grant *certiorari* in *Costco v. Omega*, despite the negative recommendation of then-Solicitor General Elena Kagan. Kagan recused herself after her appointment to the Court, and the remaining justices split 4-4 on the question of whether copies lawfully manufactured abroad with the authorization of the U.S. copyright owner are subject to the first-sale doctrine. 131 S. Ct. 565 (2010). Although this split decision left the Ninth Circuit's opinion in *Omega* intact, it also created substantial doubt as to whether the prevailing understanding of *Quality King* would survive.

The answer may come as early as 2013. The Supreme Court granted *certiorari* in *Kirtsaeng*, cited above, and oral argument was heard during the Court's October 2012 term. See the casebook's cumulative supplement for the latest update on the outcome.

What effect would you expect the rule in *Quality King* to have on international commerce in copyrighted works? In the short run, authorized distributors may be discouraged from vigorously promoting their products as competition from discounters begins to erode their profit margins. How will manufacturers respond? The alternatives are unappealing. Enforcement of contractual provisions against errant distributors abroad is, to put it mildly, impractical. Raising the price of goods sold overseas would render them uncompetitive in the foreign market. In the long run, U.S. copyright owners who consider it necessary to maintain wide price disparities between their domestic and international markets may decide to manufacture copies for the export market abroad, resulting in a loss of U.S. manufacturing jobs.

Is there an appropriate solution to this complex of problems? If so, does it lie in copyright law? Copyrighted works comprise only a small portion of all imported goods. Does it make sense to try to use copyrighted labels to try to control the international movement of goods, as in *Quality King*? Doesn't that suggest that the proper resolution of gray market problems, whatever that solution may be, should lie in other bodies of law?

The issue of parallel importation and the first-sale doctrine (generally known elsewhere as the doctrine of "exhaustion") has arisen in other countries as well. Some countries provide that exhaustion applies only to copies sold by the copyright owner in the domestic market, thereby prohibiting parallel imports without the consent of the copyright owner. Some countries provide for "international exhaustion," meaning that a sale anywhere in the world exhausts the copyright owner's distribution right, opening the door to unlimited parallel imports. In the European Union, the European Court of Justice has held that the EEC Treaty requires a rule of community-wide exhaustion, so that copies or phonorecords lawfully sold in any EU country can be imported and resold in any other EU country, but goods from other countries may be imported only with the copyright owner's consent. *See Deutsche Grammophon v. Metro*, Case No. 78/70, 1971 E.C.R. 487 (E.C.J. 1971). Because the nations of the world were unable to reconcile these competing approaches, Art. 6 of the TRIPS Agreement specifically provides that "nothing in this Agreement shall be used to address the issue of the exhaustion of intellectual property rights." Similar provisions appear in the WIPO Copyright Treaty and the WIPO Performances and Phonograms Treaty.

§ 7.05 THE PUBLIC PERFORMANCE RIGHT

Section 106(4) provides that, in the case of literary, musical, and dramatic works, pantomimes and choreographic works, and motion pictures and other audiovisual works, the copyright owner has the exclusive right "to perform the copyrighted work publicly." In this section, we will examine what it means to "perform" a work and to do so "publicly." We will discuss, as well, the numerous limitations placed on the performance right.

In order to understand the performance right provisions of the 1976 Act, one needs to know a bit about the performance right under the 1909 Act. That statute gave the copyright owner the right to perform copyrighted works "publicly for profit." In deciding what performances were "for profit," the courts construed that terminology broadly when the performance took place in a commercial setting. In *Herbert v. Shanley Co.*, 242 U.S. 591 (1917), for example, the Supreme Court found that a performance of a copyrighted musical composition in a restaurant or hotel, even without the imposition of any direct charge for the music, was a "for profit" performance: "If music did not pay, it would be given up. If it pays, it pays out of the public's pocket. Whether it pays or not, the purpose of employing it is profit, and that is enough." *Id.* at 594 (per Justice Holmes). Performances given by a church or school, on the other hand, typically were *not* construed to be "for profit." Not surprisingly, the line between the two types of performances proved difficult to draw.

The 1976 Act abrogated the "for profit" limitation, providing simply that the copyright owner has the exclusive right to do or authorize *all* "public" performance of the work, whether or not for profit. The Act did, however, retain the principle that certain nonprofit organizations should have free access to copyrighted works without authorization of the copyright owner — not on the basis of a blanket exemption as under the 1909 Act, but instead only in a limited number of circumstances specified in § 110. The following excerpt from the House Report provides further insight into the meaning and rationale of the 1976 Act approach.

[A] Public Performances

[1] Introduction

Statutory References
1976 Act: §§ 101 ("perform," "publicly"), 106(4), 109(e), 110, 116, 118
1909 Act: § 1(c), (d), and (e)

Legislative History

H.R. Rep. No. 94-1476 at 62-64,
reprinted in 1976 U.S.C.C.A.N. 5659, 5676-78

SECTION 106. EXCLUSIVE RIGHTS IN COPYRIGHTED WORKS[1]

Rights of public performance and display

Performing rights and the "for profit" limitation. — The right of public performance under section 106(4) extends to "literary, musical, dramatic, and choreographic works, pantomimes, and motion pictures and other audiovisual works . . ." and, unlike the equivalent provisions now in effect, is not limited by any "for profit" requirement. The approach of the bill . . . is first to state the public performance right in broad terms, and then to provide specific exemptions for educational and other nonprofit uses.

This approach is more reasonable than the outright exemption of the 1909 statute. The line between commercial and "nonprofit" organizations is increasingly difficult to draw. Many "nonprofit" organizations are highly subsidized and capable of paying royalties, and the widespread public exploitation of copyrighted works by public broadcasters and other noncommercial organizations is likely to grow. In addition to these trends, it is worth noting that performances and displays are continuing to supplant markets for printed copies and that in the future a broad "not for profit" exemption could not only hurt authors but could dry up their incentive to write. . . .

Definitions

Under the definitions of "perform," "display," "publicly," and "transmit" in section 101, the concepts of public performance and public display cover not only the initial rendition or showing, but also any further act by which that rendition or showing is transmitted or communicated to the public. Thus, for example: a singer is performing when he or she sings a song; a broadcasting network is performing when it transmits his or her performance (whether simultaneously or from records); a local broadcaster is performing when it transmits the network broadcast; a cable television system is performing when it retransmits the broadcast to its subscribers; and any individual is performing whenever he or she plays a phonorecord embodying the performance or communicates the performance by turning on a receiving set. Although any act by which the initial performance or display is transmitted, repeated, or made to recur would itself be a "performance" or "display" under the bill, it would not be actionable as an infringement unless it were done "publicly," as defined in section 101. Certain other performances and displays, in addition to those that are "private," are exempted or given qualified copyright control under sections 107 through [122]. . . .

---

[1] The following excerpt from the House Report discusses aspects of the § 106(4) public performance right that are shared by the § 106(5) public display right as well. You will want to refer back to this portion of the legislative history when we consider the latter right in the following section of the casebook. — *Eds.*

Under clause (1) of the definition of "publicly" in section 101, a performance or display is "public" if it takes place "at a place open to the public or at any place where a substantial number of persons outside of a normal circle of a family and its social acquaintances is gathered." One of the principal purposes of the definition was to make clear that, contrary to the decision in *Metro-Goldwyn-Mayer Distributing Corp. v. Wyatt*, 21 C.O. Bull. 203 (D. Md. 1932), performances in "semipublic" places such as clubs, lodges, factories, summer camps, and schools are "public performances" subject to copyright control. The term "a family" in this context would include an individual living alone, so that a gathering confined to the individual's social acquaintances would normally be regarded as private. Routine meetings of businesses and governmental personnel would be excluded because they do not represent the gathering of a "substantial number of persons."

Clause (2) of the definition of "publicly" in section 101 makes clear that the concepts of public performance and public display include not only performances and displays that occur initially in a public place, but also acts that transmit or otherwise communicate a performance or display of the work to the public by means of any device or process. . . .

[Section 110 of the 1976 Act contains a series of exemptions — 11, as of this writing — to the § 106(4) public performance right (and the § 106(5) public display right). These limitations, described in detail in the House Report, are considered selectively in the notes following the next case.]

[2]   Case Law

COLUMBIA PICTURES INDUSTRIES, INC. v. AVECO, INC.
United States Court of Appeals, Third Circuit
800 F.2d 59 (1986)

STAPLETON, CIRCUIT JUDGE:

Plaintiffs, appellees in this action, are producers of motion pictures ("Producers") and bring this copyright infringement action against the defendant, Aveco, Inc. Producers claim that Aveco's business, which includes renting video cassettes of motion pictures in conjunction with rooms in which they may be viewed, violates their exclusive rights under the Copyright Act of 1976. . . .

. . . The district court found that Aveco had infringed on Producers' exclusive rights to publicly perform and authorize public performances of their copyrighted works and so granted their motion for partial summary judgment. . . .

I

Among their other operations, Producers distribute video cassette copies of motion pictures in which they own registered copyrights. They do so knowing that many retail purchasers of these video cassettes, including Aveco, rent them to others for profit. Aveco also makes available private rooms of various sizes in which its customers may view the video cassettes that they have chosen from Aveco's offerings. For example, at one location, . . . Aveco has thirty viewing rooms, each containing seating, a video cassette player, and television monitor. Aveco charges a rental fee for the viewing room that is separate from the charge for the video cassette rental.

Customers of Aveco may (1) rent a room and also rent a video cassette for viewing in that room, (2) rent a room and bring a video cassette obtained elsewhere to play in the room, or (3) rent a video cassette for out of store viewing.

Aveco has placed its video cassette players inside the individual viewing rooms and, subject to a time limitation, allows the customer complete control over the playing of the video cassettes. Customers operate the video cassette players in each viewing room and Aveco's employees assist only upon request. Each video cassette may be viewed only from inside the viewing room, and is not transmitted beyond the particular room in which it is being played. Aveco asserts that it rents its viewing rooms to individual customers who may be joined in the room only by members of their families and social acquaintances. Furthermore, Aveco's stated practice is not to permit unrelated groups of customers to share a viewing room while a video cassette is being played. For purposes of this appeal we assume the veracity of these assertions.

II

. . . Producers do not, in the present litigation, allege infringement of their exclusive rights "to do and to authorize [the distribution of] copies or phonorecords of the copyrighted work to the public by sale or other transfer of ownership, or by rental, lease, or lending." Thus, Aveco's rental of video cassettes for at-home viewing is not challenged.

Producers' claim in this litigation is based on the alleged infringement of their "exclusive right . . . to perform the copyrighted work publicly" and to "authorize" such performances. Producers assert that Aveco, by renting its viewing rooms to the public for the purpose of watching Producers' video cassettes, is authorizing the public performance of copyrighted motion pictures.

Our analysis begins with the language of the Act. We first observe that there is no question that "performances" of copyrighted materials take place at Aveco's stores. "To perform" a work is defined in the Act as, "in the case of a motion picture or other audiovisual work, to show its images in any sequence or to make the sounds accompanying it audible." Section 101. As the House Report notes, this definition means that an individual is performing a work whenever he does anything by which the work is transmitted, repeated, or made to recur. . . .

Producers do not argue that Aveco itself performs the video cassettes. They acknowledge that under the Act Aveco's *customers* are the ones performing the works, for it is they who actually place the video cassette in the video cassette player and operate the controls. As we said in *Columbia Pictures Industries v. Redd Horne*, 749 F.2d 154, 158 (3d Cir. 1984), "playing a video cassette . . . constitute[s] a performance under Section 101." However, if there is a public performance, Aveco may still be responsible as an infringer even though it does not actually operate the video cassette players. In granting copyright owners the exclusive rights to "authorize" public performances, Congress intended "to avoid any questions as to the liability of contributory infringers. For example, a person who lawfully acquires an authorized copy of a motion picture would be an infringer if he or she engages in the business of renting it to others for purposes of an unauthorized public performance." H.R. Rep. No. 1476, 94th Cong., 2d Sess. 61. In our opinion, this rationale applies equally to the person who knowingly makes available other requisites of a public performance. Accordingly, we agree with the district court that Aveco, by enabling its customers to perform the video cassettes in the viewing rooms, authorizes the performances.

The performances of Producers' motion pictures at Aveco's stores infringe their copyrights, however, only if they are "public." The copyright owners' rights do not extend to control over private performances. The Act defines a public performance:

> To perform . . . a work "publicly" means —
>
> (1) to perform or display it at a place open to the public or at any place where a substantial number of persons outside of a normal circle of a family and its social acquaintances are gathered; or
>
> (2) to transmit or otherwise communicate a performance or display of the work to a place specified by clause (1) or to the public, by means of any device or process, whether the members of the public capable of receiving the performance or display receive it in the same place or in separate places and at the same or at different times.

17 U.S.C. § 101.

We recently parsed this definition in *Redd Horne*, a case similar to the one at bar. The principal factual distinction is that in Redd Horne's operation, known as Maxwell's Video Showcase, Ltd. ("Maxwell's"), the video cassette players were located in the stores' central areas, not in each individual screening room. Maxwell's customers would select a video cassette from Maxwell's stock and rent a room which they entered to watch the motion picture on a television monitor. A Maxwell's employee would play the video cassette for the customers in one of the centrally-located video cassette players and transmit the performance to the monitor located in the room. Thus, unlike Aveco's customers, Maxwell's clientele had no control over the video cassette players.

The *Redd Horne* court began its analysis with the observation that the two components of clause (1) of the definition of a public performance are disjunctive. "The first category is self-evident; it is 'a place open to the public.' The second category, commonly referred to as a semi-public place, is determined by the size and composition of the audience." 749 F.2d at 159.

The court then concluded that the performances were occurring at a place open to the public, which it found to be the entire store, including the viewing rooms:

> Any member of the public can view a motion picture by paying the appropriate fee. The services provided by Maxwell's are essentially the same as a movie theatre, with the additional feature of privacy. The relevant "place" within the meaning of Section 101 is each of Maxwell's two stores,

not each individual booth within each store. Simply because the cassettes can be viewed in private does not mitigate the essential fact that Maxwell's is unquestionably open to the public.

749 F.2d at 159.

The *Redd Horne* court reached this conclusion despite the fact that when a customer watched a movie at Maxwell's, the viewing room was closed to other members of the public. Nevertheless, Aveco asserts that factual differences between Maxwell's stores and its own require a different result in this case.

Aveco first observes that when Maxwell's employees "performed" the video cassettes, they did so in a central location, the store's main area. This lobby was undeniably "open to the public." Aveco suggests that, in *Redd Horne*, the location of the customers in the private rooms was simply irrelevant, for the performers were in a public place, the lobby. In the case at bar, Aveco continues, its employees do not perform anything, the customers do. Unlike Maxwell's employees located in the public lobby, Aveco's customers are in private screening rooms. Aveco argues that while these viewing rooms are available to anyone for rent, they are private during each rental period, and therefore, not "open to the public." The performance — the playing of the video cassette — thus occurs not in the public lobby, but in the private viewing rooms.

We disagree. The necessary implication of Aveco's analysis is that *Redd Horne* would have been decided differently had Maxwell's located its video cassette players in a locked closet in the back of the stores. We do not read *Redd Horne* to adopt such an analysis. The Copyright Act speaks of performances at a place open to the public. It does not require that the public place be actually crowded with people. A telephone booth, a taxi cab, and even a pay toilet are commonly regarded as "open to the public," even though they are usually occupied only by one party at a time. Our opinion in *Redd Horne* turned not on the precise whereabouts of the video cassette players, but on the nature of Maxwell's stores. Maxwell's, like Aveco, was willing to make a viewing room and video cassette available to any member of the public with the inclination to avail himself of this service. It is this availability that made Maxwell's stores public places, not the coincidence that the video cassette players were situated in the lobby. Because we find *Redd Horne* indistinguishable from the case at bar, we find that Aveco's operations constituted an authorization of public performances of Producers' copyrighted works.

Aveco's reliance on the first sale doctrine is likewise misplaced. The first sale doctrine, codified at 17 U.S.C. § 109(a), prevents the copyright owner from controlling future transfers of a particular copy of a copyrighted work after he has transferred its "material ownership" to another. When a copyright owner parts with title to a particular copy of his copyrighted work, he thereby divests himself of his exclusive right to vend that particular copy. . . . Accordingly, under the first sale doctrine, Producers cannot claim that Aveco's rentals or sales of lawfully acquired video cassettes infringe on their exclusive rights to vend those cassettes.

. . . [E]ven assuming, arguendo, both a waiver by Producers of their Section 106(3) distribution rights and a valid transfer of ownership of the video cassette during the rental period, the first sale doctrine is nonetheless irrelevant. The rights protected by copyright are divisible and the waiver of one does not necessarily waive any of the others. In particular, the transfer of ownership in a particular copy of a work does not affect Producers' Section 106(4) exclusive rights to do and to authorize public performances. . . . It therefore cannot protect one who is infringing Producers' Section 106(4) rights by the public performance of the copyrighted work.

III

We therefore conclude that Aveco, by renting its rooms to members of the general public in which they may view performances of Producers' copyrighted video cassettes, obtained from any source, has authorized public performances of those cassettes. This is a violation of Producers' Section 106 rights and is appropriately enjoined. We therefore will affirm the order of the district court.

NOTES AND QUESTIONS

(1) *The prima facie right.* The public performance right in § 106(4) applies to most, but not all, of the works of authorship listed in § 102(a). The performance right extends to works of literature, music, drama, pantomime, and choreography, as well as to motion pictures and other audiovisual works. What works are thereby *excluded* from the reach of § 106(4), and why? In your answer, did you treat compilations and derivative works as included or excluded? These works are not mentioned in § 106(4).

(2) To "perform" a work means "to recite, render, play, dance, or act it, either directly or by means of any device or process." § 101. As described in the legislative history, such devices and processes include "all kinds of equipment for reproducing or amplifying sounds or visual images, any sort of transmitting apparatus, any type of electronic retrieval system, and any other techniques or systems *not yet in use or even invented*" (emphasis added). Under this language, who should decide whether the use of a new technique potentially infringes the § 106(4) performance right: Congress or the courts? Specifically, in the absence of any legislative clarification, how should we regard the communication of copyrighted works over digital networks for purposes of § 106(4)? This issue will be discussed below and in § 7.05.

As an aside, is playing a copyrighted board game in public a "performance" of the game within the meaning of the Copyright Act? Why or why not? *See Allen v. Academic Games League of America, Inc.*, 89 F.3d 614, 616 (9th Cir. 1996).

(3) To violate § 106(4), of course, there must be a *public* performance. The term "publicly" is defined in § 101 to include both (1) performances in public places and (2) transmissions. (Subsection (2) will assume particular importance in the discussion of secondary transmissions (including cable TV) in § 7.05[B] below.) Each of these subsections, in turn, contains two clauses. According to *Aveco*, how are the clauses in subsection (1) related to one another? If a video is played in a rented room that is occupied by only one person, is that a "public" performance?

§ 7.05

THE PUBLIC PERFORMANCE RIGHT 533

(4) In *Redd Horne*, the earlier Third Circuit case discussed in *Aveco*, the defendant's operation included the rental of a TV monitor in a private booth, to which the defendant's employees transmitted the performance of a video pre-selected by the customer. In *Aveco* itself, the customer rented a booth containing a TV *and a VCR*, and played a video — either rented from the store or supplied by the customer himself — *in the booth*. What if, instead, the customer simply rented a cassette and recorder and took them home for viewing overnight? Would the public performance right have been infringed by anyone? If not, why the difference?

(5) If viewing rooms in videocassette stores are "public places," can the same be said for individual rooms in a hotel? Suppose a hotel equips each room with a videocassette player and maintains a "library" of videocassettes from which guests may select. After *Aveco* and *Redd Horne*, would these uses be considered public performances? *See Columbia Pictures Industries, Inc. v. Professional Real Estate Investors, Inc.*, 866 F.2d 278 (9th Cir. 1989) (no). Would the answer change if the hotel maintained a bank of video players in the lobby, linked to guest rooms by a computerized electronic switching system which allowed guests to choose from among various movies? *See On Command Video Corp. v. Columbia Pictures Industries*, 777 F. Supp. 787 (N.D. Cal. 1991) (yes). Why the different answers?

What about listening to music or watching a movie on a personal device in a public place, such as a coffee shop or airplane? If other people can hear or see the performance, is it a "public" performance? Why or why not?

(6) A public performance can occur even if the venue where the performance takes place is *not* open to all, and there is no transmission of the performance to such a place. Under § 101, a performance is public if it occurs in or is transmitted to a place "where a substantial number of persons outside of a normal circle of a family and its social acquaintances is gathered." But how many persons constitute a "substantial" number? And what is a "normal circle" of family and friends? Does a wedding reception with 200 guests qualify? *See* Cantor, *How Many Guests May Attend a Wedding Reception Before ASCAP Shows Up? Or, What Are the Limits of the Definition of Perform "Publicly" Under 17 U.S.C. § 101?*, 27 Colum. J. L. & Arts 79 (2003).

(7) Clause (2) of the definition of "publicly" encompasses transmissions to a place listed in clause (1), and transmissions directly "to the public, . . . whether the members of the public capable of receiving the performance or display receive it at the same place or in separate places and at the same time or at different times." Clause (2) is thus broad enough to encompass "asynchronous" transmissions, such as a "video on demand" ("VOD") service that transmits performances of audiovisual works to private homes.

In *Cartoon Network LP v. CSC Holdings, Inc.*, 536 F.3d 121 (2d Cir. 2008), excerpted in § 7.02 above, the court considered a "remote storage" DVR system, which allowed customers to make copies of TV programs and store them on hard drives at Cablevision's premises for later viewing. Among other claims, the plaintiffs contended that transmission of the stored programs to customers violated the public performance right, pointing to the second clause of the definition of "publicly." The Second Circuit rejected this argument. The court relied in its reasoning on the fact that Cablevision had configured its system to make and to store a separate copy each time a customer chose to record a program — even though it would have been far more efficient to simply make and store a single copy for use by multiple customers. When a customer chose to play a recorded program, Cablevision streamed the show to the customer from the copy made and stored by the customer. As a consequence, the court reasoned that this was a private performance because the "members of the public capable of receiving the performance" were limited to the household of the customer who recorded it. Following this reasoning, would streaming video on an Internet site such as YouTube be a "public" performance? Why or why not?

In responding to the Supreme Court's invitation to submit the government's views regarding the case, the Solicitor General remarked that a broad interpretation of *Cartoon Network* "could threaten to undermine copyright protection in circumstances far beyond those presented here," including VOD and online streaming. Brief for the United States as *Amicus Curiae*, in *Cable News Network, Inc. v. CSC Holdings, Inc.*, No. 08-448, at 20-21 (2009). The Solicitor General recommended a narrow reading, limited to circumstances in which "(1) each transmission would be made using a unique copy of the relevant program; and (2) each transmission would be made solely to the person who had previously made that unique copy," to avoid "casting doubt on the widespread assumption that VOD and similar services involve public performances." *Id.* at 21. Are you satisfied that this narrow interpretation avoids any potential problems created by the opinion?

(8)   A number of technology companies developing new video-delivery services have relied on *Cartoon Network*'s suggestion that a stream from a unique copy associated with the viewer is a private performance. In 2011, a company called Zediva attempted to create a virtual video-rental store. Under its model, a customer would place a rental order that would cause a Zediva employee to take a physical DVD off of its shelves and insert it into a DVD drive on Zediva's premises. The DVD would remain off the shelf during the "rental" period, and Zediva's machine would create a digital file that could be streamed to the customer under the customer's control. Hollywood studios sued. The District Court issued a preliminary injunction, which subsequently became permanent. The court distinguished *Cartoon Network*, holding that it was Zediva rather than the customer who initiated the transmission because Zediva had purchased the DVD and reused it for multiple customers. On this reasoning, the performance was to the public for reasons analogous to those stated in *Redd Horne*, discussed in the *Aveco* case above. *See Warner Bros. Entm't, Inc. v. WTV Sys., Inc.*, 824 F. Supp. 2d 1003 (C.D. Cal. 2011).

In contrast, Aereo, Inc. successfully relied upon *Cartoon Network* to defeat a motion for preliminary injunction against its service. As of the time this book went to press, Aereo operates an antenna array that can be programmed to tune in broadcast television signals. Aereo subscribers can "rent" the use of one of these antennas and Aereo's DVR-like storage capacity. Subscribers can watch "live" television by recording a temporary copy to stream to their device, or they can record a broadcast program for viewing at a later time. ABC sought a preliminary injunction only against the "live" transmission of its programs as infringing public performances. In denying the motion, the District Court held that *Cartoon Network* controlled the outcome, because subscribers control Aereo's equipment to direct the making and transmission of buffer and storage copies of broadcast programming.

See American Broadcasting Cos. v. Aereo, Inc., 103 U.S.P.Q.2d (BNA) 1774 (S.D.N.Y. 2012). Tune in to the Supplement for further developments in this case![3]

(9)   Judge Posner has suggested that the definition of "public" performance may need clarification in the Internet age. In *Flava Works, Inc. v. Gunter,* 689 F.3d 754 (7th Cir. 2012), defendants operated a website called myVidster that allowed users to "bookmark" videos found on the Internet, so that other users could watch them by clicking on an "embedded" link. (myVidster did not "host" the allegedly infringing videos; rather, those videos were uploaded by third parties and were hosted on other servers.) Judge Posner explained:

> One possible interpretation is that uploading plus bookmarking a video is a public performance because it enables a visitor to the website to receive (watch) the performance at will, and the fact that he will be watching it at a different time or in a different place from the other viewers does not affect its "publicness," as the statute makes clear. We'll call this interpretation, for simplicity, "performance by uploading." An alternative interpretation, however — call it "performance by receiving" — is that the performance occurs only when the work . . . is transmitted to the viewer's computer — in other words when it is "communicated to the public in a form in which the public can visually or aurally comprehend the work." William F. Patry, *Patry on Copyright* § 14:21, p. 14-41 (2012).

> On the first interpretation, . . . the performance of a movie in a movie theater might by analogy be said to begin not when the audience is seated and the movie begins but a bit earlier, when the operator of the projector loads the film and puts his finger on the start button; while on the second interpretation, performance by receiving, it begins when he presses the button and the reel begins to unwind. The second interpretation is certainly more plausible in the movie-theater setting. But [here] the viewer rather than the sender (the latter being the uploader of the copyrighted video) determines when the performance begins, and it is odd to think that every transmission of an uploaded video is a public performance. The first interpretation — public performance occurs when the video is uploaded and the public becomes capable of viewing it — is better at giving meaning to "public" in public performance but worse at giving meaning to "performance." Legislative clarification of the public-performance provision of the Copyright Act would therefore be most welcome. . . .

> But if the public performance is the transmission of the video when the visitor to myVidster's website clicks on the video's thumbnail (the second interpretation) and viewing begins, there is an argument that even though the video uploader is responsible for the transmitting and not myVidster, myVidster is assisting the transmission by providing the link between the uploader and the viewer, and is thus facilitating public performance.

---

[3] When interpreting the Copyright Act in light of new technologies, the courts have given significant weight to the specific design characteristics of the defendant's system. A different company seeking to transmit broadcast television signals over the Internet was enjoined because it was responsible for the transmissions and it could not qualify as a "cable system" entitled to a statutory license for such retransmissions. *See WPIX, Inc. v. ivi, Inc.,* 691 F.3d 275 (2d Cir. 2012).

Id. at 760-61. Which interpretation makes more sense? Which is most consistent with the statutory language? Which one was implicitly used in *Cartoon Network*? In *Redd Horne* and *Aveco*?

(10) As noted in the introduction to this section and in the House Report, the exclusive right to perform a work publicly is not limited by a requirement that the performance be "for profit." Any unauthorized public performance of a copyrighted work is thus a *prima facie* infringement. Unless an exemption contained in §§ 107-22 applies, the defendant will be subject to one or more of the remedies provided by the Act (discussed in Chapter 11).

(11) *The first-sale doctrine.* The Computer Software Rental Amendments Act of 1990, which we encountered in § 7.04, added § 109(e), which allowed the owner of a lawfully-made copy of a videogame to perform or display that game publicly on coin-operated equipment. Section 109(e) thus overturned *Red Baron-Franklin Park, Inc. v. Taito Corp.*, 883 F.2d 275 (4th Cir. 1989), which had held that the first-sale doctrine did not permit the operator of a video arcade, who had obtained copyrighted videogame circuit boards abroad, to perform the game publicly without the copyright owner's consent. Under a sunset provision, however, § 109(e) expired on October 1, 1995. Should § 109(e) be made permanent? Why or why not?

(12) *The § 110 limitations.* Section 110 exempts 11 types of public performances from the scope of the performance right:

(1) face-to-face teaching activities;

(2) instructional transmissions;

(3) religious services;

(4) live performances without commercial advantage to anyone;

(5) mere reception of broadcasts in a public place;

(6) annual agricultural and horticultural fairs;

(7) performances in connection with the sale of phonorecords and players, and sheet music;

(8) noncommercial broadcasts of literary works to the deaf and blind;

(9) nonprofit performances of dramatic works transmitted to the blind by radio subcarrier;

(10) certain performances conducted by veterans' and fraternal groups, and college fraternities and sororities, for charitable purposes; and

(11) making imperceptible limited portions of a motion picture during a performance in or transmitted to a private household for private home viewing.

Space does not permit discussion of all of these exemptions, but some of them are discussed in the notes that follow. Notice that the exemptions numbered (1), (2), (3), and (5) *also apply to the display right under § 106(5).*

(13) Section 110(1) exempts from copyright liability the performance (or display) of copyrighted works "by instructors or pupils in the course of face-to-face teaching activities of a nonprofit educational institution, in a classroom or similar place devoted to instruction." Does this language exempt an unauthorized performance of popular songs in the courtyard of the law school as part of an end-of-term party? What if the same songs are performed by your instructor as part of a classroom presentation illustrating how the melody from one song may infringe the copyright in another? What if, instead, the songs are performed by a local country-and-western personality whose act the instructor noticed the night before at a local bar?

(14) Does it make a difference whether the performer appears "live" from Nashville or Austin via a satellite hook-up? As originally enacted, § 110(2) accommodated "distance learning" by allowing performances or displays of nondramatic literary and musical works on broadcast or closed-circuit television for educational purposes. Those technologies were "state of the art" in 1976, but today, of course, most schools carry out such instruction using the Internet or various intranets. For example, students enrolled in "American Popular Culture 101" might log on from their dorm rooms or homes to access video clips related to their professor's lectures. Because the original § 110(2) did not allow such transmissions, many educators campaigned to revise § 110(2) to accommodate these new distance learning technologies.

In the DMCA, Congress directed the Copyright Office to investigate the problem and issue a report. *See* U.S. Copyright Office, Report on Copyright and Digital Distance Education (May 1999), available at *www.copyright.gov/reports/de_rprt.pdf*. Congress eventually adopted some of the Report's recommendations (and rejected others) in the Technology, Education and Copyright Harmonization Act of 2002.

The TEACH Act, as it is known, rewrote § 110(2) to accommodate asynchronous "distance learning" on the Internet. As amended, § 110(2) permits transmissions of performances of nondramatic literary and musical works (and "reasonable and limited portions of any other work") and displays comparable to those in a live classroom setting. The performances or displays must be "directly related" to instruction and, to the extent feasible, reception must be limited to staff and officially enrolled students. The school must reasonably attempt to prevent retention or distribution of copies other than as needed to accomplish the permitted instruction, and must not interfere with technological measures used by the copyright owner. The TEACH Act also amended § 112 to permit institutions to upload copyrighted works onto servers for later transmission to students consistent with § 110(2).

(15) Section 110(3) permits the performance and display of certain works "in the course of services at a place of worship or other religious assembly." Does this section apply if the services are also broadcast on the radio? *See Simpleville Music v Mizell*, 451 F. Supp. 2d 1293 (M.D. Ala. 2006) (no). What result in the case of a live performance of copyrighted popular music at the fellowship center of a local church? What additional facts do you need to know to answer the question?

(16) Section 110(4) exempts certain types of performances conducted "otherwise than in a transmission to the public, without any purpose of direct or indirect

commercial advantage." Obviously, this provision cuts back on the exclusive right "to perform the work publicly" under § 106(4). How do these two provisions in combination differ, in practical effect, from simply limiting the performance right itself to performances given "publicly for profit," as was done under § 1 of the 1909 Act?

Why does § 110(4) also provide that, even if the conditions quoted above are met, no "payment of any fee or other compensation for the performance [may be made] to any of its performers, promoters, or organizers"?

Assuming that the performance is without commercial advantage, results in no payment to anyone, and is live rather than part of a transmission, it still must meet one of two alternative conditions in order to be exempt. Either there must be "no direct or indirect admission charge" (§ 110(4)(A)), or the net proceeds of the performance must be "used exclusively for educational, religious, or charitable purposes and not for private financial gain" (§ 110(4)(B)). If admission is to be charged, however, the owner of the copyright may prevent the performance by serving written notice of his or her objection at least seven days before its scheduled date. Otherwise, as the House Report notes, "owners could be compelled to make involuntary donations to the fund-raising activities of causes to which they are opposed."

While pondering what sorts of works and causes might give rise to such conflicts, ask yourself how copyright owners are supposed to learn that their works are about to be performed pursuant to the § 110(4)(B) exemption. Does the Act say? The legislative history? What mechanism should be adopted, and by whom, to ensure that the right of objection afforded to owners by this provision is not an empty one? *See* 37 C.F.R. § 201.13.

(17)   Section 110(5) will be discussed in § 7.05[B] below. Subsections (6) through (10) will not be discussed in detail, but will be left for your individual consideration.

(18)   Section 110(11) was added in 2005 to permit the use of devices that skip over certain content during the playback of a motion picture. Given that this exception is limited to performances "for private home viewing," why was it necessary to enact an exemption to the right of *public* performance? Note that the exception also applies to transmissions to private households, which qualify under the definition of "publicly." Moreover, § 110(11) also implicates the right to prepare derivative works, which is not so limited. Section 110(11) is discussed in more detail in § 7.03 above.

(19)   *Other limitations on the public performance right.* Under the 1976 Act as originally passed, § 116 accorded owners of "coin-operated phonorecord players" (*i.e.*, jukeboxes) a compulsory license to perform nondramatic musical works embodied in phonorecords upon compliance with the statutory formalities and payment of required fees. But the terms of original § 116 were incompatible with the requirements of the Berne Convention. Accordingly, the Berne Convention Implementation Act of 1988 added § 116A, establishing a new system for jukebox performances based on voluntary negotiations between copyright owners and jukebox operators; and the Copyright Royalty Tribunal suspended the § 116

compulsory license. In 1993, Congress deleted original § 116 and renumbered § 116A to take its place.

(20)   Section 118 provides a statutory license for the use of published nondramatic musical works and published pictorial, graphic and sculptural works by noncommercial public broadcasting entities, which may be superseded by voluntary negotiations. The legislative history does not explain the requirement that the works be "published" in order for § 118 to apply, but it does reveal that nondramatic literary works were omitted from the provision based on assurances by interested parties that "licensing arrangements [for such works] . . . could be worked out in private negotiation." Rights in "plays, operas, ballet and other stage presentations, motion pictures and other audiovisual works" also are unaffected by § 118.

(21)   Other limitations on the public performance right involving secondary transmissions — namely, cable television (§ 111) and satellite retransmissions (§§ 119 and 122) — will be discussed in § 7.05[B] below.

[3] Performing Rights Societies

Every day, musical works are publicly performed thousands of times. Each of these performances represents a possible source of revenue for the copyright owner — but also, quite obviously, an insuperable management problem for individual copyright owners. Performing rights societies are the means by which music composers and publishers, by pooling the rights to the use of their works, are able to police, license, and otherwise administer their copyright interests.

The first performing rights society, the American Society of Composers, Authors and Publishers, or ASCAP, was formed in 1914. Its founders were Victor Herbert, the composer, and his attorney, Nathan Burkan, whose name was memorialized for many years through ASCAP's annual (but now lamentably discontinued) copyright law competition for law students. ASCAP enabled its members, for the first time, to enforce their performance rights effectively on a collective basis. The other main performing rights societies are Broadcast Music, Inc., or BMI and SESAC, Inc., formerly known as the Society of European Stage Authors and Composers. Today, ASCAP, BMI and SESAC together control access to literally millions of copyrighted musical works, license and police their use, and distribute the fees collected therefrom to tens of thousands of members.

Almost from the outset, the performing rights societies came under attack, on antitrust grounds, by both the Federal Government and various industry groups. One recurring bone of contention involves the blanket license, a single fee charged for use of the entire repertory, regardless of actual usage of individual works. Although a single fee is charged, the fee schedule varies greatly among industry groups. Generally, the wealthier are charged more: a major television network, for example, will pay a higher fee for its blanket license than a small local radio station. Discontent over the blanket license has led to suits, generally unsuccessful, by national and local broadcasters. *See, e.g., Broadcast Music, Inc. v. Columbia Broadcasting System, Inc.*, 441 U.S. 1 (1979); *Buffalo Broadcasting Co., Inc. v. American Society of Composers, Authors and Publishers*, 744 F.2d 917 (2d Cir. 1984). Both ASCAP and BMI, however, operate under consent decrees worked out over an extended period by the societies and the Department of Justice: *United*

States v. Am. Soc'y of Composers, Authors and Publishers, 1950-51 Trade Cas. ¶ 62,595 (S.D.N.Y. 1950) (ASCAP), and *United States v. Broad. Music, Inc.*, 1966 Trade Cas. ¶ 71,941 (S.D.N.Y. 1966) (BMI). Under the consent decrees, the blanket license fee must be set by the federal district court if the parties cannot agree. *See, e.g.*, *United States v. Broadcast Music, Inc.*, 426 F.3d 91 (2d Cir. 2005); *American Society of Composers, Authors and Publishers v. Showtime/The Movie Channel, Inc.*, 912 F.2d 563 (2d Cir. 1990).

There is much more that could be said concerning the performing rights societies, but too little room to say it. Readers who wish detailed information concerning the three organizations, including their membership, repertoires, licensing practices, survey and sampling techniques, clearing functions, and revenue sources by category and amount, should consult the latest edition of W. Krasilovsky & S. Shemel, *This Business Of Music*, popularly known as "the Bible of the music industry."

[4] Small and Grand Performing Rights

The performing rights societies discussed in the preceding subsection (ASCAP, BMI, and SESAC) license what are called "small" performing rights — rights to perform nondramatic musical works, and to perform individual songs from dramatic musical works separate and apart from the dramatic context in which such songs may have first appeared. By contrast, copyright owners typically retain, and license separately, so-called "grand performing" rights — rights to perform *integrated* dramatic musical works as a whole, and to perform individual songs from the larger work in a dramatic setting.

In the real world, the foregoing distinction between small and grand rights may be difficult to make. In *Robert Stigwood Group Ltd. v. Sperber*, 457 F.2d 50 (2d Cir. 1972), Stigwood, which had obtained the grand performing rights in the rock opera *Jesus Christ Superstar ("JCS")*, sued Sperber, a concert promoter. Sperber had obtained from ASCAP the right to perform each of the 23 songs contained in *JCS* and had assembled a cast, calling itself "The Original American Touring Company (OATC)," that traveled around the country presenting what it billed as "concerts." Each concert, while devoid of scenery, costumes or dialogue, consisted of performances of 20 of the 23 songs from *JCS*, presented with only one exception in the same sequence as in the stage play itself.

Jesus Christ Superstar (1973)
Corbis

Both the trial court and the Second Circuit concluded that OATC's performances violated Stigwood's rights in *JCS*. In its opinion, the Court of Appeals observed:

> There can be no question that the OATC concerts, in which singers enter and exit, maintain specific roles and occasionally make gestures, and in which the story line of the original play is preserved by the songs which are sung in almost perfect sequence using 78 of the 87 minutes of the original copyrighted score, is dramatic.

457 F.2d at 55. Accordingly, the defendant was enjoined from performing any song "in such a way as to follow another song in the same order as in the original *Jesus Christ Superstar* opera" and from the use of any accompanying dramatic action whatsoever. *Id.* at 56.

Perhaps the best way to distinguish between small and grand rights in practice is Nimmer's pithy test: "[A] performance of a musical composition is dramatic if it aids in telling a story; otherwise it is not." 3 NIMMER ON COPYRIGHT § 10.10[E] (2010). Another observer, cited by Nimmer, suggested that this standard should be implemented as follows: "Delete the proposed musical performance from the production (be it stage, motion picture, or television); if after such deletion the continuity or story line of the production is in no way impeded or obscured, then the proposed performance is non-dramatic — otherwise it is dramatic." *Id.* at 10-93 (quoting R. Monta of Metro-Goldwyn-Mayer).

For further enlightenment on this subject, see *Gershwin v. The Whole Thing Co.*, 208 U.S.P.Q. 557 (C.D. Cal. 1980) (injunction to enforce settlement between composers and theatrical company concerning performances of "Let's Call the Whole Thing Gershwin," a play depicting the composers' lives through their music).

[5] Synchronization Rights

Suppose you are producing a movie or a commercial and, rather than commission an original soundtrack, you would prefer to use preexisting compositions to supply a musical background. In the parlance of the entertainment industry, you need to obtain the "synchronization rights" (or simply "sync rights") for any copyrighted music you have chosen. The fact that synchronization rights aren't mentioned in § 106 doesn't excuse you from the duty to license them. Generally, these rights are considered to be an emanation of the § 106(1) reproduction right, but they also relate to § 106(4), because any exhibition or transmission of an audiovisual work to which music has been synchronized necessarily will entail a public performance of that music. ASCAP, BMI, and SESAC do not engage in "sync" licensing; instead, such licenses must be obtained directly from the copyright holder.

There has been a spirited debate concerning whether synchronization licenses are necessary and/or sufficient to produce karaoke products that display lyrics in conjunction with recorded music. *Compare Leadsinger, Inc. v. BMG Music Publishing*, 512 F.3d 522 (9th Cir. 2008) (display of lyrics makes product an audiovisual work, rendering it ineligible for § 115 compulsory license and necessitating a synch license), *and ABKCO Music, Inc. v. Stellar Records, Inc.*, 96 F.3d 60 (2d Cir. 1996) (§ 115 compulsory license was not sufficient without lyric reprint license), *with EMI Entertainment World v. Priddis Music*, 505 F. Supp. 2d 1217 (D. Utah 2007) (karaoke products that display only lyrics without other images are not audiovisual works and require only a § 115 compulsory license and a lyric reprint license).

[6] Digital Network Transmissions

The delivery of copyrighted content "on demand" over the Internet has enormous practical implications for the owners of copyrighted works. Important questions are raised, for example, as to whether the delivery of a digital file over the Internet constitutes a "public performance" within the meaning of § 106(4). The 1995 "White Paper" on *Intellectual Property and the National Information Infrastructure* had this to say, at p. 71:

> When a copy of a work is transmitted over wires, fiber optics, satellite signals or other modes in digital form so that it may be captured in a user's computer, without the capability of simultaneously "rendering" or "showing," it has rather clearly not been performed. Thus, for example, a file comprising the digitized version of a motion picture might be transferred from a copyright owner to an end user via the Internet without the public performance right being implicated. When, however, the motion picture is "rendered" — by showing its images in sequence — so that users with the requisite hardware and software might watch it *with or without copying the performance*, then, under the current law, a "performance" has occurred.

Notably, the just-quoted passage contains no citations to authority. Nonetheless, do you agree with it? Can you argue that an e-mail message containing copyrighted material could constitute a "public performance" if it is sent from one friend to another? What if it is sent to all the members of an extensive "listserv"? What if the work is posted to a website accessible to the public?

Note that the Digital Millennium Copyright Act of 1998 did nothing to clarify the answers to these questions. Assuming, however, that some form of permission from copyright owners is necessary before their works can be transmitted over the Internet, why is it important to know whether, in particular, such transmissions constitute performances (as distinct from reproductions and/or distributions) of those works? The answer is that different mechanisms exist for licensing different § 106 rights, and the identification of the right implicated by a particular use may determine the nature of the license the user must obtain — and the source from which he or she must obtain it.

In the case of musical works, for example, it is relatively clear that "streaming" technologies like RealAudio, which permit recorded audio files to be transmitted over the Internet and listened to in "real time," constitute public performances that must be licensed from ASCAP or BMI. But do such performances also implicate the reproduction and distribution rights? The Harry Fox Agency, which handles "mechanical licenses" for musical works (as discussed in § 7.02[C] above), has taken the position that they do. *See The Rodgers and Hammerstein Organization v. UMG Recordings, Inc.*, 60 U.S.P.Q.2d (BNA) 1354 (S.D.N.Y. 2001) (holding that temporary reproductions made to facilitate "streaming" must be separately licensed and are not covered by the § 115 compulsory license or the Harry Fox mechanical license).

And what about Internet music services like Apple's iTunes, which allow users to download digital music files for later playback? Again, it is relatively clear that such services implicate the reproduction and distribution rights, and therefore are subject to the compulsory license for musical works in § 115 or require mechanical licenses from the Harry Fox Agency. But do such "digital phonorecord deliveries" also constitute "public performances" within the meaning of § 106(4)? Despite the White Paper, ASCAP and BMI take the position that they do — and they have collected royalties from various web-based entrepreneurs who wish to avoid copyright complications. The Second Circuit, however, has rejected this contention, holding that a digital download is not a "performance" because "[t]he downloaded songs are not performed in any perceptible manner during the transfers." *United States v. ASCAP*, 627 F.3d 64, 73 (2d Cir. 2010).

In addition, there is the limited public performance right in sound recordings — as distinguished from the musical works discussed to this point — to consider. *See* §§ 106(6) and 114. Such licenses currently are being handled by another titan of the music world, the Recording Industry Association of America ("RIAA," mentioned earlier in § 7.02), and are highly controversial.

Thus, the "turf" of the Internet music industry is a crowded place, occupied by three potential tiers of licensing for a would-be music distributor to deal with. Despite the industry catch-phrase of "one-stop shopping," such convenience does not now exist, at least in this particular corner of the copyright world. The result is that Internet music distributors must weave their way through a complicated terrain fraught with risk.

Two examples will suffice to give a taste of the controversy. A tentative agreement among the National Music Publishers Association ("NMPA"), the Harry Fox Agency, and the RIAA, arrived at in October 2001, drew fire for its apparent premise that would-be providers of "streaming" audio on the Internet also must license "mechanical" rights (for temporary server reproduction, etc.). (See the comments collected at *www.copyright.gov/carp/dpd/comments.html.*) More recently, as mentioned in § 7.02[C], the Register of Copyrights has recommended to Congress that the § 115 compulsory license be eliminated, and that the Copyright Act be amended to provide that any license to publicly perform a musical work by means of digital audio transmission must include the non-exclusive right to reproduce and distribute copies of the work to facilitate such streaming. *See* Statement of Marybeth Peters before the House Subcommittee on Courts, the Internet and Intellectual Property (June 21, 2005), available at *www.copyright.gov/docs/regstat062105.html.*

For further information regarding digital network transmissions of sound recordings, see § 7.07 of this casebook. Detailed information concerning the licensing of musical works and sound recordings is available in B. Kohn & A. Kohn, KOHN ON MUSIC LICENSING (4th ed. 2009).

[7] Performance Rights in Sound Recordings

Unlike the law of most countries, American copyright law under §§ 106(4) and 114(a) specifically excludes a general performance right in sound recordings. As a result, when a radio station plays a popular song, only the copyright owner of the musical work may claim royalties for the performance of the musical composition. The owners of the sound recording copyright, whether they are the record manufacturers or the performers, have no claim. The copyright owner of the song receives all of the performance royalties, even though the song's success may be due to interpretive musicians or to the artists and technicians who capture the performance in a sound recording.

The failure to provide a performance right in sound recordings is no accident. Back in 1971, when record companies gained an amendment to the Copyright Act providing protection for recordings "fixed, published and copyrighted on and after February 15, 1972," their main concern was to obtain stronger protection against record piracy. In order to forestall the objections of broadcasters (among others) to the creation of a sound recording copyright, the record companies were willing to accept the exceptional limitations of § 114(a) (as well as those contained in § 114(b)). Since then, the recording industry has thought better of the "bargain" struck in 1971 and frequently has pointed to the illogic of the system, as well as its alleged unfairness. Pursuant to original § 114(d), the Register of Copyrights submitted a report recommending an amendment to the section to include a performance right for sound recordings. *See Report of the Register of Copyrights to the House Judiciary Comm., Performance Rights in Sound Recordings* (Comm. Print No. 15, 1978).

Despite strong support in favor of performance rights bills, economically potent forces vigorously oppose any amendment to the Copyright Act granting a general performance right in sound recordings. For one, broadcasting groups view potential legislation conferring performance rights as imposing a tax every time a record is played on the air, driving marginal stations out of business. Not only would the broadcaster have to buy a license from a performing rights society like ASCAP for the right to perform the musical work, but it would also have to obtain a similar license from SoundExchange (the collecting society for the RIAA) to perform the sound recording. There is also the thorny question of how to allocate any royalties collected.

In 1991, a Report of the Register of Copyrights, *Copyright Implications of Digital Audio Transmission Services* (Oct. 1991), restated the general arguments for a performance right in sound recordings in the special context of digital technology. The advent of ground- and satellite-based digital broadcasting fed concerns that consumers might substitute subscriptions to digital audio services for purchases of CDs. As a result, § 106 was amended in 1995 to add subsection (6), which provides an exclusive right, "in the case of sound recordings, to perform the copyrighted work publicly by means of a digital audio transmission." A new § 114(d) set forth the many details of the political compromise that brought this new right into being. Section 114(d), in turn, was revised significantly in 1998. The results are discussed at greater length in § 7.07.

The controversy over public performance rights for sound recordings resurfaced in 2009, with the introduction in the House and Senate of bills that, for the first time in U.S. history, would require terrestrial broadcasters to pay royalties for sound recordings similar to those paid by digital broadcasters. The bills received a boost in April 2010 when the Obama administration announced its support for the measure. You can follow the progress of the proposed legislation at *www.copyright.gov/legislation.*

NOTES AND QUESTIONS

(1) As already noted, broadcasters tend to regard a performance right in sound recordings as another burdensome tax on their business, and one that would greatly increase transaction costs. By contrast, the Register of Copyrights, in the report cited above, suggested the use of a statutory license to administer the system. Given that such a statutory license now exists for digital audio transmission of sound recordings, is there any compelling reason not to extend the system to all public performances of sound recordings?

(2) Would enactment of a general performance right in sound recordings necessarily redress alleged injustices to performers (as distinct from record companies)? Some argue that, in practice, the greater economic power of the record companies would allow them to claim the lion's share of the royalties in contractual arrangements with performers. What problems do you foresee in drafting an effective statute designating who will receive performance royalties, and in what percentages? When you reach § 7.07 below, you will want to consider how this problem of equitable distribution was (or wasn't) dealt with in the Digital Performance Right in Sound Recordings Act of 1995.

(3) Various international agreements address the issue of protection for sound recordings. Historically, the most important of these was the 1961 Rome Conven-

tion (or, more formally, the International Convention for the Protection of Performers, Producers of Phonograms and Broadcasting Organizations), to which the United States is not a party.

More recently, there have been two significant developments in international law. One is Article 14 of the TRIPS Agreement, which mandates protection for sound recordings in World Trade Organization countries (by means of either copyright or a neighboring right), but which carefully does *not* address the issue of the performance right. The 1996 WIPO Performances and Phonograms Treaty goes further. Article 15(1) of the treaty requires (at a minimum) a statutory licensing approach to the performance right, stating: "Performers and producers of phonograms shall enjoy the right to a single equitable remuneration for the direct or indirect use of phonograms published for commercial purposes for broadcasting or for any communication to the public." Taken alone, this language would seem to pose problems for a country (like the United States) without a general performance right. Article 15(3), however, provides a simple mechanism by which any country may opt out of the provisions of Article 15(1), in whole or in part. Such provisions are unusual (though not unknown) in international intellectual property agreements. This one was inserted primarily to accommodate the legislative situation in the United States.

(4) "Bootlegging" — the unauthorized fixation of sound and video recordings of *live* musical performances — has long presented a legal quandary for U.S. performers, not only because of the absence of a performance right under federal law but also because of the fixation requirement contained in the Copyright Act. In the past, the problem was addressed through various state anti-bootlegging and unfair competition laws, and by common-law copyright. International bootlegging has become a major economic issue, however, and has been compounded by the inability of the U.S. Customs Service to administer effective border enforcement pursuant to a uniform federal law.

The Uruguay Round Agreements Act, designed to implement U.S. obligations under the TRIPS Agreement, added federal civil and criminal remedies to combat the bootleg trade. Chapter 11 of Title 17 — a provision outside Chapters 1-8, which constitute the Copyright Act itself — gives performers a civil cause of action for the unauthorized fixation, reproduction, or distribution of bootleg sound recordings and music videos. Section 1101(a)(1) makes it illegal to fix the sound or sounds and images of a live musical performance in a copy or phonorecord without the consent of the performers, or to reproduce copies or phonorecords of such a performance from an unauthorized fixation. Section 1101(a)(2) makes it illegal to transmit or otherwise communicate a live musical performance to the public; and § 1101(a)(3) makes it illegal to distribute any copy or phonorecord embodying the unauthorized recording. Persons engaged in such activities are subject to all the remedies for infringement under copyright. Criminal penalties under 18 U.S.C. § 2319A supplement the civil cause of action. For a discussion of the constitutionality of these provisions, including recent cases, see § 2.01 above.

[B]   Secondary Transmissions

A "public" performance — that is, a performance subject to the exclusive right provided by § 106(4) — may occur in one of two ways. *See* § 101 (definition of "publicly," applicable equally to performances and displays). As we saw in the preceding section, to perform publicly means to perform a work in a public or semi-public place, or *to transmit a performance of a work to members of the public*. In general, an unauthorized transmission *or retransmission* of a copyrighted work is an infringement of copyright. In this section, we focus on the copyright owner's ability to control secondary transmissions (retransmissions) of her work to the public.

Satellite Dish
NASA

[1]   Introduction

Statutory References

1976 Act: §§ 101 ("transmission program," "transmit"), 110(5), 111 (especially definitions in subsection (f)), 119, 122

1909 Act: § 1 (c), (d), and (e)

Legislative History

H.R. Rep. No. 94-1476 at 86-87, 88-89,
reprinted in 1976 U.S.C.C.A.N. 5659, 5701-02, 5702-13

Section 110. Exemptions of Certain Performances and Displays

Mere reception in public

. . . [Section 110(5)] applies to performances and displays of all types of works, and its purpose is to exempt from copyright liability anyone who merely turns on, in a public place, an ordinary radio or television receiving apparatus of a kind commonly sold to members of the public for private use.

The basic rationale of this clause is that the secondary use of the transmission by turning on an ordinary receiver in public is so remote and minimal that no further liability should be imposed. In the vast majority of these cases no royalties are collected today, and the exemption should be made explicit in the statute. This clause has nothing to do with cable television systems and the exemptions would be denied in any case where the audience is charged directly to see or hear the transmission.

[The Report continues with a discussion of a series of Supreme Court cases beginning with *Buck v. Jewell-La Salle Realty Co.*, 283 U.S. 191 (1931), which the Report approves, and continuing with *Fortnightly Corp. v. United Artists Television, Inc*, 392 U.S. 390 (1968), *Teleprompter Corp. v. CBS*, 415 U.S. 394 (1974) and *Twentieth Century Music Corp. v. Aiken*, 422 U.S. 151 (1975), all of which departed from the reasoning of *Jewell-La Salle* — and expressly states that the 1976 Act "accepts the traditional, pre-*Aiken*, interpretation of the *Jewell-La Salle* decision, under which public communication by means other than a home receiving set, or further transmission of a broadcast to the public, is considered an infringing act." All of this is treated in detail in the Notes and Questions following the principal case below.]

Section 111. Secondary Transmissions

Introduction and general summary

The complex and economically important problem of "secondary transmissions" is considered in section 111. For the most part, the section is directed at the operation of cable television systems and the terms and conditions of their liability for the retransmission of copyrighted works. However, other forms of secondary transmissions are also considered, including apartment house and hotel systems, wired instructional systems, common carriers, nonprofit "boosters" and translators, and secondary transmissions of primary transmissions to controlled groups. . . .

In general, the committee believes that cable systems are commercial enterprises whose basic retransmission operations are based on the carriage of copyrighted program material and that copyright royalties should be paid by cable operators to the creators of such programs. The committee recognizes, however, that it would be impractical and unduly burdensome to require every cable system to negotiate with every copyright owner whose work was retransmitted by a cable system. Accordingly, . . . [the bill establishes] a compulsory copyright license [subject now to administration by the Copyright Royalty Judges] for the retransmission of those over-the-air broadcast signals that a cable system is authorized to carry pursuant to the rules and regulations of the FCC.

[The § 111 statutory license established by the 1976 Act is subject to certain requirements, limitations, and exemptions, which are contained in the Act and summarized briefly in § 7.05[B][3] below. Likewise, § 7.05[B][4] summarizes issues raised by § 119 of the Act, enacted by Congress in 1988, and § 122, enacted in 1999.]

[2]   The § 110(5) *Aiken* Exemption

NATIONAL FOOTBALL LEAGUE v.
MCBEE & BRUNO'S, INC.
United States Court of Appeals, Eighth Circuit
792 F.2d 726 (1986)

ARNOLD, CIRCUIT JUDGE.

This lawsuit, brought by the National Football League (NFL) and the St. Louis Football Cardinals (Cardinals), alleges that defendants, the owners of several St. Louis restaurants, violated federal copyright and communications law by showing Cardinals' home games which had been "blacked out" in the St. Louis area. According to plaintiffs, defendants picked up the signals for such games by means of satellite dish antennae. The District Court entered a permanent injunction against defendants after a trial on the merits. In the main, we affirm.

I.

The Cardinals, a professional football team, is one of 28 teams composing the NFL, an unincorporated non-profit association through which the member clubs schedule games and manage their affairs as a group, including contracts with the three major television networks. One provision of those television contracts is that games which are not sold out within 72 hours of game time are to be "blacked out," that is, not broadcast within a 75-mile radius of the home team's playing field. Officials of the league and club testified at trial that such a rule boosts team revenue directly by increasing ticket sales and indirectly because a full stadium contributes to a more exciting television program and therefore makes the right to broadcast games more valuable.

Witnesses also described the process by which a live football game is telecast by the networks, in this case CBS. As television cameras capture the visual portion of the game, announcers describe and discuss the action from a sound booth of some kind. Those simultaneous audio and video signals are combined at an earth station outside the stadium. This signal — called an uplink — is transmitted up to a satellite, which then sends the signal back — called a downlink — to a network control point on Long Island. Because that signal contains no images other than those from the stadium, this stage is referred to as a "clean feed." The signal is then sent by cable to CBS studios in New York; commercials and other interruptions, such as station breaks, are inserted, and it is now described as a "dirty feed." There is another uplink to the satellite, and then a downlink to local affiliates, who insert local material and finally put the live broadcast on the air. The process apparently takes far longer to describe than to occur; at argument, counsel for the NFL called the procedure "simultaneous, instantaneous," and said that the delay between the action on the field and the broadcast by local affiliates was considerably less than two seconds.

The defendants are owners, corporate or individual, of St. Louis bar-restaurants within 75 miles of Busch Stadium, the Cardinals' home field. All defendants have satellite dish antennae that enable them to receive transmissions in the so-called C-band frequency, approximately 3200-4200 megahertz, in which the satellite sends and receives transmissions.[2] There is no question that prior to November 19, 1984, all defendants but two[3] picked up the clean feed (from the satellite to CBS) and thereby showed blacked-out home games of the Cardinals. On that date, plaintiffs requested and the District Court entered a temporary restraining order, preventing defendants from intercepting and showing the home game scheduled for the following Sunday; after a hearing, the Court issued a preliminary injunction in basically the same terms, dealing with the last home game of the season. Trial on the merits was held on May 7, 1985. . . . A permanent injunction issued on September 13, 1985, prohibiting the defendants from intercepting and showing plaintiffs' programming, whether in the form of the clean or dirty feed transmissions.

II.

The owners of the defendant restaurants challenge the District Court's Copyright Act decision on a variety of grounds [including] that defendants' display of blacked-out home games falls under statutory limitations on exclusive rights of a copyright owner, 17 U.S.C. § 110(5). . . . Although some of these arguments have more substance than others, we consider all to be ultimately without merit. . . .

Defendants' . . . most considerable argument is that their display of plaintiffs' blacked-out games falls into the category of non-infringing acts under Section 110(5) of the Copyright Act. Under that provision, no copyright liability can be imposed for "communication of a transmission embodying a performance . . . by the public reception of the transmission on a single receiving apparatus of a kind commonly used in private homes. . . ." The District Court rejected this argument, finding that satellite dish antennae, which in the United States are outnumbered by television sets by more than 100-to-one, were outside the statutory exemption.

According to the defendants, this ruling ignores their theory that how "the signal was captured by the antenna outside the premises" is "irrelevant." Instead, they argue, the key to Section 110(5) is whether an alleged infringer uses commercial equipment to enhance the sound or visual quality of the performance as it is perceived inside the premises. "All published cases on Section 110(5) take this approach." This interpretation ignores both the plain language of the statute and its obvious intent.

The home-use exemption was included in the 1976 Copyright Act specifically in response to the Supreme Court's decision in *Twentieth Century Music Corp. v.*

---

[2] By contrast, the VHF or UHF frequencies used by local affiliates for public broadcasts are transmitted in frequency ranges of tens to hundreds of megahertz.

[3] Defendant Jerrald Guttmann did use his satellite dish to intercept the blacked-out home game played on 4 November 1984. However, his establishment, Guttmann's, does not have a Sunday liquor license and is not open for business on Sunday; on that date, the bar was closed and the game watched only by Guttmann and three friends. The District Court found, and we agree, that such a viewing is not a public performance under Section 101 of the Copyright Act (defining public performance as a display "at a place open to the public or at any place where a substantial number of persons outside of a normal circle of a family and its social acquaintances is gathered"). . . .

Aiken, 422 U.S. 151 (1975). *Aiken* held that the owner of a small fried-chicken restaurant was not "performing" copyright works when he played a conventional radio through four in-the-ceiling speakers for the benefit of customers and employees. According to the legislative history of the 1976 Act, an act such as Aiken's would be considered a performance; to decide whether an infringement had occurred, the critical question instead would be the type of equipment used by the putative infringer. Calling "the use of a home receiver with four ordinary loud-speakers . . . the outer limit of the exemption," the drafters then said:

> the clause would exempt small commercial establishments whose propri-
> etors merely bring onto their premises standard radio or television
> equipment and turn it on for their customers' enjoyment, but it would
> impose liability where the proprietor has a commercial 'sound system'
> installed or converts a standard home receiving apparatus . . . into the
> equivalent of a commercial sound system.

H.R. Rep. No. 94-1476 at 87, 94th Cong., 2d Sess. Common sense alone says that it does not matter how well speakers amplify a performance if a receiver cannot pick up the signal in the first place. Moreover, both the legislative history and the plain language of the statute — which speaks of a "receiving set" — contemplate that how the signal is captured will be as much at issue under the exemption as how good the captured signal sounds or looks. There is no indication that the portion of a system which receives should be considered separately from that which displays.

The factors listed in the legislative history do speak of the size of the area where the transmission will be played and "the extent to which the receiving apparatus is altered . . . for the purpose of improving the aural or visual quality of the performance." And it is true, as defendants argue, that most of the cases involving the Section 110(5) exemption deal with the enhancement factor. . . . The reason, however, is that these cases have to do not with interception of blacked-out television programming, where the difficulty is in intercepting a signal, but with the playing of music for which no royalties have been paid. In this sort of case, the question as a practical matter is whether the defendant establishment is of the size and kind that Congress would expect to obtain a license through a subscription music service. . . . In the present case, however, the NFL and Cardinals are not saying the bar owners can display their programs if a license fee is paid; these plaintiffs intend that their work not be performed at all outside their aegis, making the fact of reception rather than just its quality the primary consideration. The question in this instance, therefore, is how likely the average patron who watches a blacked-out Cardinals game at one of the defendant restaurants is to have the ability to watch the same game at home? If it is likely — that is, if such systems are the "kind commonly used in private homes" — then the Section 110(5) exemption applies.

However, as the District Court in this case stated:

> There are less than 1,000,000 dish systems in use, and many of these are
> confined to commercial establishments. The dishes do have residential use
> when the home is so situated that access to television station broadcasting
> by standard television antennae is poor. Television sets can be purchased

for $100.00 or more [while] dish systems cost no less than $1,500.00 and for desired reception, $3,000.00 to $6,000.00 or more.

621 F. Supp. [880,] 887 (citation omitted).

Given these facts, the Court's finding that satellite dishes are not "commonly found in private homes" is not clearly erroneous. There was testimony that the number of such receivers has been growing rapidly, and while some day these antennae may be commonplace, they are not now. . . .

[The defendants also claim] that no infringement took place because they intercepted the clean feed, and it was the dirty feed which was fixed under the Act and for which the plaintiffs sought copyright protection. In making the argument that the clean and dirty feeds represent separate works, defendants depend on the quoted definitions, as well as a third provision of Section 101 which states that each draft version of a work "prepared over a period of time," constitutes a separate work.

The District Court rejected this theory on two grounds. Not only could the argument rule out any protection for live broadcasting by satellite transmission but, the Court said, it also ignored the fact that the game, and not the inserted commercials and station breaks, constituted the work of authorship.

We agree. Plaintiffs testified copyright protection was obtained for "the game, the game action . . . the noncommercial elements of the game." More important, the legislative history demonstrates a clear intent on the part of Congress to "resolve, through the definition of 'fixation' . . . , the status of live broadcasts," using — coincidentally but not insignificantly — the example of a live football game. H.R. 94-1476, 94th Cong., 2d Sess. 52 . . .

Defendants' final argument is that, under Section 411(b) of the Copyright Act, the District Court could not issue a permanent injunction regarding works not yet in existence. This provision allows the copyright owner of a live broadcast to institute an action either before or after fixation only if the alleged infringer has received notice between ten and 30 days before the broadcast. By its terms, say defendants, this eliminates the possibility of permanent injunctive relief in the present case.

We disagree, and hold that permanent injunctive relief was an appropriate remedy in this situation. Defendants' argument reads Section 411(b) in a vacuum, ignoring the general grant of remedial authority in Section 502(a) of the Copyright Act, which permits a court to "grant temporary and final injunctions on such terms as it may deem reasonable to prevent or restrain infringement of a copyright." 17 U.S.C. § 502(a). In copyright actions, courts traditionally have been willing to grant permanent injunctions once liability is established and a continuing threat to the copyright exists, *Pacific & Southern Co., Inc. v. Duncan*, 744 F.2d 1490, 1499 (11th Cir. 1984). The purpose of Section 411(b) was to protect live transmissions, H.R. Rep. No. 94-1476 at 157; it would subvert the Congressional goal to deny a permanent injunction in this case, where in addition to the danger of continued infringement, the notice requirement of Section 411(b) is met as a practical matter by the fact that plaintiff's home games are scheduled and the blackout decisions made on a well-known standard.[7]

Accordingly, permanent injunctive relief was appropriate . . .

NOTES AND QUESTIONS

Secondary Transmissions and the Doctrine of Multiple Performances

(1) *Some background. McBee & Bruno's* concerns one aspect of the longstanding controversy about how to treat secondary transmissions under copyright law. But what are secondary transmissions? The Act is not entirely helpful in defining the term. Throughout § 111, the operative terms are "primary transmission" and "secondary transmission." These terms are then defined in subsection (f) entirely in relation to each other. In any particular case, the "primary" transmitter is the one whose signals are being picked up and further transmitted by a "secondary" transmitter who, in turn, is someone engaged in "the further transmitting of a primary transmission simultaneously with the primary transmission . . ."

Simply put, secondary transmissions are rebroadcasts, and the possibilities of rebroadcasting a copyrighted work are endless. They can range from the local barbershop (or boutique) that plays the radio for its clientele, to the cable system that picks up a primary signal and retransmits it to millions of listeners. Whatever their respective impact on the market for a copyrighted work, both barbershop and cable system are secondary transmitters engaging in a rebroadcast of a primary broadcast.

This raises two basic questions. Is a rebroadcast of a primary transmission a public performance? If so, should a copyright owner be entitled to enforce the performance right for every rebroadcast of a work, or should the right be limited to the first transmission or in some other way? The current Copyright Act considers secondary transmissions to be performances. It has, however, limited the copyright owner's ability to control the rebroadcast of his work in four ways. *McBee & Bruno's* illustrates an aspect of the first limitation, found in § 110(5) of the statute. Section 111 imposes a complex statutory licensing system for over-the-air broadcasts by cable television systems, and §§ 119 and 122 impose similar statutory licenses on satellite retransmissions. These provisions are discussed in more detail below.

(2) As noted in *McBee & Bruno's*, the issue of what constituted an infringing "public performance" (for profit, a qualification which the 1976 Act does not contain) had a long and vexed history under the 1909 Act. The following notes retrace the convoluted doctrinal meandering — one that reflects an inherent ambivalence, if not outright discomfort, about the authority of copyright owners to control secondary transmissions of their works.

The first case was *Buck v. Jewell-La Salle Realty Co.*, 283 U.S. 191 (1931), in

---

[7] A similar theory involving future newscasts, was advanced and rejected in *Pacific & Southern*, *supra*; we agree with the Eleventh Circuit that a permanent injunction should be granted where "the registered work and the future works are so closely related, part of series of original works created with predictable regularity and similar format and function." 744 F.2d at 1499 n.17.

which a hotel received an unauthorized broadcast of a copyrighted musical work and transmitted that broadcast to all the rooms in the hotel. In a unanimous opinion by Justice Brandeis, the Court held that the hotel had publicly performed the copyrighted work. Justice Brandeis observed that "the art of radio broadcasting was unknown at the time the Copyright Act of 1909 was passed, and the means of transmission and reception now employed is wholly unlike any then in use." But, he determined, "the novelty of the means used does not lessen the duty of the courts to give full protection to the monopoly . . . which Congress has secured . . ."

Whose responsibility is it to mitigate the rigor of the copyright laws if, logically construed, they create practical difficulties or financial hardships for businesses engaged in exploiting copyrighted works by means of inventions not contemplated by Congress when the laws were adopted?

(3)   It is fair to say that the decision in *Jewell-La Salle*, whatever its jurisprudential merits, received less than worshipful treatment in the remaining trilogy of "secondary transmission" cases — *Fortnightly, Teleprompter*, and *Aiken* — decided under the 1909 Act.

In *Fortnightly Corp. v. United Artists Television, Inc.*, 392 U.S. 390 (1968), the Court addressed cable television for the first time. The defendant in *Fortnightly* operated cable systems which received broadcast signals of copyrighted motion pictures and retransmitted those signals to its subscribers without authorization. The issue before the Court was whether such activity was or was not a "performance" of the works. Writing for a 5-1 majority, Justice Stewart drew a dichotomy between broadcasters and viewers. A broadcaster, he said, "selects and procures the program to be viewed," "converts the visible images and audible sounds of the program into electronic signals," and "broadcasts the signals . . . for public reception." Viewers, on the other hand, "receive the broadcaster's signals and reconvert them into the visible images and audible sounds of the program." In short, "Broadcasters perform. Viewers do not perform." Applying this framework, the court held that cable "falls on the viewer's side of the line," because it merely "enhances the viewer's capacity to receive the broadcaster's signals." *Jewell-La Salle* was dismissed as "a questionable 35-year-old decision that has not been applied outside its own factual context."

(4)   *Fortnightly* left unresolved a number of difficult issues concerning the potential liability of cable operators under the 1909 Act, which the Court then confronted in *Teleprompter Corp. v. Columbia Broadcasting System, Inc.*, 415 U.S. 394 (1974). What if, rather than simply making local signals more readily available to subscribers, a cable system imported "distant signals" from stations outside the subscribers' immediate area? Or originated a portion of its programming "in house," much as a network affiliate would? Or inserted its own commercials in retransmitted programming?

The Second Circuit held that such practices went beyond merely enhancing a viewer's capacity to receive the original broadcaster's signal, thereby making the cable operator a "performer." 476 F.2d 338 (1973). The Supreme Court reversed, holding that as long as the cable system did not edit the programming that it retransmitted, it was acting as a viewer. In his majority opinion, however, Justice Stewart opined that television "simply cannot be controlled by means of litigation based on copyright legislation enacted more than half a century ago, when neither broadcast television nor [cable] was yet conceived." Accordingly, "any ultimate resolution of the many sensitive and important problems in this field . . . must be left to Congress."

(5)   Clearly, the decisions in *Fortnightly* and *Teleprompter* foreclosed any application of the "multiple performances" doctrine to cable television. A year after *Teleprompter*, however, the Court virtually buried whatever remained of *Jewell-La Salle*, even as to radio transmissions, in *Twentieth Century Music Corp. v. Aiken*, 422 U.S. 151 (1975), which is discussed in *McBee & Bruno's*. In *Aiken*, a Supreme Court majority led by Justice Stewart found that Aiken's activity fell on the viewer/listener's side of the line drawn in *Fortnightly* and *Teleprompter*. Justice Blackmun concurred reluctantly, complaining of the majority's "simplistic approach" but deferring to the Court's recent precedents in *Fortnightly* and *Teleprompter*. Chief Justice Burger, joined by Justice Douglas, dissented, noting: "There can be no really satisfactory solution to the problem presented here, until Congress acts in response to longstanding proposals."

(6)   Finally, in 1976, Congress *did* act, and in so doing breathed new life into the moribund doctrine of multiple performances. The portion of the House Report explicating the § 106(4) performance right under the new Act states clearly:

> Under the definitions of "perform," . . . "publicly," and "transmit" in section 101, the concept [ ] of public performance . . . cover[s] not only the initial rendition . . . , but also any further act by which that rendition . . . is transmitted or communicated to the public. Thus, for example: a singer is performing when he or she sings a song; a broadcasting network is performing when it transmits his or her performance (whether simultaneously or from records); a local broadcaster is performing when it transmits the network broadcast; *a cable television system is performing when it retransmits the broadcast to its subscribers*; and any individual is performing whenever he or she plays a phonorecord embodying the performance or communicates the performance by turning on a receiving set. Although any act by which the initial performance . . . is transmitted, repeated, or made to recur would itself be a "performance" . . . under the bill, it would not be actionable as an infringement unless it were done "publicly," as defined in section 101. Certain other performances . . . , in addition to those that are "private," are exempted or given qualified copyright control under sections 107 through [122].

H.R. Rep. No. 94-1476 at 63 (emphasis added). Thus, Congress concluded, in effect, that *Buck v. Jewell-La Salle* had been rightly decided on the question of what constitutes a performance — but that the harshness of the results produced by that logic needed to be tempered by a series of carefully crafted exemptions for specific activities. Those targeted exemptions are the subject of the remainder of these notes.

The § 110(5) Exemption

(7)   As noted in *McBee & Bruno's*, § 110(5) was enacted in response to *Aiken*. It exempts the "public reception of [a] transmission on a single receiving apparatus

of a kind commonly used in private homes" from liability under § 106(4). Note that in 1998, Congress amended § 110(5) by adding a new paragraph (B) and redesignating original § 110(5) as § 110(5)(A). Section 110(5)(B) will be considered further below; for now, we will explore the contours of § 110(5)(A).

(8) Nothing in what is now § 110(5)(A) restricts its application to radio transmissions. Television, too, is covered, as *McBee & Bruno's* demonstrates. But note that only *transmissions* are covered. Other public performances (or displays), such as playing CDs or DVDs in public, are outside the scope of this particular limitation, although they may be covered by some other limitation or exemption in §§ 107 through 122.

(9) Most of the post-1976 Act cases which construed original § 110(5) involved background music in commercial establishments. They dealt with a number of recurrent questions such as: What constitutes a "home-style apparatus" for the purposes of § 110(5)(A)? And is a multi-store chain eligible for the exemption on a store-by-store basis? Some courts took an "economic" approach, asking whether it would have been reasonable to insist that the establishment seek a license. *See, e.g., Sailor Music v. Gap Stores, Inc.*, 668 F.2d 84 (2d Cir. 1981). Other courts hewed more closely to the statute in declining to look beyond the type of equipment used. For an excellent summary, see *Broadcast Music, Inc. v. Claire's Boutiques, Inc.*, 949 F.2d 1482 (7th Cir. 1991).

Which of these approaches is taken in *McBee & Bruno's*? Would the case be decided differently today, when satellite receivers (of one kind or another) are increasingly common in private homes? Does the court's rigorous focus on this issue obscure other important considerations?

See also *American Broadcasting Cos. v. Flying J, Inc.*, 2007 U.S. Dist. LEXIS 13252 (S.D.N.Y. 2007), which involved a chain of truck stops that received satellite TV signals but also utilized a device that switched to pre-recorded substitute advertisements whenever it detected broadcast commercials in the satellite TV signal. The District Court held that the truck stops violated the public performance right in the broadcast programming, because the commercial-switching device was not one "commonly used in private homes." Is this consistent with the *McBee & Bruno* court's conclusion that "the game, and not the inserted commercials and station breaks, constituted the work of authorship"?

(10) One of the reasons there was so much litigation concerning original § 110(5) was because ASCAP and BMI consistently took the position that the exemption was limited to stores no larger than the tiny fast-food restaurant in *Aiken*. Is there anything in the statute that warrants such a construction? As a practical matter, the size of the establishment often made a difference, although results were not always consistent. For example, in *Springsteen v. Plaza Roller Dome, Inc.*, 602 F. Supp. 1113 (M.D.N.C. 1985), the court held that performances over a radio wired to six speakers mounted on light poles dispersed over a 7,500-square-foot miniature golf course came within the exemption; but in *Sailor Music*, the exemption was held not to apply where defendant's store occupied 2,769 square feet and made use of four speakers.

(11)   Such inconsistencies were one of the reasons behind the enactment of § 110(5)(B) in the Fairness in Music Licensing Act of 1998 (or FIMLA). FIMLA was the culmination of years of complaints against ASCAP and BMI over alleged strong-arm licensing practices for bars and restaurants. Whether such complaints were justified or reflected instead the desire to get something for nothing, these businesses had enough support in Congress to hold up passage of the Sonny Bono Copyright Term Extension Act (discussed in § 5.01 of this casebook) until FIMLA was enacted.

In contrast to the flexible but uncertain language of what is now § 110(5)(A), § 110(5)(B) takes a detailed black-letter approach. It establishes an exemption (limited to nondramatic musical works) for bars and restaurants up to 3,750 square feet, and for other businesses up to 2,000 square feet (excluding dedicated customer parking spaces), or for larger establishments that use no more than six speakers (of which up to four can be in one area of the premises) to make musical broadcasts audible, and no more than four monitors of up to 55 square inches each for video portions of broadcast musical performances. As with subsection (A), § 110(5)(B) applies only if the establishment doesn't charge customers for the music and doesn't further retransmit the broadcasts.

What, then, remains of old § 110(5), now § 110(5)(A)? Of course, it continues to apply to situations like that in *McBee & Bruno*'s, where the retransmission involves works of a kind *other than* nondramatic musical works, *e.g.*, NFL games. In addition, § 110(5)(A) remains as a possible "fall-back" for establishments that rebroadcast musical works without a license but don't, for some reason, qualify for exemption under § 110(5)(B) — perhaps because their square footage is a bit too great or their speakers a trifle too numerous. How likely do you think it is that courts will look sympathetically at such defenses?

(12)   FIMLA's most innovative provision was the addition of § 513, which entitles an individual proprietor to seek a determination that the license fee being offered by ASCAP or BMI is unreasonable. The determination of disputed rates is to be made by a special master appointed by a judge of the Southern District of New York (which has jurisdiction over the consent decrees), at a hearing to be held either in New York City or "in that place of holding court of a district court that is the seat for the Federal circuit . . . in which the proprietor's establishment is located." (Pity the poor restaurant owner in Puerto Rico who has to schlep to Boston for his day in court!)

(13)   International developments have left the future of § 110(5) in considerable doubt. After the enactment of FIMLA, various countries of the European Union, led by Ireland, lodged a complaint with the World Trade Organization concerning § 110(5), based on Article 13 of the TRIPS Agreement. In 2000, a WTO dispute resolution panel affirmed that the United States was violating global rules on intellectual property protection.

The three-member panel concluded that § 110(5)(B) is inconsistent with Article 13, which confines limitations and exceptions on copyright under national law to "certain special cases which do not conflict with a normal exploitation of the work and do not unreasonably prejudice the legitimate interests of the right holder." In particular, the panel noted that § 110(5)(B) would allow 70 percent of restaurants and bars and nearly half the retail stores in the United States to avoid paying license fees for broadcast music played in their establishments. Moreover, it is unlikely that the United States could bring itself into compliance merely by reinstating the "home-style apparatus" provisions of old § 110(5). Although the WTO panel determined that § 110(5)(A) was compatible with TRIPS, this was only because the panel (somewhat dubiously) concluded that § 110(5)(A) no longer applied to nondramatic musical works. The WTO panel report (WT/DS160/R) is available at *www.wto.org/english/tratop_e/dispu_e/cases_e/ds160_e.htm*. Although the United States had the option of appealing the panel's action, it did not, with the result that the decision stands as a final determination of the WTO Dispute Settlement Body.

But what comes next? When Rep. James Sensenbrenner (R-Wis.), who was the principal sponsor of FIMLA, was the chair of the House Judiciary Committee, repeal was highly unlikely. The interim solution was a program of reparations — $1.1 million a year in compensation paid to the EU by the U.S. Government for three years. The last payment was made in 2004, however, and the matter technically remains open. If the United States fails to bring its laws into compliance, theoretically it could be subject to trade sanctions from other WTO members. Whether or not that happens, it is clear that non-compliance is harming the United States' credibility in negotiations with other countries regarding intellectual property matters.

[3] The Cable System Limitations

Section 111 ("Limitations on Exclusive Rights: Secondary Transmissions"), one of the longest and most complex sections in the Copyright Act, regulates the operations of cable television systems. Section 111(f) defines "cable system" as a "facility . . . that in whole or in part receives signals transmitted or programs broadcast by one or more television broadcast stations licensed by the Federal Communications Commission and makes secondary transmissions of such signals or programs by wire, cables, microwave, or other communications channels to subscribing members of the public who pay for such service." The statutory licensing system provided by § 111 as a whole reflects a political compromise between avoiding full copyright liability for cable retransmission and a total exemption.

Section 111 generally, and the definitions in § 111(f) particularly, make plain that an unauthorized retransmission of a signal embodying a copyrighted work is indeed a "performance" under the 1976 Act. Ironically, although the Act thus concurs with *Jewell-La Salle* on this fundamental analytical point, it then creates a specific exemption for the conduct condemned in *Jewell-La Salle*. § 111(a)(1).

The philosophy of § 111 concerning cable television systems is stated in its essentials in a single sentence in the House Report: "In general, the committee believes that cable systems are commercial enterprises whose basic retransmission operations are based on the carriage of copyrighted program material and that copyright royalties should be paid by cable operators to the creators of such programs." In order to accommodate the needs of cable operators for programming and the rights of copyright owners to royalties, § 111 creates an elaborate statutory licensing system. Detailed exploration of that system is best left to specialized courses in communications law. You may find it useful, however, to review the following summary of the structure of § 111:

Subsection (a) exempts five specified types of secondary transmissions from liability for infringing the § 106(4) performance right: (1) transmissions by hotels, motels, apartment houses, etc., to the private lodgings of their guests, if no separate charge is made for the transmission (the *Jewell-La Salle* exemption); (2) transmissions that satisfy § 110(2) of the Act (*i.e.*, instructional broadcasts); (3) transmissions by passive carriers supplying only wires, cables or other communications channels for use by others and exercising no control over the transmission's contents or recipients (*see, e.g.*, *Eastern Microwave, Inc. v. Doubleday Sports, Inc.*, 691 F.2d 125 (2d Cir. 1982)); (4) transmissions made by satellite carriers under § 119; and (5) transmissions by governmental bodies or other nonprofit organizations, charged to recipients on a cost basis and without any purpose of commercial advantage (*e.g.*, nonprofit community "translator" or "booster" services).

Subsection (b) of § 111 imposes full liability on the secondary transmitter "if the primary transmission [which is subject to the secondary transmission] is not made for reception by the public at large but is controlled and limited to reception by particular members of the public." In effect, this provision prevents the retransmission without permission of closed circuit broadcasts, pay cable, subscription television, background music, and other such services intended for limited audiences.

Subsection (c) creates a statutory license for cable television systems. Generally speaking, the license is available with respect to any primary transmission by a television station licensed by the Federal Communications Commission, provided that such retransmission is permitted under FCC rules and regulations. § 111(c)(1). In instances where such retransmission is not permitted by applicable rules and regulations, "willful or repeated" transgressions may result in full liability for infringement of the copyrights in the retransmitted broadcasts. § 111(c)(2). Similarly, the benefit of a statutory license generally will be denied if the content of the program or any accompanying commercials is altered willfully by the cable system. § 111(c)(3). The final provision of the subsection extends the availability of statutory licenses to cable systems operated in specified zones in Canada and Mexico near the American border. § 111(c)(4).

Subsection (d) governs the actual operation of the statutory licensing system: It prescribes the amounts of royalties to be paid by cable operators, describes the role of the Copyright Royalty Judges, and so on. Subsection (e) provides for tapings and retransmissions of copyrighted materials by certain off-shore cable systems. Subsection (f) is devoted to specialized definitions not contained in § 101 because of their particular applicability to the subject of secondary transmissions.

As an intricate regulatory measure, § 111 stands out from most of the rest of the Act. Its very length and complexity suggest the intense political compromise between industry participants involved in the passage of the Act. Is it an anachronism? Section 111 has not worked smoothly in practice and has led to much litigation over the distribution of royalties. *See, e.g., Program Suppliers v. Librarian of Congress*, 409 F.3d 395 (D.C. Cir. 2005). Moreover, cable television is no longer the fledgling industry it was three decades ago. Critics argue that the regulatory and technological environment that led to § 111 has changed radically, and that a market-oriented system would now be preferable. *Cf. WPIX, Inc. v. ivi, Inc.*, 691 F.3d 275 (2d Cir. 2012) (holding that an Internet retransmitter was not a "cable system" within the meaning of § 111). What do you think?

In 2009, the Copyright Office issued a report that concluded that § 111 should be significantly modified and phased out by the end of 2014. This report is discussed in § 7.05[B] below. Congress, however, has not acted on the report and has made only minor amendments to § 111.

[4] The Satellite Carrier Limitations

Cable television may have been a "state of the art" development when the 1976 Act was adopted, but retransmission technologies continued, of course, to advance in sophistication. The most notable development, in terms of its impact on the Copyright Act to date, was the introduction of various technologies for satellite home viewing. This development initially led to considerable confusion and conflict over the proper characterization of satellite systems for purposes of the § 111 statutory license.

The response was new legislation: the Satellite Home Viewer Act of 1988, creating a new statutory license, specifically tailored for satellite systems, in § 119 of the Copyright Act. Section 119 initially was enacted on an interim basis, with a sunset date of December 31, 1994. It has, however, been modified and extended for successive five-year periods, the last of which is provided for by the Satellite Television Extension and Localism Act of 2010.

Section 119 covers the retransmission of copyrighted works included in primary transmissions made by both non-network stations (so-called "superstations") and by network stations outside of their local markets. In addition, in 1999 Congress added a permanent, royalty-free statutory license in § 122 for retransmission of copyrighted works included in a primary transmission by a television broadcast station into its local market (so-called "local-to-local" satellite retransmissions). *See Satellite Broadcasting & Communications Ass'n v. FCC*, 275 F.3d 337 (4th Cir. 2001) (upholding § 122's "carry one, carry all" rule against Constitutional challenge).

As amended in 2004, § 119 treats satellite retransmissions of superstation programming and network programming in substantially different ways. Satellite retransmissions of superstation programming are subject to relatively few significant conditions other than payment of royalties. (In particular, superstations may be retransmitted for viewing in "commercial establishments" as well as for private home viewing.) By contrast, satellite retransmissions of distant network programming qualify for the statutory license only if they are made "to the public for private home viewing," and they are subject to a number of additional conditions, some of which are carried over from previous legislation.

In particular, distant network programming may only be retransmitted to so-called "unserved households," those which are unable to receive an adequate network signal from a station in their home market. The purpose of this limitation is to prevent satellite TV operators from substituting distant network affiliate signals for the signals of local network affiliates. Significant remedies are available against satellite broadcasters who persistently disregard the limitation. *See CBS Broadcasting, Inc. v. EchoStar Communication Corp.*, 450 F.3d 505 (11th Cir. 2006) (upholding finding that satellite carrier was guilty of "willful and repeated violations" of § 119, and remanding for entry of mandatory nationwide permanent injunction against use of the statutory license).

In May 2009, after months of wrangling and three temporary extensions, Congress finally reached agreement on an extension of the existing § 119 license for another five years, with more limited amendments than those recommend by the Copyright Office. The Satellite Television Extension and Localism Act (STELA) of 2010 expands the definition of "unserved households" for purposes of importing distant network signals; and it lifts an injunction previously entered against satellite provider DISH Network, on the condition that it provide local-to-local retransmission into all 210 Designated Market Areas in the United States. *See also DISH Network, Inc. v. FCC*, 636 F.3d 1139 (9th Cir. 2011) (requirement under STELA that satellite providers carry public broadcasting channels in HD as a condition of the statutory license does not violate the First Amendment). You can read the text of the legislation at *www.copyright.gov/legislation.*

[5] Current Issues in the Law of Retransmission

Retransmission consent. Before the § 122 statutory license for "local-to-local" satellite retransmissions was added in 1999, satellite providers operated under an obvious competitive disadvantage vis-à-vis cable television providers. In 1992, legislative proposals which attempted to "level the playing field" for competing systems, while phasing out the statutory license in favor of negotiation and arbitration, failed. Instead, the Cable Television Consumer Protection and Competition Act of 1992 superimposed onto the cable television statutory license the further complication of a broadcaster's "retransmission consent," provided for in the Federal Communications Act. 47 U.S.C. § 325(b). This provision required cable operators to negotiate (under certain circumstances) for the right to carry over-the-air signals — as distinct from the copyrighted programming contained in those signals, which was subject to a statutory license. If broadcasters cannot agree on terms with local cable systems, their particular signals will not be available to subscribers — although much of the same programming might be available from other sources. When § 122 was added in 1999, Congress extended the relevant provisions of the Federal Communications Act (including those relating to "retransmission consent") to satellite systems.

Retransmission consent has been criticized as a kind of "quasi-copyright" within federal communications law. How much economic or technological sense does it make to distinguish conceptually between rights in a broadcast signal, as such, and rights in broadcast programming? Do local broadcasters contribute any "value added" beyond the copyrighted works they put out over the air? Conversely, given that a broadcaster has a strong economic interest in making its signal available to as many subscribers as possible, is it likely that retransmission consent has blocked the retransmission of programming permitted by the Copyright Act for any significant period of time? Whatever its merits, "retransmission consent" seems firmly ensconced in the fabric of the Communications Act, and it is unlikely that it will be repealed anytime soon.

Future directions. In 2009, in response to a request from Congress, the Copyright Office submitted a report that concluded that "the current versions of Section 111 and Section 119 are arcane, antiquated, complicated, and dysfunctional." Accordingly, the Office recommended that Congress "adopt a new, forward looking unified statutory license, with a simplified rate structure, that takes into account marketplace conditions and recognizes the current FCC regulatory framework." The report explained:

> The principal recommendation . . . is that Congress move toward abolishing Section 111 and Section 119 of the Act. The cable and satellite industries are no longer nascent entities in need of government subsidies through a statutory licensing system. They have substantial market power and are able to negotiate private agreements with copyright owners for programming carried on distant broadcast signals. . . . [T]he Internet video marketplace is robust and is functioning well without a statutory license. . . . The Office nevertheless recommends the retention of [the Section 122] royalty-free local-into-local license, because such a license is still necessary and it promotes the general welfare of users, broadcasters, and the public.

> Despite the Office's determination that the ultimate solution should be the elimination of the existing distant signal licenses, the Office recognizes that the digital television transition in 2009 is likely to generate unanticipated signal reception problems for millions of American households. . . . The Office therefore recommends the establishment of a new statutory licensing system that would cover the retransmission of distant broadcast signals beginning on January 1, 2010 and ending on December 31, 2014. This will permit users of the license to serve the needs of their subscribers who may experience viewing disruptions. An equally important rationale for a transitional license is that it will take time for voluntary licensing arrangements to take shape and become widely available.

Alternatively, the Copyright Office recommended that if Congress wanted to maintain the existing separate cable and satellite retransmission licenses, it should enact a suite of amendments to update and modernize the licenses. In response, Congress extended the § 119 license with only minor amendments and postponed the sunset date. You can read the report in full at *www.copyright.gov/reports/section109-final-report.pdf.*

§ 7.06 THE PUBLIC DISPLAY RIGHT

Section 106(5) of the 1976 Act specifically recognizes the right of public display for the first time in American copyright law. This right applies to all categories of copyrightable subject matter other than sound recordings and architectural works.

Under § 101,

> to "display" a work means to show a copy of it, either directly or by means
> of a film, slide, television image, or any other device or process or, in the
> case of a motion picture or other audiovisual work, to show individual
> images nonsequentially.

Thus, a series of still photographs of a dancer or a pantomimist would not
infringe the performance right but might infringe the display right in the
choreographic work or pantomime. Notice also that, like the performance right, the
right of display is limited to *public* displays.

[A]   Introduction

Statutory References

1976 Act: §§ 101 ("display"), 106(5), 109(c) and (d), 110-13, 118-20, 122

1909 Act: —

Legislative History

H.R. Rep. No. 94-1476 at 62-64, 79-80,
reprinted in 1976 U.S.C.C.A.N. 5659, 5676-77, 5693-94

Section 106. Exclusive Rights in Copyrighted Works[1]

Rights of public performance and display . . .

Right of public display. — Clause (5) of section 106 represents the first explicit
statutory recognition in American copyright law of an exclusive right to show a
copyrighted work, or an image of it, to the public. The existence or extent of this
right under the [1909 Act] is uncertain and subject to challenge. The bill would give
the owners of copyright in "literary, musical, dramatic, and choreographic works,
pantomimes, and pictorial, graphic, or sculptural works," including the individual
images of a motion picture or other audiovisual work, the exclusive right "to display
the copyrighted work publicly."

Definitions

The . . . definition of "display" [in § 101] covers any showing of a "copy" of the
work, "either directly or by means of a film, slide, television image, or any other
device or process." Since "copies" are defined as including the material object "in
which the work is first fixed," the right of public display applies to original works of
art as well as to reproductions of them. With respect to motion pictures and other
audiovisual works, it is a "display" (rather than a "performance") to show their
"individual images nonsequentially." In addition to the direct showings of a copy of
a work, "display" would include the projection of an image on a screen or other
surface by any method, the transmission of an image by electronic or other means,

---

[1] See also § 7.05[A] history above. — *Eds.*

and the showing of an image on a cathode ray tube, or similar viewing apparatus connected with any sort of information storage and retrieval system. . . .

SECTION 109. EFFECT OF TRANSFER OF PARTICULAR COPY OR PHONORECORD . . .

Effect of display of copy . . .

Section 109[(c)] adopts the general principle that the lawful owner of a copy of a work should be able to put his copy on public display without the consent of the copyright owner. As in cases arising under section 109(a), this does not mean that contractual restrictions on display between a buyer and seller would be unenforceable as a matter of contract law.

The exclusive right of public display granted by section 106(5) would not apply where the owner of a copy wishes to show it directly to the public, as in a gallery or display case, or indirectly, as through an opaque projector. Where the copy itself is intended for projection, as in the case of a photographic slide, negative, or transparency, the public projection of a single image would be permitted as long as the viewers are "present at the place where the copy is located." . . .

Moreover, the exemption would extend only to public displays that are made "either directly or by the projection of no more than one image at a time." . . . For example, where each person in a lecture hall is supplied with a separate viewing apparatus, the copyright owner's permission would generally be required in order to project an image of a work on each individual screen at the same time.

[Other relevant portions of the legislative history of the 1976 Act as originally enacted appeared or were referenced earlier in this book: § 109(d), in § 7.04[A]; § 110, in § 7.05[A]; § 111, in § 7.05[B]; § 112, in § 7.02[B]; and § 118, in § 7.05[A]. In addition, you should familiarize yourself with three other provisions of the Act subsequently added by amendment: § 120, covered earlier in § 3.01[G]; and §§ 119 and 122, just discussed in § 7.05[B].]

[B]   Case Law

PERFECT 10, INC. v. AMAZON.COM, INC.
United States Court of Appeals, Ninth Circuit
508 F.3d 1146 (2007)

IKUTA, CIRCUIT JUDGE:

In this appeal, we consider a copyright owner's efforts to stop an Internet search engine from facilitating access to infringing images. Perfect 10, Inc. sued Google Inc., for infringing Perfect 10's copyrighted photographs of nude models, among other claims. Perfect 10 brought a similar action against Amazon.com and its subsidiary A9.com (collectively, "Amazon.com"). The district court preliminarily enjoined Google from creating and publicly displaying thumbnail versions of Perfect 10's images, *Perfect 10 v. Google, Inc.*, 416 F. Supp. 2d 828 (C.D. Cal. 2006), but did not enjoin Google from linking to third-party websites that display infringing full-size versions of Perfect 10's images. Nor did the district court preliminarily enjoin Amazon.com from giving users access to information provided by Google. Perfect 10 and Google both appeal the district court's order. . . . We affirm in part, reverse in part, and remand.

I. Background

. . . Computer owners can provide information stored on their computers to other users connected to the Internet through a medium called a webpage. A webpage consists of text interspersed with instructions written in Hypertext Markup Language ("HTML") that is stored in a computer. No images are stored on a webpage; rather, the HTML instructions on the webpage provide an address for where the images are stored, whether in the webpage publisher's computer or some other computer. . . .

Google operates a search engine, a software program that automatically accesses thousands of websites (collections of webpages) and indexes them within a database stored on Google's computers. . . .

The Google search engine that provides responses in the form of images is called "Google Image Search." In response to a search query, Google Image Search identifies text in its database responsive to the query and then communicates to users the images associated with the relevant text. Google's software cannot recognize and index the images themselves. Google Image Search provides search results as a webpage of small images called "thumbnails," which are stored in Google's servers. The thumbnail images are reduced, lower-resolution versions of full-sized images stored on third-party computers.

When a user clicks on a thumbnail image, the user's browser program interprets HTML instructions on Google's webpage. These HTML instructions direct the user's browser to cause a rectangular area (a "window") to appear on the user's computer screen. The window has two separate areas of information. The browser fills the top section of the screen with information from the Google webpage, including the thumbnail image and text. The HTML instructions also give the user's browser the address of the computer that stores the full-size version of the thumbnail. By following the HTML instructions to access the third-party webpage, the user's browser connects to the website publisher's computer, downloads the full-size image, and makes the image appear at the bottom of the window on the user's screen. Google does not store the images that fill this lower part of the window and does not communicate the images to the user; Google simply provides HTML instructions directing a user's browser to access a third-party website. However, the top part of the window (containing the information from the Google webpage) appears to frame and comment on the bottom part of the window. Thus, the user's window appears to be filled with a single integrated presentation of the full-size image, but it is actually an image from a third-party website framed by information from Google's website. The process by which the webpage directs a user's browser to incorporate content from different computers into a single window is referred to as "in-line linking." *Kelly v. Arriba Soft Corp.*, 336 F.3d 811, 816 (9th Cir. 2003). The term "framing" refers to the process by which information from one computer appears to frame and annotate the in-line linked content from another computer. *Perfect 10*, 416 F. Supp. 2d at 833-34.

Google also stores webpage content in its cache.[3] For each cached webpage, Google's cache contains the text of the webpage as it appeared at the time Google indexed the page, but does not store images from the webpage. Google may provide a link to a cached webpage in response to a user's search query. However, Google's cache version of the webpage is not automatically updated when the webpage is revised by its owner. So if the webpage owner updates its webpage to remove the HTML instructions for finding an infringing image, a browser communicating directly with the webpage would not be able to access that image. However, Google's cache copy of the webpage would still have the old HTML instructions for the infringing image. Unless the owner of the computer changed the HTML address of the infringing image, or otherwise rendered the image unavailable, a browser accessing Google's cache copy of the website could still access the image where it is stored on the website publisher's computer. In other words, Google's cache copy could provide a user's browser with valid directions to an infringing image even though the updated webpage no longer includes that infringing image. . . .

Perfect 10 markets and sells copyrighted images of nude models. Among other enterprises, it operates a subscription website on the Internet. Subscribers pay a monthly fee to view Perfect 10 images in a "members' area" of the site. Subscribers must use a password to log into the members' area. Google does not include these password-protected images from the members' area in Google's index or database. Perfect 10 has also licensed Fonestarz Media Limited to sell and distribute Perfect 10's reduced-size copyrighted images for download and use on cell phones.

Some website publishers republish Perfect 10's images on the Internet without authorization. Once this occurs, Google's search engine may automatically index the webpages containing these images and provide thumbnail versions of images in response to user inquiries. When a user clicks on the thumbnail image returned by Google's search engine, the user's browser accesses the third-party webpage and in-line links to the full-sized infringing image stored on the website publisher's computer. This image appears, in its original context, on the lower portion of the window on the user's computer screen framed by information from Google's webpage. . . .

III. Direct Infringement

Perfect 10 claims that Google's search engine program directly infringes [the public display right] granted to copyright holders [in § 106(5)]. . . .

The district court held that Perfect 10 was likely to prevail in its claim that Google violated Perfect 10's display right with respect to the infringing thumbnails. However, the district court concluded that Perfect 10 was not likely to prevail on its

---

[3] Generally, a "cache" is "a computer memory with very short access time used for storage of frequently or recently used instructions or data." *United States v. Ziegler*, 474 F.3d 1184, 1186 n.3 (9th Cir. 2007) (quoting MERRIAM-WEBSTER'S COLLEGIATE DICTIONARY 171 (11th ed. 2003)). There are two types of caches at issue in this case. A user's personal computer has an internal cache that saves copies of webpages and images that the user has recently viewed so that the user can more rapidly revisit these webpages and images. Google's computers also have a cache which serves a variety of purposes. Among other things, Google's cache saves copies of a large number of webpages so that Google's search engine can efficiently organize and index these webpages.

claim that Google violated either Perfect 10's display or distribution right with respect to its full-size infringing images. We review these rulings for an abuse of discretion. . . .

A. Display Right

In considering whether Perfect 10 made a prima facie case of violation of its display right, the district court reasoned that a computer owner that stores an image as electronic information and serves that electronic information directly to the user ("*i.e.,* physically sending ones and zeroes over the [I]nternet to the user's browser," *Perfect 10*, 416 F. Supp. 2d at 839) is displaying the electronic information in violation of a copyright holder's exclusive display right. . . . Conversely, the owner of a computer that does not store and serve the electronic information to a user is not displaying that information, even if such owner in-line links to or frames the electronic information. The district court referred to this test as the "server test."

Applying the server test, the district court concluded that Perfect 10 was likely to succeed in its claim that Google's thumbnails constituted direct infringement but was unlikely to succeed in its claim that Google's in-line linking to full-size infringing images constituted a direct infringement. As explained below, because this analysis comports with the language of the Copyright Act, we agree with the district court's resolution of both these issues.

We have not previously addressed the question when a computer displays a copyrighted work for purposes of section 106(5). Section 106(5) states that a copyright owner has the exclusive right "to display the copyrighted work publicly." The Copyright Act explains that "display" means "to show a copy of it, either directly or by means of a film, slide, television image, or any other device or process. . . ." 17 U.S.C. § 101. Section 101 defines "copies" as "material objects, other than phonorecords, in which a work is fixed by any method now known or later developed, and from which the work can be perceived, reproduced, or otherwise communicated, either directly or with the aid of a machine or device." *Id.* Finally, the Copyright Act provides that "[a] work is 'fixed' in a tangible medium of expression when its embodiment in a copy or phonorecord, by or under the authority of the author, is sufficiently permanent or stable to permit it to be perceived, reproduced, or otherwise communicated for a period of more than transitory duration." *Id.*

We must now apply these definitions to the facts of this case. A photographic image is a work that is " 'fixed' in a tangible medium of expression," for purposes of the Copyright Act, when embodied (*i.e.,* stored) in a computer's server (or hard disk, or other storage device). The image stored in the computer is the "copy" of the work for purposes of copyright law. *See MAI Sys. Corp. v. Peak Computer, Inc.*, 991 F.2d 511, 517-18 (9th Cir. 1993) (a computer makes a "copy" of a software program when it transfers the program from a third party's computer (or other storage device) into its own memory, because the copy of the program recorded in the computer is "fixed" in a manner that is "sufficiently permanent or stable to permit it to be perceived, reproduced, or otherwise communicated for a period of more than transitory duration" (quoting 17 U.S.C. § 101)). The computer owner shows a copy "by means of a . . . device or process" when the owner uses the computer to fill the computer screen with the photographic image stored on that computer, or by communicating the stored image electronically to another person's computer. 17 U.S.C. § 101. In sum, based on the plain language of the statute, a person displays a photographic image by using a computer to fill a computer screen with a copy of the photographic image fixed in the computer's memory. There is no dispute that Google's computers store thumbnail versions of Perfect 10's copyrighted images and communicate copies of those thumbnails to Google's users.[6] Therefore, Perfect 10 has made a prima facie case that Google's communication of its stored thumbnail images directly infringes Perfect 10's display right.

Google does not, however, display a copy of full-size infringing photographic images for purposes of the Copyright Act when Google frames in-line linked images that appear on a user's computer screen. Because Google's computers do not store the photographic images, Google does not have a copy of the images for purposes of the Copyright Act. In other words, Google does not have any "material objects . . . in which a work is fixed . . . and from which the work can be perceived, reproduced, or otherwise communicated" and thus cannot communicate a copy. 17 U.S.C. § 101.

Instead of communicating a copy of the image, Google provides HTML instructions that direct a user's browser to a website publisher's computer that stores the full-size photographic image. Providing these HTML instructions is not equivalent to showing a copy. First, the HTML instructions are lines of text, not a photographic image. Second, HTML instructions do not themselves cause infringing images to appear on the user's computer screen. The HTML merely gives the address of the image to the user's browser. The browser then interacts with the computer that stores the infringing image. It is this interaction that causes an infringing image to appear on the user's computer screen. Google may facilitate the user's access to infringing images. However, such assistance raises only contributory liability issues, *see Metro-Goldwyn-Mayer Studios, Inc. v. Grokster, Ltd.*, 545 U.S. 913, 929-30 (2005), and does not constitute direct infringement of the copyright owner's display rights.

Perfect 10 argues that Google displays a copy of the full-size images by framing the full-size images, which gives the impression that Google is showing the image within a single Google webpage. While in-line linking and framing may cause some computer users to believe they are viewing a single Google webpage, the Copyright Act, unlike the Trademark Act, does not protect a copyright holder against acts that cause consumer confusion. *Cf.* 15 U.S.C. § 1114(1) (providing that a person who uses a trademark in a manner likely to cause confusion shall be liable in a civil action to the trademark registrant).[7]

---

[6] Because Google initiates and controls the storage and communication of these thumbnail images, we do not address whether an entity that merely passively owns and manages an Internet bulletin board or similar system violates a copyright owner's display and distribution rights when the users of the bulletin board or similar system post infringing works. *Cf. CoStar Group, Inc. v. LoopNet, Inc.*, 373 F.3d 544 (4th Cir. 2004).

[7] Perfect 10 also argues that Google violates Perfect 10's right to display full-size images because Google's in-line linking meets the Copyright Act's definition of "to perform or display a work 'publicly.' " 17 U.S.C. § 101. This phrase means "to transmit or otherwise communicate a performance or display of

Nor does our ruling that a computer owner does not display a copy of an image when it communicates only the HTML address of the copy erroneously collapse the display right in section 106(5) into the reproduction right set forth in section 106(1). Nothing in the Copyright Act prevents the various rights protected in section 106 from overlapping. Indeed, under some circumstances, more than one right must be infringed in order for an infringement claim to arise. For example, a "Game Genie" device that allowed a player to alter features of a Nintendo computer game did not infringe Nintendo's right to prepare derivative works because the Game Genie did not incorporate any portion of the game itself. *See Lewis Galoob Toys, Inc. v. Nintendo of Am., Inc.*, 964 F.2d 965, 967 (9th Cir. 1992). We held that a copyright holder's right to create derivative works is not infringed unless the alleged derivative work "incorporate[s] a protected work in some concrete or permanent 'form.' " *Id.* In other words, in some contexts, the claimant must be able to claim infringement of its reproduction right in order to claim infringement of its right to prepare derivative works.

Because Google's cache merely stores the text of webpages, our analysis of whether Google's search engine program potentially infringes Perfect 10's display right is equally applicable to Google's cache. Perfect 10 is not likely to succeed in showing that a cached webpage that in-line links to full-size infringing images violates such rights. For purposes of this analysis, it is irrelevant whether cache copies direct a user's browser to third-party images that are no longer available on the third party's website, because it is the website publisher's computer, rather than Google's computer, that stores and displays the infringing image. . . .

[The Court of Appeals agreed with the trial court that Perfect 10 was unlikely to prove that Google violated its distribution rights with respect to full-size images. For reference to the appeals court's discussion of secondary liability issues, see § 9.03[D] below. For discussion of the court's conclusions regarding fair use, see § 10.04[B] below.]

VI. [Conclusion]

. . . [W]e reverse the district court's ruling and vacate the preliminary injunction regarding Google's use of thumbnail versions of Perfect 10's images. We reverse the district court's rejection of the claims that Google and Amazon.com are secondarily liable for infringement of Perfect 10's full-size images. We otherwise affirm the rulings of the district court.

---

the work to . . . the public, by means of any device or process, whether the members of the public capable of receiving the performance or display receive it in the same place or in separate places and at the same time or at different times." *Id.* Perfect 10 is mistaken. Google's activities do not meet this definition because Google transmits or communicates only an address which directs a user's browser to the location where a copy of the full-size image is displayed. Google does not communicate a display of the work itself.

NOTES AND QUESTIONS

(1) In addition to the rights of reproduction, adaptation, distribution, and performance recognized under prior law, the 1976 Act explicitly grants to copyright owners the exclusive right to "display . . . publicly" certain types of works. The public display right applies to literary, musical, dramatic, pantomime, and choreographic works, to pictorial, graphic, and sculptural works, and to the individual images contained in motion pictures and other audiovisual works. *See Michaels v. Internet Entertainment Group, Inc.*, 5 F. Supp. 2d 823 (C.D. Cal. 1998) (unauthorized display of still images from sex tape of rock singer Bret Michaels and actress Pamela Anderson Lee). What works are excluded from this list, and why? Note also that the right to "display" extends to copies but not to phonorecords (because § 101 specifies that "[t]o 'display' a work means to show a copy of it . . .").

(2) As indicated in the House Report to the 1976 Act, § 106(5) applies not only to "direct showings of a copy of the work," but also to "the projection of an image [of the work] on a screen or other surface" and to "the transmission of an image by electronic or other means." The House Report also states (in discussing § 109) that "the display of a visual image of a copyrighted work would be an infringement if the image were transmitted by any method" (including "by a computer system").

This language in the House Report was relied on in *Kelly v. Arriba Soft, Inc.*, 280 F.3d 934 (9th Cir. 2002), *superseded*, 336 F.3d 811 (9th Cir. 2003). Arriba Soft operated a visual search engine (similar to Google's) and provided links to unauthorized websites bearing Kelly's copyrighted photographs. It also framed the photos in its own website. In its initial opinion, the court held that Arriba Soft infringed Kelly's public display right by allowing the public to view the copyrighted photographs while visiting Arriba Soft's website. On reconsideration, however, the court vacated this portion of the opinion because the issue had not been raised below. It took four years for the issue that was left unresolved in *Kelly* to return to the Ninth Circuit in *Perfect 10*. (*Kelly* also inquired whether making and displaying "thumbnails" was a fair use. This portion of the amended opinion is reprinted in § 10.04 below.)

(3) Notwithstanding the language in the House Report, the *Perfect 10* court relies on the definition of "display" in § 101 to conclude that Google does not "display" the full-size images that are stored on unauthorized third-party websites by including in its image-search results an in-line link to those images. Do you agree with the court's analysis? When a user clicks on a thumbnail in Google's search engine, the user sees the full-size image in the resulting window. Google's computers supplied the link that instructed the user's browser where to find the image. Why should Google not be directly liable when the user views an unauthorized image?

Suppose a reclusive collector owns a copyrighted painting that is displayed in his own home. Suppose further that a budding entrepreneur trains a high-powered telescope at the painting through a window, and uses a projector to display the telescopic image onto a wall, where he charges viewers to see the work. Can the entrepreneur avoid liability by arguing that he "does not have a copy of the image" within the meaning of the Copyright Act? If not, why does Google avoid liability? Is the problem that Google does not possess a copy, or that it did not act with the necessary volition? Recall the *Cartoon Network* case in § 7.02 above.

(4)   Does the *Perfect 10* court implicitly assume that the third-party website is directly infringing the public display right by hosting the full-size infringing image on its own computers? What if the image was posted on the third-party website by a user? *See* footnote 6 in the opinion; *cf. Playboy Enterprises, Inc. v. Frena*, 839 F. Supp. 1552 (M.D. Fla. 1993) (operating a computer bulletin board from which users can view and download unauthorized photos posted by other users violates the public display right). Should this activity be analyzed as "direct" infringement or as "contributory" infringement of the public display right, according to the *Perfect 10* court? According to *Cartoon Network*?

(5)   Note that an unauthorized display will not infringe the copyright in the work unless it is done "publicly." *See Thomas v. Pansy Ellen Prods., Inc.*, 672 F. Supp. 237 (W.D.N.C. 1987) (display at a members-only trade show was a "public" display). Assuming posting unauthorized photos on a third-party website is a "display," are you satisfied that the image is being displayed "publicly"? Note in particular the second clause of the second paragraph of the definition of "publicly" in § 101. Recall, however, the narrow construction of this clause (in the context of the public performance right) in *Cartoon Network*. See the notes following *Columbia Pictures* in § 7.05 above.

(6)   If Google is not directly liable for publicly displaying the infringing images, should it be contributorily liable for linking to the infringing images? For maintaining the link after it learned that that the images were infringing? Those issues are addressed in § 9.03 below.

(7)   *Limitations on the right.* As with all other § 106 rights, the display right is subject to certain of the limitations set forth in §§ 107-122. For example, what is now § 109(c) recognizes clearly the right of the owner of a particular copy of a work to display it directly to the public without the consent of the copyright owner (*e.g.*, in a gallery), although it carefully restricts showings of the copy by indirect means, such as transmission by television or other electronic media from the place where the copy is located to members of the public located elsewhere. *See, e.g., Video Pipeline, Inc. v. Buena Vista Home Entertainment, Inc.*, 192 F. Supp. 2d 321, 334 (D.N.J. 2002) (first-sale doctrine does not allow Internet transmission of images), *aff'd on other grounds*, 342 F.3d 191 (3d Cir. 2003). In so doing, § 109(c) protects the copyright holder's own opportunity to exploit the work in new media.

(8)   What if the planned display of a copy of a work would otherwise be protected by § 109(c), but the copy itself was not "lawfully made under this title [*i.e.*, Title 17]"? Note also that § 109(c) also is unavailable to one who merely leases, rents or otherwise obtains possession of a copy of the work, without acquiring ownership as well. § 109(d).

(9)   Is it time to reconsider the § 109(c) limitation on the display right? The 1992 Copyright Office report on *Droit de Suite: The Artist's Resale Royalty*, while recommending against the creation of a resale royalty right, suggested the alternative of creating a broader display right, under which "museums and public galleries might pay a fee to display works of art publicly." What do you think? Would your views change if the statute stipulated a compulsory license fee, upon payment

of which the owner of a copy would be free to display the work without further negotiation with the artist?

(10)   Many of the § 110 limitations applicable to the performance right apply equally to the display right: the face-to-face teaching exemption, § 110(1); the instructional transmission exemption, § 110(2); the religious service exemption, § 110(3); and the *Aiken* exemption, § 110(5). In addition, both performances and displays are exempt under: § 111 (cable transmissions); § 112 (ephemeral recordings); § 118 (public broadcasting); § 119 (satellite retransmissions); and § 122 (local-to-local retransmissions).

(11)   Examine the § 110 exemptions that cover performances but not displays: § 110(4) (not-for-profit performances); § 110(6) (agricultural fairs); § 110(7) (record vending establishments); § 110(8) (transmissions of nondramatic literary works to the blind and handicapped); § 110(9) (transmissions of dramatic literary works to the blind and handicapped); and § 110(10) (fraternal order exemption). Why do these exemptions *not* apply to displays?

(12)   Under § 113(c), when a work has been lawfully reproduced in useful articles, the copyright owner is without authority "to prevent the . . . display of pictures or photographs of such articles in connection with advertisements or commentaries related to the . . . display of such articles, or in connection with news reports." For more on this exception, see § 3.01[D], above.

(13)   Similarly, under the Architectural Works Copyright Protection Act of 1990, copyright does not extend to "the making, distributing, or public display of pictures, paintings, photographs, or other pictorial representations of the work, if the building in which the work is embodied is located in or ordinarily visible from a public place." § 120(a). For more on this exception, see § 3.01[G], above.

(14)   *Public display and* de minimis *use.* In *Ringgold v. Black Entertainment Television, Inc.*, 126 F.3d 70 (2d Cir. 1997), a lawfully-purchased poster of plaintiff's artwork (a "story quilt" entitled "Church Picnic," consisting of a painting and handwritten text on quilting fabric) was displayed on the wall of a church fellowship hall in the background of an episode of the television series "Roc." The poster was visible (at least in part) in nine shots of a few seconds each, for a total of about 27 seconds. With little discussion, the court assumed that this action constituted a "public display" of the plaintiff's work. Can you explain why this action was not permitted under the first-sale doctrine? What other exclusive rights might also have been infringed?

The defendants (BET and HBO) defended on the ground that the use was either *de minimis* or a fair use. With regard to *de minimis* use, the court rejected the argument that "no protectible aspects of plaintiff's expression are discernable," concluding that the display was sufficient, in terms of quantity and "observability," to constitute a *prima facie* infringement. The court relied in part on the fact that the Librarian of Congress, in implementing the compulsory license for public television entities, *see* 17 U.S.C. § 118(b), requires payment of royalties for a "background" display (less than full-screen or less than three seconds) as well as for a "featured" display (substantially full-screen for more than three seconds). *See* 37 C.F.R. § 253.8 (1996). The court remarked: "Obviously, the Librarian has concluded that the use of a copyrighted visual work, even as 'background' in a television program, normally requires payment of a license fee." What is the relevance of this analogy? *See Gordon v. Nextel Communications*, 345 F.3d 922 (6th Cir. 2003) (display of plaintiff's illustrations on the wall in the background of a TV commercial, "fleetingly" and "primarily out of focus," was *de minimis* — even though the regulation would have required payment for the same use by a public broadcasting entity).

(15)   Compare *Ringgold* with *Sandoval v. New Line Cinema Corp.*, 147 F.3d 215 (2d Cir. 1998), in which some of the plaintiff's photographs appeared for less than 30 seconds as transparencies on a "light box" in the background of a scene in the motion picture "Seven." The defendants argued that the images did not constitute "legally cognizable copies" because they were: (1) severely out of focus; (2) obscured by the scene's action and set dressing; and (3) substantially reduced in size. Likewise, they contended that their use did not constitute a "public display" of plaintiff's photographs because they were not recognizable by the public. Although the district court held for the defendant on the ground of "fair use," the Court of Appeals took a different tack, finding *de minimis* use on the ground that

> the defendants' copying falls below the quantitative threshold of substantial similarity. Unlike the artwork at issue in *Ringgold*, . . . Sandoval's photographs as used in the movie are not displayed with sufficient detail for the average lay observer to identify even the subject matter of the photographs, much less the style used in creating them.

Id. at 217; *see also Gottlieb Development L.L.C. v. Paramount Pictures Corp.*, 590 F. Supp. 2d 625 (S.D.N.Y. 2008) (appearance of copyrighted pinball machine "Silver Slugger" in the background of the movie *What Women Want* was *de minimis* use as a matter of law); *Straus v. DVC Worldwide, Inc.*, 484 F. Supp. 2d 620 (S.D. Tex. 2007) (appearance of copyrighted photo on box of product for two to three seconds at end of TV commercial was *de minimis*). For more on *de minimis* use, see § 8.03 below.

(16)   A public display may occur by including a visual image of one work within another visual work, as occurred in *Ringgold. See also Woods v. Universal City Studios, Inc.*, 920 F. Supp. 62 (S.D.N.Y. 1996) (use of plaintiff's drawing as scenic design in movie "12 Monkeys"). The issue is of particular concern to the news media where copyrighted works may be incorporated into, for example, a news program. Of course, if a work is incorporated fleetingly, and in a collateral fashion, the *de minimis* doctrine might apply. If it does not, should such "cross-media" displays be treated any differently from those which occur in connection with commercial television and motion pictures? Can you think of any reason why cross-media displays should be treated any differently from others? Is there a special public interest in permitting, rather than preventing, such a use? Try to devise a legal standard that would balance the needs of journalists and third-party creators with the copyright owner's display right. You may want to think back on this challenge when you encounter the fair use privilege in Chapter 10.

§ 7.07 THE DIGITAL PERFORMANCE RIGHT IN SOUND RECORDINGS

[A] Introduction

In 1995, Congress enacted the Digital Performance Right in Sound Recordings Act (or "DPRA"), which added to the Copyright Act a sixth exclusive right — the right, "in the case of sound recordings, to perform the copyrighted work publicly by means of a digital audio transmission" (§ 106(6)) — and defined a variety of exemptions to that right, while imposing a complex regime of statutory licensing to effectuate it.

In one sense, the DPRA was a delayed legislative response to the dissatisfaction long expressed by the recording industry about the 1971 compromise which brought sound recordings within copyright.[1] In another sense, however, the DPRA was the result of technological developments — in particular, the transmission of digital audio by terrestrial means (such as cable and wireless relay), via direct broadcast satellites, and over the Internet. What all these technologies have in common is the ability to transmit commercial-free audio to subscribers, and to do so on an interactive basis — that is, in a way that permits a subscriber to order precisely the music he or she wants to hear at any time, whether it is a single cut or an entire album.

Thus, the Congressional decision to provide for the first time a performance right in sound recordings — albeit a limited one — reflected a determination that digital technology posed a special threat to the traditional market for pre-recorded music: If a consumer can select a high-quality transmission of any piece of music at any time, why would he or she ever again pay for a CD? Worse still, a digital service subscriber with consumer home audio equipment could easily download a digital transmission to a home recording format, to replay at leisure or even to resell.[2]

Congressional action on the DPRA also reflected some important political facts. Through the years, the broadcasting industry has been the strongest and most effective opponent of performance rights in sound recordings. That industry, however, decided *not* to oppose the DPRA, because that legislation imposed licensing costs on digital audio subscription services — potentially the broadcasters' most significant future commercial competitors. (Many broadcasters later came to regret that decision when they belatedly decided to enter the webcasting market themselves.) In addition, musical work copyright owners have long feared that any performance right for sound recordings may result in a smaller share of the licensing dollar for composers of the musical works embodied in those recordings. Thus, the DPRA was shaped to protect the interests of those copyright owners (and their performing rights organizations) as well.

---

[1] *See* § 7.05[A][7] above.

[2] For a description of the technology and predictions regarding its development, see generally *Copyright Implications of Digital Audio Transmission Services: A Report of the Register of Copyrights* (GPO, Oct. 1991).

In 1998, the DPRA was revisited and (in some respects) extensively revised in the Digital Millennium Copyright Act — in part to take account of some emergent technologies that had not seemed significant, to the extent they were considered at all, in 1995. The resulting provisions are extremely complex. We sketch below only a few of the (alleged) highlights.

[B]   Highlights of the DPRA

Section 106(6)

The exclusive right. The DPRA added § 106(6) to the Copyright Act. From the language of § 106(6), it follows as a general principle that unlicensed digital transmissions of sound recordings are prohibited. This principle, however, is subject to various special qualifications beyond those, like fair use, which apply to all of the § 106 exclusive rights. The most important of these are contained in § 114(d).

Section 114 Amendments

The role of exemptions. In enacting the DPRA, Congress chose to address only those uses of digital technology that promised (or threatened) to transform most dramatically the *status quo* — taking as a baseline the situation in 1971, when sound recordings were first recognized as copyrightable subject matter. The most "traditional" of the new digital technologies — over-the-air broadcasting — received an outright exemption. § 114(d)(1). The technologies that posed the greatest threat to the recording industry, so-called interactive services, can proceed only if they are expressly licensed by copyright owners (§ 114(d)(3)). Those transmission services that posed intermediate economic threats — such as subscription services (and, later, webcasting) — were made subject to a compulsory license (§ 114(d)(2)).

The broadcasting exemption. As originally enacted in 1995, § 114(d)(1) exempted various *noninteractive, nonsubscription* services. Clearly, this exemption covered, and still covers, terrestrial broadcasters of "free" (or, more accurately, advertiser-supported) radio and television programming. They will continue to perform sound recordings without licenses just as they do today, even as they migrate their operations to digital technology. Secondary transmissions of exempt primary transmissions (as well as program "feeds" directed to exempt broadcasters) also are exempt. So are transmissions within and to business establishments (for use in the ordinary course of business) — to permit background music services such as MUZAK to be carried on by digital means.

After the enactment of the original DPRA, however, there was some confusion about what other kinds of nonsubscription services, besides broadcasting, might be covered by the exemption. A particular area of concern was webcasting — the use of "streaming audio" technology to deliver sound recordings over the Internet. Under the original DPRA, "webcasting" was not clearly exempt, and — if non-exempt — it was apparently ineligible for compulsory licensing! The 1998 revisions to the DPRA narrowed the original language of § 114(d)(1)(A), which now clearly applies to terrestrial broadcasts only. Revised § 114, however, makes it clear that so-called "eligible nonsubscription transmissions" (*i.e.*, noninteractive services other than broadcasting, including but not limited to webcasting) are subject to compulsory licensing (if they comply with the statutory conditions discussed below).

New business models have raised the question of just what "noninteractive" means. In *Arista Records, LLC v. Launch Media, Inc.*, 578 F.3d 148, 162 (2d Cir. 2009), the Second Circuit confronted a digital service that allowed users to rate songs and created a customized "playlist" for each user, while still including some random selections. The court held that the service was not "interactive," because the user cannot choose particular songs, and because the playlist was not "so predictable that users will choose to listen to the webcast in lieu of purchasing music."

The compulsory license. Section 114(d)(2) provides a compulsory license for digital transmission services that function as the digital audio equivalent of cable TV — noninteractive subscription services that are generally (though not always) commercial-free — as well as "eligible nonsubscription transmissions" such as webcasting.[3] But the compulsory license is made available only under certain relatively stringent conditions, designed to minimize the impact of such services on other commercial distribution channels for recorded music. (For example, the DPRA limits the number of times a particular sound recording may be performed and prohibits a service from publishing or announcing in advance when a particular sound recording will be performed.) To make things still more complicated, the DMCA added additional conditions, with the result that the current DPRA now incorporates two sets of requirements to qualify for the statutory license — one set for "grandfathered" services that were licensed or in operation before July 31, 1998; and another, more exacting set for newer services.

A prominent example of a business that relies on the § 114 compulsory license is Pandora's streaming music service. Listeners can list a favorite song or artist, and Pandora builds a "station" — in reality, a playlist — based on the listener's request. Notably, Pandora will not play the suggested song first in order to comply with the terms of § 114(d)(2). Recall that the threshold question is whether the service is "noninteractive." Pandora takes the position that it is. Do you agree? Other countries do not have a similar statutory license, which means Pandora is unavailable in most other countries unless it has successfully negotiated licenses to stream to listeners in a particular country.

Under § 114(f), "reasonable rates and terms of royalty payments" for the statutory license are established for five-year periods. As with other statutory licenses, the Copyright Royalty Judges first initiate "voluntary negotiation proceedings" between representatives of copyright owners and transmitting entities for the purpose of setting rates. § 803(b)(3). Only if the parties are unable to reach agreement are the rates set by the CRJs themselves.

Miscellaneous protective provisions. Various additional protective provisions were built into the DPRA as the result of political compromise. Section 114(g), for

---

[3] In addition, § 112(e) provides a statutory license for the "ephemeral recordings" necessary to facilitate the digital audio performances authorized by § 114.

example, provides a formula for sharing the royalties generated by the statutory license with performers, both featured and non-featured. And § 114(h) attempts to ensure that would-be entrants into the digital audio transmission marketplace will not be blocked by existing participants and arrangements.

In addition, § 114(i) makes it clear that digital audio transmission services must license performance rights in the underlying musical works *as well as* in the sound recording itself. Section 114(i) also attempts to assuage the concerns of musical work copyright owners by expressing "the intent of Congress that royalties payable to copyright owners of musical works for the public performance of their works shall not be diminished in any respect as a result of the rights granted by section 106(6)." This hortatory statement appears not to be enforceable, however, and it remains to be seen what the real impact of the DPRA on the value of performance rights in music will be.

The webcasting controversy. One of the most contentious issues in the implementation of the DPRA has been webcasting. Royalty rates for the initial post-DMCA statutory license period were delayed by a dispute over whether AM/FM broadcasters were exempt when simulcasting their radio broadcasts on the Internet. After the Copyright Office determined that such broadcasters were *not* exempt, but were subject to the statutory license, *see Bonneville Int'l Corp. v. Peters*, 347 F.3d 485 (3d Cir. 2003) (upholding the Copyright Office's rulemaking), a Copyright Arbitration Royalty Panel (described in § 7.01[C] above) was convened to determine the webcasting rate. The CARP recommended that a per-song, per-listener royalty be adopted; and although the Librarian of Congress (advised by the Copyright Office) rejected the proposed rates in part, he retained the per-song, per-listener royalty structure.

The decision provoked considerable controversy. While recording companies expressed disappointment that the rate was not pegged higher, small webcasters were worried that the proposed licensing fees might exceed their revenues, driving them out of business. The Librarian's decision was challenged in court by both copyright owners and webcasters, but the D.C. Circuit eventually upheld the Librarian's decision on the merits. *See Beethoven.com LLC v. Librarian of Congress*, 394 F.3d 939 (D.C. Cir. 2005).

In the meantime, small and noncommercial webcasters were successful in lobbying for Congressional relief from the "onerous" rates and burdens of the compulsory license. The result was the Small Webcaster Settlement Act of 2002, Pub. L. No. 107-321, amending §§ 112 and 114. The legislation allowed SoundExchange, the royalty collecting agency for the recording industry, to enter into agreements with small webcasters that, once published in the Federal Register, were binding on *all* copyright owners of sound recordings. Such an agreement was reached, resulting in royalty rates calculated as a percentage of gross revenue, or alternatively as a percentage of expenses, subject to a minimum annual license fee.

In 2007, however, the controversy resurfaced, when the new Copyright Royalty Judges once again adopted a per-song, per-listener royalty, without any provision for blanket licenses based on webcaster revenues. Once again, webcasters complained that the new rates would drive them out of business, and once again,

Congress passed legislation that allows small webcasters to adopt alternative rates negotiated by SoundExchange and other webcasters. *See* Pub. L. No. 110-435 and Pub. L. No. 111-36. In general, the agreements negotiated under these Acts provide for a minimum annual fee of $500 per channel, with higher rates based on gross revenue for some webcasters and per-performance rates for others. See *www.copyright.gov/fedreg* for details. For webcasters who did not adopt the negotiated rates, the per-performance rates adopted by the CRJs were upheld, but the minimum annual fee of $500 was held to be arbitrary and capricious. *See Intercollegiate Broadcast System, Inc. v. Copyright Royalty Board*, 574 F.3d 748 (D.C. Cir. 2009).

Section 115 Amendments

The compulsory license for digital sound recording delivery. So far, we have examined only the new § 106(6) right and the various limitations upon it imposed by § 114. We should not overlook the amendments made by the DPRA to § 115 (the compulsory license in musical works).

The § 115 amendments were intended to facilitate the transition from traditional retail store-based distribution of sound recordings to distribution by means of "digital phonorecord delivery." Pause for a moment to be sure that you understand the key distinction between the two types of commerce involved. The DPRA amendments to § 114 concern "streaming," or the transmission of sound recordings so that they can be listened to in "real-time" by consumers — some of whom may also engage in simultaneous (and perhaps unlawful) home recording. The § 115 amendments address the sale and downloading of sound recordings for later playback — a business model that expanded exponentially following the introduction of Apple's iTunes music store in 2003.

Generally, we think of § 115 as a mechanism by which record producers can secure the rights to make new "cover" versions of compositions previously recorded under consensual license from the copyright owner, and to distribute them for private use. In fact, the potential scope of the section is somewhat broader. In addition to making a compulsory license available to company C when it wishes to re-record a song by composer A which was previously recorded by company B, § 115 dictates what is due to A if C licenses from B the right to re-release (*i.e.*, distribute) its original recording.

The DPRA amendments to § 115 make it clear that a digital delivery of a sound recording is an infringement unless it is authorized or licensed. § 115(c)(3)(G). Under amended § 115, however, services which offer their customers the ability to download digital versions of recorded music can avail themselves of a statutory license for the musical compositions in question. Here, from 2 NIMMER ON COPYRIGHT § 8.23[B][1] (2010), is a concrete example of how the process might work:

> [I]magine that Composer in 1980 authorizes Star to perform and sell copies to the public of her newly written Song. Thereafter in 1990, Upstart may invoke the compulsory license to assemble musicians to record his own version of Song; Upstart must pay compulsory license fees to Composer, with no obligation to Star. Now imagine that Techie in 1997 wishes to avail itself of the newly added compulsory license to offer digital phonorecord

delivery. Techie must remit the statutory fee to Composer for use of the music. Techie may use Star's or Upstart's sound recording only if it concludes a license agreement with either; absent successful licensing arrangements, Techie may wish to assemble its own musicians and singers (or cyberian facsimiles thereof) to record a new rendition of Song, which will then be the subject of digital phonorecord delivery. In that last instantiation, Techie will owe statutory license fees to Composer, and nothing to Star or Upstart.

The procedure for settling the practical aspects of such statutory licenses is specified by the DPRA. Section 115(c)(3)(B)–(E) provides that, under the umbrella of a limited antitrust exemption, affected parties may voluntarily negotiate terms and rates, subject to a decision by the Copyright Royalty Judges, if necessary, to resolve their differences.

NOTES AND QUESTIONS

(1)   The statutory scheme just described is an exceptionally detailed one — designed not only to regulate known technologies but also to anticipate emerging ones. As already discussed, its terms are the result of a legislative process that blended far-sighted policymaking and mundane political compromise. Is legislation of this kind built to last? Or is it likely to be overtaken by technological development? Would Congress have been wiser to adopt more general legislative language and trust the courts to work out the details? Would there have been any other alternative?

(2)   Read through the provisions that the DPRA added to §§ 114 and 115 of the Copyright Act, trying to put yourself in the position of a lay businessperson or a nonspecialist lawyer. How much of this is comprehensible (let alone relatively transparent)? Does it matter? Is the Act, among other things, a guarantee of future full employment for copyright specialists? For an aptly titled commentary on the DPRA, see Nimmer, *Ignoring the Public, Part I: On the Absurd Complexity of the Digital Audio Transmission Right*, 7 UCLA L. Rev. 189 (2000).

(3)   Can the decision to provide for a general digital performance right in sound recordings — while leaving analog performances unaddressed — be justified on any basis other than that of political expediency?

(4)   The § 111 cable statutory licensing provisions have generated tremendous controversy, with respect both to rate-setting and to the formula for sharing license fees among various kinds of copyright owners whose material is subject to cable retransmission. Will the § 114 provisions for statutory licensing prove any less productive of disputes?

(5)   The provisions of § 114(g) are designed to assure that licensing revenues will reach performers as well as record companies. How effective would you expect those provisions to be in practice? How clear is it that they apply to situations where digital transmission services negotiate consensual licenses with sound recording copyright owners, rather than relying on the statutory licensing mechanism?

(6) Are you surprised that a privately negotiated agreement concerning statutory licensing rates can become a final rule, binding on an entire industry, without further judicial or administrative scrutiny? Or is this sort of delegation of rulemaking authority appropriate in the circumstances? Is such a delegation of Congressional power to private parties — even as a one-time compromise — constitutional?

(7) Digital technology blurs traditional distinctions among the various § 106 rights — and, in particular, between the closely linked reproduction and distribution rights, on the one hand, and the public performance right, on the other. Where sound recordings are concerned, the potential for confusion is particularly acute. In the analog environment, these two sets of rights correspond fairly neatly to the two distinct modes by which sound recordings generally are exploited. In the digital environment, however, a single transmission of a sound recording may entail reproduction, distribution, and public performance. How successful is the DPRA in dealing with this problem? Section 114(d)(4)(C) provides:

> Any limitations in this section on the exclusive right under section 106(6) apply only to the exclusive right under section 106(6) and not to any other exclusive rights under section 106. Nothing in this section shall be construed to annul, limit, impair or otherwise affect in any way the ability of the owner of a copyright in a sound recording to exercise the rights under sections 106(1), 106(2) and 106(3) . . .

Is that clear? Is it helpful? Does it mean that some providers of digital audio transmission services may have to pay twice: once for the right to reproduce and distribute a work, and once for the right to perform it publicly? *Cf. SoundExchange v. Librarian of Congress*, 571 F.3d 1220 (D.C. Cir. 2009) (affirming that CRJs are required to set separate rates for ephemeral copies and public performances). For more on the "convergence" of rights in the digital environment, see 2 NIMMER ON COPYRIGHT § 8.24 (2010).

(8) The Register of Copyrights has recommended to Congress that the Copyright Act be amended to provide that any license to publicly perform a musical work by means of digital audio transmission must include the non-exclusive right to reproduce and distribute copies of the work to facilitate such streaming. *See* Statement of Marybeth Peters before the House Subcommittee on Courts, the Internet and Intellectual Property (June 21, 2005), *www.copyright.gov/docs/ regstat062105.html*. Would the proposed amendment solve the problem of "double-dipping" described in the previous note? Or are additional changes to the statutory scheme needed?

§ 7.08 MORAL RIGHTS

[A] A Comparative Overview

Generally, under the copyright law of the United States, once an author has transferred ownership of the copyright on his work, the transferee is entitled to reproduce and adapt the work and can authorize others to do so. The author, having been compensated for the transfer, can no longer control the uses of his work by the copyright owner. Somewhat similarly, under § 109(a) (the first-sale doctrine), the rightful owner of a particular copy of a copyrighted work can resell or even destroy that copy without regard to the preferences of the copyright owner.

By contrast, a number of other countries recognize a general *"droit moral"* or "moral right" that treats the author's connection to her work not as a mere economic interest, but rather as an inalienable, natural right, arising from a conception of the work as an extension of the author's personality. This continuing interest allows the author to control certain uses of the work itself (and, in some circumstances, particular copies of the work), even after transfer of the economic rights to others — a concept generally in conflict with American copyright law as it has developed over almost two centuries.

What are "moral rights"? Although the scope of moral rights legislation varies from country to country, the concept is a composite right consisting generally of several overlapping components. Most formulations include:

(1) *the right of integrity*: the right to insist that the work not be mutilated or distorted;

(2) *the right of attribution*: the right to be acknowledged as the author of the work and to prevent others from naming anyone else as the creator; and

(3) *the right of disclosure*: the right to decide when and in what form the work will be presented to the public.

Some formulations of the moral right also include: the right of withdrawal (the right to recall all existing copies of a work if, for example, the author's views on the subject matter should radically change); and, less frequently, the right to prevent excessive criticism (the right to be free from vexatious or malicious attacks on a work, on the basis that the work constitutes an extension of its creator's person).

The moral rights of attribution and integrity are recognized in Article 6[bis] of the Berne Convention, which requires all signatories to protect these moral rights in their domestic laws. But the Berne Convention Implementation Act of 1988, which restructured American law for Berne compliance, took a so-called "minimalist" approach and did not legislate in the field of moral rights. Despite this omission, the concept of moral rights has made its way into American law in two ways. First, outside of copyright, an author's integrity and attribution rights have been partially protected, in piecemeal fashion, by various bodies of state and federal law, and about a dozen states have passed statutes explicitly recognizing some moral rights for visual artists. Second, with the Visual Artists Rights Act of 1990, which added § 106A to Title 17, federal law followed the lead of state law — and at least partially displaced state law — in protecting the integrity and attribution rights of visual artists. This section of the book explores these developments in turn.

[B] Protection Outside the Copyright Act

Section 43(a) of the Lanham Act

Although the United States, for most of its history, gave no protection to authors' moral rights as such under the copyright law, legal theories not specifically denominated "moral rights" laws occasionally have produced a similar result. Theories useful for "simulating" moral rights protection include: copyright law itself (when an unauthorized modification of a work is held to violate the § 106(2) adaptation right); contract law (provided that the underlying agreement explicitly recognizes the author's continuing rights in the work, or at least contains no contrary language); unfair competition law generally and § 43(a) of the Lanham Act, 15 U.S.C. § 1125(a), in particular; defamation law; and the various rights of privacy, especially "false light" privacy. *See generally* 3 NIMMER ON COPYRIGHT § 8D (2010); Damich, *The Right of Personality: A Common-Law Basis for the Protection of the Moral Rights of Authors*, 23 Ga. L. Rev. 1 (1988).

The leading *de facto* moral rights case is *Gilliam v. American Broadcasting Cos., Inc.*, 538 F.2d 14 (2d Cir. 1976), in which the plaintiffs' right to prevent distortion of their work was protected under both the Copyright Act and § 43(a) of the Lanham Act. In *Gilliam*, defendant ABC obtained a license to broadcast several taped shows created by Monty Python, the famous British comedy group. The license provided that shows were to be broadcast in their entirety, except for minor editing to adapt the programs for commercials. ABC, however, cut 24 minutes from each 90-minute program. The court held that this truncation violated the terms of the license and likely constituted an infringement of plaintiffs' adaptation right through the creation of an unauthorized derivative work. The court also found a violation of § 43(a) of the Lanham Act, because the abridged version constituted a "false designation of origin." In effect, ABC had deformed the work and presented the plaintiffs as authors of a work which was not their own, thereby subjecting them to criticism for a work they had not created. Thus, copyright and the law of unfair competition both provided protection of artistic interests akin to the moral rights of integrity and attribution.

Gilliam demonstrates that, depending on the facts of the particular case, U.S. courts are capable of simulating an "integrity right" under a variety of theories. But thirty years later, it is apparent that the promise that *Gilliam* initially seemed to hold for greater *de facto* moral rights protection in the United States remains largely unfulfilled. One reason is that the exclusive right to prepare derivative works under § 106(2), *see* § 7.03 above, belongs to the copyright owner, whereas European moral rights are said to be "inalienable," meaning that the author retains his or her moral rights even after transferring the economic rights. *See generally* U.S. Copyright Office, *Waiver of Moral Rights in Visual Artworks* 26-56 (1996); Netanel, *Copyright Alienability Restrictions and the Enhancement of Author Autonomy: A Normative Evaluation*, 24 Rutgers L.J. 347 (1993). Another reason is that courts (and policymakers) have been reluctant to find a violation of § 43(a) of the Lanham Act in the absence of the kind of severe distortion that existed in *Gilliam*.

Suppose, for example, that a person is distributing edited versions of a motion picture without authorization. Such conduct clearly would be a violation of the *copyright owner's* exclusive rights to prepare, reproduce, and distribute derivative works; but should the *director* also have an action under § 43(a) of the Lanham Act for the use of his or her name on the edited motion picture? The issue arose in *Huntsman v. Soderbergh*, 2005 WL 1993421 (D. Colo. 2005), an action for a declaratory judgment of noninfringement brought by video retailer Clean Flicks against sixteen Hollywood directors and eight movie studios. The studios counterclaimed for copyright infringement, and the directors counterclaimed for a violation of § 43(a) of the Lanham Act. While summary judgment motions were pending, Congress intervened on behalf of some (but not all) of the alleged infringers — namely, those whose technology does not create a "fixed copy" of the allegedly infringing derivative work but instead instructs the DVD player to skip temporarily certain scenes and sounds. *See* § 110(11), discussed in § 7.03 above. Congress also amended § 32 of the Lanham Act to permit the sale of such technology so long as a "clear and conspicuous notice" of the alterations is given. 15 U.S.C. § 1114(3). While this change may eliminate (or at least mitigate) any harm caused to the directors' attribution rights, it does nothing to vindicate their alleged rights of integrity.

Now suppose a case in which, instead of abridging an audiovisual or other work, the defendant exploits the work in its entirety but with the author's name deleted from the credits. Moral rights countries would have little trouble finding a violation of the "attribution right." In the absence of applicable copyright law, would the plaintiff have any remedy under U.S. law? Suppose instead that the plaintiff at one point *had* a copyright on the work but that the copyright has *expired* — and that the defendant has removed the author credit from the work (say, a television series) and now is marketing it without attribution to the plaintiff. Is that a "false designation of origin" under the Lanham Act? In *Dastar Corp. v. Twentieth Century Fox Film Corp.*, 539 U.S. 23 (2003), reproduced in § 11.03 below, the Supreme Court unanimously answered "no." Justice Scalia's opinion for the Court states that "allowing a cause of action under § 43(a) . . . would create a species of mutant copyright law that limits the public's federal right to copy and use expired copyrights." *Id.* at 34 (internal quotations omitted). Given this decision, are you satisfied that *Gilliam* is still good law? *See* Hughes, *American Moral Rights and Fixing the* Dastar *"Gap"*, 2007 Utah L. Rev. 659.

State Art Preservation Laws

Certain aspects of the moral rights concept historically were not even arguably covered by state causes of action, federal unfair competition law, or the Copyright Act itself. One gap in the system concerned fine art. Suppose that *A* owned an original painting by *B* and decided to destroy it for whatever reason. Did *B* have a cause of action against *A* to prevent the work's destruction, or at least to recover damages? The answer, generally speaking, was no. *See generally* J. Sax, Playing Darts With a Rembrandt: Public and Private Rights in Cultural Treasures (1999). This problem led several states, including New York and California, to pass their own art preservation acts (and, as we will see below, prompted Congress in 1990 to pass the Visual Artists Rights Act).

In acting to protect the integrity and attribution rights in works by fine artists, the states have adopted varying approaches. The New York statute provides an excellent example of a state moral rights statute emphasizing *the reputational interest of the artist.* Under the Artists' Authorship Rights Act, effective January 1, 1985, no person other than the artist or someone acting under the artist's authority may display publicly or publish a work of fine art or a reproduction thereof "in an altered, defaced, mutilated or modified form if the work is displayed, published or reproduced as being the work of the artist . . . and damage to the artist's reputation is reasonably likely to occur therefrom." The statute also guarantees the artist the right to compel recognition of his or her authorship of the work. Conversely, the Act grants the artist the right to disclaim authorship for "just and valid reason[s]," including "that the work of fine art has been altered, defaced, mutilated or modified other than by the artist, without the artist's consent, and damage to the artist's reputation is reasonably likely to result or has resulted therefrom." Any artist who is aggrieved under the Act has a cause of action for legal and injunctive relief. The statute is limited in several ways, however, including its qualified exemption for works "prepared under contract for advertising or trade use" and its applicability "only to works of fine art . . . knowingly displayed in a place accessible to the public, published or reproduced" in New York State. N.Y. Arts & Cult. Aff. Law § 14.03 (2010).

In *Wojnarowicz v. American Family Assn.*, 745 F. Supp. 130 (S.D.N.Y. 1990), an artist sued to prevent the AFA from reproducing cropped images from his work in a pamphlet published as part of an effort to stop public funding of artwork the AFA deemed to be offensive. The court found that the pamphlet did not violate either the Lanham Act (because it was non-commercial) or the Copyright Act (because of fair use), but it granted an injunction under the New York statute, holding that "[e]xtracting fragmentary images from complex, multi-imaged collages clearly alters and modifies such work," and that the plaintiff's reputation was harmed because "the pamphlet impl[ied] that plaintiff's work consists primarily of explicit images of homosexual sex activity." *Id.* at 138-39. The court also rejected the defendant's First Amendment claim, noting:

> Defendants remain free to criticize and condemn plaintiff's work if they so choose. They may present incomplete reproductions labeled as such or, alternatively, without attribution of such images to plaintiff. However, they may not present as complete works by plaintiff, selectively cropped versions of his originals.

Id. at 140. Does this limited relief provide the equivalent of moral rights protection available in most European countries?

California also has a statute that affords visual artists protection for certain aspects of their moral rights. By contrast with the New York act, the California statute emphasizes not the protection of the artist's reputation but the *protection of the work of art itself* in the interest of cultural preservation. The California Art Preservation Act, effective January 1, 1980 (as amended in 1982, 1989, and 1994), prohibits intentional "physical defacement, mutilation, alteration or destruction of a work of fine art" by any person except the creating artist who owns and possesses the work, except in instances in which the work has been prepared under contract for commercial use by the purchaser.

As with the New York statute, an artist has the right to claim authorship of the work, or disclaim authorship for "just and valid reason[s]." An artist may waive these protections, but only by "an instrument in writing expressly so providing which is signed by the artist." The artist's rights may be exercised by his heirs, legatees or personal representative for 50 years after his death. Remedies under the Act include injunctive relief, actual damages, punitive damages, reasonable attorneys' and expert witness fees, and any other relief that a court deems appropriate. Cal. Civ. Code § 987 (2010).

Compare the New York and California approaches. The New York statute prohibits the public *display* of the mutilated work; it does not prohibit mutilation or destruction of a copy of the work itself. Thus, in *Wojnarowicz* the defendant could have bought all of the artist's works and burned them without violating the New York law. The California statute, on the other hand, prohibits the *destruction* of a work, not its display in a mutilated form. Would there be a violation of either the New York or the California statutes if an art critic mutilated a work in New York and publicly displayed it only in California?

Following the lead of California and New York, a handful of states have passed similar laws. Are these state statutes subject to federal preemption, at least in part, on the basis that the right to prevent deforming changes in a work under state law overlaps the right to prepare derivative works under the 1976 Act? Does it matter that the former right belongs to the creator of the work, whereas the latter right inheres in the copyright owner? *See generally* Francione, *The California Art Preservation Act and Federal Preemption by the 1976 Copyright Act — Equivalence and Actual Conflict*, 31 Copyright L. Symp. (ASCAP) 105 (1984). More generally, to what extent do these state statutes survive the specific preemption provisions of the Visual Artists Rights Act? *See* 17 U.S.C. § 301(f). This issue will be discussed in connection with the *Phillips* case below.

[C] Copyright Protection: The Visual Artists Rights Act of 1990

When the United States became a party to the Berne Convention on March 1, 1989, it did so without passing special legislation designed to comply with Article 6[bis] of Berne, which requires member nations to protect authors' rights of attribution and integrity. Article 6[bis] provides:

> Independently of the author's economic rights, and even after the transfer of the said rights, the author shall have the right to claim authorship of the work and to object to any distortion, mutilation or other modification of, or other derogatory action in relation to, the said work, which would be prejudicial to his honor or reputation.

Congress justified its decision not to adopt specific legislation implementing Article 6[bis] rights with a claim that, when the entirety of American law is considered, the United States already gives *de facto* recognition to moral rights. This argument, however, left many unpersuaded that our obligations regarding Berne membership had been met. Proponents of the latter view support further amendments to the Copyright Act explicitly recognizing moral rights. From their perspective, the Visual Artists Rights Act of 1990, which protects the rights of certain visual artists, can be viewed as a slightly deferred "down payment" on meeting U.S. responsibilities under Article 6[bis].

[1] Introduction

Statutory References

1976 Act: §§ 101 ("work of visual art"), 106A, 113(d), 301(f)

1909 Act: —

Legislative History

House Report on the Visual Artists Rights Act of 1990 (Excerpts)
H.R. REP. No. 101-514, 101st Cong., 2d Sess. at 8-9 (1990)

. . . Under the American copyright system, an artist who transfers a copy of his or her work to another may not, absent a contractual agreement, prevent that person from destroying the copy or collect damages after the fact. Further, with respect to modifications of a work, only an artist who retains the copyright in his or her work is able to invoke title 17 rights in defense of the integrity of that work, and then only where a modification amounts to the creation of a derivative work.

Visual artists, such as painters and sculptors, have complained that their works are being mutilated and destroyed, that authorship of their works is being misattributed, and that the American copyright does not enable them to share in any profits upon the resale of their works. Directors, screenwriters, and other creative contributors to motion pictures have complained that, without consent, films originally shot with the special characteristics of the wide screen in mind are being electronically recomposed for viewing on smaller television screens (panned and scanned), and films are being speeded up or slowed down (time compressed or expanded) to fit into television broadcast slots.

Where an individual creating a work typically retains the economic rights in it, such as visual artist does, an additional grant of rights such as those accorded by [VARA] will not impede distribution of the work. By contrast, those who participate in a collaborative effort, such as an audiovisual work, do not typically own the economic rights. Instead, audiovisual works are generally works-made-for-hire. Granting these artists the rights of attribution and integrity might conflict with the distribution and marketing of these works. . . .

[Such] critical factual and legal differences in the way visual arts and audiovisual works are created and disseminated have important practical consequences. They have led the Congress to consider the claims of these artists separately, and have facilitated the progress of legislation to protect the rights of visual artists.

[For a fuller excerpt from H.R. REP. No. 101-514, see Part Three of the Casebook Supplement.]

Summary of Visual Artists Rights Act of 1990

The major provisions of VARA, enacted by Congress as Pub. L. No. 101-650 (tit. VI), 104 Stat. 5089, 5128-33, on December 1, 1990 but not effective until June 1, 1991, are:

(1) *Works protected.* VARA does not cover all possible visual art works, but instead is limited, like the California and New York acts, to works of visual art. Qualifying works include paintings, drawings, prints, sculptures, and still photographic images produced for exhibition purposes only, and existing in single copies or in limited editions of 200 or fewer copies, signed by the artist. *See, e.g., Lilley v. Stout,* 384 F. Supp. 2d 83 (D.D.C. 2005) (photographic prints were not produced "for exhibition purposes only"); *Landrau v. Solis Betancourt,* 554 F. Supp. 2d 102 (D.P.R. 2007) (architectural works are not "works of visual art" under VARA). Works not covered include reproductions of qualifying works, and works destined for commercial purposes, *e.g.*, posters, maps, motion pictures, and works of applied art. *See, e.g., National Ass'n for Stock Car Auto Racing, Inc. v. Scharle,* 356 F. Supp. 2d 515 (E.D. Pa. 2005) ("technical drawings" for NASCAR Nextel Cup excluded from definition), *aff'd,* 184 Fed. Appx. 270 (3d Cir. 2006). Works made for hire are specifically excluded.

(2) *Rights of attribution and integrity.* VARA created new rights of attribution and integrity for certain visual artists. The right of attribution includes the artist's rights: (a) to claim authorship of the work; (b) to prevent the use of her name as the author of any work of visual art which she did not create; and (c) to prevent the use of her name as the author of the work in the event of a distortion, mutilation or other modification of the work which would be prejudicial to her honor or reputation. Subject to limitations described in paragraph 5 below, the right of integrity encompasses the rights: (a) to prevent any intentional distortion, mutilation or other modification of the work which would be prejudicial to the artist's honor or reputation; and (b) to prevent any destruction of a work of "recognized stature" (a term which the Act does not define) by an intentional or grossly negligent act. § 106A(a).

(3) *Scope and exercise of rights.* The author of a work of visual art, *i.e.*, the artist, has the rights provided in § 106A, whether or not she owns the copyright in the work. Persons who jointly create a work of visual art are co-owners of the § 106A rights. § 106A(b).

(4) *Exceptions.* A work is not destroyed, distorted, mutilated or modified, for purposes of the integrity right, if the modification is the result of the passage of time or the inherent nature of the materials. Likewise, the integrity right is not violated when a modification is the result of conservation measures or of public presentation, including lighting or placement, unless the modification is caused by gross negligence. *See Flack v. Friends of Queen Catherine, Inc.,* 139 F. Supp. 2d 526 (S.D.N.Y. 2001) (discussion of exceptions to integrity right). Finally, the integrity and attribution rights do not apply to reproductions or other uses of protected works in forms not themselves protected by VARA (see paragraph (1) above). § 106A(c).

(5) *Removal of works from buildings.* VARA amended § 113 to establish conditions under which a work of art incorporated as a part of a building may be removed from the building. If the work cannot be removed without being mutilated or destroyed, the owner of the building nonetheless may accomplish such removal if the artist consented to the installation before June 1, 1991, or if thereafter she consented to the possibility of mutilation or destruction in a signed instrument. If

the work can be removed without mutilation or destruction, the work is subject to the artist's attribution and integrity rights unless the owner has made a diligent, good faith attempt, without success, to notify the artist. If notice is effected, the artist has 90 days to remove the work or pay for its removal; and that copy of the work then becomes the artist's property. § 113(d).

(6) *Duration of rights.* With respect to works of visual art created on or after June 1, 1991, the effective date of VARA, the § 106A rights endure for the life of the artist (for joint works, the life of the last-surviving artist). The artist's § 106 rights (reproduction, adaptation, etc.) are unaffected and endure for the normal life-plus-70-years term.

If the work of visual art was created *before* June 1, 1991, VARA creates, in certain circumstances, what can only be described as a peculiar situation. Provided that the artist has not parted with title *to the copy/copies* of the work, she receives the life-plus-70-years term for *both* the § 106 rights *and* the § 106A rights. However, if the work was created before June 1, 1991 and the artist has sold the copy or copies to others, no § 106A rights arise at all. § 106A(d).

(7) *Transfer and waiver.* The artist's attribution and integrity rights cannot be transferred. They can, however, be waived, but only expressly in writing, through an instrument signed by the artist (or for joint works, by one of the artists), and only as to works and uses specified in that instrument. § 106A(e).

(8) *Infringement.* VARA subjects violators of the new attribution and integrity rights in works of visual art to the normal liabilities for infringement, but not to criminal penalties. §§ 501, 506.

(9) *Preemption.* VARA amended § 301 to preempt any legal or equitable rights under state law that are equivalent to those created by VARA. Nothing in VARA, however, annuls or limits any state law rights or remedies with respect to (a) causes of action arising from undertakings commenced before the Act's effective date or (b) activities violating state-created rights that are not equivalent to those created by § 106A. § 301(f).

(10) *Study on resale royalties legislation.* Congress also directed the Register of Copyrights to conduct a study on the feasibility of "allowing an author of a work of art to share monetarily in the enhanced value of that work" upon resale. The report was delivered to Congress on June 1, 1992, but no action was taken. Resale royalty rights are discussed in more detail in § 7.04 above.

[2] Case Law

PHILLIPS v. PEMBROKE REAL ESTATE, INC.
United States Court of Appeals, First Circuit
459 F.3d 128 (2006)

LIPEZ, CIRCUIT JUDGE.

This case raises important questions about the application of the Visual Artists Rights Act of 1990 ("VARA"), 17 U.S.C. § 106A, to "site-specific art", which is a subset of "integrated art". A work of "integrated art" is comprised of two or more physical objects that must be presented together as the artist intended for the work to retain its meaning and integrity. In a work of "site-specific art", one of the component physical objects is the location of the art. To remove a work of site-specific art from its original site is to destroy it.

I.

David Phillips brought suit against Pembroke Real Estate, Inc. in federal district court, asserting that the removal of any or all of his work, consisting of multiple pieces of sculpture and stonework, from Eastport Park in South Boston would violate his statutory rights under VARA and the Massachusetts Art Preservation Act ("MAPA"), Mass. Gen. Laws ch. 231, § 85S. The district court ruled . . . that most of Phillips' sculptures and stonework in the Park constituted "one integrated 'work of visual art' " — with the remaining pieces being "individual free-standing pieces of sculpture, which are not integrated into the other pieces." It also held that Phillips' integrated work of art was an example of site-specific art. But the court held that Pembroke could remove Phillips' works from the Park pursuant to VARA's so-called "public presentation" exception. See 17 U.S.C. § 106A(c)(2).

Phillips challenges that reading of the public presentation exception on appeal. Although we disagree with the district court's reasoning (we hold that VARA does not apply to site-specific art at all), we affirm the decision of the district court permitting Pembroke to remove Phillips' works from the Park.

II.

A. The artist

Phillips is a nationally recognized sculptor who works primarily with stone and bronze forms that he integrates into local environs. In many of his sculptures, the design of the stones is incorporated into the landscape — such as a private project in Ogunquit, Maine, where a band of rock was extended into a bronze tributary in the ground, which, in sunlight, glistened like a nearby stream. In some of his other works, Phillips has merged metals or polished stone with aged, naturally-shaped boulders. . . .

B. The Park

Eastport Park (the "Park"), which was completed in its current form in the spring of 2000, is located across from Boston Harbor in the South Boston Waterfront District. The Park is roughly rectangular in shape. . . . The Park is a public sculpture park with a nautical theme. . . .

Defendant Pembroke Real Estate, Inc. ("Pembroke"), a Fidelity Investments company, leases the land on which the Park is built from the Massachusetts Port Authority ("Massport"). Massport and the Boston Redevelopment Authority must approve any changes to the design of the Park. The Park is required to be open to the public, free of charge, twenty-four hours a day.

C. Phillips' work in the Park

. . . Phillips and Pembroke executed two contracts in August 1999. Under the "Eastport Park Artwork Agreement," Phillips created approximately twenty- seven sculptures for the Park, comprised of fifteen abstract bronze and granite pieces and twelve realistic bronze sculptures of various aquatic creatures, including frogs, crabs, and shrimp. Under the "Eastport Park Stonework Agreement," Phillips was responsible for the design and installation of stone walls, granite stones inlaid into the Park's walkways, and other landscape design elements. Most of Phillips' work in the Park is organized along the diagonal axis running from the northeast to the southwest corner, at the center of which is his large spherical sculpture entitled "Chords", the centerpiece of the Park, which Phillips personally carved from granite.

Phillips designed a bronze medallion with Zodiac signs, which crowns an S-shaped circular granite path, also of Phillips' design; outlying sculptures off of the main axis (many bronze crabs, frogs, and shrimp and a large seashell); and the curve motifs. He worked with a stone mason to choose and place the rough lichen-covered, Maine-quarried stone, and he selected the large granite stones that he used as part of his sculptures to mirror the large granite stones along Boston Harbor. Phillips' work in the Park is unified by a theme of spiral and circular forms.

A Portion of Phillips' Work in Eastport Park

D. Pembroke's redesign of the Park and the preliminary injunction

In 2001, Pembroke decided to alter the Park. . . . [T]he redesign plan called for the removal and relocation of Phillips' sculptures. . . . Phillips filed suit in federal district court, seeking injunctive relief under VARA and MAPA.

. . . After a two-day evidentiary hearing, the district court . . . found that Phillips had established the likelihood of showing: (1) that most, but not all, of his work in the Park constituted "one 'integrated work of visual art,' " *see Phillips v. Pembroke Real Estate, Inc.*, 288 F. Supp. 2d 89, 98 (D. Mass. 2003) (hereinafter *"Phillips I"*); [and] (2) "an artist has no right to the placement or public presentation of his sculpture under the exception in § 106A(c)(2)," VARA's public presentation exception. . . . In other words, consistent with VARA, Phillips' free-standing works could be moved; and the multi-element, integrated work of art along the northeast-southwest axis could be disassembled and moved piecemeal, so long as individual pieces comprising this integrated work of art were not altered, modified, or destroyed. However, under the broader protections of MAPA for site-specific art, the court granted a preliminary injunction preventing Pembroke from altering the Park.

E. Subsequent procedural history

Both parties filed interlocutory appeals to this court pursuant to 28 U.S.C. § 1292(a)(1). In the interim, the district court certified the question of whether MAPA protected Phillips' work in the Park to the Massachusetts Supreme Judicial Court ("SJC"), and the federal appeals were stayed pending the SJC's resolution of this state law question. *See Phillips v. Pembroke Real Estate, Inc.*, 443 Mass. 110, 819 N.E.2d 579 (Mass. 2004) (hereinafter *"Phillips II"*). . . .

The SJC concluded that MAPA did not protect site-specific art. *See id.* at 585-86. In particular, the SJC . . . [stated that] "[i]f the Legislature intended to include the type of site-specific art at issue here within MAPA's protections, it would entail a radical consequence for owners of land," *id.* [at 584.]

In light of the SJC's ruling and its own prior conclusion that it was possible for Phillips' sculptures to be removed from the Park consistent with VARA because of VARA's public presentation exception, the district court vacated the preliminary injunction it had granted and entered judgment on all counts. On appeal, . . . [Phillips] challenges only the district court's conclusion that the public presentation exception of VARA permits Pembroke to remove from the Park his large, multi-element work of art, which the district court found was both integrated and site-specific.

III.

A. Statutory Background

VARA states in relevant part that the "author of a work of visual art":

(3) subject to the limitations set forth in section 113(d), shall have the right —

    (A) to prevent any intentional distortion, mutilation, or other modification of that work which would be prejudicial to his or her honor or reputation . . . , and

    (B) to prevent any destruction of a work of recognized stature. . . .

17 U.S.C. § 106(A)(a)(3)(A) and (B). As an exception, § 106A(c)(2) states that:

> The modification of a work of visual art which is the result of conservation, or of the public presentation, including lighting and placement, of the work is not a destruction, distortion, mutilation, or other modification described in subsection (a)(3) unless the modification is caused by gross negligence.

This is the public presentation exception. A "work of visual art" is defined as including "a painting, drawing, print or sculpture, existing in a single copy" or in a limited edition. 17 U.S.C. § 101.

In *Carter v. Helmsley-Spear, Inc.*, 71 F.3d 77 (2d Cir. 1995), the Second Circuit, citing VARA's legislative history, explained that VARA:

> protects both the reputations of certain visual artists and the works of art they create. It provides these artists with the rights of "attribution" and "integrity". . . . These rights are analogous to those protected by Article 6bis of the Berne Convention, which are commonly known as "moral rights." The theory of moral rights is that they result in a climate of artistic worth and honor that encourages the author in the arduous act of creation.

Id. at 83 (citing H.R. Rep. No. 101-514, at 5, *reprinted in* 1990 U.S.C.C.A.N. 6915, 6917). "VARA grants three rights: the right of attribution, the right of integrity and, in the case of works of visual art of 'recognized stature,' the right to prevent destruction." *Id.* . . . [T]hese moral rights protect what an artist retains after relinquishing ownership (and/or copyright) of the tangible object that the artist has created. . . .

B. Site-specific art

During the preliminary injunction hearing, one of Phillips' experts . . . testified that:

> [T]oday the concept of "site specificity" is the "rallying cry" of public artists who seek to create a piece that derives enhanced meaning from its environment. Much of modern sculpture does not exist separate from its context, but rather integrates its context with the work to form, ideally, a seamless whole.

Essentially, for site-specific art, the location of the work is an integral element of the work. Because the location of the work contributes to its meaning, site-specific art is destroyed if it is moved from its original site. . . .

As [another expert] stated in an affidavit, "[t]his view contrasts with so-called 'plop-art' where a separately conceived art object is simply placed in a space."

Phillips I, 288 F. Supp. 2d at 95. A piece of plop-art does not incorporate its surroundings. . . . In summary, as the district court found below, "[t]he undisputed expert testimony is that in site-specific sculpture, the artist incorporates the environment as one of the media with which he works." *Id.*

C. The district court's opinion . . .

2. Integrated art

. . . [T]he district court . . . concluded that most of Phillips' pieces in the Park constituted a single work of integrated art, but it rejected his position that all of his pieces comprised a single work of art.

The district court then addressed [and rejected] Phillips' argument that the Park itself is an integrated work of art. . . .

Finally, the district court's conclusion that VARA applied to integrated art, and its related conclusion that Phillips had created a work of integrated art in the Park, did not prevent the removal of Phillips' works from the Park. That was so because the district court also concluded that integrated art was subject to the public presentation exception of VARA, § 106A(c)(2). Phillips' integrated work of art could still be disassembled and moved so long as the "works of visual art" are not "alter[ed], modif[ied], or destroy[ed]." *Id.* at 100.

3. Site-specific art

There remained Phillips' site-specificity argument. If Phillips could show that: (1) his work in the Park was site-specific art; (2) VARA protected site-specific art; and (3) that the public presentation exception did not apply to site-specific art, none of his work could be moved, even on a piecemeal basis.

Phillips convinced the district court that most of his work in the Park was site-specific as well as integrated.

Having made this finding on the site-specific nature of Phillips' work, the district court explained the positions of Phillips and Pembroke on site-specificity:

> [Phillips] [ ] argues that his work is so site-specific that moving it would be an intentional destruction or modification under VARA. Taking the sculpture from its current location and locating it on a private campus in Rhode Island not near the ocean . . . would be like painting over the background landscape in the Mona Lisa.

> [Pembroke] contends that the "public presentation" exclusion in § 106A(c)(2) permits it to move plaintiff's sculptures from their current placement to another, just as the statute would not prevent a curator from moving the Mona Lisa from one wall in the Louvre to another.

> Section 106A(c)(2) has been interpreted to exclude from VARA's protection "site-specific" works, works that would be modified if they were moved.

Id. at 99 (citation omitted). The district court then referenced one of the few relevant cases, see *Bd. of Managers of Soho Int'l Arts Condo. v. City of New York*, No. 01-1226, 2003 WL 21403333, at *10 (S.D.N.Y. 2003) (stating that VARA's objective "is not . . . to preserve a work of visual art *where* it is, but rather to preserve the work *as* it is"). It then found Pembroke's legal argument "more persuasive because it is rooted in the plain language of the exclusion in § 106A(c)(2) as well as the statute's legislative history." *Phillips I*, 288 F. Supp. 2d at 100; *see also id.* (" 'Generally, the removal of a work from a specific location comes within the [presentation] exclusion because the location is a matter of presentation.' ") (*quoting* H.R. Rep. No. 101-514, at 12).

Finally, the district court highlighted the fact that the public presentation exception "was crafted after the widely-publicized dispute between the General Services Administration and the artist Richard Serra over the removal of Serra's 'site-specific' piece 'Tilted Arc.' " *Id.*; *see also Serra v. United States Gen. Serv. Admin.*, 847 F.2d 1045 (2d Cir. 1988). In *Serra*, the Second Circuit rejected the plaintiff's argument that the removal of an integrated, site-specific, government-owned work of art from federal property violated the free expression and due process rights of the artist. *See Serra*, 847 F.2d at 1045. The district court inferred that because VARA and the public presentation exception were adopted after *Serra*, Congress must have been aware of site-specific art. Yet VARA says nothing that suggests special protection for site-specific art. Therefore, the district court concluded that:

> an artist has no right to the placement or public presentation of his sculpture under the exception in § 106A(c)(2). [Pembroke] is not obligated to display the works in the Park, as VARA provides no protection for a change in placement or presentation. However, under VARA, [Pembroke] is under an obligation not to alter, modify or destroy the "works of visual art" as I have defined them.

Id. at 100.

This is the conclusion that Phillips challenges on appeal. . . .

IV.

. . .

A. The district court's understanding of site-specific art and VARA

To help explain our holding that VARA does not apply to site-specific art, we must begin with a restatement of the district court's view. . . . On the one hand, the district court accepted the concept of site-specific art. It credited the unopposed testimony of Ranalli, Phillips' expert, "that for site specific art, the location of the work is a constituent element of the work." *Phillips I*, 288 F. Supp. 2d at 95. The district court understood that "[u]nder this approach, because the location defines the art, site-specific sculpture is destroyed if it is moved from the site." *Id.* The district court also found that "[t]o move Phillips' integrated work of visual art (*i.e.*, the sculptures, boulders, and granite paths along the axis . . . described in the VARA discussion) to another location . . . would be to alter it physically," *id.* at 102.

On the other hand, in the section of its opinion addressing Phillips' site-specificity argument . . . the district court found that while VARA applies to site-specific art, the public presentation exception permits the removal of site-specific art, *e.g.*, Phillips' work in the Park.

Without in any way diminishing our respect for the district court's careful handling of this difficult case, we find its analysis of VARA's relationship to site-specific art unpersuasive. By definition, site-specific art integrates its location as one of its elements. Therefore, the removal of a site-specific work from its location necessarily destroys that work of art. . . .

By concluding that VARA applies to site-specific art, and then allowing the removal of site-specific art pursuant to the public presentation exception, the district court purports to protect site-specific art under VARA's general provisions, and then permit its destruction by the application of one of VARA's exceptions. To us, this is not a sensible reading of VARA's plain meaning. Either VARA recognizes site-specific art and protects it, or it does not recognize site-specific art at all.

B. Phillips' position on appeal

Phillips recognizes the same tension in the district court's holding that we have identified, but he resolves it differently. He agrees with the district court's position that VARA applies to site-specific art . . . , but disagrees with the district court's view that the public presentation exception permits the removal of site-specific art.

1. The public presentation exception

. . . Phillips argues that VARA prevents the removal of site-specific art because the public presentation exception does not apply to site-specific art. His argument begins with a claim that the words "presentation" and "placement" in the public presentation exception are ambiguous on the issue of location. We find nothing remotely ambiguous about the word "presentation," which is modified by the word "placement." The word "placement" inescapably means location. . . .

[Next,] Phillips invokes the doctrine of *noscitur a sociis*, which counsels that words in a statute should be understood in the context of the terms around it. . . . Relying on this doctrine, Phillips asserts that "lighting and placement' must be read to be related to each other and be words of equal significance. If lighting refers to non-permanent changes in public presentation, then placement must also refer to non-permanent changes in public presentation." Phillips continues: "[b]uried within the "placement" term is the assumption that the object is moveable, and can be placed in various locations. This assumption must be examined. Site-specific artwork is a well-recognized form of art, but it is not always moveable."

We agree with Phillips that the premise of the public presentation exception is artwork that can be moved in some fashion, such as paintings or sculptures — that is, art that is not permanently affixed or "integrated" in such a way that the mere act of moving it would destroy it. The possibility of change without destruction is implicit in the public presentation exception. The public presentation exception defines the types of changes, such as those in lighting and placement, that do not constitute "destruction, distortion, or mutilation". But Phillips draws a startling conclusion from the public presentation exception's focus on permissible change in the presentation of a work of visual art: because the public presentation exception addresses itself only to "plop-art," that is, those works of art subject to temporary changes in such matters as lighting and placement, and declares further that such modifications of a work of visual art are not "destroying, distorting, or mutilating" them, [Phillips concludes that] the public presentation exception does not apply to site-specific art, which, as everyone acknowledges, cannot be removed from its location without destroying it. This approach leaves Phillips with the district court's holding that VARA applies to site-specific art, minus the court's related holding that the public presentation exception permits the removal of such art. In this way, the tension that we identified in the district court's decision disappears.

2. Dual regime

With his position on VARA and the public presentation exception, Phillips argues that VARA essentially creates a dual regime — words that mean one thing as applied to non-site-specific art have a different meaning when applied to site-specific art. Beyond his reading of the public presentation exception itself, Phillips cites only one other provision of VARA in support of his dual regime argument — § 113(d)(1)(A) of VARA, the so-called "building exception," which excludes from VARA's protection "a work of visual art [that] has been incorporated or made a part of a building in such a way that removing the work from the building will cause the destruction, distortion, mutilation, or other modification of the work as described in section 106A(a)(3)." Phillips asserts that because VARA provides an exception to VARA for artwork attached to buildings, but does not contain a similar provision for site-specific art (understood as art attached to real property), VARA must protect site-specific art.

With both . . . exceptions, Phillips is arguing that VARA's silence on a subject is actually evidence that the statute addresses that subject. To say the least, this is an odd way to read a statute. If VARA actually established such a complicated, dual regime, we would expect that the phrase "site-specific," or some equivalent, would appear in the language of the statute. There is no such phrase anywhere. Indeed, we would expect much more than just a reference to site-specific art. We would expect an elaboration of how to differentiate between site-specific and non-site-specific art (plop-art). That elaboration is nowhere to be found.

Moreover, the creation of a dual regime — which would require us, essentially, to rewrite VARA — has potentially far-reaching effects beyond the protection of Phillips' work in the Park. Once a piece of art is considered site-specific, and protected by VARA, such objects could not be altered by the property owner absent consent of the artist. Such a conclusion could dramatically affect real property interests and laws. . . .

. . . In discussing the possibility of MAPA protecting site-specific art, the SJC echoed this concern, observing that the creation of a dual regime under MAPA "would entail a radical consequence for owners of land, that the Legislature directly averted for owners of buildings. Specifically, rights afforded artists would encumber private and public land with restrictions lasting for the life of the artist plus fifty years, without the need for such restrictions to be recorded in a registry of deeds." *Phillips II*, 819 N.E.2d at 584-85. The SJC ultimately refused to:

> read such an intent into a legislative act given the recognized legislative policy of disparaging land restrictions (especially unrecorded ones), the common-law doctrine disapproving the long-term burdening of property, and the corollary judicial practice of construing statutory provisions regarding land restrictions in favor of freedom of alienation.

Id. at 585 (internal quotation marks omitted). . . .

Ultimately, we agree with Pembroke's position that "[t]here is no basis for Phillips' claim that VARA establishes two different regulatory regimes: one for free-standing works of art . . . and one for site-specific art that can never be moved and must always be displayed." VARA's plain language also requires us to reject the district court's approach to site-specific art. VARA does not protect site-specific art and then permit its destruction by removal from its site pursuant to the statute's public presentation exception. VARA does not apply to site-specific art at all.

V.

We do not denigrate the value or importance of site-specific art, which unmistakably enriches our culture and the beauty of our public spaces. We have simply concluded, for all of the reasons stated, that the plain language of VARA does not protect site-specific art. If such protection is necessary, Congress should do the job. We cannot do it by rewriting the statute in the guise of statutory interpretation.

NOTES AND QUESTIONS

(1) *Analyzing the reach of VARA.* The Visual Artists Rights Act is an initial attempt to accommodate moral rights within federal copyright law. One striking aspect of the Act is its limited scope: It applies only to "works of visual art." As defined in § 101 of the Copyright Act, the term is limited to certain works that exist in a single copy or in a limited edition of 200 copies or fewer. Do you find there to be anything peculiar about the definition? Is the idea of a "work" implicit in the definition of "work of visual art" the same as that underlying, say, the § 101 definition of a "pictorial, graphic and sculptural work"? In this connection, you may want to review what this book had to say about the concept of the "work" in Chapter 3.

What are the consequences of the definition of "work of visual art"? Under § 106A, would offensive modifications made to a reproduction of a painting (as distinct from those made to the canvas itself) violate the artist's moral right?

Note also that limited editions are covered only if they are signed and consecutively numbered by the author. Is this signing and numbering requirement consistent with Berne Article 5(2), which provides that the enjoyment and exercise of rights "shall not be subject to any formality"?

(2) The District Court opinion in *Phillips* included an interesting discussion of whether the coordinated sculptures in Eastport Park constituted one work or

several for purposes of VARA. The court concluded that the sculptures "along the northeast-southwest axis of the Park" comprised a single "work of visual art," while the remaining sculptures were separate works of art. Why was the park as a whole not considered a single "work of visual art"?

This issue also was considered in *Carter v. Helmsley-Spear, Inc.*, 71 F.3d 77 (2d Cir. 1995) (cited in *Phillips*), involving a "walk-through sculpture" that occupied most of a commercial building's lobby and consisted of "a variety of sculptural elements constructed from recycled materials . . . affixed to the walls and ceiling, and a vast mosaic made from pieces of recycled glass embedded in the floor and walls. Elements of the work include a giant hand fashioned from an old school bus, a face made up of automobile parts, and a number of interactive components." *Id.* at 80. Affirming the conclusion that although it was produced by several artists, this assemblage was, for the most part, a single "work of visual art" for VARA purposes, the Court of Appeals noted that the trial court had given weight to the method by which it had been created: "[E]ach additional element of the sculpture was based on the element preceding it so that they would mesh together. The result was a thematically consistent, interrelated work whose elements could not be separated without losing continuity and meaning." *Id.* at 84. Does this standard remind you of anything? Would the "work" described be considered a "joint work" within the meaning of § 101? Does it matter, for purposes of VARA?

The Disputed Walk-through Sculpture in *Carter*

(3) In *Carter*, the finding that the sculptors were employees meant that the work was a "work made for hire," and therefore ineligible for protection under VARA. This holding made it unnecessary for the court to reach various issues which would have been posed had VARA been held applicable. One of these arose from the

plaintiffs' claim that, under § 106A, they were entitled not only to prevent the destruction of the work, but also to be allowed to complete "unfinished" portions of it. Does such an assertion have any basis in the statute? Similar claims have been upheld under foreign moral rights statutes. *See, e.g.*, Françon & Ginsburg, *Authors' Rights in France: The Moral Right of the Creator of a Commissioned Work to Compel the Commissioning Party to Complete the Work*, 9 Colum.-VLA J.L. & Arts 381 (1985). In France and many other "authors' rights" countries, the "work made for hire" doctrine is a highly suspect notion, if not an anathema, to moral rights purists — and ownership of a copyright, subject to very limited exceptions, can only exist in natural persons.

Conversely, can an artist enjoin the owner from publicly displaying a work that he or she considers to be incomplete? *See Massachusetts Museum of Contemporary Art v. Büchel*, 593 F.3d 38 (1st Cir. 2010) (no violation for displaying unfinished work, but finding triable issue of fact whether museum made modifications that were prejudicial to the artist's honor or reputation).

(4) Should an "arrangement of living plants within two elliptical spaces" be considered a "work of visual art" within the meaning of VARA? Is such a work "fixed in a tangible medium of expression"? *See Kelley v. Chicago Park District*, 635 F.3d 290 (7th Cir. 2011) (holding that "Wildflower Works" was sufficiently original, but that it was neither "authored" nor "fixed" and was therefore not eligible for copyright protection). The court in *Kelley* suggested that the words "painting" and "sculpture" in the definition of "work of visual art" should have a narrower meaning than the phrase "pictorial, graphic or sculptural work," but it declined to rule on this ground because the defendant did not raise the issue on appeal.

(5) *"Recognized stature."* Another issue avoided in *Carter* arose from the fact that the right to prevent destruction of a work applies only to works of "recognized stature." This limitation is a radical departure in American copyright law that may force judges to make aesthetic judgments regarding highly subjective matters. Ever since *Bleistein v. Donaldson Lithographing Co.* (reproduced in Chapter 2), courts have foresworn considering artistic quality in deciding whether to protect a work. Why, then, was the "recognized stature" provision included? How is a court to decide whether a work is of recognized stature? Can you foresee problems in applying this provision to experimental or avant-garde works which may not have achieved "recognized stature" in traditional art circles?

In *Phillips*, the defendant apparently conceded that the work was one of "recognized stature," rendering it unnecessary for the court to discuss the issue. But the court endorsed a two-part test for "recognized stature" that originated in the District Court opinion in *Carter* and was applied in *Martin v. City of Indianapolis*, 192 F.3d 608 (7th Cir. 1999). *Martin* involved a large metal sculpture entitled "Symphony #1" that was erected on land donated by Martin's employer. The City promised Martin that he would be given 90 days notice to remove the sculpture in the event that the City decided to develop the land. Despite this promise, the City demolished the sculpture without notifying Martin. On appeal, the only significant question was whether the work was one of "recognized stature."

Symphony #1

The evidence pertaining to recognized stature consisted of newspaper and magazine articles and various letters about the sculpture, including a letter from the Director of the Herron School of Art at Indiana University. The City objected to the admission of this evidence on the ground that it constituted hearsay. The majority disagreed, holding that the statements were not being offered for their truth, but only to "show how art critics and the public viewed Martin's work, and [to] show that the sculpture was a matter worth reporting to the public." *Id.* at 613. One judge dissented, however, saying that "[w]hile the very publication of newspaper articles on a work of art may have bearing on the 'recognized' element, there has to be some evidence that the art had stature (*i.e.*, that it met a certain high level of quality)." *Id.* at 615. Do you agree? Does the majority implicitly conflate the two elements of "recognized stature" into one? And is it clear that a local (as distinct from national) reputation of a work is sufficient?

(6) The statutory standard of "recognized stature" continues to plague the courts, as does the tension between moral rights and the removal of big, invasive works of art in public places. In *Pollara v. Seymour*, 150 F. Supp. 2d 393 (N.D.N.Y. 2001), plaintiff's 10-foot by 30-foot mural was damaged when it was removed by state employees from Albany's Empire State Plaza the night before it was to be unveiled. On motion for summary judgment, the court held that public display of a work of art is not required in order for it to qualify as "a work of recognized stature." *Id.* at 397-98. After trial, however, the same court concluded that the work did not qualify, because "there was never any intent by the artist to preserve her work for future display." 206 F. Supp. 2d 333, 336 (N.D.N.Y. 2002). On appeal, the Second Circuit affirmed on the alternative ground that because the banner was

intended to promote a political message, it was "advertising [or] promotional material" that was expressly excluded from the definition of a "work of visual art" in § 101. 344 F.3d 265 (2d Cir. 2003). *See also Scott v. Dixon*, 309 F. Supp. 2d 395 (E.D.N.Y. 2004) (a sculpture which was kept at all times in its owner's backyard and was not visible to the public was not a "work of recognized stature" under VARA).

(7) With respect to works whose stature is not "recognized," VARA protects only against mutilations or distortions that will harm the artist's reputation. This would seem to preclude actions concerning modifications that improve the work or cause no reputational harm. Is this a wise limitation? What issues of proof do you suppose this limitation will engender?

Note also that VARA amended § 107 to make it clear that the fair use defense applies to actions under § 106A. How would you expect fair-use analysis to be applied in such cases? How big a potential "bite" may fair use take out of the artist's moral right? You may wish to revisit these questions after you have studied fair use in Chapter 10.

(8) *Site-specific sculpture.* The most contentious issue in *Phillips* is whether the artist can compel the landowner to keep the artwork where it is located, on the basis that the sculpture is "site-specific" and would effectively be destroyed (or at least distorted or mutilated) if it was moved to another location. The District Court rejected this claim under VARA, relying on an exception for modifications that result from the "public presentation" of the work.

The District Court noted that the "public presentation" exception was added following a pre-VARA controversy involving the noted artist Richard Serra. From 1986 to 1988, Serra was in and out of court seeking an injunction to prevent the dismantling of his "site-specific" sculpture "Tilted Arc" by the U.S. General Services Administration, which had installed the work in Manhattan's downtown Federal Plaza. Almost immediately upon its installation, Chief Judge Edward Re of the Court of International Trade began a letter-writing campaign urging the removal of what he termed the "rusted steel barrier" effectively bisecting the park — located adjacent to the federal courthouse. Serra lost his case, and the sculpture was dismembered and removed. (Serra recounted the story in an impassioned article in *Art in America*, May 1989, at 35.) Would the outcome have been any different if all the relevant events had occurred after the effective date of VARA?

The Court of Appeals in *Phillips* rejects reliance on the "public presentation" exception, holding instead that "VARA does not apply to site-specific art at all." Is there a meaningful difference between holding that VARA does not apply and holding that it does apply but that the work falls within an exception? *See Kelley v. Chicago Park District*, above (questioning the "all-or-nothing approach" of the *Phillips* court, noting that site-specific art is modified but not necessarily destroyed when it is moved, that site-specific art may be modified in ways that do not implicate the public presentation exception, and that the right of attribution might apply, but ultimately declining to decide the issue). More generally, should an artist have the right to insist that "site-specific" sculpture be displayed at a particular location?

(9) The sculpture in *Phillips* was built with the consent of the owner of the property on which it stood. Would the analysis be different if it had been introduced

onto the land without its owner's permission? See *English v. BFC&R East 11th Street LLC*, 1997 U.S. Dist LEXIS 19137 (S.D.N.Y., Dec. 3, 1997), concluding that an outdoor artwork created by six artists in a "community garden" on New York City property was not covered by VARA because it had been constructed illegally, "when such artwork cannot be removed from the site in question." What is the statutory basis for such a conclusion?

(10) *Duration under VARA.* The provisions of VARA concerning duration did not always read as they are summarized in the text preceding *Phillips*. As originally drafted, H.R. 2690 would have established, for works of visual art created on or after the effective date of the new Act, a (pre-Bono Act) life-plus-50 years term. This aspect of the bill was changed in response to Senate demands, resulting in a life-only term for a work of the type just described — but in a term of life-plus-50 years (later extended to life-plus-70 years) for a similar work created before the Act's effective date, where title to the copy or copies of the work was not transferred by the artist prior to such date. Is it possible, in policy terms, to make sense of § 106A as enacted?

Are the durational provisions of § 106A consistent with Art. 6bis(2) of Berne, requiring that the rights of integrity and attribution remain in force after the author's death "at least until the expiry of the economic rights"?

(11) VARA applies to works of visual art that were created on or after June 1, 1991, the effective date of the Act. But what of works that were created before the effective date? These are protected under § 106A, albeit only in the limited circumstances recited in the "Summary of Provisions" earlier. Is VARA violated if a work was mutilated before June 1, 1991, but was kept on public display in this form afterwards? In *Pavia v. 1120 Avenue of the Americas Associates*, 901 F. Supp. 620 (S.D.N.Y. 1995), a sculptor created a commissioned work in 1963 for display in a hotel. The hotel owners dismantled the work, displaying pieces of it in another location, and continued to do so despite formal complaints of the artist from 1992 to 1994. The sculptor asserted claims under VARA and the New York state act. The court dismissed the VARA claim because the only offending act — the dismantling — had taken place before VARA's effective date. The display in mutilated form, however, stated a claim under New York law.

(12) *Relief under VARA.* Under VARA, mutilation or destruction is an infringement of copyright. Injunctive relief enforcing VARA's provisions would appear to present no inherent theoretical difficulty. But what about damages? What will be the measure of damages when an artist's attribution or integrity right has been infringed? Or when her work has been destroyed intentionally?

Note also that VARA claims are exempt from the registration requirement, either as a condition of bringing suit or of recovering statutory damages and attorneys' fees. *See* §§ 411(a), 412. What explains the special treatment that VARA claims receive under these provisions?

(13) As we have seen, § 106A incorporates into U.S. law two important aspects of the *droit moral*: the rights of attribution and integrity. On the other hand, VARA fails to recognize other key components of the *droit moral* in its fullest embodiment — in particular, the rights of disclosure and of withdrawal. The right of disclosure

is simply the right to control the first public distribution of the work and is covered by § 106(3) of the Copyright Act. But what about the right of withdrawal — that is, the right of authors to remove their works from the public? Is this right protected by anything in federal law? Should it be? If so, how should such protection work? Suppose that a sculptor has sold a work that is now on display in a public building. The author decides, some years later, that it no longer represents her views and wants it removed. In France, an author can exercise the right to force removal, but has to reimburse the owner of the physical copy of the work. How often would you expect the right of withdrawal to be exercised in this country if it were recognized here?

(14)   Even within its extremely circumscribed scope of application, how well does VARA really protect the interests it is designed to safeguard? The answer may depend, in part, on how § 106A(e) — which provides that, while the right is non-transferable, it can be effectively waived by means of a specifically worded written instrument — is applied in practice. Why might this provision prove detrimental to the concept of moral rights?

The peculiar problems of works of art incorporated into buildings were anticipated in the drafting of VARA. Under § 113(d), if a work of visual art cannot be removed from a building without distorting or destroying the work, the owner can avoid liability by obtaining a waiver from the artist in advance. If you were representing a building owner who wanted to install a painting or sculpture, wouldn't you routinely demand a contractual waiver of moral rights up front? Would the artist have any more practical ability to resist such a demand than she would have had, pre-VARA, to insist on contractual stipulations limiting the manner in which the work could be displayed and reproduced? Would courts have any reason not to recognize such a waiver?

For an extended discussion of these issues, including references to relevant state laws and the laws of foreign countries, see generally U.S. Copyright Office, *Waiver of Moral Rights in Visual Artworks* (1996).

(15)   *VARA and preemption.* In *Phillips*, the District Court held that although VARA did not require the "site-specific" sculpture to be kept in its original location, the Massachusetts Art Preservation Act (MAPA) did. In so holding, the court did not discuss § 301(f) of the Copyright Act, which preempts all state law rights "equivalent" to those provided by VARA in "works of visual art" to which § 106A applies. Note, however, that § 301 does not preempt any cause of action for undertakings commenced before the effective date of the Act, for activities that violate legal or equitable rights not equivalent to those conferred by § 106A, or for activities that violate legal or equitable rights extending beyond the life of the author. Is MAPA preempted by § 301(f) in this case? More generally, how much of a role does VARA leave to state art preservation statutes? We will return to this question in § 11.02, which considers issues of preemption under § 301 generally.

In *Phillips* itself, after issuing the preliminary injunction, the District Court certified the question of MAPA's applicability to the Massachusetts Supreme Court. In *Phillips v. Pembroke Real Estate, Inc.*, 819 N.E.2d 579 (Mass. 2004), that court held that MAPA does *not* require that "site-specific" art be preserved in its original location. This holding left Phillips to the vagaries of VARA, which turned out to provide no protection either.

(16) *VARA and the future.* Some observers view VARA as merely the first step on the road to more generalized moral rights protection in the United States. If so, what's next? Moral rights protection for motion pictures? What about musical works? Literary works? Computer software? How would moral rights legislation affect the economic structure of the various industries involved? Would new rights like those created by VARA be more difficult to administer for types of works created by intensely collaborative activity? Might future applications of the moral rights concept play havoc with copyright owners' ability to exploit their § 106(2) rights to prepare derivative works? Should we hope to see Congress' first flirtation with moral rights blossom into a full-blown romance? *Compare* R. Kwall, THE SOUL OF CREATIVITY: FORGING A MORAL RIGHTS LAW FOR THE UNITED STATES (2009), *and* Bird, *Moral Rights: Diagnosis and Rehabilitation*, 4 Am. Bus. L.J. 407 (2009), *with* Adler, *Against Moral Rights*, 97 Cal. L. Rev. 263 (2009).

(17) In the 1980s, a controversy arose over the "colorization" of black-and-white films. Colorization is the process of adding color to black-and-white films by digitizing the film, assigning a color to each item in a scene, and having a computer fill in the colors for each frame in that scene. Some copyright owners believed that adding color would make older black-and-white films more marketable, while directors, cinematographers and film historians objected that colorization was a prejudicial desecration of black-and-white masterpieces.

The United States, characteristically, treated the issue in a free-market manner. In 1988, it established the National Film Registry, which each year designates 25 films deemed to be "culturally, historically or aesthetically significant," and required that anyone who distributed a "materially altered" version of any film on the Registry had to label it conspicuously as such. In France, however, the heirs of director John Huston successfully obtained an injunction against the broadcast of a colorized version of the MGM film *The Asphalt Jungle* on moral rights grounds. *See Huston v. Société de l'Exploitation de la Cinquiéme Chaine*, 149 R.I.D.A. 197 (Fr. Cour de Cassation 1991). In the end, the projected demand for colorized motion pictures failed to materialize, rendering the cost of colorizing motion pictures economically prohibitive, and the controversy subsided. (The National Film Registry survives, but the labeling requirement — its initial *raison d'être* — expired and was not renewed.) The issue of moral rights for motion pictures, however, remains very much alive (*see, e.g.*, discussion of *Huntsman v. Soderbergh* in § 7.08[B] above), and is likely to be the source of continued controversy in the future.

(18) Even in countries that are strongly protective of moral rights, such as France, there arise controversies over the scope of moral rights. Art. L. 121-1 of the French Intellectual Property Code provides that "[a]n author shall enjoy the right to respect for his name, his authorship and his work," and that this right "shall be perpetual, inalienable and imprescriptible." What does this mean in practice? In *Société Plon S.A. v. Hugo*, Arrêt No. 125 (Fr. Cour de Cassation 2007), the highest court in France held that the great-grandson of author Victor Hugo could not recover damages for the publication of two unauthorized "sequels" to the novel *Les*

Misérables, in part because the adaptation right passed into the public domain on the expiration of the copyright.

(19)   Is it possible that new international treaty commitments will push the United States toward expanding the scope of federal moral rights legislation? The 1996 WIPO Performances and Phonograms Treaty includes the following Article 5(1):

> Independently of a performer's economic rights, and even after the transfer of those rights, the performer shall, as regards his live aural performance or performances fixed in phonograms, have the right to claim to be identified as the performer of his performances, except where omission is dictated by the manner of the use of the performance, and to object to any distortion, mutilation or other modification of his performances that would be prejudicial to his reputation.

Article 5(2) permits countries bound by the treaty to limit the duration of the performer's moral right, in some instances, to his or her lifetime, while Article 5(3) gives such countries latitude in choosing "the means of redress for safeguarding" the right. The Digital Millennium Copyright Act, passed to implement the new WIPO treaties in the United States, includes no reference whatsoever to this new form of entitlement. If the goal of the DMCA was to bring U.S. law into compliance with the requirements of the new treaties, how can this be? On the other hand, were Congress to enact moral rights legislation in favor of musical performers, could it (as a matter of principle or politics) refuse to grant such rights to film directors or literary authors?

To complicate matters still further, Article 9 of the 1994 TRIPS Agreement requires World Trade Organization countries to honor all of the substantive provisions of the Berne Convention *except* for Article 6*bis* — an exception insisted upon by the United States. No similar exception was written into the 1996 WIPO Copyright Treaty. Article 1(4) thereof provides, simply, that "Contracting Parties shall comply with Articles 1 to 21 and the Appendix of the Berne Convention" — presumably including Article 6*bis* on moral rights. Thus, ratification of the treaty constituted a voluntary reobligation on the part of the United States to the obligations we assumed on March 1, 1989, and arguably have yet to fulfill.

(20)   Obviously, the WIPO treaties, which emerged from a diplomatic conference at which there was much discussion of a "digital agenda" for international copyright and neighboring rights, amounted to a reaffirmation of the importance of moral rights. But is it clear that traditional moral rights really have a place in the networked digital information environment? In what ways might universal recognition and enforcement of moral rights interfere with full realization of the potential of new technologies? *Compare* Mucinskas, *Moral Rights and Digital Art: Revitalizing the Visual Artists' Rights Act?*, 2005 U. Ill. J.L. Tech. & Pol'y 291, *with* Geller, *The Universal Electronic Archive: Issues in International Copyright*, 25 Int'l Rev. Indus. Prop. & Copyright (IIC) 54 (1994).

Chapter 8

INFRINGEMENT ACTIONS

In the preceding chapter, we explored the copyright owner's exclusive rights under the 1976 Act. Copyright infringement occurs when another party violates one or more of those rights. Thus, to infringe, the defendant must have reproduced, adapted, publicly distributed, publicly performed and/or publicly displayed the copyrighted work, or violated the digital audio transmission right in a sound recording or the attribution or integrity right in a work of visual art — and done so without either the copyright owner's authorization or the benefit of one of the limitations contained in §§ 107 through 122.

When an entire work has been used verbatim, the only contested question may be which, if any, of the exclusive rights have been infringed. But if the allegedly infringing work differs from the original, we must also consider how to determine whether the second work was "based upon" the first, and how similar the second work must be to infringe the first. As one commentator put it:

> A copy is one thing, . . . [a] resemblance another. It is indeed certain, that whoever attempts any common topic will find unexpected coincidences of his thought with those of other writers; nor can the nicest judgment always distinguish accidental similitude from artful imitation. . . . There may be a strong likeness without an identity. The question is, therefore, . . . what degree of imitation constitutes an infringement of the copyright of a particular composition?[1]

On this issue, the Statute of Anne is silent, referring only to printing "any such book or books, without the consent of the proprietor or proprietors thereof." As another commentator observed, "[t]he statute does not attempt to define what a copy is, and such rules as there are for determining whether one work is a copy of another are entirely derived from the case law on the subject."[2] The same can also be said of the 1909 and 1976 Acts.

This chapter examines the copyright owner's *prima facie* case in an action for infringement. We consider first the procedural aspects of the action (jurisdiction, standing, who may be sued, and the like). We then examine the substantive law of infringement, particularly the key issues of copying and improper appropriation. Finally, we consider extraterritorial application of U.S. law and conflicts with the laws of foreign nations. Secondary liability, including contributory infringement and vicarious liability, will be addressed in Chapter 9; and defenses, especially fair use, will be addressed in Chapter 10.

---

[1] W. Copinger, THE LAW OF COPYRIGHT 97-98 (1870).

[2] E.J. MacGillivray, A TREATISE UPON THE LAW OF COPYRIGHT 96 (1902).

§ 8.01 INTRODUCTION

Judicial Code Provisions

28 U.S.C. § 1338

(a) The district courts shall have original jurisdiction of any civil action arising under any Act of Congress relating to patents, plant variety protection, copyrights and trademarks. No State court shall have jurisdiction over any claim for relief arising under any Act of Congress relating to patents, plant variety protection, or copyrights. For purposes of this subsection, the term "State" includes any State of the United States, the District of Columbia, the Commonwealth of Puerto Rico, the United States Virgin Islands, American Samoa, Guam, and the Northern Mariana Islands.

(b) The district courts shall have original jurisdiction of any civil action asserting a claim of unfair competition when joined with a substantial and related claim under the copyright, patent, plant variety protection or trademark laws.

(c) Subsections (a) and (b) apply to exclusive rights in mask works under chapter 9 of title 17, and to exclusive rights on designs under chapter 13 of title 17, to the same extent as such subsections apply to copyrights.

28 U.S.C. § 1367

(a) Except as provided in subsections (b) and (c) or as expressly provided otherwise by Federal statute, in any civil action of which the district courts have original jurisdiction, the district courts shall have supplemental jurisdiction over all other claims that are so related to claims in the action within such original jurisdiction that they form part of the same case or controversy under Article III of the United States Constitution. Such supplemental jurisdiction shall include claims that involve the joinder or intervention of additional parties. . . .

(c) The district courts may decline to exercise supplemental jurisdiction over a claim under subsection (a) if —

(1) the claim raises a novel or complex issue of State law,

(2) the claim substantially predominates over the claim or claims over which the district court has original jurisdiction,

(3) the district court has dismissed all claims over which it has original jurisdiction, or

(4) in exceptional circumstances, there are other compelling reasons for declining jurisdiction.

(d) The period of limitations for any claim asserted under subsection (a), and for any other claim in the same action that is voluntarily dismissed at the same time as or after the dismissal of the claim under subsection (a), shall be tolled while the claim is pending and for a period of 30 days after it is dismissed unless State law provides for a longer tolling period. . . .

28 U.S.C. § 1400

(a) Civil actions, suits, or proceedings arising under any Act of Congress relating to copyrights or exclusive rights in mask works or designs may be instituted in the district in which the defendant or his agent resides or may be found. . . .

28 U.S.C. § 1498

. . .

(b) Hereafter, whenever the copyright in any work protected under the copyright laws of the United States shall be infringed by the United States, by a corporation owned or controlled by the United States, or by a contractor, subcontractor, or any person, firm, or corporation acting for the Government and with the authorization or consent of the Government, the exclusive action which may be brought for such infringement shall be an action against the United States in the Court of Federal Claims for the recovery of his reasonable and entire compensation as damages for such infringement, including the minimum statutory damages as set forth in section 504(c) of title 17, United States Code: *Provided,* That a Government employee shall have a right of action against the Government under this subsection except where he was in a position to order, influence, or induce use of the copyrighted work by the Government: *Provided, however,* That this subsection shall not confer a right of action on any copyright owner or any assignee of such owner with respect to any copyrighted work prepared by a person while in the employment or service of the United States, where the copyrighted work was prepared as a part of the official functions of the employee, or in the preparation of which Government time, material, or facilities were used: *And provided further,* That before such action against the United States has been instituted the appropriate corporation owned or controlled by the United States or the head of the appropriate department or agency of the Government, as the case may be, is authorized to enter into an agreement with the copyright owner in full settlement and compromise for the damages accruing to him by reason of such infringement and to settle the claim administratively out of available appropriations.

Except as otherwise provided by law, no recovery shall be had for any infringement of a copyright covered by this subsection committed more than three years prior to the filing of the complaint or counterclaim for infringement in the action, except that the period between the date of receipt of a written claim for compensation by the Department or agency of the Government or corporation owned or controlled by the United States, as the case may be, having authority to settle such claim and the date of mailing by the Government of a notice to the claimant that his claim has been denied shall not be counted as a part of the three years, unless suit is brought before the last-mentioned date.

(c) The provisions of this section shall not apply to any claim arising in a foreign country.

. . .

(e) Subsections (b) and (c) of this section apply to exclusive rights in mask works under chapter 9 of title 17, and to exclusive rights in designs under chapter 13 of title 17, to the same extent as such subsections apply to copyrights.

Statutory References

1976 Act: §§ 501, 511

1909 Act: § 115

Legislative History

H.R. Rep. No. 94-1476 at 158,
reprinted in 1976 U.S.C.C.A.N. 5659, 5774-75

SECTION 501. INFRINGEMENT OF COPYRIGHT

The bill, unlike the [1909 Act], contains a general statement of what constitutes infringement of copyright. Section 501(a) identifies a copyright infringer as someone who "violates any of the exclusive rights of the copyright owner as provided by sections 106 through [122]" of the bill, or who imports copies or phonorecords in violation of section 602. Under the latter section an unauthorized importation of copies or phonorecords acquired abroad is an infringement of the exclusive right of distribution under certain circumstances.

The principle of the divisibility of copyright ownership, established by section 201(d), carries with it the need in infringement actions to safeguard the rights of all copyright owners and to avoid a multiplicity of suits. Subsection (b) of section 501 enables the owner of a particular right to bring an infringement action in that owner's name alone, while at the same time insuring to the extent possible that the other owners whose rights may be affected are notified and given a chance to join the action. . . .

[For a fuller excerpt from H.R. Rep. No. 94-1476, see Part Three of the Casebook Supplement.]

§ 8.02 FRAMING THE LAWSUIT

Before an infringement lawsuit is filed, a lawyer must first consider where such actions can be brought and by and against whom they can be filed. These issues are not free from difficulty. Federal courts have exclusive jurisdiction over cases "arising under" the copyright laws, but it does not follow that every action involving a copyright falls into that category. Conversely, federal court jurisdiction encompasses some law suits that concern copyright issues but do not allege a violation of the plaintiff's exclusive rights. Moreover, some actions are vulnerable to dismissal because one or more of the plaintiffs has an insufficient interest in the copyright, failed to register its copyright, failed to join an indispensable party defendant, or because the defendant is immune to suit. The following section explores these and other issues of jurisdiction and procedure that arise at the threshold of infringement litigation.

[A]   Jurisdictional Matters

T.B. HARMS CO. v. ELISCU
United States Court of Appeals, Second Circuit
339 F.2d 823 (1964)

FRIENDLY, CIRCUIT JUDGE:

A layman would doubtless be surprised to learn that an action wherein the purported sole owner of a copyright alleged that persons claiming partial ownership had recorded their claim in the Copyright Office and had warned his licensees against disregarding their interests was not one "arising under any Act of Congress relating to . . . copyrights" over which 28 U.S.C. § 1338 gives the federal courts exclusive jurisdiction. Yet precedents going back for more than a century teach that lesson and lead us to affirm Judge Weinfeld's dismissal of the complaint.

[The litigation concerned four copyrighted songs written for the motion picture "Flying Down to Rio." The songs were composed by Vincent Youmans, with lyrics by Gus Kahn and Edward Eliscu. Youmans and Kahn assigned their rights to Max Dreyfus, principal stockholder of the T.B. Harms Co.]

Getting a Jump on the 2016 Olympics?
The Everett Collection

Allegedly — and his denial of this is a prime subject of dispute — Eliscu then entered into an agreement dated June 30, 1933, assigning his rights to the existing and renewal copyrights to Dreyfus in return for certain royalties.

When the copyrights were about to expire, proper renewal applications were made by the children of Youmans, by the widow and children of Kahn, and by Eliscu. The two former groups executed assignments of their rights in the renewal copyrights to Harms. But Eliscu, by an instrument dated February 19, 1962, recorded in the Copyright Office, assigned his rights in the renewal copyrights to

defendant Ross Jungnickel, Inc., subject to a judicial determination of his ownership. Thereafter Eliscu's lawyer advised ASCAP and one Harry Fox — respectively
the agents for the small performing rights and the mechanical recording license
fees — that Eliscu had become vested with a half interest in the renewal copyrights
and that any future payments which failed to reflect his interest would be made at
their own risk; at the same time he demanded an accounting from Harms. Finally,
Eliscu brought an action in the New York Supreme Court for a declaration that he
owned a one-third interest in the renewal copyrights and for an accounting.

Harms then began the instant action in the District Court for the Southern
District of New York for equitable and declaratory relief against Eliscu and
Jungnickel. Jurisdiction was predicated on 28 U.S.C. § 1338; plaintiff alleged its own
New York incorporation and did not allege the citizenship of the defendants, which
concededly is in New York. Defendants moved to dismiss the complaint for failure
to state a claim on which relief can be granted and for lack of federal jurisdiction;
voluminous affidavits were submitted. The district court dismissed the complaint for
want of federal jurisdiction.

In line with what apparently were the arguments of the parties, Judge Weinfeld
treated the jurisdictional issue as turning solely on whether the complaint alleged
any act or threat of copyright infringement. He was right in concluding it did not.
Infringement, as used in copyright law, does not include everything that may impair
the value of the copyright; it is doing one or more of those things which § 1 of the
Act, 17 U.S.C. § 1, reserves exclusively to the copyright owner. *See* Nimmer,
Copyright §§ 100, 141 (1963) . . . Here neither Eliscu nor Jungnickel had used or
threatened to use the copyrighted material; their various acts, as the district judge
noted, sought to establish their ownership of the copyrights by judicial and
administrative action, including notice to the parties concerned.

However, the jurisdictional statute does not speak in terms of infringement, and
the undoubted truth that a claim for infringement "arises under" the Copyright Act
does not establish that nothing else can. Simply as a matter of language, the
statutory phrasing would not compel the conclusion that an action to determine who
owns a copyright does not arise under the Copyright Act, which creates the federal
copyright with an implied right to license and an explicit right to assign. But the
gloss afforded by history and good sense leads to that conclusion as to the complaint
in this case.

Although Chief Justice Marshall, construing the "arising under" language in the
context of Article III of the Constitution, indicated in *Osborn v. Bank of the United
States*, 22 U.S. 738 (1824), that the grant extended to every case in which federal law
furnished a necessary ingredient of the claim even though this was antecedent and
uncontested, the Supreme Court has long given a narrower meaning to the "arising
under" language in statutes defining the jurisdiction of the lower federal courts.
. . .

The cases dealing with statutory jurisdiction over patents and copyrights have
taken the same conservative line. . . .

. . . [T]he federal grant of a patent or copyright has not been thought to infuse
with any national interest a dispute as to ownership or contractual enforcement

turning on the facts or on ordinary principles of contract law. Indeed, the case for an unexpansive reading of the provision conferring exclusive jurisdiction with respect to patents and copyrights has been especially strong since expansion would entail depriving the state courts of any jurisdiction over matters having so little federal significance.

In an endeavor to explain precisely what suits arose under the patent and copyright laws, Mr. Justice Holmes stated that "[a] suit arises under the law that creates the cause of action"; in the case *sub judice*, . . . involving slander of a patent, he said, "whether it is a wrong or not depends upon the law of the State where the act is done" so that the suit did not arise under the patent laws. *American Well Works Co. v. Layne & Bowler Co.*, 241 U.S. 257, 260 (1916). The Holmes "creation" test explains the taking of federal jurisdiction in a great many cases, notably copyright and patent infringement actions, both clearly authorized by the respective federal acts, and thus unquestionably within the scope of 28 U.S.C. § 1338; indeed, in the many infringement suits that depend only on some point of fact and require no construction of federal law, no other explanation may exist.

Harms' claim is not within Holmes' definition. The relevant statutes create no explicit right of action to enforce or rescind assignments of copyrights, nor does any copyright statute specify a cause of action to fix the locus of ownership. . . .

It has come to be realized that Mr. Justice Holmes' formula is more useful for inclusion than for the exclusion for which it was intended. Even though the claim is created by state law, a case may "arise under" a law of the United States if the complaint discloses a need for determining the meaning or application of such a law. . . . But Harms likewise does not meet this test. . . .

. . . The crucial issue is whether or not Eliscu executed the assignment to Dreyfus; possibly the interpretation of the initial May, 1933 contract is also relevant, but if any aspect of the suit requires an interpretation of the Copyright Act, the complaint does not reveal it.

Having thus found that appropriate pleading of a pivotal question of federal law may suffice to give federal jurisdiction even for a "state-created" claim, we cannot halt at questions hinging only on the language of the Copyright Act. . . . Even in the absence of express statute, federal law may govern what might seem an issue of local law because the federal interest is dominant. If this "federal common law" governed some disputed aspect of a claim to ownership of a copyright or for the enforcement of a license, federal jurisdiction might follow . . . But there is not the slightest reason to think that any legal question presented by Harms' complaint falls in the shadow of a federal interest suggested by the Copyright Act or any other source.

Mindful of the hazards of formulation in this treacherous area, we think that an action "arises under" the Copyright Act if and only if the complaint is for a remedy expressly granted by the Act, *e.g.*, a suit for infringement or for the statutory royalties for record reproduction, . . . or asserts a claim requiring construction of the Act, . . . or, at the very least and perhaps more doubtfully, presents a case where a distinctive policy of the Act requires that federal principles control the disposition of the claim. The general interest that copyrights, like all other forms of property, should be enjoyed by their true owners is not enough to meet this last test. . . . *Affirmed.*

NOTES AND QUESTIONS

(1) *Subject-matter jurisdiction generally.* Consider the court's threshold difficulty in defining what constituted an infringement under the 1909 Act, which contained no functional equivalent to § 501 of the 1976 Act. Judge Friendly cites an early edition of the Nimmer treatise for the proposition that "[i]nfringement . . . is doing one or more of those things which § 1 of the [old] Act . . . reserves exclusively to the copyright owner." Is this consistent with § 501(a) of the current Act?

(2) Focus now on the criteria for deciding whether a claim "aris[es] under" federal copyright law, within the meaning of 28 U.S.C. § 1338(a). Perhaps no summary of the case law in this area can truly do justice to the variety of the decisions. It is clear that under § 1338(a), "the word 'copyright' is not so compelling as to invoke federal jurisdiction upon its mere mention." *Topolos v. Caldewey,* 698 F.2d 991, 993 (9th Cir. 1983). But how much more than a "mere mention" is required?

(3) *The "classic" T.B. Harms test.* Only the first prong of Judge Friendly's three-part *Harms* test, *i.e.,* whether "the complaint is for a remedy expressly granted by the [Copyright] Act," is concerned with actual infringement of the copyright holder's rights. Is that prong too narrowly delineated? What about declaratory judgment actions relating to copyright title? If *P* alleges ownership of a copyright to the exclusion of *D*'s claimed interest, isn't that in substance an allegation that, absent a judicial declaration of *P*'s ownership, *D* will take actions inconsistent with one or more of *P*'s § 106 exclusive rights? Why try the title question first in state court, and then the infringement claim in federal court? Should the matter be treated differently if an arguable infringement already has occurred, but the plaintiff seeks only a declaratory judgment as to ownership of the copyright?

(4) Does an action for a declaratory judgment of non-infringement come within the first prong of the *Harms* test? Generally speaking, the answer is "yes"; but in order to seek declaratory relief there must be an actual "case or controversy," which requires showing that the plaintiff has "a real and reasonable apprehension of litigation." *Compare Texas v. West Publishing Co.,* 882 F.2d 171, 176 (5th Cir. 1989) ("defendant's simple assertion that they hold a copyright in certain material generally does not amount to a threat of litigation"), *with Mailer v. Zolotow,* 380 F. Supp. 894 (S.D.N.Y. 1974) ("a justiciable controversy exists even where there has been no actual threat of suit, so long as defendant has notified plaintiff that defendant claims his copyright has been infringed").

What if the claim of infringement is communicated only to a third party? In *Newmark v. Turner Broadcasting Network,* 226 F. Supp. 2d 1215 (C.D. Cal. 2002), five owners of ReplayTV digital video recorders (DVRs) sued 28 entertainment companies for a declaratory judgment of non-infringement. The plaintiffs asserted they had a "reasonable apprehension of liability" because the 28 defendants had filed suit for contributory infringement against DVR manufacturers, based on the use of DVRs by (unnamed) individual owners. The court held that these allegations were sufficient to state an actual "case or controversy" for purposes of federal subject-matter jurisdiction. After the entertainment companies settled their case against ReplayTV, however, the court dismissed the individuals' suit as moot. *Paramount Pictures Corp. v. ReplayTV*, 298 F. Supp. 2d 921 (C.D. Cal. 2004).

Must a copyright be registered before a potential defendant can file suit for a declaratory judgment of non-infringement? The question is subject to controversy. See "Registration and declaratory judgments" in the section following these notes entitled "Miscellaneous Jurisdictional Issues."

(5)   The second prong of the *Harms* test presents perhaps fewer difficulties. Federal courts have jurisdiction under § 1338(a) in cases in which the complaint "asserts a claim requiring construction of the Act." In *Harms* itself, this standard was not met because the question of ownership of the copyright depended entirely on interpretation of the contract at issue. But where the question of ownership requires an interpretation of the "work made for hire" or "joint work" provisions of the Copyright Act (*see generally* Chapter 4), federal subject-matter jurisdiction is proper. *See, e.g., Severe Records, LLC v. Rich*, 658 F.3d 571 (6th Cir. 2011); *Merchant v. Levy*, 92 F.3d 51 (2d Cir. 1996). Indeed, one court has held that there may be federal jurisdiction over state-law claims such as misappropriation of trade secrets and conversion, if the question of ownership overlaps with the "work made for hire" provisions of the federal Copyright Act. *See JustMed, Inc. v. Byce*, 600 F.3d 1118 (9th Cir. 2010).

Can a clever litigant create federal subject-matter jurisdiction by claiming that there is a threshold question as to whether the contract qualifies as a signed writing under § 204(a)? In *Jasper v. Bovina Music, Inc.*, 314 F.3d 42 (2d Cir. 2002), the court cautioned that "the line drawn in *T.B. Harms* cannot be obliterated by such verbal gymnastics. The need for interpretation of a contract does not necessarily mean that there is a bona fide issue as to whether the contract is a writing for purposes of section 204(a)." *Id.* at 47. The court found, however, that the case before it *did* present a *bona fide* issue involving the interpretation of § 204(a). *See also Sullivan v. Naturalis, Inc.*, 5 F.3d 1410, 1413 (11th Cir. 1993) (same).

(6)   The third prong of the *Harms* test concerns instances in which "a distinctive policy of the Act requires that federal principles control the disposition of the claim." The principal question under this prong is whether federal preemption permits the removal of state-law claims from state court to federal court in order to dismiss them. Although the "well-pleaded complaint" rule (discussed below) may bar consideration of defenses in determining jurisdiction, the Supreme Court has upheld removal in some cases in which state-law claims are "completely preempted" by federal law. *See, e.g., Metropolitan Life Ins. Co. v. Taylor*, 481 U.S. 58 (1987) (ERISA). Several Courts of Appeals have held that this exception applies to copyright preemption as well. *See, e.g., Rosciszewski v. Arete Associates, Inc.*, 1 F.3d 225 (4th Cir. 1993); *Briarpatch Ltd. v. Phoenix Pictures, Inc.*, 373 F.3d 296 (2d Cir. 2004); *and Ritchie v. Williams*, 395 F.3d 283 (6th Cir. 2005). *But see Dunlap v. G&L Holding Group, Inc.*, 381 F.3d 1285 (11th Cir. 2004) (exception does not apply to state-law claims for copying ideas which are not "fixed"); *accord GlobeRanger Corp. v. Software AG*, 691 F.3d 702 (5th Cir. 2012); *see also Leto v. RCA Corp.*, 341 F. Supp.

2d 1001, *on reconsideration*, 355 F. Supp. 2d 921 (N.D. Ill. 2004) (exception does not apply to copyright claims at all).

(7) *The well-pleaded complaint rule.* How important in these matters is pleading? In *Vestron, Inc. v. Home Box Office, Inc.*, 839 F.2d 1380 (9th Cir. 1988), Vestron claimed ownership of the exclusive rights to make and distribute videocassettes of two films, *Hoosiers* and *Platoon*, and alleged HBO was infringing those rights. HBO admitted it was selling videocassettes of the two films, but it contended that the producer, Hemdale, had terminated Vestron's license and had granted the rights to HBO. On appeal, the issue was whether a complaint that pleads a claim for copyright infringement properly invokes federal jurisdiction where the defendant admits the allegedly infringing use and disputes only a contractual issue concerning ownership of the copyright.

The Ninth Circuit concluded that the jurisdictional issue must be determined by reference to the "well-pleaded complaint" rule:

> [W]hether a case is one arising under . . . a law . . . of the United States . . . must be determined from what necessarily appears in the plaintiff's statement of his own claim in the [complaint], unaided by anything alleged in anticipation or avoidance of defenses . . .

839 F.2d at 1380, quoting *Franchise Tax Bd. of California v. Construction Laborers Vacation Trust*, 463 U.S. 1, 10 (1983). Because Vestron alleged infringement, the court held that federal jurisdiction was proper, and that neither the assertion of defenses by HBO nor the anticipation of those defenses by Vestron could defeat jurisdiction. *Accord Nova Design Build, Inc. v. Grace Hotels, LLC*, 652 F.3d 814 (7th Cir. 2011); *Effects Associates, Inc. v. Cohen*, 817 F.2d 72 (9th Cir. 1987).

In *Vestron*, the court stated that if the plaintiff's infringement claim later proves to be "spurious," "then the proper avenue is dismissal for failure to state a claim under federal copyright law." Is dismissal a sufficient sanction when a claim proves "spurious"? Would sanctions under Rule 11 of the Federal Rules of Civil Procedure be more appropriate?

(8) Suppose a complaint filed in state court raises exclusively state-law issues, but the defendant pleads a counterclaim alleging copyright infringement. May the state court hear and determine the counterclaim for infringement? Traditionally, the answer was clearly "no." *See, e.g., Tewarson v. Simon*, 750 N.E.2d 176 (Ohio Ct. App. 2001); *EMSA Limited Partnership v. Lincoln*, 691 So. 2d 547 (Fla. Dist. Ct. App. 1997). The Supreme Court created a potential loophole, however, when it held that under the "well-pleaded complaint" rule, a patent infringement counterclaim did not "arise under" the patent laws for purposes of § 1338(a). *Holmes Group, Inc. v. Vornado Air Circulation Sys., Inc.*, 535 U.S. 826 (2002). This holding suggested that counterclaims alleging patent and copyright infringement *could* be heard in state courts. *See Green v. Hendrickson Publishers, Inc.*, 770 N.E.2d 784 (Ind. 2002). Congress closed the loophole in the America Invents Act of 2011, by amending the second sentence of § 1338(a) to read: "No State court shall have jurisdiction over any *claim for relief* arising under any Act of Congress relating to patents, plant variety protection, or copyrights" (emphasis added).

(9) *Other bases for jurisdiction.* If an action "arises under" federal copyright law within the meaning of 28 U.S.C. § 1338(a), the District Courts have original and exclusive jurisdiction without regard to diversity of citizenship or the amount in controversy. Of course, those factors may provide an alternative basis for federal jurisdiction under 28 U.S.C. § 1332. *See, e.g., London Film Prods. v. Intercontinental Communications, Inc.,* 580 F. Supp. 47 (S.D.N.Y. 1984) (where diversity jurisdiction exists, federal court may hear claims involving copyright infringement which occurred solely in a foreign country and arose solely under that country's law).

MISCELLANEOUS JURISDICTIONAL ISSUES

Supplemental jurisdiction. By applying 28 U.S.C. § 1338(a), the federal courts determine whether they have jurisdiction to decide a case at all. If jurisdiction does lie in the federal courts but the complaint includes nonfederal as well as federal claims, it may be convenient and sensible as a matter of judicial economy to decide all of the claims in a single case in the federal forum. Under 28 U.S.C. § 1338(b), a District Court has the power to do so if three requirements are met: (1) the basis of the nonfederal claim must be "unfair competition," and the federal claim to which it is attached must be both (2) "substantial" and (3) "related." *See Conopco, Inc. v. May Dep't Stores Co.,* 46 F.3d 1556, 1571 n.14 (Fed. Cir. 1994) ("Sec. 1338(b) is a codification of the doctrine of pendent jurisdiction as it applies to patent, trademark, and copyright causes of action.").

Section 1338(b) was rendered largely redundant by the enactment in 1990 of 28 U.S.C. § 1367, which was intended to codify the judge-made doctrines of "pendent jurisdiction" and "ancillary jurisdiction" under a new heading: "supplemental jurisdiction." Section 1367(a) provides that federal courts may exercise jurisdiction over state-law claims if they arise from the same "case or controversy" as claims otherwise within their jurisdiction. There has not been much judicial discussion of the relationship between § 1338 and § 1367, but at least one decision suggests that, with regard to state "unfair competition" claims, the two statutes are coextensive in effect. *See Historical Truth Productions v. Sony Pictures Entertainment, Inc.,* 1995 U.S. Dist. LEXIS 17477 (S.D.N.Y. Nov. 22, 1995). But § 1367(a) also permits supplemental jurisdiction in copyright cases over state-law claims that could not be characterized as dealing with "unfair competition." *See, e.g., King v. Ames,* 179 F.3d 370 (5th Cir. 1999) (negligence and breach of contract). In addition, § 1367(a) expressly provides that "supplemental jurisdiction shall include claims that involve the joinder or intervention of additional parties."

Of course, pendant or supplemental jurisdiction is discretionary rather than compulsory. 28 U.S.C. § 1367(c) provides that the District Courts may decline to exercise supplemental jurisdiction over a claim under subsection (a) if:

(1) the claim raises a novel or complex issue of state law;

(2) the claim substantially predominates over the claim or claims over which the district court has original jurisdiction;

(3) the District Court has dismissed all claims over which it has original jurisdiction; or

(4) in exceptional circumstances, there are other compelling reasons for declining jurisdiction.

What happens if the federal copyright claim is dismissed on motion prior to trial — the situation addressed in § 1367(c)(3)? The usual course is to dismiss the state claims as well, without prejudice to re-filing in state court. *See, e.g., Utopia Provider Systems, Inc. v. Pro-Med Clinical Systems, LLC*, 596 F.3d 1313 (11th Cir. 2010) (District Court did not abuse its discretion in dismissing state-law claims); *but see Batiste v. Island Records, Inc.*, 179 F.3d 217, 227 (5th Cir. 1999) ("[a]lthough we have stated that our 'general rule' is to decline to exercise jurisdiction over pendent state-law claims when all federal claims are dismissed or otherwise eliminated from a case prior to trial, this rule is neither mandatory nor absolute") (reversing District Court's dismissal of remaining state-law claims).

Personal jurisdiction. Because a copyright is an intangible, incorporeal right, it has no situs other than the domicile of its proprietor and cannot be the subject of *in rem* jurisdiction. Thus, an action for copyright infringement must rest on *in personam* jurisdiction. Fed. R. Civ. P. 4(k)(1)(A) permits jurisdiction over a defendant "who could be subjected to the jurisdiction of a court . . . in the state in which the district court is located." This rule thus incorporates the limits imposed on state courts by the Due Process Clause of the Fourteenth Amendment — the familiar "minimum contacts" analysis you learned in Civil Procedure. Service of process may be made using a state "long arm" statute or by any other means specified in Fed. R. Civ. P. 4(e)–(j).

The Internet has given the law of personal jurisdiction some fascinating new twists — and, as you might expect, some of them have come in copyright cases. Although some early cases expressed skepticism about extending personal jurisdiction, *see ALS Scan, Inc. v. Digital Service Consultants, Inc.*, 293 F.3d 707 (4th Cir. 2002) (Georgia-based Internet service provider was not subject to personal jurisdiction in Maryland by enabling a website owner to publish photographs on the Internet); *Mink v. AAAA Development LLC*, 190 F.3d 333 (5th Cir. 1999) (corporate defendant's website insufficient to establish personal jurisdiction), the more recent trend has been to interpret personal jurisdiction expansively. *See Mavrix Photo, Inc. v. Brand Technologies, Inc.*, 647 F.3d 1218 (9th Cir. 2011) (Florida plaintiff could sue Ohio website operator in California, because defendant continuously and deliberately exploited the California market for its celebrity and entertainment-focused website); *Penguin Group (USA) Inc. v. American Buddha*, 640 F.3d 497 (2d Cir. 2011) (Oregon corporation with principal place of business in Arizona was subject to jurisdiction in New York, where copyright owner was located).

One issue that has arisen is whether sending a "cease-and-desist" letter or a notice of claimed infringement to a third-party website (as is required by the notice-and-take-down provisions of § 512, *see* § 9.03 of this casebook) is sufficient to permit a court to exercise personal jurisdiction over the sender, either in the state where the website operator is located or in the state of the alleged infringer's residence. Courts have reached different conclusions on the issue. *Compare Dudnikov v. Chalk & Vermillion Fine Arts, Inc.*, 514 F.3d 1063 (10th Cir. 2008) (permitting action for declaratory judgment against out-of-state copyright owner), *with Doe v. Geller*, 533 F. Supp. 2d 996 (N.D. Cal. 2008) (refusing to entertain action against foreign copyright owner).

Another interesting development is the rise of mass copyright infringement actions filed by so-called copyright "trolls." The poster child for this phenomenon was Righthaven LLC, a Nevada corporation that searched the Internet for news articles, obtained copyright assignments from the newspapers in which those articles originally appeared, and sued bloggers and websites that posted the articles. Most District Judges concluded that personal jurisdiction in Nevada was proper when the defendant knew that the articles were originally published in the Las Vegas Review-Journal. *See, e.g., Righthaven, LLC v. Virginia Citizens Defense League, Inc.*, 2011 U.S. Dist. LEXIS 67659 (D. Nev. June 23, 2011); *Righthaven, LLC v. Mostofi*, 2011 U.S. Dist. LEXIS 75810 (D. Nev. July 13, 2011); *Righthaven, LLC v. South Coast Partners, Inc.*, 2011 U.S. Dist. LEXIS 12802 (D. Nev. Feb. 5, 2011). Despite these rulings, however, Righthaven encountered serious problems with standing and on the merits, and eventually its assets were seized to satisfy judgments against it for defendants' attorneys fees. See §§ 8.02[B] and 10.04[B] below.

Venue. Copyright actions present no special venue problems, at least at a theoretical level. Under 28 U.S.C. § 1400(a), they may be instituted "in the district in which the defendant or his agent resides or may be found." Because "may be found" has been interpreted to refer to personal jurisdiction, if personal jurisdiction in a copyright case may be exercised over a corporation in a district, then venue also is proper in that district. *See, e.g., Brayton Purcell LLP v. Recordon & Recordon*, 575 F.3d 981 (9th Cir. 2009). By the same token, federal trial courts will entertain motions for change of venue under § 1404(a) in copyright cases, based on factors including the convenience of parties and witnesses, access to documents and witnesses, the locus of operative facts, and other considerations. For an example of a successful transfer motion, see *Capitol Records, LLC v. VideoEgg, Inc.*, 611 F. Supp. 2d 349 (S.D.N.Y. 2009) (change of venue to Northern District of California).

Cases concerning both patents and copyrights. In cases where a copyright infringement claim is joined in the District Court with a nonfrivolous claim (or a compulsory counterclaim) arising under the patent laws, appellate jurisdiction lies exclusively in the Federal Circuit for any or all of the counts. *See* 28 U.S.C. § 1295(a)(1); *Atari, Inc. v. JS & A Group, Inc.*, 747 F.2d 1422, 1428, 1440 (Fed. Cir. 1984) (asserting appellate jurisdiction where copyright claim was joined to patent claim below, and refusing to rule upon situations in which, *e.g.*, patent claim was withdrawn or frivolous); *Abbott Labs. v. Brennan*, 952 F.2d 1346, 1349-50 (Fed. Cir. 1991) (Federal Circuit has appellate jurisdiction even if patent count pleaded below was not on appeal, and appeal issues involved only state-law claims or nonpatent federal claims: "The path of appeal is determined by the basis of jurisdiction in the district court and is not controlled by its decision or by the substance of the issues that are appealed."). *But see Denbicare U.S.A., Inc. v. Toys "R" Us, Inc.*, 84 F.3d 1143, 1148 (9th Cir. 1996) (where all patent claims were dismissed before trial, regional circuit had jurisdiction over partial final judgment on copyright claim).

Registration and class actions. As we learned earlier, a copyright must be registered (or registration must be denied) before an infringement action may be brought, although courts disagree whether that failure may be "cured" by amendment. *See* § 6.03 above. Most courts agreed, however, that a failure to register the copyright deprived the court of subject-matter jurisdiction. As a result, in *In re Literary Works in Electronic Databases Copyright Litigation*, 509 F.3d 116 (2d Cir. 2007), a divided panel held that the District Court did not have jurisdiction to certify a class action including thousands of works for which the copyright was not registered. The Supreme Court, however, reversed, holding that lack of registration does *not* deprive the District Court of jurisdiction. *Reed Elsevier, Inc. v. Muchnick*, 130 S. Ct. 1237 (2010). The Court expressly declined to decide, however, whether "[d]istrict courts may or should enforce [§ 411(a)'s registration requirement] *sua sponte* by dismissing copyright infringement claims involving unregistered works."

On remand, a divided panel of the Second Circuit vacated the class certification, because members of the class who had not registered their copyrights were not adequately represented by those who had. *See In re Literary Works in Electronic Databases Copyright Litigation*, 654 F.3d 242 (2d Cir. 2011). *See also Palmer Kane, LLC v. Scholastic Corp.*, 103 U.S.P.Q.2d (BNA) 1632 (S.D.N.Y. 2012) (denying motion for class certification against textbook publisher because common issues were outweighed by individual questions concerning licenses). *But see Authors Guild v. Google, Inc.*, 102 U.S.P.Q.2d (BNA) 1916 (S.D.N.Y. 2012) (certifying proposed class of individual authors and their heirs whose works were reproduced in the Google Library project).

Registration and declaratory judgments. Sometimes a potential defendant will file an action seeking a declaratory judgment of non-infringement. As you may remember from first-year civil procedure, however, the statute authorizing district courts to grant declaratory judgments (28 U.S.C. § 2201) is *not* an independent basis for subject-matter jurisdiction in federal courts. Instead, courts must analyze whether they *would have* jurisdiction over a *hypothetical* action that would have been filed in the absence of § 2201.

Because federal courts have subject-matter jurisdiction over actions for infringement, most courts have found no barrier to actions seeking such a declaratory judgment. But in *Stuart Weitzman, LLC v. Microcomputer Resources, Inc.*, 542 F.3d 859 (11th Cir. 2008), the court held that because it would not have had jurisdiction over an infringement action unless the copyright was registered, it could not entertain an action for a declaratory judgment unless the copyright was registered (even though the alleged infringer has no control over registration). The Supreme Court's subsequent opinion in *Reed Elsevier* undercuts this rationale and, presumably, implicitly overrules the result. Otherwise, the ruling would create a disincentive for copyright owners to register, and it would leave alleged infringers in the Eleventh Circuit with no means of resolving a threatened infringement suit.

Arbitration. A claim for copyright infringement can be the subject of a binding agreement to arbitrate. *See, e.g., Positive Software Solutions, Inc. v. New Century Mortgage Corp.*, 476 F.3d 278 (5th Cir. 2007) (denying motion to vacate arbitration award); *1mage Software, Inc., v. Reynolds & Reynolds Co.*, 459 F.3d 1044 (10th Cir. 2006) (affirming grant of motion to compel arbitration); *Saturday Evening Post Co. v. Rumbleseat Press, Inc.*, 816 F.2d 1191 (7th Cir. 1987); *see also Packeteer, Inc. v.*

Valencia Systems, Inc., 82 U.S.P.Q.2d (BNA) 1216 (N.D. Cal. 2007) (claims for violations of anti-circumvention provisions of DMCA are arbitrable).

LIABILITY OF STATE GOVERNMENTS FOR COPYRIGHT INFRINGEMENT

Can the federal or state governments be sued for copyright infringement? The federal government has waived its immunity against liability for infringement and may be sued in the U.S. Court of Federal Claims, which can grant only monetary relief and not an injunction. *See* 28 U.S.C. § 1498(b); *O'Rourke v. Smithsonian Institution Press*, 399 F.3d 113 (2d Cir. 2005) (holding that the Smithsonian is part of the "United States" within the meaning of § 1498(b)). *But see Blueport Co. v. United States*, 533 F.3d 1374 (Fed. Cir. 2008) (holding that claims for violations of the anti-circumvention provisions of the DMCA do not fall within the waiver of sovereign immunity in § 1498(b)). There are, however, several statutory exceptions to the federal government's waiver of sovereign immunity. *See id.* at 1379-82 (plaintiff failed to demonstrate that he was not "in a position to order, influence or induce use of" the work); *Walton v. United States*, 551 F.3d 1367 (Fed. Cir. 2009) (work prepared by prison inmate under federal work program was prepared in the "service of the United States" within the meaning of the statute).

The situation with respect to state governments is, to put the matter delicately, even more complex. The matter had caused considerable controversy in the courts — *compare Johnson v. University of Virginia*, 606 F. Supp. 321 (W.D. Va. 1985) (no immunity), *with BV Engineering v. University of California, Los Angeles*, 858 F.2d 1394 (9th Cir. 1988) (immunity) — but the trend was strongly toward immunity. In 1990, however, Congress enacted the Copyright Remedy Clarification Act, Pub. L. No. 101-553, to make clear that the states, too, can be subject to liability for infringement. The Act added § 511 to Title 17, effective June 1, 1991, expressly waiving whatever immunity the states might have.

In 1995, however, the Supreme Court of the United States delivered a watershed opinion in a case which seemed, at first blush, to have little to do with the law of copyright: *Seminole Tribe of Florida v. Florida*, 517 U.S. 44 (1995). By a 5-4 majority, the Court held that Congress lacked power under the Indian Commerce Clause of the U.S. Constitution to subject states to suit in federal court for violations of federally created rights. The ruling appeared to mean that state sovereign immunity under the Eleventh Amendment trumps Congressional power under Article I, and it cast doubt on the validity of recent statutory reforms, including § 511 of the Copyright Act, that made states liable for violations of federal intellectual property laws. In dissent, Justice Stevens observed that the court's reasoning would "prevent[] Congress from providing a federal forum for a broad range of actions against States, from those sounding in copyright and patent law, to those concerning bankruptcy, environmental law, and the regulation of our vast national economy." *Id.* at 77.

Of course, *Seminole Tribe* was not a copyright case, or even an intellectual property case. In 1999, however, the Supreme Court dropped the other shoe. In *Florida Prepaid Postsecondary Education Expense Board v. College Savings Bank*, 527 U.S. 627, and *College Savings Bank v. Florida Prepaid Postsecondary*

Education Expense Board, 527 U.S. 666, the Court concluded that Congressional efforts to abrogate state sovereign immunity for patent infringement and false advertising (respectively) were unavailing, casting even greater doubt on the validity of § 511.

Both decisions followed *Seminole Tribe* in holding that the powers granted to Congress in Article I cannot constitutionally be exercised to overcome the immunity provided by the subsequently adopted Eleventh Amendment. The two majority opinions, however, took different routes in reaching that conclusion. As to the Lanham Act, the majority (per Justice Scalia) concluded that abrogation of sovereign immunity pursuant to the Fourteenth Amendment's § 1 (Due Process) Clause, which provides that no state shall "deprive any person of property . . . without due process of law," is a constitutional impossibility, because no court has recognized "a property right in freedom from a competitor's false advertising about its own products." 527 U.S. at 673.

By contrast, Chief Justice Rehnquist's majority opinion in the patent case acknowledged that abrogation of state sovereign immunity might, in certain cases, be accomplished under the Fourteenth Amendment. According to the majority opinion, however, Congress's clear and explicit attempt to subject the states to federal jurisdiction for claims of patent infringement (via the 1992 Patent and Plant Variety Protection Remedy Clarification Act) was not the type of "appropriate legislation" authorized in § 5 of the Fourteenth Amendment. In reaching this conclusion, the Court stressed that the legislation was not based on a finding of a pattern of patent infringement by the states, nor on a determination that such state patent infringements as did occur rose to the level of a Due Process violation. Lower courts likewise have concluded that the Copyright Remedy Clarification Act was not a valid exercise of Congress' power to abrogate state sovereign immunity under the Fourteenth Amendment. *See National Ass'n of Boards of Pharmacy v. Board of Regents of the University System of Georgia*, 633 F.3d 1297 (11th Cir. 2011); *Rodriguez v. Texas Comm'n on the Arts*, 199 F.3d 279 (5th Cir. 2000); *Chavez v. Arte Publico Press*, 204 F.3d 601 (5th Cir. 2000); *see also De Romero v. Institute of Puerto Rican Culture*, 466 F. Supp. 2d 410 (D.P.R. 2006) (Commonwealth of Puerto Rico is entitled to the same sovereign immunity as the states under the Eleventh Amendment).

Technically, of course, the Eleventh Amendment does not excuse states from their duties, under the Supremacy Clause, to adhere to federal law. Instead, it merely (and this is a big "merely" indeed!) forecloses the most obvious and satisfactory remedies for the violation of such duties: namely, the remedies available, by the design of federal intellectual property laws, in the exclusive jurisdiction of the federal courts. Moreover, the Supreme Court has ruled (in a different substantive context) that states may claim sovereign immunity against federal causes of action in state court as well. *See Alden v. Maine*, 527 U.S. 706 (1999).

So what will the future bring? *Seminole Tribe* also holds out the possibility that the federal government could bring suit against a state government in federal court, 517 U.S. at 71 n.14, although it is unclear how this device could operate to redress private rights. *See Federal Maritime Comm. v. South Carolina State Ports*

Authority, 535 U.S. 743 (2002) (state sovereign immunity precluded a federal agency from adjudicating a private party's complaint that a state agency had violated federal law). In addition, under the doctrine of *Ex Parte Young*, 209 U.S. 123 (1908), Congress can authorize private suits for prospective injunctions requiring state officials to uphold federal copyright law. *See National Ass'n of Boards of Pharmacy*, 633 F.3d at 1308-12 (*Ex Parte Young* action was not moot); *Cambridge Univ. Press v. Becker*, 863 F. Supp. 2d 1190 (N.D. Ga. 2012). In addition, some courts have held that actions for damages may be maintained against state officials in their individual capacity, unless it can be shown that the judgment would inevitably be paid out of the public purse. *See National Ass'n of Boards of Pharmacy*, 86 U.S.P.Q.2d (BNA) 1683, 1701 (M.D. Ga. 2008), *rev'd in part on other grounds*, 633 F.3d 1297 (11th Cir. 2011); *Marketing Information Masters, Inc. v. Board of Trustees of the California State University System*, 552 F. Supp. 2d 1088, 1095-96 (S.D. Cal. 2008). State officials are entitled to qualified immunity unless their actions violated "clearly established law." *See National Ass'n of Boards of Pharmacy*, 86 U.S.P.Q.2d at 1702-04. This may be the most meaningful option remaining after the *Florida Prepaid* cases.

It should be noted that Indian tribes also currently enjoy sovereign immunity to claims of copyright infringement. *See Bassett v. Mashantucket Pequot Tribe*, 204 F.3d 343 (2d Cir. 2000). Unlike the immunity enjoyed by state governments, however, the sovereign immunity of the tribes could be abrogated by Congress at any time.

[B] Other Procedural Matters

RIGHTHAVEN LLC v. WOLF
United States District Court, District of Colorado
813 F. Supp. 2d 1265 (2011)

JOHN L. KANE, SENIOR DISTRICT JUDGE.

The issue presented in this case, whether a party with a bare right to sue has standing to institute an action for infringement under federal copyright law, is one of first impression in the Tenth Circuit. After considering the parties' written and oral arguments and analyzing the constitutional underpinnings of federal copyright law, the legislative history of the 1909 and 1976 Copyright Acts, and the meager precedent available from analogous situations in other Circuits, I hold that the answer to that question is a forceful, yet qualified, "no" and GRANT summary judgment to Defendant Leland Wolf. . . .

FACTUAL BACKGROUND

On November 18, 2010, *the Denver Post* published a photograph of a Transportation Security Administration Agent performing an enhanced pat-down search at Denver International Airport (the "Work"). Although the copyright in this photograph was originally held by MediaNews Group, Inc., *the Denver Post*'s parent company, at some point following its original publication the copyright was purportedly transferred to Plaintiff Righthaven LLC, which registered the Work with the federal Copyright Office on December 10, 2010. Shortly thereafter, Righthaven filed fifty-seven lawsuits in this district, each alleging copyright infringement in violation of the anti-infringement provisions of federal copyright law. *See* 17 U.S.C. § 501.

Defendant Leland Wolf was among those caught up in Righthaven's enforcement dragnet. As alleged in Righthaven's complaint, on or about November 29, 2010 and February 5, 2011, Mr. Wolf displayed the Work on his website, itmakessenseblog- .com, without seeking or receiving permission to do so from Righthaven. Based on these alleged facts, Righthaven filed suit against Mr. Wolf. . . . [The court treated Wolf's motion to dismiss as a motion for summary judgment.]

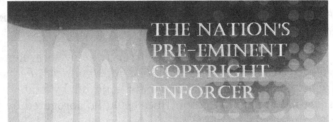

R.I.P. Righthaven LLC (2010-2012)

ANALYSIS

. . . Both parties' arguments assume the underlying legal premise that a party who holds an accrued claim for copyright infringement, but who has no beneficial or legal interest in the copyright itself, may not institute an action for infringement. Although this issue has been decided in the Ninth Circuit, it is one of first impression in the Tenth Circuit, and the parties' reliance on the Ninth Circuit's resolution of this issue in *Silvers v. Sony Pictures Entertainment, Inc.*, 402 F.3d 881 (9th Cir. 2005), is misplaced. Although that decision, and those of other circuits, are persuasive authority, they are not controlling. . . .

I begin my analysis by looking to the text of the Copyright Act. Righthaven's claim for infringement is based on 17 U.S.C. § 501, which provides that "the legal or beneficial owner of an exclusive right under a copyright is entitled, subject to the requirements of section 411, to institute an action for any infringement of that particular right committed while he or she is the owner of it." 17 U.S.C. § 501(b). Although this language is straightforward, it does not expressly limit the right to sue for infringement to a legal or beneficial owner of an exclusive right. *See Silvers*, 402 F.3d at 885. Because the statute is silent on this issue, I must determine Congress' intent in enacting this provision. . . .

Under the Copyright Act of 1909, standing to sue for copyright infringement was strictly limited to the "proprietor" of a copyright. *See* 3 Melville B. Nimmer & David Nimmer, *Nimmer on Copyright* § 10.01[A]. Furthermore, the 1909 Act prohibited the assignment of anything less than the entire copyright. *Id.* When paired with the restriction on the right to sue for infringement, this limitation on assignment, termed the doctrine of "indivisibility," promoted the public interest in the sharing of works by "protect[ing] alleged infringers from the harassment of successive law suits." *Id.*

In the years following the passage of the 1909 Act, technological developments, such as the invention of the motion picture, the television, and the phonograph, altered the fundamental nature of copyright; "as a matter of commercial reality, copyright [became] a label for a collection of diverse property rights each of which is separately marketable." *Id.* In light of these changing circumstances, courts fashioned remedies designed to circumvent the strictures of the doctrine of indivisibility. Most of these exceptions involved so-called "beneficial owners" of copyright — parties who lacked a legal interest in the copyright, but who still stood to gain financially from the legal dissemination of the copyrighted material. As explained by the Seventh Circuit:

> [C]ourts applying the 1909 Act invoked common law trust principles to hold that when a copyright owner assigned title in exchange for the right to receive royalties from the copyright's exploitation, a fiduciary relationship arose between the parties, and the assignor became a 'beneficial owner' of the copyright with standing to sue infringers should the assignee fail to do so.

Moran v. London Records, Ltd., 827 F.2d 180, 183 (7th Cir. 1987) (citations omitted); *but see Prather v. Neva Paperbacks, Inc.*, 410 F.2d 698 (5th Cir. 1969) (basing an author's, and past copyright owner's, right to sue not on trust principles but on "the effectiveness of an assignment of accrued causes of action for copyright infringement"). This principle, that a former owner of a copyright who has assigned his copyright interest in exchange for the right to receive royalties from the copyright's exploitation has the right to sue for infringement, is consistent with the guiding principles of copyright law. The former copyright owner, often the original author or creator, continues to derive an economic benefit from legal public access to the copyrighted material. The public interest in access to copyrighted materials is served, and the former copyright owner is rewarded for his efforts and encouraged to engage in further creative efforts.

In contrast, the free assignment of the right to sue for infringement, as permitted by the Fifth Circuit in *Prather* and advocated by Judge Bea in his dissent in *Silvers*, skews the delicate balance which underlies federal copyright law. *See Prather*, 410 F.2d at 700; *Silvers*, 402 F.3d at 895 (Bea, J., dissenting). A third-party who has been assigned the bare right to sue for infringement has no interest in the legal dissemination of the copyrighted material. On the contrary, that party derives its sole economic benefit by instituting claims of infringement, a course of action which necessarily limits public access to the copyrighted work.[2] This prioritizes

---

[2] Although the institution of some third-party infringement suits may protect the interest of a copyright owner, not all infringement suits are meritorious or worthwhile. Divorcing the economically beneficial interest in copyright from the right to sue for infringement eliminates the exercise of "prosecutorial" discretion by the copyright owner. The party whose only interest is in the proceeds from an action for infringement has no incentive to refrain from filing suit.

economic benefit over public access, in direct contradiction to the constitutionally mandated equilibrium upon which copyright law is based. The legislative history relating to the Copyright Act of 1976 supports this interpretation.

The Copyright Act of 1976 abandons the doctrine of indivisibility, expressly allowing for the assignment of numerous "exclusive rights" that, taken together, comprised the copyright. 17 U.S.C. § 201(d), *see also* 17 U.S.C. § 106 (enumerating the legally recognized copyright interests). As the drafters of the 1976 Act noted in discussing the import of §§ 201 and 501, "The principle of divisibility of copyright ownership, established by section 201(d), carries with it the need in infringement actions to safeguard the rights of all copyright owners and to avoid a multiplicity of suits." H.R. Rep. No. 94-1476 at 158. To achieve this result, the Act expands the right to sue for infringement to all *legal* owners of an exclusive right. 17 U.S.C. § 501(b). The 1976 Act also expands the right to sue for infringement to *beneficial* owners of an exclusive right. According to the drafters, "A 'beneficial owner' for this purpose would include, for example, an author who had parted with legal title to the copyright in exchange for percentage royalties based on sales or license fees." *See* H.R. Rep. No. 94-1476 at 159. This directly parallels the above-noted judicially created exception to the 1909 Act's strict limitation of the right to sue for infringement.

In light of the guiding principles of copyright law and the foregoing analysis of the legislative history of the 1909 and 1976 Copyright Acts, it is apparent that the 1976 Act expands standing to sue for copyright infringement to account for the divisibility of copyright ownership and to incorporate the judicially-recognized exception allowing for the assignment of the right to sue to a beneficial owner of a copyright interest. An expansive view of the right to sue for infringement, as advocated by the Fifth Circuit in *Prather* and Judge Bea in his dissent in *Silvers*, is inconsistent with these constitutional principles.[3] Accordingly, I hold that only parties with a legally recognized interest in copyright as delineated in § 106 ("legal owners"), and parties who stand to benefit from the legal dissemination of

---

Furthermore, in light of the severe statutory damages for copyright infringement and the burdensome costs of litigation, a party sued for infringement, even a party with a meritorious defense, will often agree to settlement. Thus, a party with a bare right to sue may file numerous infringement actions of questionable merit with the intention of extorting settlement agreements from innocent users. This possibility becomes even more likely when the financial viability of the entity filing suit depends upon the proceeds from settlement agreements and infringement suits. Even though copyright law expressly provides for an award of costs and reasonable attorney fees to a party prevailing in its defense of a meritless infringement action, the economic realities of securing counsel and paying in advance the costs of litigation turns this remedy into a Potemkin Village. Both fundamentally and practically, the reality is at odds with the constitutional prioritization of public access to copyrighted works.

[3] Both the Fifth Circuit and Judge Bea based their expansive views on the belief that "the assignment of an accrued cause of action for copyright infringement to an assignee is nothing more than 'simple assignment of a chose in action.' " *Silvers*, 402 F.3d at 902 (Bea, J., dissenting) (quoting *Prather*, 410 F.2d at 699-700). Although the historical common law rule prohibiting the assignment of a chose in action has largely disappeared in the context of contracts, RESTATEMENT (SECOND) OF CONTRACTS § 317 cmt. c (1981), the prohibition is much more robust in the context of torts. *See, e.g., U.S. Fax Law Ctr., Inc. v. iHire, inc.,* 362 F. Supp. 2d 1248, 1251-53 (D. Colo. 2005). The nature of a copyright injury is enigmatic. In my view, where the copyright owner is also the author or creator of the copyrighted work, the offense of infringement is arguably more analogous to a personal tort than any contract right. This issue is, however, not essential to my ruling in this case, and I decline to definitively address it.

copyrighted material ("beneficial owners") have the right to sue for infringement under § 501(b) of the Copyright Act.[4] *See Hyperquest, Inc. v. N'Site Solutions, Inc.*, 632 F.3d 377, 381 (7th Cir. 2011); *Silvers*, 402 F.3d at 885; *Silvers*, 402 F.3d at 891 (Berzon, J., dissenting) (arguing that "a complete stranger to the creative process" should not be able to institute an action for infringement). Having determined the relevant law, I now turn to the facts of this case. . . .

The Assignment purports to transfer "all rights requisite to have Righthaven recognized as the copyright owner of the Work . . ." As evidenced by the parties' arguments in this case, the transfer of a copyright interest is an issue of utmost importance in determining whether a party has standing to institute an action for infringement. A party asserting the transfer of such a right, and the concomitant standing to sue, bears the burden of establishing such a transfer. A clause purporting to transfer "all rights requisite" merely begs the question. Accordingly, I turn to the language of the Copyright Assignment Agreement to determine the nature of the "rights requisite" transferred from MediaNews Group, Inc. to Righthaven. As the Copyright Assignment Agreement states:

> *Despite any Copyright Assignment*, [Media News Group] shall *retain* (and is hereby granted by Righthaven) an exclusive license to Exploit the Publisher Assigned Copyrights for any lawful purpose whatsoever and Righthaven shall have no right or license to Exploit or participate in the receipt of royalties from the Exploitation of the Publisher Assigned Copyrights other than the right to proceeds in association with a Recovery. To the extent that Righthaven's maintenance of rights to pursue infringers of the Publisher Assigned Copyrights in any manner would be deemed to diminish Publisher's right to Exploit the Publisher Assigned Copyrights, Righthaven hereby grants an exclusive license to Publisher to the greatest extent permitted by law so that Publisher shall have unfettered and exclusive ability to Exploit the Publisher Assigned Copyrights. Righthaven shall have no obligation to protect or enforce any Work of Publisher that is not Publisher Assigned Copyrights.

Copyright Assignment Agreement, Schedule 1, Paragraph 6 (emphasis added). This document indicates that the purported assignment of "rights requisite" is meaningless. Media News Group retained all rights to exploit the Work; no legal interest ever changed hands. The usage of the term "exclusive license" does not change this analysis. As noted by the Seventh Circuit, "It is the substance of the agreement, not the labels that it uses, that controls [my] analysis." *Hyperquest, Inc.*, 632 F.3d at 383.

Righthaven's only interest in the Work is "the right to proceeds in association with a Recovery." The Copyright Assignment Agreement defines "Recovery" as "any and all sums . . . arising from an Infringement Action." Thus, when read together, the Assignment and the Copyright Assignment Agreement reveal that MediaNews Group has assigned to Righthaven the bare right to sue for infringe-

---

[4] One might ask, what of the author of a work-for-hire, who has exchanged his creative energies for a sum certain? The answer lies in the question. The author of a work-for-hire has freely bargained away his creative interest in the copyrighted work; he has no creative interest for federal copyright law to protect.

ment — no more, no less. Although the assignment of the bare right to sue is permissible, it is ineffectual. Standing alone, "[t]he right to sue for an accrued claim for infringement is not an exclusive right under § 106." *Silvers*, 402 F.3d at 884. Furthermore, neither the Assignment nor the Copyright Assignment Agreement provide Righthaven any beneficial interest in the dissemination of the Work. Accordingly, Righthaven is neither a "legal owner" or a "beneficial owner" for purposes of § 501(b), and it lacks standing to institute an action for copyright infringement. . . .

NOTES AND QUESTIONS

(1)   Section 501(b) entitles the "legal or beneficial owner of an exclusive right under a copyright" to bring an infringement action. The standards by which "legal" ownership may be proven are relatively plain and straightforward in most instances. But who is a "beneficial owner" for purposes of § 501(b)? The term is not defined in the 1976 Act, although the House Report does provide the one example cited by Judge Kane in his opinion. In applying this provision of the Act, courts reasonably assume that Congress intended the judiciary to look to the general law of trusts. *See, e.g., A. Brod, Inc. v. SK&I Co.*, 998 F. Supp. 314 (S.D.N.Y. 1998).

(2)   As the opinion notes, an author who assigns his or her copyright in exchange for a promise to pay royalties is a "beneficial owner" of the copyright and has standing to sue. *See Cortner v. Israel*, 732 F.2d 267 (2d Cir. 1984). What happens if the author assigns his or her rights *without* any promise to pay royalties? *See Maljack Prods., Inc. v. GoodTimes Home Video Corp.*, 81 F.3d 881 (9th Cir. 1996) (plaintiff was not a beneficial owner of copyright in musical works where contract assigned "any and all worldwide rights" in the music to another party).

(3)   Conversely, does a promise to pay royalties create a beneficial interest where the plaintiff did *not* previously have an ownership interest in the work? In footnote 4 of his opinion, Judge Kane states that the creator of a work for hire "who has exchanged his creative energies for a sum certain . . . has freely bargained away his creative interest in the copyrighted work . . . [and] has no creative interest for federal copyright law to protect." But what if the creator of a work for hire has bargained for royalties? *See Moran v. London Records, Ltd.*, 827 F.2d 180 (7th Cir. 1987) (performer who made TV commercial on a "work made for hire" basis was not a beneficial owner of the copyright, despite SAG agreement for royalties); *Warren v. Fox Family Worldwide, Inc.*, 328 F.3d 1136 (9th Cir. 2003) ("a grant of royalties to a creator of a work for hire, absent an express contractual provision to the contrary, does not create a beneficial ownership interest in that creator"). Is this consistent with the reasoning in *Wolf*?

(4)   The principal issue in *Wolf* is whether an accrued cause of action may be transferred by itself, without any other exclusive rights. Are you satisfied with Judge Kane's resolution of that issue? Is it consistent with the concept of "divisibility," which permits any exclusive right to be sub-divided and transferred separately?

Should it matter if the transferee is not a mere "intermeddler" like Righthaven? In *Silvers v. Sony Pictures Entertainment, Inc.*, 330 F.3d 1204 (9th Cir. 2003), *on rehearing*, 402 F.3d 881 (9th Cir. 2005) (*en banc*), the creator of a work for hire sought, and received, an assignment of an accrued cause of action against an alleged infringer that the copyright owner did not wish to sue. A panel of the Ninth Circuit initially held that the language of § 501(b) was permissive rather than exclusive, so that the assignee of an accrued cause of action also would have standing to sue. On rehearing *en banc*, however, a majority of the 11-judge panel held that Silvers was not the owner of a legal or beneficial interest in the copyright and lacked standing to sue. Does this leave any avenue for the creator of a work for hire to bring an infringement action?

(5)   Section 501(b) provides that the legal or beneficial owner of an exclusive right "is entitled . . . to institute an action for any infringement of that particular right committed *while he or she is the owner of it*" (emphasis added). What happens if the copyright is transferred after a cause of action has accrued? The general rule is that "if the accrued causes of action are not expressly included in the assignment, the assignee will not be able to prosecute them." *ABKCO Music, Inc. v. Harrisongs Music, Ltd.*, 944 F.2d 971 (2d Cir. 1991). But it has been held that "a party can cure a standing defect with a second assignment which explicitly transfers causes of action for infringements prior to the initial assignment." *Intimo, Inc. v. Briefly Stated, Inc.*, 948 F. Supp. 315 (S.D.N.Y. 1996). Should such a retroactive assignment "relate back" to the date of the original complaint for purposes of the statute of limitations? *See Co-opportunities, Inc. v. National Broadcasting Co.*, 510 F. Supp. 43 (N.D. Cal. 1981) (yes).

Does the "general rule" described above make sense? If an accrued cause of action cannot be transferred by itself, why should the assignor be able to transfer the rest of the copyright and retain only the accrued causes of action? Wouldn't that create the same imbalance of incentives that Judge Kane condemns in *Wolf*? On the other hand, is it consistent with the language of § 501(b) to allow the assignee to sue for infringements committed *before* he or she was the owner of any exclusive right?

(6)   Does the author's § 203 right to terminate his/her transfer of the copyright give the author a "remainder" interest sufficient to create standing to sue as a "beneficial owner" of an exclusive right? In effect, wouldn't such a rule confer automatic standing on virtually all authors? *See Hearn v. Meyer*, 664 F. Supp. 832 (S.D.N.Y. 1987) (mere possibility of reverter does not make the author a beneficial owner of the copyright; author must have a "present financial interest" in the exploitation of the work).

(7)   Under the 1909 Act, an exclusive licensee could bring suit, but only if the owner of the copyright itself was joined as a party plaintiff (or, in appropriate circumstances, as a party defendant). *See Goldwyn Pictures Corp. v. Howells Sales Co.*, 282 F. 9 (2d Cir. 1922). What were the deficiencies of this procedure? Obviously, the 1976 Act streamlined infringement actions by allowing suit to be brought by an exclusive licensee *without* joining the copyright holder. As explained in the opinion, the conceptual underpinning of this change was § 201(d) of the 1976 Act, which eliminated the doctrine of "indivisibility." See § 4.02[B][2] of this casebook.

(8)   Neither the 1976 Act nor the 1909 Act confers upon non-exclusive licensees standing to sue. *See, e.g., HyperQuest, Inc. v. N'Site Solutions, Inc.*, 632 F.3d 377 (7th Cir. 2011). As in *Wolf*, however, it is the substance of the agreement that

matters. In *HyperQuest*, for example, even though the agreement purported to grant a "perpetual, worldwide, exclusive" license, the court found that it conferred only a non-exclusive license, because the assignor reserved the right to license the software to others for testing and development.

In *Sybersound Records, Inc. v. UAV Corp.*, 517 F.3d 1137 (9th Cir. 2008), the court held that because a co-owner of copyright could only grant a non-exclusive license, a licensee of a co-owner did not have standing to sue competitors who allegedly lacked licenses. Why not? Does a co-owner of a copyright have standing to sue for infringement of his or her share without joining the other co-owners? *See Davis v. Blige*, 505 F.3d 90 (2d Cir. 2007) (yes). If so, why shouldn't the co-owner's successor-in-interest have the same right?

Note that even where the initial ownership or transfer of a copyright is determined by foreign law under *Itar-Tass* (*see* § 8.04 below), U.S. law still governs the issue of standing to sue for infringement. *See Saregama India Ltd. v. Mosley*, 635 F.3d 1284 (11th Cir. 2011) (plaintiff no longer owned an exclusive license and therefore lacked standing to sue).

(9)   If a non-exclusive licensee lacks standing to sue an alleged infringer, where does that leave the performing rights societies (ASCAP, BMI, and SESAC) discussed in Chapter 7? The short answer would seem to be that the societies lack standing to file suit. *See, e.g., Broadcast Music, Inc. v. CBS, Inc.*, 1983 U.S. Dist. LEXIS 15262 (S.D.N.Y. 1983). ASCAP traditionally has made it a practice to bring suit in the names of its copyright owner members. *See, e.g., Bourne Co. v. Hunter Country Club, Inc.*, 990 F.2d 934 (7th Cir. 1993) (performing rights society, as plaintiff's licensing agent, was neither a legal nor a beneficial owner of the copyright and was not required to be joined as an indispensable party). There is, however, authority to the effect that the societies may have "associational standing" to bring suit. *See* 3 NIMMER ON COPYRIGHT § 12.02 (2012), citing *Olan Mills, Inc. v. Linn Photo Co.*, 795 F. Supp. 1423, 1427 (N.D. Iowa 1991) (recognizing such standing in favor of Professional Photographers of America), *rev'd on other grounds*, 23 F.3d 1345 (8th Cir. 1994). *See also Authors Guild v. Google, Inc.*, 102 U.S.P.Q.2d 1916 (S.D.N.Y. 2012) (holding that the Authors Guild and the American Society of Media Photographers have "associational standing" to sue on behalf of their members).

(10)   As to the joinder of parties in an infringement action, notice that, under § 501(b), the court *may* require the plaintiff to serve a written notice of the action, together with a copy of the complaint, "upon any person shown, by the records of the Copyright Office or otherwise, to have or claim an interest in the copyright," and *must* require such service "upon any person whose interest is likely to be affected by a decision in the case." While the court must permit the intervention of such persons, it has discretion as to whether to require their joinder. That discretion ordinarily will be exercised in accordance with Federal Rule of Civil Procedure 19, which requires the joinder of "necessary" parties if joinder is possible, but otherwise permits the court to proceed unless nothing can be accomplished without the absent party. *See, e.g., ABKCO Music, Inc. v. LaVere*, 217 F.3d 684 (9th Cir. 2000) (beneficial owner of copyright was not an indispensable party where there was no evidence that interests diverged from or would not be adequately protected by legal owner); *Bassett v. Mashantucket Pequot Tribe*, 204 F.3d 343 (2d Cir. 2000)

(Indian tribe was not an indispensable party in infringement suit against museum located on reservation).

(11) Serial copyright plaintiff Righthaven had hoped to make a business model of suing bloggers and websites who re-posted content from newspapers from whom Righthaven had obtained "assignments." After losing several suits on the grounds of standing and/or fair use (*see* § 10.04[B] below), however, Righthaven had its assets seized to pay successful defendants' attorneys fees, effectively putting it out of business.

MISCELLANEOUS PROCEDURAL ISSUES

It may be useful here, before moving on to the substantive aspects of infringement actions, to note a few additional procedural matters of considerable importance to the practicing attorney engaged in copyright litigation for the first time:

Pleading. Like every other pleading that an attorney prepares, the complaint in a copyright infringement action requires thoughtful consideration — and, usually, a little practice — if it is to be done properly. Rule 8(a)(2) of the Federal Rules of Civil Procedure requires a short and plain statement that the pleader is entitled to relief, so as to give the opposing party fair notice of the claim. Courts typically have required the plaintiff to provide adequate allegations of the following elements: (1) a specification of the work at issue; (2) a statement that plaintiff owns the copyright in the work; (3) a statement that a registration has been obtained if required (i.e., for "United States works"); and (4) a specification of the acts by which the defendant violated the plaintiff's rights and during what time period. *See Elektra Entertainment Group, Inc. v. Barker*, 551 F. Supp. 2d 234, 238 (S.D.N.Y. 2008). Under the Supreme Court's opinions in *Bell Atlantic Corp. v. Twombly*, 550 U.S. 544 (2007) and *Ashcroft v. Iqbal*, 556 U.S. 662 (2009), however, additional facts may be required when necessary to render the claim plausible. *See, e.g., Weinstein Co. v. Smokewood Ent. Group, LLC*, 664 F. Supp. 2d 332 (S.D.N.Y. 2009) (allegation of non-exclusive license did not meet *Iqbal*'s plausibility standard); *Phillips v. Murdock*, 543 F. Supp. 2d 1219 (D. Haw. 2008) (dismissing claim based solely on statements in defendant's advertisements as impermissible speculation); *but see Arista Records, LLC v. Doe 3*, 604 F.3d 110 (2d Cir. 2010) (*Twombly* and *Iqbal* do not impose a heightened pleading standard); *CoStar Realty Info., Inc. v. Field*, 612 F. Supp. 2d 660 (D. Md. 2009) (plaintiff need only allege that it owns a valid copyright and that the defendant copied original expression). You should also note the existence of Federal Rules of Civil Procedure Form 19 ("Complaint for Copyright Infringement and Unfair Competition"),[1] as amended in 2007. The answer must, of course, plead any affirmative defenses on which the defendant intends to rely. Fed. R. Civ. P. 8(c).

---

[1] Were you not aware that the Supreme Court has promulgated a form complaint for copyright actions? You are in good company:

    CHIEF JUSTICE ROBERTS: We have forms for copyright infringement actions?

    [COUNSEL]: You do. . . .

    (Laughter.)

    CHIEF JUSTICE ROBERTS: Live and learn.

    Reed Elsevier, Inc. v. Muchnick, No. 08-103, Transcript of Argument at 16 (Oct. 7, 2009).

Burden of proof. The plaintiff in a copyright action is responsible for proving (1) *ownership* of the pertinent exclusive right(s) in the accusing work and (2) a *prima facie* case of *infringement* of the right(s) in suit by the defendant. Once a *prima facie* case has been established by the plaintiff, the defendant bears the burden of rebutting that case, including any of the limitations found in §§ 107-122, which act as affirmative defenses. As to ownership, the principal matters to be proved include: the copyrightability of the work; its authorship by the plaintiff; the plaintiff's citizenship status; compliance with any statutory formalities; and the basis of the plaintiff's claim to ownership if he or she obtained title to the right in suit subsequent to registration of the copyright.

The plaintiff's task with respect to the first four of the preceding five elements is radically simplified by § 410(c):

> In any judicial proceedings the certificate of a registration made before or within five years after first publication of the work shall constitute *prima facie* evidence of the validity of the copyright and of the facts stated in the certificate. The evidentiary weight to be accorded the certificate of a registration made thereafter shall be within the discretion of the court.

And even where a work has been registered more than five years after publication, a court had discretion to give its contents *prima facie* weight. *See Thimbleberries, Inc. v. C&F Enterprises, Inc.*, 142 F. Supp. 2d 1132, 1137 (D. Minn. 2001).

But what of the fifth element of ownership, to which the certificate does not speak? What if the plaintiff's suit concerns a right or rights in a previously registered work, so that the certificate of registration does not reflect the plaintiff's title? In such circumstances, the plaintiff "needs only to show the registration and evidence of his or her chain of title from the original copyright registrant to establish *prima facie* ownership." *Peer Int'l Corp. v. Latin American Music Corp.*, 161 F. Supp. 2d 38, 45 (D.P.R. 2001). This is, however, often easier said than done. *See, e.g., Fleischer Studios, Inc. v. A.V.E.L.A., Inc.*, 654 F.3d 958 (9th Cir. 2011) (holding plaintiffs failed to prove chain of title in famous "Betty Boop" character).

It is clear that the presumption of validity created by § 410(c) may be rebutted "[w]here other evidence in the record casts doubt on the question." *Fonar Corp. v. Domenick*, 105 F.3d 99, 104 (2d Cir. 1997), *quoting Durham Indus., Inc. v. Tomy Corp.*, 630 F.2d 905, 908 (2d Cir. 1980). *See also Ets-Hokin v. Skyy Spirits, Inc.*, 225 F.3d 1068, 1076 (9th Cir. 2000) ("To rebut the presumption, an infringement defendant must simply offer some evidence or proof to dispute or deny the plaintiff's prima facie case of infringement.").

As stated, the plaintiff also has the burden of demonstrating that there has been an infringement of his or her interest in the copyright by the defendant. The specific components of the required showing — copying and improper appropriation — are discussed in the next section of this chapter. For the moment, it is enough for you to know that, even if the plaintiff establishes the elements of a *prima facie* case, the defendant may rebut by introducing evidence that the allegedly infringing work was independently created, or was derived from a source in common with the plaintiff's work. If such evidence is introduced, "the plaintiff has the burden of proving that the defendant in fact copied the protected material." *Peel & Co., Inc. v. The Rug*

Market, 238 F.3d 391, 395 (5th Cir. 2001), citing *Miller v. Universal City Studios, Inc.*, 650 F.2d 1365, 1375 (5th Cir. 1981). The defendant also may try to show that the use was authorized by the plaintiff or was otherwise privileged (for example, under the doctrine of "fair use"). In attempting to make such showings, the defendant has the burden of proof. *See Bourne v. Walt Disney Co.*, 68 F.3d 621, 631 (2d Cir. 1995) (authorization); *Campbell v. Acuff-Rose Music, Inc.*, 510 U.S. 569, 590 (1994) (fair use).

Jury trial. In the usual case, the parties to an action for copyright infringement do not request trial by jury. In any particular case, however, one or more of the parties may desire to have the matter tried to a jury. The parties may, of course, so agree. But what if they do not, and the party seeking a jury trial — whether plaintiff or defendant — claims one *as of right*?

The determinative factor is the nature of the relief sought in the action — or, more specifically, whether the relief sought is legal, equitable, or a mixture of the two. The topic of remedies receives extensive treatment in Chapter 11. For the moment, however, the following summary will suffice:

- If the remedies in question are entirely legal in character (so-called "compensatory damages," meaning the plaintiff's own damages from the infringement and/or the infringer's profits therefrom, to the extent that the two do not overlap), either party has a right to trial by jury.

- If, hypothetically (as will rarely be the case), the remedy or remedies sought are wholly equitable in character, *e.g.*, an injunction and nothing more, such relief may be awarded by the judge alone and is not subject to a right to trial by jury.

- If, as occurs in the usual case, the relief sought involves both legal and equitable remedies (say, an injunction and an accounting, plus compensatory damages), because one or more of the remedies at issue is legal in character, the entire matter must be tried to a jury if either party so requests.

- What if, however, the relief sought is statutory damages (*i.e.*, damages awarded under § 504(c) of the Copyright Act "in lieu of" the usual combination of plaintiff's damages and infringer's profits)? In 1998, the Supreme Court supplied a definitive answer to this question: "if a party so demands, a jury must determine the actual amount of statutory damages under § 504(c) in order to preserve the substance of the common law right of trial by jury." *Feltner v. Columbia Pictures Television, Inc.*, 523 U.S. 340, 355 (1998) (internal quotes omitted).

"Statutory damages" are, as the name suggests, a creature of statute. Unfortunately, the statute — 17 U.S.C. § 504(c) — fails to describe statutory damages as "equitable" or "legal," or to provide explicitly whether they are to be awarded by the judge or the jury. In *Feltner*, the Court held, first, that the statute itself, which says "the court" shall determine statutory damages, does not provide a right to trial by jury 523 U.S. at 345-46. Finding no statutory right to jury trial, the Court considered the constitutional question. The Seventh Amendment provides:

In Suits at common law, where the value in controversy shall exceed twenty dollars, the right of trial by jury shall be preserved. . . .

Citing its own prior precedents, the Court noted that this language applies not only to common law causes of action, but also to "actions brought to enforce statutory rights that are analogous to common law causes of action ordinarily decided in English law courts in the late 18th Century, as opposed to those customarily heard by courts of equity or admiralty." *Id.* at 348. Because its examination of history revealed a number of "close analogues to actions seeking statutory damages under § 504(c)," in 18th-Century English and American practice (including actions under the Copyright Act of 1790), the Court determined that "the Seventh Amendment provides a right to a jury trial *on all issues pertinent to* the award of statutory damages under § 504(c) of the Copyright Act, *including* the amount itself." *Id.* at 355 (emphasis added). *But see Pearson Education, Inc. v. Almgren*, 685 F.3d 691 (8th Cir. 2012) (applying exception to right to jury trial for claims adjudicated in bankruptcy). We will revisit the foregoing matters in § 11.01, when we consider remedies for copyright infringement.

Forum non conveniens. As we will see in § 8.04, U.S. copyright law has no extraterritorial effect. But one reality of the global marketplace is that more and more copyright owners are attempting to invoke the jurisdiction of U.S. courts to determine whether acts that occurred outside the U.S. violate the copyright laws of the jurisdictions where they took place. The main reason why more such actions are not brought is the pesky problem of personal jurisdiction. Even when this hurdle can be overcome, however, a U.S. court may refuse to act, on the ground of *forum non conveniens.* For an interesting example, see *Creative Technology, Ltd. v. Aztech System Pte., Ltd.*, 61 F.3d 696 (9th Cir. 1995), involving a dispute between two Singaporean corporations over the manufacture — in Singapore — and the distribution — in the United States — of computer "sound cards." Remarkably, the Ninth Circuit deferred to the High Court of Singapore not only with respect to claims under the copyright laws of Singapore, but also with respect to those governed by U.S. copyright law. Is this carrying international comity too far?

Now imagine that U.S. *Company X* has licensed U.S. *Company Y* to distribute its copyrighted work in the U.S. only. Nevertheless, *Company Y* also is distributing the work in 25 foreign countries. Assume that (1) despite *Company Y*'s behavior, its license remains valid and in force with respect to the U.S. and that (2) all the manufacturing of copies for foreign distribution is done abroad. Under these circumstances, wouldn't it make more sense to litigate the entire case in a single forum instead of having 25 separate lawsuits in 25 different nations? In *Boosey & Hawkes Music Publishers, Ltd. v. Walt Disney Co.*, 145 F.3d 481 (2d Cir. 1998), the plaintiff claimed that Disney had exceeded its authority under a grant from Igor Stravinsky when it distributed videocassettes of the motion picture *Fantasia* — including sequences synchronized to "The Rite of Spring" — in at least 18 countries other than the United States. The Second Circuit reversed the trial judge's *forum non conveniens* dismissal (which had been based, among other things, on the difficulty of ascertaining and applying foreign law).

Of course, the relevant factors sometimes weigh strongly *against* the assertion of jurisdiction over foreign law claims. See, *e.g., Murray v. British Broadcasting*

Corp., 81 F.3d 287 (2d Cir. 1996), in which a British citizen sued the BBC (and its American subsidiary) for infringement of alleged rights in a character named "Mr. Blobby." According to the court, "[t]he crux of the matter . . . involves a dispute between British citizens over events that took place exclusively in the United Kingdom. Moreover, it appears that much of the dispute over the creation of Mr. Blobby implicates contract law. British law governs those issues. The United States thus has virtually no interest in resolving the truly disputed issues." *Id.* at 293.

What implications do these decisions have for the choice of forum in cases involving alleged copyright infringement in the networked digital environment — for example, the World Wide Web? For a discussion of these issues, see Jane C. Ginsburg, *Copyright Without Borders? Choice of Forum and Choice of Law for Copyright Infringement in Cyberspace*, 15 Cardozo Arts & Ent. L.J. 153 (1997).

§ 8.03 PROVING THE CLAIM

[A] Formulating a "General Test" for Infringement

Let us confess at the outset that the objective suggested by the heading above — that is, the formulation of an unvarying standard by which all infringements of copyrighted works can be judged — is unattainable. But to admit that fact, as so many cases and commentaries have not, is the beginning of wisdom. The reality is that there are not one but many types of copyrightable works, not one but many types of rights that can be infringed, and not one but several different formulations of "infringement" that the courts have announced in the various federal judicial circuits.

That said, the quest for understanding — if not for the Holy Grail of a single, one-size-fits-all formulation of what constitutes infringement — is not hopeless. The core concept of infringement is always the same: an unauthorized exercise by the defendant of a right or rights in a copyrighted work. The plaintiff must prove ownership of the copyrighted work, and conduct by the defendant that infringes one or more of the exclusive rights in that work.

Different Works and Different Rights

The rights granted in §§ 106 (and 106A) cover a broad array of activities and types of works. Many of the landmark opinions on violation of the reproduction right actually involve conduct which would also violate the right to prepare derivative works, *e.g.*, a novel or play allegedly infringed by a motion picture. These cases pose interesting and complicated questions concerning the scope of the copyright. Even infringement suits involving works in the same medium can pose such issues. For example, in *Daly v. Palmer*, 6 F. Cas. 1132 (C.C.S.D.N.Y. 1868) (No. 3,552), a claim of infringement of plaintiff's play "Under the Gaslight" by defendant's play "After Dark" was grounded not on the taking of dialogue, but instead on the "dramatic effect" of one scene. That scene, known as the railroad scene, involved tying a man onto railroad tracks as a train approached. The nature of the infringement was copying of the "dramatic effect . . . produced by what is done by movement and gesture, entirely irrespective of anything that is spoken.

. . . The spoken words in each [of the parties' works] are of but trifling consequence. . . ." *Id.* at 1136. The nature of the subject matter protected here is abstract indeed: not the words, but the action, the drama portrayed by the words. Cases involving different types of subject matter also raise such issues. Should, for example, a music infringement case be decided the same way as one concerning a painting or a computer program? Because this is an introduction to copyright and not an exhaustive review of the subject, the cases that follow present the most traditional and familiar approaches — laying, however, a solid foundation from which more "venturesome" solutions can be explored in advanced courses.

Copying/Improper Appropriation vs. Access/Substantial Similarity

The elements of a *prima facie* case of copyright infringement are generally agreed upon. Unfortunately, courts have not achieved complete consistency in the terminology they use to describe the "normal" infringement standard applied in "typical" cases. Some courts tend to ask whether the defendant had "access" to the plaintiff's work and whether the defendant's work is "substantially similar" to the plaintiff's. Many others inquire whether the defendant's work evidences "copying" of the plaintiff's, and if so whether such copying amounts to an "improper appropriation" of copyrighted matter. *See Peters v. West*, 692 F.3d 629 (7th Cir. 2012) (compiling linguistic variations from several Circuit Courts of Appeals).

The latter approach, derived mainly from *Arnstein v. Porter*, 154 F.2d 464 (2d Cir. 1946), strikes the authors of this casebook as a more accurate description of the key considerations in infringement analysis and, therefore, preferable as a general formulation. Even opinions which articulate the issues differently from *Arnstein*, however, may be trying to get at the same ultimate question: whether the defendant used a significant amount of protected material from the plaintiff's work. *Cf. Peters*, 692 F.3d at 633 ("[d]espite all of this confusing nomenclature, this strikes us as a 'pseudo-conflict' "). And, as we will see, inquiries into "access" and "substantial similarity" have an important role in the decisionmaking of courts that follow *Arnstein*.

"Copying" (the first prong of the *Arnstein* inquiry) almost always is proved by indirect — *i.e.*, circumstantial — evidence of the defendant's infringing activity, simply because direct evidence is not available. Only in the unusual case will the defendant admit copying or the plaintiff succeed in producing a witness who observed the defendant engaged in the physical act of copying. Also, the defendant often proceeds from memory rather than by contemporaneous reference to the work being copied. Accordingly, the courts are forced to presume copying upon proof that the defendant had "access" to the copyrighted work, coupled with evidence of some degree of similarity between that work and the allegedly infringing work that is "probative" of copying. If the defendant had access to the plaintiff's work and the product of the defendant's labors is somewhat similar to the plaintiff's, the probability is good that the defendant copied. The issue at this stage is not whether the defendant copied a sufficient amount to constitute infringement — only whether the defendant copied, rather than independently created. Thus, for purposes of this element of the infringement action, even proof of copying uncopyrightable features of the protected work may suffice.

"Improper appropriation" is a separate matter. Even if the defendant relied on the plaintiff's work to some degree, he or she still may escape liability if the plaintiff fails to show that the taking was impermissible as to both kind and amount. As the Supreme Court said in *Feist*, "[n]ot all copying . . . is copyright infringement." 499 U.S. at 361. Thus, the plaintiff also must demonstrate that the intended audience for the two works would find the defendant's work to be "substantially similar" to the protected expression in the plaintiff's work.

In short, if both copying and improper appropriation are demonstrated, the plaintiff has made out a *prima facie* case. Unless the defendant then successfully invokes an affirmative defense such as "fair use," a finding of infringement liability should follow. We turn now to a detailed consideration of these issues, beginning with a closer examination of how copying may be proved by indirect means.

[B]   Copying

BRIGHT TUNES MUSIC CORP. v. HARRISONGS MUSIC, LTD.
United States District Court, Southern District of New York
420 F. Supp. 177 (1976),
aff'd sub nom. ABKCO Music, Inc. v. Harrisongs Music, Ltd.,
722 F.2d 988 (2d Cir. 1983)

OWEN, DISTRICT JUDGE.

This is an action in which it is claimed that a successful song, "My Sweet Lord," listing George Harrison as the composer, is plagiarized from an earlier successful song, "He's So Fine," composed by Ronald Mack, recorded by a singing group called the "Chiffons," the copyright of which is owned by plaintiff, Bright Tunes Music Corp. "He's So Fine," recorded in 1962, is a catchy tune consisting essentially of four repetitions of a very short basic musical phrase, "sol-mi-re" (hereinafter motif A),[1] altered as necessary to fit the words, followed by four repetitions of another short basic musical phrase, "sol-la-do-la-do" (hereinafter motif B).[2] While neither motif is novel, the four repetitions of A, followed by four repetitions of B, is a highly unique pattern.[3] In addition, in the second use of the motif B series, there is a grace note inserted making the phrase go "sol-la-do-la-*re*-do."[4]

---

[1]

[2]

[3] All the experts agreed on this.

[4]

"My Sweet Lord," recorded first in 1970, also uses the same motif A (modified to suit the words) four times, followed by motif B, repeated three times, not four. In place of "He's So Fine" 's fourth repetition of motif B, "My Sweet Lord" has a transitional passage of musical attractiveness of the same approximate length, with the identical grace note in the identical second repetition.[5] The harmonies of both songs are identical.[6]

George Harrison, a former member of The Beatles, was aware of "He's So Fine." In the United States, it was No. 1 on the billboard charts for five weeks; in England, Harrison's home country, it was No. 12 on the charts on June 1, 1963, a date upon which one of the Beatle[s'] songs was, in fact, in first position. For seven weeks in 1963, "He's So Fine" was one of the top hits in England.

According to Harrison, the circumstances of the composition of "My Sweet Lord" were as follows. Harrison and his group, which include an American black gospel singer named Billy Preston,[7] were in Copenhagen, Denmark, on a singing engagement. There was a press conference involving the group going on backstage. Harrison slipped away from the press conference and went to a room upstairs and began "vamping" some guitar chords, fitting on to the chords he was playing the words "Hallelujah" and "Hare Krishna" in various ways.[8] During the course of this vamping, he was alternating between what musicians call a Minor II chord and a Major V chord.

At some point, germinating started and he went down to meet with others of the group, asking them to listen, which they did, and everyone began to join in, taking first "Hallelujah" and then "Hare Krishna" and putting them into four-part harmony. Harrison obviously started using the "Hallelujah," etc., as repeated sounds, and from there developed the lyrics, to wit, "My Sweet Lord," "Dear, Dear Lord," etc. In any event, from this very free-flowing exchange of ideas, with Harrison playing his two chords and everybody singing "Hallelujah" and "Hare Krishna," there began to emerge the "My Sweet Lord" text idea, which Harrison sought to develop a little bit further during the following week as he was playing it on his guitar. Thus developed motif A and its words interspersed with "Hallelujah" and "Hare Krishna."

Approximately one week after the idea first began to germinate, the entire group

[5] This grace note, as will be seen *infra*, has a substantial significance in assessing the claims of the parties hereto.

[6] Expert witnesses for the defendants asserted crucial differences in the two songs. These claimed differences essentially stem, however, from the fact that different words and numbers of syllables were involved. This necessitated modest alterations in the repetitions or the places of beginning a phrase, which, however, has nothing to do whatsoever with the essential musical kernel that is involved.

[7] Preston recorded the first Harrison copyrighted recording of "My Sweet Lord," of which more *infra*, and from his musical background was necessarily equally aware of "He's So Fine."

[8] These words ended up being a "responsive" interjection between the eventually copyrighted words of "My Sweet Lord." In "He's So Fine" the Chiffons used the sound "dulang" in the same places to fill in and give rhythmic impetus to what would otherwise be somewhat dead spots in the music.

flew back to London because they had earlier booked time to go to a recording studio with Billy Preston to make an album. In the studio, Preston was the principal musician. Harrison did not play in the session. He had given Preston his basic motif A with the idea that it be turned into a song, and was back and forth from the studio to the engineer's recording booth, supervising the recording "takes." Under circumstances that Harrison was utterly unable to recall, while everybody was working toward a finished song, in the recording studio, somehow or other the essential three notes of motif A reached polished form.

George Harrison
Corbis

Q. [By the Court]: . . . you feel that those three notes . . . the motif A in the record, those three notes developed somewhere in that recording session?

Mr. Harrison: I'd say those three there were finalized as beginning there. . . .

Q. [By the Court]: Is it possible that Billy Preston hit on those [notes comprising motif A]?

Mr. Harrison: Yes, but it's possible also that I hit on that, too, as far back as the dressing room, just scat singing.

Similarly, it appears that motif B emerged in some fashion at the recording session as did motif A. This is also true of the unique grace note in the second repetition of motif B.

Q. [By the Court]: All I am trying to get at, Mr. Harrison, is if you have a recollection when that [grace] note popped into existence as it ends up in the Billy Preston recording. . . .

Mr. Harrison: . . . [Billy Preston] might have put that there on every take, but it just might have been on one take, or he might have varied it on

[handwritten margin top-left: have proof of opportunity?]

different takes at different places.

The Billy Preston recording, listing George Harrison as the composer, was thereafter issued by Apple Records. The music was then reduced to paper by someone who prepared a "lead sheet" containing the melody, the words and the harmony for the United States copyright application.[9]

[handwritten margin-left: subcons.? copying?]

Seeking the wellsprings of musical composition — why a composer chooses the succession of notes and the harmonies he does — whether it be George Harrison or Richard Wagner — is a fascinating inquiry. It is apparent from the extensive colloquy between the Court and Harrison covering forty pages in the transcript that neither Harrison nor Preston were conscious of the fact that they were utilizing the "He's So Fine" theme.[10] However, they in fact were, for it is perfectly obvious to the listener that in musical terms, the two songs are virtually identical except for one phrase. There is motif A used four times, followed by motif B, four times in one case, and three times in the other, with the same grace note in the second repetition of motif B.[11]

What happened? I conclude that the composer,[12] in seeking musical materials to clothe his thoughts, was working with various possibilities. As he tried this possibility and that, there came to the surface of his mind a particular combination

[handwritten across page: independent → tried here s/c on Radio) lenders etc.]

[handwritten margin-left: independent creation?]

[9] It is of interest, but not of legal significance, in my opinion, that when Harrison later recorded the song himself, he chose to omit the little grace note, not only in his musical recording but in the printed sheet music that was issued following that particular recording. The genesis of the song remains the same, however modestly Harrison may have later altered it. Harrison, it should be noted, regards his song as that which he sings at the particular moment he is singing it and not something that is written on a piece of paper.

[10] Preston may well have been the "composer" of motif B and the telltale grace note appearing in the second use of the motif during the recording session, for Harrison testified:

> The Court: To be as careful as I can now in summing this up, you can't really say that you or Billy Preston or somebody else didn't somewhere along the line suggest these; all you know is that when Billy Preston sang them that way at the recording session, you felt they were a successful way to sing this, and you kept it?
>
> The Witness: Yes, I mean at that time we chose what is a good performance.
>
> The Court: And you felt it was a worthy piece of music?
>
> The Witness: Yes. . . .

[handwritten margin-left: strict liability doesn't matter if he intended to infringe s/c he infringed]

[11] Even Harrison's own expert witness, Harold Barlow, long in the field, acknowledged that although the two motifs were in the public domain, their use here was so unusual that he, in all his experience, had never come across this unique sequential use of these materials. He testified:

> The Court: And I think you agree with me in this, that we are talking about a basic three-note structure that composers can vary in modest ways, but we are still talking about the same heart, the same essence?
>
> The Witness: Yes.
>
> The Court: So you say that you have not seen anywhere four A's followed by three B's or four?
>
> The Witness: Or four A's followed by four B's.

The uniqueness is even greater when one considers the identical grace note in the identical place in each song.

[handwritten margin-left: question of access comes into play...]

[12] I treat Harrison as the composer, although it appears that Billy Preston may have been the composer as to part. (*See* fn. 10, *supra*.) Even were Preston the composer as to part, this is immaterial. *Peter Pan Fabrics, Inc. v. Dan River Mills, Inc.*, 295 F. Supp. 1366, 1369 (S.D.N.Y.), *aff'd*, 415 F.2d 1007 (2d Cir. 1969).

that pleased him as being one he felt would be appealing to a prospective listener; in other words, that this combination of sounds would work. Why? Because his subconscious knew it already had worked in a song his conscious mind did not remember. Having arrived at this pleasing combination of sounds, the recording was made, the lead sheet prepared for copyright and the song became an enormous success. Did Harrison deliberately use the music of "He's So Fine"? I do not believe he did so deliberately. Nevertheless, it is clear that "My Sweet Lord" is the very same song as "He's So Fine" with different words, and Harrison had access to "He's So Fine." This is, under the law, infringement of copyright, and is no less so even though subconsciously accomplished. *Sheldon v. Metro-Goldwyn Pictures Corp.*, 81 F.2d 49, 54 (2d Cir. 1936); *Northern Music Corp. v. Pacemaker Music Co., Inc.*, 147 U.S.P.Q. 358, 359 (S.D.N.Y. 1965).

Given the foregoing, I find for the plaintiff on the issue of plagiarism, and set the action down for trial . . . on the issue of damages and other relief as to which the plaintiff may be entitled. The foregoing constitutes the Court's findings of fact and conclusions of law. So ordered.

NOTES AND QUESTIONS

(1)   On rare occasions, copyright defendants may admit copying and rest their defense on the ground that their takings were insignificant or privileged. *See, e.g.*, *Nihon Keizai Shimbun, Inc. v. Comline Business Data, Inc.*, 166 F.3d 65 (2d Cir. 1999). Usually, however, the plaintiff must make a showing on the issue in order to succeed. A defendant cannot "copy" a work with which he or she is not familiar, nor can the defendant become familiar with the work allegedly copied unless he/she has access to it. But where does such access occur? Typically, in a private place such as the defendant's office or home, rather than in a public place where the plaintiff or a witness readily available to the plaintiff can directly observe the defendant reading or viewing the plaintiff's work. Even if such an incident had occurred, it seems highly unlikely that the plaintiff in *Bright Tunes* could have produced a neutral witness who would testify that he sat in the recording studio in London and watched George Harrison and Billy Preston reviewing the sheet music to, or listening to a recording of, "He's So Fine."

Nor was this a case in which copying could be proved by the presence in the defendants' work of "errors" which could be explained only by the defendants having had access to the plaintiffs' work. *See, e.g.*, *Bucklew v. Hawkins, Ash, Baptie & Co.*, 329 F.3d 923 (7th Cir. 2003) (identifying residual errors in plaintiff's spreadsheet form that were duplicated without change in defendant's form). Such telltale errors, incidentally, may originate as accidents on the plaintiff's part, *see Hassenfeld Bros., Inc. v. Mego Corp.*, 1966 U.S. Dist. LEXIS 7204 (S.D.N.Y. Aug. 5, 1966) (minor anatomical error in toy "action figures"), or may be introduced intentionally as "traps" for unwary copyists. *See Rockford Map Publishers, Inc. v. Directory Service Co. of Colo.*, 768 F.2d 145, 147 (7th Cir. 1985); Latman, *"Probative Similarity" as Proof of Copying: Toward Dispelling Some Myths in Copyright Infringement*, 90 Colum. L. Rev. 1187, 1205-06 (1990). Obviously, however, this sort of evidence of copying is unlikely to be present in a case involving alleged infringement of musical works.

How, then, is access to be established, on the way to proving copying?

(2)   Although some courts have indicated that there must be evidence that the defendant "actually viewed" the plaintiff's work, *see Herzog v. Castle Rock Entertainment*, 193 F.3d 1241, 1249 n.5 (11th Cir. 1999) (collecting cases), the "opportunity to see" approach to the problem of proving access predominates today as exemplified by *Bouchat v. Baltimore Ravens, Inc.*, 241 F.3d 350 (4th Cir. 2001), in which the court said:

> A copyright infringement plaintiff need not prove that the infringer actually saw the work in question; it is enough to prove that the infringer (or his intermediary) had the mere opportunity to see the work and that the subsequent material produced is substantially similar to the work.

241 F.3d at 354-55. In *Bouchat*, the plaintiff alleged infringement of his proposed logo for the Baltimore Ravens football team. He introduced evidence that John Moag, chairman of the Maryland Stadium Authority, offered to deliver Bouchat's drawings to the Ravens; that Bouchat faxed a drawing of the proposed logo to the MSA; that such faxes were routinely delivered to Moag's law offices; that David Modell, the owner of the Ravens, had an office "within earshot" of Moag's; and that Modell communicated with the design team that developed the team's new logo. The majority held that this evidence was sufficient to permit the jury to find that the Ravens had access to Bouchat's drawings. The dissenting judge criticized the jury's verdict as "the result of an illogical and impermissible series of inferences." Who has the better of the argument?

Compare Bouchat, with Grubb v. KMS Patriots, L.P., 88 F.3d 1 (1st Cir. 1996) (finding no infringement of plaintiff's proposed logo for the New England Patriots football team, where the designer testified that he created the defendant's logo 12 days before the plaintiff's logo was submitted). Should the court have credited the designer's testimony without submitting the issue to a jury? Is it relevant that the designer relied on written timesheets in his testimony?

(3)   How is either the "actual viewing" or the "opportunity to see" test satisfied in *Bright Tunes*? If access is defined in terms of opportunity to copy the plaintiff's work, and the plaintiff's work is a widely disseminated or performed work — a popular song, as in *Bright Tunes*, or a best-selling novel, a top-grossing motion picture, or a highly rated TV program — is there any way for a defendant with an arguably similar work to *avoid* a finding of access?

(4)   The court finds that Harrison took advantage of his access "subconsciously," not "deliberately." Why shouldn't this finding constitute a defense to the plaintiff's claim of infringement? Should it at least reduce the damages for which Harrison is liable? You may also want to read Judge Learned Hand's decision in *Fred Fisher, Inc. v. Dillingham*, 298 F. 145 (S.D.N.Y. 1924) (Jerome Kern's "Ka-lu-a"), a precursor of the later subconscious copying cases.

The doctrine of subconscious copying is alive and well. *See Three Boys Music Corp. v. Bolton*, 212 F.3d 477 (9th Cir. 2000) (upholding jury verdict that a 1991 song titled "Love is a Wonderful Thing" infringed a 1964 song of the same name). Does the theory of subconscious copying allow sufficient room for the possibility of independent creation? Is there any way a defendant could convincingly *disprove* subconscious copying?

(5)   Of course, to support a finding of access, "a plaintiff must show a reasonable possibility, not merely a bare possibility, that an alleged infringer had the chance to view the protected work." *Art Attacks Ink, LLC v. MGA Entertainment, Inc.*, 581 F.3d 1138, 1143 (9th Cir. 2009). In *Art Attacks Ink*, evidence that the plaintiff sold its "Spoiled Brats" t-shirts at the L.A. County Fair beginning in 1998, and that one of the defendant's employees attended the fair sometime between 1995 and 2005, was deemed insufficient to demonstrate access before the defendant began marketing its "Bratz" dolls in 2001. *See also Jones v. Blige*, 558 F.3d 485 (6th Cir. 2009) (affirming summary judgment for defendants; demo CD was received by employee at Universal Music, where Blige had recording contract, but no evidence of any connection between employee and Blige's work); *Armour v. Knowles*, 512 F.3d 147 (5th Cir. 2007) (affirming summary judgment for defendant where the only evidence of access was the mailing of a demo tape to a "mysterious and unidentified" alleged associate of defendant); *Jorgensen v. Epic/Sony Records*, 351 F.3d 46, 48 (2d Cir. 2003) (holding that "evidence of corporate receipt of unsolicited work is insufficient to raise a triable issue of access where there is no evidence of any connection between the individual recipients of the protected work and the [individual] alleged infringers").

(6)   Even demonstrating a "reasonable possibility" of the defendant's access to the copyrighted work, however, may not be enough for the plaintiff to prevail on the issue of copying. The plaintiff must establish, by a preponderance of the evidence, not simply access alone, but the defendant's unauthorized *use* of materials from the copyrighted work. For this reason, the plaintiff, to prevail, must also show that some similarity exists between the complaining (*i.e.*, the plaintiff's) and the accused (*i.e.*, the defendant's) works.

The showing required to prove copying need not be the same showing as will be required on the substantial similarity prong of the improper appropriation inquiry. Indeed, what is relevant for similarity that goes to proof of copying may be quite different. For example, *copying* might be suggested strongly by similarities in public domain materials that both the accused and complaining works contain; but it would not be an *improper appropriation* for the defendant to have copied such materials from the plaintiff's work, in which only matter original to the plaintiff is protected by his or her copyright. For this reason, the late Professor Latman, in the article cited in note 1, suggested that the term "probative similarity" should be employed to refer to that degree of likeness which, in connection with evidence of "access," will constitute adequate indirect proof of "copying." 90 Colum. L. Rev. at 1214. For recent Court of Appeals decisions adopting this terminology, see, *e.g.*, *Coquico, Inc. v. Rodriguez-Miranda*, 562 F.3d 62 (1st Cir. 2009); *La Resolana Architects, P.A. v. Reno, Inc.*, 555 F.3d 1171 (10th Cir. 2009); *Armour v. Knowles*, 512 F.3d 147 (5th Cir. 2007).

(7)   That said, we emphasize again that copying is an issue which turns, ultimately, on probabilities. Access and probative similarity are interactive. Often, the points of correspondence between the plaintiff's and defendant's works are so plain that the courts do not even bother to discuss similarity, focusing instead

entirely on access. But should similarities be considered *so* probative that a court may find copying even if proof of access is utterly wanting? The next case in this section explores that issue.

(8)   *Terminology alert!* Finally, it is our unhappy duty to call your attention to a particularly messy bit of terminological confusion. What Professor Latman called "probative similarity" is too often called "substantial similarity," a term also used to refer to the kind of similarity required to show improper appropriation. *See, e.g., Kamar International, Inc. v. Russ Berrie & Co.*, 657 F.2d 1059, 1062-63 (9th Cir. 1981). This may reflect the fact that, in many cases (*Bright Tunes*, for example), the evidence of similarity is in fact used to serve both purposes. But whatever the explanation, this terminology makes it considerably more difficult to make sense of a number of significant precedents relating to copyright infringement.

There is also a joker in the pack! Courts sometimes use the term "striking similarity" in their discussions of the issue of "copying." On some occasions, this usage may be no more than another synonym for "probative similarity," but on many others (as the following case illustrates) it has a more precise and specialized meaning — to the definition of which we now turn.

TY, INC. v. GMA ACCESSORIES, INC.
United States Court of Appeals, Seventh Circuit
132 F.3d 1167 (1997)

POSNER, CHIEF JUDGE.

Ty, the manufacturer of the popular "Beanie Babies" line of stuffed animals, has obtained a preliminary injunction under the Copyright Act against the sale by GMA . . . of "Preston the Pig" and "Louie the Cow." These are bean-bag animals manufactured by GMA that Ty contends are copies of its copyrighted pig ("Squealer") and cow ("Daisy"). Ty began selling the "Beanie Babies" line, including Squealer, in 1993, and it was the popularity of the line that induced GMA to bring out its own line of bean-bag stuffed animals three years later. GMA does not contest the part of the injunction that enjoins the sale of Louie, but asks us on a variety of grounds to vacate the other part, the part that enjoins it from selling Preston.

We have appended to our opinion five pictures found in the appellate record. The first shows Squealer (the darker pig, actually pink) and Preston (white). The second is a picture of two real pigs. The third and fourth are different views of the design for Preston that Janet Salmon submitted to GMA several months before Preston went into production. The fifth is a picture of the two bean-bag cows; they are nearly identical. A glance at the first picture shows a striking similarity between the two bean-bag pigs as well. The photograph was supplied by GMA and actually understates the similarity (the animals themselves are part of the record). The "real" Preston is the same length as Squealer and has a virtually identical snout. The difference in the lengths of the two animals in the picture is a trick of the camera. The difference in snouts results from the fact that the pictured Preston was a manufacturing botch. And GMA put a ribbon around the neck of the Preston in the picture, but the Preston that it sells doesn't have a ribbon.

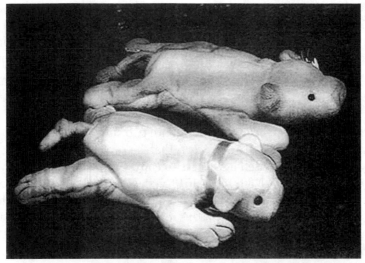

Squealer and Preston from the *Ty* court's opinion

Two Real Pigs (per Judge Posner)

The two pigs are so nearly identical that if the second is a copy of the first, the second clearly infringes Ty's copyright. But identity is not infringement. The Copyright Act forbids only copying; if independent creation results in an identical work, the creator of that work is free to sell it. *Selle v. Gibb*, 741 F.2d 896, 901 (7th Cir. 1984); *Grubb v. KMS Patriots*, L.P., 88 F.3d 1, 3 (1st Cir. 1996). The practical basis for this rule is that unlike the case of patents and trademarks, the creator of an expressive work — an author or sculptor or composer — cannot canvass the entire universe of copyrighted works to discover whether his poem or song or, as in this case, "soft sculpture" is identical to some work in which copyright subsists, especially since unpublished, unregistered works are copyrightable. 17 U.S.C. § 104(a). . . . But identity can be powerful evidence of copying. *Gaste v. Kaiser-*

man, 863 F.2d 1061, 1068 (2d Cir. 1988); *Ferguson v. National Broadcasting Co.*, 584 F.2d 111 (5th Cir. 1978). The more a work is both like an already copyrighted work and — for this is equally important — unlike anything that is in the public domain, the less likely it is to be an independent creation. As is generally true in the law, circumstantial evidence — evidence merely probabilistic rather than certain — can confer sufficient confidence on an inference, here of copying, to warrant a legal finding.

The issue of copying can be broken down into two subissues. The first is whether the alleged copier had access to the work that he is claimed to have copied; the second is whether, if so, he used his access to copy. *CMM Cable Rep, Inc. v. Ocean Coast Properties, Inc.*, 97 F.3d 1504, 1513 (1st Cir. 1996); *Fisher-Price, Inc. v. Well-Made Toy Mfg. Corp.*, 25 F.3d 119, 123 (2d Cir. 1994). It might seem that access could not be an issue where, as in this case, the allegedly copied work is a mass-produced consumer product purchasable for $5. But we shall see that GMA has attempted to make an issue of access.

Obviously, access does not entail copying. An eyewitness might have seen the defendant buy the copyrighted work; this would be proof of access, but not of copying. But copying entails access. If, therefore, two works are so similar as to make it highly probable that the later one is a copy of the earlier one, the issue of access need not be addressed separately, since if the later work was a copy its creator must have had access to the original. *Selle v. Gibb, supra*, 741 F.2d at 901; *Gaste v. Kaiserman, supra*, 863 F.2d at 1068; *Ferguson v. National Broadcasting Co., supra*. Of course the inference of access, and hence of copying, could be rebutted by proof that the creator of the later work could not have seen the earlier one or (an alternative mode of access) a copy of the earlier one. But unlike the court in *Towler v. Sayles*, 76 F.3d 579, 584-85 (4th Cir. 1996), and the authors of [NIMMER ON COPYRIGHT] . . ., we do not read our decision in *Selle* to hold or imply, in conflict with the *Gaste* decision, that no matter how closely the works resemble each other, the plaintiff must produce some (other) evidence of access. He must produce evidence of access, all right — but, as we have just said, and as is explicit in *Selle* itself, see 741 F.2d at 901, a similarity that is so close as to be highly unlikely to have been an accident of independent creation is evidence of access.

What troubled us in *Selle* but is not a factor here is that two works may be strikingly similar — may in fact be identical — not because one is copied from the other but because both are copies of the same thing in the public domain. In such a case — imagine two people photographing Niagara Falls from the same place at the same time of the day and year and in identical weather — there is no inference of access to anything but the public domain, and, equally, no inference of copying from a copyrighted work. *Id.* at 904; *Gracen v. Bradford Exchange*, 698 F.2d 300, 304 (7th Cir. 1983); *Warren Publishing, Inc. v. Microdos Data Corp.*, 115 F.3d 1509, 1516 n.19 (11th Cir. 1997); *Key Publications, Inc. v. Chinatown Today Publishing Enterprises, Inc.*, 945 F.2d 509, 514 (2d Cir. 1991). A similarity may be striking without being suspicious.

But here it is both. GMA's pig is strikingly similar to Ty's pig but not to anything in the public domain — a real pig, for example, which is why we have included in our appendix a photograph of real pigs. The parties' bean-bag pigs bear little resemblance to real pigs even if we overlook the striking anatomical anomaly of Preston — he has three toes, whereas real pigs have cloven hooves. We can imagine an argument that the technology of manufacturing bean-bag animals somehow prevents the manufacturer from imitating a real pig. But anyone even slightly familiar with stuffed animals knows that there are many lifelike stuffed pigs on the market, and whether they are stuffed with beans or other materials does not significantly affect their verisimilitude — though here we must emphasize that any factual assertions in this opinion should be treated as tentative, since the case is before us on an appeal from the abbreviated record of a preliminary-injunction proceeding and a full trial may cast the facts in a different light.

Real pigs are not the only pigs in the public domain. But GMA has not pointed to any fictional pig in the public domain that Preston resembles. Preston resembles only Squealer, and resembles him so closely as to warrant an inference that GMA copied Squealer. In rebuttal all that GMA presented was the affidavit of the designer, Salmon, who swears, we must assume truthfully, that she never looked at a Squealer before submitting her design. But it is not her design drawing that is alleged to infringe the copyright on Squealer; it is the manufactured Preston, the soft sculpture itself, which, as a comparison of the first with the third and fourth pictures in the appendix reveals, is much more like Squealer than Salmon's drawing is. And remember that the manufactured Preston in the photograph is a sport, with its stubby snout and its ribbon. Interestingly, these are features of Salmon's drawing but not of the production-model Preston, suggesting design intervention between Salmon's submission and actual production.

It is true that only a few months elapsed between Salmon's submission of the drawing to GMA and the production of Preston. But the record is silent on how long it would have taken to modify her design to make it more like Squealer. For all we know, it might have been done in hours — by someone who had bought a Squealer. The Beanie Babies are immensely popular. They are also, it is true, sometimes hard to find (though not this Christmas, in Chicago at any rate). Ty's practice, apparently, is to create a shortage (that is, to price its bean-bag animals below the market-clearing price) in order to excite the market. But it is unbelievable that a substantial company like GMA which is in the same line of business as Ty could not have located and purchased a Squealer if it wanted to copy it. A glance at the last picture in the appendix shows an identity between Louie the Cow and Ty's Daisy that is so complete (and also not explainable by reference to resemblance to a real cow or other public domain figure) as to compel an inference of copying. If GMA thus must have had access to Daisy, it is probable, quite apart from any inference from the evidence of similarity, that it had access to Squealer as well.

This discussion shows how the tension between *Gaste* and *Selle* can be resolved and the true relation between similarity and access expressed. Access (and copying) may be inferred when two works are so similar to each other and not to anything in the public domain that it is likely that the creator of the second work copied the first, but the inference can be rebutted by disproving access or otherwise showing independent creation — and in this connection GMA complains that the district judge refused to conduct an evidentiary hearing at which it might have presented evidence of independent creation. If genuine issues of material fact are created by the response to a motion for a preliminary injunction, an evidentiary hearing is indeed required. . . . But as in any case in which a party seeks an evidentiary hearing, he must be able to persuade the court that the issue is indeed genuine and material and so a hearing would be productive — he must show in other words that he has and intends to introduce evidence that if believed will so weaken the moving party's case as to affect the judge's decision on whether to issue an injunction. Here is where GMA falters. The only evidence that it seeks to present is the designer's oral testimony in support of the claim of independent creation. Her testimony would presumably have duplicated her affidavit, which was already in evidence; at least, GMA has not indicated what her testimony would add to her affidavit. Affidavits are ordinarily inadmissible at trials but they are fully admissible in summary proceedings, including preliminary-injunction proceedings. . . . So the evidence that GMA wants to put before the district judge was before him when he ruled.

Even if fully credited, the affidavit does not establish the independent creation of Preston but merely the independent creation of a drawing that resembles Squealer much less than the production model of Preston does. This is not to deny that the affidavit is some evidence of independent creation of Preston, so it was relevant evidence. No one doubts that; and since it was already part of the evidentiary record, having its contents repeated orally would not have assisted the district judge.

But this is on the assumption that the judge credited the affidavit. If he did not even though it was not contradicted — if, for example, he was laboring under the misapprehension that affidavits are inadmissible in preliminary-injunction proceedings — he would have committed an error that would have been cured by his allowing Salmon to testify in person, and his not allowing her to do so would therefore be a ground for appeal. But there is no basis for imputing such an error to the district judge. As we read his opinion, he credited Salmon's affidavit and merely concluded, as do we, that it was only weak evidence of independent creation. Silence can be pregnant; the absence of any evidence of how the designer's drawing was translated into the Squealer-resembling production model, combined with the similarity of that model to Squealer (and to nothing in the public domain) and with GMA's obviously having copied Ty's cow, overbore the weak evidence of the affidavit.

So, on the record compiled in the preliminary-injunction proceedings, Ty has indeed a strong case. . . .

We find no error of law, no clear error of fact, and no abuse of discretion in the grant of the preliminary injunction to Ty. The judgment of the district court is therefore affirmed.

NOTES AND QUESTIONS

(1)   Judge Posner relies on "striking similarity" to justify the conclusion that Ty is likely to succeed on the merits. Was proof of access lacking? Wouldn't evidence of access plus "probative similarity" (presumably a less exacting standard) have done just as well? One reason for the *Ty* court's approach may be that it wanted to "clarify" (or modify) the Seventh Circuit's previous opinion in *Selle v. Gibb*, in which the court had suggested that even if "striking similarity" was shown, "there must be at least some other evidence which would establish a reasonable possibility that the

complaining work was *available* to the alleged infringer."

For an illustration of Judge Posner's *dictum* that "[a] similarity may be striking without being suspicious," see *Mag Jewelry Co. v. Cherokee, Inc.*, 496 F.3d 108, 119 (1st Cir. 2007) ("There are only so many ways one can depict an angel. . . . [W]here the simplicity of the design makes independent creation highly plausible, similarity alone could not establish access and, in turn, copying.").

(2) *Proof of copying without evidence of access?* In *Repp v. Webber*, 132 F.3d 882, 889 (2d Cir. 1997), the Second Circuit reversed a grant of summary judgment for the defendants in a lawsuit brought by a composer alleging that Andrew Lloyd Webber's "Phantom Song" infringed the plaintiff's composition "Till You." (Lloyd Webber's counterclaim, alleging that the plaintiff's song was itself a rip-off of his own earlier tune "Close Every Door," was dismissed after trial.) The plaintiff's evidence of access was weak, because his song had been performed and distributed only in specialized religious music markets. But expert testimony demonstrating close parallels between the two works led the court to rely — in reinstating the action for trial — on its rule "permitting an inference of access where there is 'striking similarity.' " 132 F.3d at 891.

(3) Does it help to characterize the issue in terms of whether the access may be inferred from evidence of striking similarity? Would it be equally correct to say that "[i]f the two works are so strikingly similar as to preclude the possibility of independent creation, 'copying' may be proved without a showing of access"? *Ferguson v. National Broadcasting Co.*, 584 F.2d 111, 113 (5th Cir. 1978); *accord Lipton v. Nature Co.*, 71 F.3d 464, 471 (2d Cir. 1995). In *Bouchat v. Baltimore Ravens, Inc.*, 241 F.3d 350 (4th Cir. 2001), the court rejected this view, stating:

> It is clear that a showing of striking similarity does not *per se* relieve the plaintiff of his burden of establishing access. However, striking similarity is evidence of copying, thereby supporting an inference of access. What is important is that the access prong remains intact, but the level of similarity between the contested works may be used as evidence of access.

Id. at 356. Why is it "important that the access prong remains intact"? Isn't the purpose of requiring proof of access to help support an inference of copying? If striking similarity is itself evidence of copying, why must one make a further (and circular) inference of access?

Bouchat itself involved alleged infringement of the plaintiff's proposed logo for the Baltimore Ravens football team. The plaintiff's drawing and the logo adopted by the team are reproduced here. Are the drawings so strikingly similar that one could infer access (and copying) without any additional evidence?

Plaintiff's Drawing   The Accused Work

(4) The Second Circuit appears to believe that the question that troubled the court in *Bouchat* amounts to a distinction without a difference. In *Gaste v. Kaiserman*, 863 F.2d 1061 (2d Cir. 1988), the court approved a jury instruction stating "[i]f the two works . . . are what we call strikingly similar, then access does not have to be proven. . . . In other words, you are in effect presuming access from the fact of striking similarity." *Id.* at 1067-68 & n.3. Likewise, in *Repp* the court quoted *Lipton* without noting any potential inconsistency. Is there a meaningful difference between the two formulations, as the Fourth Circuit believes, or is the Second Circuit correct that they are one and the same? *See also Bucklew v. Hawkins, Ash, Baptie & Co.*, 329 F.3d 923, 926 (7th Cir. 2003) ("These cases say that access can be inferred from a sufficiently striking similarity between the two works, and that is true; but . . . it is more straightforward to say that in some cases proof of access isn't required.").

(5) How should lawyers — and courts — proceed in cases where the plaintiff's showing on probative similarity falls just short of being "striking," but is coupled with some other relevant proof, albeit weak or inconclusive? The rule that other proof of access can be dispensed with in cases of "striking similarity" probably is best viewed as a special case of the more general proposition that "the stronger the similarity between the two works in question, the less compelling the proof of access needs to be." *Ellis v. Diffie*, 177 F.3d 503, 506 (6th Cir. 1999). Should this "inverse ratio" rule also work the other way? If the plaintiff introduces compelling direct evidence of access by the defendant, does this mean that the degree of similarity required to establish copying becomes virtually nil? Some courts seem to think so. *See, e.g., Three Boys Music Corp. v. Bolton*, 212 F.3d 477, 486 (9th Cir. 2000) ("The Ninth Circuit's inverse-ratio rule requires a lesser showing of . . . similarity if there is a strong showing of access. . . . We have never held, however, that the inverse ratio rule says a weak showing of access requires a stronger showing of . . . similarity.").

The *Bolton* court's view, however, has been severely criticized. Consider the following observation: "We fear that counsel with that semantic proclivity natural to our profession have allowed themselves to be seduced by a superficially attractive apothegm which upon examination confuses more than it clarifies. The logical outcome of the claimed principle is obviously that proof of actual access will render a showing of similarities entirely unnecessary." *Arc Music Corp. v. Lee*, 296 F.2d 186, 187 (2d Cir. 1961) (Clark, J.). More straightforwardly, it has been held that "[n]o amount of proof of access will suffice to show copying if there are no similarities." *Stromback v. New Line Cinema*, 384 F.3d 283, 299 (6th Cir. 2004); *accord Funky Films Corp. v. Time Warner Ent'mt Co.*, 462 F.3d 1072, 1081 (9th Cir. 2006); *Arnstein v. Porter*, 154 F.2d 464, 468 (2d Cir. 1946).

(6) Is it relevant that the majority of the cases discussing "striking similarity" and the "inverse ratio" rule involve alleged copying of popular music? In *Gaste v. Kaiserman*, discussed above, the court observed: "[W]e are mindful of the limited number of notes and chords available to composers and the resulting fact that common themes frequently reappear in various compositions, especially in popular music. . . . Thus, striking similarity between pieces of popular music must extend beyond themes that could have been derived from a common source or themes that are so trite as to be likely to reappear in many compositions." 863 F.2d at 1068-69. *See also Benson v. Coca-Cola Co.*, 795 F.2d 973, 975 n.2 (11th Cir. 1986).

(7) Expert testimony is permitted regarding striking similarity. But should a plaintiff be *required* to produce the testimony of an expert witness in order to prove striking similarity? One case suggests the answer is "yes," at least in music infringement cases. *Testa v. Janssen*, 492 F. Supp. 198, 203 (W.D. Pa. 1980), *citing* Sherman, *Musical Copyright Infringement: The Requirement of Substantial Similarity*, 22 Copyright L. Symp. (ASCAP) 81, 96 (1977). What does *Ty* indicate? *See also Stewart v. Wachowski*, 574 F. Supp. 2d 1074, 1103 n.121 (C.D. Cal. 2005) (except in "technical" areas such as music, "the trier of fact is equipped to make this determination without expert assistance").

(8) Procedurally, what happens once the plaintiff has offered convincing indirect proof of copying, however the elements of such a showing are defined? Some courts have stated, without analysis, that "independent creation is an affirmative defense," which would imply that the defendant has the burden of persuasion at trial. *See Repp*, 132 F.3d at 889. In a more thorough analysis, however, the Fourth Circuit held that indirect evidence of copying merely shifts the burden of producing evidence ("going forward") to the defendant:

> When a plaintiff successfully creates a presumption, he not only satisfies his burden of going forward but also shifts that burden to the defendant. The defendant then must rebut the presumption to satisfy his burden of going forward. If the defendant fails to introduce sufficient evidence to rebut the presumption, the plaintiff might prevail on the strength of the presumption. When the defendant introduces sufficient rebuttal evidence, however, the fact finder then will consider all of the evidence on the issue. Regardless of these proof schemes, the burden of persuasion normally remains on the plaintiff for his claim throughout the trial. *See* Fed.R.Evid. 301. In the usual civil case, therefore, the plaintiff has the burden to persuade the trier of fact that the existence of the proposition to be proved

is more probably true than not true. . . .

Keeler Brass Co. v. Continental Brass Co., 862 F.2d 1063, 1066 (4th Cir. 1988); *accord Calhoun v. Lillenas Publishing*, 298 F.3d 1228, 1230 n.3 (11th Cir. 2002) ("[i]t should be emphasized that independent creation is *not* an affirmative defense").

(9)   Be sure, once again, that you understand the limits of "probative" similarity — that is, which elements of the plaintiff's case a showing on this matter satisfies, and which it does not. In particular, remember that proof of similarity that goes to the issue of copying (however designated) is one thing, while proof of "substantial similarity" — relevant to whether the defendant's appropriation from the plaintiff's work was improper — is something else. In what circumstances should the plaintiff's proof regarding similarity be allowed to do "double duty" as to both the copying and improper appropriation issues? When shouldn't it? See *Murray Hill Publications, Inc. v. Twentieth Century Fox Film Corp.*, 361 F.3d 312 (6th Cir. 2004), for an example of how the courts confuse the two types of similarities.

[C]   Improper Appropriation

[1]   By Way of Overview

The Classic Formulation

Once the plaintiff has proved that the defendant has copied his work, he must prove that the defendant's work appropriates an improper amount of the copyrighted matter contained in the plaintiff's work and protected by the plaintiff's copyright. The proof here has two facets. First, the plaintiff must demonstrate that what the defendant appropriated from the copyrighted work was protected expression. Second, the plaintiff must demonstrate that the intended audience will recognize substantial similarities between the two works.[1]

The first part of the test logically follows from basic copyright principles. Copyright law protects only original expression that adds to the storehouse of knowledge. Anyone can copy unprotected ideas or public domain materials that have been incorporated into a copyrighted work, so long as nothing more is copied. To meet the second part of the test — the audience test — the plaintiff must show that the intended audiences for the two works will find "substantial similarity" between the defendant's work and the protected expression in the plaintiff's work. As a matter of policy, the audience test relates directly to the economic market for the work. The fundamental question is whether, having seen, heard, read, or otherwise experienced the defendant's work, the relevant audience for the plaintiff's work would be less interested in experiencing plaintiff's work. *De minimis* takings do not interfere with the plaintiff's market and do not infringe his or her copyright. We will examine in more detail the nature of the intended audience, but we now turn to the problems involved in proving that defendant has copied an undue amount of plaintiff's protected expression.

---

[1] *See, e.g., Kohus v. Mariol*, 328 F.3d 848 (6th Cir. 2003).

Verbatim and Pattern Similarities

Many students (like many attorneys and their clients) urgently desire a simple, even mathematical, test for infringement: x number of bars of music, or x number of pages from a novel, equals infringement. Alas, no such bright line rule exists or is possible. To quote Judge Learned Hand, "wherever it is drawn [any such line] will seem arbitrary,"[2] and thus "the test for infringement of a copyright is of necessity vague."[3]

The inability to be specific is the reason that Congress chose not to define infringement in the statute, but instead to leave the matter to *ad hoc* determination by the courts. There is an almost inexhaustible variety of contexts in which the determination of substantial similarity will vary. The category of literary works, for example, includes great works of fiction, biographies, short stories, plays, telephone directories, databases, computer programs, restaurant guides, casebooks like this one, class notes like those you take, and a thousand other permutations of literary "writings." Can you think of one test that would fit equally well each of these types of works?

Additionally, the types of infringement may vary considerably. In the most easily understood instance, the defendant copies substantially word-for-word an impermissibly large portion of the plaintiff's work. This is what the late Professor Melville B. Nimmer termed "fragmented literal similarity,"[4] or what Professor Leaffer calls, more simply, "verbatim similarity."[5] Alternatively, the defendant's copying may duplicate the fundamental structure of the plaintiff's work, including perhaps the latter's selection and arrangement of contents. Such takings might be described as "comprehensive nonliteral similarity,"[6] or "pattern similarity."[7] Whether the taking is large or small, the defendant cannot be allowed to escape liability simply by the device of disguising the piracy: copyright "cannot be limited literally to the text, lest a plagiarist would escape by immaterial variation."[8]

Ultimately, whether the work is fine literature or the result of careful historical research, and whether the defendant has copied literally from the text, or has copied the overall structure of the text, infringement must be evaluated on a case-by-case basis.

Infringement and De Minimis Use

When verbatim copying is involved, it is likely that even small portions of the plaintiff's work contain at least *some* protected expression. In such cases, courts sometimes ask whether the amount of protected expression that was copied was "more than *de minimis.*" *Tufenkian Import/Export Ventures, Inc. v. Einstein*

---

[2] *Nichols v. Universal Pictures Corp.*, 45 F.2d 119, 122 (2d Cir. 1930).

[3] *Peter Pan Fabrics, Inc. v. Martin Weiner Corp.*, 274 F.2d 487, 489 (2d Cir. 1960).

[4] 4 M. Nimmer & D. Nimmer, NIMMER ON COPYRIGHT § 13.03[A][2] (2012) ("Nimmer").

[5] M. Leaffer, UNDERSTANDING COPYRIGHT LAW 425 (5th ed. 2010) ("Leaffer").

[6] 4 Nimmer, at 13.03[A][1].

[7] Leaffer, at 425-26.

[8] *Nichols v. Universal Pictures Corp.*, 45 F.2d 119, 121 (2d Cir. 1930).

Moomjy, Inc., 338 F.3d 127, 131 (2d Cir. 2003) (excerpted later in this chapter). In *Ringgold v. Black Entertainment Television, Inc.*, 126 F.3d 70 (2d Cir. 1997), however, the court explained:

> The legal maxim "*de minimis non curat lex*" (sometimes rendered, "the law does not concern itself with trifles") insulates from liability those who cause insignificant violations of the rights of others. In the context of copyright law, the concept of *de minimis* has significance in three respects, which, though related, should be considered separately.
>
> First, *de minimis* in the copyright context can mean what it means in most legal contexts: a technical violation of a right so trivial that the law will not impose legal consequences. . . .
>
> Second, *de minimis* can mean that copying has occurred to such a trivial extent as to fall below the quantitative threshold of substantial similarity, which is always a required element of actionable copying. . . .
>
> Third, *de minimis* might be considered relevant to the defense of fair use. . . . [However, if] the allegedly infringing work makes such a quantitatively insubstantial use of the copyrighted work as to fall below the threshold required for actionable copying, it makes more sense to reject the claim on that basis and find no infringement, rather than undertake an elaborate fair use analysis in order to uphold a defense.

126 F.3d at 75-76. As previously discussed in § 7.06, in *Ringgold* the court held that the use of plaintiff's artwork in the background of a television show in nine shots totalling less than 27 seconds was *not* a *de minimis* use (although it remanded for the court to consider the fair use doctrine).

In a later case, a different panel of the Second Circuit elaborated on the first meaning:

> The *de minimis* doctrine is rarely discussed in copyright opinions because suits are rarely brought over trivial instances of copying. Nonetheless, it is an important aspect of the law of copyright. Trivial copying is a significant part of modern life. Most honest citizens in the modern world frequently engage, without hesitation, in trivial copying that, but for the *de minimis* doctrine, would technically constitute a violation of law. We do not hesitate to make a photocopy of a letter from a friend to show to another friend, or of a favorite cartoon to post on the refrigerator. Parents in Central Park photograph their children perched on José de Creeft's Alice in Wonderland sculpture. . . . Waiters at a restaurant sing "Happy Birthday" at a patron's table. When we do such things, it is not that we are breaking the law but [are] unlikely to be sued given the high cost of litigation. Because of the *de minimis* doctrine, in trivial instances of copying, we are in fact not breaking the law.

On Davis v. The Gap, Inc., 246 F.3d 152, 173 (2d Cir. 2001). Other courts, however, have expressed a more skeptical view of the first meaning:

> That the copying involved only a small portion of the plaintiff's work does not by itself make the copying permissible. Indeed, "even if the similar

material is quantitatively small, if it is qualitatively important, the trier of fact may properly find substantial similarity." 4 [Nimmer] § 13.03[A][2][a], at 13-55. As a result, *de minimis* copying is best viewed not as a separate defense to copyright infringement but rather as a statement regarding the strength of the plaintiff's proof of substantial similarity. Where substantial similarity exists and the fair use doctrine, as here, is inapplicable, "the overwhelming thrust of authority upholds liability even under circumstances in which the use of the copyrighted work is of minimal consequence." 2 [Nimmer] § 8.01[G], at 8-26.

Situation Mgmt. Sys., Inc. v. ASP Consulting LLC, 560 F.3d 53, 59 (1st Cir. 2009).

The argument that any copying was merely *de minimis* is frequently made but is only rarely successful. In addition to the cases cited in § 7.06, see *Knickerbocker Toy Co. v. Azrak-Hamway Int'l, Inc.*, 668 F.2d 699 (2d Cir. 1982) (photo of plaintiff's toy was reproduced on display card for competitor's product, but display card was never used commercially); *Newton v. Diamond*, 349 F.3d 591 (9th Cir. 2003) (sampling of a three-note sequence from a musical work, where the sound recording of the work had been licensed). *But see Bridgeport Music, Inc. v. Dimension Films*, 410 F.3d 792 (6th Cir. 2005) (holding, based on a dubious interpretation of § 114(b), that *any* sampling of a sound recording is infringement *per se*, without regard to *de minimis* use or substantial similarity).

The "Subtractive" and "Totality" Approaches

Because liability attaches only for substantial unauthorized reproduction of copyrightable material, it is important to distinguish between the protectible and nonprotectible elements of the complaining work which may have been copied in the accused work. *See Feist Publications, Inc. v. Rural Telephone Service Co.*, 499 U.S. 340, 361 (1991) ("Not all copying . . . is copyright infringement.").

Over time, various courts have devised different "tests" for determining whether unlawful appropriation has occurred, or — to use a shorthand shared by most of the opinions on this subject — whether the accused work is "substantially" similar to protected expression in the plaintiff's work. Below, we will explore some of these particular formulations and suggest that the differences among them may sometimes be more apparent than real. At base, however, one might conceptualize two general approaches to the issue.

The "subtractive" approach. One possible approach might be called the "subtractive" approach (also known as "analytic dissection"). In this approach, the allegedly infringed work is analyzed first to determine which of its elements are protected by copyright and which are not. After "subtracting" the unprotected elements, the finder-of-fact proceeds to determine whether substantial similarities exist between what remains of the allegedly infringed work, on the one hand, and the various elements of the allegedly infringing work, on the other.

To illustrate this approach, suppose that the defendant's work resembles the plaintiff's work in structure and in many of the particular components of that structure, but that a number of those components, standing alone, would not be copyrightable: *e.g.*, historical events, which often provide a backdrop to the dramatic action of a motion picture or play, and *scènes à faire*, usually defined as "incidents, characters or settings which are as a practical matter indispensable, or at least standard, in the treatment of a given topic." *Alexander v. Haley*, 460 F. Supp. 40, 45 (S.D.N.Y. 1978) (rejecting the claim that "Roots," a personal history of black slavery in the United States, infringed an earlier historical novel dealing with similar subject matter). In determining whether improper appropriation has occurred, a court applying the "subtractive" approach would exclude from its analysis any consideration of the noncopyrightable components of the two works.

Many courts do rigorously disqualify all noncopyrightable elements from consideration and only then compare what remains of the complaining and accused works. *See, e.g., Benay v. Warner Bros. Entertainment, Inc.*, 607 F.3d 620, 625-29 (9th Cir. 2010) (although screenplay titled *The Last Samurai* shared a common premise with film of the same name, in which "an American war veteran travels to Japan in the 1870s to train the Imperial Army in modern Western warfare in order to combat a samurai uprising," similarities that arose from the common premise were either historical facts or *scènes à faire* and were unprotected). Is success in applying the "subtractive" approach as likely when the finder-of-fact is a *jury*? Consider the following list of nonprotectible elements, found in *Haley*, 460 F. Supp. at 44-46:

   a. matters of historical or contemporary fact;

   b. material traceable to common sources, the public domain, or folk custom;

   c. *scènes à faire*;

   d. clichéd language, metaphors and the very words of which the language is constructed (*e.g.*, "poor white trash"); and

   e. theme or setting.

Obviously, rigorous application of the "subtractive" approach to the plaintiff's work runs the real risk of missing the protectible forest for the nonprotectible trees. Or, to paraphrase another cliche, the sum of the parts is not the same as the parts.

Thus, for any given work, there may be an important distinction to be made between the nonprotectible *components* and the possibly protectible *selection and arrangement* of those components within the work. The former, it would seem, should be subtracted; the latter should not. As we know, selection and organization are protected components of certain kinds of works: compilations, for example. In fact, however, the proposition can be generalized. At the extreme, every literary work is made up of unprotected words, and every artistic work of unprotected forms and colors. It is the manner of their arrangement that justifies the extension of copyright protection, and any application of the "subtractive approach" which ignores the fact that arrangement, in and of itself, is protectible would be unacceptably reductionistic. *See, e.g., Metcalf v. Bochco*, 294 F.3d 1069, 1074 (9th Cir. 2002) ("The particular sequence in which an author strings a significant number of unprotectable elements can itself be a protectable element."); *Warner Bros., Inc. v. American Broadcasting Cos.*, 720 F.2d 231, 243 (2d Cir. 1983) (individual elements, although perhaps not protectible in isolation, contribute to "the expressive aspect of the combination").

The "totality" approach. Copyrightability, as we know from § 3.02, may inhere in the way in which elements unprotected in and of themselves are selected and arranged. In infringement actions, this basic proposition of protectibility has been adapted to create what may be called the "totality" approach. The approach is particularly well illustrated by cases decided in the Ninth Circuit.

A good starting place is *Roth Greeting Cards v. United Card Co.*, 429 F.2d 1106 (9th Cir. 1970). *Roth* involved two competing groups of card designs, each featuring combinations of simple art work and trite sentiments — elements which would have been largely (if not entirely) unprotectible standing on their own. Although the specifics of the designs of the plaintiff's and defendant's cards differed, there was a close resemblance between the works as to the *configuration* of the artworks and the brief messages characterizing each. In explaining its decision to uphold a finding that the defendant had infringed, the court noted that the two sets of cards had the same "total concept and feel." Is this turn of phrase helpful in explaining the basis for the holding? One might inquire, for example, whether a "concept" is anything more than an idea and whether the term "feel" means anything at all.

The "totality" approach was further developed in *Sid & Marty Krofft Television Productions, Inc. v. McDonald's Corp.*, 562 F.2d 1157 (9th Cir. 1977). In concluding that a series of television commercials portraying the imaginary kingdom of "McDonaldland" infringed the plaintiffs' "H.R. Pufnstuf" television programs, the Ninth Circuit said: "We have viewed representative samples of both the H.R. Pufnstuf show and McDonaldland commercials. It is clear to us that defendants' works are substantially similar to plaintiff's. They have captured the 'total concept and feel' of the Pufnstuf show." *Id.* at 1167 (citing *Roth*).

A footnote to the preceding passage helps make clear the extent to which the court's analysis depended on general similarities going to atmosphere or overall approach, rather than particular points of likeness in the way the two groups of works were organized or structured:

> The "Living Island" locales of Pufnstuf and "McDonaldland" are both imaginary worlds inhabited by anthropomorphic plants and animals and other fanciful creatures. The dominant topographical features of the locales are the same: trees, caves, a pond, a road, and a castle. Both works feature a forest with talking trees that have human faces and characteristics.

> The characters are also similar. Both lands are governed by mayors who have disproportionately large round heads dominated by long wide mouths. They are assisted by "Keystone cop" characters. Both lands feature strikingly similar crazy scientists and a multi-armed evil creature.

Id. at 1167 n.9.

In the decade or so after *Krofft* was decided, the "totality" approach to infringement enjoyed a remarkable vogue, in and out of the Ninth Circuit, and in cases involving all sorts of copyrightable works. Although for a time it seemed to have waned as an analytic tool, even in the circuit of its birth, at least where certain types of works are concerned, *see, e.g., Cooling Systems and Flexibles, Inc. v. Stuart Radiator, Inc.*, 777 F.2d 485, 491 (9th Cir. 1985) (catalogue case, holding "total concept and feel" unimportant where works at issue are "factual" as distinguished from "artistic": "similarity of expression may have to amount to verbatim reproduction or very close paraphrasing before a factual work will be deemed infringed"), other panels of the same court have signaled their continued allegiance to the "totality" approach in cases involving works in more traditional creative media. *See, e.g., Cavalier v. Random House, Inc.*, 297 F.3d 815 (9th Cir. 2002) (reversing summary judgment for defendant as to certain illustrations in children's books).

Even the "totality" approach can, of course, be a two-edged sword. Some courts have used it as a basis for finding a *lack* of substantial similarity. *See, e.g., Cavalier* (affirming summary judgment for defendant as to the works as a whole); *Williams v. Crichton*, 84 F.3d 581 (2d Cir. 1996) (affirming summary judgment for defendant where the "total concept and feel of the two works differ substantially").

As we try to demonstrate below, the messy reality of infringement decisionmaking is that courts often attempt to combine the various alternative approaches to assessing substantial similarity. No matter how they do so in the illustrative cases that will appear shortly, the goal is always the same: to determine whether the defendant has appropriated an improper amount of the plaintiff's copyrightable expression.

The inquiry into improper appropriation, both at trial and on appeal, remains one of the most contentious (and, not coincidentally, least precisely delineated) exercises in all of copyright law. As you read the following cases, try to identify the competing interests at play (including the public interest). Ask yourself whether the courts have formulated, or can formulate, any completely satisfactory method of reconciling those interests. Note that all of the major cases below are from the Second Circuit, where, over the years, courts have experimented with most of the possible approaches to assessing substantial similarity and encountered most of the difficulties that those approaches entail.

[2] Illustrative Cases

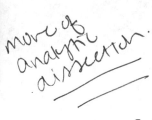

NICHOLS v. UNIVERSAL PICTURES CORP.
United States Court of Appeals, Second Circuit
45 F.2d 119 (1930)

L. HAND, CIRCUIT JUDGE.

The plaintiff is the author of a play, "Abie's Irish Rose," which it may be assumed was properly copyrighted under section five, subdivision (d), of the Copyright Act, 17 USCA § 5(d). The defendant produced publicly a motion picture play, "The Cohens and The Kellys," which the plaintiff alleges was taken from it. As we think the defendant's play too unlike the plaintiff's to be an infringement, we may assume, *arguendo*, that in some details the defendant used the plaintiff's play, as will subsequently appear, though we do not so decide. It therefore becomes necessary to give an outline of the two plays.

"Abie's Irish Rose" presents a Jewish family living in prosperous circumstances in New York. The father, a widower, is in business as a merchant, in which his son and only child helps him. The boy has philandered with young women, who to his father's great disgust have always been Gentiles, for he is obsessed with a passion that his daughter-in-law shall be an orthodox Jewess. When the play opens the son, who has been courting a young Irish Catholic girl, has already married her secretly before a Protestant minister, and is concerned to soften the blow for his father, by securing a favorable impression of his bride, while concealing her faith and race. To accomplish this he introduces her to his father at his home as a Jewess, and lets it appear that he is interested in her, though he conceals the marriage. The girl somewhat reluctantly falls in with the plan; the father takes the bait, becomes infatuated with the girl, concludes that they must marry, and assumes that of course they will, if he so decides. He calls in a rabbi, and prepares for the wedding according to the Jewish rite.

Judge Learned Hand
Courtesy of Harvard Law School Art Collection

Meanwhile the girl's father, also a widower, who lives in California, and is as intense in his own religious antagonism as the Jew, has been called to New York, supposing that his daughter is to marry an Irishman and a Catholic. Accompanied by a priest, he arrives at the house at the moment when the marriage is being celebrated, but too late to prevent it, and the two fathers, each infuriated by the proposed union of his child to a heretic, fall into unseemly and grotesque antics. The priest and the rabbi become friendly, exchange trite sentiments about religion, and agree that the match is good. Apparently out of abundant caution, the priest celebrates the marriage for a third time, while the girl's father is inveigled away. The second act closes with each father, still outraged, seeking to find some way by which the union, thus trebly insured, may be dissolved.

The last act takes place about a year later, the young couple having meanwhile been abjured by each father, and left to their own resources. They have had twins, a boy and a girl, but their fathers know no more than that a child has been born. At Christmas each, led by his craving to see his grandchild, goes separately to the young folks' home, where they encounter each other, each laden with gifts, one for a boy, the other for a girl. After some slapstick comedy, depending upon the insistence of each that he is right about the sex of the grandchild, they become reconciled when they learn the truth, and that each child is to bear the given name of a grandparent. The curtain falls as the fathers are exchanging amenities, and the Jew giving evidence of an abatement in the strictness of his orthodoxy.

"The Cohens and The Kellys" presents two families, Jewish and Irish, living side by side in the poorer quarters of New York in a state of perpetual enmity. The wives in both cases are still living, and share in the mutual animosity, as do two small sons, and even the respective dogs. The Jews have a daughter, the Irish a son; the Jewish father is in the clothing business; the Irishman is a policeman. The children are in love with each other, and secretly marry, apparently after the play opens. The Jew, being in great financial straits, learns from a lawyer that he has fallen heir to a large fortune from a great-aunt, and moves into a great house, fitted luxuriously. Here he and his family live in vulgar ostentation, and here the Irish boy seeks out his Jewish bride, and is chased away by the angry father. The Jew then abuses the Irishman over the telephone, and both become hysterically excited. The extremity of his feelings makes the Jew sick, so that he must go to Florida for a rest, just before which the daughter discloses her marriage to her mother.

On his return the Jew finds that his daughter has borne a child; at first he suspects the lawyer, but eventually learns the truth and is overcome with anger at such a low alliance. Meanwhile, the Irish family, who have been forbidden to see the grandchild, go to the Jew's house, and after a violent scene between the two fathers, in which the Jew disowns his daughter, who decides to go back with her husband, the Irishman takes her back with her baby to his own poor lodgings. The lawyer, who had hoped to marry the Jew's daughter, seeing his plan foiled, tells the Jew that his fortune really belongs to the Irishman, who was also related to the dead woman, but offers to conceal his knowledge, if the Jew will share the loot. This the Jew repudiates, and, leaving the astonished lawyer, walks through the rain to his enemy's house to surrender the property. He arrives in great dejection, tells the truth, and abjectly turns to leave. A reconciliation ensues, the Irishman agreeing to share with him equally. The Jew shows some interest in his grandchild, though this is at most a minor motive in the reconciliation, and the curtain falls while the two are in their cups, the Jew insisting that in the firm name for the business, which they are to carry on jointly, his name shall stand first.

It is of course essential to any protection of literary property, whether at common-law or under the statute, that the right cannot be limited literally to the text, else a plagiarist would escape by immaterial variations. That has never been the law, but, as soon as literal appropriation ceases to be the test, the whole matter is necessarily at large. . . . When plays are concerned, the plagiarist may excise a separate scene or he may appropriate part of the dialogue. Then the question is whether the part so taken is "substantial," and therefore not a "fair use" of the copyrighted work; it is the same question as arises in the case of any other copyrighted work. But when the plagiarist does not take out a block *in situ*, but an abstract of the whole, decision is more troublesome. Upon any work, and especially upon a play, a great number of patterns of increasing generality will fit equally well, as more and more of the incident is left out. The last may perhaps be no more than the most general statement of what the play is about, and at times might consist only of its title; but there is a point in this series of abstractions where they are no longer protected, since otherwise the playwright could prevent the use of his "ideas," to which, apart from their expression, his property is never extended. . . . Nobody has ever been able to fix that boundary, and nobody ever can. In some cases the question has been treated as though it were analogous to lifting a portion out of the copyrighted work but the analogy is not a good one, because, though the skeleton is a part of the body, it pervades and supports the whole. In such cases we are rather concerned with the line between expression and what is expressed. As respects plays, the controversy chiefly centers upon the characters and sequence of incident, these being the substance.

We did not in *Dymow v. Bolton*, 11 F.(2d) 690, hold that a plagiarist was never liable for stealing a plot. . . . We found the plot of the second play was too different to infringe, because the most detailed pattern, common to both, eliminated so much from each that its content went into the public domain; and for this reason we said, "this mere subsection of a plot was not susceptible of copyright." But we do not doubt that two plays may correspond in plot closely enough for infringement. How far that correspondence must go is another matter. Nor need we hold that the same may not be true as to the characters, quite independently of the "plot" proper, though, as far as we know, such a case has never arisen. If *Twelfth Night* were copyrighted, it is quite possible that a second comer might so closely imitate Sir Toby Belch or Malvolio as to infringe, but it would not be enough that for one of his characters he cast a riotous knight who kept wassail to the discomfort of the household, or a vain and foppish steward who became amorous of his mistress. These would be no more than Shakespeare's "ideas" in the play, as little capable of monopoly as Einstein's Doctrine of Relativity, or Darwin's theory of the *Origin of Species*. It follows that the less developed the characters, the less they can be copyrighted; that is the penalty an author must bear for marking them too indistinctly.

In the two plays at bar we think both as to incident and character, the defendant took no more — assuming that it took anything at all — than the law allowed. The stories are quite different. One is of a religious zealot who insists upon his child's marrying no one outside his faith; opposed by another who is in this respect just like him, and is his foil. Their difference in race is merely an *obbligato* to the main theme, religion. They sink their differences through grandparental pride and affection. In the other, zealotry is wholly absent; religion does not even appear. It is true that the parents are hostile to each other in part because they differ in race; but the marriage of their son to a Jew does not apparently offend the Irish family at all, and it exacerbates the existing animosity of the Jew, principally because he has become rich, when he learns it. They are reconciled through the honesty of the Jew and the generosity of the Irishman; the grandchild has nothing whatever to do with it. The only matter common to the two is a quarrel between a Jewish and an Irish father, the marriage of their children, the birth of grandchildren and a reconciliation.

If the defendant took so much from the plaintiff, it may well have been because her amazing success seemed to prove that this was a subject of enduring popularity. Even so, granting that the plaintiff's play was wholly original, and assuming that novelty is not essential to a copyright, there is no monopoly in such a background. Though the plaintiff discovered the vein, she could not keep it to herself; so defined, the theme was too generalized an abstraction from what she wrote. It was only a part of her "ideas."

Nor does she fare better as to her characters. It is indeed scarcely credible that she should not have been aware of those stock figures, the low comedy Jew and Irishman. The defendant has not taken from her more than their prototypes have contained for many decades. If so, obviously so to generalize her copyright would allow her to cover what was not original with her. But we need not hold this as matter of fact, much as we might be justified. Even though we take it that she devised her figures out of her brain *de novo*, still the defendant was within its rights.

There are but four characters common to both plays, the lovers and the fathers. The lovers are so faintly indicated as to be no more than stage properties. They are loving and fertile; that is really all that can be said of them, and anyone else is quite within his rights if he puts loving and fertile lovers in a play of his own, wherever he gets the cue. The plaintiff's Jew is quite unlike the defendant's. His obsession is his religion, on which depends such racial animosity as he has. He is affectionate, warm and patriarchal. None of these fit the defendant's Jew, who shows affection for his daughter only once, and who has none but the most superficial interest in his grandchild. He is tricky, ostentatious and vulgar, only by misfortune redeemed into honesty. Both are grotesque, extravagant and quarrelsome; both are fond of display; but these common qualities make up only a small part of their simple pictures, no more than any one might lift if he chose. The Irish fathers are even more unlike; the plaintiff's a mere symbol for religious fanaticism and patriarchal pride, scarcely a character at all. Neither quality appears in the defendant's, for while he goes to get his grandchild, it is rather out of a truculent determination not to be forbidden, than from pride in his progeny. For the rest he is only a grotesque hobbledehoy, used for low comedy of the most conventional sort, which any one might borrow, if he chanced not to know the exemplar.

The defendant argues that the case is controlled by my decision in *Fisher v. Dillingham* (D.C.) 298 F. 145. Neither my brothers nor I wish to throw doubt upon the doctrine of that case, but it is not applicable here. We assume that the plaintiff's play is altogether original, even to an extent that in fact it is hard to believe. We assume further that, so far as it has been anticipated by earlier plays of which she knew nothing, that fact is immaterial. Still, as we have already said, her copyright did not cover everything that might be drawn from her play; its content went to some extent into the public domain. We have to decide how much, and while we are as aware as any one that the line, wherever it is drawn, will seem arbitrary, that is no excuse for not drawing it; it is a question such as courts must answer in nearly all cases. Whatever may be the difficulties *a priori*, we have no question on which side of the line this case falls. A comedy based upon conflicts between Irish and Jews, into which the marriage of their children enters, is no more susceptible of copyright than the outline of Romeo and Juliet.

The plaintiff has prepared an elaborate analysis of the two plays, showing a "quadrangle" of the common characters, in which each is represented by the emotions which he discovers. She presents the resulting parallelism as proof of infringement, but the adjectives employed are so general as to be quite useless. Take for example the attribute of "love" ascribed to both Jews. The plaintiff has depicted her father as deeply attached to his son, who is his hope and joy; not so, the defendant, whose father's conduct is throughout not actuated by any affection for his daughter, and who is merely once overcome for the moment by her distress when he has violently dismissed her lover. "Anger" covers emotions aroused by quite different occasions in each case; so do "anxiety," "despondency" and "disgust." It is unnecessary to go through the catalogue, for emotions are too much colored by their causes to be a test when used so broadly. This is not the proper approach to a solution; it must be more ingenuous, more like that of a spectator, who would rely upon the complex of his impressions of each character. . . . Decree affirmed.

[handwritten margin note: cannot have protection for universal idea]

[handwritten margin note: see Sheldon]

PETER PAN FABRICS, INC. v. MARTIN WEINER CORP.
United States Court of Appeals, Second Circuit
274 F.2d 487 (1960)

HAND, CIRCUIT JUDGE.

[Both the plaintiffs and the defendant were "converters" of textiles used in the manufacture of women's dresses. Converters buy uncolored cloth, imprint the cloth with ornamental designs, and then sell the cloth to dressmakers. The defendant appealed an injunction issued by the trial court to prevent it from copying one of the plaintiff's designs.]

The test for infringement of a copyright is of necessity vague. In the case of verbal "works," it is well settled that, although the "proprietor's" monopoly extends beyond an exact reproduction of the words, there can be no copyright in the "ideas" disclosed but only in their "expression." Obviously, no principle can be stated as to when an imitator has gone beyond copying the "idea," and has borrowed its "expression." Decisions must therefore inevitably be *ad hoc*. In the case of designs, which are addressed to the aesthetic sensibilities of an observer, the test is, if possible, even more intangible. No one disputes that the copyright extends beyond a photographic reproduction of the design, but one cannot say how far an imitator must depart from an undeviating reproduction to escape infringement. In deciding that question one should consider the uses for which the design is intended, especially the scrutiny that observers will give to it as used. In the case at bar we must try to estimate how far its overall appearance will determine its aesthetic appeal when the cloth is made into a garment. Both designs have the same general color, and the arches, scrolls, rows of symbols, etc., on one resemble those on the other though they are not identical. Moreover, the patterns in which these figures are distributed to make up the design as a whole are not identical. However, the ordinary observer, unless he set out to detect the disparities, would be disposed to overlook them, and regard their aesthetic appeal as the same. That is enough; and indeed, it is all that can be said, unless protection against infringement is to be denied because of variants irrelevant to the purpose for which the design is intended. . . . Order affirmed.

NOTES AND QUESTIONS

(1)   One of Judge Hand's major contributions to the tableaux of copyright law is the "spectator" (as she is described in *Nichols*) or "ordinary observer" (per *Peter Pan Fabrics*). For reasons that will become clear, we defer consideration of that worthy individual to the notes following later cases. The present notes concentrate on the actual substance of what the ordinary observer is to observe.

(2)   According to Judge Hand, "all that can be said" is that, wherever the line is drawn between substantial similarity, which is actionable, and insubstantial taking, which is not, "[it] will seem arbitrary," and that decisions in this area "must . . . inevitably be *ad hoc*." Harking back to first principles again, why is it that the line must be drawn at all? Why not just punish all unauthorized copying? Isn't any such use of the plaintiff's creation, by hypothesis, wrong?

(3)   Judge Hand's method of separating protected expression from unprotectible ideas was his famous "abstractions" test, which is to be distinguished (but not much) from Prof. Zachariah Chafee's later "pattern" test:

> [I]f we protect more than precise words, where shall we stop? The line is sometimes drawn between an idea and its expression. This does not solve the problem, because "expression" has too wide a range. To some extent, the expression of an abstract idea should be free for use by others. No doubt, the line does lie somewhere between the author's idea and the precise form in which he wrote it down. I like to say that the protection covers the "pattern" of the work. This is not a solution, but I find it helpful as an imaginative description of what should not be imitated.

Chafee, *Reflections on the Law of Copyright*, 45 Colum. L. Rev. 503, 513 (1945). Chafee says that, given the theme in *Nichols*, "some resemblance in characters and situations" was inevitable and permissible, but that "the pattern of the play — the sequence of events and the development of the interplay of the characters — [could] not be followed scene by scene" without constituting an infringement. *Id.* at 513-14.

What, if anything, does the "pattern" test add to the "abstractions" test? In this connection, you may want to review *Williams v. Crichton*, 84 F.3d 581 (2d Cir. 1996), in which the court relies on Hand's and Chafee's tests in holding that the sci-fi novel and movie "Jurassic Park" did not infringe the plaintiff's "Dinosaur World" children's books.

(4)   Consider the following scenario, suggested by an observation that appears in the next-to-last paragraph of *Nichols*:

a. A boy and a girl are members of hostile groups.

b. They meet at a dance.

c. One night, the boy climbs up to the girl's room and they profess their love.

d. The girl is betrothed to another, against her will.

e. The boy and the girl secretly pledge themselves to one another in marriage.

f. In an encounter between the hostile groups, the boy restrains his best friend in order to avoid violence.

g. As a result, one of the girl's relatives succeeds in killing the friend.

h. The boy kills the girl's relative in retaliation.

i. The boy flees.

j. A message is sent to the boy at his hideaway, explaining a plan for him to rendezvous with the girl.

k. The message never reaches the boy.

l. The boy receives erroneous information that the girl is dead.

m. The boy's grief leads, tragically, to his own death.

Was what you just read the basic plot outline of William Shakespeare's "Romeo and Juliet," mentioned by Judge Hand in the next-to-last paragraph of *Nichols*? Or was it Leonard Bernstein's "West Side Story," the Broadway musical? Applying the test of your choice, do you find the works to be substantially similar? Isn't every one of the items on the preceding list an "idea," rather than an "expression"?

(5)   In compiling lists of similarities, one must proceed with care. Anyone familiar with "Romeo and Juliet" and "West Side Story" will agree that the incidents recited in the preceding note were judiciously chosen to reflect the major structural elements of each work. The Ninth Circuit, however, has cautioned that lists of similarities are "inherently subjective and unreliable," and may be employed to distort the degree of coincidence between the works in suit by "emphasiz[ing] random similarities [in plot, theme, dialogue, mood, setting, pace and sequence] scattered throughout the works." *Litchfield v. Spielberg*, 736 F.2d 1352, 1356 (9th Cir. 1984) (holding that "E.T. — The Extra Terrestrial" did not infringe "Lokey from Maldemar"). *See also Peters v. West*, 692 F.3d 629 (7th Cir. 2012) (two songs titled "Stronger," with lyrics based on the public-domain quote "what does not kill me, makes me stronger" and featuring words that rhyme with "stronger" and a reference to Kate Moss, "share only small cosmetic similarities" as a matter of law).

(6)   After *Nichols*, Judge Hand's most famous copyright opinion is probably *Sheldon v. Metro-Goldwyn Pictures Corp.*, 81 F.2d 49, 56 (2d Cir. 1936), a *tour de force* of legal writing marked by a high degree of sheer "entertainment value." Among other things, *Sheldon* is famous for Judge Hand's observation that "no plagiarist can excuse the wrong by showing how much of his work he did not pirate" — which has become a fountainhead of later judicial generalizations about the significance (or insignificance) of differences between works under scrutiny in infringement litigation. Was Judge Hand correct in suggesting that only similarities matter, and that differences are of no account in the reckoning of substantial

similarity? Is this what Hand is saying in *Peter Pan Fabrics*? Or has he retreated to a more guarded position on the significance of differences?

(7)   Suppose that the defendant has begun with a copy of the plaintiff's work, all of the components of which are copyrightable, and has selectively substituted new elements, and revised the language here and there, to produce a second work that is strongly reminiscent, albeit no longer an exact duplicate, of its predecessor. Isn't it clear that the resulting work is an infringement by any standard? Suppose that the process of substitution continues. At what point in that process does the defendant's end product become anything less (or more) than an infringement? Should nonliability be recognized at *any* point, considering the character of the defendant's activity? One commentator has opined that "a defendant may legitimately avoid infringement by intentionally making sufficient changes in a work that would otherwise be regarded as substantially similar to the plaintiff's." 4 NIMMER ON COPYRIGHT § 13.03[B][1][b] (2012); *accord Knitwaves, Inc. v. Lollytogs Ltd.*, 71 F.3d 996 (2d Cir. 1995); *Sportsmans Warehouse, Inc. v. Fair*, 576 F. Supp. 2d 1175 (D. Colo. 2008). Can this statement be reconciled with Hand's observation in *Sheldon*? Does it matter whether the revisions in question are wholesale additions or instead mere emendations? Should the test be the number or percentage of similarities avoided by this process of substitution, or the significance of the similarities that remain?

(8)   For an example of a case in which differences made the difference, see *Kerr v. The New Yorker Magazine, Inc.*, 63 F. Supp. 2d 320 (S.D.N.Y. 1999) (summary judgment for defendant in case involving two graphic works — the plaintiff's "New York Hairline" and the defendant's "Manhattan Mohawk"):

> Although both images do include a male figure with a skyline Mohawk, the expressions of this idea are completely different. Kerr's black-and-white image is made with pen and ink and cross-hatching. The figure appears in three-quarters profile, with two eyes visible, and meets the viewer's eyes. His leather jacket and goatee give him an aggressive and street-smart appearance. Kunz's image, in contrast, has very smooth lines and rounded contours. The buildings that make up the skyline appear in a different order, and they are more differentiated than Kerr's buildings. Kunz's picture is in color, with a fully-realized background. Her figure appears in a true profile, with one eye visible, and the figure looks downward. Moreover, Kunz's figure wears four earrings and a chain stretching from a pierced nostril to its ear, and has bare, non-realistically sloped shoulders. . . . The two figures have an entirely different "concept and feel."

Id. at 325. *See also Warner Bros. Inc. v. American Broadcasting Cos.*, 720 F.2d 231 (2d Cir. 1983) (rights in "Superman" television series were not infringed by defendant's series "Greatest American Hero," because "numerous differences tend to undercut substantial similarity," at least where graphic or three-dimensional works are concerned).

New York Hairline

Manhattan Mohawk

(9)   The fabric design cases, of which *Peter Pan Fabrics* is an example, often call for particularly difficult applications of the principles of substantial similarity. Suppose that the plaintiff claims copyright in a fabric featuring an Argyle or bias plaid in a brown, beige and white color combination. What if the defendant varies the color scheme but preserves the lines, spacings, juxtapositions, etc., of the plaintiff's design? Or vice versa? How is substantial similarity, or the lack thereof, to be determined in this context? *See L.A. Printex Indus., Inc. v. Aeropostale, Inc.*, 676 F.3d 841 (9th Cir. 2012).

(10)   Courts have applied the "total concept and feel" approach across the entire range of copyrightable subject matter, but perhaps more readily when dealing with works that contain visual elements. Is there a good reason why this should be the case? For an example of "total concept and feel" as applied to architectural works, see *Sturdza v. United Arab Emirates*, 281 F.3d 1287 (D.C. Cir. 2002). The Court of Appeals determined that various individual elements of the plaintiff's design — "domes, wind-towers, parapets, and arches" — were unprotectible ideas, and that certain "Islamic patterns" were *scènes à faire. Id.* at 1297. But the court held that the expression of certain elements, as well as the "overall look and feel" of the two designs, was sufficiently similar to remand for trial on the issue of substantial similarity. *Id.* at 1298-99. In the accompanying illustrations, check out the accused and accusing works for yourself. Do you agree with the court's assessment?

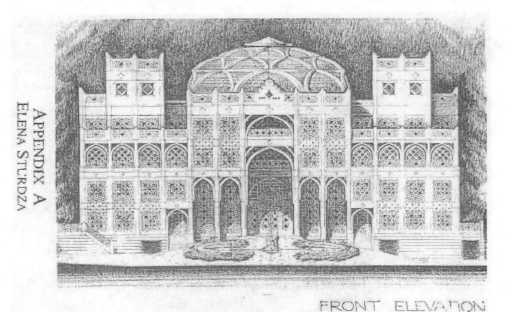

Sturdza Appendix A: Plaintiff's Design

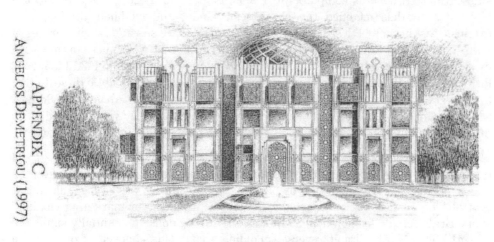

APPENDIX C
ANGELOS DEMETRIOU (1997)

FRONT ELEVATION

Sturdza Appendix C: Defendant's Design

Not all courts agree, however, that the "totality" approach is appropriate for architectural works. For an example of a particularly aggressive application of the "subtractive" or "analytic dissection" approach, see *Trek Leasing, Inc. v. United States*, 66 Fed. Cl. 8 (2005) (dismissing the vast majority of similarities as arising from the common use of a standard building design and the Bureau of Indian Affairs Pueblo Revival style). *See also Oravec v. Sunny Isles Luxury Ventures, L.C.*, 527 F.3d 1218 (11th Cir. 2008) (affirming summary judgment for defendant because common elements were "similar only at the broadest level of generality"); *Intervest Construction, Inc. v. Canterbury Estate Homes, Inc.*, 554 F.3d 914 (11th Cir. 2008) (treating architectural work as a compilation of unprotected elements).

(11) *The role of expert witnesses.* In *Arnstein v. Porter*, 154 F.2d 464, 468 (2d Cir. 1946), the Second Circuit opined that while expert testimony was appropriate in determining "copying," expert testimony was "irrelevant" in determining improper appropriation because, with respect to the latter issue, substantial similarity is judged from the viewpoint of the "ordinary observer" or the "intended audience" (much like the "reasonably prudent person" standard in tort law). *Accord La Resolana Architects, P.A. v. Reno, Inc.*, 555 F.3d 1171, 1180-81 (10th Cir. 2009) (excluding testimony of lay witness on issue of "substantial similarity" of architectural plans). These individuals, collectively considered, are the yardstick because they are the actual or potential consumers of the parties' works.

By contrast, the Ninth Circuit's opinion in *Krofft* set forth a bifurcated extrinsic/intrinsic test for infringement. *Krofft* contemplated that expert testimony was appropriate under its "extrinsic test," which addressed whether the defendant copied the *ideas* of the plaintiff's work. If the plaintiff succeeded in making this showing, a further inquiry — the "intrinsic test" — was in order. At this second stage, designed to determine the degree of similarity of *expression*, expert testimony was, as in *Arnstein*, inappropriate.

Nowadays, expert testimony increasingly is used when specialized, technical subject matter, such as computer programs, is at issue. Perhaps as a result, the Ninth Circuit has modified the *Krofft* test. Under the modified version, "the extrinsic test now objectively considers whether there are substantial similarities in both ideas and expression, whereas the intrinsic test continues to measure expression subjectively." *Apple Computer Inc. v. Microsoft Corp.*, 35 F.3d 1435, 1442 (9th Cir. 1994). As part of the objective "extrinsic" test, both "analytic dissection of a work and expert testimony" often are required. *Swirsky v. Carey*, 376 F.3d 841, 845 (9th Cir. 2004). Thus, the modified *Krofft* test apparently requires courts to discriminate between protected and unprotected material in a copyrighted work.

(12) For example, in *Mattel, Inc. v. MGA Entertainment, Inc.*, 616 F.3d 904 (9th Cir. 2010), the jury found that Carter Bryant had created preliminary sketches and a prototype for MGA's line of "Bratz" dolls while he was still employed at Mattel. The District Court enjoined MGA "from producing or marketing virtually every Bratz female fashion doll, as well as any future dolls substantially similar to [them]." The Ninth Circuit reversed, holding that "[t]he concept of depicting a young, fashion-forward female with exaggerated features, including an oversized head and feet, is [both] unoriginal as well as an unprotectable idea." Accordingly, "MGA's Bratz dolls can't be considered substantially similar to Bryant's preliminary sketches simply because the dolls and sketches depict young, stylish girls with big heads and an attitude." While "[i]t might have been reasonable to hold that some of the Bratz dolls were substantially similar to Bryant's sketches, . . . we fail to see how the district court could have found the vast majority of Bratz dolls . . . substantially similar — even though their fashions and hair styles are nothing like anything Bryant drew — unless it was relying on similarities in ideas."

(13) Some commentators have expressed the opinion that the *Krofft* court simply misread *Arnstein*, which it cites (and later quotes) with seeming approval. *See* Latman, *"Probative Similarity" as Proof of Copying: Towards Dispelling Some Myths About Copyright Infringement*, 90 Colum. L. Rev. 1187, 1203 (1990). Perhaps for that reason, the *Krofft* extrinsic/intrinsic analysis has been confined largely to the Ninth Circuit. Occasionally, however, *Krofft*'s bifurcated analysis has made an appearance in other Circuits as well. *See, e.g., Rottlund Co. v. Pinnacle Corp.*, 452 F.3d 726 (8th Cir. 2006). Other courts have expressed their *dis*approval of the *Krofft* test. *See, e.g., Oravec v. Sunny Isles Luxury Ventures, L.C.*, 527 F.3d 1218, 1224 n.5 (11th Cir. 2008); *Positive Black Talk, Inc. v. Cash Money Records, Inc.*, 394 F.3d 357, 374 n.13 (5th Cir. 2004). While the Second Circuit has so far remained immune to the *Krofft* methodology, and the gap between the two has narrowed over the years, lawyers should be aware that the modified *Krofft* test continues to hold sway in the Ninth Circuit.

LAUREYSSENS v. IDEA GROUP, INC.
United States Court of Appeals, Second Circuit
964 F.2d 131 (1992)

Oakes, Chief Judge:

At issue in this trade dress and copyright infringement case are the similarities between two sets of foam rubber puzzles. The puzzles produced by the parties contain six pieces with a variety of notches cut into each of their four edges. By interlocking the notched edges, the puzzles can be assembled either in a flat form in a rectangular frame or into a three-dimensional hollow cube. The more intrepid puzzler can piece together more challenging multi-puzzle combinations such as a larger cube or other three-dimensional figures including a beam of two or three cubes joined in a line, a cross of five cubes, and a star comprised of pieces from six cube puzzles.

One set of puzzles is marketed under the name HAPPY CUBE. The HAPPY CUBE puzzles were designed by Dirk Laureyssens and are produced, distributed, exported from Europe, and marketed in the United States through a number of entities including I Love Love Company, N.V., Creative City Limited, and Extar Corporation (collectively "Laureyssens"). The competing set is marketed under the name SNAFOOZ by Idea Group, Inc., a California corporation ("Idea Group").

Idea Group appeals from an order . . . granting a preliminary injunction [on trade dress infringement and unfair competition claims]. In addition, Laureyssens cross-appeals from the district court's denial of a preliminary injunction against Idea Group for copyright infringement, which, if granted, would have forced Idea Group to cease all activities relating to the SNAFOOZ puzzles. . . .

I.

Dirk Laureyssens, a designer of various toys and puzzles, first began creating cube puzzles in 1985. Over the next few years, he refined his cube puzzle designs by selecting puzzle pieces which would not only permit assembly in flat and cube form, but which also were aesthetically pleasing. Six puzzle designs emerged, each of which contains pieces with edges that are five notch-widths to a side.[1]

By 1991, Laureyssens had filed certificates of copyright registration with the Copyright Office in Washington for each of his six designs. The certificates indicate that the nature of authorship claimed consists of the shape of the pieces; the certificates also refer to earlier filings with the Copyright Office in 1987 and 1988 which also covered his puzzle designs. . . .

Following the original appearance at the 1988 American International Toy Fair in New York, Laureyssens exhibited the puzzles at toy and novelty shows across the country. . . .

The first conflict between Laureyssens and Idea Group arose at the 1990 American International Toy Fair in New York City. During the fair, Dirk Laureyssens discovered that Idea Group was manufacturing and marketing identical puzzles called SNAFOOZ. After receiving cease and desist letters from Laureyssens' counsel, Idea Group acknowledged on March 19, 1990 that "our puzzle apparently was copied from a sample obtained through your French distributor or licensee and, in its present form, cannot be marketed in the U.S. without your permission."

---

[1] A notch-width is equal to the thickness of the puzzle material. The notch-width must be equal to the thickness of the puzzle material in order to join two pieces smoothly in the perpendicular alignment.

The president of Idea Group was approached by Mr. Berkien of Extar Corporation approximately one month after the Toy Fair about the possibility of Idea Group marketing the Laureyssens puzzles in the United States. . . . After a few weeks of negotiations, however, the parties failed to reach an agreement.

HAPPY CUBE Puzzle

SNAFOOZ Puzzle

Following the breakdown of negotiations, Idea Group decided to develop its own version of the flat-to-cube puzzle series, utilizing pieces whose edges were six notch-widths in length rather than five. Late in July 1990, an executive vice president of Idea Group contacted a graduate student in computer science at the Massachusetts Institute of Technology, Eric Brewer, and described the new series of puzzle designs that Idea Group was hoping to market. Brewer then met with the executive vice president who provided him with two of the old SNAFOOZ Puzzles and discussed the nature of the computer program Idea Group desired. An agreement was reached in August 1990, and the graduate student completed the work for Idea Group a few weeks later. Brewer stated in an affidavit that he designed the new series entirely from scratch, utilizing the old SNAFOOZ Puzzles only to gain an understanding of the desired product and to calibrate the difficulty of his puzzle designs against the five notch-width designs of the Laureyssens puzzles. . . .

II.

[The court's discussions of the trade dress and unfair competition issues are omitted.]

C. Copyright Infringement

In order to establish a claim for copyright infringement, a plaintiff must show ownership of a valid copyright and the defendant's infringement by unauthorized copying. . . .

In this cross-appeal by Laureyssens, the parties do not take issue with the district court's conclusion that Laureyssens owns valid copyrights in the HAPPY CUBE puzzle designs. Therefore, we will focus our review on Laureyssens' claim that the district court erred in its analysis of whether the SNAFOOZ puzzles raise a serious question of actionable copying.

It is now an axiom of copyright law that actionable copying can be inferred from the defendant's access to the copyrighted work and substantial similarity between the copyrighted work and the alleged infringement. . . . We have recently explained this recitation to mean that a plaintiff must first show that his work was actually copied by proving "access and substantial similarity between the works." *See Folio Impressions*, 937 F.2d at 765. The plaintiff then must show that the copying amounts to an "improper" or "unlawful" appropriation, *Arnstein v. Porter*, 154 F.2d 464, 468 (2d Cir. 1946), by demonstrating that substantial similarities relate to protectible material. *See Folio Impressions*, 937 F.2d at 765; *see also* Latman, *"Probative Similarity" as Proof of Copying: Toward Dispelling Some Myths in Copyright Infringement*, 90 Colum. L. Rev. 1187, 1191-1204 (1990) (clarifying that copyright infringement claims involve consideration of similarity at two different stages of the analysis — actual copying and improper appropriation).

The presence of a "substantial similarity" requirement in both prongs of the analysis — actual copying and whether the copying constitutes an improper appropriation — creates the potential for unnecessary confusion, especially because a plaintiff need not prove substantial similarity in every case in order to prove actual copying. *Cf. Universal Athletic Sales Co. v. Salkeld*, 511 F.2d 904, 907 (3d Cir. 1975) ("Substantial similarity to show that the original work has been copied is not the same as substantial similarity to prove infringement. As the *Arnstein* case points out, dissection and expert testimony in the former setting are proper but are irrelevant when the issue turns to unlawful appropriation. While 'a rose is a rose is a rose is a rose,' substantial similarity is not always substantial similarity."). As Professor Latman explains:

Copying in the first instance may be established by direct or indirect proof. Though direct proof may not be routinely available, its potential should not be overlooked.

A common form of indirect proof of copying — but far from the only form — is a showing of defendant's opportunity to come into contact with plaintiff's work and such similarities between the works which, under all the circumstances, make independent creation unlikely. *Such similarities may or may not be substantial.* They are not, however, offered for their own sake in satisfaction of the requirement that defendant has taken a substantial amount of protected material from the plaintiff's work. Rather, they are offered as probative of the act of copying and may accordingly for the sake of clarity conveniently be called "probative similarity."

Latman, *supra*, at 1214 (emphasis added). . . .

For these reasons, we wish to restate some of our previous explanations of the requirements for proving actionable copying in copyright infringement cases. A plaintiff must first show that his or her work was actually copied. Copying may be established either by direct evidence of copying or by indirect evidence, including access to the copyrighted work, similarities that are probative of copying between the works, and expert testimony. If actual copying is established, a plaintiff must then show that the copying amounts to an improper appropriation by demonstrating that substantial similarity to protected material exists between the two works.

In the case at hand, with respect to proof of actual copying, Idea Group does not dispute that it had access to the HAPPY CUBE puzzles.[8] Furthermore, after examining pieces of the HAPPY CUBE and SNAFOOZ puzzles, we find similarities in their shapes which are probative of copying and which at least raise a question of actual copying.[9] The central concern in this appeal, then, is whether the district court properly determined that no serious question exists of unlawful appropriation of protected material.

The test for unlawful appropriation to prove infringement of another's copyright asks whether substantial similarity as to protectible material exists between the works at issue. *Folio Impressions*, 937 F.2d at 765. To that end, we determine in most cases whether "the ordinary observer, unless he set out to detect the disparities, would be disposed to overlook them, and regard their aesthetic appeal as the same." *Peter Pan Fabrics, Inc. v. Martin Weiner Corp.*, 274 F.2d 487, 489 (2d Cir. 1960). However, where a design contains both protectible and unprotectible elements, we have held that the observer's inspection must be more "discerning," ignoring those aspects of a work that are unprotectible in making the comparison. *Folio Impressions*, 937 F.2d at 765-66.

The district court applied the more discerning ordinary observer test for

---

[8] Idea Group, in fact, gave two of their original SNAFOOZ puzzles, which admittedly were copies of the HAPPY CUBE puzzles, to the graduate student hired to design the new SNAFOOZ puzzles.

[9] No expert testimony was included in the record pertaining to the ability of an individual to create a series of puzzles with six notch-widths per edge based on a visual inspection of puzzle pieces with five notch-widths per edge, which would help to resolve whether a question of actual copying has been shown. *See Arnstein*, 154 F.2d at 468.

substantial similarity of *Folio Impressions*, concluding that this was the appropriate test because only the shapes of the HAPPY CUBE puzzle pieces are protected by Laureyssens' copyrights. In doing so, the district court excluded from its consideration of substantial similarity the fact that both sets of designs involve "a hollow cube puzzle formed from six pieces with rectilinear interlocking projections which can also be assembled into a flat three-piece-by-two-piece form."

Laureyssens argues that it was clearly erroneous for the district court to exclude any portion of the Laureyssens design because Laureyssens created the puzzles independently, thereby rendering the entire puzzle design "original" under the standard of *Feist Publications, Inc. v. Rural Tel. Serv. Co.*, 499 U.S. 340, 345-47 (1991). We disagree. "The protection granted to a copyrightable work extends only to the particular expression of an idea and never to the idea itself." *Durham Industries, Inc. v. Tomy Corp.*, 630 F.2d 905, 912 (2d Cir. 1980) (quoting *Reyher v. Children's Television Workshop*, 533 F.2d 87, 90 (2d Cir. 1976)). In the case at hand, in order to express the idea of a perfect hollow cube puzzle that can also be assembled in flat form, a designer must use pieces that interlock through fingers and notches cut at right angles. Indeed, Idea Group presented evidence of two different patents that were obtained for flat-to-cube puzzles in 1974 and 1975; both were created prior to Laureyssens' work. Therefore, we think the district court was correct in concluding that the Laureyssens copyright extends only to his particular expression of the idea of a flat-to-cube puzzle, manifested in the particular shapes of his puzzle pieces. *Cf. Mattel, Inc. v. Azrak-Hamway Intern., Inc.*, 724 F.2d 357, 360 (2d Cir. 1983) (5" "Warlord" action figure toy doll did not infringe Mattel's copyright in 5" "Masters of the Universe" action figure toy doll because both are different expressions of the same unprotectible idea of a superhuman muscleman crouching in a fighting pose).

Finally, Laureyssens argues that the district court misapplied even the more discerning ordinary observer test for substantial similarity because Laureyssens contends that any differences between the shapes of the puzzle pieces reflect only a proportional enlargement of the puzzle pieces.

As Judge Learned Hand pointed out in *Peter Pan Fabrics*, "No principle can be stated as to when an imitator has gone beyond copying the 'idea' and has borrowed its 'expression.'" 274 F.2d at 489. However, he explained that in deciding whether unlawful appropriation has taken place, "one should consider the uses for which the design is intended, especially the scrutiny that observers will give to it as used." *Id.*

Here, the designs of the puzzle pieces at issue have as their purpose the creation of a puzzle which can be assembled in either cube or flat form. The question, then, is whether the ordinary observer would consider a design change in the shapes of the pieces from five notch-widths per edge to six notch-widths per edge as effectuating essentially the same puzzle challenge with pieces that have somewhat wider notches and fingers, or as effectuating a completely different expression of a flat-to-cube puzzle.

We think that an ordinary observer would conclude that the design change to six notch-widths per edge in the shapes of the SNAFOOZ puzzle pieces results in a qualitatively different challenge to the puzzler. A side-by-side visual comparison of the pieces comprising the green HAPPY CUBE and the purple SNAFOOZ — the two puzzles with the most pieces that are supposedly similar — provides the clearest evidence of the different ways in which the HAPPY CUBE and SNAFOOZ puzzles express the idea of a flat-to-cube: three of the six pieces in each puzzle share some similarities, none are virtually identical, and the remaining three are quite different. Based on this observation, we think the ordinary observer comparing the shapes of the pieces would conclude that SNAFOOZ is a *bona fide* redesign of the idea of a flat-to-cube puzzle. If the ordinary observer were asked to compare side-by-side two common cardboard 500-piece jigsaw puzzles depicting the American flag where the two puzzles were configured differently, and assuming that the copyright did not protect the particular depiction of the flag, we certainly think the observer would conclude that the allegedly infringing jigsaw puzzle was simply a different expression of the idea of a jigsaw puzzle.

Our belief that the SNAFOOZ puzzles are not unlawful appropriations of the HAPPY CUBE designs is reinforced by the testimony of the graduate student who designed the SNAFOOZ puzzles. He stated in his affidavit that he generated a computer program from scratch to create flat-to-cube puzzles that could also be assembled in multi-puzzle combinations with six notch-widths per edge. *Declaration of Eric Brewer* ("I can state without equivocation that I designed the SNAFOOZ Puzzles, along with their solutions and the solutions for all of the complex shapes . . . without any reference to the Five-Segment Puzzles (other than to play with them); I started from scratch.").

For these reasons, we conclude that the district court did not abuse its discretion in deciding that the SNAFOOZ puzzles pose no serious question of unlawful appropriation, and accordingly, of copyright infringement with respect to the protectible elements of Laureyssens' copyrights in his HAPPY CUBE designs.

III.

. . . [T]he district court's decision to grant a preliminary injunction based on trade dress infringement under section 43(a) of the Lanham Act and under the New York common law of unfair competition is reversed, the district court's denial of a preliminary injunction based on copyright infringement is affirmed, and costs are awarded to Idea Group.

NOTES AND QUESTIONS

(1) *The function of "substantial similarity."* The two premier appeals courts in the field of copyright — the Second and the Ninth — continue to differ about the place of "substantial similarity" in infringement analysis. In *Laureyssens*, the Second Circuit distinguishes carefully between the two different kinds of "substantial similarity" inquiry that may be involved in an infringement action: "[A] plaintiff must first show that his work was actually copied by proving 'access and substantial similarity between the works' . . . and then must show that copying amounts to an 'improper' or 'unlawful' appropriation . . . by demonstrating that the substantial similarities relate to protectible material." In passing, the court refers approvingly to both *Arnstein v. Porter* and Professor Latman's article on "probative similarity." *See also Johnson v. Gordon*, 409 F.3d 12 (1st Cir. 2005) (carefully distinguishing

between "probative similarity" to prove copying and "substantial similarity" to prove improper appropriation). Clearly, as the *Laureyssens* court acknowledges, "potential for unnecessary confusion" exists when "substantial similarity" is required to prove not only the second prong of the substantive infringement test, but also the first, especially because "a plaintiff need not prove substantial similarity in every case in order to prove actual copying." In some cases, of course, copying may be admitted, or can be proved by direct (rather than indirect) means.

(2) An instance of such confusion may have occurred in *Norse v. Henry Holt & Co.*, 991 F.2d 563 (9th Cir. 1993), in which a Ninth Circuit panel concluded that no "substantial similarity" inquiry was in order because "appellees admit that they in fact copied phrases from Norse's letters." The determinative issue on remand, the panel continued, should be whether any "protectible expression" was copied, and not (to quote *Laureyssens*) whether there was a "substantial similarity relat[ing] to protectible material." Does Norse represent something other than terminological confusion? Taking the opinion at face value, how radical a departure from the *Arnstein*-based approach to infringement analysis would it represent, if adopted more generally? *See also Range Road Music, Inc. v. East Coast Foods, Inc.*, 668 F.3d 1148 (9th Cir. 2012) ("substantial similarity" is not an element of copyright infringement, but a doctrine that helps determine whether copying of original expression occurred "when an allegedly infringing work appropriates elements of an original [work] without reproducing it *in toto*"; where direct testimony existed that defendant had publicly performed copyrighted works, issue of "substantial similarity" was irrelevant).

(3) *The "ordinary observer" test.* The pivot point of the improper appropriation inquiry is the creature of law most often described as the "ordinary observer." Recall *Nichols*, in which Judge Hand suggested that the trier-of-fact should approach the inquiry much like "a spectator, who would rely upon the complex of his impressions. . . ." Hand developed this test further in *Peter Pan Fabrics*, saying that there is substantial similarity when "the ordinary observer, unless he set out to detect the disparities, would be disposed to overlook them, and regard [the two works'] aesthetic appeal as the same." As we discuss possible variations in this standard below, bear in mind that the "ordinary observer" remains the most common. *See, e.g., Coquico, Inc. v. Rodriguez-Miranda*, 562 F.3d 62 (1st Cir. 2009).

Other decisions have referred to the "ordinary observer," in the alternative, as the "ordinary reasonable observer," *Jada Toys, Inc. v. Mattel, Inc.*, 518 F.3d 628 (9th Cir. 2008); the "ordinary reasonable person," *JCW Investments, Inc. v. Novelty, Inc.*, 482 F.3d 910 (7th Cir. 2007); the "ordinary lay person," *Kay Berry, Inc. v. Taylor Gifts, Inc.*, 421 F.3d 199 (8th Cir. 2005); the "average lay observer" (see the next case in the book); or even the "more discerning ordinary observer" (*Laureyssens*, invoking the fabric cases as the appropriate frame of reference for an alleged attempt to knock off foam rubber puzzles).

Should it matter whether this obviously fictional person is a generalized embodiment of reasonableness or a more particularized hypothetical representative of an audience with specialized tastes? Is the latter more likely than the former to appreciate certain kinds of similarities? To overlook certain kinds of differences?

(4) The argument for particularization of the "ordinary observer" standard was made with special force in *Dawson v. Hinshaw Music, Inc.*, 905 F.2d 731 (4th Cir. 1990), in which the works were two musical arrangements of the familiar spiritual "Ezekiel Saw De Wheel." Rejecting the "ordinary *lay* observer" as the proper focus of the inquiry into "substantial similarity" (and referring specifically to *Krofft* as the basis for its analysis), the Fourth Circuit stated:

> When conducting the second prong of the substantial similarity inquiry, a district court must consider the nature of the *intended audience* of the plaintiff's work. If, as will most often be the case, the lay public fairly represents the intended audience, the court should apply the lay observer formulation of the ordinary observer test. However, if the intended audience is more narrow in that it possesses specialized expertise, relevant to the purchasing decision, that lay people would lack, the court's inquiry should focus on whether a member of the intended audience would find the two works to be substantially similar. Such an inquiry may include, and no doubt in many cases will require, admission of testimony from members of the intended audience or, possibly, from those who possess expertise with reference to the tastes and perceptions of the intended audience. . . .

> . . . [I]n any given case, a court should be hesitant to find that the lay public does not fairly represent a work's intended audience. . . . To warrant departure from the lay characterization of the ordinary observer test, "specialized expertise" must go beyond mere differences in taste and instead must rise to the level of the possession of knowledge that the lay public lacks.

> We believe that, [with that caveat,] "intended audience" should supplant "ordinary observer" as the label for the appropriate test.

905 F.2d at 736-737. The trial court therefore was directed to consider, on remand, whether the "intended audience" for the plaintiff's musical arrangement was the "general, undifferentiated lay public" or "choral directors who possess specialized expertise relevant to their selection of one [spiritual] arrangement rather than another." *Id.* at 737.

(5) The *Dawson* court's reliance on *Krofft* is not unusual. Like so many other developments in the law of copyright infringement, the redefinition of the "ordinary observer" standard received much of its impetus from *Krofft*. There, in adjusting the infringement inquiry to take account of children's presumably lesser powers of discrimination (rather than ratcheting it upward, as in *Dawson*, to account for the specialized expertise of professionals), the Ninth Circuit noted: "[B]oth plaintiffs' and defendants' works are directed to an audience of children. This raises the particular factual issue of the impact of the respective works upon the minds and imaginations of young people." 562 F.2d at 1166. Isn't there a close, if implicit, connection between *Krofft's* "totality" approach to assessing substantial similarity and its view of how the "ordinary observer" standard should be applied? Or would the arguments for adjusting that definition to fit the circumstances of the particular works involved in litigation be as strong — or stronger — if the "subtractive" approach to determining ultimate similarity were being employed?

(6) In *Dawson*, the Fourth Circuit remanded for a determination of the "intended audience" for the work because it was "quite possible that spiritual arrangements are *purchased* primarily by choral directors who possess specialized expertise." 905 F.2d at 737 (emphasis added). In *Lyons Partnership, L.P. v. Morris Costumes, Inc.*, 243 F.3d 789 (4th Cir. 2001), however, a different panel of the same court reversed the District Court's holding that the intended audience for a purple dragon costume (alleged to resemble the plaintiff's famous purple dinosaur "Barney") was "the average adult renter or purchaser of those costumes because that person is the one who would actually decide whether to obtain the costumes." 243 F.3d at 802. Instead, the court held that "the similarity of child-oriented works must be viewed from the perspective of the child audience for which the products were intended." *Id.* Is this consistent with *Dawson*? The court explained that "even though children were not present during any of the purchases or rentals testified to at trial, their impressions and views were the primary influences on the purchase decision." *Id.* at 803. Are you convinced?

(7) Should copyright law credit arguments that some target audiences are more likely to be impressed by gross similarities and less attuned to differences between works? Isn't there an obvious danger here, especially when the "totality" approach to infringement analysis is employed? Note that children aren't the only group whom the courts have characterized as "fairly undiscriminating." In *C. Blore & D. Richman, Inc. v. 20/20 Advertising, Inc.*, 674 F. Supp. 671, 679 (D. Minn. 1987), the same characterization is applied to the target audiences for television commercials. Isn't that all of us? Are you insulted? And how true is it, anyway, that children are less attuned to subtle differences between works directed to them as a target audience? This assertion is made in *Krofft* and *Lyons*, but is it borne out by your personal experience? What happened the last time you tried to satisfy a five-year-old consumer with a product which was "almost like" the one advertised on TV? Of how much use are assumptions and conventional wisdom in resolving such questions?

(8) Some litigants have tried to get beyond assumption and anecdote, and to place the definition of the relevant "ordinary observer" on a scientific footing. The "Cabbage Patch Kids" case, *Original Appalachian Artworks, Inc. v. Blue Box Factory (USA) Ltd.*, 577 F. Supp. 625 (S.D.N.Y. 1983), featured expert testimony from well-known columnist Dr. Joyce Brothers, exploring her opinion concerning how the works in questions would be perceived by juvenile consumers. Does such evidence violate the conventional prohibition on using expert testimony on the ultimate issue of substantial similarity? Or does that bar apply only where it is the expert's own opinion as to similarity which is elicited?

Also in *Appalachian Artworks*, the plaintiff introduced into evidence a survey of consumer reactions to the defendant's allegedly infringing dolls, called "Flower Kids." The survey tested shopping mall consumers who were planning to buy gifts for girls under 12 years of age. The shoppers were taken individually to a room containing nothing but a Flower Kid doll and an interviewer, who asked them: "What is this doll called?" The survey found that 64% of those expressing an opinion thought that the doll was a Cabbage Patch Kid. 577 F. Supp. at 630. Is evidence of this sort an appropriate means of determining the reaction of the "ordinary observer" to the works in suit? How reliable and probative is it on the issue of substantial similarity? The "Cabbage Patch Kids" court said that such surveys should "carry little weight." *Id.* Why? Isn't this evidence better than mere supposition?

(9)   Just how far can one go in defining specialized versions of the "ordinary observer" standard without lapsing into absurdity? Consider *Data East USA, Inc. v. Epyx, Inc.*, 862 F.2d 204 (9th Cir. 1988), where the Ninth Circuit (applying the "subtractive" approach to substantial similarity analysis) summed up its conclusion in these words: "a discerning 17.5 year-old boy could not regard the works as substantially similar." A "discerning 17.5 year-old boy"? According to a footnote, "[t]he district court found that the average age of individuals purchasing 'Karate Champ' is 17.5 years, that the purchasers are predominantly male, and comprise a knowledgeable, critical, and discerning group." Putting aside the implicit sexism, what do you think of this analysis? Would this specialized perspective differ materially from that of an "ordinary observer"? Compare *Data East* to *Atari, Inc. v. North American Philips Consumer Electronics Corp.*, 672 F.2d 607, 619 (7th Cir. 1982), in which the court opined that videogames, "unlike an artist's painting or even other audiovisual works, appeal to an audience that is fairly undiscriminating insofar as their concern about more subtle differences in artistic expression." Apart from being ungrammatical, isn't this assertion snobbery, pure and simple? And doesn't it fly in the face of all anecdotal evidence?

(10)   In the Second Circuit, where the "ordinary observer" got his or her start in life, some courts seem to be having second thoughts about this venerable construct's utility. It is not only that the "more discerning ordinary observer" has become a staple of the Circuit's infringement jurisprudence in cases where the plaintiff's work has both protectible and unprotectible components. *See, e.g., Boisson v. Banian, Ltd.*, 273 F.3d 262, 273 (2d Cir. 2001). In some cases, the court has gone further still in distancing itself from Judge Hand's creation. For example, in *Ringgold v. Black Entertainment Television, Inc.*, 126 F.3d 70 (2d Cir. 1997), which was discussed briefly in § 7.06 of this casebook, Judge Newman observed that "substantial similarity"

> requires that the copying is quantitatively and qualitatively sufficient to support the legal conclusion that infringement (actionable copying) has occurred. The qualitative component concerns the copying of expression, rather than ideas, a distinction that often turns on the level of abstraction at which the works are compared. The quantitative component generally concerns the amount of the copyrighted work that is copied, a consideration that is especially pertinent to exact copying. . . . Thus, as in this case, a copyrighted work might be copied as a factual matter, yet a serious dispute might remain as to whether the copying that occurred was actionable.

126 F.3d at 75 (citations and footnotes omitted). Perhaps because of the procedural posture of the appeal, no mention was made of the perspective or point of view from which the quantitative or qualitative components are to be assessed.

But in a subsequent decision, *Castle Rock Entertainment, Inc. v. Carol Publishing Group, Inc.*, 150 F.3d 132, 138–39 (2d Cir. 1998), the court concluded that a trivia quiz book, *The Seinfeld Aptitude Test*, infringed the copyright in the popular television series using the "quantitative/qualitative" standard, without any reference to either the "ordinary observer" or the "more discerning ordinary observer." It then briefly reviewed how the dispute might have been analyzed under various "other" tests, including the "ordinary observer" test and the "total concept and feel" test. 150 F.3d at 139-40. Is this merely an aberration? Compare *Castle Rock* with *Nihon Keizai Shimbun, Inc. v. Comline Business Data, Inc.*, 166 F.3d 65, 70 (2d Cir. 1999), in which the court combines the "ordinary observer" test with the "quantitative/qualitative" standard.

(11)   But first, it is time to test yourself on what you have learned to this point about the proper approaches to deciding an action for infringement. Imagine a case in which an artist whose fame derives in significant part from works he has drawn for *The New Yorker* magazine discovers that one of his most famous covers, widely known as "A New Yorker's View of the World," apparently has provided the inspiration for a motion picture company's poster for its movie "Moscow on the Hudson." Indeed, there is such a case. Here is a passage from the front page obituary of the artist, Saul Steinberg, in the May 13, 1999 edition of the *New York Times* that may help you put the problem "in perspective":

> Mr. Steinberg's place in the art world was always in question, as he well knew: "I don't quite belong to the art, cartoon or magazine world, so the art world doesn't quite know where to place me." Nonetheless, he made a splash in all three. . . . He did 85 covers and 642 drawings for *The New Yorker*. He published several books . . . From the start his work was often exhibited in the best museums and galleries.

> . . . Still, people never stopped asking, "But is it art?" And for many Americans he remained the man who drew the Manhattanite's view of the world, which first appeared on *The New Yorker* cover of March 29, 1976. It was subsequently copied in knockoffs made for London, Paris, Rome, Venice, Kansas City, Durango, wherever. "I could have retired on this painting," if royalties had been paid, he once mused. But they weren't, and he didn't. Finally, sick of the many knockoffs, he sued Columbia Pictures for an unauthorized version of the painting used as an advertisement for the 1984 movie "Moscow on the Hudson."

On neighboring pages are reproductions of Steinberg's cover and Columbia's poster. Infringement? When you have finished your analysis of this case, have a look at the actual decision: *Steinberg v. Columbia Pictures Industries, Inc.*, 663 F. Supp. 706 (S.D.N.Y. 1987).

Artwork © 1976 Saul Steinberg
Cover Reprinted by Special Permission of Saul Steinberg and The New Yorker
All Rights Reserved
The litigation involved also certain similarities in color not reproducible here.

In the end, ask yourself whether consideration of the problem in *Steinberg* leaves you confident that you — or the courts — have perfected the tools necessary to handle the complex issues associated with the substantive aspects of copyright infringement. If not, two aspirin and a careful reading of the software infringement cases below may help. Or maybe not.

The Everett Collection

(12)   Is the methodology explored in the above cases appropriate for old media, *e.g.*, plays, fabrics, and foam rubber puzzles, only? Is software so fundamentally different as to require a different approach? Or should the following decision be read as a "general corrective" to law shaped in the pre-digital era?

COMPUTER ASSOCIATES INT'L, INC. v. ALTAI, INC.
United States Court of Appeals, Second Circuit
982 F.2d 693 (1992)

WALKER, CIRCUIT JUDGE

. . . [T]his case deals with the challenging question of whether and to what extent the "non-literal" aspects of a computer program, that is, those aspects that are not reduced to written code, are protected by copyright. While a few other courts have already grappled with this issue, this case is one of first impression in this circuit. As we shall discuss, we find the results reached by other courts to be less than satisfactory. Drawing upon longstanding doctrines of copyright law, we take an approach that we think better addresses the practical difficulties embedded in these types of cases. In so doing, we have kept in mind the necessary balance between creative incentive and industrial competition.

. . . [At trial,] Judge Pratt found that defendant Altai, Inc.'s ("Altai") OSCAR 3.4 computer program had infringed plaintiff Computer Associates' ("CA") copyrighted computer program entitled CA-SCHEDULER. . . . With respect to CA's second claim for copyright infringement, Judge Pratt found that Altai's OSCAR 3.5 program was not substantially similar to a portion of CA-SCHEDULER called ADAPTER, and thus denied relief. . . .

BACKGROUND . . .

I. COMPUTER PROGRAM DESIGN . . .

II. FACTS

CA-SCHEDULER is a job scheduling program designed for IBM mainframe computers. Its primary functions are straightforward: to create a schedule specifying when the computer should run various tasks, and then to control the computer as it executes the schedule. CA-SCHEDULER contains a sub-program entitled ADAPTER, also developed by CA. ADAPTER is not an independently marketed product of CA; it is a wholly integrated component of CA-SCHEDULER and has no capacity for independent use.

Nevertheless, ADAPTER plays an extremely important role. It is an "operating system compatibility component," which means, roughly speaking, it serves as a translator. An "operating system" is itself a program that manages the resources of the computer, allocating those resources to other programs as needed. The IBM System 370 family of computers, for which CA-SCHEDULER was created, is, depending upon the computer's size, designed to contain one of three operating systems: DOS/VSE, MVS, or CMS. As the district court noted, the general rule is that "a program written for one operating system, *e.g.*, DOS/VSE, will not, without modification, run under another operating system such as MVS." *Computer Assocs.*, 775 F. Supp. at 550. ADAPTER's function is to translate the language of a given program into the particular language that the computer's own operating system can understand.

The district court succinctly outlined the manner in which ADAPTER works within the context of the larger program. In order to enable CA-SCHEDULER to function on different operating systems, CA divided the CA-SCHEDULER into two components:

— a first component that contains only the task-specific portions of the program, independent of all operating system issues, and

— a second component that contains all the interconnections between the first component and the operating system.

In a program constructed in this way, whenever the first, task-specific, component needs to ask the operating system for some resource through a "system call", it calls the second component instead of calling the operating system directly.

The second component serves as an "interface" or "compatibility component" between the task-specific portion of the program and the operating system. It receives the request from the first component and translates it into the appropriate system call that will be recognized by whatever operating system is installed on the computer, *e.g.*, DOS/VSE, MVS, or CMS. Since the first, task-specific component calls the adapter component rather than the operating system, the first component need not be customized to use any specific operating system. The second, interface, component insures that all the system calls are performed properly for the particular operating system in use. ADAPTER serves as the second, "common system interface" component referred to above.

A program like ADAPTER, which allows a computer user to change or use multiple operating systems while maintaining the same software, is highly desirable. It saves the user the costs, both in time and money, that otherwise would be expended in purchasing new programs, modifying existing systems to run them, and gaining familiarity with their operation. . . .

[In 1983, Altai recruited a Computer Associates employee to work on the program which was to become OSCAR. Unbeknownst to Altai, the employee brought with him and used the code of CA's ADAPTER. On discovering this, Altai rewrote the OSCAR program to eliminate literal duplications of code, an apparently successful effort that resulted in OSCAR 3.5. CA sued, the matter was tried to and decided by Judge Pratt, and this appeal followed.]

DISCUSSION

[The excerpt below concerns only CA's appeal from the district court's ruling that Altai was not liable for copyright infringement in developing OSCAR 3.5.]

For the purpose of analysis, the district court assumed that Altai had access to the ADAPTER code when creating OSCAR 3.5. Thus, in determining whether Altai had unlawfully copied protected aspects of CA's ADAPTER, the district court narrowed its focus of inquiry to ascertaining whether Altai's OSCAR 3.5 was substantially similar to ADAPTER. Because we approve Judge Pratt's conclusions regarding substantial similarity, our analysis will proceed along the same assumption.

As a general matter, and to varying degrees, copyright protection extends beyond a literary work's strictly textual form to its non-literal components. As we have said, "[i]t is of course essential to any protection of literary property . . . that the right cannot be limited literally to the text, else a plagiarist would escape by immaterial variations." *Nichols v. Universal Pictures Co.*, 45 F.2d 119, 121 (2d Cir. 1930) (L. Hand, J.). Thus, where "the fundamental essence or structure of one work is duplicated in another," 3 NIMMER ON COPYRIGHT, § 13.03[A][1], at 13-24 (1991), courts have found copyright infringement. . . .

A. *Copyright Protection for the Non-literal Elements of Computer Programs*

It is now well settled that the literal elements of computer programs, i.e., their source and object codes, are the subject of copyright protection. [*Whelan Assocs. v. Jaslow Dental Laboratory, Inc.*, 797 F.2d 1222 (3d Cir. 1986); *Apple Computer, Inc. v. Franklin Computer Corp.*, 714 F.2d 1240 (3d Cir. 1983) (reproduced in Chapter 3).] Here, as noted earlier, Altai admits having copied approximately 30% of the OSCAR 3.4 program from CA's ADAPTER source code, and does not challenge the district court's related finding of infringement.

In this case, the hotly contested issues surround OSCAR 3.5. . . . OSCAR 3.5 is the product of Altai's carefully orchestrated rewrite of OSCAR 3.4. After the purge, none of the ADAPTER source code remained in the 3.5 version; thus, Altai made sure that the literal elements of its revamped OSCAR program were no longer substantially similar to the literal elements of CA's ADAPTER.

. . . CA argues that, despite Altai's rewrite of the OSCAR code, the resulting program remained substantially similar to the structure of its ADAPTER program. As discussed above, a program's structure includes its non-literal components such as general flow charts as well as the more specific organization of inter-modular relationships, parameter lists, and macros. In addition to these aspects, CA contends that OSCAR 3.5 is also substantially similar to ADAPTER with respect to the list of services that both ADAPTER and OSCAR obtain from their respective operating systems. We must decide whether and to what extent these elements of computer programs are protected by copyright law.

. . . The Copyright Act affords protection to "original works of authorship fixed in any tangible medium of expression. . . ." 17 U.S.C. § 102(a). This broad category of protected "works" includes "literary works," *id.* at § 102(a)(1), which are defined by the Act as

> works, other than audiovisual works, expressed in words, numbers, or other verbal or numerical symbols or indicia, regardless of the nature of the material objects, such as books, periodicals, manuscripts, phonorecords, film tapes, disks, or cards, in which they are embodied.

17 U.S.C. § 101. While computer programs are not specifically listed as part of the above statutory definition, the legislative history leaves no doubt that Congress intended them to be considered literary works. *See* H.R. Rep. No. 1476, 94th Cong.,

2d Sess. 54 (hereinafter "House Report"); *Whelan*, 797 F.2d at 1234; *Apple Computer*, 714 F.2d at 1247.

The syllogism that follows from the foregoing premises is a powerful one: if the non-literal structures of literary works are protected by copyright; and if computer programs are literary works, as we are told by the legislature; then the non-literal structures of computer programs are protected by copyright. *See Whelan*, 797 F.2d at 1234 ("By analogy to other literary works, it would thus appear that the copyrights of computer programs can be infringed even absent copying of the literal elements of the program."). We have no reservation in joining the company of those courts that have already [sub]scribed to this logic. . . . However, that conclusion does not end our analysis. We must determine the scope of copyright protection that extends to a computer program's non-literal structure. . . .

(1) Idea vs. Expression Dichotomy

It is a fundamental principle of copyright law that a copyright does not protect an idea, but only the expression of the idea. *See Baker v. Selden*, 101 U.S. 99 (1879); *Mazer v. Stein*, 347 U.S. 201 (1954). This axiom of common law has been incorporated into the governing statute. Section 102(b) of the Act provides:

> In no case does copyright protection for an original work of authorship extend to any idea, procedure, process, system, method of operation, concept, principle, or discovery, regardless of the form in which it is described, explained, illustrated, or embodied in such work.

17 U.S.C. § 102(b). *See also* House Report, [1976 U.S.C.C.A.N.] at 5670 ("Copyright does not preclude others from using ideas or information revealed by the author's work.").

Congress made no special exception for computer programs. To the contrary, the legislative history explicitly states that copyright protects computer programs only "to the extent that they incorporate authorship in programmer's expression of original ideas, as distinguished from the ideas themselves." *Id.* at 5667. . . .

. . . The essentially utilitarian nature of a computer program further complicates the task of distilling its idea from its expression. . . . In order to describe both computational processes and abstract ideas, its content "combines creative and technical expression." *See* Spivack, [35 UCLA L. Rev. 723] at 755. The variations of expression found in purely creative compositions, as opposed to those contained in utilitarian works, are not directed towards practical application. For example, a narration of Humpty Dumpty's demise, which would clearly be a creative composition, does not serve the same ends as, say, a recipe for scrambled eggs — which is a more process-oriented text. Thus, compared to aesthetic works, computer programs hover even more closely to the elusive boundary line described in § 102(b).

The doctrinal starting point in analyses of utilitarian works, is the seminal case of *Baker v. Selden*. . . .

To the extent that an accounting text and a computer program are both "a set of statements or instructions . . . to bring about a certain result," 17 U.S.C. § 101, they are roughly analogous. In the former case, the processes are ultimately conducted by human agency; in the latter, by electronic means. In either case, as already stated, the processes themselves are not protectible. But the holding in *Baker* goes farther. The Court concluded that those aspects of a work, which "must necessarily be used as incident to" the idea, system or process that the work describes, are also not copyrightable. 101 U.S. at 104. Selden's ledger sheets, therefore, enjoyed no copyright protection because they were "necessary incidents to" the system of accounting that he described. *Id.* at 103. From this reasoning, we conclude that those elements of a computer program that are necessarily incidental to its function are similarly unprotectible.

While *Baker v. Selden* provides a sound analytical foundation, it offers scant guidance on how to separate idea or process from expression, and moreover, on how to further distinguish protectible expression from that expression which "must necessarily be used as incident to" the work's underlying concept. In the context of computer programs, the Third Circuit's noted decision in *Whelan* has, thus far, been the most thoughtful attempt to accomplish these ends.

The court in *Whelan* faced substantially the same problem as is presented by this case. There, the defendant was accused of making off with the non-literal structure of the plaintiff's copyrighted dental lab management program, and employing it to create its own competitive version. In assessing whether there had been an infringement, the court had to determine which aspects of the programs involved were ideas, and which were expression. In separating the two, the court settled upon the following conceptual approach:

> [T]he line between idea and expression may be drawn with reference to the end sought to be achieved by the work in question. In other words, *the purpose or function of a utilitarian work would be the work's idea, and everything that is not necessary to that purpose or function would be part of the expression of the idea.* . . . Where there are various means of achieving the desired purpose, then the particular means chosen is not necessary to the purpose; hence, there is expression, not idea.

797 F.2d at 1236 (citations omitted). The "idea" of the program at issue in *Whelan* was identified by the court as simply "the efficient management of a dental laboratory." *Id.* at n.28.

So far, in the courts, the *Whelan* rule has received a mixed reception. . . .

Whelan has fared even more poorly in the academic community, where its standard for distinguishing idea from expression has been widely criticized for being conceptually overbroad. . . . The leading commentator in the field has stated that, "[t]he crucial flaw in [*Whelan*'s] reasoning is that it assumes that only one 'idea,' in copyright law terms, underlies any computer program, and that once a separable idea can be identified, everything else must be expression." 3 Nimmer § 13.03[F], at 13-62.34. This criticism focuses not upon the program's ultimate purpose but upon the reality of its structural design. As we have already noted, a computer program's ultimate function or purpose is the composite result of interacting subroutines. Since each subroutine is itself a program, and thus, may be said to have its own "idea," *Whelan*'s general formulation that a program's overall purpose equates with the program's idea is descriptively inadequate.

Accordingly, we think that Judge Pratt wisely declined to follow *Whelan*. . . .

(2) Substantial Similarity Test for Computer Program Structure: Abstraction-Filtration-Comparison

We think that *Whelan*'s approach to separating idea from expression in computer programs relies too heavily on metaphysical distinctions and does not place enough emphasis on practical considerations. . . .

. . . [D]istrict courts would be well-advised to undertake a three-step procedure, based on the abstractions test utilized by the district court, in order to determine whether the non-literal elements of two or more computer programs are substantially similar. This approach breaks no new ground; rather, it draws on such familiar copyright doctrines as merger, *scènes à faire*, and public domain. In taking this approach, however, we are cognizant that computer technology is a dynamic field which can quickly outpace judicial decisionmaking. Thus, in cases where the technology in question does not allow for a literal application of the procedure we outline below, our opinion should not be read to foreclose the district courts of our circuit from utilizing a modified version.

In ascertaining substantial similarity under this approach, a court would first break down the allegedly infringed program into its constituent structural parts. Then, by examining each of these parts for such things as incorporated ideas, expression that is necessarily incidental to those ideas, and elements that are taken from the public domain, a court would then be able to sift out all non-protectible material. Left with a kernel, or possible kernels, of creative expression after following this process of elimination, the court's last step would be to compare this material with the structure of an allegedly infringing program. The result of this comparison will determine whether the protectible elements of the programs at issue are substantially similar so as to warrant a finding of infringement. It will be helpful to elaborate a bit further.

Step One: Abstraction

As the district court appreciated, the theoretic framework for analyzing substantial similarity expounded by Learned Hand in the *Nichols* case is helpful in the present context. . . . [See the Hand "abstractions" test, described earlier in the present section of the casebook. — *Eds.*]

While the abstractions test was originally applied in relation to literary works such as novels and plays, it is adaptable to computer programs. In contrast to the *Whelan* approach, the abstractions test "implicitly recognizes that any given work may consist of a mixture of numerous ideas and expressions." 3 Nimmer § 13.03[F], at 13-62.34-63.

As applied to computer programs, the abstractions test will comprise the first step in the examination for substantial similarity. Initially, in a manner that resembles reverse engineering on a theoretical plane, a court should dissect the allegedly copied program's structure and isolate each level of abstraction contained within it. This process begins with the code and ends with an articulation of the program's ultimate function. Along the way, it is necessary essentially to retrace and map each of the designer's steps — in the opposite order in which they were taken during the program's creation. . . .

As an anatomical guide to this procedure, the following description is helpful:

> At the lowest level of abstraction, a computer program may be thought of in its entirety as a set of individual instructions organized into a hierarchy of modules. At a higher level of abstraction, the instructions in the lowest-level modules may be replaced conceptually by the functions of those modules. At progressively higher levels of abstraction, the functions of higher-level modules conceptually replace the implementations of those modules in terms of lower-level modules and instructions, until finally, one is left with nothing but the ultimate function of the program. . . . A program has structure at every level of abstraction at which it is viewed. At low levels of abstraction, a program's structure may be quite complex; at the highest level it is trivial.

Englund, [88 Mich. L. Rev. 866] at 897-98. *Cf.* Spivack, at 774.

Step Two: Filtration

Once the program's abstraction levels have been discovered, the substantial similarity inquiry moves from the conceptual to the concrete. Professor Nimmer suggests, and we endorse, a "successive filtering method" for separating protectible expression from non-protectible material. *See generally* 3 Nimmer § 13.03[F]. This process entails examining the structural components at each level of abstraction to determine whether their particular inclusion at that level was "idea" or was dictated by considerations of efficiency, so as to be necessarily incidental to that idea; required by factors external to the program itself; or taken from the public domain and hence is non-protectible expression. . . . The structure of any given program may reflect some, all, or none of these considerations. Each case requires its own fact specific investigation.

Strictly speaking, this filtration serves "the purpose of defining the scope of plaintiff's copyright." *Brown Bag Software v. Symantec Corp.*, 960 F.2d 1465, 1475 (9th Cir. 1992). . . .

(a) *Elements Dictated by Efficiency*

The portion of *Baker v. Selden*, discussed earlier, which denies copyright protection to expression necessarily incidental to the idea being expressed, appears to be the cornerstone for what has developed into the doctrine of merger. . . .

CONTU recognized the applicability of the merger doctrine to computer programs. In its report to Congress, it stated that:

> [C]opyrighted language may be copied without infringing when there is but a limited number of ways to express a given idea. . . . In the computer context, this means that when specific instructions, even though previously copyrighted, are the only and essential means of accomplishing a given task, their later use by another will not amount to infringement.

CONTU Report at 20. While this statement directly concerns only the application of merger to program code, that is, the textual aspect of the program, it reasonably suggests that the doctrine fits comfortably within the general context of computer programs.

Furthermore, when one considers the fact that programmers generally strive to create programs "that meet the user's needs in the most efficient manner," Menell, [41 Stan. L. Rev. 1045] at 1052, the applicability of the merger doctrine to computer programs becomes compelling. In the context of computer program design, the concept of efficiency is akin to deriving the most concise logical proof or formulating the most succinct mathematical computation. Thus, the more efficient a set of modules are, the more closely they approximate the idea or process embodied in that particular aspect of the program's structure.

While, hypothetically, there might be a myriad of ways in which a programmer may effectuate certain functions within a program — *i.e.*, express the idea embodied in a given subroutine — efficiency concerns may so narrow the practical range of choice as to make only one or two forms of expression workable options. . . . It follows that in order to determine whether the merger doctrine precludes copyright protection [for] an aspect of a program's structure that is so oriented, a court must inquire "whether the use of this particular set of modules is necessary efficiently to implement that part of the program's process" being implemented. Englund, at 992. If the answer is yes, then the expression represented by the programmer's choice of a specific module or group of modules has merged with their underlying idea and is unprotected. . . .

Another justification for linking structural economy with the application of the merger doctrine stems from a program's essentially utilitarian nature and the competitive forces that exist in the software marketplace. . . . Working in tandem, these factors give rise to a problem of proof which merger helps to eliminate.

Efficiency is an industry-wide goal. Since, as we have already noted, there may be only a limited number of efficient implementations for any given program task, it is quite possible that multiple programmers, working independently, will design the identical method employed in the allegedly infringed work. Of course, if this is the case, there is no copyright infringement. . . .

. . . [S]ince evidence of similarly efficient structure is not particularly probative of copying, it should be disregarded in the overall substantial similarity analysis. . . .

(b) *Elements Dictated by External Factors*

We have stated that where "it is virtually impossible to write about a particular historical era or fictional theme without employing certain 'stock' or standard literary devices," such expression is not copyrightable. . . . This is known as the *scènes à faire* doctrine, and like "merger," it has its analogous application to computer programs. . . .

Professor Nimmer points out that "in many instances it is virtually impossible to write a program to perform particular functions in a specific computing environment without employing standard techniques." 3 Nimmer § 13.03[F][3], at 13-65.

This is a result of the fact that a programmer's freedom of design choice is often circumscribed by extrinsic considerations such as: (1) the mechanical specifications of the computer on which a particular program is intended to run; (2) compatibility requirements of other programs with which a program is designed to operate in conjunction; (3) computer manufacturers' design standards; (4) demands of the industry being serviced; and (5) widely accepted programming practices within the computer industry. *Id.* at 13-65-71.

Courts have already considered some of these factors in denying copyright protection to various elements of computer programs. In [*Plains Cotton Coop. Assoc. v. Goodpasture Computer Serv., Inc.*, 807 F.2d 1256 (5th Cir. 1987)], the Fifth Circuit refused to reverse the district court's denial of a preliminary injunction against an alleged program infringer because, in part, "many of the similarities between the . . . programs [were] dictated by the externalities of the cotton market." 807 F.2d at 1262. . . .

Building upon this existing case law, we conclude that a court must also examine the structural content of an allegedly infringed program for elements that might have been dictated by external factors.

(c) *Elements Taken from the Public Domain*

Closely related to the non-protectibility of *scènes à faire* is material found in the public domain. Such material is free for the taking and cannot be appropriated by a single author even though it is included in a copyrighted work. . . . We see no reason to make an exception to this rule for elements of a computer program that have entered the public domain by virtue of freely accessible program exchanges and the like. *See* 3 Nimmer § 13.03[F][4]. . . . Thus, a court must also filter out this material from the allegedly infringed program before it makes the final inquiry in its substantial similarity analysis.

Step Three: Comparison

The third and final step of the test for substantial similarity that we believe appropriate for non-literal program components entails a comparison. Once a court has sifted out all elements of the allegedly infringed program which are "ideas" or are dictated by efficiency or external factors, or taken from the public domain, there may remain a core of protectible expression. In terms of a work's copyright value, this is the golden nugget. . . . At this point, the court's substantial similarity inquiry focuses on whether the defendant copied any aspect of this protected expression, as well as an assessment of the copied portion's relative importance with respect to the plaintiff's overall program. . . .

(3) *Policy Considerations*

. . . CA and some *amici* argue against the type of approach that we have set forth on the grounds that it will be a disincentive for future computer program research and development. At bottom, they claim that if programmers are not guaranteed broad copyright protection for their work, they will not invest the extensive time, energy and funds required to design and improve program structures. While they have a point, their argument cannot carry the day. The interest of the copyright law is not in simply conferring a monopoly on industrious persons, but in advancing the public welfare through rewarding artistic creativity, in a manner that permits the free use and development of non-protectible ideas and processes. . . .

Feist [*Publications, Inc. v. Rural Tel. Serv. Co.*, 499 U.S. 340 (1991)] teaches that substantial effort alone cannot confer copyright status on an otherwise uncopyrightable work. As we have discussed, despite the fact that significant labor and expense often goes into computer program flow-charting and debugging, that process does not always result in inherently protectible expression. Thus, *Feist* implicitly undercuts the *Whelan* rationale, "which allow[ed] copyright protection beyond the literal computer code . . . [in order to] provide the proper incentive for programmers by protecting their most valuable efforts . . ." *Whelan*, 797 F.2d at 1237 (footnote omitted). We note that *Whelan* was decided prior to *Feist* when the "sweat of the brow" doctrine still had vitality. In view of the Supreme Court's recent holding, however, we must reject the legal basis of CA's disincentive argument.

Furthermore, we are unpersuaded that the test we approve today will lead to the dire consequences for the computer program industry that plaintiff and some *amici* predict. To the contrary, serious students of the industry have been highly critical of the sweeping scope of copyright protection engendered by the *Whelan* rule, in that it "enables first comers to 'lock up' basic programming techniques as implemented in programs to perform particular tasks." Menell, at 1087 . . .

To be frank, the exact contours of copyright protection for non-literal program structure are not completely clear. We trust that as future cases are decided, those limits will become better defined. Indeed, it may well be that the Copyright Act serves as a relatively weak barrier against public access to the theoretical interstices behind a program's source and object codes. This results from the hybrid nature of a computer program, which, while it is literary expression, is also a highly functional, utilitarian component in the larger process of computing. . . .

B. *The District Court Decision*

We turn now to our review of the district court's decision in this particular case. At the outset, we must address CA's claim that the district court erred by relying too heavily on the court appointed expert's "personal opinions on the factual and legal issues before the court."

(1) *Use of Expert Evidence in Determining Substantial Similarity Between Computer Programs*

Pursuant to Fed. R. Evid. 706, and with the consent of both Altai and CA, Judge Pratt appointed and relied upon Dr. Randall Davis of the Massachusetts Institute of Technology as the court's own expert witness on the issue of substantial similarity. Dr. Davis submitted a comprehensive written report that analyzed the various aspects of the computer programs at issue and evaluated the parties' expert evidence. At trial, Dr. Davis was extensively cross-examined by both CA and Altai.

The well-established general rule in this circuit has been to limit the use of expert opinion in determining whether works at issue are substantially similar. As a threshold matter, expert testimony may be used to assist the fact finder in ascertaining whether the defendant had copied any part of the plaintiff's work. . . . To this end, "the two works are to be compared in their entirety . . . [and] in making such comparison resort may properly be made to expert analysis . . ." 3 Nimmer § 13.03[E][2], at 13-62.16.

However, once some amount of copying has been established, it remains solely for the trier of fact to determine whether the copying was "illicit," that is to say, whether the "defendant took from plaintiff's works so much of what is pleasing to [lay observers] who comprise the audience for whom such [works are] composed, that defendant wrongfully appropriated something which belongs to the plaintiff." [*Arnstein v. Porter*, 154 F.2d 464, 473 (2d Cir. 1946).] Since the test for illicit copying is based upon the response of ordinary lay observers, expert testimony is thus "irrelevant" and not permitted. *Id.* at 468, 473. We have subsequently described this method of inquiry as "merely an alternative way of formulating the issue of substantial similarity." *Ideal Toy Corp. v. Fab-Lu Ltd.*, 360 F.2d 1021, 1023 n.2 (2d Cir. 1966).

. . . *Arnstein*'s ordinary observer standard . . . may well have served its purpose when the material under scrutiny was limited to art forms readily comprehensible and generally familiar to the average lay person. However, in considering the extension of the rule to the present case, we are reminded of Holmes' admonition that, "[t]he life of the law has not been logic: it has been experience." O.W. Holmes, Jr., The Common Law 1 (1881).

. . . [In] deciding the limits to which expert opinion may be employed in ascertaining the substantial similarity of computer programs, we cannot disregard the highly complicated and technical subject matter at the heart of these claims. Rather, we recognize the reality that computer programs are likely to be somewhat impenetrable by lay observers — whether they be judges or juries — and, thus, seem to fall outside the category of works contemplated by those who engineered the *Arnstein* test. *Cf. Dawson v. Hinshaw Music Inc.*, 905 F.2d 731, 737 (4th Cir. 1990) ("departure from the lay characterization is warranted only where the intended audience possesses 'specialized expertise' "). As Judge Pratt correctly observed:

> In the context of computer programs, many of the familiar tests of similarity prove to be inadequate, for they were developed historically in the context of artistic and literary, rather than utilitarian, works.

775 F. Supp. at 558.

In making its finding on substantial similarity with respect to computer programs, we believe that the trier of fact need not be limited by the strictures of its own lay perspective. . . . Rather, we leave it to the discretion of the district court to decide to what extent, if any, expert opinion, regarding the highly technical nature of computer programs, is warranted in a given case. . . .

In this case, Dr. Davis' opinion was instrumental in dismantling the intricacies of computer science so that the court could formulate and apply an appropriate rule of law. While Dr. Davis' report and testimony undoubtedly shed valuable light on the subject matter of the litigation, Judge Pratt remained, in the final analysis, the trier of fact. The district court's use of the expert's assistance, in the context of this case, was entirely appropriate.

(2) *Evidentiary Analysis*

The district court had to determine whether Altai's OSCAR 3.5 program was substantially similar to CA's ADAPTER. We note that Judge Pratt's method of analysis effectively served as a road map for our own, with one exception: Judge Pratt filtered out the non-copyrightable aspects of OSCAR 3.5 rather than those found in ADAPTER, the allegedly infringed program. We think that our approach — *i.e.*, filtering out the unprotected aspects of an allegedly infringed program and then comparing the end product to the structure of the suspect program — is preferable, and therefore believe that district courts should proceed in this manner in future cases. . . .

The fact that the district court's analysis proceeded in the reverse order, however, had no material impact on the outcome of this case. Since Judge Pratt determined that OSCAR effectively contained no protectible expression whatsoever, the most serious charge that can be leveled against him is that he was overly thorough in his examination. The district court took the first step in the analysis set forth in this opinion when it separated the program by levels of abstraction. The district court stated:

> As applied to computer software programs, this abstractions test would progress in order of "increasing generality" from object code, to source code, to parameter lists, to services required, to general outline. In discussing the particular similarities, therefore, we shall focus on these levels.

775 F. Supp. at 560. While the facts of a different case might require that a district court draw a more particularized blueprint of a program's overall structure, this description is a workable one for the case at hand.

Moving to the district court's evaluation of OSCAR 3.5's structural components, we agree with Judge Pratt's systematic exclusion of non-protectible expression. With respect to code, the district court observed that after the rewrite of OSCAR 3.4 to OSCAR 3.5, "there remained virtually no lines of code that were identical to ADAPTER." Accordingly, the court found that the code "present[ed] no similarity at all."

Next, Judge Pratt addressed the issue of similarity between the two programs' parameter lists and macros. He concluded that, viewing the conflicting evidence most favorably to CA, it demonstrated that "only a few of the lists and macros were similar to protected elements in ADAPTER; the others were either in the public domain or dictated by the functional demands of the program." As discussed above, functional elements and elements taken from the public domain do not qualify for copyright protection. With respect to the few remaining parameter lists and macros, the district court could reasonably conclude that they did not warrant a finding of infringement given their relative contribution to the overall program. . . . In any event, the district court reasonably found that, for lack of persuasive evidence, CA failed to meet its burden of proof on whether the macros and parameter lists at issue were substantially similar.

The district court also found that the overlap exhibited between the list of services required for both ADAPTER and OSCAR 3.5 was "determined by the demands of the operating system and of the applications program to which it [was] to be linked through ADAPTER or OSCAR. . . ." In other words, this aspect of the program's structure was dictated by the nature of other programs with which it was designed to interact and, thus, is not protected by copyright.

Finally, in his infringement analysis, Judge Pratt accorded no weight to the similarities between the two programs' organizational charts, "because [the charts were] so simple and obvious to anyone exposed to the operation of the program[s]." CA argues that the district court's action in this regard "is not consistent with copyright law" — that "obvious" expression is protected, and that the district court erroneously failed to realize this. However, to say that elements of a work are "obvious," in the manner in which the district court used the word, is to say that they "follow naturally from the work's theme rather than from the author's creativity." 3 Nimmer § 13.03 [F][3], at 13-65. This is but one formulation of the *scènes à faire* doctrine, which we have already endorsed as a means of weeding out unprotectible expression.

CA argues, at some length, that many of the district court's factual conclusions regarding the creative nature of its program's components are simply wrong. Of course, we are limited in our review of factual findings to setting aside only those that we determine are clearly erroneous. *See* Fed. R. Civ. P. 52. Upon a thorough review of the voluminous record in this case, which is comprised of conflicting testimony and other highly technical evidence, we discern no error on the part of Judge Pratt, let alone clear error. . . .

CONCLUSION

In adopting the above three-step analysis for substantial similarity between the non-literal elements of computer programs, we seek to insure two things: (1) that programmers may receive appropriate copyright protection for innovative utilitarian works containing expression; and (2) that non-protectible technical expression remains in the public domain for others to use freely as building blocks in their own work. At first blush, it may seem counter-intuitive that someone who has benefitted to some degree from illicitly obtained material can emerge from an infringement suit relatively unscathed. However, so long as the appropriated material consists of non-protectible expression, "[t]his result is neither unfair nor unfortunate. It is the means by which copyright advances the progress of science and art." *Feist*, 499 U.S. at 350.

NOTES AND QUESTIONS

Software Infringement: the Ascendance of Altai

(1)   The cases in this chapter help to illustrate that there are many ways to infringe the copyright in traditional copyrighted works without copying them word-for-word and in their entirety. With respect to traditional literary works, infringement may occur, for example, by copying of protected matter that rises to the level of either "verbatim" or "pattern" similarity.

As we saw in § 3.01, however, software programs have very distinctive differences from traditional copyrighted works, including the other "literary works" with which the 1976 Act groups them. Arguably, the result should be that computer programs are *not* treated like other types of works for purposes of infringement analysis. Specifically, the exclusive rights of their copyright owners might be deemed to apply only in cases of slavish literal copying (and perhaps translation from one computer language to another), rather than in cases involving freer, less faithful sorts of adaptation. Such a regime would, in some respects, resemble the limited protection given to sound recordings.

(2)   *The* Whelan *misadventure.* Whatever the merits of such analyses, however, they initially fared poorly in what we referred to in Chapter 3 as the "second generation" software cases. The prime example, cited in *Altai*, is *Whelan Associates, Inc. v. Jaslow Dental Laboratory, Inc.*, 797 F.2d 1222 (3d Cir. 1986). There, the principal of the plaintiff company (herself a computer expert) had worked closely with defendants (data-processing neophytes engaged in running a dental laboratory) to develop a specialized business management program, under a contract calling for profit-sharing. When the defendants decided to "go it alone," marketing a program designed to perform the same specialized functions, they terminated the contract, and the plaintiff sued. Reviewing these facts, it is difficult to escape the feeling that, whether legally relevant or not, defendants had enjoyed something of a "free ride."

Against this background, the Third Circuit faced a clear problem. At the level of literal code, the plaintiff's and defendants' programs were by no means identical. To find for the plaintiff, then, required the court to articulate a standard that would afford legal weight to the similarities which *did* exist between the programs. As identified at trial by expert witnesses, these included similarities as to "file structure," "screen outputs," and certain "subroutines" used in the programming, as well as "overall structural similarities" (a.k.a. "structure, sequence, and organization").

In considering and rejecting a number of defenses — in particular, the argument that a program's structure was so integrally related to its unprotected "idea" that the former could not be protected without permitting indirect monopolization of the latter — the *Whelan* court relied on the premise that "copyright principles derived from other areas are applicable in the field of computer programs." Not surprisingly, because the Copyright Act categorizes computer programs as literary works, the court felt free to draw upon decisions involving protection for the plots of literary works. More controversially, it also relied on decisions finding infringement of one audiovisual work by another where the two display the same "total concept and feel."

The result suggested by *Whelan*'s language was that, far from being *less* extensive, the scope of copyright protection for computer programs might actually *exceed* that afforded to traditional literary works, which are not protected insofar as their atmosphere and style — or the overall impression they create in readers' minds — are concerned.

Likewise vulnerable to criticism was the reasoning employed by the *Whelan* court to demonstrate that the defendant had copied protected "expression" that was independent of the unprotected "idea" of plaintiffs' program: "[T]he idea is the efficient organization of a dental laboratory. . . . Because there are a variety of program structures through which that idea can be expressed, the structure is not a necessary incident to the idea." Obviously, the unexamined first premise of this syllogism more or less determined the result.

(3) *The* Altai *course correction.* Most of what we have just discussed was swept away by the tide of case law released by the Second Circuit's decision in *Altai. Altai* announced both standards and procedures for assessing "substantial similarity" in software infringement cases which could hardly mark a more dramatic departure from the line taken in *Whelan.* The essence of that departure is captured in the Second Circuit's comment that "[w]e think that *Whelan*'s approach to separating idea from expression in computer programs relies too heavily on metaphysical distinctions and does not place enough emphasis on practical considerations."

Obviously, the decision in *Altai* was informed by the Supreme Court's rejection of the "sweat of the brow" theory of copyright protection in *Feist v. Rural Telephone*, which you studied in § 3.02 on compilations. But the Second Circuit's opinion also reflected considerable skepticism about the *appropriateness* of copyright protection for computer software: "[W]e think that copyright . . . is not ideally suited to deal with the highly dynamic technology of computer science." Perhaps as a result, the court, while it ultimately took copyright protection for software as a statutory given, also took very seriously the notion that copyright principles which limit the scope of protection for certain works — such as the "merger" and *scènes à faire* doctrines — should be applied to software. As a result, *Altai* imposed its now-famous three-step procedure for evaluating claims of substantial similarity in such cases: The plaintiff's work is first put through processes of "abstraction" and "filtration," designed to "sift out all elements of the allegedly infringed program which are 'ideas' or are dictated by efficiency or external factors, or taken from the public domain"; then, and only *if* "there [remains] a core of copyrighted material," this "golden nugget" is put through the final process of "comparison" with the allegedly infringing work.

Altai provides a "new paradigm" for thinking about the troublesome question of software copyright infringement. Clearly, the *Altai* "three-step" has largely supplanted the more amorphous "structure, sequence, and organization" analysis of *Whelan* as the courts' preferred method of analysis. Turnabout being fair play, however, it seems fair to ask: How useful — in practical terms — is the method of analysis which *Altai* prescribes?

(4) Take, for example, the first step: "abstraction." For Judge Pratt, in the District Court, this exercise posed little difficulty, because he had already concluded that the OSCAR 3.5 program contained little or no protectible expression. But how difficult would the "abstraction" exercise be in a case where something actually depended upon it? Is the District Court's proposed description of the levels of abstraction in terms of increasing generality — "from object code, to source code, to parameter lists, to services required, to general outline" — a reliable approach? Or do some of these terms describe functional elements of a program rather than levels of abstraction? Would you expect that computer programmers would agree on a generic description of software in terms of levels of abstraction? And if they couldn't agree, how successful might we expect courts to be in developing a consistent, coherent approach to the issue?

(5) If "abstraction" poses problems, so does "filtration." As we know, the application of the "merger" doctrine, especially in the domain of computer software, is controversial in itself. What, exactly, does it mean to say that program features dictated by "efficiency" should be "filtered out"? Many programmers would claim that all programs strive toward efficiency, but that the goal can be defined in a number of different ways: A program may be efficient because it runs quickly, for example, or because it uses the fewest system resources; but these two forms of efficiency are likely to be incompatible. What kinds of efficiency should count?

Similarly, we might ask how broadly (or narrowly) the decision's command to filter out "elements dictated by external factors" should be taken. Just how far can a programmer go in borrowing what might otherwise be protected material from an existing program in the interests of "compatibility"? Suppose a programmer desires to create an application that will run in the Microsoft "Windows" operating environment. Does *Altai* mean that that programmer is free to borrow as much code from the Windows program itself as is required to achieve that result? *See Dun & Bradstreet Software Services, Inc. v. Grace Consulting, Inc.*, 307 F.3d 197 (3d Cir. 2002) (rejecting argument that interoperability required copying certain command codes). And what is the significance of the court's reference to "widely accepted programming practices within the computer industry" — *de facto* standards, in effect? Does it mean that if the owner of a program licenses routines from it often enough, to enough other programmers, it may lose its proprietary interest in that material? Would such a rule penalize success? If so, would such a penalty be acceptable? And more generally, what do the references in the opinion to the *scènes à faire* doctrine add to our understanding of "elements dictated by external factors"?

(6) Once "filtration" is complete, what is left to be employed in "comparison" with the defendant's work? Will the plaintiff's work more closely resemble a "golden nugget" — or a piece of Swiss cheese? And is anything likely to have been lost along the way? *Altai* insists that public domain elements of programs should be "filtered out" of the analysis. Ultimately, however, all copyrightable works, in all media, are simply combinations of public domain elements (be they individual words, or musical notes, or simple shapes). That brings us back to the question addressed (however rashly) in *Whelan*: the availability of protection for "non-literal program structure" (that is, the ways in which the public domain components are arranged and sequenced to create the work). The Second Circuit's opinion is sufficiently

candid to admit that "the exact contours of copyright protection for non-literal program structure are not completely clear," while suggesting that, because of the "highly functional, utilitarian" character of programs, they should not receive as much protection for "non-literal structure" as do other kinds of copyrightable works. There is no "level of abstraction" in the *Altai* list, however, that corresponds neatly with those aspects of computer software which might be analogized to the *protectible elements of compilations*. So what's the solution?

Consider *Softel, Inc. v. Dragon Medical & Scientific Communications, Inc.*, 118 F.3d 955 (2d Cir. 1997), in which the plaintiff claimed protection for four "design elements" of a computer program: "(1) an external file structure, (2) English language commands, (3) functional modules, specifically including those to operate the hardware, and (4) a hierarchical series of menus with a touchscreen." *Id.* at 966. Applying *Altai*, the District Judge had determined that (for various reasons) each of these elements was to be filtered out in the second step, leaving nothing to compare. The Court of Appeals sent the case back for further consideration of how to "apply the *Altai* test to the interrelationship among the design elements," leaving open the questions of "whether the manner in which Softel combined the various design elements in its software was protectible expression, and, if it was, whether Dragon infringed that expression." *Id.* at 967. Is there a risk that courts applying the *Altai* test to program structure in this way will recreate the *Whelan* approach by other means?

(7) At least courts that follow *Altai* have help in seeking the appropriate levels of protection for particular aspects of particular works. The methodology approved by the Second Circuit is one in which *expert testimony* plays an extensive role at all stages of the inquiry, including the ultimate inquiry into substantial similarity. Indeed, Professor Randall Davis of M.I.T., the court-appointed expert at the *Altai* trial, undoubtedly had an influence in shaping not only the court's conclusion but its mode of decision as well. What do you think of this significant deviation from the general rule that the role of experts in copyright infringement litigation should be severely limited? Is it a transitional measure, the need for which will disappear as the federal bench is enriched by more and more "computer-literate" judges? Or should this liberalized approach to the use of experts be generalized throughout copyright litigation?

(8) *Reactions to Altai. Altai* can be criticized as being overly restrictive in its vision of software copyright, as well as for doing a better job of articulating standards and procedures than of applying them. All the same, the criteria articulated in *Altai* apparently satisfied a previously unmet need. Since 1992, each circuit newly confronting the choice between the *Whelan* and *Altai* approaches has adopted the latter, in one form or another. *See, e.g., Gates Rubber Co. v. Bando Chemical Indus., Ltd.*, 9 F.3d 823 (10th Cir. 1993); *Apple Computer, Inc. v. Microsoft Corp.*, 35 F.3d 1435 (9th Cir. 1994) (similar standard "differently articulated"); *Engineering Dynamics, Inc., v. Structural Software, Inc.*, 26 F.3d 1335 (5th Cir. 1994); *MiTek Holdings, Inc. v. Arce Engineering Co.*, 89 F.3d 1548 (11th Cir. 1996); *Mitel, Inc. v. Iqtel, Inc.*, 124 F.3d 1366 (10th Cir. 1997); *Computer Mgmt. Assistance Co. v. Robert F. DeCastro, Inc.*, 220 F.3d 396 (5th Cir. 2000); and *General Universal Sys., Inc. v. Lee*, 379 F.3d 131 (5th Cir. 2004); *cf. R.C. Olmstead, Inc. v. CU Interface, LLC*, 606 F.3d 262 (6th Cir. 2010) ("All of the evidence offered

by Olmstead clearly lacks the abstraction and filtration elements."). Only the Third Circuit stubbornly clings to *Whelan*, rejecting an argument based on *Altai* that interoperability justifies a certain amount of copying. *See Dun & Bradstreet Software Services, Inc. v. Grace Consulting, Inc.*, 307 F.3d 197 (3d Cir. 2002).

(9) For a careful and thoughtful application of *Altai's* three-part test, see *Oracle America, Inc. v. Google, Inc.*, 103 U.S.P.Q.2d (BNA) 1023 (N.D. Cal. 2012). Oracle's predecessor, Sun Microsystems, developed the Java programming language and invited all comers to use it. Sun also developed and licensed an "Application Programming Interface" (or API) that consisted of 166 software packages, divided into more than 600 program classes and subdivided into more than 6,000 subroutines, or methods. The purpose of the API is to provide a "library" of pre-written programs to execute simple tasks that a programmer can use in writing more complex programs. In developing the Android software platform, Google wrote its own code to perform the same functions, but it copied the "structure, sequence, and organization" of 37 of the software packages, including the exact names of the classes and methods contained in them.

District Judge William Alsup held that the names of the classes and methods were individually not copyrightable, and because the Java language requires that commands be written in the format "java.package.class.method()," the organization of methods into classes and packages was itself a method of operation and was also not protected. To hold otherwise, he said, would "allow anyone to copyright one version of code to carry out a system of commands and thereby bar all others from writing their own different versions to carry out all or part of the same commands." *Id.* at 1045.

(10) Although the *Altai* "abstraction-filtration-comparison" test originally was formulated in a case involving nonliteral copying, it has since been extended by some courts to encompass the copying of literal code, as well. *See, e.g., Lee*, 379 F.3d at 142; *Bateman v. Mnemonics, Inc.*, 79 F.3d 1532 (11th Cir. 1996). Other courts, however, have resisted employing *Altai*-type analysis in cases where there has been literal duplication of code. *See, e.g., Stenograph LLC v. Bossard Associates, Inc.*, 144 F.3d 96 (D.C. Cir. 1998).

Who has the better of this divergence between the Circuits? *Should* copying of literal code utilize the three-step approach?

User Interfaces

(11) Altai *and Second Generation issues.* After *Altai* ascended to its present position as the "leading case" on software infringement, questions arose about what implications its approach might have for some of the other "second generation" copyright issues previewed in § 3.01 of this book. In particular, commentators wondered about its implications for the issue of protection for computer user interfaces. Two prominent types of user interfaces that have made their way into the case law are graphical user interfaces and menu command hierarchies. A graphical user interface or GUI, such as Microsoft Windows, takes advantage of the computer's graphic abilities to make a program easier to use. A typical GUI consists of visual images, such as icons, pointers, a desktop, windows, and menus. Menu command hierarchies allow users to implement a program through a series of menu

commands (and tree structure) such as "file," "save," "print," etc. In both instances, these two forms of user interfaces may contain copyrightable subject matter (e.g., pictorial or literary), but they often are dictated to some extent by market standards and functional considerations.

(12) *Graphical user interfaces.* Between *Whelan* and *Altai*, courts had developed two approaches for trying to deal with screen displays. In one line of cases, screen displays which function as "graphical user interfaces" (or GUIs) were treated as separate works, whether or not subject to separate copyright registration, and in particular as "compilations" of terms and symbols. *See, e.g., Digital Communications Associates, Inc. v. Softklone Distributing Corp.*, 659 F. Supp. 449 (N.D. Ga. 1987); *Manufacturers Technologies, Inc. v. Cams, Inc.*, 706 F. Supp. 984 (D. Conn. 1989). In the other line of decisions, screen displays were treated as protected aspects of the computer program. Examples of this approach include *Broderbund Software, Inc. v. Unison World, Inc.*, 648 F. Supp. 1127 (N.D. Cal. 1986), and Judge Keeton's scholarly and voluminous decision in *Lotus Development Corp. v. Paperback Software Int'l*, 740 F. Supp. 37 (D. Mass. 1990).

Following *Altai*, the former approach appears to have gained the upper hand. In *Apple Computer, Inc. v. Microsoft Corp.*, 35 F.3d 1435 (9th Cir. 1994), the court held that "analytic dissection" was an appropriate method of analyzing the GUIs of two competing operating systems. The court noted that Apple had licensed certain elements of its GUI to Microsoft in settling an earlier claim of infringement, and that other elements were "filtered out" because of merger or *scènes à faire*. "Thus, any claim of infringement that Apple may have against Microsoft must rest on the copying of Apple's unique selection and arrangement of all of those features." *Id.* at 1446. "Having correctly found that almost all the similarities sprang either from the license or from basic ideas and their obvious expression, [the District Court] correctly concluded that illicit copying could occur only if the works as a whole are virtually identical." *Id.* at 1447. *See also MiTek Holdings, Inc. v. Arce Engineering Co.*, 89 F.3d 1548 (11th Cir. 1996) (analyzing user interface as a compilation and adopting the "virtually identical" standard); *Dream Games of Arizona, Inc. v. PC Onsite*, 561 F.3d 983 (9th Cir. 2009) (although individual elements of electronic bingo videogame screen displays are unprotected, jury may properly consider whether a combination of unprotected elements warrants protection); *Real View, LLC v. 20-20 Technologies, Inc.*, 683 F. Supp. 2d 147 (D. Mass. 2010) (user interface for computer-aided design (CAD) software, consisting of a gray grid bounded by horizontal and vertical tool bars, was a copyrightable compilation).

(13) *Menu command hierarchies.* The other principal user interface issue confronted by the courts in the aftermath of *Altai* concerned menu command hierarchies.

In *Lotus Development Corp. v. Borland International, Inc.*, 49 F.3d 807 (1st Cir. 1995), *aff'd by an equally divided Court*, 516 U.S. 233 (1996), Lotus, the copyright owner of the popular Lotus 1-2-3 spreadsheet software, sued Borland, which had attempted to win over Lotus 1-2-3 users to a new spreadsheet program, Quattro Pro. The underlying code that drove the two programs was different, but, in an effort to make Lotus users feel at home, Borland had copied the words and structure of Lotus's "menu command hierarchy": hundreds of commands arranged in multiple menus and submenus, within each of which particular commands could be invoked by clicking on a highlighted on-screen item or typing in the command's initial letter. This Lotus-like interface was provided by Borland to Quattro Pro users as an elective alternative to its own very different command structure.

This was not a dispute about "non-literal copying" of the structure of a copyrighted computer program. Rather, the issue was literal and exact copying of the menu command structure (but not the visual appearance) of the program's screen interface.

A Windows Version of Lotus 1-2-3

On appeal, the First Circuit held that the entire menu command structure was an uncopyrightable "method of operation": "We think that 'method of operation,' as that term is used in § 102(b), refers to the means by which a person operates something, whether it be a car, a food processor, or a computer." Thus, no infringement analysis was required in order to absolve Borland of liability. Without expressly disagreeing with the finding that Lotus had made "some expressive choices" in selecting and arranging the menu terms, the Court of Appeals held that the expression in the menus was not copyrightable because those commands provided the "means" by which users controlled and operated the program.

In so holding, the court analogized the menu commands to the buttons on a video cassette recorder, which are the " 'method of operating' the VCR." Such a method could be protected, if at all, only by a patent. The opinion also invoked the principle of program compatibility, or "interoperability." Copyright protection for the menu command structure, the court said, would prevent competing software manufacturers from offering compatible products, thus forcing software users to learn multiple interfaces and to write multiple sets of macros.

Judge Boudin, in a concurring opinion, wondered why customers of Lotus who had devised macros using 1-2-3 should remain "captives of Lotus because of an investment in learning made by the users and not by Lotus." He noted that a new menu may involve creative work, but that over time the value of the menu resides primarily in the investment of users in learning to use it. He drew an analogy to the familiar QWERTY keyboard, which "dominates the market because that is what everyone has learned to use." But rather than eliminate all protection for such menus by categorizing them as "methods of operation," Judge Boudin proposed instead what he described as a "privileged use" doctrine, under which competitors would be precluded from copying such menus without contributing something important of its own to the resulting product.

When the Supreme Court agreed to review *Lotus v. Borland*, expectations were raised that the scope of copyright in user interfaces might finally be clarified. But such hopes were dashed when the Court affirmed the First Circuit by a 4-4 vote (Justice Stevens not participating). The effect of the Court's "non-decision" is that the result stands: The opinion in *Lotus* remains as a binding precedent in the First Circuit, and a potentially influential one beyond its borders. In a subsequent case with similar facts, the Tenth Circuit declined to follow *Lotus* on this point, although ultimately it arrived at a similar conclusion, using *Altai*'s three-step abstraction-filtration-comparison approach. *See Mitel, Inc. v. Iqtel, Inc.*, 124 F.3d 1366 (10th Cir. 1997).

(14) *Videogames.* Do the principles applicable to user interfaces of operating systems and application programs apply to videogames? While complex role-playing games are more like motion pictures, some videogames consist of little more than manipulation of basic geometric shapes. Consider Tetris, in which game pieces (each consisting of four rectangles) fall from the top of the screen, while the user tries to maneuver them to fit with pieces already on the screen. In *Tetris Holding, LLC v. Xio Interactive, Inc.*, 863 F. Supp. 2d 394 (D.N.J. 2012), the court found that Xio had copied "almost all of visual look of Tetris," including the visual appearance and motion of the pieces, the dimensions of the playing field, the use of "garbage" lines and "ghost" pieces, the "preview" of the next piece, and the way the pieces change color when "locked" into place. Are any of these things "rules" of the game that should have been "filtered out"?

Altai *as the Future of Infringement Analysis Generally?*

(15) We return now to *Altai* itself, and to the interesting question of the future of infringement analysis generally. It is fair to say that the influence of the *Altai* test has been felt well beyond the original context of that decision. For example, in the Tenth Circuit (whose decision in *Gates Rubber* we discussed above), the abstraction-filtration-comparison procedure has been adopted as the general approach to substantial similarity analysis in copyright infringement litigation:

> The "abstraction-filtration-comparison" test, or the "successive filtration" test, was developed for use in the context of alleged infringement of computer software, and it is exclusively in that context that we have previously applied the test. *See, e.g., Gates Rubber*, 9 F.3d at 834-39. . . . However, we see no reason to limit the abstraction-filtration-comparison approach to cases involving computer programs.

Country Kids 'N City Slicks, Inc. v. Sheen, 77 F.3d 1280, 1285 n.5 (10th Cir. 1996) (dolls); *see also Fisher v. United Feature Syndicate, Inc.*, 37 F. Supp. 2d 1213 (D. Colo. 1999), *aff'd mem.*, 203 F.3d 834 (10th Cir. 2000) (cartoon dogs). *But see*

Jacobsen v. Deseret Book Co., 287 F.3d 936 (10th Cir. 2002) (noting that "[w]hile abstraction-filtration-comparison analysis is useful in a variety of copyright cases, not every case requires extensive analysis").

Indeed, one leading treatise has urged that *Altai*-style analysis be employed by courts across the board, in place of the "audience" test, in the wake of *Feist v. Rural Telephone* (reproduced in § 3.02):

> [The *Feist* Court] defined the essential element of an infringement claim . . . as follows: "copying of constituent elements of the work that are original." That definition purports to apply across the board, not merely to the type of factual compilation at issue in *Feist*. . . .

> [T]here was no hint that the Court deemed relevant the effect "upon the public," any "spontaneous and immediate" impression, or reactions reached "without any aid or suggestion or critical analysis." Indeed, to focus on the precise scope of defendant's admitted copying and to detail how said copying was limited to unprotected expression, it would seem that critical analysis is essential. The Court's approach in *Feist*, on the facts there presented, is therefore inhospitable to an unadorned audience test.

> . . . [While] the courts can contort and distend the audience test such that it will not fall directly afoul of *Feist* [,] . . . the mere fact that the exercise is possible hardly proves it to be desirable. . . .

> But what to offer in its stead? . . . "[S]uccessive filtering[,]" the method [employed in *Altai*,] is sound and has been applied, at least *sub silentio*, by courts in a variety of contexts. In the wake of *Feist*, it should be considered not only for factual compilations and computer programs, but across the gamut of copyright law. . . . The result[s] of that test may or may not match the outcomes of the various cases applying the so-called audience test and its innumerable variants.

4 NIMMER ON COPYRIGHT § 13.03[E][1][b] (2012) (footnotes omitted).

Is this the wave of the future? Do *Altai* and its progeny, and the Nimmer proposal above, allay any concerns you may previously have harbored that protecting software under copyright might have been a mistake? Or do they reinforce them?

(16) It is worth noting also that the emphasis on "filtration" of unprotected material in *Altai* bears more than a passing resemblance to the "subtractive" approach described earlier, at least in its attention to "fragmented literal" or "verbatim" similarity. Thus, even if *Altai* does not replace the "audience" test as a general matter, it undoubtedly has contributed to a revival of a rigorous "analytic dissection" approach in other cases. *See, e.g., Kohus v. Mariol*, 328 F.3d 848 (6th Cir. 2003) (adopting a modified version of the *Altai* test as a general infringement standard); *Trek Leasing, Inc. v. United States*, 66 Fed. Cl. 8 (2005) (adopting same approach for architectural works).

Despite this revival, however, the "totality" approach — which arguably, when properly deployed, corresponds to the "comprehensive non-literal" or "pattern" aspects of the subtractive approach — continues to influence courts in infringement cases. As an example, we offer one more Second Circuit case for your consideration before moving on to other matters.

TUFENKIAN IMPORT/EXPORT VENTURES INC. v. EINSTEIN MOOMJY, INC.

United States Court of Appeals, Second Circuit
338 F.3d 127 (2003)

CALABRESI, CIRCUIT JUDGE

This copyright infringement case involves two textile designs, each of which combines, with modifications, the "primary border" and the "half field" of two unrelated public domain carpets, one a classical Indian Agra and the other a Persian antique. . . . The district court found no infringement, concluding as a matter of law that whatever substantial similarity there may be emerges from unprotected public domain materials in the allegedly infringed design. We disagree.

Floral Heriz

BACKGROUND

In March 1995, James Tufenkian, a designer and manufacturer of Tibetan style carpets, filed a copyright registration for the "Floral Heriz" ("Heriz") carpet design that is the subject of this lawsuit. He had composed the Heriz two years earlier by scanning into his computer two public domain images, one of the "Battilossi" carpet (a Persian antique), the other of the "Blau" carpet (an Indian Agra, designed by Dorris Blau). The field of the Battilossi rug is a dense, bilateral symmetrical design of stylized branching-vine, leaf and flower motifs. Tufenkian selected roughly the central third of the upper half of this Battilossi field. From this dense pattern, he culled out a number of motifs. He then stretched the field slightly in one direction and used the thus modified design as the entire field of the Heriz. In the process, Tufenkian created an asymmetrical pattern, for he used only an off-center portion of what had been a symmetrical design. From the Blau, he took the principal border, which, with modifications, became the major border of the Heriz. Finally, he added two minor borders of his own creation. . . .

Bromley

Tufenkian describes his principal creative contributions as: (1) combining two unrelated rug styles; (2) designing and adding the minor borders; (3) selectively removing entire design motifs from the Battilossi so as to create a more 'open' aesthetic from those remaining; (4) converting the symmetrical Battilossi image into a design "with no central focus" (by copying from only half of the Battilossi field); and (5) elongating the Battilossi pattern.

Sometime in 1995, Appellee Bashian retained Appellee Nichols-Marcy, who had worked for Tufenkian, to oversee the designing of the "Bromley 514" ("Bromley").

Nichols-Marcy and his Nepalese contractors began work on the Bromley in early 1996, two years after the Heriz was first marketed. These designers were familiar with the Heriz, and the appellees do not challenge the district court's determination that some copying of the Heriz actually occurred.

Nonetheless, the appellees contend that the Heriz's extensive use of designs taken from the public domain combined with the Bromley's distinctiveness precludes a finding of infringement. In the latter regard, they point to the following as instances of their own creative work that distinguishes the Bromley from the Heriz: (1) addition of a second "beetle" (or "flower") element to the field, placed in a roughly symmetrical position to an existing "beetle" shape so as to give the Bromley a more balanced feel than the Heriz; (2) retention of a "leaf shape" from the Battilossi that Tufenkian did not include in the Heriz; (3) removal of a vine-like line segment from the Battilossi that Tufenkian had retained; and (4) greater modification of the Blau border design, with different shapes at different angles.

In November 1999, Tufenkian initiated this lawsuit, claiming copyright infringement and seeking various injunctive and monetary remedies. . . . [The district court granted summary judgment to Bashian, holding that the Bromley was not substantially similar to protected expression in the Heriz.]

The district court evaluated infringement by comparing the two designs' "total concept and feel" (or "overall aesthetic"). In so doing the court applied what we have called the "more discerning observer" test, . . . a test intended to emphasize that substantial similarity must exist between the defendant's allegedly infringing design and the *protectible* elements in the plaintiff's design. . . . [The district court gave special attention to public domain elements incorporated into Floral Heriz, factoring out those elements from the substantial similarity comparison. Having identified the plaintiff's and the defendants' original contributions, the district court concluded that there was no infringement.]

DISCUSSION

I.

. . .

B. The Test for Copyright Infringement

"Copyright infringement is established when the owner of a valid copyright demonstrates unauthorized copying." *Castle Rock Entm't, Inc. v. Carol Publ'g Group, Inc.*, 150 F.3d 132, 137-38 (2d Cir. 1998). To demonstrate unauthorized copying, the plaintiff must first "show that his work was actually copied"; second, he must establish "substantial similarity" or that "the copying amounts to an improper or unlawful appropriation," i.e., (i) that it was protected expression in the earlier work that was copied and (ii) that the amount that was copied is "more than de minimis." . . .

C. The Scope of Copyright Protection: Original Expression

. . . It is universally true . . . that even works which express enough originality to be protected [under *Feist*] also contain material that is not original, and hence that may be freely used by other designers. This is not simply an artifact of some rather lenient caselaw on the originality requirement. . . . The principle is more fundamental: all creative works draw on the common wellspring that is the public domain.

In this pool are not only elemental "raw materials," like colors, letters, descriptive facts, and the catalogue of standard geometric forms, but also earlier works of art that, due to the passage of time or for other reasons, are no longer copyright protected. Thus the public domain includes, for example, both the generic shape of the letter "L" and all of the elaborately more specific "L's" from the hundreds of years of font designs that have fallen into the public domain. . . .

D. Conundrums of Infringement by Inexact Copies

It has long been settled that "no plagiarist can excuse the wrong by showing how much of his work he did not pirate," *Sheldon v. Metro-Goldwyn Pictures Corp.*, 81 F.2d 49, 56 (2d Cir. 1936) (Hand, *J.*), and this aphorism applies equally to exact reproduction of visual works. As a result, a would-be appropriator who wishes to test the limits of copyright law gains nothing from "adding on" to what she has precisely reproduced. But she might prevail insofar as her work transforms the copied expression into a design that in some respects resembles the original, yet does not actually excerpt ("cut and paste") a more-than-de-minimis protected portion of the original. Such designs may be termed "inexact copies," in recognition of the fact that they alter the prior image yet mimic its structure in some fashion.[5] Jurists have long been vexed by the task of precisely identifying that which separates inexact copies that infringe from those that do not.

In recent years we have often found it productive to assess claims of inexact-copy infringement by comparing the contested design's "total concept and overall feel" with that of the allegedly infringed work. Because this was the method used by the district court, and because the appellant sharply disputes the district court's "total concept and feel" analysis, a few remarks on the history and application of this test are in order.

Our circuit first employed the "total feel" nomenclature in a case involving children's books. *See Reyher v. Children's Television Workshop*, 533 F.2d 87, 91-92 (2d Cir. 1976). *Reyher* characterized this Court's previous treatment of inexact copying of books, movies, and plays as concerned with the "the 'pattern' of the work[, i.e.,] the sequence of events and the development of the interplay of characters." *Id.* at 91. . . . But the children's books at issue in *Reyher* were

---

[5] Our intention in using the term "inexact copies" is to describe a manner of visual copying analogous to the textual copying that is described in Nimmer as "non-literal." Melville B. Nimmer & David Nimmer, 4 Nimmer on Copyright § 13.03[A][1] (2003). We recognize, of course, that these designs may feature much that is new, in addition to whatever may be said to be original in the "inexact copy." Terming such a design an "inexact copy" is simply a means of drawing attention to the portion of the design that is relevant to a charge of infringement.

"necessarily less complex" than the works we had previously submitted to "pattern" analysis, and, moreover, the sequence of events in the plaintiff's book consisted of little more than "*scènes à faire*" attendant to an underlying idea that was shared with the defendant's work. In all respects other than the sequence of events, the works were very different . . .

Some commentators have worried that the "total concept and feel" standard may "invite[ ] an abdication of analysis," because "feel" can seem a "wholly amorphous referent." Melville B. Nimmer & David Nimmer, 4 Nimmer on Copyright § 13.03[A][1][c] (2003). Likewise, one may wonder whether a copyright doctrine whose aspiration is to protect a work's "concept" could end up erroneously protecting "ideas." But our caselaw is not so incautious. Where we have described possible infringement in terms of whether two designs have or do not have a substantially similar "total concept and feel," we generally have taken care to identify precisely the particular aesthetic decisions — original to the plaintiff and copied by the defendant — that might be thought to make the designs similar . . .

Essentially, the total-concept-and-feel locution functions as a reminder that, while the infringement analysis must *begin* by dissecting the copyrighted work into its component parts in order to clarify precisely what is not original, infringement analysis is not *simply* a matter of ascertaining similarity between components viewed in isolation. For the defendant may infringe on the plaintiff's work not only through literal copying of a portion of it, but also by parroting properties that are apparent only when numerous aesthetic decisions embodied in the plaintiff's work of art — the excerpting, modifying, and arranging of public domain compositions, if any, together with the development and representation of wholly new motifs and the use of texture and color, etc. — are considered in relation to one another. The court, confronted with an allegedly infringing work, must analyze the two works closely to figure out in what respects, if any, they are similar, and then determine whether these similarities are due to protected aesthetic expressions original to the allegedly infringed work, or whether the similarity is to something in the original that is free for the taking.

II.

The appellant charges that, in comparing the two designs' total concept and feel, the district court improperly factored out public domain elements from the Heriz and the Bromley. As the above discussion of doctrine indicates, however, the court was surely correct to factor such elements out. For copying is not unlawful if what was copied from the allegedly infringed work was not protected, for example, if the copied material had itself been taken from the public domain. This principle applies, moreover, whether the copied, unprotected expression at issue is a selection, coordination, or arrangement of elements, or whether it is the exact design itself.

But in its comparison of the two rugs, the district court failed to consider — apart from total concept and feel — whether *material portions* of the Bromley infringed on corresponding parts of the Heriz. Here the court erred. . . .

What makes this case perplexing is that, to the judicial observer who has a passing familiarity with carpet design, many of the plaintiff's expressive choices may seem to be rather mechanical or conventional acts, which might be deemed to be either non-original or else so weakly original that their copying would appropriate no more than a de minimis amount of protected expression. . . .

Whether the Bromley infringes on the Heriz, however, need not depend on variation between the primary borders, or on a determination of the extent to which various features of the Heriz design are conventions. There is one substantial respect in which the creator of the Heriz made distinctly idiosyncratic and particular design decisions — decisions whose effect permeates the entire field of the Heriz — and in this respect the Bromley is a virtually exact copy of the Heriz. The plaintiff not only cropped and elongated the Battillossi half-field, he also *selectively eliminated* numerous design motifs, creating a more open, less busy aesthetic.

Of course, mere simplification of an ornate public domain carpet into a mass market knock-off may not be protectible. But the plaintiff's half-field modification was not a uniform or homogeneous simplification akin to removing all serifs from a font, blurring the petals on all flowers, or eliminating every third leaf on a stem. Rather, the plaintiff seems to have engaged in a selective and particularized culling of a leaf here, a complex of leaves and flowers there, and so forth. And close visual inspection of the two rugs confirms that the Bromley precisely mimics the Heriz in nearly all of these choices.

This non-mechanical adaptation of individually unprotectible elements from the public domain is precisely the type of "original selection" that the Supreme Court indicated was protectible expression in *Feist*. . . . The Court cautioned, however, that the protection given is "thin, because the scope of the copyright is limited to the particular selection or arrangement," and a "subsequent [author] remains free to use [the public domain elements] to aid in preparing a competing work, so long as the competing work does not feature the same selection and arrangement." 499 U.S. at 349-51.

We conclude that this is one of those relatively unusual cases in which the infringing work has copied the original and "particular" or "same" selections embodied in the allegedly infringed upon work. The number of motifs present (or absent) in the Bromley field which mirror those the Heriz selected (or deleted) in an original way from the Battilossi is overwhelming. And the structural layout of these elements is essentially the same in both designs. . . .

III.

For the for[e]going reasons, we hold that the Bromley is substantially similar to the Heriz. We therefore VACATE the judgment of the district court and REMAND for further proceedings.

NOTES AND QUESTIONS

(1) *Tufenkian* provides another example of the difficulties of determining improper appropriation where the allegedly copyrightable components of the plaintiff's work involve decisions about selecting, excerpting, modifying, and

arranging preexisting matter that would not individually constitute original expression. The court reminds us that infringement analysis must begin by dissecting the work into component parts to determine what constitutes original authorship, but that infringement analysis is more than evaluating those components in isolation. From *Tufenkian*, we see that "total concept and feel" need not be a boundless inquiry informed by visceral reactions. *Tufenkian* involves rug designs, which typically rearrange public domain materials. But other varieties of copyrighted works also involve selecting and arranging from the public domain. Clearly, architectural works are good examples that would lend themselves to the *Tufenkian* court's methodology. Can you think of any other examples?

(2)   According to the Second Circuit, the District Court was correct in factoring out any public domain elements when considering substantial similarity but erred in failing to consider "whether *material portions* of the Bromley infringed on corresponding parts of the Heriz." Can you specify which aspects of the rugs constitute the "material portions" referred to by Judge Calabresi?

(3)   *Tufenkian*, with its modest reintroduction of "total concept and feel" analysis, provides a good place to review the various Second Circuit cases that have tackled the question of improper appropriation. Can the approaches in *Nichols, Peter Pan, Laureyssens, Altai,* and *Tufenkian* be reconciled? Obviously, the *Tufenkian* court is not buying into the Nimmer "successive filtration" proposal that would generalize abstraction-filtration-comparison to all infringement actions, which also would have involved tossing out the "more discerning observer" baby with the audience test bathwater. But then, abstraction-filtration-comparison (perhaps improperly overlooking any compilation aspects of the plaintiff's work) *was* the analytical methodology employed in *Altai* (cited in a footnote in *Tufenkian*) a decade earlier. What gives here? Does the methodology appropriate in a particular case still depend, in the Second Circuit, on the category of the work involved? The procedural setting of the case?

(4)   *The role of summary judgment.* In addition to its method of determining improper appropriation, *Tufenkian* illustrates the changing role of summary judgment in copyright infringement litigation. Much has changed since *Arnstein v. Porter*, where Judge Jerome Frank stated that summary judgment should be granted in copyright cases only in the face of outlandish claims as to which there is not the "slightest doubt about the facts." 154 F.2d at 468. As we have just seen, however, courts these days often decline to follow *Arnstein* in this matter; and, although summary judgment in favor of copyright plaintiffs remains highly unusual, grants of summary judgment for defendants are relatively commonplace, if far from routine. *See, e.g., Johnson v. Gordon*, 409 F.3d 12 (1st Cir. 2005); *Stromback v. New Line Cinema*, 384 F.3d 283 (6th Cir. 2004); *Schoolhouse, Inc. v. Anderson*, 275 F.3d 726 (8th Cir. 2002). Indeed, some courts have held that where the works in question are attached to the complaint, a court may properly determine lack of substantial similarity as a matter of law. *See Peters v. West*, 692 F.3d 629 (7th Cir. 2012); *Peter F. Gaito Architecture, LLC v. Simone Development Corp.*, 602 F.3d 57 (2d Cir. 2010).

(5)   The Circuits vary in their approach to summary judgment. As you recall, the Ninth Circuit has broken down the improper appropriation inquiry into two elements: an extrinsic test that determines "objectively" which ideas and expression

have been copied, and an intrinsic test in which the works are compared subjectively as to their overall concept and feel. That Circuit has held that only extrinsic similarity is relevant in connection with a defendant's motion for summary judgment. *Shaw v. Lindheim,* 919 F.2d 1353, 1359 (9th Cir. 1990); *Kouf v. Walt Disney Pictures & Television,* 16 F.3d 1042, 1045 (9th Cir. 1994). This version of the Ninth Circuit *Krofft* test clearly militates against summary judgment, because the original extrinsic test is an exam that relatively few plaintiffs will flunk. It is not clear, however, whether this limitation applies to works of visual art. *See Cavalier v. Random House, Inc.,* 297 F.3d 815, 826 (9th Cir. 2002). In addition, there is authority that *Krofft* "does not hold that summary judgment is always inappropriate on the issue of substantial similarity of expression if there is a substantial similarity of ideas. . . . Summary judgment is proper if reasonable minds could not differ as to the presence or absence of substantial similarity of expression." *See v. Durang,* 711 F.2d 141, 143 (9th Cir. 1983) (*per curiam*). Moreover, courts in other circuits adopting the *Krofft* analysis have held that summary judgment may be granted on intrinsic as well as extrinsic similarity. *See, e.g., Schoolhouse, Inc.,* 275 F.3d at 729; *Herzog v. Castle Rock Entertainment,* 193 F.3d 1241, 1257 (11th Cir. 1999). These developments, together with the later modifications of the *Krofft* test referenced above, open up a greater potential for successful summary judgment motions in the Ninth Circuit.

(6) In contrast to the limited role for summary judgment outlined above, the Eleventh Circuit has expressed a preference for summary judgment in cases involving compilations and other works containing both protected and unprotected elements:

> [W]hen the crucial question in a dispute . . . is substantial similarity at the level of protected expression, it is often more reliably and accurately resolved in a summary judgment proceeding. This is so because a judge is better able to separate original expression from the non-original elements of a work. . . . The judge understands the concept of the idea/expression dichotomy and how it should be applied in the context of the works before him. . . . Because a judge will more readily understand that not all copying is infringement, . . . the "substantial similarity" test is more often correctly administered by a judge rather than a jury — even one provided proper instruction.

Intervest Construction, Inc. v. Canterbury Estate Homes, Inc., 554 F.3d 914, 920 (11th Cir. 2008). Do you agree that judges are better suited to these tasks than juries? If so, what role will this leave for juries in copyright cases? Don't all works contain both protected and unprotected elements?

(7) *The standard of review.* What standard of review should the Courts of Appeal apply in reviewing District Court determinations relating to copyright infringement? The answer would seem to be straightforward. Infringement is an issue of fact (or, at worst, a "mixed" issue of fact and law), so that an appeals court should disturb a trial court decision only if it is "clearly erroneous." And, as a practical matter, the appeals court will be poorly situated to reconsider the appropriateness of findings relating to the issue of copying. Where substantial similarity is concerned, however, the works at issue form part of the record on

appeal, so the practical potential for closer appellate oversight obviously is present. As *Tufenkian* illustrates, the Second Circuit takes the position that *de novo* review of substantial similarity is appropriate on appeals from bench trials, but that, when reviewing a jury's findings, the more deferential "clearly erroneous" standard is required because of the Seventh Amendment's guarantee of a right to a jury trial. *See, e.g., Boisson v. Banian, Ltd.*, 273 F.3d 262, 272 (2d Cir. 2001); *Yurman Design, Inc. v. PAJ, Inc.*, 262 F.3d 101 (2d Cir. 2001).

(8)   Most courts outside the Second Circuit, claiming to reject *de novo* review, pledge general allegiance to the "clearly erroneous" standard. It is common to see the arguments on appeal from jury verdicts in copyright cases focus on the legal sufficiency of the court's instructions relating to substantial similarity, rather than on the determination itself. *See, e.g., Harper House, Inc. v. Thomas Nelson, Inc.*, 889 F.2d 197 (9th Cir. 1989). In other cases, however, the "clearly erroneous" standard, while still saluted, has been employed to second-guess the District Court's findings on substantial similarity, based on the appellate panel's own "side-by-side" and "ocular" comparisons. *See, e.g., Wildlife Express Corp. v. Carol Wright Sales, Inc.*, 18 F.3d 502, 506 n.1 (7th Cir. 1994); *see also Krofft*, 562 F.2d at 1167 ("It is clear to us that the defendants' works are substantially similar to plaintiffs'. . . . We would so conclude even if we were sitting as the triers of fact. There is no doubt that the findings of the jury in the case are not clearly erroneous.").

§ 8.04   EXTRATERRITORIALITY AND CONFLICTS OF LAWS

The major treaties involving intellectual property are all premised on the concept of territoriality, meaning that each nation is entitled to police the use of intellectual property within its own borders. But in an increasingly global society, works created and published in one nation are frequently exploited in other nations as well. The global nature of the Internet and other communications technologies exacerbates the problem, sometimes making it difficult even to identify where infringing conduct takes place. When conduct in one country contributes to the use of a work in another country, national courts and legislatures have to decide how far their laws will reach and which nation's laws should be applied to determine the legality of such actions. In this section, we examine to what extent U.S. law applies to alleged infringements that cross borders, and how U.S. courts decide what law applies in such cases.

[A]   Extraterritoriality

SUBAFILMS, LTD. v. MGM-PATHE COMMUNICATIONS CO.
United States Court of Appeals, Ninth Circuit
24 F.3d 1088 (1994)

D.W. NELSON, CIRCUIT JUDGE

In this case, we consider the "vexing question" of whether a claim for infringement can be brought under the Copyright Act when the assertedly infringing conduct consists solely of the authorization within the territorial boundaries of the United States of acts that occur entirely abroad. We hold that such allegations do not state a claim for relief under the copyright laws of the United States.

Factual and Procedural Background

In 1966, the musical group The Beatles, through Subafilms, Ltd., entered into a joint venture with the Hearst Corporation to produce the animated motion picture entitled "Yellow Submarine" (the "Picture"). Over the next year, Hearst, acting on behalf of the joint venture (the "Producer"), negotiated an agreement with United Artists Corporation ("UA") to distribute and finance the film. Separate distribution and financing agreements were entered into in May, 1967. Pursuant to these agreements, UA distributed the Picture in theaters beginning in 1968 and later on television.

In the early 1980s, with the advent of the home video market, UA entered into several licensing agreements to distribute a number of its films on videocassette. Although one company expressed interest in the Picture, UA refused to license "Yellow Submarine" because of uncertainty over whether home video rights had been granted by the 1967 agreements. Subsequently, in 1987, UA's successor company, MGM/UA Communications Co. ("MGM/UA"), over the Producer's objections, authorized its subsidiary, MGM/UA Home Video, Inc., to distribute the Picture for the domestic home video market, and, pursuant to an earlier licensing agreement, notified Warner Bros., Inc. ("Warner") that the Picture had been cleared for international videocassette distribution. Warner, through its wholly owned subsidiary, Warner Home Video, Inc., in turn entered into agreements with third parties for distribution of the Picture on videocassette around the world.

In 1988, Subafilms and Hearst ("Appellees") brought suit against MGM/UA, Warner, and their respective subsidiaries (collectively the "Distributors" or "Appellants"), contending that the videocassette distribution of the Picture, both foreign and domestic, constituted copyright infringement and a breach of the 1967 agreements. . . . The special master found for Appellees on both claims. . . . [T]he district court adopted all of the special master's factual findings and legal conclusions. Appellees were awarded [an injunction and] $2,228,000.00 in compensatory damages, split evenly between the foreign and domestic home video distributions. . . .

Yellow Submarine (1968)
The Everett Collection

A panel of this circuit, in an unpublished disposition, affirmed the district court's judgment on the ground that both the domestic and foreign distribution of the Picture constituted infringement under the Copyright Act. With respect to the foreign distribution of the Picture, the panel concluded that it was bound by this court's prior decision in *Peter Starr Prod. Co. v. Twin Continental Films, Inc.*, 783 F.2d 1440 (9th Cir. 1986), which it held to stand for the proposition that, although "'infringing actions that take place entirely outside the United States are not actionable' [under the Copyright Act, an] 'act of infringement within the United States' [properly is] alleged where the illegal *authorization* of international exhibitions *t[akes] place in the United States*," *Subafilms*, slip op. at 4917-18 (quoting *Peter Starr*, 783 F.2d at 1442, 1443 (emphasis in original) (alterations added)). Because the Distributors had admitted that the initial authorization to distribute the Picture internationally occurred within the United States, the panel affirmed the district court's holding with respect to liability for extraterritorial home video distribution of the Picture.

We granted Appellants' petition for rehearing *en banc* to consider whether the panel's interpretation of *Peter Starr* conflicted with our subsequent decision in *Lewis Galoob Toys, Inc. v. Nintendo of Am., Inc.*, 964 F.2d 965 (9th Cir.1992), which held that there could be no liability for authorizing a party to engage in an infringing act when the authorized "party's use of the work would not violate the

Copyright Act," *id.* at 970; *see also Columbia Pictures Indus., Inc. v. Professional Real Estate Investors, Inc.*, 866 F.2d 278, 279-81 (9th Cir. 1989) (holding that a hotel was not liable under the Copyright Act for making available videodisc players for in-room viewing), *rev'd on other grounds*, 508 U.S. 49 (1993). Because we conclude that there can be no liability under the United States copyright laws for authorizing an act that itself could not constitute infringement of rights secured by those laws, and that wholly extraterritorial acts of infringement are not cognizable under the Copyright Act, we overrule *Peter Starr* insofar as it held that allegations of an authorization within the United States of infringing acts that take place entirely abroad state a claim for infringement under the Act. Accordingly, we vacate the panel's decision in part and return the case to the panel for further proceedings.

DISCUSSION

I. The Mere Authorization of Extraterritorial Acts of Infringement Does Not State a Claim Under the Copyright Act

As the panel in this case correctly concluded, *Peter Starr* held that the authorization within the United States of entirely extraterritorial acts stated a cause of action under the "plain language" of the Copyright Act. Observing that the Copyright Act grants a copyright owner "the *exclusive rights* to do and *to authorize*" any of the activities listed in 17 U.S.C. § 106(1)–(5), and that a violation of the "authorization" right constitutes infringement under section 501 of the Act, the *Peter Starr* court reasoned that allegations of an authorization within the United States of extraterritorial conduct that corresponded to the activities listed in section 106 "allege[d] an act of infringement within the United States." . . .

The *Peter Starr* court accepted, as does this court, that the acts authorized from within the United States themselves could not have constituted infringement under the Copyright Act because "[i]n general, United States copyright laws do not have extraterritorial effect," and therefore, "infringing actions that take place entirely outside the United States are not actionable." *Peter Starr*, 783 F.2d at 1442 (citing *Robert Stigwood Group, Ltd. v. O'Reilly*, 530 F.2d 1096, 1101 (2d Cir. 1976)). The central premise of the *Peter Starr* court, then, was that a party could be held liable as an "infringer" under section 501 of the Act merely for authorizing a third party to engage in acts that, had they been committed within the United States, would have violated the exclusive rights granted to a copyright holder by section 106.

Since *Peter Starr*, however, we have recognized that, when a party authorizes an activity not proscribed by one of the five section 106 clauses, the authorizing party cannot be held liable as an infringer. In *Lewis Galoob*, we rejected the argument that "a party can unlawfully authorize another party to use a copyrighted work even if that party's use of the work would not violate the Copyright Act," *Lewis Galoob*, 964 F.2d at 970, and approved of Professor Nimmer's statement that " 'to the extent that an activity does not violate one of th[e] five enumerated rights [found in 17 U.S.C. § 106], authorizing such activity does not constitute copyright infringement,' " *id.* (quoting 3 David Nimmer & Melville B. Nimmer, NIMMER ON COPYRIGHT § 12.04[A][3][a], at 12-80 n.82 (1991)). Similarly, in *Columbia Pictures*, we held that no liability attached under the Copyright Act for providing videodisc players to hotel guests when the use of that equipment did not constitute a "public" performance within the meaning of section 106 of the Act, *see Columbia Pictures*, 866 F.2d at 279-81.

The apparent premise of *Lewis Galoob* was that the addition of the words "to authorize" in the Copyright Act was not meant to create a new form of liability for "authorization" that was divorced completely from the legal consequences of authorized conduct, but was intended to invoke the preexisting doctrine of contributory infringement. . . . We agree.

Contributory infringement under the 1909 Act developed as a form of third party liability. Accordingly, there could be no liability for contributory infringement unless the authorized or otherwise encouraged activity itself could amount to infringement. . . .

As the Supreme Court noted in [*Sony Corp. of Am. v. Universal City Studios, Inc.*, 464 U.S. 417 (1984)], and this circuit acknowledged in *Peter Starr*, under the 1909 Act courts differed over the degree of involvement required to render a party liable as a contributory infringer. . . . Viewed with this background in mind, the addition of the words "to authorize" in the 1976 Act appears best understood as merely clarifying that the Act contemplates liability for contributory infringement, and that the bare act of "authorization" can suffice. . . .

Consequently, we believe that " 'to authorize' [wa]s simply a convenient peg on which Congress chose to hang the antecedent jurisprudence of third party liability." 3 Nimmer, *supra*, § 12.04[A][3][a], at 12-84 n.81.

Although the *Peter Starr* court recognized that the addition of the authorization right in the 1976 Act "was intended to remove the confusion surrounding contributory . . . infringement," it did not consider the applicability of an essential attribute of the doctrine identified above: that contributory infringement, even when triggered solely by an "authorization," is a form of third party liability that requires the authorized acts to constitute infringing ones. We believe that the *Peter Starr* court erred in not applying this principle to the authorization of acts that cannot themselves be infringing because they take place entirely abroad. . . .

Appellees resist the force of this logic, and argue that liability in this case is appropriate because, unlike in *Lewis Galoob* and *Columbia Pictures*, in which the alleged primary infringement consisted of acts that were entirely outside the purview of 17 U.S.C. § 106(1)–(5) (and presumably lawful), the conduct authorized in this case was precisely that prohibited by section 106, and is only uncognizable because it occurred outside the United States. Moreover, they contend that the conduct authorized in this case would have been prohibited under the copyright laws of virtually every nation. . . .

Even assuming *arguendo* that the acts authorized in this case would have been illegal abroad, we do not believe the distinction offered by Appellees is a relevant one. Because the copyright laws do not apply extraterritorially, each of the rights conferred under the five section 106 categories must be read as extending "no farther than the [United States'] borders." [2 Paul Goldstein, Copyright: Principles, Law and Practice § 16.0, at 675 (1989) (hereinafter *Goldstein*)] . . . In light of our above conclusion that the "authorization" right refers to the doctrine of contributory infringement, which requires that the authorized act itself could violate one of the exclusive rights listed in section 106(1)–(5), we believe that "[i]t is simply not possible to draw a principled distinction" between an act that does not violate a copyright because it is not the type of conduct proscribed by section 106, and one that does not violate section 106 because the illicit act occurs overseas. *Danjaq, S.A. v. MGM/UA Communications, Co.*, 773 F. Supp. 194, 203 (C.D. Cal. 1991), *aff'd on other grounds*, 979 F.2d 772 (9th Cir. 1992). In both cases, the authorized conduct could not violate the exclusive rights guaranteed by section 106. In both cases, therefore, there can be no liability for "authorizing" such conduct. . . .

To hold otherwise would produce the untenable anomaly, inconsistent with the general principles of third party liability, that a party could be held liable as an infringer for violating the "authorization" right when the party that it authorized could not be considered an infringer under the Copyright Act. Put otherwise, we do not think Congress intended to hold a party liable for merely "authorizing" conduct that, had the authorizing party chosen to engage in itself, would have resulted in no liability under the Act. . . .[8]

Appellees rely heavily on the Second Circuit's doctrine that extraterritorial application of the copyright laws is permissible "when the type of infringement permits further reproduction abroad." *Update Art, Inc. v. Modiin Publishing, Ltd.*, 843 F.2d 67, 73 (2d Cir. 1988). Whatever the merits of the Second Circuit's rule, and we express no opinion on its validity in this circuit, it is premised on the theory that the copyright holder may recover damages that stem from a direct infringement of its exclusive rights that occurs within the United States. . . . [The cases supporting the Second Circuit rule] simply are inapplicable to a theory of liability based merely on the authorization of noninfringing acts.

Accordingly, accepting that wholly extraterritorial acts of infringement cannot support a claim under the Copyright Act, we believe that the *Peter Starr* court, and thus the panel in this case, erred in concluding that the mere authorization of such acts supports a claim for infringement under the Act.

II. The Extraterritoriality of the Copyright Act

Appellees additionally contend that, if liability for "authorizing" acts of infringement depends on finding that the authorized acts themselves are cognizable under the Copyright Act, this court should find that the United States copyright laws do extend to extraterritorial acts of infringement when such acts "result in adverse effects within the United States." Appellees buttress this argument with the contention that failure to apply the copyright laws extraterritorially in this case will have a disastrous effect on the American film industry, and that other remedies, such as suits in foreign jurisdictions or the application of foreign copyright laws by American courts, are not realistic alternatives.

We are not persuaded by Appellees' parade of horribles. More fundamentally, however, we are unwilling to overturn over eighty years of consistent jurisprudence

---

[8] We express no opinion on whether liability might attach when a party authorizes an act that could constitute copyright infringement, but the "attempted" infringement fails.

on the extraterritorial reach of the copyright laws without further guidance from Congress.

The Supreme Court recently reminded us that "[i]t is a long-standing principle of American law 'that legislation of Congress, unless a contrary intent appears, is meant to apply only within the territorial jurisdiction of the United States.'" *EEOC v. Arabian American Oil Co. (Aramco)*, 499 U.S. 244 (1991). . . . Because courts must "assume that Congress legislates against the backdrop of the presumption against extraterritoriality," unless "there is 'the affirmative intention of the Congress clearly expressed'" congressional enactments must be presumed to be "'primarily concerned with domestic conditions.'" *Id.*, 499 U.S. at 248. . . .

. . . There is no clear expression of congressional intent in either the 1976 Act or other relevant enactments to alter the preexisting extraterritoriality doctrine. Indeed, the *Peter Starr* court itself recognized the continuing application of the principle that "infringing actions that take place entirely outside the United States are not actionable in United States federal courts."

Furthermore, we note that Congress chose in 1976 to expand one specific "extraterritorial" application of the Act by declaring that the unauthorized importation of copyrighted works constitutes infringement even when the copies lawfully were made abroad. *See* 17 U.S.C.A. § 602(a) (West Supp. 1992). Had Congress been inclined to overturn the preexisting doctrine that infringing acts that take place wholly outside the United States are not actionable under the Copyright Act, it knew how to do so. . . .

. . . Extraterritorial application of American law would be contrary to the spirit of the Berne Convention, and might offend other member nations by effectively displacing their law in circumstances in which previously it was assumed to govern. Consequently, an extension of extraterritoriality might undermine Congress's objective of achieving "'effective and harmonious' copyright laws among all nations." *House Report* [H.R. Rep. No. 100-609], at 20. Indeed, it might well send the signal that the United States does not believe that the protection accorded by the laws of other member nations is adequate, which would undermine two other objectives of Congress in joining the convention: "strengthen[ing] the credibility of the U.S. position in trade negotiations with countries where piracy is not uncommon" and "rais[ing] the like[li]hood that other nations will enter the Convention." [S. Rep. No. 100-352, at] 4-5. . . .

Accordingly, because an extension of the extraterritorial reach of the Copyright Act by the courts would in all likelihood disrupt the international regime for protecting intellectual property that Congress so recently described as essential to furthering the goal of protecting the works of American authors abroad, . . . we conclude that the *Aramco* presumption must be applied. . . . Because the presumption has not been overcome, we reaffirm that the United States copyright laws do not reach acts of infringement that take place entirely abroad. It is for Congress, and not the courts, to take the initiative in this field. . . .

CONCLUSION

We hold that the mere authorization of acts of infringement that are not cognizable under the United States copyright laws because they occur entirely outside of the United States does not state a claim for infringement under the Copyright Act. *Peter Starr* is overruled insofar as it held to the contrary. . . . Vacated in Part and Remanded.

NOTES AND QUESTIONS

(1) Do you perceive any irony in the fact that the *Subafilms* decision was handed down at a moment of unprecedented public concern over foreign "piracy" of American copyrighted works? Doesn't this reading of § 106 "tie the hands" of American copyright owners seeking practical remedies against such "piracy"? What justification exists, at the level of copyright policy, for effectively immunizing from liability individuals and companies in the United States who abet and promote foreign "piracy"?

For a very different "take" on these issues, see *Curb v. MCA Records, Inc.*, 898 F. Supp. 586, 594-95 (M.D. Tenn. 1995) ("This interpretation, tying the authorization right solely to a claim of justiciable contributory infringement, appears contrary . . . to well-reasoned precedent, statutory text, and legislative history. . . . [P]iracy has changed since the Barbary days. Today, the raider need not grab the bounty with his own hands; he need only transmit his go-ahead by wire or telefax to start the presses in a distant land. . . . Under [the *Subafilms*] view, a phone call to Nebraska results in liability; the same phone call to France results in riches. In a global marketplace, it is literally a distinction without a difference."). *See also Expediters International of Washington, Inc. v. Direct Line Cargo Management Services, Inc.*, 995 F. Supp. 468 (D.N.J. 1998) ("*Curb* . . . appear[s] more closely adapted to our modern age of telefaxes, Internet communication, and electronic mail systems [than does *Subafilms*]").

(2) In particular, are you persuaded by the *Subafilms* court's interpretation of the legislative history of the decision to include the words "to authorize" in § 106? Again, *Curb v. MCA* has something to say about this: "A better view . . . would be to hold that domestic violation of the authorization right is an infringement, sanctionable under the Copyright Act, whenever the authorizee has committed an act that would violate the copyright owner's § 106 rights." 898 F. Supp. at 595.

The court in *Curb* also suggested in passing a way in which the question of the proper interpretation of § 106's "authorization" language might often be finessed in practice — one which the *Subafilms* opinion does not choose to explore. Can you imagine what it might be? Hint: Ask yourself how Warner Brothers obtained a copy of the film in order to manufacture the videotapes distributed abroad.

(3) *Subafilms* relied in part on *Robert Stigwood Group, Ltd. v. O'Reilly*, 530 F.2d 1096, 1100-01 (2d Cir. 1976), in which the Second Circuit excluded public performances in Canada when calculating statutory damages, despite the argument that "the defendants assembled and arranged in the United States all the necessary elements for the performances in Canada, and then simply travelled to Canada to

complete the performances." For an interesting application of *Stigwood*, see *Jacobs v. Carnival Corp.*, 2009 U.S. Dist. LEXIS 31374 (S.D.N.Y. Mar. 25, 2009) (allegation that "within the United States [defendants] planned, prepared, authorized, [and] developed" public performances of Broadway shows on cruise ships were insufficient to state a claim without specifically alleging that the performances occurred in the United States' territorial waters). Does that mean that public performances in international waters are beyond the reach of any nation's laws?

(4)   While taking an agnostic position on its merits, *Subafilms* nevertheless notes the Second Circuit rule that where there has been a "predicate act" of infringement in the U.S., damages may be recovered for losses abroad that stem from it. *Update Art, Inc. v. Modiin Publishing, Ltd.*, 843 F.2d 67, 73 (2d Cir. 1988) (distribution in Israel of infringing copies manufactured in U.S.). What practical problems can you see this rule posing for copyright plaintiffs seeking to invoke U.S. law?

The Ninth Circuit has expressed contradictory views concerning the *Update Art* rule. In *Los Angeles News Service v. Reuters Television Int'l, Ltd.*, 149 F.3d 987 (9th Cir. 1998), the plaintiff's work was copied on videotape in the U.S. before being transmitted by satellite overseas, where it was retransmitted to Reuters' subscribers. The Ninth Circuit initially held that "LANS is entitled to recover damages flowing from exploitation abroad of the domestic acts of infringement committed by defendants." 149 F.3d at 992. On appeal after remand, however, the circuit reversed course, holding that recovery under the *Update Art* rule was limited to defendant's profits, under a constructive trust theory, and that plaintiff could not recover actual damages. 340 F.3d 926 (9th Cir. 2003).

In *Tire Eng'g & Dist., LLC v. Shandong Linglong Rubber Co.*, 682 F.3d 292 (4th Cir. 2012), the Fourth Circuit adopted the *Update Art* rule, where the defendants copied the plaintiff's blueprints in the United States and used them to manufacture allegedly infringing articles in China. (See § 3.01[D] above for more details.) The court said: "Absent the predicate-act doctrine, a defendant could convert a plaintiff's intellectual property in the United States, wait for the Copyright Act's three-year statute of limitations to expire, and then reproduce the property abroad with impunity." Oddly, the court cited only the Ninth Circuit's initial decision in *LANS v. Reuters*, without noting the subsequent restriction of that decision.

(5)   Neither *Subafilms* nor *Update Art* directly addresses situations in which an act of infringement itself begins in the United States and is completed in a foreign jurisdiction. Subsequently, however, the Ninth Circuit held that unless an infringing copy is created within U.S. borders, later foreign use of a work is beyond the reach of U.S. copyright law. *See Allarcom Pay Television, Ltd. v. General Instrument Corp.*, 69 F.3d 381, 387 (9th Cir. 1995) (no liability under U.S. law where there was no domestically "completed act of infringement" and "potential infringement was only completed in Canada once the [scrambled satellite] signal [decoded using defendant's device] was received and viewed"). Does this rule make sense, in the era of global wired (and wireless) communication? What if a defendant's business consists of receiving U.S. TV signals and retransmitting them via satellite to audiences outside the country, for whom they are not intended? *See National Football League v. PrimeTime 24 Joint Venture*, 211 F.3d 10, 13 (2d Cir. 2000)

(rejecting *Allarcom*; upholding liability based on "PrimeTime's uplink transmission of signals captured in the United States").

Other courts have taken the position that "a distinction should be drawn between purely extraterritorial conduct, which is itself nonactionable, and conduct that crosses borders, so that at least a part of the offense takes place within the United States. . . . U.S. courts may entertain such multiterritorial infringement claims." *Litecubes, LLC v. Northern Light Prods., Inc.*, 523 F.3d 1353, 1371 (Fed. Cir. 2008) (quoting 4 NIMMER ON COPYRIGHT § 17.02). In *Litecubes*, a seller located outside the U.S. sold infringing goods to a U.S. buyer "f.o.b." ("free on board"), meaning that the title and the risk of loss passes to the buyer as soon as the goods are loaded for shipping in the foreign country. The court nonetheless held that this was a public distribution of goods in the United States for purposes of applying § 106(3).

Is it relevant in any of these cases that in 2008 Congress amended § 602(a) to add "exportation from the United States" to the list of acts that violate the § 106(3) distribution right? See § 7.04 above for a discussion of the importation and exportation rights.

(6)   What about the converse of the *Subafilms* situation? May a foreign defendant be held liable for contributory infringement under U.S. law, based on authorization in a foreign country of infringing acts which occur in the U.S.? *See Armstrong v. Virgin Records, Ltd.*, 91 F. Supp. 2d 628, 635-36 (S.D.N.Y. 2000) (yes); *accord Trustees of Columbia University v. Roche Diagnostics, GmbH*, 150 F. Supp. 2d 191, 205 n.37 (S.D.N.Y. 2001) (collecting cases). *But see* 7 PATRY ON COPYRIGHT § 25.87 n.10 (2012) ("acts outside the United States authorizing conduct which is infringing in the United States cannot rise to infringement in the United States apart from unauthorized importation").

(7)   If a complaint alleges conduct that occurred outside the United States, is the proper response a motion to dismiss for lack of subject-matter jurisdiction or a motion to dismiss for failure to state a claim? In *Litecubes*, the court followed *Subafilms* in holding that allegations of extraterritorial conduct fail to state a claim under the Copyright Act, but do not deprive the trial court of subject-matter jurisdiction. 523 F.3d at 1366-68. *But see Palmer v. Braun*, 376 F.3d 1254 (11th Cir. 2004) (assuming, without analysis, that extraterritoriality is jurisdictional).

(8)   As noted in § 8.02, claims for infringement of foreign copyright law may be heard in federal district court if they are supplemental to a federal claim — or there is some other basis for subject-matter jurisdiction, such as diversity of citizenship. *See, e.g., Armstrong v. Virgin Records, Ltd.*, 91 F. Supp. 2d 628, 637-38 (S.D.N.Y. 2000); *Carell v. Shubert, Inc.*, 104 F. Supp. 2d 236, 257-58 (S.D.N.Y. 2000). In light of these cases, is there any reason why the court in *Subafilms* should not have asserted supplemental jurisdiction and adjudicated the overseas infringements under foreign law? *See also Boosey & Hawkes Music Publishers, Ltd. v. Walt Disney Co.*, 145 F.3d 481, 491-92 (2d Cir. 1998) (reversing District Court's dismissal of foreign infringement claims under doctrine of *forum non conveniens*).

(9)   Obviously, one concern of the *Subafilms* court is a sensitivity about American courts intruding — or appearing to intrude — on the sovereignty of foreign nations. Is this concern well-placed? Would a complete adjudication of the

claims in such a case necessarily involve any interpretation or application of foreign law?

[B] Conflict of Laws

ITAR-TASS RUSSIAN NEWS AGENCY v. RUSSIAN KURIER, INC.
United States Court of Appeals, Second Circuit
153 F.3d 82 (1998)

JON O. NEWMAN, CIRCUIT JUDGE:

This appeal primarily presents issues concerning the choice of law in international copyright cases and the substantive meaning of Russian copyright law as to the respective rights of newspaper reporters and newspaper publishers. The conflicts issue is which country's law applies to issues of copyright ownership and to issues of infringement. The primary substantive issue under Russian copyright law is whether a newspaper publishing company has an interest sufficient to give it standing to sue for copying the text of individual articles appearing in its newspapers, or whether complaint about such copying may be made only by the reporters who authored the articles. Defendants . . . appeal from [a judgment] . . . enjoining them from copying articles that have appeared or will appear in publications of the plaintiffs-appellees, mainly Russian newspapers and a Russian news agency, and awarding the appellees substantial damages for copyright infringement.

On the conflicts issue, we conclude that, with respect to the Russian plaintiffs, Russian law determines the ownership and essential nature of the copyrights alleged to have been infringed and that United States law determines whether those copyrights have been infringed in the United States and, if so, what remedies are available. We also conclude that Russian law, which explicitly excludes newspapers from a work-for-hire doctrine, vests exclusive ownership interests in newspaper articles in the journalists who wrote the articles, not in the newspaper employers who compile their writings. We further conclude that to the extent that Russian law accords newspaper publishers an interest distinct from the copyright of the newspaper reporters, the publishers' interest, like the usual ownership interest in a compilation, extends to the publishers' original selection and arrangement of the articles, and does not entitle the publishers to damages for copying the texts of articles contained in a newspaper compilation. We therefore reverse the judgment to the extent that it granted the newspapers relief for copying the texts of the articles. However, because one non-newspaper plaintiff-appellee is entitled to some injunctive relief and damages and other plaintiffs-appellees may be entitled to some, perhaps considerable, relief, we also remand for further consideration of this lawsuit.

BACKGROUND

The lawsuit concerns Kurier, a Russian language weekly newspaper with a circulation in the New York area of about 20,000. It is published in New York City by defendant Kurier. Defendant Pogrebnoy is president and sole shareholder of Kurier and editor-in-chief of Kurier. The plaintiffs include corporations that publish, daily or weekly, major Russian language newspapers in Russia and Russian language magazines in Russia or Israel; Itar-Tass Russian News Agency ("Itar-Tass"), formerly known as the Telegraph Agency of the Soviet Union (TASS), a wire service and news gathering company centered in Moscow, functioning similarly to the Associated Press; and the Union of Journalists of Russia ("UJR"), the professional writers union of accredited print and broadcast journalists of the Russian Federation.

The Kurier defendants do not dispute that Kurier has copied about 500 articles that first appeared in the plaintiffs' publications or were distributed by Itar-Tass. The copied material, though extensive, was a small percentage of the total number of articles published in Kurier. *See Itar-Tass Russian News Agency v. Russian Kurier, Inc.*, 1997 U.S. Dist. LEXIS 2717 (S.D.N.Y. Mar. 10, 1997) (*"Itar-Tass II"*). The Kurier defendants also do not dispute how the copying occurred: articles from the plaintiffs' publications, sometimes containing headlines, pictures, bylines, and graphics, in addition to text, were cut out, pasted on layout sheets, and sent to Kurier's printer for photographic reproduction and printing in the pages of Kurier.

Most significantly, the Kurier defendants also do not dispute that, with one exception, they had not obtained permission from any of the plaintiffs to copy the articles that appeared in Kurier. . . .

DISCUSSION

I. Choice of Law

The threshold issue concerns the choice of law for resolution of this dispute. That issue was not initially considered by the parties, all of whom turned directly to Russian law for resolution of the case. Believing that the conflicts issue merited consideration, we requested supplemental briefs from the parties and appointed Professor William F. Patry as Amicus Curiae. Prof. Patry has submitted an extremely helpful brief on the choice of law issue.

Choice of law issues in international copyright cases have been largely ignored in the reported decisions and dealt with rather cursorily by most commentators. . . .

The Nimmer treatise briefly (and perhaps optimistically) suggests that conflicts issues "have rarely proved troublesome in the law of copyright." Nimmer on Copyright § 17.05 (1998) ("Nimmer") (footnote omitted). Relying on the "national treatment" principle of the Berne Convention[6] and the Universal Copyright Convention[7] ("U.C.C."), Nimmer asserts, correctly in our view, that "an author who

---

[6] *See* Berne Convention Art. 5(1) (Paris text 1971). . . .

[7] *See* Universal Copyright Convention [Art. II] (Paris text 1971). . . .

is a national of one of the member states of either Berne or the U.C.C., or one who first publishes his work in any such member state, is entitled to the same copyright protection in each other member state as such other state accords to its own nationals." *Id.* (footnotes omitted). Nimmer then somewhat overstates the national treatment principle: "The applicable law is the copyright law of the state in which the infringement occurred, not that of the state of which the author is a national, or in which the work is first published." *Id.* (footnote omitted). The difficulty with this broad statement is that it subsumes under the phrase "applicable law" the law concerning two distinct issues — ownership and substantive rights, *i.e.*, scope of protection.[8] Another commentator has also broadly stated the principle of national treatment, but described its application in a way that does not necessarily cover issues of ownership. "The principle of national treatment also means that both the question of whether the right exists and the question of the scope of the right are to be answered in accordance with the law of the country where the protection is claimed." S.M. Stewart, International Copyright and Neighboring Rights § 3.17 (2d ed. 1989). We agree with the view of the Amicus that the Convention's principle of national treatment simply assures that if the law of the country of infringement applies to the scope of substantive copyright protection, that law will be applied uniformly to foreign and domestic authors. . . .

Source of conflicts rules. Our analysis of the conflicts issue begins with consideration of the source of law for selecting a conflicts rule. Though Nimmer turns directly to the Berne Convention and the U.C.C., we think that step moves too quickly past the Berne Convention Implementation Act of 1988, Pub. L. 100-568, 102 Stat. 2853. Section 4(a)(3) of the Act amends Title 17 to provide: "No right or interest in a work eligible for protection under this title may be claimed by virtue of . . . the provisions of the Berne Convention. . . . Any rights in a work eligible for protection under this title that derive from this title . . . shall not be expanded or reduced by virtue of . . . the provisions of the Berne Convention."[9] 17 U.S.C. § 104(c).

We start our analysis with the Copyrights Act itself, which contains no provision relevant to the pending case concerning conflicts issues.[10] We therefore fill the

---

[8] Prof. Patry's brief, as Amicus Curiae, helpfully points out that the principle of national treatment is really not a conflicts rule at all; it does not direct application of the law of any country. It simply requires that the country in which protection is claimed must treat foreign and domestic authors alike. Whether U.S. copyright law directs U.S. courts to look to foreign or domestic law as to certain issues is irrelevant to national treatment, so long as the scope of protection would be extended equally to foreign and domestic authors.

[9] Other pertinent provisions are:

Section 2(2), which provides: "The obligations of the United States under the Berne Convention may be performed only pursuant to appropriate domestic law."

Section 3(a)(2), which provides: "The provisions of the Berne Convention . . . shall not be enforceable in any action brought pursuant to the provisions of the Berne Convention itself."

Section 3(b)(1), which provides: "The provisions of the Berne Convention . . . do not expand or reduce the right of any author of a work, whether claimed under Federal, State, or the common law . . . to claim authorship of the work."

[10] The recently added provision concerning copyright in "restored works," those that are in the public domain because of noncompliance with formalities of United States copyright law, contains an explicit

interstices of the Act by developing federal common law on the conflicts issue. . . . In doing so, we are entitled to consider and apply principles of private international law, which are "part of our law." *Maxwell Communication Corp. v. Société Générale*, 93 F.3d 1036, 1047 (2d Cir. 1996) (quoting *Hilton v. Guyot*, 159 U.S. 113, 143 (1895)).

The choice of law applicable to the pending case is not necessarily the same for all issues. See Restatement (Second) of Conflict of Laws § 222 ("The courts have long recognized that they are not bound to decide all issues under the local law of a single state."). We consider first the law applicable to the issue of copyright ownership.

Conflicts rule for issues of ownership. Copyright is a form of property, and the usual rule is that the interests of the parties in property are determined by the law of the state with "the most significant relationship" to the property and the parties. *See id.* The Restatement recognizes the applicability of this principle to intangibles such as "a literary idea." *Id.* Since the works at issue were created by Russian nationals and first published in Russia, Russian law is the appropriate source of law to determine issues of ownership of rights. That is the well-reasoned conclusion of the Amicus Curiae, Prof. Patry, and the parties in their supplemental briefs are in agreement on this point. In terms of the United States Copyrights Act and its reference to the Berne Convention, Russia is the "country of origin" of these works, *see* 17 U.S.C. § 101 (definition of "country of origin" of Berne Convention work); Berne Convention, Art. 5(4), although "country of origin" might not always be the appropriate country for purposes of choice of law concerning ownership.[11]

To whatever extent we look to the Berne Convention itself as guidance in the development of federal common law on the conflicts issue, we find nothing to alter our conclusion. The Convention does not purport to settle issues of ownership, with one exception not relevant to this case.[12] *See* Jane C. Ginsburg, *Ownership of*

---

subsection vesting ownership of a restored work "in the author or initial rightholder of the work as determined by the law of the source country of the work." 17 U.S.C. § 104A(b) (emphasis added); *see id.* § 104A(h)(8) (defining "source country").

This provision could be interpreted to be an example of the general conflicts approach we take in this opinion to copyright ownership issues, or an exception to some different approach. *See* Jane C. Ginsburg, *Ownership of Electronic Rights and the Private International Law of Copyright*, 22 Colum.-VLA J.L. & Arts 165, 171 (1998). We agree with Prof. Ginsburg and with the amicus, Prof. Patry, that section 104A(b) should not be understood to state an exception to any otherwise applicable conflicts rule. *See* Ginsburg, *id.*; Brief for Amicus Curiae at 14-17.

[11] In deciding that the law of the country of origin determines the ownership of copyright, we consider only initial ownership, and have no occasion to consider choice of law issues concerning assignments of rights.

[12] The Berne Convention expressly provides that "[o]wnership of copyright in a cinematographic work shall be a matter for legislation in the country where protection is claimed." Berne Convention, Art. 14[bis] (2)(a). With respect to other works, this provision could be understood to have any of three meanings. First, it could carry a negative implication that for other works, ownership is not to be determined by legislation in the country where protection is claimed. Second, it could be thought of as an explicit assertion for films of a general principle already applicable to other works. Third, it could be a specific provision for films that was adopted without an intention to imply anything about other works. In the absence of any indication that either the first or second meanings were intended, we prefer the third understanding.

Electronic Rights and the Private International Law of Copyright, 22 Colum.-VLA J.L. & Arts 165, 167-68 (1998) (The Berne Convention "provides that the law of the country where protection is claimed defines what rights are protected, the scope of the protection, and the available remedies; the treaty does not supply a choice of law rule for determining ownership.") (footnote concerning Art. 14bis (2)(a) omitted).

Selection of Russian law to determine copyright ownership is, however, subject to one procedural qualification. Under United States law, an owner (including one determined according to foreign law) may sue for infringement in a United States court only if it meets the standing test of 17 U.S.C. § 501(b), which accords standing only to the legal or beneficial owner of an "exclusive right."

Conflicts rule for infringement issues. On infringement issues, the governing conflicts principle is usually *lex loci delicti*, the doctrine generally applicable to torts. *See Lauritzen v. Larsen*, 345 U.S. 571, 583 (1953). We have implicitly adopted that approach to infringement claims, applying United States copyright law to a work that was unprotected in its country of origin. *See Hasbro Bradley, Inc. v. Sparkle Toys, Inc.*, 780 F.2d 189, 192-93 (2d Cir. 1985). In the pending case, the place of the tort is plainly the United States. To whatever extent *lex loci delicti* is to be considered only one part of a broader "interest" approach, *see Carbotrade S.p.A. v. Bureau Veritas*, 99 F.3d 86, 89-90 (2d Cir. 1996), United States law would still apply to infringement issues, since not only is this country the place of the tort, but also the defendant is a United States corporation.

The division of issues, for conflicts purposes, between ownership and infringement issues will not always be as easily made as the above discussion implies. If the issue is the relatively straightforward one of which of two contending parties owns a copyright, the issue is unquestionably an ownership issue, and the law of the country with the closest relationship to the work will apply to settle the ownership dispute. But in some cases, including the pending one, the issue is not simply who owns the copyright but also what is the nature of the ownership interest. Yet as a court considers the nature of an ownership interest, there is some risk that it will too readily shift the inquiry over to the issue of whether an alleged copy has infringed the asserted copyright. Whether a copy infringes depends in part on the scope of the interest of the copyright owner. Nevertheless, though the issues are related, the nature of a copyright interest is an issue distinct from the issue of whether the copyright has been infringed. *See, e.g., Kregos v. Associated Press*, 937 F.2d 700, 709-10 (2d Cir. 1991) (pointing out that although work survives summary judgment on issue of copyrightability of compilation, scope of protection against claim of infringement might be limited). The pending case is one that requires consideration not simply of who owns an interest, but, as to the newspapers, the nature of the interest that is owned.

II. Determination of Ownership Rights Under Russian Law

Since United States law permits suit only by owners of "an exclusive right under a copyright," 17 U.S.C. § 501(b), we must first determine whether any of the plaintiffs own an exclusive right. That issue of ownership, as we have indicated, is to be determined by Russian law.

Determination of a foreign country's law is an issue of law. *See* Fed.R.Civ.P. 44.1. . . . Even though the District Court heard live testimony from experts from both sides, that Court's opportunity to assess the witnesses' demeanor provides no basis for a reviewing court to defer to the trier's ruling on the content of foreign law. In cases of this sort, it is not the credibility of the experts that is at issue, it is the persuasive force of the opinions they expressed. . . .

[The court concluded that the defendant's interpretation of Art. 11(2) of the 1993 Russian Copyright Law, which gives the authors of contributions to newspapers the exclusive power to control their separate use — including the sole right to sue when they are used without authorization — was persuasive.]

Relief. Our disagreement with the District Court's interpretation of Article 11 does not mean, however, that the defendants may continue copying with impunity. In the first place, Itar-Tass, as a press agency, is within the scope of Article 14, and, unlike the excluded newspapers, enjoys the benefit of the Russian version of the work-for-hire doctrine. Itar-Tass is therefore entitled to injunctive relief to prevent unauthorized copying of its articles and to damages for such copying, and the judgment is affirmed as to this plaintiff.

Furthermore, the newspaper plaintiffs, though not entitled to relief for the copying of the text of the articles they published, may well be entitled to injunctive relief and damages if they can show that Kurier infringed the publishers' ownership interests in the newspaper compilations. Because the District Court upheld the newspapers' right to relief for copying the text of the articles, it had no occasion to consider what relief the newspapers might be entitled to by reason of Kurier's copying of the newspapers' creative efforts in the selection, arrangement, or display of the articles. Since Kurier's photocopying reproduced not only the text of articles but also headlines and graphic materials as they originally appeared in the plaintiffs' publication, it is likely that on remand the newspaper plaintiffs will be able to obtain some form of injunctive relief and some damages. On these infringement issues, as we have indicated, United States law will apply.

[The court's discussion of the claims for relief of the remaining plaintiffs is omitted.]

CONCLUSION

Accordingly, we affirm the judgment to the extent that it granted relief to Itar-Tass, we reverse to the extent that the judgment granted relief to the other plaintiffs, and we remand for further proceedings. . . .

NOTES AND QUESTIONS

(1)   It took a bit of time for the courts to absorb the *Itar-Tass* doctrine. Compare, for example, the two opinions in *Bridgeman Art Library, Ltd. v. Corel Corp.*, 25 F. Supp. 2d 421 (S.D.N.Y. 1998) and 36 F. Supp. 2d 191 (S.D.N.Y. 1999). Eventually, the District Judge got around to making the right call, applying U.S. law to determine whether a work created in Great Britain and allegedly infringed here contained sufficient original expression to deserve copyright protection. Is

resorting to *Itar-Tass* really necessary, however, in *Bridgeman*? In its *Itar-Tass* opinion, the Second Circuit seems to distinguish between the well-settled principle of national treatment embodied in the Berne Convention (and other international arrangements) and a choice-of-law principle to be applied where the subsistence or scope of rights is at issue. But isn't this a distinction without a difference? Having elected to endorse Professor Stewart's understanding of "national treatment," did the court need to separately address the proper "conflicts rule for infringement purposes"?

(2)   The place of a work's first publication is an important factor in determining what national law applies to issues of copyright ownership under *Itar-Tass. See Cranston Print Works Co. v. J. Mason Prods.*, 1998 U.S. Dist. LEXIS 18004 (S.D.N.Y. 1998) (U.S. law applies where fabric design based on artwork created in Italy was first published in the U.S.). But *Itar-Tass* should not be misunderstood to hold that issues of copyright ownership will always be governed by the law of the country where the works were first published. In some cases, ownership will be appropriately determined by the law of another state, if it has "the most significant relationship to the property and the parties." 153 F.3d at 90. What might be examples of circumstances in which the place of publication would be overshadowed by other considerations? *See Shaw v. Rizzoli Int'l Pubs., Inc.*, 1999 U.S. Dist. LEXIS 3233 (S.D.N.Y. 1999) (U.S. law applies where all plaintiffs except one were U.S. citizens, and 60 of 105 photos were first published in U.S.).

(3)   An interesting application of *Itar-Tass*, demonstrating how difficult the tasks set by the Second Circuit may sometimes be to perform, appears in *Films by Jove, Inc. v. Berov*, 154 F. Supp. 2d 432 (E.D.N.Y. 2001). There, the court was called upon to track the ownership of a group of Russian animated films as the studio that had produced them passed through various transformations "as part of the [property] ownership liberalization trend that accompanied Glasnost and Perestroika." In reaching its conclusions, the court dealt with battling U.S. academic experts on Russian law and with a number of Russian court decisions.

Nearly two years later, the defendants moved for reconsideration, citing a decision by a Russian court that overturned some of the precedents on which the District Court had relied (and, in addition, a French decision between the same parties construing Russian law). The court denied the motion, relying in part on an affidavit from a Russian judge condemning the Russian decision as the product of corruption. *See Films by Jove, Inc. v. Berov*, 250 F. Supp. 2d 156 (E.D.N.Y. 2003). The French decision was rejected because it was inconsistent with a previous French decision between the same parties that had reached a different result.

Eighteen months later, the defendants again moved for reconsideration, this time citing a 2003 Directive of the Russian Federation (purporting to clarify an earlier Directive that the U.S. court had held transferred only real property and not intangible property) and a new decision of a Russian court that the Directive was constitutional under Russian law. The defendants argued that the "act of state" doctrine — under which the courts of one nation will decline to review the validity of the governmental acts of another nation — barred the District Court from rejecting the applicability of the Directive. The District Court again disagreed, holding that "the act of state doctrine does not extend to takings of property located outside the territory of the acting state at the time of the taking, even if the property belonged to an enterprise based in that state." *Films by Jove, Inc. v. Berov*, 341 F. Supp. 2d 199, 207 (E.D.N.Y. 2004).

Does this extended battle suggest that the *Itar-Tass* court made the wrong decision in requiring U.S. courts to apply the law of a foreign country to determine the ownership of U.S. copyrights?

(4)   In footnote 11 of *Itar-Tass*, the court says "we have no occasion to consider choice of law issues concerning assignments of rights." Five years earlier, however, the Second Circuit decided *Corcovado Music Corp. v. Hollis Music, Inc.*, 981 F.2d 679 (2d Cir. 1993), a case involving competing claims to renewal copyrights in works of the Brazilian composer Antonio Carlos Jobim. The crucial question was whether assignments executed by Jobim during the initial term of copyright were sufficient to convey his renewal interest. The parties to the original assignments were Brazilian, the contracts were written in Portuguese, and they contained a forum selection clause specifying the jurisdiction of Brazilian courts. On the other hand, as discussed in § 5.01, there is a strong presumption in U.S. copyright law against the conveyance of renewal rights. Should Brazilian or U.S. law have been applied to the interpretation of the contracts in question? How do you think the issue would be analyzed under *Itar-Tass*? When you have decided, you may want to compare your analysis with that of the court in *Corcovado*. And another question: Given the source of law to be applied, should the action be heard in Brazil or in the United States? For discussion of the doctrine of *forum non conveniens*, see § 8.02.

What law applies if the defendant claims the use was licensed? In *Corbello v. DeVito*, 844 F. Supp. 2d 1136 (D. Nev. 2012), the producers of musical *Jersey Boys* received a license from one joint author of an unpublished manuscript. The court held that the license was valid under U.S. law; and that under *Itar-Tass*, U.S. law should be applied to authorize productions in the United Kingdom, Canada, and Australia as well, even if the license would not have been valid under the law of those countries. Does this decision violate the sovereignty of other nations to decide what constitutes a valid license? Conversely, would it make sense for the parties to have to negotiate individual licenses for each country in which a work is to be used?

(5)   The choice-of-law principle announced in *Itar-Tass* means, among other things, that issues of infringement (and related ones concerning remedies) arising out of uses of works that occur on foreign soil generally will be governed by foreign law. Despite (or perhaps because of) this rule, however, copyright owners are increasingly asking U.S. courts to pass on questions of foreign copyright. See § 8.02 and the notes following *Subafilms*, above, for a discussion of when federal courts have jurisdiction to hear such claims.

(6)   Domestic courts also may be asked to enforce a judgment against a U.S. defendant that was obtained in a foreign country under that country's laws. Such judgments generally will be enforced unless they violate the fundamental public policy of the forum state. *See Sarl Louis Feraud Int'l v. Viewfinder, Inc.*, 489 F.3d 474 (2d Cir. 2007) (mere fact that U.S. law does not extend copyright to dress designs does not render French default judgment repugnant to First Amendment; remanding to determine whether conduct involved would have qualified for fair use under U.S. law).

(7) *Itar-Tass* notes that ownership of a restored copyright vests "in the author or initial rightholder of the work as determined by the law of the source country of the work." 17 U.S.C. § 104A(b). For two cases in which this provision was determinative, see *Alameda Films S.A. de C.V. v. Authors Rights Restoration Corp.*, 331 F.3d 472 (5th Cir. 2003) (under Mexican law, movie production companies, rather than directors and writers, were the "authors" of the films at issue); *La Parade v. Ivanova*, 387 F.3d 1099 (9th Cir. 2004) (same).

Chapter 9

SECONDARY LIABILITY

When infringing activity is widely dispersed, it may be a practical impossibility for the copyright holder to sue the individual infringers. This fact, and the usual search for "deep-pocket" defendants, has led copyright owners to try to impose liability on various intermediaries — such as manufacturers of copying equipment, Internet service providers, and software designers — instead of, or in addition to, the individuals who are directly infringing.

Society's concern with purveyors of copying technologies is hardly new. Before the Statute of Anne, English monarchs attempted to control the use of the printing press through a series of licensing acts, which forbade anyone to operate a printing press unless he or she had royal approval — either in the form of a printing patent for a specific book or books, or through membership in the Stationers' Company. The expiration of the licensing acts, and the enactment of the Statute of Anne, changed this approach. Copyright law focused on the infringing acts themselves, rather than the technology used to reproduce copyrighted works. As described by a federal district judge:

> There was a time when copyright infringement could be dealt with quite adequately by focusing on the infringing act. If someone wished to make and sell high quality but unauthorized copies of a copyrighted book, for example, the infringer needed a printing press. The copyright holder, once aware of the appearance of infringing copies, usually was able to trace the copies up the chain of distribution, find and prosecute the infringer, and shut off the infringement at the source.[1]

The ever-increasing availability of copying technology has challenged this assumption. Photocopiers made it possible for individuals to reproduce printed materials on a large scale. VCRs made it possible to reproduce motion pictures without a film laboratory. Personal computers and the Internet have made it possible to copy and disseminate works in digital form quickly and at a fraction of the cost of traditional publishing.

This chapter discusses various legal theories under which such intermediaries may be held liable for the infringing conduct of others, together with statutory provisions that expand or limit such liability. In particular, we will examine provisions of the Digital Millennium Copyright Act that support the ability of the copyright holder to engage in "self-help" measures, which may suppress both lawful and unlawful copying; and those that limit the liability of Internet service providers.

---

[1] *Universal City Studios, Inc. v. Reimerdes*, 111 F. Supp. 2d 294, 331-32 (S.D.N.Y. 2000).

§ 9.01 CONTRIBUTORY INFRINGEMENT AND VICARIOUS LIABILITY

[A] Introduction

Statutory References
  1976 Act: § 106, 501
  1909 Act: —

Legislative History

H.R. Rep. No. 94-1476 at 61, 159-60,
reprinted in 1976 U.S.C.C.A.N. 5659, 5674, 5775-76

Section 106. Exclusive Rights in Copyrighted Works

The exclusive rights accorded to a copyright owner under section 106 are "to do and to authorize" any of the activities specified in the [six] numbered clauses. Use of the phrase "to authorize" is intended to avoid any questions as to the liability of contributory infringers. For example, a person who lawfully acquires an authorized copy of a motion picture would be an infringer if he or she engages in the business of renting it to others for purposes of unauthorized public performance.

Section 501. Infringement of Copyright

Vicarious liability for infringing performances

The committee has considered and rejected an amendment to this section intended to exempt the proprietors of an establishment, such as a ballroom or night club, from liability for copyright infringement committed by an independent contractor, such as an orchestra leader. A well-established principle of copyright law is that a person who violates any of the exclusive rights of the copyright owner is an infringer, including persons who can be considered related or vicarious infringers. To be held a related or vicarious infringer in the case of performing rights, a defendant must either actively operate or supervise the operation of the place wherein the performances occur, or control the content of the infringing program, and expect commercial gain from the operation and either direct or indirect benefit from the infringing performance. The committee has decided that no justification exists for changing existing law, and causing a significant erosion of the public performance right.

[For a fuller excerpt from H.R. Rep. No. 94-1476, see Part Three of the Casebook Supplement.]

[B]   Case Law

FONOVISA, INC. v. CHERRY AUCTION, INC.
United States Court of Appeals, Ninth Circuit
76 F.3d 259 (1996)

SCHROEDER, CIRCUIT JUDGE:

This is a copyright and trademark enforcement action against the operators of a swap meet, sometimes called a flea market, where third-party vendors routinely sell counterfeit recordings that infringe on the plaintiff's copyrights and trademarks. The district court dismissed on the pleadings, holding that the plaintiffs, as a matter of law, could not maintain any cause of action against the swap meet for sales by vendors who leased its premises. We reverse.

Background

The plaintiff and appellant is Fonovisa, Inc., a California corporation that owns copyrights and trademarks to Latin/Hispanic music recordings. Fonovisa filed this action in district court against defendant-appellee, Cherry Auction, Inc., and its individual operators (collectively "Cherry Auction"). For purposes of this appeal, it is undisputed that Cherry Auction operates a swap meet in Fresno, California, similar to many other swap meets in this country where customers come to purchase various merchandise from individual vendors. . . . The vendors pay a daily rental fee to the swap meet operators in exchange for booth space. Cherry Auction supplies parking, conducts advertising and retains the right to exclude any vendor for any reason, at any time, and thus can exclude vendors for patent and trademark infringement. In addition, Cherry Auction receives an entrance fee from each customer who attends the swap meet.

There is also no dispute for purposes of this appeal that Cherry Auction and its operators were aware that vendors in their swap meet were selling counterfeit recordings in violation of Fonovisa's trademarks and copyrights. Indeed, it is alleged that in 1991, the Fresno County Sheriff's Department raided the Cherry Auction swap meet and seized more than 38,000 counterfeit recordings. The following year, after finding that vendors at the Cherry Auction swap meet were still selling counterfeit recordings, the Sheriff sent a letter notifying Cherry Auction of the on-going sales of infringing materials, and reminding Cherry Auction that they had agreed to provide the Sheriff with identifying information from each vendor. In addition, in 1993, Fonovisa itself sent an investigator to the Cherry Auction site and observed sales of counterfeit recordings.

A Swap Meet
Corbis

. . . [T]he district court granted defendants' motion to dismiss pursuant to Federal Rule of Civil Procedure 12(b)(6). In this appeal, Fonovisa does not challenge the district court's dismissal of its claim for direct copyright infringement, but does appeal the dismissal of its claims for contributory copyright infringement, vicarious copyright infringement and contributory trademark infringement.

. . . Although the Copyright Act does not expressly impose liability on anyone other than direct infringers, courts have long recognized that in certain circumstances, vicarious or contributory liability will be imposed. *See Sony Corp. of America v. Universal City Studios, Inc.*, 464 U.S. 417, 435 (1984). . . .

. . . [This is] the first case to reach a federal appeals court raising issues of contributory and vicarious copyright infringement in the context of swap meet or flea market operations. . . .

Vicarious Copyright Infringement

The concept of vicarious copyright liability was developed in the Second Circuit as an outgrowth of the agency principles of *respondeat superior*. The landmark case on vicarious liability for sales of counterfeit recordings is *Shapiro, Bernstein and Co. v. H.L. Green Co.*, 316 F.2d 304 (2d Cir. 1963). In *Shapiro*, the court was faced with a copyright infringement suit against the owner of a chain of department stores where a concessionaire was selling counterfeit recordings. Noting that the normal agency rule of *respondeat superior* imposes liability on an employer for copyright infringements by an employee, the court endeavored to fashion a principle for enforcing copyrights against a defendant whose economic interests were intertwined with the direct infringer's, but who did not actually employ the direct infringer.

The *Shapiro* court looked at the two lines of cases it perceived as most clearly relevant. In one line of cases, the landlord-tenant cases, the courts had held that a landlord who lacked knowledge of the infringing acts of its tenant and who exercised no control over the leased premises was not liable for infringing sales by its tenant. *See, e.g., Deutsch v. Arnold,* 98 F.2d 686 (2d Cir. 1938); *cf. Fromont v. Aeolian Co.,* 254 F. 592 (S.D.N.Y. 1918). In the other line of cases, the so-called "dance hall cases," the operator of an entertainment venue was held liable for infringing performances when the operator (1) could control the premises and (2) obtained a direct financial benefit from the audience, who paid to enjoy the infringing performance. *See, e.g., Buck v. Jewell-LaSalle Realty Co.,* 283 U.S. 191, 198-199 (1931); *Dreamland Ball Room, Inc. v. Shapiro, Bernstein & Co.,* 36 F.2d 354 (7th Cir. 1929).

. . . [T]he *Shapiro* court determined that the relationship between the store owner and the concessionaire . . . was closer to the dance-hall model than to the landlord-tenant model. It imposed liability even though the defendant was unaware of the infringement. *Shapiro* deemed the imposition of vicarious liability neither unduly harsh nor unfair because the store proprietor had the power to cease the conduct of the concessionaire, and because the proprietor derived an obvious and direct financial benefit from the infringement. 316 F.2d at 307. The test was more clearly articulated in a later Second Circuit case as follows: "even in the absence of an employer-employee relationship one may be vicariously liable if he has the right and ability to supervise the infringing activity and also has a direct financial interest in such activities." *Gershwin Publishing Corp. v. Columbia Artists Management, Inc.,* 443 F.2d 1159, 1162 (2d Cir. 1971). . . .

The district court in this case agreed with defendant Cherry Auction that Fonovisa did not, as a matter of law, meet either the control or the financial benefit prong of the vicarious copyright infringement test articulated in *Gershwin, supra.* Rather, the district court concluded that based on the pleadings, "Cherry Auction neither supervised nor profited from the vendors' sales." 847 F. Supp. at 1496. In the district court's view, with respect to both control and financial benefit, Cherry Auction was in the same position as an absentee landlord who has surrendered its exclusive right of occupancy in its leased property to its tenants.

This analogy to absentee landlord is not in accord with the facts as alleged in the district court and which we, for purposes of appeal, must accept. The allegations below were that vendors occupied small booths within premises that Cherry Auction controlled and patrolled. According to the complaint, Cherry Auction had the right to terminate vendors for any reason whatsoever and through that right had the ability to control the activities of vendors on the premises. In addition, Cherry Auction promoted the swap meet and controlled the access of customers to the swap meet area. In terms of control, the allegations before us are strikingly similar to those in *Shapiro* and *Gershwin.*

In *Shapiro*, for example, the court focused on the formal licensing agreement between defendant department store and the direct infringer-concessionaire. There, the concessionaire selling the bootleg recordings had a licensing agreement with the department store (H.L. Green Company) that required the concessionaire and its employees to "abide by, observe and obey all regulations promulgated from time to time by the H.L. Green Company," and H.L. Green Company had the "unreviewable discretion" to discharge the concessionaires' employees. In practice, H.L. Green Company was not actively involved in the sale of records and the concessionaire controlled and supervised the individual employees. Nevertheless, H.L. Green's ability to police its concessionaire — which parallels Cherry Auction's ability to police its vendors under Cherry Auction's similarly broad contract with its vendors — was sufficient to satisfy the control requirement.

In *Gershwin*, the defendant lacked the formal, contractual ability to control the direct infringer. Nevertheless, because of defendant's "pervasive participation in the formation and direction" of the direct infringers, including promoting them (*i.e.*, creating an audience for them), the court found that defendants were in a position to police the direct infringers and held that the control element was satisfied. As the promoter and organizer of the swap meet, Cherry Auction wields the same level of control over the direct infringers as did the *Gershwin* defendant. *See also Polygram Int'l Publ., Inc. v. Nevada/TIG, Inc.*, 855 F. Supp. 1314, 1329 (D. Mass. 1994) (finding that the control requirement was satisfied because the defendant (1) could control the direct infringers through its rules and regulations; (2) policed its booths to make sure the regulations were followed; and (3) promoted the show in which direct infringers participated).

The district court's dismissal of the vicarious liability claim in this case was therefore not justified on the ground that the complaint failed to allege sufficient control.

We next consider the issue of financial benefit. The plaintiff's allegations encompass many substantive benefits to Cherry Auction from the infringing sales. These include the payment of a daily rental fee by each of the infringing vendors; a direct payment to Cherry Auction by each customer in the form of an admission fee[;] and incidental payments for parking, food and other services by customers seeking to purchase infringing recordings.

Cherry Auction nevertheless contends that these benefits cannot satisfy the financial benefit prong of vicarious liability because a commission, directly tied to the sale of particular infringing items, is required. They ask that we restrict the financial benefit prong to the precise facts presented in *Shapiro*, where defendant H.L. Green Company received a 10 or 12 per cent commission from the direct infringers' gross receipts. Cherry Auction points to the low daily rental fee paid by each vendor, discounting all other financial benefits flowing to the swap meet, and asks that we hold that the swap meet is materially similar to a mere landlord. The facts alleged by Fonovisa, however, reflect that the defendants reap substantial financial benefits from admission fees, concession stand sales and parking fees, all of which flow directly from customers who want to buy the counterfeit recordings at bargain basement prices. The plaintiff has sufficiently alleged direct financial benefit.

Our conclusion is fortified by the continuing line of cases, starting with the dance hall cases, imposing vicarious liability on the operator of a business where infringing performances enhance the attractiveness of the venue to potential customers. In

Polygram, for example, direct infringers were participants in a trade show who used infringing music to communicate with attendees and to cultivate interest in their wares. The court held that the trade show participants "derived a significant financial benefit from the attention" that attendees paid to the infringing music. *Id.*; *see also Famous Music Corp. v. Bay State Harness Horse Racing and Breeding Ass'n*, 554 F.2d 1213, 1214 (1st Cir. 1977) (race track owner vicariously liable for band that entertained patrons who were not "absorbed in watching the races"); *Shapiro*, 316 F.2d at 307 (dance hall cases hold proprietor liable where infringing "activities provide the proprietor with a source of customers and enhanced income"). In this case, the sale of pirated recordings at the Cherry Auction swap meet is a "draw" for customers, as was the performance of pirated music in the dance hall cases and their progeny.

Plaintiffs have stated a claim for vicarious copyright infringement.

Contributory Copyright Infringement

Contributory infringement originates in tort law and stems from the notion that one who directly contributes to another's infringement should be held accountable. *See Sony v. Universal City*, 464 U.S. at 417; 1 Neil Boorstyn, BOORSTYN ON COPYRIGHT § 10.06[2], at 10-21 (1994) ("In other words, the common law doctrine that one who knowingly participates in or furthers a tortious act is jointly and severally liable with the prime tortfeasor, is applicable under copyright law"). Contributory infringement has been described as an outgrowth of enterprise liability, . . . and imposes liability where one person knowingly contributes to the infringing conduct of another. The classic statement of the doctrine is in *Gershwin*, 443 F.2d 1159, 1162: "[O]ne who, with knowledge of the infringing activity, induces, causes or materially contributes to the infringing conduct of another, may be held liable as a 'contributory' infringer." *See also Universal City Studios v. Sony Corp. of America*, 659 F.2d 963, 975 (9th Cir. 1981), *rev'd on other grounds*, 464 U.S. 417 (1984) (adopting *Gershwin* in this circuit).

There is no question that plaintiff adequately alleged the element of knowledge in this case. The disputed issue is whether plaintiff adequately alleged that Cherry Auction materially contributed to the infringing activity. We have little difficulty in holding that the allegations in this case are sufficient to show material contribution to the infringing activity. Indeed, it would be difficult for the infringing activity to take place in the massive quantities alleged without the support services provided by the swap meet. These services include, *inter alia*, the provision of space, utilities, parking, advertising, plumbing, and customers.

Here again Cherry Auction asks us to ignore all aspects of the enterprise described by the plaintiffs, to concentrate solely on the rental of space, and to hold that the swap meet provides nothing more. Yet Cherry Auction actively strives to provide the environment and the market for counterfeit recording sales to thrive. Its participation in the sales cannot be termed "passive," as Cherry Auction would prefer.

The district court apparently took the view that contribution to infringement should be limited to circumstances in which the defendant "expressly promoted or encouraged the sale of counterfeit products, or in some manner protected the identity of the infringers." 847 F. Supp. 1492, 1496. Given the allegations that the local sheriff lawfully requested that Cherry Auction gather and share basic, identifying information about its vendors, and that Cherry Auction failed to comply, the defendant appears to qualify within the last portion of the district court's own standard that posits liability for protecting infringers' identities. Moreover, we agree with the Third Circuit's analysis in *Columbia Pictures Industries, Inc. v. Aveco, Inc.*, 800 F.2d 59 (3rd Cir. 1986) that providing the site and facilities for known infringing activity is sufficient to establish contributory liability. *See* 2 William F. Patry, Copyright Law & Practice 1147 ("Merely providing the means for infringement may be sufficient" to incur contributory copyright liability).

[The court's discussion of contributory trademark infringement is omitted.]

The judgment of the district court is REVERSED and the case is REMANDED FOR FURTHER PROCEEDINGS.

NOTES AND QUESTIONS

(1)   The *Fonovisa* court says that "the Copyright Act does not expressly impose liability on anyone other than direct infringers," citing *Sony Corp. v. Universal City Studios, Inc.*, 464 U.S. 417, 434 (1984). But is this really so? Section 106 gives copyright owners the right "to do and to authorize" any of the exclusive rights provided by that section. The House Report indicates that the phrase "to authorize" was "intended to avoid any questions as to the liability of contributory infringers." Is this information relevant to the analysis of a case such as *Fonovisa*? *See Soc'y of Holy Transfiguration Monastery, Inc. v. Archbishop Gregory of Denver, Colo.*, 689 F.3d 29 (1st Cir. 2012) (holding that "a principal . . . may be held liable for the authorized acts of its agent" and finding defendant *directly* liable for "authorizing" subordinate to infringe). You may wish to consider again the discussion in the notes to *Subafilms, Ltd. v. MGM-Pathe Communications Co.*, 24 F.3d 1088 (9th Cir. 1994), in § 8.04 above.

(2)   The opinion notes that *vicarious liability* is "an outgrowth of the agency principles of *respondeat superior*." The vendors are not employees of the swap meet; but is it fair to characterize them as "agents" of the swap meet, under traditional agency law principles? Is vicarious liability appropriate in the absence of a finding of agency? *Compare Fonovisa with Adobe Systems, Inc. v. Canus Productions, Inc.*, 173 F. Supp. 2d 1044 (C.D. Cal. 2001) (requiring a showing that "the vendor's infringement constitutes a draw to the venue to the extent that the economic interests of the direct infringer and those of the landlord become closely intertwined").

The other prong of the test for vicarious liability is financial benefit to the defendant. In *Monotype Imaging, Inc., v. Bitstream, Inc.*, 2005 U.S. Dist. LEXIS 7410 (N.D. Ill. Apr. 21, 2005), it was alleged that the usefulness of the defendants' computer program (which facilitates the display of typeface designs) for copying the digital code of plaintiffs' fonts was "a tremendous draw for customers." Should this have been enough to withstand a motion for summary judgment?

It is important to remember that vicarious liability, like direct infringement, does *not* require a showing of knowledge or intent. *See Lowry's Reports, Inc. v. Legg Mason, Inc.*, 271 F. Supp. 2d 737 (D. Md. 2003) (holding defendant vicariously liable despite the fact that the copying contravened express company policy and violated a direct order prohibiting copying).

(3)   The opinion in *Fonovisa* observes that "providing the site and facilities for known infringing activity is sufficient to establish" *contributory liability*. Is this consistent with the principle that a landlord is not vicariously liable for infringement occurring on leased premises? If a landlord is notified of alleged infringing activity, do the "landlord" cases become irrelevant? *See Adobe*, 173 F. Supp. 2d at 1056 (questioning trade show sponsor's knowledge that a small number of vendors were offering infringing items).

What kind of knowledge suffices for contributory liability? Is it enough that the defendant knows that the infringing activity is occurring, or must he also have reason to know that the activity is infringing? The analogy to criminal conspiracy would suggest that the third party need only know of the activity; but at least two trial courts have suggested that the defendant also must have reason to believe that it is likely the activity is infringing. *See Faulkner v. National Geographic Society*, 211 F. Supp. 2d 450, 474 (S.D.N.Y. 2002); *Religious Tech. Ctr. v. Netcom On-Line Communication Services, Inc.*, 907 F. Supp. 1361, 1374 (N.D. Cal. 1995).

(4)   How easy is it to distinguish the two forms of secondary liability? For example, what if you are going after an employee/officer/director of a small incorporated business that has been engaging in widespread infringements of your client's product line? What are the potential strengths and weaknesses of "vicarious" and "contributory" liability in these circumstances? *See Softel, Inc. v. Dragon Medical & Scientific Communications, Inc.*, 118 F.3d 955, 971 (2d Cir. 1997) (derivative claims against defendant company's president dismissed); *Arista Records LLC v. Lime Group LLC*, 784 F. Supp. 2d 398, 437-39 (S.D.N.Y. 2011) (defendant's CEO and sole Director directed and benefitted from infringing activity); *MDY Industries, LLC v. Blizzard Entertainment, Inc.*, 616 F. Supp. 2d 958, 971-73 (D. Ariz. 2009) (principal of MDY supervised infringing activities and personally profited from their success), *vacated on other grounds*, 629 F.3d 928, 958 & n.25 (9th Cir. 2010); *Burdick v. Koerner*, 988 F. Supp. 1206 (E.D. Wis. 1998) (contributory and vicarious liability claims against defendant company's board members dismissed on various grounds).

(5)   From the copyright litigator's standpoint, it is sometimes highly desirable to be able to reach the parent corporation of an allegedly infringing subsidiary. Under which version of derivative liability are you most likely to be able to accomplish this result? *See Goes Lithography Co. v. Banta Corp.*, 26 F. Supp. 2d 1042 (N.D. Ill. 1998) (distinguishing and criticizing *Broadcast Music, Inc. v. Hartmarx Corp.*, 1988 U.S. Dist. LEXIS 13298 (N.D. Ill. Nov. 17, 1988), which presumes the parent corporation's right to control the subsidiary's infringing activities as part of a contributory infringement analysis). *See also UMG Recordings, Inc. v. Shelter Capital Partners, LLC*, 667 F.3d 1022 (9th Cir. 2011) (claims against investors in video-sharing website Veoh Networks dismissed; allegations that investors controlled a majority of the board of directors were insufficient absent allegations that

those directors acted in concert); *Arista Records v. Lime Group* (although formally separate, parent and subsidiary were operated as a single company).

(6) In *Demetriades v. Kaufmann*, 690 F. Supp. 289, 291 (S.D.N.Y. 1988), the court found no contributory infringement on the part of defendants who brokered a real estate transaction that led to the construction of a house that allegedly infringed plaintiff's architectural plans. The court stated: "We are familiar with no concept of justice that would permit extension of third-party liability . . . on so attenuated a basis. Something more — deriving from one's substantial involvement — is needed." *Id.* at 294 (citing Restatement (Second) of Torts § 876(b) (1977)). Is this consistent with the discussion of contributory infringement in *Fonovisa*? If not, which court has the better of the argument?

For a post-*Demetriades* case applying a "substantial" participation test, see *Faulkner v. National Geographic Society*, 211 F. Supp. 2d 450, 473-74 (S.D.N.Y. 2002) (advertising an infringing product is a material contribution, but advertising a non-infringing product in a magazine that contains infringing photographs is not), *aff'd on other grounds*, 409 F.3d 26 (2d Cir. 2005).

(7) New technology has given the law of derivative liability some interesting twists. In *Alcatel USA, Inc. v. DGI Technologies, Inc.*, 166 F.3d 772 (5th Cir. 1999), for example, the Fifth Circuit concluded that the rights of the plaintiff company, which sold telephone switching equipment and licensed its customers to use its copyrighted operating system software to run them, were infringed by the defendant, who sold compatible microprocessor cards designed to expand the call-handling capacity of the plaintiff's equipment. Among other things, the court concluded that the defendant had committed contributory infringement because "[t]he evidence shows that each time a DGI microprocessor card is booted up it downloads (makes a copy of) the DSC operating system," which was not authorized by the end-user license agreement. *Id.* at 791.

In the next chapter, we will return to the *Alcatel* case and discover the basis on which — after all — the defendant escaped liability. You may also want to examine *Adobe Systems, Inc. v. Southern Software, Inc.*, 45 U.S.P.Q.2d (BNA) 1827 (N.D. Cal. 1998), involving a claim of contributory infringement against a third-party defendant who provided the original defendant with the software required to permit him to copy fonts from the plaintiff's copyrighted programs. In that case, the third-party defendant "worked with [defendant] to achieve his purpose in using the software." What if it the defendant had merely supplied the software in question, knowing its capabilities but not the particular use to which it would be put?

§ 9.02 COPYING DEVICES AND SOFTWARE

As novel as the fact pattern in *Fonovisa* may be (and diligent research confirms it is indeed "the first case to reach a federal appeals court raising issues of contributory and vicarious copyright infringement in the context of swap meet or flea market operations"), the decision represents a decidedly old-style "low-tech" — or "no tech" — setting in which to consider secondary liability. Increasingly, the setting in which the courts encounter such issues is neither a parking lot nor a dance hall, but the high-tech venues of consumer electronics, personal computers, and the

Internet. The present section examines the histories of three such technologies: videocassettes, digital audio tapes, and file-sharing software.

We begin with a case that pre-dates the World Wide Web, not to mention the decision in *Fonovisa*: *Sony v. Universal City Studios* (the "Betamax" case), which we first encountered in Chapter 7.

In the excerpt below, the Supreme Court considers the copyright/new technology interface in the context of the alleged liability, not of primary infringers (*i.e.*, consumers using the Betamax to record copyrighted works for later home viewing), but of the manufacturer and distributors of the copying devices themselves.

[A] Case Law

SONY CORP. OF AMERICA v.
UNIVERSAL CITY STUDIOS, INC.
Supreme Court of the United States
464 U.S. 417 (1984)

JUSTICE STEVENS delivered the opinion of the Court.

Petitioners manufacture and sell home video tape recorders. Respondents own the copyrights on some of the television programs that are broadcast on the public airwaves. Some members of the general public use video tape recorders sold by petitioners to record some of these broadcasts, as well as a large number of other broadcasts. The question presented is whether the sale of petitioners' copying equipment to the general public violates any of the rights conferred upon respondents by the Copyright Act.

Respondents commenced this copyright infringement action against petitioners in the United States District Court for the Central District of California in 1976. Respondents alleged that some individuals had used Betamax video tape recorders (VTR's) to record some of respondents' copyrighted works which had been exhibited on commercially sponsored television and contended that these individuals had thereby infringed respondents' copyrights. Respondents further maintained that petitioners were liable for the copyright infringement allegedly committed by Betamax consumers because of petitioners' marketing of the Betamax VTR's. Respondents sought no relief against any Betamax consumer. Instead, they sought money damages and an equitable accounting of profits from petitioners, as well as an injunction against the manufacture and marketing of Betamax VTR's. . . .

. . . [The District Court's] findings reveal that the average member of the public uses a VTR principally to record a program he cannot view as it is being televised and then to watch it once at a later time. This practice, known as "time-shifting," enlarges the television viewing audience. For that reason, a significant amount of television programming may be used in this manner without objection from the owners of the copyrights on the programs. For the same reason, even the two respondents in this case, who do assert objections to time-shifting in this litigation, were unable to prove that the practice has impaired the commercial value of their copyrights or has created any likelihood of future harm. Given these findings, there is no basis in the Copyright Act upon which respondents can hold petitioners liable for distributing VTR's to the general public. The Court of Appeals' holding that respondents are entitled to enjoin the distribution of VTR's, to collect royalties on the sale of such equipment, or to obtain other relief, if affirmed, would enlarge the scope of respondents' statutory monopolies to encompass control over an article of commerce that is not the subject of copyright protection. Such an expansion of the copyright privilege is beyond the limits of the grants authorized by Congress.

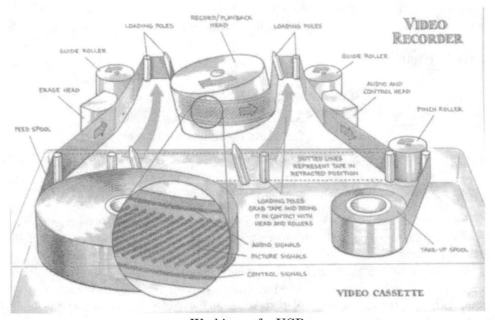

Workings of a VCR

[Having heard a reargument, "since we had not completed our study of the case last Term," the Supreme Court reverses.]

I

. . . The respondents and Sony both conducted surveys of the way the Betamax machine was used by several hundred owners during a sample period in 1978. Although there were some differences in the surveys, they both showed that the primary use of the machine for most owners was "time-shifting," the practice of recording a program to view it once at a later time, and thereafter erasing it. . . . Both surveys also showed, however, that a substantial number of interviewees had accumulated libraries of tapes. . . .

Sony introduced considerable evidence describing television programs that could be copied without objection from any copyright holder, with special emphasis on sports, religious, and educational programming. For example, their survey indicated that 7.3% of all Betamax use is to record sports events, and representatives of professional baseball, football, basketball, and hockey testified that they had no objection to the recording of their televised events for home use. . . .

The District Court concluded that noncommercial home use recording of material broadcast over the public airwaves was a fair use of copyrighted works and did not constitute copyright infringement. . . .

As an independent ground of decision, the District Court also concluded that Sony could not be held liable as a contributory infringer even if the home use of a VTR was considered an infringing use. The District Court noted that Sony had no direct involvement with any Betamax purchasers who recorded copyrighted works off the air. Sony's advertising was silent on the subject of possible copyright infringement, but its instruction booklet contained the following statement:

> "Television programs, films, videotapes and other materials may be copyrighted. Unauthorized recording of such material may be contrary to the provisions of the United States copyright laws." . . .

The District Court assumed that Sony had constructive knowledge of the probability that the Betamax machine would be used to record copyrighted programs, but found that Sony merely sold a "product capable of a variety of uses, some of them allegedly infringing." . . .

The Court of Appeals reversed the District Court's judgment on respondents' copyright claim. It did not set aside any of the District Court's findings of fact. Rather, it concluded as a matter of law that the home use of a VTR was not a fair use . . .

On the issue of contributory infringement, the Court of Appeals first rejected the analogy to staple articles of commerce such as tape recorders or photocopying machines. It noted that such machines "may have substantial benefit for some purposes" and do not "even remotely raise copyright problems." VTR's, however, are sold "for the primary purpose of reproducing television programming" and "virtually all" such programming is copyrighted material. The Court of Appeals concluded, therefore, that VTR's were not suitable for any substantial noninfringing use even if some copyright owners elect not to enforce their rights.

The Court of Appeals also rejected the District Court's reliance on Sony's lack of knowledge that home use constituted infringement. Assuming that the statutory provisions defining the remedies for infringement applied also to the non-statutory tort of contributory infringement, the court stated that a defendant's good faith would merely reduce his damages liability but would not excuse the infringing conduct. It held that Sony was chargeable with knowledge of the homeowner's infringing activity because the reproduction of copyrighted materials was either "the most conspicuous use" or "the major use" of the Betamax product. . . .

II

. . . The two respondents in this case do not seek relief against the Betamax users who have allegedly infringed their copyrights. Moreover, this is not a class action on behalf of all copyright owners who license their works for television broadcast, and respondents have no right to invoke whatever rights other copyright holders may have to bring infringement actions based on Betamax copying of their works. As was made clear by their own evidence, the copying of the respondents' programs represents a small portion of the total use of VTR's. It is, however, the taping of respondents own copyrighted programs that provides them with standing to charge Sony with contributory infringement. . . .

III

The Copyright Act does not expressly render anyone liable for infringement committed by another. In contrast, the Patent Act expressly brands anyone who "actively induces infringement of a patent" as an infringer, 35 U.S.C. § 271(b), and further imposes liability on certain individuals labeled "contributory" infringers, § 271(c). The absence of such express language in the copyright statute does not preclude the imposition of liability for copyright infringements on certain parties who have not themselves engaged in the infringing activity.[17] For vicarious liability is imposed in virtually all areas of the law, and the concept of contributory infringement is merely a species of the broader problem of identifying the circumstances in which it is just to hold one individual accountable for the actions of another. . . .

. . . [T]he label "contributory infringement" has been applied in a number of lower court copyright cases involving an ongoing relationship between the direct infringer and the contributory infringer at the time the infringing conduct occurred. In such cases, as in other situations in which the imposition of vicarious liability is manifestly just, the "contributory" infringer was in a position to control the use of copyrighted works by others and had authorized the use without permission from the copyright owner. This case, however, plainly does not fall in that category. The only contact between Sony and the users of the Betamax that is disclosed by this record occurred at the moment of sale. The District Court expressly found that "no employee of Sony, Sonam or DDBI had either direct involvement with the allegedly infringing activity or direct contact with purchasers of Betamax who recorded copyrighted works off-the-air." 480 F. Supp., at 460. And it further found that "there was no evidence that any of the copies made by Griffiths or the other individual witnesses in this suit were influenced or encouraged by [Sony's] advertisements." *Ibid.*

If vicarious liability is to be imposed on Sony in this case, it must rest on the fact that it has sold equipment with constructive knowledge of the fact that its customers may use that equipment to make unauthorized copies of copyrighted material. There is no precedent in the law of copyright for the imposition of vicarious liability on such a theory. The closest analogy is provided by the patent law cases to which

---

[17] As the District Court correctly observed, however, "the lines between direct infringement, contributory infringement and vicarious liability are not clearly drawn. . . ." The lack of clarity in this area may, in part, be attributable to the fact that an infringer is not merely one who uses a work without authorization by the copyright owner, but also one who authorizes the use of a copyrighted work without actual authority from the copyright owner.

We note the parties' statements that the questions of petitioners' liability under the "doctrines" of "direct infringement" and "vicarious liability" are not nominally before this Court. . . . We also observe, however, that reasoned analysis of respondents' unprecedented contributory infringement claim necessarily entails consideration of arguments and case law which may also be forwarded under the other labels . . .

it is appropriate to refer because of the historic kinship between patent law and copyright law.

In the Patent Act both the concept of infringement and the concept of contributory infringement are expressly defined by statute. The prohibition against contributory infringement is confined to the knowing sale of a component especially made for use in connection with a particular patent. There is no suggestion in the statute that one patentee may object to the sale of a product that might be used in connection with other patents. Moreover, the Act expressly provides that the sale of a "staple article or commodity of commerce suitable for substantial noninfringing use" is not contributory infringement. 35 U.S.C. § 271(c).

When a charge of contributory infringement is predicated entirely on the sale of an article of commerce that is used by the purchaser to infringe a patent, the public interest in access to that article of commerce is necessarily implicated. A finding of contributory infringement does not, of course, remove the article from the market altogether; it does, however, give the patentee effective control over the sale of that item. Indeed, a finding of contributory infringement is normally the functional equivalent of holding that the disputed article is within the monopoly granted to the patentee.[21]

For that reason, in contributory infringement cases arising under the patent laws the Court has always recognized the critical importance of not allowing the patentee to extend his monopoly beyond the limits of his specific grant. These cases deny the patentee any right to control the distribution of unpatented articles unless they are "unsuited for any commercial noninfringing use." *Dawson Chemical Co. v. Rohm & Hass Co.*, 448 U.S. 176, 198 (1980). Unless a commodity "has no use except through practice of the patented method," *id.*, at 199, the patentee has no right to claim that its distribution constitutes contributory infringement. "To form the basis for contributory infringement the item must almost be uniquely suited as a component of the patented invention." P. Rosenberg, Patent Law Fundamentals § 17.02[2] (2d ed. 1982). "[A] sale of an article which though adapted to an infringing use is also adapted to other and lawful uses, is not enough to make the seller a contributory infringer. Such a rule would block the wheels of commerce." *Henry v. A. B. Dick Co.*, 224 U.S. 1, 48 (1912), overruled on other grounds, *Motion Picture Patents Co. v. Universal Film Mfg. Co.*, 243 U.S. 502, 517 (1917).

We recognize there are substantial differences between the patent and copyright laws. But in both areas the contributory infringement doctrine is grounded on the recognition that adequate protection of a monopoly may require the courts to look beyond actual duplication of a device or publication to the products or activities that make such duplication possible. The staple article of commerce doctrine must strike a balance between a copyright holder's legitimate demand for effective — not

---

[21] It seems extraordinary to suggest that the Copyright Act confers upon all copyright owners collectively, much less the two respondents in this case, the exclusive right to distribute VTR's simply because they may be used to infringe copyrights. That, however, is the logical implication of their claim. The request for an injunction below indicates that respondents seek, in effect, to declare VTR's contraband. Their suggestion in this Court that a continuing royalty pursuant to a judicially created compulsory license would be an acceptable remedy merely indicates that respondents, for their part, would be willing to license their claimed monopoly interest in VTR's to Sony in return for a royalty.

merely symbolic — protection of the statutory monopoly, and the rights of others freely to engage in substantially unrelated areas of commerce. Accordingly, the sale of copying equipment, like the sale of other articles of commerce, does not constitute contributory infringement if the product is widely used for legitimate, unobjectionable purposes. Indeed, it need merely be capable of substantial noninfringing uses.

IV

The question is thus whether the Betamax is capable of commercially significant noninfringing uses. In order to resolve that question, we need not explore *all* the different potential uses of the machine and determine whether or not they would constitute infringement. Rather, we need only consider whether on the basis of the facts as found by the District Court a significant number of them would be noninfringing. Moreover, in order to resolve this case we need not give precise content to the question of how much use is commercially significant. For one potential use of the Betamax plainly satisfies this standard, however it is understood: private, noncommercial time-shifting in the home. It does so both (A) because respondents have no right to prevent other copyright holders from authorizing it for their programs, and (B) because the District Court's factual findings reveal that even the unauthorized home time-shifting of respondents' programs is legitimate fair use. . . .

[The Court's discussion of "fair use" appears in Chapter 10 of this book.]

V

One may search the Copyright Act in vain for any sign that the elected representatives of the millions of people who watch television every day have made it unlawful to copy a program for later viewing at home, or have enacted a flat prohibition against the sale of machines that make such copying possible.

It may well be that Congress will take a fresh look at this new technology, just as it so often has examined other innovations in the past. But it is not our job to apply laws that have not yet been written. Applying the copyright statute, as it now reads, to the facts as they have been developed in this case, the judgment of the Court of Appeals must be reversed. *It is so ordered.*

JUSTICE BLACKMUN, with whom JUSTICE MARSHALL, JUSTICE POWELL, and JUSTICE REHNQUIST join, dissenting.

. . . In absolving Sony from liability, the District Court reasoned that Sony had no direct involvement with individual Betamax users, did not participate in any off-the-air copying, and did not know that such copying was an infringement of the Studios' copyright. I agree with the *Gershwin* court that contributory liability may be imposed even when the defendant has no formal control over the infringer. . . . Moreover, a finding of contributory infringement has never depended on actual knowledge of particular instances of infringement; it is sufficient that the defendant have reason to know that infringement is taking place. . . .

The District Court found that Sony has advertised the Betamax as suitable for off-the-air recording of "favorite shows," "novels for television," and "classic movies," with no visible warning that such recording could constitute copyright infringement. It is only with the aid of the Betamax or some other VTR that it is possible today for home television viewers to infringe copyright by recording off-the-air. Off-the-air recording is not only a foreseeable use for the Betamax, but indeed is its intended use. Under the circumstances, I agree with the Court of Appeals that if off-the-air recording is an infringement of copyright, Sony has induced and materially contributed to the infringing conduct of Betamax owners. . . .

I recognize, however, that many of the concerns underlying the "staple article of commerce" doctrine are present in copyright law as well. . . .

I therefore conclude that if a *significant* portion of the product's use is *noninfringing*, the manufacturers and sellers cannot be held contributorily liable for the product's infringing uses. If virtually all of the product's use, however, is to infringe, contributory liability may be imposed; if no one would buy the product for noninfringing purposes alone, it is clear that the manufacturer is purposely profiting from the infringement, and that liability is appropriately imposed. In such a case, the copyright owner's monopoly would not be extended beyond its proper bounds; the manufacturer of such a product contributes to the infringing activities of others and profits directly thereby, while providing no benefit to the public sufficient to justify the infringement.

. . . The proportion of VTR recording that is infringing is ultimately a question of fact, and the District Court specifically declined to make findings on the "percentage of legal versus illegal home-use recording." In light of my view of the law, resolution of this factual question is essential. I therefore would remand the case for further consideration of this by the District Court.

NOTES AND QUESTIONS

(1)   In reading *Sony*, one must first get a handle on the Court's frustratingly fluid use of terminology. Note first that the Court prefers the term "vicarious liability" to "vicarious infringement." At times, however, the Court appears to use "vicarious liability" as an umbrella term for all types of secondary liability, including "contributory infringement"; at other times, the Court seems to treat the two terms as synonyms. *Fonovisa*, by contrast, distinguishes systematically between "contributory" and "vicarious" infringement as two separate doctrines. The parties in *Sony*, as indicated in footnote 17, briefed and argued the case (at the Supreme Court level) as a case of contributory infringement only.

(2)   The Court is frustratingly imprecise in other ways, as well. For example, what is the Court's standard for determining whether a piece of copying equipment is a "staple article of commerce"? That the article is "widely used for legitimate, unobjectionable purposes"? That it is "capable of commercially significant noninfringing uses"? That it is "capable of substantial noninfringing uses"? Does "commercially significant" mean the same thing as "substantial"? Does "capable of substantial noninfringing uses" (plural) mean the same thing as "suitable for substantial noninfringing use" (singular) in 35 U.S.C. § 271(c)?

(3)   The dissent's proposed standard isn't much clearer. Justice Blackmun states that he would not impose liability "if a *significant* portion of the product's use is noninfringing," but that he would impose liability if "virtually all of the product's use . . . is to infringe." Is the word "significant" the converse of the phrase "virtually all"? Is "significant" a larger or smaller quantity than "substantial"? If the District Court found that 40% of the Betamax's usage was noninfringing, would that be enough to avoid liability? 20%? 10%?

(4)   More generally, should contributory liability for selling copying equipment be based on the uses of which a product is capable, as the majority holds, or on the product's actual use by consumers, as the dissent would prefer? The dissent's standard has the virtue of being quantifiable. But how could a manufacturer determine a product's "actual use" until the product was sold (at which time it would be too late to avoid liability)? And if "actual use" was the standard, what would happen if consumer behavior changed over time?

(5)   The outcome of the *Sony* case may have been significantly affected by the District Court's refusal to grant a preliminary injunction. According to the respondents' unsuccessful petition for rehearing, at the time of trial there were only 800,000 VTRs (what we now call VCRs) in the entire United States; but by the time the Supreme Court rendered its decision, there were 10 million. Is it possible that the Court was influenced by the widespread adoption of VTRs by consumers? If so, is that a good thing or a bad thing? By contrast, the music "file-sharing" website Napster was preliminarily enjoined despite having millions of users.

(6)   Both the majority and the dissent in *Sony* expressed the hope that Congress would study the situation and come up with a legislative solution. Which outcome would have made it more likely that Congress would act? If the Court had affirmed, isn't it likely that Congress would have quickly passed legislation permitting off-the-air home recording, perhaps imposing a royalty on the sale of VTRs and blank tapes? By reversing, did the Supreme Court make it politically impossible for copyright owners to obtain home-taping royalty legislation?

(7)   Although the motion picture industry forecasted dire consequences if it lost the *Sony* case, the result turned out to be a win-win proposition for everyone. The widespread availability of VTRs led to an entirely new market for exploiting motion pictures: namely, the home-video market. By 1986, movie studios made more money from rentals and sales of videotapes (and later, DVDs) than they did from theatrical releases. Does this outcome indicate that courts should be cautious about granting injunctions where new technology is involved? Or, on the contrary, are the reproductive capabilities of new technologies so potentially devastating to plaintiffs not as well financed as Universal and Disney as to counsel a need to protect such copyright holders from harm until the legal niceties of defendants' technological advances can be sorted out by the courts (or Congress)?

(8)   For an enlightening account of *Sony*'s background, doctrine, and continuing importance to the law, see Litman, *The Story of* Sony v. Universal City Studios: *Mary Poppins Meets the Boston Strangler, in* INTELLECTUAL PROPERTY STORIES (J. Ginsburg & R. Dreyfuss eds., 2005).

(9)   How should the *Sony* doctrine be applied to the current generation of digital video recorders (DVRs)? Should it matter whether the recording is stored in the consumer's home on a set-top box, or whether it is stored on a server at the cable company's premises at an individual user's request? In *Cartoon Network LP v. CSC Holdings, Inc.*, 536 F.3d 121 (2d Cir. 2008), reproduced in part in Chapter 7, the plaintiffs did not plead contributory infringement. What would have happened if they had?

[B]   The Audio Home Recording Act

[1]   Introduction

In the 1980s, the recording industry moved away from conventional "analog" recording formats (like vinyl discs and magnetic tapes) and toward the new "digital format" of compact discs ("CDs"). But just as consumers began to accept the new format, an even newer format was being launched in Japan: Digital Audio Tape ("DAT"). Although less durable than CDs, DATs offered customers several apparent advantages. They (and the equipment on which they were played) were more portable, and home users of DAT technology could record in the new format, as well as play back prerecorded DAT tapes.

From the viewpoint of the American recording industry, home taping of prerecorded discs was always problematic, but the near-perfect fidelity of multi-generational digital copies added new dimensions to that problem. While the risk to sales posed by home taping in "analog" format was limited by the fact that sound quality degrades noticeably with each "generation" of copies, a key characteristic of digital media is that there is little appreciable difference between the sound quality of, say, a CD and that of a DAT recording (or MP3 file) copied from it. When and if DAT technology became widely available to American consumers, the recording companies feared the resultant increase in home copying might pose a threat to the market in prerecorded CDs.

The industry's response was to threaten (and, in at least one instance, to sue) manufacturers and importers of DAT recording and playback devices, based on their alleged contributory liability for private acts of copyright infringement which would be committed using the devices. Whether actions brought on this basis would have succeeded in the face of *Sony* is a moot question. In effect, the possibility of *Sony*-like litigation was enough to delay the introduction of the technology in this country until a legislative solution could be devised.

The Audio Home Recording Act ("AHRA"), enacted in 1992, broke new ground in American intellectual property law. Not only did it create a new compulsory license, but it imposed legal limitations *on copying technology itself*, rather than solely on the uses to which that technology may be put; and it created a new cause of action, *apart from copyright infringement*, for violations of its regulatory scheme. Significantly, the Act was codified outside the Copyright Act — in Chapter 10 of Title 17.

[2] Highlights of the AHRA

The scope of the Act. The AHRA avoids any use of the term "phonorecord" to describe the material objects to which its provisions apply. Instead, the Act uses the term "digital musical recording," which is defined to exclude "audio books" and computer hard drives. Notably, however, coverage is *not* limited to DAT tapes alone, even though DAT is the recording format which prompted the legislation.

Anti-serial copying technology. The AHRA requires the use of built-in devices or mechanisms to prevent "serial copying" on digital audio recording devices made, imported into, or sold in the United States, and bars the marketing of equipment designed to frustrate the devices. The Act also bars encoding inaccurate information about the copyright status of a sound recording or musical composition on a digital recording — although it does not affirmatively require that any information of this kind be encoded.

Royalty payments. The AHRA creates an obligation on the part of importers and manufacturers of digital audio equipment to pay royalties, and to file periodic reports with the Copyright Office. The royalties are based on the "transfer price" of equipment distributed, with special provisions for audio systems which have digital and nondigital components. Royalties are also due on the "transfer price" of "digital audio recording media" (such as DAT tapes). "Transfer price" is the price charged by the domestic manufacturer of digital equipment or media, or the price entered for customs purposes (in the case of imported items). Significantly, no provision for adjustment of royalty rates had to be built into the AHRA, because the royalty formula is based on a percentage of transfer price.

Royalty distributions. The AHRA defines a class of persons who have stakes in the funds generated by the new statutory license, and who have standing to enter into negotiations and agreements (and, if necessary, to sue) with respect to the distribution of those funds. These "interested copyright parties" include: so-called "featured recording artists" (who have a 40% share of the 66-2/3% of overall royalties that flow into the so-called Sound Recording Fund, calculated after the deduction of 4% for nonfeatured artists); the owners of copyright in the sound recordings (who share the rest of the Sound Recording Fund); and the owners of the musical works copyrights (music publishers and songwriters, who share equally the 33-1/3% of overall royalties which go into the Musical Works Fund).

Dispute resolution. The AHRA grants an antitrust exemption allowing the "interested copyright parties" to appoint common agents to collect and distribute the funds, and to negotiate distribution of the funds within the group. As enacted, the legislation looked to the Copyright Royalty Tribunal to resolve intra-group disputes concerning distribution which cannot be negotiated successfully. Like the other statutory licenses, this function now has been transferred to the Copyright Royalty Judges. *See* § 7.01[C].

Independent remedies for independent wrongs. The AHRA provides for civil actions to recover actual and statutory damages, as well as for injunctive relief, in case of a failure to observe the serial copying regulation requirements or to pay the required royalties, with repeat offenders subject to enhanced penalties. The AHRA also makes it clear that there can be no liability for copyright infringement in

connection with noncommercial home recording by consumers using digital recording equipment and media — or for contributory infringement based on the
manufacture, importation or distribution of such equipment or media. *See* § 1008.
The meaning of this language was clarified (if not narrowed) by § 115(c)(3)(I),
enacted as part of the DPRA (discussed in § 7.07).

NOTES AND QUESTIONS

(1) The exemption from copyright infringement liability in certain circumstances in § 1008 represents a central innovation of the amendments contained in
the AHRA. Not only did these amendments define a new set of obligations and
enforcement mechanisms, distinct from the Copyright Act of 1976, but, in turn, they
limited the rights of copyright owners under § 106. Do you find it odd that *sui
generis* legislation — legislation codified in Title 17, but not a part of the Copyright
Act — limits rights under the Copyright Act? Is this the result of Congressional
indifference to formal distinctions between copyright and legislation designed to
regulate new technology? Or does the technique employed by Congress in crafting
the AHRA reflect instead a concern for the integrity of the Copyright Act, and a
judgment that carving out the subject matter of the AHRA for special treatment
was preferable to tinkering more intrusively with the Copyright Act itself?

(2) Another innovation is the requirement imposed on manufacturers and
importers to build safeguards against serial copying into digital recording equipment. Is this a wise approach? Suppose that, in the 1800s, it had been possible to
impose a technical "fix" on printing presses to make it physically impossible to
engage in the kind of wholesale book piracy to which the first copyright statute was
a response. Would the results have been desirable?

Turning to the present day, should computer manufacturers be required to build
"anti-copy" chips (which would shut down attempts to copy software carrying a
digital indicator of copyright status) into the hardware systems they build and sell?
Why or why not? Does your answer depend on the nature of any penalties imposed
for circumvention of anti-copying devices? Should there be substantial fines or
prison terms for the development of means to evade such technology? Should it
matter whether the circumvention device has legitimate non-infringing uses?

Should we be concerned that intellectual property legislation will degenerate into
Congressional endorsement of private technological solutions, which may be too
broad and/or outdated? Why should Congress be involved at all in enforcing such
marketplace maneuverings?

(3) Under the terms of the AHRA, performers enjoy a statutorily prescribed
share in the distribution of royalties. (In this connection, remember that many
artists who participate in the making of sound recordings do so as "employees for
hire," or assign away copyright in their employment agreements.) Moreover, the
portion of the Sound Recording Fund allocated to these performers is to be paid out
directly, rather than through the recording companies. Is this innovation good
intellectual property policy? Is it transferable to other rights or technologies?

(4) The scheme for the distribution of royalties under the AHRA has proved
problematic, in part because small individual claimants to disbursements from the

various funds have the power to frustrate agreements among the agents who represent the overwhelming bulk of the individuals entitled to share in the funds deposited with the Copyright Office. Thus, for example, it was not until February 1997 that the distribution of 1992–1994 royalties was resolved, after a CARP was appointed at the insistence of two songwriters who were the only holdouts from a settlement agreed to in early 1995 by organizations representing thousands of other claimants — from whose royalties were deducted the lion's share of the costs of the protracted determination. *See* 62 Fed. Reg. 6558. Similarly, it was not until February 2001 that the Copyright Office announced the results of a CARP to distribute the 1995-1998 royalties. *See* 66 Fed. Reg. 9360. These examples illustrate how much trouble a few stubborn individuals can generate in such proceedings. Is this process too cumbersome? Is the Government's role too large?

(5)   Despite the promise of DAT for consumers, the technology failed in the marketplace. Few consumers bought DAT equipment, and recording companies issued only small numbers of prerecorded DAT tapes. Some consumer advocates contend that this failure can be attributed to the incremental increased cost attributable to the statutory royalty. Another possible explanation is that there were two competing DAT formats, and consumers were reluctant to invest in either until a single standard emerged. Finally, with the rise of the Internet, DAT was largely supplanted by computer-based digital technologies, such as MP3.

(6)   MP3 technology makes possible the authorized and unauthorized distribution of music over the Internet in the form of compressed digital files. Inexpensive portable MP3 players can be loaded with music files previously downloaded from the Internet to a personal computer, thus allowing for their playback anywhere and anytime. Even before the first such device — the "Rio" — had come to market, several recording industry associations sued its manufacturer for (among other things) violation of the AHRA. In June 1999, the Ninth Circuit concluded that computers do not constitute "digital audio recording devices" within the meaning of the statute; and because players like the Rio merely allow consumers to "space-shift" digital music files for personal use, it is consistent with both the letter and the spirit of the AHRA to exempt them from its coverage. *See Recording Industry Association of America v. Diamond Multimedia Systems, Inc.*, 180 F.3d 1072 (9th Cir. 1999). The decision is discussed in useful detail in a student note by Ines G. Gonzalez in 15 Berkeley Tech. L.J. 67 (2000).

(7)   The exclusion of computers from the AHRA does not always favor consumers. In the *Napster* case (discussed in the next subsection), for example, the Ninth Circuit rejected an affirmative defense based on the home-recording exemption in § 1008. The court said:

> We agree with the district court that the Audio Home Recording Act does not cover the downloading of MP3 files to computer hard drives. First, "under the plain meaning of the Act's definition of digital audio recording devices, computers (and their hard drives) are not digital audio recording devices because their 'primary purpose' is not to make digital audio copied recordings." *Recording Indus. Ass'n of Am. v. Diamond Multimedia Sys., Inc.*, 180 F.3d 1072, 1078 (9th Cir. 1999). Second, notwithstanding Napster's claim that computers are "digital audio recording devices," computers do

not make "digital music recordings" as defined by the Audio Home Recording Act. *Id.* at 1077 (citing S. Rep. 102-294) ("There are simply no grounds in either the plain language of the definition or in the legislative history for interpreting the term 'digital musical recording' to include songs fixed on computer hard drives.").

239 F.3d at 1024. In other words, because the AHRA was defined narrowly to keep computer manufacturers from paying royalties, the recording industry was able to reconsider the "grand bargain" that allowed home recording in exchange for royalties on equipment.

The *Napster* defendants also took comfort from *Diamond Rio* in asserting that the "space-shifting" activities of Napster users should be considered privileged fair use. For the fate of that contention, see the discussion in Chapter 10.

(8) In 2006, XM Satellite Radio announced that it would provide a new receiver, called the "Inno," which would enable subscribers to record and playback individual songs that were broadcast on the XM service. When sued by the major record labels, XM defended itself on the ground that the Inno was a "digital audio recording device" that was exempt from liability under § 1008. How should the court have ruled on this defense? *See Atlantic Recording Corp. v. XM Satellite Radio, Inc.*, 81 U.S.P.Q.2d (BNA) 1407 (S.D.N.Y. 2007).

[C] Peer-to-Peer File Sharing

In June 1999, a new website called Napster allowed users to search for MP3 files contained on other users' computers. Napster's software uploaded file names — but not the files themselves — to the Napster website and indexed them. When a user clicked on a file name, the software initiated a transfer of the file from the host computer to the user's computer over the Internet — without going through the Napster website. Napster quickly became enormously popular: at its height, it had some 75 million users exchanging 10,000 MP3 files per second.

Major record labels sued Napster for contributory and vicarious infringement. In *A&M Records v. Napster*, 239 F.3d 1004 (9th Cir. 2001), the court affirmed the District Court's findings that Napster had ample notice of how its website was being used, and that the centralized architecture of the system made it possible for Napster to exercise control over those uses. Ultimately, the District Court ordered Napster to suspend operations until it could install a new filtering mechanism, which searched user files for specific "audio fingerprints," and the Ninth Circuit upheld this modified preliminary injunction. 284 F.3d 1091 (9th Cir. 2002). Unable to comply, Napster filed for bankruptcy in June 2002.[1]

After a long-running dispute over whether companies which invested in Napster bore any responsibility for its conduct, *see UMG Recordings, Inc. v. Bertelsmann AG*, 222 F.R.D. 408 (N.D. Cal. 2004) (denying motion to dismiss), settlements were reached between the investors and copyright owners. For more on investor

---

[1] Napster's assets were sold to a Silicon Valley software firm, Roxio, Inc., which relaunched Napster as an authorized, fee-based service. Napster merged with the online music service Rhapsody in December 2011.

liability, see *UMG Recordings, Inc. v. Shelter Capital Partners, LLC*, 667 F.3d 1022 (9th Cir. 2011) (investors are not liable for exercising power to select a majority of the Board of Directors without proof that those directors acted in concert).

Following the original Napster's demise, attention shifted to other peer-to-peer file sharing services. In *In re Aimster Copyright Litigation*, 334 F.3d 643 (7th Cir. 2003), Judge Posner affirmed a preliminary injunction against Aimster, a Napster-like service, noting there was no evidence that anyone had actually used Aimster for noninfringing purposes. Perhaps more significantly, in April 2003, a federal district judge granted partial summary judgment in favor of Grokster and Streamcast, whose "second-generation" file-sharing software enabled users to search for files on other users' computers *without* maintaining an index on a centralized website.

Following the District Court's ruling in *Grokster*, the recording industry embarked on a controversial campaign of filing suits against individuals alleged to have made music files available for sharing on peer-to-peer networks. But the campaign ran into an unexpected snag when the D.C. Circuit ruled that subpoenas seeking to compel Internet service providers to identify individual file-sharers would no longer be available as a matter of course. *See Recording Industry Ass'n of America v. Verizon Internet Services, Inc.*, 351 F.3d 1229 (D.C. Cir. 2003) (discussed in § 9.03[B] below). As a result, the industry must now file "John Doe" lawsuits before attempting to obtain the identities of alleged infringers from service providers.

In December 2004, the Supreme Court granted certiorari to review the Ninth Circuit's affirmance in *Grokster*. The Court's opinion follows.

METRO-GOLDWYN-MAYER STUDIOS, INC. v. GROKSTER, LTD.
Supreme Court of the United States
545 U.S. 913 (2005)

JUSTICE SOUTER delivered the opinion of the Court.

The question is under what circumstances the distributor of a product capable of both lawful and unlawful use is liable for acts of copyright infringement by third parties using the product. We hold that one who distributes a device with the object of promoting its use to infringe copyright, as shown by clear expression or other affirmative steps taken to foster infringement, is liable for the resulting acts of infringement by third parties.

I A

Respondents, Grokster, Ltd., and StreamCast Networks, Inc., defendants in the trial court, distribute free software products that allow computer users to share electronic files through peer-to-peer networks, so called because users' computers communicate directly with each other, not through central servers.

. . . [U]sers of peer-to-peer networks include individual recipients of Grokster's and StreamCast's software, and although . . . the software can be used to share any type of digital file, they have prominently employed [the software] in sharing copyrighted music and video files without authorization. A group of copyright holders (MGM for short, but including motion picture studios, recording companies, songwriters, and music publishers) sued Grokster and StreamCast for their users' copyright infringements, alleging that they knowingly and intentionally distributed their software to enable users to reproduce and distribute the copyrighted works in violation of the Copyright Act. MGM sought damages and an injunction.

. . . Grokster's eponymous software employs what is known as FastTrack technology. . . . [StreamCast's] software, called Morpheus, relies on what is known as Gnutella technology. A user who downloads and installs either software [may] send requests for files directly to the computers of others using software compatible with FastTrack or Gnutella. On the FastTrack network opened by the Grokster software, the user's request goes to a computer given an indexing capacity by the software and designated a supernode. . . . If the file is found, the supernode discloses its location to the computer requesting it, and the requesting user can download the file directly from the computer located. . . .

. . . [I]n some versions of the Gnutella protocol there are no supernodes. In these versions, . . . [w]hen a user enters a search request into the Morpheus software, it sends the request to computers connected with it, which in turn pass the request along to other connected peers. The search results are communicated to the requesting computer, and the user can download desired files directly from peers' computers. As this description indicates, Grokster and StreamCast use no servers to intercept the content of the search requests or to mediate the file transfers conducted by users of the software. . . .

Although Grokster and StreamCast do not therefore know when particular files are copied, . . . [a study by plaintiffs' expert] showed that nearly 90% of the files available for download on the FastTrack system were copyrighted works. Grokster and StreamCast dispute this figure. . . . They also argue that potential noninfringing uses of their software are significant in kind, even if infrequent in practice. Some musical performers, for example, have gained new audiences by distributing their copyrighted works for free across peer-to-peer networks, and some distributors of unprotected content have used peer-to-peer networks to disseminate files. . . .

As for quantification, . . . no one can say how often the software is used to obtain copies of unprotected material. But MGM's evidence gives reason to think that the vast majority of users' downloads are acts of infringement, and because well over 100 million copies of the software in question are known to have been downloaded, and billions of files are shared across the FastTrack and Gnutella networks each month, the probable scope of copyright infringement is staggering.

Grokster and StreamCast concede the infringement in most downloads, and it is uncontested that they are aware that users employ their software primarily to download copyrighted files. . . . [In addition,] [t]he record is replete with evidence that from the moment Grokster and StreamCast began to distribute their free software, each one clearly voiced the objective that recipients use it to download copyrighted works, and each took active steps to encourage infringement.

After the notorious file-sharing service, Napster, was sued by copyright holders for facilitation of copyright infringement, *A & M Records, Inc. v. Napster, Inc.*, 114 F. Supp. 2d 896 (N.D. Cal. 2000), *aff'd in part, rev'd in part*, 239 F.3d 1004 (9th Cir. 2001), . . . [both Grokster and StreamCast took steps to encourage the former users of Napster to download and use their software as an alternative to Napster for making copies of copyrighted music files. Other evidence of intent is summarized in Part III.A. below.] . . .

II A

MGM and many of the *amici* fault the Court of Appeals's holding for upsetting a sound balance between the respective values of supporting creative pursuits through copyright protection and promoting innovation in new communication technologies by limiting the incidence of liability for copyright infringement. . . .

The tension between the two values is the subject of this case, with its claim that digital distribution of copyrighted material threatens copyright holders as never before, because every copy is identical to the original, copying is easy, and many people (especially the young) use file-sharing software to download copyrighted works. . . . [Indeed,] the indications are that the ease of copying songs or movies using software like Grokster's and Napster's is fostering disdain for copyright protection. As the case has been presented to us, these fears are said to be offset by the different concern that imposing liability, not only on infringers but on distributors of software based on its potential for unlawful use, could limit further development of beneficial technologies.

The argument for imposing indirect liability in this case is, however, a powerful one, given the number of infringing downloads that occur every day using StreamCast's and Grokster's software. When a widely shared service or product is used to commit infringement, it may be impossible to enforce rights in the protected work effectively against all direct infringers, the only practical alternative being to go against the distributor of the copying device for secondary liability on a theory of contributory or vicarious infringement. . . .

One infringes contributorily by intentionally inducing or encouraging direct infringement, see *Gershwin Pub. Corp. v. Columbia Artists Management, Inc.*, 443 F.2d 1159, 1162 (2d Cir. 1971), and infringes vicariously by profiting from direct infringement while declining to exercise a right to stop or limit it, *Shapiro, Bernstein & Co. v. H. L. Green Co.*, 316 F.2d 304, 307 (2d Cir. 1963). Although "the Copyright Act does not expressly render anyone liable for infringement committed by another," *Sony Corp. v. Universal City Studios*, 464 U.S., at 434, these doctrines of secondary liability emerged from common law principles and are well established in the law. . . .

B

. . . In *Sony Corp. v. Universal City Studios, supra*, . . . there was no evidence that Sony had expressed an object of bringing about taping in violation of copyright or had taken active steps to increase its profits from unlawful taping. Although Sony's advertisements urged consumers to buy the VCR to "record favorite shows" or "build a library" of recorded programs, neither of these uses was necessarily infringing. . . .

On those facts, with no evidence of stated or indicated intent to promote infringing uses, the only conceivable basis for imposing liability was on a theory of contributory infringement arising from its sale of VCRs to consumers with knowledge that some would use them to infringe. But because the VCR was "capable of commercially significant noninfringing uses," we held the manufacturer could not be faulted solely on the basis of its distribution.

This analysis reflected patent law's traditional staple article of commerce doctrine, now codified, that distribution of a component of a patented device will not violate the patent if it is suitable for use in other ways. 35 U.S.C. § 271(c). The doctrine was devised to identify instances in which it may be presumed from distribution of an article in commerce that the distributor intended the article to be used to infringe another's patent, and so may justly be held liable for that infringement. . . .

In sum, where an article is "good for nothing else" but infringement, there is no legitimate public interest in its unlicensed availability, and there is no injustice in presuming or imputing an intent to infringe. Conversely, the doctrine absolves the equivocal conduct of selling an item with substantial lawful as well as unlawful uses. . . . It leaves breathing room for innovation and a vigorous commerce.

The parties and many of the *amici* in this case think the key to resolving it is the *Sony* rule and, in particular, what it means for a product to be "capable of commercially significant noninfringing uses." . . . MGM says [that 10% noninfringing use] should not qualify as "substantial," and the Court should quantify *Sony* to the extent of holding that a product used "principally" for infringement does not qualify. . . .

We agree with MGM that the Court of Appeals misapplied *Sony*, which it read as limiting secondary liability quite beyond the circumstances to which the case applied. *Sony* barred secondary liability based on presuming or imputing intent to cause infringement solely from the design or distribution of a product capable of substantial lawful use, which the distributor knows is in fact used for infringement. The Ninth Circuit read *Sony* . . . to mean that whenever a product is capable of substantial lawful use, the producer can never be held contributorily liable for third parties' infringing use of it . . . , unless the distributors had "specific knowledge of infringement at a time at which they contributed to the infringement, and failed to act upon that information." 380 F.3d at 1162. . . .

This view of *Sony*, however, was error, converting the case from one about liability resting on imputed intent to one about liability on any theory. Because *Sony* did not displace other theories of secondary liability, and because we find below that it was error to grant summary judgment to the companies on MGM's inducement claim, we do not revisit *Sony* further, as MGM requests, to add a more quantified description of the point of balance between protection and commerce when liability rests solely on distribution with knowledge that unlawful use will occur. It is enough to note that the Ninth Circuit's judgment rested on an erroneous understanding of

Sony and to leave further consideration of the *Sony* rule for a day when that may be required.

C

Sony's rule limits imputing culpable intent as a matter of law from the characteristics or uses of a distributed product. But nothing in *Sony* requires courts to ignore evidence of intent if there is such evidence, and the case was never meant to foreclose rules of fault-based liability derived from the common law.[10] Thus, where evidence goes beyond a product's characteristics or the knowledge that it may be put to infringing uses, and shows statements or actions directed to promoting infringement, *Sony*'s staple-article rule will not preclude liability.

The classic case of direct evidence of unlawful purpose occurs when one induces commission of infringement by another, or "entices or persuades another" to infringe, as by advertising. . . .

For the same reasons that *Sony* took the staple-article doctrine of patent law as a model for its copyright safe-harbor rule, the inducement rule, too, is a sensible one for copyright. We adopt it here, holding that one who distributes a device with the object of promoting its use to infringe copyright, as shown by clear expression or other affirmative steps taken to foster infringement, is liable for the resulting acts of infringement by third parties. We are, of course, mindful of the need to keep from trenching on regular commerce or discouraging the development of technologies with lawful and unlawful potential. Accordingly, . . . mere knowledge of infringing potential or of actual infringing uses would not be enough here to subject a distributor to liability. Nor would ordinary acts incident to product distribution, such as offering customers technical support or product updates, support liability in themselves. The inducement rule, instead, premises liability on purposeful, culpable expression and conduct, and thus does nothing to compromise legitimate commerce or discourage innovation having a lawful promise.

III A

The only apparent question about treating MGM's evidence as sufficient to withstand summary judgment under the theory of inducement goes to the need on MGM's part to adduce evidence that StreamCast and Grokster communicated an inducing message to their software users. The classic instance of inducement is by advertisement or solicitation that broadcasts a message designed to stimulate others to commit violations. . . . It is undisputed that StreamCast . . . [distributed ads to] patrons of Napster, then under attack in the courts for facilitating massive infringement. Those who accepted . . . were offered software to perform the same services, which a fact-finder could conclude would readily have been understood in the Napster market as the ability to download copyrighted music files. Grokster distributed an electronic newsletter containing links to articles promoting its software's ability to access popular copyrighted music. . . .

---

[10] Nor does the Patent Act's exemption from liability for those who distribute a staple article of commerce, 35 U.S.C. § 271(c), extend to those who induce patent infringement, § 271(b).

In StreamCast's case, . . . the evidence just described was supplemented by other unequivocal indications of unlawful purpose in the internal communications and advertising designs aimed at Napster users. Whether the messages were communicated is not to the point. . . . The function of the message in the theory of inducement is to prove by a defendant's own statements that his unlawful purpose disqualifies him from claiming protection. . . . Proving that a message was sent out, then, is the preeminent but not exclusive way of showing that active steps were taken with the purpose of bringing about infringing acts. . . . Here, the summary judgment record is replete with other evidence that Grokster and StreamCast, unlike the manufacturer and distributor in *Sony*, acted with a purpose to cause copyright violations by use of software suitable for illegal use.

Three features of this evidence of intent are particularly notable. First, each company showed itself to be aiming to satisfy a known source of demand for copyright infringement, the market comprising former Napster users. . . . Grokster and StreamCast's efforts to supply services to former Napster users, deprived of a mechanism to copy and distribute what were overwhelmingly infringing files, indicate a principal, if not exclusive, intent on the part of each to bring about infringement.

Second, . . . neither company attempted to develop filtering tools or other mechanisms to diminish the infringing activity using their software. While the Ninth Circuit treated the defendants' failure to develop such tools as irrelevant because they lacked an independent duty to monitor their users' activity, we think this evidence underscores Grokster's and StreamCast's intentional facilitation of their users' infringement.[12]

Third, . . . StreamCast and Grokster make money by selling advertising space, by directing ads to the screens of computers employing their software. As the record shows, the more the software is used, the more ads are sent out and the greater the advertising revenue becomes. Since the extent of the software's use determines the gain to the distributors, the commercial sense of their enterprise turns on high-volume use, which the record shows is infringing.[13] This evidence alone would not justify an inference of unlawful intent, but viewed in the context of the entire record its import is clear.

The unlawful objective is unmistakable.

---

[12] Of course, in the absence of other evidence of intent, a court would be unable to find contributory infringement liability merely based on a failure to take affirmative steps to prevent infringement, if the device otherwise was capable of substantial noninfringing uses. Such a holding would tread too close to the *Sony* safe harbor.

[13] Grokster and StreamCast contend that any theory of liability based on their conduct is not properly before this Court because the rulings in the trial and appellate courts dealt only with the present versions of their software, not "past acts . . . that allegedly encouraged infringement or assisted . . . known acts of infringement." This contention misapprehends the basis for their potential liability. It is not only that encouraging a particular consumer to infringe a copyright can give rise to secondary liability for the infringement that results. Inducement liability goes beyond that, and the distribution of a product can itself give rise to liability where evidence shows that the distributor intended and encouraged the product to be used to infringe. In such a case, the culpable act is not merely the encouragement of infringement but also the distribution of the tool intended for infringing use.

B

In addition to intent to bring about infringement and distribution of a device suitable for infringing use, the inducement theory of course requires evidence of actual infringement by recipients of the device, the software in this case. As the account of the facts indicates, there is evidence of infringement on a gigantic scale, and there is no serious issue of the adequacy of MGM's showing on this point. . . .

There is substantial evidence in MGM's favor on all elements of inducement, and summary judgment in favor of Grokster and StreamCast was error. On remand, reconsideration of MGM's motion for summary judgment will be in order.

The judgment of the Court of Appeals is vacated, and the case is remanded for further proceedings consistent with this opinion. . . .

The United States Supreme Court unanimously confirmed that using this service to trade copyrighted material is illegal. Copying copyrighted motion picture and music files using unauthorized peer-to-peer services is illegal and is prosecuted by copyright owners.

There are legal services for downloading music and movies. This service is not one of them.

YOUR IP ADDRESS IS ▆▆ ▌ ▆▆ ▆▆ AND HAS BEEN LOGGED. Don't think you can't get caught. You are not anonymous.

In the meantime, please visit www.respectcopyrights.com and www.musicunited.org to learn more about copyright.

Goodbye, Grokster!

JUSTICE GINSBURG, with whom the CHIEF JUSTICE and JUSTICE KENNEDY join, concurring.

I concur in the Court's decision, which vacates in full the judgment of the Court of Appeals for the Ninth Circuit, and write separately to clarify why I conclude that the Court of Appeals misperceived, and hence misapplied, our holding in *Sony* . . .

This case differs markedly from *Sony*. Here, there has been no finding of any fair use and little beyond anecdotal evidence of noninfringing uses. . . . Review of these declarations [submitted by defendants] reveals mostly anecdotal evidence, sometimes obtained second-hand, of authorized copyrighted works or public domain works available online and shared through peer-to-peer networks, and general statements about the benefits of peer-to-peer technology. . . . These declarations do not support summary judgment in the face of evidence, proffered by MGM, of overwhelming use of Grokster's and StreamCast's software for infringement.

Even if the absolute number of noninfringing files copied using the Grokster and StreamCast software is large, it does not follow that the products are therefore put to substantial noninfringing uses and are thus immune from liability. The number of noninfringing copies may be reflective of, and dwarfed by, the huge total volume of files shared. Further, the District Court and the Court of Appeals did not sharply distinguish between uses of Grokster's and StreamCast's software products (which this case is about) and uses of peer-to-peer technology generally (which this case is not about).

In sum, . . . there was evidence that Grokster's and StreamCast's products were . . . overwhelmingly used to infringe, and that this infringement was the overwhelming source of revenue from the products. Fairly appraised, the evidence was insufficient to demonstrate, beyond genuine debate, a reasonable prospect that substantial or commercially significant noninfringing uses were likely to develop over time. . . .

JUSTICE BREYER, with whom JUSTICE STEVENS and JUSTICE O'CONNOR join, concurring.

I agree with the Court that the distributor of a dual-use technology may be liable for the infringing activities of third parties where he or she actively seeks to advance the infringement. I further agree that, in light of our holding today, we need not now "revisit" *Sony* . . . Other Members of the Court, however, take up the *Sony* question. . . . And they answer that question by stating that the Court of Appeals was wrong when it granted summary judgment on the issue in Grokster's favor. I write to explain why I disagree with them on this matter. . . .

. . . When measured against *Sony*'s underlying evidence and analysis, the evidence now before us shows that Grokster passes *Sony*'s test — that is, whether the company's product is capable of substantial or commercially significant noninfringing uses. For one thing, MGM's own expert declared that 75% of current files available on Grokster are infringing and 15% are "likely infringing." That leaves some number of files near 10% that apparently are noninfringing, a figure very similar to the 9% or so of authorized time-shifting uses of the VCR that the Court faced in *Sony*. . . .

Importantly, *Sony* also used the word "*capable*," asking whether the product is "capable of" substantial noninfringing uses. . . . [This] language indicates the appropriateness of looking to potential future uses of the product to determine its "capability."

Here the record reveals a significant future market for noninfringing uses of Grokster-type peer-to-peer software. Such software permits the exchange of *any* sort of digital file — whether that file does, or does not, contain copyrighted material. As more and more uncopyrighted information is stored in swappable form, it seems a likely inference that lawful peer-to-peer sharing will become increasingly prevalent. . . .

The real question here . . . is whether we should modify the *Sony* standard, as MGM requests, or interpret *Sony* more strictly, as . . . JUSTICE GINSBURG [suggests]. . . . [T]o determine whether modification, or a strict interpretation, of *Sony* is needed, I would ask . . . (1) Has *Sony* worked to protect new technology? (2) If so, would modification or strict interpretation significantly weaken that protection? (3) If so, would new or necessary copyright-related benefits outweigh any such weakening?

[JUSTICE BREYER's opinion then (1) praises the *Sony* rule as "clear," "strongly technology protecting," "forward looking," and "mindful of the limitations facing judges where matters of technology are concerned"; (2) predicts that changing the *Sony* standard would greatly increase the legal uncertainty facing developers of new technology; and (3) suggests that copyright owners have other methods of reducing infringement, including suits against individual infringers and making lawful distribution cheaper and easier.]

For these reasons, I disagree with JUSTICE GINSBURG, but I agree with the Court and join its opinion.

NOTES AND QUESTIONS

(1)   The *Grokster* litigation was significantly shaped by an unusual procedural circumstance. In the District Court, defendants moved only for *partial* summary judgment with respect to *future* distribution of the current versions of the defendants' software, apparently conceding that there were triable issues of fact concerning liability for damages for past infringement. Believing that evidence of inducement went only to liability for damages for past infringement, the lower courts never considered the proffered evidence of inducement. Thus, once the Supreme Court determined that past activities could give rise to an inference of improper intent that also would taint future distribution of the software (see footnote 13), reversal was all but assured.

(2)   The concurring opinions reveal that the Court remains deeply divided over the proper interpretation of *Sony*'s "capable of substantial noninfringing use" standard. Justice Ginsburg's opinion (joined by Chief Justice Rehnquist and Justice Kennedy) finds little more than anecdotal evidence of noninfringing use, and indicates that this evidence is outweighed by the fact that the vast majority of actual use was infringing. Justice Breyer (joined by Justice Stevens and Justice O'Connor) emphasizes that *Sony* appeared to find authorized time-shifting to be "significant" even though it represented only 9% of actual use of the VCR at the time of trial. Which of the two concurring opinions do you think has the better of the argument?

(3)   The unanimous opinion of the *Grokster* Court by Justice Souter sidesteps the contentious issue of the proper interpretation of *Sony* entirely, finding *Sony* inapplicable where there is evidence that the defendant distributed a device "with the object of promoting its use to infringe copyright." This new standard shifts the focus away from the characteristics of the product or device itself to the intent of the person who distributes it. Do you foresee any difficulties in applying the Court's new inducement standard? Can you imagine any circumstances under which a future defendant could distribute similar file-sharing software without raising an inference of improper intent?

(4)   The Court says that inducement liability must be supported by "clear expression or other *affirmative* steps taken to foster infringement" (emphasis added). Yet one of the three categories of evidence that the Court relies on to

demonstrate the defendants' intent is the *failure* to take any affirmative steps to prevent infringing use, such as attempting to develop filtering tools. Does this suggest that technology developers now have an affirmative duty to attempt to minimize infringement? After *Grokster*, would you be comfortable advising a technology developer that it need not take any steps to attempt to minimize infringement? What if a technology company could design safeguards against copyright infringement into a product — but does not (fearing, perhaps, that it would make the product less attractive in the marketplace)? Footnote 12 of the *Grokster* opinion states that "a court would be unable to find contributory infringement liability merely based on a failure to take affirmative steps to prevent infringement." How significant is this limitation? How often will a claim of secondary liability be based on such a failure alone?

(5)   The Court also relied on the fact that both defendants aimed to capture the former users of Napster (implicitly assuming, despite fierce academic debate, that *Napster* was correctly decided). Does that fact, by itself, demonstrate an intent to encourage infringement? Aren't the developers of authorized music-downloading services also trying to capture the same market? Moreover, as demonstrated by *Sony*, it will rarely be clear at the outset whether the use of a new technology will or will not be held to be infringing. Suppose a technology developer encourages a use that it honestly believes to be noninfringing, but that is later held to be infringing. Should it be held liable for inducement?

(6)   The Court notes that the defendants gave away their software and made money instead by selling advertising, so that their revenue depended on how frequently the software was used (for both infringing and noninfringing purposes). Suppose instead that a subsequent software developer sells copies of similar software outright, without any advertising revenue. Will that be seen as a legitimate business model or as a devious attempt to circumvent legal restrictions on a product that has already been enjoined? What if an individual decides to give similar software away for free? Is that an act of altruism, or an act of piracy?

(7)   How long does the taint of active inducement last? If a defendant distributed a device that is capable of noninfringing uses, but did so with unlawful intent, should it be enjoined from distributing the device permanently? If not, how long should the injunction last? Would it matter whether there are any parties distributing a similar device without any unlawful intent?

(8)   Justices Ginsburg and Kennedy (along with the late Chief Justice) seem open to a fundamental reconsideration of the *Sony* standard that Justice Breyer (in his concurrence) commends as "clear," "strongly technology protecting," "forward looking," and "mindful of the limitations facing judges where matters of technology are concerned." But is such a fundamental reconsideration to occur anytime soon? And if *Grokster*'s articulation of the "inducement" concept has saved *Sony*, at what cost? In the future, how great is the risk that companies providing the new technologies that Justice Breyer believes *Sony* has sheltered will be tagged with liability for "inducement"? And how would you expect those companies to adapt to their new legal exposure, however great or small?

(9)   As we saw above, the *Sony* standard can be understood as applied to both contributory *and* vicarious liability — or to contributory liability only. In *Grokster*,

the Ninth Circuit relied on *Sony* to absolve the defendants of both. Given its ruling on "inducement," however, the Supreme Court did not reach the issue of vicarious liability. After *Grokster*, how should a court deal with a case in which the issue of a technology provider's vicarious liability is inescapably presented? In *Arista Records LLC v. Lime Group LLC*, 715 F. Supp. 2d 481 (S.D.N.Y. 2010), the District Court refused to extend *Sony* to vicarious liability. Should it have?

In *Arista Records*, the District Court held that defendant LimeWire was liable for inducement under *Grokster* for creating and distributing file-sharing software. The court systematically reviewed evidence that LimeWire was aware of substantial infringement by users, purposefully marketed LimeWire to former Napster users, optimized its features to facilitate searches for copyrighted music recordings, depended on infringement for its economic success, and considered but failed to implement filtering to mitigate infringement. Despite this evidence, however, the court held that there was a genuine issue of material fact with regard to contributory infringement, because it was unclear whether LimeWire was "capable of substantial non-infringing use" under *Sony*. Did *Grokster* establish inducement as a separate category of secondary liability, or is it more properly viewed as a type of contributory infringement? If the former, does *Sony* still apply without change to the category of contributory infringement?

(10)   In *Fonovisa* (in § 9.01 above), liability for contributory infringement turned on the defendant (1) knowing of the infringing activity and (2) providing the means that made it possible. Bad intent was not part of the equation, nor has it typically been in the case law exploring this branch of secondary liability. But intent clearly *is* a factor in Justice Souter's explication of "inducement." Can we expect that a plaintiff now will be required, as a general matter, to demonstrate the defendant's *mens rea* in order to make a case for contributory liability?

(11)   The Court makes a point of noting that, like contributory infringement and vicarious liability, active inducement requires evidence of actual infringement by recipients of the device. Whether users of peer-to-peer file sharing software are directly infringing depends in part on whether making individual copies for personal use is a fair use. On what considerations might this depend? The issue is discussed in § 10.03[A] below. For purposes of summary judgment, it is sufficient to note that defendants did not contest the allegation that a large percentage of their users were engaging in direct infringement. Should they have done so?

(12)   After the Supreme Court's decision, Grokster settled, leaving StreamCast as the only remaining defendant. The District Court then accepted the Supreme Court's invitation and granted summary judgment against StreamCast on the inducement theory. *See Metro-Goldwyn-Mayer Studios, Inc. v. Grokster, Ltd.*, 454 F. Supp. 2d 966 (C.D. Cal. 2006). The scope and terms of the permanent injunction are discussed extensively at 518 F. Supp. 2d 1197 (C.D. Cal. 2007).

On remand, should the District Court have revisited the question of personal use? Is personal reproduction expressly permitted by § 1008, which provides that "no action may be brought under this title alleging infringement of copyright based on the manufacture, importation, or distribution of a digital audio recording device . . . or based on the noncommercial use by a consumer of such a device"? For an affirmative answer (as to reproduction, not distribution), see Schaumann, *Direct*

Infringement on Peer-to-Peer Networks, http://papers.ssrn.com/sol3/papers.cfm? abstract_id=703882.

(13)   There is some reason to think that, after *Napster* and *Grokster*, peer-to-peer users migrated to other, less easily regulated platforms rather than giving up the practice. *See* Opderbeck, *Peer-to-Peer Networks, Technological Evolution, and Intellectual Property Reverse Private Attorney General Litigation*, 20 Berkeley Tech. L.J. 1685 (2005). Is there, perhaps, an alternative to costly and frustrating copyright enforcement campaigns? For a provocative proposal to turn file-sharing into a new source of revenues for content industries, through an "alternative compensation" system employing collectively administered blanket licenses, see W. Fisher, PROMISES TO KEEP: TECHNOLOGY, LAW, AND THE FUTURE OF ENTERTAINMENT (2004).

§ 9.03   INTERNET SERVICE PROVIDERS

[A]   Introduction

What role should contributory infringement and vicarious liability play in the regulation of the Internet? To what standards should providers of Internet access and web-hosting services be held? As will be discussed below, the Digital Millennium Copyright Act of 1998 attempted to provide some answers to these questions by giving certain kinds of providers a qualified immunity if they comply with its "notice-and-take-down" scheme. The case law on this subject still matters, however. It provides important background for the interpretation of the DMCA provisions, and it states the principles that will apply in cases where — for one reason or another — no immunity under the DMCA is available. *See* § 512(l) (failure to qualify for limitation of liability under § 512 does not adversely affect any other defenses); *CoStar Group, Inc. v. LoopNet, Inc.*, 373 F.3d 544 (4th Cir. 2004) (concluding that prior case law was not preempted by passage of the DMCA).

The leading case is *Religious Technology Center v. Netcom On-line Communication Services, Inc.*, 907 F. Supp. 1361 (N.D. Cal. 1995), in which it was alleged that Netcom had provided Internet access for a computer bulletin board operated by one Klemesrud, over which Dennis Erlich, a former member of the Church of Scientology, had made proprietary Church documents available. The bulk of the court's opinion concerned Netcom's potential liability for direct infringement, contributory infringement, and vicarious liability.

As noted in § 7.02[D] above, the court held that Netcom was not directly liable for copyright infringement for designing or implementing a system that automatically makes and stores temporary copies absent some element of volition or causation. 907 F. Supp. at 1368-71; *see also CoStar*, 373 F.3d at 548-55 (approving and applying this holding from *Netcom*).

With regard to contributory infringement, the court found that there was a genuine issue of material fact concerning whether Netcom "knew or should have known that Erlich has infringed plaintiffs' copyrights":

Although a mere unsupported allegation of infringement by a copyright owner may not automatically put a defendant on notice of infringing activity, Netcom's position that liability must be unequivocal is unsupportable. . . . The court is more persuaded by the argument that it is beyond the ability of a [provider] to quickly and fairly determine when a use is not infringement where there is at least a colorable claim of fair use. Where a [provider] cannot reasonably verify a claim of infringement, either because of a possible fair use defense, the lack of copyright notices on the copies, or the copyright holder's failure to provide the necessary documentation . . . , the operator's lack of knowledge will be found reasonable and there will be no liability for contributory infringement for allowing the continued distribution of the works on its system.

. . . Given the context of a dispute between a former minister and a church he is criticizing, Netcom may be able to show that its lack of knowledge that Erlich was infringing was reasonable. However, Netcom admits that it did not even look at the postings once given notice and that had it looked at the copyright notice and statements regarding authorship it would have triggered an investigation into whether there was infringement. . . . These facts are sufficient to raise a question as to Netcom's knowledge once it received a letter from plaintiffs. . . .

907 F. Supp. at 1374-75. The court also concluded that "[p]roviding a service that allows for the automatic distribution of all Usenet postings, infringing and noninfringing," constituted "substantial participation" in the infringing activity. It therefore declined to grant summary judgment to Netcom on the issue of contributory infringement.

With regard to vicarious liability, the court found that there was a genuine issue of fact as to whether Netcom had the right and ability to supervise the conduct of its subscribers. The court continued:

Plaintiffs cannot provide any evidence of a direct financial benefit received by Netcom from Erlich's infringing postings. Unlike *Shapiro, Bernstein,* and like *Fonovisa,* Netcom receives a fixed fee. There is no evidence that infringement by Erlich, or any other user of Netcom's services, in any way enhances the value of Netcom's services to subscribers or attracts new subscribers. . . . Plaintiffs point to Netcom's advertisements that, compared to competitors like CompuServe and America Online, Netcom provides easy, regulation-free Internet access. Plaintiffs assert that Netcom's policy attracts copyright infringers to its system, resulting in a direct financial benefit. The court is not convinced that such an argument, if true, would constitute a direct financial benefit to Netcom from Erlich's infringing activities. *See Fonovisa,* 847 F. Supp. at 1496 (finding no direct financial benefit despite argument that lessees included many vendors selling counterfeit goods and that clientele sought "bargain basement prices"). . . .

Id. at 1377. Accordingly, the court held that Netcom was not vicariously liable for any infringement committed by Erlich.

Note that *Netcom* was decided before the Court of Appeals reversed the District Court's decision in *Fonovisa*. How much of the *Netcom* court's reasoning is now in question as a result of that reversal?

In *Ellison v. Robertson*, 357 F.3d 1072 (9th Cir. 2004), the Ninth Circuit rejected an argument that AOL could not be vicariously liable under the *Netcom* analysis because any infringing activity was an insubstantial portion of its business. The court said: "The essential aspect of the 'direct financial benefit' inquiry is whether there is a causal relationship between the infringing activity and any financial benefit a defendant reaps, regardless of *how substantial* the benefit is in proportion to a defendant's overall profits." 357 F.3d at 1079. The court nonetheless affirmed a summary judgment in favor of AOL on the issue of vicarious liability, because "[t]he record lacks evidence that AOL attracted or retained subscriptions because of the infringement or lost subscriptions because of AOL's eventual obstruction of the infringement." *Id. See also Perfect 10, Inc. v. Cybernet Ventures, Inc.*, 213 F. Supp. 2d 1146, 1171-72 (C.D. Cal. 2002) (distinguishing *Netcom* where "[t]he income derived from each website is directly based on the site's initial popularity").

After the Supreme Court's ruling in the *Grokster* case (discussed in § 9.02[C] above), the Ninth Circuit decided a trio of cases involving secondary liability brought by Perfect 10, a purveyor of soft-core pornography. In *Perfect 10, Inc. v. CCBill LLC*, 488 F.3d 1102 (9th Cir. 2007), the court addressed a number of issues concerning the statutory immunity for internet service providers. See § 9.03[B] below. In *Perfect 10, Inc. v. Amazon.com, Inc.*, 508 F.3d 1146 (9th Cir. 2007), the court addressed both direct liability for violation of the public display right and secondary liability for linking to allegedly infringing images. See § 7.06[B] above and § 9.03[D] below. Finally, in *Perfect 10, Inc. v. VISA Int'l Service Ass'n*, 494 F.3d 788 (9th Cir. 2007), the court considered whether defendants could be held liable for processing credit-card payments to allegedly infringing websites.

In *VISA*, the court held that the credit-card companies did not "materially contribute" to the alleged infringement, because payment did not directly assist in the reproduction, distribution or display of the infringing copies. It distinguished *Amazon.com*, in which search engines "provided links to specific infringing images," and *Napster* and *Grokster*, in which the software "allowed users to locate and obtain infringing material." 494 F.3d at 796. The court also held that defendants could not be held liable for inducing infringement, distinguishing *Napster* and *Grokster* where the software was "engineered, disseminated, and promoted explicitly for the purpose of facilitating piracy." *Id.* at 801-02.

The ruling drew a strong dissent from Judge Kozinski, who wrote that payment "is not just an economic incentive for infringement; it's an essential step in the infringement process," because the infringing images were not distributed until payment was made. *Id.* at 812 (Kozinski, J., dissenting). Judge Kozinski also noted that search engines such as Google were not designed to facilitate piracy, but that they could still be held liable for knowingly linking to infringing images (as discussed in § 9.03[C] below). *Id.* at 811 n.4.

Do you agree with the majority that credit-card payments can meaningfully be distinguished from search engines? Are there other policy reasons for limiting the liability of credit-card companies? If so, should that judgment be made by the courts or by Congress?

Note that two bills introduced in the 112th Congress, dubbed "SOPA" and "PIPA," would have allowed the U.S. Attorney General to seek a court order that would require Internet service providers, search engines, payment processing services, and advertising services to cease doing business with or linking to a foreign website accused of infringing activity. For more on these bills, see § 11.01[F] below.

[B]   Limitation of Liability for Service Providers

In the months and years preceding enactment of the DMCA, Internet service providers ranging from AOL to local public libraries expressed concern that, on one basis or another, they might be left holding the bag for the infringing online activities of those to whom they provided Internet connections. One concern was about liability for temporary reproductions of digital works made, in the course of their transmission over the Internet, on various servers and routers maintained by service providers. Another concern was liability for "hosting" the webpages of others — *i.e.*, providing them with server capacity to use as they see fit. *See Marobie-FL, Inc. v. National Association of Fire Equipment Distributors*, 983 F. Supp. 1167 (N.D. Ill. 1997) (applying *Netcom* and finding potential liability for contributory infringement).

Having failed to obtain a comprehensive solution in the 1996 WIPO treaties (see § 7.02[D] above), service providers sought a legislative solution in Congress. The result was Title II of the DMCA, the Online Copyright Infringement Liability Limitation Act ("OCILLA"), codified in 17 U.S.C. § 512. Section 512 limits the liability of service providers in four common situations, if certain specific conditions are met. The four situations are:

§ 512(a) — Transitory digital network communications. As long as someone other than the service provider initiated a transmission and chose its recipient, and the service provider does not interfere with its content, no liability can attach to the service provider in connection with that transmission. This includes liability for transitory reproductions, so long as they are not "maintained on the system or network . . . for a longer period than is reasonably necessary for the transmission, routing, or provision of connections." As it turns out, the "intermediate or transient storage" exempted under § 512(a) can be relatively long-lived. One District Court found that its provisions were satisfied even though AOL maintained messages on its servers for as long as 14 days. *See Ellison v. Robertson*, 189 F. Supp. 2d 1051, 1068-70 (C.D. Cal. 2002) (holding that the statute was designed to codify the rule in *Netcom*, where messages had been maintained for 11 days). Although the Ninth Circuit reversed *Ellison* on other grounds, it specifically approved this portion of the District Court's holding. 357 F.3d at 1081.

§ 512(b) — System caching. Service providers are not liable for the "intermediate and temporary storage of material" posted online by another person, as long as the storage is carried out through an automatic technical process; the service provider complies with industry standards for refreshing, reloading, and

updating the material; and the service provider does not interfere with password protections and other security measures. The service provider must also comply with the "notice-and-take-down" provisions of subsection (c), if the material has been removed or disabled on the originating website. The distinction between subsections (a) and (b) is that the former applies to the pass-through and storage of directed transmissions, such as e-mail, while the latter applies to the temporary local storage of the contents of frequently visited websites, to speed or simplify user access. *See Field v. Google Inc.*, 412 F. Supp. 2d 1106 (D. Nev. 2006) (upholding Google's use of caching on a number of grounds, including § 512(b) and fair use).

§ 512(c) — "Hosting" services. This subsection limits the liability of service providers who provide "hosting" services by allocating server space to customers or clients who wish to make information available to others, typically by way of the World Wide Web. Web-hosting activities pose a range of potential copyright concerns for service providers, including potential liability for direct infringement of the reproduction and distribution rights, and for contributory infringement or vicarious liability by assisting or abetting the online activities of customers. Section 512(c) cuts across these various doctrines of infringement to provide a qualified defense against any and all financial liability (and some, though not all, forms of injunctive relief) for service providers who meet a series of statutory conditions: they must not know or have reason to know that the material posted to websites they host is infringing; they must either be unable to control what their customers post to those sites or get no direct financial benefits from those postings (as they would, for example, if they charged a specified fee for each item posted); they must adopt and implement a policy for terminating service to repeat infringers; they must not undercut the effectiveness of standard technological protection measures (such as encryption); and, crucially, they must comply with the "notice-and-take-down" provisions described below.

§ 512(d) — Information location tools. Likewise, service providers are not liable for referring or linking users to an online location containing infringing material, or for providing the means to locate infringing material, such as a directory, index, or search engine. All of the same conditions and limitations applicable to subsection (c) including the "notice-and-take-down" provisions, apply to subsection (d) as well. *See, e.g., Perfect 10 v. Amazon.com, Inc.*, 508 F.3d 1146 (9th Cir. 2007) (remanding for further fact-finding on this issue).

The "hosting" exemption in § 512(c) was the major focus in a $1 billion infringement suit filed against YouTube by Viacom, parent company of Paramount Pictures, MTV, and Comedy Central, among others. The Second Circuit's opinion in the case follows.

VIACOM INTERNATIONAL, INC. v. YOUTUBE, INC.
United States Court of Appeals for the Second Circuit
676 F.3d 19 (2012)

JOSE A. CABRANES, CIRCUIT JUDGE:

This appeal requires us to clarify the contours of the "safe harbor" provision of the Digital Millennium Copyright Act (DMCA) that limits the liability of online service providers for copyright infringement that occurs "by reason of the storage at the direction of a user of material that resides on a system or network controlled or operated by or for the service provider." 17 U.S.C. § 512(c). . . .

[Plaintiffs are Viacom, the Football Association Premier League, and "various film studios, television networks, music publishers, and sports leagues." They sued YouTube and its parent company, Google, alleging "direct and secondary copyright infringement based on the public performance, display, and reproduction of approximately 79,000 audiovisual 'clips' that appeared on the YouTube website between 2005 and 2008." The District Court granted summary judgment to defendants based on the § 512(c) safe harbor.]

BACKGROUND

. . . [Founded in 2005, YouTube operates a website that "allows people to watch, upload, and share personal video clips."] In November 2006, Google acquired YouTube in a stock-for-stock transaction valued at $1.65 billion. By March 2010, at the time of summary judgment briefing in this litigation, site traffic on YouTube had soared to more than 1 billion daily video views, with more than 24 hours of new video uploaded to the site every minute.

The basic function of the YouTube website permits users to "upload" and view video clips free of charge. Before uploading a video to YouTube, a user must register and create an account with the website. The registration process requires the user to accept YouTube's Terms of Use agreement, which provides, *inter alia*, that the user "will not submit material that is copyrighted . . . unless [he is] the owner of such rights or ha[s] permission from their rightful owner to post the material and to grant YouTube all of the license rights granted herein." . . .

Uploading a video to the YouTube website triggers a series of automated software functions. During the upload process, YouTube makes one or more exact copies of the video in its original file format. YouTube also makes one or more additional copies of the video in "Flash" format,[4] a process known as "transcoding." . . . The YouTube system allows users to gain access to video content by "streaming" the video to the user's computer in response to a playback request. YouTube uses a computer algorithm to identify clips that are "related" to a video the user watches and display links to the "related" clips . . . .

DISCUSSION

A. Actual and "Red Flag" Knowledge: § 512(c)(1)(A)

1. The Specificity Requirement

"As in all statutory construction cases, we begin with the language of the statute." . . . Under § 512(c)(1)(A), safe harbor protection is available only if the service provider:

> (i) does not have actual knowledge that the material or an activity using the material on the system or network is infringing;

> (ii) in the absence of such actual knowledge, is not aware of facts or circumstances from which infringing activity is apparent; or

> (iii) upon obtaining such knowledge or awareness, acts expeditiously to remove, or disable access to, the material.

17 U.S.C. § 512(c)(1)(A). . . . [T]he District Court held that the statutory phrases "actual knowledge that the material . . . is infringing" and "facts or circumstances from which infringing activity is apparent" refer to "knowledge of specific and identifiable infringements." *Viacom*, 718 F. Supp. 2d at 523. For the reasons that follow, we substantially affirm that holding.

. . . [I]t is the text of the statute that compels our conclusion. . . . Under § 512(c)(1)(A), knowledge or awareness alone does not disqualify the service provider; rather, the provider that gains knowledge or awareness of infringing activity retains safe-harbor protection if it "acts expeditiously to remove, or disable

---

[4] The "Flash" format "is a highly compressed streaming format that begins to play instantly. Unlike other delivery methods, it does not require the viewer to download the entire video file before viewing.". . .

access to, the material." 17 U.S.C. § 512(c)(1)(A)(iii). Thus, the nature of the removal obligation itself contemplates knowledge or awareness of specific infringing material, because expeditious removal is possible only if the service provider knows with particularity which items to remove. Indeed, to require expeditious removal in the absence of specific knowledge or awareness would be to mandate an amorphous obligation to "take commercially reasonable steps" in response to a generalized awareness of infringement. Such a view cannot be reconciled with the language of the statute, which requires "expeditious[ ]" action to remove or disable *the material* at issue. 17 U.S.C. § 512(c)(1)(A)(iii) (emphasis added).

On appeal, the plaintiffs dispute this conclusion by drawing our attention to § 512(c)(1)(A)(ii), the so-called "red flag" knowledge provision. . . . In their view, the use of the phrase "facts or circumstances" demonstrates that Congress did not intend to limit the red flag provision to a particular type of knowledge. The plaintiffs contend that requiring awareness of specific infringements in order to establish "aware[ness] of facts or circumstances from which infringing activity is apparent," 17 U.S.C. § 512(c)(1)(A)(ii), renders the red flag provision superfluous, because that provision would be satisfied only when the "actual knowledge" provision is also satisfied. For that reason, the plaintiffs urge the Court to hold that the red flag provision "requires less specificity" than the actual knowledge provision.

. . . [C]ontrary to the plaintiffs' assertions, construing § 512(c)(1)(A) to require actual knowledge or awareness of specific instances of infringement does not render the red flag provision superfluous. The phrase "actual knowledge," which appears in § 512(c)(1)(A)(i), is frequently used to denote subjective belief. By contrast, courts often invoke the language of "facts or circumstances," which appears in § 512(c)(1)(A)(ii), in discussing an objective reasonableness standard. . . .

The difference between actual and red flag knowledge is thus not between specific and generalized knowledge, but instead between a subjective and an objective standard. In other words, the actual knowledge provision turns on whether the provider actually or "subjectively" knew of specific infringement, while the red flag provision turns on whether the provider was subjectively aware of facts that would have made the specific infringement "objectively" obvious to a reasonable person. . . . Both provisions do independent work, and both apply only to specific instances of infringement.

The limited body of case law interpreting the knowledge provisions of the § 512(c) safe harbor comports with our view of the specificity requirement. Most recently, a panel of the Ninth Circuit addressed the scope of § 512(c) in *UMG Recordings, Inc. v. Shelter Capital Partners, LLC*, 667 F.3d 1022 (9th Cir. 2011), a copyright infringement case against Veoh Networks, a video-hosting service similar to YouTube. As in this case, various music publishers brought suit against the service provider, claiming direct and secondary copyright infringement based on the presence of unauthorized content on the website, and the website operator sought refuge in the § 512(c) safe harbor. The Court of Appeals affirmed the district court's determination on summary judgment that the website operator was entitled to safe harbor protection. With respect to the actual knowledge provision, the panel . . . [held] that the safe harbor "[r]equir[es] specific knowledge of particular infringing activity," *id.* at 1037. The Court of Appeals "reach[ed] the same conclusion" with respect to the red flag provision, noting that "[w]e do not place the burden of determining whether [materials] are actually illegal on a service provider." *Id.* at 1038 (alterations in original) (quoting *Perfect 10, Inc. v. CCBill, LLC*, 488 F.3d 1102, 1114 (9th Cir.2007)).

Although *Shelter Capital* contains the most explicit discussion of the § 512(c) knowledge provisions, other cases are generally in accord. . . . [N]o court has embraced the contrary proposition — urged by the plaintiffs — that the red flag provision "requires less specificity" than the actual knowledge provision.

Based on the text of § 512(c)(1)(A), as well as the limited case law on point, we affirm the District Court's holding that actual knowledge or awareness of facts or circumstances that indicate specific and identifiable instances of infringement will disqualify a service provider from the safe harbor.

2. The Grant of Summary Judgment . . .

i. Specific Knowledge or Awareness

The plaintiffs argue that, even under the District Court's construction of the safe harbor, the record raises material issues of fact regarding YouTube's actual knowledge or "red flag" awareness of specific instances of infringement. To that end, . . . Viacom cites evidence that YouTube employees conducted website surveys and estimated that 75-80% of all YouTube streams contained copyrighted material. . . . But such estimates are insufficient, standing alone, to create a triable issue of fact as to whether YouTube actually knew, or was aware of facts or circumstances that would indicate, the existence of particular instances of infringement.

Beyond the survey results, the plaintiffs rely upon internal YouTube communications that do refer to particular clips or groups of clips. . . . [Here the court summarizes an internal report and several e-mails discussing particular items. All of the material pre-dates Google's acquisition of YouTube in 2006.]

Upon a review of the record, we are persuaded that the plaintiffs may have raised a material issue of fact regarding YouTube's knowledge or awareness of specific instances of infringement. . . . The March 2006 report indicates Karim's awareness of specific clips [of Viacom shows] that he perceived to be "blatantly illegal." Similarly, the . . . e-mails refer to particular clips in the context of correspondence about whether to remove infringing material from the website. On these facts, a reasonable juror could conclude that YouTube had actual knowledge of specific infringing activity, or was at least aware of facts or circumstances from which specific infringing activity was apparent. See § 512(c)(1)(A)(i)-(ii). Accordingly, we hold that summary judgment to YouTube on all clips-in-suit, especially in the absence of any detailed examination of the extensive record on summary judgment, was premature.

We hasten to note, however, that . . . it is unclear whether the clips referenced therein are among the current clips-in-suit. . . . Accordingly, we vacate the order granting summary judgment and instruct the District Court to determine on remand whether any specific infringements of which YouTube had knowledge or awareness correspond to the clips-in-suit in these actions.

ii. "Willful Blindness"

The plaintiffs further argue that the District Court erred in granting summary judgment to the defendants despite evidence that YouTube was "willfully blind" to specific infringing activity. On this issue of first impression, we consider the application of the common law willful blindness doctrine in the DMCA context.

"The principle that willful blindness is tantamount to knowledge is hardly novel." *Tiffany (NJ) Inc. v. eBay, Inc.*, 600 F.3d 93, 110 n.16 (2d Cir. 2010) (collecting cases); *see In re Aimster Copyright Litig.*, 334 F.3d 643, 650 (7th Cir. 2003) ("Willful blindness is knowledge, in copyright law . . . as it is in the law generally."). A person is "willfully blind" or engages in "conscious avoidance" amounting to knowledge where the person " 'was aware of a high probability of the fact in dispute and consciously avoided confirming that fact.' " *United States v. Aina-Marshall*, 336 F.3d 167, 170 (2d Cir.2003); *cf. Global-Tech Appliances, Inc. v. SEB S.A.*, 131 S. Ct. 2060, 2070-71 (2011) (applying the willful blindness doctrine in a patent infringement case). Writing in the trademark infringement context, we have held that "[a] service provider is not . . . permitted willful blindness. When it has reason to suspect that users of its service are infringing a protected mark, it may not shield itself from learning of the particular infringing transactions by looking the other way." *Tiffany*, 600 F.3d at 109.

The DMCA does not mention willful blindness. As a general matter, we interpret a statute to abrogate a common law principle only if the statute "speak[s] directly to the question addressed by the common law." . . . The DMCA provision most relevant to the abrogation inquiry is § 512(m), which provides that safe harbor protection shall not be conditioned on "a service provider monitoring its service or affirmatively seeking facts indicating infringing activity . . . ." 17 U.S.C. § 512(m)(1). Section 512(m) is explicit: DMCA safe harbor protection cannot be conditioned on affirmative monitoring by a service provider. For that reason, § 512(m) is incompatible with a broad common law duty to monitor or otherwise seek out infringing activity based on general awareness that infringement may be occurring. That fact does not, however, dispose of the abrogation inquiry. . . . Because the statute does not "speak[ ] directly" to the willful blindness doctrine, § 512(m) limits — but does not abrogate — the doctrine. Accordingly, we hold that the willful blindness doctrine may be applied, in appropriate circumstances, to demonstrate knowledge or awareness of specific instances of infringement under the DMCA.

The District Court cited § 512(m) for the proposition that safe harbor protection does not require affirmative monitoring, *Viacom*, 718 F. Supp. 2d at 524, but did not expressly address the principle of willful blindness or its relationship to the DMCA safe harbors. As a result, whether the defendants made a "deliberate effort to avoid guilty knowledge," *In re Aimster*, 334 F.3d at 650, remains a fact question for the District Court to consider in the first instance on remand.

B. Control and Benefit: § 512(c)(1)(B)

Apart from the foregoing knowledge provisions, the § 512(c) safe harbor provides that an eligible service provider must "not receive a financial benefit directly attributable to the infringing activity, in a case in which the service provider has the right and ability to control such activity." 17 U.S.C. § 512(c)(1)(B). The District Court . . . conclude[ed] that "[t]he 'right and ability to control' the activity requires knowledge of it, which must be item-specific." *Viacom*, 718 F. Supp. 2d at 527. For the reasons that follow, we hold that the District Court erred by importing a specific knowledge requirement into the control and benefit provision, and we therefore remand for further fact-finding on the issue of control.

1. "Right and Ability to Control" Infringing Activity

On appeal, the parties advocate two competing constructions of the "right and ability to control" infringing activity. 17 U.S.C. § 512(c)(1)(B). Because each is fatally flawed, we reject both proposed constructions in favor of a fact-based inquiry to be conducted in the first instance by the District Court.

The first construction, pressed by the defendants, is the one adopted by the District Court, which held that "the provider must know of the particular case before he can control it." *Viacom*, 718 F. Supp. 2d at 527. The Ninth Circuit recently agreed, holding that "until [the service provider] becomes aware of specific unauthorized material, it cannot exercise its 'power or authority' over the specific infringing item. In practical terms, it does not have the kind of ability to control infringing activity the statute contemplates." *UMG Recordings, Inc. v. Shelter Capital Partners, LLC*, 667 F.3d 1022, 1041 (9th Cir. 2011). The trouble with this construction is that importing a specific knowledge requirement into § 512(c)(1)(B) renders the control provision duplicative of § 512(c)(1)(A). Any service provider that has item-specific knowledge of infringing activity and thereby obtains financial benefit would already be excluded from the safe harbor under § 512(c)(1)(A) for having specific knowledge of infringing material and failing to effect expeditious removal. No additional service provider would be excluded by § 512(c)(1)(B) that was not already excluded by § 512(c)(1)(A). Because statutory interpretations that render language superfluous are disfavored, . . . we reject the District Court's interpretation of the control provision.

The second construction, urged by the plaintiffs, is that the control provision codifies the common law doctrine of vicarious copyright liability. The common law imposes liability for vicarious copyright infringement "[w]hen the right and ability to supervise coalesce with an obvious and direct financial interest in the exploitation of copyrighted materials . . . ." *Shapiro, Bernstein & Co. v. H.L. Green Co.*, 316 F.2d 304, 307 (2d Cir. 1963); *cf. Metro-Goldwyn-Mayer Studios Inc. v. Grokster, Ltd.*, 545 U.S. 913, 930 n.9 (2005). To support their codification argument, the plaintiffs rely on a House Report relating to a preliminary version of the DMCA: "The 'right and ability to control' language . . . codifies the second element of vicarious liability . . . . Subparagraph (B) is intended to preserve existing case law that examines all relevant aspects of the relationship between the primary and secondary infringer." H.R. Rep. No. 105-551(I), at 26 (1998). In response, YouTube notes that the codification reference was omitted from the committee reports describing the final legislation, and that Congress ultimately abandoned any attempt to "embark[ ] upon a wholesale clarification" of vicarious liability, electing instead "to create a series of 'safe harbors' for certain common activities of service providers." S. Rep. No. 105-190, at 19.

Happily, the future of digital copyright law does not turn on the confused legislative history of the control provision. The general rule with respect to common law codification is that when "Congress uses terms that have accumulated settled meaning under the common law, a court must infer, unless the statute otherwise dictates, that Congress means to incorporate the established meaning of those terms." *Neder v. United States*, 527 U.S. 1, 21 (1999). . . . Under the common law vicarious liability standard, " '[t]he ability to block infringers' access to a particular environment for any reason whatsoever is evidence of the right and ability to supervise.' " *Arista Records LLC v. Usenet.com, Inc.*, 633 F. Supp. 2d 124, 157 (S.D.N.Y. 2009) (alteration in original) (quoting *A&M Records, Inc. v. Napster, Inc.*, 239 F.3d 1004, 1023 (9th Cir. 2001)). To adopt that principle in the DMCA context, however, would render the statute internally inconsistent. Section 512(c) actually presumes that service providers have the ability to "block . . . access" to infringing material. *Id.* at 157; *see Shelter Capital*, 667 F.3d at 1042-43. Indeed, a service provider who has knowledge or awareness of infringing material or who receives a takedown notice from a copyright holder is required to "remove, or disable access to, the material" in order to claim the benefit of the safe harbor. 17 U.S.C. §§ 512(c)(1)(A)(iii) & (C). But in taking such action, the service provider would — in the plaintiffs' analysis — be admitting the "right and ability to control" the infringing material. Thus, the prerequisite to safe harbor protection under §§ 512(c)(1)(A)(iii) & (C) would at the same time be a disqualifier under § 512(c)(1)(B).

Moreover, if Congress had intended § 512(c)(1)(B) to be coextensive with vicarious liability, "the statute could have accomplished that result in a more direct manner." *Shelter Capital*, 667 F.3d at 1045.

> It is conceivable that Congress . . . intended that [service providers] which receive a financial benefit directly attributable to the infringing activity would not, under any circumstances, be able to qualify for the subsection (c) safe harbor. But if that was indeed their intention, it would have been far simpler and much more straightforward to simply say as much.

Id. (alteration in original). . . .

In any event, the foregoing tension . . . is sufficient to establish that the control provision "dictates" a departure from the common law vicarious liability standard, *Neder*, 527 U.S. at 21. Accordingly, we conclude that the "right and ability to control" infringing activity under § 512(c)(1)(B) "requires something more than the ability to remove or block access to materials posted on a service provider's website." [*Capitol Records, Inc. v.*] *MP3tunes, LLC*, 821 F. Supp. 2d [637,] 645 [(S.D.N.Y. 2011)]; *accord*, . . . *Io Group, Inc. v. Veoh Networks, Inc.*, 586 F. Supp. 2d 1132, 1151 (N.D. Cal. 2008); . . . . The remaining — and more difficult — question is how to define the "something more" that is required.

To date, only one court has found that a service provider had the right and ability to control infringing activity under § 512(c)(1)(B). In *Perfect 10, Inc. v. Cybernet Ventures, Inc.*, 213 F. Supp. 2d 1146 (C.D. Cal. 2002), the court found control where the service provider instituted a monitoring program by which user websites received "detailed instructions regard[ing] issues of layout, appearance, and content." *Id.* at 1173. The service provider also forbade certain types of content and refused access to users who failed to comply with its instructions. *Id.* Similarly, inducement of copyright infringement under *Metro-Goldwyn-Mayer Studios Inc. v. Grokster, Ltd.*, 545 U.S. 913 (2005), which "premises liability on purposeful, culpable expression and conduct," *id.* at 937, might also rise to the level of control under § 512(c)(1)(B). Both of these examples involve a service provider exerting substantial influence on the activities of users, without necessarily — or even frequently — acquiring knowledge of specific infringing activity.

In light of our holding that § 512(c)(1)(B) does not include a specific knowledge requirement, we think it prudent to remand to the District Court to consider in the first instance whether the plaintiffs have adduced sufficient evidence to allow a reasonable jury to conclude that YouTube had the right and ability to control the infringing activity and received a financial benefit directly attributable to that activity.

C. "By Reason of" Storage: § 512(c)(1)

The § 512(c) safe harbor is only available when the infringement occurs "by reason of the storage at the direction of a user of material that resides on a system or network controlled or operated by or for the service provider." 17 U.S.C. § 512(c)(1). In this case, the District Court held that YouTube's software functions fell within the safe harbor for infringements that occur "by reason of" user storage, noting that a contrary holding would "confine[ ] the word 'storage' too narrowly to meet the statute's purpose." *Viacom*, 718 F. Supp. 2d at 526. For the reasons that follow, we affirm that holding with respect to three of the challenged software functions — the conversion (or "transcoding") of videos into a standard display format, the playback of videos on "watch" pages, and the "related videos" function. We remand for further fact-finding with respect to a fourth software function, involving the third-party syndication of videos uploaded to YouTube.

As a preliminary matter, we note that "the structure and language of OCILLA indicate that service providers seeking safe harbor under [§]512(c) are not limited to merely storing material." *Io Group*, 586 F. Supp. 2d at 1147. The structure of the statute distinguishes between so-called "conduit only" functions under § 512(a) and the functions addressed by § 512(c) and the other subsections. . . . Most notably, OCILLA contains two definitions of "service provider." 17 U.S.C. § 512(k)(1)(A)-(B). The narrower definition, which applies only to service providers falling under § 512(a), is limited to entities that "offer[ ] the transmission, routing or providing of connections for digital online communications, between or among points specified by a user, of material of the user's choosing, *without modification to the content of the material* as sent or received." *Id.* § 512(k)(1)(A) (emphasis added). No such limitation appears in the broader definition, which applies to service providers — including YouTube — falling under § 512(c). Under the broader definition, "the term 'service provider' means a provider of online services or network access, or the operator of facilities therefor, and includes an entity described in subparagraph (A)." *Id.* § 512(k)(1)(B). In the absence of a parallel limitation on the ability of a service provider to modify user-submitted material, we conclude that § 512(c) "is clearly meant to cover more than mere electronic storage lockers." *UMG Recordings, Inc. v. Veoh Networks, Inc.*, 620 F. Supp. 2d 1081, 1088 (C.D. Cal. 2008) ("*UMG I*")[, *aff'd sub nom. UMG Recordings, Inc. v. Shelter Capital Partners, LLC*, 667 F.3d 1022 (9th Cir. 2011)].

The relevant case law makes clear that the § 512(c) safe harbor extends to software functions performed "for the purpose of facilitating access to user-stored material." *Id.; see Shelter Capital*, 667 F.3d at 1031-35. Two of the software functions challenged here — transcoding and playback — were expressly considered by our sister Circuit in *Shelter Capital*, which held that liability arising from these functions occurred "by reason of the storage at the direction of a user." 17 U.S.C. § 512(c); *see Shelter Capital*, 667 F.3d at 1027-28, 1031. . . . Transcoding involves "[m]aking copies of a video in a different encoding scheme" in order to render the video "viewable over the Internet to most users." Supp. Joint App'x [at] 236. The playback process involves "deliver[ing] copies of YouTube videos to a user's browser cache" in response to a user request. *Id.* at 239. The District Court correctly found that to exclude these automated functions from the safe harbor would eviscerate the protection afforded to service providers by § 512(c). *Viacom*, 718 F. Supp. 2d at 526-27.

A similar analysis applies to the "related videos" function, by which a YouTube computer algorithm identifies and displays "thumbnails" of clips that are "related" to the video selected by the user. The plaintiffs claim that this practice constitutes content promotion, not "access" to stored content, and therefore falls beyond the scope of the safe harbor. . . . But even if the plaintiffs are correct that § 512(c) incorporates a principle of proximate causation — a question we need not resolve here — the indexing and display of related videos retain a sufficient causal link to the prior storage of those videos. The record makes clear that the related videos algorithm "is fully automated and operates solely in response to user input without the active involvement of YouTube employees." Supp. Joint App'x [at] 237. Furthermore, the related videos function serves to help YouTube users locate and gain access to material stored at the direction of other users. Because the algorithm "is closely related to, and follows from, the storage itself," and is "narrowly directed toward providing access to material stored at the direction of users," *UMG I*, 620 F. Supp. 2d at 1092, we conclude that the related videos function is also protected by the § 512(c) safe harbor.

The final software function at issue here — third-party syndication — is the closest case. In or around March 2007, YouTube transcoded a select number of videos into a format compatible with mobile devices and "syndicated" or licensed the videos to Verizon Wireless and other companies. The plaintiffs argue — with some force — that business transactions do not occur at the "direction of a user" within the meaning of § 512(c)(1) when they involve the manual selection of copyrighted material for licensing to a third party. The parties do not dispute, however, that none of the clips-in-suit were among the approximately 2,000 videos provided to Verizon Wireless. In order to avoid rendering an advisory opinion on the outer boundaries of the storage provision, we remand for fact-finding on the question of whether any of the clips-in-suit were in fact syndicated to any other third party.

D. Other Arguments

. . . Finally, the plaintiffs argue that the District Court erred in denying summary judgment to the plaintiffs on their claims for direct infringement, vicarious liability, and contributory liability under *Metro-Goldwyn-Mayer Studios Inc. v. Grokster, Ltd.*, 545 U.S. 913 (2005). In granting summary judgment to the defendants, the District Court held that YouTube "qualif[ied] for the protection of . . . § 512(c)," and therefore denied the plaintiffs' cross-motion for summary judgment without comment. *Viacom*, 718 F. Supp. 2d at 529.

The District Court correctly determined that a finding of safe harbor application necessarily protects a defendant from all affirmative claims for monetary relief. 17 U.S.C. § 512(c)(1); *see* H.R. Rep. No. 105-551(II), at 50; S. Rep. No. 105-190, at 20; *cf.* 17 U.S.C. § 512(j) (setting forth the scope of injunctive relief available under § 512). For the reasons previously stated, further fact-finding is required to determine whether YouTube is ultimately entitled to safe harbor protection in this case. Accordingly, we vacate the order denying summary judgment to the plaintiffs and remand the cause without expressing a view on the merits of the plaintiffs' affirmative claims. . . .

NOTES AND QUESTIONS

(1) There are number of requirements that an entity like YouTube must meet to qualify for the safe harbors. First, the defendant must be a "service provider." Second, the service provider must have "adopted and reasonably implemented" a policy for terminating repeat infringers. Third, the service provider must designate an agent to receive notices of alleged infringement from copyright owners. Fourth, all but § 512(a) service providers must comply with the "notice-and-takedown" provisions of § 512(c). These requirements were not contested on appeal in *YouTube* and are discussed below. Instead, the appeal in *YouTube* focused on additional requirements that are specific to § 512(c) (although some of the same language appears in § 512(d) as well).

(2) The first issue addressed in *YouTube* is what kind of knowledge will disqualify a service provider from relying on the § 512(c) safe harbor. What does it mean that the service provider "does not have actual knowledge" of infringement and "is not aware of facts or circumstances from which infringing activity is apparent"? The dispute here centers on the fact that service providers like YouTube often have general knowledge that some infringing material is available on their system, even though they dutifully comply with the notice-and-takedown provisions when they receive compliant notices. The court holds that such general knowledge is insufficient, and instead requires knowledge of "specific and identifiable instances of infringement" to disqualify YouTube from the safe harbor. Do you think this is what Congress intended? If so, do you think Congress struck the proper balance?

(3) The court also considered the effect of § 512(m), which says that a service provider does not have an obligation to "monitor[ ] its service or affirmatively seek[ ]

facts indicating infringing activity." Is the "willful blindness" doctrine consistent with § 512(m)? If a service provider was "aware of a high probability" that specific infringing material was on its system, how could it respond to the obligation in § 512(c) "to remove, or disable access to, the material" without "affirmatively seeking" out the infringing activity? Is there some other way to interpret the statute to reconcile these two sections?

(4)   What happens on remand if the District Court finds that YouTube had actual knowledge of specific infringing videos back in 2005-2006, but that after they were removed it lacked such knowledge (except with respect to videos that were timely removed)? Will such a finding disqualify YouTube from reliance on the safe harbor altogether? Or it will only disqualify YouTube for the time period in which actual knowledge existed? Does the language of the statute answer the question?

(5)   The second issue addressed is whether YouTube complied with the requirement that it "does not receive a financial benefit directly attributable to the infringing activity, in a case in which [it] has the right and ability to control such activity." YouTube did not dispute that it receives a financial benefit (because its video-sharing service is supported by advertising), so the parties focused on the second element.

What positions did the parties take on the meaning of "the right and ability to control such [infringing] activity? Why did the court reject those positions? The court agrees that YouTube's ability to remove videos from its service was not, by itself, sufficient, and that "something more" is needed to show that YouTube had "control." Under what circumstances will "something more" be found to exist? Do you think the court gives sufficient guidance to lower courts in resolving this question?

(6)   The third issue addressed is what is meant by the phrase "by reason of the storage . . . of material." Does this include providing public access to the material? Given that the purpose was to enable web hosting services, the phrase must include at least public display of the material. Assuming that is the case, is there a meaningful distinction between public display of allegedly infringing material and public performance of allegedly infringing material, as facilitated by YouTube? What about making the material available for downloading? Alternatively, if these things were not intended to be covered, how could any website that permits users to post content manage to avoid infringement?

(7)   A related issue is what is meant by "at the direction of a user." YouTube automatically processes uploaded videos into a format that can easily be shared with others. Is this type of automated processing "at the direction of a user"? The user uploaded the video, but YouTube's programmers decided what to do with that video. Alternatively, would it make sense to construe the statute to require individual users to do their own "format" conversions to use video-sharing or photo-sharing websites?

(8)   YouTube also recommends "related" websites to its users, relying on a software algorithm to identify "related" videos. Does this activity occur "by reason of storage at the direction of a user"? How do these "related" videos differ from the videos that YouTube "syndicated" to third parties? If the lower court finds that some

of those "syndicated" videos were owned by Viacom, does that disqualify YouTube from reliance on the safe harbor at all, or only just for those specific videos?

(9)   Moving beyond YouTube, what other kinds of service providers potentially can benefit from the four "safe harbors" in § 512? Clearly, a wide range of different business models may fall within § 512(k)(1)(B). These include an online auction site, *see Hendrickson v. eBay, Inc.*, 165 F. Supp. 2d 1082 (C.D. Cal. 2001), and a service for real estate brokers that hosts descriptions and images of commercial real estate, *see CoStar Group, Inc. v. LoopNet, Inc.*, 164 F. Supp. 2d 688 (D. Md. 2001), *aff'd*, 373 F.3d 544 (4th Cir. 2004). *But see Perfect 10, Inc. v. Cybernet Ventures, Inc.*, 213 F. Supp. 2d 1146 (C.D. Cal. 2002) (expressing doubt whether an age-verification service for adult websites qualifies).

(10)   To qualify for the safe harbors, a service provider must have "adopted and reasonably implemented . . . a policy that provides for the termination in appropriate circumstances of subscribers . . . who are repeat infringers." 17 U.S.C. § 512(i)(1)(A). This section already has proven to be difficult for some service providers to overcome. *See Ellison v. Robertson*, 357 F.3d 1072, 1080 (9th Cir. 2004) (finding a triable issue of fact as to whether AOL "reasonably implemented" its policy); *Cybernet Ventures*, 213 F. Supp. 2d at 1175-79 (concluding defendant had not complied with § 512(i)). But because Congress required only "reasonable" implementation, and not perfect implementation, individual instances of non-enforcement are not sufficient to overcome evidence of a general policy of enforcement. *See, e.g., UMG Recordings, Inc. v. Veoh Networks*, 620 F. Supp. 2d 1081 (C.D. Cal. 2008) (hypothetical possibility that a rogue infringer might reappear under a different user name did not defeat reasonableness); *Corbis Corp. v. Amazon.com, Inc.*, 351 F. Supp. 2d 1090 (W.D. Wash. 2004). In addition, a service provider has no independent duty to monitor its system to identify repeat infringers; instead, it need only respond to notices that comply with the "notice-and-take-down" provisions of § 512(c). *See Perfect 10, Inc. v. CCBill, LLC*, 488 F.3d 1102 (9th Cir. 2007).

Notice-and-Take-Down Provisions

To qualify for three of the four safe harbors, a service provider must comply with the "notice-and-take-down" provisions of § 512(c). Those provisions require that every service provider designate an agent to receive notices of alleged infringement from copyright owners, by filing with the U.S. Copyright Office *and* by posting the agent's name and address (including an e-mail address) on a publicly accessible website. § 512(c)(2). The function of this agent is to receive notices of claimed infringement from copyright owners. Under § 512(c)(3)(A), such a notice must:

- be sworn and physically or virtually signed;

- be based on a good faith belief that the allegedly infringing material is being used without permission (although not, apparently, that the use is in fact infringing, rather than, say, a "fair use");

- identify the work allegedly infringed; and (perhaps most importantly)

- identify the infringing material and provide "information reasonably sufficient to permit the service provider to locate the material."

Copyright owners have a strong motivation to provide notices that comply with the statutory requirements. A service provider is entitled to ignore any notice which is not in "substantial" compliance; and if it does, its receipt of the non-complying notice cannot be used against it in a subsequent effort to prove its "knowledge" of infringing activity. § 512(c)(3)(B). As to what constitutes "substantial" compliance, compare *ALS Scan, Inc. v. RemarQ Communities, Inc.*, 239 F.3d 619, 625 (4th Cir. 2001) (plaintiff substantially complied by identifying two sites and alleging that "virtually all" the images were infringing), with *CCBill*, 488 F.3d at 1112-13 ("Compliance is not 'substantial' if the notice provided complies with only some of the requirements of § 512(c)(3)(A)"; and defendant may not "cobble together adequate notice from separately defective notices"). A service provider may also choose to ignore even a fully compliant notice; but if it does, it loses the limitation on liability that § 512 provides, and the notice may be used to prove secondary liability.

The timing of the notice also has been the subject of litigation. In *Hendrickson v. Amazon.com, Inc.*, 298 F. Supp. 2d 914 (C.D. Cal. 2003), the court held that although a blanket notice that all DVDs of a motion picture were infringing was adequate with respect to all copies then available on the service provider's website, the notice was not sufficient with respect to other copies of the same movie which were posted several months later. The court specifically held that imposing on a service provider a continuing duty to monitor its site was contrary to the intent of Congress in enacting § 512(m).

To secure the exemption, a service provider must "respond[ ] expeditiously to remove, or disable access to, the material that is claimed to be infringing." The person whose material was removed may then serve a "counter notification," including a sworn statement that he or she believes in good faith "that the material was removed or disabled as a result of mistake or misidentification." If the person does so, the service provider must pass this counter-notification along to the copyright owner, which has 10 working days in which to seek judicial relief. If the owner does not file a lawsuit, the service provider has four working days in which to restore the material. If the service provider complies with this procedure in good faith, § 512(g) immunizes the service provider against claims by anyone whose material is "taken down."

The "notice-and-take-down" procedure has come under some criticism from consumer advocates who charge that copyright owners are abusing the procedure by sending § 512(c) notices to request removal of material that is merely embarrassing or unflattering, rather than infringing. For example, in *Online Policy Group v. Diebold, Inc.*, 337 F. Supp. 2d 1195 (N.D. Cal. 2004), Diebold sent § 512(c) notices to ISPs that were hosting copies of internal Diebold e-mails that discussed security problems with Diebold electronic voting machines.

But users who receive overreaching notices are not entirely without recourse: They can seek affirmative relief under § 512(f), which imposes liability on "any person who knowingly materially misrepresents under this section . . . that material or activity is infringing." Thus, in *Diebold*, the District Court granted summary judgment to the plaintiffs, holding as a matter of law that posting the e-mails online for the purpose of informing the public about potential problems with Diebold electronic voting machines was a fair use, and that no reasonable copyright owner could have believed otherwise. 337 F. Supp. 2d at 1203-05; *see also Lenz v. Universal Music Group*, 572 F. Supp. 2d 1150 (N.D. Cal. 2008) (denying motion to dismiss claim under § 512(f) alleging improper removal of video of plaintiff's baby dancing to a song played on the radio).

No description of the "notice-and-take-down" provisions would be complete without a reference to § 512(h), which allows any copyright owner who has served a compliant notice on a service provider to obtain an automatic *ex parte* court order requiring the service provider to identify the individual subscriber whose material or conduct was the subject of the original notice. Two courts of appeals have held that this section is limited to those service providers subject to the "notice-and-take-down" provisions of § 512(c), pointing to the statutory requirement that the subpoena request contain a notification that "satisfies the provisions of subsection (c)(3)(A)." *See Recording Industry Ass'n. of America v. Verizon Internet Services, Inc.*, 351 F.3d 1229 (D.C. Cir. 2003); *accord In re Charter Communications, Inc. Subpoena Enforcement Matter*, 393 F.3d 771 (8th Cir. 2005).

[C] Other Online Issues

One of the distinguishing features of the World Wide Web is the ability to move automatically from one website to another via "hyperlinks" — icons or highlighted text that, when clicked on, instruct the user's browser to request a copy of the data residing at another website and to display that data on the user's monitor. Ordinary hyperlinks direct the user's browser to the "home page" of another website. But so-called "deep-linking" directs the user's browser to an interior page of the destination website — thus bypassing any advertising or terms and conditions contained on the home page of the destination website. Further complicating the analysis is the fact that the destination site may contain either authorized or unauthorized material.

Most commentators agree that unauthorized linking to a website containing authorized material is not a violation of the Copyright Act. While the data on the destination website is copied into the RAM of the user's machine, such copying must be considered to have been done with the authorization of the copyright owner. Otherwise, anyone browsing the authorized website would be deemed to be an infringer. *See Ticketmaster Corp. v. Tickets.com, Inc.*, 54 U.S.P.Q.2d (BNA) 1344, 1346 (C.D. Cal. 2000) ("hyperlinking does not itself involve a violation of the Copyright Act").[1] In a later proceeding, however, the *Ticketmaster* court held that unauthorized linking might constitute a breach of contract under certain circumstances. 2003 U.S. Dist. LEXIS 6483 (C.D. Cal., Mar. 7, 2003). In addition, at least one District Court has reached a different conclusion, holding that a website which linked to an authorized live broadcast of a motorcycle race without

---

[1] The *Ticketmaster* case clearly is incorrect, however, in observing that "no copying is involved." *Id.* All browsing on the Internet involves the copying of data from the website where the material is stored into the RAM of the user's computer.

permission was a *direct* infringer. *See Live Nation Motor Sports, Inc. v. Davis*, 81 U.S.P.Q.2d (BNA) 1826 (N.D. Tex. 2007).

Linking to a website containing infringing material is another matter. In this situation, the theory is that users who browse the destination website are infringers, because a copy of the infringing material is downloaded into the RAM of their computers, and that the linking site may be held liable for contributory infringement for providing the link. *See Intellectual Reserve, Inc. v. Utah Lighthouse Ministry, Inc.*, 75 F. Supp. 2d 1290 (D. Utah 1999). There is also the possibility that linking without permission may violate foreign law.

Both hyperlinking and deep-linking should be distinguished from so-called "inline linking," by which an individual image from another website is displayed in the context of the linking site. In *Kelly v. Arriba Soft Corp.*, 280 F.3d 934 (9th Cir. 2002), the court initially held that in-line linking was an infringement of the plaintiff's public display right and was not a fair use. On reconsideration, however, the court vacated its earlier opinion and declined to address the issue on procedural grounds. 336 F.3d 811 (9th Cir. 2003). An edited version of this opinion is reproduced in § 10.04[B].

The issue left unresolved in *Kelly* was addressed in *Perfect 10, Inc. v. Amazon.com, Inc.*, 508 F.3d 1146 (9th Cir. 2007), in which the court held that although Google did not publicly "display" infringing images merely by including an in-line link to those images in its search results (see § 7.06 above), Google could be contributorily liable for the infringing actions of third-party websites by maintaining the link after being notified that it was infringing:

> . . . [W]e hold that a computer system operator can be held contributorily liable if it has *actual* knowledge that *specific* infringing material is available using its system, and can take simple measures to prevent further damage to copyrighted works, yet continues to provide access to infringing works.

Id. at 1172 (internal quotes and citations omitted; emphasis in original). The court remanded for further fact-finding regarding "the adequacy of Perfect 10's notices to Google and Google's responses to these notices," and "whether there are reasonable and feasible means for Google to refrain from providing access to infringing images." On the issue of vicarious liability, however, the court affirmed the District Court's ruling that Google did not have the right and ability to control the infringing conduct of third-party websites. *Id.* at 1173-75.

Judge Posner took a somewhat similar approach in vacating a preliminary injunction against myVidster, a "social bookmarking" website, in *Flava Works, Inc. v. Gunter*, 689 F.3d 754 (7th Cir. 2012). myVidster allowed users to "bookmark" videos found on the Internet and share them with others. When myVidster received a bookmark request, its software would obtain the "embed" code from the server that hosted the video, so that myVidster users could view the video by clicking on a thumbnail. (An "embed" is the video version of an "inline link" for images.) Like Google (and unlike YouTube), however, myVidster did not "host" the videos; it only provided a means by which they could be viewed by others.

The court held that there was insufficient evidence to hold myVidster liable as a secondary infringer. myVidster was not contributing to any reproduction or distribution of the videos, because users who viewed the videos were not making fixed "copies" (recall the discussion of *Cartoon Network* in § 7.02 above), and myVidster did not encourage or assist the people who uploaded the videos. myVidster also was not contributing to public performance of the videos, because there was no evidence that Flava's videos were actually being viewed via the myVidster bookmarks. The court distinguished *Fonovisa*, on the ground that myVidster did not provide a "market" for infringing works (nothing was being sold), so myVidster did not have a profit motive for encouraging the performance of infringing videos.

In light of these cases, are you satisfied that the existing Copyright Act is flexible enough to deal with the problem of online infringement? Should questions of secondary liability turn on the details of the technology involved? Are there "self-help" measures that copyright owners can use to help protect their works from infringement? If so, should copyright owners have legal recourse if hackers circumvent those self-help measures? That is the topic to which we now turn.

§ 9.04   TECHNOLOGICAL PROTECTION MEASURES AND CIRCUMVENTION DEVICES

[A]   Anti-Circumvention Measures

In the 1980s, when personal computers first became widely available, manufacturers of computer software became concerned that it would be impossible to combat widespread copying with infringement lawsuits alone. As a result, many software manufacturers tried to prevent copying through technological means, including encryption and password protection. These measures were largely unsuccessful, for three reasons. First, hackers were able to defeat each new technological measure almost as soon as it was released. Second, some courts held that it was lawful to sell products which helped consumers to circumvent such measures, because consumers had a right under § 117 to make a backup or archival copy of a program. *See, e.g., Vault Corp. v. Quaid. Software, Ltd.*, 847 F.2d 255, 263-67 (5th Cir. 1988). Third, technological measures often rendered software inconvenient to use, which harmed the software in the marketplace. By the end of the decade, many software makers had decided that copy-protection measures were simply not worth the effort.

The commercial development of the Internet revived interest in technological protection measures. In August 1995, the "White Paper" on *Intellectual Property and the National Information Infrastructure* (see § 7.01[D] above) proposed that "[t]he public will . . . have access to more copyright works via the NII if they are not vulnerable to the defeat of protection systems" and called for a ban on the importation, manufacture and sale of devices (and device components) "the primary purpose or effect of which" is to defeat such systems. *Id.* at 230.

The Administration carried a similar proposal to the WIPO Diplomatic Conference in December 1996, where, after heated debate, a compromise was struck, under which the new treaties called for national legislation to "provide adequate legal protection and effective legal remedies against the circumvention of effective technological measures that are used by authors in connection with the exercise of their rights." WIPO Copyright Treaty, art. 11. Obviously, this formulation leaves a great deal to the discretion of national legislatures.

In the United States, the WIPO Copyright Treaty was implemented in Title I of the Digital Millennium Copyright Act of 1998, which added a new Chapter 12 to Title 17. Before summarizing its provisions, we should make an overarching point: Chapter 12 is *not* copyright legislation — strictly, or even not so strictly, speaking. Rather, it is what has been termed "paracopyright" legislation: a new and independent set of prohibitions on activities related to the use of copyrighted works, in addition to those of copyright law itself. In what follows, the distinction between copyright and "paracopyright" will be important. For example, the exceptions and limitations in §§ 107-122 of the Copyright Act do not necessarily apply to the new "paracopyright" provisions in § 1201. Thus, we must pay special attention to those exceptions and limitations which are — and are not — built into § 1201 itself.

Section 1201 contains three new causes of action: a prohibition on the circumvention of technological measures which control access to a copyrighted work, in § 1201(a)(1); a prohibition on trafficking in technology that helps circumvent such access-control measures, in § 1201(a)(2); and a prohibition on trafficking in technology that helps circumvent copy-protection measures, in § 1201(b).

What sorts of technological measures are these provisions designed to protect against circumvention? The House Commerce Committee Report on the DMCA states that "effective" technological measures would include those "based on encryption, scrambling, authentication, or some other measure that requires the use of a 'key' provided by a copyright owner." H.R. Rep. No. 105-551 (Pt. 2), at 39-40 (1998). The requisite threshold of effectiveness apparently is quite low, so that even simple "password"-based systems are included. *But see I.M.S. Inquiry Mgmt. Sys., Ltd. v. Berkshire Info. Sys. Inc.*, 307 F. Supp. 2d 521 (S.D.N.Y. 2004) (although password protection constitutes an effective technological protection measure, unauthorized use of a password belonging to another does not constitute "circumvention" within the meaning of the DMCA). With this general qualification, § 1201 extends protection to two kinds of technological safeguards: those which control access to works, and those which control the exercise of rights with respect to works. The former are "gatekeeper" technologies which must be bypassed (lawfully or otherwise) if a user is to read, see, hear, or otherwise perceive a work to which they have been applied; the latter are technologies (usually, in fact, the same technologies) which limit the further uses which can potentially be made of works to which access has been obtained, i.e., reproduction, adaptation, distribution, public performance, and public display. In what follows, we will refer to these safeguards, collectively, as "technological protection measures," or "TPMs."[1]

---

[1] For a catalogue of such measures, see Schlachter, *The Intellectual Property Renaissance in Cyberspace: Why Copyright Law Could be Unimportant on the Internet*, 12 Berkeley Tech. L. J. 15 (1997).

Section 1201(a)(1), which prohibits circumvention conduct (rather than circumvention technology), applies only to access-control TPMs. This limitation was described as an effort to assure that the public will be able to make fair use of copyrighted works. The contention is that, while § 1201 prohibits circumventing technological measures that prevent unauthorized access, it does not apply to those that prevent copying. The reality is not so straightforward. The statute does not define "access," and there is nothing in law or technology to bar copyright owners from imposing "persistent" access controls, *i.e.*, measures that not only regulate a consumer's initial access to works, but also effectively control the subsequent utilization of those works by requiring new permission for "access" each time the work is used. In other words, the "access/use" distinction tends to collapse under pressure.

The specific exceptions to § 1201(a)(1) include a broadly worded "law enforcement" privilege (§ 1201(e)) and a "browsing privilege" in favor of libraries, archives, and schools (§ 1201(d)), which are permitted to circumvent TPMs solely for the purpose of making a good-faith determination as to whether they wish to acquire the protected works. Section 1201(f) permits reverse engineering, if undertaken solely to achieve interoperability. For more on the limits of this exception, see *Davidson & Assocs. v. Jung*, 422 F.3d 630 (8th Cir. 2005). Encryption research received a carefully circumscribed exemption in § 1201(g), while computer security testing is covered in § 1201(j). Section 1201(i) provides a personal privacy exception when a TPM is capable of collecting or disseminating personally identifying information about the online activities of an individual — which may or may not be an issue of real practical importance.

In contrast to these specific exceptions stands one that was most controversial in the forging of the DMCA. Every three years, the Librarian of Congress must conduct a formal rulemaking proceeding to inquire whether users have been, or in the ensuing three years are likely to be, adversely affected in their ability to make otherwise lawful uses of particular "classes" of copyright works. If the inquiry finds this is the case, the Librarian is authorized to make corresponding exceptions to the § 1201(a)(1) prohibitions on circumvention conduct, which remain in effect for a three-year period.

In the initial rulemaking, a key dispute concerned the meaning of "classes" of works. Some users proposed, for example, that "works embodied in copies which have been lawfully acquired by users who subsequently seek to made non-infringing uses thereof" constituted an eligible "class" of works. The Copyright Office rejected this suggestion, because it did not refer primarily to the qualities of the works themselves. *See* 65 Fed. Reg. 64555 (2000). In the third rulemaking in 2006, however, the Copyright Office took a more flexible view, stating that "in certain circumstances, it will also be permissible to refine the description of a class of works by reference to the type of user who may take advantage of the exemption or by reference to the type of use of the work that may be made pursuant to the exemption." 71 Fed. Reg. 68,472. Thus, in 2010 the Copyright Office approved an exemption for

> Motion pictures on DVDs . . . when circumvention is accomplished solely
> in order to accomplish the incorporation of short portions of motion

pictures into new works for the purpose of criticism or comment, and where the person engaging in circumvention believes and has reasonable grounds for believing that circumvention is necessary to fulfill the purpose of the use in . . . (i) Educational uses by college and university professors and by college and university film and media studies students; (ii) Documentary filmmaking; and (iii) Noncommercial videos.

75 Fed. Reg. 43,827. Four additional classes of copyrighted works were exempted from § 1201(a)(1)'s prohibition of circumvention for three years: computer programs on cell phones that execute so-called "apps," "for the sole purpose of enabling interoperability" of such apps with the phone's software; computer programs in cells phones, "solely in order to connect to a wireless telecommunications network" with authorization of the network operator; video games, "solely for the purpose of good faith testing for, investigating, or correcting security flaws and vulnerabilities"; and computer programs protected by damaged and obsolete access control mechanisms, or "dongles." *Id.* at 43,828-33. Six other proposed classes were considered and rejected.

The fifth rulemaking concluded in early 2013 and will be described in the casebook Supplement. Documents pertaining to the rulemaking are available on the Copyright Office website, *www.copyright.gov/1201*. If nothing else, this triennial rulemaking process has provided a forum for a robust, continuing public discussion of the fate of "fair use" under a regime of "paracopyright."

Of course, even if the scope of § 1201(a)(1) is limited as the result of the Librarian's rulemaking, the practical ability of consumers to exercise their circumvention privileges may still be severely restricted by the non-availability of devices and services to assist them. Sections 1201(a)(2) and 1201(b) cover more than just "black boxes" designed specifically to facilitate electronic copyright piracy. Instead, they prohibit trafficking in "any technology, product, service, device, component, or part thereof" that can be used to circumvent access to copyright works or limit the exercise of rights with respect to such works, if any of a series of conditions, stated in the disjunctive, is met. The prohibitions apply if the item or service is primarily designed or made for circumvention, if it has only "limited commercially significant purpose" other than circumvention, or if it is marketed for circumvention purposes. The fact that a circumvention device or service might be made or sold to aid circumvention conduct that is lawful under the statute, or that is found to be exempt in the course of the Librarian of Congress's rulemaking, does not in itself save the device or service from the sweep of these prohibitions. *See, e.g., RealNetworks, Inc. v. DVD Copy Control Ass'n*, 641 F. Supp. 2d 913 (N.D. Cal. 2009) (although it may be a fair use for consumers to make a backup copy of a DVD, it is illegal to make or sell a device that permits a consumer to make such copies).

NOTES AND QUESTIONS

(1) Is the DMCA's delegation of what appears to be legislative power to the Librarian of Congress constitutional? *See* Jiles, *Copyright Protection in the New Millennium: Amending the Digital Millennium Copyright Act to Prevent Constitutional Challenges*, 52 Admin. L. Rev. 443 (2000).

(2)   Note that the exceptions to the anti-circumvention provisions and the exceptions to the anti-trafficking provisions often do not mesh with one another. For example, law enforcement personnel and software designers engaged in qualifying reverse engineering activities may develop circumvention hardware and software to counteract all kinds of TPMs, while encryption researchers and computer security testers may do so to circumvent TPMs which control access, but not those that control copying. "Browsing" libraries and computer users engaging in self-help to protect their personal privacy apparently have to do without the equipment and services they require to exercise their circumvention privileges. And while there is no exemption to the anti-circumvention provisions for parents seeking to protect their children from harmful online content, § 1201(h) allows a court to excuse from liability the maker of a hardware or software component designed for this purpose. Does this hodgepodge of mismatched exemptions make any sense from a policy point of view? Or does it merely reflect the reality of legislative politics, negotiation among affected interest groups, and last-minute amendments?

(3)   Consider the "anti-trafficking" provisions of § 1201(a)(2) and (b). Both sections prohibit technology which has "only limited commercially significant purpose or use other than to circumvent a technological measure." Is this a codification of the "capable of substantial non-infringing uses" standard of *Sony*? Or is it more similar to the proposed standard in the dissenting opinion in *Sony*? Has *Sony* been legislatively overruled with respect to circumvention devices?

(4)   In addition, § 1201(a)(2) and (b) also prohibit technology which is "primarily designed or produced for the purpose of circumventing a technological measure," and technology which is "marketed . . . for use in circumventing a technological measure," even if the circumvention technology is capable of legitimate uses. By their wording (and richly supported in the legislative history of the DMCA), § 1201(a)(2) and (b) may not reach general-purpose consumer electronics devices (such as VCRs and PCs) and telecommunications equipment that may incidentally perform some circumvention functions. Moreover, § 1201(c)(3) specifically provides that such manufacturers are not required to design their products to respond affirmatively to (or facilitate the effectiveness of) any particular type of TPM — whether now in existence or to be developed in the future. This so-called "no mandate" provision represented a hard-won victory for the consumer electronics and hardware industries, and it was won (in part) through compromise: § 1201(k) modifies the general "no mandate" provision by requiring that all new analog VCRs must conform with certain "copy-protection" technologies — generally referred to as "Macrovision" — that are commonly applied to prerecorded videotapes offered for sale and rental.

Over the long haul, another portion of § 1201(k) actually may turn out to be among the most important features of the DMCA. That portion prohibits the application of Macrovision technology to prevent consumer copying of free over-the-air television broadcasts. In a world of "paracopyright," "encoding rules" barring the application of TPMs in certain circumstances may represent the most realistic legislative option for assuring the meaningful continuation of the traditional user privileges embedded in the copyright law itself.

(5)   Would it have been possible to design the DMCA to give greater scope to consumer interests (including, but not limited to "fair use")? This issue is squarely posed by the European Union "Directive on the harmonisation of certain aspects of copyright and related rights in the information society" (2001/29/EC). That document was designed to serve multiple, seemingly contradictory, purposes. In effect, Article 5 invites each European legislature to define specific limitations and exceptions to copyright protection in digital (as well as non-digital) works. Indeed, it even supplies a long list of permissible exceptions. But Article 6 then mandates that European countries implement the 1996 WIPO treaties by adopting DMCA-style prohibitions on circumvention conduct and devices. In an effort at reconciliation, Article 6(4) then commands (in part) that "[m]ember states shall take appropriate measures to ensure that rightsholders make available to the beneficiar[ies of certain] limitation[s] and exception[s] provided for in national law . . . the means of benefitting from that exception or limitation." But how?

For information on implementation of the Directive, and a flavor of the debate over the meaning of Article 6(4), see *http://cyber.law.harvard.edu/media/eucd_materials*, and Hart, *The Copyright in the Information Society Directive: An Overview*, 24 Eur. Intell. Prop. Rev. 58, 62-63 (2002). Note in particular § 75d of the Danish Consolidated Act on Copyright (2003), which allows the Copyright License Tribunal to order that a copyright owner make the "key" to a technological protection measure available to a deserving applicant within 4 weeks — after which circumvention by the user is permitted. *See www.kum.dk/sw4550.asp* (Denmark). *See also* Peter K. Yu, *Anticircumvention and Anti-anticircumvention*, 84 Denv. U. L. Rev. 13 (2006).

(6)   Other countries also have faced the problem of how to reconcile consumer use privileges and anti-circumvention protection. For the controversial approach adopted in Australia's Copyright Amendment (Digital Agenda) Act 2000 (only to be discarded in the aftermath of the U.S-Australia Free Trade Agreement of 2004) see Aplin, *Contemplating Australia's Digital Future*, 23 Eur. Intell. Prop. Rev. 565 (2001).

[B]   Case Law

UNIVERSAL CITY STUDIOS, INC. v. CORLEY
United States Court of Appeals, Second Circuit
273 F.3d 429 (2001)

JON O. NEWMAN, CIRCUIT JUDGE.

When the Framers of the First Amendment prohibited Congress from making any law "abridging the freedom of speech," they were not thinking about computers, computer programs, or the Internet. But neither were they thinking about radio, television, or movies. Just as the inventions at the beginning and middle of the 20th [C]entury presented new First Amendment issues, so does the cyber revolution at the end of that century. This appeal raises significant First Amendment issues concerning one aspect of computer technology — encryption to protect materials in digital form from unauthorized access. . . .

Introduction

. . . This appeal concerns the anti-trafficking provisions of the DMCA, which Congress enacted in 1998 to strengthen copyright protection in the digital age. Fearful that the ease with which pirates could copy and distribute a copyrightable work in digital form was overwhelming the capacity of conventional copyright enforcement to find and enjoin unlawfully copied material, Congress sought to combat copyright piracy in its earlier stages, before the work was even copied. The DMCA therefore backed with legal sanctions the efforts of copyright owners to protect their works from piracy behind digital walls such as encryption codes or password protections. In so doing, Congress targeted not only those pirates who would circumvent these digital walls (the "anti-circumvention provisions," contained in 17 U.S.C. § 1201(a)(1)), but also anyone who would traffic in a technology primarily designed to circumvent a digital wall (the "anti-trafficking provisions," contained in 17 U.S.C. § 1201(a)(2), (b)(1)).

[Defendant-Appellant] Corley publishes a print magazine and maintains an affiliated web site geared towards "hackers," a digital-era term often applied to those interested in techniques for circumventing protections of computers and computer data from unauthorized access. The so-called hacker community includes serious computer-science scholars conducting research on protection techniques, computer buffs intrigued by the challenge of trying to circumvent access-limiting devices or perhaps hoping to promote security by exposing flaws in protection techniques, mischief-makers interested in disrupting computer operations, and thieves, including copyright infringers who want to acquire copyrighted material (for personal use or resale) without paying for it.

In November 1999, Corley posted a copy of the decryption computer program "DeCSS" on his web site, *www.2600.com* ("2600.com"). DeCSS is designed to circumvent "CSS," the encryption technology that motion picture studios place on DVDs to prevent the unauthorized viewing and copying of motion pictures. Corley also posted on his web site links to other web sites where DeCSS could be found.

Plaintiffs-Appellees are eight motion picture studios that brought an action in the Southern District of New York seeking injunctive relief against Corley under the DMCA. Following a full non-jury trial, the District Court entered a permanent injunction barring Corley from posting DeCSS on his web site or from knowingly linking via a hyperlink to any other web site containing DeCSS. . . .

Corley renews his constitutional challenges on appeal. . . .

Background

. . . [T]he improved quality of a movie in [DVD] format brings with it the risk that a virtually perfect copy, *i.e.*, one that will not lose perceptible quality in the copying process, can be readily made at the click of a computer control and instantly distributed to countless recipients throughout the world over the Internet. This case arises out of the movie industry's efforts to respond to this risk by invoking the anti-trafficking provisions of the DMCA. . . .

I. CSS

. . . The [studios] enlisted the help of members of the consumer electronics and computer industries, who in mid-1996 developed the Content Scramble System ("CSS"). CSS is an encryption scheme that employs an algorithm configured by a set of "keys" to encrypt a DVD's contents. The algorithm is a type of mathematical formula for transforming the contents of the movie file into gibberish; the "keys" are . . . strings of 0's and 1's that serve as values for the mathematical formula. Decryption . . . requires a set of "player keys" contained in compliant DVD players, as well as an understanding of the CSS encryption algorithm. Without the player keys and the algorithm, a DVD player cannot access the contents of a DVD. With the player keys and the algorithm, a DVD player can display the movie on a television or a computer screen, but does not give a viewer the ability . . . to copy the movie or to manipulate the digital content of the DVD.

The studios developed a licensing scheme for distributing the technology to manufacturers of DVD players. . . . With encryption technology and licensing agreements in hand, the studios began releasing movies on DVDs in 1997. . . . In 1998, the studios secured added protection against DVD piracy when Congress passed the DMCA . . . .

II. DeCSS

In September 1999, Jon Johansen, a Norwegian teenager, . . . reverse-engineered a licensed DVD player designed to operate on the Microsoft operating system, and culled from it the player keys and other information necessary to decrypt CSS. The record suggests that Johansen was trying to develop a DVD player operable on Linux, an alternative operating system that did not support any licensed DVD players at that time. In order to accomplish this task, Johansen wrote a decryption program executable on Microsoft's operating system. That program was called, appropriately enough, "DeCSS.". . .

Johansen posted the executable object code, but not the source code, for DeCSS on his web site. . . . Within months of its appearance in executable form on Johansen's web site, DeCSS was widely available on the Internet, in both object code and various forms of source code. . . .

In November 1999, Corley wrote and placed on his web site, 2600.com, an article about the DeCSS phenomenon. . . .

Corley's article about DeCSS detailed how CSS was cracked, and described the movie industry's efforts to shut down web sites posting DeCSS. It also explained that DeCSS could be used to copy DVDs. At the end of the article, the Defendants posted copies of the object and source code of DeCSS. In Corley's words, he added the code to the story because "in a journalistic world, . . . you have to show your evidence . . ." . . . Corley also added to the article links that he explained would take the reader to other web sites where DeCSS could be found.

2600.com was only one of hundreds of web sites that began posting DeCSS near the end of 1999. The movie industry tried to stem the tide by sending cease-and-desist letters to many of these sites. These efforts met with only partial success; a number of sites refused to remove DeCSS. In January 2000, the studios filed this lawsuit.

Examples of DeCSS Art
DeCSS Haiku (top left); DeCSS T-Shirt (top right);
DeCSS Tie (bottom left); DeCSS DVD (bottom right)

III. The DMCA

[The court describes the history and provisions of the DMCA.]

IV. Procedural History

Invoking [17 U.S.C.] subsection 1203(b)(1), the Plaintiffs sought an injunction against the Defendants, alleging that the Defendants violated the anti-trafficking provisions of the statute. On January 20, 2000, after a hearing, the District Court issued a preliminary injunction barring the Defendants from posting DeCSS.

The Defendants complied with the preliminary injunction, but continued to post links to other web sites carrying DeCSS, an action they termed "electronic civil disobedience." Under the heading "Stop the MPAA [(Motion Picture Association of America)]," Corley urged other web sites to post DeCSS lest "we . . . be forced into submission."

The Plaintiffs then sought a permanent injunction barring the Defendants from both posting DeCSS and linking to sites containing DeCSS. After a trial on the merits, the Court . . . granted a permanent injunction. . . .

The Court's injunction barred the Defendants from: "posting on any Internet web site" DeCSS; "in any other way . . . offering to the public, providing, or otherwise trafficking in DeCSS"; violating the anti-trafficking provisions of the DMCA in any other manner, and finally "knowingly linking any Internet web site operated by them to any other web site containing DeCSS, or knowingly maintaining any such link, for the purpose of disseminating DeCSS."

The Appellants have appealed from the permanent injunction. . . .

Discussion

I. Narrow Construction to Avoid Constitutional Doubt

The Appellants first argue that, because their constitutional arguments are at least substantial, we should interpret the statute narrowly so as to avoid constitutional problems. They identify three different instances of alleged ambiguity in the statute that they claim provide an opportunity for such a narrow interpretation.

First, they contend that subsection 1201(c)(1), which provides that "nothing in this section shall affect rights, remedies, limitations or defenses to copyright infringement, including fair use, under this title," can be read to allow the circumvention of encryption technology protecting copyrighted material when the material will be put to "fair uses" exempt from copyright liability. [On the contrary,] subsection 1201(c)(1) . . . simply clarifies that the DMCA targets the circumvention of digital walls guarding copyrighted material (and trafficking in circumvention tools), but does not concern itself with the use of those materials after circumvention has occurred. Subsection 1201(c)(1) ensures that the DMCA is not read to prohibit the "fair use" of information just because that information was obtained in a manner made illegal by the DMCA. . . .

Second, the Appellants urge a narrow construction of the DMCA because of subsection 1201(c)(4), which provides that "nothing in this section shall enlarge or diminish any rights of free speech or the press for activities using consumer electronics, telecommunications, or computing products." This language is clearly precatory: Congress could not "diminish" constitutional rights of free speech even if it wished to . . .

Third, the Appellants argue that an individual who buys a DVD has the "authority of the copyright owner" to view the DVD, and therefore is exempted from the DMCA pursuant to subsection 1201(a)(3)(A) when the buyer circumvents an encryption technology in order to view the DVD on a competing platform (such as Linux). The basic flaw in this argument is that it misreads subsection 1201(a)(3)(A). . . . In any event, the Defendants offered no evidence that the Plaintiffs have either explicitly or implicitly authorized DVD buyers to circumvent encryption technology to support use on multiple platforms.[16]

We conclude that the anti-trafficking and anti-circumvention provisions of the DMCA are not susceptible to the narrow interpretations urged by the Appellants. We therefore proceed to consider the Appellants' constitutional claims.

II. Constitutional Challenge Based on the Copyright Clause

In a footnote to their brief, the Appellants appear to contend that the DMCA, as construed by the District Court, exceeds the constitutional authority of Congress to grant authors copyrights for a "limited time," U.S. Const. art. I, § 8, cl. 8 . . . For two reasons, the argument provides no basis for disturbing the judgment of the District Court.

First, we have repeatedly ruled that arguments presented to us only in a footnote are not entitled to appellate consideration. . . . Although an amicus brief can be helpful in elaborating issues properly presented by the parties, it is normally not a method for injecting new issues into an appeal, at least in cases where the parties are competently represented by counsel. . . .

Second, to whatever extent the argument might have merit at some future time in a case with a properly developed record, the argument is entirely premature and speculative at this time on this record. There is not even a claim, much less evidence, that any Plaintiff has sought to prevent copying of public domain works, or that the injunction prevents the Defendants from copying such works. . . .

III. Constitutional Challenges Based on the First Amendment

A. Applicable Principles

[The Court held that communication of a computer program is a form of speech protected under the First Amendment, and that laws regulating such communications may be permissible "content-neutral" restrictions. To qualify, such laws must

---

[16] Even if the Defendants had been able to offer such evidence, and even if they could have demonstrated that DeCSS was "primarily designed . . . for the purpose of" playing DVDs on multiple platforms (and therefore not for the purpose of "circumventing a technological measure"), a proposition questioned by Judge Kaplan, the Defendants would defeat liability only under subsection 1201(a)(2)(A). They would still be vulnerable to liability under subsection 1201(a)(2)(C), because they "marketed" DeCSS for the copying of DVDs, not just for the playing of DVDs on multiple platforms.

serve a substantial governmental interest, the interest must be unrelated to the suppression of free expression, and the regulations must be narrowly tailored, which "in this context requires . . . that the means chosen do not 'burden substantially more speech than is necessary to further the government's legitimate interests'" (quoting *Turner Broadcasting System, Inc. v. FCC*, 512 U.S. 622, 662 (1994)). The Court then determined that the DMCA was "content-neutral" because its purpose was to forestall massive abuse of copyright owners' rights. DeCSS, it observed, "is like a skeleton key that . . . enables anyone to gain access to a DVD movie without using a DVD player," a development potentially very damaging to copyright owners because the advent of the Internet creates the potential for instantaneous worldwide distribution of the copied material.]

. . . [DeCSS] also is a form of communication, albeit written in a language not understood by the general public. . . . [Thus,] it has a claim to being protected by the First Amendment. But just as the realities of what any computer code can accomplish must inform the scope of its constitutional protection, so the capacity of a decryption program like DeCSS to accomplish unauthorized — indeed, unlawful — access to materials in which the Plaintiffs have intellectual property rights must inform and limit the scope of its First Amendment protection. . . .

B. First Amendment Challenge

The District Court's injunction applies the DMCA to the Defendants by imposing two types of prohibition, both grounded on the anti-trafficking provisions of the DMCA. The first prohibits posting DeCSS or any other technology for circumventing CSS on any Internet web site. The second prohibits knowingly linking any Internet web site to any other web site containing DeCSS. The validity of the posting and linking prohibitions must be considered separately.

1. Posting

The initial issue is whether the posting prohibition is content-neutral, since, as we have explained, this classification determines the applicable constitutional standard. The Appellants['] . . . argument fails to recognize that the target of the posting provisions of the injunction — DeCSS — has both a non-speech and a speech component, and that the DMCA, as applied to the Appellants, and the posting prohibition of the injunction target only the nonspeech component. . . .

. . . The Government's interest in preventing unauthorized access to encrypted copyrighted material is unquestionably substantial, and the regulation of DeCSS by the posting prohibition plainly serves that interest. Moreover, that interest is unrelated to the suppression of free expression. . . .

. . . Appellants have not suggested, much less shown, any technique for barring them from making this instantaneous worldwide distribution of a decryption code that makes a lesser restriction on the code's speech component. It is true that the Government has alternative means of prohibiting unauthorized access to copyrighted materials. For example, it can create criminal and civil liability for those who gain unauthorized access, and thus it can be argued that the restriction on posting DeCSS is not absolutely necessary to preventing unauthorized access to copyrighted materials. But a content-neutral regulation need not employ the least restrictive means of accomplishing the governmental objective. It need only avoid burdening "substantially more speech than is necessary to further the government's legitimate interests." *Turner Broadcasting*, 512 U.S. at 662 (internal quotation marks and citation omitted). The prohibition on the Defendants' posting of DeCSS satisfies that standard.[30]

2. Linking

. . . A hyperlink is a cross-reference (in a distinctive font or color) appearing on one web page that, when activated by the point-and-click of a mouse, brings onto the computer screen another web page. . . . Or the hyperlink can appear as an image, for example, an icon depicting a person sitting at a computer watching a DVD movie and text stating "click here to access DeCSS and see DVD movies for free!" . . . With a hyperlink on a web page, the linked web site is just one click away.

In applying the DMCA to linking (via hyperlinks), Judge Kaplan recognized, as he had with DeCSS code, that a hyperlink has both a speech and a nonspeech component. It conveys information, the Internet address of the linked web page, and has the functional capacity to bring the content of the linked web page to the user's computer screen . . . As he had ruled with respect to DeCSS code, he ruled that application of the DMCA to the Defendants' linking to web sites containing DeCSS is content-neutral because it . . . applies whether or not the hyperlink contains any information, comprehensible to a human being, as to the Internet address of the web page being accessed. The linking prohibition is justified solely by the functional capability of the hyperlink.

. . . Judge Kaplan then ruled that the DMCA, as applied to the Defendants' linking, served substantial governmental interests and was unrelated to the suppression of free expression. We agree. He then carefully considered the "closer call" as to whether a linking prohibition would satisfy the narrow tailoring requirement. In an especially carefully considered portion of his opinion, he observed that strict liability for linking to web sites containing DeCSS would risk two impairments of free expression. Web site operators would be inhibited from displaying links to various web pages for fear that a linked page might contain DeCSS, and a prohibition on linking to a web site containing DeCSS would curtail access to whatever other information was contained at the accessed site.

To avoid applying the DMCA in a manner that would "burden substantially more speech than is necessary to further the government's legitimate interests," *Turner Broadcasting*, 512 U.S. at 662 (internal quotation marks and citation omitted), Judge Kaplan adapted the standards of *New York Times Co. v. Sullivan*, 376 U.S. 254, 283 (1964), to fashion a limited prohibition against linking to web sites

---

[30] We have considered the opinion of a California intermediate appellate court in *DVD Copy Control Ass'n v. Bunner*, 93 Cal. App. 4th 648 (Cal. Ct. App. 2001), declining, on First Amendment grounds, to issue a preliminary injunction under state trade secrets law prohibiting a web site operator from posting DeCSS. To the extent that *DVD Copy Control* disagrees with our First Amendment analysis, we decline to follow it. [The judgment in *Bunner* was later reversed by the California Supreme Court. 31 Cal. 4th 864, 75 P.3d 1, 4 Cal. Rptr. 3d 69, (2003). See the notes following *Corley*. — Eds.]

containing DeCSS. He required clear and convincing evidence

> that those responsible for the link (a) know at the relevant time that the offending material is on the linked-to site, (b) know that it is circumvention technology that may not lawfully be offered, and (c) create or maintain the link for the purpose of disseminating that technology.

[*Universal City Studios, Inc. v. Reimerdes*, 111 F. Supp. 2d 294, 341 (S.D.N.Y. 2000)]. He then found that the evidence satisfied his three-part test by his required standard of proof. . . .

. . . [W]e see no need on this appeal to determine whether a test as rigorous as Judge Kaplan's is required to respond to First Amendment objections to the linking provision of the injunction that he issued. It suffices to reject the Appellants' contention that an intent to cause harm is required and that linking can be enjoined only under circumstances applicable to a print medium. As they have throughout their arguments, the Appellants ignore the reality of the functional capacity of decryption computer code and hyperlinks to facilitate instantaneous unauthorized access to copyrighted materials by anyone anywhere in the world. . . .

This reality obliges courts considering First Amendment claims in the context of the pending case to choose between two unattractive alternatives: either tolerate some impairment of communication in order to permit Congress to prohibit decryption that may lawfully be prevented, or tolerate some decryption in order to avoid some impairment of communication. . . . [T]he fundamental choice between impairing some communication and tolerating decryption cannot be entirely avoided.

In facing this choice, we are mindful that it is not for us to resolve the issues of public policy implicated by the choice we have identified. Those issues are for Congress. Our task is to determine whether the legislative solution adopted by Congress, as applied to the Appellants . . . , is consistent with the limitations of the First Amendment, and we are satisfied that it is.

IV. Constitutional Challenge Based on Claimed Restriction of Fair Use

> [The portion of the opinion discussing "fair use" is considered in Chapter 10.]

Conclusion

We have considered all the other arguments of the Appellants and conclude that they provide no basis for disturbing the District Court's judgment. Accordingly, the judgment is affirmed.

NOTES AND QUESTIONS

(1)   Obviously, lawyers usually must take the clients they are given. But if you were constructing a case to test the "device" provisions of the DMCA's prohibitions on circumvention, would you have chosen these defendants?

(2)   Begin with an issue addressed below that the defendants chose *not* to appeal. Is CSS a technological measure that "effectively controls access to a work"? *See* 17 U.S.C. § 1201(a)(3)(B). Is it relevant that Johansen was able to defeat CSS so easily? If not, what is the meaning of the word "effectively"? *See Agfa Monotype Corp. v. Adobe Sys.*, 404 F. Supp. 2d 1030 (N.D. Ill. 2005) (embedded "bits" encoding permissions do not by themselves constitute an "effective" technological protection measure).

(3)   Why did the court reject the defendants' reliance on § 1201(c)(1)? Could the defendants have relied instead on § 1201(c)(2)? Both subsections purport to leave unaffected certain legal doctrines applicable to "copyright infringement." But "copyright infringement" is governed entirely by the Copyright Act, which comprises only Chapters 1-8 of Title 17. Section 1201, like the rest of Chapter 12, is "paracopyright" legislation which imposes new legal restrictions *in addition to* those of copyright. Do subsections (c)(1) and (c)(2) impose *any* substantive limits on circumvention, or are they merely tautologies?

(4)   The defendants contended that Johansen was trying to develop a way to view lawfully-purchased DVDs on a computer using the Linux operating system, rather than the more common Microsoft Windows operating system. If that could be proved to the court's satisfaction, would the defendants qualify for the exemption in § 1201(f)?

(5)   Metaphors matter. One of the most prominent comparisons made by advocates of the DMCA's Chapter 12 was between devices (and services) that enable circumvention, on the one hand, and "'skeleton keys" or "burglar tools," on the other. The court in *Corley* seems to find this metaphor compelling. Do you?

(6)   The opinion states that "[o]wners of all property rights are entitled to prohibit access to their property by unauthorized persons." If consumers have a right to make a "fair use" of a copyrighted work, are they "unauthorized" persons? If the public has an established easement over a parcel of real property, could the property owner install a fence to keep the public out?

(7)   The DCMA creates a new kind of secondary liability (for circumvention "conduct") on top of copyright infringement itself, and even a sort of tertiary liability (for supplying circumvention "devices") on top of that. How clear is it that the Act also was intended to penalize conduct — *i.e.*, linking — yet one step *further* removed from any actual harm to a protected intellectual property interest? How successful do you think the court's efforts to prevent chilling effects on legitimate "linkers" will be? How easy will it be for individuals to conform their conduct to this standard?

(8)   The co-authors of the casebook are not First Amendment specialists — but you (or your professor) may be. How representative of the mainstream jurisprudence of freedom of expression are the court's views as expressed in this opinion? How consistent are they with contemporary cases that consider the expressive content of computer code?

(9)   In January 2003, Johansen was acquitted of criminal charges by a Norwegian court, and the Court of Appeal upheld the acquittal. For an English translation of the decision, see *www.ipjustice.org/johansen/DVD-Jon-Borgarting-1-eng.doc.*

Meanwhile, the campaign against DeCSS continued on various fronts. In *DVD Copy Control Association v. Bunner*, 113 Cal. Rptr. 2d 338 (2001) (noted in the *Corley* opinion), the California Court of Appeal reversed a preliminary injunction in a trade secret action brought against an individual who posted DeCSS on his website. The court held that the preliminary injunction was an impermissible prior restraint that violated the First Amendment. The California Supreme Court reversed, holding that the First Amendment was not a bar *if* a valid trade secret existed. 31 Cal. 4th 864, 4 Cal. Rptr. 3d 69, 75 P.3d 1 (2003). On remand, the Court of Appeal again denied the preliminary injunction, this time on the substantive merits of the claim. 116 Cal. App. 4th 241 (2004).

(10)   In a related development, 321 Studios, which made and sold a product that enables users to make unencrypted backup copies of DVDs, sued the major motion picture studios for a declaratory judgment that its product, DVD-X Copy, did not violate the anti-trafficking provisions of the DMCA. In February 2004, the court granted summary judgment in favor of the studios on their counterclaim. *321 Studios v. Metro-Goldwyn-Mayer Studios, Inc.*, 307 F. Supp. 2d 1085 (N.D. Cal. 2004). Three weeks later, another federal court granted a preliminary injunction in another suit by the studios against 321. *Paramount Pictures Corp. v. 321 Studios*, 2004 U.S. Dist. LEXIS 3306 (S.D.N.Y., Mar. 4, 2004). Both decisions relied heavily on the analysis in *Corley*. *See also RealNetworks, Inc. v. DVD Copy Control Ass'n*, 641 F. Supp. 2d 913 (N.D. Cal. 2009) (granting a preliminary injunction against backup software RealDVD).

(11)   *"Plugging the analog hole."* The "no mandate" compromise embodied in § 1201(c)(3) may be unraveling. Some content-owners have had discussions with major consumer electronics manufacturers to develop a voluntary standard that, when implemented in software and hardware, would provide additional security against copying. The MPAA's "Content Protection Status Report," of April 25, 2002, with its now-notorious reference to the importance of "plugging the analog hole" (*i.e.*, making it impossible for digital electronic devices to generate analog outputs), has been a special target of criticism from consumer organizations.

With the advent of "BluRay" high-definition video players, the MPAA may yet get its wish. BluRay license agreements now require consumer electronics manu-facturers to "phase out" analog outputs after December 31, 2013. For more information, see the materials collected by the Electronic Frontier Foundation at *www.eff.org/issues/analog-hole.*

(12)   *"Broadcast flag" and beyond.* The Federal Communications Commission has regulatory jurisdiction over high definition television ("HDTV") in the U.S. market. In 2003, the FCC adopted regulations requiring set-top boxes to respond to a so-called "broadcast flag" which permits content providers to limit (but not eliminate) copying by consumers. The FCC's report is available at *http:// hraunfoss.fcc.gov/edocs_public/attachmatch/FCC-03-273A1.pdf.*

After several parties challenged the broadcast flag regulation in court, the D.C. Circuit held that the FCC "acted outside the scope of its delegated authority when it adopted the disputed broadcast flag regulations." *American Library Ass'n v. FCC*, 406 F.3d 689 (D.C. Cir. 2005). The court noted that the FCC only has statutory authority to regulate "interstate communication by wire or radio," and it held that the FCC's ancillary jurisdiction did not extend to technology (such as the "broadcast flag") that acts only after a communication has been received, and does not directly affect the communication itself. *Id.* at 703.

Evidence has emerged, however, that despite the lack of a legal mandate, Microsoft voluntarily built broadcast-flag recognition into its Vista operating system. For more information, see *www.eff.org/issues/broadcast-flag.*

Additional Litigation Under the DMCA's Anti-Circumvention Provisions

A few other lawsuits involving the anti-circumvention provisions of the DMCA are worth noting in particular.

In 1999, RealNetworks, Inc., whose products deliver "streamed" audio and video content over the Internet, brought suit against Streambox, Inc., for offering software usable for downloading RealNetworks' feeds in various data storage formats, including MP3, WAV, and Windows Media. Because "streamed" audio and video technology is designed to safeguard content by preventing downloading, RealNetworks regarded Streambox's products as prohibited "circumvention" technologies and sued to bar their use — despite the fact that it was not the owner of copyright in the music and video content in question. In an opinion reported at 2000 U.S. Dist. LEXIS 1889 (W.D. Wash., Jan. 18, 2000), a federal judge agreed that some of RealNetwork's claims had enough merit to justify a preliminary injunction. Ten years later, RealNetworks found itself on the other side of the issue, when its RealDVD copying software was preliminarily enjoined as a circumvention device. *See* 641 F. Supp. 2d 914 (N.D. Cal. 2009).

Another high-profile case, involving criminal enforcement of the "device" provisions of § 1201, began with the widely-publicized arrest of a Russian computer scientist, Dmitry Sklyarov, who had helped devise a computer program that allows consumers to avoid restrictions (like limits on copying, printing, and lending) embedded in the Adobe Acrobat eBook Reader software. Charges against Sklyarov were dismissed in exchange for his testimony against his employer, a Russian company which distributed the allegedly offending product. *See United States v. Elcom Ltd.*, 203 F. Supp. 2d 1111 (N.D. Cal. 2002) (denying motion to dismiss indictment on constitutional grounds). In the end, Elcom was acquitted by a jury, which concluded that the Russian company had not intentionally violated the statute. *See* Healey, *Russian Firm Cleared in Digital-Piracy Trial*, L.A. Times, Dec. 18, 2002, at C1.

Next, consider the Secure Digital Music Initiative ("SDMI"), an effort by recording companies and consumer electronics firms to come up with an industry standard for anti-copying protection. In an attempt to publicly demonstrate its effectiveness, the organization invited computer scientists to try to "hack" its prototype security system. When a team of researchers announced that it had successfully done so, a lawyer for the RIAA threatened them with suit under the DMCA if they delivered an academic paper describing their strategy and thus exposing SDMI's shortcomings. An action for a declaratory judgment brought by the computer scientists (including Professor Edward Felten of Princeton) was dismissed after the recording industry (and the U.S. Government) offered assurances that the original threats had been misconceived and would not be repeated.

For details, see the documents available at *www.eff.org/cases/felten-et-al-v-riaa-et-al*.

Multi-user online games and gold farming. The DMCA also has been applied to combat automated "gold farming" in online video games. "Gold farming" refers to the practice of performing repetitive actions in online games for hours on end, accumulating virtual money that is sold to other players in exchange for real money. Players who buy virtual gold typically are seeking to accumulate wealth in the game faster than they otherwise could, and to skip "boring" or repetitive tasks while still participating in more exciting parts of the game. Game providers typically discourage or prohibit gold farming because it forces them to provide new levels and new experiences at a faster rate, increasing their development costs; and because it angers other users who see it as a form of cheating.

The legal skirmish began when MDY Industries developed a computer program called "Glider" that automated play in the online game *World of Warcraft*, allowing a user's computer to accumulate gold while the user was away. After receiving a cease-and-desist warning from WoW's developer Blizzard, MDY sued for a declaratory judgment of non-infringement. Blizzard counterclaimed, arguing that (1) the program was licensed, not sold, so that loading the program into RAM without authorization was infringing; (2) any use of Glider was unauthorized and therefore infringing, because the end-user license agreement prohibited automated play; and (3) Glider was designed to circumvent "Warden," a "technological measure" that attempts to detect automated play, thereby controlling "access" to the copyrighted game.

On appeal, the Ninth Circuit affirmed the District Court's findings that Warden did not control access to the software code or to the individual non-literal elements (visual images and recorded sounds) of the game because the purchaser could access those elements without encountering Warden. *MDY Industries, LLC v. Blizzard Entertainment, Inc.*, 629 F.3d 928, 952-53 (9th Cir. 2010). It also, however, upheld the District Court's finding that Warden did control access to the dynamic non-literal elements of the game (the combination of the visual images and recorded sounds into an audiovisual work), and that Glider was designed to circumvent Warden. *Id.* at 953-54. Do you think this is an appropriate application of the DMCA's anti-circumvention provisions? Why or why not?

Anti-Circumvention: Unintended Consequences and Continuing Controversy

Creative lawyers look for good opportunities to use new legislation for their clients' benefit, even when these applications probably were never contemplated by the legislature. If you have ever lost the remote control to a household appliance, you may have wondered about the high cost of a manufacturer-supplied replacement. If you explored alternatives, were you contemplating a violation of the DMCA?

In *Chamberlain Group, Inc. v. Skylink Technologies, Inc.*, 381 F.3d 1178 (Fed. Cir. 2004), the plaintiff, a manufacturer of garage door systems, asserted that the "embedded" security software in its remote garage-door openers was copyrighted, and that a third-party manufacturer of "universal" remote controls was wrongfully enabling purchasers of the plaintiff's doors to "access" that software. Consider the following language from the Federal Circuit's opinion turning back this clever — but almost certainly unanticipated — application of the DMCA:

> Under . . . Chamberlain's proposed construction . . . , the owners of a work protected by *both* copyright *and* a technological measure that effectively controls access to that work per § 1201(a) would possess *unlimited* rights to hold circumventors liable under § 1201(a) *merely for accessing that work*, even if that access enabled *only* rights that the Copyright Act grants to the public. This . . . regime would be problematic for a number of reasons. First, as the Supreme Court recently explained, "Congress' exercise of its Copyright Clause authority must be rational." *Eldred v. Ashcroft*, 537 U.S. 186 (2003). . . .
>
> Chamberlain's proposed construction of § 1201(a) implies that in enacting the DMCA, Congress attempted to "give the public appropriate access" to copyrighted works by allowing copyright owners to deny all access to the public. Even under the substantial deference due Congress, such a redefinition borders on the irrational.
>
> That apparent irrationality, however, is not the most significant problem that this . . . regime implies. Such a regime would be hard to reconcile with the DMCA's statutory prescription that "nothing in this section shall affect rights, remedies, limitations, or defenses to copyright infringement, including fair use, under this title." 17 U.S.C. § 1201(c)(1). A provision that prohibited access without regard to the rest of the Copyright Act would clearly affect rights and limitations, if not remedies and defenses. . . .
>
> Chamberlain's proposed construction of § 1201(a) would flatly contradict § 1201(c)(1) — a simultaneously enacted provision of the same statute. We are therefore bound, if we can, to obtain an alternative construction that leads to no such contradiction. . . .
>
> . . . We conclude that 17 U.S.C. § 1201 prohibits only forms of access that bear a reasonable relationship to the protections that the Copyright Act otherwise affords copyright owners. While such a rule of reason may create some uncertainty and consume some judicial resources, it is the only meaningful reading of the statute. . . .
>
> . . . The courts must decide where the balance between the rights of copyright owners and those of the broad public tilts[,] subject to a fact-specific rule of reason. Here, Chamberlain can point to no protected property right that Skylink imperils. The DMCA cannot allow Chamberlain to retract the most fundamental right that the Copyright Act grants consumers: the right to use the copy of Chamberlain's embedded software that they purchased.
>
> The proper construction of § 1201(a)(2) therefore makes it clear that Chamberlain cannot prevail. A plaintiff alleging a violation of § 1201(a)(2) must prove: (1) ownership of a valid *copyright* on a work, (2) effectively controlled by a *technological measure*, which has been circumvented, (3) that third parties can now *access* (4) *without authorization*, in a manner that (5) infringes or facilitates infringing a right *protected* by the Copyright

Act, because of a product that (6) the defendant either (i) *designed or produced* primarily for circumvention; (ii) made available despite only *limited commercial significance* other than circumvention; or (iii) *marketed* for use in circumvention of the controlling technological measure. A plaintiff incapable of establishing any one of elements (1) through (5) will have failed to prove a prima facie case. A plaintiff capable of proving elements (1) through (5) need prove only one of (6)(i), (ii), or (iii) to shift the burden back to the defendant. At that point, the various affirmative defenses enumerated throughout § 1201 become relevant. . . .

Chamberlain . . . has failed to show not only the requisite lack of authorization, but also the necessary fifth element of its claim, the critical nexus between access and protection. Chamberlain neither alleged copyright infringement *nor explained how the access provided by the Model 39 transmitter facilitates the infringement of any right that the Copyright Act protects.* There can therefore be no reasonable relationship between the access that homeowners gain to Chamberlain's copyrighted software when using Skylink's Model 39 transmitter and the protections that the Copyright Act grants to Chamberlain. The Copyright Act authorized Chamberlain's customers to use the copy of Chamberlain's copyrighted software embedded in the GDOs [garage door openers] that they purchased. Chamberlain's customers are therefore immune from § 1201(a)(1) circumvention liability. In the absence of allegations of either copyright infringement or § 1201(a)(1) circumvention, Skylink cannot be liable for § 1201(a)(2) trafficking. The District Court's grant of summary judgment in Skylink's favor was correct. . . .

381 F.3d at 1200-04 (emphasis in original).

At one level, the message of this decision is pretty clear. But how far-reaching is the principle the court announces? Does it reach, for example, to consumer "fair use"? For example, can a teacher who wants to use short film clips from a DVD in a class circumvent CSS with impunity? Can someone go into business supplying such teachers with circumvention services? Consider this question after you have studied the materials on "fair use" in Chapter 10.

In *MDY Industries, LLC v. Blizzard Entertainment, Inc.*, 629 F.3d 928, 943-52 (9th Cir. 2010), the Ninth Circuit expressly disagreed with the Federal Circuit's conclusion that § 1201(a)(2) requires a "nexus" between the circumvention and infringing activity. Instead, the court concluded that only § 1201(b), which prohibits trafficking in devices that permit circumvention of measures "that effectively protect a right of a copyright owner," requires such a nexus. Accordingly, it held that MDY's "Glider" program, which was designed to circumvent "Warden," a program that controlled online access to Blizzard's *World of Warcraft* videogame, violated § 1201(a)(2), even though users did not commit copyright infringement when they used the "Glider" program to automate game play. If the Federal Circuit had adopted this interpretation, would the universal remote control in *Chamberlain* likewise have violated § 1201(a)(2)?

Another case involving so-called "embedded" software is *Lexmark Int'l, Inc. v. Static Control Components, Inc.*, 253 F. Supp. 2d 943 (E.D. Ky. 2003), *vacated and remanded*, 387 F.3d 522 (6th Cir. 2004). The plaintiff, which manufactures printers and toner cartridges, sued a competitor for including in its less-expensive reconditioned cartridges software that allegedly "circumvents" Lexmark's "authentication" protocol. The District Court granted a preliminary injunction, holding that an anti-circumvention violation had occurred. On appeal, however, the Sixth Circuit vacated the preliminary injunction. It held that while Lexmark's "authentication" protocol controlled the *use* of the computer program contained in the printer, it did not control *access* to that program, because anyone purchasing the printer could read the (unencrypted) program directly from the printer's memory. It also reversed the District Court's conclusion that the interoperability defense of § 1201(f) did not apply. For more on *Lexmark* and *Chamberlain*, see § 10.06.

A particularly piquant example of criticism of the DMCA's anticircumvention provisions from the think tank sector is the Cato Institute's 2006 policy study, *Circumventing Competition: The Perverse Consequences of the Digital Millennium Copyright Act*. Here is the Executive Summary:

> The courts have a proven track record of fashioning balanced remedies for the copyright challenges created by new technologies. But when Congress passed the Digital Millennium Copyright Act in 1998, it cut the courts out of this role and instead banned any devices that "circumvent" digital rights management (DRM) technologies, which control access to copyrighted content.

> The result has been a legal regime that reduces options and competition in how consumers enjoy media and entertainment. Today, the copyright industry is exerting increasing control over playback devices, cable media offerings, and even Internet streaming. Some firms have used the DMCA to thwart competition by preventing research and reverse engineering. Others have brought the weight of criminal sanctions to bear against critics, competitors, and researchers.

> The DMCA is anti-competitive. It gives copyright holders — and the technology companies that distribute their content — the legal power to create closed technology platforms and exclude competitors from interoperating with them. Worst of all, DRM technologies are clumsy and ineffective; they inconvenience legitimate users but do little to stop pirates.

> Fortunately, repeal of the DMCA would not lead to intellectual property anarchy. Prior to the DMCA's enactment, the courts had already been developing a body of law that strikes a sensible balance between innovation and the protection of intellectual property. That body of law protected competition, consumer choice, and the important principle of fair use without sacrificing the rights of copyright holders. And because it focused on the actions of people rather than on the design of technologies, it gave the courts the flexibility they needed to adapt to rapid technological change.

Interested? For more, see *http://cato.org/pub_display.php?pub_id=6025*.

Chapter 10

FAIR USE AND AFFIRMATIVE DEFENSES

There are many ways for the defendant to prevail in an infringement action. First, if the plaintiff fails on the jurisdictional issues, or in proving ownership or actionable copying, or in proving the defendant's secondary liability, the plaintiff loses. *See* Chapters 8 and 9. Second, and of primary interest to us in this chapter, copyright — being a unique body of law — offers a *sui generis* defense: fair use.

There is no doctrine that compares closely with fair use to be found in other national laws around the world (or, indeed, elsewhere in U.S. intellectual property law) — nor, as we will see below, was it anticipated by the Statute of Anne or cases construing it, except through the much more narrow doctrine of "fair abridgment." On occasion today, the term is used journalistically, as shorthand for all the various copyright doctrines that work to promote reasonable levels of public access to copyrighted works (such as the idea/expression distinction, for example). In this chapter, however, we use the term in the more technical sense, as bounded (more or less!) by 17 U.S.C. § 107.

Fair use under § 107 has been criticized as vague and unpredictable: "[n]othing more than the right to hire a lawyer," in Lawrence Lessig's memorable phrase. But despite — or perhaps because of — such critiques, the doctrine seems to be coming into its own. Recent scholarship suggests that this is not actually a new phenomenon, but one that was set in motion by the Congressional decision to codify the doctrine as part of the 1976 Copyright Act. Pamela Samuelson's article, *Unbundling Fair Uses*, 77 FORDHAM L. REV. 2537 (2009), documents how fair use has been elaborated in a variety of contexts over three decades of case decisions, suggesting that the doctrine now has more to offer than ever — both in litigation and for planning business and cultural ventures. Clearly, it is an essential part of the contemporary copyright lawyer's toolkit.

We examine various aspects of fair use in §§ 10.01 through 10.05 below. Potentially significant though it may be, fair use is considered an affirmative defense that comes into play only after the plaintiff has made out a *prima facie* case. Other defenses beyond fair use, including copyright misuse, the statute of limitations, and traditional equitable doctrines found in other areas of law, receive brief treatment in § 10.06.

§ 10.01   INTRODUCTION: THE FAIR USE DOCTRINE

Statutory References
  1976 Act: § 107
  1909 Act: —

Legislative History

H.R. Rep. No. 94-1476 at 65-66,
reprinted in 1976 U.S.C.C.A.N. 5659, 5678-80

Section 107. Fair Use

General background of the problem

The judicial doctrine of fair use, one of the most important and well-established limitations on the exclusive right of copyright owners, would be given express statutory recognition for the first time in section 107. . . . The examples enumerated [in] the Register's 1961 Report, while by no means exhaustive, give some idea of the sort of activities the courts might regard as fair use under the circumstances: "quotation of excerpts in a review or criticism for purposes of illustration or comment; quotation of short passages in a scholarly or technical work, for illustration or clarification of the author's observations; use in a parody of some of the content of the work parodied; summary of an address or article, with brief quotations, in a news report; reproduction by a library of a portion of a work to replace part of a damaged copy; reproduction by a teacher or student of a small part of a work to illustrate a lesson; reproduction of a work in legislative or judicial proceedings or reports; incidental and fortuitous reproduction, in a newsreel or broadcast, of a work located in the scene of an event being reported." . . .

The statement of the fair use doctrine in section 107 offers some guidance to users in determining when the principles of the doctrine apply. However, the endless variety of situations and combinations of circumstances that can [a]rise in particular cases precludes the formulation of exact rules in the statute. The bill endorses the purpose and general scope of the judicial doctrine of fair use, but there is no disposition to freeze the doctrine in the statute, especially during a period of rapid technological change. Beyond a very broad statutory explanation of what fair use is and some of the criteria applicable to it, the courts must be free to adapt the doctrine to particular situations on a case-by-case basis. . . .

[Noting that "most of the discussion of section 107 has centered around questions of classroom reproduction, particularly photocopying," the Committee also included in the Report a discussion of the bill's intention with respect to that topic. The issue of copying for classroom use is considered in § 10.03 below.]

[For a fuller excerpt from H.R. Rep No. 94-1476, see Part Three of the Casebook Supplement.]

§ 10.02   THE FUNDAMENTALS OF FAIR USE

As noted in the House Report, the fair use privilege was created and developed by the courts. So it seems appropriate to begin by looking back at the doctrine's very beginnings in *Folsom v. Marsh*, the 1841 Circuit Court decision by Justice Story which introduced the doctrine into American jurisprudence. After looking at its codification by Congress in 1976 (an act billed by the House Report as merely a statutory recognition of the privilege, intended only "to restate the present judicial doctrine of fair use, not to change, narrow, or enlarge it in any way"), we then consider the Supreme Court's 1994 decision in *Campbell v. Acuff-Rose Music, Inc.*, the leading modern case on the meaning of fair use as codified.

[A] Judicial Origins

FOLSOM v. MARSH

United States Circuit Court, District of Massachusetts

9 F. Cas. 342 (No. 4,901), 13 Copr. Dec. 991 (1841)

STORY, J.

This is one of those intricate and embarrassing questions, arising in the administration of civil justice, in which it is not, from the peculiar nature and character of the controversy, easy to arrive at any satisfactory conclusion, or to lay down any general principles applicable to all cases. Patents and copyrights approach, nearer than any other class of cases belonging to forensic discussions, to what may be called the metaphysics of the law, where the distinctions are, or at least may be, very subtle and refined, and, sometimes, almost evanescent. . . . [I]n cases of copyright, it is often exceedingly obvious, that the whole substance of one work has been copied from another, with slight omissions and formal differences only, which can be treated in no other way than as studied evasions; whereas, in other cases, the identity of the two works in substance, and the question of piracy, often depend upon a nice balance of the comparative use made in one of the materials of the other; the nature, extent, and value of the materials thus used; the objects of each work; and the degree to which each writer may be fairly presumed to have resorted to the same common sources of information, or to have exercised the same common diligence in the selection and arrangement of the materials. Thus, for example, no one can doubt that a reviewer may fairly cite largely from the original work, if his design be really and truly to use the passages for the purposes of fair and reasonable criticism. On the other hand, it is as clear, that if he thus cites the most important parts of the work, with a view, not to criticise, but to supersede the use of the original work, and substitute the review for it, such a use will be deemed in law a piracy. A wide interval might, of course, exist between these two extremes, calling for great caution and involving great difficulty, where the court is approaching the dividing middle line which separates the one from the other. So, it has been decided that a fair and bona fide abridgment of an original work, is not a piracy of the copyright of the author. See Dodsley v. Kinnersley, 1 Amb. 403; Whittingham v. Wooler, 2 Swanst. 428, 430, 431, note; Tonson v. Walker, 3 Swanst. 672-679, 681. But, then, what constitutes a fair and bona fide abridgment, in the sense of the law, is one of the most difficult points, under particular circumstances, which can well arise for judicial discussion. It is clear, that a mere selection, or different arrangement of parts of the original work, so as to bring the work into a smaller compass, will not be held to be such an abridgment. There must be real, substantial condensation of the materials, and intellectual labor and judgment bestowed thereon; and not merely the facile use of the scissors; or extracts of the essential parts, constituting the chief value of the original work. See Gyles v. Wilcox, 2 Atk. 141. . . .

Justice Joseph Story
Library of Congress

[The case involved the use of letters of George Washington, originally published as a multi-volume appendix to the plaintiff's narrative of the former President's life — an "original work" which Justice Story describes as being of "very great, and, I may almost say, of inestimable value." Selected letters were republished in part by the defendant, interspersed in the text of a two-volume biography. "The gravamen is, that [the defendant] used the letters of Washington, and inserted, verbatim, copies thereof from the collection of [the plaintiff]." The opinion first considers and rejects various objections to the protectibility of the plaintiff's work.]

The question, then, is, whether this is a justifiable use of the original materials, such as the law recognizes as no infringement of the copyright of the plaintiffs. It is said, that the defendant has selected only such materials, as suited his own limited purpose as a biographer. That is, doubtless, true; and he has produced an exceedingly valuable book. But that is no answer to the difficulty. It is certainly not necessary, to constitute an invasion of copyright, that the whole of a work should be copied, or even a large portion of it, in form or in substance. If so much is taken, that the value of the original is sensibly diminished, or the labors of the original author are substantially to an injurious extent appropriated by another, that is sufficient, in point of law, to constitute a piracy *pro tanto*. The entirety of the copyright is the property of the author; and it is no defen[s]e, that another person has appropriated a part, and not the whole, of any property. Neither does it necessarily depend upon the quantity taken, whether it is an infringement of the copyright or not. It is often affected by other considerations, the value of the materials taken, and the importance of it to the sale of the original work. . . . In short, we must often, in deciding questions of this sort, look to the nature and objects of the selections made, the quantity and value of the materials used, and the degree in which the use may prejudice the sale, or diminish the profits, or supersede the objects, of the original work. . . .

In the present case, I have no doubt whatever, that there is an invasion of the plaintiffs' copyright; I do not say designedly, or from bad intentions; on the contrary, I entertain no doubt, that it was deemed a perfectly lawful and justifiable use of the plaintiffs' work. . . . [E]very one must see, that the work of the defendants is mainly founded upon these letters, constituting more than one third of their work, and imparting to it its greatest, nay, its essential value. Without those letters, in its present form the work must fall to the ground. It is not a case, where abbreviated or select passages are taken from particular letters; but the entire letters are taken, and those of most interest and value to the public, as illustrating the life, the acts, and the character of Washington. It seems to me, therefore, that it is a clear invasion of the right of property of the plaintiffs, if the copying of parts of a work, not constituting a major part, can ever be a violation thereof; as upon principle and authority, I have no doubt it may be. If it had been the case of a fair and *bona fide* abridgment of the work of the plaintiffs, it might have admitted of a very different consideration. . . .

NOTES AND QUESTIONS

(1) Fair use had its origins in the 18th-Century concept of "fair abridgment" in English law. In *Folsom*, Justice Story recognized an alternative device for balancing the interests of a copyright owner and a later author wishing to "borrow" from the former's protected works: a "privilege in others than the owner of the copyright," as it would later be described, "to use the copyrighted material in a reasonable manner without his consent, notwithstanding the monopoly granted to the owner of the copyright." H. Ball, THE LAW OF COPYRIGHT AND LITERARY PROPERTY 260 (1944). Some scholars contend that in so doing, Story enlarged rather than limited the rights of copyright owners, by redefining infringement in terms of a natural property right, subject only to restricted and limited exceptions. *See* Patterson, Folsom v. Marsh *and Its Legacy*, 5 J. Intell. Prop. L. 431 (1998); Tehranian, *Et tu, Fair Use? The Triumph of Natural Law Copyright*, 38 U.C. Davis L. Rev. 465 (2005). In any event, the fair abridgment doctrine is long forgotten, having been abolished officially by the 1909 Act. Today, whether any particular defendant's use is "fair" depends, as we will see, almost wholly on the circumstances of the case.

To read the fascinating tale behind the "case that started it all," see Reese, *The Story of* Folsom v. Marsh: *Distinguishing Between Infringing and Legitimate Uses, in* INTELLECTUAL PROPERTY STORIES 259 (J. Ginsburg & R. Dreyfuss eds., 2006).

(2) Subsequent 19th-Century cases followed and elaborated upon *Folsom*. *Story v. Holcombe*, 23 F. Cas. 171 (C.C.D. Ohio 1847) (No. 13,497), was decided shortly after Justice Story's death and, ironically, involved protection of Story's COMMENTARIES ON EQUITY JURISPRUDENCE against condensation by another. The court

opined that abridgments "do[ ], to some extent in all cases, and not infrequently to a great extent, impair the rights of the author — a right secured by law," *id.* at 172-73, and denied the claim of fair use.

A later case, *Lawrence v. Dana*, 15 F. Cas. 26 (C.C.D. Mass. 1869) (No. 8,136), gave "fair use" its name. Like *Story*, *Lawrence* emphasized the impact of the second work on the market for the first. The defendant, drawing upon an earlier edition of a treatise by the noted scholar and Supreme Court Reporter Henry Wheaton, "[had] not merely use[d the plaintiff's] work as a storehouse of facts, but [had] reproduced [his] selection, combination, and arrangement." *Id.* at 44. The later edition, designed for the same class of readers and serving the same general purpose as the first, infringed it.

(3)   Twentieth-Century cases sharpened several aspects of the fair use doctrine as enunciated in *Folsom*, *Lawrence*, and subsequent decisions. The courts took explicit notice, for example, of the character of the plaintiff's and defendant's works, thereby establishing that (1) "the privilege is more narrowly restricted in cases of rival publications treating of the same subject, than in the case of two works dissimilar in scope, content and purpose," H. Ball, THE LAW OF COPYRIGHT AND LITERARY PROPERTY 261 (1944), and (2) defendants typically may borrow more freely from certain types of works (*e.g.*, compilations) than from others (*e.g.*, more scholarly or creative works). *See* Latman, *Fair Use of Copyrighted Works*, Copyright Law Revision Study No. 14, at 15 (1960).

(4)   Another significant 20th-Century development, notable particularly in the Second Circuit, was a more determined attempt to express the rationale of the fair use privilege in terms of policies embedded in the Copyright Clause. As noted in *Berlin v. E.C. Publications, Inc.*, 329 F.2d 541, 544 (2d Cir. 1964):

> [C]opyright protection is designed "To promote the Progress of Science and useful Arts," and the financial reward guaranteed to the copyright holder is but an incident of this general objective, rather than an end in itself. As a result, courts in passing upon particular claims of infringement must occasionally subordinate the copyright holder's interest in a maximum financial return to the greater public interest in the development of art, science and industry.

Accord Rosemont Enterprises, Inc. v. Random House, Inc., 366 F.2d 303 (2d Cir. 1966); *Meeropol v. Nizer*, 417 F. Supp. 1201 (S.D.N.Y. 1976), *aff'd in part, rev'd in part*, 560 F.2d 1061 (2d Cir. 1977).

(5)   Along the way, the doctrine also hit some rough patches, none rougher than the Ninth Circuit decision in *Benny v. Loew's, Inc.*, 239 F.2d 532 (9th Cir. 1956), *aff'd by an equally divided Court*, 356 U.S. 43 (1958), which denied the defense for a radio "burlesque" or "parody" of a popular movie melodrama, stating that "the so-called doctrine of fair use of copyrighted material appears in cases in federal courts having to do with compilations, listings, digests, and the like, and is concerned with the use made of prior compilations, listings, and digests," before eventually concluding that "[w]hether the audience is gripped with tense emotion in viewing the original drama, or, on the other hand, laughs at the burlesque, does not absolve the copier. Otherwise, any individual or corporation could appropriate, in its

entirety, a serious and famous dramatic work . . ." Viewed with the benefit of hindsight, what is the fallacy of this reasoning?

(6)　During the legislative deliberations that led up to the enactment of the 1976 Copyright Act, codification of the fair use doctrine was a frequent topic of discussion. Vigorous debate occurred over the wisdom of trying to capture, in any fixed formulation, a doctrine that was intended to be, in the words of the 1976 House Report, "an equitable rule of reason." In the end, Congress settled on a general statement of principle — "Notwithstanding the provisions of section 106 [on exclusive rights], . . . the fair use of a copyrighted work is not an infringement of copyright" — accompanied by two sources of interpretive guidance: a list of six illustrative purposes in the preamble, and the four factors that follow. (The last sentence of § 107 was not added until 1992.) While one can trace the evolution of this statutory language in the legislative record, the discussions of the intent behind the provision are not as enlightening as one would like. Other than insisting that it was doing no more than codifying preexisting judicial precedents, Congress provided the courts with surprisingly little guidance about how to interpret the new provision that emerged as § 107 of the 1976 Act.

[B]　Analyzing Fair Use Today

Since the codification by Congress of the fair use privilege in the 1976 Act, it has been the subject of four major Supreme Court decisions. The first, *Sony Corp. of America v. Universal City Studios, Inc.*, 464 U.S. 417 (1984), sufficiently perplexed the Court that it resolved the case only after hearing reargument of the issues — and then only on a 5-4 vote. The outcome in *Sony* appears to have been strongly influenced by the presence of "new technology" considerations, and the doctrine of the majority opinion has been the object of delicate restatement by the Court in subsequent opinions, as we will see below. *Harper & Row, Publishers, Inc. v. Nation Enterprises*, 471 U.S. 539 (1985), which we will read in § 10.03 of this chapter, was itself decided on unusual facts involving an unpublished manuscript "purloined" on its way to market. Nor was the Court's third encounter with fair use — *Stewart v. Abend*, 495 U.S. 207 (1990) (discussed in Chapter 5 with respect to ownership rights in derivative works) — exactly a meat-and-potatoes fair use case, either. Not until *Campbell v. Acuff-Rose Music, Inc.*, 510 U.S. 569 (1994), did the Court finally confront the doctrine of fair use, and the legacy of *Folsom v. Marsh*, in a reasonably typical setting: parody.

CAMPBELL v. ACUFF-ROSE MUSIC, INC.
Supreme Court of the United States
510 U.S. 569 (1994)

JUSTICE SOUTER delivered the opinion of the Court.

We are called upon to decide whether 2 Live Crew's commercial parody of Roy Orbison's song, "Oh, Pretty Woman," may be a fair use within the meaning of the Copyright Act of 1976, 17 U.S.C. § 107. Although the District Court granted summary judgment for 2 Live Crew, the Court of Appeals reversed, holding the defense of fair use barred by the song's commercial character and excessive borrowing. Because we hold that a parody's commercial character is only one element to be weighed in a fair use enquiry, and that insufficient consideration was given to the nature of parody in weighing the degree of copying, we reverse and remand.

I

In 1964, Roy Orbison and William Dees wrote a rock ballad called "Oh, Pretty Woman" and assigned their rights in it to respondent Acuff-Rose Music, Inc. *See* Appendix A, *infra*. Acuff-Rose registered the song for copyright protection.

Petitioners Luther R. Campbell, Christopher Wongwon, Mark Ross, and David Hobbs are collectively known as 2 Live Crew, a popular rap music group. In 1989, Campbell wrote a song entitled "Pretty Woman," which he later described in an affidavit as intended, "through comical lyrics, to satirize the original work. . . ." On July 5, 1989, 2 Live Crew's manager informed Acuff-Rose that 2 Live Crew had written a parody of "Oh, Pretty Woman," that they would afford all credit for ownership and authorship of the original song to Acuff-Rose, Dees, and Orbison, and that they were willing to pay a fee for the use they wished to make of it. Enclosed with the letter were a copy of the lyrics and a recording of 2 Live Crew's song. *See* Appendix B, *infra*. Acuff-Rose's agent refused permission, stating that "I am aware of the success enjoyed by 'The 2 Live Crews [sic]', but I must inform you that we cannot permit the use of a parody of 'Oh, Pretty Woman.' " Nonetheless, in June or July 1989, 2 Live Crew released records, cassette tapes, and compact discs of "Pretty Woman" in a collection of songs entitled "As Clean As They Wanna Be." The albums and compact discs identify the authors of "Pretty Woman" as Orbison and Dees and its publisher as Acuff-Rose.

Almost a year later, after nearly a quarter of a million copies of the recording had been sold, Acuff-Rose sued 2 Live Crew and its record company, Luke Skywalker Records, for copyright infringement. The District Court granted summary judgment for 2 Live Crew . . .

The Court of Appeals for the Sixth Circuit reversed and remanded. Although it assumed for the purpose of its opinion that 2 Live Crew's song was a parody of the Orbison original, the Court of Appeals thought the District Court had put too little emphasis on the fact that "every commercial use . . . is presumptively . . . unfair," *Sony Corp. of America v. Universal City Studios, Inc.*, 464 U.S. 417, 451 (1984), and it held that "the admittedly commercial nature" of the parody "requires the conclusion" that the first of four factors relevant under the statute weighs against a finding of fair use. Next, the Court of Appeals determined that, by "taking the heart of the original and making it the heart of a new work," 2 Live Crew had, qualitatively, taken too much. Finally, after noting that the effect on the potential market for the original (and the market for derivative works) is "undoubtedly the single most important element of fair use," *Harper & Row, Publishers, Inc. v. Nation Enterprises*, 471 U.S. 539, 566 (1985), the Court of Appeals faulted the District Court for "refusing to indulge the presumption" that "harm for purposes of the fair use analysis has been established by the presumption attaching to commercial uses." In sum, the court concluded that its "blatantly commercial purpose . . . prevents this parody from being a fair use."

Roy Orbison

We granted certiorari to determine whether 2 Live Crew's commercial parody could be a fair use.

II

It is uncontested here that 2 Live Crew's song would be an infringement of Acuff-Rose's rights in "Oh, Pretty Woman," under 17 U.S.C. § 106, but for a finding of fair use through parody.[4] From the infancy of copyright protection, some opportunity for fair use of copyrighted materials has been thought necessary to fulfill copyright's very purpose, "to promote the Progress of Science and useful Arts . . ." U.S. Const., Art. I, § 8, cl. 8. For as Justice Story explained, "in truth, in literature, in science and in art, there are, and can be, few, if any, things, which in an abstract sense, are strictly new and original throughout. Every book in literature, science and art, borrows, and must necessarily borrow, and use much which was well known and used before." *Emerson v. Davies*, 8 F. Cas. 615, 619 (No. 4,436) (CCD Mass. 1845). Similarly, Lord Ellenborough expressed the inherent tension in the need simultaneously to protect copyrighted material and to allow others to build upon it when he wrote: "[W]hile I shall think myself bound to secure

---

[4] 2 Live Crew concedes that it is not entitled to a compulsory license under § 115 because its arrangement changes "the basic melody or fundamental character" of the original. § 115(a)(2).

every man in the enjoyment of his copy-right, one must not put manacles upon science." *Carey v. Kearsley*, 4 Esp. 168, 170, 170 Eng. Rep. 679, 681 (K.B. 1803). In copyright cases brought under the Statute of Anne of 1710, English courts held that in some instances "fair abridgments" would not infringe an author's rights, *see* W. Patry, THE FAIR USE PRIVILEGE IN COPYRIGHT LAW 6-17 (1985) (hereinafter *Patry*); Leval, *Toward a Fair Use Standard*, 103 Harv. L. Rev. 1105 (1990) (hereinafter *Leval*), and although the First Congress enacted our initial copyright statute, Act of May 31, 1790, 1 Stat. 124, without any explicit reference to "fair use," as it later came to be known, the doctrine was recognized by the American courts nonetheless.

In *Folsom v. Marsh*, Justice Story distilled the essence of law and methodology from the earlier cases: "look to the nature and objects of the selections made, the quantity and value of the materials used, and the degree in which the use may prejudice the sale, or diminish the profits, or supersede the objects, of the original work." 9 F. Cas. 342, 348 (No. 4,901) (CCD Mass. 1841). Thus expressed, fair use remained exclusively judge-made doctrine until the passage of the 1976 Copyright Act, in which Story's summary is discernible . . .

Congress meant § 107 "to restate the present judicial doctrine of fair use, not to change, narrow, or enlarge it in any way" and intended that courts continue the common-law tradition of fair use adjudication. H.R. Rep. No. 94-1476, p. 66 (1976) (hereinafter *House Report*); S. Rep. No. 94-473, p. 62 (1975) (hereinafter *Senate Report*). The fair use doctrine thus "permits [and requires] courts to avoid rigid application of the copyright statute when, on occasion, it would stifle the very creativity which that law is designed to foster." *Stewart v. Abend*, 495 U.S. 207, 236 (1990) (internal quotation marks and citation omitted).

The task is not to be simplified with bright-line rules, for the statute, like the doctrine it recognizes, calls for case-by-case analysis. . . . Nor may the four statutory factors be treated in isolation, one from another. All are to be explored, and the results weighed together, in light of the purposes of copyright. *See Leval* 1110-1111. . . .[10]

A

The first factor in a fair use enquiry is "the purpose and character of the use, including whether such use is of a commercial nature or is for nonprofit educational purposes." § 107(1). This factor draws on Justice Story's formulation, "the nature and objects of the selections made." *Folsom v. Marsh*, 9 F. Cas., at 348. The enquiry here may be guided by the examples given in the preamble to § 107, looking to whether the use is for criticism, or comment, or news reporting, and the like. *See* § 107. The central purpose of this investigation is to see, in Justice Story's words, whether the new work merely "supersedes the objects" of the original creation, *Folsom v. Marsh, supra*, at 348; *accord, Harper & Row, supra*, at 562 ("supplanting"

---

[10] Because the fair use enquiry often requires close questions of judgment as to the extent of permissible borrowing in cases involving parodies (or other critical works), courts may also wish to bear in mind that the goals of the copyright law, "to stimulate the creation and publication of edifying matter," *Leval* 1134, are not always best served by automatically granting injunctive relief when parodists are found to have gone beyond the bounds of fair use. . . .

the original), or instead adds something new, with a further purpose or different character, altering the first with new expression, meaning, or message; it asks, in other words, whether and to what extent the new work is "transformative." *Leval* 1111. Although such transformative use is not absolutely necessary for a finding of fair use, *Sony, supra*, at 455, n.40,[11] the goal of copyright, to promote science and the arts, is generally furthered by the creation of transformative works. Such works thus lie at the heart of the fair use doctrine's guarantee of breathing space within the confines of copyright, and the more transformative the new work, the less will be the significance of other factors, like commercialism, that may weigh against a finding of fair use.

This Court has only once before even considered whether parody may be fair use, and that time issued no opinion because of the Court's equal division. *Benny v. Loew's Inc.*, 239 F.2d 532 (CA9 1956), *aff'd sub nom. Columbia Broadcasting System, Inc. v. Loew's Inc.*, 356 U.S. 43 (1958). Suffice it to say now that parody has an obvious claim to transformative value, as Acuff-Rose itself does not deny. Like less ostensibly humorous forms of criticism, it can provide social benefit, by shedding light on an earlier work, and, in the process, creating a new one. We thus line up with the courts that have held that parody, like other comment or criticism, may claim fair use under § 107. *See, e.g., Fisher v. Dees*, 794 F.2d 432 (CA9 1986) ("When Sonny Sniffs Glue," a parody of "When Sunny Gets Blue," is fair use); *Elsmere Music, Inc. v. National Broadcasting Co.*, 482 F. Supp. 741 (S.D.N.Y.), *aff'd*, 623 F.2d 252 (CA2 1980) ("I Love Sodom," a "Saturday Night Live" television parody of "I Love New York," is fair use); *see also House Report*, p. 65; *Senate Report*, p. 61 ("Use in a parody of some of the content of the work parodied" may be fair use).

The germ of parody lies in the definition of the Greek *parodeia* as "a song sung alongside another." 972 F.2d, at 1440, quoting 7 ENCYCLOPEDIA BRITANNICA 768 (15th ed. 1975). Modern dictionaries accordingly describe a parody as a "literary or artistic work that imitates the characteristic style of an author or a work for comic effect or ridicule,"[12] or as a "composition in prose or verse in which the characteristic turns of thought and phrase in an author or class of authors are imitated in such a way as to make them appear ridiculous."[13] For the purposes of copyright law, the nub of the definitions, and the heart of any parodist's claim to quote from existing material, is the use of some elements of a prior author's composition to create a new one that, at least in part, comments on that author's work. . . . If, on the contrary, the commentary has no critical bearing on the substance or style of the original composition, which the alleged infringer merely uses to get attention or to avoid the drudgery in working up something fresh, the claim to fairness in borrowing from another's work diminishes accordingly (if it does not vanish), and other factors, like the extent of its commerciality, loom larger.[14] Parody needs to

---

[11] The obvious statutory exception to this focus on transformative uses is the straight reproduction of multiple copies for classroom distribution.

[12] THE AMERICAN HERITAGE DICTIONARY 1317 (3d ed. 1992).

[13] 11 THE OXFORD ENGLISH DICTIONARY 247 (2d ed. 1989).

[14] A parody that more loosely targets an original than the parody presented here may still be sufficiently aimed at an original work to come within our analysis of parody. If a parody whose wide

mimic an original to make its point, and so has some claim to use the creation of its victim's (or collective victims') imagination, whereas satire can stand on its own two feet and so requires justification for the very act of borrowing.[15] . . .

The fact that parody can claim legitimacy for some appropriation does not, of course, tell either parodist or judge much about where to draw the line. Like a book review quoting the copyrighted material criticized, parody may or may not be fair use, and petitioner's suggestion that any parodic use is presumptively fair has no more justification in law or fact than the equally hopeful claim that any use for news reporting should be presumed fair. . . . The Act has no hint of an evidentiary preference for parodists over their victims, and no workable presumption for parody could take account of the fact that parody often shades into satire when society is lampooned through its creative artifacts, or that a work may contain both parodic and non-parodic elements. Accordingly, parody, like any other use, has to work its way through the relevant factors, and be judged case by case, in light of the ends of the copyright law. . . .

We have less difficulty in finding [criticism of Orbison's original] in 2 Live Crew's song than the Court of Appeals did, although having found it we will not take the further step of evaluating its quality. The threshold question when fair use is raised in defense of parody is whether a parodic character may reasonably be perceived. Whether, going beyond that, parody is in good taste or bad does not and should not matter to fair use. . . .

While we might not assign a high rank to the parodic element here, we think it fair to say that 2 Live Crew's song reasonably could be perceived as commenting on the original or criticizing it, to some degree. 2 Live Crew juxtaposes the romantic musings of a man whose fantasy comes true, with degrading taunts, a bawdy demand for sex, and a sigh of relief from paternal responsibility. The later words can be taken as a comment on the naivete of the original of an earlier day, as a rejection of its sentiment that ignores the ugliness of street life and the debasement that it signifies. It is this joinder of reference and ridicule that marks off the author's choice of parody from the other types of comment and criticism that traditionally have had a claim to fair use protection as transformative works.

The Court of Appeals, however, immediately cut short the enquiry into 2 Live Crew's fair use claim by confining its treatment of the first factor essentially to one relevant fact, the commercial nature of the use. The court then inflated the significance of this fact by applying a presumption ostensibly culled from *Sony*, that "every commercial use of copyrighted material is presumptively . . . unfair. . . ."

---

dissemination in the market runs the risk of serving as a substitute for the original or licensed derivatives (see *infra*, discussing factor four), it is more incumbent on one claiming fair use to establish the extent of transformation and the parody's critical relationship to the original. By contrast, when there is little or no risk of market substitution, whether because of the large extent of transformation of the earlier work, the new work's minimal distribution in the market, the small extent to which it borrows from an original, or other factors, taking parodic aim at an original is a less critical factor in the analysis, and looser forms of parody may be found to be fair use, as may satire with lesser justification for the borrowing than would otherwise be required.

[15] Satire has been defined as a work "in which prevalent follies or vices are assailed with ridicule," 14 THE OXFORD ENGLISH DICTIONARY 500 (2d ed. 1989), or are "attacked through irony, derision, or wit." THE AMERICAN HERITAGE DICTIONARY 1604 (3d ed. 1992).

Sony, 464 U.S., at 451. In giving virtually dispositive weight to the commercial nature of the parody, the Court of Appeals erred.

The language of the statute makes clear that the commercial or nonprofit educational purpose of a work is only one element of the first factor enquiry into its purpose and character. Section 107(1) uses the term "including" to begin the dependent clause referring to commercial use, and the main clause speaks of a broader investigation into "purpose and character." As we explained in *Harper & Row*, Congress resisted attempts to narrow the ambit of this traditional enquiry by adopting categories of presumptively fair use, and it urged courts to preserve the breadth of their traditionally ample view of the universe of relevant evidence. 471 U.S., at 561; *House Report*, p. 66. Accordingly, the mere fact that a use is educational and not for profit does not insulate it from a finding of infringement, any more than the commercial character of a use bars a finding of fairness. If, indeed, commerciality carried presumptive force against a finding of fairness, the presumption would swallow nearly all of the illustrative uses listed in the preamble paragraph of § 107, including news reporting, comment, criticism, teaching, scholarship, and research, since these activities "are generally conducted for profit in this country." *Harper & Row, supra*, at 592 (BRENNAN, J., dissenting). Congress could not have intended such a rule. . . .

Sony itself called for no hard evidentiary presumption. . . . Rather, as we explained in *Harper & Row*, *Sony* stands for the proposition that the "fact that a publication was commercial as opposed to nonprofit is a separate factor that tends to weigh against a finding of fair use." 471 U.S., at 562. But that is all, and the fact that even the force of that tendency will vary with the context is a further reason against elevating commerciality to hard presumptive significance. . . .[18] . . .

B

The second statutory factor, "the nature of the copyrighted work," § 107(2), draws on Justice Story's expression, the "value of the materials used." *Folsom v. Marsh*, 9 F. Cas., at 348. This factor calls for recognition that some works are closer to the core of intended copyright protection than others, with the consequence that fair use is more difficult to establish when the former works are copied. . . . We agree with both the District Court and the Court of Appeals that the Orbison original's creative expression for public dissemination falls within the core of the copyright's protective purposes. . . . This fact, however, is not much help in this case, or ever likely to help much in separating the fair use sheep from the infringing goats in a parody case, since parodies almost invariably copy publicly known, expressive works.

---

[18] Finally, . . . we reject Acuff-Rose's argument that 2 Live Crew's request for permission to use the original should be weighed against a finding of fair use. Even if good faith were central to fair use, 2 Live Crew's actions do not necessarily suggest that they believed their version was not fair use; the offer may simply have been made in a good-faith effort to avoid this litigation. If the use is otherwise fair, then no permission need be sought or granted. Thus, being denied permission to use a work does not weigh against a finding of fair use. *See Fisher v. Dees*, 794 F.2d 432, 437 (CA9 1986).

C

The third factor asks whether "the amount and substantiality of the portion used in relation to the copyrighted work as a whole," § 107(3) (or, in Justice Story's words, "the quantity and value of the materials used," *Folsom v. Marsh, supra*, at 348) are reasonable in relation to the purpose of the copying. Here, attention turns to the persuasiveness of a [defendant]'s justification for the particular copying done, and the enquiry will harken back to the first of the statutory factors, for, as in prior cases, we recognize that the extent of permissible copying varies with the purpose and character of the use. *See Sony*, 464 U.S., at 449-450 (reproduction of entire work "does not have its ordinary effect of militating against a finding of fair use" as to home videotaping of television programs); *Harper & Row*, 471 U.S., at 564 ("Even substantial quotations might qualify as fair use in a review of a published work or a news account of a speech" but not in a scoop of a soon-to-be-published memoir). The facts bearing on this factor will also tend to address the fourth, by revealing the degree to which the parody may serve as a market substitute for the original or potentially licensed derivatives . . .

. . . [T]his factor calls for thought not only about the quantity of the materials used, but about their quality and importance, too. In *Harper & Row*, for example, The Nation had taken only some 300 words out of President Ford's memoirs, but we signalled the significance of the quotations in finding them to amount to "the heart of the book," the part most likely to be newsworthy and important in licensing serialization. 471 U.S., at 564-566, 568 (internal quotation marks omitted). . . . [W]hether "a substantial portion of the infringing work was copied verbatim" from the copyrighted work [also] is a relevant question, *see id.*, at 565, for it may reveal a dearth of transformative character or purpose under the first factor, or a greater likelihood of market harm under the fourth; a work composed primarily of an original, particularly its heart, with little added or changed, is more likely to be a merely superseding use, fulfilling demand for the original.

. . . Parody presents a difficult case. Parody's humor, or in any event its comment, necessarily springs from recognizable allusion to its object through distorted imitation. Its art lies in the tension between a known original and its parodic twin. When parody takes aim at a particular original work, the parody must be able to "conjure up" at least enough of that original to make the object of its critical wit recognizable. . . . What makes for this recognition is quotation of the original's most distinctive or memorable features, which the parodist can be sure the audience will know. Once enough has been taken to assure identification, how much more is reasonable will depend, say, on the extent to which the song's overriding purpose and character is to parody the original or, in contrast, the likelihood that the parody may serve as a market substitute for the original. But using some characteristic features cannot be avoided.

We think the Court of Appeals was insufficiently appreciative of parody's need for the recognizable sight or sound when it ruled 2 Live Crew's use unreasonable as a matter of law. It is true, of course, that 2 Live Crew copied the characteristic opening bass riff (or musical phrase) of the original, and true that the words of the first line copy the Orbison lyrics. But if quotation of the opening riff and the first line may be said to go to the "heart" of the original, the heart is also what most readily conjures up the song for parody, and it is the heart at which parody takes aim. Copying does not become excessive in relation to parodic purpose merely because the portion taken was the original's heart. If 2 Live Crew had copied a significantly less memorable part of the original, it is difficult to see how its parodic character would have come through.

This is not, of course, to say that anyone who calls himself a parodist can skim the cream and get away scot free. In parody, as in news reporting, context is everything, and the question of fairness asks what else the parodist did besides go to the heart of the original. It is significant that 2 Live Crew not only copied the first line of the original, but thereafter departed markedly from the Orbison lyrics for its own ends. 2 Live Crew not only copied the bass riff and repeated it, but also produced otherwise distinctive sounds, interposing "scraper" noise, overlaying the music with solos in different keys, and altering the drum beat. This is not a case, then, where "a substantial portion" of the parody itself is composed of a "verbatim" copying of the original. It is not, that is, a case where the parody is so insubstantial, as compared to the copying, that the third factor must be resolved as a matter of law against the parodists.

Suffice it to say here that, as to the lyrics, we think the Court of Appeals correctly suggested that "no more was taken than necessary," but just for that reason, we fail to see how the copying can be excessive in relation to its parodic purpose, even if the portion taken is the original's "heart." As to the music, we express no opinion whether repetition of the bass riff is excessive copying, and we remand to permit evaluation of the amount taken, in light of the song's parodic purpose and character, its transformative elements, and considerations of the potential for market substitution sketched more fully below.

D

The fourth fair use factor is "the effect of the use upon the potential market for or value of the copyrighted work." § 107(4). It requires courts to consider not only the extent of market harm caused by the particular actions of the alleged infringer, but also "whether unrestricted and widespread conduct of the sort engaged in by the defendant . . . would result in a substantially adverse impact on the potential market" for the original. [3 NIMMER ON COPYRIGHT § 13.05[A][4] (1993)]; *accord, Harper & Row*, 471 U.S., at 569. . . . The enquiry "must take account not only of harm to the original but also of harm to the market for derivative works." *Harper & Row, supra*, at 568.

Since fair use is an affirmative defense, its proponent would have difficulty carrying the burden of demonstrating fair use without favorable evidence about relevant markets. In moving for summary judgment, 2 Live Crew left themselves at just such a disadvantage when they failed to address the effect on the market for rap derivatives, and confined themselves to uncontroverted submissions that there was no likely effect on the market for the original. They did not, however, thereby subject themselves to the evidentiary presumption applied by the Court of Appeals. In assessing the likelihood of significant market harm, the Court of Appeals quoted from language in *Sony* that " 'if the intended use is for commercial gain, that likelihood may be presumed. But if it is for a noncommercial purpose, the likelihood must be demonstrated.' " 972 F.2d, at 1438, quoting *Sony*, 464 U.S., at 451. The court reasoned that because "the use of the copyrighted work is wholly commercial, . . . we presume a likelihood of future harm to Acuff-Rose exists." 972 F.2d, at 1438. In so doing, the court resolved the fourth factor against 2 Live Crew, just as it had the first, by applying a presumption about the effect of commercial use, a presumption which as applied here we hold to be error.

No "presumption" or inference of market harm that might find support in *Sony* is applicable to a case involving something beyond mere duplication for commercial purposes. *Sony*'s discussion of a presumption contrasts a context of verbatim copying of the original in its entirety for commercial purposes, with the noncommercial context of *Sony* itself (home copying of television programming). In the former circumstances, what *Sony* said simply makes common sense: when a commercial use amounts to mere duplication of the entirety of an original, it clearly "supersedes the objects," *Folsom v. Marsh*, 9 F. Cas., at 348, of the original and serves as a market replacement for it, making it likely that cognizable market harm to the original will occur. *Sony*, 464 U.S., at 451. But when, on the contrary, the second use is transformative, market substitution is at least less certain, and market harm may not be so readily inferred. Indeed, as to parody pure and simple, it is more likely that the new work will not affect the market for the original in a way cognizable under this factor, that is, by acting as a substitute for it. . . .

We do not, of course, suggest that a parody may not harm the market at all, but when a lethal parody, like a scathing theater review, kills demand for the original, it does not produce a harm cognizable under the Copyright Act. Because "parody may quite legitimately aim at garroting the original, destroying it commercially as well as artistically," B. Kaplan, An Unhurried View of Copyright 69 (1967), the role of the courts is to distinguish between "[b]iting criticism [that merely] suppresses demand [and] copyright infringement[, which] usurps it." *Fisher v. Dees*, 794 F.2d, at 438.

This distinction between potentially remediable displacement and unremediable disparagement is reflected in the rule that there is no protectible derivative market for criticism. The market for potential derivative uses includes only those that creators of original works would in general develop or license others to develop. Yet the unlikelihood that creators of imaginative works will license critical reviews or lampoons of their own productions removes such uses from the very notion of a potential licensing market. . . . Thus, to the extent that the opinion below may be read to have considered harm to the market for parodies of "Oh, Pretty Woman," the court erred. . . .

In explaining why the law recognizes no derivative market for critical works, including parody, we have, of course, been speaking of the later work as if it had nothing but a critical aspect (*i.e.*, "parody pure and simple"). But the later work may have a more complex character, with effects not only in the arena of criticism but also in protectible markets for derivative works, too. In that sort of case, the law looks beyond the criticism to the other elements of the work, as it does here. 2 Live Crew's song comprises not only parody but also rap music, and the derivative market for rap music is a proper focus of enquiry. Evidence of substantial harm to it would weigh against a finding of fair use, because the licensing of derivatives is an important economic incentive to the creation of originals. *See* 17 U.S.C. § 106(2) (copyright owner has rights to derivative works). Of course, the only harm to derivatives that need concern us, as discussed above, is the harm of market substitution. The fact that a parody may impair the market for derivative uses by the very effectiveness of its critical commentary is no more relevant under copyright than the like threat to the original market.

Although 2 Live Crew submitted uncontroverted affidavits on the question of market harm to the original, neither they nor Acuff-Rose introduced evidence or affidavits addressing the likely effect of 2 Live Crew's parodic rap song on the market for a non-parody, rap version of "Oh, Pretty Woman." And while Acuff-Rose would have us find evidence of a rap market in the very facts that 2 Live Crew recorded a rap parody of "Oh, Pretty Woman" and another rap group sought a license to record a rap derivative, there was no evidence that a potential rap market was harmed in any way by 2 Live Crew's parody, rap version. The fact that 2 Live Crew's parody sold as part of a collection of rap songs says very little about the parody's effect on a market for a rap version of the original, either of the music alone or of the music with its lyrics. . . . [I]t is impossible to deal with the fourth factor except by recognizing that a silent record on an important factor bearing on fair use disentitled the proponent of the defense, 2 Live Crew, to summary judgment. The evidentiary hole will doubtless be plugged on remand.

III

It was error for the Court of Appeals to conclude that the commercial nature of 2 Live Crew's parody of "Oh, Pretty Woman" rendered it presumptively unfair. No such evidentiary presumption is available to address either the first factor, the character and purpose of the use, or the fourth, market harm, in determining whether a transformative use, such as parody, is a fair one. The court also erred in holding that 2 Live Crew had necessarily copied excessively from the Orbison original, considering the parodic purpose of the use. We therefore reverse the judgment of the Court of Appeals and remand for further proceedings consistent with this opinion.

Appendix A
"Oh, Pretty Woman" by Roy Orbison and William Dees

Pretty Woman, walking down the street,
Pretty Woman, the kind I like to meet,
Pretty Woman, I don't believe you, you're not the truth,
No one could look as good as you Mercy

Pretty Woman, won't you pardon me,
Pretty Woman, I couldn't help but see,
Pretty Woman, that you look lovely as can be
Are you lonely just like me?

Pretty Woman, stop a while,
Pretty Woman, talk a while,
Pretty Woman, give your smile to me

Pretty woman, yeah, yeah, yeah
Pretty Woman, look my way,
Pretty Woman, say you'll stay with me
'Cause I need you, I'll treat you right
Come to me baby, Be mine tonight

Pretty Woman, don't walk on by,
Pretty Woman, don't make me cry,
Pretty Woman, don't walk away,
Hey, O. K.
If that's the way it must be, O. K.
I guess I'll go on home, it's late
There'll be tomorrow night, but wait!

What do I see
Is she walking back to me?
Yeah, she's walking back to me!
Oh, Pretty Woman.

Appendix B
"Pretty Woman" as Recorded by 2 Live Crew

Pretty woman walkin' down the street
Pretty woman girl you look so sweet
Pretty woman you bring me down to that knee
Pretty woman you make me wanna beg please
Oh, pretty woman

Big hairy woman you need to shave that stuff
Big hairy woman you know I bet it's tough
Big hairy woman all that hair it ain't legit
'Cause you look like 'Cousin It'
Big hairy woman

Bald headed woman girl your hair won't grow
Bald headed woman you got a teeny weeny afro
Bald headed woman you know your hair could look nice
Bald headed woman first you got to roll it with rice
Bald headed woman here, let me get this hunk of biz for ya
Ya know what I'm saying you look better than rice a roni
Oh bald headed woman

Big hairy woman come on in
And don't forget your bald headed friend
Hey pretty woman let the boys Jump in

Two timin' woman girl you know you ain't right
Two timin' woman you's out with my boy last night
Two timin' woman that takes a load off my mind
Two timin' woman now I know the baby ain't mine
Oh, two timin' woman
Oh pretty woman

JUSTICE KENNEDY, concurring.

. . . [P]arody may qualify as fair use only if it draws upon the original composition to make humorous or ironic commentary about that same composition. It is not enough that the parody use the original in a humorous fashion, however creative that humor may be. The parody must target the original, and not just its general style, the genre of art to which it belongs, or society as a whole (although if it targets the original, it may target those features as well). *See Rogers v. Koons*, 960 F.2d 301, 310 (CA2 1992) ("Though the satire need not be only of the copied work and may . . . also be a parody of modern society, the copied work must be, at least in part, an object of the parody"); *Fisher v. Dees*, 794 F.2d 432, 436 (CA9 1986) ("[A] humorous or satiric work deserves protection under the fair-use doctrine only if the copied work is at least partly the target of the work in question"). . . .

. . . As future courts apply our fair use analysis, they must take care to ensure that not just any commercial take-off is rationalized *post hoc* as a parody. . . .

NOTES AND QUESTIONS

(1)   Justice Souter identifies fair use as one — but only one — of the doctrines of copyright law designed to achieve copyright's overriding goal of "promot[ing] the Progress of Science and useful Arts." Footnote 5 points out that the exclusion of facts and ideas from copyright protection, particularly following the Court's 1991 decision in *Feist v. Rural Telephone* (see Chapter 3 of this casebook), serves the same purpose. Look back at the facts in *Folsom v. Marsh*. Notwithstanding its other merits, would you expect *Folsom* to be decided the same way today?

Campbell *and § 107 Analysis Generally*

(2)   Under *Campbell*, what is the function of the *preamble* to § 107? To what degree is a court constrained by the specific examples in the list? To what degree are the examples helpful in applying the four factors that follow the preamble in the statute? The opinion in *Campbell* itself treats the preamble in conjunction with the first factor, to which it is closely tied, but otherwise has little to say about the former — not surprisingly, perhaps, given that "parody" is *not* one of the examples specifically provided there. We will return to the preamble shortly in *Harper & Row*, a case concerning an example that *is*: news reporting.

(3)   With respect to the *first factor*, how significant is it that the defendants' use in *Campbell* was "commercial"? Obviously, that fact wasn't significant enough to preclude victory. But, just as certainly, it gave the Court pause. Justice Souter adopts at this point in his opinion the criterion of "transformativeness" as a critical guide to fair use analysis. The growing significance of this concept is explored in depth in § 10.03 below. But it may not be too soon to ask: Was this additional, non-statutory criterion needed to iron out wrinkles — perhaps even Court-made wrinkles — that had developed in the fair use doctrine since the 1976 Act?

The Court says in *Campbell* that, although a finding of transformative use "is not absolutely necessary, . . . the more transformative the new work, the less will be the significance of other factors, like commercialism, that may weigh against" fair use. It is difficult to appreciate the subtlety of that formulation without understanding that, in *Sony v. Universal City Studios*, a 5-4 majority of the Court had declined to approve the lower courts' long-time embrace of "productive use" (a quality, at a minimum, very similar to "transformative use"). In addition, the *Sony* majority had observed flatly that "every commercial use of copyrighted material is presumptively an unfair exploitation of the monopoly privilege that belongs to the owner of the copyright . . ." 464 U.S. at 451. The latter "presumption," when added to a further presumption (also created by the *Sony* majority) that a purpose of commercial gain creates a likelihood of harm to the copyright holder's economic interests under § 107's fourth factor, had produced an unwarranted "double whammy" against commercial uses of copyrighted works in pre-*Campbell* cases (most notably, the Sixth Circuit's 2-1 decision in *Campbell* itself). The Supreme Court's own decision in *Campbell* "presumptively" puts all that to rest.

(4) Issues having to do with "good faith" (or the lack thereof) on the user's part often are dealt with under the first factor, although they could be treated just as easily as an unenumerated factor (remembering that § 107 itself says only that the fair use calculus "shall *include*" the four factors specified). *See NXIVM Corp. v. Ross Institute*, 364 F.3d 471 (2d Cir. 2004) (finding bad faith where defendants knew access to plaintiff's work was unauthorized, but nonetheless holding that the use of selected excerpts for the purpose of criticism was a fair use). Are you satisfied with Justice Souter's discussion in footnote 18 of the significance of 2 Live Crew's failed attempt to secure consent?

(5) The *second factor* is dealt with quite summarily in Justice Souter's opinion, but the quoted language suggests that if the work copied was soon-to-be-published, on the one hand, or predominantly "factual" (rather than "expressive"), on the other, this might affect the analysis. How? For the significance of a work's unpublished status, see *Harper & Row*, and the accompanying Notes and Questions, in § 10.03 below. As to the distinction between kinds of works, consider the Court's statement in *Harper & Row*: "The law generally recognizes a greater need to disseminate factual works than works of fiction or fantasy." 471 U.S. at 563. How generalizable is this principle?

Courts typically apply the second factor by determining whether a copyrighted work is factual/creative or published/unpublished. Are there any other opportunities to apply the second factor besides these well-trodden dichotomies? For example, what if the copyrighted work is an orphan work, that is, a work whose owner cannot be determined or cannot be found? We discussed both orphan works and possible legislative solutions to that problem in Chapter 4. Some have argued that another's use of an orphan work should invariably be considered a fair use because of the "orphaned" *nature* of the work being used. Moreover, from the standpoint of the fourth factor, an orphan work represents a market failure. After all, a prospective user cannot strike up a deal with a copyright owner who cannot be found. Knowing what you know about orphan works, do you think that fair use solution, utilizing the second and fourth factors of § 107, is preferable to a legislative remedy?

(6) The *third factor*, going to the quantity of the taking, has some particular ramifications in parody cases, which are discussed below. In general, as Justice Souter notes, this factor tends to be subsumed in (or at least strongly influenced by)

other § 107 considerations. But this is as good a place as any to state that there is no absolute rule against treating the use of all (or virtually all) of a work as a "fair use" — although such wholesale copying is disfavored. You will find more on this topic in the discussion of the "conjure up" test for parody fair use, immediately below, and in the notes to the *Bill Graham Archives* case in § 10.03[C]. Obvious examples include home videotaping for time-shifting purposes (the specific activity approved in *Sony*) and reproduction for use in a judicial proceeding. *See Bond v. Blum*, 317 F.3d 385 (4th Cir. 2003) (reproducing unpublished manuscript for use as evidence in a state-court child custody proceeding was a fair use). Other, perhaps more controversial examples, are so-called intermediate copying in connection with software development (which we will address in § 10.04) and incidental reproduction of an artwork in the background of a TV show or motion picture. What all of these instances have in common, of course, is that they involve uses that can be argued to be non-substitutional (or, to harken back to *Folsom*, non-supplanting) uses.

(7)   The problem of possible substitution effects also informs the consideration of the *fourth factor*, the effect on the plaintiff's potential market. Justice Souter's *Campbell* opinion notes at the outset the Sixth Circuit's reliance on a well-known passage from *Harper & Row* that describes this factor as "undoubtedly the most important element of fair use." Is the rest of Justice Souter's opinion — particularly its actual consideration of factor four — consistent with that observation? If not, what is the message? And what kind of proof would you have expected to be offered at the trial on remand, in light of the Supreme Court opinion? In fact, the case was not heard of again, presumably because the parties came to terms!

Campbell *and Parody*

(8)   *Parody and satire.* The Capitol Steps, a Washington, D.C.-based political parody group, submitted an *amicus* brief in *Campbell*, arguing for a presumption in favor of political parodies. The group takes well-known songs and substitutes new lyrics targeting contemporary political events. The Capitol Steps are quite successful, selling tapes and compact discs throughout the country. How should a lower court analyze a case brought against the Capitol Steps after *Campbell*? Is Justice Souter's distinction between *parody* and *satire* relevant here? What is the import of Justice Kennedy's concurrence? Should a defendant be allowed to appropriate someone else's copyrighted work solely in order to make a political statement? For another example, *see MasterCard Int'l, Inc. v. Nader 2000 Primary Committee*, 70 U.S.P.Q.2d (BNA) 1046 (S.D.N.Y. 2004) (TV advertisement for Ralph Nader's presidential campaign which mimicked MasterCard's "Priceless" advertising campaign was a fair use).

(9)   Since *Campbell*, the lower courts have had several opportunities to consider what is and is not a parody. Perhaps the most entertaining case to date is *Dr. Seuss Enterprises, L.P. v. Penguin Books U.S.A., Inc.*, 924 F. Supp. 1559 (S.D. Cal. 1996), *aff'd*, 109 F.3d 1394 (9th Cir. 1997). The District Court described the defendants' work as follows:

> Defendant Alan Katz conceived and wrote *The Cat NOT in the Hat!, A Parody by Dr. Juice*, a work poised to supply a "fresh new look" at the O.J. Simpson double-murder trial. Katz's rhymes, the illustrations . . . and the

book's packaging . . . mimic the distinctive style of the family of works created by Theodore S. Geisel, better known as Dr. Seuss.

924 F. Supp. at 1561. While acknowledging that "a general satire of social conditions is certainly a creative work having social value . . . ," the District Court discerned no "attempt to comment upon the text or themes of" *The Cat in the Hat. Id.* at 1569.

The Cat NOT in the Hat

On appeal, the Ninth Circuit agreed with the District Court that the defendants' work "is 'pure shtick' and that their *post-hoc* characterization of the work is 'completely unconvincing.'" 109 F.3d at 1403. The court interpreted *Campbell* as requiring that a parody comment, at least in part, on the first author's work. In contrast, the court said, *The Cat NOT in the Hat* "simply retell[s] the Simpson tale," evidencing "no effort to create a new transformative work. . . ." *Id.* at 1401. Do you agree?

If you wished to argue that *The Cat NOT in the Hat* did comment on the work of Dr. Seuss, how would your argument run? Is the relevant question the intent of the purported parodist or the perception of the typical audience member? Is there a tension between asking a court to determine the "target" of a parody and the aesthetic non-discrimination principle of *Bleistein*, discussed in § 2.02? For a critique of the *Dr. Seuss* opinion, drawing into question the parody/satire distinction, see Ochoa, *Dr. Seuss, The Juice and Fair Use: How the Grinch Silenced a Parody*, 45 J. Copr. Soc'y 546 (1998).

For an interesting follow-up to *Dr. Seuss*, compare *Leibovitz v. Paramount Pictures Corp.*, 137 F.3d 109 (2d Cir. 1998) (poster for the film "Naked Gun 33-1/3," in which the head of actor Leslie Nielsen was superimposed on a photograph of a model posed to resemble Annie Leibovitz's well-known *Vanity Fair* portrait of the nude, pregnant Demi Moore, was a fair use), with *Columbia Pictures Indus., Inc. v. Miramax Films Corp.*, 11 F. Supp. 2d 1179 (C.D. Cal. 1998) (enjoining posters for Michael Moore's satiric documentary "The Big One," which imitated the poster for the hit comedy science-fiction film "Men in Black").

(10)   *What's in a name?* How far afield did the lawyers and judges in *Campbell* have to go in order to characterize the 2 Live Crew song as a parodic commentary on Orbison's naïve rock 'n roll world view? And was that trip really necessary? It is worth remembering that parody is really just a special case of criticism, which (in turn) is simply an example of transformative use. Even though the defendant's works in some fair use decisions are hard to categorize in terms of their precise *genre*, it may not matter.

For example, in *Mattel, Inc. v. Walking Mountain Prods.*, 353 F.3d 792 (9th Cir. 2003), photographer Thomas Forsythe created a series of photos featuring naked Barbie dolls being menaced by kitchen appliances, baked in enchiladas, and in various other absurd (and often sexualized) positions. Forsythe described his photos as an attempt to "critique the objectification of women associated with [Barbie], and to lambast [sic] the conventional beauty myth and the societal acceptance of women as objects because this is what Barbie embodies." One of the photos is reproduced below. The Ninth Circuit affirmed summary judgment in favor of Forsythe on fair use grounds, rejecting Mattel's argument that Forsythe could have made his statements about consumerism, gender roles and sexuality without using Barbie. Is this parody or satire?

Enchilada Barbie

Likewise, in *Lennon v. Premise Media Corp.*, 556 F. Supp. 2d 310 (S.D.N.Y. 2008), Yoko Ono, John Lennon's widow, challenged the use of a 15-second clip from the Beatles' song "Imagine" in the documentary film *Expelled: No Intelligence Allowed.* The court held that the use was fair, because the movie sought "to criticize what the filmmakers see as the naïveté of John Lennon's views." A companion case in state court applied the fair use defense to a state-law claim for infringement of the common-law copyright in the pre-1972 sound recording. *EMI Records Ltd. v. Premise Media Corp.*, 89 U.S.P.Q.2d (BNA) 1593 (N.Y. Sup. Ct. 2008).

(11)   TV shows that are well-known for parody and satire seem to get a break. In *Brownmark Films, LLC v. Comedy Partners*, 682 F.3d 687 (7th Cir. 2012), for example, the court held that *South Park's* imitation of a viral video was fair use, despite extensive copying. *See also Bourne Co. v. Twentieth Century Fox Film Corp.*, 602 F. Supp. 2d 499 (S.D.N.Y. 2009) ("When You Wish Upon a Weinstein" episode of *The Family Guy* evoked song "When You Wish Upon a Star," but reasonably could be perceived as commenting on original work's "fantasy of stardust and magic" and Walt Disney's alleged anti-Semitism); *Burnett v. Twentieth Century Fox Film Corp.*, 491 F. Supp. 2d 962 (C.D. Cal. 2007) (*The Family Guy's* brief use of Carol Burnett's "Charwoman" character was fair use.).

(12)   *"Conjuring up": how much is too much?* Prior to *Campbell*, an important line of cases suggested that the fair use defense would be available to a parody only when the defendant took no more from the original than was necessary to "conjure up" that work. *See, e.g., Walt Disney Prods. v. Air Pirates*, 581 F.2d 751, 757-58 (9th Cir. 1978). Does the majority opinion in *Campbell* (which uses the "conjure up" language) depart from this restrictive test? If so, how? If a parodist is sometimes permitted to use more than this minimum amount needed to identify the work parodied, how much more will it be and how will a court know? And what meaning does the Court's discussion have for fair use in non-parody contexts? See the discussion to come in § 10.03.

(13)   For an example of a work that went well beyond merely "conjuring up" the original, consider *SunTrust Bank v. Houghton Mifflin Co.*, 268 F.3d 1257 (11th Cir. 2001). Alice Randall wrote *The Wind Done Gone*, which re-tells the story of Margaret Mitchell's novel *Gone with the Wind* from the point of view of a mulatto half-sister to Scarlett O'Hara, to critique the novel's depiction of slavery in the Civil War-era American South. Randall's book includes all of the major characters and plot elements of Mitchell's novel. Reversing a preliminary injunction, the Eleventh Circuit held that *The Wind Done Gone* was a parody and a fair use.

Are there any limits to the holding in *SunTrust*? Should Randall now be permitted to produce a "faithful" film version of *The Wind Done Gone*? Would the Eleventh Circuit allow a fair use defense for a feminist retelling of a James Bond story through one of its female characters? Are all such "sequels" fair game, or does the special status of Mitchell's book somehow set it apart as a target for parody? *See* Udovich, *Lo.Lee.Ta.*, N.Y. Times Book Review, Oct. 31, 1999 (reviewing *Lo's Diary*, a retelling of Vladimir Nabokov's *Lolita* from the point of view of the title character, which was temporarily shelved until a copyright dispute was resolved).

Vivian Leigh and Hattie McDaniel in "Gone With the Wind" (1939)

For a contrary view, see *Salinger v. Colting*, 641 F. Supp. 2d 250 (S.D.N.Y. 2009) (preliminarily enjoining U.S. publication of defendant's novel, *60 Years Later: Coming Through the Rye*, in which a senior citizen known simply as "Mr. C." escapes from a retirement home and reencounters a world of "phonies," including a reclusive, self-protective character named "Salinger"), *vacated on other grounds*, 607 F.3d 68 (2d Cir. 2010) (agreeing that "[d]efendants are not likely to prevail in their fair use defense"). In concluding that the defendant was unlikely to show that the new work transformed *The Catcher in the Rye*, the District Court placed considerable weight on the fact that defendant's marketing materials described the book as a "sequel" instead of a "parody" or "critique."

(14) *The economics of fair use.* A number of law-and-economics scholars contend that American copyright law is best understood as a body of law that creates private rights in order to facilitate voluntary market transactions. In their view, the role of fair use is to allow the dissemination of copyrighted works in situations of market failure — that is, where transactions costs, i.e., the costs of negotiation, are so high that an otherwise mutually beneficial exchange would not take place. *See, e.g.*, Landes & Posner, *An Economic Analysis of Copyright Law*, 18 J. Legal Stud. 325 (1989) (fair use arises where "costs of a voluntary exchange are so high relative to the benefits that no such exchange is feasible between a user of a copyrighted work and its owner"). Does this analysis have any bearing on the situation in *Campbell*? Is there a "transaction costs" problem with clearing "parody rights"? Or is the difficulty of another kind?

(15)   The market approach, however, has been criticized for failing to comprehend basic premises of copyright law. *See* Yen, *When Authors Won't Sell: Parody, Fair Use, and Efficiency in Copyright Law*, 62 U. Colo. L. Rev. 79 (1991); Winslow, *Rapping on a Revolving Door: An Economic Analysis of Parody and* Campbell v. Acuff-Rose Music, Inc., 69 S. Cal. L. Rev. 767 (1996). Specifically, critics of a mechanistic economic approach say that fair use is important to assuring the continued creation of new works incorporating preexisting materials — and in promoting the wide dissemination of works to end users. In other words, fair use serves the non-economic interests of both creators and consumers — two groups that are becoming more and more difficult to distinguish in the new technological environment.

At the heart of many of these critiques is the proposition that fair use embodies cultural values as well as economic ones, as Wendy Gordon recognized in her famous article, *Fair Use as Market Failure: A Structural and Economic Analysis of the* Betamax *Case and Its Predecessors*, 82 Colum. L. Rev. 1600 (1982) (arguing that "[f]air use should be awarded . . . to the defendant when: (1) market failure is present; (2) transfer of the use to defendant is socially desirable; and (3) an award of fair use would not cause substantial injury to the incentives of the plaintiff copyright owner"). Twenty-five years later, Gordon made the point even more emphatically: "On the *general* question of commodification, we know that there are some things (like the freedom to criticize) that simply shouldn't be sold on any commercial market, whether or not such a market could feasibly arise. . . . [E]ven if all ideas could be bought and sold, that wouldn't make you want to force the public to pay before using them. . . . [I]ncursions of commercialism and bureaucracy can dampen creativity in many domains." *The "Why" of Markets: Fair Use and Circularity*, 116 Yale L.J. Pocket Part 371 (2007), *http://yalelawjournal.org/2007/4/25/gordon.html*.

(16)   *Fair use and moral rights.* Section 106A makes the limited moral rights provisions of U.S. law explicitly subject to fair use — but without saying how the two concepts might interact in case of conflict. Not infrequently, as apparently occurred in *Campbell*, the copyright owner is unwilling to license the work at any price, because the use is seen as offensive or because allowing it would create some sort of reputational harm. Should fair use be utilized by the courts to overrule such decisions, and, if so, on what grounds? *See* Gordon, 82 Colum. L. Rev. at 1632-35 (finding "market failure" where "antidissemination motives" cause the copyright owner to refuse to license socially desirable comment or criticism). Or should we give greater consideration to the feelings of the author — assuming it is he or she, rather than an assignee of economic rights, who has made the decision to withhold? Should it matter whether the author has transferred the copyright to a publisher, as in *Campbell*?

On the facts of *Campbell*, one might think that Roy Orbison would have had a "sure winner" in a country such as France that takes moral rights seriously. In fact, however, Orbison would have had a tough go in France, too. Article L.122-5(4) of the French Intellectual Property Code allows "parodies, pastiches, and caricatures, with due consideration for the laws of this genre." To benefit from this exception to copyright, comic intent must be proved — even though a comic result may not have been accomplished. The French have allowed wide scope for sarcasm, ridicule and disrespect in applying the parody exception, but they have drawn the line against excessive distortions of the work. *See* Geller, *Toward an Overriding Norm in Copyright Law: Sign Wealth*, 159 R.I.D.A. 3, 91-93 (1994). How does the "line" provided by U.S. copyright law compare?

(17)   While reminding us of the ultimately situational nature of fair use analysis, *Campbell* does explain a lot. It also leaves a number of questions unanswered. We turn now to a consideration of some remaining areas of uncertainty.

§ 10.03   CONCEPTUAL ISSUES IN FAIR USE

[A]   Copyright and the First Amendment

Are the Copyright Act and the First Amendment in conflict? Put another way, does copyright inhibit free traffic in the "marketplace of ideas"? Does the First Amendment free up all expression from ownership claims of any kind? If, as we saw in Chapter 2, copyright protection extends only to expression and not to ideas, and the First Amendment is not inherently hostile to ownership of intellectual property rights in expression, where is the conflict? The answer lies in the fact that sometimes the creators of new expression want (or need) to make use of more than just the ideas of those who have gone before. This is where fair use comes in.

As we will see below in *Harper & Row*, one can argue that copyright and the First Amendment reinforce each other rather than conflict. Copyright provides the financial security necessary for investment in the creation of new works. Without that financial security, there would be fewer works, and thus less speech. Still, it is always possible to have too much of a good thing — and copyright (when considered in relation to the First Amendment) is no exception. This case, and the Notes and Questions that follow, explore the role of fair use in accommodating the potential tension between rights in information and freedom of expression.

HARPER & ROW, PUBLISHERS, INC. v. NATION ENTERPRISES
Supreme Court of the United States
471 U.S. 539 (1985)

Justice O'Connor delivered the opinion of the Court.

This case requires us to consider to what extent the "fair use" provision of the Copyright Revision Act of 1976, 17 U.S.C. § 107 (hereinafter the Copyright Act), sanctions the unauthorized use of quotations from a public figure's unpublished manuscript. In March 1979, an undisclosed source provided The Nation magazine with the unpublished manuscript of "A Time to Heal: The Autobiography of Gerald R. Ford." Working directly from the purloined manuscript, an editor of The Nation produced a short piece entitled "The Ford Memoirs — Behind the Nixon Pardon." The piece was timed to "scoop" an article scheduled shortly to appear in Time magazine. Time had agreed to purchase the exclusive right to print prepublication excerpts from the copyright holders, Harper & Row, Publishers, Inc. (hereinafter

Harper & Row) and Reader's Digest Association, Inc. (hereinafter Reader's Digest). As a result of The Nation article, Time canceled its agreement. Petitioners brought a successful copyright action against The Nation. On appeal, the Second Circuit reversed the lower court's finding of infringement, holding that The Nation's act was sanctioned as a "fair use" of the copyrighted material. We granted certiorari, 467 U.S. 1214 (1984), and we now reverse.

I

In February 1977, shortly after leaving the White House, former President Gerald R. Ford contracted with petitioners Harper & Row and The Reader's Digest to publish his as yet unwritten memoirs. . . . Two years later, as the memoirs were nearing completion, petitioners negotiated a prepublication licensing agreement with Time, a weekly news magazine. Time agreed to pay $25,000, $12,500 in advance and an additional $12,500 at publication, in exchange for the right to excerpt 7,500 words from Mr. Ford's account of the Nixon pardon. The issue featuring the excerpts was timed to appear approximately one week before shipment of the full length book version to bookstores. . . .

Two to three weeks before the Time article's scheduled release, an unidentified person secretly brought a copy of the Ford manuscript to Victor Navasky, editor of The Nation, a political commentary magazine. Mr. Navasky knew that his possession of the manuscript was not authorized and that the manuscript must be returned quickly to his "source" to avoid discovery. 557 F. Supp. 1067, 1069 (S.D.N.Y. 1983). He hastily put together what he believed was "a real hot news story" composed of quotes, paraphrases and facts drawn exclusively from the manuscript. Mr. Navasky attempted no independent commentary, research or criticism, in part because of the need for speed if he was to "make news" by "publish[ing] in advance of publication of the Ford book." The 2,250 word article appeared on April 3, 1979. As a result of The Nation's article, Time canceled its piece and refused to pay the remaining $12,500.

[Petitioners brought suit, alleging copyright infringement and various state law claims. The District Court found that "A Time to Heal" was protected by copyright at the time of The Nation's publication and that respondents' use of the copyrighted material constituted an infringement under § 106(1),(2), and (3) of the Copyright Act, rejected respondents' argument that The Nation's piece was a "fair use," and awarded actual damages of $12,500.]

A divided panel of the Court of Appeals for the Second Circuit reversed. . . .

II

We agree with the Court of Appeals that copyright is intended to increase and not to impede the harvest of knowledge. But we believe the Second Circuit gave insufficient deference to the scheme established by the Copyright Act for fostering the original works that provide the seed and substance of this harvest. The rights conferred by copyright are designed to assure contributors to the store of knowledge a fair return for their labors. *Twentieth Century Music Corp. v. Aiken*, 422 U.S. 151, 156 (1975).

Nixon's Farewell
Corbis

. . . This principle applies equally to works of fiction and nonfiction. . . .

. . . [T]here is no dispute that the unpublished manuscript of "A Time to Heal," as a whole, was protected by § 106 from unauthorized reproduction. Nor do respondents dispute that verbatim copying of excerpts of the manuscript's original form of expression would constitute infringement unless excused as fair use. . . .

. . . The Nation has admitted to lifting verbatim quotes of the author's original language totaling between 300 and 400 words and constituting 13% of The Nation article. In using generous verbatim excerpts of Mr. Ford's unpublished manuscript to lend authenticity to its account of the forthcoming memoirs, The Nation effectively arrogated to itself the right of first publication, an important marketable subsidiary right. . . .

IIIA

. . . Professor Latman, in a study of the doctrine of fair use commissioned by [the Copyright Office] for the revision effort, . . . summarized prior law as turning on the "importance of the material copied or performed from the point of view of the reasonable copyright owner. In other words, would the reasonable copyright owner have consented to the use?" [A. Latman, FAIR USE OF COPYRIGHTED WORKS (1958), reprinted as Study No. 14 in Copyright Law Revision Studies Nos. 14-16, Prepared for the Senate Committee on the Judiciary, 86th Cong., 2d Sess., 7 (1960) (hereinafter *Latman*)] at 15. . . .

Perhaps because the fair use doctrine was predicated on the author's implied consent to "reasonable and customary" use when he released his work for public consumption, fair use traditionally was not recognized as a defense to charges of copying from an author's as yet unpublished works. Under common-law copyright, "the property of the author . . . in his intellectual creation [was] absolute until he voluntarily part[ed] with the same. *American Tobacco Co. v. Werckmeister*, 207 U.S. 284, 299 (1907). . . . This absolute rule, however, was tempered in practice by the equitable nature of the fair use doctrine. . . .

. . . The right of first publication implicates a threshold decision by the author whether and in what form to release his work. First publication is inherently different from other § 106 rights in that only one person can be the first publisher; as the contract with Time illustrates, the commercial value of the right lies primarily in exclusivity. Because the potential damage to the author from judicially enforced "sharing" of the first publication right with unauthorized users of his manuscript is substantial, the balance of equities in evaluating such a claim of fair use inevitably shifts. . . .

. . . We conclude that the unpublished nature of a work is "[a] key, though not necessarily determinative, factor" tending to negate a defense of fair use. *Senate Report*, at 64.

. . . The author's control of first public distribution implicates not only his personal interest in creative control but his property interest in exploitation of prepublication rights, which are valuable in themselves and serve as a valuable adjunct to publicity and marketing. . . . Under ordinary circumstances, the author's right to control the first public appearance of his undisseminated expression will outweigh a claim of fair use.

B

Respondents, however, contend that First Amendment values require a different rule under the circumstances of this case. . . . Respondents advance the substantial public import of the subject matter of the Ford memoirs as grounds for excusing a use that would ordinarily not pass muster as a fair use — the piracy of verbatim quotations for the purpose of "scooping" the authorized first serialization. Respondents explain their copying of Mr. Ford's expression as essential to reporting the news story it claims the book itself represents. In respondents' view, not only the facts contained in Mr. Ford's memoirs, but "the precise manner in which [he] expressed himself was as newsworthy as what he had to say." Respondents argue that the public's interest in learning this news as fast as possible outweighs the right of the author to control its first publication.

The Second Circuit noted, correctly, that copyright's idea/expression dichotomy "strike[s] a definitional balance between the First Amendment and the Copyright Act by permitting free communication of facts while still protecting an author's expression." 723 F.2d, at 203. No author may copyright his ideas or the facts he narrates. 17 U.S.C. § 102(b). *See, e.g., New York Times Co. v. United States,* 403 U.S. 713, 726, n.* (1971) (BRENNAN, J., concurring) (copyright laws are not restrictions on freedom of speech as copyright protects only form of expression and not the ideas expressed). . . . As this Court long ago observed: "[T]he news element — the information respecting current events contained in the literary production — is not the creation of the writer, but is a report of matters that ordinarily are *publici juris;* it is the history of the day." *International News Service v. Associated Press,* 248 U.S. 215, 234 (1918). But copyright assures those who write and publish factual narratives such as "A Time to Heal" that they may at least enjoy the right to market the original expression contained therein as just compensation for their investment. . . .

Respondents' theory, however, would expand fair use to effectively destroy any expectation of copyright protection in the work of a public figure. Absent such protection, there would be little incentive to create or profit in financing such memoirs and the public would be denied an important source of significant historical information. The promise of copyright would be an empty one if it could be avoided merely by dubbing the infringement a fair use "news report" of the book.

Nor do respondents assert any actual necessity for circumventing the copyright scheme with respect to the types of works and users at issue here. Where an author and publisher have invested extensive resources in creating an original work and are poised to release it to the public, no legitimate aim is served by preempting the right of first publication. The fact that the words the author has chosen to clothe his narrative may of themselves be "newsworthy" is not an independent justification for unauthorized copying of the author's expression prior to publication. . . .

In our haste to disseminate news, it should not be forgotten that the Framers intended copyright itself to be the engine of free expression. By establishing a marketable right to the use of one's expression, copyright supplies the economic incentive to create and disseminate ideas. This Court stated . . . in *Twentieth Century Music Corp. v. Aiken:*

> The immediate effect of our copyright law is to secure a fair return for an "author's" creative labor. But the ultimate aim is, by this incentive, to stimulate [the creation of useful works] for the general public good.

422 U.S., at 156.

It is fundamentally at odds with the scheme of copyright to accord lesser rights in those works that are of greatest importance to the public. Such a notion ignores the major premise of copyright and injures author and public alike. "[T]o propose that fair use be imposed whenever the 'social value [of dissemination] . . . outweighs any detriment to the artist' would be to propose depriving copyright owners of their right in the property precisely when they encounter those users who could afford to pay for it." Gordon, *Fair Use as Market Failure: A Structural and Economic Analysis of the* Betamax *Case and its Predecessors,* 82 Colum. L. Rev. 1600, 1615 (1982). . . .

Moreover, freedom of thought and expression "includes both the right to speak freely and the right to refrain from speaking at all." *Wooley v. Maynard,* 430 U.S. 705, 714 (1977) (BURGER, C.J.). We do not suggest this right not to speak would sanction abuse of the copyright owner's monopoly as an instrument to suppress facts. But in the words of New York's Chief Judge Fuld:

> The essential thrust of the First Amendment is to prohibit improper restraints on the *voluntary* public expression of ideas; it shields the man who wants to speak or publish when others wish him to be quiet. There is necessarily, and within suitably defined areas, a concomitant freedom *not* to speak publicly, one which serves the same ultimate end as freedom of speech in its affirmative aspect.

Estate of Hemingway v. Random House, 244 N.E.2d 250, 255 (N.Y. 1968). . . . [C]opyright, and the right of first publication in particular, serve this countervailing First Amendment value. . . .

In view of the First Amendment protections already embodied in the Copyright Act's distinction between copyrightable expression and uncopyrightable facts and ideas, and the latitude for scholarship and comment traditionally afforded by fair use, we see no warrant for expanding the doctrine of fair use to create what amounts to a public figure exception to copyright. Whether verbatim copying from a public figure's manuscript in a given case is or is not fair must be judged according to the traditional equities of fair use.

IV

. . . [W]hether The Nation article constitutes fair use under § 107 must be reviewed in light of the principles discussed above [and the statutory factors]. . . .

Purpose of the Use. The Second Circuit correctly identified news reporting as the general purpose of The Nation's use. News reporting is one of the examples enumerated in § 107 to "give some idea of the sort of activities the courts might regard as fair use under the circumstances." *Senate Report*, at 61. This listing was not intended to be exhaustive, . . . or to single out any particular use as presumptively a "fair" use. . . . The fact that an article arguably is "news" and therefore a productive use is simply one factor in a fair use analysis. . . .

The fact that a publication was commercial as opposed to nonprofit is a separate factor that tends to weigh against a finding of fair use. . . . In arguing that the purpose of news reporting is not purely commercial, The Nation misses the point entirely. The crux of the profit/nonprofit distinction is not whether the sole motive of the use is monetary gain but whether the user stands to profit from exploitation of the copyrighted material without paying the customary price. . . .

. . . Also relevant to the "character" of the use is "the propriety of the defendant's conduct." 3 *Nimmer* § 13.05[A], at 13-72. "Fair use presupposes 'good faith' and 'fair dealing.' " *Time Inc. v. Bernard Geis Associates*, 293 F. Supp. 130, 146 (S.D.N.Y. 1968), quoting Schulman, *Fair Use and the Revision of the Copyright Act*, 53 Iowa L. Rev. 832 (1968). The trial court found that The Nation knowingly exploited a purloined manuscript. . . .

Nature of the Copyrighted Work. . . . The law generally recognizes a greater need to disseminate factual works than works of fiction or fantasy. *See* Gorman, *Fact or Fancy? The Implications for Copyright*, 29 J. Copyright Soc. 560, 561 (1982).

. . . Some of the briefer quotes from the memoir are arguably necessary adequately to convey the facts. . . . But The Nation did not stop at isolated phrases and instead excerpted subjective descriptions and portraits of public figures whose power lies in the author's individualized expression. Such use, focusing on the most expressive elements of the work, exceeds that necessary to disseminate the facts.

The fact that a work is unpublished is a critical element in its "nature." . . . Our prior discussion establishes that the scope of fair use is narrower with respect to unpublished works. While even substantial quotations might qualify as fair use in a review of a published work . . . , the author's right to control the first public appearance of his expression weighs against such use of the work before its release. The right of first publication encompasses not only the choice of whether to publish at all, but also the choices of when, where, and in what form first to publish a work. . . .

Amount and Substantiality of the Portion Used. . . . In absolute terms, the words actually quoted were an insubstantial portion of "A Time to Heal." The district court, however, found that "[T]he Nation took what was essentially the heart of the book." We believe the Court of Appeals erred in overruling the district judge's evaluation of the qualitative nature of the taking. . . .

As the statutory language indicates, a taking may not be excused merely because it is insubstantial with respect to the *infringing* work. . . . Conversely, the fact that a substantial portion of the infringing work was copied verbatim is evidence of the qualitative value of the copied material, both to the originator and to the plagiarist who seeks to profit from marketing someone else's copyrighted expression.

Stripped to the verbatim quotes, the direct takings from the unpublished manuscript constitute at least 13% of the infringing article. . . . The Nation article is structured around the quoted excerpts which serve as its dramatic focal points. In view of the expressive value of the excerpts and their key role in the infringing work, we cannot agree with the Second Circuit that the "magazine took a meager, indeed an infinitesimal amount of Ford's original language."

Effect on the Market. . . . This last factor is undoubtedly the single most important element of fair use.[9] *See 3 Nimmer* § 13.05[A], at 13-76, and cases cited therein. "Fair use, when properly applied, is limited to copying by others which does not materially impair the marketability of the work which is copied." 1 *Nimmer* § 1.10[D], at 1-87. The trial court found not merely a potential but an actual effect on the market. Time's cancellation of its projected serialization and its refusal to pay the $12,500 were the direct effect of the infringement. . . .

More important, to negate fair use one need only show that if the challenged use "should become widespread, it would adversely affect the *potential* market for the copyrighted work." *Sony Corp. v. Universal City Studios, Inc.*, 464 U.S. [417], at 451 [(1984)] (emphasis added); *id.*, at 484, and n.36 (collecting cases) (dissenting opinion). This inquiry must take account not only of harm to the original but also of

---

[9] Economists who have addressed the issue believe the fair use exception should come into play only in those situations in which the market fails or the price the copyright holder would ask is near zero. . . . In [their] view, permitting "fair use" to displace normal copyright channels disrupts the copyright market without a commensurate public benefit.

harm to the market for derivative works. . . .

It is undisputed that the factual material in the balance of The Nation's article, besides the verbatim quotes at issue here, was drawn exclusively from the chapters on the pardon. The excerpts were employed as featured episodes in a story about the Nixon pardon — precisely the use petitioners had licensed to Time. . . . Thus it directly competed for a share of the market for prepublication excerpts. . . .

V

. . . The Nation conceded that its verbatim copying of some 300 words of direct quotation from the Ford manuscript would constitute an infringement unless excused as a fair use. Because we find that The Nation's use of these verbatim excerpts from the unpublished manuscript was not a fair use, the judgment of the Court of Appeals is reversed and remanded for further proceedings consistent with this opinion.

JUSTICE BRENNAN, with whom JUSTICE WHITE and JUSTICE MARSHALL join, dissenting.

The Court holds that The Nation's quotation of 300 words from the unpublished 200,000-word manuscript of President Gerald R. Ford infringed the copyright in that manuscript, even though the quotations related to an historical event of undoubted significance — the resignation and pardon of President Richard M. Nixon. Although the Court pursues the laudable goal of protecting "the economic incentive to create and disseminate ideas," this zealous defense of the copyright owner's prerogative will, I fear, stifle the broad dissemination of ideas and information copyright is intended to nurture. Protection of the copyright owner's economic interest is achieved in this case through an exceedingly narrow definition of the scope of fair use. The progress of arts and sciences and the robust public debate essential to an enlightened citizenry are ill served by this constricted reading of the fair use doctrine. . . .

NOTES AND QUESTIONS

The Fair Use/Free Speech Interface

(1)   Does the Court's opinion, with its emphasis on the four factors and the essential compatibility of copyright and free expression, do justice to the tension that seems to the dissenters to exist between these principles on the facts of this case? Can we imagine variations on the facts that would make that tension arguably more acute? What if the Ford memoirs had been a document not destined for publication anytime in the near future, and the previously unknown information they contained was charged with more urgent historical or political importance?

(2)   Justice Brennan seems greatly concerned in his dissent that the Court's analysis and result impede "the progress of arts and sciences and the robust public debate essential to an enlightened citizenry." Realistically, is this decision likely to chill the media's willingness to report the news? Has it? How would we know the answer?

On the other hand, would the outcome urged by Justice Brennan actually have dampened the creativity of future memoir writers? Are public figures like Ford and Nixon — or Hillary or Bill Clinton — motivated to recount the stories of their stewardships to a waiting world *solely* by the prospect of monetary reward? If not, what harm if that prospect is snatched away from them? The public will still get their "take" on events, won't it? Do we care *how many* of the public get to read their accounts, whether in *Time* or *The Nation*?

(3)　Since *Harper & Row*, a formidable literature has developed around the relationship between copyright and the First Amendment, with many, but not all, commentators concluding that copyright — particularly the right to prepare derivative works — restricts free speech and ought to be limited by the First Amendment to some degree. *See, e.g.*, Benkler, *Free as the Air to Common Use: First Amendment Constraints on Enclosure of the Public Domain*, 74 N.Y.U. L. Rev. 354 (1999); Netanel, *Locating Copyright Within the First Amendment Skein*, 54 Stan. L. Rev. 1 (2001); Rubenfeld, *The Freedom of Imagination: Copyright's Constitutionality*, 112 Yale L.J. 1 (2002); Baker, *First Amendment Limits on Copyright*, 55 Vand. L. Rev. 891 (2002); Tushnet, *Copy This Essay: How Fair Use Doctrine Harms Free Speech and How Copying Serves It*, 114 Yale L.J. 535 (2004); *cf.* Patterson & Joyce, *Copyright in 1791: An Essay*, 52 Emory L.J. 909 (2003). To date, however, such work has not brought about any fundamental recalibration of the balance struck in *Harper & Row*.

(4)　Did *Harper & Row* in effect decide that *authors* have a First Amendment right *to remain silent* — and that the First Amendment rights (if any) of users must be determined exclusively by a fair use analysis? The Supreme Court's *Eldred* decision, which we read in § 5.01, confirms the proposition that, in general, free expression and copyright are compatible, thanks in part to the fair use doctrine. This, in turn, led to the conclusion (already implicit in *Harper & Row*) that the courts need recognize no First Amendment defense to copyright infringement liability, independent of or beyond fair use itself. But *Eldred* also sent a warning, as the Notes and Questions following that opinion emphasized: copyright can escape additional First Amendment scrutiny only so long as it remains within its "traditional contours." What if (for example) Congress invented a new form of copyright and chose not to build in fair use, or worse, actively to exclude it? Arguably, this is just what occurred when the "paracopyright" provisions of the 1998 Digital Millennium Copyright Act (discussed in § 9.04) were enacted. In § 10.04 below, we will examine some of the implications of that enactment.

Harper & Row *and the Fair Use Factors*

(5)　Quite apart from its relevance to the relationship between copyright and the First Amendment, what does *Harper & Row* have to say about § 107's "four factor" analysis? In *Harper & Row*, *The Nation* argued that, because its purpose — news reporting — was enumerated in the *preamble* to § 107, the first factor should automatically be weighed in its favor. The Court rejected this construction of the statute. This, however, leaves open the important question of what significance should be accorded to the fact that a defendant's use is one of those enumerated in the preamble. Is this just verbiage, or does the mention of "news reporting" add something (although, in *Harper & Row*, not enough) to the defendant's case? Two settings in which the doctrine frequently is invoked successfully are news reporting and scholarship. *See Video-Cinema Films, Inc. v. Cable News Network, Inc.*, 60 U.S.P.Q.2d (BNA) 1415 (S.D.N.Y. 2001) (use of film clips by television news networks to report actor Robert Mitchum's death was a fair use), and *Williamson v. Pearson Education, Inc.*, 60 U.S.P.Q.2d (BNA) 1723 (S.D.N.Y. 2001) (book that included quotations by and passages about George S. Patton from another book made fair use of the material).

Of course, a claim of "news reporting" may sometimes be just a pretext. In *Murphy v. Millennium Radio Group LLC*, 650 F.3d 295 (3d Cir. 2011), the court held that it was not fair use for a radio station to post a photo of two of its anchors receiving a "Best of New Jersey" award, without any accompanying commentary, and to invite users to alter the image using photo-manipulation software, without paying the photographer. *See also Balsley v. LFP, Inc.*, 691 F.3d 747 (6th Cir. 2012) (reprinting wet t-shirt photo of TV newswoman in *Hustler* magazine's "Hot News Babes" feature was not a fair use); *Monge v. Maya Magazines, Inc.*, 688 F.3d 1164 (9th Cir. 2012) (publishing photos of celebrity pop singer's clandestine wedding in celebrity gossip magazine was not a fair use).

(6) What about socially desirable uses of copyrighted works that didn't make it into the preamble? Should they receive lesser consideration? Not necessarily. In *Sony Computer Entertainment America, Inc. v. Bleem, LLC*, 214 F.3d 1022 (9th Cir. 2000), for example, the court held that copying video game "screen shots" from a television display for comparative advertising purposes was a fair use, opining that comparative advertising, when truthful and nondeceptive, "assists [consumers] in making rational purchase decisions[,] . . . encourages product improvement and innovation, and can lead to lower prices in the marketplace." *Id.* at 1027.

(7) In discussing the *first factor*, Justice O'Connor's opinion in *Harper & Row* carefully characterizes *The Nation*'s commercial use of the plaintiff's copyrighted material as only "a separate factor that tends to weigh against a finding of fair use" (not as having the presumptive effect that *Sony* had seemed to recognize). The opinion also describes the "crux of the profit/nonprofit distinction" as "not whether the sole motive of the use is monetary gain but whether the user stands to profit from exploitation of the copyrighted material without paying the customary price." Where does this distinction lead? Is it helpful in all cases? And what is "exploitation of the copyrighted material"? You may want to consider that question after reading the *Bill Graham Archives* decision below.

(8) Turning to the *second factor*, the majority in *Harper & Row* refuses to allow *The Nation* to employ fair use, the First Amendment, or any other defense to justify its usurpation of the plaintiff's § 106(3) right of first publication. Under principles of "moral rights" applicable in, for example, French law, the author has the right to determine the circumstances in which her work first will be disclosed to the public: the so-called *"droit de divulgation."* Does *Harper & Row* endow American authors with the functional equivalent? Suppose that *The Nation* had published its article, still without authorization, *after* the plaintiff had published Ford's memoirs. Same result?

(9) *Harper & Row*'s careful treatment of fair use of unpublished works proved to be the jumping-off point for an extraordinary series of cases in the Second

Circuit. The sequence of decisions follows:

In *Salinger v. Random House, Inc.*, 650 F. Supp. 413 (S.D.N.Y. 1986) (Leval, J.), *rev'd*, 811 F.2d 90 (2d Cir. 1987), defendant's unauthorized biography of reclusive author J.D. Salinger quoted from letters written by Salinger that, unbeknownst to him, had been deposited by the recipients (or their estates) in various university libraries. Interpreting *Harper & Row* as holding that unpublished works "normally enjoy complete protection against copying any protected expression," 811 F.2d at 97, the Court of Appeals reversed the District Court's finding of fair use, venturing that, if a biographer copies more than minimal amounts of protected unpublished material, "he deserves to be enjoined." *Id.* at 96.

In *New Era Publications Int'l, ApS v. Henry Holt & Co.*, 684 F. Supp. 808, 695 F. Supp. 1493 (S.D.N.Y. 1988), *aff'd on other grounds*, 873 F.2d 576, *reh'g en banc denied*, 884 F.2d 659 (2d Cir. 1989), the unpublished works were letters by L. Ron Hubbard, founder of the Church of Scientology. The District Court found fair use, only to be chastised by the Court of Appeals in an extended *dictum* — after affirming the lower court's denial of an injunction, on the ground of laches. A petition for rehearing *en banc*, filed by the prevailing party (complaining about the *dictum!*), was denied.

In *Wright v. Warner Books, Inc.*, 748 F. Supp. 105 (S.D.N.Y. 1990), *aff'd*, 953 F.2d 731 (2d Cir. 1991), however, the District Court declined to lump all "unpublished" materials into one category for fair use analysis purposes. The court noted that the biographer was also the addressee of some of the unpublished letters in which the plaintiff claimed copyright, and that the biographer's subject had sold other unpublished material to a research library without restricting access to others. The Second Circuit, while disagreeing with the District Court's factor two analysis, nonetheless affirmed.

In the end, in 1992, Congress enacted legislation to make it clear that fair use does apply, at least to some extent, to unpublished works. The amendment consisted of a single sentence tacked onto the end of § 107: "The fact that a work is unpublished shall not itself bar a finding of fair use if such finding is made upon consideration of all the above factors."

How does amended § 107 work in practice? *See Sundeman v. The Seajay Society*, 142 F.3d 194 (4th Cir. 1998), which involved a scholarly article quoting portions (four to six percent) of an unpublished first novel by the late Marjorie Kinnan Rawlings. Although the second factor was found to cut against the claim of fair use, ultimately that factor was outweighed by the other three. But for the amendment, would this case have been decided differently? Or are the facts distinguishable from *Harper & Row* and the Second Circuit biography cases?

(10)   The *third factor* under § 107 is, perhaps, the most problematic in *Harper & Row.* The taking of 300-400 words out of a full-length (*at least* full-length!) Presidential autobiography does not seem excessive, especially when we consider that those 300-400 words were not exactly bristling with creativity. Did *Harper & Row*'s treatment of the third factor rely too heavily on the unpublished nature of the work, thereby collapsing the second and third factors?

(11)   Finally, consider the *fourth factor*, which the *Harper & Row* majority describes as "undoubtedly the single most important element of fair use." Is this still the law after *Campbell?* Does it matter? Again, you may want to return to this question after reading the note on "Actual and Potential Market Effect" in § 10.03[C] below.

(12)   *Fair use and custom: virtuous and vicious circles.* The Court's opinion (referring to Alan Latman's *Copyright Revision Study* on fair use) reminds us of the important role that custom can play in adding specificity to other otherwise sometimes vague contours of fair use. *See also Wall Data, Inc., v. L.A. County Sheriff's Dep't*, 447 F.3d 769, 778 (2006) (fair use may be appropriate "where the 'custom or public policy' at the time would have defined the use as reasonable"). Beginning in 2005, there have been efforts to harness this aspect of the doctrine by articulating standards of "Best Practices" in fair use for different communities (filmmakers, teachers, archivists, and so forth). *See* Jaszi, *Copyright, Fair Use and Motion Pictures*, 2007 UTAH L. REV. 715, and the materials collected at *www.centerforsocialmedia.org/resources/fair_use*. But does documentation of custom always work reliably to expand the horizons of fair use? In *Risk Aversion and Rights Accretion in Intellectual Property Law*, 116 Yale L.J. 882 (2007), James Gibson makes a strong argument that, under some circumstances, custom may have a constrictive effect on the doctrine. Imagine, for example, that in a given part of the entertainment industry, it has become conventional to license the rights to make uses that — as a doctrinal matter — may actually be fair ones. See *Bridgeport Music, Inc. v. UMG Recordings, Inc.*, 585 F.3d 267 (6th Cir. 2009), holding that the defendant's imitation of certain musical elements was "transformative" but not fair use, because the copyright owner stood to lose "substantial licensing revenue" from this and similar uses. *See also* Rothman, *The Questionable Use of Custom in Intellectual Property*, 93 Va. L. Rev. 1899 (2007).

(13)   *Fair use — beyond the four factors?* In *Time, Inc. v. Bernard Geis Associates*, 293 F. Supp. 130 (S.D.N.Y. 1968), the plaintiff challenged an historian's unauthorized use of still frames from its copyrighted Zapruder film of President John F. Kennedy's assassination in Dallas. The court approved the taking as a fair use, on the ground that "the public interest in having the fullest information available on the murder of President Kennedy" outweighed the copyright owner's interest in the work. What information was the defendant prohibited from conveying? Is the "public interest" a separate concern that § 107 somehow neglects?

A Frame From the Zapruder Film

(14) *Fair use and media reporting.* Obviously, "facts" are free for the taking. But sometimes it is difficult or downright undesirable to report just the facts and leave the associated words and images behind. If "a picture is worth a thousand words," does that justify using the image itself in reporting the news? *Compare Los Angeles News Service v. Reuters Television Int'l, Ltd.,* 149 F.3d 987 (9th Cir. 1998) (holding that Reuters' use of plaintiff's footage of Reginald Denny's beating during the 1992 L.A. riots was not a fair use) *with Los Angeles News Service v. CBS Broadcasting, Inc.,* 305 F.3d 924 (9th Cir. 2002) (holding that Court TV's use of a short clip of the same footage as part of "a video montage" introducing its "Prime Time Justice" program was a fair use). Does it make sense that the use of the footage for news reporting was disapproved, while the use of the footage for what was essentially commercial promotion was approved?

If you read both opinions, you will see that they place different emphasis on the issue of "transformative use," to which we now turn.

[B] The Meaning of "Transformative Use"

We know, of course, the pedigree of the "transformative use" standard that the Supreme Court elevated to special status in fair use analysis in the *Campbell* decision. It had its beginnings (leaving aside its "productive use" forebear) in the writings of Judge Pierre Leval of the Second Circuit, especially his influential article, *Toward a Fair Use Standard,* 103 Harv. L. Rev. 1105 (1990). Here, however,

we are less concerned with the origins than with the destiny of this standard —
which some have likened to a hardy invasive plant that, once established, threatens
to take over the entire garden. Is this really the future of fair use analysis?

BILL GRAHAM ARCHIVES v.
DORLING KINDERSLEY LTD.
United States Court of Appeals, Second Circuit
448 F.3d 605 (2006)

RESTANI, JUDGE:

This appeal concerns the scope of copyright protection afforded artistic concert
posters reproduced in reduced size in a biography of the musical group the Grateful
Dead. Asserted copyright holder Bill Graham Archives, LLC ("BGA") appeals from
a judgment of the District Court . . . dismissing, on motion for summary judgment,
its copyright infringement action against Dorling Kindersley Limited, Dorling
Kindersley Publishing, Inc., and R.R. Donnelley & Sons Company (collectively
"DK"). We review the district court's grant of summary judgment *de novo*, and we
agree with the court that DK's reproduction of BGA's images is protected by the fair
use exception to copyright infringement.

BACKGROUND

In October of 2003, DK published *Grateful Dead: The Illustrated Trip* ("*Illustrated Trip*"), in collaboration with Grateful Dead Productions, intended as a
cultural history of the Grateful Dead. The resulting 480-page coffee table book tells
the story of the Grateful Dead along a timeline running continuously through the
book, chronologically combining over 2000 images representing dates in the
Grateful Dead's history with explanatory text. A typical page of the book features
a collage of images, text, and graphic art designed to simultaneously capture the eye
and inform the reader. Plaintiff BGA claims to own the copyright to seven images
displayed in *Illustrated Trip*, which DK reproduced without BGA's permission.

Initially, DK sought permission from BGA to reproduce the images. In May of
2003, the CEO of Grateful Dead Productions sent a letter to BGA seeking
permission for DK to publish the images. BGA responded by offering permission in
exchange for Grateful Dead Productions' grant of permission to BGA to make CDs
and DVDs out of concert footage in BGA's archives. Next, DK directly contacted
BGA seeking to negotiate a license agreement, but the parties disagreed as to an
appropriate license fee. Nevertheless, DK proceeded with publication of *Illustrated
Trip* without entering a license fee agreement with BGA. Specifically, DK reproduced seven artistic images originally depicted on Grateful Dead event posters and
tickets. BGA's seven images are displayed in significantly reduced form and are
accompanied by captions describing the concerts they represent.

An Illustrative Page from *The Illustrated Trip*

When DK refused to meet BGA's post-publication license fee demands, BGA filed suit for copyright infringement. BGA sought to enjoin further publication of *Illustrated Trip*, the destruction of all unsold books, and actual and statutory damages. The parties cross-moved for summary judgment, with the primary issue before the district court being whether DK's use of BGA's images constituted fair use under the Copyright Act of 1976. After applying the statutory fair use balancing test, the district court . . . granted DK's motion for summary judgment.

DISCUSSION

. . . Whether . . . "fair use" exists involves a case-by-case determination using four non-exclusive, statutorily provided factors in light of the purposes of copyright. . . . "The ultimate test of fair use . . . is whether the copyright law's goal of promoting the Progress of Science and useful Arts would be better served by allowing the use than by preventing it." *Castle Rock Entm't, Inc. v. Carol Publ'g Group*, 150 F.3d 132, 141 (2d Cir. 1998). . . .

I. Purpose and Character of Use

We first address "the purpose and character of the use, including whether such use is of a commercial nature or is for nonprofit educational purposes." 17 U.S.C. § 107(1). Most important to the court's analysis of the first factor is the "transformative" nature of the work. *See* Pierre N. Leval, *Toward a Fair Use Standard*, 103 Harv. L. Rev. 1105, 1111 (1990). The question is "whether the new work merely supersede[s] the objects f the original creation, or instead adds something new, with a further purpose or different character, altering the first with new expression, meaning, or message." *Campbell v. Acuff-Rose Music, Inc.*, 510 U.S. 569, 579 (1994).

Here, the district court determined that *Illustrated Trip* is a biographical work, and the original images are not, and therefore accorded a strong presumption in favor of DK's use. In particular, the district court concluded that DK's use of images placed in chronological order on a timeline is transformatively different from the mere expressive use of images on concert posters or tickets. Because the works are displayed to commemorate historic events, arranged in a creative fashion, and displayed in significantly reduced form, the district court held that the first fair use factor weighs heavily in favor of DK.

Appellant challenges the district court's strong presumption in favor of fair use based on the biographical nature of *Illustrated Trip*. . . . Moreover, Appellant argues that as a matter of law merely placing poster images along a timeline is not a transformative use. Appellant asserts that each reproduced image should have been accompanied by comment or criticism related to the artistic nature of the image.

We disagree with Appellant's limited interpretation of transformative use and we agree with the district court that DK's actual use of each image is transformatively different from the original expressive purpose. Preliminarily, we recognize, as the district court did, that *Illustrated Trip* is a biographical work documenting the 30-year history of the Grateful Dead. While there are no categories of presumptively fair use, . . . courts have frequently afforded fair use protection to the use of copyrighted material in biographies, recognizing such works as forms of historic scholarship, criticism, and comment that require incorporation of original source material for optimum treatment of their subjects. . . . No less a recognition of biographical value is warranted in this case simply because the subject made a mark in pop culture rather than some other area of human endeavor. . . .

In the instant case, DK's purpose in using the copyrighted images at issue in its biography of the Grateful Dead is plainly different from the original purpose for which they were created. Originally, each of BGA's images fulfilled the dual purposes of artistic expression and promotion. The posters were apparently widely distributed to generate public interest in the Grateful Dead and to convey information to a large number people about the band's forthcoming concerts. In contrast, DK used each of BGA's images as historical artifacts to document and represent the actual occurrence of Grateful Dead concert events featured on *Illustrated Trip*'s timeline.

In some instances, it is readily apparent that DK's image display enhances the reader's understanding of the biographical text.[3] In other instances, the link between image and text is less obvious; nevertheless, the images still serve as historical artifacts graphically representing the fact of significant Grateful Dead concert events selected by the *Illustrated Trip*'s author for inclusion in the book's timeline.[4] We conclude that both types of uses fulfill DK's transformative purpose of enhancing the biographical information in *Illustrated Trip*, a purpose separate and distinct from the original artistic and promotional purpose for which the images were created. . . . In sum, . . . we agree with the district court that DK was not required to discuss the artistic merits of the images to satisfy this first factor of fair use analysis.

This conclusion is strengthened by the manner in which DK displayed the images. First, DK significantly reduced the size of the reproductions. *See Kelly v. Arriba Soft Corp.*, 336 F.3d 811, 818-20 (9th Cir. 2003) (finding online search engine's use of thumbnail-sized images to be highly transformative). While the small size is sufficient to permit readers to recognize the historical significance of the posters, it is inadequate to offer, more than a glimpse of their expressive value. In short, DK used the minimal image size necessary to accomplish its transformative purpose.

Second, DK minimized the expressive value of the reproduced images by

---

[3] For example, BGA claims copyright infringement of a concert poster image, reproduced on page 254 of *Illustrated Trip*, depicting two skeletons flanking the Warfield Theatre. The reader is expected to view this image together with the text on pages 254 and 255 under the caption, "The Warfield/Radio City Shows," and with a non-contested image on page 255, depicting two skeletons flanking the Radio City Music Hall. In this instance, the text specifically comments on the poster image, explaining:

> . . . The [Dead's] otherwise brilliant Radio City run was marred by a bizarre dispute between the band and Radio City's management. The latter objected to promotional posters showing the inevitable skeletons flanking the venerable venue. . . . The misunderstanding was quickly cleared up.

The author uses [these] images to enhance the reader's understanding of the statement that Radio City Music Hall executives were unfamiliar with Grateful Dead iconography by displaying nearly identical concert promotion posters for the Warfield Theatre and the Radio City Music Hall.

[4] For example, BGA claims copyright infringement of a concert poster image, reproduced on page 103. . . . While the concert poster image does not necessarily enhance the reader's understanding of the text, it serves as a recognizable representation of the concert. It also documents concert information and provides notable historic details, such as the fact that, at this relatively early stage of its career, the Grateful Dead received second billing to Jefferson Airplane.

combining them with a prominent timeline, textual material, and original graphical artwork, to create a collage of text and images on each page of the book. To further this collage effect, the images are displayed at angles and the original graphical artwork is designed to blend with the images and text. Overall, DK's layout ensures that the images at issue are employed only to enrich the presentation of the cultural history of the Grateful Dead, not to exploit copyrighted artwork for commercial gain. . . .

Third, BGA's images constitute an inconsequential portion of *Illustrated Trip*. The extent to which unlicensed material is used in the challenged work can be a factor in determining whether a biographer's use of original materials has been sufficiently transformative to constitute fair use. . . . Although our circuit has counseled against considering the percentage the allegedly infringing work comprises of the copyrighted work in conducting *third-factor* fair use analysis, several courts have done so, *see, e.g.,* [*Harper & Row*], 471 U.S. 539, at 565–66. . . . We find this inquiry more relevant in the context of first-factor fair use analysis.

In the instant case, the book is 480 pages long, while the BGA images appear on only seven pages. . . . And no BGA image takes up more than one-eighth of a page in a book or is given more prominence than any other image on the page. In total, the images account for less than one-fifth of one percent of the book. This stands in stark contrast to the wholesale takings in cases such as those described above, and we are aware of no case where such an insignificant taking was found to be an unfair use of original materials.

Finally, as to this first factor, we briefly address the commercial nature of *Illustrated Trip*. . . . Even though *Illustrated Trip* is a commercial venture, we recognize that "nearly all of the illustrative uses listed in the preamble paragraph of § 107 . . . are generally conducted for profit . . ." *Campbell*, 510 U.S. at 584. Moreover, "[t]he crux of the profit/nonprofit distinction is not whether the sole motive of the use is monetary gain but whether the user stands to profit from exploitation of the copyrighted material without paying the customary price." *Harper*, 471 U.S. at 562. Here, *Illustrated Trip* does not exploit the use of BGA's images as such for commercial gain. Significantly, DK has not used any of BGA's images . . . to promote the sale of the book. *Illustrated Trip* merely uses pictures and text to describe the life of the Grateful Dead. By design, the use of BGA's images is incidental to the commercial biographical value of the book.

Accordingly, we conclude that the first fair use factor weighs in favor of DK because DK's use of BGA's images is transformatively different from the images' original expressive purpose and DK does not seek to exploit the images' expressive value for commercial gain.

II. Nature of the Copyrighted Work

The second factor in a fair use determination is "the nature of the copyrighted work." 17 U.S.C. § 107(2). To resolve this inquiry the court considers "the protection of the reasonable expectations of one who engages in the kinds of creation/authorship that the copyright seeks to encourage." Leval, *supra*, at 1122. "[C]reative expression for public dissemination falls within the core of the copyright's

[handwritten margin note: Purpose in the book was different then the poster in general. Didn't make a difference then they took the whole poster]

protective purposes." *Campbell*, 510 U.S. at 586.

The district court determined that the second factor weighs against DK because the images are creative artworks, which are traditionally the core of intended copyright protection. Nevertheless, the court limited the weight it placed on this factor because the posters have been published extensively. Appellant agrees that the district court properly weighed the second factor against DK, although it questions the lesser protection given to published works. Appellees counter that because the images are mixed factual and creative works and have been long and extensively published, the second factor tilts toward fair use.

. . . We recognize . . . that the second factor may be of limited usefulness where the creative work of art is being used for a transformative purpose. . . . This is not a case such as *Ringgold v. Black Entm't Television, Inc.*, 126 F.3d 70 (2d Cir. 1997), in which we held that the creative work was being used for the same decorative purpose as the original. Here, we conclude that DK is using BGA's images for the transformative purpose of enhancing the biographical information provided in *Illustrated Trip*. Accordingly, we hold that even though BGA's images are creative works, which are a core concern of copyright protection, the second factor has limited weight in our analysis because the purpose of DK's use was to emphasize the images' historical rather than creative value.

III. Amount and Substantiality of the Portion Used

The third fair use factor asks the court to examine "the amount and substantiality of the portion used in relation to the copyrighted work as a whole." 17 U.S.C. § 107(3). We review this factor with reference to the copyrighted work, not the infringing work. The court must examine the quantitative and qualitative aspects of the portion of the copyrighted material taken. *Campbell*, 510 U.S. at 586. . . .

. . . Neither our court nor any of our sister circuits has ever ruled that the copying of an entire work *favors* fair use. At the same time, however, courts have concluded that such copying does not necessarily weigh against fair use because copying the entirety of a work is sometimes necessary to make a fair use of the image. . . . Adopting this reasoning, we conclude that the third-factor inquiry must take into account that "the extent of permissible copying varies with the purpose and character of the use." *Campbell*, 510 U.S. at 586–87.

Here, DK used BGA's images because the posters and tickets were historical artifacts that could document Grateful Dead concert events and provide a visual context for the accompanying text. . . . We conclude that such use by DK is tailored to further its transformative purpose because DK's reduced size reproductions of BGA's images in their entirety displayed the minimal image size and quality necessary to ensure the reader's recognition of the images. . . . Accordingly, the third fair use factor does not weigh against fair use.

IV. Effect of the Use upon the Market for or Value of the Original

The fourth factor is "the effect of the use upon the potential market for or value of the copyrighted work." 17 U.S.C. § 107(4). The court looks to not only the market harm caused by the particular infringement, but also to whether, if the challenged use becomes widespread, it will adversely affect the potential market for the copyrighted work. . . . This analysis requires a balancing of "the benefit the public will derive if the use is permitted and the personal gain the copyright owner will receive if the use is denied." *MCA, Inc. v. Wilson*, 677 F.2d 180, 183 (2d Cir. 1981).

In the instant case, the parties agree that DK's use of the images did not impact BGA's primary market for the sale of the poster images. Instead, we look to whether DK's unauthorized use usurps BGA's potential to develop a derivative market. Appellant argues that DK interfered with the market for licensing its images for use in books. Appellant contends that there is an established market for licensing its images and it suffered both the loss of royalty revenue directly from DK and the opportunity to obtain royalties from others.

"It is indisputable that . . . the impact on potential licensing revenues is a proper subject for consideration in assessing the fourth factor." [*American Geophysical Union v.*] *Texaco, Inc.*, 60 F.3d [913 (2d. Cir. 1995)], at 929. We have noted, however, that "were a court automatically to conclude in every case that potential licensing revenues were impermissibly impaired simply because the secondary user did not pay a fee for the right to engage in the use, the fourth fair use factor would always favor the copyright holder." *Id.* at 930 n.17 (emphasis added) . . . Accordingly, we do not find a harm to BGA's license market merely because DK did not pay a fee for BGA's copyrighted images.

Instead, we look at the impact on potential licensing revenues for "traditional, reasonable, or likely to be developed markets." *Texaco*, 60 F.3d at 930. In order to establish a traditional license market, Appellant points to the fees paid to other copyright owners for the reproduction of their images in *Illustrated Trip*. Moreover, Appellant asserts that it established a market for licensing its images, and in this case expressed a willingness to license images to DK. Neither of these arguments shows impairment to a traditional, as opposed to a transformative market.[5] *See* Leval, *supra*, at 1125 (explaining that "[t]he fourth factor disfavors a finding of fair use only when the market is impaired because the . . . material serves the consumer as a substitute, or, . . . supersedes the use of the original").

Here, unlike in *Texaco*, we hold that DK's use of BGA's images is transformatively different from their original expressive purpose.[6] In a case such as this, a copyright holder cannot prevent others from entering fair use markets merely "by developing or licensing a market for parody, news reporting, educational or other transformative uses of its own creative work. . . . [C]opyright owners may not preempt exploitation of transformative markets. . . ." *Castle Rock*, 150 F.3d at 146

---

[5] To the contrary, had the book been commercially successful — which it was not — it might have garnered interest in the original images in full size because the reduced images have such minimal expressive impact. An afficionado might seek more than a "peek."

[6] *Texaco* may also be distinguished because . . . [that case] involved direct evidence that the allegedly infringing use would cause the owner to lose license revenues derived from a substantially similar use. Here, in contrast, BGA's direct evidence of its license revenues involves a use that is markedly different from the use by DK. The licenses BGA sold to other publishers were for substantially less transformative uses of its posters: full-page, prominently displayed reproductions of BGA's images, with little discussion of the images or their historical context. . . .

n.11. Moreover, a publisher's willingness to pay license fees for reproduction of images does not establish that the publisher may not, in the alternative, make fair use of those images. *Campbell*, 510 U.S. at 585 n.18 (stating that "being denied permission to use [or pay license fees for] a work does not weigh against a finding of fair use"). Since DK's use of BGA's images falls within a transformative market, BGA does not suffer market harm due to the loss of license fees.

V. Balance of Factors

On balance, we conclude, as the district court did, that the fair use factors weigh in favor of DK's use. For the first factor, we conclude that DK's use of concert posters and tickets as historical artifacts of Grateful Dead performances is transformatively different from the original expressive purpose of BGA's copyrighted images. While the second factor favors BGA because of the creative nature of the images, its weight is limited because DK did not exploit the expressive value of the images. Although BGA's images are copied in their entirety, the third factor does not weigh against fair use because the reduced size of the images is consistent with the author's transformative purpose. Finally, we conclude that DK's use does not harm the market for BGA's sale of its copyrighted artwork, and we do not find market harm based on BGA's hypothetical loss of license revenue from DK's transformative market.

CONCLUSION

For the foregoing reasons, we conclude that DK's use of BGA's copyrighted images in its book *Illustrated Trip* is fair use. Accordingly, we affirm.

NOTES AND QUESTIONS

(1) *Some preliminary technicalities.* The *Bill Graham Archives* opinion characterizes the challenged book as a "biography" of the band. What's the relationship of this characterization to the examples ("criticism, commentary . . ." and so forth) in the preamble to this section of the Act? And how much does it really matter? Would the analysis be any different if the book were a "history" of the Grateful Dead? And what should we make of the court's discussion, in connection with the first factor, of what a small part of the *Illustrated Trip* the unlicensed images actually are? Clearly, this doesn't belong in a consideration of the third factor. But is it more than a make-weight argument here?

Not all courts agree that "historical" context makes a use fair. In *Bouchat v. Baltimore Ravens Ltd. Partnership*, 619 F.3d 301 (4th Cir. 2010) ("*Bouchat IV*"), the court held that a display of memorabilia featuring the team's former logo, which had been held to infringe the plaintiff's design, was a fair use; but a majority held that the sale of highlight films containing actual game footage from previous seasons when the logo was used was not a fair use. Is this distinction consistent with *Campbell*, which disapproved a presumption against "commercial" uses? One suspects that the majority might have been swayed by sympathy for the plaintiff, who previously was unsuccessful in proving that any of the team's profits from merchandising were "attributable" to the infringing logo. Is this a case where two wrongs make a right?

(2) *A § 107(2) renaissance?* Long the poor step-child of fair use analysis, the second factor may be emerging from the shadows. The *Bill Graham Archives* opinion, for example, suggests that just as unpublished works may be entitled to special solicitude when fair use is assessed, much-published ones may be entitled to less and that, in any event, the poster and tickets were of a "mixed factual and creative" character. Are you impressed? Was the court? And what does this have to do with transformative use? For a thoughtful discussion of the factor's untapped potential, see Kasunic, *Is That All There Is? Reflections on the Nature of the Second Fair Use Factor*, 31 Colum. J.L. & Arts 529 (2008).

(3) *The mystery of transformative use.* Is the *Bill Graham Archives* court clear about how "transformative use" in fair use analysis differs from the statutory usage of the word "transformed" in the § 101 definition of "derivative work"? Does the potential for confusion suggest that Judge Leval made an unfortunate choice in christening this standard? Or perhaps the culprit is the Supreme Court majority in *Sony* for having quashed the "productive use" terminology favored by the Ninth Circuit? What term might best convey the core concept that the first factor weighs in the defendant's favor to the extent that the defendant's use "adds value" to the underlying work in advancing public welfare?

(4) So what is a "transformative use" after all? Is it in the eye of the beholder? And how easy is it to tell, in advance, whether a particular use will or will not qualify? How would you advise a publisher that wanted to ride the commercial wave of a new hit TV show with an unauthorized "companion" volume? This was the situation in the *Castle Rock* case, on which the court relies in *Bill Graham Archives* — and there, the fair use defense failed because the claimed "transformation" was seen as more pretextual than real: "Any transformative purpose possessed by *The SAT* [the defendants' "Seinfeld Aptitude Test" trivia quiz book] is slight to non-existent. We reject the argument that *The SAT* was created to educate *Seinfeld* viewers or to criticize, 'expose,' or otherwise comment upon *Seinfeld*." *See also Toho Co., Ltd. v. William Morrow & Co.*, 33 F. Supp. 2d 1206 (C.D. Cal. 1998) (enjoining distribution of the defendant's Godzilla compendium book, which contained "commentary, critique, and trivia," as well as plot summaries and still pictures of each Godzilla film).

(5) Clearly, a transformative use need not be a critical use. Nor is it necessary that the new work comment directly on the one from which an unlicensed quotation has been taken. In fact, *Bill Graham Archives* suggests that merely illustrative uses also may be transformative, at least if they truly add new value. In what other situations will a work that reproduces an existing work verbatim be held to be transformative because of a different purpose or context? *See* Zimmerman, *The More Things Change The Less They Seem "Transformed": Some Reflections on Fair Use*, 46 J. Copr. Soc'y 261 (1998). Consider the following:

- Defendant allows subscribers to listen to radio stations around the country over telephone lines — a service for which advertisers wishing to check up on their on-air advertising are willing to pay. Some, but not all, of the plaintiff broadcast stations offer similar "listen lines" for free to certain advertisers. Can you craft an argument that this is a transformative use? *See Infinity Broadcast Corp. v. Kirkwood*, 150 F.3d 104 (2d Cir. 1998).

- "Appropriation art" attempts to recontextualize famous (or not-so-famous) images by juxtaposing them with new material. Should this be considered a transformative use? *Compare Rogers v. Koons*, 960 F.2d 301 (2d Cir. 1992) (no), *with Blanch v. Koons*, 467 F.3d 244 (2d Cir. 2006) (yes). *See also* Jaszi, *Is There a Postmodern Copyright?*, 12 Tul. J. Tech. & Intell. Prop. 105 (2009); Heymann, *Everything Is Transformative: Fair Use and Reader Response*, 31 Colum. J.L. & Arts 445 (2008); Landes, *Copyright, Borrowed Images and Appropriation Art: An Economic Approach*, 9 Geo. Mason L. Rev. 1, 10 (2000).

  [handwritten margin note: Blanch different purpose than the pr of magazine]

- Suppose a client wishes to create a visual time line of 20th-Century American clothing design by compiling a series of copyrighted fashion photographs, without textual commentary? Or suppose the client's project involves juxtaposing fashion photographs from various eras with news photographs illustrating the social/political/economic conditions in which those fashion trends arose, again with any "commentary" being implied rather than expressed? In each case, the client explains that it would cost too much, or take too much time, to license the use of the photographs. Would you advise the client to desist or proceed? What does *Bill Graham Archives* teach? Documentary filmmakers often justify claims of fair use by pointing out that they have provided voice-over narration or lead-ins by "talking heads" to put the unlicensed copyrighted material they quote into context. But how necessary is this practice to the successful invocation of the doctrine?

(6)   These questions matter because what arguably began as an attempt to justify the application of fair use to a range of commercial activities has become the gold standard of fair use analysis in general. How many of the four fair use factors in *Bill Graham Archives* seem to turn, at least in part, on whether the use is "transformative"? If this criterion now constitutes a double, triple, or even quadruple "whammy" in fair use analysis, what, if anything, has been lost from the discussion? For a discussion of the meaning of *Bill Graham Archives* for the future of factor four, see § 10.03[C] below.

(7)   *Transformativeness, § 107(3), and the nexus between purpose and use.* One of the contributions of *Bill Graham Archives* is that it lays to rest, once and for all, a persistent shibboleth of copyright: the oft-repeated adage that it is never fair to copy an entire work. More interesting — and uncertain — is the question of how the quantitative appropriateness of any unlicensed copying should be assessed. In *Campbell*, you were introduced to the "conjure up" standard for parody fair use, which is linked to an inquiry into whether the user took "no more than was necessary" from the copyrighted work. But "necessary" for what? And whatever may be true of parody, is this a workable general standard? The *Bill Graham*

Archives opinion suggests that the question may be whether the actual use was appropriately "tailored to further its transformative purpose." And it appears to bless at least some uses that "require incorporation of original source material for optimum treatment of their subjects." Suppose your filmmaker client claims that while a 2-second clip from a music video would do an adequate job of illustrating how hip-hop music objectifies women, a 7-second one would really drive the point home. What advice would you give?

In this connection, consider *Warner Bros. Entertainment, Inc. v. RDR Books*, 575 F. Supp. 2d 513 (S.D.N.Y. 2008), involving *The Lexicon*, an unauthorized encyclopedia-style guide to the Harry Potter books series. The court held that the purpose of creating an A-to-Z guide was transformative and that many of the allegedly infringing quotations were appropriate in kind and quantity. But while noting that "to fulfill its purpose as a reference guide to the Harry Potter works, it is reasonably necessary for *The Lexicon* to make considerable use of the original works," the opinion concluded that some verbatim copying and close paraphrasing went too far. Also, while concluding that the guide would not harm sales of the seven Harry Potter novels, the court found possible harm to sales of two companion works — *Fantastic Beasts And Where To Find Them* and *Quidditch Through The Ages* — which were themselves published in the form of reference works. Guided by the District Court's opinion, RDR Books decided to go forward with publication of a revised version of *The Lexicon*.

(8) *A backlash against transformative use?* In *Ty, Inc. v. Publications Int'l, Ltd.*, 292 F.3d 512 (7th Cir. 2002), the Seventh Circuit addressed the issue of whether the copyrights in Ty's popular "Beanie Babies" line of beanbag-like stuffed animals were infringed by two books published by the defendant. Writing for the court, Judge Posner characteristically recast the problem in economic terms, drawing a distinction between *complementary uses* of a work, such as a book review or parody, and *substitutional uses* that usurp the market for the copyrighted work or licensed derivatives. 292 F.3d at 517-18.

Applying this analysis, the court suggested that *For the Love of Beanie Babies*, a children's book featuring posed photographs of various Beanie Babies, was probably not a fair use, because each photograph was nothing more than a derivative work based on Ty's works. But the *Beanie Babies Collector's Guide*, which featured a photograph of each Beanie Baby along with its release date, its retired date, its estimated value, and other information relevant to a collector, was analyzed differently, as a valuable instance of "complementary" use.

"Kitty Korner" (from For the Love of Beanie Babies)

What is the relationship of this analysis to "transformative use"? Judge Posner remarks that "the distinction between complementary and substitutional copying [is] sometimes — though as it seems to us, confusingly — said to be between 'transformative' and 'superseding' copies." *Id.* at 518. Do you agree that these concepts are equivalent? Does Judge Posner's preferred terminology advance the discussion? Would you characterize *Illustrated Trip* as complementary or substitutional? Why?

(9)   In addition to critiquing the vocabulary of "transformative use," Judge Posner's opinion is generally dismissive of four-factor fair use analysis:

We have thus far discussed the application of the fair-use doctrine in terms of the purpose of the doctrine rather than its statutory definition, which though extensive is not illuminating. . . . Factors (1) and (2) are empty, except that (1) suggests a preference for noncommercial educational uses. . . . Factor (3) is inapplicable to Beanie Babies, each one of which is copyrighted separately . . . (no one, we imagine, wants a photograph of part of a Beanie Baby). Factor (4) at least glances at the distinction we noted earlier between substitute and complementary copying, since the latter does not impair the potential market or value of the copyrighted work except insofar as it criticizes the work, which is the opposite of taking a free ride on its value.

The important point is simply that . . . the four factors are a checklist of things to be considered rather than a formula for decision; and likewise the list of statutory purposes. . . . Because the factors and purposes are not exhaustive, Ty can get nowhere in defending the judgment by arguing that some or even all of them lean against the defense of fair use. The question is whether . . . the use of the photos is a fair use because it is the only way to prepare a collectors' guide.

292 F.3d at 522.

Is it proper for a judge, even one as distinguished as Judge Posner, essentially to dismiss the statutory text and the efforts of courts over the years to invest the factors with content, however imperfect those efforts have been? Or is Judge Posner simply being candid? If the statutory factors (or some of them) are "empty," as Judge Posner suggests, what then? Does inquiring whether the challenged use is the "only way" to accomplish a legitimate end threaten a diminution of fair use, denying application of the doctrine where the defendant's taking was convenient, or added real value, but wasn't absolutely necessary?

[C] Actual and Potential Market Effect

Clearly, from 2 Live Crew to *Seinfeld* to Beanie Babies, fair use law has taken a "cultural turn" (of sorts) in recent years. But at the end of the day, the way of the world remains as it always has. Money still talks — at least, sometimes. And so it seems fair to ask: Whither factor four?

Campbell v. Acuff-Rose, as we have seen, pays lip service to *Harper & Row*'s "undoubtedly the most important element" dictum. Operationally, however, disproportionate weighting of the impact of the defendant's use on the plaintiff's market (actual or potential) is nowhere to be found in the *Campbell* analysis. Nonetheless, not all lower courts have abandoned the habit of according factor four primacy of place in the § 107 pecking order. As Barton Beebe has pointed out, market effect continues to play an important role in judicial decision-making:

> [Among post-*Campbell*] opinions, 26.5% [have] continued explicitly to state that factor four was the most important factor. . . .

> The conventional wisdom is that regardless of what the Supreme Court has said, the fourth factor analysis remains the most influential on the outcome of the overall test. The data support a different account, however, one which suggests that we have failed to appreciate the true role of the fourth factor analysis in the section 107 test as applied. The fourth factor essentially constitutes a metafactor under which courts integrate their analyses of the other three factors and, in doing so, arrive at the outcome not simply of the fourth factor, but of the overall test.

See An Empirical Study of U.S. Copyright Fair Use Opinions, 1978-2005, 156 U. PA. L. REV. 549, 617 (2007).

Many courts, however, appear to have gotten the message that factor four is no longer to be treated as "the fairest of them all" (think Snow White) in the kingdom of fair use. Perhaps the leading post-*Campbell* decision on the subject is *American Geophysical Union v. Texaco, Inc.*, 60 F.3d 913 (2d Cir. 1995). There, the majority of a Second Circuit panel, in an opinion by Judge Newman affirming a decision by Judge Leval (before the latter's ascension to the Court of Appeals), pointedly observed:

Prior to *Campbell*, the Supreme Court had characterized the fourth factor as "the single most important element of fair use" [citing *Harper & Row*]. . . . However, *Campbell*'s discussion of the fourth factor conspicuously omits this phrasing. Apparently abandoning the idea that any factor enjoys primacy, *Campbell* instructs that "[a]ll [four factors] are to be explored, and the results weighed together, in light of the purposes of copyright."

Id. at 926.

Two considerations helped to produce the decision in *Texaco*. One was that that the defendant's practice of photocopying articles from scientific journals to which its library subscribed, for the use of scientist-employees (between 400 and 500 in number) was deemed not to be meaningfully transformative: "Texaco's photocopying merely transforms the material object embodying the intangible article that is the copyrighted original work," but the uses to which the copied articles were put were like those that could be made of the original published versions. One particular area of disagreement between the judges was whether to treat all research alike. Judge Jacob, in dissent, would not have distinguished applied research by an oil company chemist from theoretical research done by a university professor.

The other consideration apparently critical to the *Texaco* majority's decision was the existence of an established system for licensing the rights to make such photocopies: "Though the publishers still have not established a conventional market for the direct sale and distribution of individual articles, they have created, primarily through the Copyright Clearance Center, a workable market for institutional users to obtain licenses for the right to produce their own copies of individual articles via photocopying." The fourth factor may no longer rule, but clearly it is relevant when the first factor also favors the plaintiff!

If nothing else, *Texaco* (like *Campbell*) illustrates that sensitive factor four analysis needs to take into account the possibility that one work may have value in both primary and secondary markets. But there is another twist in § 107's approach to the market. The version of what was to become § 107(4) in the original 1963 Preliminary Draft referred to "the effect of the use upon the potential value of the copyrighted work," which by 1964 had been recast as "the effect of the use upon the potential market for or value of the copyrighted work" — the final formulation. So the emphasis on *potential* as distinct from *actual* market value always has been part of the statutory design. That emphasis creates an essentially insoluble analytic conundrum: Just how unlikely or attenuated must a possible source of revenue from the exploitation of a work be before it ceases to qualify as a "potential market"?

In the end, it seems likely that *Campbell* and *Harper & Row* may mean much the same thing: What determines fair use is a delicate balancing of the impact of the defendant's use on the plaintiff's legitimate market expectations against the contribution that the defendant has made to the progress of science and art by his borrowing.

NOTES AND QUESTIONS

(1) *Transformativeness in* Texaco. What do you think of Judge Jacobs's view (in dissent) that Texaco should be insulated from liability because its scientists' use of photocopies "is integral to transformative and productive ends"? The majority's response, basically, is that the argument proves too much. Judge Newman says that "[i]t would be equally extravagant for a newspaper to contend that because its business is 'news reporting' it may line the shelves of its reporters with photocopies of books on journalism or that schools engaged in 'teaching' may supply [their] faculty members with personal photocopies of books on educational techniques or substantive fields."

So is there some more specific use you can imagine a scientist making of a photocopy from a professional journal (other than tucking it into a file for reference) that might fare better when judged by the vague but increasingly important standard of transformative use? What if the scientist had written notes in the margin? What if she had taken a photocopy into the lab (which is a lot easier and safer than hefting a bound journal volume) to verify or repeat the experiment described in an article?

(2) Texaco *and lost revenue.* Suppose that the Copyright Clearance Center hadn't been a real entity, but merely a hypothetical project under discussion by journal (and other) publishers? Would or should that have affected the fair use analysis in *Texaco*? The existence of well-established markets for lyric reprint licenses and synchronization licenses (*see* § 7.05[A] above) has led two Courts of Appeals to conclude that making and selling karaoke products that display lyrics in conjunction with sound recordings of musical works is not a fair use. *See Leadsinger, Inc. v. BMG Music Publishing*, 512 F.3d 522 (9th Cir. 2008); *Zomba Enterprises, Inc. v. Panorama Records, Inc.*, 491 F.3d 574 (6th Cir. 2007). Note also that the music industry has developed a complex system of licenses for sample clearance, as detailed in K. McLeod & P. DiCola, CREATIVE LICENSE: THE LAW AND CULTURE OF DIGITAL SAMPLING (2011).

(3) *Sec. 107(4) beyond* Texaco. Remember that the plaintiff in *Bill Graham Archives* was very much in the licensing business. Does that decision, with its pronouncement that "copyright owners may not prevent the exploitation of transformative markets" by others, change the rules of the game? Could the editor of a future "biography" of another band in the same format simply forego licensing altogether? Conversely, are there cases in which a copyright owner could claim the right to profit by licensing uses in "transformative markets," and (if so) what would they be? Remember that the court in *Bill Graham Archives* concluded that the copyright images were being used for their "historical" rather than their "creative" value, and that the use of those images on internal pages of the volume was "incidental" to the commercial value of the book. What if they had been used on the cover instead?

See also Warren Publ'g Co. v. Spurlock, 645 F. Supp. 2d 402 (E.D. Pa. 2009), in which the defendant employed copyrighted art work from the plaintiff's magazines in a book entitled *Famous Monster Movie Art of Basil Gogos*. The court found that the challenged use was transformative, such that factor one "weigh[ed] heavily" in favor of fair use, but went on to analyze factor four anyway, concluding that while it "slightly favor[ed]" the plaintiff, the defendant had the best of the four factors overall. Note that, as in *Bill Graham Archives*, the defendant's book in *Spurlock* was produced in cooperation with the artist.

(4) What should be the result when there is only a market of one? In *Gaylord v. United States*, 85 Fed. Cl. 59 (2008), *rev'd*, 595 F.3d 1364 (Fed. Cir. 2010), the sculptor of the Korean War Veterans Memorial sued the U.S. Postal Service for using a photograph of his sculpture on a postage stamp. The trial court found that the use would have little effect on the market for the work, because Gaylord "has made only limited attempts to commercialize his copyright." In so holding, did the court ignore a potential market for licensing an image of the sculpture for the stamp itself? Ultimately, the Federal Circuit held that the use was not fair, *despite* affirming the finding that there was no adverse effect on the potential market.

(5) *Cumulation of harm.* The parties in *Texaco* agreed to focus, for analytic convenience, on the activities of one scientist out of all those employed by the company. The court seems justified, then, in assuming that whatever market harm this individual's activities might generate would, in practice, be multiplied several hundred-fold. Even with that multiplier, however, the resulting estimate (in dollar terms) wouldn't necessarily have been all that impressive. Perhaps this is one reason why Judge Jacobs remained unconvinced that a showing of more than *de minimis* harm had been made. But what about all the other companies (not parties to the action) that were engaging in similar photocopying practices, and presumably would continue to do so unless warned off by the courts? Should information (or speculation) along these lines be relevant to the § 107(4) determination?

(6) *Burden of proof.* Fair use is an affirmative defense, and normally the burden associated with such defenses is on the party asserting them. It is pretty straightforward to say that this rule applies to fair use, and that it makes sense as far as factors one through three of § 107 are concerned. But what about factor four? Is it realistic to ask the defendant to make a showing of "no harm" when the information relating to the plaintiff's business model and sales is within that party's exclusive control? Will discovery under the Federal Rules of Civil Procedure suffice to make up the difference? Should the defendant be permitted to make a threshold showing to shift the burden back to the plaintiff? Remember that, in *Campbell*, the Supreme Court remanded the case so that the "hole" in the record on the § 107(4) issue could be "plugged." How could the defendant do this in actual practice?

On the flip side, some courts have shown a remarkable willingness to grant summary judgment to the defendants on the issue of fair use, based solely on comparing the two works. Indeed, the Seventh Circuit has suggested that fair use might properly be decided on a motion for judgment *on the pleadings*, if the two works are incorporated by reference. *See Brownmark Films, LLC v. Comedy Partners*, 682 F.3d 687 (7th Cir. 2012).

(7) *Varieties of economic harm.* For § 107(4) purposes, not just any economic harm will do. *Campbell* teaches, for example, that the loss of sales stemming from a devastating book review doesn't make the quotations from the work included by the reviewer any less "fair." Generally speaking, courts have hewed to the principle that only economic losses resulting from the supplanting of demand for the work will count where factor four is concerned.

But what, then, are we to make of the statutory reference to harm to the "potential market for *or value of*" the plaintiff's work? Do the italicized words have any independent significance? Do they open up new vistas in economic fair use analysis, allowing plaintiffs to show that the value of their intellectual property has been harmed other than by a substitution effect? A fair argument can be made that the language is a vestigial remnant from the original 1963 Preliminary Draft of the copyright revision legislation, which used "value" (rather than "market") to express the idea of the copyright owner's interest that is threatened by substitutional uses. But statutory provisions have a way of taking on their own life. In *Clean Flicks of Colorado, LLC v. Soderbergh*, 433 F. Supp. 2d 1236 (D. Colo. 2006), the declaratory judgment plaintiff claimed that, even though it was making and distributing edited copies of motion pictures for "family viewing," there was no harm to the copyright owner's market because it had bought an authorized copy for each copy it made. The District Court said that this argument had "superficial appeal, but [that] it ignores the intrinsic value of the right to control the content of the copyrighted work." Is this a form of moral rights for corporate copyright owners, rather than for individual artists? Is this the sort of "value" the drafters of § 107 had in mind? We will consider this question again in connection with *Kelly v. Arriba Soft* in § 10.04.

(8) *Photocopying — a perennial challenge.* As we note below, Congress was very much aware of the photocopying issue when it was debating what became the Copyright Act of 1976. Even today, when a range of technological developments challenge fair use, the courts (and, as we will see shortly, others as well) continue to grapple with the "great granddaddy" of the new reproductive technologies. So some background may be in order.

[D] Photocopying, Guidelines, and "Personal Reproduction"

[1] Photocopying

In the 1960s and 1970s, photocopying placed in the hands of ordinary people, for the first time, the capacity to multiply wholesale the physical representations of works of their choice. Shortly before passage of the 1976 Act, the judiciary confronted photocopying head-on in *Williams & Wilkins Co. v. United States*, 487 F.2d 1345 (Ct. Cl. 1973). The case involved the National Institutes of Health ("NIH") and the National Library of Medicine ("NLM"). Their practice was to photocopy and distribute articles to those requesting them, but generally to limit requests to no more than one article per journal, no more than 50 pages, and no more than a single copy of an article per request.

The Court of Claims held that the photocopying of an entire article from a specialized, low-circulation medical journal, at least when carried out by the NIH and the NLM, constituted fair use. The decision was affirmed by an equally divided Supreme Court, 420 U.S. 376 (1975), without the doctrinal clarification that would have flowed from a decision on the merits. Not surprisingly, the exact status of new technology in the fair use context has remained a subject of vigorous debate ever since.

Photocopying in education was the next focus of concern — with little direct precedent to turn to for guidance. There is remarkably little case law on fair use in and around schools, colleges and universities, perhaps because the invulnerability of many educational activities to copyright challenge has been generally assumed. In any event, the publishing industry proceeded cautiously in challenging institutional photocopying practices. In fact, no case has ever actually been brought to trial challenging the users with the strongest potential fair use defenses: nonprofit educational institutions that photocopy material in-house for classroom use and make it available to students at no extra charge or at cost.

"It's the new Copyright Clearance Center. We used to call it a library."
Courtesy of Bion Smalley

In the early 1980s, however, nine publishers did sue New York University and some of its faculty, alleging illegal use of copies in the school's classes. That case, *Addison-Wesley Publishing v. New York University*, 1983 Copr. L. Dec. (CCH) ¶ 25,554 (S.D.N.Y. 1983), was settled, with the university adopting a new school-wide photocopying policy that required prior approval of all photocopying that exceeded the very restrictive brevity, spontaneity and cumulative effect criteria of the so-called "Classroom Guidelines" for educational photocopying that were part of the legislative history of the 1976 Copyright Act (more on this below). Although the settlement obviously had no precedential value, it received extensive publicity — and was "voluntarily" adopted by some other institutions. *See* Brandfonbrener, *Fair Use and University Photocopying*, 19 Mich. J.L. Reform 669 (1986).

Thereafter, the publishing industry concentrated on suits targeting for-profit copy shops that reproduced "course packs" or "anthologies" (sets of readings selected by teachers from a range of published sources) for use by schools. In the copy shop lawsuits, fair use defenses have not prospered, thanks largely to the overtly commercial nature of the defendants' activities. *See Princeton University*

Press v. Michigan Document Services, Inc., 99 F.3d 1381 (6th Cir. 1996) (*en banc*); *Blackwell Publishing, Inc. v. Excel Research Group, LLC*, 661 F. Supp. 2d 786 (E.D. Mich. 2009); *Basic Books, Inc. v. Kinko's Graphics Corp.*, 758 F. Supp. 1522 (S.D.N.Y. 1991).

On the "front lines" of education, controversies regarding fair use have expanded beyond photocopying to include electronic reproduction and distribution. For example, Cambridge University Press and other publishers filed an infringement suit against Georgia State University for "pervasive, flagrant, and ongoing unauthorized distribution of copyrighted materials" by means of its "electronic course reserves service, its . . . electronic course management system, and its departmental web pages and hyperlinked online syllabi available on websites and computer servers controlled by GSU." The court held largely in favor of Georgia State. *See Cambridge University Press v. Becker*, 863 F. Supp. 2d 1190 (N.D. Ga. 2012).

As you read what follows, ask yourself whether the flexible, situation-specific doctrine of fair use can survive when it is pressed from one direction by increasingly aggressive copyright owners and from the other by academic institutions with an understandable craving for certainty!

[2]   The Role of Guidelines

Fair Use Guidelines and the 1976 Copyright Act

The folklore of copyright is replete with purported "rules of thumb" for gauging the fairness of various kinds of unauthorized uses. Most of us have heard, for example, that it is permissible to take so many notes or bars from a piece of copyrighted music, or so many words from a copyrighted text. The prevalence of these quantitative "bright-line" tests reflects the frustratingly unpredictable, and even seemingly *ad hoc*, quality of the process of fair use analysis, when viewed from the standpoint of would-be users. Unfortunately, however, such easy-to-apply criteria do not reflect the reality of copyright doctrine, as a general matter. But (as always with generalizations) there is one partial exception.

One of the more curious innovations of the 1976 Copyright Act is one which left no trace in the text of Title 17 itself. Rather, it is contained in the legislative history relating to § 107. There, among other things, one finds two sets of so-called "fair use guidelines," negotiated (under the aegis of Congress and the Copyright Office) among various representatives of proprietor and user groups, and then ambiguously enshrined in legislative history, where they were endorsed as "a reasonable interpretation of the minimum standards of fair use." H.R. Rep. No. 94-1476, at 72 (1976). The presence of the Guidelines in the House Report reflects a concern by various user groups — especially schools and colleges — that § 107 offered too little predictability (and thus, too little security) with respect to educational uses of copyrighted materials. Even the express enumeration of educational uses in the text of § 107 itself — as "teaching (including multiple copies for classroom use), scholarship, or research" — could not assuage uneasiness about how the inherently vague four-factor test would be applied to such uses.

The stakeholder negotiations ultimately produced two sets of "guidelines" (both reproduced in the Supplement to this casebook): the "Agreement on Guidelines for

Classroom Copying in Not-For-Profit Educational Institutions," relating to teacher photocopying, and a less well-known set of "Guidelines for Educational Uses of Music." Most, but not all, of the groups that had participated in the negotiations ultimately subscribed to the guidelines. The Association of American Law Schools and the American Association of University Professors, for example, were conspicuously absent from the list of signatories to the Classroom Guidelines, stating that they found the provisions relating to classroom photocopying "too restrictive with respect to classroom situations at the university and graduate level."

Subsequently, the Classroom Guidelines became the focus of considerable controversy, both as to their proper interpretation, and as to their very utility. In particular, proprietors and user groups have disagreed about whether the Guidelines should be viewed merely as defining a set of practices which, among others, constitute fair use, or whether, on the other hand, uses which fall beyond their scope should be viewed as at least presumptively unfair.

At least visibly, the Guidelines have had only limited impact on judicial decision making. Mentioned in only a handful of decisions, they have been treated with considerable respect. For example, in *Marcus v. Rowley*, 695 F.2d 1171 (9th Cir. 1993), the court applied the § 107 factors and, while declining to accept the Classroom Guidelines as "law," found the defendant's behavior wanting on that alternative basis as well. And in the *Michigan Document Services* case, the Sixth Circuit described the Classroom Guidelines as "evok[ing] a general idea, at least, of the type of educational copying Congress had in mind," and determined that the fact that the defendant's copying "[wa]s light years away from the safe harbor of the guidelines weigh[ed] against a finding of fair use." 99 F.3d at 1390. In *Basic Books v. Kinko's*, however, although the court described the Classroom Guidelines as "compelling," it refused to treat them as an outer limit on permissible educational practice in this area. Instead, it interpreted the legislative history to mean that the highly restricted activities explicitly authorized by the Guidelines were merely a "safe harbor" (that is, activities that presumptively qualified as fair use). In fact, this determination did the defendant little good, because the overtly commercial nature of its business militated strongly against a fair use finding.

Perhaps more importantly, the Classroom Guidelines have had a profound impact on the actual practices of educational establishments, many of which have adopted internal "fair use policies" which employ the quantitative criteria of the Guidelines to define the extent of institutionally permissible copying — following the model of the 1983 *Addison-Wesley* NYU settlement.[3]

The CONFU Process

Despite the mixed reception given the Classroom Guidelines incorporated into the legislative history of the 1976 Act, September 1994 saw the launch of the so-called Conference on Fair Use (or "CONFU"), a new effort to devise agreements

---

[3] For a discussion of this tendency, see generally Kenneth Crews, *Copyright, Fair Use, and the Challenge for Universities: Promoting the Progress of Higher Education* (1993). Several major universities have articulated new internal fair use policies which do not depend so closely on the Classroom Guidelines, and which reject those guidelines as a source of outer limits on fair use. *See* Crews, *The Law of Fair Use and the Illusion of Fair Use Guidelines*, 62 Ohio St. L. J.601 (2001).

along similar lines dealing with emerging issues concerning the scope of "fair use" in digitized materials. "Facilitated" by the U.S. Patent and Trademark Office, this shifting group of copyright industry companies and trade associations, on the one hand, and representatives of educational, library and other not-for-profit cultural organizations, on the other, labored for two and a half years over such topics as distance learning, electronic reserves, and the educational use of digital images.[4]

Some of the issues confronting CONFU proved so difficult and contentious that no meaningful progress toward the formulation of guidelines took place. As to other issues, even the draft guidelines which finally did emerge from the CONFU process proved controversial. Many feared that whatever certainty these guidelines might provide would come at too high a price, and the reception accorded them was extremely mixed.

Although its real work was effectively completed in May 1997, CONFU met for a final time in May 1998 to prepare its Final Report. That report reflects the fact that the working groups on guidelines for Digital Images and Distance Education had ceased to meet without reaching consensus; the guidelines on Electronic Multimedia and Electronic Reserve Systems ultimately had not commanded consensus support within CONFU itself, although some institutions might nevertheless choose to adopt them.[5] Although fair use is relied upon heavily in the digital age, the failure of the CONFU process demonstrated that attempts to draft widely supported guidelines often will be complicated by the competing interests of the copyright owner and user communities.

[3] Modern Technology and "Personal Reproduction"

Texaco had to do with photocopying in the institutional setting of the for-profit company. The discussions of guidelines above related to the use of photocopiers (and other, newer technologies) to multiply copies for the use of students in nonprofit schools and universities. Copying by individuals, for their own purposes, may be another matter. As Judge Newman put it, early in the *Texaco* opinion, 60 F.3d at 916:

> We do not deal with the question of copying by an individual, for personal use in research or otherwise (not for resale), recognizing that under the fair use doctrine or the *de minimis* doctrine, such a practice by an individual might well not constitute an infringement. In other words, our opinion does not decide the case that would arise if Chickering were a professor or an independent scientist engaged in copying and creating files for independent research, as opposed to being employed by an institution in the pursuit of his research on the institution's behalf.

---

[4] Detailed information about the process can be found in *The Conference on Fair Use: Report to the Commissioner on the Conclusion of the First Phase of the Conference on Fair Use* (Sept. 1997) ("*First Phase Report*"), *www.uspto.gov/web/offices/dcom/olia/confu/conclu1.html*.

[5] *See* Bruce A. Lehman, *The Conference on Fair Use: Final Report to the Commissioner on the Conclusion of the Conference on Fair Use* (Nov. 1998), *www.uspto.gov/web/offices/dcom/olia/confu/ confurep.pdf*.

There is a reason for this. Personal uses of copyrighted materials, even those that didn't qualify as *de minimis*, often have been presumed to be "fair." For example, when sound recordings were first added to the Copyright Act in 1972, Congress recognized that home tape recording of recorded performances was a "common and unrestrained" practice, and it specifically expressed an intent not to limit such recording "where the home recording is for private use and with no purpose of reproducing or otherwise capitalizing commercially on it." H.R. Rep. No. 92-487, reprinted in U.S.C.C.A.N. 1566, 1572. Similarly, in the famous "Betamax" case, *Sony Corp. of America v. Universal City Studios, Inc.*, 464 U.S. 417 (1984), much of which we read back in § 9.02, the motion picture studios' secondary liability claims against the makers and sellers of VCRs collapsed because the primary conduct of the equipment's users was found to be, at least in significant part, noninfringing. The various noninfringing uses of the VCR adduced by the defendants included (for example) authorized home taping of children's television programming: no less a figure than the late Fred Rogers had appeared at trial to testify that viewers were welcome to record episodes of his show, *Mr. Rogers' Neighborhood.* But by far the most significant use of the VCR was unauthorized home taping for "time-shifting" purposes, which the defendants claimed was a fair use. Considering this argument, the Supreme Court majority first embraced the District Court's finding that "[n]o likelihood of harm was shown at trial, and plaintiffs admitted that there had been no actual harm to date," 480 F. Supp. 429, 468-69, and then it added some observations of its own:

> The District Court's conclusions are buttressed by the fact that to the extent time-shifting expands public access to freely broadcast television programs, it yields societal benefits. . . .
>
> Congress has plainly instructed us that fair use analysis calls for a sensitive balancing of interests. The distinction between "productive" and "unproductive" uses may be helpful in calibrating the balance, but it cannot be wholly determinative. Although copying to promote a scholarly endeavor certainly has a stronger claim to fair use than copying to avoid interrupting a poker game, the question is not simply two-dimensional. For one thing, it is not true that all copyrights are fungible. Some copyrights govern material with broad potential secondary markets. Such material may well have a broader claim to protection because of the greater potential for commercial harm. Copying a news broadcast may have a stronger claim to fair use than copying a motion picture. And, of course, not all uses are fungible. Copying for commercial gain has a much weaker claim to fair use than copying for personal enrichment. But the notion of social "productivity" cannot be a complete answer to this analysis. A teacher who copies to prepare lecture notes is clearly productive. But so is a teacher who copies for the sake of broadening his personal understanding of his specialty. Or a legislator who copies for the sake of broadening her understanding of what her constituents are watching; or a constituent who copies a news program to help make a decision on how to vote.

464 U.S. at 454-55. In other words (or so many commentators have suggested), "personal uses" of copyrighted materials deserve special solicitude in judicial "fair use" analysis.

That understanding began to unravel in 1992, when the Audio Home Recording Act ("AHRA")was enacted (see § 9.02[B]). In the AHRA, Congress included an express exemption in § 1008 for noncommercial use by a consumer of a digital audio recording device or medium (or an analog recording device or medium) for making digital or analog musical recordings — but only in exchange for imposing a levy on digital audio recording devices and media for the benefit of copyright owners. This compromise suggested to some that "personal uses" were not themselves a beneficial end to be encouraged, but were merely an unjustified exception for which copyright owners deserved to be compensated. *But see Recording Industry Assn. of America v. Diamond Multimedia Systems, Inc.*, 180 F.3d 1072, 1079 (9th Cir. 1999) (indicating that "space-shifting" digital music files from a computer to a portable MP3 player was a "paradigmatic noncommercial personal use" that was "entirely consistent with the purposes of" the AHRA).

The debate concerning personal copies was reignited in 1998, when Napster introduced software that enabled peer-to-peer file sharing of music files in the MP3 digital format. Ultimately, as we know from *Metro-Goldwyn-Mayer Studios, Inc. v. Grokster, Ltd.*, 545 U.S. 913 (2005) (discussed in § 9.03 above), the U.S. Supreme Court assumed (and the defendants conceded) that downloading a copyrighted sound recording for personal use was an infringement and was not a fair use. Despite some academic criticism, courts that have analyzed the issue have unanimously agreed. *See Arista Records LLC v. Doe 3*, 604 F.3d 110 (2d Cir. 2010); *BMG Music v. Gonzalez*, 430 F.3d 888 (7th Cir. 2005); *Sony BMG Music Entm't v. Tenenbaum*, 672 F. Supp. 2d 217 (D. Mass. 2009). *But see* Lunney, *Brief of Amici Curiae Law Professors in Support of Respondents in Metro-Goldwyn-Mayer Studios, Inc. v. Grokster, Ltd.*, 545 U.S. 913 (2005), available on LEXIS at 2004 U.S. Briefs 480 (contending that "[t]he predominant use of P2P file-sharing software . . . appears to be fair"); Schaumann, *Copyright Infringement and Peer-to-Peer Technology*, 28 Wm. Mitchell L. Rev. 1001, 1028-39 (2002) (concluding that making music files available to others is an unlawful distribution, but that downloading music files for personal use is either a fair use or immunized by § 1008).

Given these developments, what has become of the notion that "personal uses" are presumptively fair? Was that a mistaken understanding all along? Have the courts simply changed direction? Or, as Rebecca Tushnet asserted in *Copy This Essay: How Fair Use Doctrine Harms Free Speech and How Copying Serves It*, 114 Yale L.J. 535 (2004), is there something about the new emphasis on "transformative" fair uses that may obscure the social value of copying for personal use? Finally, is there something about new technology in general, and the partial erasure of the public/private distinction by digital networks in particular, that makes the general principle inapplicable in some situations? If the Supreme Court had expressly analyzed the fair use issue in *Grokster*, might that have affected the outcome on the question of Grokster's secondary liability?

Revisiting the *Betamax* case itself, we see that there are now real questions about how far the principles announced in *Sony* should be extended beyond the factual context of that decision. In 2001, 28 entertainment industry companies sued ReplayTV, seeking to enjoin a digital video recorder that allowed consumers to delete commercials from recorded programs automatically and to send recorded programs to other ReplayTV owners over the Internet. The District Court initially allowed several individual ReplayTV users, represented by the Electronic Frontier Foundation, to assert a claim for a declaratory judgment of noninfringement. *Newmark v. Turner Broadcasting Network*, 226 F. Supp. 2d 1215 (C.D. Cal. 2002). In the end, however, ReplayTV agreed to remove the offending features, and the court dismissed the individuals' suit as moot. *Paramount Pictures Corp. v. ReplayTV*, 298 F. Supp. 2d 921 (C.D. Cal. 2004).

In 2008, the Second Circuit decided *Cartoon Network LP v. CSC Holdings, Inc.*, *Cartoon Network LP v. CSC Holdings, Inc. (Cablevision)*, 536 F.3d 121 (2d Cir. 2008) (excerpted in § 7.02 above), addressing a cable system's operation of a "remote-storage digital video recorder" ("RS-DVR") on its own servers on behalf of its subscribers (who controlled what programs would be recorded for their use). In absolving the DVR operators of liability for direct infringement, the court answered a number of interesting questions in the negative, including (1) whether buffer copies are infringing reproductions; (2) whether the company has legal responsibility for "playback" copies made on its own servers; and (3) whether the transmission of those copies to users at a time of their choosing constituted "public performance." The parties agreed to exclude a number of issues, including third-party liability and fair use, from the agenda for decision. In addressing the question of responsibility for the making of the playback copy, the court opined:

> [M]ost copyright disputes . . . turn on whether the conduct in question does, in fact, infringe the plaintiff's copyright. In this case, however, the core of the dispute is over the authorship of the infringing conduct. . . . In the case of a VCR, it seems clear — and we know of no case holding otherwise — that the operator of the VCR, the person who actually presses the button to make the recording, supplies the necessary element of volition, not the person who manufactures, maintains, or, if distinct from the operator, owns the machine. We do not believe that an RS-DVR customer is sufficiently distinguishable from a VCR user to impose liability as a direct infringer on a different party for copies that are made automatically upon that customer's command.

Was the Second Circuit here simply following the rationale of the Supreme Court's 1984 *Sony* decision, with its emphasis on safeguarding private choices about information consumption? You may wish to read the opinion and consider whether it suggests any shift away from the *Sony* rule that private copying for time-shifting purposes is fair.

For now, an uneasy stalemate prevails here in the United States. Most countries of the world, however, have enacted a "personal use" exemption of some kind, often in exchange for a levy on recording equipment and blank media. Although the U.S.'s lone experiment with such a compromise (the AHRA) now is considered by many to have been a failure, the door remains open for the United States to adopt a more general compromise along those lines in the future. For a visionary treatment of a proposed "win-win" solution based on private ordering, see W. Fisher, III, PROMISES TO KEEP. TECHNOLOGY, LAW, AND THE FUTURE OF ENTERTAINMENT (2004).

§ 10.04   FAIR USE AND TECHNOLOGY

Obviously, we have already embarked on this topic in the preceding series of notes. But there is more to the fair use/technology relationship than the issues raised by consumer uses of copyrighted materials. Fair use is also important — and controversial — among companies that compete to offer high technology products and services.

[A]   Fair Use and Decompilation

As we saw in § 8.03, computer programs contain a great deal of unprotected material that is "filtered out" in assessing substantial similarity, including elements dictated by efficiency, and elements dictated by external factors, such as the need to interoperate with both hardware and software. These elements of a computer program may therefore be copied with impunity. Unlike with most other copyrighted works, however, the unprotected elements of computer programs ordinarily are not visible to inspection. Instead, the unprotected elements of a computer program usually can be copied only through a laborious process of reverse engineering.

Computer programs are written in specialized alphanumeric languages, or "source code." In order to operate a computer, source code must be translated into computer readable form, or "object code." Object code uses only two symbols, 0 and 1, combinations of which represent the alphanumeric characters of the source code. A program written in source code is translated into object code using computer programs called "assemblers" and "compilers." Devices called "disassemblers" and "decompilers" can reverse this process by "reading" the electronic signals for "0" and "1" that are produced while the program is being run, storing the resulting object code in computer memory and translating the object code into something resembling source code. (It is usually not possible to completely reconstruct the original source code from the object code.)

In order to reverse engineer a computer program, a competitor must first transform the machine-readable object code contained in a commercially available program into human-readable code through disassembly or decompilation. Engineers can then study the decompiled code in order to determine how the computer program functions. The functional aspects of the program, including any interface specifications required for interoperability, can then be incorporated into a new computer program. In order to fend off accusations of unlawful copying, the engineers who analyze the existing program often are kept separate from the engineers who are writing the new computer program, so that the only information that passes between them is a written set of functional specifications that is preserved for use in the event of litigation.

The first step of this process, disassembly (or decompilation), entails copying of the entire computer program, including whatever protected expression it may contain. Even though this copying is "intermediate," and the protected expression is not incorporated into the final product, we know from § 7.02 that "intermediate" copying falls within the exclusive right to reproduce the copyrighted work. Owners of copyright in computer software therefore have attempted to use copyright in order to prevent competitors from reverse engineering their programs. Competitors, in turn, have argued that copying for the purpose of reverse engineering is a fair use.

Sega Enterprises, Ltd. v. Accolade, Inc., 977 F.2d 1510 (9th Cir. 1993), the leading case in this area, squarely addressed the issue presented by the process just described. In the process of reverse engineering the Sega Genesis video game console, Accolade decompiled (or disassembled) three video game programs written by Sega. Accolade then studied the decompiled programs and used the information to make its own video games compatible with the Sega console. Sega sued Accolade for copyright infringement. In the first step of its analysis, the *Sega* court held without blinking that Accolade's intermediate copying presented a *prima facie* violation of Sega's reproduction right. The court then turned its attention to the issue of fair use, concluding ultimately that "[because] disassembly is the only means of gaining access to [unprotected ideas and functional concepts embodied in Sega's code], and because Accolade has a legitimate interest in gaining such access (in order to determine how to make its cartridges compatible with the Genesis console)," Accolade's activity constituted "a fair use that is privileged by section 107 of the [Copyright] Act."

Accolade's "Ishido" Game

The court's detailed examination of the § 107 factors is instructive." The opinion began its discussion by noting with respect to factor one that any commercial "exploitation" of the Sega's copyrighted code was merely "indirect or derivative," emphasizing that Accolade's goal (which it achieved) was to write noninfringing interoperable software "based on what it had learned through disassembly" about the Sega system's functional requirements. Still on the first factor, the court observed that there was a clear "public interest" served by permitting such disassembly, namely, "an increase in the number of independently designed video game programs offered for use with the Genesis console." In the court's view (citing *Feist* in support), "It is precisely this growth in creative expression . . . that the Copyright Act was intended to promote."

Sega's analysis of the second factor turned on the "functional" nature of the protected software (and, presumably, of software in general), with the court noting that most functional works — one example given is accounting textbooks (shades of *Baker v. Selden!*) — can be analyzed with the human eye. With machine-readable software, that is not the case, so to treat disassembly as a *per se* unfair use would, in the court's reading of 17 U.S.C. § 102(b), give the copyright owner "a *de facto* monopoly over the functional aspects of his work — aspects that were expressly denied copyright protection by Congress."

Assessing the impact of factor three, the court acknowledged that the plaintiff's entire work had copied, but indicated that "where the ultimate (as opposed to direct) use is as limited as it was here, th[is] factor is of very little weight."

By now, the pattern of the opinion may be clear: a heavy reliance on fair use analysis to address market distortions in the gaming software industry. This emphasis became even more apparent in the *Sega* court's discussion of the fourth factor, which distinguished between market harm from illegitimate competition and losses that legitimate competitors may suffer at one another's hands in a functioning marketplace: "By facilitating the entry of a new competitor, the first lawful one that is not a Sega licensee, Accolade's disassembly of Sega's software undoubtedly 'affected' the market for Genesis-compatible games in an indirect fashion" (although the extent of those losses is unclear). "In any event," said the court, "an attempt to monopolize the market by making it impossible for others to compete runs counter to the statutory purpose of promoting creative expression and cannot constitute a strong equitable basis for resisting the invocation of the fair use doctrine."

With three factors weighing in favor of the defendant, and one tilting only slightly against, the court concluded that

> where disassembly is the *only way* to gain access to the ideas and functional elements embodied in a copyrighted computer program and where there is a *legitimate reason* for seeking such access, disassembly is a fair use of the copyrighted work, *as a matter of law.* Our conclusion does not, of course, insulate Accolade from a claim of copyright infringement with respect to its finished products. Sega has reserved the right to raise such a claim, and it may do so on remand.

977 F.2d at 1520-29 (emphasis added).

You may want to compare and contrast *Sega* with *Atari Games, Inc. v. Nintendo of America Inc.*, 975 F.2d 832 (Fed. Cir. 1992). Both treat the "deprocessing" of lawfully purchased computer chips, in an effort to understand the functioning of a video game manufacturer's security program, as a form of "fair use." There is, however, at least one major difference between the two cases: In *Atari*, the defendant loses anyway. There, the court concluded that while its intermediate copying may have been privileged, the "key" program that Atari finally produced to fit Nintendo's "lock" was "substantially similar" to the plaintiff's own. For this separate and distinct instance of ultimate (rather than intermediate) copying, no defense of "fair use" was available.

Although *Sega* clearly established that reverse engineering of software would qualify as fair use under certain circumstances, the decision left several questions unanswered. *Sega* seemed to indicate that reverse engineering would be considered fair use only to the extent that it was necessary to identify and understand the unprotected elements of a copyrighted software program. The court, however, gave no guidance as to how literally this requirement was to be interpreted. The problem is that reverse engineering frequently is imprecise and may involve false starts and blind alleys. Would such acts be considered strictly "necessary" to the analysis of a competitor's software? In addition, what about the situation where alternative methods of analysis are available? Would the fair use defense apply only to the method which entailed the least amount of copying? And what if, during the reverse engineering process, some or all of the original program is used to test the validity of the information obtained to that point? Would such use still constitute fair use?

One decision declining to extend *Sega* is *DSC Communications Corp. v. Pulse Communications, Inc.*, 170 F.3d 1354 (Fed. Cir. 1999). There, the dispute was over interface cards designed to operate with the plaintiff's telephone switching systems. The court found that using the defendant's competing interface card in conjunction with the plaintiff's system inevitably entailed copying plaintiff's software into the resident memory of the card. In rejecting the defendant's *Sega*-based fair use defense, the court said:

> [Plaintiff]'s evidence showed that [defendant] made copies of [the] software as part of the ordinary operation of [plaintiff's interface] cards, not as part of an effort to determine how the . . . system worked. Rather than being part of an attempt at reverse engineering, the copying appears to have been done after [defendant] had determined how the system worked and merely to demonstrate the interchangeability of [its] cards with those made and sold by [the plaintiff].

Id. at 1363.

In *Sony Computer Entertainment, Inc. v. Connectix Corp.*, 203 F.3d 596 (9th Cir. 2000), however, the Ninth Circuit read *Sega* expansively, permitting extensive intermediate copying in the reverse engineering context even where other, more limited methods existed for gaining access to plaintiff's unprotectible ideas. The court held that once the necessity of the defendant's method was established, the number of times that method was applied was not relevant. Because the defendant in *Connectix* had to make at least one copy of the Sony code to study it, it was permitted to make and use hundreds of copies to make the disassembly process more expedient. In addition, the court held that the new game platform was transformative because the defendant created its own new expression rather than just repackaging the plaintiff's code.

In addition, at least one District Court has applied *Sega* outside the context of reverse engineering to permit automated temporary copying of interior web pages in order to extract the factual information contained in them. *See Ticketmaster Corp. v. Tickets.com, Inc.*, 2003 U.S. Dist. LEXIS 6483 (C.D. Cal. 2003). In *Ticketmaster*, however, the unprotected factual information was visible to the naked eye. Should automated copying always be permissible whenever manual copying would be permitted?

Would you expect to see large numbers of post-*Sega*, post-*Connectix* decisions in which their fair use analysis is invoked by copyright defendants? Why or why not? To date, most of the practical consequences of *Sega* have been invisible from the perspective of reported copyright litigation. Under the authority of *Sega*, commercial software developers presumably have continued, in their day-to-day practice, to use reverse engineering techniques, which were common to the field long before the Ninth Circuit ruling. For a comprehensive overview of the reverse engineering issue (covering the entirety of intellectual property), see Samuelson & Scotchmer, *The Law and Economics of Reverse Engineering*, 111 Yale L. J. 1575 (2002).

Many of the problems dealt with by case law in the U.S. were addressed by the European Union in its May 14, 1991 *Directive on the Legal Protection of Computer Programs*, 91/250/EEC, O.J. (L 22). Article 6 of the *Directive* enumerates the rules governing the right to reverse-engineer computer software for the purpose of interoperability (principally, that the reproduction of the copyrighted work is indispensable to achieve interoperability).

Article 6

1. The authorization of the rightholder shall not be required where reproduction of the code and translation of its form . . . are indispensable to obtain the information necessary to achieve the interoperability of an independently created computer program with other programs, provided that the following conditions are met:

(a) these acts are performed by the licensee or by another person having a right to use a copy of a program, or on their behalf by a person authorized to do so;

(b) the information necessary to achieve interoperability has not previously been readily available to the persons referred to in subparagraph (a); and

(c) these acts are confined to the parts of the original program which are necessary to achieve interoperability. . . .

For your further information, the preamble to the *Directive* defines "interoperability" as "the ability to exchange information and mutually to use the information which has been exchanged"; and the reference to the Berne Convention invokes Article 9(2) thereof, which authorizes countries of the Berne Union "to permit the reproduction of . . . works in certain special cases, provided that such reproduction does not conflict with a normal exploitation of the work and does not unreasonably prejudice the legitimate interests of the author." (We consider this provision hereafter in § 10.05.)

While the EU *Directive* was the combined result of considerable lobbying, of political considerations reflective of the state of software development in Europe, and of civil law traditions, it appears to include a number of considerations that U.S. courts might want to weigh in attempting to distinguish, under fair use analysis, between chiselers and those who seek to promote the progress of science. Would it be better for the United States to continue to address such issues through the fair use decisions of the courts, or should the U.S. adopt legislation addressing the considerations included in the European Union *Directive*?

[B]　Fair Use and the Internet

A new kind of technological challenge to the fair use doctrine is posed by certain capabilities of the Internet. Back in § 7.06 of this casebook, we introduced the facts of *Kelly v. Arriba Soft Corp.*, 336 F.3d 811 (9th Cir. 2003), involving a defendant who trawled the web for photographic images using an automated robotic program and then posted the results on its own website. The images appeared on the site as "thumbnails," but also could be viewed in enlarged form by visitors to the site, by means of inline links back to their originating websites. The Court of Appeals' opinion is excerpted below.

KELLY v. ARRIBA SOFT CORP.
United States Court of Appeals, Ninth Circuit
336 F.3d 811 (2003)

T.G. NELSON, CIRCUIT JUDGE:

This case involves the application of copyright law to the vast world of the internet and internet search engines. The plaintiff, Leslie Kelly, is a professional photographer who has copyrighted many of his images of the American West. Some of these images are located on Kelly's web site or other web sites with which Kelly has a license agreement. The defendant, Arriba Soft Corp.,[1] operates an internet search engine that displays its results in the form of small pictures rather than the more usual form of text. Arriba obtained its database of pictures by copying images from other web sites. By clicking on one of these small pictures, called "thumbnails," the user can then view a large version of that same picture within the context of the Arriba web page.

When Kelly discovered that his photographs were part of Arriba's search engine database, he brought a claim against Arriba for copyright infringement. The District Court found that Kelly had established a prima facie case of copyright infringement based on Arriba's unauthorized reproduction and display of Kelly's works, but that this reproduction and display constituted a non-infringing "fair use" under Section 107 of the Copyright Act. Kelly appeals that decision, and we affirm in part and reverse in part. The creation and use of the thumbnails in the search engine is a fair use. However, the District Court should not have decided whether the display of the larger image is a violation of Kelly's exclusive right to publicly

---

[1] Arriba Soft has changed its name since the start of this litigation. It is now known as "Ditto.com."

display his works. Thus, we remand for further proceedings consistent with this opinion.

Arriba Soft a.k.a. "Ditto.com" Website

I.

The search engine at issue in this case is unconventional in that it displays the results of a user's query as "thumbnail" images. When a user wants to search the internet for information on a certain topic, he or she types a search term into a search engine, which then produces a list of web sites that have information relating to the search term. Normally, the list of results is in text format. The Arriba search engine, however, produces its list of results as small pictures.

To provide this functionality, Arriba developed a computer program that "crawls" the web looking for images to index. This crawler downloads full-sized copies of the images onto Arriba's server. The program then uses these copies to generate smaller, lower-resolution thumbnails of the images. Once the thumbnails are created, the program deletes the full-sized originals from the server. Although a user could copy these thumbnails to his computer or disk, he cannot increase the resolution of the thumbnail; any enlargement would result in a loss of clarity of the image.

The second component of the Arriba program occurs when the user double-clicks on the thumbnail. From January 1999 to June 1999, clicking on the thumbnail produced the "Images Attributes" page. This page used in-line linking to display the original full-sized image, surrounded by text describing the size of the image, a link to the originating web site, the Arriba banner, and Arriba advertising.

In-line linking allows one to import a graphic from a source website and incorporate it in one's own website, creating the appearance that the in-lined graphic is a seamless part of the second web page. The in-line link instructs the user's browser to retrieve the linked-to image from the source website and display it on the user's screen, but does so without leaving the linking document.[3] Thus, the linking party can incorporate the linked image into its own content. As a result, although the image in Arriba's Images Attributes page came directly from the originating web site and was not copied onto Arriba's server, the user would not realize that the image actually resided on another web site.

From July 1999 until sometime after August 2000, the results page contained thumbnails accompanied by two links: "Source" and "Details." The "Details" link produced a screen similar to the Images Attributes page but with a thumbnail rather than the full-sized image. Alternatively, by clicking on the "Source" link or the thumbnail from the results page, the site produced two new windows on top of the Arriba page. The window in the forefront contained solely the full-sized image. This window partially obscured another window, which displayed a reduced-size version of the image's originating web page. Part of the Arriba web page was visible underneath both of these new windows.

In January 1999, Arriba's crawler visited web sites that contained Kelly's photographs. The crawler copied thirty-five of Kelly's images to the Arriba database. Kelly had never given permission to Arriba to copy his images and objected when he found out that Arriba was using them. Arriba deleted the thumbnails of images that came from Kelly's own web sites and placed those sites on a list of sites that it would not crawl in the future. Several months later, Arriba received Kelly's complaint of copyright infringement, which identified other images of his that came from third-party web sites. Arriba subsequently deleted those thumbnails and placed those third-party sites on a list of sites that it would not crawl in the future.

The district court granted summary judgment in favor of Arriba . . . [, finding] that the character and purpose of Arriba's use was significantly transformative and the use did not harm the market for or value of Kelly's works. Kelly now appeals this decision.

II.

. . . The district court's decision in this case involves two distinct actions by Arriba that warrant analysis. The first action consists of the reproduction of Kelly's images to create the thumbnails and the use of those thumbnails in Arriba's search engine. The second action involves the display of Kelly's larger images when the

---

[3] Stacey L. Dogan, *Infringement Once Removed: The Perils of Hyperlinking to Infringing Content*, 87 Iowa L. Rev. 829, 839 n.32 (2002).

user clicks on the thumbnails. We conclude that, as to the first action, the district court correctly found that Arriba's use was fair. However, as to the second action, we conclude that the district court should not have reached the issue because neither party moved for summary judgment as to the full-size images and Arriba's response to Kelly's summary judgment motion did not concede the prima facie case for infringement as to those images.

A.

[The court began by characterizing the "thumbnails" as potential violations of the reproduction right.]

A claim of copyright infringement is subject to certain statutory exceptions, including the fair use exception. . . . The statute sets out four factors to consider in determining whether the use in a particular case is a fair use. . . .

1. *Purpose and character of the use.*

[The court cites *Campbell*'s general treatment of "commercialism" and "transformative use." *See Campbell v. Acuff-Rose Music, Inc.*, 510 U.S. 569, 579 (1994).]

. . . There is no dispute that Arriba operates its web site for commercial purposes and that Kelly's images were part of Arriba's search engine database. As the district court found, while such use of Kelly's images was commercial, it was more incidental and less exploitative in nature than more traditional types of commercial use. Arriba was neither using Kelly's images to directly promote its web site nor trying to profit by selling Kelly's images. Instead, Kelly's images were among thousands of images in Arriba's search engine database. Because the use of Kelly's images was not highly exploitative, the commercial nature of the use only slightly weighs against a finding of fair use.

The second part of the inquiry as to this factor involves the transformative nature of the use. We must determine if Arriba's use of the images merely superseded the object of the originals or instead added a further purpose or different character. We find that Arriba's use of Kelly's images for its thumbnails was transformative.

Although Arriba made exact replications of Kelly's images, the thumbnails were much smaller, lower-resolution images that served an entirely different function than Kelly's original images. Kelly's images are artistic works intended to inform and to engage the viewer in an aesthetic experience. His images are used to portray scenes from the American West in an aesthetic manner. Arriba's use of Kelly's images in the thumbnails is unrelated to any aesthetic purpose. Arriba's search engine functions as a tool to help index and improve access to images on the internet and their related web sites. In fact, users are unlikely to enlarge the thumbnails and use them for artistic purposes because the thumbnails are of much lower resolution than the originals; any enlargement results in a significant loss of clarity of the image, making them inappropriate as display material.

Kelly asserts that because Arriba reproduced his exact images and added nothing to them, Arriba's use cannot be transformative. Courts have been reluctant to find fair use when an original work is merely retransmitted in a different medium. Those cases are inapposite, however, because the resulting use of the copyrighted work in those cases was the same as the original use. For instance, reproducing music CD's into computer MP3 format does not change the fact that both formats are used for entertainment purposes. Likewise, reproducing news footage into a different format does not change the ultimate purpose of informing the public about current affairs. . . .

This case involves more than merely a retransmission of Kelly's images in a different medium. . . . Because Arriba's use is not superseding Kelly's use but, rather, has created a different purpose for the images, Arriba's use is transformative.

Comparing this case to . . . recent cases in the Ninth and First Circuits reemphasizes the functionality distinction. . . .

. . . [I]n *Núñez v. Caribbean International News Corp.*,[24] the First Circuit found that copying a photograph that was intended to be used in a modeling portfolio and using it instead in a news article was a transformative use. By putting a copy of the photograph in the newspaper, the work was transformed into news, creating a new meaning or purpose for the work. The use of Kelly's images in Arriba's search engine is . . . analogous to the situation in *Nunez* because Arriba has created a new purpose for the images and is not simply superseding Kelly's purpose.

. . . The thumbnails do not stifle artistic creativity because they are not used for illustrative or artistic purposes and therefore do not supplant the need for the originals. In addition, they benefit the public by enhancing information gathering techniques on the internet.

. . . [Thus,] this first factor weighs in favor of Arriba due to the public benefit of the search engine and the minimal loss of integrity to Kelly's images.

2. *Nature of the copyrighted work.*

"Works that are creative in nature are closer to the core of intended copyright protection than are more fact-based works."[30] Photographs that are meant to be viewed by the public for informative and aesthetic purposes, such as Kelly's, are generally creative in nature. The fact that a work is published or unpublished also is a critical element of its nature. Published works are more likely to qualify as fair use because the first appearance of the artist's expression has already occurred. Kelly's images appeared on the internet before Arriba used them in its search image. When considering both of these elements, we find that this factor only slightly weighs in favor of Kelly.

---

[24] 235 F.3d 18 (1st Cir. 2000).

[30] *A&M Records*, 239 F.3d at 1016 (citing *Campbell*, 510 U.S. at 586) (internal quotation marks omitted).

3. *Amount and substantiality of portion used.*

"While wholesale copying does not preclude fair use per se, copying an entire work militates against a finding of fair use."[33] However, the extent of permissible copying varies with the purpose and character of the use. If the secondary user only copies as much as is necessary for his or her intended use, then this factor will not weigh against him or her.

This factor will neither weigh for nor against either party because, although Arriba did copy each of Kelly's images as a whole, it was reasonable to do so in light of Arriba's use of the images. It was necessary for Arriba to copy the entire image to allow users to recognize the image and decide whether to pursue more information about the image or the originating web site. If Arriba only copied part of the image, it would be more difficult to identify it, thereby reducing the usefulness of the visual search engine.

4. *Effect of the use upon the potential market for or value of the copyrighted work.*

This last factor requires courts to consider "not only the extent of market harm caused by the particular actions of the alleged infringer, but also 'whether unrestricted and widespread conduct of the sort engaged in by the defendant . . . would result in a substantially adverse impact on the potential market for the original.' "[35] A transformative work is less likely to have an adverse impact on the market of the original than a work that merely supersedes the copyrighted work.

Kelly's images are related to several potential markets. One purpose of the photographs is to attract internet users to his web site, where he sells advertising space as well as books and travel packages. In addition, Kelly could sell or license his photographs to other web sites or to a stock photo database, which then could offer the images to its customers.

Arriba's use of Kelly's images in its thumbnails does not harm the market for Kelly's images or the value of his images. By showing the thumbnails on its results page when users entered terms related to Kelly's images, the search engine would guide users to Kelly's web site rather than away from it. Even if users were more interested in the image itself rather than the information on the web page, they would still have to go to Kelly's site to see the full-sized image. The thumbnails would not be a substitute for the full-sized images because the thumbnails lose their clarity when enlarged. . . .

Arriba's use of Kelly's images also would not harm Kelly's ability to sell or license his full-sized images. Arriba does not sell or license its thumbnails to other parties. Anyone who downloaded the thumbnails would not be successful selling full-sized images enlarged from the thumbnails because of the low-resolution of the thumbnails. . . . Therefore, Arriba's creation and use of the thumbnails does not harm the market for or value of Kelly's images. This factor weighs in favor of Arriba.

---

[33] *Worldwide Church of God v. Philadelphia Church of God*, 227 F.3d 1110, 1118 (9th Cir. 2000) (internal quotation marks omitted).

[35] [*Campbell*, 510 U.S.] at 590 (quoting 3 M. Nimmer & D. Nimmer, *Nimmer on Copyright* § 13.05[A][4] (1993)) (ellipses in original).

Having considered the four fair use factors and found that two weigh in favor of Arriba, one is neutral, and one weighs slightly in favor of Kelly, we conclude that Arriba's use of Kelly's images as thumbnails in its search engine is a fair use.

B.

As mentioned above, the district court granted summary judgment to Arriba as to the full-size images as well. However, because the court broadened the scope of both the parties' motions for partial summary judgment and Arriba's concession on the prima facie case, we must reverse this portion of the court's opinion.

With limited exceptions that do not apply here, a district court may not grant summary judgment on a claim when the party has not requested it. The parties did not move for summary judgment as to copyright infringement of the full-size images. Further, Arriba had no opportunity to contest the prima facie case for infringement as to the full-size images. Accordingly, we reverse this portion of the district court's opinion and remand for further proceedings.

CONCLUSION

We hold that Arriba's reproduction of Kelly's images for use as thumbnails in Arriba's search engine is a fair use under the Copyright Act. However, we hold that the district court should not have reached whether Arriba's display of Kelly's full-sized images is a fair use because the parties never moved for summary judgment on this claim and Arriba never conceded the prima facie case as to the full-size images. The district court's opinion is affirmed as to the thumbnails and reversed as to the display of the full-sized images. We remand for further proceedings consistent with this opinion.

NOTES AND QUESTIONS

(1) *A funny thing happened* . . . When the Ninth Circuit originally announced its decision in *Kelly* in February 2002, the opinion included in Part II.B. an extended analysis of Arriba's display of full-sized images on its website (accomplished by an inline link to Kelly's website and framing of the resulting image), in which the court concluded that Arriba had violated Kelly's exclusive right of public display, and that the display of full-sized images (in contrast to thumbnails) was not a fair use. 280 F.3d 934 (9th Cir. 2002). In response to Arriba's petition for rehearing, more than one year later (in July 2003) the court withdrew its original opinion and substituted the revised opinion that appears above. The superseded portion of the opinion is no longer precedential, and the court's public display analysis has been superseded by *Perfect 10 v. Amazon.com, Inc.*, 508 F.3d 1146 (9th Cir. 2007) (see § 7.06 above).

(2) *Fair use analysis.* What do you make of the Court of Appeals' conclusion that Arriba's activities (or some of them) are only "slightly" commercial? Is this important inquiry one that should take place on a sliding scale rather than a binary one? And is the portion of the opinion dealing with the "fair use" and "thumbnails" as noncontroversial as the Court of Appeals (which here follows the approach of the

District Court) seems to think? How novel — and how compelling — is the vision of "transformative use" that it adopts? *See also Field v. Google, Inc.*, 412 F. Supp. 2d 1106 (D. Nev. 2006) (holding that search-engine "caching" of authorized websites is a fair use under *Kelly*).

Changes in technology have overtaken the issue in *Kelly*. Today, search engine providers (like Google) no longer reproduce or save thumbnail images on their servers. Instead, the web-crawler software reproduces and saves only a link to the image, and the search engine software generates a "script" that instructs the user's browser to make and display a thumbnail image in response to a search. Because Google does not itself reproduce the image, Google can argue that it is liable (if at all) only for contributory infringement (which requires a showing of knowledge), rather than direct infringement. Is this "indirect" method of generating a thumbnail any more or less likely to be a fair use than the method used in *Kelly*?

(3) *Fair use and "linking."* The withdrawn portion of the opinion, which found fair use inapplicable to the second aspect of Kelly's claim — Arriba's provision of links to the high-resolution versions of the photographer's images — had sparked considerable controversy, as has the larger topic of liability for linking in general. In its revised opinion, the court retreated to an agnostic position regarding whether Arriba's linking even constituted copyright infringement (a proposition that seems clear enough where the use of the "thumbnails" is concerned). Assuming for the moment that there may be some liability for linking, is it "direct" liability rather than "contributory" or "vicarious" liability? Should it matter? There are, of course, different ways to accomplish hyperlinks and display their results. In fact, as the revised opinion explains, at various times Arriba used different methods. Should the method chosen affect the legal analysis? *See Perfect 10 v. Amazon.com, Inc.*, 508 F.3d 1146 (9th Cir. 2007) (in-line linking); *Ticketmaster Corp. v. Tickets.com, Inc.*, 2003 U.S. Dist. LEXIS 6483 (C.D. Cal., Mar. 7, 2003) (deep linking).

The District Court in *Perfect 10* distinguished *Kelly* on the ground that Google's search engine was more "commercial" than Arriba's, in part because Google's thumbnails potentially were competing with authorized thumbnails offered by Perfect 10 for use on cell phones. The Ninth Circuit reversed, noting that Perfect 10 had not offered any evidence that anyone had ever downloaded a thumbnail from Google. For more on this case, see §§ 7.06[B] and 9.03[D] above.

(4) *Arriba's activities and § 107(4).* In discussing this aspect of Arriba's "fair use" defense, the court notes that, in addition to the obvious potential for consumer sales of downloaded copies, there were at last two other dimensions to the photographer's economic interest: "Kelly's markets for his images include using them to attract advertisers and buyers to his web site, and selling or licensing the images to other web sites or stock photo databases." It then proceeds to conclude that Arriba's display of thumbnails did not compromise either of these secondary potential markets. Do you agree with the analysis?

(5) *Implications of the* Kelly *analysis.* Is Kelly's use of his images to "attract advertisers and buyers" really a "market" at all, in the sense that the term is used in § 107(4)? Or does that factor, at least as it conventionally has been understood, direct courts to inquire only about substitution effect: whether the alleged

infringements actually supersede sales or licenses for the works that are being used without permission?

(6)   The academic question just suggested was implicated in the *Kelly* court's analysis of the "linking" issue in its earlier, now superseded, opinion — in which it assumed that loss of promotional value should be weighed against a finding of fair use. The question also was raised in *Video Pipeline, Inc. v. Buena Vista Home Entertainment, Inc.*, 342 F.3d 191 (3d Cir. 2003) (preliminary injunction affirmed). Video Pipeline was in the business of providing Internet sites that rent or sell videos and DVDs with short clips from its large cross-referenced database. When a customer requested a "preview" at one of these sites, the images (and accompanying sound) that he or she received were actually being streamed from Video Pipeline's central servers.

Video Pipeline argued that its use was "transformative" because it was providing a database for informational rather than entertainment purposes. Most motion picture companies welcomed this service and cooperated to make it possible. A few, including Disney, first refused to supply their own clips and then objected to Video Pipeline's practice of generating clips from purchased copies of their tapes and DVDs. As plaintiffs, they admitted that they had no market for brief promotional video clips, as such. But they argued that, nevertheless, they should be entitled to funnel all consumers seeking previews of their films through their own (or associated) proprietary websites. The court evidently sympathized with their view of § 107(4), and cited *Kelly* to justify its conclusion:

> Disney introduced evidence that it has entered an agreement to cross-link its trailers with the Apple Computer home page and that it uses on its own websites "the draw of the availability of authentic trailers to advertise, cross-market and cross-sell other products, and to obtain valuable marketing information from visitors who chose [sic] to register at the site or make a purchase there." App. 945; *see also Kelly*, 336 F.3d at 821 ("Kelly's images are related to several potential markets. . . .") . . . In light of Video Pipeline's commercial use of the clip previews and Disney's use of its trailers as described by the record evidence, we easily conclude that there is a sufficient market for, *or other value in*, movie previews such that the use of an infringing work could have a harmful effect cognizable under the fourth factor.

342 F.3d at 202 (emphasis added).This reading, giving independent meaning to the "value" language in § 107(4) is almost certainly ahistorical. Even as a matter of policy, can it be right? If the concept of "value" is completely unmoored from the competitive marketplace, where will it float next? How much of a threat does this mode of analysis pose to the future of the fair use doctrine generally, or to fair use in the digital environment?

(7)   *Google Book Project.* In December 2004, Internet search engine Google announced that it had signed agreements with the New York Public Library and the libraries of Harvard, Stanford, Michigan and Oxford Universities to scan all of the books in their collections and to make them available for full-text searching on the Internet. Books published before 1923 would be displayed to users in their entirety; but for books published after 1923 (and therefore presumptively still under

copyright), Google would display only basic bibliographic information about the book (title, author, publisher, date of publication, and number of pages) and a few brief excerpts from the book (a few lines apiece) surrounding the user's search terms.

The announcement provoked a storm of criticism from authors and publishers, who objected to the fact that Google makes money from advertisements that are displayed next to the searches. In response, Google announced that it would allow any copyright owner to "opt out" by having its books excluded from the Google Book Search project. The change did not mollify the Authors Guild, which filed a class-action lawsuit in September 2005 charging Google with "massive copyright infringement at the expense of the rights of individual writers." Five publishers filed a similar lawsuit the following month, and several photographers' associations followed suit (so to speak) in 2010.

In October 2008, the parties announced a settlement, under which Google would have paid $45 million to copyright owners for books already scanned, and an additional $35 million to create a Book Rights Registry — a collective licensing organization for authors and publishers. Google could then have offered to paying subscribers (institutions and individuals) the full text of books under copyright (with an opt-out mechanism), and 63% of future revenues from such displays would go to the Registry to be distributed to authors and publishers. Some of the strongest objections to the settlement (by the U.S. Department of Justice, among others) were related to its potential anticompetitive effects. Specifically, many objected that the settlement would provide Google with an advantage in utilizing many so-called "orphan works." Objections also were raised on the ground that the settlement represented an unprecedented extension of the Rule 23 class action mechanism — going beyond settling outstanding claims to creating a new business model. Still further objections were raised by foreign governments which did not want their authors and publishers embroiled in the settlement at all — on cultural as well as economic grounds.

In March 2011, the District Court held that a revised proposed settlement (excluding non-English language books) was not "fair, adequate, and reasonable." *Authors Guild v. Google Inc.*, 770 F. Supp. 2d 666 (S.D.N.Y. 2011). Although the District Court found that notice to the class was reasonable and that counsel were experienced, it found that many members of the proposed class had different interests from the named plaintiffs. It also held that orphan works legislation was a matter for Congress; that the proposed settlement exceeded the scope of the original controversy; that the "opt-out" mechanism might violate § 201(e) (which forbids seizure of copyrights by "any governmental body or other official or organization"); and that the settlement raised serious antitrust, privacy, and international law concerns. The court suggested that many of the concerns could be alleviated by converting the settlement to an "opt-in" agreement.

Following rejection of the settlement, the District Court granted the plaintiffs' motions for class certification, finding that "[i]t is, without question, more efficient and effective than requiring thousands of authors to sue individually." 282 F.R.D. 384 (S.D.N.Y. 2012). If the parties are unable to reach a settlement that addresses the District Court's concerns, then the original lawsuit concerning display of "snippets" will go forward. Rejection of the settlement, however, may encourage Congress to adopt some kind of "orphan works" legislation, as discussed in § 4.02[F] in the casebook.

(8) Before signing off the World Wide Web, we would like to direct your attention to a case that is cited in a number of the opinions excerpted in this chapter: *Los Angeles Times v. Free Republic*, 54 U.S.P.Q.2d (BNA) 1453 (C.D. Cal. 2000). The defendants there operated a so-called "bulletin board" website, where they posted news stories from mainstream media (including the plaintiffs L.A. Times and Washington Post) and invited commentary from visitors to the site. The defendants lost, on summary judgment, primarily because they could not persuade the court that their use of copyrighted news articles was significantly "transformative" — and because the court credited the plaintiffs' claims that the Free Republic had the potential to reduce traffic to their own web sites.

Today, of course, posting entire articles is no longer necessary. Instead, one links to the news article on the publisher's website. Google News, for example, typically copies the headline and the first sentence of a news article and generates a link to that article. Assuming the amount of copying is not *de minimis*, should it be considered a fair use? How would you go about crafting arguments for such a defendant? The exercise may be a good way to review some of the issues about fair use and technology that we have treated so far. Note also the possibility of a state-law misappropriation claim, which may survive preemption by federal copyright law. *See Associated Press v. All-Headline News Corp.*, 608 F. Supp. 2d 454 (S.D.N.Y. 2009) (denying motion to dismiss). Misappropriation is discussed in more detail in § 11.02.

The issue of fair use was raised in a number of cases filed by serial copyright plaintiff Righthaven LLC, which searched the internet for news articles, obtained assignments of copyright from the newspapers in which those articles originally appeared, and sued bloggers and websites that posted the articles. Critics claimed that Righthaven's business model amounted to near-extortion, because the cost of litigating a fair use claim vastly exceeds the nuisance value of a settlement (especially given the threat of statutory damages). *See, e.g., Righthaven LLC v. Choudhry*, 99 U.S.P.Q.2d (BNA) 1225 (2011) (denying defendant's motion for summary judgment despite finding that fourth factor weighed in defendant's favor). After losing several cases on fair use grounds, however, Righthaven went out of business. *See Righthaven, LLC v. Hoehn*, 792 F. Supp. 2d 1138 (D. Nev. 2011) (summary judgment for defendant); *Righthaven, LLC v. Jama*, 2011 U.S. Dist. LEXIS 43952 (D. Nev. Apr. 22, 2011) (same); *Righthaven LLC v. Realty One Group, Inc.*, 96 U.S.P.Q.2d (BNA) 1516 (D. Nev. 2010) (granting motion to dismiss). Does copyright law need some kind of "small claims" procedure to deal with mass infringement lawsuits? *See* Lemley & Reese, *A Quick and Inexpensive System for Resolving Peer-to-Peer Copyright Disputes*, 23 Cardozo Arts & Ent. L.J. 1 (2005).

(9) For good or ill, this section's principal case, *Kelly v. Arriba Soft*, represents an attempt to adapt copyright law to the rich and unruly electronic information environment. Back in § 9.04, we reviewed one of the other legal initiatives designed to accomplish a similar end: the insertion of "anti-circumvention" provisions into Title 17, courtesy of the 1998 Digital Millennium Copyright Act. Of course, the

DMCA's title was, in part, a misnomer. As we already noted, the new prohibitions and penalties in Chapter 12 of Title 17 are not expansions of copyright as such, but something else: "paracopyright." And that sets up some interesting conflicts between these new provisions, on the one hand, and traditional copyright doctrines like fair use, on the other.

[C]   Fair Use and Technological Protection Measures Under the DMCA

As the material above may suggest, there is considerable uncertainty — if not outright disagreement — about how the fair use doctrine should apply in cases involving the use of copyrighted works on digital networks. Academic and scholarly "users" insist that the change in technology ought not to affect the scope of their statutory privilege under § 107, and that the traditional "balance" of rights and privileges in copyright should be maintained in the new information environment. With equal vigor, copyright owners assert that, while fair use may continue to be a legal factor in the digital environment, its significance can be expected to dwindle over time, as the line between "private" and "public" uses of information becomes increasingly blurred, and electronic commerce over digital networks become more prevalent.[1]

The disagreement is not a merely technical one. Rather, it represents a clash of cultures. In the view of the "user" community, the fair use doctrine is not merely a matter of economics. Instead, it facilitates re-uses of copyrighted material which are themselves socially, academically, or even commercially valuable — and which might not occur if every use were subject to licensing. In the contrary view of the "content providers," fair use is largely an historic artifact of the particular economic conditions of the print marketplace, in which the transaction costs associated with clearing rights sometimes exceeded the value of the proposed use. In the new information environment, the range of cognizable fair use claims could therefore be drastically restricted.

The conflict just described will not be resolved easily. The debates leading to the enactment of the Digital Millennium Copyright Act saw legislative proposals to amend § 107 to make clear that "fair use" would apply with full force in the digital network environment. These proposals, in turn, were endorsed as essential by various user organizations, and loudly denounced as both unnecessary and potentially mischievous by content providers. In the end, the DMCA contained no amendments to § 107, although its legislative history is replete with statements referring to both the importance of "fair use" and the technologically neutral character of the doctrine.

The question, of course, is whether these statements were more than rhetorical window-dressing. And it is an important question. If copyrighted content is effectively under electronic lock and key thanks to digital rights management ("DRM") technology, with access available only by agreeing to electronically

---

[1] This is the position of the 1995 "White Paper," which concluded that "it may be that technological means of tracking transactions and licensing will lead to reduced application and scope of the fair use doctrine" (at p. 82, citing the *Texaco* case discussed in § 10.03 above).

mediated terms and conditions, access for the kind of unauthorized use which the fair use doctrine exists to shelter is at risk. Indeed, content providers could lock up content consisting of public domain material, such as noncopyrightable facts, or works whose terms of protection have expired, and demand access fees as the price of providing a key.

While some forms of access traditionally enabled by fair use were specifically safeguarded, at least in part, as the DMCA moved through Congress (*see, e.g.*, the treatment of reverse engineering and decompilation in § 1201(f)), the final legislation did not grapple directly with the larger issue: that legislation could jeopardize creativity, education, and research by frustrating the fair use principle (and other access-promotion provisions of the Act, including those found in § 110). Consideration of this larger issue was, in effect, deferred and delegated to the rulemaking called for in new §§ 1201(a)(1)(B)–(E) of Title 17. However, as we know from the discussion in § 9.04, even when the rulemaking produces additional useful exemptions to the § 1201(a)(1) circumvention prohibitions, information users continue to face major difficulties.

And even if the contemplated use *is* one allowed under § 1201(a)(1), the ordinary would-be user won't have the means to make it — thanks to §§ 1201(a)(2) and (b). These sections prohibit making available hardware, software or services that can be used to accomplish circumvention, subject to a much narrower range of exceptions. So what hope does this would-be user have? Is it possible to argue that old-fashioned § 107-type "fair use" *does* apply in the realm of "paracopyright"? After all, § 1201(c)(1) provides that "nothing in this section shall affect rights, remedies, limitations or defenses to copyright infringement, including fair use, under this title."

Currently, courts are divided about the implications of § 1201(c)(1). As you saw in § 9.04 above, *Universal City Studios, Inc. v. Corley*, 273 F.3d 429 (2d Cir. 2001), dismissed the provision as irrelevant to the proper application of § 1201, while *Chamberlain Group, Inc. v. Skylink Technologies, Inc.*, 381 F.3d 1178, 1202 (Fed. Cir. 2004) struggled to effectuate it by applying a "rule of reason" when specifying the necessary elements of a valid § 1201(a)(2) claim. If *Corley* is correct about the meaning of § 1201(c)(1), courts may yet be called upon to invent a new exceptional doctrine, rooted in constitutional values of free expression and specifically applicable to "paracopyright." *See* Nimmer, *A Riff on Fair Use in the Digital Millennium Copyright Act*, 148 U. Pa. L. Rev. 673 (2000). Such a course might be supported by § 1201(c)(4), which provides that "nothing in this section shall enlarge or diminish any rights of free speech or the press for activities using consumer electronics, telecommunications, or computing products." *Corley*, however, rejected such an argument, saying: "This language is clearly precatory: Congress could not 'diminish' constitutional rights of free speech even if it wished to . . ." 273 F.3d at 444.

Corley went on to consider whether enforcement of the DMCA against the defendants would impermissibly burden the fair use rights of third parties — namely, the Linux users who could have employed the DeCSS patch on their computer systems. Here's what the court had to say about this "vicarious" fair use defense:

Asserting that fair use "is rooted in and required by both the Copyright Clause and the First Amendment," the Appellants contend that the DMCA, as applied by the District Court, unconstitutionally "eliminates fair use" of copyrighted materials. We reject this extravagant claim.

Preliminarily, we note that the Supreme Court has never held that fair use is constitutionally required, although some isolated statements in its opinions might arguably be enlisted for such a requirement. . . .

We need not explore the extent to which fair use might have constitutional protection, grounded on either the First Amendment or the Copyright Clause. . . . In the first place, the Appellants do not claim to be making fair use of any copyrighted materials, and nothing in the injunction prohibits them from making such fair use. They are barred from trafficking in a decryption code that enables unauthorized access to copyrighted materials.

Second, as the District Court properly noted, to whatever extent the anti-trafficking provisions of the DMCA might prevent others from copying portions of DVD movies in order to make fair use of them, "the evidence as to the impact of the anti-trafficking provisions of the DMCA on prospective fair users is scanty and fails adequately to address the issues." *Universal I*, 111 F. Supp. 2d at 338 n.246.

Third, the Appellants have provided no support for their premise that fair use of DVD movies is constitutionally required to be made by copying the original work in its original format. Their examples of the fair uses that they believe others will be prevented from making all involve copying in a digital format those portions of a DVD movie amenable to fair use, a copying that would enable the fair user to manipulate the digitally copied portions. One example is that of a school child who wishes to copy images from a DVD movie to insert into the student's documentary film. We know of no authority for the proposition that fair use, as protected by the Copyright Act, much less the Constitution, guarantees copying by the optimum method or in the identical format of the original. Although the Appellants insisted at oral argument that they should not be relegated to a "horse and buggy" technique in making fair use of DVD movies, the DMCA does not impose even an arguable limitation on the opportunity to make a variety of traditional fair uses of DVD movies, such as commenting on their content, quoting excerpts from their screenplays, and even recording portions of the video images and sounds on film or tape by pointing a camera, a camcorder, or a microphone at a monitor as it displays the DVD movie. . . . Fair use have never been held to be a guarantee of access to copyrighted material in order to copy it by the fair user's preferred technique or in the format of the original.

273 F.3d at 458-59. On reading these passages, one may suspect that the court's distaste for the 2600.com defendants pushed it toward adopting a more dismissive approach to fair use than the case law clearly justified. In fact, the Supreme Court's decision in *Eldred v. Ashcroft* (considered in § 5.01) seems to reinforce the proposition that some sort of fair use doctrine probably is a constitutional necessity.

Even so, the Second Circuit seems to be saying that the courts are not required to keep fair use technologically *au courant*, Even if some kind of fair use may perhaps be a necessity, the *Corley* court appears to say, the "best" fair use isn't.

Such reasoning would appear to have implications well beyond the digital environment. Could courts in the 1960s and '70s have refused, for example, to recognize personal-use photocopying as fair use, noting that students and scholars can always copy material "the old-fashioned way," by hand? Could a court today decide that TV viewers should not have the right to use digital video recorders because analog ones are still available?

One more point about *Eldred* may be in order. There, the Court suggests that copyright escapes serious First Amendment scrutiny, in part because of fair use, but only so long as "Congress has not altered the traditional contours of copyright protection." Perhaps, however, Congress *has* altered the "traditional contours" of copyright by enacting the anti-circumvention provisions. If *Corley* is correct, "paracopyright" has no place for fair use. Nor, for that matter, does it recognize the "idea/expression" distinction: so long as any *part* of a work (even a small part) is protectible, the *entire* work can be locked away behind a digital fence and all fence jumpers treated as outlaws. Perhaps, then, *Eldred* signals that the Court may be willing to subject the anti-circumvention provisions to more exacting First Amendment scrutiny.

While we wait for the courts to sort this out — and it could be a long wait — digital consumers and others may have to seek elsewhere for relief. The conjunction of digital distribution, technological safeguards and broad-brush legal sanctions against circumvention may permit copyright owners to enjoy the benefits of making a work public without bearing any of the traditionally associated costs or providing the traditionally expected public benefits. If so, does this rearrangement represent better information policy than that expressed in the familiar pattern of owners' and users' rights that is woven through the law of copyright itself? This, ultimately, may be an issue for Congress rather than the courts.

§ 10.05   FAIR USE IN COMPARATIVE PERSPECTIVE

[A]   The Singularity of U.S. Fair Use

In the end, the fate of the fair use doctrine in the United States may be affected, if not determined, by outside influences. As the United States participates increasingly in both the global market in information products and the international intellectual property system, it is ever more difficult to ignore the fact that, where limitations and exceptions on copyright are concerned, we "do things differently" than most of the rest of the world.

United States law, as you know from Chapter 7 and the preceding materials in Chapter 10, contains both specific exemptions from copyright — like those contained in §§ 108 and 110 of the Act — and a general, residuary provision — fair use under § 107 — that is designed to reach specific cases of worthy, unauthorized uses that do not fall within any of the exemptions.

Elsewhere, the situation is different. In civil law countries, exceptions and limitations are spelled out in considerable statutory detail. As Dr. Adolf Dietz, a leading expert on German law, has written:

> No concept as broad as fair use or dealing exists in German law, although doctrines of free utilization and freedom of artistic expression, as explained below, may be invoked to limit copyright in appropriate cases. Otherwise, as a general rule, exceptions and limitations should be strictly interpreted, except in rare and rather technical cases.

Dietz, *Germany*, *in* INTERNATIONAL COPYRIGHT LAW AND PRACTICE § 8[2][a], at GER-100 (P. Geller & M. Nimmer eds., 2008). Some of the specific exemptions to which Dietz refers have long been part of German law, while others were enacted in, response to the 2001 European Union *Directive on Copyright and Related Rights in the Information Society* (2001/29/EC). They include (among others) certain non-commercial private copying (mainly by analog means) and, subject to additional restrictions, copying for use within organizations; quotations (including music, but generally permissible only to the extent required by the purpose); some nonprofit, educational, and religious uses; uses by libraries (including making collection materials electronically available on their own premises); uses for the benefit of the disabled; private and social uses; reproduction of portraits by their subject; uses in connection with news reporting; home taping of broadcasts; reverse engineering of lawfully acquired copies of software to achieve interoperability; and so forth. Some of these exceptions are available without strings, but most can be invoked only upon payment of a so-called "equitable remuneration" to the pertinent collecting society (for art, or music, or text, as the case may be), for eventual distribution to copyright owners whom the society represents. In addition, as indicated above, there also are "cultural" exceptions for uses in which entire works are "transformed creatively" and a right of "free utilization" which sometimes allows for parody and artistic reference.

Questions of form aside, how different is the German system of specific exemptions buttressed by "free utilization" from U.S.-style fair use? From your reading of the preceding sections of this chapter, you should be able to satisfy yourself that the privileges secured by fair use *are* significantly broader than their German counterparts. Even more to the point, however, fair use is by its nature a dynamic rather than a static doctrine. As patterns of exploitation and consumption for copyrighted works change, courts can adapt the fair use doctrine to new copying technologies such as photocopying, videotaping, and the Internet. Thus, the doctrine has the capacity to retain its relevance without the need for constant Congressional tinkering. By contrast, parliamentary action is required to keep the German law abreast of current developments. Many civil law countries take the same general approach to limitations and exceptions as does Germany.

Similarly, even countries of the common law tradition rely heavily these days on enumerated statutory exemptions, although the lists are far from uniform from country to country. For example, the United Kingdom recognizes an exception for "incidental" copying of all kinds, while the law of South Africa restricts its equivalent exception to copying of texts and works of visual art. On the other hand, South Africa has one of the broadest exceptions for "quotation" in any national law anywhere.[1] Even educational and library exceptions differ significantly from one Commonwealth country to another. Whereas most also recognize an affirmative defense of "fair dealing," they do not give it the scope that the fair use doctrine enjoys in the United States. In particular, fair dealing generally applies only to private study or research, criticism and review, and news reporting. When that threshold has been satisfied, the manner of its application differs from place to place. The United Kingdom's courts interpret the fair dealing provisions of the Copyright, Designs and Patents Act of 1988 (§§ 29, 30) quite restrictively.[2]

By contrast, §§ 29.1–29.3 of the Canadian Copyright Act have been more liberally construed by the Supreme Court of Canada since its landmark decision in a photocopying case, *CCH Canadian Ltd. v. Law Society of Upper Canada*, [2004] 1 S.C.R. 339. *CCH* held that fair dealing should be analyzed in a two-step manner, asking first whether the use fits into one of the eligible categories. If it does, then the court balances the dealing's purpose, character, amount, and effect as well as the nature of the work and alternatives to the dealing, to determine whether the use is fair.[3]

CCH received a ringing endorsement in 2012, a watershed for Canadian copyright law, in which the Supreme Court of Canada decided *five* copyright cases, and the Parliament passed the Copyright Modernization Act, Bill C-11, a significant revision to the law. Both developments moved fair dealing in Canada closer to fair use. In light of the Court's determination that fair dealing is a user right that forms an integral part of copyright law, the Court held that use for "research or private study" should be understood capaciously to include previews of songs on iTunes (consumer research) and photocopying for classroom use (to facilitate students' research and private study). *See* SOCAN v. Bell Canada [2012] S.C.C. 36; *and* Alberta v. Access Copyright [2012] S.C.C. 37, respectively. The Copyright Modernization Act adds educational use, parody, and satire to the list of eligible uses. Whether other Commonwealth countries will follow Canada's lead, and whether Canada's Copyright Board and its courts will balance these factors in a manner that resembles fair use analysis, remains to be seen.

There are, to be sure, isolated examples in other countries of a fair use provision similar to § 107 of Title 17. For some time, § 185 of the Intellectual Property Code

---

[1] *See* Tobias Schonwetter. *Summary of the Evolution, Current State, and Potential Future Developments of the Fair or Flexible Dealing Norms in South Africa that Allow the Use of Copyrighted Material, Especially in Documentary Films, Without Permission of the Copyright Holder*, www.wcl.american.edu/pijip/go/filmmakerpapers.

[2] For an interesting example of a "fair dealing" case that might well have been decided differently had it arisen under the U.S. law's fair use doctrine, see *Hyde Park Residence Ltd. v. Yelland*, [2001] 2 Ch. 143 (Ct. App. 2000) (involving unauthorized press reproductions of security camera photos taken of Diana, Princess of Wales, during the final hours of her life).

[3] Something similar was achieved by statutory means in the copyright law of Hong Kong, shortly before the return of the territory to China. Section 38 of the law (entitled "Research and Private Study") directs courts to consider (a) the purpose and nature of the dealing; (b) the nature of the work; and (c) the amount and substantiality of the portion dealt with in relation to the work as a whole. For the background and implications of the provision, see Band, *Gunboat Diplomacy on the Pearl River: The Tortuous History of the Software Reverse Engineering Provisions of Hong Kong's New Copyright Bill*, 15 Computer L. 8 (1998).

of the Philippines has included fair use language derived from U.S. law; and in 2007, as part of a general revision of its copyright law, Israel joined the club with its new § 19, which tracks § 107 of Title 17.[4] See, *e.g.*, the Tel Aviv District Court decision in *Football Association Premier League Ltd. v. Ploni and Others* (Case No. 1636/08, Sept. 2, 2009), finding that unauthorized streaming of football (*i.e.*, soccer) broadcasts was fair use because, among other things, the social importance of the alleged infringement overrode its commercial purpose.

These few counterexamples notwithstanding, where fair use is concerned, the United States presently stands apart, if no longer alone, in the world intellectual property community. In an era when "harmonization" has become the watchword in international copyright, the potential significance of these differences should not be ignored. In the meantime, is this an area where the United States *should* be open to harmonization, even if that might mean sacrificing the uniqueness of its home-grown fair use doctrine?

[B] International Treaties and the Future of Fair Use

Whether the United States will be able to maintain its singular set of limitations and exceptions may depend on how the governing instruments in the field of international intellectual property law are interpreted. Here, as with so many other aspects of global copyright, the inquiry begins with the Berne Convention.

Article 9(2) of the 1971 Paris Act, to which the United States and most other countries are parties, provides the following standard for granting exceptions to the reproduction right:

> It shall be a matter for legislation in the countries of the Union to permit the reproduction of [literary and artistic] works in certain special cases, provided that such reproduction does not conflict with a normal exploitation of the work and does not unreasonably prejudice the legitimate interests of the author.

This so-called "three-part test" — the first part being the "special cases" limitation, the second the requirement of "no conflict with normal exploitation," and the third the "avoidance of unreasonable prejudice" standard — had, at the time of its adoption by the 1967 Stockholm Conference, a very specific purpose. Its point was to provide a general formulation, suitable for enactment into the national laws of Berne's member countries, which would balance public and private interests in the use of copyrighted works in the face of the then-looming problem of photocopying (or reprography).[8] The test's open-ended quality, however, clearly promised controversy to come — both in its application to national laws creating exceptions to the reproduction right for technologies other than photocopying, and in relation to the flexible and dynamic U.S. doctrine of fair use.

---

[4] *See* Neil Netanel, *Israeli Fair Use from an American Perspective, in* CREATING RIGHTS: READINGS IN COPYRIGHT LAW (Birnhack & Pessach eds., 2009).

[8] For a fascinating review of the "three-step" test, see Daniel Gervais' comment submitted in response to the Copyright Office's Notice of Inquiry and Request for Comments on the Topic of Facilitating Access to Copyrighted Works for the Blind or Other Persons With Disabilities, *www.copyright.gov/docs/sccr/comments/2009/comments-2/daniel-gervais-vanderbilt-university-law-school.pdf.*

Under Berne, every would-be party is the final arbiter of the conformity of its own laws to the requirements of the treaty. When the United States became a party to the Convention in 1989, the question of whether various judicial applications of fair use could be viewed as fully consistent with Article 9(2) was, for the most part, finessed.

Subsequently, doubts have been raised about the conformity of U.S. fair use law with the three-part test, especially for new technologies. The international law challenge to fair use may be of negligible significance where analog means of distribution and reproduction are concerned, but one might argue that a different calculus should apply in the digital environment. In particular, it seems reasonable to ask whether "normal exploitation," as contemplated by the three-part test, presupposed the media and market conditions which obtained when Article 9(2) was adopted — a quarter-century ago, and in response to a very different technology.

Concerns about the compliance of U.S. fair use case law with the three-part test are all the more important in light of the successful U.S.-led effort, in the Uruguay Round of GATT negotiations, to stem the potential proliferation of exceptions and limitations in the national laws of nations with poor records of copyright enforcement. That campaign produced Article 13 of the TRIPS agreement:

> Members shall confine limitations or exceptions to exclusive rights to certain special cases which do not conflict with a normal exploitation of the work and do not unreasonably prejudice the legitimate interests of the author.

Article 13 is a reformulation of Berne's Article 9(2), but with two fundamental differences. First, unlike Article 9(2), the TRIPS formulation of the three-part test applies to *all exclusive rights*. Second, the TRIPS test is *restrictive in intent*: where Article 9(2) merely permits nations to provide for limitations on copyright in certain circumstances, leaving open the possibility that others may be allowable on the basis on other treaty provisions, Article 13 expressly limits allowable limitations and exceptions to those which comply with its standards.

Apart from these differences in formulation, the TRIPS agreement, unlike the Berne Convention, has teeth. The dispute-resolution mechanisms of the World Trade Organization stand ready to entertain allegations that the national laws of WTO countries do not comply with Article 13. This consideration, as one observer has noted, will become increasingly important as protected works and sound recordings are transmitted on advanced computer networks, "and unauthorized copying by the recipient — arguably justified under a private copying exemption — is challenged by copyright owners as incompatible with . . . 'normal exploitation' . . ."[10]

Another battle over U.S. fair use and its relationship with international norms, this time in the Berne context, was fought at the December 1996 WIPO Diplomatic Conference, which concentrated on new international agreements in the fields of

---

[10] Smith, *Impact of the TRIPS Agreement on Specific Disciplines: Copyrightable Literary and Artistic Works*, 29 Vand. J. Transnat'l L. 559, 578 n.36 (1996). For more on the compatibility — or incompatibility — of fair use with the three-step test, see Chon, *Intellectual Property and the Development Divide*, 27 Cardozo L. Rev. 2821 n.57 (2006).

copyright and neighboring rights With special reference to the digital information environment, the issue of limitations and exceptions, including those such as fair use, received considerable attention.

The negotiating history of the WIPO treaties is complex.[11] In short, the draft language would have involved a further and more restrictive reformulation of the TRIPS three-part test, with differences that would have alarmed the proponents of traditional U.S. fair use. Most threatening to the continued good health of fair use, the accompanying commentary offered by the Chairman noted that it was "clear that not all limitations currently included in various national legislations would correspond to the conditions now being imposed." Had the proposed language been adopted, the potential for challenges to U.S. law was palpable.

As the Conference proceeded, however, sufficient support emerged to revise the proposed language of the new WIPO Copyright Treaty to conform to that previously employed in Article 13 of TRIPS. *See* WIPO Copyright Treaty Article 10. Of critical importance, the Conference ultimately decided to adopt the following agreed-upon statements in both the WIPO Copyright Treaty and the Performances and Phonograms Treaty:

> It is understood that the provisions of [this treaty] permit Contracting Parties to carry forward and appropriately extend into the digital environment limitations and exceptions in their national laws which have been considered acceptable under the Berne Convention. Similarly, these provisions should be understood to permit Contracting Parties to devise new exceptions and limitations that are appropriate in the digital network environment.

In other words, the Conference agreed to preserve existing privileges in national laws, including fair use, and to permit the evolution of new exceptions in the digital environment.

On the other hand, the outcome of the WTO Dispute Settlement Body panel on the TRIPS-compliance of § 110(5) of the U.S. Copyright Act (described in § 7.05[B]) seems to heighten the risk of future attacks on at least some aspects of "fair use." Suppose, for example, that the WTO were asked to consider whether the *Sony* approach to personal off-air videotaping for "time-shifting" purposes measures up to Article 13. What would be the likely result? In most of the world, this issue has long been handled through laws that authorize private taping while imposing fees on equipment and blank media, so as to assure remuneration to copyright owners. *See* Kreile, *Collection and Distribution of the Statutory Remuneration for Private Copying with Respect to Recorders and Blank Cassettes in Germany*, 23 Int'l Rev. Indus. Prop. & Copyright 449 (1992). Moreover, the European Union has imposed this approach as a mandatory minimum for Europe as a whole in Article 5(2)(b) of its "Directive on the harmonisation of certain aspects of copyright and neighboring rights in the information society" (2001/29/EC), reproduced in the supplement to this casebook.

---

[11] *See* Paula Samuelson, *The U.S. Digital Agenda at WIPO*, 37 Va. J. Int'l L. 369 (1997) (hereinafter *"Digital Agenda"*).

But for now, fair use survives — and perhaps even prospers!

§ 10.06 AFFIRMATIVE COPYRIGHT DEFENSES

Clearly, fair use is a major defense to actions for copyright infringement, but it is only one means by which a defendant may prevail. As you know from Chapter 8, the plaintiff will lose if she fails to establish jurisdiction, or fails to prove ownership of a valid copyright and impermissible copying. Issues covered in other chapters of this book may be relevant here, as well. For example, the defendant might be able to show an assignment or licensing of rights by the plaintiff or by a joint owner. *See* Chapter 4. Or, the term of protection for the plaintiff's rights could have expired. *See* Chapter 5. The statutory formalities might also, in certain circumstances, prove a fatal pitfall in the path to recovery. *See* Chapter 6. The plaintiff's rights under the Copyright Act could be subject to an exemption or statutory license contained in §§ 108-22. *See* Chapter 7. Or the claim might fall victim to any of a host of traditional defenses, including *res judicata* or collateral estoppel.

In addition, defendants in copyright cases frequently attempt to interpose several more specialized legal and equitable defenses, ranging from copyright misuse (an equitable case law doctrine) to the statute of limitations (provided by the Copyright Act itself) to innocent intent (which is really no defense at all). This section briefly discusses some of these less frequently encountered defenses to copyright infringement.

Copyright Misuse. The doctrine of copyright misuse "forbids the use of the [copyright] to secure an exclusive right or limited monopoly not granted by the [Copyright] Office and which it is contrary to public policy to grant." *Lasercomb America, Inc. v. Reynolds*, 911 F.2d 970, 972 (4th Cir. 1990) (holding that a license prohibiting the licensee from developing competing software is copyright misuse). Copyright misuse has its roots in the equitable doctrine of "unclean hands," which holds that a party who seeks an equitable remedy must not itself have acted in bad faith or engaged in inequitable conduct. Thus, a finding of copyright misuse does not invalidate the plaintiff's copyright; instead, the copyright owner "is free to bring a suit for infringement once it has purged itself of the misuse." *Id.* at 979 n.22. The copyright misuse defense is analogous to the patent misuse defense recognized by the Supreme Court. *See, e.g., Morton Salt Co. v. G. S. Suppiger Co.*, 314 U.S. 488 (1942) (license requiring that patented machine be used only with salt purchased from licensor was patent misuse).

In *Lasercomb*, the Fourth Circuit became the first Court of Appeals to uphold a defense of copyright misuse. Other circuits have since followed suit. *See, e.g., DSC Communications Corp. v. DGI Technologies, Inc.*, 81 F.3d 597 (5th Cir. 1996); *Alcatel USA, Inc. v. DGI Technologies, Inc.*, 166 F.3d 772 (5th Cir. 1999). In *DSC* and *Alcatel*, the plaintiff manufactured telephone switching systems consisting of microprocessor cards and operating system software. The plaintiff's end-user license agreement stipulated that the software was licensed for use only with equipment manufactured by the plaintiff. The defendant made compatible micro-processor cards in competition with the plaintiff and was found to have infringed the plaintiff's copyright in testing and using the replacement cards. After remanding for consideration of the misuse defense in *DSC*, the Fifth Circuit in *Alcatel* affirmed a jury finding that "DSC has used its copyrights to indirectly gain commercial control over products DSC does not have copyrighted" and declined to grant relief because of the misuse. 166 F.3d at 793.

Copyright misuse often is asserted by parties who also claim that their adversaries have violated the antitrust laws. But while the two theories have obvious conceptual connections, the proof of each involves somewhat different elements. The showing necessary to make out an antitrust claim presumably will be sufficient to demonstrate misuse as well. *See* 4 NIMMER ON COPYRIGHT, § 13.09[A] (2012). It is possible, however, to lose on an antitrust claim while succeeding with a misuse defense. *See, e.g., Practice Management Information Corp. v. American Medical Association*, 121 F.3d 516 (9th Cir. 1997) (holding that the AMA misused its copyright by licensing its medical procedure coding system to the federal Health Care Financing Administration in exchange for the agency's agreement not to use any competing system and to require the use of AMA system by applicants for Medicaid reimbursement). See also *Omega S.A. v. Costco Wholesale Corp.*, 2011 U.S. Dist. LEXIS 155893 (E.D. Cal. Nov. 9, 2011), holding that Omega's use of a copyrighted logo to try to prevent "gray market" importation of genuine Omega watches was copyright misuse.

Like most of the defenses considered in this section, copyright misuse fails far more often than it succeeds. *See, e.g., Video Pipeline, Inc. v. Buena Vista Home Entertainment, Inc.*, 342 F.3d 191 (3d Cir. 2003). One article, however, suggests that the misuse defense may be well adapted for dealing with overreaching by plaintiffs asserting claims not under conventional copyright law, but under the new "para-copyright" anti-circumvention provisions of § 1201. *See* Burk, *Anticircumvention Misuse*, 50 UCLA L. Rev. 1095 (2003). For example, in *Lexmark International, Inc. v. Static Control Components, Inc.*, 253 F. Supp. 2d 943 (E.D. Ky. 2003), the defendant allegedly circumvented an electronic "handshake" protocol that the plaintiff used to ensure that its laser printers would not be used with reconditioned toner cartridges. The defendant claimed copyright misuse, alleging that the plaintiff was attempting to monopolize the market in replacement toner cartridges. The District Court rejected the defense and granted a preliminary injunction. *Id.* at 956, *citing Data Gen. Corp. v. Gruman Sys. Support Corp.*, 36 F.3d 1147 (1st Cir. 1994), and *Sony Computer Entm't Am. Inc. v. Gamemasters*, 87 F. Supp. 2d 976 (N.D. Cal. 1999) (also a DMCA case). The preliminary injunction was overturned on other grounds, *see* 387 F.3d 522 (6th Cir. 2004); but in a factually similar case (involving replacement remote controls for garage door openers), the Federal Circuit interpreted the anti-circumvention provisions of the DMCA narrowly, in part because "[plaintiff's] construction of the DMCA would allow virtually any company to attempt to leverage its sales into aftermarket monopolies — a practice that both the antitrust laws and the doctrine of copyright misuse normally prohibit." *Chamberlain Group, Inc. v. Skylink Technologies, Inc.*, 381 F.3d 1178, 1201 (Fed. Cir. 2004). For more on these cases, see § 9.04 above.

Copyright misuse is discussed at length in *Apple Inc. v. Psystar Corp.*, 658 F.3d 1150 (9th Cir. 2011) and in Cross, *Competition Law and Copyright Misuse*, 56 Drake L. Rev. 427 (2008).

The Statute of Limitations. Copyright infringement is a tort, but it is a tort with its own statutory provision for limitation of actions. Under § 507 of the Copyright Act, the limitation period is three years for civil actions and five years for criminal actions. In criminal actions, the statute runs from the date on which "the cause of action arose." § 507(a). In civil actions, it runs from the date on which "the claim accrued." § 507(b). If there is any practical consequence attached to the differing terminology of the two subsections, it has yet to surface in the case law.

If you think back to your first year torts course, you probably will recall a series of cases involving doctors who left sponges or other such paraphernalia inside their patients when sewing them up after surgery. When does the patient's claim "accrue," thus triggering the statute of limitations? In general, statutes of limitation begin to run when the wrongful act or the injury occurs; but in many circumstances (such as the medical malpractice described above), the statute does not begin to run until the victim learns of the tortious wrong or could have learned of it through the exercise of reasonable diligence (a doctrine known as the "discovery" rule). Courts have been fairly consistent, with some exceptions, in their view that the "discovery" rule applies to copyright infringement. *See, e.g., Roley v. New World Pictures, Ltd.,* 19 F.3d 479 (9th Cir. 1994) (claim accrues "when one has knowledge of a violation or is chargeable with such knowledge"); *Polar Bear Prods. Inc. v. Timex Corp.,* 384 F.3d 700 (9th Cir. 2004); *but see Bridgeport Music, Inc. v. Diamond Time, Ltd.,* 371 F.3d 883 (6th Cir. 2004) (quoting *Roley* but nonetheless applying a "wrongful act" rule without discussion).

In *Auscape Int'l v. National Geographic Soc'y,* 71 U.S.P.Q.2d 1874 (S.D.N.Y. 2004), however, U.S. District Judge Lewis Kaplan held that the "wrongful act" rule applied. Judge Kaplan noted that earlier cases had relied on a presumption that Congress intended the discovery rule to apply unless it expressly stated otherwise, a presumption that the Supreme Court subsequently rejected in *TRW, Inc. v. Andrews,* 534 U.S. 19 (2001). Judge Kaplan also relied on the legislative history of the 1957 amendment that adopted the three-year period, in which many members of Congress assumed the wrongful act rule would apply. It remains to be seen whether Judge Kaplan's careful analysis will find favor with courts in other circuits.

Equally controversial is the "continuing infringement" theory of *Taylor v. Meirick,* 712 F.2d 1112 (7th Cir. 1983). In *Taylor,* the defendant made and began selling nearly exact copies of the plaintiff's copyrighted maps in 1976. The resulting infringement action was not filed, however, until 1980. The unauthorized copies were still being peddled by the defendant himself, or by others with his encouragement, as late as 1979. In an opinion by Judge Posner, the court initially held that the statute of limitations was tolled as to the defendant's 1976 infringements until the plaintiff discovered them in 1979. 712 F.2d at 1119. Alternatively, the court opined that "[t]he initial copying was not a separate and completed wrong but simply the first step in a course of wrongful conduct that continued till the last copy of the infringing map was sold. . . ." *Id.* Other courts, however, have distinguished or rejected Judge Posner's "continuing infringement" theory. *See, e.g., Roley,* 19 F.3d at 481 (damages limited to acts that accrued within three years of date suit was filed), and *Bridgeport Music, Inc. v. Chrysalis Songs,* 2002 U.S. Dist. LEXIS 26200, at *19-*20 (M.D. Tenn. Oct. 23, 2002) (stating that Posner's "theory of tolling the limitations period for continuing infringement has been rejected by just about every other circuit court that has considered it" and citing cases).

Interestingly, several courts have held that the statute of limitations in the Copyright Act is not limited to infringement claims, but extends as well to claims seeking declarations of copyright ownership. *See, e.g., Merchant v. Levy*, 92 F.3d 51, 55-56 (2d Cir. 1996) (plaintiffs claiming to be co-authors were time-barred three years after accrual of their claim "from seeking a declaration of copyright co-ownership rights and any remedies that would flow from such a declaration"); *accord Kwan v. Schlein*, 634 F.3d 224 (2d Cir. 2011); *Santa-Rosa v. Combo Records*, 471 F.3d 224 (1st Cir. 2006) (claim of sole ownership of sound recordings was time-barred; claim accrued when recordings were made, or at latest, when copies were sold without payment of royalties). *But see Pritchett v. Pound*, 473 F.3d 217 (5th Cir. 2006) (action for declaratory judgment not barred where party seeks no affirmative relief and only asserts ownership as a defense). When does a claim for a declaratory judgment of co-ownership accrue? Does the analogy to "adverse possession" in real property law counsel a discovery rule in these situations? *See Gaiman v. McFarlane*, 360 F.3d 644 (7th Cir. 2004) (neither publication nor registration of alleged joint work with copyright notice in name of one author only was sufficient to place alleged co-author on notice of adverse claim and commence running of three-year limitations period); *Ritchie v. Williams*, 395 F.3d 283 (6th Cir. 2005) (claim based on alleged assignment was time-barred where claim had been expressly repudiated more than three years before suit filed). *But see Advance Magazine Publishers, Inc. v. Leach*, 466 F. Supp. 2d 628 (D. Md. 2006) (doctrine of adverse possession does not apply to copyright).

Finally, what happens if the plaintiff files the complaint in the action within three years after the infringement, but somehow fails to register the copyright in the work until the § 507(b) period has expired? *Compare Co-Opportunities, Inc. v. National Broadcasting Co.*, 510 F. Supp. 43 (N.D. Cal. 1981) (recordation of assignment relates back to date of filing), *with Brewer-Giorgio v. Producers Video, Inc.*, 216 F.3d 1281 (11th Cir. 2000) (refusing to allow amendment to add related claim where copyright was not registered before limitation period expired).

Laches. An equitable doctrine that serves the same policies as statutes of limitations, laches permits dismissal for unreasonable delay that prejudices the defendant. In *Petrella v. Metro-Goldwyn-Mayer, Inc.*, 695 F.3d 946 (9th Cir. 2012), for example, plaintiff brought a claim based on *Stewart v. Abend* (*see* § 5.01[C] above), alleging that the plaintiff owned the renewal rights in one of the sources for the 1980 movie *Raging Bull*. The majority held that the plaintiff's 19-year delay in bringing suit after first contacting an attorney, and MGM's investment in continuing to distribute the movie during that period, justified the denial of all relief.

Should a court apply the doctrine of laches to bar an action that is brought within the period of the statute of limitations? The Courts of Appeals are divided on this issue. *Compare Lyons Partnership v. Morris Costumes, Inc.*, 243 F.3d 789, 797 (4th Cir. 2001) (laches cannot bar claims brought within the statute of limitations), *and Peter Letterese & Assocs. v. World Institute of Scientology Enterprises, Int'l*, 533 F.3d 1287 (11th Cir. 2008) (laches can bar only claims for damages, and not for prospective relief), *with Danjaq LLC v. Sony Corp.*, 263 F.3d 942, 954 (9th Cir. 2001) (laches held to bar claim of co-ownership in James Bond character, even though brought within statutory period), *Jacobsen v. Deseret Book Co.*, 287 F.3d 936, 951 (10th Cir. 2002) (accepting *Lyons* as a general rule, but permitting exceptions in "rare cases"), *and Chirco v. Crosswinds Communities, Inc.*, 474 F.3d 227 (6th Cir. 2007) (same; applying laches to bar destruction of infringing building).

In *Petrella*, Circuit Judge William Fletcher concurred on the basis of the *Danjaq* precedent but called for *en banc* review, contending that Congress intended to eliminate the laches defense when it enacted a statute of limitations and taking the majority to task for failing to distinguish laches from equitable estoppel. 695 F.3d at 952-53.

Estoppel. In *HGI Assocs., Inc. v. Wetmore Printing Co.*, 427 F.3d 867, 875 (11th Cir. 2005), the court defined this equitable doctrine as follows:

> Copyright estoppel applies when the alleged infringer can show that (1) the copyright owner knew the facts of the infringement, (2) the copyright owner intended its conduct to be acted upon or the copyright owner acted such that the alleged infringer has a right to believe it was so intended, (3) the alleged infringer is ignorant of the true facts, and (4) the alleged infringer relies on the copyright owner's conduct to his detriment.

The court found this four-part test was satisfied when Wetmore, acting as an agent of Microsoft Corp., offered to sell Microsoft software to HGI, even though it knew that HGI was not an authorized Microsoft distributor. The court found that Microsoft encouraged the deception (allegedly in an attempt to ensnare a suspected software pirate), and that HGI at all times intended and believed that it was buying authorized software for which royalties had been paid. Accordingly, Wetmore was estopped from claiming infringement as a defense to HGI's action for breach of contract. *Id.* at 875-76. *See also Carson v. Dynegy, Inc.*, 344 F.3d 446, 453-55 (5th Cir. 2003) (former employee was estopped from claiming infringement by his former employer when he encouraged the creation of a derivative program for other employees to use and never informed his employer that he was claiming sole ownership of the underlying program or any modifications); *Field v. Google, Inc.*, 412 F. Supp. 2d 1106 (D. Nev. 2006) (author was estopped from claiming infringement by search engine when he intentionally failed to use standard "no-archive" Internet protocol on his website).

Abandonment or Forfeiture of Copyright. The plaintiff's assertion of copyright ownership can be countered, and the claim of infringement defeated, where the plaintiff (or the plaintiff's predecessor) has abandoned or forfeited the copyright. The nomenclature employed in the cases sometimes is less than precise, but abandonment must not be confused with forfeiture. Forfeiture usually occurred, in the older cases, as a consequence of publication without proper notice. The copyright owner's intent was irrelevant: the forfeiture occurred by operation of law. *See Donald Frederick Evans & Assocs., Inc. v. Continental Homes, Inc.*, 785 F.2d 897 (11th Cir. 1986).

Abandonment, on the other hand, requires *intent* by the copyright owner to surrender rights in the work and normally is proved by an *overt act* evidencing such intent (for example, a statement relinquishing any copyright interest in a work or an act destroying the only existing copy of the work). *See, e.g., Seshadri v.*

Kasraian, 130 F.3d 798 (7th Cir. 1997); *Pacific & Southern Co., Inc. v. Duncan*, 572 F. Supp. 1186 (N.D. Ga. 1983), *aff'd in part and rev'd in part*, 744 F.2d 1490 (11th Cir. 1984); *Paramount Pictures Corp. v. Carol Publ'g Group*, 11 F. Supp. 2d 329 (S.D.N.Y. 1998), *aff'd*, 181 F.3d 83 (2d Cir. 1999) ("Star Trek" television series and motion pictures). To say that these defenses succeed infrequently would be an understatement. Very occasionally, however, one does come up trumps. *See, e.g., Stuff v. E.C. Publ'ns, Inc.*, 342 F.2d 143 (2d Cir. 1965), involving the "Alfred E. Newman" character adopted as a mascot (but, as it turns out, not originated) by Mad Magazine; the court concluded that the original artist's long acquiescence in the widespread use of his drawing amounted to a forfeiture.

MAD Magazine's Alfred E. Newman

Fraud on the Copyright Office. Like misuse of copyright, this defense has roots both in the traditional equitable doctrine of unclean hands and in patent law. The gist of the defense is that the plaintiff, in his or her application for registration of the work in suit, willfully misstated or failed to state facts which, if known to the Copyright Office, would have constituted reason for rejecting the application. *See, e.g., Fonar Corp. v. Domenick*, 105 F.3d 99 (2d. Cir. 1997). In addition, some courts have required that a party alleging fraud on the Copyright Office show that it was prejudiced by the alleged fraud. *See, e.g., S.O.S., Inc. v. Payday, Inc.*, 886 F.2d 1081 (9th Cir. 1989). The penalty imposed by the courts is, at the least, a determination that the registration is invalid and incapable of supporting an infringement action. Indeed, it may even be argued that, as a result of the claimant's fraudulent actions, the copyright should be considered void, thus precluding the possibility of re-registration and subsequent enforcement. In addition, fraud on the Copyright Office may be an alternate basis for the equitable defense of "unclean hands" (discussed in *Alcatel*).

An illustration of the problem may help. In *Whimsicality, Inc. v. Rubie's Costume Co.*, 891 F.2d 452 (2d Cir. 1989), the plaintiff, a designer and manufacturer of high-quality costumes for children and adults, succeeded in registering six of its creations — the Pumpkin, Bee, Penguin, Spider, Hippo Ballerina, and Tyrannosaurus Rex — not as mere utilitarian wearing apparel, but rather as "soft sculptures." Concluding that no reasonable observer could in fact believe the works to be soft sculptures and that the plaintiff had purposely deceived the Copyright Office as to the character of the works, the court held the copyrights invalid and thus incapable of enforcement. (In fact, the Office knowingly registers costumes as "soft sculptures" when such works contain original aspects; and, subsequent to decision in the case, it filed an affidavit stating that it had not been defrauded in this instance. The court, however, refused further consideration of the matter.)

The result in *Whimsicality* presumably would have been different under an amendment made to the Copyright Act in 2008, which provides that a registration certificate is valid, even if it contains inaccurate information, unless the information was both knowingly inaccurate and material to the Copyright Office's registration decision. In such cases, "the court shall request the Register of Copyrights to advise the court whether the inaccurate information, if known, would have caused the Register of Copyrights to refuse registration." 17 U.S.C. § 411(b)(1).

Innocent Intent. In general, and laying aside the particularized provisions of § 406(a) (good faith reliance on error in name in notice on certain copies or phonorecords), infringement with innocent intent is *not* a defense to a finding of liability. If proved, however, there is authority (although not extensive) to the effect that such intent on the part of the defendant, as well as the potential harm to the public, may be taken into account by the court in fashioning the remedy for infringement. *See, e.g., Cadence Design Sys., Inc. v. Avant! Corp.*, 125 F.3d 824 (9th Cir. 1997); *Cybermedia, Inc. v. Symantec Corp.*, 19 F. Supp. 2d 1070 (N.D. Cal. 1998); §§ 401(d), 402(d) & 405(b) (discussed in Chapter 6); § 504(c)(2) (discussed in Chapter 11).

Chapter 11

REMEDIES, PREEMPTION, AND RELATED BODIES OF LAW

In this chapter, we consider the relief available to the plaintiff in an action for copyright infringement. The origins of these remedies lie, of course, in English history. Like the Licensing Acts that preceded it, the Statute of Anne authorized courts to seize and destroy infringing copies (instead of unlicensed books) and to impose statutory damages (instead of fines). These remedies are available under the current U.S. Copyright Act, along with temporary and permanent injunctions, other monetary remedies, criminal penalties, and additional remedies reflecting the challenges of the digital era. These remedies are the subject of § 11.01.

In addition, the plaintiff may (or may not) be able to obtain relief under various state-law theories. The availability of that relief depends on application of the doctrine of federal preemption, which is the subject of § 11.02. While the law of federal remedies is fairly straightforward, you will see that preemption law is substantially more problematic.

Assuming that the plaintiff escapes federal preemption, a variety of related bodies of law may offer opportunities for relief beyond copyright. These include trademark and trade dress protection under § 43(a) of the Lanham Act, idea protection (under a variety of state-law theories), and the right of publicity — all covered in § 11.03 below.

§ 11.01   REMEDIES UNDER FEDERAL LAW

The remedies available for copyright infringement are prescribed in §§ 502 through 513 of the Copyright Act (supplemented by remedies under other titles of the U.S. Code, including declaratory judgment actions). We begin this chapter by considering the various kinds of non-monetary relief available to copyright plaintiffs, including (but not limited to) preliminary and permanent injunctions. We then explore the monetary awards that a successful plaintiff might recover, including the plaintiff's actual damages and the defendant's profits, to the extent that the two do not overlap; and, as an alternative to these familiar measures of recovery, statutory damages. Finally, we deal with awards of costs and attorneys' fees, new sanctions for unauthorized "circumvention" of technical measures and interference with "copyright management information," and criminal sanctions.

Immediately below, as is our custom, we reproduce excerpts from the legislative history of the 1976 Copyright Act relating to remedial issues. Bear in mind that some major additions to Chapter 5 of Title 17 have taken place since that time. For example, in 1990, Congress added § 511 to the Copyright Act, "clarifying" its intent to subject states and state officials to suit in federal court for copyright infringement. As we noted in § 8.02 above (in our discussion of the Supreme Court's *Florida Prepaid* decisions), there is now good reason to think that this Congressional effort was unavailing.

Section 512, added as part of the Digital Millennium Copyright Act of 1998, created an elaborate scheme limiting the situations in which "internet service providers" can be held legally accountable for copyright infringement. It was codified in Chapter 5 of the Copyright Act because it operates as a restriction on various forms of relief. This section was discussed in § 9.03[B] above.

Section 513 is another 1998 addition, this one accompanying the Sonny Bono Copyright Term Extension Act. As we noted in § 7.05 above, term extension was enacted through a political compromise that included various concessions to business owners which had complained of the high cost of licensing "background music" from performing rights organizations like ASCAP and BMI. The most important of these concessions were those contained in § 110(5) of the Act as amended. But § 513 gives restaurants and other small businesses yet another legal resource: a right to bring an action in federal district court to determine a "reasonable" license fee in cases of disagreement.

Finally, 1998 also saw other significant additions to the remedial provisions of Title 17, including the various penalties provided for various "paracopyright" violations in new Chapter 12. These are discussed below.

[A]   Introduction

Statutory References
   1976 Act: §§ 502-13
   1909 Act: §§ 101-16

Legislative History

H.R. REP. No. 94-1476 at 160-64,
reprinted in 1976 U.S.C.C.A.N. 5659, 576-80

SECTION 502. INJUNCTIONS

Section 502(a) reasserts the discretionary power of courts to grant injunctions and restraining orders, whether "preliminary," "temporary," "interlocutory," "permanent," or "final," to prevent or stop infringements of copyright. . . .

SECTION 503. IMPOUNDING AND DISPOSITION OF INFRINGING ARTICLES

The two subsections of section 503 deal respectively with the courts' power to impound allegedly infringing articles during the time an action is pending, and to order the destruction or other disposition of articles found to be infringing. In both cases the articles affected include "all copies or phonorecords" which are claimed or found "to have been made or used in violation of the copyright owner's exclusive rights," and also "all plates, molds, matrices, masters, tapes, film negatives, or other articles by means of which such copies of phonorecords may be reproduced." . . .

Section 504. Damages and Profits

In general

. . . Subsection (a) . . . establish[es] the liability of a copyright infringer for either "the copyright owner's actual damages and any additional profits of the infringer," or statutory damages. Recovery of actual damages and profits under section 504(b) or of statutory damages under section 504(c) is alternative and for the copyright owner to elect. . . .

Actual damages and profits

In allowing the plaintiff to recover "the actual damages suffered by him or her as a result of the infringement," plus any of the infringer's profits "that are attributable to the infringement and are not taken into account in computing the actual damages," section 504(b) recognizes the different purposes served by awards of damages and profits. Damages are awarded to compensate the copyright owner for losses from the infringement, and profits are awarded to prevent the infringer from unfairly benefiting from a wrongful act. Where the defendant's profits are nothing more than a measure of the damages suffered by the copyright owner, it would be inappropriate to award damages and profits cumulatively, since in effect they amount to the same thing. However, in cases where the copyright owner has suffered damages not reflected in the infringer's profits, or where there have been profits attributable to the copyrighted work but not used as a measure of damages, subsection (b) authorizes the award of both. . . .

Statutory damages

Subsection (c) of section 504 makes clear that the plaintiff's election to recover statutory damages may take place at any time during the trial before the court has rendered its final judgment. The remainder of clause (1) of the subsection represents a statement of the general rates applicable to awards of statutory damages. Its principal provisions may be summarized as follows:

1. As a general rule, where the plaintiff elects to recover statutory damages, the court is obliged to award between $250 and $10,000 [now $750 and $30,000, respectively, as a result of statutory amendments adopted by Congress in 1999]. . . .

2. Although, as explained below, an award of minimum statutory damages may be multiplied if separate works and separately liable infringers are involved in the suit, a single award in the $[750] to $[30,000] range is to be made "for all infringements involved in the action." . . .

3. Where the suit involves infringement of more than one separate and independent work, minimum statutory damages for each work must be awarded. For example, if one defendant has infringed three copyrighted works, the copyright owner is entitled to statutory damages of at least $[2,250] and may be awarded up to $[90,000]. Sub-section (c)(1) makes clear, however, that, although they are regarded as independent works for other purposes, "all the parts of a compilation or derivative work constitute one

work" for this purpose. . . .

4. Where the infringements of one work were committed by a single infringer acting individually, a single award of statutory damages would be made. Similarly, where the work was infringed by two or more joint tortfeasors, the bill would make them jointly and severally liable for an amount in the $[750] to $[30,000] range. However, where separate infringements for which two or more defendants are not jointly liable are joined in the same action, separate awards of statutory damages would be appropriate.

Clause (2) of section 504(c) provides for exceptional cases in which the maximum award of statutory damages could be raised from $[30,000] to $[150,000], and in which the minimum recovery could be reduced from $[750] to $[200]. The basic principle underlying this provision is that the courts should be given discretion to increase statutory damages in cases of willful infringement and to lower the minimum where the infringer is innocent. . . .

SECTIONS 505 THROUGH 5[10]. MISCELLANEOUS PROVISIONS ON INFRINGEMENT AND REMEDIES

. . . Under section 505 the awarding of costs and attorney's fees is left to the court's discretion, and the section also makes clear that neither costs nor attorney's fees can be awarded to or against "the United States or an officer thereof."

[Subsection (a) of § 506, makes it a criminal offense to infringe a copyright "willfully and for purposes of commercial advantage or private financial gain." Under 18 U.S.C. § 2319, the penalty for criminal infringement may in some circumstances be quite severe: a fine of up to $250,000, imprisonment for up to five years, or both. In addition, subsection (b) of § 506 provides for mandatory forfeiture and destruction of all infringing copies or phonorecords and the devices used to produce them. Subsections (c), (d) and (e) also outlaw fraudulent use of a copyright notice, fraudulent removal of a notice, and false representations in connection with a copyright application. The penalty, in each case, is a fine of up to $2,500.]

Section 507 . . . establishes a three-year statute of limitations for [civil actions and, owing to subsequent amendment, a five-year period for criminal proceedings].

Section 508 . . . establish[es] a method for notifying the Copyright Office and the public of the filing and disposition of copyright cases. . . .

[What is now § 509 of the Act provides for seizure and forfeiture to the United States in certain instances of criminal infringement.]

Section 5[10] [deals exclusively with remedies] for alteration of programming by cable systems. . . .

[New §§ 511–13 are discussed in the text note at the beginning of this section of the casebook.]

[For a fuller excerpt from H.R. REP. No. 94-1476, see Part Three of the Casebook Supplement.]

[B]   Non-Monetary Relief

Under § 502(a) of the Copyright Act, a District Court may grant both temporary and final injunctive relief "on such terms as it may deem reasonable to prevent or restrain infringement of a copyright." Often, a copyright owner may need immediate relief against current or threatened infringing activity in order to avoid irreparable harm. Temporary relief may include a temporary restraining order, a preliminary injunction, and/or an impoundment order. Although the grant of preliminary relief is conferred at the court's discretion, traditionally such relief was granted generously in copyright cases when the plaintiff was able to make a showing of irreparable harm. As you will see, however, the landscape has changed considerably in recent years. The following case and notes examines the substantive and procedural issues in the grant of a preliminary injunction.

[1]   Preliminary and Permanent Injunctions

SALINGER v. COLTING
United States Court of Appeals, Second Circuit
607 F.3d 68 (2010)

CALABRESI, CIRCUIT JUDGE:

Defendants-Appellants . . . appeal from an order . . . granting Plaintiff-Appellee J.D. Salinger's[1] motion for a preliminary injunction. The District Court's judgment is VACATED and REMANDED.

BACKGROUND

I.

Salinger published *The Catcher in the Rye* in 1951. Catcher is a coming-of-age story about a disaffected sixteen-year-old boy, Holden Caulfield, who after being expelled from prep school wanders around New York City for several days before returning home. . . .

Catcher was an instant success. It was on the *New York Times* best-seller list for over seven months and sold more than one million copies in its first ten years. To date it has sold over 35 million copies, influenced dozens of literary works, and been the subject of "literally reams of criticism and comment." . . .

---

[1] We note that Plaintiff-Appellee J.D. Salinger died during the pendency of this appeal. . . . Colleen M. Salinger and Matthew R. Salinger, trustees of the J.D. Salinger Literary Trust, [have been] substituted for Salinger as Appellees. For reasons of convenience, however, we will continue to refer to Salinger as "Plaintiff" or "Appellee" in this opinion.

J.D. Salinger
Corbis

Inseparable from the *Catcher* mystique is the lifestyle of its author, Salinger. . . . Salinger has not published since 1965 and has never authorized any new narrative involving Holden or any work derivative of *Catcher*. . . . Salinger has never permitted, and has explicitly instructed his lawyers not to allow, adaptations of his works. He has, however, remained in the public spotlight through a series of legal actions to protect his intellectual property. Salinger has registered and duly renewed his copyright in *Catcher* with the U.S. Copyright Office.

II.

Defendant-Appellant Fredrik Colting wrote *60 Years Later: Coming Through the Rye* under the pen name "John David California." Colting published *60 Years Later* . . . in England on May 9, 2009. Copies were originally scheduled to be available in the United States on September 15, 2009. Colting did not seek Salinger's permission to publish *60 Years Later.*

60 Years Later tells the story of a 76-year-old Holden Caulfield, referred to as "Mr. C," in a world that includes Mr. C's 90-year-old author, a "fictionalized Salinger." . . . [Despite Colting's claim that *60 Years Later* was a post-modern commentary on or criticism of *Catcher* and/or Salinger, the District Court noted that the cover of the U.K. edition describes the novel as "a marvelous sequel to one of our most beloved classics."]

III.

On July 1, 2009, the District Court granted Salinger's motion for a preliminary injunction, barring Defendants from "manufacturing, publishing, distributing, shipping, advertising, promoting, selling, or otherwise disseminating any copy of [*60 Years Later*], or any portion thereof, in or to the United States." *Salinger v. Colting*, 641 F. Supp. 2d 250, 269 (S.D.N.Y. 2009). In doing so, it found that (1) Salinger has a valid copyright in *Catcher* and the Holden Caulfield character, (2) absent a successful fair use defense, Defendants have infringed Salinger's copyright in both

Catcher and the Holden Caulfield character, (3) Defendants' fair use defense is likely to fail, and (4) a preliminary injunction should issue. . . .

. . . Because Salinger had established a *prima facie* case of copyright infringement, and in light of how the District Court, understandably, viewed this Court's precedents, the District Court presumed irreparable harm without discussion. *Id.* at 268 (citing *ABKCO Music, Inc. v. Stellar Records, Inc.*, 96 F.3d 60, 66 (2d Cir. 1996)).

DISCUSSION

We hold that, although the District Court applied our Circuit's longstanding standard for preliminary injunctions in copyright cases, our Circuit's standard is inconsistent with the "test historically employed by courts of equity" and has, therefore, been abrogated by *eBay, Inc. v. MercExchange, LLC*, 547 U.S. 388, 390 (2006). . . .

I.

The Copyright Act of 1976 authorizes courts to "grant temporary and final injunctions on such terms as [they] may deem reasonable to prevent or restrain infringement of a copyright." 17 U.S.C. § 502(a). And, as the District Court stated, this Court has long issued preliminary injunctions in copyright cases upon a finding of (a) irreparable harm and (b) either (1) likelihood of success on the merits or (2) sufficiently serious questions going to the merits to make them a fair ground for litigation and a balance of hardships tipping decidedly toward the party requesting the preliminary relief. *See, e.g., NXVIM Corp. v. Ross Inst.*, 364 F.3d 471, 476 (2d Cir. 2004). . . .

Thus, once a plaintiff establishes a likelihood of success on the merits, the only additional requirement is a showing that the plaintiff will be irreparably harmed if the preliminary injunction does not issue. And traditionally, this Court has presumed that a plaintiff likely to prevail on the merits of a copyright claim is also likely to suffer irreparable harm if an injunction does not issue. *See, e.g., Richard Feiner & Co. v. Turner Entm't Co.*, 98 F.3d 33, 34 (2d Cir. 1996). . . .

This Court has applied this presumption in several ways. Some decisions have interpreted the presumption to mean that a plaintiff likely to prevail on the merits does not need to make a detailed showing of irreparable harm. Other cases have discussed the presumption as though it applies automatically and is irrebuttable. A few decisions, by contrast, have found the presumption rebuttable where the plaintiff delayed in bringing the action seeking an injunction. . . .

Under any of these articulations, however, this Court has nearly always issued injunctions in copyright cases as a matter of course upon a finding of likelihood of success on the merits. *Cf.* Mark A. Lemley & Eugene Volokh, *Freedom of Speech and Injunctions in Intellectual Property Cases*, 48 Duke L.J. 147, 19 (1998) ("The ostensibly four-factor test collapses . . . to a simple inquiry into likelihood of success on the merits. If that can be demonstrated, a preliminary injunction is the expected remedy.") . . .

II.

Defendants do not claim that the District Court failed to apply this Circuit's longstanding preliminary injunction standard. Rather, they argue both that this standard is an unconstitutional prior restraint on speech and that it is in conflict with the Supreme Court's decision in by *eBay, Inc. v. MercExchange, LLC*, 547 U.S. 388 (2006). We agree that *eBay* abrogated parts of this Court's preliminary injunction standard in copyright cases, and accordingly, this case must be remanded to the District Court to reevaluate Salinger's preliminary injunction motion. In light of that holding, we need not decide whether the preliminary injunction issued by the District Court constituted an unconstitutional prior restraint on speech.

eBay involved the propriety of a permanent injunction after a finding of patent infringement. . . . [The District Court held] that "the evidence of the plaintiff's willingness to license its patents, its lack of commercial activity in practicing the patents, and its comments to the media as to its intent with respect to enforcement of its patent rights, are sufficient to rebut the presumption that it will suffer irreparable harm if an injunction does not issue." 275 F. Supp. 2d at 712. The Federal Circuit reversed on appeal, applying a "general rule . . . that a permanent injunction will issue once infringement and validity have been adjudged." *MercExchange, LLC v. eBay, Inc.*, 401 F.3d 1323, 1338 (Fed. Cir. 2005). The court cited for this rule *Richardson v. Suzuki Motor Co.*, which equates the "general rule" with a rule that "[i]n matters involving patent rights, irreparable harm has been presumed when a clear showing has been made of patent validity and infringement." 868 F.2d 1226, 1246-47 (Fed. Cir. 1989). . . .

Writing for a unanimous Court, Justice Thomas held that neither the district court nor the Federal Circuit correctly applied the equitable factors:

> According to well-established principles of equity, a plaintiff seeking a permanent injunction must satisfy a four-factor test before a court may grant such relief. A plaintiff must demonstrate: (1) that it has suffered an irreparable injury; (2) that remedies available at law, such as monetary damages, are inadequate to compensate for that injury; (3) that, considering the balance of hardships between the plaintiff and defendant, a remedy in equity is warranted; and (4) that the public interest would not be disserved by a permanent injunction.

eBay, 547 U.S. at 391. Although the courts below had articulated the correct standard, they had both, albeit in different ways, applied "broad classifications" that were inconsistent with traditional equitable principles. *Id.* at 393. . . .

We hold today that *eBay* applies with equal force (a) to preliminary injunctions (b) that are issued for alleged copyright infringement. First, nothing in the text or the logic of *eBay* suggests that its rule is limited to patent cases. On the contrary, *eBay* strongly indicates that the traditional principles of equity it employed are the presumptive standard for injunctions in any context. . . .

Moreover, the Court expressly relied upon copyright cases in reaching its conclusion. In response to the Federal Circuit's reasoning that the Patent Act's right to exclude justifies the preference for injunctive relief, . . . the Court emphasized that it "has consistently rejected invitations to replace traditional equitable considerations with a rule that an injunction automatically follows a determination that a copyright has been infringed." Id. at 392-93 (citing *New York Times Co. v. Tasini*, 533 U.S. 483, 505 (2001); *Campbell*, 510 U.S. at 578 n.10; *Dun v. Lumberman's Mutual Credit Ass'n*, 209 U.S. 20, 23-24 (1908)). Whatever the underlying issues and particular circumstances of the cases cited by the Court in *eBay*, it seems clear that the Supreme Court did not view patent and copyright injunctions as different in kind, or as requiring different standards.

Nor does *eBay* . . . permit an easier grant of a preliminary than of a permanent injunction. First, as mentioned above, one of the two cases *eBay* relied upon in stating the traditional equitable test involved a preliminary injunction. *See Amoco Prod.*, 480 U.S. at 542; *see also id.* at 546 n.12 ("The standard for a preliminary injunction is essentially the same as for a permanent injunction with the exception that the plaintiff must show a likelihood of success on the merits rather than actual success."). Second, in *Winter* [*v. Natural Resources Defense Counsel*, 129 S. Ct. 365 (2008)], the Supreme Court in fact applied *eBay* in a case involving a preliminary injunction. Reversing the Ninth Circuit, . . . the Court stated: "Issuing a preliminary injunction based only on a possibility of irreparable harm is inconsistent with our characterization of injunctive relief as an extraordinary remedy that may only be awarded upon a clear showing that the plaintiff is entitled to such relief." *Winter*, 129 S. Ct. at 375-76. And, using broad, unqualified language, the Court discussed the preliminary injunction standard as follows:

> A preliminary injunction is an extraordinary remedy never awarded as of right. In each case, courts must balance the competing claims of injury and must consider the effect on each party of the granting or withholding of the requested relief. In exercising their sound discretion, courts of equity should pay particular regard for the public consequences in employing the extraordinary remedy of injunction.

Id. at 376-77. . . .

III.

This Court's pre-*eBay* standard for when preliminary injunctions may issue in copyright cases is inconsistent with the principles of equity set forth in *eBay*. . . . Therefore, in light of *Winter* and *eBay*, we hold that a district court must undertake the following inquiry in determining whether to grant a plaintiff's motion for a preliminary injunction in a copyright case. First, as in most other kinds of cases in our Circuit, a court may issue a preliminary injunction in a copyright case only if the plaintiff has demonstrated "either (a) a likelihood of success on the merits or (b) sufficiently serious questions going to the merits to make them a fair ground for litigation and a balance of hardships tipping decidedly in the [plaintiff]'s favor." *NXIVM Corp.*, 364 F.3d at 476 . . . Second, the court may issue the injunction only if the plaintiff has demonstrated "that he is likely to suffer irreparable injury in the absence of an injunction." *Winter*, 129 S. Ct. at 374. The court must not adopt a "categorical" or "general" rule or presume that the plaintiff will suffer irreparable harm (unless such a "departure from the long tradition of equity practice" was intended by Congress). *eBay*, 547 U.S. at 391, 393-94. Instead, the court must actually consider the injury the plaintiff will suffer if he or she loses on the preliminary injunction but ultimately prevails on the merits, paying particular attention to whether the "remedies available at law, such as monetary damages, are inadequate to compensate for that injury." *eBay*, 547 U.S. at 391 . . . Third, a court must consider the balance of hardships between the plaintiff and defendant and issue the injunction only if the balance of hardships tips in the plaintiff's favor. *Winter*, 129 S. Ct. at 374; *eBay*, 547 U.S. at 391. Finally, the court must ensure that the "public interest would not be disserved" by the issuance of a preliminary injunction. *eBay*, 547 U.S. at 391; *accord Winter*, 129 S. Ct. at 374.

A.

The first consideration in the preliminary injunction analysis is the probability of success on the merits. In gauging this, we emphasize that courts should be particularly cognizant of the difficulty of predicting the merits of a copyright claim at a preliminary injunction hearing. *See* Lemley & Volokh, *supra*, at 201-02 ("When deciding whether to grant a TRO or a preliminary injunction, the judge has limited time for contemplation. The parties have limited time for briefing. Preparation for a typical copyright trial, even a bench trial, generally takes many months; the arguments about why one work isn't substantially similar in its expression to another, or about why it's a fair use of another, are often sophisticated and fact-intensive, and must be crafted with a good deal of thought and effort."). This difficulty is compounded significantly when a defendant raises a colorable fair use defense. . . .

B.

Next, the court must consider whether the plaintiff will suffer irreparable harm in the absence of a preliminary injunction, and the court must assess the balance of hardships between the plaintiff and defendant. Those two items, both of which consider the harm to the parties, are related. The relevant harm is the harm that (a) occurs to the parties' legal interests and (b) cannot be remedied after a final adjudication, whether by damages or a permanent injunction. The plaintiff's interest is, principally, a property interest in the copyrighted material. But as the Supreme Court has suggested, a copyright holder might also have a First Amendment interest in not speaking. *See Harper & Row Publishers, Inc. v. Nation Enterprises*, 471 U.S. 539, 559 (1985). The defendant to a copyright suit likewise has a property interest in his or her work to the extent that work does not infringe the plaintiff's copyright. And a defendant also has a core First Amendment interest in the freedom to express him or herself, so long as that expression does not infringe the plaintiff's copyright.

But the above-identified interests are relevant only to the extent that they are not remediable after a final adjudication. Harm might be irremediable, or irreparable, for many reasons, including that a loss is difficult to replace or difficult to measure, or that it is a loss that one should not be expected to suffer. In the context of copyright infringement cases, the harm to the plaintiff's property interest has often been characterized as irreparable in light of possible market confusion. And courts have tended to issue injunctions in this context because "to prove the loss of sales due to infringement is . . . notoriously difficult." *Omega Importing Corp. v.*

Petri-King Camera Co., 451 F.2d 1190, 1195 (2d Cir. 1971) (Friendly, C.J.). Additionally, "[t]he loss of First Amendment freedoms," and hence infringement of the right *not* to speak, "for even minimal periods of time, unquestionably constitutes irreparable injury." *Elrod v. Burns*, 427 U.S. 347, 373 (1976).

After *eBay*, however, courts must not simply presume irreparable harm. Rather, plaintiffs must show that, on the facts of their case, the failure to issue an injunction would actually cause irreparable harm. This is not to say that most copyright plaintiffs who have shown a likelihood of success on the merits would not be irreparably harmed absent preliminary injunctive relief. As an empirical matter, that may well be the case, and the historical tendency to issue preliminary injunctions readily in copyright cases may reflect just that. *See* H. Tomás Gómez-Arostegui, *What History Teaches Us About Copyright Injunctions and the Inadequate-Remedy-at-Law Requirement*, 81 S. Cal. L. Rev. 1197, 1201 (2008) (concluding, after a thorough historical analysis, that "the historical record suggests that in copyright cases, legal remedies were deemed categorically inadequate"). As Chief Justice Roberts noted, concurring in *eBay*:

> From at least the early 19th century, courts have granted injunctive relief upon a finding of infringement in the vast majority of patent cases. This "long tradition of equity practice" is not surprising, given the difficulty of protecting a right to *exclude* through monetary remedies. . . . This historical practice, as the Court holds, does not *entitle* a patentee to [an] . . . injunction or justify a *general rule* that such injunctions should issue. . . . At the same time, there is a difference between exercising equitable discretion pursuant to the established four-factor test and writing on an entirely clean slate. . . . When it comes to discerning and applying those standards, in this area as others, a page of history is worth a volume of logic.

547 U.S. at 395 (quotation marks omitted).

But by anchoring the injunction standard to equitable principles, albeit with one eye on historical tendencies, courts are able to keep pace with innovation in this rapidly changing technological area. Justice Kennedy, responding to Justice Roberts, made this very point as to patent injunctions in his *eBay* concurrence. . . . Justice Kennedy concluded that changes in the way parties use patents may now mean that "legal damages [are] sufficient to compensate for the infringement." *Id.*

C.

Finally, courts must consider the public's interest. The object of copyright law is to promote the store of knowledge available to the public. But to the extent it accomplishes this end by providing individuals a financial incentive to contribute to the store of knowledge, the public's interest may well be already accounted for by the plaintiff's interest.

The public's interest in free expression, however, is significant and is distinct from the parties' speech interests. *See Pacific Gas & Elec. Co. v. Public Utilities Commission of Cal.*, 475 U.S. 1, 8 (1986). "By protecting those who wish to enter the marketplace of ideas from government attack, the First Amendment protects the public's interest in receiving information." *Id.* Every injunction issued before a final adjudication on the merits risks enjoining speech protected by the First Amendment. Some uses, however, will so patently infringe another's copyright, without giving rise to an even colorable fair use defense, that the likely First Amendment value in the use is virtually nonexistent.

IV.

Because the District Court considered only the first of the four factors that, under *eBay* and our holding today, must be considered before issuing a preliminary injunction, we vacate and remand the case. But in the interest of judicial economy, we note that there is no reason to disturb the District Court's conclusion as to the factor it did consider — namely, that Salinger is likely to succeed on the merits of his copyright infringement claim.

Most of the matters relevant to Salinger's likelihood of success on the merits are either undisputed or readily established in his favor. Thus, Defendants do not contest either that Salinger owns a valid copyright in *Catcher* or that they had actual access to *Catcher.* And while they argue only that *60 Years Later* and *Catcher* are not substantially similar, that contention is manifestly meritless. . . .

More serious is Defendants' assertion of a fair use defense. And at this preliminary stage, we agree with the District Court that Defendants will not likely be able to make out such a defense. The District Court . . . found that "[i]t is simply not credible for Defendant Colting to assert now that his primary purpose was to critique Salinger and his persona, while he and his agents' previous statements regarding the book discuss no such critique, and in fact reference various other purposes behind the book." *Salinger,* 641 F. Supp. 2d at 262. Such a finding is not clear error. . . . [W]hen we consider the District Court's credibility finding together with all the other facts in this case, we conclude, with the District Court, that Defendants are not likely to prevail in their fair use defense.

CONCLUSION

In this preliminary injunction case, the District Court erred by not applying the equitable standard outlined by the Supreme Court in *eBay, Inc. v. MercExchange, LLC* and *Winter v. Natural Resources Defense Counsel.* Accordingly, we vacate and remand for further proceedings consistent with this opinion. . . .

NOTES AND QUESTIONS

(1) *Permanent injunctions.* Section 502(a) provides that a court *may* "grant temporary and final injunctions on such terms as it may deem reasonable to prevent or restrain infringement of a copyright." Despite the permissive language of the statute, however, virtually all courts were willing to presume the existence of irreparable harm. "[T]he traditional formulation [was] to characterize as an abuse of discretion the denial of a permanent injunction when liability has been established and there is a threat of continuing infringement." 4 NIMMER ON COPYRIGHT § 14.06[B] (2012). Only occasionally did one see suggestions that "where great

public injury would be worked by an injunction . . . the courts could follow cases in other areas of property law, and award damages or a continuing royalty [*i.e.*, what would amount to a judicially created compulsory license] instead of an injunction in such special circumstances." *Id.*

(2)   As the Second Circuit indicates in *Salinger*, the Supreme Court's opinion in *eBay v. MercExchange*, 547 U.S. 388 (2006), a patent case, has changed the game entirely. As stated in *Salinger, eBay* held that it was improper to presume irreparable harm in patent cases. Three other circuits already had held, prior to *Salinger*, that the *eBay* standard applies with equal force in copyright cases. *See CoxCom, Inc. v. Chaffee*, 536 F.3d 101, 112 (1st Cir. 2008); *Peter Letterese & Assocs. v. World Institute of Scientology Enters. Int'l*, 533 F.3d 1287, 1323 (11th Cir. 2008); *Christopher Phelps & Assocs. v. Galloway*, 492 F.3d 532, 543 (4th Cir. 2007). All three of those cases, however, involved *permanent* injunctions. *Salinger* was the first appellate opinion to address how *eBay* should be applied in considering a *preliminary* injunction in a copyright case. The Ninth Circuit subsequently indicated its agreement with *Salinger. See Flexible Lifeline Systems, Inc. v. Precision Lift, Inc.*, 654 F.3d 989 (9th Cir. 2011); *Perfect 10, Inc. v. Google, Inc.*, 653 F.3d 976 (9th Cir. 2011).

(3)   *Preliminary injunctions.* Even before the Supreme Court's opinion in *eBay*, a majority of the Circuits were using the standard four-part preliminary injunction test familiar to you from other areas of the law. They considered:

(a)   the significance of the threat of irreparable harm to the plaintiff if the injunction is not granted;

(b)   the balance between this harm and the injury that granting the injunction would inflict on the defendant;

(c)   the probability that the plaintiff will succeed on the merits; and

(d)   promotion of the public interest.

For an example of the four-part test applied in a copyright case, see *Lakedreams v. Taylor*, 932 F.2d 1103 (5th Cir. 1991) (dispute over the design of a T-shirt illustrating the genealogy of the mythical Schitt family, "whose members had names that evoked one or another inelegant image").

(4)   How is the traditional four-factor test affected by *eBay*? At the least, *eBay* seems to require an affirmative showing of irreparable harm (or at least the probability of irreparable harm). It seems that a mere "possibility" of irreparable harm is no longer sufficient, even if the other factors weigh in the movant's favor. Second, because *eBay* involved a permanent injunction, success on the merits was already established and was not expressly discussed. Instead, the *eBay* court lists an inadequate remedy at law as the second factor (moving the balance of hardships to the third factor). Does that mean an inadequate remedy at law is now a factor *in addition* to probable success on the merits? How is an inadequate remedy at law different from irreparable harm? Isn't it the lack of an adequate remedy at law that makes any likely harm "irreparable"?

(5)   By contrast, prior to *eBay*, the Second and Ninth Circuits, the nation's two premier copyright courts, both employed a "streamlined" preliminary injunction

standard that specified more precisely how the various factors would be weighed against one another. *Salinger* notes the standard formerly employed by the Second Circuit: The movant must show (a) a possibility of irreparable harm *and* (b) either (1) a likelihood of success on the merits or (2) sufficiently serious questions going to the merits to make them a fair ground of litigation *and* a balance of hardships tipping decidedly in the movant's favor.

The Ninth Circuit used a slightly different standard, requiring that "a plaintiff seeking preliminary injunctive relief must demonstrate 'either a likelihood of success on the merits and the possibility of irreparable injury . . . or that serious questions going to the merits were raised and that the balance of hardships tips sharply in its favor.'" *Cadence Design Sys., Inc. v. Avant! Corp.*, 125 F.3d 824, 826 (9th Cir. 1997), quoting *Sega Enters. Ltd. v. Accolade, Inc.*, 977 F.2d 1510, 1517 (9th Cir. 1992). Was there really any significant difference between the Second and Ninth Circuit standards? What was the role of the public interest in the Second and Ninth Circuits?

(6)   Despite the holding in *eBay*, the Second Circuit seems reluctant to abandon its previous standard entirely. Thus, in adapting the *eBay* standard to preliminary injunctions, the *Salinger* court expressly retains the second half of its pre-*eBay* formula, requiring "either (a) a likelihood of success on the merits or (b) sufficiently serious questions going to the merits to make them a fair ground for litigation and a balance of hardships tipping decidedly in the [plaintiff]'s favor." But then, under its third factor, the *Salinger* court states that a court may "issue the injunction only if the balance of hardships tips in the plaintiff's favor." What is the point of retaining the "balance of hardships" formulation in two different places in the test?

(7)   *Irreparable injury.* Following *eBay* and *Salinger*, irreparable harm may no longer be presumed, but must be proven. In what circumstances will irreparable injury be found to be lacking? Some guidance may be found in those few pre-*eBay* cases in which the presumption of irreparable harm was found to be rebutted. Suppose, for example, that the plaintiff had known of the defendant's infringing uses for an extended period but had taken no legal steps until the present filing to bring them to an end. *See Bourne Co. v. Tower Records, Inc.*, 976 F.2d 99 (2d Cir. 1992) (no injunction regarding Disney's use of songs from movie "Pinocchio" in videocassette trailer advertisements); *Richard Feiner & Co. v. Turner Entertainment Co.*, 98 F.3d 33 (2d Cir. 1996) (delay in suing is "suggestive of a lack of irreparable harm"). The Ninth Circuit has stated (in *Cadence Design*) that there may be other situations, as well, *e.g.*, "[w]here the plaintiff has not been harmed, where any harm is *de minimis*, or where the defendant acted with innocent intent, relying on lack of copyright notice; *cf. Belushi v. Woodward*, 598 F. Supp. 36, 37 (D.D.C 1984) (denying injunction where one photograph in the defendant's book infringed the plaintiff's copyright)." 125 F.3d at 829.

The plaintiff must also demonstrate a causal connection between the alleged infringement and the irreparable harm. "While being forced into bankruptcy qualifies as a form of irreparable harm, Perfect 10 has not established that the requested injunction would forestall that fate." *Perfect 10 v. Google*, 653 F.3d at 981. Where plaintiff had never been profitable, its images were available on other search engines, and there was no evidence that anyone had stopped paying for its service as a result of Google's indexing, the District Court did not abuse its discretion in denying a preliminary injunction.

(8)   *Balance of hardships.* Under the third factor in *Salinger*, the court must consider the balance of hardships, and find that the probable harm to the plaintiff if the injunction is not issued outweighs the probable harm to the defendant if the injunction is issued wrongfully. Under what circumstances will a court find that this factor weighs in the defendant's favor? Note that prior to *eBay*, many courts were reluctant to rely on this factor. *See, e.g., Apple Computer, Inc. v. Franklin Computer Corp.*, 714 F.2d 1240, 1255 (3d Cir. 1983) (if the balance of harm were given too much weight, "a knowing infringer would be permitted to construct its business around its infringement").

(9)   *The public interest.* Generally, the "public interest" factor has not figured prominently in decisions about preliminary injunctive relief in copyright cases, even in those circuits which retained it as an element of the four-part test. As one Circuit stated, "[s]ince Congress has elected to grant certain exclusive rights to the owner of a copyright in a protected work, it is virtually axiomatic that the public interest can only be served by upholding copyright protections and, correspondingly, preventing the misappropriation of the skills, creative energies, and resources which are invested in the protected work." *Apple v. Franklin* at 1254.

Sometimes, however, the "public interest" factor (closely linked to considerations of copyright policy) may come into play. *See, e.g., Silverstein v. Penguin Putnam, Inc.*, 368 F.3d 77 (2d Cir. 2004) (even if plaintiff's selection of poems by Dorothy Parker was original, it would be an abuse of discretion to grant an injunction against publication of a book of Parker's complete poems that infringed that selection); *Abend v. MCA, Inc.*, 863 F.2d 1465, 1479 (9th Cir. 1988) (despite a finding of infringement, withdrawal of film *Rear Window* would cause public injury as well as injustice to the film's owners, and an award of damages would vindicate the plaintiff's interests), *aff'd on other grounds sub nom. Stewart v. Abend*, 495 U.S. 207 (1990) (discussed in § 5.01 above) (carefully describing the Court of Appeals' discussion of remedies as "not relevant to the issue on which we granted *certiorari*"); *and Greenberg v. National Geographic Society*, 244 F.3d 1267, 1275 (11th Cir. 2001) (discussed in § 4.01 above) (urging the District Court "to consider alternatives, such as mandatory license fees, in lieu of foreclosing the public's computer-aided access to" *The Complete National Geographic* on CD-ROM).

(10)   For the most practical of reasons, many copyright infringement cases are never litigated beyond the preliminary injunction stage. Perhaps for this reason, opinions on motions for preliminary injunctions sometimes seem difficult to distinguish from opinions on the merits. If *Salinger* goes to trial, what will be left to decide?

Does the frequency with which litigation is wound up, one way or another, after a grant of preliminary injunctive relief pose any risks to the integrity of copyright law? Can you identify any aspects of the infringement or fair use analysis in the *Salinger* opinion which seem controversial to you? Is a District Court more likely to "stretch" its legal analysis in a preliminary injunction opinion than in a final decision on the merits?

(11) *Burden of proof.* In *Perfect 10, Inc. v. Amazon.com, Inc.*, 487 F.3d 701, 714 (9th Cir. 2007), the court initially held that although defendant Google had the burden of introducing evidence on its affirmative defenses of fair use and § 512, Perfect 10 retained the ultimate burden of demonstrating a likelihood of overcoming those defenses in order to obtain a preliminary injunction. Several months later, however, the court amended its opinion to hold that once Perfect 10 had satisfied its burden of demonstrating a likelihood of success on the merits, the burden shifted to Google to demonstrate a likelihood of success on its affirmative defense. 508 F.3d 1146, 1158 (9th Cir. 2007). Which party *should* bear the burden when an affirmative defense is raised in defense to a motion for a preliminary injunction?

(12) *Scope of the injunction.* The *Perfect 10* court also held that even though § 411(a) requires registration before an infringement suit may be commenced, a preliminary injunction could issue as to both registered and unregistered works. *Id.* at 1154 n.1, citing *Olan Mills, Inc. v. Linn Photo Co.*, 23 F.3d 1345, 1349 (8th Cir. 1994). This holding is consistent with the Supreme Court's subsequent ruling in *Reed Elsevier, Inc. v. Muchnick*, 130 S. Ct. 1237 (2010), that failure to register a work does not deprive the court of subject-matter jurisdiction. See § 6.03 above. May a court also enjoin copying of works that have not yet been created? In answering, consider the language of the statute itself, which empowers a court to issue injunctions "on such terms as it may deem reasonable to prevent or restrain infringement of *a copyright*." § 502(a) (emphasis added). *See Pacific & Southern Co. v. Duncan*, 572 F. Supp. 1186 (N.D. Ga. 1983) (videotaping of future news broadcasts by clipping service enjoined); *Walt Disney Co. v. Powell*, 897 F.2d 565 (D.C. Cir. 1990) (in view of "history of continuing infringement and a significant threat of future infringement," trial court properly enjoined future infringement of works owned by plaintiff but not in suit); *accord Apple, Inc. v. Psystar Corp.*, 658 F.3d 1150 (9th Cir. 2011).

(13) *Injunctions and technology.* Should grants of preliminary injunctive relief be granted more sparingly in cases involving dissemination of expression through new technologies? For example, the trial court in the *Betamax* case, *Universal City Studios, Inc. v. Sony Corp. of America*, 480 F. Supp. 429, 464 (C.D. Cal. 1979), *rev'd*, 659 F.2d 963 (9th Cir. 1981), *rev'd*, 464 U.S. 417 (1984), denied the plaintiffs' request for a preliminary injunction, stating that "[t]his is a doubtful case [and a]n injunction would deprive the public of a new technology capable of noninfringing uses." The result was that VCRs were widely adopted by the public before the Supreme Court rendered its decision. But in *A&M Records, Inc. v. Napster, Inc.*, 239 F.3d 1004 (9th Cir. 2001), the Ninth Circuit dismissed the defendant's suggestion that it should impose a compulsory royalty payment schedule rather than restricting the scope of its services.

(14) *Prior restraint.* Are preliminary injunctions in copyright cases constitutionally permissible, in any case? See the provocative article by Mark Lemley & Eugene Volokh, *Freedom of Speech and Injunctions in Intellectual Property Cases*, 48 Duke L.J. 147 (1998), cited in *Salinger*, questioning preliminary injunctions in copyright cases under the "prior restraint" doctrine. How — if at all — should courts take account of the professors' argument? Should it matter if the injunction in question is being sought in an effort to silence speech with which the plaintiff disagrees for political or ideological reasons? *See, e.g., Religious Tech. Ctr. v.*

F.A.C.T.NET, Inc., 901 F. Supp. 1519 (D. Colo. 1995) (action brought by the Church of Scientology against critics distributing its proprietary scriptures on the Internet).

Consider the initial ruling in *SunTrust Bank v. Houghton Mifflin Co.*, 252 F.3d 1165 (11th Cir. 2001). After hearing the appeal from the grant of preliminary injunctive relief, an Eleventh Circuit panel ruled, from the bench, that "the entry of a preliminary injunction in this copyright case was an abuse of discretion in that it represents an unlawful prior restraint in violation of the First Amendment." In its subsequent written opinion at 268 F.3d 1257, however, the court did not mention the prior restraint doctrine.

(15) *Miscellaneous.* By virtue of § 502(a)'s express reference to 28 U.S.C. § 1498, neither a preliminary nor a permanent injunction may issue against the United States. Once issued, an injunction may be served and enforced anywhere in the United States. § 502(b).

[2] Impoundment and Disposition

In addition to temporary and/or permanent injunctive relief, equitable remedies available to the successful plaintiff under the Copyright Act include impoundment and eventual disposition of the defendant's infringing copies and the equipment used to produce them, up to and including possible confiscation and destruction.

Impoundment

Under § 503(a) of the 1976 Act, the court may order the impounding of all copies and phonorecords claimed to have been used to violate the copyright owner's exclusive rights. This remedy extends as well to "all plates, molds, matrices, masters, tapes, film negatives, or other articles by means of which such copies or phonorecords may be reproduced." Should this include a personal computer that is used for non-infringing as well as infringing purposes?

It may also be applied against items "which, though reproduced and acquired lawfully, have been used for infringing purposes such as rentals, performances and displays." H.R. Rep. No. 94-1476, at 160 (1976). These provisions may be particularly important when the defendant, rather than being a reputable publisher acting in good faith but with dubious judgment, is a fly-by-night operator whose counterfeit products may reappear at any moment in a different form or in a different market.

Whether impoundment orders can be issued in summary or *ex parte* proceedings at which the applicant need only make a *prima facie* showing of infringement, or whether the defendant has a right to an adversarial hearing, was for many years a controversial issue. The Rules of Practice in Copyright Cases, adopted by the Supreme Court under the 1909 Act, appeared to permit *ex parte* orders on a routine basis, even when notice could be given. *See* Rules 3-6 of the Rules of Practice for Copyright Cases, 214 U.S. 533 (1909), as amended by 307 U.S. 652 (1959) and 383 U.S. 1031 (1966). Those Rules, however, were inconsistent with both Rule 65 of the later-adopted Federal Rules of Civil Procedure, and with § 503 of the 1976 Act. In addition, several courts suggested that *ex parte* seizures might violate the Due

Process Clauses of the Fifth and Fourteenth Amendments. *See, e.g., Paramount Pictures Corp. v. Doe*, 821 F. Supp. 82 (E.D.N.Y. 1993); *WPOW, Inc. v. MRLJ Enterprises*, 584 F. Supp. 132 (D.D.C. 1984). As a result, in 2001 the Supreme Court abrogated the obsolete Copyright Rules and amended Rule 65 to expressly govern impoundment proceedings. Under Fed. R. Civ. P. 65(b), impoundment may be ordered on an *ex parte* basis only when "giving the defendant notice of the application . . . could result in an inability to provide any relief at all," *Adobe Systems, Inc. v. South Sun Prods., Inc.*, 187 F.R.D. 636, 640 (S.D. Cal. 1999), and may last "only for so long as is necessary to hold a hearing." *First Tech. Safety Sys., Inc. v. Depinet*, 11 F.3d 641, 650 (6th Cir. 1993).

Unlike many of the other remedies we have studied, impoundment offers a mercifully small annual output of opinions by the courts. Some interesting examples include: *Playboy Enterprises, Inc. v. Sanfilippo*, 46 U.S.P.Q.2d (BNA) 1350 (S.D. Cal. 1998) (court ordered pre-trial seizure of 7,745 computer files containing infringing photographs); *Richard J. Zitz, Inc. v. Pereira*, 965 F. Supp. 350 (E.D.N.Y. 1997) (§ 503 did not authorize seizure of house claimed to be infringing "copy" of plaintiff's architectural designs); and *Devils Films, Inc. v. Nectar Video, Inc.*, 29 F. Supp. 2d 174 (S.D.N.Y. 1998) (in view of strong public policy against obscenity, court declined to order U.S. Marshal to seize unlicensed copies of plaintiff's copyrighted "hard core" films).

Note that impoundment may only be ordered against an infringer. Impoundment *cannot* be ordered against an innocent third party who purchased an infringing item in good faith, because mere possession of an infringing item does not violate any of the copyright owner's exclusive rights. *See Société Civile Succession Richard Guino v. Int'l Foundation for Anticancer Drug Discovery*, 460 F. Supp. 2d 1105 (D. Ariz. 2006).

Disposition

In addition to the possibility of impoundment during the pendency of the action, § 503(b) provides that, as part of its final judgment or decree, a court may order "the destruction or other reasonable disposition" of both the infringing articles and the equipment used to produce them. What is "other reasonable disposition"? Under § 101(d) of the 1909 Act, a court could order only that the infringing articles and equipment be delivered up for destruction. As the House Report points out, present § 503(b) permits the court to order that such products and devices be "sold, delivered to the plaintiff, or disposed of in some other way that would avoid needless waste and best serve the ends of justice." H.R. REP. No. 94-1476, at 160 (1976). In *M.S.R. Imports, Inc. v. R.E. Greenspan*, 220 U.S.P.Q. (BNA) 361 (E.D. Pa. 1983), for example, the court suggested that the infringing toy wagons be donated to charity for distribution to poor children.

A time-honored variant on the § 503(b) order requiring the destruction of infringing materials is the "turnover" order, under which the defendant must surrender the articles in question to the plaintiff. Such orders may raise delicate questions of fairness. In *Richard Feiner & Co. v. Turner Entertainment Co.*, 47 U.S.P.Q.2d (BNA) 1539 (S.D.N.Y. 1998), the plaintiff held a court-ordered license of certain Laurel and Hardy screenplay copyrights, due to expire in 2001. The defendant was required to hand over copies of its compilation film, *The Laughing 20's*, despite the fact that it included noninfringing as well as infringing materials: "It is only correct," the judge reasoned, "that the infringer . . . suffer the loss of the inextricable material." At the same time, however, the defendant was permitted to retain a master copy of its film, for "use after [the plaintiff's] license expires." Is this Solomonic, or what?

[C] Damages

Damages are the "pot of gold at the end of the rainbow" that motivate many litigants to seek relief in the courts. Under the 1909 Act, unfortunately, there was much "confusion and uncertainty" concerning the relationship among the various possible elements of recovery: the plaintiff's actual damages, the infringer's profits, and statutory damages. As you will see below, the 1976 Act is, by contrast, extremely straightforward, at least on that subject.

[1] Plaintiff's Damages and Defendant's Profits

POLAR BEAR PRODUCTIONS, INC. v. TIMEX CORPORATION
United States Court of Appeals, Ninth Circuit
384 F.3d 700 (2004)

McKEOWN, CIRCUIT JUDGE:

This intellectual property case pits the sport of extreme kayaking against the iconic American timepiece, Timex. In an effort to update its image, Timex Corporation ("Timex") arranged with Polar Bear Productions ("Polar Bear") to produce film footage featuring some of the stars of whitewater kayaking, paddling through exotic locales in North and South America and using equipment bearing the Timex logo. The promotion was so popular with Timex that it just kept on ticking and continued using the footage well beyond any permission to do so. . . .

. . . On th[e copyright] claim, the jury awarded Polar Bear $2.4 million in damages for actual damages and indirect profits stemming from Timex's infringement. . . .

These appeals provide the opportunity to reiterate the principle that a plaintiff in a copyright infringement action must establish a sufficient causal connection between the infringement and the infringer's profits it seeks to recover. Because the evidence at trial was insufficient to support a finding that the lost and indirect profits resulted from Timex's infringements, we vacate the jury award. We also conclude the district court erred in barring prejudgment interest. . . .

I. FACTUAL AND PROCEDURAL BACKGROUND

In an effort to market its line of "Expedition" brand watches to outdoor sports enthusiasts, Timex, the Connecticut-based watch company, entered into a contract with Polar Bear, a Montana-based film production company. Timex agreed to sponsor Polar Bear's production of an extreme-kayaking film entitled "Paddle-Quest." Under the terms of the sponsorship agreement, Timex paid Polar Bear a $25,000 fee and provided assistance in promoting and showing the film. In return, Timex received an exclusive one-year license to use the film in its promotional materials, and the Timex logo was featured prominently on the film's packaging and posters, as well as on equipment used in the film itself. The "PaddleQuest" promotion was, in Timex's words, "an unqualified success." Apparently, Timex enjoyed its association with "PaddleQuest" so much that it continued to use images from the film in its promotion of the Expedition line of watches after the license expired.

The most significant acts of infringement occurred when Timex used "Paddle-Quest" materials at twelve different trade shows between 1995 and 1998. These materials included a ten minute promotional "loop tape" — so named because it is shown continuously — displayed at Timex's presentation booth at the trade shows. . . . Polar Bear warned Timex that it had no right to use images from "Paddle-Quest" without permission, and Timex agreed not to produce the tape. Neverthe-less, without Polar Bear's knowledge or permission, Timex proceeded to create the video, one-third of which consisted of images from "PaddleQuest."

Polar Bear first learned of Timex's infringement approximately two years later when the producer of "PaddleQuest," one of Polar Bear's two shareholders, witnessed the Timex-produced loop tape playing continuously at a trade show. . . .

Polar Bear later discovered that Timex used Polar Bear's copyrighted images on two other occasions — in a promotional campaign associated with the soft drink Mountain Dew and in videos used to train salespeople at a large national retailer. In all three instances, Polar Bear expressly denied Timex permission to use the images, and Timex deleted any reference to Polar Bear's copyright. Timex does not dispute that it used the copyrighted images without permission and beyond the period of time allowed by the license.

Polar Bear brought suit against Timex, alleging claims for copyright infringe-ment under the Copyright Act, 17 U.S.C. § 101 et seq., [and] removal of copyright management information under the Digital Millennium Copyright Act ("DMCA"), 17 U.S.C. § 1202. . . . [Discussion of non-copyright claims is omitted throughout.] Before the first trial, the district court disposed of a number of Polar Bear's claims in a series of oral rulings, [precluding, *inter alia*, on procedural grounds,] Polar Bear's effort to claim attorney's fees under the DMCA, 17 U.S.C. § 1203. . . .

[At the second of two trials, the jury returned a copyright infringement] verdict of $2,415,00.00 — $315,000 in actual damages and $2.1 million in indirect profits related to Timex's infringements.[3]

---

[3] Although the jury did not specify the components of the actual damages award, the $315,000 figure appears to reflect the $115,000 in lost license fees and $200,000 in lost profits that Polar Bear requested at trial. We also note that Polar Bear estimated the range of indirect profits to be between $1.7 million and $3.2 million.

II. COPYRIGHT ACT

A. DAMAGES AWARD

1. STATUTE OF LIMITATIONS

The first issue we confront is Timex's claim that Polar Bear is barred from recovering monetary relief for infringements occurring more than three years prior to the commencement of its copyright action. Section 507(b) of the Copyright Act provides that copyright claims must be "commenced within three years after the claim accrued." 17 U.S.C. § 507(b).

In copyright litigation, the statute of limitations issue that often arises is that the plaintiff filed its copyright claim more than three years after it discovered or should have discovered infringement. Here, Timex makes a different, novel argument and asks us to rule that § 507(b) prohibits copyright plaintiffs from obtaining any damages resulting from infringement occurring more than three years before filing the copyright action, regardless of the date the plaintiff discovered the infringement. . . . We conclude that § 507(b) permits damages occurring outside of the three-year window, so long as the copyright owner did not discover — and reasonably could not have discovered — the infringement before the commencement of the three-year limitation period. . . .

Our decision in *Roley v. New World Pictures, Ltd.*, 19 F.3d 479 (9th Cir. 1994), illustrates the way the statute of limitations in § 507(b) operates. Roley, a screen writer, argued that he was entitled to recover damages for infringement that occurred before the three-year period prior to filing suit because the infringement was continuous — that is, there was an instance of at least one infringement within the three-year window. We rejected this theory, reasoning that "in a case of continuing copyright infringements, an action may be brought for all acts that accrued within the three years preceding the filing of suit." *Id.* at 481. The copyright plaintiff cannot, however, reach back beyond the three-year limit and sue for damages or other relief for infringing acts that he knew about at the time but did not pursue. *Id.*. . .

Importantly, *Roley* also signals that this general rule does not erect an impenetrable wall preventing recovery for infringement occurring prior to the three-year window. *Roley* interpreted the term "accrue," as it is used in § 507(b), to be the moment when the copyright holder "has knowledge of a violation or is chargeable with such knowledge." . . .

Thus, under *Roley*, the statute of limitations does not prohibit recovery of damages incurred more than three years prior to the filing of suit if the copyright plaintiff was unaware of the infringement, and that lack of knowledge was reasonable under the circumstances. Without the benefit of tolling in this situation, a copyright plaintiff who, through no fault of its own, discovers an act of infringement more than three years after the infringement occurred would be out of luck. Such a harsh rule would distort the tenor of the statute. Section 507(b), like all statutes of limitations, is primarily intended to promote the timely prosecution of grievances and discourage needless delay. It makes little sense, then, to bar damages recovery by copyright holders who have no knowledge of the infringement, particularly in a case like this one, in which much of the infringing material is in the control of the defendant. . . .

. . . Timex presented no evidence that Polar Bear was aware of the infringement prior to attending a trade show on August 9, 1997, and we therefore see no reason to disturb the district court's finding regarding the date of discovery. . . .

2. STATUTORY FRAMEWORK

[Because Polar Bear did not register its copyright before infringement, it could recover only actual damages and infringer's profits under § 504(b), not statutory damages under § 504(c).]

Congress explicitly provides for two distinct monetary remedies — actual damages and recovery of wrongful profits. These remedies are two sides of the damages coin — the copyright holder's losses and the infringer's gains. "Actual damages are usually determined by the loss in the fair market value of the copyright, measured by the profits lost due to the infringement or by the value of the use of the copyrighted work to the infringer." *McRoberts Software, Inc. v. Media 100, Inc.*, 329 F.3d 557, 566 (7th Cir. 2003); *see also Mackie v. Rieser*, 296 F.3d 909, 914 (9th Cir. 2002) (approving of recovery of reasonable license fee).

To take away incentives for would-be infringers and "to prevent the infringer from unfairly benefiting from a wrongful act," the statute also provides for the recovery of wrongfully obtained profits resulting from the infringement. H.R. Rep. No. 94-1476, § 504, at 161 (1976). . . .

Under § 504(b), actual damages must be suffered "as a result of the infringement," and recoverable profits must be "attributable to the infringement." From the statutory language, it is apparent that a causal link between the infringement and the monetary remedy sought is a predicate to recovery of both actual damages and profits. We take this opportunity to reaffirm the principle that a plaintiff in a § 504(b) action must establish this causal connection, and that this requirement is akin to tort principles of causation and damages. *See Mackie*, 296 F.3d at 915 & n.6, 916-17 (applying tort principles to evaluate the claim for indirect profits and assessing the quantum of actual damages). We now turn to the damages award.

3. ACTUAL DAMAGES

The jury awarded Polar Bear $315,000 in actual damages, a figure apparently consisting of lost license and renewal fees and lost profits. . . . Although we conclude that the portion of the award related to the license and renewal fees is supported by the evidence, we remand the actual damages award for remission of the excess by Polar Bear because the lost profits portion is speculative.

In our review of Timex's challenge to the actual damages award, we must assess whether the award is non-speculative — that is, whether it is sufficiently supported by evidence. The relevant inquiry is whether the evidence, construed in the light most favorable to the non-moving party, permits only one reasonable conclusion, and that conclusion is contrary to the jury verdict . . .

Applying this deferential standard, we conclude that sufficient evidence supports the portion of the award related to the license fee. The jury heard the testimony of one of Polar Bear's expert witnesses, Paul Sepp, a certified public accountant, who calculated a reasonable production and license fee by determining their fair market value. His valuation, predicated on the price Polar Bear quoted to produce the loop tape for Timex in 1995, was justified as being within the range of the fair market value. . . .

Timex argues that Polar Bear cannot recover the amount of Sepp's estimate because Polar Bear never charged that rate. But having taken the copyrighted material, Timex is in no better position to haggle over the license fee than an ordinary thief and must accept the jury's valuation unless it exceeds the range of the reasonable market value. The proposed license fee was proffered before Timex's infringement. Nothing suggests that the fee was contrived or artificially inflated.

Timex also challenges the license fee award as speculative because Sepp based his valuations, in part, on consultations with the principals of Polar Bear. Common sense dictates that an expert may confer with the copyright holder and that the background data may be factored into calculations of actual damages. . . .

. . . The jury was not required to adopt Timex's view, nor do we substitute our view for the jury's verdict where the award is supported by substantial evidence. We therefore conclude that the district court did not err in denying the motion for judgment as a matter of law as to Polar Bear's lost license fee.

The award for lost profits is a different story. At trial, witnesses for Polar Bear testified that the company's losses during the period of Timex's infringement totaled $200,000. Polar Bear advanced the theory that it could have sold at least 10,000 to 15,000 copies of "PaddleQuest" at a profit of between $20 to $30 per copy, but was unable to do so because it had overextended itself and lacked the financial wherewithal to sell the additional videos. Polar Bear concluded that, but for Timex's failure to pay for its use of "PaddleQuest," it would have had the necessary funds to produce these tapes, thus reaping the profits from its would-be sales.

This theory of liability is too "pie-in-the-sky." *Cf. MindGames, Inc. v. Western Pub. Co.*, 218 F.3d 652, 658 (7th Cir. 2000) (holding that in a breach of contract context, "a start-up company should not be permitted to obtain pie-in-the-sky damages upon allegations that it was snuffed out before it could begin to operate . . . capitalizing fantasized earnings into a huge present value sought as damages. . . . Damages must be proved, and not just dreamed"). Although it is hypothetically possible that Polar Bear's business venture would have been more successful if it had greater access to cash, Timex's failure to pay license fees for the use of the footage was not the cause of Polar Bear's inability to put 10,000 copies of "PaddleQuest" on the market. . . .

. . . It is too speculative to say that Timex's failure to pay a modest license fee was the cause of Polar Bear's business failure. Thus, it was error for the district court to deny Timex's motion for judgment as a matter of law on the claim for lost profits.

. . . We therefore affirm the lost license and renewal fee award but remand to the district court to order a remission of the excess by the plaintiff for the remaining portion of the award.

4. INDIRECT PROFITS

Section 504(b) provides recovery for "any profits of the infringer that are attributable to the infringement." 17 U.S.C. § 504(b). "On its face, § 504(b) does not differentiate between 'direct profits' — those that are generated by selling an infringing product — and 'indirect profits' — revenue that has a more attenuated nexus to the infringement." *Mackie*, 296 F.3d at 914. Consequently, we have held that, like its predecessor [in the 1909 Act], § 504(b) is "expansive enough to afford parties an indirect profits remedy under certain conditions." *Id.*

. . . [B]ecause the amount of profits attributable to the infringement in an indirect profits case is not always clear, "we have held that a copyright holder must establish the existence of a causal link before indirect profits damages can be recovered." *Mackie*, 296 F.3d at 914. . . .

. . . § 504(b) creates a two-step framework for recovery of indirect profits: 1) the copyright claimant must first show a causal nexus between the infringement and the gross revenue; and 2) once the causal nexus is shown, the infringer bears the burden of apportioning the profits that were not the result of infringement.

This appeal requires us to apply the fundamental standard articulated in our decision in *Mackie*: that a copyright infringement plaintiff seeking to recover indirect profit damages "must proffer some evidence . . . [that] the infringement at least partially caused the profits that the infringer generated as a result of the infringement." *Mackie*, 296 F.3d at 911. Thus, a copyright owner is required to do more initially than toss up an undifferentiated gross revenue number; the revenue stream must bear a legally significant relationship to the infringement.[8] . . .

. . . Otherwise, the plaintiff in a copyright action against a multi-division, multi-product company such as General Mills, would need to do nothing more than offer an overall gross revenue number — like $11.5 billion — and sit back. . . .

With these requirements in mind, we address Timex's challenge to the $2.1 million indirect profit award. At trial, Polar Bear estimated that it was entitled to recover between $1.7 and $3.2 million in Timex's profits allegedly gained from its unauthorized use of Polar Bear's copyrighted material. Polar Bear's request was based on the testimony of its expert witness, Professor Robert Hansen, who arrived at his estimate by aggregating the purported profit resulting from three sources: 1) Timex's direct sales at trade shows; 2) its use of a still image in a promotion affiliated with the soft drink Mountain Dew; and 3) the overall enhancement of brand prestige resulting from Timex's association with the sport of extreme kayaking.

. . . Hansen calculated that Timex yielded an average of $30,000 in sales per show, for a total of $360,000 in gross revenue. Based on his experience evaluating

---

[8] Like us, our sister circuits have taken the statute's general reference to "gross revenue" to mean the gross revenue associated with the infringement, as opposed to the infringer's overall gross sales resulting from all streams of revenue. *See Davis v. The Gap*, 246 F.3d 152, 160 (2d Cir. 2001) . . .

trade shows, he concluded that approximately 10% to 25% of trade show sales are the result of excitement created by the booth promotion, of which the "Paddle-Quest" materials were a substantial part.

Hansen's testimony established the requisite causal connection between the category of profits sought — revenue from trade booth sales — and the infringement. Under § 504(b), Polar Bear was not required to separate the gross profits resulting from the infringement from the profits resulting from other sources, but it undertook to do so anyway. Using a profit margin determined from Timex's invoices, Hansen estimated that Timex gained between approximately $20,000 and $50,000 in net profit from the infringement. . . . Polar Bear more than satisfied the sole requirement of "a reasonable approximation" in assessing the amount of profits attributable to the infringing material. *Id.* (quoting *Sheldon v. Metro-Goldwyn Pictures Corp.*, 309 U.S. 390, 408 (1940)).

Sufficient circumstantial evidence also supports Polar Bear's argument that the use of "PaddleQuest" images contributed to sales of Expedition watches in Timex's promotional efforts with Mountain Dew. The Mountain Dew promotional materials offered consumers the opportunity to purchase a Timex Expedition watch at a discounted price. . . . Polar Bear satisfied its burden of establishing the infringer's relevant gross revenue, as required by § 504(b), by presenting sales figures from Timex's press releases stating that the Mountain Dew promotion generated $564,000 in sales. Although it was not required to apportion the gross profit figure, Polar Bear claimed only $242,520 in Timex's profits, based on an estimated profit rate of 43%. Under § 504(b), the primary responsibility for further apportionment of profits fell to Timex.

. . . In the absence of evidence to the contrary, we presume that the jury fulfilled its duty to apportion profits.

Our deferential review of the verdict cannot, however, insulate the basis for the overwhelming bulk of the indirect profits claim, namely, Timex's purported revenue derived from the enhanced prestige of the Expedition line of watches. Substantial evidence does not support the required causal link between the infringement and the revenue derived from enhanced brand prestige. Because the other damages claims — trade show sales and the Mountain Dew promotion — cannot total to the overall $2.1 million verdict, nor can they be fairly segregated from the total, we are left with no choice but to vacate the award.

Using a method called "brand premium analysis," Hansen posited that a significant portion of the price increase for Expedition watches during a four-year period was the result of customers' favorable feelings generated by Timex's promotional efforts involving "PaddleQuest" materials. Multiplying the increase in the average watch price with the number of watches sold, Hansen determined that Timex's enhanced brand premium was worth approximately $10 million in gross revenue, translating to a $6 million gain in net profits. Finally, Hansen attributed between one-quarter and one-half of that profit to the cumulative effect of the copyright infringement at the twelve trade shows, resulting in approximately $1.5 million and $3 million in indirect profits. . . .

To recover indirect profits under its brand premium theory, Polar Bear shoulders the burden of demonstrating that the infringement is causally linked to the revenues from the sales of all Expedition watches. Polar Bear's theory is that the infringement at the trade shows created excitement about the product and an association between Expedition watches and outdoor sports, that the excitement and association generated at the trade shows somehow translated into consumers purchasing Timex's products, and that consumer enthusiasm permitted Timex to increase prices and generate more revenue. According to Polar Bear, the necessary causal link is evidenced by Timex's statement that the "PaddleQuest" promotion was an unqualified success, as well as evidence that "PaddleQuest" images formed a significant part of Timex's promotion at the twelve trade shows. Polar Bear's theory stretches the causation rubber band to its breaking point.

A comparison of indirect profits cases illustrates why the evidence fails to support this element of the award. In its recent decision in *Andreas v. Volkswagen of Am., Inc.*, 336 F.3d 789 (8th Cir. 2003), . . . the Eighth Circuit held that a copyright plaintiff adequately established the causal nexus between an automobile manufacturer's use of infringing material in a widely-aired commercial and a portion of profits from the sale of the automobile. *Andreas*, 336 F.3d at 797-98. Reversing the district court's grant of a motion for judgment as a matter of law, the Eighth Circuit relied on evidence that the infringing material "was the centerpiece of a commercial that essentially showed nothing but [the advertised product] . . . that [the infringer] enthusiastically presented the commercial to its dealers as an important and integral part of its launch of [the product] . . . sales of the [product] during the period that the commercial aired were above [infringer's] projections; the [ ] commercials received high ratings on . . . surveys that rated consumer recall of the commercials; and [infringer] paid [the advertising company that created the commercial] a substantial bonus based on the success of the commercials." *Id.* at 796-97.

Although *Andreas* does not necessarily set the bar for what is sufficient evidence of a causal nexus, comparing Polar Bear's claim vividly highlights its deficiencies. Missing is the link between the infringement and revenue resulting from sales. In contrast to *Andreas*, no evidence establishes that the infringement may have actually influenced the purchasing decisions of those that bought Timex's watches at retail stores or other outlets — the decisions that lead to increased sales revenue, which is the foundation of profits recoverable under § 504(b).

. . . [There was no] evidence that vendors at the trade shows somehow transmitted enthusiasm to retail customers. Timex's statement of satisfaction with the initial "PaddleQuest" promotion and its use of "PaddleQuest" images do not suffice as the links because they do not explain how the infringement influenced the purchasing decisions that lead to increased prices and ultimately to increased profits. . . .

Polar Bear's claim to the profits Timex allegedly derived from brand prestige is less like *Andreas*, which dealt with revenue from actual sales, and is more like cases involving claims to indirect profits purportedly resulting from enhanced good will, a theory generally rejected by courts. *See, e.g., Deltak Inc. v. Advanced Sys., Inc.*, 574 F. Supp. 400 (N.D. Ill. 1983), *vacated on other grounds*, 767 F.2d 357 (7th Cir. 1985) (rejecting as speculative claim for defendant's profits on increased product sales due to infringing sales pamphlet). . . . [I]t is impossible to connect the dots of Polar Bear's theory because there is a gap between the infringement and actual sales revenue — and thus, the alleged profits. . . .

. . . Only then would Timex bear the responsibility for apportioning profits. *Cf. Frank Music Corp. v. Metro-Goldwyn-Mayer, Inc.*, 886 F.2d 1545, 1554 (9th Cir. 1989) ("Frank II") (holding that percentage increase in stock value of parent company too speculative and attenuated).

Because Polar Bear failed to demonstrate a non-speculative causal link between the trade show promotion and the increased revenue from Expedition watches, we conclude that the district court erred in allowing the jury to consider the claim of profits associated with the brand premium calculation.

The jury did not detail how it arrived at the $2.1 million indirect profits figure. We are therefore unable to determine how much of the award the jury attributed to the brand premium effect. It is evident from the record, however, that the elements of the award that were supported by substantial evidence — namely, the booth sales and the Mountain Dew promotion — could conceivably comprise only a small fraction of the $2.1 million total for indirect profits. . . . Because the total award cannot be supported in light of the evidence as a whole, and because the record does not provide a sufficient basis for appellate review of specific portions of the award, we vacate the entire indirect profits damages award. . . .

AFFIRMED in part, REVERSED in part, and REMANDED. Each party shall bear its own costs on appeal.

NOTES AND QUESTIONS

(1)   Section 504 of the 1976 Act contains three subsections. Subsection (a) provides that the successful plaintiff in an infringement action may recover *either* (1) his/her actual damages *and* the infringer's profits (subject, however, to § 504(b)) *or* (2) statutory damages. As the House Report points out, there was substantial "confusion and uncertainty" in cases decided under the prior Act regarding the relationship among these measures of damages. *See, e.g., Sid & Marty Krofft Television Productions, Inc. v. McDonald's Corp.*, 562 F.2d 1157 (9th Cir. 1977). Subsection (b), with which the present Notes and Questions are primarily concerned, regulates awards of actual damages and profits. It also allocates the burden of proof on the issue of profits. Subsection (c) concerns the awards of statutory damages and will be dealt with in the next section of the book.

Plaintiff's Damages

(2)   The term "actual damages" is not defined in the Act but, as we see in *Polar Bear*, the award of actual damages — as in any tort action — is designed to compensate the copyright owner for the harm caused by the infringement. This compensatory principle is illustrated in cases involving partial takings of a copyrighted work. If an advertiser uses a fraction of a copyrighted song, and in so doing it utterly destroys the song's ad licensing potential, the proper award is the full value of the lost revenue. *See Cream Records, Inc. v. Jos. Schlitz Brewing Co.,*

754 F.2d 826 (9th Cir. 1985) ("The Theme from Shaft").

(3) *Substitute license fees.* What if the best a plaintiff can do is to claim that, by virtue of the defendant's infringements, it lost out on licensing fees that the defendant itself otherwise would have paid? Is the form of this argument too circular to withstand pressure? Or does it make some commercial sense? More and more copyright cases involve damage claims of this kind, and whether they are honored will depend, in part, on the certainty with which the plaintiff can demonstrate the amount of the hypothetical license fee. In *Polar Bear*, the proof was relatively straightforward because the plaintiff actually had proposed a license fee before the infringement occurred. But what if there had been no such proposal? *See On Davis v. The Gap, Inc.*, 246 F.3d 152 (2d Cir. 2001) (extensive discussion noting that the Nimmer and Goldstein treatises are in conflict on the point but concluding that "the decisions in this and other courts support the view that the owner's actual damages may include in appropriate cases the reasonable license fee on which a willing buyer and a willing seller would have agreed for the use taken by the infringer"). *Accord Jarvis v. K2 Inc.*, 486 F.3d 526 (9th Cir. 2007).

Some courts have held, however, that in order to recover a hypothetical license fee, there must be some evidence (such as existing "benchmark" licenses) that the plaintiff would have been willing to license the work. In a case where the plaintiff had never licensed its software and would not have licensed its software to a direct competitor, one court overturned a $1.3 billion jury verdict and granted a remittitur to $272 million (the estimated amount of harm due to lost sales), or in the alternative, a new trial on damages. *See Oracle USA, Inc. v. SAP AG*, 100 U.S.P.Q.2d (BNA) 1450 (N.D. Cal. 2011). *But see Gaylord v. United States*, 678 F.3d 1339 (Fed. Cir. 2012) (rejecting argument that hypothetical license for use of photo on postage stamp was limited to what Postal Service had paid in the past).

(4) *Speculativeness.* Often plaintiff claims that it lost profits from the sale of copies of the work that it would have made if the defendant had not infringed. In such a case, the plaintiff bears the burden of demonstrating both what its gross revenue would have been and what its costs would have been, to arrive at net profit. *See Taylor v. Meirick*, 712 F.2d 1112 (7th Cir. 1983) (reversing award based on lost revenue rather than lost profit). *Polar Bear* illustrates a common pitfall in the proof of such damages (and damages in general): "undue speculation." What, if anything, could Polar Bear have done to improve its proof that the infringement had led to its business failure? Note, however, that avoiding speculativeness does not mean offering proof to an exact certainty.

(5) *Double counting.* Although the Act allows recovery of both actual damages and defendant's profits, plaintiff can only recover profits that are not taken into account when computing actual damages. Sometimes, a plaintiff will have to *choose between* its actual damages and the defendant's profits because those elements of recovery represent the same harm.

In *Taylor v. Meirick*, the defendant made and sold maps nearly identical to the plaintiff's. Taylor claimed damages of $19,300, which he said he would have earned from the sale of his maps but for Meirick's infringement, plus $3,300 made by Meirick from sales of the infringing maps — and the trial court allowed both. By Judge Posner's calculations, however, Taylor had both produced defective figures to start with and failed to make the set-off required to avoid double-counting. Result: a remand for a new trial on damages.

In some cases, the infringer's profits will be greater than the plaintiff's losses — perhaps because the infringer is a better businessperson, or just lucky! Imagine, for example, that a successful movie has been based (without authorization) on the work of a struggling young novelist who had no prospects of making a movie sale. Wouldn't awarding the novelist a share confer an undeserved windfall, while penalizing the infringer for his/her superior efficiency? Yes. Wouldn't it also discourage infringements — and encourage licenses? Again, yes. In *Taylor*, Judge Posner opted hypothetically for permitting recovery: To do otherwise would encourage the user to "bypass the market by stealing the copyright and forcing the owner to seek compensation from the courts for his loss. Since the infringer's gain might exceed the owner's loss, . . . limiting damages to that loss would not effectively deter this kind of forced exchange." 712 F.2d at 1120.

(6)　How should courts deal with cases in which there are no profits or losses, as those conventionally understood? Suppose, for example, that the plaintiff isn't in the business of using (or licensing others to use) its work in the way the infringing defendant has used it. And suppose further that the defendant's use is a business disaster, yielding nothing but losses. The usual answer is that, in such a situation, the plaintiff is remitted to statutory damages, but (as we will see when we cover that species of damages below) there will be situations in which this solution is not available. Is this situation then one of a right — and a wrong! — without a remedy?

Not necessarily, as it turns out. *In extremis*, some courts have fashioned an alternative "value of use" or "saved acquisition costs" measure of actual damages, reasoning that the value of whatever costs the defendant might have saved by virtue of its infringement ought to accrue to the plaintiff. *See, e.g., Deltak, Inc. v. Advanced Systems, Inc.*, 767 F.2d 357 (7th Cir. 1985). This approach has been limited to situations in which statutory damages are unavailable. *See, e.g., Storm Impact, Inc. v. Software of the Month Club*, 13 F. Supp. 2d 782 (N.D. Ill. 1998).

Another possibility would be to consider damages for reputational harm to the plaintiff. In *Rainey v. Wayne State University*, 26 F. Supp. 2d 963 (E.D. Mich. 1998), one of the plaintiff's claims (not adjudicated in the reported opinion) was that her artistic reputation had suffered as the result of the upside-down reproduction of her painting in an infringing sales brochure for automobiles. Would this be overreaching? *See Graham v. James*, 144 F.3d 229, 238-39 (2d Cir. 1998) (remanding on other grounds), where the availability of damages for non-attribution is linked to non-speculative proof of lost economic opportunities.

(7)　What if the defendant's domestic infringing activities have given rise to revenues from foreign markets? The Second Circuit has for some time followed a rule which permits awards of infringer's profits in such situations, starting with *Sheldon v. Metro-Goldwyn Pictures Corp.*, 106 F.2d 45 (2d Cir. 1939), *aff'd*, 309 U.S. 390 (1940). The Ninth Circuit, however, has held that the *Sheldon* rule should be limited to an award of profits (on a constructive trust theory) and should not extend to an award of actual damages, in order to avoid applying the Copyright Act extraterritorially. *Los Angeles News Serv. v. Reuters Television Int'l, Ltd.*, 340 F.3d 926 (9th Cir. 2003). For details, see the discussion in § 8.04 above.

Infringer's Profits

(8) *Opportunities and risks. Polar Bear* illustrates both why many plaintiffs concentrate on recovering defendants' profits — and some of the pitfalls they face in doing so. Why does § 504(b) allocate burdens of proof as it does? Literally, the section requires the plaintiff to prove "*only* the infringer's gross revenue," after which the defendant must then show "his or her deductible expenses and the elements of profit attributable to factors other than the copyrighted work." (For an example of what happens when a defendant fails to do so, see *Johnson v. Jones,* 149 F.3d 494 (6th Cir. 1998).) But will just any proof of gross revenues do? Why did Polar Bear's proof fall short?

(9) The requirement of a "causal link" is illustrated in *Mackie v. Rieser,* 296 F.3d 909 (9th Cir. 2002) (artist whose work was infringed in season brochure of Seattle Symphony could not recover a percentage of the Symphony's gross revenues), on which the *Polar Bear* court relied, and by *Bouchat v. Baltimore Ravens Football Club, Inc.,* 346 F.3d 514 (4th Cir. 2003) (plaintiff failed to offer non-speculative evidence that revenues from ticket sales, broadcast licenses, game programs, parking, and food concessions were attributable to infringing logo design). By way of contrast, note the *Polar Bear* court's discussion of *Andreas v. Volkswagen of America, Inc.,* 336 F.3d 789 (8th Cir. 2003), in which the defendant had "the burden of establishing that its profit was attributable to factors other than the infringing [advertisement]," *id.* at 797, and the plaintiff ended up with 10% of the profits from the new car model in question. Are you satisfied by the distinction that the *Polar Bear* opinion draws? *See also Balsley v. LFP, Inc.,* 691 F.3d 747 (6th Cir. 2012) (plaintiff does not have the burden of proving a causal link; upholding an award of 12% of gross revenue for magazine issue, despite the fact that magazine was sold in shrink-wrap and infringing photo was not advertised on cover); *Bonner v. Dawson,* 404 F.3d 290 (4th Cir. 2005) (affirming jury verdict that profit from construction and leasing of building was not attributable to infringing exterior design).

(10) In calculating awards of infringer's profits, courts generally allow defendants to deduct only their "variable" (or "incremental") costs, and not their "fixed" ones. *See, e.g., Kamar Int'l, Inc. v. Russ Berrie & Co.,* 752 F.2d 1326 (9th Cir. 1984). For an extensive review of the cases classifying various kinds of expenditures according to these categories, see *In re Independent Service Organizations Antitrust Litigation,* 23 F. Supp. 2d 1242 (D. Kan. 1998). *See also Taylor v. Meirick,* 712 F.2d at 1121 ("[c]osts that would be incurred anyway should not be subtracted, because by definition they cannot be avoided by curtailing the profit-making activity").

(11) When an infringer's profits are attributable to factors in addition to use of the plaintiff's work, an apportionment of profits is proper. One pattern occurs, as in *Frank Music Corp. v. Metro-Goldwyn-Mayer, Inc.,* 772 F.2d 505 (9th Cir. 1985), when infringing materials are commingled with other materials. In that case, an abbreviated version of plaintiff's musical comedy, *Kismet,* was incorporated into defendant's Las Vegas revue. Proof that the defendant's successful venture was attributable to aspects other than the copyrighted work can reduce drastically the percentage of recoverable profits. The leading case is *Sheldon v. Metro-Goldwyn*

Pictures Corp., 309 U.S. 390 (1940). In *Sheldon*, the Supreme Court allowed a 20% recovery of defendant's profits from the motion picture *Letty Lyndon* as attributable to plaintiff's copyrighted play. The motion picture's success was due in large part to aspects unrelated to the copyrighted work, such as famous movie stars and the MGM screenplay. Despite the virtually impossible task of exact apportionment, *Sheldon* stands for the proposition, affirmed in *Frank Music*, that the court should attempt to apportion when there is a reasonable basis for doing so. *See also John G. Danielson, Inc. v. Winchester-Conant Properties, Inc.*, 322 F.3d 26 (1st Cir. 2003) (District Court erred in holding that apportionment was unavailable where infringing plans were "intertwined" with noninfringing contributions). For a recent and unusually detailed judicial application of apportionment principles, see *Caffey v. Cook*, 409 F. Supp. 2d 484 (S.D.N.Y. 2006).

Miscellaneous Matters

(12) *Prejudgment interest.* Under the current Copyright Act (which is silent on the issue), whether the plaintiff should be awarded prejudgment interest on damages and/or profits under § 504(b) is a matter of conflict among the circuits. Compare the treatment of the issue in *Polar Bear* (holding in an omitted portion of the opinion that prejudgment interest is available and may be awarded on remand) *and William A. Graham Co. v. Haughey*, 646 F.3d 138 (3d Cir. 2011) (affirming award of prejudgment interest) with *Robert R. Jones Assocs. v. Nino Homes*, 858 F.2d 274 (6th Cir. 1988) (vacating award of prejudgment interest), and *Danielson* (affirming denial of prejudgment interest). Can you articulate the rationale (in terms of deterrence, compensation, or both) for such interest awards?

(13) *Tax expense.* Should taxes paid on income from sales of infringing products be deductible? In general, income tax paid on profits is not deductible where infringement was conscious and deliberate. For non-willful infringers, however, income tax deduction is appropriate. For a discussion of these issues, see *In Design v. K-Mart Apparel Corp.*, 13 F.3d 559 (2d Cir. 1994).

(14) *Pretrial Settlements.* Should the amount of pre-trial settlements with other defendants be deducted from the amount of damages found by the jury at trial? In *BUC Int'l Corp. v. Int'l Yacht Council Ltd.*, 517 F.3d 1271 (11th Cir. 2008), the court held that such a deduction was proper under the "one satisfaction" rule, an equitable doctrine that "operates to prevent double recovery, or the overcompensation of a plaintiff for a single injury." *Id.* at 1277; *accord TMTV Corp. v. Mass Prods., Inc.*, 645 F.3d 464 (1st Cir. 2011).

[2]   Statutory or "In Lieu" Damages

COLUMBIA PICTURES TELEVISION v. KRYPTON BROADCASTING OF BIRMINGHAM, INC.
United States Court of Appeals, Ninth Circuit
106 F.3d 284 (1997), *rev'd and remanded sub nom.*
Feltner v. Columbia Pictures Television, Inc.,
523 U.S. 340 (1998)

BRUNETTI, CIRCUIT JUDGE:

C. Elvin Feltner is the owner of Krypton International Corporation, which in turn owns three television stations in the southeast. Columbia Pictures Television licensed several television shows to the three stations, including "Who's the Boss?," "Silver Spoons," "Hart to Hart," and "T.J. Hooker." After the stations became delinquent in paying royalties, Columbia attempted to terminate the licensing agreements. The stations continued to broadcast the programs, and Columbia filed suit. During the course of the litigation, Columbia dropped all causes of action except its copyright claims against Feltner. The district court found Feltner vicariously and contributorily liable for copyright infringement on the part of the Krypton defendants, granted summary judgment in favor of Columbia on liability, and, after a bench trial, awarded Columbia $8,800,000 in statutory damages and over $750,000 in attorneys' fees and costs. In this appeal, Feltner and Krypton International challenge several of the district court's rulings. . . .

IV. COURT TRIAL ON STATUTORY DAMAGES

Section 504(c)(1) of the Act allows a copyright holder to elect statutory damages in lieu of actual damages. If statutory damages have been elected, and a defendant is found to have infringed, damages are to be awarded "in a sum of not less than $500 or more than $20,000 as the court considers just." 17 U.S.C. § 504(c)(1). Additionally, if the "court finds . . . that infringement was committed willfully, the court in its discretion may increase the award of statutory damages to a sum of not more than $100,000," and if the court finds that the infringement was committed innocently "the court [in] its discretion may reduce the award of statutory damages to a sum of not less than $200." *Id.* § 504(c)(2). Columbia elected statutory damages. Over Feltner's objection, the district court held a bench trial on damages, found Feltner's infringement to be willful, and fixed the statutory damages at $20,000 per violation.

Feltner argues that the district court's denial of his request for a jury trial on the issue of statutory damages was erroneous, both as a matter of statutory interpretation and because it deprived him of his Seventh Amendment right to a jury trial. We reject Feltner's argument.

[On this issue, the U.S. Supreme Court reversed and remanded the case, *sub nom. Feltner v. Columbia Pictures Television, Inc.*, 523 U.S. 340 (1998). See § 8.02 above, and the Notes and Questions hereafter, for discussion.]

Heather Locklear and William Shatner in "T.J. Hooker"
The Everett Collection

V. WILLFULNESS FINDING

"Willful" within the meaning of § 504(c)(2) means "with knowledge that the defendant's conduct constitutes copyright infringement." *Peer Int'l Corp. v. Pausa Records, Inc.*, 909 F.2d 1332, 1335 n.3 (9th Cir. 1990) (quoting 4 NIMMER ON COPYRIGHT § 14.04[B], at 14.40.2–.3 (1989)). "To refute evidence of willful infringement, [the defendant] must not only establish its good faith belief in the innocence of its conduct, it must also show that it was reasonable in holding such a belief." *Id.* at 1336.

Feltner contends that the district court's findings of willfulness are unsupported by the evidence. In support of this contention, Feltner presents his version of how the evidence should be interpreted. Feltner, however, neglects to mention that the district court's finding is reviewed for clear error. *See* Fed. R. Civ. P. 52(a). Feltner's arguments, at best, demonstrate that the facts presented to the district court were susceptible to more than one interpretation. Considering that all 440 of the infringing episodes were broadcast after Columbia's clear termination of the licensing agreements on October 17, 1991, and 415 of them were broadcast after the complaint in this action was filed, we cannot say that the district court's finding was clearly erroneous. . . .

VII. CALCULATION OF THE NUMBER OF INFRINGEMENTS

A. The Stations Were Separate Infringers

Section 504(c)(1) of the Act provides that statutory damages may be awarded "for all infringements involved in the action, with respect to any one work, for which any one infringer is liable individually, or for which any two or more infringers are liable jointly and severally. . . ." Thus, when statutory damages are assessed against one defendant or a group of defendants held to be jointly and severally liable, each work infringed may form the basis of only one award, regardless of the number of separate infringements of that work. . . . However, "where separate infringements for which two or more defendants are not jointly liable are joined in the same action, separate awards of statutory damages would be appropriate." H.R. Rep. No. 94-1476, 94th Cong., 2d Sess., at 162 . . .

By finding that "the 'Who's the Boss?' episodes broadcast by WNFT are separate acts of infringement from the episodes broadcast by WTVX," the district court impliedly found that WNFT and WTVX were not joint tortfeasors with respect to the broadcasting of these episodes. Feltner, relying on *RCA/Ariola International, Inc. v. Thomas & Grayston Co.*, 845 F.2d 773, 778-779 (8th Cir. 1988), argues that this finding was erroneous because Columbia had repeatedly alleged in its complaint that all of the defendants acted together and should be treated as one.

RCA/Ariola is distinguishable. In that case, the district court had found a group of defendants to be jointly and severally liable. *Id.* at 778. On appeal, the Eighth Circuit rejected the plaintiff's argument that the district court's finding was erroneous. Because the plaintiff asserted in its summary judgment papers that the defendants were jointly and severally liable, the plaintiff "invited any error and ha[d] no grounds to complain." *Id.* at 779. In contrast to *RCA/Ariola*, the district court's finding was contrary to the allegations in the complaint and it is the defendant who is challenging the findings. Feltner has not presented sufficient facts to develop a "judicial estoppel" argument. . . . Thus, despite the fact that the district court's finding on this issue was both favorable to the plaintiff and contrary to the complaint, Feltner has failed to demonstrate that the finding was erroneous.

B. Each Episode Was a Separate Work

As mentioned, § 504(c)(1) of the Act provides that statutory damages may be awarded "for all infringements involved in the action, with respect to any one work." Section 504(c)(1) further provides that "for purposes of this subsection, all the parts of a compilation or derivative work constitute one work." The district court found that each infringed episode of the television series constituted a separate work for purposes of § 504(c)(1). Feltner argues that each series, and not each episode, constitutes a work.

The two courts to have addressed whether each episode of a television series constitutes a separate work have both held in the affirmative. *Gamma Audio & Video, Inc. v. Ean-Chea*, 11 F.3d 1106, 1116-17 (1st Cir. 1993); *Twin Peaks Prods., Inc. v. Publications Int'l, Ltd.*, 996 F.2d 1366, 1380-81 (2d Cir. 1993). Feltner attempts to distinguish these cases by arguing that the episodes at issue are not separate works because they do not have independent economic value.

While Feltner correctly states the proper test to apply in analyzing whether each episode is a separate work, *see Gamma Audio*, 11 F.3d at 1117 (focusing on whether each television episode "has an independent economic value and is, in itself, viable"); *Walt Disney Co. v. Powell*, 897 F.2d 565, 569 (D.C. Cir. 1990) (stating that "separate copyrights are not distinct unless they can 'live their own copyright life' ") (quoting *Robert Stigwood Group Ltd. v. O'Reilly*, 530 F.2d 1096, 1105 (2d Cir. 1976)), the facts upon which Feltner bases his argument — that the episodes are licensed as a series — were addressed and rejected in *Gamma Audio*.

In *Gamma Audio*, the district court found that the episodes were a single work because the copyright holder sold only complete sets of the series to video stores. 11 F.3d at 1117. The First Circuit found this unpersuasive. Instead, the court found significant "the fact that (1) viewers who rent the tapes from their local video stores may rent as few or as many tapes as they want, may view one, two, or twenty episodes in a single setting, and may never watch or rent all of the episodes; and (2) each episode in the . . . series was separately produced." *Id.*

In this case, the different episodes were broadcast over the course of weeks, months, and years. From this fact, it was reasonable for the district court to conclude that, as in *Gamma Audio*, viewers may watch as few or as many episodes as they want, and may never watch all of the episodes. Additionally, it was clear from the record that the episodes could be repeated and broadcast in different orders. Nor does Feltner contest that the episodes were separately written, produced, and registered. Thus, this case comes squarely within the holdings of *Gamma Audio* and *Twin Peaks*.

Feltner also contends that each series was an anthology, a type of "compilation" under § 504(c). *See* § 101 (defining "compilation" as including "collective works"); *id.* (defining "collective work" as "a work, such as a periodical issue, anthology, or encyclopedia, in which a number of contributions, constituting separate and independent works in themselves, are assembled into a collective whole"). Feltner argues that the question of whether the episodes amounted to a "collective whole" was a factual one. Thus, argues Feltner, the district court's refusal to allow Feltner to produce evidence on the issue, which would have consisted of a license agreement and expert testimony that "programs of this nature are considered to be anthologies," was error.

Even were Feltner allowed to prove that the programs were considered to be "anthologies," he would still have to show that they consisted of "separate and independent works . . . assembled into a collective whole." As mentioned, the evidence was uncontroverted that the episodes were broadcast over the course of weeks, months, or even years, and could be repeated and rearranged at the option of the broadcaster. Because this evidence supports the conclusion that the episodes were not "assembled into a collective whole," it was not error for the district court to reject Feltner's contention that each series was a "compilation" under § 504(c).

The district court did not err in calculating the number of infringements.

VIII. AMOUNT OF STATUTORY DAMAGES AWARDED

"The court has wide discretion in determining the amount of statutory damages to be awarded, constrained only by the specified maxima and minima." *Harris v. Emus Records Corp.*, 734 F.2d 1329, 1335 (9th Cir. 1984). "Within these limits the court's discretion and sense of justice are controlling." *Peer International*, 909 F.2d at 1336 (quoting *F.W. Woolworth Co. v. Contemporary Arts*, 344 U.S. 228, 232 (1952)). Feltner argues that the court's award was erroneous because it failed to take into account certain factors and because it failed to articulate its reasons for the award. However, considering the numerous willful infringements involved, for which the maximum award is $100,000 per work infringed, the district court's award of $20,000 per work infringed is well within the statutory limits and is not an abuse of discretion. . . .

CONCLUSION

[Except on the issue of the attorneys' fees discretionarily awarded by the District Court to Columbia, as to which the matter was remanded for explanation, the Court of Appeals affirmed in all respects.]

NOTES AND QUESTIONS

(1) As *Krypton* illustrates, § 504(c) of the Copyright Act entitles a prevailing copyright owner who has timely complied with the Act's registration requirements to recover statutory damages, within prescribed minimum and maximum amounts (now $750 to $30,000, or $150,000 in cases of willfulness) instead of actual damages and profits. The allowance of statutory damages is unique to copyright law. Statutory damages cannot be recovered for patent, trademark, or trade secret infringement.

(2) *Right to jury trial. Krypton* is significant for a number of other reasons, as well. Most importantly, as we saw in § 8.02 above, the decision reproduced above was reversed and remanded by the Supreme Court of the United States, *sub nom. Feltner v. Columbia Pictures Television, Inc.*, 523 U.S. 340 (1998), on the basis that the Seventh Amendment to the U.S. Constitution affords either party the right to a jury trial, on demand, in an action in which the relief sought includes statutory damages. We will return to the "fall-out" from *Feltner* in this regard after considering other § 504(c) issues raised by the Ninth Circuit's own decision in the case (which, for the sake of clarity, we will continue to refer to here as *Krypton*).

(3) *Willfulness.* According to the *Krypton* court, the defendant's act is willful if he/she proceeds with knowledge that the conduct in question constitutes an infringement. Can a lesser degree (or different kind) of culpability satisfy the willfulness standard? In some instances, a reckless disregard for the plaintiff's rights may provide sufficient evidence of willfulness. *Yurman Design, Inc. v. PAJ, Inc.*, 262 F.3d 101, 112 (2d Cir. 2001). Note also that 504(c)(3), added in 2005, provides a rebuttable presumption of willfulness if the infringer "knowingly provided or knowingly caused to be provided materially false contact information . . . in registering, maintaining, or renewing a domain name used in connection with

the infringement." But merely determining that the defendant's infringing act was willful does not establish the amount of statutory damages to be awarded. Rather, § 504(c)(2) provides that the court may then "in its discretion" increase the award.

Note that under §§ 401(d) and 402(d), a defendant cannot claim to be an "innocent" infringer for purposes of calculating statutory damages if proper notice appears on the copies or phonorecords of the work to which the defendant had access. *See, e.g., Maverick Recording Co. v. Harper*, 598 F.3d 193 (5th Cir. 2010) (rule satisfied if published CDs bore proper notice, even though infringing audio files which defendant downloaded did not; subjective intent is irrelevant); *BMG Music v. Gonzalez*, 430 F.3d 888 (7th Cir. 2005) (same).

(4) *Setting the award.* What factors should be considered in fixing the exact amount of statutory damages per infringed work? *See, e.g., Curet-Velazquez v. ACEMLA de Puerto Rico, Inc.*, 656 F.3d 47, 58 (1st Cir. 2011) (factors to be considered include "the expenses saved and profits reaped by the defendants in connection with the infringements, the revenues lost by the plaintiff as a result of the defendant's conduct, and the state of mind of the infringers"); *NFL v. PrimeTime 24 Joint Venture*, 131 F. Supp. 2d 458 (S.D.N.Y. 2001) (adding "the deterrent effect on the defendant and third parties, the defendant's cooperation in providing evidence concerning the value of the infringing material, and the conduct and attitude of the parties").

Some courts have held that statutory damages should bear some discernible relationship to the compensatory damages that the plaintiff otherwise would have been awarded. *See, e.g., RSO Records, Inc. v. Peri*, 596 F. Supp. 849 (S.D.N.Y. 1984); *Milene Music, Inc. v. Gotauco*, 551 F. Supp. 1288 (D.R.I. 1982). That said, "[c]ourts have . . . focused largely on the element of intent, and the per-infringement award tends understandably to escalate, in direct proportion to the blameworthiness of the infringing conduct." *Milene Music*, 551 F. Supp. at 1296. Thus, where the infringer had been a defendant in six similar actions in the previous three years and the court concluded that "the business of encroaching [on] others' copyrights [was] not unfamiliar to [him]," the plaintiff received in statutory damages an amount approximately eight times as great as its actual damages. *Lauratex Textile Corp. v. Allton Knitting Mills, Inc.*, 519 F. Supp. 730, 733 (S.D.N.Y. 1981).

(5) In *Feltner*, the Supreme Court stated that "[s]tatutory damages may serve purposes traditionally associated with legal relief, such as compensation and punishment." 523 U.S. at 352. It is conventional wisdom that punitive damages, as such, are not available under the Copyright Act. *See, e.g., On Davis v. The Gap, Inc.*, 246 F.3d 152, 172 (2d Cir. 2001); *Bucklew v. Hawkins, Ash, Baptie & Co.*, 329 F.3d 923, 933-34 (7th Cir. 2003). Notwithstanding some ill-considered dicta to the contrary, this conventional wisdom recently has been reaffirmed. *See Viacom Int'l, Inc. v. YouTube, Inc.*, 540 F. Supp. 2d 461 (S.D.N.Y. 2008); *Calio v. Sofa Express, Inc.*, 368 F. Supp. 2d 1290 (M.D. Fla. 2005). Note, however, that punitive damages may be available in state-law actions for infringement of common-law copyright in pre-Feb. 15, 1972 sound recordings. *See Bridgeport Music, Inc. v. Justin Combs Publishing*, 507 F.3d 470 (6th Cir. 2007) (holding award of $3.5 million in punitive damages unconstitutionally excessive under the Due Process Clause).

How do awards of statutory damages for willful infringement differ from awards of punitive damages? That statutory damages may sometimes serve the same purpose as punitive damages is borne out by the case law, such as the $8.8 million in *Krypton. See also UMG Recordings, Inc. v. MP3.com, Inc.*, 56 U.S.P.Q.2d (BNA) 1376 (S.D.N.Y. 2000). After a three-day trial, the court found MP3 to have willfully infringed Universal's musical copyrights and imposed statutory damages of $25,000 per CD. Judgment eventually was entered for a total of $53.4 million. 2000 U.S. Dist. LEXIS 17907 (S.D.N.Y., Nov. 16, 2000).

(6) An interesting debate has developed over whether the constitutional limitations in *BMW of North America, Inc. v. Gore*, 517 U.S. 559 (1996) and *State Farm Mutual Auto. Inc. Co. v. Campbell*, 538 U.S. 408 (2003), which imposed a presumptive maximum ratio between punitive damages and actual damages under the Due Process Clause, apply to statutory damages under the Copyright Act. The issue has arisen in the context of peer-to-peer file sharing.

In *Capitol Records, Inc. v. Thomas-Rasset*, 680 F. Supp. 2d 1045 (D. Minn. 2010), defendant was found to have willfully infringed 24 songs. The first jury awarded statutory damages of $9,250 per song, for a total award of $222,000. After the court ordered a new trial (for incorrect jury instructions on liability), the second jury awarded statutory damages of $80,000 per song, for a total award of $1,920,000. The trial judge held that the award was grossly excessive, and it granted a remittitur to $2,250 per song (three times the minimum amount of statutory damages), for a total award of $54,000. Plaintiffs rejected the remittitur, and a third jury awarded statutory damages of $62,500 per song, for a total award of $1,500,000. The trial judge found that the award violated the Due Process Clause and ordered it reduced to $2,250 per song. 799 F. Supp. 2d 999 (D. Minn. 2011).

On appeal, however, the Eighth Circuit held that the District Court erred in applying *Gore* and *Campbell*. Instead, it held that statutory damages should be overturned only if they are "so severe and oppressive as to be wholly dispropor-tioned to the offense and obviously unreasonable," *St. Louis, I. M. & S. Ry. Co. v. Williams*, 251 U.S. 63 (1919), and it reinstated the original verdict of $222,000. 692 F.3d 899 (8th Cir. 2012).

See also Sony BMG Music Entertainment v. Tenenbaum, 721 F. Supp. 2d 85 (D. Mass. 2010) (holding award of $22,500 per song, for a total of $675,000, violated the Due Process Clause), *vacated and remanded*, 660 F.3d 487 (1st Cir. 2011) (ordering court to consider remittitur instead); *Zomba Enterprises, Inc. v. Panorama Records, Inc.*, 491 F.3d 574, 586-88 (6th Cir. 2007) (upholding ratio of statutory damages to actual damages of 44:1 under *Williams*); *but cf. Parker v. Time Warner Entertainment Co.*, 331 F.3d 13, 22 (2d Cir. 2003) (suggesting in dicta that *Gore* and *Campbell* might apply to statutory damages under Cable Communications Policy Act).

(7) *The number of infringements.* In addition to assessing damages for a willful infringement, the court in *Krypton* was confronted with the problem of deciding the number of infringements that would serve as the basis for statutory damages. In this regard, consider those portions of § 504(c)(1) and its legislative history that concern multiple infringements. Are they intended to govern situations in which the copyright holder joins, in a single action, a series of claims for infringements of

his/her rights in multiple works? If not, what situations are governed by § 504(c)(1)? *See Bryant v. Media Right Prods.*, 603 F.3d 135 (2d Cir. 2010) (one award of statutory damages per album, as a "compilation," rather than per song). *But see WB Music Corp. v. RTV Communication Group, Inc.*, 445 F.3d 538 (2d Cir. 2006) (§ 504(c)(1) applies only to a compilation made by the copyright owner, and does not apply to a new compilation of 13 songs made by the defendant, so separate awards of statutory damages per song was appropriate). What if eight registrations are obtained for eight episodes of a popular television program, where the basic plot continues throughout all eight episodes? Would your answer change if a book written as a unitary work was later adapted for television as a series of eight episodes? *See Twin Peaks Prods., Inc. v. Publ'ns Int'l, Ltd.*, 996 F.2d 1366, 1381 (2d Cir. 1993). You also may wish to consider a later episode in the *Feltner* saga itself: *MCA Television Ltd. v. Feltner*, 89 F.3d 766 (11th Cir. 1996) (TV series episodes considered as separate works for statutory damages purposes, leading to a total award of $9 million and a vigorous dissent).

What if the plaintiff's copyright in a single work has been infringed by several different acts, all committed by the same infringer? The House Report is quite emphatic: "A single infringer of a single work is liable for a single amount between $[750] and $[30,000], no matter how many acts of infringement are involved in the action and regardless of whether the acts were separate, isolated, or occurred in a related series." Moreover, as *Krypton* indicates, only one award per work may be made against defendants who are jointly and severally liable. *See Louis Vuitton Malletier S.A. v. Akanoc Solutions, Inc.*, 658 F.3d 936 (9th Cir. 2011). If, however, two or more defendants are individually liable, as in *Krypton*, then separate awards are appropriate.

(8) In *Walt Disney Co. v. Powell*, 897 F.2d 565 (D.C. Cir. 1990), defendant Powell sold shirts that bore the famous Disney characters, Mickey and Minnie Mouse, in various poses. The District Court held that six works were willfully infringed, supporting an assessment of six statutory damages recoveries. The Court of Appeals found that only two works had been infringed, observing "that where separate copyrights 'have no separate economic value, whatever their artistic value they must be considered part of a work for purposes of the copyright statute.'" The court continued: "While Mickey and Minnie are certainly distinct, viable works with separate economic value and copyright lives of their own, . . . Mickey is still Mickey whether he is smiling or frowning, running or walking, waving his left hand or his right. Thus, we find that Powell's mouse-face shirts infringed only two of Disney's works." *Id.* at 569.

Do you agree that economic viability should be the standard? What does it mean to say that a work is economically viable? And who should make this determination? *See also Bryant* (refusing to recognize an exception to the "one award per compilation" rule for parts of a compilation having independent economic value).

More fundamentally still, how sound is the court's math? Are characters "works"? Is it important to know that Mickey and Minnie were both introduced to a waiting world in the same "short": *Steamboat Willie* (1928)? What if defendant has made a faithful but unauthorized film of plaintiff's epic novel, which features a gallery of literally dozens of colorful and "distinctly marked" literary characters?

How many awards of statutory damages are appropriate?

(9) *Statutory damages and copyright registration.* Section 412 of the Copyright Act provides that no award of statutory damages — or attorneys' fees — "shall be made for . . . any infringement of copyright commenced after first publication of the work and before the effective date of its registration, unless such registration is made within three months after the first publication of the work." Consider the impact of § 412 in the following situations:

(a) What if, prior to filing suit, the plaintiff had not attempted to register his or her copyright with the Copyright Office?

(b) What if the copyright was registered (or registration was refused) six months after the commencement of the defendant's allegedly infringing course of action, and six months prior to the initiation of suit?

(c) What if the work was published in month 1, the infringing conduct was begun in month 2, and registration occurred in month 3?

And what about the oft-heard argument that where there has been a continuing course of infringing conduct, commencing before registration and continuing thereafter, post-registration acts should be available as a basis for an award of statutory damages? *See Johnson v. Jones*, 149 F.3d 494, 505 (6th Cir. 1998) ("infringement 'commences' for the purposes of § 412 when the first act in a series of acts constituting continuing infringement occurs."); *accord Derek Andrew, Inc. v. Poof Apparel Corp.*, 528 F.3d 696 (9th Cir. 2008); *Bouchat v. Bon-Ton Dept. Stores, Inc.*, 506 F.3d 315 (4th Cir. 2007).

(10) *The fallout from* Feltner. In reversing and remanding the Ninth Circuit's *Krypton Broadcasting* decision on the ground that the District Court's denial of a jury trial on statutory damages offended the Seventh Amendment, the Supreme Court in *Feltner* held that the Federal Constitution "provides a right to a jury trial *on all issues pertinent to* an award of statutory damages under § 504(c) of the Copyright Act, including the amount itself" (emphasis added). What does the emphasized language mean for future litigation?

For example, if one of the parties requests a jury, must the jury decide not only the amount of the award within the normal $750 to $30,000 range, but also whether willfulness or lack of awareness exists, within the meaning of § 504(c)(2), so as to raise or lower the normal limits? Does the jury have to decide the number of infringements, including the number of works in suit? If so, what evidence should the jury be allowed to consider, particularly on the issue of willfulness?

What happens in such cases if the trial court grants a copyright owner's motion for summary judgment on liability issues? Does there, nevertheless, have to be a jury trial on the award of statutory damages? *See BMG Music v. Gonzalez*, 430 F.3d 888 (7th Cir. 2005) (jury trial not required if copyright owner seeks only the minimum award of $750 per work infringed).

(11) Section 504(c)(1) provides that, if the copyright owner wishes to recover statutory damages in lieu of actual damages and profits, she may "elect" to do so "at any time before final judgment is rendered." What is the interaction between the copyright owner's right of election, under § 504(c)(1), and the prerogative of either

the plaintiff or the defendant, under *Feltner*, to exercise the right to jury trial? Courts have held that "a plaintiff may submit both actual damages and statutory damages to the trier of fact as alternatives and wait until the verdict is rendered to select which one it prefers." *Curet-Velazquez*, 656 F.3d at 58, quoting 6 PATRY ON COPYRIGHT § 22.171 (2011). A plaintiff may even elect statutory damages after a trial limited to actual damages and profits only, although in such a case, the plaintiff's right to jury trial on the issue of statutory damages will be deemed to have been waived, for failure to make a timely demand. *See* Fed. R. Civ. P. 38; *Ortiz-Gonzalez v. Fonovisa*, 277 F.3d 59, 63 & n.6 (1st Cir. 2002).

(12)   By the way, are you curious what happened in *Krypton* itself on remand? The jury awarded nearly $32 million in statutory damages against Feltner, about four times more than the $8.8 million the court had awarded before he demanded his right to jury trial. The award was upheld in a subsequent appeal by the Ninth Circuit. *Columbia Pictures Television, Inc. v. Krypton Broadcasting of Birmingham, Inc.*, 259 F.3d 1186 (9th Cir. 2001). The ultimate moral may be: "Be careful what you ask for. You may get it!"

[D]   Costs and Attorneys' Fees

Costs and attorneys' fees are available in a suit for copyright infringement and are entirely at the court's discretion. Under 17 U.S.C. § 412, the copyright must be registered in order for the plaintiff to recover fees (but not costs), just as preregistration is a requisite for recovery of statutory damages. The 1976 Act does not expressly provide for punitive damages, and most courts have held that punitive damages are *not* available in a copyright infringement action. See the Notes and Questions following *Krypton* above. In some cases, however, the assessment of costs and attorneys' fees (perhaps accompanied by statutory damages of up to $150,000 for willful infringement), can serve much the same deterrent purpose as punitive damages in an infringement action.

Costs

Under § 505 of the 1976 Act, "the court in its discretion may allow the recovery of full costs by or against any party other than the United States or an officer thereof." Full costs are generally not assessed, however, unless some degree of fault or bad faith is shown. Costs recovered may include amounts for filing fees, marshal's fees, transcripts, service of process, depositions, photocopying, and postage.

Fees

Reasonable attorneys' fees may be awarded to the "prevailing party." The prevailing party can be either the plaintiff or the defendant, and is the party who was successful at the conclusion of all proceedings, not just the trial on the merits. Appeals courts sometimes reverse grants and denials of attorneys' fees not for an abuse of discretion, but because their reconsideration of the substantive issues affects the determination of who is the "prevailing" party.

Unlike patent law, which limits attorneys' fees to exceptional cases, copyright has seen frequent awards of fees to prevailing plaintiffs. When the prevailing party was the defendant, however, courts formerly tended to allow recovery of attorneys' fees only if the plaintiff brought the action frivolously or in bad faith. *See Jaszi, 505 and All That — the Defendant's Dilemma*, 55 Law & Contemp. Probs. 107 (1992).

In *Fogerty v. Fantasy Inc.*, 510 U.S. 517 (1994), the Supreme Court declined to follow lower court precedent supporting favored treatment for plaintiffs on the issue of attorneys' fees. The Court held that Congress intended no such disparity between plaintiffs and defendants when, in the 1976 Act, it permitted judges to award reasonable fees to the prevailing party.

Writing for the Court, Chief Justice Rehnquist declared that the policies underlying federal copyright law are served not only by vigorous prosecution of copyright claims, but also by vigorous defense against them. Because the boundaries of the copyright monopoly should be demarcated as clearly as possible, the law should encourage defendants to litigate meritorious defenses as vigorously as it should encourage plaintiffs to advance their claims for infringement. Thus, a system that favors plaintiffs in awarding attorney's fees distorts this boundary-making function of copyright litigation and, as such, conflicts with the underlying goals of copyright law.

In addition to abrogating the double standard for plaintiffs and defendants, the Court in *Fogerty* rejected the notion that attorneys' fees should be automatic for any prevailing party. Rather, the award of attorneys' fees is in the District Court's discretion. Among the factors that may be considered in determining whether to award attorney's fees to the prevailing party are, "frivolousness, motivation, objective unreasonableness (both in the factual and legal components of the case) and the need in particular circumstances to advance considerations of compensation and deterrence." *Id.* at 534 n.19. See also *Lieb v. Topstone Indus. Inc.*, 788 F.2d 151 (3d Cir. 1986) (cited favorably in *Fogerty*), for a discussion of the various factors.

Despite the Supreme Court's emphasis on discretion, some courts have established presumptions to guide (or constrain?) that discretion. Judge Posner, in *Gonzales v. Transfer Technologies, Inc.*, 301 F.3d 608 (7th Cir. 2002), found the (non-exclusive) *Fogerty* factors "rather miscellaneous and ill-sorted," and vacated the District Court's denial of attorneys' fees to a prevailing plaintiff for failure to explain adequately its rationale. The court held that, in the case of willful infringements involving small amounts of money, attorneys' fees should be presumed in order to optimally deter willful infringement. Without the specter of attorneys' fees, willful infringement could be committed with impunity. After all, who can prosecute a copyright infringement for $3,000? In a subsequent opinion, *Assessment Technologies of Wisconsin, LLC v. WIREdata, Inc.*, 361 F.3d 434 (7th Cir. 2004), Judge Posner established a similar presumption in favor of prevailing defendants, because "without the prospect of such an award, the party might be forced into a nuisance settlement or deterred altogether from enforcing his rights."

An interesting disagreement has developed over whether and when it is appropriate to award fees to a prevailing defendant when the plaintiff's claim was not "objectively unreasonable." *Compare Virgin Records America, Inc. v.*

Thompson, 512 F.3d 724 (5th Cir. 2008) (affirming denial of attorneys' fees where dismissed action was neither frivolous nor objectively unreasonable), *Fogerty v. MGM Group Holdings, Inc.*, 379 F.3d 348 (6th Cir. 2004) (reversing award of attorneys' fees where plaintiff's claims were not objectively unreasonable), *and Matthew Bender & Co., Inc. v. West Publ'g Co.*, 240 F.3d 116 (2d Cir. 2001) ("imposition of a fee award against a copyright holder with an objectively reasonable litigation position *generally* will not promote the purposes of the Copyright Act") (emphasis added), *with Bridgeport Music, Inc. v. WB Music Corp.*, 520 F. 3d 588 (6th Cir. 2008) (affirming award of attorneys' fees despite fact that plaintiff's legal theory was objectively reasonable). Does this trend threaten to re-impose the "double standard" that was disapproved by the Supreme Court in *Fogerty?*

Fogerty notwithstanding, the availability of costs and attorneys' fees remains subject to the limitations of § 412 — yet another reason to encourage your clients to register their copyrights! The registration requirement for copyright owners reveals one weakness with *Fogerty*'s "balanced policy" in the recovery of attorneys' fees. The problem is that copyright owners must register to recover attorneys' fees, whereas defendants, of course, labor under no such requirement. *Latin American Music Co. v. ASCAP*, 642 F.3d 87 (1st Cir. 2011). Thus *Fogerty*, in dismantling one double standard, may have erected another.

As for the amount of the award, courts typically use what is known as the "lodestar" method. "This approach requires the district court to ascertain the number of hours productively expended and multiply that time by reasonable hourly rates." *Spooner v. EEN, Inc.*, 644 F.3d 62, 68 (1st Cir. 2011). The party seeking fees must support the request with adequate documentation, consisting of "contemporaneous time and billing records and information establishing the usual and customary rates in the marketplace for comparably credentialed counsel." *Id.* (Yet another reason to keep those time sheets!) The court will delete any "duplicative, unproductive, or excessive hours" in arriving at the lodestar; and it may also adjust the amount awarded for other factors, such as "a significant gap between the relief requested and the result obtained." *Id. See also Martin v. City of Indianapolis*, 28 F. Supp. 2d 1098, 1106 & n.4 (S.D. Ind. 1998) (listing 12 adjustment factors), *aff'd*, 192 F.3d 608 (7th Cir. 1999).

Incidentally, the fees (and costs) ultimately awarded to Fogerty himself, following remand of the case to the trial court, amounted to almost $1.35 million. 94 F.3d 553 (9th Cir. 1996). Other defendants also have obtained handsome awards in post-*Fogerty* actions. *See, e.g., Compaq Computer Corp. v. Ergonome, Inc.*, 387 F.3d 403 (5th Cir. 2004) ($2,765,026 to prevailing defendant, in part because the plaintiff's attorneys would have received a contingent fee of 120 times that had their client's $800 million claim prevailed).

[E]   Federal Remedies and Rights Management

The Digital Millennium Copyright Act of 1998 created new rights against interference with "rights management" mechanisms — and new federal remedies for the violation of those rights. These mechanisms consist of two elements: (1) technological protection measures (TPMs), such as encryption systems, designed to block access to copyrighted works (discussed in § 9.04) and (2) copyright management information (or CMI) accompanying copies of protected works, including information about copyright ownership and licensing terms (discussed in § 7.01).

Significantly, the new prohibitions contained in §§ 1201 and 1202 of the DMCA are not aspects of copyright law, as such. Thus, the preexisting remedies of Title 17 do not apply to violators. Instead, Chapter 12 contains its own remedies. Under the civil remedies section (§ 1203), a person injured by a violation of either § 1201 or § 1202 can seek a range of equitable and statutory remedies modeled on those in the Copyright Act. With respect to the anti-circumvention provisions of § 1201, the DMCA provides for statutory damages of from $200 to $2,500 for each act of circumvention, prohibited device, or wrongful offer or provision of service. For violations of the § 1202 CMI provisions, the range is from $2,500 to $25,000. Treble damages are available against repeat offenders (defined as persons who commit another violation within three years). Courts have discretion to reduce or waive damages in cases of innocent infringement and are required to remit them fully where the defendant is a nonprofit library, archive, or educational institution which demonstrates that it did not know, and should not have known, that its act was a violation.

Where criminal sanctions are concerned, § 1204 of the DMCA envisions fines of up to $500,000 or up to five years in prison or both for first-time offenders, and up to $1,000,000 or 10 years or both for recidivists. No criminal penalties are available against nonprofit libraries, archives, or educational institutions — although the exemption does not appear to extend to their employees, faculty, and students.

Does any of this seem to you to be overkill?

[F] Criminal Penalties

In addition to the remedies available to the copyright owner in a civil action, you should be aware that the Government may subject an infringer to criminal penalties. These penalties apply to direct infringers, and also to those who aid or abet copyright infringement. *See U.S. v. Schmidt*, 15 F. Supp. 804 (M.D. Pa. 1936); 18 U.S.C. § 2(a) (2003).

Under former § 506(a) (now § 506(a)(1)(A)), anyone who infringes a copyright "willfully and for purposes of commercial advantage or private financial gain" is subject to felony or misdemeanor punishment, as specified in 18 U.S.C. § 2319. The commercial development of the Internet, however, revealed a perceived "loophole" in this statute. In *U.S. v. La Macchia*, 871 F. Supp. 535 (D. Mass. 1994), the court quashed the prosecution of a computer bulletin board operator who provided free unauthorized copies of commercial software programs to his subscribers, on the ground that his activity lacked the then-essential element of commercial advantage or private financial gain.

In response to *La Macchia*, Congress enacted the "No Electronic Theft Act" (or NET Act) in 1997, to provide that willful infringement can be a crime even when undertaken without a profit motive. The NET Act added what is now § 506(a)(1)(B), which penalizes "the reproduction or distribution, including by electronic means, during any 180-day period, of 1 or more copies or phonorecords of 1 or more copyrighted works, which have a total retail value of more than $1,000." For a discussion of how to calculate retail value, see *United States v. Armstead*, 524 F.3d 442 (4th Cir. 2008) (when retail copies were not lawfully available at the time of infringement, only evidence of retail value was actual price at which infringing copies were sold in the market).

The Family Entertainment and Copyright Act of 2005 added an additional violation for "pre-release" infringement in § 506(a)(1)(C), criminalizing "the distribution of a work being prepared for commercial distribution, by making it available on a computer network accessible to members of the public, if such person knew or should have known that the work was intended for commercial distribution." Although added in response to the problem of movies being distributed on the Internet before their official release in theaters, the amendment applies to any class of works designated by the Register of Copyrights, including literary works. 37 C.F.R. § 202.16(b)(1). Would this amendment have criminalized the conduct in *Harper & Row, Publishers, Inc. v. Nation Enterprises* (back in Chapter 10) if the article held not to qualify for fair use had been posted on the Internet?

As originally enacted, the 1976 Act made criminal copyright infringement a misdemeanor, punishable by a $10,000 fine or imprisonment for one year. (If movies or sound recordings were infringed, the maximum punishment was $25,000 or one year for the first offense, or $50,000 or two years for repeat offenders.).

The criminal penalties were substantially overhauled in 1992. Felony liability now arises where, during any 180-day period, at least 10 copies or phonorecords of one or more copyrighted works having a retail value of more than $2,500 are reproduced or distributed without the authorization of the copyright owner. The maximum penalty for such a violation is:

- imprisonment for not more than five years for first offenders and ten years for repeat offenders, if the infringement is done for commercial advantage or private financial gain;

- imprisonment for not more than three years for first offenders and six years for repeat offenders, if the infringement is *not* for commercial advantage or private financial gain; and

- a fine as specified in either 18 U.S.C. § 3571(b) (individuals — up to $250,000) or 18 U.S.C. § 3571(c) (organizations — up to $500,000).

Where the requisite number of copies are not made within the specified time periods, or the infringing acts are acts other than reproduction or distribution, misdemeanor liability will lie (imprisonment of up to one year).

The remainder of § 506 of the Copyright Act provides additional criminal penalties. Under § 506(b), forfeiture and disposition (usually by destruction) of the infringer's copies and the equipment used in the infringement are mandatory. The final three subsections of § 506 criminalize, with appropriate punishments, the fraudulent use of copyright notice, the fraudulent removal of such notice, and the fraudulent representation of material facts in connection with copyright registration. §§ 506(c), (d) and (e), respectively.

Further criminal violations are provided in Title 18. 18 U.S.C. § 2319A penalizes unauthorized fixation of a live musical performance, when done "knowingly and for purposes of commercial advantage or private financial gain," by imprisonment up to five years for the first offense and up to ten years for the second offense. (See the notes in § 2.01[B] above for case law concerning this provision.) In addition, 18 U.S.C. § 2319B, added in 2005, makes it a felony to knowingly use or attempt to use a camcorder or other recording device to record a motion picture in a theater without authorization from the copyright owner. Violators may be imprisoned for up to three years for a first offense, and up to six years for a subsequent offense.

Criminal penalties for violations of the new prohibitions contained in Chapter 12 of the Digital Millennium Copyright Act of 1998 are discussed in § 11.01[E] above.

The Supreme Court has ruled that criminal copyright infringement, while a violation of § 506, may not also be prosecuted by the Government under the National Stolen Property Act ("NSPA") (18 U.S.C. § 2314). The Court reasoned that the latter statute contemplates punishment for the theft, conversion or fraud of *physical* goods, but not of intangible rights in intellectual property. *Dowling v. United States*, 473 U.S. 207 (1985) (NSPA not applicable to interstate transportation of "bootleg" records embodying performances by Elvis Presley of copyrighted musical works).

Criminal Enforcement of Copyright in Foreign Countries

A common complaint of U.S. copyright owners is that foreign countries do not provide adequate remedies to enforce their rights in those countries. One of the goals of the TRIPS Agreement was to provide a minimum level of enforcement that adhering countries must agree to, so that inadequate enforcement would be considered a trade violation that could be addressed through the dispute resolution procedure of the World Trade Organization. In 2007, the U.S. tested those procedures when it filed a complaint alleging that China was in violation of three of the enforcement provisions in the TRIPS Agreement. The WTO Panel announced its ruling in 2009, exonerating China on all but one of the allegations.

Art. 61 of TRIPS states reads: "Members shall provide for criminal procedures and penalties to be applied at least in cases of willful trademark counterfeiting or copyright piracy on a commercial scale." The U.S. alleged that China violated this article by announcing "thresholds" of infringement, in terms of the number of copies and monetary value, below which criminal penalties would not be applied. The Panel held that the United States did not provide enough evidence to show that these thresholds were too high to punish piracy "on a commercial scale." The Panel also held that Chinese officials had "the authority to order the destruction or disposal of infringing articles . . . outside the channels of commerce," as required by Articles 59 and 46 of TRIPS, and that TRIPS did not require that they exercise that authority. The Panel did find that Article 4 of the Chinese Copyright Law violated the TRIPS Agreement by denying any copyright protection to works that could not lawfully be distributed in China. China promptly complied with the ruling by amending Article 4 to allow infringement suits and criminal punishment against those who copy banned works.

SOPA and PIPA

Frustration with ineffective copyright enforcement against websites in foreign countries had led U.S. copyright owners (such as the MPAA) to seek legislative relief. In the 112th Congress, Sen. Patrick Leahy introduced S. 968, the Protect IP Act (PIPA), and Rep. Lamar Smith introduced H.R. 3261, the Stop Online Piracy Act (SOPA). These parallel bills authorized the Attorney General to commence an action against a "foreign infringing site" and to obtain a court order against domestic Internet service providers, search engines, payment processing services, and advertising services that would require them to cease doing business with or linking to the accused website. Proponents, including the MPAA and other copyright owners, contended that the bills were aimed only at shutting down foreign websites that were flagrantly committing large-scale, criminal copyright infringement. Opponents, including Google, Facebook, and other service providers, contended that the bills would permit a site to be shut down entirely on a mere accusation of infringement, even if the site contained a large amount of legitimate content and only a small amount of allegedly infringing content; and that the bills targeted four types of service providers on whom copyright owners had unsuccessfully sought to impose secondary liability through litigation. Opponents were particularly concerned about a provision that required service providers to take measures "to prevent the domain name of the foreign infringing site . . . from resolving to that domain name's Internet protocol address," contending that it would "break the Internet" and interfere with a proposed upgrade to the domain name system that was designed to provide greater security against malicious "redirection" of Internet traffic.

Despite these concerns, it appeared that the bills were headed toward passage until they were derailed by an extraordinary event. On January 18, 2012, over 115,000 Internet sites joined together in an online protest against SOPA and PIPA. Some sites, including Wikipedia, blacked out access to their content for the day, to simulate the potential effect of a shutdown. Others, including Google, altered their home pages and encouraged users to contact Congress. After Congress received millions of phone calls and e-mails opposing the legislation, several co-sponsors withdrew their support, and the leaders of the House and Senate announced that further consideration of the bills would be postponed until a greater consensus could be reached.

You may wish to compare SOPA and PIPA with the Online Protection and Enforcement of Digital Trade Act (or OPEN Act), an alternative measure introduced by Sen. Ron Wyden as S. 2029 and by Rep. Darrell Issa as H.R. 3782. The OPEN Act would allow expedited enforcement actions against foreign infringing websites to be brought to the U.S. International Trade Commission. The sponsors have established a website at *www.keepthewebopen.com*, through which members of the public can submit comments and proposed improvements to the legislation.

Assuming there is a problem with foreign infringing websites, what is the best approach to solving the problem? Is there a solution that would provide meaningful relief to U.S. copyright owners without imposing unreasonable costs on legitimate Internet businesses?

Perhaps not coincidentally, on January 19, 2012, the U.S. Justice Department unsealed an indictment against Hong Kong-based file-hosting website megaupload.com and several individuals, including its founder, Kim Dotcom. The Justice Department "seized" the website's domain name and posted an anti-piracy warning on the site. The next day, police in New Zealand arrested Dotcom and authorities in New Zealand and Hong Kong seized his assets. In January 2013, Dotcom founded another cloud-storage website, Mega, and he continues to fight his extradition to the United States.

Does this action suggest that the U.S. government has sufficient tools to combat foreign infringing websites, even without SOPA and PIPA? Or does the lengthy two-year investigation suggest that more streamlined tools are needed? Should users who lost access to legitimate material stored on megaupload.com (including several famous recording artists who were using the site to distribute content) be able to seek compensation? From whom? For more information on the seizure issue, see *www.megaretrieval.com*.

§ 11.02 PREEMPTION AND STATE LAW REMEDIES

An extensive system of state law protection of intangibles always has coexisted with federal intellectual property law. State trade secret, "common-law copyright," and unfair competition laws overlap federal patent, copyright, and trademark laws both in the subject matter involved and in the rights protected. This overlap, however, creates tensions within the federal system. The vehicle for regulating these tensions is the Supremacy Clause of the Constitution, which dictates that a federal statute preempts (*i.e.*, displaces) state law when the state law "stands as an obstacle to the accomplishment and execution of the full purposes and objectives of Congress." *Hines v. Davidowitz*, 312 U.S. 52, 67 (1941). As applied to forms of intellectual property protection, the issue under the Supremacy Clause is not whether states have the power to protect intellectual property, but rather under what circumstances state protection unduly interferes with the policies of federal protection. Resolving this difficult problem often has led to irreconcilable results and conflicting doctrine — as, for example, in copyright law, where the preemption doctrine was in disarray under the 1909 Act. One objective of Congress in promulgating the new Copyright Act in 1976 was to clarify preemption doctrine. Unfortunately, as we will discuss below, the 1976 Act has done little, if anything, to solve the problem.

Some of the confusion may be simply a "hangover" from case law decided under the 1909 Act. State law (so-called "common-law copyright") protected unpublished works until publication, and federal copyright began (if it did at all) when a work was first published with proper notice. But after the work was published, it was never quite clear to what degree the states could, under non-copyright state-law doctrines, continue in effect to protect the writings of authors.

Effective January 1, 1978, the Copyright Act of 1976 eliminated the dual system of federal and state copyright protection, replacing it with a single national system under which virtually all works of authorship, whether published or unpublished, were made exclusively the subject of federal law. Partly in anticipation of conflicts between federal and state law, and partly to avoid the uncertainties of the pre-1976 preemption cases, § 301 of the 1976 Act sets forth specific criteria for preemption. Under § 301, state law is preempted when two conditions are met: first, the state law must protect the same rights as are conferred by § 106; and second, the state law must protect the same subject matter as is provided for by §§ 102 and 103. But although § 301 was intended to clarify preemption doctrine as it applied to copyright law, it has instead superimposed another set of problems on this already complicated and confusing subject.

We have organized the present section as follows. After the usual Introduction (statutory references and legislative history), we examine preemption doctrine as it developed before the 1976 Act. Much of the controversy, as we will see, concerned the misappropriation doctrine, a broad, amorphous, and basically equitable concept used by courts to protect intangible property that failed to meet federal intellectual property standards. We consider next the history of preemption under the Supremacy Clause of the U.S. Constitution, as the Supreme Court has attempted to harmonize state law not just with federal copyright law, but also with federal law in related areas of intellectual property, particularly federal patent law. Finally, we turn to preemption analysis under § 301 of the 1976 Copyright Act itself. Here, we observe the valiant struggles of the federal courts to try to administer the statutory "dividing line" between federal and state protections. As you will see, sorting out the impact of § 301 on the wide variety of possible state-created causes of action — from unfair competition to breach of contract — has proven not to be the easy task that the framers of the 1976 Act envisioned.

[A]   Introduction

Statutory References
   1976 Act: § 301
   1909 Act: § 2

Legislative History

H.R. REP. No. 94-1476 at 130-33,
reprinted in 1976 U.S.C.C.A.N. 5659, 5746-49

SECTION 301. FEDERAL PREEMPTION OF RIGHTS EQUIVALENT TO COPYRIGHT

Preemption of State Law

The intention of section 301 is to preempt and abolish any rights under the common law or statutes of a State that are equivalent to copyright and that extend to works coming within the scope of the Federal copyright law. The declaration of this principle in section 301 is intended to be stated in the clearest and most unequivocal language possible, so as to foreclose any conceivable misinterpretation of its unqualified intention that Congress shall act preemptively, and to avoid the development of any vague borderline areas between State and Federal protection.

Under section 301(a), all "legal or equitable rights that are equivalent to any of the exclusive rights within the general scope of copyright as specified by section

106" are governed exclusively by the Federal copyright statute if the works involved are "works of authorship that are fixed in a tangible medium of expression and come within the subject matter of copyright as specified by sections 102 and 103." All corresponding State laws, whether common law or statutory, are preempted and abrogated. Regardless of when the work was created and whether it is published or unpublished, disseminated or undisseminated, in the public domain or copyrighted under the Federal statute, the States cannot offer it protection equivalent to copyright. . . . The preemptive effect of section 301 is limited to State laws; as stated expressly in subsection (d) of section 301, there is no intention to deal with the question of whether Congress can or should offer the equivalent of copyright protection under some constitutional provision other than the patent-copyright clause of article 1, section 8.

As long as a work fits within one of the general subject matter categories of sections 102 and 103, the bill prevents the States from protecting it even if it fails to achieve Federal statutory copyright because it is too minimal or lacking in originality to qualify, or because it has fallen into the public domain. On the other hand, section 301(b) explicitly preserves common-law copyright protection for one important class of works: works that have not been "fixed in any tangible medium of expression." [This category includes extemporaneous speeches and improvised music that is not notated or recorded.] . . .

In a general way subsection (b) of section 301 represents the obverse of subsection (a). It sets out, in broad terms and without necessarily being exhaustive, some of the principal areas of protection that preemption would not prevent the States from protecting. Its purpose is to make clear, consistent with the 1964 Supreme Court decisions in *Sears, Roebuck & Co. v. Stiffel Co.*, 376 U.S. 225, and *Compco Corp. v. Day-Brite Lighting, Inc.*, 376 U.S. 234, that preemption does not extend to causes of action, or subject matter outside the scope of the revised Federal copyright statute. . . .

A unique and difficult problem is presented with respect to the status of sound recordings fixed before February 15, 1972, the effective date of the amendment bringing recordings fixed after that date under Federal copyright protection. [Congress decided not to preempt state law protections for pre-1972 sound recordings. See current 17 U.S.C. § 301(c). . . .]

Subsection [(d)] makes clear that nothing contained in Title 17 annuls or limits any rights or remedies under any other Federal statute.

[For a fuller excerpt from H.R. Rep. No. 94-1476, see Part Three of the Casebook Supplement.]

[B]   Misappropriation and the General Problem of Preemption

Through the years, two general attitudes have been expressed about how expansive state law should be in protecting the valuable intangibles that we call intellectual property. The "expansive" view would permit an active role for state law in filling gaps in protection left by federal law. This view would allow states to regulate intellectual property except in clear instances of conflict with federal law.

The opposing "minimalist" view would treat common-law protection for intellectual property with much suspicion because of its tendency to take information out of the public domain. This view favors federal intellectual property law and the public domain over an active regime of state regulation of intellectual property.

Our story begins with a case that did *not* concern statutory copyright under federal law *or* the Supremacy Clause, but in which the Supreme Court gave classic expression to the foregoing divergent views of intellectual property protection in a federal system. Along the way, the Court applied (or invented) a federal common-law tort of misappropriation — a tort extinguished, along with federal common law generally, in *Erie R.R. v. Tompkins*, 304 U.S. 64 (1938), but which has lived on under state law to bedevil the federal courts, in varying degrees, ever since.

The case was *International News Service v. Associated Press*, 248 U.S. 215 (1918), a case whose background and reception receives a vivid accounting in Baird, *The Story of* INS v. AP: *Property, Natural Monopoly, and the Uneasy Legacy of a Concocted Controversy, in* INTELLECTUAL PROPERTY STORIES 9-35 (J. Ginsburg & R. Dreyfuss eds., 2006). AP and INS were rival organizations, both engaged in gathering and distributing news for publication in newspapers throughout the United States. The controversy arose during World War I, when the AP was seeking ways to establish a property right in the news from Europe and chose to make an example of the Cleveland bureau of Hearst-owned INS — which had been diverting the content of AP dispatches for its own use, in a scheme that involved, *inter alia*, outright copying and corruption of AP staff. As Professor Baird explains,"[o]nce INS admitted to copying bulletins, AP would claim that copying public material also violated its rights." In the District Court, Judge Augustus Hand enjoined INS from obtaining the news reports by certain specific unfair means, including bribery, leaving it to the Court of Appeals to make new law by broadening the injunction to restrain INS from copying news from early editions and publicly posted copies of such papers. INS sought and obtained *certiorari*. Baird describes how, at this point, INS lawyers pulled a number of their best punches, because Hearst (himself a news monopolist) had no interest in unsettling the basic principle of common-law property in information — or invoking antitrust principles.

In its decision, a majority of the Supreme Court approved broad common-law power to regulate intangible interests by recognizing the misappropriation doctrine as a vehicle for protecting intellectual property. "Passing off" — unfair competition in the traditional sense of the term — was not involved, because INS was not trying to deceive consumers about the origin of the stories. It simply took valuable information from AP without permission or payment. The news stories themselves did not qualify for copyright protection, having been published without notice (and perhaps also because as news stories, they would have run afoul of the fact/expression dichotomy). Nonetheless, the Court held that INS's acts constituted a "misappropriation" because "he who has fairly paid the price should have the beneficial use of the property." 248 U.S. 215, 240 (1918). Writing for the majority, Justice Pitney based his opinion on a natural rights theory, recognizing the right of an individual to the fruits of his labor:

. . . The right of the purchaser of a single newspaper to spread knowledge of its contents gratuitously, for any legitimate purpose not unreasonably interfering with complainant's right to make merchandise of it, may be admitted; but to transmit that news for commercial use, in competition with complainant — which is what defendant has done and seeks to justify — is a very different matter. In doing this defendant, by its very act, admits that it is taking material that has been acquired by complainant as the result of organization and the expenditure of labor, skill, and money, and which is salable by complainant for money, and that defendant in appropriating it and selling it as its own is endeavoring to reap where it has not sown, and by disposing of it to newspapers that are competitors of complainant's members is appropriating to itself the harvest of those who have sown. Stripped of all disguises, the process amounts to an unauthorized interference with the normal operation of complainant's legitimate business precisely at the point where the profit is to be reaped. . . . The transaction speaks for itself and a court of equity ought not to hesitate long in characterizing it as unfair competition in business. . . .

It is said that the elements of unfair competition are lacking because there is no attempt by defendant to palm off its goods as those of the complainant, characteristic of the most familiar, if not the most typical, cases of unfair competition. . . . But we cannot concede that the right to equitable relief is confined to that class of cases. In the present case[,] . . . instead of selling its own goods as those of complainant, [defendant] substitutes misappropriation in the place of misrepresentation, and sells complainant's goods as its own.

Id. at 221-22.

Justice Brandeis, in dissent, eloquently stated the case for a narrower field of protection:

[T]he fact that a product of the mind has cost its producer money and labor, and has a value for which others are willing to pay, is not sufficient to ensure to it this legal attribute of property. The general rule of law is, that the noblest of human productions — knowledge, truths ascertained, conceptions, and ideas — become, after voluntary communication to others, free as the air to common use. Upon these incorporeal productions the attribute of property is continued after such communication only in certain classes of cases where public policy has seemed to demand it. . . .

Id. at 250. To Brandeis, then, any protection conferred on intellectual property should be limited, and, except in narrow circumstances, should be a matter of federal statutory law. Brandeis, and Justice Holmes, however, were in the minority. The *INS* majority's more expansive view of protection prevailed.

Thus was born the far-reaching equitable doctrine of "misappropriation," soon further developed under state law and providing broad, although vaguely defined, protection against the taking of intangible values. The elements of that elusive doctrine can stated as follows:

1. The plaintiff has created an intangible product through extensive time, labor, skill, and money.

2. The free-riding defendant, a competitor, makes use of that product and gains a special advantage because the defendant is not burdened with the same costs of production.

3. The plaintiff suffers commercial damage.

See Synercom Tech., Inc. v. University Computing Co., 474 F. Supp. 37, 39 (N.D. Tex. 1979). Some courts do not require a competitive relationship but rather have focused on the unjust enrichment aspect of defendant's actions. *See, e.g., Metropolitan Opera Ass'n v. Wagner-Nichols Recorder Corp.*, 101 N.Y.S.2d 483, 492 (N.Y. Sup. Ct. 1950), *aff'd*, 107 N.Y.S.2d 795 (N.Y. App. Div. 1951) (misappropriation claim upheld where defendant recorded radio broadcasts of plaintiff's operatic performances and sold them to the retail market). Other courts have added further elements, such as a requirement that the information be time-sensitive, and that the freeriding would "so reduce the incentive to produce the product or service that its existence or quality would be substantially threatened." *National Basketball Ass'n v. Motorola, Inc.*, 105 F.3d 841, 845 (2d Cir. 1997). Meantime, judges and scholars (and sometimes someone who is both) have suggested abolishing the tort altogether. *See* Posner, *Misappropriation: A Dirge*, 40 Hous. L. Rev. 621 (2003).

The misappropriation doctrine has waxed and waned. Beginning in the 1930s, the pendulum began to swing against permitting broad state protection of intangibles. See, *e.g., Cheney Bros. v. Doris Silk Corp.*, 35 F.2d 279 (2d Cir. 1929), in which Judge Learned Hand refused to extend the *INS* rationale to protect dress designers. *See also RCA Mfg. Co. v. Whiteman*, 114 F.2d 86 (2d Cir. 1940) (restrictive legend on a phonograph record cannot prevent subsequent broadcast of the record). But the misappropriation tort itself, not to mention other state-based claims that coexist uneasily with federal intellectual property protection, was never extinguished. Most recently, the doctrine has again been invoked by the Associated Press, this time against online news "aggregators" that systematically copy headlines, lead sentences and facts from AP news reports. *See Associated Press v. All-Headline News Corp.*, 608 F. Supp. 2d 454 (S.D.N.Y. 2009) (denying motion to dismiss "hot news" misappropriation claim).

The breadth of the problem can be suggested by a series of examples that actually arose prior to the passage of the 1976 Act. Suppose that plaintiffs had brought actions under state unfair competition law for copying product shapes, *e.g.*, pole lamps and fluorescent lighting fixtures, neither of which qualified for either utility or design patent protection nor had subsisting protection under federal copyright law. Were the state-based claims valid, or preempted? Suppose (prior to the sound recording amendments of 1971, effective the following year, that brought such works under federal protection via the 1909 Act) that a state sought to protect record producers against the unauthorized duplication of tape and records. Until that time, Congress could have provided such protection, but hadn't. Preemption of state law? Or suppose that a plaintiff had developed a process that was potentially patentable under statutes that Congress *had* already enacted, but that the plaintiff, choosing not to seek such protection, tried to enforce its rights to the process under state trade secret law. Preempted, or not?

These are the sorts of questions that the Supreme Court of the United States sought to answer, beginning in 1964, by resort to the Supremacy Clause of the Constitution. A brief overview of that effort follows.

[C] Preemption Under the Supremacy Clause

Prior to January 1, 1978, the law of preemption was defined not primarily by statute, but rather by four major decisions of the Supreme Court: *Sears, Roebuck & Co. v. Stiffel Co.*, 376 U.S. 225, and *Compco Corp. v. Day-Brite Lighting Inc.*, 376 U.S. 234, two cases decided on the same day in 1964; *Goldstein v. California*, 412 U.S. 546, decided in 1973; and *Kewanee Oil Co. v. Bicron Corp.*, 416 U.S. 470, decided in 1974. Only *Goldstein* directly concerned the relationship between federal law regarding *copyright* (as distinguished from other branches of intellectual property) and state law. But all four decisions addressed generally the supremacy of federal law where rights and remedies in intellectual property are concerned, and all four were treated by the courts as governing the interface between the Copyright Act and the laws of the several states. *See, e.g., Synercom Tech., Inc. v. University Computing Co.*, 474 F. Supp. 37 (N.D. Tex. 1979). In 1989, the U.S. Supreme Court undertook to summarize its previous Supremacy Clause rulings, and to delineate again the sometimes wavering line between preemption and non-preemption. That decision follows.

BONITO BOATS, INC. v. THUNDER CRAFT BOATS, INC.
Supreme Court of the United States
489 U.S. 141 (1989)

Justice O'Connor delivered the opinion of the Court.

We must decide today what limits the operation of the federal patent system places on the States' ability to offer substantial protection to utilitarian and design ideas which the patent laws leave otherwise unprotected. In *Interpart Corp. v. Italia*, 777 F.2d 678 (1985), the Court of Appeals for the Federal Circuit concluded that a California law prohibiting the use of the "direct molding process" to duplicate unpatented articles posed no threat to the policies behind the federal patent laws. In this case, the Florida Supreme Court came to a contrary conclusion. It struck down a Florida statute which prohibits the use of the direct molding process to duplicate unpatented boat hulls, finding that the protection offered by the Florida law conflicted with the balance struck by Congress in the federal patent statute between the encouragement of invention and free competition in unpatented ideas. *See* 515 So. 2d 220 (1987). We granted *certiorari* to resolve the conflict, and we now affirm the judgment of the Florida Supreme Court.

. . . [O]ur past decisions have made clear that state regulation of intellectual property must yield to the extent that it clashes with the balance struck by Congress in our patent laws. The tension between the desire to freely exploit the full potential of our inventive resources and the need to create an incentive to deploy those resources is constant. Where it is clear how the patent laws strike that balance in a particular circumstance, that is not a judgment the States may second guess.
. . .

In our decisions in *Sears, Roebuck & Co. v. Stiffel Co.*, 376 U.S. 225 (1964), and *Compco Corp. v. Day-Brite Lighting, Inc.*, 376 U.S. 234 (1964), we found that publicly known design and utilitarian ideas which were unprotected by patent occupied much the same position as the subject matter of an expired patent. The *Sears* case involved a pole lamp originally designed by the plaintiff Stiffel, who had secured both design and mechanical patents on the lamp. Sears purchased unauthorized copies of the lamps, and was able to sell them at a retail price practically equivalent to the wholesale price of the original manufacturer. Stiffel brought an action against Sears in federal District Court, alleging infringement of the two federal patents and unfair competition under Illinois law. The District Court found that Stiffel's patents were invalid due to anticipation in the prior art, but nonetheless enjoined Sears from further sales of the duplicate lamps based on a finding of consumer confusion under the Illinois law of unfair competition. The Court of Appeals affirmed, coming to the conclusion that the Illinois law of unfair competition prohibited product simulation even in the absence of evidence that the defendant took some further action to induce confusion as to source.

This Court reversed, finding that the unlimited protection against copying which the Illinois law accorded an unpatentable item whose design had been fully disclosed through public sales conflicted with the federal policy embodied in the patent laws. The Court stated:

> In the present case the "pole lamp" sold by Stiffel has been held not to be entitled to the protection of either a mechanical or a design patent. An unpatentable article, like an article on which the patent has expired, is in the public domain and may be made and sold by whoever chooses to do so. What Sears did was to copy Stiffel's design and sell lamps almost identical to those sold by Stiffel. This it had every right to do under the federal patent laws.

376 U.S., at 231.

A similar conclusion was reached in *Compco*, where the District Court had extended the protection of Illinois' unfair competition law to the functional aspects of an unpatented fluorescent lighting system. The injunction against copying of an unpatented article, freely available to the public, impermissibly "interfere[d] with the federal policy, found in Art. I, § 8, cl. 8, of the Constitution and in the implementing federal statutes, of allowing free access to copy whatever the federal patent and copyright laws leave in the public domain." *Compco, supra*, 376 U.S., at 237.

. . . Read at their highest level of generality, the two decisions could be taken to stand for the proposition that the States are completely disabled from offering any form of protection to articles or processes which fall within the broad scope of patentable subject matter. Since the potentially patentable includes "anything under the sun that is made by man," *Diamond v. Chakrabarty*, 447 U.S. 303, 309 (1980) (citation omitted), the broadest reading of *Sears* would prohibit the States from regulating the deceptive simulation of trade dress or the tortious appropriation of private information.

That the extrapolation of such a broad pre-emptive principle from *Sears* is inappropriate is clear from the balance struck in *Sears* itself. The *Sears* Court made it plain that the States "may protect businesses in the use of their trademarks, labels, or distinctive dress in the packaging of goods so as to prevent others, by imitating such markings, from misleading purchasers as to the source of the goods." *Sears, supra*, 376 U.S., at 232 (footnote omitted). Trade dress is, of course, potentially the subject matter of design patents. . . . Yet our decision in *Sears* clearly indicates that the States may place limited regulations on the circumstances in which such designs are used in order to prevent consumer confusion as to source. Thus, while *Sears* speaks in absolutist terms, its conclusion that the States may place some conditions on the use of trade dress indicates an implicit recognition that all state regulation of potentially patentable but unpatented subject matter is not *ipso facto* pre-empted by the federal patent laws.

What was implicit in our decision in *Sears*, we have made explicit in our subsequent decisions concerning the scope of federal pre-emption of state regulation of the subject matter of patent. Thus, in *Kewanee Oil Co. v. Bicron Corp.*, 416 U.S. 470 (1974), we held that state protection of trade secrets did not operate to frustrate the achievement of the congressional objectives served by the patent laws. Despite the fact that state law protection was available for ideas which clearly fell within the subject matter of patent, the Court concluded that the nature and degree of state protection did not conflict with the federal policies of encouragement of patentable invention and the prompt disclosure of such innovations.

Several factors were critical to this conclusion. First, because the public awareness of a trade secret is by definition limited, the Court noted that "the policy that matter once in the public domain must remain in the public domain is not incompatible with the existence of trade secret protection." *Id.*, at 484. Second, the *Kewanee* Court emphasized that "[t]rade secret law provides far weaker protection in many respects than the patent law." *Id.*, at 489-490. . . . The public at large remained free to discover and exploit the trade secret through reverse engineering of products in the public domain or by independent creation. Thus, the possibility that trade secret protection would divert inventors from the creative effort necessary to satisfy the rigorous demands of patent protection was remote indeed. Finally, certain aspects of trade secret law operated to protect non-economic interests outside the sphere of congressional concern in the patent laws. As the Court noted, "[a] most fundamental human right, that of privacy, is threatened when industrial espionage is condoned or is made profitable." *Id.*, at 487 (footnote omitted). There was no indication that Congress had considered this interest in the balance struck by the patent laws, or that state protection for it would interfere with the policies behind the patent system. . . .

At the heart of *Sears* and *Compco* is the conclusion that the efficient operation of the federal patent system depends upon substantially free trade in publicly known, unpatented design and utilitarian conceptions. . . . [While] our decisions since *Sears* have taken a decidedly less rigid view of the scope of federal pre-emption under the patent laws, . . . we believe that the *Sears* Court correctly concluded that the States may not offer patent-like protection to intellectual creations which would otherwise remain unprotected as a matter of federal law. . . . We understand this to be the reasoning at the core of our decisions in *Sears* and *Compco* and we reaffirm that reasoning today. . . .

Our decisions since *Sears* and *Compco* have made it clear that the Patent and Copyright Clauses do not, by their own force or by negative implication, deprive the States of the power to adopt rules for the promotion of intellectual creation within their own jurisdictions. *See Aronson* [v. *Quick Point Pencil Co.]*, 440 U.S., [257] at 262 [(1979)]; *Goldstein v. California*, 412 U.S. 546, 552-561 (1973); *Kewanee*, 416 U.S., at 478-479. Thus, where "Congress determines that neither federal protection nor freedom from restraint is required by the national interest," *Goldstein, supra*, 412 U.S., at 559, the States remain free to promote originality and creativity in their own domains.

Nor does the fact that a particular item lies within the subject matter of the federal patent laws necessarily preclude the States from offering limited protection which does not impermissibly interfere with the federal patent scheme. . . . Both the law of unfair competition and state trade secret law have co-existed harmoniously with federal patent protection for almost 200 years, and Congress has given no indication that their operation is inconsistent with the operation of the federal patent laws. . . .

Indeed, there are affirmative indications from Congress that both the law of unfair competition and trade secret protection are consistent with the balance struck by the patent laws [*e.g.*, § 43(a) of the Lanham Act]. . . . The case for federal pre-emption is particularly weak where Congress has indicated its awareness of the operation of state law in a field of federal interest, and has nonetheless decided to "stand by both concepts and to tolerate whatever tension there [is] between them." *Silkwood v. Kerr-McGee Corp.*, 464 U.S. 238, 256 (1984). The same cannot be said of the Florida statute at issue here, which offers protection beyond that available under the law of unfair competition or trade secret, without any showing of consumer confusion, or breach of trust or secrecy.

The Florida statute is aimed directly at the promotion of intellectual creation by substantially restricting the public's ability to exploit ideas which the patent system mandates shall be free for all to use. . . . It thus enters a field of regulation which the patent laws have reserved to Congress. The patent statute's careful balance between public right and private monopoly to promote certain creative activity is a "scheme of federal regulation . . . so pervasive as to make reasonable the inference that Congress left no room for the States to supplement it." *Rice v. Santa Fe Elevator Corp.*, 331 U.S. 218, 230 (1947).

. . . We therefore agree with the majority of the Florida Supreme Court that the Florida statute is preempted by the Supremacy Clause and the judgment of that court is hereby affirmed. *It is so ordered.*

NOTES AND QUESTIONS

(1)   You will recall from § 3.01 above that the specific problem addressed in the foregoing case — namely, the protection of vessel hull designs against knock-offs produced using "plug molding" or "hull splashing" techniques — was resolved by Congress in favor of hull designers in Title V of the Digital Millennium Copyright Act. The Vessel Hull Design Protection Act ("VHDPA") raises at least two major questions (quite apart from the issue of whether Congress will subsequently pour

into this at-present nearly empty vessel a raft of protections for other types of ornamental designs). First: Why doesn't such legislation to protect subpatentable or subcopyrightable subject matter raise preemption concerns of its own? Perhaps, after reading the materials that follow, you will be able to tell us the answer to that question. Second: Does passage of the VHDPA overrule *Bonito Boats*, and with it the whole *Sears-Compco-Goldstein-Kewanee* line of Supremacy Clause preemption cases? This one, we will answer for you: no. The VHDPA does not purport to overrule the Supreme Court's general jurisprudence in this area, nor would Congress have had the power to do so if it wanted. So both *Bonito Boats* and the prior line of cases it elaborates and explains remain relevant for your study of the law of preemption.

(2)   *Bonito Boats* itself (at least, in terms of its facts) is a patent preemption case. Clearly, *Sears* and *Compco* were patent cases — and clearly, in those decisions, the Supreme Court refused to distinguish between patent and copyright for preemption purposes. Should the reasoning of *Bonito Boats* likewise be applied to copyright? Why? Is there a principled basis on which courts could distinguish between the Patent and Copyright Clauses for Supremacy Clause purposes?

(3)   Both *Sears* and *Compco* were authored by Justice Hugo L. Black, whose literalist philosophy of constitutional construction already may be familiar to you from other courses. But what exactly did Justice Black say in *Sears/Compco*? That state laws protecting intellectual property are invalid insofar as they conflict with federal statutory law? Insofar as they overlap the power granted to Congress by Art. I, § 8, cl. 8 of the Constitution? Insofar as they may impede the accomplishment of "federal policy" (including a deliberate policy of non-protection for certain types of works), as the courts divine such policy by examining the constitutional grant regarding copyrights and patents as well as relevant provisions of the United States Code? Can you tell from the opinion in *Bonito Boats* which of these formulations the Supreme Court today prefers? Does it make a difference which formulation the courts embrace?

(4)   Justice Black used to carry a copy of the Constitution with him at all times. In case you have misplaced your own copy, here is the text of the Supremacy Clause: "This Constitution, and the Laws of the United States which shall be made in Pursuance thereof . . . , shall be the supreme Law of the Land; and the Judges in every State shall be bound thereby, any Thing in the Constitution or Laws of any State to the Contrary notwithstanding." U.S. Const., Art. VI.

(5)   If applied rigorously in the domain of copyright today, would the holding of *Sears/Compco* require preemption of statutory or decisional law adopted by a state to protect unoriginal works or works not fixed in a tangible medium of expression? What if the state law in question sought to protect a work that otherwise satisfied the prerequisites for federal copyright but whose subject matter had not yet been anointed by Congress as a "work of authorship" under § 102 or 103? What if the state law merely afforded the successful plaintiff in an action on a federally copyrightable work a remedy not already provided by Congress?

As you read further in these notes, try to answer the same questions by reference to the holdings in *Goldstein* and *Kewanee*.

(6) In *Goldstein v. California*, 412 U.S. 546 (1973), cited but not discussed extensively in *Bonito Boats*, the Supreme Court substantially narrowed the broad preemptive thrust of *Sears* and *Compco* (at least where copyright is concerned), holding 5-4 that states have concurrent power with the federal government to protect works of authorship, at least where Congress has chosen to leave an area of potential protection "unattended." The case involved a criminal statute prohibiting the unauthorized copying of sound recordings. At the time the cause of action arose, sound recordings were not protected under federal copyright law, and record piracy was rife. The criminal statute in *Goldstein* attempted to protect an important state industry threatened by widespread piracy. But was this California statute preempted by federal law? Nothing in the Copyright Clause of the Constitution explicitly indicated that Congress had been granted exclusive power to protect the writings of authors. Moreover, the Court said, the power given to Congress to protect authors' writings was not a matter of such national interest that state legislation in the field would inevitably lead to conflicts with federal law. The Court also held that the California statute was not preempted under the Supremacy Clause: It found no conflict between federal copyright policy and California's protection of sound recordings. The opinion distinguished *Sears* and *Compco* as cases involving patent policy, where the need for uniform national protection of limited duration is greater than in copyright.

(7) *Kewanee Oil Co. v. Bicron Corp.*, 416 U.S. 470 (1974), discussed at some length in *Bonito Boats*, was decided one year after *Goldstein*. In *Kewanee*, the Supreme Court took a similar position on the power of the states to protect trade secrets, further narrowing the preemption doctrine as articulated in *Sears* and *Compco*. The plaintiff had developed a process for synthesizing a new crystal for use in detecting ionizing radiation. The process was potentially patentable, but the plaintiff decided not to seek patent protection. Instead, it tried to enforce its rights in the process under Ohio's trade secret law. The Court found that state trade secret law was not preempted by federal patent law because the state law neither clashed with the objectives of federal patent law nor "conflict[ed] with the operation of the laws in this area passed by Congress."

(8) Clearly, the *Goldstein/Kewanee* approach erased the bright line presumption favoring preemption set forth in *Sears* and *Compco*. The new approach focused on whether state and federal law could exist harmoniously in the same field, and whether Congress had a clearly stated policy in favor of preemption. This trend away from *Sears/Compco* was reinforced in *Aronson v. Quick Point Pencil Co.*, 440 U.S. 257 (1979) (federal patent law does not preempt state contract law so as to preclude enforcement of a contract to pay royalties to a patent applicant on sales of articles embodying the putative invention for so long as the contracting party sells them, even though a patent is not granted).

(9) Is *Bonito Boats* a retreat from the more expansive role for state intellectual property law articulated in *Goldstein* and *Kewanee*? Is it a return to the stricter preemption analysis of *Sears/Compco*? Certainly, some of the observations in *Bonito Boats* seem sweeping: for example, "States may not offer patent-like protection to intellectual creations which would otherwise remain unprotected as a matter of federal law." But how comprehensive is this standard, in fact? Does it mean that all state laws conferring protection on any products of the mind are

preempted under federal law — *e.g.*, rights of publicity, trademark and anti-dilution laws, and state misappropriation laws? Or should the preemptive effect of *Bonito Boats* properly be viewed as being limited to state law that provides patent-like protection to design and utilitarian aspects of products, rather than applying to the entire range of intellectual creation? For an interesting discussion of these issues, see Wiley, Bonito Boats: *Uninformed But Mandatory Innovation Policy*, 1989 Sup. Ct. Rev. 283.

(10) *Varieties of preemption.* The uncertainty left by *Sears, Compco, Goldstein,* and *Kewanee* led Congress to attempt to clarify preemption doctrine in the Copyright Act of 1976. Section 301 abolished common-law copyright for fixed works and sets forth explicit criteria to resolve preemption issues arising out of conflicts between state law and copyright law as enacted. We take up § 301 and its legislative background immediately following this note.

First, however, we should point out that Supremacy Clause analysis of the kind involved in the cases just reviewed is still a potential part of the overall picture of preemption analysis. Theoretically, at least, some state laws that do not technically fall within the scope of § 301's provisions for "express statutory preemption" nevertheless might operate to frustrate the policies behind the copyright system, which are rooted in Article I, § 8, cl. 8 of the Constitution. In such a situation, there would still exist what might be called "constitutional preemption." Of perhaps more practical importance is "implied statutory preemption," which applies where state laws that are technically not contrary to § 301 nevertheless severely burden or interfere with the choices made by Congress and embodied in Title 17. An instructive case is *Orson, Inc. v. Miramax Film Corp.*, 189 F.3d 377 (3rd Cir. 1999), involving a Pennsylvania state law designed to promote competition in motion picture exhibition. Under its terms (according to the court), "a distributor who exercises its federal right to grant an exclusive license to an exhibitor of choice will be subject to liability . . . for refusing to grant licences to other exhibitors in the same geographic area after the forty-second day." Such a statute is preempted, the court concluded, because it "conflicts with the Copyright Act's grant of an exclusive right to distribute and license a work . . ." *Id.* at 385-86.

How would you analyze the assertion that the application of Louisiana community property law (to find an artist's former wife entitled as a matter of law to a half-share in the copyrights to his paintings) conflicts with the federal copyright statute, which sets up specific and exclusive conditions for the transfer of rights under copyright? See the very thoughtful opinion in *Rodrigue v. Rodrigue*, 218 F.3d 432 (5th Cir. 2000).

Also, consider how you would apply preemption analysis to the following situations:

(a) A state statute requires any publisher whose hardcover books are distributed within the state to cause an "inexpensive softcover version to be distributed within six months thereof," specifying criminal and civil penalties in the event of violation.

(b) A state statute provides a private performance right for sound recordings.

(c) A state statute gives motion picture copyright owners the right to prohibit the rental of their movies by video stores that legally obtained copies of their films.

(11) As discussed in § 7.04 above, the California Resale Royalties Act gives artists the right to receive a percentage of the sales price when original works of fine art are resold. In *Morseburg v. Balyon*, 621 F.2d 972 (9th Cir. 1980), the Ninth Circuit followed *Goldstein* in holding that the CRRA was not preempted by the 1909 Act. If a similar case arose today, how should the case be resolved under § 301 of the 1976 Act? In *Estate of Graham v. Sotheby's, Inc.*, 860 F. Supp. 2d 1117 (C.D. Cal. 2012), the District Court avoided the statutory preemption question by holding that the CRRA was preempted under the dormant Commerce Clause, because it impermissibly attempts to regulate commercial transactions that occur entirely outside the boundaries of California.

The possibilities of "constitutional preemption" and "implied statutory preemption" notwithstanding, § 301 dominates most judicial opinions on the topic today. To that provision, we now turn.

[D]   Preemption Under the 1976 Act

[1]   Section 301: A Study in Confusion

On the whole, the Copyright Act of 1976 is an example of clear, comprehensible draftsmanship (as indeed any piece of legislation that was 21 years in the making *should* be). To this happy generalization, however, there is one notably unhappy exception: § 301.

The purposes of the provision are plain enough. First, § 301 replaces the old, dual system of common-law copyright in unpublished works, complemented by federal statutory copyright for published works, with a new, unitary system of copyright affording the author immediate protection under federal law from the instant that the work is created. See Chapter 6. Second, § 301 was intended, as the House Report states, "to preempt and abolish any rights under the common law or statutes of a State that are equivalent to copyright and that extend to works coming within the scope of the Federal copyright law." The drafters of the Act were only too familiar with the legacy of *Sears/Compco* and the Supreme Court's Supremacy Clause analysis. As part of their second objective, they hoped to infuse into the law of preemption a measure of predictability previously unimagined in that troublesome frontier of federalism. Again, in the words of the House Report: "The declaration of [the principle quoted immediately above] in section 301 is intended to be stated in the clearest and most unequivocal language possible, so as to foreclose any conceivable misinterpretation of its unqualified intention that Congress shall act preemptively, and to avoid the development of any vague borderline areas between State and Federal protection."

It was not to be. Even on a first reading of § 301, one is immediately (if perhaps only vaguely) aware that something is not quite right. Subsection (a) states the intended effect of the entire provision with admirable directness, although obviously certain key terms and concepts are left without precise definition. Subsections (c) and (d) are essentially housekeeping provisions: § 301(c) deals with the *sui generis* problem of sound recordings, which prior to February 15, 1972 had been ineligible for federal copyright, while § 301(d) clarifies that nothing in the 1976 Act abridges rights or remedies under the patent, trademark, or other federal statutes. Subsections (e) and (f) clarify the preemption effects of two later-passed pieces of legislation: the Berne Convention Implementation Act of 1988 (no preemption) and the Visual Artists Rights Act of 1990 (preemption specified).

But what is the purpose of § 301(b)? Does it add anything at all that could not readily be inferred from subsection (a)? If the two subsections are merely the obverse of one another, what considerations might have prompted the drafters to include § 301(b), other than a misplaced love of symmetry?

The answer is that subsection (b), as ultimately enacted by Congress in 1976, is but a pale shadow of its former self. The history of § 301(b) as it made its way through Congress in the decade or so prior to enactment provides an instructive instance concerning the nature of the legislative process, even if, in the end, it affords us little certainty in divining the legislative intent.

The explanation lies in what happened to § 301(b)(3) between 1966 and 1976. The initial draft of § 301 had been preceded by the Supreme Court's decisions in *Sears* and *Compco* in 1964. *Goldstein* was handed down in 1973, and *Kewanee* in 1974. Apparently influenced by what it took to be the trend of these decisions, the Senate in 1975 approved a long list of non-equivalent rights for inclusion in § 301:

> (b) Nothing in this title annuls or limits any rights or remedies under the common law or statutes of any State with respect to — . . .

> (3) activities violating legal or equitable rights that are not equivalent to any of the exclusive rights within the general scope of copyright as specified by section 106, including *rights against misappropriation not equivalent to any of such exclusive rights*, breaches of contract, breaches of trust, *trespass, conversion*, invasion of privacy, defamation, and deceptive trade practices such as passing off and false representation.

S. 22, 94th Cong., 2d Sess. (1975) (emphasis added).

By far the most controversial of the causes of action in the "non-equivalent rights" list was our old friend, of *INS v. AP* fame, "misappropriation" — by now, a vaguely delimited expansion of traditional state unfair competition law, with no definition in the proposed legislation. The Department of Justice had grave misgivings concerning its addition to the bill, which it communicated to Rep. Robert Kastenmeier, as Chairman of the House Judiciary Subcommittee on Courts, Civil Liberties, and the Administration of Justice, on July 27, 1976. In the Department's view, the exclusion of misappropriation was both highly anti-competitive and, by reason of the doctrine's amorphous nature, "almost certain to nullify preemption." In fact, the Department's letter suggested that the other causes of action listed in the Senate draft "m[ight also] be construed to have the same effect." Accordingly, the Department recommended that the *entire list* be deleted, "[i]n order to more clearly delineate [for] the courts the area to be preempted . . ."

Apparently, the Department's plea was unconvincing (or, as Representative Kastenmeier later indicated, arrived too late to receive full consideration). In its discussion of proposed § 301(b), the House Report of September 3, 1976 set forth the views of the full Judiciary Committee in these words:

> The examples in Clause (3), while not exhaustive, are intended to illustrate rights and remedies that are different in nature from the rights comprised in a copyright and that may continue to be protected under State common law or statute. The evolving common law rights of "privacy," "publicity," and trade secrets, and the general laws of defamation and fraud, would remain unaffected as long as the causes of action contain elements, such as an invasion of personal rights or a breach of trust or confidentiality, that are different in kind from copyright infringement. Nothing in the bill derogates from the rights of parties to contract with each other and to sue for breaches of contract; however, to the extent that the unfair competition concept known as "interference with contract relations" is merely the equivalent of copyright protection, it would be preempted.

> The last example listed in clause (3) — "deceptive trade practices such as passing off and false representation" — represents an effort to distinguish between those causes of action known as "unfair competition" that the copyright statute is not intended to preempt and those that it is. Section 301 is not intended to preempt common law protection in cases involving activities such as false labeling, fraudulent representation, and passing off, even where the subject matter involved comes within the scope of the copyright statute.

> "Misappropriation" is not necessarily synonymous with copyright infringement, and thus a cause of action labeled as "misappropriation" is not preempted if it is in fact based neither on a right within the general scope of copyright as specified by section 106 nor on a right equivalent thereto. For example, state law should have the flexibility to afford a remedy (under traditional principles of equity) against a consistent pattern of unauthorized appropriation by a competitor of the facts (*i.e.*, not the literary expression) constituting "hot" news, whether in the traditional mold of *International News Service v. Associated Press*, 248 U.S. 215 (1918), or in the newer form of data updates from scientific, business, or financial data bases. . . .

> Nothing contained in section 301 precludes the owner of a material embodiment of a copy or a phonorecord from enforcing a claim of conversion against one who takes possession of a copy or phonorecord without consent.

H.R. REP. No. 94-1476 at 129-33.

On the eve of the bill's passage, however, the examples listed in clause (3) were deleted — leaving § 301 as it now reads. There was little justification for this important modification made at the eleventh hour, except for a unenlightening exchange between Congressmen Seiberling, Railsback, and Kastenmeier on the

House floor. 122 Cong. Rec. H10910 (daily ed. Sept. 22, 1976).

So how should courts interpret § 301 as enacted in emasculated form? No one would contend that the deletion of the list of non-equivalent rights and remedies included in earlier drafts of that section means that all of the causes of action enumerated there should now be considered preempted. Congress clearly did not mean, for example, to preempt the state laws of libel and slander. But how much more can be said with confidence? The reality is that the courts have been left to their own resources. The following cases demonstrate some of the problems in applying § 301's supposed "bright line" preemption test when a court is confronted with state claims such as unfair competition and breach of contract.

[2] The Struggle in the Courts

KATZ, DOCHTERMANN & EPSTEIN, INC. v. HOME BOX OFFICE

United States District Court, Southern District of New York
50 U.S.P.Q.2d (BNA) 1957 (1999)

GRIESA, DISTRICT JUDGE:

Plaintiff Katz, Dochtermann & Epstein ("KDE") is an advertising agency and brings this action for copyright infringement and related state law claims against Home Box Office ("HBO"), a cable television network and division of Time Warner Entertainment Company, and against BBDO Worldwide ("BBDO"), a rival advertising agency. Defendants move under Rule 12(b)(6) to dismiss claims two, three and four from the complaint, on grounds that these state law causes of action are preempted by federal copyright law.

The motion is granted in part and denied in part.

The Complaint

The original complaint filed in this action asserted a claim for copyright infringement under 17 U.S.C. § 501, and a claim for misappropriation under state law. Defendants' motion, when initially filed, sought dismissal of the misappropriation claim.

Subsequent to the filing of defendants' motion, KDE properly exercised its right to file an amended complaint. The amended complaint omits the misappropriation claim and asserts four causes of action: the first for copyright infringement under 17 U.S.C. § 501; and the second, third and fourth claims under state law, for unfair competition, breach of implied-in-fact contract, and unjust enrichment.

The parties have agreed to construe the motion as seeking dismissal of KDE's second, third and fourth claims contained in the amended complaint and have provided the court with supplemental briefing to that effect.

The amended complaint ("the complaint") alleges that in June of 1992, HBO contacted KDE to request advertising ideas to help HBO reverse sagging business and subscription cancellations among its subscribers.

In response to HBO's request, KDE conceived an ad campaign focused on the theme "It's Not TV, It's HBO," designed to distinguish HBO from other TV stations. KDE alleges that it conceived and created sample print ads, storyboards and advertising copy ("the literary work"), and recorded an original music composition, all based on the marketing concept, "It's Not TV, It's HBO."

The complaint states that a meeting was then held at HBO's offices on June 30, 1992, at which KDE executives presented their marketing concept to HBO executives, and exhibited the literary work and played the original music composition. The complaint states that all the literary work exhibited at the meeting was clearly marked with copyright and agency identification stamps.

KDE alleges that the HBO executives expressed interest in the campaign idea, but told KDE that they would get back to them. A copy of the literary work was left with the HBO executives for their review.

KDE thereafter followed up with HBO periodically for over a year. HBO executives allegedly expressed continued interest but said that they wanted more time to make a final decision.

The complaint states that on August 15, 1996, Time Warner announced that it would run a new ad campaign for HBO around the concept, "It's Not TV, It's HBO," and that the new ad campaign began running around September 5, 1996, and has run continuously ever since.

KDE alleges that when it contacted Time Warner and HBO about the advertising, Time Warner responded that the "It's Not TV, It's HBO" ad concept was created independently by HBO's advertising agency, BBDO, without any knowledge of the KDE presentation to HBO executives.

The complaint states that on August 8, 1997, KDE duly registered its claim to a copyright in the literary work with the Register of Copyrights in Washington, D.C., but that Time Warner and HBO continued on a daily basis, without the consent of KDE, to publish and exhibit the "It's Not TV, It's HBO" ad campaign to the public.

Discussion

HBO argues that KDE's state law claims of unfair competition, breach of contract implied in fact, and unjust enrichment are preempted by 17 U.S.C. § 301(a), which provides:

> On and after January 1, 1978, all legal or equitable rights that are equivalent to any of the exclusive rights within the general scope of copyright as specified by section 106 in works of authorship that are fixed in a tangible medium of expression and come within the subject matter of copyright as specified by sections 102 and 103, whether created before or after that date and whether published or unpublished, are governed exclusively by this title. Thereafter, no person is entitled to any such right or equivalent right in any such work under the common law or statutes of any state.

Courts hold that a state law claim is preempted under § 301 when two conditions are satisfied: (1) the "subject matter" of the work in which the state law rights are asserted comes within the subject matter of the copyright law, as defined in 17 U.S.C. §§ 102 and 103; and (2) the state law rights asserted in the work are equivalent to the exclusive rights protected by federal copyright under 17 U.S.C. § 106. *See, e.g., Harper & Row, Publishers, Inc. v. Nation Enterprises*, 723 F.2d 195, 200 (2d Cir. 1983).

Subject Matter of KDE's State Law Claims

With respect to the first condition for preemption, KDE contends that its state law claims collectively "concern the misappropriation of an idea for a marketing concept and strategy," and that ideas themselves, as distinguished from their expression, do not constitute subject matter covered by federal copyright law.

It is well established, however, that the scope of preemption under § 301 is not the same as the scope of copyright protection, and the former is in fact broader than the latter. *United States ex rel. Berge v. Board of Trustees of Univ. of Alabama*, 104 F.3d 1453, 1463 (4th Cir. 1997); *Markogianis v. Burger King Corp.*, 42 U.S.P.Q.2d (BNA) 1862 (S.D.N.Y. 1997).

Courts have made clear, for instance, that although the Copyright Act does not protect mere ideas alone, the scope of § 301 preemption includes state law claims with respect to uncopyrightable as well as copyrightable material, precisely because if the law was otherwise, "states would be free to expand the perimeters of copyright protection to their own liking, on the theory that preemption would be no bar to state protection of material not meeting federal statutory standards." *Harper & Row Publishers*, 723 F.2d at 200.

KDE carefully attempts to plead its state law claims to allege that HBO misappropriated the "idea" of the ad campaign concept, as distinguished from KDE's federal claim for misappropriation of the copyrighted literary work.

Despite these efforts, the idea at issue here cannot, on the facts alleged, meaningfully be separated from their tangible expression. Under KDE's allegations, HBO did not learn of KDE's idea and therefore have opportunity to misappropriate it except as it was expressed during KDE's presentation to HBO through the alleged copyrightable literary work.

Even if KDE had alleged facts which provided some meaningful distinction between the defendant's misappropriation of the idea versus misappropriation of the idea's expression, it is the court's view that this still cannot be the determinative test for when a particular state law claim falls outside the Copyright Act's preemption. Such a test would undermine one of the Copyright Act's central purposes, to "avoid the development of any vague borderline areas between State and Federal protection." *Harper & Row Publishers*, 723 F.2d at 200 (quoting H.R. Rep. No. 1476, 94th Cong., 2d Sess. 131 (1976)).

The court finds that both the copyrightable expression, and the uncopyrightable idea that underlies it, fall within the "subject matter of copyright" for preemption purposes.

Equivalency of the State Protected Rights to
Rights Protected by Federal Copyright

The second condition for preemption requires that the state law rights asserted in the work must be equivalent to the exclusive rights protected by federal copyright under 17 U.S.C. § 106. Section 106 provides in pertinent part:

> Subject to sections 107 through 120, the owner of copyright under this title has the exclusive rights to do and to authorize any of the following:
>
> (1) to reproduce the copyrighted work in copies or phonorecords;
>
> (2) to prepare derivative works based upon the copyrighted work;
>
> (3) to distribute copies or phonorecords of the copyrighted work to the public by sale or other transfer of ownership, or by rental, lease, or lending . . .

The Second Circuit has explained that a state law claim is not equivalent to any of the exclusive rights protected in § 106 if it includes an "extra element" instead of or in addition to acts of reproduction, performance, distribution or display, which "changes the nature of the action so that it is qualitatively different from a copyright infringement claim." *Computer Assoc. Int'l v. Altai, Inc.*, 982 F.2d 693, 716 (2d Cir. 1992).

In applying the "extra element" test, the court must consider "what plaintiff seeks to protect, the theories in which the matter is thought to be protected and the rights sought to be enforced. . . . An action will not be saved from preemption by elements such as awareness or intent, which alter the action's scope but not its nature." *Id.* at 716-17.

KDE's first state law claim is for unfair competition. The essence of an unfair competition claim under New York law is that the defendant misappropriated the fruit of plaintiff's labors and expenditures by obtaining access to plaintiff's business idea either through fraud or deception, or an abuse of a fiduciary or confidential relationship. *See Werlin v. Reader's Digest Assoc., Inc.*, 528 F. Supp. 451, 464 (S.D.N.Y. 1981).

KDE's theory of liability on this particular claim is that HBO misappropriated the idea for the ad campaign, as distinguished from its tangible expression, by means of an implicit and fraudulent promise to pay for it. KDE contends that the allegation of fraud provides an "extra element" which qualitatively distinguishes its unfair competition claim from a copyright infringement claim.

On the facts alleged in the complaint, however, there is no meaningful distinction between KDE's idea and its tangible expression in terms of HBO's act of alleged misappropriation. As discussed above, the idea was presented to HBO through the copyrightable literary work displayed at the June 1992 meeting. There was no opportunity for HBO to have misappropriated KDE's idea except as it was presented to HBO through the copyrighted literary work.

The distinction between state law protection against misappropriation of the unexpressed idea, and federal protection against misappropriation of the idea as expressed, on these alleged facts, is not a qualitative one. KDE's allegation of fraudulent intent simply alters the scope of the state action but not the equivalency of its nature to a copyright infringement claim. The claim of unfair competition is therefore dismissed.

KDE's second state law claim is for breach of implied-in-fact contract. Under New York law, a contract will be implied in fact when the parties clearly intended payment to the extent of the use of the plaintiff's idea, though they did not set forth that intention in express language. *See Werlin*, 528 F. Supp. at 465.

KDE alleges that HBO solicited KDE for an ad campaign idea, and that implicit in this request was a promise to compensate KDE for its time, talent and effort, should HBO choose to use KDE's idea.

Whereas the facts alleged in the complaint make it impossible to separate a claim of misappropriation of KDE's idea from a claim of misappropriation of the copyrightable literary work through which that idea was expressed to HBO, KDE's contract claim seeks to enforce a promise to pay for the use of the idea alone, regardless of any subsequent rights KDE may have acquired under the Copyright Act to the storyboards, sample print ads, and other copyrightable work it prepared. Thus, KDE's allegation that HBO made an implied promise to pay for its idea is entirely separate and apart from any claim for copyright infringement involving the literary work. The court finds that KDE's claim for breach of implied promise to pay is not preempted. The motion to dismiss KDE's breach of contract claim is denied.

KDE's third state law claim is for unjust enrichment. In order to recover for unjust enrichment under New York law, a plaintiff must show that the defendant was enriched by plaintiff and that the circumstances were such that it would be unjust, in equity and good conscience, to permit defendants to refuse to make any restitution to the plaintiff. *Werlin*, 528 F. Supp. at 465.

KDE's cause of action for unjust enrichment is simply an alternative claim asserted in equity, to the claims KDE asserts at law. The court will allow the unjust enrichment claim to remain in the case in so far as it asserts an alternative equitable remedy to KDE's claim for breach of implied in fact contract. The claim is dismissed, however, as an alternative ground for recovery on KDE's copyright infringement and unfair competition claims.

Conclusion

For the above reasons, HBO's motion to dismiss is granted as to KDE's claim for unfair competition, but is denied as to the claim for breach of implied in fact contract, and denied to the extent that the claim for unjust enrichment asserts an alternative, equitable remedy for the remaining breach of contract claim. So ordered.

NOTES AND QUESTIONS

(1) Under the Copyright Act of 1976, when does federal law preempt state-created causes of action? The thorny issues presented by § 301 and its troubled history have prompted a spate of decisions, many of which are difficult to reconcile fully as to either result or rationale. Unfortunately, opinions in preemption cases

are not always as clear or straightforward as the one in *Katz, Dochtermann & Epstein.*

(2) *Subject matter equivalency.* Section 301(b)(1) provides that "[n]othing in [the Copyright Act] annuls or limits any rights or remedies under the common law or statutes of any State with respect to . . . subject matter that does not come within the subject matter of copyright as specified by sections 102 and 103. . . ." Does this mean that states *can* provide copyright-like protection for subject matter that fails to achieve copyright protection because it lacks originality or has fallen into the public domain, or has been denied protection by § 102(b), which excludes ideas, concepts, discoveries, etc.?

Katz answers that question in the negative, and its analysis finds support in the House Report on the 1976 Act, which observes that otherwise the states could confer unlimited protection on subject matter that is unfit for even limited protection under federal law. *See* H.R. Rep. No. 94-1476, at 131 (1976). A majority of appellate decisions agree. In *Ho v. Taflove*, 648 F.3d 489, 501 (7th Cir. 2011), for example, two professors allegedly copied a mathematical model simulating the behavior of electrons without attribution. The court held that the subject-matter element of preemption was met, because "Congress sought to ensure that a state will not provide copyright-like protections in materials that should remain uncopyrighted or uncopyrightable" (internal quotes omitted). *See also, e.g., Barclays Capital, Inc. v. Theflyonthewall.com, Inc.*, 650 F.3d 876, 892-93 (2d Cir. 2011); *Montz v. Pilgrim Films & Television, Inc.*, 649 F.3d 975, 979-80 (9th Cir. 2011) (en banc); and *R.W. Beck, Inc. v. E3 Consulting, LLC*, 577 F.3d 1133, 1146-47 (10th Cir. 2009).

(3) Some courts disagree with the approach just outlined, applying instead a more literal interpretation of § 301(b)(1). In *Dunlap v. G & L Holding Group Inc.*, 381 F.3d 1285 (11th Cir. 2004), for example, the plaintiff alleged misappropriation of his idea (fixed in a proposed business plan) for "an Internet-based bank that would cater to the gay and lesbian community." The court concluded "that the subject matter of copyright, in terms of preemption, includes only those elements that are substantively qualified for copyright protection." *Id.* at 1295. *See also GlobeRanger Corp. v. Software AG*, 691 F.3d 702 (5th Cir. 2012) (state-law claims based on copying of RFID "procedures, processes, systems, and methods of operation were not preempted); *Dun & Bradstreet Software Servs., Inc. v. Grace Consulting, Inc.*, 307 F.3d 197, 218 (3d Cir. 2002) ("Grace does not dispute that the customer lists are not subject to copyright and presumably escape preemption for that reason pursuant to § 301(b)(1)"). For a scholarly argument that § 301 does not preempt state protection of the categories listed in § 102(b), see P. Goldstein, 3 COPYRIGHT § 15.2.3 (2006).

(4) Is it *possible*, and would it be desirable, to carve out a middle position, in which state law protection is tolerated for some noncopyrightable ideas and barred for others? What form would such a "carve-out" take? Should a state law conferring exclusive rights in the "themes and general plots" of published (or unpublished) works of fiction be analyzed differently from a state law creating property rights in "concepts for exercise, diet and self-help programs"? *See Baltimore Orioles v. Major League Baseball Players Ass'n*, 805 F.2d 663, 676 (7th Cir. 1986) (players'

right of publicity claims in connection with performances embodied in copyrighted game broadcasts held preempted); *Keane v. Fox Television Stations, Inc.*, 297 F. Supp. 2d 921 (S.D. Tex. 2004) (idea for "American Idol" TV show "is the type of material covered by the copyright laws even though it probably would not have qualified for protection under those laws . . .")

(5) The House Report expressly recognizes the possibility of state-law protection for unfixed works. As a result, there is widespread agreement that state-law protection for unfixed works is not preempted. This doesn't mean, of course, that all states affirmatively protect unfixed works. One — California — does so by statute, in Cal. Civ. Code § 980(a)(1). In many others, there is simply no significant jurisprudence relating to common-law copyright and, in some others, the case law places in doubt the question of protection for unfixed works. *See, e.g., Estate of Hemingway v. Random House, Inc.*, 23 N.Y.2d 341, 296 N.Y.S.2d 771 (1968).

(6) *Equivalent rights.* Under § 301(b)(3), federal law does not preempt state law with respect to "activities violating legal or equitable rights that are not equivalent to any of the exclusive rights within the general scope of copyright as specified by section 106." One thing is clear: This is not a formalistic inquiry, and the names of the state-created rights are not necessarily determinative of the outcome. In *Computer Associates International, Inc. v. Altai, Inc.*, 982 F.2d 693 (2d Cir. 1992), for example, the court noted that state "trade secret" claims that turn on an allegation of mere unauthorized "copying" are subject to preemption, while those which allege wrongful acquisition of a trade secret are not. This said, courts have persistent difficulties in determining whether a state-created right has met the § 301(b)(3) test.

There are several reasons for these problems. First, the term "equivalent" has no stable meaning. Second, the legislative history, as revealed in "Section 301: A Study in Confusion" above, is particularly unhelpful in interpreting the scope of preemption. Thus, the courts are forced to fall back on their own resources in determining whether a state law confers "equivalent" rights. As *Katz* indicates, the prevailing standard is the "extra element" test. A right which is equivalent to copyright is one which is infringed by acts of reproduction, adaptation, public distribution, public performance, public display or, in the case of sound recordings, digital audio transmission. Alternatively, if proving an alleged violation of a state law necessitates a showing of elements other than those required to show infringement of the exclusive rights provided by § 106, the conditions for preemption are not present. Courts frequently add that the extra element must change the *nature* of the action, rendering it "qualitatively" different from an action for copyright infringement.

How conclusive is the "extra element" test? Try restating the difference between elements that alter the "nature" of an action (thus preserving the action from the preemptive effect of § 301) and those that alter only its "scope" (thereby leaving the action subject to preemption).

(7) *The "extra element" test applied.* Squirrely legislative history notwithstanding, courts generally find (as in *Katz*) that straight-up misappropriation claims are preempted when they are applied to copyrighted or copyrightable material. *See, e.g., Stromback v. New Line Cinema*, 384 F.3d 283 (6th Cir. 2004). In limited circumstances, however, a "hot news" misappropriation claim of the type alleged in

INS v. AP may survive. *See National Basketball Ass'n v. Motorola, Inc.*, 105 F.3d 841 (2d Cir. 1997) (claim based on real-time reporting of sports scores is preempted, but explaining exception); *Barclays Capital, Inc. v. Theflyonthewall.com*, 650 F.3d 876 (2d Cir. 2011) (despite exception, claim based on real-time reporting of recommendations made in research reports for investors was preempted). State courts may be somewhat more likely to hold that a misappropriation claim is *not* preempted. *See, e.g., Chicago Bd. Options Exch., Inc. v. Int'l Securities Exch., LLC*, 973 N.E.2d 390 (Ill. App. 2012) (claims based on use of Dow Jones Industrial Average and S&P 500 Index to offer index options were not preempted).

(8)   Beyond misappropriation, the *Katz* court deals with several different state law claims under § 301(b)(3). One is for "breach of implied-in-fact contract." How inevitable is the court's "equivalency" analysis? Consider *Wrench LLC v. Taco Bell Corp.*, 256 F.3d 446 (6th Cir. 2001), involving plaintiffs' allegations that their "Psycho Chihuahua" character was the source of Taco Bell's ad campaign featuring a live Chihuahua "with a taste for Taco Bell food and known for the line 'Yo quiero Taco Bell' ('I want some Taco Bell')." Specifically, the plaintiffs complained that, after they had shared their idea with Taco Bell, the company took it without compensating them. The District Court concluded that preemption applied, holding that an implied promise not to use another's ideas and concepts without paying for them is equivalent to the protection provided by § 106 of the Copyright Act.

The Court of Appeals reversed. While refusing to make any blanket proclamations regarding non-preemption and state contract law, the court held that the implied-in-fact contract in suit was not preempted because the implied promise to pay made the claim qualitatively different from a copyright claim. However, the court declined to hold that *all* state law contract claims survive preemption simply because they involve the additional element of a promise:

> If the promise amounts only to a promise to refrain from reproducing, performing, distributing or displaying the work, then the contract claim is preempted. The contrary result would clearly violate the rule that state law rights are preempted when they would be abridged by an act which in and of itself would infringe one of the exclusive rights of § 106.

Id. at 457-458.

Compare the *Wrench* courts' characterizations of preemption for implied-in-fact contracts with *Katz*. Which court do you think articulates the issue in the most coherent manner? For more variations on this theme, see *Forest Park Pictures v. Universal Television Network, Inc.*, 683 F.3d 424 (2d Cir. 2012) (implied-in-fact contract claim not preempted); *Grosso v. Miramax Film Corp.*, 383 F.3d 965 (9th Cir. 2004), *amended* 400 F.3d 658 (9th Cir. 2005) (same); and *Montz v. Pilgrim Films & Television, Inc.*, 649 F.3d 975 (9th Cir. 2011) (en banc) (claims for breach of implied contract and breach of confidence not preempted).

The other principal claim in *Katz*, for "unfair competition," fares poorly in the court's analysis. Will claims so denominated always flunk the "extra element" test? Again, a blanket disposition of claims, based on labeling, cannot pass the test of common sense. What matters is the substance of the state law claim, not its label.

(9)   Often a plaintiff will launch a barrage of state actions, hoping that one or more of them will manifest sufficient nonequivalency to elude preemption. This raises a practical problem: Does a court analyze the elements of each claim, or can it expedite matters by looking at the conduct involved? In *Daboub v. Gibbons*, 42 F.3d 285 (5th Cir. 1995), a rock group, the Nightcaps, claimed that the defendant band, ZZ Top, had copied a song they had recorded in the 1960s. Their state law claims included conversion, misappropriation, plagiarism, disparagement, and defamation. Without analyzing each specific claim, the court found the state causes of action were preempted because the "core" of each of the claims was the same: the wrongful copying, distribution, and performance of the lyrics of plaintiff's song.

Suppose instead that, as part of their claim for "defamation," the Nightcaps had claimed that the ZZ Top version was so poorly executed that it tended to bring the band which originated the tune into disrepute? Would this constitute an extra element that would make the conduct complained of qualitatively different from mere copyright infringement?

(10)   Two hardy perennials in the garden of state-law claims considered in preemption cases are "unjust enrichment" and its close cousin "*quantum meruit.*" In *Katz*, unjust enrichment is treated strictly as an adjunct to the plaintiff's other legal theories; but in many opinions these theories of recovery receive independent consideration with varying results. Generally, such claims are treated as mere restatements of copyright-based causes of action. *See, e.g., Weber v. Geffen Records, Inc.*, 63 F. Supp. 2d 458 (S.D.N.Y. 1999) ("Any 'enrichment' of the Defendants as a result of the exploitation . . . is 'unjust' only by virtue of [the plaintiff's] co-authorship interest under federal Copyright law, under which he is entitled to an accounting, precisely the remedy he seeks in this claim."). *See also Rainey v. Wayne State University*, 26 F. Supp. 2d 963 (E.D. Mich. 1998). Contrast these cases with *Schuchart & Associates, Professional Engineers, Inc. v. Solo Serve Corp.*, 540 F. Supp. 928 (W.D. Tex. 1982) (recovery under a *quantum meruit* theory for the use of plaintiffs copyrighted architectural plans was not preempted).

For a creative (and, so far, successful) attempt to avoid preemption by pleading "fraud," see *Bean v. McDougal Littell*, 538 F. Supp. 2d 1196 (D. Ariz. 2008) and *Shuptrine v. McDougal Littell*, 535 F. Supp. 2d 892 (E.D. Tenn. 2008), in which the plaintiffs alleged that the defendant publisher deliberately sought a license to print a small number of copies, knowing that its actual use would greatly exceed that number, in order to obtain access to the work at a lower cost. Other courts, however, have held that state-law fraud claims are merely improper attempts to obtain punitive damages, which are not available under the Copyright Act. *See, e.g., Bucklew v. Hawkins, Ash, Baptie & Co.*, 329 F.3d 923, 933-34 (7th Cir. 2004).

(11)   What about "conversion"? In general, such a claim will escape preemption only if it contains the extra element of unlawful interference with the physical object embodying the work at issue. *See, e.g., Tire Engineering & Dist., LLC v. Shandong Linglong Rubber Co.*, 682 F.3d 292 (4th Cir. 2012); *GlobeRanger*, 691 F.3d at 709-10. What if the plaintiff claims, instead, that the extra elements in a conversion claim is the "unauthorized use" of intangible property, or the "breach of trust" that led to that use? *See United States ex rel. Berge v. Bd. of Trustees of Univ. of Alabama*, 104 F.3d 1453, 1463 (4th Cir. 1997). *See also Briarpatch Limited v. Phoenix Pictures,*

Inc., 373 F.3d 296 (2d Cir. 2004) ("breach of fiduciary duty" claim not preempted).

(12)   How do claims involving the so-called "right of publicity" fare in terms of preemption analysis? *Baltimore Orioles*, cited earlier in these notes, sometimes has been cited for the proposition that such state-law claims are broadly preempted. In *Toney v. L'Oreal USA, Inc.*, 406 F.3d 905 (2005), however, the Seventh Circuit vacated its own 2004 decision upholding the dismissal of a model's right of publicity claim, and in the process "clarified" (and narrowed) its *Baltimore Orioles* precedent by stating that state laws are preempted only when they "intrude on the domain of copyright." How's that for clarification? What about a claim that a new use of part of a vocalist's recording, licensed by the company for which she created it but not by her, violated state laws prohibiting misappropriation of name and voice? *See Laws v. Sony Music Entertainment, Inc.*, 448 F.3d 1134 (9th Cir. 2006). See also the cases cited in the notes following *White v. Samsung Elecs. America, Inc.*, in § 11.03[C] below.

(13)   *Preemption of criminal law.* Section 301(c) expressly preserves state-law claims for reproduction of sound recordings fixed before February 15, 1972. For recordings fixed after that date, are state criminal laws prohibiting record piracy preempted, on the ground that they are "equivalent" to federal criminal copyright law? *See Crow v. Wainwright*, 720 F.2d 1224 (11th Cir. 1983) (yes). Many states avoid the issue by clever drafting. *See Anderson v. Nidorf*, 26 F.3d 100 (9th Cir. 1994) (California statute criminalizing "failure to disclose the origin of a recording or audiovisual work" is not preempted); *Powell v. State*, 72 So. 3d 1268 (Ala. Crim. App. 2011) (state law making it illegal to transport unauthorized recordings was not preempted, because "transport" is not equivalent to distribution).

(14)   *Miscellaneous preemption issues.* As you will recall from § 8.04, the courts — particularly in the Ninth Circuit — have imposed strict limits on the extraterritorial application of federal copyright laws. What if the complaint in an action pending in the Ninth Circuit incorporated various California state law claims (like unfair competition, interference with contract, or interference with economic advantage) that were potentially applicable to actions occurring beyond the borders of the United States? See *Allarcom Pay Television, Ltd. v. General Instrument Corp.*, 69 F.3d 381 (9th Cir. 1995), where a Canadian company complained that the defendants had assisted Canadian viewers in decoding satellite signals intended for the U.S. market only, and which contained programming to which the plaintiff had exclusive subscription TV rights in Canada. Is such an action barred by preemption? And is § 301(b)(3) helpful in thinking about the answer to this question?

(15)   Recall the discussion of artists' moral rights, including *Phillips v. Pembroke Real Estate Co.* in § 7.08. In the Visual Artists Rights Act of 1990, Congress included a preemption provision, codified as § 301(f). Under this section, all causes of action arising after the effective date of the Act under state statutes conferring equivalent rights on equivalent subject matter arising will be preempted.

Clearly, many of the same questions concerning preemption that have arisen under § 301(a) and (b) will arise in connection with § 301(f). For example, the Massachusetts statute, Mass. Gen. Laws Ann. ch. 231 § 85S (2003), contains a much broader definition of "fine art" than § 101 of the Copyright Act (as amended by VARA). Massachusetts's definition could include movies and television productions.

By comparison, the § 101 definition limits fine art to works of painting, graphic arts, and sculpture. Does the Massachusetts provision clearly interfere with the federal act? The court in *Phillips* failed even to discuss the issue.

According to the House Report accompanying an earlier version of VARA, Congress did not intend to preempt state art preservation acts which confer protection on such subject matter as audiovisual works and photographs. *See* H.R. Rep. No. 101-514, at 21 (1990). Should state statutes conferring protection on categories of works that are broader than federal law escape preemption? What if a state statute does not require the artist's signature, as does the federal act, or extends protection beyond the limited editions protected federally, or provides a different statute of limitations and/or different remedies?

Although certain protections conferred by VARA are limited in duration to the life of the author, the states are explicitly given the right to extend *their* protection beyond the life of the author. *See* 17 U.S.C. § 301(f)(2)(C). This last-minute amendment to the Act was explained by Representative Kastenmeier as follows: "[The new subsection] clarifies that Congress does not intend to preempt section 989 of the California Civil Code, the 'cultural heritage protection,' or any other similar State code. I believe that, in light of the Senate's limitation on the duration of the rights afforded by the act, this amendment is necessary to ensure compatibility with the Berne Convention." *See* 136 Cong. Rec. H13314 (daily ed. Oct. 27, 1990). Does this mean that such state laws are preempted during the artist's life, or not at all? How does this question affect the general preemption issue?

(16)   The Architectural Works Copyright Protection Act, enacted on the same date as VARA, also takes preemption into account, specifically limiting what might otherwise be the effect of recognizing protection for architectural works by revising § 301 to provide:

> (b) Nothing in this title annuls or limits any rights or remedies under the common law or statutes of any State with respect to —

> . . .

> (4) *State and local landmarks, historic preservation, zoning or building codes, relating to architectural works protected under section 102(a)(8).*

(Emphasis added.) What issues does this provision raise?

BOWERS v. BAYSTATE TECHNOLOGIES, INC.
United States Court of Appeals, Federal Circuit
320 F.3d 1317 (2003)

RADER, CIRCUIT JUDGE. . . .

I.

Harold L. Bowers (Bowers) created a template [Cadjet] to improve computer aided design (CAD) software . . . Mr. Bowers filed a patent application for his template on February 27, 1989. On June 12, 1990, United States Patent No. 4,933,514 ('514 patent) issued from that application. . . .

. . . [Bowers later bundled Cadjet together with other software in a product called Designer's Toolkit.] Mr. Bowers sold the Designer's Toolkit with a shrink-wrap license that, inter alia, prohibited any reverse engineering. . . .

In 1990, Mr. Bowers released Designer's Toolkit. By January 1991, Baystate had obtained copies of that product. Three months later, Baystate introduced the substantially revised [version of its own software,] Draft-Pak version 3, incorporating many of the features of Designer's Toolkit. . . .

On May 16, 1991, Baystate sued Mr. Bowers for declaratory judgment that 1) Baystate's products do not infringe the '514 patent, 2) the '514 patent is invalid, and 3) the '514 patent is unenforceable. Mr. Bowers filed counterclaims for copyright infringement, patent infringement, and breach of contract.

Following trial, the jury found for Mr. Bowers and awarded $1,948,869 for copyright infringement, $3,831,025 for breach of contract, and $232,977 for patent infringement. The district court, however, set aside the copyright damages as duplicative of the contract damages and entered judgment for $5,270,142 (including pre-judgment interest). Baystate filed timely motions for judgment as a matter of law (JMOL), or for a new trial, on all of Mr. Bowers' claims. Baystate appeals the district court's denial of its motions for JMOL or a new trial, while Mr. Bowers appeals the district court's denial of copyright damages. This court has jurisdiction under 28 U.S.C. § 1295(a)(1) (2000).

II.

[The court first determined that the law applicable to the copyright claim, and to arguments concerning preemption of state law, was that of the United States Court of Appeals for the First Circuit.]

A.

Baystate contends that the Copyright Act preempts the prohibition of reverse engineering embodied in Mr. Bowers' shrink-wrap license agreements. Swayed by this argument, the district court considered Mr. Bowers' contract and copyright claims coextensive. The district court instructed the jury that "reverse engineering violates the license agreement only if Baystate's product that resulted from reverse engineering infringes Bowers' copyright because it copies protectable expression." This court holds that, under First Circuit law, the Copyright Act does not preempt or narrow the scope of Mr. Bowers' contract claim.

Courts respect freedom of contract and do not lightly set aside freely-entered agreements. Nevertheless, at times, federal regulation may preempt private contract. The Copyright Act provides that "all legal or equitable rights that are equivalent to any of the exclusive rights within the general scope of copyright . . . are governed exclusively by this title." 17 U.S.C. § 301(a) (2000). The First Circuit does not interpret this language to require preemption as long as "a state cause of action requires an extra element, beyond mere copying, preparation of derivative works, performance, distribution or display." *Data Gen. Corp. v. Grumman Sys. Support Corp.*, 36 F.3d 1147, 1164 (1st Cir. 1994) (quoting *Gates Rubber Co. v. Bando Chem. Indus.*, 9 F.3d 823, 847 (10th Cir. 1993)). Nevertheless, "not every 'extra element' of a state law claim will establish a qualitative variance between the rights protected by federal copyright law and those protected by state law." *Id.*

In *Data General*, Data General alleged that Grumman misappropriated its trade secret software. Grumman obtained that software from Data General's customers and former employees who were bound by confidentiality agreements to refrain from disclosing the software. In defense, Grumman argued that the Copyright Act preempted Data General's trade secret claim. The First Circuit held that the Copyright Act did not preempt the state law trade secret claim. Beyond mere copying, that state law claim required proof of a trade secret and breach of a duty of confidentiality. These additional elements of proof . . . made the trade secret claim qualitatively different from a copyright claim. In contrast, the First Circuit noted that claims might be preempted whose extra elements are illusory, being "mere labels attached to the same odious business conduct." *Id.* at 1165 (quoting *Mayer v. Josiah Wedgwood & Sons, Ltd.*, 601 F. Supp. 1523, 1535 (S.D.N.Y. 1985)). For example, the First Circuit observed that "a state law misappropriation claim will not escape preemption . . . simply because a plaintiff must prove that copying was not only unauthorized but also commercially immoral." *Id.*

The First Circuit has not addressed expressly whether the Copyright Act preempts a state law contract claim that restrains copying. This court perceives, however, that *Data General*'s rationale would lead to a judgment that the Copyright Act does not preempt the state contract action in this case. Indeed, most courts to examine this issue have found that the Copyright Act does not preempt contractual constraints on copyrighted articles. *See, e.g., ProCD, Inc. v. Zeidenberg*, 86 F.3d 1447 (7th Cir. 1996) (holding that a shrink-wrap license was not preempted by federal copyright law); *Wrench LLC v. Taco Bell Corp.*, 256 F.3d 446, 457 (6th Cir. 2001) (holding a state law contract claim not preempted by federal copyright law); *Nat'l Car Rental Sys., Inc. v. Computer Assocs. Int'l, Inc.*, 991 F.2d 426, 433 (8th Cir. 1993) . . .; *but see Lipscher v. LRP Publs., Inc.*, 266 F.3d 1305, 1312 (11th Cir. 2001).

In *ProCD*, for example, the court found that the mutual assent and consideration required by a contract claim render that claim qualitatively different from copyright infringement. Consistent with *Data General*'s reliance on a contract element, the court in *ProCD* reasoned: "A copyright is a right against the world. Contracts, by contrast, generally affect only their parties; strangers may do as they please, so contracts do not create 'exclusive rights.' " 86 F.3d at 1454. This court believes that the First Circuit would follow the reasoning of *ProCD* and the majority of other courts to consider this issue. This court, therefore, holds that the Copyright Act does not preempt Mr. Bowers' contract claims.

In making this determination, this court has left untouched the conclusions reached in *Atari Games v. Nintendo* regarding reverse engineering as a statutory fair use exception to copyright infringement. *Atari Games Corp. v. Nintendo of Am., Inc.*, 975 F.2d 832, (Fed. Cir. 1992). In *Atari*, this court stated that, with respect to 17 U.S.C. § 107 (fair use section of the Copyright Act), "the legislative history of section 107 suggests that courts should adapt the fair use exception to accommodate new technological innovations." *Atari*, 975 F.2d at 843. This court noted "[a] prohibition on all copying whatsoever would stifle the free flow of ideas without serving any legitimate interest of the copyright holder." *Id.* Therefore, this court held "reverse engineering object code to discern the unprotectable ideas in a computer program is a fair use." Application of the First Circuit's view distinguishing a state law contract claim having additional elements of proof from a copyright claim does not alter the findings of *Atari*. . . .

Moreover, while the Fifth Circuit has held a state law prohibiting all copying of a computer program is preempted by the federal Copyright Act, *Vault Corp. v. Quaid Software, Ltd.*, 847 F.2d 255 (5th Cir. 1988), no evidence suggests the First Circuit would extend this concept to include private contractual agreements supported by mutual assent and consideration. . . . Thus, case law indicates the First Circuit would find that private parties are free to contractually forego the limited ability to reverse engineer a software product under the exemptions of the Copyright Act. Of course, a party bound by such a contract may elect to efficiently breach the agreement in order to ascertain ideas in a computer program unprotected by copyright law. Under such circumstances, the breaching party must weigh the benefits of breach against the arguably de minimus damages arising from merely discerning non-protected code. . . .

In this case, the contract unambiguously prohibits "reverse engineering." That term means ordinarily "to study or analyze (a device, as a microchip for computers) in order to learn details of design, construction, and operation, perhaps to produce a copy or an improved version." Random House Unabridged Dictionary (1993). . . . Thus, the contract in this case broadly prohibits any "reverse engineering" of the subject matter covered by the shrink-wrap agreement.

The record amply supports the jury's finding of a breach of that agreement. . . . In view of the breadth of Mr. Bowers' contracts, this court perceives that substantial evidence supports the jury's breach of contract verdict relating to both the DOS and Windows versions of Draft-Pak. . . .

Baystate does not contest the contract damages amount on appeal. Thus, this court sustains the district court's award of contract damages. Mr. Bowers, however, argues that the district court abused its discretion by dropping copyright damages from the combined damage award. To the contrary, this court perceives no abuse of discretion.

The shrink-wrap license agreement prohibited, *inter alia*, all reverse engineering of Mr. Bowers' software, protection encompassing but more extensive than copyright protection, which prohibits only certain copying. Mr. Bowers' copyright and contract claims both rest on Baystate's copying of Mr. Bowers' software. Following the district court's instructions, the jury considered and awarded damages on each separately. This was entirely appropriate. The law is clear that the jury may award separate damages for each claim, "leaving it to the judge to make appropriate adjustments to avoid double recovery." *Britton v. Maloney*, 196 F.3d 24, 32 (1st Cir. 1999). . . . Because this court affirms the district court's omission of the copyright damages, this court need not reach the merits of Mr. Bowers' copyright infringement claim.

B.

[Here, the court discusses the patent claims.] In sum, this court perceives no basis upon which a reasonable jury could find that Baystate's accused templates infringe claim 1 of the '514 patent. Hence, this court reverses the district court's denial of Baystate's motion for JMOL of non-infringement.

Conclusion

Because substantial evidence supports the jury's verdict that Baystate breached its contract with Mr. Bowers, this court affirms that verdict. This court holds also that the district court did not abuse its discretion in omitting as duplicative copyright damages from the damage award. Because no reasonable jury could find that Baystate infringes properly construed claim 1, this court reverses the verdict of patent infringement. . . .

DYK, Circuit Judge, concurring in part and dissenting in part.

I join the majority opinion except insofar as it holds that the contract claim is not preempted by federal law. Based on the petition for rehearing and the opposition, I have concluded that our original decision on the preemption issue, reaffirmed in today's revision of the majority opinion, was not correct. By holding that shrinkwrap licenses that override the fair use defense are not preempted by the Copyright Act, 17 U.S.C. §§ 101 *et seq.*, the majority has rendered a decision in conflict with the only other federal court of appeals decision that has addressed the issue — the Fifth Circuit decision in *Vault Corp. v. Quaid Software Ltd.*, 847 F.2d 255 (5th Cir. 1988). The majority's approach permits state law to eviscerate an important federal copyright policy reflected in the fair use defense, and the majority's logic threatens other federal copyright policies as well. I respectfully dissent.

I

Congress has made the Copyright Act the exclusive means for protecting copyright. The Act provides that "all legal or equitable rights that are equivalent to any of the exclusive rights within the general scope of copyright . . . are governed exclusively by this title." 17 U.S.C. § 301(a) (2000). All other laws, including the common law, are preempted. "No person is entitled to any such right or equivalent right in any such work under the common law or statutes of any State."

The test for preemption by copyright law, like the test for patent law preemption, should be whether the state law "substantially impedes the public use of the otherwise unprotected" material. *Bonito Boats, Inc. v. Thunder Craft Boats, Inc.*, 489 U.S. 141, 157, 167 (1989) (state law at issue was preempted because it "substantially restricted the public's ability to exploit ideas that the patent system mandates shall be free for all to use."); *Sears, Roebuck & Co. v. Stiffel Co.*, 376 U.S. 225, 231-32 (1964). . . . In the copyright area, the First Circuit has adopted an "equivalent in substance" test to determine whether a state law is preempted by the Copyright Act. *Data Gen. Corp. v. Grumman Sys. Support Corp.* 36 F.3d 1147, 1164-65 (1st Cir. 1994). That test seeks to determine whether the state cause of action contains an additional element not present in the copyright right, such as scienter. If the state cause of action contains such an extra element, it is not preempted by the Copyright Act. *Id.* However, "such an action is equivalent in substance to a copyright infringement claim [and thus preempted by the Copyright Act] where the additional element merely concerns *the extent to which* authors and their licensees can prohibit unauthorized copying by third parties." *Id.* at 1165 (emphasis in original).

II

The fair use defense is an important limitation on copyright. Indeed, the Supreme Court has said that "from the infancy of copyright protection, some opportunity for fair use of copyrighted materials has been thought necessary to fulfill copyright's very purpose, 'to promote the Progress of Science and useful Arts. . . .' U.S. Const., Art. I, § 8, cl.8." *Campbell v. Acuff-Rose Music, Inc.*, 510 U.S. 569, 575 (1994). The protective nature of the fair use defense was recently emphasized by the Court in the *Eldred* case, in which the Court noted that "copyright law contains built-in accommodations," including "the 'fair use' defense [which] allows the public to use not only facts an[d] ideas contained in the copyrighted work, but also expression itself in certain circumstances." [*Eldred v. Ashcroft*, 537 U.S. 186, 220 (2003)].

We correctly held in *Atari Games Corp. v. Nintendo of America, Inc.*, 975 F.2d 832, 843 (Fed. Cir. 1992), that reverse engineering constitutes a fair use under the Copyright Act. The Ninth and Eleventh Circuits have also ruled that reverse engineering constitutes fair use. *Bateman v. Mnemonics, Inc.*, 79 F.3d 1532, 1539 n.18 (11th Cir. 1996); *Sega Enters. Ltd. v. Accolade, Inc.*, 977 F.2d 1510, 1527-28 (9th Cir. 1992). No other federal court of appeals has disagreed.

We emphasized in *Atari* that an author cannot achieve protection for an idea simply by embodying it in a computer program. "An author cannot acquire patent-like protection by putting an idea, process, or method of operation in an unintelligible format and asserting copyright infringement against those who try to understand that idea, process, or method of operation." 975 F.2d at 842. Thus, the fair use defense for reverse engineering is necessary so that copyright protection does not "extend to any idea, procedure, process, system, method of operation, concept, principle, or discovery, regardless of the form in which it is described, explained, illustrated, or embodied in such work," as proscribed by the Copyright Act. 17 U.S.C. § 102(b) (2000).

III

A state is not free to eliminate the fair use defense. Enforcement of a total ban on reverse engineering would conflict with the Copyright Act itself by protecting otherwise unprotectable material. If state law provided that a copyright holder could bar fair use of the copyrighted material by placing a black dot on each copy of the work offered for sale, there would be no question but that the state law would be preempted. A state law that allowed a copyright holder to simply label its products so as to eliminate a fair use defense would "substantially impede" the public's right to fair use and allow the copyright holder, through state law, to protect material that the Congress has determined must be free to all under the Copyright Act. *See Bonito Boats*, 489 U.S. at 157.

I nonetheless agree with the majority opinion that a state can permit parties to contract away a fair use defense or to agree not to engage in uses of copyrighted material that are permitted by the copyright law, if the contract is freely negotiated. *See, e.g., Nat'l Car Rental Sys., Inc. v. Computer Assocs. Int'l, Inc.*, 991 F.2d 426 (8th Cir. 1993) . . . *But see Wrench LLC v. Taco Bell Corp.*, 256 F.3d 446, 457 (6th Cir. 2001) ("If the promise amounts only to a promise to refrain from reproducing, performing, distributing or displaying the work, then the contract claim is preempted."). A freely negotiated agreement represents the "extra element" that prevents preemption of a state law claim that would otherwise be identical to the infringement claim barred by the fair use defense of reverse engineering. . . .

However, state law giving effect to shrinkwrap licenses is no different in substance from a hypothetical black dot law. Like any other contract of adhesion, the only choice offered to the purchaser is to avoid making the purchase in the first place. *See Fuentes v. Shevin*, 407 U.S. 67, 95 (1972). State law thus gives the copyright holder the ability to eliminate the fair use defense in each and every instance at its option. In doing so, as the majority concedes, it authorizes "shrinkwrap agreements . . . [that] are far broader than the protection afforded by copyright law."

IV

There is, moreover, no logical stopping point to the majority's reasoning. The amici [which included the Electronic Frontier Foundation] rightly question whether under our original opinion the first sale doctrine and a host of other limitations on copyright protection might be eliminated by shrinkwrap licenses in just this fashion. If by printing a few words on the outside of its product a party can eliminate the fair use defense, then it can also, by the same means, restrict a purchaser from asserting the "first sale" defense, embodied in 17 U.S.C. § 109(a), or any other of the protections Congress has afforded the public in the Copyright Act. That means that, under the majority's reasoning, state law could extensively undermine the protections of the Copyright Act.

V

The Fifth Circuit's decision in *Vault* directly supports preemption of the shrinkwrap limitation. The majority states that *Vault* held that "a state law prohibiting all copying of a computer program is preempted by the federal Copyright Act" and then states that "no evidence suggests the First Circuit would extend this concept to include private contractual agreements supported by mutual assent and consideration." *Ante* at 11. But, in fact, the Fifth Circuit held that the specific provision of state law that authorized contracts prohibiting reverse engineering, decompilation, or disassembly of computer programs was preempted by federal law because it conflicted with a portion of the Copyright Act and because it " 'touched upon an area' of federal copyright law." 847 F.2d at 269-70 (quoting *Sears,*

Roebuck, 376 U.S. at 229). From a preemption standpoint, there is no distinction between a state law that explicitly validates a contract that restricts reverse engineering (*Vault*) and general common law that permits such a restriction (as here). On the contrary, the preemption clause of the Copyright Act makes clear that it covers "any such right or equivalent right in any such work *under the common law or statutes of any State*." 17 U.S.C. § 301(a) (2000) (emphasis added).

I do not read *ProCD, Inc. v. Zeidenberg*, 86 F.3d 1447 (7th Cir. 1996), the only other court of appeals shrinkwrap case, as being to the contrary, even though it contains broad language stating that "a simple two-party contract is not 'equivalent to any of the exclusive rights within the general scope of copyright.' " *Id.* at 1455. In *ProCD*, the Seventh Circuit validated a shrinkwrap license that restricted the use of a CD-ROM to non-commercial purposes, which the defendant had violated by charging users a fee to access the CD-ROM over the Internet. The court held that the restriction to non-commercial use of the program was not equivalent to any rights protected by the Copyright Act. Rather, the "contract reflected private ordering, essential to efficient functioning of markets." *Id.* at 1455. The court saw the licensor as legitimately seeking to distinguish between personal and commercial use. "ProCD offers software and data for two prices: one for personal use, a higher prices for commercial use," the court said. The defendant "wants to use the data without paying the seller's price." *Id.* at 1454. The court also emphasized that the license "would not withdraw any information from the public domain" because all of the information on the CD-ROM was publicly available. *Id.* at 1455.

The case before us is different from *ProCD*. The Copyright Act does not confer a right to pay the same amount for commercial and personal use. It does, however, confer a right to fair use, 17 U.S.C. § 107, which we have held encompasses reverse engineering.

ProCD and the other contract cases are also careful not to create a blanket rule that all contracts will escape preemption. The court in that case emphasized that "we think it prudent to refrain from adopting a rule that anything with the label 'contract' is necessarily outside the preemption clause." 86 F.3d at 1455. It also noted with approval another court's "recogni[tion of] the possibility that some applications of the law of contract could interfere with the attainment of national objectives and therefore come within the domain" of the Copyright Act. *Id.* The Eighth Circuit too cautioned in *National Car Rental* that a contractual restriction could impermissibly "protect rights equivalent to the exclusive copyright rights." 991 F.2d at 432.

I conclude that *Vault* states the correct rule; that state law authorizing shrinkwrap licenses that prohibit reverse engineering is preempted; and that the First Circuit would so hold because the extra element here "merely concerns *the extent to which* authors and their licensees can prohibit unauthorized copying by third parties." *Data Gen.*, 36 F.3d at 1165 (emphasis in original). I respectfully dissent.

NOTES AND QUESTIONS

(1)   Can you articulate clearly the understanding of the "extra element" test on which the majority opinion in *Baystate* relied? How is it similar to — or different from — the dissent's view of the same criterion?

(2)   In *Baystate*, the majority relied on an earlier decision from the Seventh Circuit, *ProCD, Inc. v. Zeidenberg*, 86 F.3d 1447 (7th Cir. 1996), for the proposition that a contract claim arising from the restrictive "shrink-wrap contract" was not preempted. Judge Dyk's characterization of *ProCD* notwithstanding, that decision does state a fairly sweeping conclusion on the preemption issue, reasoning that rights under private contract and copyright simply aren't equivalent. Other decisions, including some relied upon by the majority in *Baystate*, take more nuanced approaches considering the specific nature of the contract and the kinds of acts that would constitute the breach. For example, in *National Car Rental Systems*, cited in the opinions above, the court found that the Copyright Act did not preempt a state breach of contract action alleging that the licensee of computer software exceeded the limitations of use contained in license agreements. After scrutinizing the contract terms at issue, the court concluded that the contractual restriction on use of the licensed programs constituted an extra element that made the state cause of action qualitatively different from one for copyright infringement:

> A use of an authorized copy of copyrighted subject matter ordinarily is not infringing. . . . Therefore, applicable limitations on [defendant's] use of the programs, if any, must be derived initially from the license agreements, not copyright law.

991 F.2d at 432 (quoting *Computer Associates Int'l, Inc. v. State St. Bank & Trust*, 789 F. Supp. 470 (D. Mass. 1992)). How would a contract which barred the purchaser of a copy from making any unauthorized adaptation (or performance) of the work fare under this sort of preemption analysis? Under that of *Baystate*? Similarly, is it possible that the *Baystate* majority's confidence in the authority of *Wrench* (the Taco Bell chihuahua case) was misplaced?

(3)   Some courts have differed with the principal case on the contract/preemption question. For example, in *American Movie Classics Co. v. Turner Entertainment Co.*, 922 F. Supp. 926 (S.D.N.Y. 1996), the court found that § 301 would preempt an exclusive license to transmit certain films within a specified time because there was no extra element in the contract claim that was qualitatively different from the licensee's copyright claims. Similarly, in *Wolff v. Inst. of Elec. & Electronics Engineers Inc.*, 768 F. Supp. 66 (S.D.N.Y. 1991), a photographer's contract claim arising from a license to a magazine for one-time use of a photo was preempted because the contract claim was equivalent to the photographer's exclusive right of reproduction.

(4)   Although the majority in *Baystate* does not attach much significance to the fact that the agreement in question was a "shrink-wrap," Judge Dyk obviously does in his dissent. Indeed, he is quite clear in saying that if this had been a typical bargained-for agreement, he would have reached a different conclusion on the preemption issue. What makes "shrink-wraps" arguably different? The *Baystate* majority quotes, with approval, Judge Easterbrook's reasoning: "A copyright is a

right against the world. Contracts, by contrast, generally affect only their parties," not those who are strangers to the agreement. But how meaningful is this distinction in today's world?

Imagine that a particular work is available only on-line, and can be accessed only by those who accept the restrictive terms of a "click-through" license. The terms of the license limit them to personal use only and prohibit any copying or retransmission of the work, even to the extent that this might otherwise be justified as "fair use." If these terms are enforceable, the net effect is that the only *lawful* source from which the work can be acquired by a third party is the copyright owner. Aren't the "options" of "strangers" effectively restricted as a result? *See* Lemley, *Intellectual Property and Shrinkwrap Licenses*, 68 S. Cal. L. Rev. 1239 (1995) (challenging the assumption that contract terms affect only the parties to the contract); *see also* O'Rourke, *Drawing the Boundaries Between Copyright and Contract: Copyright Preemption of Software License Terms*, 45 Duke L.J. 479 (1995) (antitrust principles should govern the analysis of software licenses restricting conduct such as decompilation).

(5) Writing for the *Baystate* majority, Judge Rader distinguishes the Fifth Circuit precedent in *Vault v. Quaid*. Judge Dyk, on the other hand, sees it as controlling. Who has the better of this argument, and why? Is there a meaningful distinction between the quality of the "state action" involved in the two situations?

(6) There is no small irony in the fact that the Court of Appeals for the Federal Circuit was an early champion (in its 1992 *Atari Games* decision) of a "fair use" right to engage in software decompilation for purposes of reverse engineering. Judge Rader is emphatic in saying that the *Baystate* decision is not inconsistent with that principle. But, again, is the distinction wholly convincing? Aren't the same policy issues raised in both instances?

(7) *Is that all there is?* Before there was § 301, courts did preemption analysis in copyright cases by analyzing whether the state law conflicted with the scheme established by the federal statute and the fundamental policies it expresses. Is there still room for such an approach today? In *Baystate*, the majority confined its analysis to the contours of § 301, but should the judges have looked further and broadened the preemption inquiry? In this connection, you may want to review the relevant discussion in the *Bonito Boats* notes earlier, especially the reference to the *Orson* case from the Third Circuit. To what extent was Judge Dyk's dissent in *Baystate* specifically tied to § 301? Why does he make so much of the fact that the "fair use" rights limited by the agreement are affirmatively granted by the copyright statute? And does the issue have larger constitutional dimensions? Again, Judge Dyk points out "fair use" doctrine traces its pedigree, in part, to the First Amendment. Why should this matter?

(8) In *Davidson & Assocs. v. Jung*, 422 F.3d 630 (8th Cir. 2005), the defendants were participants in a commercial multi-player on-line gaming environment, Battle.net, for games owned by the plaintiffs. On first joining, the defendants gave assent (by clicking "I agree") to a uniform "end user license agreement" and a set of "terms of use." Later, the defendants jumped ship in order to create an alternative platform for playing plaintiffs' games on line — and along the way they breached their undertaking not to reverse engineer the Battle.net software. A

lawsuit followed, and the Court of Appeals opinion contained this passage:

> This case concerns conflict preemption. Conflict preemption applies when there is no express preemption but (1) it is impossible to comply with both the state and federal law or when (2) the state law stands as an obstacle to the accomplishment and execution of the full purposes and objectives of Congress. . . . Appellants, relying upon *Vault* . . . , argue that the federal Copyright Act preempts Blizzard's state law breach-of-contract claims. We disagree. . . .

> Unlike in *Vault*, the state law at issue here . . . [does not] restrict[ ] rights given under federal law. Appellants contractually accepted restrictions on their ability to reverse engineer by their agreement to the terms of the TOU and EULA. "[P]rivate parties are free to contractually forego the limited ability to reverse engineer a software product under the exemptions of the Copyright Act[,]" *Bowers v. Baystate Techs, Inc.*, 320 F.3d 1317, 1325-26 (Fed. Cir. 2003), and "a state can permit parties to contract away a fair use defense or to agree not to engage in uses of copyrighted material that are permitted by the copyright law if the contract is freely negotiated." *Id.* at 1337 (Dyk, J., dissenting). While *Bowers* and *Nat'l Car Rental* were express preemption cases rather than conflict preemption, their reasoning applies here with equal force. By signing the TOUs and EULAs, Appellants expressly relinquished their rights to reverse engineer. . . .

422 F.3d at 638-39.

Is this the end of the line? Or does the *Davidson* analysis leave something to be desired? What do you make of the *Davidson* court's use of Judge Dyk's *Baystate* dissent as authority? *See also MDY Industries, LLC v. Blizzard Entertainment, Inc.*, 629 F.3d 928 (9th Cir. 2010) (state-law action for tortious interference with contract was not preempted because Terms of Use were "contract-enforceable covenants rather than copyright-enforceable conditions").

(9)   Preemption issues aside, do shrink-wrap, "click-through," and other forms of "mass market" copyright licenses satisfy contract law requirements for the formation of a binding agreement? For a comprehensive selection of views on this topic, see the symposium issues of the Berkeley Technology Law Journal (Vol. 13, No. 3, Fall 1998) and the California Law Review (Vol. 87, No. 1, Jan. 1999) (which includes McManis, *The Privatization (or "Shrink-Wrapping") of American Copyright Law*). For a judicial meditation on the topic, see *Specht v. Netscape Communications Corp.*, 150 F. Supp. 2d 585 (S.D.N.Y. 2001), *aff'd*, 306 F.3d 17 (2d Cir. 2002).

(10)   *Trespass, etc.* In *eBay, Inc. v. Bidder's Edge, Inc.*, 100 F. Supp. 2d 1058 (N.D. Cal. 2000), the plaintiff, an on-line auctioneer, objected to the activities of the defendant, an auction aggregator whose website displayed information about on-going sales at various primary auction sites, with links to those sites. This information was collected, in turn, by using software "robots" (or "web crawlers") that scanned the Internet in search of relevant data items. In granting preliminary injunctive relief, the court did not, for obvious reasons, rely on copyright. Instead,

it resorted to a number of state-law theories, including (notably) trespass to chattels. The theory was that the use of the defendant's web crawlers deprived eBay of the use of some of the capacity of a physical asset (its computer servers). While one aggregator's robots may not interfere substantially with eBay's operations, the use of this data collection technique by multiple aggregators could have such an effect.

Putting to one side the internal problems with this theory of recovery — which are admirably treated in Burk, *The Trouble With Trespass*, 4 J. Small & Emerging Bus. L. 27 (2000) — what about preemption? The court concluded that "the right to exclude others from using physical personal property is not equivalent to any rights protected by copyright and therefore constitutes an extra element that makes trespass qualitatively different from a copyright infringement claim." 100 F. Supp. 2d at 1071. Courts agree, however, that "trespass to chattels" claims will be preempted when they involve alleged interference with intangible property, such as facts and ideas. *See Gary Friedrich Enterprises, LLC v. Marvel Enterprises, Inc.*, 713 F. Supp. 2d 215 (S.D.N.Y. 2010) (collecting cases).

Note also that state law may require proof of damage, such as actual interference with the plaintiff's computer operations, in order to sustain a claim of trespass to chattels. *See, e.g., Intel Corp. v. Hamidi*, 30 Cal. 4th 1342 (2003); *Ticketmaster Corp. v. Tickets.com, Inc.*, 2003 U.S. Dist. LEXIS 6483 (C.D. Cal. Mar. 6, 2003).

(11) *State protection of sound recordings under § 301(c)*. Section 301(c) stipulates that state record piracy laws protecting sound recordings fixed before February 15, 1972 are not preempted. This provision continues the rule of *Goldstein v. California*, 412 U.S. 546 (1973), that insulated state anti-piracy laws against preemption by the 1909 Act. Under § 301(c), in contrast to *Goldstein*, state protection will not run in perpetuity but rather will terminate on February 15, 2067.

In 1994, as part of the more general extension of retroactive copyright protection to qualifying foreign works in the Uruguay Round Agreements Act, Congress conferred federal protection on sound recordings fixed before February 15, 1972 by certain foreign authors. *See* § 104A(h)(6). Unfortunately, Congress did not amend § 301(c). Thus, it would seem that pre-1972 restored foreign sound recordings can be protected under *both* state and federal law — an industrial-strength right which Congress almost certainly did not intend. *See, e.g., Capitol Records, Inc. v. Naxos of America, Inc.*, 4 N.Y.3d 540 (2005). Per *Naxos*, pre-1972 sound recordings receive New York common-law copyright protection (usually reserved, of course, for unpublished works) *even if* they are in the public domain in their country of origin and thus ineligible for copyright restoration under § 104A.

In December 2011, the Copyright Office issued a report recommending that pre-1972 sound recordings be brought under federal law, with ownership vesting in the person who was entitled to the recording under state law. The report concluded that "[f]ederalization would best serve the interest of libraries, archives and others in preserving old sound recordings and in increasing the availability to the public of old sound recordings." As of this writing, Congress has yet to act on the recommendation. For the full report, see *www.copyright.gov/docs/sound*.

§ 11.03 RELATED BODIES OF FEDERAL AND STATE LAW

In the previous section, we considered the preemption of state law under the Supremacy Clause and the Copyright Act. Here, we turn to some of the neighboring bodies of federal and state law that coexist, more or less comfortably, with copyright. These related bodies of law merit coverage because, as we have already seen, plaintiffs often, along with their claims for copyright infringement, plead claims under such theories as § 43(a) of the Lanham Act (passing off), idea protection, or the right of publicity. Today, the federal law of unfair competition, and a variety of state-law doctrines, are being interpreted to grant to the proprietors of various imaginative creations significant rights which lie outside copyright's ambit. The question is whether this ever-expanding protection circumvents the considerations of intellectual property policy which are expressed in the various constraints on protection operative within copyright itself. When reading the following materials, consider whether, the technicalities of preemption aside, the protection conferred by these bodies of law is consistent with the spirit of copyright law — and why that might matter.

[A] Passing Off and the Protection of Trade Dress Under Federal Law

DASTAR CORPORATION v. TWENTIETH CENTURY FOX FILM CORPORATION
Supreme Court of the United States
539 U.S. 23 (2003)

Justice Scalia delivered the opinion of the Court.

In this case, we are asked to decide whether § 43(a) of the Lanham Act, 15 U.S.C. § 1125(a), prevents the unaccredited copying of a work.

In 1948, three and a half years after the German surrender at Reims, General Dwight D. Eisenhower completed *Crusade in Europe*, his written account of the allied campaign in Europe during World War II. Doubleday published the book, registered it with the Copyright Office in 1948, and granted exclusive television rights to an affiliate of respondent Twentieth Century Fox Film Corporation (Fox). Fox, in turn, arranged for Time, Inc., to produce a television series, also called *Crusade in Europe*, based on the book, and Time assigned its copyright in the series to Fox. The television series, consisting of 26 episodes, was first broadcast in 1949. It combined a soundtrack based on a narration of the book with film footage from the United States Army, Navy, and Coast Guard, the British Ministry of Information and War Office, the National Film Board of Canada, and unidentified "Newsreel Pool Cameramen." In 1975, Doubleday renewed the copyright on the book as the "proprietor of copyright in a work made for hire." Fox, however, did not renew the copyright on the *Crusade* television series, which expired in 1977, leaving the television series in the public domain.

In 1988, Fox reacquired the television rights in General Eisenhower's book, including the exclusive right to distribute the *Crusade* television series on video and to sub-license others to do so. Respondents SFM Entertainment and New Line Home Video, Inc., in turn, acquired from Fox the exclusive rights to distribute *Crusade* on video. SFM obtained the negatives of the original television series, restored them, and repackaged the series on videotape; New Line distributed the videotapes.

Enter petitioner Dastar. In 1995, . . . Dastar released a video set entitled *World War II Campaigns in Europe.* To make *Campaigns,* Dastar purchased eight beta cam tapes of the *original* version of the *Crusade* television series, which is in the public domain, copied them, and then edited the series. Dastar's *Campaigns* series is slightly more than half as long as the original *Crusade* television series. Dastar substituted a new opening sequence, credit page, and final closing for those of the *Crusade* television series; inserted new chapter-title sequences and narrated chapter introductions; moved the "recap" in the *Crusade* television series to the beginning and retitled it as a "preview"; and removed references to and images of the book. Dastar created new packaging for its *Campaigns* series and (as already noted) a new title.

Eisenhower on D-Day
Corbis

Dastar manufactured and sold the *Campaigns* video set as its own product. The advertising states: "Produced and Distributed by: Entertainment Distributing" (which is owned by Dastar), and makes no reference to the *Crusade* television series. Similarly, the screen credits state "DASTAR CORP presents" and "an ENTERTAINMENT DISTRIBUTING Production," and list as executive producer, producer, and associate producer, employees of Dastar. The *Campaigns* videos themselves also make no reference to the *Crusade* television series, New Line's *Crusade* videotapes, or the book. Dastar sells its *Campaigns* videos to Sam's

Club, Costco, Best Buy, and other retailers and mail-order companies for $25 per set, substantially less than New Line's video set.

In 1998, respondents Fox, SFM, and New Line brought this action alleging that Dastar's sale of its *Campaigns* video set infringes Doubleday's copyright in General Eisenhower's book and, thus, their exclusive television rights in the book. Respondents later amended their complaint to add claims that Dastar's sale of *Campaigns* "without proper credit" to the *Crusade* television series constitutes "reverse passing off"[1] in violation of § 43(a) of the Lanham Act, 15 U.S.C. § 1125(a), and in violation of state unfair-competition law. On cross-motions for summary judgment, the District Court found for respondents on all three counts, treating its resolution of the Lanham Act claim as controlling on the state-law unfair-competition claim because "the ultimate test under both is whether the public is likely to be deceived or confused." The court awarded Dastar's profits to respondents and doubled them pursuant to § 35 of the Lanham Act, 15 U.S.C. § 1117(a), to deter future infringing conduct by petitioner.

The Court of Appeals for the Ninth Circuit affirmed the judgment for respondents on the Lanham Act claim, but reversed as to the copyright claim. (It said nothing with regard to the state-law claim.) With respect to the Lanham Act claim, the Court of Appeals reasoned that "Dastar copied substantially the entire *Crusade in Europe* series created by Twentieth Century Fox, labeled the resulting product with a different name and marketed it without attribution to Fox [, and] therefore committed a 'bodily appropriation' of Fox's series." It concluded that "Dastar's 'bodily appropriation' of Fox's original [television] series is sufficient to establish the reverse passing off." The court also affirmed the District Court's award under the Lanham Act of twice Dastar's profits. We granted certiorari.

II

The Lanham Act was intended to make "actionable the deceptive and misleading use of marks," and "to protect persons engaged in . . . commerce against unfair competition." 15 USC § 1127. While much of the Lanham Act addresses the registration, use, and infringement of trademarks and related marks, § 43(a) is one of the few provisions that goes beyond trademark protection. . . . [E]very Circuit to consider the issue found § 43(a) broad enough to encompass reverse passing off. . . .[4] . . . The Trademark Law Revision Act of 1988 . . . is amply inclusive,

---

[1] Passing off (or palming off, as it is sometimes called) occurs when a producer misrepresents his own goods or services as someone else's. "Reverse passing off," as its name implies, is the opposite: The producer misrepresents someone else's goods or services as his own. *Williams v. Curtiss-Wright Corp.*, 691 F.2d 168, 172 (CA3 1982).

[4] Section 43(a) of the Lanham Act now provides:

Any person who, on or in connection with any goods or services, or any container for goods, uses in commerce any word, term, name, symbol, or device, or any combination thereof, or any false designation of origin, false or misleading description of fact, or false or misleading representation of fact, which —

(A) is likely to cause confusion, or to cause mistake, or to deceive as to the affiliation, connection, or association of such person with another person, or as to the origin, sponsorship, or approval of his or her goods, services, or commercial activities by another person, or

moreover, of reverse passing off . . .

. . . Th[e respondents'] claim would undoubtedly be sustained if Dastar had bought some of New Line's *Crusade* videotapes and merely repackaged them as its own. Dastar's alleged wrongdoing, however, is vastly different: it took a creative work in the public domain — the *Crusade* television series — copied it, made modifications (arguably minor), and produced its very own series of videotapes. If "origin" refers only to the manufacturer or producer of the physical "goods" that are made available to the public (in this case the videotapes), Dastar was the origin. If, however, "origin" includes the creator of the underlying work that Dastar copied, then someone else (perhaps Fox) was the origin of Dastar's product. At bottom, we must decide what § 43(a)(1)(A) of the Lanham Act means by the "origin" of "goods."

III

The dictionary definition of "origin" is "the fact or process of coming into being from a source," and "that from which anything primarily proceeds; source." Webster's New International Dictionary 1720-1721 (2d ed. 1949). And the dictionary definition of "goods" (as relevant here) is "[w]ares; merchandise." *Id.*, at 1079. We think the most natural understanding of the "origin" of "goods" — the source of wares — is the producer of the tangible product sold in the marketplace, in this case the physical *Campaigns* videotape sold by Dastar. . . . [The 1988 amendments to § 43(a) now expressly extend] the concept to include not only the actual producer, but also the trademark owner who commissioned or assumed responsibility for ("stood behind") production of the physical product. But as used in the Lanham Act, the phrase "origin of goods" is in our view incapable of connoting the person or entity that originated the ideas or communications that "goods" embody or contain. Such an extension would not only stretch the text, but it would be out of accord with the history and purpose of the Lanham Act and inconsistent with precedent.

Section 43(a) of the Lanham Act prohibits actions like trademark infringement that deceive consumers and impair a producer's goodwill. It forbids, for example, the Coca-Cola Company's passing off its product as Pepsi-Cola or reverse passing off Pepsi-Cola as its product. But the brand-loyal consumer who prefers the drink that the Coca-Cola Company or PepsiCo sells, while he believes that that company produced (or at least stands behind the production of) that product, surely does not necessarily believe that that company was the "origin" of the drink in the sense that it was the very first to devise the formula. The consumer who buys a branded product does not automatically assume that the brand-name company is the same entity that came up with the idea for the product, or designed the product — and typically does not care whether it is. The words of the Lanham Act should not be stretched to cover matters that are typically of no consequence to purchasers.

It could be argued, perhaps, that the reality of purchaser concern is different for

---

(B) in commercial advertising or promotion, misrepresents the nature, characteristics, qualities, or geographic origin of his or her or another person's goods, services, or commercial activities, shall be liable in a civil action by any person who believes that he or she is or is likely to be damaged by such act."

15 U.S.C. § 1125(a)(1).

what might be called a communicative product — one that is valued not primarily for its physical qualities, such as a hammer, but for the intellectual content that it conveys, such as a book or, as here, a video. The purchaser of a novel is interested not merely, if at all, in the identity of the producer of the physical tome (the publisher), but also, and indeed primarily, in the identity of the creator of the story it conveys (the author). And the author, of course, has at least as much interest in avoiding passing-off (or reverse passing-off) of his creation as does the publisher. For such a communicative product (the argument goes) "origin of goods" in § 43(a) must be deemed to include not merely the producer of the physical item (the publishing house Farrar, Straus and Giroux, or the video producer Dastar) but also the creator of the content that the physical item conveys (the author Tom Wolfe, or — assertedly — respondents).

The problem with this argument according special treatment to communicative products is that it causes the Lanham Act to conflict with the law of copyright, which addresses that subject specifically. The right to copy, and to copy without attribution, once a copyright has expired, like "the right to make [an article whose patent has expired] — including the right to make it in precisely the shape it carried when patented — passes to the public." *Sears, Roebuck & Co. v. Stiffel Co.*, 376 U.S. 225, 230 (1964). The rights of a patentee or copyright holder are part of a "carefully crafted bargain," *Bonito Boats, Inc. v. Thunder Craft Boats, Inc.*, 489 U.S. 141 (1989), under which, once the patent or copyright monopoly has expired, the public may use the invention or work at will and without attribution. Thus, in construing the Lanham Act, we have been "careful to caution against misuse or over-extension" of trademark and related protections into areas traditionally occupied by patent or copyright. *TrafFix Devices, Inc. v. Marketing Displays, Inc.*, 532 U.S. 23, 29 (2001). "The Lanham Act," we have said, "does not exist to reward manufacturers for their innovation in creating a particular device; that is the purpose of the patent law and its period of exclusivity." *Id.*, at 34. Federal trademark law "has no necessary relation to invention or discovery," *Trade-Mark Cases*, 100 U.S. 82, 94 (1879), but rather, by preventing competitors from copying "a source-identifying mark," "reduces the customer's costs of shopping and making purchasing decisions," and "helps assure a producer that it (and not an imitating competitor) will reap the financial, reputation-related rewards associated with a desirable product," *Qualitex Co. v. Jacobson Products* Co., 514 U.S. 159 (1995) (internal quotation marks and citation omitted). Assuming for the sake of argument that Dastar's representation of itself as the "Producer" of its videos amounted to a representation that it originated the creative work conveyed by the videos, allowing a cause of action under § 43(a) for that representation would create a species of mutant copyright law that limits the public's "federal right to 'copy and to use,'" expired copyrights, *Bonito Boats, supra*, at 165.

When Congress has wished to create such an addition to the law of copyright, it has done so with much more specificity than the Lanham Act's ambiguous use of "origin." The Visual Artists Rights Act of 1990, § 603(a), 104 Stat 5128, provides that the author of an artistic work "shall have the right . . . to claim authorship of that work." 17 U.S.C. § 106A(a)(1)(A). That express right of attribution is carefully limited and focused: It attaches only to specified "works of visual art," § 101, is personal to the artist, §§ 106A(b) and (e), and endures only for "the life of the author," at § 106A(d)(1). Recognizing in § 43(a) a cause of action for misrepresentation of authorship of noncopyrighted works (visual or otherwise) would render these limitations superfluous. A statutory interpretation that renders another statute superfluous is of course to be avoided. *E.g., Mackey v. Lanier Collection Agency & Service, Inc.*, 486 U.S. 825 (1988).

Reading "origin" in § 43(a) to require attribution of uncopyrighted materials would pose serious practical problems. Without a copyrighted work as the basepoint, the word "origin" has no discernable limits. A video of the MGM film *Carmen Jones*, after its copyright has expired, would presumably require attribution not just to MGM, but to Oscar Hammerstein II (who wrote the musical on which the film was based), to Georges Bizet (who wrote the opera on which the musical was based), and to Prosper Merimee (who wrote the novel on which the opera was based). In many cases, figuring out who is in the line of "origin" would be no simple task. Indeed, in the present case it is far from clear that respondents have that status. Neither SFM nor New Line had anything to do with the production of the *Crusade* television series — they merely were licensed to distribute the video version. While Fox might have a claim to being in the line of origin, its involvement with the creation of the television series was limited at best. Time, Inc., was the principal if not the exclusive creator, albeit under arrangement with Fox. And of course it was neither Fox nor Time, Inc., that shot the film used in the *Crusade* television series. Rather, that footage came from the United States Army, Navy, and Coast Guard, the British Ministry of Information and War Office, the National Film Board of Canada, and unidentified "Newsreel Pool Cameramen." If anyone has a claim to being the *original* creator of the material used in both the *Crusade* television series and the *Campaigns* videotapes, it would be those groups, rather than Fox. We do not think the Lanham Act requires this search for the source of the Nile and all its tributaries.

Another practical difficulty of adopting a special definition of "origin" for communicative products is that it places the manufacturers of those products in a difficult position. On the one hand, they would face Lanham Act liability for *failing* to credit the creator of a work on which their lawful copies are based; and on the other hand they could face Lanham Act liability for *crediting* the creator if that should be regarded as implying the creator's "sponsorship or approval" of the copy, 15 U.S.C. § 1125(a)(1)(A). . . .

Finally, reading § 43(a) of the Lanham Act as creating a cause of action for, in effect, plagiarism — the use of otherwise unprotected works and inventions without attribution — would be hard to reconcile with our previous decisions. For example, in *Wal-Mart Stores, Inc. v. Samara Brothers, Inc.*, 529 U.S. 205 (2000), we considered whether product-design trade dress can ever be inherently distinctive. Wal-Mart produced "knockoffs" of children's clothes designed and manufactured by Samara Brothers, containing only "minor modifications" of the original designs. We concluded that the designs could not be protected under § 43(a) without a showing that they had acquired "secondary meaning" so that they " 'identify the source of the product rather than the product itself' " (quoting *Inwood Laboratories, Inc. v. Ives Laboratories, Inc.*, 456 U.S. 844, 851, n.11 (1982)). This carefully considered limitation would be entirely pointless if the "original" producer could turn around and pursue a reverse-passing-off claim under exactly the same provision of the

Lanham Act. Samara would merely have had to argue that it was the "origin" of the designs that Wal-Mart was selling as its own line. It was not, because "origin of goods" in the Lanham Act referred to the producer of the clothes, and not the producer of the (potentially) copyrightable or patentable designs that the clothes embodied.

Similarly under respondents' theory, the "origin of goods" provision of § 43(a) would have supported the suit that we rejected in *Bonito Boats*, where the defendants had used molds to duplicate the plaintiff's unpatented boat hulls (apparently without crediting the plaintiff). And it would have supported the suit we rejected in *TrafFix*: The plaintiff, whose patents on flexible road signs had expired, and who could not prevail on a trade-dress claim under § 43(a) because the features of the signs were functional, would have had a reverse-passing-off claim for unattributed copying of his design.

In sum, reading the phrase "origin of goods" in the Lanham Act in accordance with the Act's common-law foundations (which were *not* designed to protect originality or creativity), and in light of the copyright and patent laws (which *were*), we conclude that the phrase refers to the producer of the tangible goods that are offered for sale, and not to the author of any idea, concept, or communication embodied in those goods. *Cf.* 17 USC § 202 (distinguishing between a copyrighted work and "any material object in which the work is embodied"). To hold otherwise would be akin to finding that § 43(a) created a species of perpetual patent and copyright, which Congress may not do. *See Eldred v. Ashcroft*, 537 U.S. 186, 208 (2003).

The creative talent of the sort that lay behind the *Campaigns* videos is not left without protection. The original film footage used in the *Crusade* television series could have been copyrighted, see 17 U.S.C. 102(a)(6), as was copyrighted (as a compilation) the *Crusade* television series, even though it included material from the public domain, see § 103(a). Had Fox renewed the copyright in the *Crusade* television series, it would have had an easy claim of copyright infringement. And respondents' contention that *Campaigns* infringes Doubleday's copyright in General Eisenhower's book is still a live question on remand. If, moreover, the producer of a video that substantially copied the *Crusade* series were, in advertising or promotion, to give purchasers the impression that the video was quite different from that series, then one or more of the respondents might have a cause of action — not for reverse passing off under the "confusion . . . as to the origin" provision of § 43(a)(1)(A), but for misrepresentation under the "misrepresents the nature, characteristics [or] qualities" provision of § 43(a)(1)(B). For merely saying it is the producer of the video, however, no Lanham Act liability attaches to Dastar.

Because we conclude that Dastar was the "origin" of the products it sold as its own, respondents cannot prevail on their Lanham Act claim. We thus have no occasion to consider whether the Lanham Act permitted an award of double petitioner's profits. The judgment of the Court of Appeals for the Ninth Circuit is reversed, and the case is remanded for further proceedings consistent with this opinion. *It is so ordered.*

Justice BREYER took no part in the consideration or decision of this case.

NOTES AND QUESTIONS

(1)   All federal laws are created equal, so this is not an example of "preemption" analysis, as described in § 11.02 above. Doctrinally speaking, what sort of analysis is it?

(2)   Back in 1988, when the United States decided to join the Berne Convention, the obvious deficiencies of U.S. relating to moral rights were rationalized, in part, on the basis that the Lanham Act provided meaningful federal protection for authors' reputational interests. Since then, of course, Congress enacted the Visual Artists Rights Act, which (as we know from § 7.08) amounts to only a partial codification of the European-style doctrine. Does Dastar put the issue of U.S. compliance with Berne Art. 6bis back into play? Does it matter? *See* Ginsburg, *The Right to Claim Authorship in U.S. Copyright and Trademark Law*, 41 Hous. L. Rev. 263 (2004).

(3)   Exactly how categorical is the conclusion of the *Dastar* opinion? Does "reverse passing off" have any role left to play in the arts or entertainment? Might it still provide relief for an actor who finds that credit for his or her screen role has been assigned to another person? *See Smith v. Montoro*, 648 F.2d 602 (9th Cir. 1981) (motion picture "Convoy Buddies"), cited in *Dastar*. Note that virtually every lower court to consider the issue after *Dastar* has concluded that a "reverse passing off" claim based on alleged copying (rather than mislabeling of tangible goods) is unavailable. *See, e.g., Zyla v. Wadsworth*, 360 F.3d 243 (1st Cir. 2004); *General Universal Sys., Inc. v. Lee*, 379 F.3d 131 (5th Cir. 2004).

(4)   On the way to his conclusion, Justice Scalia describes the classic doctrine of "passing off." In the United States, passing off began as a state-law doctrine; and, despite the federal legislation under which the principal case was decided, it remains an important part of the law of unfair competition in every state jurisdiction. Obviously, the federal law of passing off is not preempted by copyright. *See, e.g.*, 17 U.S.C. § 301(d). But why have so many courts also held that state-law causes of action in the nature of passing off are immune from either constitutional or statutory preemption?

(5)   The passing off concept traditionally has been applied to protect names, words and symbols (including artwork like logos) associated with particular firms or their products. In addition, it has been extended to apply to other indicia of commercial identity, such as trade dress — *i.e.* distinctive packaging, product configuration and labeling, sometimes including the total image, advertising materials, and marketing techniques by which the product or service is presented to customers.

(6)   The major vehicle for the protection of trade dress, in particular, has been federal law: to be precise, § 43 (a) of the Lanham Act (15 U.S.C. § 1125(a)). *Sears/Compco*, discussed in the preceding section of this chapter, threw much of existing state law in this area into doubt and enhanced interest in § 43(a). The last two decades of the twentieth century brought a vast increase in the number of suits brought under § 43(a). *Two Pesos, Inc. v. Taco Cabana, Inc.*, 505 U.S. 763 (1992) (discussed in *Dastar*), concerned the protection of the overall décor of a Mexican style restaurant under § 43(a). The Supreme Court, continuing an expansive trend,

held that inherently distinctive trade dress may be protected without proof of secondary meaning — *i.e.*, a demonstration that the public would associate the design with a particular source of goods or services.   After *Two Pesos*, courts struggled to devise a workable standard for discerning "inherent distinctiveness." For one attempt, see *Duraco Products, Inc. v. Joy Plastic Enterprises, Ltd.*, 40 F.3d 1431 (3d Cir. 1994) (to be inherently distinctive, the product feature or arrangement of features must be unusual and memorable, conceptually separable from the product, and likely to serve primarily as an indicator of origin). Perhaps because this proved so difficult, in *Wal-Mart Stores, Inc. v. Samara Brothers, Inc.*, 529 U.S. 205 (2000), the Court retrenched by requiring a proof of secondary meaning for the protection of *product design* trade dress (as distinguished from other forms of trade dress). Are you convinced that the distinction between packaging and décor of a restaurant and product design such as a bottle configuration will be easy to make? *See also Knitwares, Inc. v. Lollytogs, Ltd.*, 71 F.3d 996 (2d Cir. 1995) (holding that a sweater design was merely aesthetic and not origin-indicating); *Landscape Forms, Inc. v. Columbia Cascade Co.* 113 F.3d 373 (2d Cir. 1997) (holding that overall configuration of outdoor furniture line is not an indicator of source).

Model of TWO PESOS Building

Model of TACO CABANA Building

(7)   Labels can be original literary or artistic works, and some product designs may survive "useful articles" analysis. Thus, claims of passing off and copyright infringement often overlap. But trademark or trade dress protection goes further than copyright protection in some respects. First, protectible trademarks and arrays of trade dress may enjoy perpetual protection, so long as they are used and maintain their ability to indicate source. Second, independent creation is not a defense to an action in the nature of passing off. Conversely, trademark and trade dress protection is limited in some ways in which copyright is not. For example, distinctive trade dress will only be protected when third-party use creates a likelihood of confusion. To what extent will the analysis of "inherent distinctiveness" in a trade dress case (like *Two Pesos*) track the copyrightibility analysis that might be applied to the same designs?

(8)   In addition to secondary meaning (or, where appropriate, inherent distinctiveness), another prerequisite for trade dress protection is the non-functionality requirement. Like various doctrines of copyright law (including the § 102(b) exclusions and the "useful articles" doctrine), this aspect of § 43(a) doctrine operates, among other things, to prevent the law of trademark from encroaching upon the domain of patent law. The usual test is that a product feature is functional if it is essential to the use or purpose of the article or if it affects the cost or quality of the article. *See Inwood Laboratories, Inc. v. Ives Laboratories, Inc.*, 456 U.S. 844, 850 n.10 (1982); *see also Merchant & Evans, Inc. v. Roosevelt Building Products, Co.* 963 F.2d 628 (3d Cir. 1992) (roofing seam design held functional where it improved impermeability and was one of two basic designs on the market).

The Supreme Court, in *TrafFix Devices, Inc. v. Marketing Displays, Inc.*, 532 U.S. 23 (2001), reaffirmed the functionality doctrine, creating an apparently bright-line rule against the protection of product features that previously enjoyed patent protection. *TrafFix* concerned the protection of dual-spring design mechanism for keeping outdoor signs upright in adverse wind conditions. The Court held that the existence of expired utility patents on a product feature created a strong evidentiary inference of the design's functionality. As it did in *Wal-Mart*, the Supreme Court in *TrafFix* continued the trend of erecting a more rigorous standard for the protection of product designs than for ornamental non-utilitarian forms of trade dress, such as the décor of a restaurant or fanciful packaging.

(9)   Some courts have gone further and found an aesthetic feature functional if it is an important ingredient in the success of a product, so that trade dress protection would hinder competition or impinge upon the rights of others to compete effectively. *See W.T. Rogers Co. v. Keene*, 778 F.2d 334, 343 (7th Cir. 1985); *Keene Corp. v. Paraflex Industries, Inc.*, 653 F.2d 822 (3d Cir. 1981) (plaintiff's design for its outdoor wall-mounted luminaire was so architecturally compatible with modern structures that the grant of a trademark monopoly would stifle competition). How similar or different is this test from copyright law's restrictions on the protection of utilitarian designs? And how did the design elements in *Two Pesos* (see the illustration above, which lamentably cannot be reproduced in color here) escape being characterized as aesthetically "functional"?

In *Fleischer Studios, Inc. v. A.V.E.L.A., Inc.*, 636 F.3d 1115, *opinion withdrawn and superseded*, 654 F.3d 958 (9th Cir. 2011), the defendant reproduced the cartoon character "Betty Boop" on t-shirts. After holding that the plaintiff failed to prove ownership of a valid copyright, the court initially rejected the trademark claim because the defendant "is not using Betty Boop as a trademark . . . The name and [Betty Boop image] were functional aesthetic components of the product." The court added: "If we ruled that [defendant's] depictions of Betty Boop infringed Fleischer's trademarks, the Betty Boop character would essentially never enter the public domain. Such a result would run directly contrary to *Dastar.*" After a storm of controversy, however, the court withdrew its original opinion, holding instead that Fleischer had failed to prove secondary meaning in the image of Betty Boop, but remanding the claim for infringement of the "Betty Boop" word mark.

Do you agree with either of the court's opinions on this issue? Isn't Mickey Mouse a trademark of the Walt Disney Company as well as a copyrighted character? How should those interests be reconciled after the copyright in *Steamboat Willie* has expired?

(10)   Trade dress litigation is not the only example of expansive tendencies in the federal law of passing off. For example, it has been held that a color associated with a product line could be protected under § 43(a) of the Lanham Act against use by a competitor. *Qualitex Co. v. Jacobson Products Co.*, 514 U.S. 159 (1995). There may, however, be some limits on this trend. In *Rock & Roll Hall of Fame & Museum, Inc. v. Gentile Productions*, 134 F.3d 749 (6th Cir. 1998), the appellate court reversed a preliminary injunction, expressing skepticism about whether the plaintiff would succeed in showing that the distinctive architectural design of its headquarters building qualified for protection under § 43(a): "In reviewing the

Museum's disparate uses of several different perspectives of its building design, we cannot conclude that they create a consistent and distinct commercial impression as an indicator of a single source of origin or sponsorship." Should the availability of protection for architectural designs under current copyright law have had any impact on the court's reasoning in this case?

(11) Whatever the outer limits on the scope of federal passing off doctrine ultimately may prove to be, there is also an observable tendency toward liberalization of criteria for the *registration* of trademarks under the Lanham Act — as the Supreme Court decision in *Qualitex* indicates. Today, the universe of registrable marks embraces not only colors but container shapes, architectural structures, and sounds. (For the distinction between the federal law of passing off and that relating to registered marks, see § 1.02 of this book.) Registrability has been extended even to fragrances. *See In re Clark*, 17 U.S.P.Q.2d (BNA) 1238 (T.T.A.B. 1990). And the Harley-Davidson company even tried (unsuccessfully) to register as a trademark the characteristic sounds of its motorcycles' exhaust pipes! Do consumers or competitors have any reason to be concerned about these developments?

(12) A well-known axiom maintains that copyright does not protect artistic style *per se*. Can the federal law of unfair competition — § 43(a) of the Lanham Act — protect against the imitation of an artistic style? *Romm Art Creations Ltd. v. Simcha International, Inc.*, 786 F. Supp. 1126 (E.D.N.Y. 1992), applied the law of trade dress to artistic style. Romm Art was the exclusive licensee for the distribution of posters of original art works of Itzchak Tarkay, whose collection was known as "Women and Cafes." Defendant distributed a line of pictures that simulated the Tarkay style. The court found that the plaintiff had priority, that the style of the works had attained secondary meaning, and that the defendant's works caused likelihood of confusion. Would *Romm Art* support an action by Picasso against Braque, if Picasso could have shown priority in using the distinctive Cubist style? Does *Romm Art* survive the ruling in *Dastar*?

(13) *Beyond passing off: dilution.* The action for passing off is based on the concept of consumer confusion about the origin of products or services. Thus, if the trademark TIDE is used on a detergent, a third party might still be able to use the trademark on an unrelated product — for example, on a line of fruit juices or dog food. Owners of strong marks — *i.e.*, ones that are widely recognized by consumers — have often argued that third-party use on unrelated products could dilute the distinctive quality of their mark and detract from their positive image. Anti-dilution statutes are found in about half the states and have been applied to protect strong (if not always famous) marks against third-party use. *See, e.g., Wedgwood Homes, Inc. v. Lund*, 659 P.2d 377 (Or. 1993); *Deere & Co. v. MTD Products, Inc.*, 41 F.3d 39 (2d Cir. 1994) (use of altered, animated form of John Deere logo in advertisement found to constitute trademark dilution under New York law).

(14) In 1995, Congress enacted the Federal Trademark Dilution Act to provide relief against the blurring and tarnishment of famous marks. The FTDA generated a number of splits in the federal Courts of Appeals. *See generally* D. Welkowitz, TRADEMARK DILUTION: FEDERAL, STATE AND INTERNATIONAL LAW (2002). The first Supreme Court case in this area involved lingerie giant Victoria's Secret, which sued a shop selling adult toys under the name Victor's Little Secret. The Court

unanimously held that the FTDA requires proof of actual dilution, not merely a likelihood of dilution. *See Moseley v. V Secret Catalogue, Inc.*, 537 U.S. 418 (2003).

In 2006, the result in *Moseley* was overturned by the enactment of the Trademark Dilution Revision Act (TDRA), codified at 15 U.S.C. § 1125(c), which explicitly extends anti-dilution protection to cases in which only a likelihood of dilution is shown. As with the FDTA, the TDRA limits anti-dilution protection to "famous" marks only, and it lists four factors for courts to consider in determining whether a mark is famous. *See* 15 U.S.C. § 1125(c)(2)(A). The TDRA clarified that the statute protects only marks that are "widely recognized by the general consuming public of the United States," such as KODAK, EXXON and CADIL-LAC, thus eliminating marks that are well-known only in a limited market segment or geographic area. The TDRA also expressly recognized two categories of dilution — "dilution by blurring" and "dilution by tarnishment" — and it established definitions for each.

The TDRA contains several enumerated exceptions, including any "fair use" (a term that is defined very differently in trademark law than in copyright law) for purposes such as comparative advertising and parody; all forms of news reporting and news commentary; and any non-commercial use of a mark. *See* 15 U.S.C. § 1125(c)(3). Are you satisfied that these exceptions are adequate to reconcile this expanded version of federal anti-dilution law with the First Amendment? Does the availability of federal or state anti-dilution protection for material which potentially falls within the universe of copyrightable subject matter raise any special intellectual property concerns? Or are you satisfied that the rationale for protection is sufficiently different from that of copyright so that no conflicts should arise?

(15)   In § 3.02 of this book, we reviewed a series of attempts, so far unsuccessful, to extend federal protection to non-original databases that reflect the investment of labor or capital. Obviously, such protection wouldn't be constitutionally available within copyright as such, under the rule of *Feist*. Proponents and opponents of database protection have disputed, however, whether the Commerce Clause could provide Congress with an alternative source of power to enact such legislations. *Compare* Bender, *The Constitutionality of Proposed Federal Database Protection Legislation*, 28 U. Dayton L. Rev. 143 (2002), *with* Heald & Sherry, *Implied Limits on the Legislative Power: The Intellectual Property Clause as an Absolute Constraint in Congress*, 2000 U. Ill. L. Rev. 1119 (2000). Does *Dastar* add anything to our understanding of this controversy? (In considering the last question, bear in mind that federal trademark law, including § 43(a), is a creature of the Commerce Clause.)

[B] Idea Protection

MURRAY v. NATIONAL BROADCASTING CO., INC.
United States Court of Appeals, Second Circuit
844 F.2d 988 (1988)

ALTIMARI, CIRCUIT JUDGE:

[In the 1960s, Bill Cosby became the first African-American entertainer to star in a major network television series. In a 1965 interview, Cosby expressed his desire to create a situation comedy, located in a middle-class black neighborhood. Plaintiff Hwesu Murray, an employee of defendant NBC, claimed that, in 1980, he had proposed to NBC a "new" idea for a half-hour situation comedy starring Bill Cosby. In a written proposal submitted to NBC, Murray described his series, called *Father's Day*, as "wholesome . . . entertainment" which "will focus upon the family life of a Black American family." The leading character was to be the father, "a devoted family man and a compassionate, proud, authority figure." Murray was asked to flesh out his proposal and did, indicating that he expected to be named executive producer and to receive compensation. Murray also allegedly told NBC that his ideas were being submitted in confidence. NBC rejected the proposal on November 21, 1980.

[In 1984, NBC launched *The Cosby Show*, starring Bill Cosby, about ordinary life in an upper middle-class black family. Murray wrote to NBC, asserting that *The Cosby Show* had been derived from his idea for *Father's Day.* NBC responded that the show was an outgrowth of the humor and style developed by Bill Cosby throughout his career, and further maintained that the show was developed and produced by an independent production company.

[The District Court considered whether Murray's idea was "property" that could be subject to legal protection under the rule articulated in *Downey v. General Foods Corp.*, 286 N.E.2d 257 (N.Y. 1972), that "[l]ack of novelty in an idea is fatal to *any* cause of action for its unlawful use" (emphasis in original). In focusing on the novelty of plaintiff's proposal, the District Court determined that Murray's idea was not subject to legal protection from unauthorized use because *Father's Day* merely combined two ideas which had been circulating in the industry for a number of years — namely, the family situation comedy, which was a standard formula, and the casting of black actors in non-stereotypical roles. The District Court granted the defendants' motion for summary judgment.]

DISCUSSION

I.

. . . As the district court recognized, the dispositive issue in this case is whether plaintiff's idea is entitled to legal protection. Plaintiff points to "unique" — even "revolutionary" — aspects of his "Father's Day" proposal that he claims demonstrate "genuine novelty and invention," *see Educational Sales Programs, Inc. v.*

Dreyfus Corp., 317 N.Y.S.2d 840, 844 (Sup. Ct. N.Y. Cty. 1970), which preclude the entry of summary judgment against him. Specifically, plaintiff contends that his idea suggesting the non-stereotypical portrayal of black Americans on television is legally protectible because it represents a real breakthrough. . . . Murray claims that the novelty of his idea subsequently was confirmed by the media and the viewing public which instantly recognized the "unique" and "revolutionary" portrayal of a black family on *The Cosby Show.*

We certainly do not dispute the fact that the portrayal of a non-stereotypical black family on television was indeed a breakthrough. Nevertheless, that breakthrough represents the achievement of what many black Americans, including Bill Cosby and plaintiff himself, have recognized for many years — namely, the need for a more positive, fair, and realistic portrayal of blacks on television. While NBC's decision to broadcast *The Cosby Show* unquestionably was innovative in the sense that an intact, non-stereotypical black family had never been portrayed on television before, the mere fact that such a decision had not been made before does not necessarily mean that the idea for the program is itself novel. *See Educational Sales Programs*, 317 N.Y.S.2d at 843 ("[n]ot every 'good idea' is a legally protectible idea"). . . .

We recognize of course that even novel and original ideas to a greater or lesser extent combine elements that are themselves not novel. Originality does not exist in a vacuum. Nevertheless, where, as here, an idea consists in essence of nothing more than a variation on a basic theme — in this case, the family situation comedy — novelty cannot be found to exist. . . . The addition to this basic theme of the portrayal of blacks in non-stereotypical roles does not alter our conclusion, especially in view of the fact that Bill Cosby previously had expressed a desire to do a situational comedy about a black family and that, as the district court found, Cosby's entire career has been a reflection of the positive portrayal of blacks and the black family on television.

Appellant would have us believe that by interpreting New York law as we do, we are in effect condoning the theft of ideas. On the contrary, ideas that reflect "genuine novelty and invention" are fully protected against unauthorized use. *Educational Sales Programs*, 317 N.Y.S.2d at 844. But those ideas that are not novel "are in the public domain and may freely be used by anyone with impunity." *Ed Graham Productions*, [*Inc. v. National Broadcasting Co.*,] 347 N.Y.S.2d [766,] at 769 [(Sup. Ct. N.Y. Cty. 1973)]. Since such non-novel ideas are not protectible as property, they cannot be stolen. . . .

Finally, as an alternative attack on the propriety of the district court's order granting summary judgment, plaintiff posits that even if his idea was not novel as a matter of law, summary judgment still was inappropriate because his proposal was solicited by defendants and submitted to them in confidence. In this regard, Murray relies on *Cole v. Phillips H. Lord, Inc.*, 28 N.Y.S.2d 404 (1st Dep't 1941). Murray contends that *Cole* stands for the proposition that when an idea is protected by an agreement or a confidential relationship, a cause of action arises for unauthorized use of that idea irrespective of the novelty of the subject matter of the contract. Plaintiff's reliance on *Cole* is misplaced in light of subsequent cases, particularly the New York Court of Appeals decision in *Downey v. General Foods*

Corp., 286 N.E.2d 257 (N.Y. 1972). *See also Ferber v. Sterndent Corp.*, 412 N.E.2d 1311 (N.Y. 1980) ("[a]bsent a showing of novelty, plaintiff's action to recover damages for illegal use of 'confidentially disclosed ideas' must fail as a matter of law"). . . .

Consequently, we find that New York law requires that an idea be original or novel in order for it to be protected as property. *See Downey*, 286 N.E.2d at 259. Since, as has already been shown, plaintiff's proposal for "Father's Day" was lacking in novelty and originality, we conclude that the district court correctly granted defendants' motion for summary judgment.

II.

. . . "[W]hen one submits an idea to another, no promise to pay for its use may be implied, and no asserted agreement enforced, if the elements of novelty and originality are absent. . . ." *Downey*, 286 N.E.2d at 259. As the district court recognized, non-novel ideas do not constitute property. As a result, there can be no cause of action for unauthorized use of Murray's proposal since it was not unlawful for defendants to use a non-novel idea. We conclude, therefore, that the district court properly dismissed plaintiff's state law claims for breach of implied contract, misappropriation, conversion, and unjust enrichment. . . .

Similarly, plaintiff's fraud claim also fails, since, as the district court recognized, plaintiff "cannot be defrauded of property that he does not own." . . .

Lastly, we find that Judge Cedarbaum correctly determined that plaintiff's claim for false designation of origin, *see* Lanham Act § 43(a), 15 U.S.C. § 1125(a), regarding the credits to *The Cosby Show*, cannot survive in light of the court's granting of summary judgment against plaintiff on the issue of novelty. Even assuming defendants used plaintiff's idea, NBC's failure to designate Murray as the creator of The Cosby Show does not mean that the credits to the program are false, since ideas in the public domain may be used with impunity and thus do not require attribution. . . . Affirmed.

GEORGE C. PRATT, CIRCUIT JUDGE, dissenting:

Today this court holds that the idea underlying what may well be the most successful situation comedy in television history was, in 1980, so unoriginal and so entrenched in the public domain that, as a matter of law, it did not constitute intellectual property protected under New York law. Because I am convinced that the novelty issue in this case presents a factual question subject to further discovery and ultimate scrutiny by a trier of fact, I respectfully dissent.

. . . Novelty, by its very definition, is highly subjective. As fashion, advertising, and television and radio production can attest, what is novel today may not have been novel 15 years ago, and what is commonplace today may well be novel 15 years hence. In this instance, where Cosby expressed the concept almost a decade and a half before Murray submitted his proposal, where it was Murray's idea that NBC actually used, where there is no evidence indicating NBC knew anything of the program idea until Murray submitted it, . . . and where substantial conflicting evidence exists as to the "novelty" of the idea under New York law, there seems to be at least a triable issue.

The majority's decision prematurely denies Murray a fair opportunity to establish his right to participate in the enormous wealth generated by *The Cosby Show.* Accordingly, I would reverse the district court judgment and remand the case for further consideration.

NOTES AND QUESTIONS

(1)   As a fundamental proposition, copyright law protects the expression of ideas, but not ideas *per se.* State law, however, has protected ideas under several legal theories: express contract, implied-in-fact contract, unjust enrichment (or quasi-contract), breach of confidential relationship (akin to trade secret), and even, occasionally, simply an inchoate notion of so-called "property" in ideas. Among these theories, plaintiffs seem to have had the best results with express or implied contract. On which theory or theories was the plaintiff in *Murray* relying? How easy is it to tell? Certainly, the fact that NBC allegedly solicited the submission would seem to be of importance. Should industry custom be considered in deciding the viability of various theories of liability? *See Whitfield v. Lear,* 751 F.2d 90 (2d Cir. 1984).

(2)   It appears that the *Murray* court attached a great deal of importance to the fact that Cosby revealed a similar idea for a television series in a 1965 interview, some fifteen years before Murray's submission to NBC. Why is this significant? Does it mean that Murray's submission to NBC was valueless? The answers to these questions reflect the fact that an implied rather than an express contract was in issue. When confronted with theories of recovery other than express contract, the courts of most states traditionally have imposed two general preconditions for idea protection: novelty and concreteness. Courts have varied on the meaning of novelty in the idea context, but they generally require more than originality: that is, the idea must manifest innovative qualities. For a comprehensive overview, see Barrett, *The Law of Ideas Reconsidered,* 71 J. Pat. & Trademark Off. Soc'y 691 (1989).

As the principal case indicates, lack of novelty in an idea (however defined) can be fatal to a cause of action for its unlawful use. Such a threshold requirement may be understandable in cases where the plaintiff's claim amounts to an assertion of intellectual property rights under state law (*i.e.,* quasi-contract). But why should it apply here if Murray is claiming that, under the circumstances, NBC should be understood to have committed itself to pay him for his idea submission if it were used? Does this rule reflect some uncertainty about whether implied-in-fact contracts are real contracts or mere judicial fictions?

After *Murray* was decided, the New York Court of Appeals held that "novelty" was not an absolute requirement in an action for breach of an *express* contract to use another's idea. *Apfel v. Prudential-Bache Securities, Inc.,* 616 N.E.2d 1095 (N.Y. 1993). Murray moved to reopen his case under Federal Rule of Civil Procedure 60(b), but the court denied the motion. 1993 U.S. Dist. LEXIS 16745 (S.D.N.Y.), *aff'd mem.,* 29 F.3d 621 (2d Cir. 1994). *See also Nadel v. Play-by-Play Toys & Novelties, Inc.,* 208 F.3d 368 (2d Cir. 2000) (discussing *Apfel* and distinguishing absolute novelty required for misappropriation claims from "novelty to the buyer" required for contract claims). *Apfel* brings New York law closer to that of other states (in particular, California), which have rejected the novelty requirement in cases of express contracts related to ideas. *See, e.g., Aliotti v. R. Dakin & Co.*, 831 F.2d 898 (9th Cir. 1987); *see also Wrench LLC v. Taco Bell Corp.*, 256 F.3d 446 (6th Cir. 2001) (Michigan law) (discussed in § 11.02 above). Nevertheless, *Wrench* notes, "many courts do require novelty in an action based upon an implied contract theory on the ground that there can be no consideration for an implied promise to pay if the idea does not constitute 'property.'" *Id.* at 461.

Even in situations where a qualitative threshold standard makes sense as a precondition for idea protection, why should the standard be "novelty" rather than something else? Wouldn't "originality" (in the copyright sense) be enough? *See* D. Nimmer & M. Nimmer, 4 NIMMER ON COPYRIGHT § 19D.06 (2012).

(3) As already noted, in addition to demanding novelty, courts have required that the idea be concrete. As with novelty, the concreteness requirement has been varyingly defined. Some courts require that the idea be embodied in tangible form, *e.g.*, as a written document, whereas others would insist that the idea be developed in sufficient detail to be of practical use. As one court expressed the notion, "we think . . . that in the field of radio broadcasting concreteness may lie between the boundaries of mere generality on the one hand and, on the other, a full script containing the words to be uttered and delineating the action to be portrayed." *See Hamilton Nat. Bank v. Belt*, 210 F.2d 706, 708 (D.C. Cir. 1953). Suppose Murray were to overcome the novelty barrier. Does it appear from the facts that his submission would have met the concreteness standard? What is the rationale justifying the concreteness standard? Is it more appropriate to some legal theories for idea protection than to others?

(4) Generally, if disclosure occurs before it is known that compensation is a condition for the use of an idea, no contract will be implied. *See Desny v. Wilder*, 299 P.2d 257, 270 (Cal. 1956) (holding, by contrast, that prior disclosure will not bar an action based on express contract). Assume now that Murray had no prior relationship with NBC. What if Murray had sent his idea to NBC, expressly stating that he expected compensation for its use? Suppose further that NBC had implemented the series without acknowledging Murray's submission. Assuming that applicable threshold standards (such as novelty or concreteness) are satisfied, should a contract be implied under these circumstances? The fact is that companies constantly receive idea submissions and have developed a series of practices to avoid becoming embroiled in legal suits involving these unsolicited submissions. Some companies will return the submission unopened. Others have developed a standard release form, requiring the signature of the idea submitter before they will proceed with the idea. For an example of these company practices, see *Sylvania Electric Prods., Inc. v. Brainerd*, 166 U.S.P.Q. (BNA) 387 (D. Mass. 1970).

(5) In the world of cinema, an obligation to pay for an idea for a movie will often be contingent on whether the movie is based on the plot idea. What constitutes "based on" has provided some difficult questions of interpretation. This issue arose in *Buchwald v. Paramount Pictures Corp.*, 1990 Cal. App. LEXIS 634 (Cal. App. Dep't Super. Ct. 1990), where the humorist Art Buchwald submitted an outline for

a motion picture built around the character of an African prince who comes to the United States, loses his money and title, has to work in a fast food restaurant, and finds true love. Buchwald entered into an agreement with Paramount that he was entitled to payment only if Paramount produced "a feature-length motion picture based upon" the author's work. Paramount, after a series of meetings with Buchwald, decided not to make the film. Three years later, however, Paramount released a film (*Coming to America*, starring Eddie Murphy) whose plot included, along with certain additions, the elements indicated above.

To determine whether the movie was "based on" the Buchwald treatment, the court used an analysis similar to that encountered in copyright cases. It compared the plots of the two works, and, despite some significant differences, found them to be "substantially similar." *See also Landsberg v. Scrabble Crossword Game Players, Inc.*, 802 F.2d 1193 (9th Cir. 1986) (recovery for breach of implied-in-fact contract against recipient of manuscript on Scrabble strategy who later created a "substantially similar" work "based on" plaintiff's manuscript). Is it appropriate to use the notion of substantial similarity in this circumstance? Does it necessarily indicate that the state law of idea protection is impinging on the territory of copyright?

(6) Where there is a pre-existing duty of trust and confidence (as between employee and employer, or lawyer and client), a number of jurisdictions will provide an equitable remedy for the wrongful disclosure or use of an idea disclosed within the confidential relationship, without engaging in implied contract analysis as such. *See Davies v. Krasna*, 245 Cal. App. 2d 535, 54 Cal. Rptr. 37 (1966). But isn't such a claim nevertheless based on the notion that certain confidential relationships necessarily entail implied agreements to preserve information in confidence?

State courts are less consistent in their application of the confidential relationship theory to situations involving idea submissions by strangers. If a court were to impose liability in such a situation, however, wouldn't the result be akin to a finding of quasi-contractual liability — *i.e.*, liability imposed to avoid an unfair or unjust result? Why should the answer to the questions just posed matter? *See* D. Nimmer & M. Nimmer, 4 NIMMER ON COPYRIGHT § 19D.05[B] (2010) (discussing distinctions among the applicable preconditions to liability, and the available defenses and remedies, in various kinds of actions).

[C] The Right of Publicity

WHITE v. SAMSUNG ELECTRONICS AMERICA, INC.
United States Court of Appeals, Ninth Circuit
971 F.2d 1395 (1992)

GOODWIN, CIRCUIT JUDGE:

This case involves a promotional "fame and fortune" dispute. In running a particular advertisement without Vanna White's permission, defendants Samsung Electronics America, Inc. (Samsung) and David Deutsch Associates, Inc. (Deutsch) attempted to capitalize on White's fame to enhance their fortune. . . .

Plaintiff Vanna White is the hostess of "Wheel of Fortune," one of the most popular game shows in television history. An estimated forty million people watch the program daily. Capitalizing on the fame which her participation in the show has bestowed on her, White markets her identity to various advertisers.

The dispute in this case arose out of a series of advertisements prepared for Samsung by Deutsch. The series ran in at least half a dozen publications with widespread, and in some cases national, circulation. Each of the advertisements in the series followed the same theme. Each depicted a current item from popular culture and a Samsung electronic product. Each was set in the twenty-first century and conveyed the message that the Samsung product would still be in use by that time. By hypothesizing outrageous future outcomes for the cultural items, the ads created humorous effects. For example, one lampooned current popular notions of an unhealthy diet by depicting a raw steak with the caption: "Revealed to be health food. 2010 A.D." Another depicted irreverent "news"-show host Morton Downey Jr. in front of an American flag with the caption: "Presidential candidate. 2008 A.D."

The advertisement which prompted the current dispute was for Samsung video-cassette recorders (VCRs). The ad depicted a robot, dressed in a wig, gown, and jewelry which Deutsch consciously selected to resemble White's hair and dress. The robot was posed next to a game board which is instantly recognizable as the Wheel of Fortune game show set, in a stance for which White is famous. The caption of the ad read: "Longest-running game show. 2012 A.D." Defendants referred to the ad as the "Vanna White" ad. Unlike the other celebrities used in the campaign, White neither consented to the ads nor was she paid.

Following the circulation of the robot ad, White sued Samsung and Deutsch in federal district court under: (1) California Civil Code § 3344; (2) the California common law right of publicity; and (3) § 43(a) of the Lanham Act, 15 U.S.C. § 1125(a). The district court granted summary judgment against White on each of her claims. White now appeals.

[The Ninth Circuit agreed with the District Court that "the robot at issue here was not White's 'likeness' within the meaning" of the California statute but concluded, as to § 43(a) that there remained a genuine issue of material fact as to whether the ad created a likelihood of confusion concerning White's endorsement of the product.]

Vanna White

Right of Publicity

White next argues that the district court erred in granting summary judgment to defendants on White's common law right of publicity claim. In *Eastwood v. Superior Court*, 149 Cal. App. 3d 409 (1983), the California court of appeal stated that the common law right of publicity cause of action "may be pleaded by alleging (1) the defendant's use of the plaintiff's identity; (2) the appropriation of plaintiff's name or likeness to defendant's advantage, commercially or otherwise; (3) lack of consent; and (4) resulting injury." *Id.* at 417 (citing Prosser, Law of Torts (4th ed. 1971) § 117, pp. 804-807). The district court dismissed White's claim for failure to satisfy Eastwood's second prong, reasoning that defendants had not appropriated White's "name or likeness" with their robot ad. We agree that the robot ad did not make use of White's name or likeness. However, the common law right of publicity is not so confined. . . .

Ms. C3PO?

In [*Midler v. Ford Motor Co.*, 849 F.2d 460 (9th Cir. 1988)], this court held that, even though the defendants had not used [singer Bette] Midler's name or likeness [in a Ford television commercial employing a "sound-alike" to sing a song that Midler had made famous], Midler had stated a claim for violation of her California common law right of publicity because "the defendants . . . for their own profit in selling their product did appropriate part of her identity" by using a Midler sound-alike. *Id.* at 463-64.

In *Carson v. Here's Johnny Portable Toilets, Inc.*, 698 F.2d 831 (6th Cir. 1983), the defendant had marketed portable toilets under the brand name "Here's Johnny" — Johnny Carson's signature "Tonight Show" introduction — without Carson's permission. The district court had dismissed Carson's Michigan common law right of publicity claim because the defendants had not used Carson's "name or likeness." *Id.* at 835. In reversing the district court, the sixth circuit found "the district court's conception of the right of publicity . . . too narrow" and held that the right was implicated because the defendant had appropriated Carson's identity by using, *inter alia*, the phrase "Here's Johnny." *Id.* at 835-37.

These cases teach not only that the common law right of publicity reaches means of appropriation other than name or likeness, but that the specific means of appropriation are relevant only for determining whether the defendant has in fact appropriated the plaintiff's identity. . . . As the *Carson* court explained:

> [T]he right of publicity has developed to protect the commercial interest of celebrities in their identities. The theory of the right is that a celebrity's identity can be valuable in the promotion of products, and the celebrity has an interest that may be protected from the unauthorized commercial exploitation of that identity. . . . If the celebrity's identity is commercially exploited, there has been an invasion of his right whether or not his "name or likeness" is used.

Carson, 698 F.2d at 835. It is not important how the defendant has appropriated the plaintiff's identity, but whether the defendant has done so. . . .

Viewed separately, the individual aspects of the advertisement in the present case say little. Viewed together, they leave little doubt about the celebrity the ad is meant to depict. The female-shaped robot is wearing a long gown, blond wig, and large jewelry. Vanna White dresses exactly like this at times, but so do many other women. The robot is in the process of turning a block letter on a game-board. Vanna White dresses like this while turning letters on a game-board but perhaps similarly attired Scrabble-playing women do this as well. The robot is standing on what looks to be the Wheel of Fortune game show set. Vanna White dresses like this, turns letters, and does this on the Wheel of Fortune game show. She is the only one. Indeed, defendants themselves referred to their ad as the "Vanna White" ad. We are not surprised.

Television and other media create marketable celebrity identity value. Considerable energy and ingenuity are expended by those who have achieved celebrity value to exploit it for profit. The law protects the celebrity's sole right to exploit this value whether the celebrity has achieved her fame out of rare ability, dumb luck, or a combination thereof. We decline Samsung and Deutsch's invitation to permit the evisceration of the common law right of publicity through means as facile as those in this case. Because White has alleged facts showing that Samsung and Deutsch had appropriated her identity, the district court erred by rejecting, on summary judgment, White's common law right of publicity claim. . . .

The Parody Defense

[The defendants also argued] that their robot ad constituted protected speech. . . . This case involves a true advertisement run for the purpose of selling Samsung VCRs. The ad's spoof of Vanna White and Wheel of Fortune is subservient and only tangentially related to the ad's primary message: "buy Samsung VCRs." Defendants' parody arguments are better addressed to non-commercial parodies. The difference between a "parody" and a "knock-off" is the difference between fun and profit. . . .

Conclusion

In remanding this case, we hold only that White has pleaded claims which can go to the jury for its decision. . . .

WHITE v. SAMSUNG ELECTRONICS AMERICA, INC.
United States Court of Appeals, Ninth Circuit
989 F.2d 1512 (1993)

DISSENT FROM REJECTION OF SUGGESTION FOR REHEARING EN BANC

KOZINSKI, CIRCUIT JUDGE, with whom CIRCUIT JUDGES O'SCANNLAIN and KLEINFELD join, dissenting from the order rejecting the suggestion for rehearing en banc.

I

Saddam Hussein wants to keep advertisers from using his picture in unflattering contexts.[1] Clint Eastwood doesn't want tabloids to write about him.[2] Rudolph Valentino's heirs want to control his film biography.[3] The Girl Scouts don't want their image soiled by association with certain activities.[4] George Lucas wants to keep Strategic Defense Initiative fans from calling it "Star Wars."[5] Pepsico doesn't want singers to use the word "Pepsi" in their songs.[6] Guy Lombardo wants an exclusive property right to ads that show big bands playing on New Year's Eve.[7] Uri Geller thinks he should be paid for ads showing psychics bending metal through telekinesis.[8] Paul Prudhomme, that household name, thinks the same about ads featuring corpulent bearded chefs.[9] And scads of copyright holders see purple when

---

[1] *See* Eben Shapiro, *Rising Caution on Using Celebrity Images*, N.Y. Times, Nov. 4, 1992, at D20 (Iraqi diplomat objects on right of publicity grounds to ad containing Hussein's picture and caption "History has shown what happens when one source controls all the information").

[2] *Eastwood v. Superior Court*, 149 Cal. App. 3d 409, 198 Cal. Rptr. 342 (1983).

[3] *Guglielmi v. Spelling-Goldberg Prods.*, 25 Cal. 3d 860, 160 Cal. Rptr. 352, 603 P.2d 454 (1979) (Rudolph Valentino).

[4] *Girl Scouts v. Personality Posters Mfg.*, 304 F. Supp. 1228 (S.D.N.Y. 1969) (poster of a pregnant girl in a Girl Scout uniform with the caption "Be Prepared").

[5] *Lucasfilm Ltd. v. High Frontier*, 622 F. Supp. 931 (D.D.C. 1985).

[6] Pepsico Inc. claimed the lyrics and packaging of grunge rocker Tad Doyle's "Jack Pepsi" song were "offensive to [it] and [are] likely to offend [its] customers," in part because they "associate [Pepsico] and its Pepsi marks with intoxication and drunk driving." Russell, *Doyle Leaves Pepsi Thirsty for Compensation*, Billboard, June 15, 1991, at 43. Conversely, the Hell's Angels recently sued Marvel Comics to keep it from publishing a comic book called "Hell's Angel," starring a character of the same name. Marvel settled by paying $35,000 to charity and promising never to use the name "Hell's Angel" again in connection with any of its publications. *Marvel, Hell's Angels Settle Trademark Suit*, L.A. Daily J., Feb. 2, 1993, § II, at 1.

[7] *Lombardo v. Doyle, Dane & Bernbach, Inc.*, 58 A.D.2d 620, 396 N.Y.S.2d 661 (1977).

[8] *Geller v. Fallon McElligott*, No. 90-Civ-2839 (S.D.N.Y. July 22, 1991) (involving a Timex ad).

[9] *Prudhomme v. Procter & Gamble Co., 800 F. Supp. 390 (E.D. La. 1992).*

their creations are made fun of. . . .

Something very dangerous is going on here. Private property, including intellectual property, is essential to our way of life. It provides an incentive for investment and innovation; it stimulates the flourishing of our culture; it protects the moral entitlements of people to the fruits of their labors. But reducing too much to private property can be bad medicine. Private land, for instance, is far more useful if separated from other private land by public streets, roads and highways. Public parks, utility rights-of-way and sewers reduce the amount of land in private hands, but vastly enhance the value of the property that remains.

So too it is with intellectual property. Overprotecting intellectual property is as harmful as underprotecting it. Creativity is impossible without a rich public domain. Nothing today, likely nothing since we tamed fire, is genuinely new: Culture, like science and technology, grows by accretion, each new creator building on the works of those who came before. Overprotection stifles the very creative forces it's supposed to nurture.[11]

The panel's opinion is a classic case of overprotection. Concerned about what it sees as a wrong done to Vanna White, the panel majority erects a property right of remarkable and dangerous breadth: Under the majority's opinion, it's now a tort for advertisers to *remind* the public of a celebrity. Not to use a celebrity's name, voice, signature or likeness; not to imply the celebrity endorses a product; but simply to evoke the celebrity's image in the public's mind. This Orwellian notion withdraws far more from the public domain than prudence and common sense allow. It conflicts with the Copyright Act and the Copyright Clause. It raises serious First Amendment problems. It's bad law, and it deserves a long, hard second look.

II

. . . The district judge quite reasonably held that, because Samsung didn't use White's name, likeness, voice or signature, it didn't violate her right of publicity. Not so, says the panel majority: The California right of publicity can't possibly be limited to name and likeness. If it were, a "clever advertising strategist" could avoid using White's name or likeness but nevertheless remind people of her with impunity, "effectively eviscerating" her rights. To prevent this "evisceration," the panel majority holds that the right of publicity must extend beyond name and likeness, to any "appropriation" of White's "identity" — anything that "evokes" her personality.

III

But what does "evisceration" mean in intellectual property law? Intellectual property rights aren't like some constitutional rights, absolute guarantees protected against all kinds of interference, subtle as well as blatant. They cast no penumbras, emit no emanations: The very point of intellectual property laws is that they protect only against certain specific kinds of appropriation. I can't publish unauthorized copies of, say, Presumed Innocent; I can't make a movie out of it. But

---

[11] *See* Wendy J. Gordon, *A Property Right in Self Expression: Equality and Individualism in the Natural Law of Intellectual Property*, 102 Yale L.J. 1533 (1993).

I'm perfectly free to write a book about an idealistic young prosecutor on trial for a crime he didn't commit. So what if I got the idea from PRESUMED INNOCENT? So what if it reminds readers of the original? Have I "eviscerated" Scott Turow's intellectual property rights? Certainly not. All creators draw in part on the work of those who came before, referring to it, building on it, poking fun at it; we call this creativity, not piracy.

The majority isn't, in fact, preventing the "evisceration" of Vanna White's existing rights; it's creating a new and much broader property right, a right unknown in California law. . . .

. . . The panel is giving White an exclusive right not in what she looks like or who she is, but in what she does for a living.

This is entirely the wrong place to strike the balance. Intellectual property rights aren't free: They're imposed at the expense of future creators and of the public at large. Where would we be if Charles Lindbergh had an exclusive right in the concept of a heroic solo aviator? If Arthur Conan Doyle had gotten a copyright in the idea of the detective story, or Albert Einstein had patented the theory of relativity? If every author and celebrity had been given the right to keep people from mocking them or their work? Surely this would have made the world poorer, not richer, culturally as well as economically.

This is why intellectual property law is full of careful balances between what's set aside for the owner and what's left in the public domain for the rest of us: The relatively short life of patents; the longer, but finite, life of copyrights; copyright's idea-expression dichotomy; the fair use doctrine; the prohibition on copyrighting facts; the compulsory license of television broadcasts and musical compositions; federal preemption of overbroad state intellectual property laws; the nominative use doctrine in trademark law; the right to make soundalike recordings. All of these diminish an intellectual property owner's rights. All let the public use something created by someone else. But all are necessary to maintain a free environment in which creative genius can flourish.

The intellectual property right created by the panel here has none of these essential limitations: No fair use exception; no right to parody; no idea-expression dichotomy. It impoverishes the public domain, to the detriment of future creators and the public at large. Instead of well-defined, limited characteristics such as name, likeness or voice, advertisers will now have to cope with vague claims of "appropriation of identity," claims often made by people with a wholly exaggerated sense of their own fame and significance. . . .

IV

The panel, however, does more than misinterpret California law: By refusing to recognize a parody exception to the right of publicity, the panel directly contradicts the federal Copyright Act. Samsung didn't merely parody Vanna White. It parodied Vanna White appearing in "Wheel of Fortune," a copyrighted television show, and parodies of copyrighted works are governed by federal copyright law. . . .

The majority's decision decimates this federal scheme. It's impossible to parody a movie or a TV show without at the same time "evoking" the "identities" of the actors. You can't have a mock Star Wars without a mock Luke Skywalker, Han Solo and Princess Leia, which in turn means a mock Mark Hamill, Harrison Ford and Carrie Fisher. You can't have a mock Batman commercial without a mock Batman, which means someone emulating the mannerisms of Adam West or Michael Keaton. . . . The public's right to make a fair use parody and the copyright owner's right to license a derivative work are useless if the parodist is held hostage by every actor whose "identity" he might need to "appropriate." . . .

V

[Judge Kozinski concludes also that the majority's decision, owing to the breadth of the protection it affords, conflicts with the U.S. Constitution's "dormant Copyright Clause," under which state intellectual property laws can stand only so long as they do not "prejudice the interests of other States" (citing, Goldstein v. California, 412 U.S. 546, 558 (1973).]

VI

Finally, I can't see how giving White the power to keep others from evoking her image in the public's mind can be squared with the First Amendment. Where does White get this right to control our thoughts? The majority's creation goes way beyond the protection given a trademark or a copyrighted work, or a person's name or likeness. All those things control one particular way of expressing an idea, one way of referring to an object or a person. But not allowing *any* means of reminding people of someone? That's a speech restriction unparalleled in First Amendment law.[28]

What's more, I doubt even a name-and-likeness-only right of publicity can stand without a parody exception. The First Amendment isn't just about religion or politics — it's also about protecting the free development of our national culture. Parody, humor, irreverence are all vital components of the marketplace of ideas. The last thing we need, the last thing the First Amendment will tolerate, is a law that lets public figures keep people from mocking them, or from "evoking" their images in the mind of the public.

The majority dismisses the First Amendment issue out of hand. . . .

---

[28] Just compare the majority's holding to the intellectual property laws upheld by the Supreme Court. The Copyright Act is constitutional precisely because of the fair use doctrine and the idea-expression dichotomy, *Harper & Row v. Nation Enterprises*, 471 U.S. 539, 560 (1985), two features conspicuously absent from the majority's doctrine. The right of publicity at issue in *Zacchini v. Scripps-Howard Broadcasting Co.*, 433 U.S. 562, 576 (1977), was only the right to "broadcast of petitioner's entire performance," not "the unauthorized use of another's name for purposes of trade." *Id.* Even the statute upheld in *San Francisco Arts & Athletics, Inc. v. United States Olympic Comm.*, 483 U.S. 522, 530 (1987), which gave the USOC sweeping rights to the word "Olympic," didn't purport to protect all expression that reminded people of the Olympics.

VII

For better or worse, we *are* the Court of Appeals for the Hollywood Circuit. Millions of people toil in the shadow of the law we make, and much of their livelihood is made possible by the existence of intellectual property rights. But much of their livelihood — and much of the vibrancy of our culture — also depends on the existence of other intangible rights: the right to draw ideas from a rich and varied public domain, and the right to mock, for profit as well as fun, the cultural icons of our time.

In the name of avoiding the "evisceration" of a celebrity's rights in her image, the majority diminishes the rights of copyright holders and the public at large. In the name of fostering creativity, the majority suppresses it. Vanna White and those like her have been given something they never had before, and they've been given it at our expense. I cannot agree.

NOTES AND QUESTIONS

(1)   Relative to other doctrines in state intellectual property law (for example, passing off), the right of publicity is the new kid on the block, born in the 1950s through the midwifery of legal scholarship — the critical article being Melville Nimmer's *The Right of Publicity*, 19 L. & Contemp. Probs. 203 (1954). Today, about half the states have recognized the right of publicity by either legislation or judicial decision.

As originally conceived, the right of publicity was a property interest in an individual's persona, *i.e.*, name, image, and likeness. But *White* suggests that today the scope of the right has expanded considerably, at least in some states, going beyond the use of name or likeness to protect against more indirect evocation of a celebrity's identity. *See, e.g., Hirsch v. S.C. Johnson & Sons, Inc.*, 280 N.W.2d 129 (Wisc. 1979) (use of the nickname "Crazylegs"); *Carson v. Here's Johnny Portable Toilets, Inc.*, 698 F.2d 831 (6th Cir. 1983) (use of "Here's Johnny" on portable toilets violated Johnny Carson's right of publicity); *Newcombe v. Adolf Coors Co.*, 157 F.3d 686 (9th Cir. 1998) (drawing for a beer advertisement focusing on a baseball pitcher in a windup position could be the basis of right of publicity claim if it readily identified the plaintiff's distinctive pitching stance).

In his dissent from the denial of the petition for rehearing in *White*, Judge Kozinski suggests that "the panel is giving White an exclusive right not in what she looks like or who she is, but in what she does for a living." Are you convinced by this characterization of the holding? Can you suggest an alternative which might be somewhat less far-reaching? Does the expansion of the right to various secondary indicia of personality put it on a collision course with the law of copyright?

(2)   Early judicial acknowledgments of the right of publicity treated it — like its older cousin, the right of privacy — as a strictly personal entitlement. As *White* demonstrates, however, the right of publicity is a dynamic rather than a static legal category, and its contours are being further elaborated even as we write.

For example, most states now explicitly recognize the descendibility of the right of publicity after the death of the individual to whose persona it first attached. The duration of the post-mortem right under the statutes varies widely: 100 years (Indiana, where the Curtis Management Group, the largest management company specializing in celebrity merchandising, is located); 70 years (California); 40 years (Florida); as long as continuously used (Tennessee, home of Elvis Presley, the once-and-future King of Publicity Rights); or, most simply but least helpfully, no stated duration (Nebraska). In addition, some states have recognized the post-mortem right by case law. *See* J.T. McCarthy, THE RIGHTS OF PUBLICITY AND PRIVACY § 9:1 to 9:37 (2012).

What is the rationale for the descendible right of publicity? Recall the arguments for the life-plus-70 term for copyright. Are the justifications the same for the right of publicity? If so, does the similarity raise any questions about possible preemption of this burgeoning state law doctrine?

A fascinating battle has been waged over the post-mortem rights to exploit Marilyn Monroe's image. Two federal district courts initially held that CMG did not have standing to sue, because Monroe could not devise property in her will that did not exist at the time of her death in 1962. *See Shaw Family Archives, Ltd. v. CMG Worldwide, Inc.*, 486 F. Supp. 2d 309 (S.D.N.Y. 2007). After California amended its statute to make its post-mortem right expressly retroactive, both courts ruled that Monroe was domiciled in New York at the time of her death, rather than California. *See Milton H. Greene Archives, Inc. v. CMG Worldwide, Inc.*, 568 F. Supp. 2d 1152 (C.D. Cal. 2008), *aff'd sub nom. Milton H. Green Archives, Inc. v. Marilyn Monroe LLC*, 692 F.3d 983 (9th Cir. 2012). Because New York does not recognize a post-mortem right of publicity, the rulings have cast Monroe's likeness into the public domain.

(3) Is the *White* majority's analysis advanced by its assertion that Samsung "appropriated" something of White's? Doesn't the question of whether there has been an "appropriation" depend on how broadly White's rights are defined? If so, how can that characterization help us to understand how great the scope of those rights should be? Does your answer depend on whether you view the right of publicity in economic terms — or in moral rights terms (that is, in terms of the protection of an individual's interest in personal dignity and autonomy)? Does the majority opinion leave much space for a dignitary conception of the right? Is it important, in the words of Justice Pitney in the *INS* case we saw in § 11.02, that the defendant is reaping where he has not sown? Or is this also a circular argument? Does it matter whether a third-party use is deceiving the public?

(4) Why do we need a right of publicity to enable celebrities to appropriate the pecuniary value of their fame? To provide them the economic incentive to produce their intellectual and creative work? Does the invocation of this rationale suggest that state publicity rights may have the potential to duplicate (or interfere with) the work of the federal copyright laws? For a comprehensive analysis of the rationale of the right of publicity from a skeptical point of view, see Madow, *Private Ownership of Public Image: Popular Culture and Publicity Rights*, 81 Cal. L. Rev. 125 (1993).

(5) Judge Kozinski points out in his *White* dissent that "intellectual property rights aren't free." But will the losses to the public domain he foresees resulting from the extension of publicity rights be offset by public benefits? For an attempt

to justify the right of publicity from an economic welfare standpoint, see Grady, *A Positive Economic Theory of the Right of Publicity*, 1 UCLA Ent. L. Rev. 97 (1994).

Grady analogizes the right of publicity to the economic problem of the common pool (sometimes called "the tragedy of the commons"). The argument for private property rights goes like this: Absent property rights in a fish pond (for example), anglers would exhaust the entire stock, and thus destroy the resource, in an effort to grab as much value as possible for themselves as quickly as possible. By contrast, the argument runs, assigning property rights to the resource encourages a socially optimal resource use. When applied to intangible creations, how does this argument differ from the usual "incentive" rationale for intellectual property rights? Does the common pool analysis apply with full force (or at all) to products of the mind? Are there significant differences between celebrity personae and fish? For criticism of this approach, see Lemley, *Ex Ante Versus Ex Post Justifications for Intellectual Property*, 71 U. Chi. L. Rev. 129 (2004).

(6) *Limitations on the right of publicity.* Judge Kozinski makes the point that publicity rights may actually pose a greater threat to the public domain than does copyright, because the former are not subject to the same limitations and exceptions (for example, fair use). In *Groucho Marx Productions, Inc. v. Day and Night Co.*, 523 F. Supp. 485 (S.D.N.Y. 1981), *rev'd on other grounds*, 689 F.2d 317 (2d Cir. 1982), which held the right of publicity infringed by a new play featuring the Marx Brothers' characters, the court discussed the possibility of limiting publicity rights by a "fair use" privilege in appropriate situations. What criteria would you use to determine what those situations might be?

In *Comedy III Prods. Inc. v. Gary Saderup, Inc.*, 21 P.3d 797 (Cal. 2001), the California Supreme Court held that the defendant's lithograph of the Three Stooges violated their post-mortem right of publicity. Borrowing the concept of "transformative use" from copyright law, the court indicated that uses which were "transformative" would be protected by the First Amendment, but that a "literal depiction or imitation of a celebrity for commercial gain" would not be protected. *Id.* at 808. Other courts have disagreed, holding that an artistic depiction of a celebrity is entitled to broader — though not absolute — First Amendment protection. *See, e.g.*, *ETW Corp. v. Jireh Publ'g, Inc.*, 332 F.3d 915 (6th Cir. 2003) (public interest balancing test). *But see Doe v. TCI Cablevision, Inc.*, 110 S.W.3d 363 (Mo. 2003) (criticizing both *Comedy III* and *ETW* as not sufficiently protective of celebrity rights).

Will it be any easier to apply the "transformative" use test in right of publicity cases than in copyright cases? Early indications are that the answer is "no." In *Winter v. DC Comics*, the plaintiffs alleged that they were depicted in a comic book as sadistic, half-worm, half-human villains. The California Court of Appeal held there was a genuine issue of material fact as to whether the work was "transformative"! 121 Cal. Rptr. 2d 431 (Ct. App. 2002). The California Supreme Court unanimously reversed, instructing lower courts that summary judgment should be readily granted in such cases. 30 Cal. 4th 881 (2003).

(7) Because values of free speech and press do sometimes clash with people's desire to control the use of their names or likenesses, state courts and legislatures have tried to limit application of the publicity right to situations involving the

commercial exploitation of an individual's persona. Thus, use of an individual's name or likeness in news reporting and similar contexts is permitted. Moreover, such communicative uses may be privileged under the First Amendment. *See Rosemont Enterprises, Inc. v. Random House, Inc.*, 294 N.Y.S.2d 122 (1968), *aff'd*, 301 N.Y.S.2d 948 (1969) (biography of Howard Hughes); *Tyne v. Time Warner Entertainment Co.*, 901 So. 2d 802 (Fla. 2005) (fact-based movie *The Perfect Storm*). For better or worse, the privilege may apply to some crassly commercial uses. For example, in *C.B.C. Distr. & Mktg., Inc. v. Major League Baseball Advanced Media, L.P.*, 505 F.3d 818 (8th Cir. 2007), the court held that the use of baseball players' names and statistics for commercial fantasy baseball leagues was protected under the First Amendment.

Should the use of likenesses of professional and student athletes in videogames also be protected by the First Amendment? *Compare Hart v. Electronic Arts, Inc.*, 808 F. Supp. 2d 757 (D.N.J. 2011) (yes), *with Keller v. Electronic Arts, Inc.*, 94 U.S.P.Q.2d (BNA) 1130 (N.D. Cal. 2010) (no).

(8)   There are limits to the privilege to use information relating to an individual's identity in news reporting and related contexts. In *Zacchini v. Scripps-Howard Broadcasting Co.*, 433 U.S. 562 (1977), the Supreme Court held that a television station which filmed a 15-second human cannonball act at a county fair and played it on the evening news violated the performer's state-law right of publicity. The Court pointed to three factors in rejecting a claim of First Amendment privilege: the damage to plaintiff was considerable; the station could have accomplished the same journalistic purpose without showing the entire act; and the plaintiff was seeking damages rather than trying to enjoin the defendant's activity.

(9)   *Zacchini* is an important case from another standpoint as well. In its decision, the Supreme Court refused to preempt the state right of publicity under the Supremacy Clause. One warning is in order, however: *Zacchini* is hardly a garden variety right-of-publicity case involving name or likeness. Can you think of any other basis on which the cannonball act could be protected? What about common-law copyright? See the lower court's opinion at 351 N.E.2d 454 (Ohio 1976).

(10)   What are the differences between right of publicity and passing off? For a passing off action to lie, one must prove likelihood of confusion. By contrast, in a right of publicity action, the unauthorized commercial use of an individual's persona is the issue. The two causes of action, however, clearly overlap and are closely related. For example, in the *Carson* case noted above, the court sustained the right of publicity claim but rejected the § 43(a) cause of action for the use of "Here's Johnny." But in *Allen v. National Video, Inc.*, 610 F. Supp. 612 (S.D.N.Y. 1985), where a Woody Allen look-alike was used in a video store advertisement, the court rejected the publicity claim, but allowed the § 43(a) claim based on a finding of likelihood of confusion. *See also ETW Corp.* (rejecting both § 43(a) and Ohio right of publicity claims in a case involving art prints depicting golfer Tiger Woods); *and Parks v. LaFace Records*, 329 F.3d 437 (6th Cir. 2003) (reversing First Amendment dismissal of Rosa Parks' Lanham Act and publicity right action against Outkast's song, *Rosa Parks*, the lyrics of which were substantially unrelated to the life of the civil rights figure).

(11)   Consider also the various theories used to protect against the imitation of famous voices in commercial contexts. In *Waits v. Frito-Lay, Inc.*, 978 F.2d 1093 (9th Cir. 1992), the court sustained a $2.6 million award for imitation of singer Tom Waits' voice in a snack food ad, based on a publicity rights claim as well one under § 43(a) of the Lanham Act. The leading case, however, remains *Midler v. Ford Motor Co.*, 849 F.2d 460 (9th Cir. 1988), a straightforward common-law right of publicity action brought successfully against the imitation of Bette Midler's singing voice in a commercial.

Does this result implicate the preemption doctrine? Remember that copyright law has always resisted protecting artistic style *per se*. Moreover, copyright law expressly allows the creation of "sound-alike" recordings. § 114(b). By bringing these voice imitation cases under a right of publicity, are these plaintiffs making an end run around the constraints of copyright law? In *Waits*, the court makes a distinction between the protection of a famous voice as opposed to a singing style. Is this is valid distinction?

(12)   *Preemption*. The courts remain divided as to whether the right of publicity is preempted by the Copyright Act. Courts finding no preemption are in the majority. *See Brown v. Ames*, 201 F.3d 654 (5th Cir. 2000); *Landham v. Lewis Galoob Toys, Inc.*, 227 F.3d 619 (6th Cir. 2000); *Wendt v. Host International, Inc.*, 125 F.3d 806 (9th Cir. 1997), *rehearing en banc denied*, 197 F.3d 1284 (9th Cir. 1999) (a remarkable decision involving actors' claims against the distributors of animatronic figures representing the recurring characters in the TV series *Cheers*, decided over a sharp dissent by Judge Kozinski). *But see Laws v. Sony Music Entertainment, Inc.*, 448 F.3d 1134 (9th Cir. 2006) (holding singer's right publicity claim was preempted by licensed use of copyrighted sound recording). *See also Jules Jordan Video, Inc. v. 144942 Canada, Inc.*, 617 F.3d 1146 (9th Cir. 2010) (actor's right of publicity claim based on reproduction and sale of videos was preempted, even where defendant was not authorized by the copyright owner).

(13)   *The persistence of publicity rights*. What becomes of the rights to a name that a celebrity hasn't used in 25 years? *See Abdul-Jabbar v. GMC*, 85 F.3d 407 (9th Cir. 1996) (considering right of publicity — and Lanham Act — claims in the plaintiff's former name "Lew Alcindor"). By the same token, it may be possible (at least under New Jersey law) for the heirs of an actor to enjoy a post-mortem right of publicity in the name of a character with which the decedent was strongly associated in the public mind. *See McFarland v. Miller*, 14 F.3d 912 (3rd Cir. 1994) ("Spanky McFarland").

Chapter 12

EPILOGUE: THE HORIZON OF COPYRIGHT

By the time you read these few concluding observations, the 300th Anniversary of the Statute of Anne will have come and gone. But while the official commemoration of this momentous event in copyright history was April 10, 2010, the importance of the Statute of Anne — as a measure for where copyright has been, what it has become, and what it may yet be — continues.

In 1710 (had anyone given the point any thought), the likelihood that this newly-minted statutory scheme would someday assume an important position in the *corpus juris* could not have seemed very high. Essentially, the first copyright act represented a modest regulatory response to a specialized social problem of less than earth-shaking proportions: the growing insecurity of capital investments in the burgeoning London-based publishing business. Many means might have been chosen to address this problem. In fact, Parliament elected to stabilize the market in printed books by recognizing a portable legal right in texts which vested initially in their creators — while acknowledging the existence of a "public interest" in access to information. These choices, as we know, proved to be fateful. Unbeknownst to its members, the Parliament of 1710 managed to invent a formula which has been flexible enough to serve as the primary vehicle for more than three centuries of legal responses to changes in the way information is made, stored, sold, and used.

Considered as a whole, the history of Anglo-American copyright law has been a remarkable one, driven, in significant part, by the waves of innovation in information technology which are a hallmark of the late modern period. But the relationship between ever-accelerating technological progress and the development of copyright doctrine has not been simple. Technology itself does not drive the development of copyright law. Rather, copyright is driven by the changes in social life, economic organization, and cultural outlook which technology inspires. To complicate the pattern further, copyright law has helped to shape these changes, even as it has been shaped by them.

In the United States at least, where the basic framework of law laid down by the Statute of Anne has persisted the longest, the story of copyright now has entered a new era — one in which this body of law is being remade more radically and more rapidly than at any other point in its history. In retrospect, at least, we can see the process of law revision which began in the early 1960s and culminated in the Copyright Act of 1976 — a tectonic shifting of the plates — as the crucial episode in the modern transformation of copyright, paving the way for future efforts at harmonization and the development of international norms. But if the 1976 Act represented a critical reconsideration of historic theory and practice in this branch of the law, events since the Act took effect in 1978 have been even more dramatic. Today, copyright law is subject to extraordinary new pressures. As never before, the globalization of information commerce has subjected U.S. copyright law to a variety of external forces, including international legal norms and the ideological influences of foreign laws of literary and artistic property. Meanwhile, copyright law is being pressed to adapt to the new realities of the digital condition — and to do so without the delay associated with its past accommodations to technological developments. What can be guessed, then, about the vectors of change along which these pressures will direct the law of copyright in years to come?

To frame the speculations that follow, it may be worthwhile to point out that, although U.S. copyright always has had many features in common with the analogous laws of other countries, it also has maintained a somewhat distinct identity, not least where thinking about goals and purposes is concerned. Like all laws of literary and artistic property, ours has been affected by a deep-seated vision of inherent authorial entitlement. Unlike most other national laws, however, U.S. copyright has not developed primarily from a discourse dominated by that vision. Instead, the discussion of copyright policy in the United States has been characterized largely, at least for most of its history, by a shared rhetoric of *public purpose*. Like the laws of other countries which inherited the British legal tradition, U.S. copyright law is explicitly premised on a vision in which grants of information monopolies to individuals are rationalized as incentives to the creation and distribution of information for the benefit of all. Unlike some other national laws rooted in the Statute of Anne, U.S. copyright has remained mostly faithful to that vision. Put differently, U.S. copyright law has been conceived as an instrument of national cultural policy, rather than a mere scheme of private rights. From its inception, it has been the vehicle for the balancing of private proprietary claims and the public interest in access to information resources.

The concept of purpose just described has been of more than merely rhetorical significance. Where copyright doctrine is concerned, it has had an important generative influence. It explains the "limited Times" language of the constitutional Copyright Clause (a limitation notably relaxed, as we have seen, by recent decisions of the Supreme Court). It helps account for the historical commitment of U.S. copyright law to the various "formalities" which formed part of the public price rightsholders were expected to pay for their private privileges. And it informs many of the most characteristic and distinct features of U.S. law as it stands today, including its insistence on the exclusion of protection for factual and governmental information and its broad conception of a residual "fair use" exception to claims of copyright infringement.

Intimately related to U.S. copyright's special vision of purpose (and its cognate doctrinal peculiarities) is its unusual position of primacy in the field of information law. As we know, copyright shares the field of federal intellectual property with other bodies of rules. Where proprietary rights and use privileges in intangible expression are concerned, however, it stands more or less entirely alone. Until very recently indeed, Congress had not seen fit to enact *any* "neighboring rights" legislation of the sort that is common abroad, displaying instead a positive antipathy toward the notion of specialized protections of lesser scope and duration than those afforded by copyright. In the United States, policy choices regarding the recognition of federal proprietary rights for new forms of expression historically have been framed in quite singular fashion: protection under copyright, or no protection at all.

Similarly, the preemption doctrine has kept the underbrush of state laws relating to rights in information under fairly rigorous check. In the United States, then, copyright law consistently has represented more than a mere set of default rules for interest-balancing in the domain of cultural production. Instead, it has represented the definitive expression of a collective social judgment about what forms such balancing should take.

The preceding paragraphs represent an effort to articulate the basis for our persistent sense of the "special character" of U.S. copyright law. It is precisely those features of the law, however, which have been under pressure for most of the last half-century, and are under ever-increasing pressure today. The next decade or so of developments will provide at least a tentative answer to this question, among others: As we enter the fourth century of statutory copyright law, what remains of the special copyright tradition, first engendered by the Statute of Anne, of which the United States is arguably the preeminent inheritor?

Imagine a Rip Van Winkle of intellectual property (or, indeed, Good Queen Anne herself!), who dozed off in 1710, only to awaken now, more than three centuries later. How easily would he (or she) recognize copyright doctrine — or copyright discourse — in this post-tricentennial era? And if the answer is "only with difficulty," does it really matter?

Rip Van Winkle
Corbis

Where *copyright doctrine* is concerned, U.S. law has been substantially remade by the Copyright Law of 1976, subsequent legislative revisions, and the explosive growth of copyright case law. That process of revision is likely to continue unabated in the decade to come. Of course, some of the most peculiar — even anomalous — features of U.S. copyright doctrine are unlikely to be displaced. The work-for-hire doctrine, for example, represents too great a convenience to corporate copyright owners to be lightly discarded (although U.S. efforts to persuade the *rest* of the world to adopt or at least defer to it have been less than wholly successful).

In other respects, however, our sleeper would be in for a rude awakening. Getting over his first shock at the sheer volume and density of our increasingly muscle-bound (and consequently inflexible) copyright statute, with all its new, exquisitely qualified specialized provisions, he might reflect on the end of the dream of a "unified field" theory of copyright. Almost certainly, he would marvel at the range of new subject matter categories (including "works" resolutely unintelligible to the ordinary information consumer) — as well as the proliferation of "rights," and the reflexive growth in the complexity and sophistication of infringement analysis. Likewise, he might note the remarkable punitive turn reflected in the trend toward the criminalization of copyright remedies and the decoupling of civil remedies from ideas of actual harm and benefit. But of all the intervening developments, perhaps none would appear as so dramatic a break with the past as the unseating of "publication" as the triggering event for the attachment of copyright and the enthronement of "fixation" in its place — the "big bang" of 1978, by which statutory copyright expanded to embrace our private letters, laundry lists, and doodles, as well as our undying literary and artistic effusions.

Presumably, changes in the calculus of copyright term — including, in particular, the life-plus-70 regime — also would come as a surprise to our newly awakened sleeper. Even more surprising, one suspects, would be the breach of the once-axiomatic principle that a work once in the public domain should remain in the public domain — a principle first set aside in 1994 where various works of foreign origin are concerned and perhaps to be challenged, in due course, with respect to domestic works as well.

The familiar © notice might seem to offer a comfortingly stable point of reference when the sleeper wakes. But when he inspected it more closely, that sense of comfort would be likely to fade with the realization that copyright formalities are not what they used to be. And while the fair use doctrine — that monument to the singularity of U.S. copyright law — still looms large over the much changed landscape of copyright today, an attentive listener can hear rumblings emanating from the growing influence of the "three-part test" of the TRIPs Article 13.

No doubt our sleeper also would be stunned by the speed and ubiquity of modern digital communications networks, and in their ability to facilitate both authorized and unauthorized distribution of copyrighted works. Our sleeper might be surprised, too, to discover a tremendous amount of non-commercial authorship online, in the form of collaborative projects such as open-source software and Wikipedia, and the large amount of content offered for free, such as fan fiction and YouTube videos.

Extrapolation from today's situation suggests that, whatever the changes in doctrine, *copyright discourse* in the 21st century may be even more dramatically different than that produced in the decades just past. Hearing longer, stronger protection justified in microeconomic terms, as promoting the efficient allocation of information resources, and the public domain derided as a wasteland of abandoned interests, our sleeper might wonder what had become of the once-dominant notion of a "public-private bargain" at the heart of copyright. Likewise, he probably would be struck by the continuing viability of the rhetoric of "misappropriation" — once associated only with various obscure and suspect state-law doctrines — in mainstream discussions of copyright itself. He would be moved to wonder how limitations and exceptions to copyright, seen in his time as a fully integrated part of the distribution of rights and privileges in the overall copyright system, could now be widely characterized as burdens or impositions on the rights of owners. And he would be puzzled to hear so much said about the centrality of copyright to the U.S. foreign balance of payments and to the welfare of information-owning corporations — and so little about its importance in the working lives of individual creators.

It seems entirely possible, however, that the greatest surprise of all might be the gathering demise of copyright's historical — and sometimes splendid — isolation. In the not-too-distant future, for example, it is reasonable to expect renewed pressure for *sui generis* legislation outside copyright law, extending protection under a Commerce Clause-based scheme of neighboring rights to subject matter excluded from copyright for various reasons — following the path blazed by the introduction of special design rights for boat hulls in 1998. Even today, various state-law doctrines, such as the "right of publicity," are giving copyright a run for its money, while enjoying widespread immunity from preemption. Our waking sleeper would see a world in which "shrink-wrap" and "click-through" licenses, enforceable under state laws, have increasingly reduced the norms of copyright to an easily overridden "default setting" where the distribution of works in digital formats is concerned.

Already, under the Digital Millennium Copyright Act, information use is regulated by elaborate systems of "technological safeguards," themselves backed up by the new non-copyright provisions of Title 17 imposing various pains and penalties on those who circumvent them or enable their circumvention. Indeed, our sleeper is waking to an unforeseen world in which information consumers are required to secure licenses for more and more uses of proprietary content, no matter how trivial in amount and no matter how fully justified in terms of traditional copyright categories such as fair use. It is something of a paradox that, in such a brave new world, the best hopes for safeguarding a vestige of a "public interest" in access to information may lie outside copyright itself, in doctrines of competition law which impinge on the law of intellectual property.

However the just-sketched scenario of copyright's possible "marginalization" plays out, it is clear today that — in yet another sense — the historic isolation of U.S. copyright law already is a thing of the past. Whether we locate the decisive shift in 1891 (passage of the Chace Act) or 1988 (U.S. adherence to the Berne Convention), the United States now is enmeshed irrevocably with the larger world where copyright is concerned — and copyright itself is no longer an independent category in the international legal order in this post-TRIPs era. In years to come, we will hear still more calls to revise domestic copyright law in the cause of "harmonization" with the intellectual property norms of other nations, reinforced by reminders that only harmonization can protect us from being haled before the World Trade Organization to justify the peculiarities of our own regime.

The elegiac tone of the preceding passages is quite intentional — but it may or may not be justified. Even as we continue to celebrate the adoption of the world's first-ever copyright statute more than three centuries ago, our duty to those joining in the celebration vicariously through these pages is to be accurate, informed, clear, insightful, and at least occasionally provocative. We need to acknowledge, too, the possibility that our own attachment to many of the old ways of U.S. copyright, so many of them derived so directly from Anne's landmark legislation, *may* be a matter of mere sentimentality or antiquarian taste. Perhaps, after all, the changes that have been underway since the mid-1960s, and which have continued beyond the 2010 celebrations, will prove to have been all for the good — or, at least, inevitable in the great scheme of history. And yet . . .

We should not forget that the law of copyright, particularly as it has been developed in the United States from its English antecedents, has made a remarkable contribution to the development not only of the U.S. economy, but of American culture and freedoms as well. In particular, the profound alliance between the Copyright Clause and the First Amendment — stretching from the idea/expression dichotomy to our broadly formulated principle of fair use, with deference throughout to the concept of a vital public domain — affords to at least parts of traditional U.S. copyright law a deep and abiding appeal. In a world increasingly linked by a system of commerce of which the United States has been the principal proponent — a world in which America's political and cultural ideas likewise have continued (despite occasional missteps) to gain adherents — it is perhaps not too much to hope that the modest republican virtues of our copyright law may yet survive.

As a reawakened Rip Van Winkle might remind us from his knowledge of U.S. history, copyright's long record of carefully calibrated encouragement for learning requires no resort to jingoism to justify its continuance. American copyright law, whatever its failings, has played an indisputably central role in making the United States today the world's preeminent creator and exporter of intangible information products. We would suggest that copyright has been able to play this role precisely because of, rather than in spite of, its doctrinal and theoretical peculiarities — and, specifically, because of its success over time in balancing proprietary rights and public access. Through the process of successive approximation which is the special genius of a common law system, the United States has managed to negotiate a course between overprotection and underprotection, and to strike at least a rough balance between the social interest in securing capital investment, on the one hand, and encouraging both innovation and free expression, on the other. Perhaps, in years to come, we will be able to recalibrate that balance without overcompensating. If not, perhaps the entailed consequences of our collective failure to do so will make us wish eventually that we had left well enough alone.

At the end of the day — and of this book — what should we make of the trends and tendencies according to which copyright law is being remade from its ancient antecedents? The truest answer is also the ultimate proverbial cop-out: Only time will tell. Whatever may lie beyond the horizon for this venerable body of law, your challenge, should you choose to accept it, is to help constitute the new generation of copyright lawyers who will shape our law in the post-tricentennial period. And our plea to you is a simple one: In the pursuit of the goals of rationalization and harmonization with the cognate laws of other lands, do not be too ready to discard whatever remains of the traditions of Anglo-American copyright law. After all, they may yet come in handy.

TABLE OF CASES

[References are to pages.]

A

A&M Records v. Napster. 755; 758; 778; 920
A. Brod, Inc. v. SK&I Co.. 628
Aalmuhammed v. Lee. 293
Abbott Labs. v. Brennan. 619
Abdul-Jabbar v. GMC 1021
Abend v. MCA, Inc.. . . . . 347; 353; 919
ABKCO Music, Inc. v. Harrisongs Music, Ltd. . 629; 637
ABKCO Music, Inc. v. LaVere 412; 630
ABKCO Music, Inc. v. Stellar Records, Inc.. . .542; 911
Academy of Motion Picture Arts & Sciences v. Creative House Promotions, Inc.. 403
Action Tapes, Inc. v. Mattson 520
Acuff-Rose Music, Inc. v. Jostens, Inc. . 87; 91; 171; 172
Addison-Wesley Publishing Co. v. Brown 498
Adobe Systems, Inc. v. Canus Productions, Inc.. .740, 741
Adobe Systems, Inc. v. South Sun Prods., Inc.. .922
Adobe Systems, Inc. v. Southern Software, Inc. . 742
Advance Magazine Publishers, Inc. v. Leach. . .900
Advanced Computer Services of Michigan, Inc. v. MAI Systems Corp.. 80
Advanz Behavioral Management Resources, Inc. v. Miraflor. 124
Aerospace Servs. Int'l v. LPA Group 414
Agfa Monotype Corp. v. Adobe Sys.. 801
Aimster Copyright Litigation, In re 756; 776
Aina-Marshall; United States v.. 776
Alameda Films S.A. de C.V. v. Authors Rights Restoration Corp.. . . . . .358; 732
Alappat, In re. 167
Alaska Airlines, Inc. v. Brock. 271
Alberto-Culver Co. v. Andrea Dumon, Inc. 87
Alcatel USA, Inc. v. DGI Technologies, Inc.. . .742; 897
Alden v. Maine. 622
Aldon Accessories Ltd. v. Spiegel, Inc.. . .267, 268; 272
Alexander v. Haley. 656
Alfred Bell & Co. v. Catalda Fine Arts, Inc. . 90, 91; 116; 232
Aliotti v. R. Dakin & Co. 1007
Allarcom Pay Television, Ltd. v. General Instrument Corp.. . . . . .722; 977

Allen v. Academic Games League of America, Inc.. . . . . .128; 532
Allen v. National Video, Inc.. 1020
ALS Scan, Inc. v. Digital Service Consultants, Inc.. 618
ALS Scan, Inc. v. RemarQ Communities, Inc.. . . 784
Altera Corp. v. Clear Logic, Inc.. 170
Am. Library Ass'n v. FCC. 802, 803
Amato v. Wilentz. 201
American Broadcasting Cos. v. Aereo, Inc.. . . .535
American Broadcasting Cos. v. Flying J, Inc.. . .556
American Dental Ass'n v. Delta Dental Plans Ass'n. 87
American Geophysical Union v. Texaco, Inc.. . . 854; 860
American Movie Classics Co. v. Turner Entertainment Co.. .986
American Tobacco Co. v. Werckmeister. . .411; 838
American Visuals Corp. v. Holland. 409
American Vitagraph v. Levy . . . 404; 406, 407; 411
American Well Works Co. v. Layne & Bowler Co.. 613
Amoco Prod. Co. v. Vill. of Gambell. 913
A & M Records, Inc. v. Napster, Inc.. 758
Amsterdam v. Triangle Publications, Inc.. 174
Anderson v. Nidorf. 977
Anderson v. Stallone. 235; 497
Andreas v. Volkswagen of Am., Inc.. . . . .930; 934
Ansehl v. Puritan Pharmaceutical Co 102, 103
AP v. All Headline News Corp.. . . . . . . .887; 957
Apfel v. Prudential-Bache Securities, Inc.. . . . 1006
Apple Barrel Productions, Inc. v. Beard. 442
Apple Computer, Inc. v. Formula International, Inc.. . . . . .161; 164
Apple Computer, Inc. v. Franklin Computer Corp.. . . . . 154; 157; 164; 686, 687; 919
Apple Computer, Inc. v. Microsoft Corp.. .129; 670; 700; 702
Apple Inc. v. Psystar Corp.. . . . . .898; 920
Application of (see name of party) . . . .
Arc Music Corp. v. Lee 651
Archie Comics Publications, Inc. v. DeCarlo. . .153
Architectronics, Inc. v. Control Sys.. 316
Arista Records, LLC v. Doe 3. . . . . . . .631; 870
Arista Records, LLC v. Launch Media, Inc. . . . 576
Arista Records LLC v. Lime Group LLC . .741; 766
Arista Records LLC v. Usenet.com, Inc.. 778

[References are to pages.]

Armour v. Knowles 643

Armstead; United States v.. 949

Armstrong v. Virgin Records, Ltd. 723

Arnstein v. Porter . . .636, 637; 651; 669; 673, 674; 694

Aronson v. Quick Point Pencil Co. 961; 963

Art Attacks Ink, LLC v. MGA Entertainment, Inc.. 643

ASCAP v. Showtime/Movie Channel. 540

ASCAP; United States v. 543

Ashcroft v. Iqbal. 631

Ashton-Tate Corp. v. Ross. 285

Assessment Technologies of Wisconsin, LLC v. WIREdata, Inc.. . . . . 251; 946

Asset Marketing Systems, Inc. v. Gagnon. 311

Atari Games Corp. v. Oman. 86; 104; 203

Atari Games, Inc. v. Nintendo of America Inc. . 874; 980, 981; 983

Atari, Inc. v. North American Philips Consumer Electronics Corp.. 680

Atari, Inc. v. JS & A Group, Inc.. . . . . . 485; 619

ATC Distrib. Group, Inc. v. Whatever It Takes Transmissions & Parts, Inc.. . . 87; 113, 114; 137; 252

Atlantic Recording Corp. v. Howell . . 413; 516, 517

Atlantic Recording Corp. v. XM Satellite Radio, Inc.. 755

Attia v. Society of the New York Hospital . 175; 212

Auscape Int'l v. National Geographic Soc'y . . . 899

Authors Guild v. Google, Inc.. . . . . 620; 630; 886

Autoskill, Inc. v. National Educational Support Systems, Inc.. 280

Avtec Systems, Inc. v. Peiffer 275

Aymes v. Bonelli. 274

B

Bagdadi v. Nazar. 426

Baisden v. I'm Ready Prods., Inc.. 311

Baker v. Libbie. 271; 301

Baker v. Selden . . 90; 118; 126, 127; 159; 241; 248; 687

Balsley v. LFP, Inc.. . . . . .844; 934

Baltimore Orioles v. Major League Baseball Players Ass'n 973

Banco Popular de Puerto Rico, Inc. v. Latin American Music Co.. 317

Banks v. Manchester. 136

Barbour v. Head 128

Barclays Capital, Inc. v. Theflyonthewall.com, Inc.. . . . . .15; 973; 975

Barefoot Architect, Inc. v. Bunge 308

Baron v. Leo Feist, Inc.. 172

Bartok v. Boosey & Hawkes, Inc.. 346

Bartsch v. Metro-Goldwyn-Mayer, Inc.. 314

Basic Books, Inc. v. Kinko's Graphics Corp.. . . .866

Bassett v. Mashantucket Pequot Tribe. . . .623; 630

Bateman v. Mnemonics, Inc.. . . . . .701; 983

Batiste v. Island Records, Inc.. . . . . . . .291; 618

Batjac Prods., Inc. v. GoodTimes Home Video Corp.. . . . . .353; 415

Bd. of Managers of Soho Int'l Arts Condo. v. City of New York. 594

Bean v. McDougal Littell 976

Beauregard, In re. 167

Beethoven.com LLC v. Librarian of Congress . . 577

Bell v. E. Davis International, Inc. 149

Bell Atlantic Corp. v. Twombly 631

Bellsouth Advertising Publishing Corp. v. Donnelly Information Publishing, Inc.. 251

Belushi v. Woodward 918

Benay v. Warner Bros. Entertainment, Inc.. . . .656

Benny v. Loew's, Inc. 814; 819

Benson v. Coca-Cola Co. 651

Berge, United States ex rel. v. Board of Trustees of Univ. of Alabama 970; 976

Berkic v. Crichton 468

Berlin v. E. C. Publs. 814

Bibbero Systems, Inc. v. Colwell Systems, Inc. . 124

Bieg v. Hovnanian Enterprises, Inc.. 308

Bill Graham Archives v. Dorling Kindersley Ltd.. . . . . .479; 848

Billy-Bob Teeth, Inc. v. Novelty, Inc.. 308

Bilski v. Kappos. 7; 167

Blackwell Publishing, Inc. v. Excel Research Group, LLC. 866

Blanch v. Koons. 857

Bleistein v. Donaldson Lithographing Co.. . .66; 99; 107; 226; 273

Blueport Co. v. United States 621

BMG Music v. Gonzalez. 427; 870; 941; 944

BMW of North America, Inc. v. Gore. 942

Board of Trade v. Dow Jones & Co.. 15

Bobbs-Merrill Co. v. Straus 517

Boisson v. Banian, Ltd.. . . . . . .91; 213; 680; 714

Bond v. Blum. 829

Bonito Boats, Inc. v. Thunder Craft Boats, Inc.. . 188; 198; 958; 982; 984; 994

Bonner v. Dawson. 934

Bonneville Int'l Corp. v. Peters 577

[References are to pages.]

Boosey & Hawkes Music Publishers, Ltd. v. Walt Disney Co. 314; 634; 723

Bouchat v. Baltimore Ravens Football Club, Inc. 642; 649; 934

Bouchat v. Baltimore Ravens Ltd. Partnership . . 855

Bouchat v. Bon-Ton Dep't Stores, Inc. 944

Bourne v. Walt Disney Co. 313; 633

Bourne Co. v. Hunter Country Club, Inc. 630

Bourne Co. v. Tower Records, Inc. 918

Bourne Co. v. Twentieth Century Fox Film Corp. 832

Bowers v. Baystate Technologies, Inc. 168; 978; 988

Brandir Int'l, Inc. v. Cascade Pac. Lumber Co. . 184; 195

Brayton Purcell LLP v. Recordon & Recordon . .619

Brewer v. Hustler Magazine, Inc. 407, 408

Brewer-Giorgio v. Producers Video, Inc. 900

Briarpatch Ltd. v. Phoenix Pictures, Inc. . . 615; 976

Bridgeman Art Library, Ltd. v. Corel Corp. 113; 116; 225; 729

Bridgeport Music, Inc. v. Chrysalis Songs 899

Bridgeport Music, Inc. v. Diamond Time, Ltd. . .899

Bridgeport Music, Inc. v. Dimension Films . 504; 655

Bridgeport Music, Inc. v. Justin Combs Publishing. 941

Bridgeport Music, Inc. v. UMG Recordings, Inc..846

Bridgeport Music, Inc. v. WB Music Corp. 947

Bright Tunes Music Corp. v. Harrisongs Music, Ltd. 637

Brilliance Audio, Inc. v. Haights Cross Comms., Inc. 520

Britton v. Maloney. 981

Broadcast Music, Inc. v. CBS, Inc. . . . 539; 541; 630

Broadcast Music, Inc. v. Claire's Boutiques, Inc..556

Broadcast Music, Inc. v. Hartmarx Corp. 741

Broadcast Music, Inc. v. Hirsch. 315

Broadcast Music, Inc. v. Roger Miller Music, Inc. 348

Broadcast Music, Inc.; United States v. 540

Broderbund Software, Inc. v. Unison World, Inc..702

Brooks-Ngwenya v. Indianapolis Public Schools 123; 443

Brooktree Corp. v. Advanced Micro Devices, Inc. 170

Brown v. Ames. 1021

Brown v. Tabb 409

Brown Bag Software v. Symantec Corp. 690

Brownmark Films, LLC v. Comedy Partners. . .832; 863

Brunswick Beacon, Inc. v. Schock-Hopchas Publishing Co. 267

Bryant v. Gordon. 518

Bryant v. Media Right Prods. 943

BTE v. Bonnecaze 295

BUC Int'l Corp. v. Int'l Yacht Council Ltd..252; 935

Buchwald v. Paramount Pictures Corp. 1007

Buck v. Jewell-La Salle Realty Co. . . 548; 553; 737

Bucklew v. Hawkins, Ash, Baptie & Co., LLP . 224; 227, 228; 641; 650; 941; 976

Buffalo Broadcasting Co., Inc. v. American Society of Composers, Authors and Publishers 539

Building Officials & Code Admins. Int'l v. Code Technology, Inc. 137

Burdick v. Koerner. 741

Burke v. National Broadcasting Co. 406; 411

Burnett v. Twentieth Century Fox Film Corp. . . 832

Burroughs v. Metro-Goldwyn-Mayer, Inc. . 153; 389; 393

Burrow-Giles Lithographic Co. v. Sarony . . 85, 86; 91; 99; 111; 144, 145; 240; 247; 362

BV Engineering v. University of California, Los Angeles. 621

C

C. Blore & D. Richman, Inc. v. 20/20 Advertising, Inc. 679

C.B.C. Distr. & Mktg., Inc. v. Major League Baseball Advanced Media, L.P. 1020

Cadence Design Sys., Inc. v. Avant! Corp. . 903; 918

Caffey v. Cook 236; 935

Calhoun v. Lillenas Publishing 652

Calio v. Sofa Express, Inc. 941

Cambridge Univ. Press v. Becker 623; 866

Campbell v. Acuff-Rose Music, Inc.. .335; 353; 633; 815; 850; 852; 853; 855; 880; 881; 913; 983

Capitol Records, Inc. v. MP3tunes, LLC 778

Capitol Records, Inc. v. Naxos of America, Inc. . 15; 205, 206; 344; 357; 412; 989

Capitol Records, Inc. v. Thomas-Rasset. . .516; 942

Capitol Records, LLC v. VideoEgg, Inc. 619

Carbotrade S.p.A. v. Bureau Veritas. 728

Carell v. Shubert, Inc. 723

Carey v. Kearsley 818

Carol Barnhart Inc. v. Economy Cover Corp. . . 184; 191; 193; 445

Carson v. Dynegy, Inc. 901

Carson v. Here's Johnny Portable Toilets, Inc. . 1011, 1012; 1017

[References are to pages.]

Carter v. Helmsley-Spear, Inc. 274; 592; 598

Cartoon Network v. CSC Holdings, Inc.. . .80; 478; 517; 533; 751; 871

Castle Rock Entertainment, Inc. v. Carol Publishing Group, Inc.. . . . . .680; 708; 850; 854

Cavalier v. Random House, Inc.. . . . . . .658; 713

CBS Broadcasting, Inc. v. EchoStar Communication Corp.. 561

CCC Information Services, Inc. v. Maclean Hunter Market Reports, Inc. 133; 252

CDN Inc. v. Kapes. 133; 252

Chamberlain Group, Inc. v. Skylink Technologies, Inc.. . . . . 804; 806; 889; 898

Chambers v. Time Warner, Inc.. 314

Charles Garnier, Paris v. Andin International, Inc.. 425

Charter Oak Fire Ins. Co. v. Hedeen & Cos.. . . .149

Chase-Riboud v. Dreamworks, Inc.. 148

Chavez v. Arte Publico Press 622

Cheney Bros. v. Doris Silk Corp.. . . . . . .15; 957

Chicage Bd. Options Exch., Inc v. Int'l Securities Exch., LLC,. 975

Childress v. Taylor 273; 281; 294

Chirco v. Crosswinds Communities, Inc.. 901

Chosun Int'l v. Chrisha Creations, Ltd.. 190

Christopher Phelps & Assocs., LLC v. Galloway.. . . . . .519; 917

Cincom Systems, Inc. v. Novelis Corp.. . . . 309; 311

City of (see name of city). . . . .

Clarke, In re.. 1001

Clarkstown v. Reeder 267

Classic Media, Inc. v. Mewborn. 395

Clean Flicks of Colorado, LLC v. Soderbergh . . 864

CMM Cable Rep., Inc. v. Ocean Coast Properties, Inc.. . . . . 88; 646

Cohen v. Paramount Pictures Corp.. 314

Cole v. Phillips H. Lord, Inc.. 1004

Coles v. Wonder 439

College Savings Bank v. Florida Prepaid Postsecondary Education Expense Board . . . 621

Columbia Broadcasting System, Inc. v. Teleprompter Corp.. 554

Columbia Broadcasting System, Inc. v. Loew's Inc.. . . . . .814; 819

Columbia Pictures Indus., Inc. v. Miramax Films Corp.. 831

Columbia Pictures Industries v. Redd Horne . . .529

Columbia Pictures Industries, Inc. v. Aveco, Inc.. . . . . .528; 740

Columbia Pictures Industries, Inc. v. Professional Real Estate Investors, Inc.. . . . . .533; 717, 718

Columbia Pictures Television, Inc. v. Krypton Broadcasting of Birmingham, Inc.. . . . .936; 945

Comedy III Prods., Inc. v. Gary Saderup, Inc. . . 14; 1019

Comedy Partners v. Street Players Holding Corp.. 116

Community for Creative Non-Violence v. Reid . 263; 280; 289; 305

Compaq Computer Corp. v. Ergonome, Inc..88; 278; 947

Compco Corp. v. Day-Brite Lighting, Inc.. .15; 954; 958, 959

Computer Assocs. Int'l, Inc. v. Altai, Inc. . 164; 684; 971; 974

Computer Assoc. Int'l, Inc. v. State Street Bank & Trust Co.. 986

Computer Mgmt. Assistance Co. v. Robert F. DeCastro, Inc.. 700

Compuware Corp. v. Serena Software Int'l, Inc.. 439

Conopco, Inc. v. May Dep't Stores Co.. 617

Consulting, LLC 128; 973

Cooling Systems and Flexibles, Inc. v. Stuart Radiator, Inc.. .657

Co-Opportunities, Inc. v. National Broadcasting Co.. . . . . 315; 629; 646; 900

Coquico, Inc. v. Rodriguez-Miranda . .129; 643; 677

Corbello v. DeVito.. 731

Corbis Corp. v. Amazon.com, Inc. 783

Corcovado Music Corp. v. Hollis Music, Inc. . . 731

Cordon Art B.V. v. Walker. 357

Cordon Holding, C.B. v. Northwest Publ. Corp. . 358

Cortner v. Israel 628

Cosmetic Ideas, Inc. v. IAC/Interactive Corp. . . 442

CoStar Group Inc. v. LoopNet, Inc.. .481; 483; 487; 568; 767; 783

CoStar Realty Info., Inc. v. Field 631

County of (see name of county). . . . .

Courier Lithographing Co. v. Donaldson Lithographing Co.. 102

Coventry Ware, Inc. v. Reliance Picture Frame Co.. .423

CoxCom, Inc. v. Chaffee. 917

Cramer v. Crestar Financial Corp.. 275

Cranston Print Works Co. v. J. Mason Prods.. . .730

Cream Records, Inc. v. Jos. Schlitz Brewing Co..931

Creative Technology, Ltd. v. Aztech System Pte., Ltd.. 634

Crow v. Wainwright 977

Curb v. MCA Records, Inc.. 721

Curet-Velazquez v. ACEMLA de Puerto Rico, Inc.. . . . . .941; 945

[References are to pages.]

Cybermedia, Inc. v. Symantec Corp. 903

CyberSource Corp. v. Retail Decisions, Inc. 167

D

Daboub v. Gibbons. 976

Daly v. Palmer. 635

Danjaq L.L.C. v. Sony Corp. 900

Danjaq, S.A. v. MGM/UA Communications, Co..719

Danjaq, S.A. v. Pathe Communications Corp. . . . 719

Darden v. Peters 175; 443

Dastar Corp. v. Twentieth Century Fox Film
  Corp.. . . . . .583; 990

Data Cash Systems, Inc. v. JS&A Group, Inc. . . . 74;
  413

Data East USA, Inc. v. Epyx, Inc.. 680

Data Gen. Corp. v. Gruman Sys. Support Corp..898;
  980; 982; 985

Davidson & Associates v. Jung. 168; 789; 987

Davies v. Krasna 1008

Davis v. Blige. 309, 310; 630

Dawson v. Hinshaw Music, Inc. 678; 694, 695

Dawson Chemical Co. v. Rohm & Haas Co. 747

De Romero v. Institute of Puerto Rican Culture . 622

Dean v. Burrows. 308

Deere & Co. v. MTD Prods.. 1001

Deltak Inc. v. Advanced Sys., Inc.. . . . . .930; 933

Demetriades v. Kaufmann 742

Denbicare U.S.A., Inc. v. Toys R Us, Inc. . 518; 524;
  619

Denmark v. Russ Berrie & Co. 359

Derek Andrew, Inc. v. Poof Apparel Corp. 944

Design v. K-Mart Apparel Corp. 935

Desny v. Wilder. 1007

DeSylva v. Ballentine 347

Deutsch v. Arnold 737

Devils Films, Inc. v. Nectar Video. 104; 922

Diamond v. Chakrabarty 7; 959

Diamond v. Diehr 7; 159; 166

Digital Communications Associates, Inc. v. Softklone
  Distributing Corp.. 702

DISH Network, Inc. v. FCC. 561

Dobson v. NBA Properties, Inc. 86

Dodsley v. Kinnersley. 811

Doe v. Geller. 619

Doe v. TCI Cablevision, Inc.. 1019

Dolman v. Agee 409

Donald Frederick Evans & Associates, Inc. v.
  Continental Homes, Inc. 426; 901

Doran v. Sunset House Distributing Corp. 235

Dowling v. United States 950

Downey v. General Foods Corp. 1003–1005

Dr. Seuss Enterprises, L.P. v. Penguin Books U.S.A.,
  Inc.. . . . . .829, 830

Dream Games of Arizona, Inc. v. PC Onsite . . . 702

Dreamland Ball Room, Inc. v. Shapiro, Bernstein &
  Co.. 737

DSC Communs. Corp. v. DGI Techs.. 897

DSC Communs. Corp. v. Pulse Communs., Inc. . 875

Dudnikov v. Chalk & Vermilion Fine Arts 618

Dumas v. Gommerman. 267; 269; 305

Dun v. Lumberman's Mutual Credit Ass'n 913

Dun & Bradstreet Software Services, Inc. v. Grace
  Consulting, Inc. 699; 701; 973

Dunlap v. G&L Holding Group, Inc. 615; 973

Duraco Prods. v. Joy Plastic Enters.. 998

Durham Indus., Inc. v. Tomy Corp.. . .226; 233; 632;
  675

DVD Copy Control Ass'n v. Bunner. .167; 799; 802

Dymow v. Bolton. 160; 661

E

Earth Flag, Ltd. v. Alamo Flag Co. 237

Easter Seal Society for Crippled Children & Adults of
  Louisiana, Inc. v. Playboy Enterprises. 267

Eastern Microwave, Inc. v. Doubleday Sports,
  Inc. 559

Eastwood v. Superior Court. 1010; 1013

eBay, Inc. v. Bidder's Edge, Inc.. . . .988, 989; 993

eBay, Inc. v. MercExchange, LLC. . .911, 912; 917

Eckert v. Hurley Chicago Co., Inc. 286

Eckes v. Card Prices Update. 249

Ed Graham Productions, Inc. v. National Broadcasting
  Co.. 1004

Eden Toys, Inc. v. Florelee Undergarment Co.. .226;
  308; 468

Educational Sales Programs, Inc. v. Dreyfus
  Corp.. . . . . 1003, 1004

Educational Testing Services v. Katzman. 447

Edward B. Marks Music Corp. v. Charles K. Harris
  Music Publishing Co.. 349

Edward B. Marks Music Corp. v. Jerry Vogel Music
  Co.. . . . . .285; 291

EEOC v. Arabian American Oil Co. (Aramco) . .720

Effects Associates, Inc. v. Cohen 303; 616

Egyptian Goddess Inc. v. Swisa Inc. 197

Einhorn v. Mergatroyd Prods.. 413

Elcom Ltd.; United States v.. 803

[References are to pages.]

Eldred v. Ashcroft . 64; 66; 123; 329; 333; 805; 983; 996

Elektra Entertainment Group, Inc. v. Barker. . .516; 631

Ellis v. Diffie. 650

Ellison v. Robertson. 769, 770; 783

Elrod v. Burns 915

Elsevier, B.V. v. UnitedHealth Group, Inc.. . . . 446

Elsmere Music, Inc. v. National Broadcasting Co.. 819

Eltra Corp. v. Ringer. 450

Emerson v. Davies. 88; 817

EMI Entertainment World v. Priddis Music. . . .542

EMI Entertainment World, Inc. v. Karen Records, Inc.. 477

EMSA Limited Partnership v. Lincoln 616

Engineering Dynamics, Inc. v. Structural Software, Inc.. 700

English v. BFC&R East 11th Street LLC. 602

Entertainment Research Group, Inc. v. Genesis Creative Group, Inc.. . . . . .234; 444

Epoch Producing Corp. v. Killiam Shows, Inc. . 203; 349

Erickson v. Blake. 131

Erickson v. Trinity Theatre, Inc.. 291

Erie Railroad Co. v. Tompkins 14; 955

Esquire, Inc. v. Ringer 183; 189; 192

Estate of (see name of party) . . . .

Ets-Hokin v. Skyy Spirits, Inc. . . 96; 105; 112; 131; 225; 235; 632

ETW Corp. v. Jireh Publishing, Inc., ... 14; 1019

Evans Newton, Inc. v. Chicago Systems Software. 267

Ewer v. Coxe. 416

Ex parte (see name of relator). . . . .

Ex rel. (see name of relator). . . . .

Expediters International of Washington, Inc. v. Direct Line Cargo Management Services, Inc.. 721

F

F. Gaito Architecture LLC v. Simone Development Corp.. . . . . .175; 712

F.W. Woolworth Co. v. Contemporary Arts. . . .940

Falwell v. Penthouse International, Ltd.. 82

Famous Music Corp. v. Bay State Harness Horse Racing and Breeding Ass'n. 739

Fantasy, Inc. v. Fogerty 947

Faulkner v. Nat'l Geographic Enters. . 299; 741, 742

Faulkner Press, LLC v. Class Notes, LLC 463

Federal Maritime Comm. v. South Carolina State Ports Authority 622

Feist Publications, Inc. v. Rural Telephone Service Company, Inc.. . .85, 86; 111; 113; 237; 333; 655; 675; 693; 696

Feltner v. Columbia Pictures Television, Inc. . . . 633; 936; 940

Ferber v. Sterndent Corp.. 1005

Ferguson v. National Broadcasting Co.. . . . 646; 649

Ferris v. Frohman. 406; 411

Field v. Google, Inc. 489; 771; 884; 901

Films by Jove, Inc. v. Berov. 730, 731

First Tech. Safety Sys., Inc. v. Depinet. 922

Fisher v. Dees. 819; 821; 824; 827

Fisher v. United Feature Syndicate, Inc.. 704

Fisher-Price, Inc. v. Well-Made Toy Mfg. Corp. . 646

Flack v. Friends of Queen Catherine, Inc.. 587

Flava Works, Inc. v. Gunter 535; 786

Fleischer Studios, Inc. v. A.V.E.L.A., Inc. . 152; 632; 1000

Fleurimond v. New York University. 276

Flexible Lifeline Systems, Inc. v. Precision Lift, Inc.. 917

Florida Prepaid Postsecondary Education Expense Board v. College Savings Bank 621

Foad Consulting Group, Inc. v. Musil Govan Azzalino. 311

Fogerty v. Fantasy Inc.. 946

Fogerty v. MGM Group Holdings, Inc.. 947

Folio Impressions, Inc. v. Byer California 214

Folsom v. Marsh 1; 811; 818; 821, 822; 824

Fonar Corp. v. Domenick. 444; 632; 902

Fonovisa, Inc. v. Cherry Auction, Inc.. . . . .735; 740

Football Ass'n Premier League Ltd. v. YouTube, Inc.. 446

Foraste v. Brown Univ.. 278

Ford Motor Co. v. Summit Motor Products, Inc.. . 517

Forest Park Pictures v. Universal Television Network, Inc.. 975

Forry, Inc. v. Neundorfer, Inc.. 424

Fortnightly Corp. v. United Artists Television, Inc 548; 554

Forward v. Thorogood. 279

Franchise Tax Bd. of California v. Construction Laborers Vacation Trust 616

Frank Music Corp. v. Metro-Goldwyn-Mayer, Inc.. . . . . .931; 934

Franklin Mint Corp. v. National Wildlife Art Exchange, Inc.. . . . . .107; 160

[References are to pages.]

Fred Ahlert Music Corp. v. Warner/Chappell Music, Inc. 398

Fred Fisher, Inc. v. Dillingham 642; 662

Fred Fisher Music Co. v. M. Witmark & Sons. .348; 385; 390

Frederick Music Co. v. Sickler 354

Frederick Warne & Co. v. Book Sales, Inc.. . . .153

Freedman v. Grolier Enterprises Inc. 161

Fromont v. Aeolian Co.. 737

Fuentes v. Shevin. 984

Funky Films Corp. v. Time Warner Entmt Co.. .651

G

Gaiman v. McFarlane 150; 230; 290; 900

Galiano v. Harrah's Operating Co.. . . . . .191; 196

Gamma Audio & Video, Inc. v. Ean-Chea. .938, 939

Gardner v. Nike, Inc.. 310

Gary Friedrich Enters., LLC v. Marvel Enters.. .989

Gaste v. Kaiserman 214; 645; 646; 650

Gates Rubber Co. v. Bando Chemical Indus., Ltd.. . . . . .700; 704; 980

Gaylord v. U.S.. . . . . 292; 863; 932

General Universal Sys., Inc. v. Lee . . 700, 701; 997

Georgia v. Harrison Co.. 136

Gershwin v. The Whole Thing Co. 541

Gershwin Publishing Corp. v. Columbia Artists Management, Inc.. . . . . 737; 739; 758

Getaped.com, Inc. v. Cangemi. 413

Gilliam v. American Broadcasting Companies, Inc.. . . . . .496; 582

Girl Scouts v. Personality Posters Mfg. 1013

Global-Tech Appliances, Inc. v. SEB S.A. 776

GlobeRanger Corp. v. Software AG . . 615; 973; 976

Goes Lithography Co. v. Banta Corp.. 741

Golan v. Gonzales 360

Golan v. Holder. 64; 123; 356; 360

Golden Books Family Entertainment, Inc., In re . 310

Goldman v. Healthcare Mgmt. Systems, Inc.. . . .164

Goldstein v. California . . 14; 66; 86; 958; 961; 963; 989; 1016

Goldwyn Pictures Corp. v. Howells Sales Co. . . 629

Gonzales v. Transfer Technologies, Inc.. 946

Goodis v. United Artists Television, Inc. . . 302; 428

Gordon v. Nextel Communs.. . . . . .463; 573

Gottlieb Development L.L.C. v. Paramount Pictures Corp.. .573

Gottschalk v. Benson. 166

Gracen v. Bradford Exchange . . 223; 227; 229; 493; 646

Graham v. James 311; 933

Graham v. John Deere Co.. . . . . .8; 66; 333

Graham, Estate of v. Sotheby's, Inc.. . . . .522; 965

Grand Upright Music Ltd. v. Warner Bros. Records, Inc.. 504

Grandma Moses Properties, Inc. v. This Week Magazine 410

Green v. Hendrickson Publishers, Inc. 616

Greenberg v. National Geographic Society . 299; 919

Gross v. Seligman 105

Grosso v. Miramax Film Corp. 975

Groucho Marx Productions, Inc. v. Day and Night Co.. 1019

Group Mgmt. Servs., Ltd. v. Bloomberg L.P. . . . 81

Grove Press, Inc. v. Greenleaf Publishing Co.. .415; 498

Grubb v. KMS Patriots, L.P.. . . . . .642; 645

Guglielmi v. Spelling-Goldberg Prods.. 1013

H

Haelan Laboratories, Inc. v. Topps Chewing Gum, Inc.. 13

Halicki Films, LLC v. Sanderson Sales & Marketing. 152

Hamilton Nat'l Bank v. Belt. 1007

Hamilton; United States v.. 175

Harper v. Maverick Recording Co. 427

Harper & Row, Publishers, Inc. v. Nation Enterprises . 54; 85; 239; 243; 335; 815; 816; 818; 821; 835; 852; 914; 970; 1016

Harper House, Inc. v. Thomas Nelson, Inc.. . . .714

Harris v. Emus Records Corp.. 940

Hart v. Dan Chase Taxidermy Supply Co.. 131; 182; 191

Hart v. Electronic Arts, Inc. 1020

Hasbro Bradley, Inc. v. Sparkle Toys, Inc. . 425; 728

Hassenfeld Bros., Inc. v. Mego Corp.. 641

Hays v. Sony Corp. of America 277

Health Grades, Inc. v. Robert Wood Johnson University Hospital, Inc.. 252

Hearn v. Meyer. 629

Heim v. Universal Pictures Corp., Inc.. . . . .87; 424

Hemingway, Estate of v. Random House, Inc. . . . 16; 81; 840; 974

Hendrickson v. Amazon.com, Inc.. 784

Hendrickson v. eBay, Inc.. 783

Henry v. A. B. Dick Co.. 747

Herbert v. Shanley Co.. 526

Herbert Rosenthal Jewelry Corp. v. Grossbardt. .129

[References are to pages.]

Herbert Rosenthal Jewelry Corp. v. Kalpakian. .129; 160

Herzog v. Castle Rock Entertainment 642; 713

Hevia, Estate of v. Portrio Corp. 311

HGI Assocs. v. Wetmore Printing Co.. 901

Hilton v. Guyot. 727

Hines v. Davidowitz 952

Hirsch v. S.C. Johnson & Son, Inc.. . . . .13; 1017

Hirshon v. United Artists Corp. 407; 409

Historical Truth Productions v. Sony Pictures Entertainment, Inc.. 617

Ho v. Taflove 128; 131; 973

Hodel v. Virginia Surface Mining & Reclamation Ass'n 342

Hoehling v. Universal City Studios, Inc.. 146

Hoepker v. Kruger 359

Hogarth, Estate of v. Edgar Rice Burroughs, Inc.. . . . . .280; 347; 444

Holmes Group, Inc. v. Vornado Air Circulation Sys., Inc.. 616

Holt v. Winpisinger 272

Home Design Services, Inc. v. Starwood Const., Inc.. 220

Horgan v. MacMillan, Inc.. . . . . .173; 499

Hotaling v. Church of Jesus Christ of Latter-Day Saints 510

Hunt v. Pasternack. 217

Huntsman v. Soderbergh. 503; 582

Hutchins v. Zoll Medical Corp.. 123

Hutchinson Telephone Co. v. Fronteer Directory Co.. 250

Hyperquest, Inc. v. N'Site Solutions, Inc.. .627; 629

I

I.M.S. Inquiry Mgmt. Sys., Ltd. v. Berkshire Info. Sys. Inc.. 788

Ideal Toy Corp. v. Fab-Lu Ltd. 694

Illinois Bell Tel. Co. v. Haines & Co.. 250

Imperial Residential Design, Inc. v. Palms Development Group, Inc.. 308

In re Marriage of (see name of party). . . . .

In re (see name of party) . . . .

Incredible Techs., Inc. v. Virtual Techs, Inc.. . . . 87

Independent Service Organizations Antitrust Litigation, In re 934

Infinity Broadcast Corp. v. Kirkwood. 857

Intel Corp. v. Hamidi 989

Intellectual Reserve, Inc. v. Utah Lighthouse Ministry, Inc.. . . . . .488; 786

Intercollegiate Broad. Sys. v. Copyright Royalty Bd.. . . . . .450; 458; 578

International News Service v. Associated Press. . .14; 52; 145; 243; 839; 955, 956; 967

Interpart Corp. v. Italia. 958

Intervest Construction, Inc. v. Canterbury Estate Homes, Inc.. . . . . 132; 137; 669; 713

Intimo, Inc. v. Briefly Stated, Inc.. 629

Inwood Laboratories, Inc. v. Ives Laboratories, Inc.. . . . . .995; 999

Io Group, Inc. v. Veoh Networks, Inc.. . . . .778, 779

IQ Group, Ltd. v. Wiesner Publishing, LLC . . . 462

Itar-Tass Russian News Agency v. Russian Kurier, Inc.. . . . . .724, 725

ITOFCA, Inc. v. Mega Trans Logistics, Inc.. . . .312

J

Jacobs v. Carnival Corp.. 722

Jacobsen v. Deseret Book Co.. . . . . . . .705; 901

Jacobsen v. Katzer. 312

Jada Toys, Inc. v. Mattel, Inc.. 677

Janky v. Lake County Convention & Visitors Bureau. .294

Jartech, Inc. v. Clancy. 104

Jarvis v. A&M Records 504

Jarvis v. K2, Inc.. . . . . .236; 932

Jasper v. Bovina Music, Inc.. 615

Javelin Investments, LLC v. McGinnis 219

JCW Investments, Inc. v. Novelty, Inc.. 677

Jeweler's Circular Pub. Co. v. Keystone Pub. Co.. . . . . .97; 242, 243

Jim Henson Prods. v. John T. Brady & Assocs. . 150

John G. Danielson, Inc. v. Winchester-Conant Properties, Inc.. . . . . 414; 935

John Muller & Co. v. New York Arrows Soccer Team, Inc.. 87

John Wiley & Sons v. Kirtsaeng. 524

Johnson v. Gordon 676; 692; 712

Johnson v. Jones 934; 944

Johnson v. University of Virginia 621

Jones v. Blige. 643

Jorgensen v. Epic/Sony Records. 643

Jules Jordan Video, Inc. v. 144942 Canada, Inc.. .1021

JustMed, Inc. v. Byce 275; 615

K

Kahle v. Gonzales 344

Kamar Int'l, Inc. v. Russ Berrie & Co. . . . 644; 934

Kasten v. Jerrytone. 277

Katz Dochrermann & Epstein, Inc. v. HBO. . . .968

Kay Berry, Inc. v. Taylor Gifts, Inc.. 677

Keane v. Fox Television Stations, Inc. 974

Keeler Brass Co. v. Continental Brass Co. 652

Keene Corp. v. Paraflex Industries, Inc. 1000

Keller v. Electronic Arts, Inc. 1020

Kelley v. Chicago Park District . . 80; 90; 117; 599; 601

Kelly v. Arriba Soft Corp. . 463; 490; 565; 570; 786; 851; 877; 883; 885

Keogh v. Big Lots Corp. 463

Kern River Gas Transmission Co. v. Coastal Corp. 128; 131; 175

Kernal Records Oy v. Mosley 413; 446

Kerr v. The New Yorker Magazine, Inc. 666

Kewanee Oil Co. v. Bicron Corp. . . .958; 960, 961; 963

Key Publications, Inc. v. Chinatown Today Publishing Enterprises, Inc. 251; 646

Kieselstein-Cord v. Accessories by Pearl, Inc. . .184; 192

King v. Ames. 617

King v. Mister Maestro, Inc. 408, 409

King Features Syndicate, Inc. v. Fleischer 149

Kirk v. Harter. 275

Kirtsaeng v. John Wiley & Sons, Inc. 524

Kiss Catalog, Ltd. v. Passport Int'l Prods. . . .83, 84; 207

Knickerbocker Toy Co. v. Azrak-Hamway Int'l, Inc. 655

Knitwaves, Inc. v. Lollytogs Ltd. . . . 214; 666; 998

Kodadek v. MTV Networks, Inc. 439

Kohler Co. v. Moen, Inc. 198

Kohus v. Mariol 652; 705

Konigsberg Int'l v. Rice. 308

Kootenia Homes, Inc. v. Reliable Homes, Inc. . .216

Korman v. HBC Florida, Inc. 372

Kouf v. Walt Disney Pictures & Television. . . .713

Krause v. Titleserv, Inc. 486; 504; 519

Kregos v. Associated Press 124; 131; 250; 728

KSR Int'l Co. v. Teleflex, Inc. 8

Kwan v. Schlein 900

L

L.A. Printex Indus., Inc. v. Aeropostale, Inc. . . .668

L.A. Times v. Free Republic. 887

L. Batlin & Son, Inc. v. Snyder . 226, 227; 230; 234; 493

L.C. Page & Co. v. Fox Film Corp. 313

La Cienega Music Co. v. ZZ Top 412

La Macchia; U.S. v. 948

La Parade v. Ivanova. 358; 732

La Resolana Architects, P.A. v. Reno, Inc. . .643; 669; 674; 684

Ladd v. Law & Technology Press. 437

Lakedreams v. Taylor 917

Landham v. Lewis Galoob Toys, Inc. 1021

Landrau v. Solis-Betancourt. 587

Landsberg v. Scrabble Crossword Game Players, Inc. 148; 1008

Landscape Forms, Inc. v. Columbia Cascade Co. .998

LaResolana Architects v. Clay Realtors Angel Fire 443

Larry Spier, Inc. v. Bourne Co. 394

Lasercomb America, Inc. v. Reynolds. 897

Latimer v. Roaring Toyz, Inc. 235; 311

Latin American Music Co. v. Archdiocese of San Juan .317

Latin American Music Co. v. ASCAP. . . .309; 947

Lauratex Textile Corp. v. Allton Knitting Mills, Inc. 941

Laureyssens v. Idea Group, Inc. 670; 673

Lauritzen v. Larsen. 728

Lawrence v. Dana 814

Laws v. Sony Music Entertainment, Inc. . .977; 1021

Leadsinger, Inc. v. BMG Music Publishing . 542; 862

Lee v. A.R.T. Co. 492; 498

Lee v. Deck the Walls 492

Leibovitz v. Paramount Pictures Corp. 830

Leicester v. Warner Bros. 217

Leigh v. Warner Bros., Inc. 96

Lennon v. Premise Media Corp. 832

Lenz v. Universal Music Group. 785

Leon v. Pacific Telephone & Telegraph Co. .242; 249

Leto v. RCA Corp. 615, 616

Letter Edged in Black Press, Inc. v. Public Building Commission of Chicago 411

Levy v. Rutley. 285

Lewis Galoob Toys, Inc. v. Nintendo of America, Inc. 500; 569; 716, 717

Lexmark Int'l, Inc. v. Static Control Components, Inc. 806; 898

Lieb v. Topstone Indus. Inc. 946

Lifshitz v. Walter Drake & Sons, Inc. 425

Lilley v. Stout 587

Lipscher v. LRP Publs., Inc. 980

Lipton v. Nature Co. 649

Litchfield v. Spielberg 665

Litecubes, LLC v. Northern Light Prods., Inc. . . 723

Literary Works in Electronic Databases Copyright Litigation, In re 298; 620

Liu v. Price Waterhouse LLP. 223; 228; 236

Live Nation Motor Sports, Inc. v. Davis 786

Lombardo v. Doyle, Dane & Bernbach, Inc. . . 1013

London Film Prods. v. Intercontinental Communications, Inc.. 617

London-Sire Records, Inc. v. Doe 1 . . . . .413; 508

Lone Ranger Television, Inc. v. Program Radio Corp.. .494

Los Angeles News Serv. v. Reuters TV Int'l. . .722; 847; 933

Los Angeles News Service v. CBS Broadcasting, Inc.. 847

Los Angeles News Service v. KCAL-TV. 96

Los Angeles News Service v. Tullo 88, 89; 96

Lotus Dev. Corp. v. Paperback Software Int'l . . 132; 702

Lotus Development Corp. v. Borland International, Inc.. . . . . .165; 702

Louis Vuitton Malletier S.A. v. Akanoc Solutions, Inc. 943

Lowry's Reports, Inc. v. Legg Mason, Inc.. . . .741

Lucasfilm Ltd. v. High Frontier 1013

Lulirama Ltd. v. Axcess Broadcast Services, Inc..277

Lyons Partnership, L.P. v. Morris Costumes, Inc.. . . . . .679; 900

M

M.B. Schnapper Public Affairs Press v. Foley . . 136

M.G.B. Homes, Inc. v. Ameron Homes, Inc.. . . .443

M.S.R. Imports, Inc. v. R.E. Greenspan. 922

Mackey v. Lanier Collection Agency & Service, Inc.. 995

Mackie v. Rieser 926; 928; 934

Mag Jewelry Co. v. Cherokee, Inc.. 649

Magnussen Furniture, Inc. v. Collezione Europa USA, Inc.. 196

MAI Systems Corp. v. Peak Computer Inc. . 79; 480; 486; 567

Mailer v. Zolotow 614

Maljack Prods., Inc. v. GoodTimes Home Video Corp.. .628

Manners v. Morosco. 313

Mannion v. Coors Brewing Co.. 97

Manufacturers Technologies, Inc. v. Cams, Inc. . 702

Marascalco v. Fantasy, Inc.. . . . . 64; 354

Marcus v. Rowley. 867

Marketing Information Masters, Inc. v. Board of Trustees of the California State University System. 623

Markogianis v. Burger King Corp.. 970

Marobie-FL, Inc. v. National Association of Fire Equipment Distributors. 770

Martha Graham Sch. & Dance Found., Inc. v. Martha Graham Ctr. of Contemporary Dance, Inc.. . .173; 276; 309; 354; 411

Martignon; United States v.. . . . . .83; 207

Martin v. City of Indianapolis 599; 947

Martin Luther King, Jr., Center for Social Change, Inc. v. American Heritage Products, Inc.. 13

Martin Luther King, Jr., Inc., Estate of v. CBS, Inc.. 410

Marvel Characters, Inc. v. Simon 396

Marvel Enterprises, Inc. v. NCSoft Corp.. 152

Marvel Worldwide, Inc. v. Kirby 280; 396

Mason v. Montgomery Data, Inc.. . . . . . 128; 175

Masquerade Novelty, Inc. v. Unique Industries, Inc.. 190

Massachusetts Museum of Contemporary Art v. Büchel. 599

MasterCard Int'l Inc. v. Nader 2000 Primary Comm., Inc.. 829

Mattel, Inc. v. Azrak-Hamway Intern., Inc.. . . .675

Mattel, Inc. v. Goldberger Doll Manufacturing Co.. . . . . 186, 187

Mattel, Inc. v. MGA Entertainment, Inc. . . 276; 670

Mattel, Inc. v. Walking Mountain Prods.. 831

Matthew Bender & Co., Inc. v. West Publishing Co.. . . . . .75; 88; 89; 135; 255; 947

Matthews v. Freedman. 132

Maverick Boat Co. v. American Marine Holdings, Inc.. 200

Maverick Recording Co. v. Harper 427; 941

Mavrix Photo, Inc. v. Brand Technologies, Inc. . 618

Maxwell Communication Corp. v. Socit Gnrale, .727

May v. Morganelli-Heumann & Associates. . . .277

Mayer v. Josiah Wedgwood & Sons, Ltd.. 980

Mayhew v. Allsup 412

Mayhew v. Gusto Records, Inc.. 346

Mayo Collaborative Servs. v. Prometheus Labs., Inc.. 7

Mazer v. Stein . . 142; 160; 175, 176; 183; 367; 687

MCA, Inc. v. Wilson. 854

MCA Television Ltd. v. Feltner 943

McFarland v. Miller. 1021

McRoberts Software, Inc. v. Media 100, Inc.. . . .926

MDY Industries. LLC v. Blizzard Entertainment, Inc.. . . . . 311; 741; 804; 806; 988

Meade v. United States. 91; 95

Meeropol v. Nizer. 814

Meltzer v. Zoller. 285

MercExchange, LLC v. eBay, Inc.. 912

Merchant v. Levy. 615; 900

[References are to pages.]

Merchant & Evans, Inc. v. Roosevelt Building Products, Co. 999
Meshwerks, Inc. v. Toyota Motor Sales U.S.A.. .107
Metcalf v. Bochco 656
Metro-Goldwyn-Mayer, Inc. v. American Honda Motor Co.. 152
Metro-Goldwyn-Mayer, Inc. v. Showcase Atlanta Cooperative Productions, Inc.. 498
Metro-Goldwyn-Mayer Studios, Inc. v. Grokster, Ltd.. . . .568; 756; 759; 766; 777; 779; 781; 870
Metropolitan Life Ins. Co. v. Taylor. 615
Metropolitan Opera Association v. Wagner-Nichols Recorder Corp.. . . . . 14; 957
Michaels v. Internet Entertainment Group, Inc.. .570
Micro Star v. Formgen Inc. 174; 501
Microdecisions, Inc. v. Skinner 136
Midler v. Ford Motor Co.. . . . . .1011; 1021
Midway Manufacturing Co. v. Artic International, Inc.. . . . . 75; 78; 496
Milene Music, Inc. v. Gotauco 941
Miller v. California. 104
Miller v. Universal City Studios, Inc.. .86; 143; 240; 250; 633
Miller Music Corp. v. Charles N. Daniels, Inc. . 349; 351
Mills Music, Inc. v. Snyder 269; 397
Milne v. Stephen Slesinger, Inc.. 395
Milton H. Greene Archives, Inc. v. CMG Worldwide, Inc.. .1018
Milton H. Greene Archives, Inc. v. Marilyn Monroe LLC .1018
MindGames, Inc. v. Western Pub. Co. 927
Mink v. AAAA Development LLC 618
Mirage Editions, Inc. v. Albuquerque A.R.T. Co..492
Mitchell Bros. Film Group v. Cinema Adult Theater 104
MiTek Holdings, Inc. v. Arce Engineering Co.. .700; 702
Mitel, Inc. v. Iqtel, Inc. 87; 700; 704
Moberg v. 33T, LLC 413; 446
Moghadam; United States v.. . . . . .83; 207
Monge v. Maya Magazines, Inc.. 844
Monotype Imaging, Inc. v. Bitstream, Inc.. . . . 740
Montgomery v. Noga 88; 447
Montz v. Pilgrim Films & Television, Inc. . 973; 975
Moran v. London Records, Ltd.. . . . . . . 625; 628
Morgan v. Hanna Holdings, Inc.. 443
Morris v. Business Concepts, Inc.. 447
Morrissey v. Procter & Gamble Co.. . . . .126; 161
Morseburg v. Balyon. 522; 965

Morton Salt Co. v. G. S. Suppiger Co.. 897
Moseley v. V Secret Catalogue, Inc.. . . . . .11; 1002
Motion Picture Patents Co. v. Universal Film Mfg. Co.. .747
Muller v. Walt Disney Prods.. 313
Munoz v. Albuquerque A.R.T. Co. 492
Murphy v. Millennium Radio Group, LLC . 462; 844
Murray v. British Broadcasting Corp.. 634
Murray v. National Broadcasting Co.. . .1003; 1006
Murray v. Schooner Charming Betsy 516
Murray Hill Publ'ns, Inc. v. ABC Communs., Inc.. 447
Murray Hill Publications, Inc. v. Twentieth Century Fox Film Corp.. 652
Music Sales Corp. v. Morris. 348; 394

N

N City Slicks, Inc. v. Sheen. 704
Nadel v. Play-by-Play Toys & Novelties, Inc.. .1006
NASCAR v. Scharle. 587
National Ass'n of Boards of Pharmacy v. Board of Regents of the University System of Georgia.622, 623
National Bank of Commerce v. Shaklee Corp.. . .498
National Basketball Ass'n v. Motorola, Inc..957; 975
National Car Rental Systems, Inc. v. Computer Associates Int'l, Inc.. . . . . .516; 980; 984
National Council of Young Israel, Inc. v. Feit, Co.. .415
National Football League v. McBee & Bruno's, Inc.. . . . . .549; 552
National Football League v. PrimeTime 24 Joint Venture. 722; 941
NEC Corp. v. Intel Corp.. 165
Neder v. United States. 778
New Era Publs. Int'l v. Henry Holt & Co.. . . .845
New York Mercantile Exchange, Inc. v. IntercontinentalExchange, Inc.. . . . . . 133; 253
New York Times Co. v. Sullivan 799
New York Times Co. v. Tasini. .297; 314; 428; 512; 913
New York Times Co. v. United States. 839
New York Trust Co. v. Eisner. 331
Newcombe v. Adolf Coors Co.. 1017
Newmark v. Turner Broadcasting Network . 614; 871
Newton v. Diamond 87, 88; 171; 504; 655
Nichols v. Ruggles. 416
Nichols v. Universal Pictures Corp.. .150; 653; 658; 686

Niemi v. American Axle Mfg. & Holding, Inc.. . 196

Nihon Keizai Shimbun, Inc. v. Comline Business
Data, Inc. 641; 681

NLRB v. Amax Coal Co. 267

Norse v. Henry Holt & Co. 677

North Coast Indus. v. Jason Maxwell, Inc.. 88

Northern Music Corp. v. Pacemaker Music Co.,
Inc. 641

Nova Design Build, Inc. v. Grace Hotels, LLC . 439;
616

Nova Stylings, Inc. v. Ladd 443

Nunez v. Caribbean Int'l News Corp.. 881

NXIVM Corp. v. Ross Institute 828; 911; 913

O

O'Neill Dev., Inc. v. Galen Kilburn, Inc.. 425

O'Rourke v. Smithsonian Inst. Press 621

Oddo v. Ries 296; 306

OddzOn Prods., Inc. v. Oman 104, 105

Olan Mills, Inc. v. Eckerd Drug of Texas, Inc.. . .99

Olan Mills, Inc. v. Linn Photo Co.. . .517; 630; 920

Olson v. National Broadcasting Co.. 152

Omega Importing Corp. v. Petri-King Camera
Co.. 914

Omega S.A. v. Costco Wholesale Corp.. . .524; 898

On Command Video Corp. v. Columbia Picture
Industries 533

On Davis v. The Gap, Inc.. . . . 654; 928; 932; 941

1-800 Contacts, Inc. v. WhenU.com, Inc.. . .79; 502

Open Source Yoga Unity v. Choudhury. 173

Oracle America, Inc. v. Google, Inc. 701

Oracle USA, Inc. v. SAP AG 932

Oravec v. Sunny Isles Luxury Ventures, L.C. . . 215;
220; 447; 669, 670

Oriental Art Printing, Inc. v. Goldstar Printing
Corp.. 97

Original Appalachian Artworks, Inc. v. Blue Box
Factory (USA) Ltd.. 679

Original Appalachian Artworks, Inc. v. Toy Loft,
Inc.. 426

Orson, Inc. v. Miramax Film Corp.. 964

Ortiz-Gonzalez v. Fonovisa 945

Osborn v. Bank of the United States 612

P

P.C. Films Corp. v. MGM/UA Home Video Inc. . 349

Pacific & Southern Co., Inc. v. Duncan. . .552; 553;
902; 920

Pacific Gas & Elec. Co. v. Public Utilities
Commission of Cal.. 915

Packeteer, Inc. v. Valencia Systems, Inc.. 620

Palladium Music, Inc. v. EatSleepMusic, Inc.. . . 204;
235

Palmer v. Braun 723

Palmer Kane, LLC v. Scholastic Corp.. 620

Papa's-June Music v. McLean. 308

Paramount Pictures Corp. v. Carol Publ'g Group.902

Paramount Pictures Corp. v. Doe 922

Paramount Pictures Corp. v. ReplayTV . . . 615; 871

Paramount Pictures Corp. v. 321 Studios 802

Paramount Pictures Corp. v. Video Broadcasting
Systems, Inc.. 498

Parker v. Google, Inc.. 489

Parker v. Time Warner Entertainment Co.. 942

Parks v. LaFace Records 1020

Paul Morelli Design, Inc. v. Tiffany & Co.. . 89; 91;
104; 443

Pavia v. 1120 Avenue of the Americas
Associates. 602

Pearson Education, Inc. v. Almgren. 634

Peel & Co., Inc. v. The Rug Market 632

Peer Int'l Corp. v. Latin Am. Music Corp.. 632

Peer Int'l Corp. v. Pausa Records, Inc. . . . 937, 938

Peliculas y Videos Internacionales, S.A. de C.V. v.
Harriscope of Los Angeles, Inc.. 358

Penguin Group (USA) Inc. v. American Buddha. 618

Penguin Group (USA) Inc. v. Steinbeck 395

Peregrine v. Lauren Corp.. 267

Peregrine Entertainment, Ltd., In re. 317

Perfect 10, Inc. v. Amazon.com, Inc. . 564; 769; 771;
786; 883, 884; 920

Perfect 10, Inc. v. CCBill LLC . .769; 775; 783, 784

Perfect 10, Inc. v. Cybernet Ventures, Inc.. 769; 779;
783

Perfect 10, Inc. v. Google, Inc.. . . . .564; 917, 918

Perfect 10, Inc. v. Visa Int'l Serv. Ass'n 769

Peter Letterese & Assocs. v. World Institute of
Scientology Enterprises, Int'l. 900; 917

Peter Pan Fabrics, Inc. v. Dan River Mills, Inc. . 640

Peter Pan Fabrics, Inc. v. Martin Weiner Corp. . 212;
653; 663; 674

Peter Starr Prod. Co. v. Twin Continental Films,
Inc.. . . . . .716, 717

Peters v. West. 636; 665; 712

Petrella v. Metro-Goldwyn-Mayer, Inc.. 900

Philadelphia Orchestra Ass'n v. Walt Disney Co..293

Phillips v. Murdock 631

Phillips v. Pembroke Real Estate, Inc..588; 591; 593,
594; 597; 603

[References are to pages.]

Pivot Point Int'l v. Charlene Prods., Inc.. . 180, 181; 191

Plains Cotton Coop. Assoc. v. Goodpasture Computer Serv., Inc.. 692

Platt & Munk Co. v. Republic Graphics, Inc.. . .518

Playboy Enterprises, Inc. v. Dumas 278; 308

Playboy Enterprises, Inc. v. Frena. 571

Playboy Enterprises, Inc. v. Sanfilippo 922

Poe v. Missing Persons 196

Polar Bear Prods. Inc. v. Timex Corp.. . . .899; 923

Pollara v. Seymour. 600

Polygram Int'l Publishing v. Nevada/TIG, Inc.. . .738

Positive Black Talk, Inc. v. Cash Money Records, Inc.. .443; 670

Positive Software Solutions, Inc. v. New Century Mortgage Corp.. 620

Powell v. State. 977

Practice Mgmt. Info. Corp. v. AMA. 137; 898

Prather v. Neva Paperbacks, Inc.. . . . . . .625, 626

Princeton Univ. Press v. Mich. Document Servs.. . . . . 483; 865

Pritchett v. Pound. 275; 900

ProCD, Inc. v. Zeidenberg 980; 985, 986

Professional Real Estate Investors v. Columbia Pictures Indus.. 717

Program Suppliers v. Librarian of Congress . . . 560

Prudhomme v. Proctor & Gamble Co.. 1013

Public Affairs Associates v. Rickover 136; 413

Publications Int'l, Ltd. v. Meredith Corp.. 128

Pushman v. New York Graphic Society, Inc.. . . 301

Q

Qualitex Co. v. Jacobson Products Co.. . .994; 1000

Quality King Distribs. v. L'anza Research Int'l . 514; 523

R

R.C. Olmstead, Inc. v. CU Interface, LLC 700

Radio Television Espanola S.A. v. New World Entertainment, Ltd.. 308

Rainey v. Wayne State University. 933; 976

Random House, Inc. v. Rosetta Books LLC . . . 314

Range Road Music, Inc. v. East Coast Foods, Inc.. 677

Range Road Music, Inc. v. Music Sales Corp.. . . 394

Rano v. Sipa Press, Inc.. 372

RCA/Ariola International, Inc. v. Thomas & Grayston Co.. .938

RCA Mfg. Co. v. Whiteman. 957

Real View, LLC v. 20-20 Technologies, Inc.. . . 702

RealNetworks, Inc. v. DVD Copy Control Ass'n. 790; 802, 803

RealNetworks, Inc. v. Streambox, Inc.. 803

Recording Indus. Ass'n of Am. v. Copyright Royalty Tribunal. 457

Recording Indus. Ass'n of Am. v. Diamond Multimedia Sys.. . . . . .754, 755; 870

Recording Indus. Ass'n of Am. v. Verizon Internet Services, Inc.. . . . . 756; 785

Red Baron-Franklin Park, Inc. v. Taito Corp.. . . .536

Reed Elsevier, Inc. v. Muchnick . 298; 443; 620; 920

Registrability of Costume Designs 190

Reinhardt v. Wal-Mart Stores, Inc.. 314

Religious Tech. Ctr. v. F.A.C.T.NET, Inc.. . . .920

Religious Technology Center v. Netcom On-Line Communication Services.483, 484; 489; 741; 767

Repp v. Webber. 649; 651

Reyher v. Children's Television Workshop . 675; 709

Rice v. Fox Broadcasting Co.. 152

Rice v. Santa Fe Elevator Corp.. 961

Richard Feiner & Co. v. Turner Entertainment Co.. . . . . 911; 918; 922

Richard J. Zitz, Inc. v. Dos Santos Pereira 217

Richard J. Zitz, Inc. v. Pereira. 922

Richardson v. Suzuki Motor Co.. 912

Richlin v. Metro-Goldwyn-Mayer Pictures, Inc. . 293

Richmond Homes Management, Inc. v. Raintree, Inc.. 216

Righthaven, LLC v. Choudhry. 887

Righthaven, LLC v. Hoehn 887

Righthaven, LLC v. Jama 887

Righthaven, LLC v. Mostofi. 619

Righthaven, LLC v. Realty One Group, Inc.. . . . 887

Righthaven, LLC v. South Coast Partners, Inc.. . .619

Righthaven, LLC v. Virginia Citizens Defense League, Inc.. 619

Righthaven, LLC v. Wolf 623

Ringgold v. Black Entertainment Television, Inc.. . . . . 572; 654; 680; 853

Ritchie v. Williams. 615; 900

Robert R. Jones Assocs v. Nino Homes. 935

Robert Stigwood Group v. O'Reilly . . 717; 721; 939

Robert Stigwood Group Ltd. v. Sperber. 540

Rock & Roll Hall of Fame & Museum, Inc. v. Gentile Prods.. . . . . .219; 1000

Rockford Map Publishers, Inc. v. Directory Service Co. of Colorado, Inc.. . . . . 175; 185; 641

The Rodgers and Hammerstein Organization v. UMG Recordings, Inc.. 543

Rodrigue v. Rodrigue. 295; 964

Rodriguez v. Texas Comm'n on the Arts 622

[References are to pages.]

Roger Miller Music, Inc. v. Sony/ATV Publishing, LLC 349; 354

Rogers v. Koons 827; 857

Rohauer v. Friedman. 351

Rohauer v. Killiam Shows. 352

Roley v. New World Pictures, Ltd. 899; 925

Romm Art Creations Ltd v. Simcha International, Inc.. 1001

Rosciszewski v. Arete Associates, Inc. 615

Rosemont Enterprises, Inc. v. Random House, Inc. 146; 243; 814; 1020

Rosette v. Rainbo Record Mfg. Corp.. 412

Ross, Brovins & Oehmke v. Lexis Nexis Group . 251

Roth v. Pritikin. 280

Roth Greeting Cards v. United Card Co.. 657

Rottlund Co. v. Pinnacle Corp. 670

Rouse v. Walter & Assocs., LLC 277

RSO Records, Inc. v. Peri 941

Rural Telephone Service Co. v. Feist Publications, Inc.. 239

Rushton v. Vitale. 415

S

S.A.R.L. Louis Feraud Int'l v. Viewfinder, Inc.. .731

S.O.S., Inc. v. Payday, Inc.. . . . . .290; 902

Sailor Music v. Gap Stores, Inc.. 556

Salinger v. Colting. 833; 909; 910; 916

Salinger v. Random House, Inc.. . . . . . .301; 845

Sampson & Murdock Co. v. Seaver-Radford Co..127

San Francisco Arts & Athletics, Inc. v. United States Olympic Comm'n 1016

Sandoval v. New Line Cinema Corp.. 573

Santa Clara, County of v. Superior Court. 136

Santa-Rosa v. Combo Records. 900

Saregama India Ltd. v. Mosley 630

Saroyan v. William Saroyan Foundation 347

Satava v. Lowry 129

Satellite Broadcasting & Communications Ass'n v. FCC. .560

Saturday Evening Post Co. v. Rumbleseat Press, Inc.. . . . . .230; 620

Scherr v. Universal Match Co.. . . . . . . .136; 273

Schiller & Schmidt, Inc. v. Nordisco Corp.. . . .278

Schmid Brothers, Inc. v. W. Goebel Porzellanfabrik KG. 347

Schmidt; U.S. v.. 948

Scholz Design, Inc. v. Sard Custom Homes, LLC. .215

Schoolhouse, Inc. v. Anderson 712, 713

Schrock v. Learning Curve Int'l, Inc.. . . . 115; 222

Schuchart & Associates, Professional Engineers, Inc. v. Solo Serve Corp.. 976

SCO Group, Inc. v. Novell, Inc.. 308

Scorpio Music S.A. v. Willis 373

Scott v. Dixon 601

Seago v. Horry County. 136

Sears, Roebuck & Co. v. Stiffel Co.. . 15; 188; 954; 958–960; 982; 984; 994

See v. Durang 713

Sega Enterprises Ltd. v. Accolade, Inc.. . .165; 470; 873; 918; 983

Seiler v. Lucasfilm, Ltd.. 439

Self-Realization Fellowship Church v. Ananda Church of Self-Realization 347

Selle v. Gibb 645, 646

Seminole Tribe of Florida v. Florida. 621, 622

Serra v. United States Gen. Serv. Admin.. 594

Seshadri v. Kasraian 901

Severe Records, LLC v. Rich 615

Shapiro & Son Bedspread Corp. v. Royal Mills Associates. 425

Shapiro, Bernstein & Co. v. H.L. Green Co.. . .736; 739; 758; 777

Shapiro, Bernstein & Co., Inc. v. Jerry Vogel Music Co., Inc. 291; 309; 429; 432

Shaul v. Cherry Valley-Springfield Central School Dist.. .277

Shaw v. Lindheim 149; 713

Shaw v. Rizzoli Int'l Publs., Inc.. 730

Shaw Family Archives, Ltd. v. CMG Worldwide, Inc.. .1018

Sheldon v. Metro-Goldwyn Pictures Corp.. .90; 641; 665; 709; 929; 933, 934

Shine v. Childs. 209

SHL Imaging, Inc. v. Artisan House, Inc.. 226

Shoptalk, Ltd. v. Concorde-New Horizons Corp.. . . . . .353; 415

Shuptrine v. McDougal Littell. 976

Sid & Marty Krofft Television Productions, Inc. v. McDonald's Corp.. . . . . 468; 657; 678; 714; 931

Siegel v. National Periodical Publications, Inc. . 153; 385

Siegel v. Warner Bros. Entm't, Inc. . . 383; 392; 416

Silkwood v. Kerr-McGee Corp.. 961

Silverman v. CBS, Inc.. 149

Silverman v. Sunrise Pictures Corp.. 348

Silvers v. Sony Pictures Entertainment, Inc. . . . 624

Silverstein v. Penguin Putnam, Inc.. . . . . 251; 919

Simpleville Music v. Mizell 537

SimplexGrinnell LP v. Integrated Systems & Power, Inc. 487

Situation Mgmt. Sys., Inc. v. ASP Consulting LLC. 90; 655

Smith v. Montoro. 997

Smith; United States v.. 301

Soc'y of the Holy Transfiguration Monastery, Inc. v. Archbishop Gregory of Denver, Colo. . 312; 409; 740

Société Civile Succession Richard Guino v. Int'l Foundation for Anticancer Drug Discovery . . 922

Société Civile Succession Richard Guino v. Renoir. 424

Softel, Inc. v. Dragon Medical & Scientific Communications, Inc.. . . . . .700; 741

Softman Products Co. v. Adobe Systems, Inc. . . 519

Software, Inc. v. Reynolds & Reynolds Co. . . . 620

Sony BMG Music Entertainment v. Tenenbaum.870; 942

Sony Computer Entertainment America, Inc. v. Bleem, LLC 844

Sony Computer Entertainment, Inc. v. Connectix Corp.. .875

Sony Computer Entm't Am., Inc. v. GameMasters 898

Sony Corp. of America v. Universal City Studios, Inc. . . .367; 455; 468; 718; 736; 739; 740; 743; 758; 815; 816; 819; 821; 822; 824; 841; 869; 920

SoundExchange v. Librarian of Congress. 580

Southco, Inc. v. Kanebridge Corp. 87

Southeast Bank v. Lawrence 13

Southern Bell Telephone & Telegraph Co. v. Associated Telephone Directory Publishers . . 250

Sparaco v. Lawler, Matusky, Skelly, Engineers LLP 175; 212

Specht v. Netscape Communications Corp. . 168; 988

Specialized Seating, Inc. v. Greenwich Industries, L.P.. 198

Spooner v. EEN, Inc.. 947

Sportsmans Warehouse, Inc. v. Fair. 666

Springsteen v. Plaza Roller Dome, Inc.. 556

St. Louis, I. M. & S. Ry. Co. v. Williams. . . .942

Staggers v. Real Authentic Sound. 279

State Farm Mutual Auto. Inc. Co. v. Campbell. .942

State of (see name of state). . . . .

State Street Bank & Trust Co. v. Signature Financial Group, Inc. 167

Steinberg v. Columbia Pictures Industries, Inc.. .681

Stenograph L.L.C. v. Bossard Associates, Inc. . . 80; 486; 701

Stern Electronics, Inc. v. Kaufman 78; 201

Stewart v. Abend. 153; 347; 351; 355; 815; 818; 919

Stewart v. Wachowski 651

Stone v. Williams. 347

Storage Technology Corp. v. Custom Hardware Engineering & Consulting, Inc. 486

Storm Impact, Inc. v. Software of the Month Club. 933

Story v. Holcombe. 813

Stowe v. Thomas. 496

Straus v. DVC Worldwide, Inc. 573

Streetwise Maps, Inc. v. Vandam, Inc.. . . .175; 447

Stromback v. New Line Cinema 651; 712; 974

Stuart Weitzman, LLC v. Microcomputer Resources, Inc.. 620

Stuff v. E. C. Publications, Inc.. 902

Sturdza v. United Arab Emirates 668

Subafilms, Ltd. v. MGM-Pathe Communications Co.. . . . . .715; 740

Suffolk, County of v. First American Real Estate Solutions. 136; 175

Sullivan v. Naturalis, Inc.. 615

Sun Microsystems, Inc. v. Microsoft Corp.. . . .311

Sundeman v. The Seajay Society 845

Sunset House Distributing Corp. v. Doran 234

SunTrust Bank v. Houghton Mifflin Co.. . .832; 921

Superior Form Builders, Inc. v. Dan Chase Taxidermy Supply Co., Inc.. . . . . .88; 129; 182; 191

Swirsky v. Carey. 670

Sybersound Records, Inc. v. UAV Corp. 630

Sylvania Electric Prods., Inc. v. Brainerd 1007

Synercom Tech., Inc. v. University Computing Co.. . . . . .957, 958

Syntek Semiconductor Co. v. Microchip Technology, Inc 105; 165; 185

T

T. B. Harms Co. v. Eliscu 611

Tasini v. N.Y. Times Co.. 296

Taylor v. Meirick 899; 932; 934

Teleprompter Corp. v. CBS 548; 554

Tempo Music, Inc. v. Famous Music Corp.. . . .171

Testa v. Janssen 651

Tetris Holding, LLC v. Xio Interactive, Inc.. . . 704

Tewarson v. Simon. 616

Texas v. West Publishing Co.. 614

Textile Secrets Int'l v. Ya-Ya Brand, Inc.. 462

Thimbleberries, Inc. v. C&F Enterprises, Inc. . . 632

Thomas v. Pansy Ellen Prods., Inc.. 571

Thompkins v. Lil' Joe Records, Inc. 312

Thomson v. Larson. 292; 295

Thornton v. J Jargon Co.. 251

[References are to pages.]

Three Boys Music Corp. v. Bolton 642; 650

321 Studios v. Metro-Goldwyn-Mayer Studios, Inc. 802

Ticketmaster Corp. v. Tickets.com. . .490; 785; 876; 884; 989

Tiffany (NJ) Inc. v. eBay, Inc. 776

Tiffany Design, Inc v. Reno-Tahoe Specialty, Inc..80

Time, Inc. v. Bernard Geis Associates. .96; 840; 846

Tire Engineering & Distribution, LLC v. Shandong Linglong Rubber Co. 196; 722; 976

TMTV Corp. v. Mass Prods., Inc.. 935

Toho Co. v. William Morrow & Co.. . . . .152; 856

Toney v. L'Oreal USA, Inc.. 977

Topolos v. Caldewey. 614

Toro Co. v. R & R Products Co.. 87

Towler v. Sayles 646

T-Peg, Inc. v. Vermont Timber Works, Inc.. . . .220

Trade-Mark Cases. 9; 85; 240; 994

TrafFix Devices, Inc. v. Marketing Displays, Inc.. . . . . 188; 994; 1000

Traicoff v. Digital Media, Inc.. 310

TransWestern Publ'g Co. LP v. Multimedia Mktg. Assocs.. . . . . .251; 428

Trek Leasing, Inc. v. United States. . .216; 669; 705

Troll Co. v. Uneeda Doll Co.. 358

Trustees of Columbia University v. Roche Diagnostics, GmbH. 723

TRW, Inc. v. Andrews. 899

Tufenkian Import/Export Ventures, Inc. v. Einstein Moomjy, Inc.. . . . . 653; 706

Turner Broadcasting System, Inc. v. FCC. .798, 799

Twentieth Century Fox Film Corp. v. Cablevision Sys. Corp.. .478

Twentieth Century Fox Film Corp. v. Entertainment Distributing 280; 347

Twentieth Century Music Corp. v. Aiken . . 54; 241; 367; 548; 550; 555; 836

Twin Books Corp. v. Walt Disney Co. 424

Twin Peaks Prods., Inc. v. Publications Int'l, Ltd.. . . . . .938; 943

Two Pesos, Inc. v. Taco Cabana, Inc.. 997

24/7 Records, Inc. v. Sony Music Entm't, Inc.. . .477

Ty, Inc. v. GMA Accessories 644

Ty, Inc. v. Publ'ns Int'l 498, 499; 858–860

Tyne v. Time Warner Entm't Co., L.P.. 1020

U

U.S. v. (see name of defendant). . . . .

U.S. Auto Parts Network, Inc. v. Parts Geek, LLC. 276

U.S. Golf Association v. St. Andrews Systems, Inc.. 15

U-Haul Int'l, Inc. v. WhenU.com, Inc.. 502

Ulloa v. Universal Music & Video Distrib. Corp . 91; 279

UMG Recordings, Inc. v. Augusto 518

UMG Recordings, Inc. v. Bertelsmann AG. . . .755

UMG Recordings, Inc. v. MP3.com, Inc.. 942

UMG Recordings, Inc. v. Shelter Capital Partners, LLC. 741; 756; 774; 777, 778; 780

UMG Recordings, Inc. v. Veoh Networks, Inc. .780; 783

United States v. (see name of defendant). . . . . .

Universal Athletic Sales Co. v. Salkeld. 673

Universal City Studios, Inc. v. Corley. . . .792; 889

Universal City Studios, Inc. v. Reimerdes . 733; 755; 800

Universal City Studios, Inc. v. Sony Corp. of America 455; 739; 920

Universal Furniture Int'l, Inc. v. Collezione Europa USA, Inc.. . . . . 192; 195

Update Art, Inc. v. Modiin Publishing, Ltd..719; 722

US Fax Law Ctr., Inc. v. iHire, Inc.. 626

Utopia Provider Systems, Inc. v. Pro-Med Clinical Systems, LLC. 124; 618

V

Vanderhurst v. Colorado Mountain College District. .277

Vault Corp. v. Quaid Software Ltd.. .485; 505; 787; 981, 982

Veeck v. S. Bldg. Code Cong. Int'l, Inc.. 137

Venegas-Hernandez v. Asociacion de Compositores y Editores de Musica Latinoamericana. . .348; 509

Vernor v. Autodesk, Inc.. 518

Vestron, Inc. v. Home Box Office, Inc.. 616

Viacom Int'l, Inc. v. YouTube, Inc.. . 772, 773; 776, 777; 779; 941

Video Pipeline, Inc. v. Buena Vista Home Entertainment, Inc.. . . . . .571; 885; 898

Video-Cinema Films, Inc. v. Cable News Network, Inc.. 844

Virgin Records America, Inc. v. Thompson. . . .946

W

W.T. Rogers Co. v. Keene 1000

Waits v. Frito-Lay, Inc.. 1021

Wallace v. Int'l Business Machines Corp.. 312

WallData, Inc. v. Los Angeles County Sheriff's Dept.. . . . . .486; 846

Wal-Mart Stores, Inc. v. Samara Bros., Inc. . . . 198; 995; 998

Walt Disney Co. v. Powell. 920; 939; 943

Walt Disney Productions v. Air Pirates. . .151; 468; 832

Walt Disney Productions v. Filmation Associates.465

Walthal v. Rusk. 372

Walton v. United States 621

Warner Bros. Entertainment, Inc. v. RDR Books. 499; 858

Warner Bros. Entertainment, Inc. v. WTV Sys., Inc.. 534

Warner Bros. Entertainment, Inc. v. X One X Prods.. . . . . .153; 409; 416

Warner Bros., Inc. v. American Broadcasting Cos.. . . . . 153; 656; 666

Warner Bros. Pictures, Inc. v. Columbia Broadcasting System, Inc.. 150

Warren v. Fox Family Worldwide, Inc.. 628

Warren Publ'g Co. v. Spurlock 862

Warren Publishing, Inc. v. Microdos Data Corp..251; 646

Washington Mint, LLC; United States v.. 136

Washingtonian Publishing Co. v. Pearson. 429

Watkins v. Chesapeake Custom Homes. 216

WB Music Corp. v. RTV Communication Group, Inc.. 943

Weber v. Geffen Records, Inc.. 976

Wedgwood Homes, Inc. v. Lund. 1001

Weinstein v. University of Illinois. 277

Weinstein Co. v. Smokewood Ent. Group, LLC . 631

Weissmann v. Freeman 214; 286; 292; 294

Welles v. Turner Entm't Co.. 313

Well-Made Toy Mfg. Corp. v. Goffa Int'l Corp. . 447

Wells Fargo & Co. v. WhenU.com, Inc. 502

Wendt v. Host Int'l, Inc. 153; 1021

Werlin v. Reader's Digest Assoc., Inc., . . . 971, 972

West Publishing Co. v. Mead Data Central, Inc..253; 256

WGN Continental Broadcasting Co. v. United Video. 202; 496

Wheaton v. Peters. 21; 135; 253; 417

Whelan Assocs. v. Jaslow Dental Laboratory, Inc.. . . . . 686; 687; 693; 697

Whimsicality, Inc. v. Rubie's Costume Co..190; 446; 902

White v. Kimmell 407

White v. Samsung Electronics America, Inc. . . . 13; 153; 1008; 1013

White-Smith Music Publishing Co. v. Apollo Co..67, 68; 157; 412

Whitfield v. Lear 1006

Wilchombe v. Tee VeeToons, Inc.. 311

Wildlife Express Corp. v. Carol Wright Sales, Inc.. 714

William A. Graham Co. v. Haughey 935

Williams v. Crichton 658; 664

Williams v. Curtiss-Wright Corp.. 992

Williams & Wilkins Co. v. United States . . 472; 864

Williams Electronics, Inc. v. Artic International, Inc.. . . . . 78; 157

Williamson v. Pearson Education, Inc.. 844

Winter v. DC Comics. 1019

Winter v. Natural Resources Defense Counsel. .913, 914

Wisconsin, State of v. Law Office Info. Systems, Inc.. 135

Wise; United States v.. 518

Wojnarowicz v. American Family Ass'n 584

Wolff v. Inst. of Elec. & Electronics Engineers Inc.. 986

Woods v. Bourne Co. 87; 398

Woods v. Universal City Studios, Inc.. 573

Wooley v. Maynard 839

World Auxiliary Power Co., In re 317

Worlds of Wonder, Inc. v. Vector Intercontinental, Inc.. 503

Worlds of Wonder, Inc. v. Veritel Learning Systems, Inc.. 503

Worldwide Church of God v. Philadelphia Church of God 882

Worth v. Selchow & Righter Co. 249

Worth, In re Marriage of. 295

WPIX, Inc. v. IVI, Inc.. . . . . .535; 560

WPOW, Inc. v. MRLJ Enterprises. 922

Wrench LLC v. Taco Bell Corp.. . . .975; 980; 984; 1007

Wright v. Warner Books, Inc.. 845

X

Xoom, Inc. v. Imageline, Inc.. 447

Y

Yankee Candle Co. v. New England Candle Co..215

Yardley, Application of. 197

Young, Ex Parte 623

Yurman Design, Inc. v. PAJ, Inc. 714; 940

[References are to pages.]

Z

Zacchini v. Scripps-Howard Broadcasting Co . 1016; 1020

Ziegler; United States v.. 566

Zomba Enterprises, Inc. v. Panorama Records, Inc.. . . . . .862; 942

Zyla v. Wadsworth. 997

TABLE OF PRINCIPAL DISCUSSIONS
OF PROVISIONS OF THE
COPYRIGHT ACT OF 1976 AS AMENDED

[References are to sections.]

UNITED STATES CODE

Provision	Section
17 U.S.C. § 1	.8.02[A]
17 U.S.C. § 4	.1.03[C][1]
17 U.S.C. § 5(a)	.3.01[B]
17 U.S.C. § 5(d)	.8.03[C][2]
17 U.S.C. § 10	1.03[C][1]; 2.03[C]
17 U.S.C. § 24	.1.03[C][1]; 5.02[A][1]
17 U.S.C. § 26	.4.01[B]
17 U.S.C. § 101	1.03[D][1]; 2.01[B]; 2.02[E]; 3.01[B], [D], [G]; 3.02[B], [C]; 4.01[B], [C]; 4.02[C]; 7.02[B]–[D]; 7.03[B]; 7.04[B]; 7.05[A][2]; 7.06[B]; 7.08[C][2]; 8.03[C][2]; 8.04[B]; 11.01[C][1]; 11.02[D][2]
17 U.S.C. §§ 101 to 914	.7.02[B]
17 U.S.C. § 101	11.01[C][1]
17 U.S.C. § 102	3.01[G]; 11.02[D][2]
17 U.S.C. § 102(5)	.3.01[G]
17 U.S.C. § 102(a)	1.02[C][2]; 1.03[D][1]; 2.01[B]; 3.01[B]; 3.02[C]; 8.03[C][2]
17 U.S.C. § 102(a)(6)	.11.03[A]
17 U.S.C. § 102(b)	3.01[E]; 5.01[B]; 8.03[C][2]; 10.03[A]; 10.04[A]; 11.02[D][2]
17 U.S.C. § 103	3.01[B]; 3.02[C]; 11.02[D][2]
17 U.S.C. § 103(a)	.3.02[B]
17 U.S.C. § 103(b)	.3.02[B]
17 U.S.C. § 104A(b)	.8.04[B]
17 U.S.C. § 104A(g)	.5.01[D]
17 U.S.C. § 104(a)	.8.03[B]
17 U.S.C. § 104(b)	.6.01[B]
17 U.S.C. § 104(c)	.8.04[B]
17 U.S.C. § 105	.2.02[D]
17 U.S.C. § 106	1.03[D][1]; 2.02[F]; 3.01[F]; 4.02[C]; 8.02[B]; 8.04[A]; 10.02[B]; 11.02[D][2]
17 U.S.C. § 106(1)	7.02[B], [D]; 7.04[B]
17 U.S.C. § 106(1) to (5)	.8.04[A]
17 U.S.C. § 106(2)	3.02[B]; 7.03[B]; 10.02[B]
17 U.S.C. § 106(3)	.7.04[B]
17 U.S.C. § 106(4)	.7.02[D]
17 U.S.C. § 106A	7.03[B]; 7.08[C][2]
17 U.S.C. § 106A(a)(1)(A)	.11.03[A]
17 U.S.C. § 106(A)(a)(3)(A)	.7.08[C][2]
17 U.S.C. § 106A(c)(2)	.7.08[C][2]
17 U.S.C. § 106(B)	.7.08[C][2]

UNITED STATES CODE

Provision	Section
17 U.S.C. § 107	. .; 10.02[B]; 10.03[A]; 11.02[D][2]
17 U.S.C. § 107(1)	.10.03[B]
17 U.S.C. § 107(2)	.10.03[B]
17 U.S.C. § 107(3)	.10.03[B]
17 U.S.C. § 107(4)	.10.03[B]
17 U.S.C. §§ 107 to 122	.1.03[D][1]
17 U.S.C. § 109	.7.04[B]
17 U.S.C. § 109(a)	7.03[B]; 7.05[A][2]; 11.02[D][2]
17 U.S.C. § 110(5)	.7.05[B][2]
17 U.S.C. § 114	.1.03[D][1]
17 U.S.C. § 115	.7.04[B]
17 U.S.C. § 117	.3.01[B]
17 U.S.C. § 117(c)	.2.01[B]
17 U.S.C. § 118(b)	.7.06[B]
17 U.S.C. § 201(a)	.4.01[B], [C]
17 U.S.C. § 201(b)	.4.01[B], [C]
17 U.S.C. § 201(d)	1.03[D][1]; 4.01[C]; 8.02[B]
17 U.S.C. § 202	1.03[D][1]; 11.03[A]
17 U.S.C. § 203	.1.03[D][1]
17 U.S.C. § 204(a)	.4.02[C]
17 U.S.C. § 301	1.02[C][2]; 1.03[D][1]
17 U.S.C. § 301(a)	.4.01[B]; 11.02[D][2]
17 U.S.C. § 301(c)	.11.02[A]
17 U.S.C. § 301(d)	.11.03[A]
17 U.S.C. § 301(f)	.7.08[B]
17 U.S.C. § 301(f)(2)(C)	11.02[D][2]
17 U.S.C. § 302	.5.01[B]
17 U.S.C. §§ 302 to 304	.5.01[B]
17 U.S.C. § 302(a)	1.03[D][1]; 5.01[B]
17 U.S.C. § 302(c)	1.03[D][1]; 5.01[B]
17 U.S.C. § 303	.5.01[B]
17 U.S.C. § 303(b)	.6.01[B]
17 U.S.C. § 304	4.01[C]; 5.01[B]
17 U.S.C. § 304(a)(2)	.5.01[C][3]
17 U.S.C. § 304(a)(4)(A)	.5.01[C][3]
17 U.S.C. § 304(a)(4)(B)	.5.01[C][3]
17 U.S.C. § 304(c)	1.03[D][1]; 5.02[D][2]
17 U.S.C. § 304(c)(3)	.5.02[D][2]
17 U.S.C. § 304(c)(4)	.5.02[D][2]
17 U.S.C. § 304(c)(4)(B)	.5.02[D][2]
17 U.S.C. § 304(c)(6)(E)	.5.02[D][2]

[References are to sections.]

UNITED STATES CODE

Provision	Section
17 U.S.C. § 401(c).	6.02[B]
17 U.S.C. § 405	5.01[D]
17 U.S.C. § 408(a)	1.03[D][1]
17 U.S.C. § 410(c).	3.01[G]
17 U.S.C. § 411(b)(1)	10.06
17 U.S.C. § 412.	11.01[D]
17 U.S.C. § 501	8.02[B]; 11.02[D][2]
17 U.S.C. § 501(b).	3.01[D]; 8.02[B]; 8.04[B]
17 U.S.C. § 502(a)	7.05[B][2]; 11.01[B][1]
17 U.S.C. § 504(b).	11.01[C][1]
17 U.S.C. § 504(c).	8.01; 8.02[B]
17 U.S.C. § 504(c)(1)	11.01[C][2]
17 U.S.C. § 507(b).	11.01[C][1]
17 U.S.C. § 512	2.01[B]; 9.03[B]
17 U.S.C. § 512(C)	9.03[B]
17 U.S.C. § 512(c).	9.03[B]
17 U.S.C. § 512(c)(1)	9.03[B]
17 U.S.C. § 512(c)(1)(A)	9.03[B]
17 U.S.C. § 512(c)(1)(A)(ii).	9.03[B]

UNITED STATES CODE

Provision	Section
17 U.S.C. § 512(c)(1)(A)(iii)	9.03[B]
17 U.S.C. § 512(c)(1)(B)	9.03[B]
17 U.S.C. § 512(i)(1)(A).	9.03[B]
17 U.S.C. § 512(j).	9.03[B]
17 U.S.C. § 512(k)(1)(A) to (B).	9.03[B]
17 U.S.C. § 512(m)(1).	9.03[B]
17 U.S.C. § 601	5.01[D]
17 U.S.C. § 602(a).	8.04[A]
17 U.S.C. § 802(a)(1)	7.01[C]
17 U.S.C. § 904	5.01[B]
17 U.S.C. § 1101.	3.01[F]
17 U.S.C. § 1201.	9.04[B]
17 U.S.C. § 1201(a)(3)(B).	9.04[B]
17 U.S.C. § 1201(c)(1).	9.04[B]
17 U.S.C. § 1202	11.01[C][1]
17 U.S.C. § 1202(c)(3).	6.02[B]
17 U.S.C. § 1203	11.01[C][1]
17 U.S.C. § 1305.	5.01[B]

TABLE OF LEGISLATIVE HISTORY
EXCERPTS

[References are to sections.]

Legislative History	Section
H.R. Rep. 1976 Act § 101	7.08[C][1]
H.R. Rep. 1976 Act § 102	2.01[A]; 2.02[A]; 3.01[A], [G]
H.R. Rep. 1976 Act § 103	3.02[A]
H.R. Rep. 1976 Act § 106	7.01[A]; 7.02[A]; 7.03[A]; 7.04[A]; 7.05[A][1]; 7.06[A]; 9.01[A]
H.R. Rep. 1976 Act § 107	10.01
H.R. Rep. 1976 Act § 109	7.04[A]; 7.06[A]
H.R. Rep. 1976 Act § 110	7.05[B][1]
H.R. Rep. 1976 Act § 111	7.05[B][1]
H.R. Rep. 1976 Act § 201	4.01[A]; 4.02[A]
H.R. Rep. 1976 Act § 203	5.02[A][1]
H.R. Rep. 1976 Act § 204	4.02[A]
H.R. Rep. 1976 Act § 205	4.02[A]
H.R. Rep. 1976 Act § 301	6.01[A]; 11.02[A]
H.R. Rep. 1976 Act § 302	5.01[A]
H.R. Rep. 1976 Act § 303	5.01[A]
H.R. Rep. 1976 Act § 304	5.01[A]
H.R. Rep. 1976 Act § 304	5.02[B][1]
H.R. Rep. 1976 Act § 305	5.01[A]
H.R. Rep. 1976 Act § 401	6.02[A]
H.R. Rep. 1976 Act § 407	6.03[A]
H.R. Rep. 1976 Act § 408	6.03[A]
H.R. Rep. 1976 Act § 410	6.03[A]
H.R. Rep. 1976 Act § 411	6.03[A]
H.R. Rep. 1976 Act § 412	6.03[A]
H.R. Rep. 1976 Act § 501	8.01; 9.01[A]
H.R. Rep. 1976 Act § 502	11.01[A]
H.R. Rep. 1976 Act § 503	11.01[A]
H.R. Rep. 1976 Act § 504	11.01[A]
H.R. Rep. 1976 Act §§ 505–10	11.01[A]
H.R. Rep. 1976 Act § 602	7.04[A]
H.R. Rep. 1976 Act § 701	6.04[A]

INDEX

[References are to pages.]

A

AFFIRMATIVE COPYRIGHT DEFENSES
Generally . . . 897
Fair use (See FAIR USE)

AHRA (See AUDIO HOME RECORDING ACT (AHRA))

ANGLO-AMERICAN COPYRIGHT LAW, HISTORY OF
Generally . . . 16
Copyright Act of 1909 (See COPYRIGHT ACT OF 1909)
Copyright Act of 1976 (See COPYRIGHT ACT OF 1976)
Donaldson v. Beckett (1774), beginnings to . . . 16

ARCHITECTURAL WORKS
Copyrightability . . . 207

ART WORKS
Pictorial, graphic, and sculptural works . . . 174
Visual Artists Rights Act
    Generally . . . 585; 586
    Case law . . . 588

ASSIGNMENT OF RIGHTS (See OWNERSHIP AND TRANSFERS)

ATTORNEYS' FEES
Remedies under federal law . . . 945

AUDIO HOME RECORDING ACT (AHRA)
Secondary liability . . . 751

AUDIOVISUAL WORKS
Copyrightability . . . 201

AUTHORSHIP
Generally . . . 140
Architectural works . . . 207
Audiovisual works . . . 201
Choreographic works . . . 171
Compilations
    Generally . . . 221; 237
    Notice of copyright . . . 427
Computer software (See SOFTWARE)
Dramatic works . . . 171
Graphic works . . . 174
Literary works
    Generally . . . 142
    Computer software (See SOFTWARE)
Motion pictures . . . 201
Musical works . . . 171
Original works
    Generally . . . 141
    Architectural . . . 207
    Audiovisual . . . 201
    Choreographic . . . 171
    Computer software . . . 142

AUTHORSHIP—Cont.
Original works—Cont.
    Dramatic . . . 171
    Graphic . . . 174
    Literary
        Generally . . . 142
        Computer software (See SOFTWARE)
    Motion pictures . . . 201
    Musical . . . 171
    Pantomimes . . . 171
    Pictorial . . . 174
    Sculptural . . . 174
    Sound recordings . . . 203
Pantomimes . . . 171
Pictorial works . . . 174
Sculptural works . . . 174
Software (See SOFTWARE)
Sound recordings . . . 203

B

BERNE CONVENTION
Generally . . . 34
Berne Convention Implementation Act of 1988
    Generally . . . 38
    Unfinished business of . . . 38
Copyright Act of 1909, effect on . . . 22
Implementation Act of 1988 . . . 432
Incentives for United States entry . . . 37
Registration . . . 432
Trade-related Aspects of Intellectual Property Rights (TRIPS), and . . . 42
United States entry
    Implementation Act of 1988 . . . 38
    Incentives for entry . . . 37
Updating . . . 43

BERNE CONVENTION IMPLEMENTATION ACT OF 1988
Generally . . . 419; 432
Unfinished business . . . 38
United States entry . . . 38

BUNDLE OF RIGHTS
Transfers of ownership . . . 302

C

CHOREOGRAPHIC WORKS
Copyrightability . . . 171

COLLECTIVE WORKS
Initial ownership . . . 296
Notice of copyright . . . 427
Registration . . . 447

COMPILATIONS
Generally . . . 221; 237
Notice of copyright . . . 427

[References are to pages.]

"COMPULSORY" LICENSES
Exclusive rights . . . 456

COMPUTER SOFTWARE
Commission on New Technological Uses of Copyrighted Works (CONTU), final report of . . . 162
Copyrightability . . . 142

CONTRIBUTORY INFRINGEMENT
Secondary liability . . . 734

COPYRIGHT ACT OF 1909
Generally . . . 22
Berne Convention, effect of . . . 22
Constitution to, from . . . 20
Importance of . . . 23
Renewal (See DURATION AND TERMINATION, subhead: Renewal under Copyright Act of 1909)
Revision, legislative attempts . . . 23

COPYRIGHT ACT OF 1976
Changes made by . . . 23
Preemption (See PREEMPTION OF STATE LAWS)
Subsequent developments under . . . 25
Trends in copyright legislation . . . 27

COPYRIGHT (GENERALLY)
Generally . . . 3
Anglo-American copyright law, history of (See ANGLO-AMERICAN COPYRIGHT LAW, HISTORY OF)
Berne Convention (See BERNE CONVENTION)
Changing world, in a
Generally . . . 28
Comparative law overview . . . 28
Intellectual property and international trade (See subhead: Intellectual property and international trade)
International trade, intellectual property and (See subhead: Intellectual property and international trade)
International treaties involving copyright (See INTERNATIONAL TREATIES)
Neighboring and related rights conventions . . . 39
Related rights conventions, neighboring and . . . 39
United States entry into Berne (See BERNE CONVENTION, subhead: United States entry)
Comparative law overview . . . 28
Contemporary copyright discourse, other rhetorics . . . 60
Copyright management information (CMI) . . . 461
Devices and software (See SECONDARY LIABILITY, subhead: Copying devices and software)
Digital challenge, and (See DIGITAL TECHNOLOGY)
Federal intellectual property law (See FEDERAL INTELLECTUAL PROPERTY LAW)
Future trends . . . 1023
History of Anglo-American copyright law (See ANGLO-AMERICAN COPYRIGHT LAW, HISTORY OF)
Importance of . . . 1

COPYRIGHT (GENERALLY)—Cont.
Intellectual property and international trade
Berne Convention, updating . . . 43
North American Free Trade Agreement (NAFTA) . . . 40
Trade-related Aspects of Intellectual Property Rights (TRIPS)
Berne Convention, and . . . 42
North American Free Trade Agreement (NAFTA) and . . . 40
United States participation in new order . . . 44
WTO implementing legislation . . . 42
Interest analysis and . . . 53
International trade, intellectual property and (See subhead: Intellectual property and international trade)
International treaties involving (See INTERNATIONAL TREATIES)
Natural law conception of copyright . . . 54
Neighboring and related rights conventions . . . 39
1909 Act (See COPYRIGHT ACT OF 1909)
1976 Act (See COPYRIGHT ACT OF 1976)
Patent law, relationship to . . . 4
Related rights conventions, neighboring and . . . 39
Rhetorics of copyright jurisprudence
Generally . . . 54
Contemporary copyright discourse, other rhetorics . . . 60
Natural law conception of copyright . . . 54
Utilitarian conception of copyright . . . 54
State Intellectual Property Law (See STATE INTELLECTUAL PROPERTY LAW)
Thinking and talking about copyright law
Generally . . . 52; 64
Interest analysis and copyright . . . 53
Rhetorics of copyright jurisprudence (See subhead: Rhetorics of copyright jurisprudence)
United States entry into Berne (See BERNE CONVENTION, subhead: United States entry)
Utilitarian conception of copyright . . . 54

COPYRIGHT OFFICE
Generally . . . 448
Functions of . . . 448
History of . . . 448
Patent and Trademark Office, combined with . . . 450

COPYRIGHT TERM EXTENSION ACT (CTEA)
Generally . . . 327

CRIMINAL PENALTIES
Remedies under federal law . . . 948

CTEA (See COPYRIGHT TERM EXTENSION ACT (CTEA))

D

DAMAGES UNDER FEDERAL LAW (See REMEDIES UNDER FEDERAL LAW, subhead: Damages)

DEFENSES
Affirmative copyright defenses . . . 897
Fair use defense (See FAIR USE)

DERIVATIVE WORKS
Copyrightability . . . 221; 222
Publication and public domain . . . 415
Registration . . . 447
Renewal and . . . 351
Termination of transfer, exception from . . . 396

DIGITAL PERFORMANCE RIGHT IN SOUND RECORDINGS ACT (DPRA)
Exclusive rights . . . 574

DIGITAL TECHNOLOGY
Generally . . . 45
Audio Home Recording Act (AHRA) . . . 751
Digital copyright at home and abroad . . . 48
Digital network transmissions . . . 47; 542
Digital Performance Right in Sound Recordings Act (DPRA) . . . 574
Future issues . . . 50
Information processing, digitization and revolution in . . . 45
Issues in context . . . 50
Public performances . . . 542

DISPLAY RIGHTS
Generally . . . 562; 563
Case law . . . 564

DISPOSITION
Remedies under federal law . . . 921

DISTRIBUTION RIGHTS
Generally . . . 505; 506
Domestic distribution . . . 508
Exported goods . . . 522
Imported goods . . . 522

DPRA (See DIGITAL PERFORMANCE RIGHT IN SOUND RECORDINGS ACT (DPRA))

DRAMATIC WORKS
Copyrightability . . . 171

DURATION AND TERMINATION
Generally . . . 323; 324
Automatic renewal . . . 354
Copyright Term Extension Act (CTEA) . . . 327
Derivative works
    Renewal . . . 351
    Termination of transfer, exception from . . . 396
Renewal under Copyright Act of 1909
    Generally . . . 344; 345
    Automatic renewal . . . 354
    Derivative works . . . 351
Restored copyrights . . . 355
Terminations of transfers
    Generally . . . 370
    Derivative works, exception for . . . 396
    Mechanics of termination
        Generally . . . 380
        Decisional law . . . 383

DURATION AND TERMINATION—Cont.
Terminations of transfers—Cont.
    § 203 terminations: post-1977 transfers
        Generally . . . 371
        Provisions, summary of . . . 372
    § 304(c) terminations: pre-1978 transfers
        Generally . . . 375; 376
        Provisions, summary of . . . 377
    §304(d) terminations . . . 379

E

ELECTRONIC REPRODUCTION RIGHTS
Generally . . . 478

EXCLUSIVE RIGHTS
Generally . . . 454
Adaptation rights
    Generally . . . 490; 491
    Case law . . . 492
Architecture of rights and limitations . . . 455
Compulsory licenses . . . 456
Copyright management information (CMI) . . . 461
Digital Performance Right in Sound Recordings Act (DPRA) . . . 574
Display rights
    Generally . . . 562; 563
    Case law . . . 564
Distribution rights (See DISTRIBUTION RIGHTS)
Miscellaneous rights
    Generally . . . 460
    Copyright management information (CMI) . . . 461
Moral rights (See MORAL RIGHTS)
Networked information environment . . . 459
Performance rights (See PERFORMANCE RIGHTS)
Reproduction rights (See REPRODUCTION RIGHTS)

EXPORTED GOODS
Distribution rights . . . 522

F

FAIR USE
Generally . . . 809
Actual and potential market effect . . . 860
Comparative perspective
    International treaties and future of fair use . . . 894
    United States, singularity of fair use in . . . 891
Conceptual issues in fair use
    Actual and potential market effect . . . 860
    First Amendment issues . . . 835
    Guidelines, role of . . . 866
    Market effect, actual and potential . . . 860
    Modern technology and personal reproduction . . . 868
    Personal reproduction, modern technology and . . . 868
    Photocopying . . . 864

[References are to pages.]

FAIR USE—Cont.
Conceptual issues in fair use—Cont.
    Potential market effect, actual and . . . 860
    Role of guidelines . . . 866
    Transformative use . . . 847
Copyright issues . . . 835
Decompilation and fair use . . . 872
First Amendment issues . . . 835
Fundamentals of fair use
    Generally . . . 810
    Analyzing fair use today . . . 815
    Judicial origins . . . 811
Guidelines, role of . . . 866
International treaties and future of fair use . . . 894
Market effect, actual and potential . . . 860
Modern technology . . . 868
Personal reproduction . . . 868
Photocopying . . . 864
Potential market effect, actual and . . . 860
Technology and
    Decompilation and fair use . . . 872
    Internet issues . . . 877
    Photocopying . . . 864; 868
    Technological protection measures under
        DMCA . . . 888
Transformative use . . . 847
United States, singularity of fair use in . . . 891

FEDERAL INTELLECTUAL PROPERTY LAW
Generally . . . 4
Patent law . . . 4
Trademark law . . . 9

FILMS
Copyrightability . . . 201

FIXATION REQUIREMENT
Generally . . . 66; 67
Current law, development of . . . 67

FOR-HIRE WORKS
Initial ownership . . . 263

G

GRAPHIC WORKS
Copyrightability . . . 174

H

**HISTORY OF ANGLO-AMERICAN COPY-
RIGHT LAW** (See ANGLO-AMERICAN COPY-
RIGHT LAW, HISTORY OF)

I

IDEAS
Idea/expression dichotomy . . . 118
Protection of . . . 1003

IMPORTED GOODS
Distribution rights . . . 522

IMPOUNDMENT AND DISPOSITION
Remedies under federal law . . . 921

INFRINGEMENT ACTIONS
Generally . . . 608
Affirmative copyright defenses . . . 897
Conflict of laws . . . 714; 724
Copying . . . 637
Defenses
    Affirmative copyright defenses . . . 897
    Fair use defense (See FAIR USE)
Extraterritoriality . . . 714; 715
Fair use defense (See FAIR USE)
Framing the lawsuit
    Generally . . . 610
    Jurisdictional matters . . . 611
    Procedural matters, other . . . 623
General test for infringement, formulation of
    . . . 635
Improper appropriation
    Generally . . . 652
    Illustrative cases . . . 658
Jurisdictional matters . . . 611
Procedural matters, other . . . 623
Proving the claim
    Copying . . . 637
    General test for infringement, formulation of
        . . . 635
    Improper appropriation
        Generally . . . 652
        Illustrative cases . . . 658

INITIAL OWNERSHIP (See OWNERSHIP AND
TRANSFERS)

INJUNCTIONS
Preliminary and permanent . . . 909

INTERNATIONAL TRADE (See COPYRIGHT
(GENERALLY), subhead: Intellectual property
and international trade)

INTERNATIONAL TREATIES
Generally . . . 31
Berne Convention . . . 34
United States and international copyright . . . 33

INTERNET
Fair use, technology and . . . 877
Internet service providers (See SECONDARY LI-
ABILITY, subhead: Internet service providers)
Peer-to-peer file sharing . . . 755
Secondary liability
    Copying devices and software (See SECOND-
        ARY LIABILITY, subhead: Copying devices
        and software)
    Internet service providers (See SECONDARY
        LIABILITY, subhead: Internet service pro-
        viders)
Service providers (See SECONDARY LIABILITY,
    subhead: Internet service providers)

[References are to pages.]

J

JOINT WORKS
Initial ownership . . . 281

JURISDICTION
Infringement actions . . . 611

L

LICENSES
Statutory (or compulsory) licenses . . . 456

LITERARY WORKS
Computer software (See SOFTWARE)
Copyrightability . . . 142

M

MISAPPROPRIATION
Preemption of state law . . . 954

MORAL RIGHTS
Generally . . . 580
Protection outside Copyright Act . . . 581
Visual Artists Rights Act
    Generally . . . 585; 586
    Case law . . . 588

MOTION PICTURES
Copyrightability . . . 201

MUSICAL WORKS
Copyrightability . . . 171
Performance rights in music videos . . . 544

MUSIC VIDEOS
Performance rights in . . . 544

N

NAFTA (See NORTH AMERICAN FREE TRADE
    AGREEMENT (NAFTA))

1909 ACT (See COPYRIGHT ACT OF 1909)

1976 ACT (See COPYRIGHT ACT OF 1976)

**NORTH AMERICAN FREE TRADE AGREE-
    MENT (NAFTA)**
International trade, intellectual property and . . . 40

NOTICE
Generally . . . 416; 418
Berne Convention Implementation Act of 1988, ex-
    cerpts from House Report on . . . 419
Compilations and collective works . . . 427
Concepts . . . 420
Copyright Office, Circular 3: Copyright Notice Au-
    gust 2011 . . . 420
Procedures . . . 420

NOVELTY
Originality distinguished . . . 89

O

ORIGINALITY
Generally . . . 84
Authors and their writings . . . 91
Basic concepts . . . 85
Idea/expression dichotomy . . . 118
Merger doctrine . . . 126
National origin . . . 134
Novelty distinguished . . . 89
Preliminary considerations, other
    National origin . . . 134
    Statutory formalities, role of . . . 137
    United States Government works . . . 135
Revisited . . . 107
Statutory formalities, role of . . . 137
United States Government works . . . 135
Writings . . . 91

ORPHAN WORKS
Transfers of rights . . . 318

OWNERSHIP AND TRANSFERS
Initial ownership
    Generally . . . 261; 262
    Collective works and *Tasini* case . . . 296
    Joint works . . . 281
    Works made for hire . . . 263
Transfers of rights
    Generally . . . 299
    Bundle of rights . . . 302
    Decisional law . . . 303
    Material object, distinction between copyright
        and . . . 301
    New media problem . . . 313
    Orphan works . . . 318
    Preliminary concepts
        Bundle of rights . . . 302
        Material object, distinction between copy-
            right and . . . 301
    Recordation . . . 315

P

PANTOMIMES
Copyrightability . . . 171

PATENT AND TRADEMARK OFFICE
Copyright office, combined with . . . 450

PATENT LAW
Relation to copyright . . . 4

PEER-TO-PEER FILE SHARING
Secondary liability . . . 755

PERFORMANCE RIGHTS
Generally . . . 526
Case law . . . 528
Digital network transmissions . . . 542
Digital Performance Right in Sound Recordings Act
    (DPRA) . . . 574
Grand performing rights . . . 540
Music videos . . . 544
Performing rights societies . . . 539

[References are to pages.]

PERFORMANCE RIGHTS—Cont.
Secondary transmissions (See SECONDARY TRANSMISSIONS)
Small performing rights . . . 540
Sound recordings and music videos . . . 544
Synchronization rights . . . 542

PHONORECORD REPRODUCTION RIGHTS
Sound recordings . . . 474

PHOTOCOPYING
Generally . . . 864

PICTORIAL WORKS
Copyrightability . . . 174

PREEMPTION OF STATE LAWS
Generally . . . 952; 953
Copyright Act of 1976
    Court rulings . . . 968
        Section 301: A study in confusion . . . 965
Misappropriation . . . 954
Publicity rights . . . 1008
Supremacy Clause, under . . . 958

PUBLICATION
Generally . . . 400; 402
Court decisions . . . 403
Derivative works and public domain . . . 415

PUBLIC DISPLAY
Generally . . . 562; 563
Case law . . . 564

PUBLIC DISTRIBUTION (See DISTRIBUTION RIGHTS)

PUBLIC DOMAIN
Derivative works and . . . 415

PUBLICITY RIGHTS
Preemption of state law . . . 1008

PUBLIC PERFORMANCE (See PERFOR-MANCE RIGHTS)

R

RECORDATION
Transfers of rights . . . 315

REGISTRATION
Berne Convention Implementation Act of 1988 . . . 432
Copyright Office, Circular 1: Copyright Basics May 2012 . . . 433
Joint explanatory statement on amendment to S. 1301 [Berne Convention Implementation Act of 1988] . . . 432
Procedures . . . 433

REGISTRATION, DEPOSIT AND
Generally . . . 428; 430
Collective works . . . 447
Concepts . . . 433
Derivative works . . . 447
Procedures . . . 433

REMEDIES UNDER FEDERAL LAW
Generally . . . 906
Attorneys' fees . . . 945
Costs . . . 945
Damages
    Generally . . . 923; 947
    Defendant's profits, plaintiff's damages and . . . 923
    "In lieu" damages . . . 936
    Plaintiff's damages and defendant's profits . . . 923
    Statutory or "in lieu" damages . . . 936
Defendant's profits, plaintiff's damages and . . . 923
Impoundment and disposition . . . 921
Injunctions, preliminary and permanent . . . 909
"In lieu" damages . . . 936
Non-monetary relief
    Generally . . . 909
    Impoundment and disposition . . . 921
    Injunctions, preliminary and permanent . . . 909
Plaintiff's damages and defendant's profits . . . 923
Rights management and . . . 947
State law, related bodies of
    Generally . . . 990
    Idea protection . . . 1003
    Passing off . . . 990
    Trade dress, protection of . . . 990
Statutory or "in lieu" damages . . . 936

RENEWAL (See DURATION AND TERMINA-TION)

REPRODUCTION RIGHTS
Generally . . . 464
Copies . . . 465
Electronic . . . 478
Fair use (See FAIR USE)
Phonorecords . . . 474

RESTORED COPYRIGHTS
Generally . . . 355

S

SATELLITE TRANSMISSIONS
Carrier limitations . . . 560

SCULPTURAL WORKS
Copyrightability . . . 174

SECONDARY LIABILITY
Generally . . . 733
Anti-circumvention measures . . . 787
Audio Home Recording Act (AHRA) . . . 751
Circumvention devices, technological protection measures and
    Anti-circumvention measures . . . 787
    Case law . . . 792
Contributory infringement and vicarious liability . . . 734
Copying devices and software
    Generally . . . 742

[References are to pages.]

SECONDARY LIABILITY—Cont.
Copying devices and software—Cont.
    Audio Home Recording Act (AHRA) . . . 751
    Case law . . . 743
    Peer-to-peer file sharing . . . 755
Internet service providers
    Generally . . . 767
    Liability for service providers, limitation of . . . 770
    Online issues, other . . . 785
Peer-to-peer file sharing . . . 755
Software (See subhead: Copying devices and software)
Technological protection measures and circumvention devices
    Anti-circumvention measures . . . 787
    Case law . . . 792
Vicarious liability, contributory infringement and . . . 734

SECONDARY TRANSMISSIONS
Generally . . . 547
Aiken exemption . . . 549
Cable system limitations . . . 558
Current issues in law of retransmission . . . 561
Satellite carrier limitations . . . 560
§ 110(5) *Aiken* exemption . . . 549

SOFTWARE
Generally . . . 142
Commission on New Technological Uses of Copyrighted Works (CONTU), final report of . . . 162
Secondary liability (See SECONDARY LIABILITY, subhead: Copying devices and software)

SOUND RECORDINGS
Copyrightability . . . 203
Digital Performance Right in Sound Recordings Act (DPRA) . . . 574
Performance rights . . . 544
Phonorecord reproduction rights . . . 474

STATE INTELLECTUAL PROPERTY LAW
Generally . . . 11
Federal law, related bodies of (See REMEDIES UNDER FEDERAL LAW)
Preemption of (See PREEMPTION OF STATE LAWS)
State law theories, other . . . 12
Trade secrets, unfair competition and . . . 11
Unfair competition and trade secrets . . . 11

STATUTORY (OR COMPULSORY) LICENSES
Generally . . . 456

T

TERMINATION (See DURATION AND TERMINATION)

THIRD-PARTY LIABILITY (See SECONDARY LIABILITY)

TRADE DRESS
Protection of . . . 990

TRADEMARK LAW
Relation to copyright . . . 9

TRADE-RELATED ASPECTS OF INTELLECTUAL PROPERTY RIGHTS (TRIPS)
Berne Convention and . . . 42
International trade . . . 40

TRANSFERS OF OWNERSHIP (See OWNERSHIP AND TRANSFERS)

"TRANSFORMATIVE" USE
Fair use . . . 847

TRIPS (See TRADE-RELATED ASPECTS OF INTELLECTUAL PROPERTY RIGHTS (TRIPS))

U

UNFAIR COMPETITION
Trade secrets and . . . 11

V

VICARIOUS LIABILITY, CONTRIBUTORY INFRINGEMENT AND
Generally . . . 734
Case law . . . 735

VIDEOS
Performance rights in music videos . . . 544

VISUAL ARTISTS RIGHTS ACT
Generally . . . 585; 586
Case law . . . 588

W

WORKS MADE FOR HIRE
Initial ownership . . . 263

WORKS OF AUTHORSHIP (See AUTHORSHIP)

WORLD TRADE ORGANIZATION (WTO)
International trade, copyright protection in . . . 42

WTO (See WORLD TRADE ORGANIZATION (WTO))